LUMBER MEN

LUMBER MEN

Nontraditional Statistical Measurements of the Batting Careers of Over 900 Major League Regulars from 1876 to 1992

by Leo Leahy

McFarland & Company, Inc., Publishers
Jefferson, North Carolina, and London

Frontispiece: George Kelly toughens up the lumber, 1922. Courtesy National Baseball Library, Cooperstown, NY.

British Library Cataloguing-in-Publication data are available

Library of Congress Cataloguing-in-Publication Data

Leahy, Leo.
  Lumber men : nontraditional statistical measurements of the
batting careers of over 900 major league regulars from 1876 to 1992
present / by Leo Leahy.
    p. cm.
  Includes index.
  ISBN 0-89950-925-8 (lib. bdg.: 50# alk. paper) ∞
  1. Batting (Baseball) — Statistical methods.   2. Baseball — United
States — Records.   3. Baseball players — United States — Rating of.
I. Title.
GV869.L43   1994
796.357′26 — dc20   93-40431
                                                                          CIP

©1994 Leo Leahy. All rights reserved

Manufactured in the United States of America

McFarland & Company, Inc., Publishers
  Box 611, Jefferson, North Carolina 28640

Acknowledgments

In 1989 I was enjoying life in the Fiji Islands. Every day brings baseball weather to Melanesia, but no one plays the game. Rugby and soccer are the team sports of choice. While I lived in Fiji I met just one other baseball fan, Ross Thrasher, an Ontario native who grew up cheering for the Tigers. Ross would retrieve the Vancouver newspapers that flight attendants left at the Canadian Air office in Suva when passing through. In these crumpled pages we followed the pennant races in North America.

We couldn't play, watch, or listen to baseball, so we talked about the game. Over a sunset, a soothing trade wind, and a cool drink, Ross and I evoked the memories of great players we had seen and speculated about the famous names of yesteryear. A baseball hero's feats do not disappear, for statistical records measure and preserve them. With time to study the statistics, I became convinced that the raw numbers are an insufficient evaluative aid. The traditional statistics do not reveal a vital dimension: *context*. But I discovered, to my excitement, that they could be manipulated to do so.

Ross was there when the idea of the OQ emerged. Now a resident of Toronto, he has been steadfast in his encouragement of this project. The same is true of other friends with whom I shared this material: Joe Gluck in New York, Enrico Edagiata in New Orleans, Paul Jenkins and Richard L. Miller in Cincinnati, and, in the Hague, Dr. Ignacio de Areta.

This book could not have been published without the efforts of Jim Krailler at the College of Mount Saint Joseph in Cincinnati. His expertise was vital, and he gave freely of his time whenever I needed it. Mike Shannon and Steve Simurda offered valuable advice, and Bill Hugo provided important research assistance. I wish also to thank Harald Aardman, Chuck Abbe, Bob Bailey, Susan Hettinger, Carmen B. Lane, Dale Meyers, Mike Warden, and Rod Wenz.

This book is dedicated to the memory of Raymond H. Greenlaw.

Contents

Introduction

This book compiles the batting records of baseball's greatest stars, and in doing so provides the argument-settler that baseball fans have always craved: a simple, meaningful yardstick for comparing the accomplishments of any of the great players, regardless of the era they played in. Was Reggie Jackson a better hitter than Joe Jackson? Was Jim Rice the equal of Zack Wheat? Was King Kelly any good? Was Harvey Kuenn more valuable than Rocky Colavito? Does George Brett stack up against Eddie Mathews or Pie Traynor? The answers are in this book.

The Urge to Compare

Roger Maris' quest for the single-season home run record in 1961 is generally regarded today as heroic. But while it was happening, Maris, to his bewilderment and frustration, found himself more denigrated than praised. Maris' talents were substantial; he was a skilled and intelligent defensive player, a dangerous hitter, and a major all-round contributor to a championship team. That he was no Babe Ruth was self-evident, for nobody ever was or will be. Yet many of the sportswriting experts of the day felt they needed to underscore the point by belittling Maris' accomplishments. The Yankee right fielder, they wrote, was just a mediocre ballplayer. The proof? His .269 batting average!

Implicit in this judgment was the notion that one could reasonably compare the players of the present to those of the past by merely checking the AVG column in the table of batting statistics. There were giants on the earth in *those* days, the scribes wrote in 1961, referring to the 1920s and 1930s. Maris? Colavito? Killebrew? Don't mention them in the same breath as Al Simmons or Paul Waner or Ki Ki Cuyler!

Since then the conventional wisdom has changed. Now one hears the assertion that players of different eras cannot be compared; playing conditions were different in the old days, so it's a case of apples and oranges. Ironically this refrain, too, is employed to disparage the modern crop of baseball stars. One hears that although Hank Aaron hit more home runs than Babe Ruth and Pete Rose banged out more hits than Ty Cobb, comparisons are not possible. The old stars, after all, had to travel by train, wear flannel uniforms, play doubleheaders and day games...

Until now no effective statistical yardstick has existed to measure performance consistently in the face of evolving and fluctuating playing conditions. The issue is important because baseball fans want to compare. They want to know whether Pete Rose was a modern Ty Cobb. They look at today's players and ask, who are the best of them, and how good are they?

Baseball is competition, which is another way of saying comparison. Teams compete for supremacy, and managers, seeking a competitive edge, compare players every day as they choose their lineups. Who plays? Who sits on the bench? Who gets sent to the minors? Who gets called up? Fans second-guess these decisions, agreeing or disagreeing. All-Star selections are hotly argued, and opinion is rarely unanimous on the relative merits of contemporary third basemen or center fielders. Comparison is essential to fan interest, and particularly so in the area of batting, the most essential of all baseball skills.

The Allure of Batting

Players who never make it to the big leagues are usually those who can't hit; there is always a place for a good hitter. Hits and runs stimulate and satisfy the appetites of baseball fans because they signify success. Scoring is more exciting than failing to score in a game like baseball, where an approximate equilibrium has always existed between offense and defense.

Most baseball games are decided by just a few runs, many by one. A team is rarely so far behind that it cannot catch up with some judicious batting. Runs are not scored so frequently that they become meaningless, nor so infrequently that action and drama are wanting. The potential for scoring is always present, but not always fulfilled. Batting skill produces runs, but there is only so much of that skill to go around. As pundits often point out, even .300 hitters fail 70 percent of the time. A hitter's job is to *make* something happen, and the great hitters are always bigger stars, more fascinating to the public, than the great pitchers, whose job it is to *prevent* something from happening. As General Francis A. Walker commented about the Civil War, "The sword is ever of higher honor than the shield."

It is true, of course, that playing conditions have changed. Stadium dimensions, the height of the pitcher's mound, and the size of the strike zone have often been altered. Night games and hard artificial surfaces are modern phenomena which affect the physical environment of the game. Equipment has changed over the years, too. Even slight variations in the manufacture of the baseball have profound effects on baseball offense, and such changes have occurred many times in the game's history. Meanwhile improved glove design has led to better fielding.

New strategies have evolved. At one time managers expected their pitchers to go nine innings; later it became acceptable to remove pitchers who got tired. Today starting pitchers are relieved as a matter of course, and a batter may see a different pitcher every time he comes to bat. And there have been important rule changes, most notably including the legalization of overhand pitching (1884), the lengthening of the pitching distance (1893), the foul-strike rule (1901 in the National League, 1903 in the American), the banning of the spitball (1920), and the introduction of the designated hitter (American League, 1973).

Home Run Baker hit 9 home runs for the Philadelphia Athletics in 1914 and led the American League. The entire league hit 148 home runs that year in 631 games, with a batting average of .248. The explanation for these low totals is not that the American League hitters that year were a bunch of weaklings. They weren't. In 1914 the baseball was wound more loosely than today's article, and old balls were kept in the game much longer, even if battered and discolored. It was so difficult to hit one of these balls out of the park that few batters attempted such a low-percentage play, preferring instead to choke up on the bat and punch the ball to precise areas of the field.

But every season has its dominant players, the ones who rise above the competition. The Offensive Quotient, or OQ, is a statistic that reveals who they were and are. It enables baseball fans to compare the productivity of players from different eras. Baker's OQ of 141 (fifth in the league) shows that he was a greater offensive force in 1914 than Reggie Jackson was in 1975, when "Mr. October" led the American League with 36 home runs (129 OQ, tenth in the league). Fans can use the OQ, introduced in this book, to answer questions about the batting abilities of all of baseball's great stars.

Measuring Batting Skill

How do we measure batting skill? How do we know how well a man is hitting, or how well he has hit over the course of a six-month season? The easiest way is to count the hits. The man with the most hits is the best hitter. Or is he?

Very early in the history of the game, fans adopted what they regarded as a fairer standard for batting. This was the batting average, the ratio of success to opportunity. The batting average (BA) is calculated by a simple mathematical operation:

$$\text{Batting Average} = \frac{\text{Hits}}{\text{At Bats}}$$

A problem with the batting average is that it regards all hits as equal in value, when every fan knows that this is not so. A double is better than a single; in fact, it is twice as valuable. From this truth the slugging average (SA) was invented. From the four categories of hit (single, double, triple, and home run), a player's total bases are tabulated, then used to compute another percentage:

$$\text{Slugging Average} = \frac{\text{Total Bases}}{\text{At Bats}}$$

Both these formulas overlook the offensive contribution of a player's ability to reach base on balls. The on-base average (OBA) grew out of the recognition that drawing walks is a legitimate offensive skill whose result is more baserunners and in turn more runs scored.

$$\text{On-Base Average} = \frac{(\text{Hits} + \text{Walks})}{(\text{At Bats} + \text{Walks})}$$

The batting average has proved to be the most popular and durable of these three computation-based measurements. The reason it endures is that the average fan believes he knows what a good batting average is: .300, or "three hundred," as it is universally known. The notion that a .300 hitter is a good hitter is taken for granted by players, sportswriters, and fans. The slugging average is a less widely accepted measurement because nobody is sure how to identify a good one. The same is true of the on-base average. Every year, the batting championship is awarded to the player who has achieved the highest batting average.

Hits, Outs, and Time

None of these statistics is useful for comparing batting skill across time, that is, in different seasons. The batting skill of the average batter has varied significantly, up and down, throughout the history of the game.

First baseman Jim Bottomley of the St. Louis Cardinals hit .304 in 1930, which looks impressive until one learns that the National League as a whole batted .303 that year. In terms of batting average, Bottomley was just a run-of-the-mill performer in 1930. Curt Flood's .301 average for the 1968 Cardinals was a more commendable feat by far, for that year the National League batted only .243. Hits were much harder to come by in 1968 than in 1930, but the simple batting average does not reveal what either man accomplished in relation to his peers.

This book introduces a different statistic for measuring batting skill. This is the Offensive Quotient (OQ). The OQ is as simple to calculate as the BA, the SA, and the OBA, and it has two distinct advantages: its value remains fixed over time, and it is easy to identify a good one.

To determine a player's OQ, we add a player's total bases and walks, then divide that sum by the number of outs he made (step 1). This is his Base-To-Out Ratio (BTOR). This figure we divide by the figure for the league as a whole (step 2).

$$1. \ BTOR = \frac{Total \ Bases + Walks}{Outs}$$

$$2. \ OQ = \frac{Player \ BTOR}{League \ BTOR}$$

A player whose Base-To-Out-Ratio is exactly the same as the league's would be, by definition, an average batter. His OQ would be 1.00, or 100 when we drop the decimal point. The OQ, then, uses the figure of 100 to indicate average batting skill. A player with an OQ of 100 is an average batter. Above 100, above average. Below 100, below average.

The OQ measures a batter's offensive efficiency. More important, it measures his ability to dominate his league. While doing so it incorporates all of the values of the old statistics. Like the BA, the OQ compares success to opportunity. It recognizes the value of hitting for extra bases, like the SA does, and the value of simply getting on base, like the OBA does. But only the OQ enables the fan to appreciate a player's batting record in its proper context.

A Fair Comparison

The table on page 489 reveals that the season base-to-out ratio in the American League has been as low as .493 in 1908 and as high as .749 in 1936. The latter total is over 50 percent higher than the former, indicating that there was over 50 percent more offense in the American League in 1936 than in 1908. We cannot, then, compare with any fairness or accuracy a 1908 batter to a 1936 batter, at least not by using the traditional measures of batting average, slugging average, or on-base average. These statistics do not take into account the wide variation in playing conditions that made hits and runs so much more commonplace in 1936. What was different in

1936? Was it the pitching? The ball? The parks? The weather? We can't be entirely certain, but we can quantify the change, and adjust for it using the OQ formula.

	G	AB	R	H	2B	3B	HR	RBI	AVG	BB	OQ
Jerry Freeman, 1908	154	531	45	134	15	5	1	45	.252	36	101
Moose Solters, 1936	152	628	100	183	45	7	17	134	.291	41	100

These seasons do not appear to be at all comparable, but the OQs indicate that each of them represents average batting skill for that year. Amazingly, Freeman's season was slightly better!

Now consider two different players.

	G	AB	R	H	2B	3B	HR	RBI	AVG	BB	OQ
Sam Crawford, 1908	152	591	102	184	33	16	7	80	.311	37	153
Joe DiMaggio, 1936	138	637	132	206	44	15	29	125	.323	24	121

Both these men are now in the Hall of Fame, but Sam Crawford did not compete with Joe DiMaggio. They did not face the same pitchers. Crawford competed in the American League of his time, DiMaggio in his. The 1908 Crawford was a better hitter than the 1936 DiMaggio, more dominant, rising higher above his peers. DiMaggio was a rookie in 1936. He would improve; this was his lowest OQ until his final year, 1951.

The OQ Explained

A player fails at bat by making an out. His team gets only three outs an inning, and each out that is made diminishes the team's chances to score runs. A player succeeds at bat by getting on base. A player who reaches base may score a run (although his chances of doing so depend largely on the actions of the players who follow him in the batting order), and he has not made an out. Anything he does to get on base and avoid making an out is desirable, and the more bases he earns, the better.

A player can reach base by hitting safely, drawing a walk, getting hit by a pitched ball, or by benefiting from catcher's interference. He may also reach base when an opponent makes an error or chooses to retire another baserunner. The OQ counts hits and walks because they are earned by the batter, and because they are statistically significant events for which individual player totals are available all the way back to 1876. Likewise, the OQ's formula for outs is uncomplicated:

$$\text{Outs} = \text{At Bats minus Hits}$$

Runs scored and driven in, while meaningful to record, are situational statistics that are less directly under the control of the individual batter. If there is no one on base, his hit will not produce an RBI; if no one drives him in, he won't score a run. But whether he gets on base or makes an out depends largely on his own abilities. This is what the OQ considers. Stolen base/caught stealing data are also ignored. Baserunning, although it is offensive in nature, is a separate skill from batting, in much the same way that pitching and fielding are separate facets of defensive play.

A baseball maxim (not universally endorsed) is that a walk is as good as a hit. The OQ accepts this principle as true. The player who has the patience to let four wide balls go by helps his team in two ways. He gets on base (from which position he may score a run), and he does not make an out. Hitting coaches who counsel players to "wait for their pitch" know that swinging at bad balls is, in general, a low-percentage play. Batters get few hits swinging at pitches outside the strike zone; they are more likely to make outs.

The OQ begins, then, by comparing a batter's bases with his outs. How many bases did he earn per out, it asks, or, how many outs did his bases cost him?

$$\frac{\text{Player Total Bases} + \text{Walks}}{\text{Outs}}$$

Let's look closely at Jim Bottomley's 1930 batting record.

	G	AB	R	H	2B	3B	HR	RBI	AVG	BB	OQ
Jim Bottomley, 1930	131	487	92	148	33	7	15	97	.304	44	110

If we add Bottomley's doubles, triples, and home runs, and subtract the total from his hits, we find that we hit 93 singles. We calculate his total bases this way:

$$
\begin{array}{ll}
93 \text{ singles} & \times 1 = 93 \\
33 \text{ doubles} & \times 2 = 66 \\
7 \text{ triples} & \times 3 = 21 \\
15 \text{ home runs} & \times 4 = 60 \\
\hline
& 240 \text{ total bases.}
\end{array}
$$

Total Bases + Walks = 284.

Bottomley made 339 outs (487 minus 148 = 339), and 284 divided by 339 yields a ratio of .83775811. For ease of computation the OQ employs 3-digit numbers, so we round this to .838.

The base-to-out ratio for the National League in 1930 was .764. Dividing 838 by 764 according to the OQ formula, we get 1.09685864, or 1.10. Expressed without the decimal point, this becomes 110. Thus 110 is Bottomley's 1930 OQ.

This means that in 1930 Jim Bottomley was 1.10 times as good a hitter as the average National Leaguer. To put it another way, he was 10 percent better than the average National League batter. The National League player with the highest OQ in 1930 was Hack Wilson of the Chicago Cubs.

	G	AB	R	H	2B	3B	HR	RBI	AVG	BB	OQ
Hack Wilson, 1930	155	585	146	208	35	6	56	190	.356	105	183

Wilson made 377 outs (585 minus 208). His 208 hits were good for 423 bases, and he walked 105 times. 423 + 105 = 528. Divide 528 by 377 outs and you get 1.401. Divide 1.401 by the National League figure (again, .764), and you get 1.83, so Wilson's 1930 OQ was 183. Wilson, then, was 83 percent better than the average National League batter in 1930.

Bill Terry of the New York Giants, whose .401 was the highest batting average in the National League that year, recorded an OQ of 155. This is an excellent figure, but the OQ enables us to make two points about Terry's season. Terry was a less efficient batter than Wilson, compiling more outs per bases earned. And Terry did not dominate the league to the extent that Wilson did.

Let's reconsider Jim Bottomley. If a player in the National League in 1968 had put up Bottomley's 1930 numbers, he would have recorded an OQ of 151. He would have been a standout in a league whose base-to-out ratio was just .554. What Bottomley achieved in 1930 was not particularly remarkable by the standards of that year, but it would have been in 1968. The term ".300 hitter" gives a less accurate picture of Bottomley's accomplishments in 1930 than his 110 OQ, which shows him to have been better than average, but not by much.

Because the OQ measures dominance, we can use it to compare players across time. Bottomley's 110 OQ season in 1930 is exactly comparable to each of the following:

	G	AB	R	H	2B	3B	HR	RBI	AVG	BB	OQ
Bug Holliday, 1890	131	518	93	140	18	14	4	75	.270	49	110
George Van Haltren, 1897	129	564	117	186	22	9	3	64	.330	40	110
Tommy Leach, 1906	133	476	66	136	10	7	1	39	.286	33	110
Jake Daubert, 1910	144	552	67	146	15	15	8	50	.264	47	110
Cy Williams, 1915	151	518	59	133	22	6	13	64	.257	26	110
Bob Elliott, 1941	141	527	74	144	24	10	3	76	.273	64	110
Vince DiMaggio, 1942	143	496	57	118	22	3	15	75	.238	52	110
Pee Wee Reese, 1955	145	553	99	156	29	4	10	61	.282	78	110
Charlie Neal, 1957	128	448	62	121	13	7	12	62	.270	53	110
Johnny Lewis, 1965	148	477	64	117	15	3	15	45	.245	59	110
Mike Lum, 1971	145	454	56	122	14	1	13	55	.269	47	110
Dan Driessen, 1979	150	515	72	129	24	3	18	75	.250	62	110
Keith Moreland, 1984	140	495	59	138	17	3	16	70	.279	34	110
Johnny Ray, 1986	155	579	67	174	33	0	7	78	.301	58	110

Consider these equivalents:

	G	AB	R	H	2B	3B	HR	RBI	AVG	BB	OQ
Bill Terry, 1930	154	633	139	254	39	15	23	129	.401	57	155
Orlando Cepeda, 1963	156	579	100	183	33	4	34	97	.316	37	155
Eddie Murray, 1990	155	558	96	184	22	3	26	95	.330	82	155

Hack Wilson's great 1930 season is similar to two others:

	G	AB	R	H	2B	3B	HR	RBI	AVG	BB	OQ
Honus Wagner, 1904	132	490	97	171	44	14	4	75	.349	59	185
Kevin Mitchell, 1989	154	543	100	158	34	6	47	125	.291	87	184

From the Beginning

Major league baseball as we know it began in 1876, the National League's first year of operation. Though there are differences between today's game and the game of 1876, it was the same game: 9 men on a side, 9 innings, 3 outs, 4 bases separated by 90 feet of infield. Runs were scored and outs registered in just the same way as today. The variations are minor, the similarities preponderant.

Old newspaper accounts reveal that nineteenth century fans followed the game with the same fervor, and they argued and speculated about the same issues we do. It is unfortunate and unfair that nineteenth century players are overlooked in so many of the modern popular histories of baseball. It is possible, for instance, to buy a book entitled *The Greatest First Basemen of All Time* and find no mention in it of Cap Anson, Dan Brouthers, or Roger Connor.

Be assured that the pre-1901 stars are in this book. They are no less worthy of consideration than their successors, and because their accomplishments were also measured statistically, they are no harder to get to know. The OQ is just as useful for evaluating Buck Ewing as it is for Johnny Bench. When 2001 arrives, do the panjandrums of baseball intend again to declare all prior-century records invalid? Will fans be asked to say goodbye to Babe Ruth and Willie Mays?

The Men in the Book

Here are the batting records of 986 major league players. In these pages one can trace the flow and ebb of great careers. Included is everyone who played as a regular for at least five seasons. A man who was in the lineup every day for five or more years has made his mark in the history of the game and deserves to have his offensive contributions taken seriously. Our definition of a regular is a player with at least three at bats plus walks for every game his team played that year.

About a dozen catchers are included who do not meet this criterion. The unique physical demands of this position have historically rendered it difficult for catchers to play as many games per season as other nonpitchers. The records of some catchers who had long major league careers appear here although they do not qualify in terms of plate appearances per season. Unless we allowed this, catchers as a group would be under-represented in these pages. Furthermore, any player who led his league in OQ is included, whether or not he achieved the status of a five-year regular.

The player records are listed chronologically, beginning with those of the men who were playing during the first National League season of 1876. This arrangement enables players who were contemporaries to appear in the same section of the book. Heinie Manush, for example, is listed not next to Mickey Mantle as alphabetical order would dictate but instead among all the players who reached the major leagues in 1923. It is hoped that the chronological order of presentation will impart a sense of each individual's own era of activity.

The index at the back of the book locates specific player records. The first year of major league service determines the order in which players are listed. Within these groupings, player records are arranged so that they can appear complete on a single page, their visual unity undisturbed. The book is organized in this admittedly unorthodox way in order to satisfy the eye as well as the mind.

Baseball has evolved and changed, and it will continue to do so, but the fans of the game view its history as one of continuity. Fans may know little or much about the bygone days of baseball, but they are never unaware of the game's past and rarely uninterested in it. The OQ was developed to illuminate this continuum. It will always be a valid evaluative tool. The men in the beginning of this book have been dead for decades, and no one is alive who saw them play. Yet the numbers remain, loyal to their memory. Each season's record is the summary of individual afternoons and evenings enjoyed by multitudes of fascinated onlookers.

Whatever the future holds for baseball, the game will have its stars. Professional baseball derives a great measure of its appeal from the charisma of those players whose feats exceed the common, the average, the mediocre. Those players shine brighter, and baseball, unique among sports, allows us to capture the luster of their performance in numbers which can be studied, savored, and appreciated in years to come.

Data Included

Every man's record contains the following special information:

• **POS.** Included in each year's totals is the player's position in the field. A second position is listed if he appeared there in more than 10 percent of his games. An outfielder is listed at the specific position he played most frequently.

• **LEAGUE.** Only major league statistics are listed. This book follows the decision of the Special Baseball Records Committee in 1968 that designated the following leagues as major:

National League	(1876–present)
American Association	(1882–1891)
Union Association	(1884)
Players' League	(1890)
American League	(1901–present)
Federal League	(1914–1915)

This book does not include player records from the National Association (1871–1875). The NA was certainly a major league in one important sense: it was the organization in which the best professional players competed. But a league exists to ensure fair competition, and the NA perished because it failed in this purpose. The zany scheduling arrangements, lack of a standard ball, and widespread hippodroming that characterized the NA prevent a precise evaluation of the productivity of individual players. For the record, statistics indicate that the dominant offensive players of the NA years were Cap Anson, Ross Barnes, Cal McVey, Levi Meyerle, Lip Pike, Deacon White, and George Wright. Baseball fans are directed to William J. Ryczek's superb study of the NA, *Blackguards and Red Stockings* (McFarland, 1992).

•**FIN.** This measure indicates the performance of each player's team in a given year. The number preceding the hyphen in this column is the order in which the team finished in the league standings. The number after the hyphen is the number of teams that were in the league. A designation of 10–12, then, would indicate that the team finished tenth in a twelve-team league. If the team competed in the era of divisional play (1969–present), it is listed according to its standings within the division. If the player played for two or three teams in one league during a single year, only the teams' standings are listed in this column, separated by a slash mark (/).

• **RANK.** Players who were regulars are ranked according to their OQs. Every player whose total of at bats and walks equaled or exceeded three times the number of games his team played that year is considered a regular, and his OQ is followed by a ranking. The number preceding the hyphen is the player's individual rank. The number after the hyphen is the number of players who qualified that year. A designation of 9-41 in this column indicates that the player's OQ was the ninth highest of 41 qualifiers. If no rank is listed, the player did not have enough at bats and walks to qualify that season. However, OQs are calculated for every player having 100 or more at bats and walks in a given year.

• **TOTALS.** A player's lifetime OQ is the simple average of his OQs for all the years he qualified as a regular. Lifetime OQs are listed only for players who were regulars for five or more seasons.

For some seasons RBIs are not available.

Total Baseball (Warner Books, 1991) is the sourcebook for the raw figures used in *Lumber Men*. Of the comprehensive record books available today, *Total Baseball* is the most accurate and dependable.

Team Abbreviations

ALT	Altoona		MON	Montreal
ATL	Atlanta		NWK	Newark
BAL	Baltimore		NY	New York
BOS	Boston		OAK	Oakland
BRO	Brooklyn		PHI	Philadelphia
BUF	Buffalo		PIT	Pittsburgh
CAL	California		PRO	Providence
CHI	Chicago		RIC	Richmond
CIN	Cincinnati		ROC	Rochester
CLE	Cleveland		SD	San Diego
COL	Columbus		SEA	Seattle
COR	Colorado		SF	San Francisco
DET	Detroit		SL	St. Louis
FLA	Florida		SYR	Syracuse
HAR	Hartford		TEX	Texas
HOU	Houston		TOL	Toledo
IND	Indianapolis		TOR	Toronto
KC	Kansas City		TRO	Troy
LA	Los Angeles		WAS	Washington
LOU	Louisville		WIL	Wilmington
MIL	Milwaukee		WOR	Worcester
MIN	Minnesota			

Roscoe Charles Barnes   Born May 8, 1850 Lima, NY
5'8 145 lbs Batted right   Died Feb 5, 1915 Chicago, IL

YR	POS	TEAM	LG	FIN	G	AB	R	H	2B	3B	HR	RBI	AVG	BB	TB	OO	RANK
1876	2B	CHI	NL	1-8	66	322	126	138	21	14	1	59	.429	20	190	249	1-61
1877	2B	CHI	NL	5-6	22	92	16	25	1	0	0	5	.272	7	26	99	—
1879	SS-2B	CIN	NL	5-8	77	323	55	86	9	2	1	30	.266	16	102	106	30-62
1881	SS-2B	BOS	NL	6-8	69	295	42	80	14	1	0	17	.271	16	96	101	33-56
MAJOR LEAGUE TOTALS					234	1032	239	329	45	17	2	111	.319	59	414	—	—

Adrian Constantine Anson   Born Apr 11, 1852 Marshalltown, IA
6'0 227 lbs Batted right   Died Apr 14, 1922 Chicago, IL

YR	POS	TEAM	LG	FIN	G	AB	R	H	2B	3B	HR	RBI	AVG	BB	TB	OO	RANK
1876	3B	CHI	NL	1-8	66	309	63	110	9	7	2	59	.356	12	139	165	3-61
1877	3B-C	CHI	NL	5-6	59	255	52	86	19	1	0	32	.337	9	107	138	7-45
1878	LF-2B	CHI	NL	4-6	60	261	55	89	12	2	0	40	.341	13	105	147	6-49
1879	1B	CHI	NL	4-8	51	227	40	72	20	1	0	34	.317	2	94	132	—
1880	1B-3B	CHI	NL	1-8	86	356	54	120	24	1	1	74	.337	14	149	149	4-58
1881	1B	CHI	NL	1-8	84	343	67	137	21	7	1	82	.399	26	175	190	1-56
1882	1B	CHI	NL	1-8	82	348	69	126	29	8	1	83	.362	20	174	172	3-57
1883	1B	CHI	NL	2-8	98	413	70	127	36	5	0	68	.308	18	173	124	16-60
1884	1B	CHI	NL	4-8	112	475	108	159	30	3	21	102	.335	29	258	173	3-54
1885	1B	CHI	NL	1-8	112	464	100	144	35	7	7	108	.310	34	214	154	5-46
1886	1B	CHI	NL	1-8	125	504	117	187	35	11	10	147	.371	55	274	189	3-48
1887	1B	CHI	NL	3-8	122	472	107	164	33	13	7	102	.347	60	244	158	3-49
1888	1B	CHI	NL	2-8	134	515	101	177	20	12	12	84	.344	47	257	180	1-46
1889	1B	CHI	NL	3-8	134	518	100	161	32	7	7	117	.311	86	228	142	6-53
1890	1B	CHI	NL	2-8	139	504	95	157	14	5	7	107	.312	113	202	153	1-48
1891	1B	CHI	NL	2-8	136	540	81	157	24	8	8	120	.291	75	221	131	7-52
1892	1B	CHI	NL	7-12	146	559	62	152	25	9	1	74	.272	67	198	116	25-72
1893	1B	CHI	NL	9-12	103	398	70	125	24	2	0	91	.314	68	153	120	25-80
1894	1B	CHI	NL	8-12	83	340	82	132	28	4	5	99	.388	40	183	138	—
1895	1B	CHI	NL	4-12	122	474	87	159	23	6	2	91	.335	55	200	116	26-75
1896	1B-C	CHI	NL	5-12	108	402	72	133	18	2	2	90	.331	49	161	117	25-73
1897	1B-C	CHI	NL	9-12	114	424	67	121	17	3	3	75	.285	60	153	106	39-69
MAJOR LEAGUE TOTALS			2276		9101	1719	2995	528	124	97	1879	.329	952	4062	147	20 yrs

David W Force   Born Jul 27, 1849   New York, NY
5'4 130 lbs Batted right   Died Jun 21, 1918   Englewood, NJ

YR	POS	TEAM	LG	FIN	G	AB	R	H	2B	3B	HR	RBI	AVG	BB	TB	OQ	RANK
1876	SS	PH/NY	NL	6/7	61	287	48	66	6	0	0	17	.230	5	72	76	49-61
1877	SS-3B	SL	NL	4-6	58	225	24	59	5	3	0	22	.262	11	70	98	24-45
1879	SS	BUF	NL	3-8	79	316	36	66	5	2	0	8	.209	13	75	75	51-62
1880	2B-SS	BUF	NL	7-8	81	290	22	49	10	0	0	17	.169	10	59	62	58-58
1881	2B-SS	BUF	NL	3-8	75	278	21	50	9	1	0	15	.180	11	61	61	55-56
1882	SS-3B	BUF	NL	3-8	73	278	39	67	10	1	1	28	.241	12	82	87	43-57
1883	SS-3B	BUF	NL	5-8	96	378	40	82	11	3	0	35	.217	12	99	69	58-60
1884	SS	BUF	NL	3-8	106	403	47	83	13	3	0	36	.206	27	102	77	49-54
1885	2B-SS	BUF	NL	7-8	71	253	20	57	6	1	0	15	.225	13	65	79	—
1886	SS-2B	WAS	NL	8-8	68	242	26	44	5	1	0	16	.182	17	51	62	—
MAJOR LEAGUE TOTALS					768	2950	323	623	80	15	1	209	.211	131	736	76	8 yrs

James Laurie White   Born Dec 7, 1847   Caton, NY
5'11 175 lbs Batted left   Died Jul 7, 1939   Aurora, IL

YR	POS	TEAM	LG	FIN	G	AB	R	H	2B	3B	HR	RBI	AVG	BB	TB	OQ	RANK
1876	C	CHI	NL	1-8	66	303	66	104	18	1	1	60	.343	7	127	147	7-61
1877	1B-RF	BOS	NL	1-6	59	266	51	103	14	11	2	49	.387	8	145	189	1-45
1878	C-RF	CIN	NL	2-6	61	258	41	81	4	1	0	29	.314	10	87	117	15-49
1879	C-RF	CIN	NL	5-8	78	333	55	110	16	6	1	52	.330	6	141	140	8-62
1880	RF	CIN	NL	8-8	35	141	21	42	4	2	0	7	.298	9	50	128	—
1881	1B-2B	BUF	NL	3-8	78	319	58	99	24	4	0	53	.310	9	131	124	13-56
1882	3B-C	BUF	NL	3-8	83	337	51	95	17	0	1	33	.282	15	115	106	29-57
1883	3B-C	BUF	NL	5-8	94	391	62	114	14	5	0	47	.292	23	138	108	26-60
1884	3B	BUF	NL	3-8	110	452	82	147	16	11	5	74	.325	32	200	145	10-54
1885	3B	BUF	NL	7-8	98	404	54	118	6	6	0	57	.292	12	136	103	30-46
1886	3B	DET	NL	2-8	124	491	65	142	19	5	1	76	.289	31	174	107	23-48
1887	3B	DET	NL	1-8	111	449	71	136	20	11	3	75	.303	26	187	109	26-49
1888	3B	DET	NL	5-8	125	527	75	157	22	5	4	71	.298	21	201	120	13-46
1889	3B	PIT	NL	5-8	55	225	35	57	10	1	0	26	.253	16	69	82	—
1890	3B-1B	BUF	PL	8-8	122	439	62	114	13	4	0	47	.260	67	135	93	43-57
MAJOR LEAGUE TOTALS					1299	5335	849	1619	217	73	18	756	.303	292	2036	124	13 yrs

John Edgar Clapp
5'7 194 lbs Batted right

Born Jul 17, 1851 Ithaca, NY
Died Dec 18, 1904 Ithaca, NY

YR	POS	TEAM	LG	FIN	G	AB	R	H	2B	3B	HR	RBI	AVG	BB	TB	OQ	RANK
1876	C	SL	NL	2-8	64	298	60	91	4	2	0	29	.305	8	99	113	21-61
1877	C-RF	SL	NL	4-6	60	255	47	81	6	6	0	34	.318	8	99	123	12-45
1878	LF-1B	IND	NL	5-6	63	263	42	80	10	2	0	29	.304	13	94	125	14-49
1879	C-RF	BUF	NL	3-8	70	292	47	77	12	5	1	36	.264	11	102	112	23-62
1880	C-CF	CIN	NL	8-8	80	323	33	91	16	4	1	20	.282	21	118	129	13-58
1881	C-LF	CLE	NL	7-8	68	261	47	66	12	2	0	25	.253	35	82	117	20-56
1883	C-CF	NY	NL	6-8	20	73	6	13	0	0	0	5	.178	5	13	—	—
MAJOR LEAGUE TOTALS					425	1765	282	499	60	21	2	178	.283	101	607	120	6 yrs

James Henry O'Rourke
5'8 185 lbs Batted right

Born Sep 1, 1850 Bridgeport, CT
Died Jan 8, 1919 Bridgeport, CT

YR	POS	TEAM	LG	FIN	G	AB	R	H	2B	3B	HR	RBI	AVG	BB	TB	OQ	RANK
1876	CF	BOS	NL	4-8	70	312	61	102	17	3	2	43	.327	15	131	151	6-61
1877	CF	BOS	NL	1-6	61	265	68	96	14	4	0	23	.362	20	118	164	2-45
1878	CF	BOS	NL	1-6	60	255	44	71	17	7	1	29	.278	5	105	128	12-49
1879	RF-1B	PRO	NL	1-8	81	362	69	126	19	9	1	46	.348	13	166	161	5-62
1880	CF-1B	BOS	NL	6-8	86	363	71	100	20	11	6	45	.275	21	160	148	5-58
1881	3B-LF	BUF	NL	3-8	83	348	71	105	21	7	0	30	.302	27	140	134	8-56
1882	CF	BUF	NL	3-8	84	370	62	104	15	6	2	37	.281	13	137	111	24-57
1883	LF-C	BUF	NL	5-8	94	436	102	143	29	8	1	38	.328	15	191	130	12-60
1884	LF-1B	BUF	NL	3-8	108	467	119	162	33	7	5	63	.347	35	224	162	5-54
1885	CF	NY	NL	2-8	112	477	119	143	21	16	5	42	.300	40	211	149	7-46
1886	CF-C	NY	NL	3-8	105	440	106	136	26	6	1	34	.309	39	177	130	11-48
1887	C-3B	NY	NL	4-8	103	397	73	113	15	13	3	88	.285	36	163	112	22-49
1888	LF-C	NY	NL	1-8	107	409	50	112	16	6	4	50	.274	24	152	119	15-46
1889	LF	NY	NL	1-8	128	502	89	161	36	7	3	81	.321	40	220	123	15-53
1890	RF	NY	PL	3-8	111	478	112	172	37	5	9	115	.360	33	246	136	8-57
1891	LF-C	NY	NL	3-8	136	555	92	164	28	7	5	95	.295	26	221	107	29-52
1892	LF	NY	NL	8-12	115	448	62	136	28	5	0	56	.304	30	174	117	23-72
1893	LF-1B	WAS	NL	12-12	129	547	75	157	22	5	2	95	.287	49	195	92	60-80
1904	C	NY	NL	1-8	1	4	1	1	0	0	0	0	.250	0	1	—	—
MAJOR LEAGUE TOTALS					1774	7435	1446	2304	414	132	50	1010	.310	481	3132	132	18 yrs

Robert V Ferguson   Born Jan 31, 1845 Brooklyn, NY
5'9 149 lbs Batted both   Died May 3, 1894 Brooklyn, NY

YR	POS	TEAM	LG	FIN	G	AB	R	H	2B	3B	HR	RBI	AVG	BB	TB	OQ	RANK
1876	3B	HAR	NL	3-8	69	310	48	82	8	5	0	32	.265	2	100	97	30-61
1877	3B	HAR	NL	3-6	58	254	40	65	7	2	0	35	.256	3	76	84	34-45
1878	SS	CHI	NL	4-6	61	259	44	91	10	2	0	39	.351	10	105	147	8-49
1879	3B-2B	TRO	NL	8-8	30	123	18	31	5	2	0	4	.252	4	40	102	—
1880	2B	TRO	NL	4-8	82	332	55	87	9	0	0	22	.262	24	96	106	31-58
1881	2B	TRO	NL	5-8	85	339	56	96	13	5	1	35	.283	29	122	121	17-56
1882	2B	TRO	NL	7-8	81	319	44	82	15	2	0	32	.257	23	101	103	32-57
1883	2B	PHI	NL	8-8	86	329	39	85	9	2	0	27	.258	18	98	88	44-60
1884	RF-1B	PIT	AA	10-12	10	41	2	6	0	0	0		.146	0	6	—	—
MAJOR LEAGUE TOTALS					562	2306	346	625	76	20	1		.271	113	744	107	7 yrs

John Joseph Burdock   Born 1851   Brooklyn, NY
5'9 158 lbs Batted right   Died Nov 28, 1931 Brooklyn, NY

YR	POS	TEAM	LG	FIN	G	AB	R	H	2B	3B	HR	RBI	AVG	BB	TB	OQ	RANK
1876	2B	HAR	NL	3-8	69	309	66	80	9	1	0	23	.259	13	91	99	29-61
1877	2B	HAR	NL	3-6	58	277	35	72	6	0	0	9	.260	2	78	78	39-45
1878	2B	BOS	NL	1-6	60	246	37	64	12	6	0	25	.260	3	88	107	20-49
1879	2B	BOS	NL	2-8	84	359	64	86	10	3	0	36	.240	9	102	87	42-62
1880	2B	BOS	NL	6-8	86	356	58	90	17	4	2	35	.253	8	121	105	32-58
1881	2B	BOS	NL	6-8	73	282	36	67	12	4	1	24	.238	7	90	88	45-56
1882	2B	BOS	NL	3-8	83	319	36	76	6	7	0	27	.238	9	96	85	49-57
1883	2B	BOS	NL	1-8	96	400	80	132	27	8	5	88	.330	14	190	141	8-60
1884	2B	BOS	NL	2-8	87	361	65	97	14	4	6	49	.269	15	137	110	24-54
1885	2B	BOS	NL	5-8	45	169	18	24	5	0	0	7	.142	8	29	51	—
1886	2B	BOS	NL	5-8	59	221	26	48	6	1	0	25	.217	11	56	70	—
1887	2B	BOS	NL	5-8	65	237	36	61	6	0	0	29	.257	18	67	77	—
1888	2B	BOS	NL	4-8	22	79	5	16	0	0	0	4	.203	2	16	—	—
1888	2B	BRO	AA	2-8	70	246	15	30	1	2	1	8	.122	8	38	42	—
1891	2B	BRO	NL	6-8	3	12	1	1	0	0	0	1	.083	1	1	—	—
MAJOR LEAGUE TOTALS					960	3873	578	944	131	40	15	390	.244	128	1200	100	9 yrs

Charles Wesley Jones Born Apr 30, 1850 Alamance County, NC
5'11 202 lbs Batted right Date and place of death unknown

YR	POS	TEAM	LG	FIN	G	AB	R	H	2B	3B	HR	RBI	AVG	BB	TB	OO	RANK
1876	CF	CIN	NL	8-8	64	276	40	79	17	4	4	38	.286	7	116	136	11-61
1877	LF	CN/CH	NL	6/5	57	240	53	75	12	10	2	38	.313	15	113	156	3-45
1878	LF	CIN	NL	2-6	61	261	50	81	11	7	3	39	.310	4	115	142	9-49
1879	LF	BOS	NL	2-8	83	355	85	112	22	10	9	62	.315	29	181	184	1-62
1880	LF	BOS	NL	6-8	66	280	44	84	15	3	5	37	.300	11	120	144	6-58
1883	CF	CIN	AA	3-8	90	391	84	115	15	11	11		.294	20	185	149	4-56
1884	LF	CIN	AA	5-12	112	472	117	148	19	17	7		.314	37	222	165	5-59
1885	LF	CIN	AA	2-8	112	487	108	157	19	17	4		.322	21	222	145	5-49
1886	LF	CIN	AA	5-8	127	500	87	135	22	11	5		.270	61	194	131	9-48
1887	LF-CF	CN/NY	AA	2/7	103	400	58	111	18	7	5		.278	31	158	105	27-49
1888	LF	KC	AA	8-8	6	25	2	4	0	1	0	5	.160	1	6	—	—
MAJOR LEAGUE TOTALS					881	3687	728	1101	170	98	55		.299	237	1632	146	10 yrs

Ezra Ballou Sutton Born Sep 17, 1850 Palmyra, NY
5'8 153 lbs Batted right Died Jun 20, 1907 Braintree, MA

YR	POS	TEAM	LG	FIN	G	AB	R	H	2B	3B	HR	RBI	AVG	BB	TB	OO	RANK
1876	1B-2B	PHI	NL	7-8	54	236	45	70	12	7	1	31	.297	3	99	134	12-61
1877	SS-3B	BOS	NL	1-6	58	253	43	74	10	6	0	39	.292	4	96	112	17-45
1878	3B	BOS	NL	1-6	60	239	31	54	9	3	1	29	.226	2	72	86	34-49
1879	SS-3B	BOS	NL	2-8	84	339	54	84	13	4	0	34	.248	2	105	89	38-62
1880	SS-3B	BOS	NL	6-8	76	288	41	72	9	2	0	25	.250	7	85	92	38-58
1881	3B	BOS	NL	6-8	83	333	43	97	12	4	0	31	.291	13	117	107	28-56
1882	3B	BOS	NL	3-8	81	319	44	80	8	1	2	38	.251	24	96	99	36-57
1883	3B	BOS	NL	1-8	94	414	101	134	28	15	3	73	.324	17	201	144	6-60
1884	3B	BOS	NL	2-8	110	468	102	162	28	7	3	61	.346	29	213	151	8-54
1885	3B-SS	BOS	NL	5-8	110	457	78	143	23	8	4	47	.313	17	194	134	12-46
1886	LF-SS	BOS	NL	5-8	116	499	83	138	21	6	3	48	.277	26	180	104	26-48
1887	SS-LF	BOS	NL	5-8	77	326	58	99	14	9	3	46	.304	13	140	108	—
1888	3B	BOS	NL	4-8	28	110	16	24	3	1	1	16	.218	7	32	91	—
MAJOR LEAGUE TOTALS					1031	4281	739	1231	190	73	21	518	.288	164	1630	114	11 yrs

John Paul Peters   Born Apr 8, 1850   Louisiana, MO
5'7   180 lbs   Batted right   Died Jan 4, 1924   St Louis, MO

YR	POS	TEAM	LG	FIN	G	AB	R	H	2B	3B	HR	RBI	AVG	BB	TB	OQ	RANK
1876	SS	CHI	NL	1-8	66	316	70	111	14	2	1	47	.351	3	132	144	9-61
1877	SS	CHI	NL	5-6	60	265	45	84	10	3	0	41	.317	1	100	112	18-45
1878	2B-SS	MIL	NL	6-6	55	246	33	76	6	1	0	22	.309	5	84	112	17-49
1879	SS	CHI	NL	4-8	83	379	45	93	13	2	1	31	.245	1	113	85	44-62
1880	SS	PRO	NL	2-8	86	359	30	82	5	0	0	24	.228	5	87	72	55-58
1881	SS	BUF	NL	3-8	54	229	21	49	8	1	0	25	.214	3	59	67	—
1882	SS	PIT	AA	4-6	78	333	46	96	10	1	0		.288	4	108	103	23-37
1883	SS	PIT	AA	7-8	8	28	3	3	0	0	0		.107	0	3	—	—
1884	SS	PIT	AA	10-12	1	4	0	0	0	0	0		.000	0	0	—	—
MAJOR LEAGUE TOTALS					491	2159	293	594	66	10	2		.275	22	686	105	6 yrs

Charles N Snyder   Born Oct 6, 1854   Washington, DC
5'11   184 lbs   Batted right   Died Oct 29, 1924   Washington, DC

YR	POS	TEAM	LG	FIN	G	AB	R	H	2B	3B	HR	RBI	AVG	BB	TB	OQ	RANK
1876	C	LOU	NL	5-8	56	224	21	44	4	1	1	9	.196	2	53	67	56-61
1877	C	LOU	NL	2-6	61	248	23	64	7	2	2	28	.258	3	81	92	29-45
1878	C	BOS	NL	1-6	60	226	21	48	5	0	0	14	.212	1	53	65	44-49
1879	C	BOS	NL	2-8	81	329	42	78	16	3	2	35	.237	5	106	94	34-62
1881	C	BOS	NL	6-8	62	219	14	50	8	0	0	16	.228	3	58	70	—
1882	C	CIN	AA	1-6	72	309	49	90	12	2	1		.291	9	109	117	10-37
1883	C	CIN	AA	3-8	58	250	38	64	14	6	0		.256	8	90	106	—
1884	C	CIN	AA	5-8	67	268	32	69	9	9	0		.257	7	96	107	—
1885	C	CIN	AA	2-8	39	152	13	36	4	3	1		.237	6	49	94	—
1886	C-1B	CIN	AA	5-8	60	220	33	41	8	3	0		.186	13	55	71	—
1887	C-1B	CLE	AA	8-8	74	282	33	72	12	6	0		.255	9	96	80	—
1888	C	CLE	AA	6-8	64	237	22	51	7	3	0	14	.215	6	64	74	—
1889	C	CLE	NL	6-8	22	83	5	16	3	0	0	12	.193	2	19	—	—
1890	C	CLE	PL	7-8	13	48	5	9	1	0	0	12	.188	1	10	—	—
1891	1B-C	WAS	AA	8-8	8	27	4	5	0	1	0	2	.185	0	7	—	—
MAJOR LEAGUE TOTALS					797	3122	355	737	110	39	7		.236	75	946	87	5 yrs

John P Cassidy   Born 1857   Brooklyn, NY
5'8 168 lbs   Died Jul 2, 1891   Brooklyn, NY

YR	POS	TEAM	LG	FIN	G	AB	R	H	2B	3B	HR	RBI	AVG	BB	TB	OQ	RANK
1876	RF-1B	HAR	NL	3-8	12	47	6	13	2	0	0	8	.277	1	15	—	—
1877	RF	HAR	NL	3-6	60	251	43	95	10	5	0	27	.378	3	115	152	5-45
1878	RF	CHI	NL	4-6	60	256	33	68	7	1	0	29	.266	9	77	98	27-49
1879	RF	TRO	NL	8-8	9	37	4	7	1	0	0	1	.189	2	8	—	—
1880	CF	TRO	NL	4-8	83	352	40	89	14	8	0	29	.253	12	119	107	28-58
1881	CF	TRO	NL	5-8	85	370	57	82	13	3	1	11	.222	18	104	82	48-56
1882	CF-3B	TRO	NL	7-8	29	121	14	21	3	1	0	9	.174	3	26	57	—
1883	RF	PRO	NL	3-8	89	366	46	87	16	5	0	42	.238	9	113	81	51-60
1884	RF	BRO	AA	9-12	106	433	57	109	11	6	2		.252	19	138	100	40-59
1885	RF	BRO	AA	5-8	54	221	36	47	6	2	1		.213	8	60	77	—
MAJOR LEAGUE TOTALS					587	2454	336	618	83	31	4		.252	84	775	103	6 yrs

John Joseph Gerhardt   Born Feb 14, 1855 Washington, DC
6'0 160 lbs Batted right   Died Mar 11, 1922 Middletown, NY

YR	POS	TEAM	LG	FIN	G	AB	R	H	2B	3B	HR	RBI	AVG	BB	TB	OQ	RANK
1876	1B	LOU	NL	5-8	65	292	33	76	10	3	2	18	.260	3	98	102	28-61
1877	2B	LOU	NL	2-6	59	250	41	76	6	5	1	35	.304	5	95	115	15-45
1878	2B	CIN	NL	2-6	60	259	46	77	7	2	0	28	.297	7	88	112	18-49
1879	2B-3B	CIN	NL	5-8	79	313	22	62	12	3	1	39	.198	3	83	73	54-62
1881	2B	DET	NL	4-8	80	297	35	72	13	6	0	36	.242	7	97	90	42-56
1883	2B	LOU	AA	5-8	78	319	56	84	11	9	0		.263	14	113	108	24-56
1884	2B	LOU	AA	3-12	106	404	39	89	7	8	0		.220	13	112	82	54-59
1885	2B	NY	NL	2-8	112	399	43	62	12	2	0	33	.155	24	78	60	46-46
1886	2B	NY	NL	3-8	123	426	44	81	11	7	0	40	.190	22	106	68	46-48
1887	2B	NY	NL	4-8	1	4	0	0	0	0	0	0	.000	0	0	—	—
1887	2B	NY	AA	7-8	85	307	40	68	13	2	0		.221	24	85	73	—
1890	2B-3B	BR/SL	AA	8/3	136	494	49	107	10	4	3		.217	39	134	77	40-42
1891	2B	LOU	AA	7-8	2	6	0	0	0	0	0	0	.000	1	0	—	—
MAJOR LEAGUE TOTALS					986	3770	448	854	112	51	7		.227	162	1089	89	10 yrs

John E Manning
5'8 158 lbs Batted right

Born Dec 20, 1853 Braintree, MA
Died Aug 15, 1929 Boston, MA

YR	POS	TEAM	LG	FIN	G	AB	R	H	2B	3B	HR	RBI	AVG	BB	TB	OQ	RANK
1876	RF-P	BOS	NL	4-8	70	288	52	76	13	0	2	25	.264	7	95	105	26-61
1877	SS-1B	CIN	NL	6-6	57	252	47	80	16	7	0	36	.317	5	110	134	8-45
1878	RF	BOS	NL	1-6	60	248	41	63	10	1	0	23	.254	10	75	98	25-49
1880	RF	CIN	NL	8-8	48	190	20	41	6	3	2	17	.216	7	59	95	—
1881	LF	BUF	NL	3-8	1	1	0	0	0	0	0	0	.000	0	0	—	—
1883	RF	PHI	NL	8-8	98	420	60	112	31	5	0	37	.267	20	153	104	33-60
1884	RF	PHI	NL	6-8	104	424	71	115	29	4	5	52	.271	40	167	128	16-54
1885	RF	PHI	NL	3-8	107	445	61	114	24	4	3	40	.256	37	155	115	22-46
1886	RF	BAL	AA	8-8	137	556	78	124	18	7	1		.223	50	159	90	38-48
MAJOR LEAGUE TOTALS					682	2824	430	725	147	31	13		.257	176	973	111	7 yrs

John Francis Morrill
5'10 155 lbs Batted right

Born Feb 19, 1855 Boston, MA
Died Apr 2, 1932 Boston, MA

YR	POS	TEAM	LG	FIN	G	AB	R	H	2B	3B	HR	RBI	AVG	BB	TB	OQ	RANK
1876	2B-C	BOS	NL	4-8	66	278	38	73	5	2	0	26	.263	3	82	90	38-61
1877	3B-1B	BOS	NL	1-6	61	242	47	73	5	1	0	28	.302	6	80	102	22-45
1878	1B	BOS	NL	1-6	60	233	26	56	5	1	0	23	.240	5	63	82	38-49
1879	3B-1B	BOS	NL	2-8	84	348	56	98	18	5	0	49	.282	14	126	119	19-62
1880	1B-3B	BOS	NL	6-8	86	342	51	81	16	8	2	44	.237	11	119	107	29-58
1881	1B	BOS	NL	6-8	81	311	47	90	19	3	1	39	.289	12	118	114	23-56
1882	1B	BOS	NL	3-8	83	349	73	101	19	11	2	54	.289	18	148	131	11-57
1883	1B	BOS	NL	1-8	97	404	83	129	33	16	6	68	.319	15	212	153	3-60
1884	1B-2B	BOS	NL	2-8	111	438	80	114	19	7	3	61	.260	30	156	109	25-54
1885	1B-2B	BOS	NL	5-8	111	394	74	89	20	7	4	44	.226	64	135	130	16-46
1886	SS-1B	BOS	NL	5-8	117	430	86	106	25	6	7	69	.247	56	164	124	13-48
1887	1B	BOS	NL	5-8	127	504	79	141	32	6	12	81	.280	37	221	114	21-49
1888	1B	BOS	NL	4-8	135	486	60	96	18	7	4	39	.198	55	140	100	26-46
1889	1B	WAS	NL	8-8	44	146	20	27	5	0	2	16	.185	30	38	92	—
1890	1B-SS	BOS	PL	1-8	2	7	1	1	0	0	0	2	.143	2	1	—	—
MAJOR LEAGUE TOTALS					1265	4912	821	1275	239	80	43	643	.260	358	1803	113	13 yrs

Thomas J York Born Jul 13, 1851 Brooklyn, NY
5'9 165 lbs Batted left Died Feb 17, 1936 New York, NY

YR	POS	TEAM	LG	FIN	G	AB	R	H	2B	3B	HR	RBI	AVG	BB	TB	OQ	RANK
1876	LF	HAR	NL	3-8	67	263	47	68	12	7	1	39	.259	10	97	120	18-61
1877	LF	HAR	NL	3-6	56	237	43	67	16	7	1	37	.283	3	100	122	13-45
1878	LF	PRO	NL	3-6	62	269	56	83	19	10	1	26	.309	8	125	153	3-49
1879	LF	PRO	NL	1-8	81	342	69	106	25	5	1	50	.310	19	144	147	7-62
1880	LF	PRO	NL	2-8	53	203	21	43	9	2	0	18	.212	8	56	86	—
1881	LF	PRO	NL	2-8	85	316	57	96	23	5	2	47	.304	29	135	145	4-56
1882	LF	PRO	NL	2-8	81	321	48	86	23	7	1	40	.268	19	126	121	17-57
1883	LF	CLE	NL	4-8	100	381	56	99	29	5	2	46	.260	37	144	119	22-60
1884	LF	BAL	AA	6-12	83	314	64	70	14	7	1		.223	34	101	114	26-59
1885	RF	BAL	AA	8-8	22	87	6	23	4	2	0		.264	8	31	—	—

| MAJOR LEAGUE TOTALS | | | | | 690 | 2733 | 467 | 741 | 174 | 57 | 10 | | .271 | 175 | 1059 | 130 | 8 yrs |

George Washington Bradley Born Jul 13, 1852 Reading, PA
5'10 175 lbs Batted right Died Oct 2, 1931 Philadelphia, PA

YR	POS	TEAM	LG	FIN	G	AB	R	H	2B	3B	HR	RBI	AVG	BB	TB	OQ	RANK
1876	P	SL	NL	2-8	64	265	29	66	7	6	0	28	.249	3	85	96	31-61
1877	P-3B	CHI	NL	5-6	55	214	31	52	7	3	0	12	.243	6	65	88	32-45
1879	P	TRO	NL	8-8	63	251	36	62	9	5	0	23	.247	1	81	92	36-62
1880	3B-P	PRO	NL	2-8	82	309	32	70	7	6	0	23	.227	5	89	85	45-58
1881	3B-SS	DE/CL	NL	4/7	61	245	21	60	10	1	2	18	.245	4	78	86	—
1882	P-LF	CLE	NL	5-8	30	115	16	21	5	0	0	6	.183	4	26	63	—
1883	SS	CLE	NL	4-8	4	16	0	5	0	1	0	1	.313	0	7	—	—
1883	3B-P	PHI	AA	1-8	76	312	47	73	8	5	1		.234	8	94	86	46-56
1884	P-RF	CIN	UA	2-8	58	226	31	43	4	7	0		.190	7	61	79	—
1886	SS	PHI	AA	6-8	13	48	1	4	0	1	0		.083	1	6	—	—
1888	SS	BAL	AA	5-8	1	3	0	0	0	0	0	0	.000	0	0	—	—

| MAJOR LEAGUE TOTALS | | | | | 507 | 2004 | 244 | 456 | 57 | 35 | 3 | | .228 | 39 | 592 | 89 | 5 yrs |

Alonzo P Knight   Born Jun 16, 1853   Philadelphia, PA
5'11   165 lbs   Batted right   Died Apr 23, 1932   Philadelphia, PA

YR	POS	TEAM	LG	FIN	G	AB	R	H	2B	3B	HR	RBI	AVG	BB	TB	OQ	RANK
1876	P-1B	PHI	NL	7-8	55	240	32	60	9	3	0	24	.250	2	75	93	32-61
1880	RF	WOR	NL	5-8	49	201	31	48	11	3	0	21	.239	5	65	99	—
1881	RF	DET	NL	4-8	83	340	67	92	16	3	1	52	.271	23	117	110	26-56
1882	RF	DET	NL	6-8	86	347	39	72	12	6	0	24	.207	16	96	80	52-57
1883	RF	PHI	AA	1-8	97	429	98	108	23	9	1		.252	21	152	108	25-57
1884	RF	PHI	AA	7-12	108	484	94	131	18	12	1		.271	10	176	109	29-59
1885	RF	PHI	AA	4-8	29	119	17	25	1	1	0		.210	9	28	78	—
1885	RF	PRO	NL	4-8	25	81	8	13	1	0	0	8	.160	11	14	—	—
MAJOR LEAGUE TOTALS					532	2241	386	549	91	37	3		.245	97	723	100	5 yrs

Paul A Hines   Born Mar 1, 1852   Washington, DC
5'9   173 lbs   Batted right   Died Jul 10, 1935   Hyattsville, MD

YR	POS	TEAM	LG	FIN	G	AB	R	H	2B	3B	HR	RBI	AVG	BB	TB	OQ	RANK
1876	CF	CHI	NL	1-8	64	305	62	101	21	3	2	59	.331	1	134	144	8-61
1877	RF-2B	CHI	NL	5-6	60	261	44	73	11	7	0	23	.280	1	98	106	20-45
1878	CF	PRO	NL	3-6	62	257	42	92	13	4	4	50	.358	2	125	165	1-49
1879	CF	PRO	NL	1-8	85	409	81	146	25	10	2	52	.357	8	197	166	4-62
1880	CF	PRO	NL	2-8	85	374	64	115	20	2	3	35	.307	13	148	134	9-58
1881	CF	PRO	NL	2-8	80	361	65	103	27	5	2	31	.285	13	146	120	18-56
1882	CF	PRO	NL	2-8	84	379	73	117	28	10	4	34	.309	10	177	140	7-57
1883	CF	PRO	NL	3-8	97	442	94	132	32	4	4	45	.299	18	184	121	19-60
1884	CF	PRO	NL	1-8	114	490	94	148	36	10	3	41	.302	44	213	143	11-54
1885	CF	PRO	NL	4-8	98	411	63	111	20	4	1	35	.270	19	142	107	27-46
1886	CF-3B	WAS	NL	8-8	121	487	80	152	30	8	9	56	.312	35	225	141	7-48
1887	CF	WAS	NL	7-8	123	478	83	147	32	5	10	72	.308	48	219	129	11-49
1888	CF	IND	NL	7-8	133	513	84	144	26	3	4	58	.281	41	188	124	12-46
1889	1B-CF	IND	NL	7-8	121	486	77	148	27	1	6	72	.305	49	195	117	18-53
1890	CF-1B	PT/BO	NL	8/5	100	394	52	94	13	3	2	57	.239	43	119	91	37-48
1891	CF-1B	WAS	AA	8-8	54	206	25	58	7	5	0	31	.282	21	75	107	—
MAJOR LEAGUE TOTALS					1481	6253	1083	1881	368	84	56	751	.301	366	2585	130	15 yrs

Joseph Start
5'9 165 lbs Batted left

Born Oct 14, 1842 New York, NY
Died Mar 27, 1927 Providence, RI

YR	POS	TEAM	LG	FIN	G	AB	R	H	2B	3B	HR	RBI	AVG	BB	TB	OQ	RANK
1876	1B	NY	NL	6-8	56	264	40	73	6	0	0	21	.277	1	79	91	35-61
1877	1B	HAR	NL	3-6	60	271	55	90	3	6	1	21	.332	6	108	127	10-45
1878	1B	CHI	NL	4-6	61	285	58	100	12	5	1	27	.351	2	125	147	5-49
1879	1B	PRO	NL	1-8	66	317	70	101	11	5	2	37	.319	7	128	133	10-62
1880	1B	PRO	NL	2-8	82	345	53	96	14	6	0	27	.278	13	122	117	18-58
1881	1B	PRO	NL	2-8	79	348	56	114	12	6	0	29	.328	9	138	122	15-56
1882	1B	PRO	NL	2-8	82	356	58	117	8	10	0	48	.329	11	145	128	13-57
1883	1B	PRO	NL	3-8	87	370	63	105	16	7	1	57	.284	22	138	112	24-60
1884	1B	PRO	NL	1-8	93	381	80	105	10	5	2	32	.276	35	131	114	22-54
1885	1B	PRO	NL	4-8	101	374	47	103	11	4	0	41	.275	39	122	118	20-46
1886	1B	WAS	NL	8-8	31	122	10	27	4	1	0	17	.221	5	33	73	—
MAJOR LEAGUE TOTALS					798	3433	590	1031	107	55	7	357	.300	150	1269	121	10 yrs

Michael Cornelius Dorgan
5'9 180 lbs Batted right

Born Oct 2, 1853 Middletown, CT
Died Apr 26, 1909 Syracuse, NY

YR	POS	TEAM	LG	FIN	G	AB	R	H	2B	3B	HR	RBI	AVG	BB	TB	OQ	RANK
1877	LF-C	SL	NL	4-6	60	266	45	82	9	7	0	23	.308	9	105	124	11-45
1879	1B-RF	SYR	NL	7-8	59	270	38	72	11	5	1	17	.267	4	96	107	28-62
1880	RF	PRO	NL	2-8	79	321	45	79	10	1	0	31	.246	10	91	90	39-58
1881	RF-1B	WO/DE	NL	8/4	59	254	41	69	6	0	0	23	.272	9	75	88	43-56
1883	RF	NY	NL	6-8	64	261	32	61	11	3	0	27	.234	2	78	74	—
1884	RF-P	NY	NL	4-8	83	341	61	94	11	6	1	48	.276	13	120	102	29-54
1885	RF	NY	NL	2-8	89	347	60	113	17	8	0	46	.326	11	146	133	13-46
1886	RF	NY	NL	3-8	118	442	61	129	19	4	2	79	.292	29	162	111	20-48
1887	RF	NY	NL	4-8	71	283	41	73	10	0	0	34	.258	15	83	75	—
1890	RF	SYR	AA	6-8	33	139	19	30	8	0	0		.216	16	38	85	—
MAJOR LEAGUE TOTALS					715	2924	443	802	112	34	4		.274	118	994	108	7 yrs

William Michael Crowley   Born Apr 8, 1857   Philadelphia, PA
5'7 159 lbs Batted right   Died Jul 14, 1891   Gloucester, NJ

YR	POS	TEAM	LG	FIN	G	AB	R	H	2B	3B	HR	RBI	AVG	BB	TB	OQ	RANK
1877	CF	LOU	NL	2-6	61	238	30	67	9	3	1	23	.282	4	85	104	21-45
1879	RF-C	BUF	NL	3-8	60	261	41	75	9	5	0	30	.287	6	94	114	21-62
1880	CF-C	BUF	NL	7-8	85	354	57	95	16	4	0	20	.268	19	119	115	21-58
1881	CF	BOS	NL	6-8	72	279	33	71	12	0	0	31	.254	14	83	91	39-56
1883	CF	PHI	AA	1-8	23	96	16	24	4	3	0		.250	3	34	—	—
1883	RF	CLE	NL	4-8	11	41	3	12	5	0	0	5	.293	1	17	—	—
1884	RF	BOS	NL	2-8	108	407	50	110	14	6	6	61	.270	33	154	120	18-54
1885	LF	BUF	NL	7-8	92	344	29	83	14	1	1	36	.241	21	102	94	35-46
MAJOR LEAGUE TOTALS					512	2020	259	537	83	22	8		.266	101	688	106	6 yrs

George Shaffer   Born 1852   Philadelphia, PA
5'9 165 lbs Batted left   Date and place of death unknown

YR	POS	TEAM	LG	FIN	G	AB	R	H	2B	3B	HR	RBI	AVG	BB	TB	OQ	RANK
1877	RF	LOU	NL	2-6	61	260	38	74	9	5	3	34	.285	9	102	120	14-45
1878	RF	IND	NL	5-6	63	266	48	90	19	6	0	30	.338	13	121	163	2-49
1879	RF	CHI	NL	4-8	73	316	53	96	13	0	0	35	.304	6	109	111	25-62
1880	RF	CLE	NL	3-8	83	338	62	90	14	9	0	21	.266	17	122	121	15-58
1881	RF	CLE	NL	7-8	85	343	48	88	13	6	1	34	.257	23	116	106	31-56
1882	RF	CLE	NL	5-8	84	313	37	67	14	2	3	28	.214	27	94	97	39-57
1883	RF	BUF	NL	5-8	95	401	67	117	11	3	0	41	.292	27	134	105	29-60
1884	RF	SL	UA	1-8	106	467	130	168	40	10	2		.360	30	234	189	2-33
1885	RF	SL	NL	8-8	69	257	30	50	11	2	0	18	.195	19	65	81	—
1885	RF	PHI	AA	4-8	2	9	1	2	0	1	0		.222	1	4	—	—
1886	RF	PHI	AA	6-8	21	82	15	22	3	3	0		.268	8	31	—	—
1890	RF	PHI	AA	7-8	100	390	55	110	15	5	1		.282	47	138	114	20-42
MAJOR LEAGUE TOTALS					842	3442	584	974	162	52	10		.283	227	1270	125	9 yrs

Frank Edward Hankinson

5'11 168 lbs Batted right

Born Apr 29, 1856 New York, NY
Died Apr 5, 1911 Palisades Park, NJ

YR	POS	TEAM	LG	FIN	G	AB	R	H	2B	3B	HR	RBI	AVG	BB	TB	OQ	RANK
1878	3B	CHI	NL	4-6	58	240	38	64	8	3	1	27	.267	5	81	105	22-49
1879	P-CF	CHI	NL	4-8	44	171	14	31	4	0	0	8	.181	2	35	56	—
1880	3B-CF	CLE	NL	3-8	69	263	32	55	7	4	1	19	.209	1	73	77	51-58
1881	3B	TRO	NL	5-8	85	321	34	62	15	0	1	19	.193	10	80	68	54-56
1883	3B	NY	NL	4-8	94	337	40	74	13	6	2	30	.220	19	105	87	47-60
1884	3B	NY	NL	5-8	105	389	44	90	16	7	2	43	.231	23	126	95	36-54
1885	3B	NY	AA	2-8	94	362	43	81	12	2	2		.224	12	103	81	44-49
1886	3B	NY	AA	7-8	136	522	66	126	14	5	2		.241	49	156	97	33-48
1887	3B	NY	AA	7-8	127	512	79	137	29	11	1		.268	38	191	98	34-49
1888	2B-SS	KC	AA	8-8	37	155	20	27	4	1	1	20	.174	11	36	73	—
MAJOR LEAGUE TOTALS					849	3272	410	747	122	39	13		.228	170	986	89	8 yrs

Charles Wesley Bennett

5'11 180 lbs Batted right

Born Nov 21, 1854 New Castle, PA
Died Feb 24, 1927 Detroit, MI

YR	POS	TEAM	LG	FIN	G	AB	R	H	2B	3B	HR	RBI	AVG	BB	TB	OQ	RANK
1878	C-CF	MIL	NL	6-6	49	184	16	45	9	0	1	12	.245	10	57	103	24-49
1880	C-CF	WOR	NL	5-8	51	193	20	44	9	3	0	18	.228	10	59	100	—
1881	C	DET	NL	4-8	76	299	44	90	18	7	7	64	.301	18	143	150	3-56
1882	C-3B	DET	NL	6-8	84	342	43	103	16	10	5	51	.301	20	154	143	6-57
1883	C-2B	DET	NL	7-8	92	371	56	113	34	7	5	55	.305	26	176	145	5-60
1884	C	DET	NL	8-8	90	341	37	90	18	6	3	40	.264	36	129	125	17-54
1885	C-LF	DET	NL	6-8	91	349	49	94	24	13	5	60	.269	47	159	161	4-46
1886	C	DET	NL	2-8	72	235	37	57	13	5	4	34	.243	48	92	143	—
1887	C	DET	NL	1-8	46	160	26	39	6	5	3	20	.244	30	64	124	—
1888	C	DET	NL	5-8	74	258	32	68	12	4	5	29	.264	31	103	141	—
1889	C	BOS	NL	2-8	82	247	42	57	8	2	4	28	.231	21	81	87	—
1890	C	BOS	NL	5-8	85	281	59	60	17	2	3	40	.214	72	90	124	—
1891	C	BOS	NL	1-8	75	256	35	55	9	3	5	39	.215	42	85	107	—
1892	C	BOS	NL	1-12	35	114	19	23	4	0	1	16	.202	27	30	112	—
1893	C	BOS	NL	1-12	60	191	34	40	6	0	4	27	.209	40	58	96	—
MAJOR LEAGUE TOTALS					1062	3821	549	978	203	67	55	533	.256	478	1480	138	6 yrs

Frank Sylvester Flint
6'0 180 lbs Batted right

Born Aug 3, 1855 Philadelphia, PA
Died Jan 14, 1892 Chicago, IL

YR	POS	TEAM	LG	FIN	G	AB	R	H	2B	3B	HR	RBI	AVG	BB	TB	OQ	RANK
1878	C-LF	IND	NL	5-6	63	254	23	57	7	0	0	18	.224	2	64	72	43-49
1879	C	CHI	NL	4-8	79	324	46	92	22	6	1	41	.284	6	129	124	14-62
1880	C-RF	CHI	NL	1-8	74	284	30	46	10	4	0	17	.162	5	64	63	57-58
1881	C-RF	CHI	NL	1-8	80	306	46	95	18	0	1	34	.310	6	116	112	24-56
1882	C-RF	CHI	NL	1-8	81	331	48	83	18	8	4	44	.251	2	129	104	31-57
1883	C-RF	CHI	NL	2-8	85	332	57	88	23	4	0	32	.265	3	119	93	41-60
1884	C	CHI	NL	4-8	73	279	35	57	5	2	9	45	.204	7	93	86	—
1885	C	CHI	NL	1-8	68	249	27	52	8	2	1	17	.209	2	67	70	—
1886	C	CHI	NL	1-8	54	173	30	35	6	2	1	13	.202	12	48	79	—
1887	C	CHI	NL	3-8	49	187	22	50	8	6	3	21	.267	4	79	97	—
1888	C	CHI	NL	2-8	22	77	6	14	3	0	0	3	.182	1	17	—	—
1889	C	CHI	NL	3-8	15	56	6	13	1	0	1	9	.232	3	17	—	—
MAJOR LEAGUE TOTALS					743	2852	376	682	129	34	21	294	.239	53	942	95	6 yrs

Abner Frank Dalrymple
5'10 175 lbs Batted left

Born Sep 9, 1857 Warren, IL
Died Jan 25, 1939 Warren, IL

YR	POS	TEAM	LG	FIN	G	AB	R	H	2B	3B	HR	RBI	AVG	BB	TB	OQ	RANK
1878	LF	MIL	NL	6-6	61	271	52	96	10	4	0	15	.354	6	114	147	7-49
1879	LF	CHI	NL	4-8	71	333	47	97	25	1	0	23	.291	4	124	115	20-62
1880	LF	CHI	NL	1-8	86	382	91	126	25	12	0	36	.330	3	175	150	3-58
1881	LF	CHI	NL	1-8	82	362	72	117	22	4	1	37	.323	15	150	131	10-56
1882	LF	CHI	NL	1-8	84	397	96	117	25	11	1	36	.295	14	167	127	14-57
1883	LF	CHI	NL	2-8	80	363	78	108	24	4	2	37	.298	11	146	114	23-60
1884	LF	CHI	NL	4-8	111	521	111	161	18	9	22	69	.309	14	263	146	9-54
1885	LF	CHI	NL	1-8	113	492	109	135	27	12	11	61	.274	46	219	148	8-46
1886	LF	CHI	NL	1-8	82	331	62	77	7	12	3	26	.233	33	117	108	—
1887	LF	PIT	NL	6-8	92	358	45	76	18	5	2	31	.212	45	110	88	42-49
1888	LF	PIT	NL	6-8	57	227	19	50	9	2	0	14	.220	6	63	78	—
1891	LF	MIL	AA	5-8	32	135	31	42	7	5	1	22	.311	7	62	122	—
MAJOR LEAGUE TOTALS					951	4172	813	1202	217	81	43	407	.288	204	1710	130	9 yrs

George W Creamer   Born 1855   Philadelphia, PA
6'2 Batted right   Died Jun 27, 1886 Philadelphia, PA

YR	POS	TEAM	LG	FIN	G	AB	R	H	2B	3B	HR	RBI	AVG	BB	TB	OQ	RANK
1878	2B-CF	MIL	NL	6-6	50	193	30	41	7	3	0	15	.212	5	54	83	37-49
1879	2B-SS	SYR	NL	7-8	15	60	3	13	2	0	0	3	.217	1	15	—	—
1880	2B	WOR	NL	5-8	85	306	40	61	6	3	0	27	.199	4	73	68	56-58
1881	2B	WOR	NL	8-8	80	309	42	64	9	2	0	25	.207	11	77	70	53-56
1882	2B	WOR	NL	8-8	81	286	27	65	16	6	1	29	.227	14	96	98	38-57
1883	2B	PIT	AA	7-8	91	369	54	94	7	9	0		.255	20	119	101	31-56
1884	2B	PIT	AA	10-12	98	339	38	62	8	5	0		.183	16	80	72	58-59
MAJOR LEAGUE TOTALS					500	1862	234	400	55	28	1		.215	71	514	82	6 yrs

Michael Joseph Kelly   Born Dec 31, 1857 Troy, NY
5'10 170 lbs Batted right   Died Nov 8, 1894   Boston, MA

YR	POS	TEAM	LG	FIN	G	AB	R	H	2B	3B	HR	RBI	AVG	BB	TB	OQ	RANK
1878	RF-C	CIN	NL	2-6	60	237	29	67	7	1	0	27	.283	7	76	104	23-49
1879	3B-RF	CIN	NL	5-8	77	345	78	120	20	12	2	47	.348	8	170	168	3-62
1880	RF-C	CHI	NL	1-8	84	344	72	100	17	9	1	60	.291	12	138	133	11-58
1881	RF-C	CHI	NL	1-8	82	353	84	114	27	3	2	55	.323	16	153	138	7-56
1882	SS-RF	CHI	NL	1-8	84	377	81	115	37	4	1	55	.305	10	163	130	12-57
1883	RF-C	CHI	NL	2-8	98	428	92	109	28	10	3	61	.255	16	166	106	27-60
1884	RF-C	CHI	NL	4-8	108	452	120	160	28	5	13	95	.354	46	237	185	1-54
1885	RF-C	CHI	NL	1-8	107	438	124	126	24	7	9	75	.288	46	191	151	6-46
1886	RF-C	CHI	NL	1-8	118	451	155	175	32	11	4	79	.388	83	241	214	1-48
1887	RF-2B	BOS	NL	5-8	116	484	120	156	34	11	8	63	.322	55	236	142	6-49
1888	C-RF	BOS	NL	4-8	107	440	85	140	22	11	9	71	.318	31	211	161	5-46
1889	RF-C	BOS	NL	2-8	125	507	120	149	41	5	9	78	.294	65	227	132	12-53
1890	C-SS	BOS	PL	1-8	89	340	83	111	18	6	4	66	.326	52	153	133	10-57
1891	C	CN/BO	AA	5/1	86	298	58	88	15	7	2	57	.295	51	123	136	—
1891	C-RF	BOS	NL	1-8	16	52	7	12	1	0	0	5	.231	6	13	—	—
1892	C	BOS	NL	1-12	78	281	40	53	7	0	2	41	.189	39	66	82	—
1893	C	NY	NL	5-12	20	67	9	18	1	0	0	15	.269	6	19	—	—
MAJOR LEAGUE TOTALS					1455	5894	1357	1813	359	102	69	950	.308	549	2583	146	13 yrs

William Henry McClellan   Born Mar 22, 1856 Chicago, IL
156 lbs   Batted left   Died Jul 3, 1929   Chicago, IL

YR	POS	TEAM	LG	FIN	G	AB	R	H	2B	3B	HR	RBI	AVG	BB	TB	OQ	RANK
1878	2B-SS	CHI	NL	4-6	48	205	26	46	6	1	0	29	.224	2	54	75	40-49
1881	SS-RF	PRO	NL	2-8	68	259	30	43	3	1	0	16	.166	15	48	57	56-56
1883	SS	PHI	NL	8-8	80	326	42	75	21	4	1	33	.230	19	107	93	39-60
1884	SS	PHI	NL	6-8	111	450	71	116	13	2	3	33	.258	28	142	97	34-54
1885	3B-2B	BRO	AA	5-8	112	464	85	124	22	7	0		.267	28	160	109	19-49
1886	2B	BRO	AA	3-8	141	595	131	152	33	9	1		.255	56	206	110	22-48
1887	2B	BRO	AA	6-8	136	548	109	144	24	6	1		.263	80	183	105	28-49
1888	2B-RF	BR/CL	AA	2/6	96	350	39	73	7	3	0	26	.209	46	86	94	—
MAJOR LEAGUE TOTALS					792	3197	533	773	129	33	6		.242	274	986	92	7 yrs

John Montgomery Ward   Born Mar 3, 1860   Bellefonte, PA
5'9   165 lbs   Batted left   Died Mar 4, 1925   Augusta, GA

YR	POS	TEAM	LG	FIN	G	AB	R	H	2B	3B	HR	RBI	AVG	BB	TB	OQ	RANK
1878	P	PRO	NL	3-6	37	138	14	27	5	4	1	15	.196	2	43	87	—
1879	P-3B	PRO	NL	1-8	83	364	71	104	9	4	2	41	.286	7	127	110	26-62
1880	P-3B	PRO	NL	2-8	86	356	53	81	12	2	0	27	.228	6	97	81	49-58
1881	RF-P	PRO	NL	2-8	85	357	56	87	18	6	0	53	.244	5	117	88	44-56
1882	RF-P	PRO	NL	2-8	83	355	58	87	10	3	1	39	.245	13	106	87	44-57
1883	CF-P	NY	NL	6-8	88	380	76	97	18	7	7	54	.255	8	150	103	34-60
1884	CF-2B	NY	NL	4-8	113	482	98	122	11	8	2	51	.253	28	155	97	35-54
1885	SS	NY	NL	2-8	111	446	72	101	8	9	0	37	.226	17	127	83	41-46
1886	SS	NY	NL	3-8	122	491	82	134	17	5	2	81	.273	19	167	95	35-48
1887	SS	NY	NL	4-8	129	545	114	184	16	5	1	53	.338	29	213	107	27-49
1888	SS	NY	NL	1-8	122	510	70	128	14	5	2	49	.251	9	158	87	37-46
1889	SS	NY	NL	1-8	114	479	87	143	13	4	1	67	.299	27	167	93	38-53
1890	SS	BRO	PL	2-8	128	561	134	189	15	12	4	60	.337	51	240	117	21-57
1891	SS-2B	BRO	NL	6-8	105	441	85	122	13	5	0	39	.277	36	145	96	36-52
1892	2B	BRO	NL	3-12	148	614	109	163	13	3	1	47	.265	82	185	106	39-72
1893	2B	NY	NL	5-12	135	588	129	193	27	9	2	77	.328	47	244	109	36-80
1894	2B	NY	NL	2-12	136	540	100	143	12	5	0	77	.265	34	165	64	76-77
MAJOR LEAGUE TOTALS					1825	7647	1408	2105	231	96	26	867	.275	420	2606	95	16 yrs

Joseph L Quest
5'6 150 lbs Batted right

Born Nov 3, 1851 New Castle, PA
Date and place of death unknown

YR	POS	TEAM	LG	FIN	G	AB	R	H	2B	3B	HR	RBI	AVG	BB	TB	OQ	RANK
1878	2B	IND	NL	5-6	62	278	45	57	3	2	0	13	.205	12	64	74	42-49
1879	2B	CHI	NL	4-8	83	334	38	69	16	1	0	22	.207	9	87	77	49-62
1880	2B	CHI	NL	1-8	82	300	37	71	12	1	0	27	.237	8	85	88	41-58
1881	2B	CHI	NL	1-8	78	293	35	72	6	0	1	26	.246	2	81	73	50-56
1882	2B	CHI	NL	1-8	42	159	24	32	5	2	0	15	.201	8	41	76	—
1883	2B	DET	NL	7-8	37	137	22	32	8	2	0	25	.234	10	44	95	—
1883	2B	SL	AA	2-8	19	78	12	20	3	1	0		.256	1	25	—	—
1884	2B	SL/PT	AA	4/10	93	353	48	73	12	5	0		.207	19	95	84	53-59
1885	2B-SS	DET	NL	6-8	55	200	24	39	8	2	0	21	.195	14	51	80	—
1886	SS	PHI	AA	6-8	42	150	14	31	4	1	0		.207	20	37	90	—
MAJOR LEAGUE TOTALS					593	2282	299	496	77	17	1		.217	103	610	79	5 yrs

Edward Nagle Williamson
5'11 170 lbs Batted right

Born Oct 24, 1857 Philadelphia, PA
Died Mar 3, 1894 Willow Springs, AR

YR	POS	TEAM	LG	FIN	G	AB	R	H	2B	3B	HR	RBI	AVG	BB	TB	OQ	RANK
1878	3B	IND	NL	5-6	63	250	31	58	10	2	1	19	.232	5	75	89	31-49
1879	3B	CHI	NL	4-8	80	320	66	94	20	13	1	36	.294	24	143	157	6-62
1880	3B-C	CHI	NL	1-8	75	311	65	78	20	2	0	31	.251	15	102	108	27-58
1881	3B	CHI	NL	1-8	82	343	56	92	12	6	1	48	.268	19	119	107	29-56
1882	3B	CHI	NL	1-8	83	348	66	98	27	4	3	60	.282	27	142	133	10-57
1883	3B	CHI	NL	2-8	98	402	83	111	49	5	2	59	.276	22	176	126	14-60
1884	3B	CHI	NL	4-8	107	417	84	116	18	8	27	84	.278	42	231	173	4-54
1885	3B	CHI	NL	1-8	113	407	87	97	16	5	3	65	.238	75	132	133	14-46
1886	SS	CHI	NL	1-8	121	430	69	93	17	8	6	58	.216	80	144	121	15-48
1887	SS	CHI	NL	3-8	127	439	77	117	20	14	9	78	.267	73	192	132	9-49
1888	SS	CHI	NL	2-8	132	452	75	113	9	14	8	73	.250	65	174	141	9-46
1889	SS	CHI	NL	3-8	47	173	16	41	3	1	1	30	.237	23	49	88	—
1890	3B-SS	CHI	NL	4-8	73	261	34	51	7	3	2	26	.195	36	70	75	—
MAJOR LEAGUE TOTALS					1201	4553	809	1159	228	85	64	667	.255	506	1749	129	11 yrs

George F Gore   Born May 3, 1857 Saccarappa, ME
5'11 195 lbs Batted left   Died Sep 16, 1933 Utica, NY

YR	POS	TEAM	LG	FIN	G	AB	R	H	2B	3B	HR	RBI	AVG	BB	TB	OQ	RANK
1879	CF-1B	CHI	NL	4-8	63	266	43	70	17	4	0	32	.263	8	95	112	24-62
1880	CF	CHI	NL	1-8	77	322	70	116	23	2	2	47	.360	21	149	178	1-58
1881	CF	CHI	NL	1-8	73	309	86	92	18	9	1	44	.298	27	131	142	6-56
1882	CF	CHI	NL	1-8	84	367	99	117	15	7	3	51	.319	29	155	145	5-57
1883	CF	CHI	NL	2-8	92	392	105	131	30	9	2	16	.334	27	185	150	4-60
1884	CF	CHI	NL	4-8	103	422	104	134	18	4	5	34	.318	61	175	156	6-54
1885	CF	CHI	NL	1-8	109	441	115	138	21	13	5	57	.313	68	200	176	3-46
1886	CF	CHI	NL	1-8	118	444	150	135	20	12	6	63	.304	102	197	176	5-48
1887	CF	NY	NL	4-8	111	459	95	133	16	5	1	49	.290	42	162	100	34-49
1888	CF	NY	NL	1-8	64	254	37	56	4	4	2	17	.220	30	74	105	—
1889	CF	NY	NL	1-8	120	488	132	149	21	7	7	54	.305	84	205	138	7-53
1890	CF	NY	PL	3-8	93	399	132	127	26	8	10	55	.318	77	199	151	3-57
1891	CF	NY	NL	3-8	130	528	103	150	22	7	2	48	.284	74	192	120	19-52
1892	CF	NY/SL	NL	8/11	73	266	56	64	11	3	0	15	.241	67	81	131	—
MAJOR LEAGUE TOTALS					1310	5357	1327	1612	262	94	46	582	.301	717	2200	145	12 yrs

John A Farrell   Born Jul 5, 1857   Newark, NJ
5'9 165 lbs Batted right   Died Feb 10, 1914 Overbrook, NJ

YR	POS	TEAM	LG	FIN	G	AB	R	H	2B	3B	HR	RBI	AVG	BB	TB	OQ	RANK
1879	2B	SY/PR	NL	7/1	66	292	45	86	8	2	1	26	.295	3	101	107	29-62
1880	2B	PRO	NL	2-8	80	339	46	92	12	5	3	36	.271	10	123	116	20-58
1881	2B	PRO	NL	2-8	84	345	69	82	16	5	5	36	.238	29	123	112	25-56
1882	2B	PRO	NL	2-8	84	366	67	93	21	6	2	31	.254	16	132	106	27-57
1883	2B	PRO	NL	3-8	95	420	92	128	24	11	3	61	.305	15	183	126	15-60
1884	2B	PRO	NL	1-8	111	469	70	102	13	6	1	37	.217	35	130	86	44-54
1885	2B	PRO	NL	4-8	68	257	27	53	7	1	1	19	.206	10	65	73	—
1886	2B	PH/WA	NL	4/8	64	231	31	52	11	5	2	21	.225	18	79	99	—
1887	SS-2B	WAS	NL	7-8	87	339	40	75	14	9	0	41	.221	20	107	77	—
1888	SS-2B	BAL	AA	5-8	103	398	72	81	19	5	4	36	.204	26	122	92	35-47
1889	SS	BAL	AA	5-8	42	157	25	33	3	0	1	26	.210	15	39	71	—
MAJOR LEAGUE TOTALS					884	3613	584	877	148	55	23	370	.243	197	1204	106	7 yrs

Peter James Hotaling Born Dec 16, 1856 Mohawk, NY
5'8 166 lbs Batted right Died Jul 3, 1928 Cleveland, OH

YR	POS	TEAM	LG	FIN	G	AB	R	H	2B	3B	HR	RBI	AVG	BB	TB	OQ	RANK
1879	CF	CIN	NL	5-8	81	369	64	103	20	9	1	27	.279	12	144	125	13-62
1880	CF	CLE	NL	3-8	78	325	40	78	17	8	0	41	.240	10	111	106	30-58
1881	CF	WOR	NL	8-8	77	317	51	98	15	3	1	35	.309	18	122	124	12-56
1882	CF	BOS	NL	3-8	84	378	64	98	16	5	0	28	.259	16	124	98	37-57
1883	CF	CLE	NL	4-8	100	417	54	108	20	8	0	30	.259	12	144	94	38-60
1884	CF	CLE	NL	7-8	102	408	69	99	16	6	3	27	.243	28	136	101	31-54
1885	CF	BRO	AA	5-8	94	370	73	95	9	5	1		.257	49	117	119	15-49
1887	CF	CLE	AA	8-8	126	505	108	151	28	13	3		.299	53	214	121	13-49
1888	CF	CLE	AA	6-8	98	403	67	101	7	6	0	55	.251	26	120	96	34-47
MAJOR LEAGUE TOTALS					840	3492	590	931	148	63	9		.267	224	1232	109	9 yrs

Dennis Joseph Brouthers Born May 8, 1858 Sylvan Lake, NY
6'2 207 lbs Batted left Died Aug 2, 1932 East Orange, NJ

YR	POS	TEAM	LG	FIN	G	AB	R	H	2B	3B	HR	RBI	AVG	BB	TB	OQ	RANK
1879	1B	TRO	NL	8-8	39	168	17	46	12	1	4	17	.274	1	72	127	—
1880	1B	TRO	NL	4-8	3	12	0	2	0	0	0	1	.167	1	2	—	—
1881	LF-1B	BUF	NL	3-8	65	270	60	86	18	9	8	45	.319	18	146	173	2-56
1882	1B	BUF	NL	3-8	84	351	71	129	23	11	6	63	.368	21	192	188	1-57
1883	1B	BUF	NL	5-8	98	425	85	159	41	17	3	97	.374	16	243	180	1-60
1884	1B	BUF	NL	3-8	94	398	82	130	22	15	14	79	.327	33	224	183	2-54
1885	1B	BUF	NL	7-8	98	407	87	146	32	11	7	59	.359	34	221	194	1-46
1886	1B	DET	NL	2-8	121	489	139	181	40	15	11	72	.370	66	284	207	2-48
1887	1B	DET	NL	1-8	123	500	153	169	36	20	12	101	.338	71	281	170	1-49
1888	1B	DET	NL	5-8	129	522	118	160	33	11	9	66	.307	68	242	171	4-46
1889	1B	BOS	NL	2-8	126	485	105	181	26	9	7	118	.373	66	246	166	4-53
1890	1B	BOS	PL	1-8	123	460	117	152	36	9	1	97	.330	99	209	149	4-57
1891	1B	BOS	AA	1-8	130	486	117	170	26	19	5	109	.350	87	249	175	1-48
1892	1B	BRO	NL	3-12	152	588	121	197	30	20	5	124	.335	84	282	167	2-72
1893	1B	BRO	NL	6-12	77	282	57	95	21	11	2	59	.337	52	144	155	—
1894	1B	BAL	NL	1-12	123	525	137	182	39	23	9	128	.347	67	294	135	11-77
1895	1B	BA/LO	NL	1/12	29	120	15	36	12	1	2	20	.300	12	56	116	—
1896	1B	PHI	NL	8-12	57	218	42	75	13	3	1	41	.344	44	97	147	—
1904	1B	NY	NL	1-8	2	5	0	0	0	0	0	0	.000	0	0	—	—
MAJOR LEAGUE TOTALS					1673	6711	1523	2296	460	205	106	1296	.342	840	3484	174	13 yrs

Sargent Perry Houck   Born 1856   Washington, DC
5'7 151 lbs Batted right   Died May 26, 1919 Washington, DC

YR	POS	TEAM	LG	FIN	G	AB	R	H	2B	3B	HR	RBI	AVG	BB	TB	OQ	RANK
1879	RF-SS	BOS	NL	2-8	80	356	69	95	24	9	2	49	.267	4	143	120	16-62
1880	LF	BO/PR	NL	6/2	61	231	29	44	7	7	1	24	.190	3	68	82	—
1881	SS	DET	NL	4-8	75	308	43	86	16	6	1	36	.279	6	117	108	27-56
1883	SS	DET	NL	7-8	101	416	52	105	18	12	0	40	.252	9	147	93	40-60
1884	SS	PHI	AA	7-12	108	472	93	140	19	14	0		.297	7	187	120	19-59
1885	SS	PHI	AA	4-8	93	388	74	99	10	9	0		.255	10	127	94	36-49
1886	SS	BAL	AA	8-8	61	260	29	50	8	1	0		.192	4	60	57	—
1886	SS	WAS	NL	8-8	52	195	14	42	3	0	0	14	.215	2	45	56	—
1887	SS-2B	NY	AA	7-8	10	33	3	5	1	0	0		.152	3	6	—	—
MAJOR LEAGUE TOTALS					641	2659	406	666	106	58	4		.250	48	900	107	5 yrs

John Wesley Glasscock   Born Jul 22, 1859 Wheeling, WV
5'8 160 lbs Batted right   Died Feb 24, 1947 Wheeling, WV

YR	POS	TEAM	LG	FIN	G	AB	R	H	2B	3B	HR	RBI	AVG	BB	TB	OQ	RANK
1879	2B-3B	CLE	NL	6-8	80	325	31	68	9	3	0	29	.209	6	83	74	53-62
1880	SS	CLE	NL	3-8	77	296	37	72	13	3	0	27	.243	2	91	89	40-58
1881	SS	CLE	NL	7-8	85	335	49	86	9	5	0	33	.257	15	105	94	36-56
1882	SS	CLE	NL	5-8	84	358	66	104	27	9	4	46	.291	13	161	135	8-57
1883	SS	CLE	NL	4-8	96	383	67	110	19	6	0	46	.287	13	141	104	32-60
1884	SS	CLE	NL	7-8	72	281	45	70	4	4	1	22	.249	25	85	99	—
1884	SS	CIN	UA	2-8	38	172	48	72	9	5	2		.419	8	97	224	—
1885	SS	SL	NL	8-8	111	446	66	125	18	3	1	40	.280	29	152	112	24-46
1886	SS	SL	NL	6-8	121	486	96	158	29	7	3	40	.325	38	210	138	8-48
1887	SS	IND	NL	8-8	122	483	91	142	18	7	0	40	.294	41	174	101	33-49
1888	SS	IND	NL	7-8	113	442	63	119	17	3	1	45	.269	14	145	98	29-46
1889	SS	IND	NL	7-8	134	582	128	205	40	3	7	85	.352	31	272	130	13-53
1890	SS	NY	NL	6-8	124	512	91	172	32	9	1	66	.336	41	225	132	9-48
1891	SS	NY	NL	3-8	97	369	46	89	12	6	0	55	.241	36	113	90	—
1892	SS	SL	NL	11-12	139	566	83	151	27	5	3	72	.267	44	197	104	43-72
1893	SS	SL/PT	NL	10/2	114	488	81	156	15	12	2	100	.320	42	201	108	37-80
1894	SS	PIT	NL	7-12	86	332	46	93	10	7	1	63	.280	31	120	81	—
1895	SS-1B	LO/WA	NL	12/10	43	174	29	48	5	1	1	16	.276	10	58	78	—
MAJOR LEAGUE TOTALS					1736	7030	1163	2040	313	98	27		.290	439	2630	109	13 yrs

Warren William Carpenter
5'11 186 lbs Batted right

Born Aug 16, 1855 Grafton, MA
Died Apr 18, 1937 San Diego, CA

YR	POS	TEAM	LG	FIN	G	AB	R	H	2B	3B	HR	RBI	AVG	BB	TB	OQ	RANK
1879	1B-3B	SYR	NL	7-8	65	261	30	53	6	0	0	20	.203	2	59	62	60-62
1880	3B-1B	CIN	NL	8-8	77	300	32	72	6	4	0	23	.240	2	86	83	48-58
1881	3B	WOR	NL	8-8	83	347	40	75	12	2	2	31	.216	3	97	72	52-56
1882	3B	CIN	AA	1-6	80	351	78	120	15	5	1		.342	10	148	148	3-37
1883	3B	CIN	AA	3-8	95	436	99	129	18	4	3		.296	18	164	119	15-56
1884	3B	CIN	AA	5-12	108	474	80	121	16	2	4		.255	6	153	93	46-59
1885	3B	CIN	AA	2-8	112	473	89	131	12	8	2		.277	9	165	101	30-49
1886	3B	CIN	AA	5-8	111	458	67	101	8	5	2		.221	18	125	75	46-48
1887	3B	CIN	AA	2-8	127	498	70	124	12	6	1		.249	19	151	73	48-49
1888	3B	CIN	AA	4-8	136	551	68	147	14	5	3	67	.267	5	180	91	36-47
1889	3B	CIN	AA	4-8	123	486	67	127	23	6	0	63	.261	18	162	82	46-51
1892	3B	SL	NL	11-12	1	3	0	1	0	0	0	0	.333	1	1	—	—
MAJOR LEAGUE TOTALS					1118	4638	720	1201	142	47	18		.259	121	1491	91	11 yrs

John Charles Rowe
5'8 170 lbs Batted left

Born Dec 8, 1856 Harrisburg, PA
Died Apr 25, 1911 St Louis, MO

YR	POS	TEAM	LG	FIN	G	AB	R	H	2B	3B	HR	RBI	AVG	BB	TB	OQ	RANK
1879	C-RF	BUF	NL	3-8	8	34	8	12	1	0	0	8	.353	0	13	—	—
1880	C-RF	BUF	NL	7-8	79	326	43	82	10	6	1	36	.252	6	107	100	35-58
1881	C-SS	BUF	NL	3-8	64	246	30	82	11	11	1	43	.333	1	118	141	—
1882	C-SS	BUF	NL	3-8	75	308	43	82	14	5	1	42	.266	12	109	105	30-57
1883	C-LF	BUF	NL	5-8	87	374	65	104	18	7	1	38	.278	15	139	106	28-60
1884	C-LF	BUF	NL	3-8	93	400	85	126	14	14	4	61	.315	23	180	141	12-54
1885	SS-C	BUF	NL	7-8	98	421	62	122	28	8	2	51	.290	13	172	123	18-46
1886	SS	DET	NL	2-8	111	468	97	142	21	9	6	87	.303	26	199	126	12-48
1887	SS	DET	NL	1-8	124	537	135	171	30	10	6	96	.318	39	239	122	16-49
1888	SS	DET	NL	5-8	105	451	62	125	19	8	2	74	.277	19	166	113	20-46
1889	SS	PIT	NL	5-8	75	317	57	82	14	3	2	32	.259	22	108	89	—
1890	SS	BUF	PL	8-8	125	504	77	126	22	7	2	76	.250	48	168	85	48-57
MAJOR LEAGUE TOTALS					1044	4386	764	1256	202	88	28	644	.286	224	1718	113	9 yrs

Michael Joseph Hornung   Born Jun 12, 1857   Carthage, NY
5'8 164 lbs Batted right   Died Oct 30, 1931   Howard Beach, NY

YR	POS	TEAM	LG	FIN	G	AB	R	H	2B	3B	HR	RBI	AVG	BB	TB	OQ	RANK
1879	LF	BUF	NL	3-8	78	319	46	85	18	7	0	38	.266	2	117	108	27-62
1880	LF-1B	BUF	NL	7-8	85	342	47	91	8	11	1	42	.266	8	124	113	22-58
1881	LF	BOS	NL	6-8	83	324	40	78	12	8	2	25	.241	5	112	93	37-56
1882	LF	BOS	NL	3-8	85	388	67	117	14	11	1	50	.302	2	156	115	19-57
1883	LF	BOS	NL	1-8	98	446	107	124	25	13	8	66	.278	8	199	119	20-60
1884	LF	BOS	NL	2-8	115	518	119	139	27	10	7	51	.268	17	207	113	23-54
1885	LF	BOS	NL	5-8	25	109	14	22	4	1	1	7	.202	1	31	73	—
1886	LF	BOS	NL	5-8	94	424	67	109	12	2	2	40	.257	10	131	82	43-48
1887	LF	BOS	NL	5-8	98	437	85	118	10	6	5	49	.270	17	155	86	43-49
1888	LF	BOS	NL	4-8	107	431	61	103	11	7	3	53	.239	16	137	93	32-46
1889	LF	BAL	AA	5-8	135	533	73	122	13	9	1	78	.229	22	156	71	51-51
1890	LF-1B	NY	NL	6-8	120	513	62	122	18	5	0	65	.238	12	150	70	46-48

MAJOR LEAGUE TOTALS   1123 4784 788 1230 172 90 31 564 .257 120 1675 97 11 yrs

William Aloysius Purcell   Born Mar 16, 1854   Paterson, NJ
5'9 159 lbs Batted right   Died Feb 20, 1912   Trenton, NJ

YR	POS	TEAM	LG	FIN	G	AB	R	H	2B	3B	HR	RBI	AVG	BB	TB	OQ	RANK
1879	RF-P	SY/CN	NL	7/5	75	327	42	83	6	3	0	29	.254	3	95	86	43-62
1880	CF-P	CIN	NL	8-8	77	325	48	95	13	6	1	24	.292	5	123	120	16-58
1881	LF-P	CL/BF	NL	7/3	50	193	18	47	9	3	0	21	.244	13	62	100	—
1882	LF	BUF	NL	3-8	84	380	79	105	18	6	2	40	.276	14	141	111	25-57
1883	3B-LF	PHI	NL	8-8	97	425	70	114	20	5	1	32	.268	13	147	95	37-60
1884	LF	PHI	NL	6-8	103	428	67	108	11	7	1	31	.252	29	136	98	33-54
1885	LF	PHI	AA	4-8	66	304	71	90	15	5	0		.296	16	115	121	—
1885	LF	BOS	NL	5-8	21	87	9	19	1	1	0	3	.218	3	22	—	—
1886	LF	BAL	AA	8-8	26	85	17	19	0	1	0		.224	17	21	108	—
1887	RF	BAL	AA	3-8	140	567	101	142	25	8	4		.250	46	195	91	44-49
1888	RF	BA/PH	AA	5/3	119	472	63	107	12	5	2	45	.227	32	135	91	38-47
1889	RF	PHI	AA	3-8	129	507	72	160	19	7	0	85	.316	50	193	115	13-51
1890	LF	PHI	AA	7-8	110	463	110	128	28	3	2		.276	43	168	109	24-42

MAJOR LEAGUE TOTALS   1097 4563 767 1217 177 60 13   .267 284 1553 102 9 yrs

William B Phillips
202 lbs Batted right

Born 1857   St John, NB
Died Oct 7, 1900   Chicago, IL

YR	POS	TEAM	LG	FIN	G	AB	R	H	2B	3B	HR	RBI	AVG	BB	TB	OQ	RANK
1879	1B-C	CLE	NL	6-8	81	365	58	99	15	4	0	29	.271	2	122	99	32-62
1880	1B	CLE	NL	3-8	85	334	41	85	14	10	1	36	.254	6	122	111	25-58
1881	1B	CLE	NL	7-8	85	357	51	97	18	10	1	44	.272	5	138	107	29-56
1882	1B	CLE	NL	5-8	78	335	40	87	17	7	4	47	.260	7	130	108	26-57
1883	1B	CLE	NL	4-8	97	382	42	94	29	8	2	40	.246	8	145	98	36-60
1884	1B	CLE	NL	7-8	111	464	58	128	25	12	3	46	.276	18	186	116	21-54
1885	1B	BRO	AA	5-8	99	391	65	118	16	11	3		.302	27	165	139	8-49
1886	1B	BRO	AA	3-8	141	585	68	160	26	15	0		.274	33	216	110	24-48
1887	1B	BRO	AA	6-8	132	533	82	142	34	11	2		.266	45	204	102	31-49
1888	1B	KC	AA	8-8	129	509	57	120	20	10	1	56	.236	27	163	97	32-47

MAJOR LEAGUE TOTALS | | | | | 1038 | 4255 | 562 | 1130 | 214 | 98 | 17 | | .266 | 178 | 1591 | 109 | 10 yrs

Abram Harding Richardson
5'9 170 lbs Batted right

Born Apr 21, 1855 Clarksboro, NJ
Died Jan 14, 1931   Utica, NY

YR	POS	TEAM	LG	FIN	G	AB	R	H	2B	3B	HR	RBI	AVG	BB	TB	OQ	RANK
1879	3B	BUF	NL	3-8	79	336	54	95	18	10	0	37	.283	16	133	131	11-62
1880	3B	BUF	NL	7-8	83	343	48	89	18	8	0	17	.259	14	123	116	19-58
1881	CF	BUF	NL	3-8	83	344	62	100	18	9	2	53	.291	12	142	123	14-56
1882	2B	BUF	NL	3-8	83	354	61	96	20	8	2	57	.271	11	138	114	21-57
1883	2B	BUF	NL	5-8	92	399	73	124	34	7	1	56	.311	22	175	133	11-60
1884	2B-CF	BUF	NL	3-8	102	439	85	132	27	9	6	60	.301	22	195	135	15-54
1885	2B-CF	BUF	NL	7-8	96	426	90	136	19	11	6	44	.319	20	195	147	9-46
1886	LF-2B	DET	NL	2-8	125	538	125	189	27	11	11	61	.351	46	271	165	6-48
1887	2B-LF	DET	NL	1-8	120	543	131	178	25	18	8	94	.328	31	263	129	12-49
1888	2B	DET	NL	5-8	58	266	60	77	18	2	6	32	.289	17	117	142	—
1889	2B-LF	BOS	NL	2-8	132	536	122	163	33	10	6	79	.304	48	234	122	16-53
1890	LF	BOS	PL	1-8	130	555	126	181	26	14	13	146	.326	52	274	130	12-57
1891	LF-3B	BOS	AA	1-8	74	278	45	71	9	4	7	52	.255	40	109	118	—
1892	2B-LF	WA/NY	NL	10/8	74	285	38	57	11	5	2	34	.200	26	84	86	—

MAJOR LEAGUE TOTALS | | | | | 1331 | 5642 | 1120 | 1688 | 303 | 126 | 70 | 822 | .299 | 377 | 2453 | 131 | 11 yrs

Charles Marvin Smith   Born Oct 12, 1856 Digby, NS
5'11 170 lbs Batted right   Died Apr 18, 1927 Boston, MA

YR	POS	TEAM	LG	FIN	G	AB	R	H	2B	3B	HR	RBI	AVG	BB	TB	OQ	RANK
1880	2B	CIN	NL	8-8	83	334	35	69	10	9	0	27	.207	6	97	84	47-58
1881	3B-CF	Cl/Bf/Wo	NL	7/3/8	24	86	5	7	0	0	0	6	.081	6	7	—	—
1882	SS-CF	BA/LO	AA	6/3	4	14	1	2	0	0	0		.143	0	2	—	—
1883	2B-3B	COL	AA	6-8	97	405	82	106	14	17	4		.262	22	166	126	9-56
1884	2B	COL	AA	2-12	108	445	78	106	18	10	6		.238	20	162	111	28-59
1885	2B	PIT	AA	3-8	106	453	85	113	11	13	0		.249	25	150	102	28-49
1886	SS-2B	PIT	AA	2-8	126	483	75	105	20	9	2		.217	42	149	94	35-48
1887	2B-SS	PIT	NL	6-8	122	456	69	98	12	7	2	54	.215	30	130	72	48-49
1888	SS-2B	PIT	NL	6-8	131	481	61	99	15	2	4	52	.206	22	130	80	42-46
1889	SS	PT/BO	NL	5/2	131	466	47	108	23	6	5	59	.232	47	158	93	39-53
1890	2B	BOS	NL	5-8	134	463	82	106	16	12	1	53	.229	80	149	108	31-48
1891	2B-SS	WAS	AA	8-8	27	90	13	16	2	2	0	13	.178	13	22	78	—

MAJOR LEAGUE TOTALS   1093 4176 633 935 141 87 24   .224 313 1322 97 9 yrs

George A Wood   Born Nov 9, 1858 Boston, MA
5'10 175 lbs Batted left   Died Apr 4, 1924 Harrisburg, PA

YR	POS	TEAM	LG	FIN	G	AB	R	H	2B	3B	HR	RBI	AVG	BB	TB	OQ	RANK
1880	LF	WOR	NL	5-8	81	327	37	80	16	5	0	28	.245	10	106	101	34-58
1881	LF	DET	NL	4-8	80	337	54	100	18	9	2	32	.297	19	142	132	9-56
1882	LF	DET	NL	6-8	84	375	69	101	12	12	7	29	.269	14	158	123	16-57
1883	LF	DET	NL	7-8	99	441	81	133	26	11	5	47	.302	25	196	133	10-60
1884	LF	DET	NL	8-8	114	473	79	119	16	10	8	29	.252	39	179	117	20-54
1885	LF-3B	DET	NL	6-8	82	362	62	105	19	8	5	28	.290	13	155	130	15-46
1886	LF	PHI	NL	4-8	106	450	81	123	18	15	4	50	.273	23	183	115	18-48
1887	LF	PHI	NL	2-8	113	491	118	142	22	19	14	66	.289	40	244	130	10-49
1888	LF	PHI	NL	3-8	106	433	67	99	19	6	6	15	.229	39	148	112	21-46
1889	LF	PHI	NL	4-8	97	422	77	106	21	4	5	53	.251	53	150	104	28-53
1889	RF	BAL	AA	5-8	3	10	1	2	0	0	0	1	.200	0	2	—	—
1890	LF	PHI	PL	5-8	132	539	115	156	20	14	9	102	.289	51	231	110	30-57
1891	LF	PHI	AA	4-8	132	528	105	163	18	14	3	61	.309	72	218	131	11-48
1892	RF-LF	BA/CN	NL	12/5	51	183	19	38	3	5	0	24	.208	20	51	87	—

MAJOR LEAGUE TOTALS   1280 5371 965 1467 228 132 68 565 .273 418 2163 120 12 yrs

Frederick C Dunlap
5'8 165 lbs Batted right

Born May 21, 1859 Philadelphia, PA
Died Dec 1, 1902 Philadelphia, PA

YR	POS	TEAM	LG	FIN	G	AB	R	H	2B	3B	HR	RBI	AVG	BB	TB	OQ	RANK
1880	2B	CLE	NL	3-8	85	373	61	103	27	9	4	30	.276	7	160	133	10-58
1881	2B	CLE	NL	7-8	80	351	60	114	25	4	3	24	.325	18	156	143	5-56
1882	2B	CLE	NL	5-8	84	364	68	102	19	4	0	28	.280	23	129	114	20-57
1883	2B	CLE	NL	4-8	93	396	81	129	34	2	4	37	.326	22	179	139	9-60
1884	2B	SL	UA	1-8	101	449	160	185	39	8	13		.412	29	279	249	1-33
1885	2B	SL	NL	8-8	106	423	70	114	11	5	2	25	.270	41	141	117	21-46
1886	2B	SL/DE	NL	6/2	122	481	85	132	23	5	7	69	.274	44	186	120	16-48
1887	2B	DET	NL	1-8	65	272	60	72	13	10	5	45	.265	25	120	116	—
1888	2B	PIT	NL	6-8	82	321	41	84	12	4	1	36	.262	16	107	104	—
1889	2B	PIT	NL	5-8	121	451	59	106	19	0	2	65	.235	46	131	83	48-53
1890	2B	PIT	NL	8-8	17	64	9	11	1	1	0	3	.172	7	14	—	—
1890	2B	NY	PL	3-8	1	4	1	2	0	0	0	0	.500	0	2	—	—
1891	2B	WAS	AA	8-8	8	25	4	5	1	1	0	4	.200	5	8	—	—

MAJOR LEAGUE TOTALS   965 3974 759 1159 224 53 41   .292 283 1612 137   8 yrs

Edward Hugh Hanlon
5'9 170 lbs Batted left

Born Aug 22, 1857 Montville, CT
Died Apr 14, 1937 Baltimore, MD

YR	POS	TEAM	LG	FIN	G	AB	R	H	2B	3B	HR	RBI	AVG	BB	TB	OQ	RANK
1880	LF	CLE	NL	3-8	73	280	30	69	10	3	0	32	.246	11	85	98	36-58
1881	CF	DET	NL	4-8	76	305	63	85	14	8	2	28	.279	22	121	126	11-56
1882	CF	DET	NL	6-8	82	347	68	80	18	6	5	38	.231	26	125	111	23-57
1883	CF	DET	NL	7-8	100	413	65	100	13	2	1	40	.242	34	120	91	42-60
1884	CF	DET	NL	8-8	114	450	86	119	18	6	5	39	.264	40	164	117	19-54
1885	CF	DET	NL	6-8	105	424	93	128	18	8	1	29	.302	47	165	142	11-46
1886	CF	DET	NL	2-8	126	494	105	116	6	6	4	60	.235	57	146	98	31-48
1887	CF	DET	NL	1-8	118	471	79	129	13	7	4	69	.274	30	168	93	38-49
1888	CF	DET	NL	5-8	109	459	64	122	6	8	5	39	.266	15	159	103	24-46
1889	CF	PIT	NL	5-8	116	461	81	110	14	10	2	37	.239	58	150	96	35-53
1890	CF	PIT	PL	6-8	118	472	106	131	16	6	1	44	.278	80	162	106	34-57
1891	CF	PIT	NL	8-8	119	455	87	121	12	8	0	60	.266	48	149	100	34-52
1892	LF	BAL	NL	12-12	11	43	3	7	1	1	0	2	.163	3	10	—	—

MAJOR LEAGUE TOTALS   1267 5074 930 1317 159 79 30 517 .260 471 1724 107 12 yrs

John Good Reilly   Born Oct 5, 1858   Cincinnati, OH
6'3   178 lbs   Batted right   Died May 31, 1937   Cincinnati, OH

YR	POS	TEAM	LG	FIN	G	AB	R	H	2B	3B	HR	RBI	AVG	BB	TB	OQ	RANK
1880	1B	CIN	NL	8-8	73	272	21	56	8	4	0	16	.206	3	72	75	52-58
1883	1B	CIN	AA	3-8	98	437	103	136	21	14	9		.311	9	212	147	5-56
1884	1B	CIN	AA	5-12	105	448	114	152	24	19	11		.339	5	247	175	2-59
1885	1B	CIN	AA	2-8	111	482	92	143	18	11	5		.297	11	198	122	12-49
1886	1B	CIN	AA	5-8	115	441	92	117	12	11	6		.265	31	169	115	19-48
1887	1B	CIN	AA	2-8	134	551	106	170	35	14	10		.309	22	263	120	15-49
1888	1B	CIN	AA	4-8	127	527	112	169	28	14	13	103	.321	17	264	155	3-47
1889	1B	CIN	AA	4-8	111	427	84	111	24	13	5	66	.260	34	176	109	23-51
1890	1B	CIN	NL	4-8	133	553	114	166	25	26	6	86	.300	16	261	121	17-48
1891	1B	CIN	NL	7-8	135	546	60	132	20	13	4	64	.242	9	190	82	47-52
MAJOR LEAGUE TOTALS					1142	4684	898	1352	215	139	69		.289	157	2052	122	10 yrs

Roger Connor   Born Jul 1, 1857   Waterbury, CT
6'3   220 lbs   Batted left   Died Jan 4, 1931   Waterbury, CT

YR	POS	TEAM	LG	FIN	G	AB	R	H	2B	3B	HR	RBI	AVG	BB	TB	OQ	RANK
1880	3B	TRO	NL	4-8	83	340	53	113	18	8	3	47	.332	13	156	160	2-59
1881	1B	TRO	NL	5-8	85	367	55	107	17	6	2	31	.292	15	142	118	19-56
1882	1B-CF	TRO	NL	7-8	81	349	65	115	22	18	4	42	.330	13	185	166	4-57
1883	1B	NY	NL	6-8	98	409	80	146	28	15	1	50	.357	25	207	163	2-60
1884	2B-CF	NY	NL	4-8	116	477	98	151	28	4	4	82	.317	38	199	138	13-54
1885	1B	NY	NL	2-8	110	455	102	169	23	15	1	65	.371	51	225	192	2-46
1886	1B	NY	NL	3-8	118	485	105	172	29	20	7	71	.355	41	262	176	4-48
1887	1B	NY	NL	4-8	127	471	113	134	26	22	17	104	.285	75	255	157	4-49
1888	1B	NY	NL	1-8	134	481	98	140	15	17	14	71	.291	73	231	178	2-46
1889	1B	NY	NL	1-8	131	496	117	157	32	17	13	130	.317	93	262	169	2-53
1890	1B	NY	PL	3-8	123	484	133	169	24	15	14	103	.349	88	265	167	1-57
1891	1B	NY	NL	3-8	129	479	112	139	29	13	7	94	.290	83	215	149	4-52
1892	1B	PHI	NL	4-12	155	564	123	166	37	11	12	73	.294	116	261	169	1-72
1893	1B	NY	NL	5-12	135	511	111	156	25	8	11	105	.305	91	230	134	11-80
1894	1B	NY/SL	NL	2/9	121	462	93	146	35	25	8	93	.316	59	255	128	16-77
1895	1B	SL	NL	11-12	103	398	78	131	29	9	8	77	.329	63	202	143	10-75
1896	1B	SL	NL	11-12	126	483	71	137	21	9	11	72	.284	52	209	113	29-73
1897	1B	SL	NL	12-12	22	83	13	19	3	1	1	12	.229	13	27	—	—
MAJOR LEAGUE TOTALS					1997	7794	1620	2467	441	233	138	1322	.317	1002	3788	154	17 yrs

Peter Patrick Gillespie   Born Nov 30, 1851 Carbondale, PA
6'1 178 lbs Batted left   Died May 5, 1910 Carbondale, PA

YR	POS	TEAM	LG	FIN	G	AB	R	H	2B	3B	HR	RBI	AVG	BB	TB	OQ	RANK
1880	LF	TRO	NL	4-8	82	346	50	84	20	5	2	24	.243	17	120	113	23-58
1881	LF	TRO	NL	5-8	84	348	43	96	14	3	0	41	.276	9	116	96	35-56
1882	LF	TRO	NL	7-8	74	298	46	82	5	4	2	33	.275	9	101	100	35-57
1883	LF	NY	NL	6-8	98	411	64	129	23	12	1	62	.314	9	179	124	17-60
1884	LF	NY	NL	4-8	101	413	75	109	7	4	2	44	.264	19	130	93	38-54
1885	LF	NY	NL	2-8	102	420	67	123	17	6	0	52	.293	15	152	112	25-46
1886	LF	NY	NL	3-8	97	396	65	108	13	8	0	58	.273	16	137	97	32-48
1887	LF	NY	NL	4-8	76	295	40	78	9	3	3	37	.264	12	102	84	—
MAJOR LEAGUE TOTALS					714	2927	450	809	108	45	10	351	.276	106	1037	105	7 yrs

William Ewing   Born Oct 17, 1859 Hoaglands, OH
5'10 188 lbs Batted right   Died Oct 20, 1906 Cincinnati, OH

YR	POS	TEAM	LG	FIN	G	AB	R	H	2B	3B	HR	RBI	AVG	BB	TB	OQ	RANK
1880	C-RF	TRO	NL	4-8	13	45	1	8	1	0	0	5	.178	1	9	—	—
1881	C-SS	TRO	NL	5-8	67	272	40	68	14	7	0	25	.250	7	96	98	34-56
1882	3B-C	TRO	NL	7-8	74	328	67	89	16	11	2	29	.271	10	133	117	18-57
1883	C-CF	NY	NL	6-8	88	376	90	114	11	13	10	41	.303	20	181	142	7-60
1884	C-RF	NY	NL	4-8	94	382	90	106	15	20	3	41	.277	28	170	137	14-54
1885	C-RF	NY	NL	2-8	81	342	81	104	15	12	6	63	.304	13	161	145	10-46
1886	C-CF	NY	NL	3-8	73	275	59	85	11	7	4	31	.309	16	122	132	—
1887	3B-2B	NY	NL	4-8	77	318	83	97	17	13	6	44	.305	30	158	136	—
1888	C-3B	NY	NL	1-8	103	415	83	127	18	15	6	58	.306	24	193	151	6-46
1889	C	NY	NL	1-8	99	407	91	133	23	13	4	87	.327	37	194	136	11-53
1890	C	NY	PL	3-8	83	352	98	119	19	15	8	72	.338	39	192	148	—
1891	2B-C	NY	NL	3-8	14	49	8	17	2	1	0	18	.347	5	21	—	—
1892	1B-C	NY	NL	8-12	105	393	58	122	10	15	8	76	.310	38	186	147	—
1893	RF	CLE	NL	3-12	116	500	117	172	28	15	6	122	.344	41	248	130	14-80
1894	RF	CLE	NL	6-12	53	211	32	53	12	4	2	39	.251	24	79	84	—
1895	1B	CIN	NL	8-12	105	434	90	138	24	13	5	94	.318	30	203	113	31-75
1896	1B	CIN	NL	3-12	69	263	41	73	14	4	1	38	.278	29	98	100	—
1897	1B	CIN	NL	4-12	1	1	0	0	0	0	0	0	.000	0	0	—	—
MAJOR LEAGUE TOTALS					1315	5363	1129	1625	250	178	71	883	.303	392	2444	130	9 yrs

Arthur Wilson Whitney　　　　　Born Jan 16, 1858　Brockton, MA
5'8　155 lbs　Batted right　　　　　Died Aug 15, 1943　Lowell, MA

YR	POS	TEAM	LG	FIN	G	AB	R	H	2B	3B	HR	RBI	AVG	BB	TB	OQ	RANK
1880	3B	WOR	NL	5-8	76	302	38	67	13	5	1	36	.222	9	93	94	37-58
1881	3B	DET	NL	4-8	58	214	23	39	7	5	0	9	.182	7	56	70	—
1882	3B-SS	PR/DE	NL	2/6	42	155	12	24	0	0	0	5	.155	3	24	40	—
1884	3B	PIT	AA	10-12	23	94	10	28	4	0	0		.298	1	32	—	—
1885	SS	PIT	AA	3-8	90	373	53	87	10	4	0		.233	16	105	84	43-49
1886	3B-SS	PIT	AA	2-8	136	511	70	122	13	4	0		.239	51	143	93	36-48
1887	3B	PIT	NL	6-8	119	431	57	112	11	4	0	51	.260	55	131	93	36-49
1888	3B	NY	NL	1-8	90	328	28	72	1	4	1	28	.220	8	84	72	—
1889	3B	NY	NL	1-8	129	473	71	103	12	2	1	59	.218	56	122	78	51-53
1890	3B-SS	NY	PL	3-8	119	442	71	97	12	3	0	45	.219	64	115	77	53-57
1891	3B	CN/SL	AA	5/2	96	358	42	69	6	1	3	33	.193	32	86	67	—
MAJOR LEAGUE TOTALS					978	3681	475	820	89	32	6		.223	302	991	87	6 yrs

Walter Arlington Latham　　　　Born Mar 15, 1860　West Lebanon, NH
5'8　150 lbs　Batted right　　　　　Died Nov 29, 1952　Garden City, NJ

YR	POS	TEAM	LG	FIN	G	AB	R	H	2B	3B	HR	RBI	AVG	BB	TB	OQ	RANK
1880	SS-RF	BUF	NL	7-8	22	79	9	10	3	1	0	3	.127	1	15	—	—
1883	3B	SL	AA	2-8	98	406	86	96	12	7	0		.236	18	122	91	41-56
1884	3B	SL	AA	4-12	110	474	115	130	17	12	1		.274	19	174	116	24-59
1885	3B	SL	AA	1-8	110	485	84	100	15	3	1		.206	18	124	73	49-49
1886	3B	SL	AA	1-8	134	578	152	174	23	8	1		.301	55	216	125	13-48
1887	3B	SL	AA	1-8	136	627	163	198	35	10	2		.316	45	259	114	20-49
1888	3B	SL	AA	1-8	133	570	119	151	19	5	2	31	.265	43	186	108	24-47
1889	3B	SL	AA	2-8	118	512	110	126	13	3	4	49	.246	42	157	85	45-51
1890	3B	CHI	PL	4-8	52	214	47	49	7	2	1	20	.229	22	63	77	—
1890	3B	CIN	NL	4-8	41	164	35	41	6	2	0	15	.250	23	51	102	—
1891	3B	CIN	NL	7-8	135	533	119	145	20	10	7	53	.272	74	206	123	14-52
1892	3B	CIN	NL	5-12	152	622	111	148	20	4	0	44	.238	60	176	89	56-72
1893	3B	CIN	NL	6-12	127	531	101	150	18	6	2	49	.282	62	186	96	54-80
1894	3B	CIN	NL	10-12	129	524	129	164	23	6	4	60	.313	60	211	97	51-77
1895	3B	CIN	NL	8-12	112	460	93	143	14	6	2	69	.311	42	175	98	44-75
1896	3B	SL	NL	11-12	8	35	3	7	0	0	0	5	.200	4	7	—	—
1899	2B-LF	WAS	NL	11-12	6	6	1	1	0	0	0	0	.167	1	1	—	—
1909	2B	NY	NL	3-8	4	2	1	0	0	0	0	0	.000	0	0	—	—
MAJOR LEAGUE TOTALS					1627	6822	1478	1833	245	85	27		.269	589	2329	101	12 yrs

Thomas Everett Burns
5'7   152 lbs   Batted right

Born Mar 30, 1857 Honesdale, PA
Died Mar 19, 1902 Jersey City, NJ

YR	POS	TEAM	LG	FIN	G	AB	R	H	2B	3B	HR	RBI	AVG	BB	TB	OQ	RANK
1880	SS-3B	CHI	NL	1-8	85	333	47	103	17	3	0	43	.309	12	126	129	12-58
1881	SS	CHI	NL	1-8	84	342	41	95	20	3	4	42	.278	14	133	116	22-56
1882	2B-SS	CHI	NL	1-8	84	355	55	88	23	6	0	48	.248	15	123	102	33-57
1883	SS-2B	CHI	NL	2-8	97	405	69	119	37	7	2	67	.294	13	176	122	18-60
1884	SS	CHI	NL	4-8	83	343	54	84	14	2	7	44	.245	13	123	100	32-54
1885	SS	CHI	NL	1-8	111	445	82	121	23	9	7	71	.272	16	183	122	19-46
1886	3B	CHI	NL	1-8	112	445	64	123	18	10	3	65	.276	14	170	104	25-48
1887	3B	CHI	NL	3-8	115	424	57	112	20	10	3	60	.264	34	161	100	35-49
1888	3B	CHI	NL	2-8	134	483	60	115	12	6	3	70	.238	26	148	95	31-46
1889	3B	CHI	NL	3-8	136	525	64	127	27	6	4	66	.242	32	178	85	44-53
1890	3B	CHI	NL	2-8	139	538	86	149	17	6	5	86	.277	57	193	108	30-48
1891	3B	CHI	NL	2-8	59	243	36	55	8	1	1	17	.226	21	68	80	—
1892	3B-RF	PIT	NL	6-12	12	39	7	8	0	0	0	4	.205	3	8	—	—

MAJOR LEAGUE TOTALS					1251	4920	722	1299	236	69	39	683	.264	270	1790	108	11 yrs

Arthur Albert Irwin
5'8   158 lbs   Batted left

Born Feb 14, 1858 Toronto, ON
Died Jul 16, 1921 Atlantic Ocean

YR	POS	TEAM	LG	FIN	G	AB	R	H	2B	3B	HR	RBI	AVG	BB	TB	OQ	RANK
1880	SS	WOR	NL	5-8	85	352	53	91	19	4	1	35	.259	11	121	109	26-58
1881	SS	WOR	NL	8-8	50	206	27	55	8	2	0	24	.267	7	67	95	—
1882	3B-SS	WOR	NL	8-8	84	333	30	73	12	4	0	30	.219	14	93	81	51-57
1883	SS	PRO	NL	3-8	98	406	67	116	22	7	0	44	.286	12	152	105	30-60
1884	SS	PRO	NL	1-8	102	404	73	97	14	3	2	44	.240	28	123	94	37-54
1885	SS	PRO	NL	4-8	59	218	16	39	2	1	0	14	.179	14	43	63	—
1886	SS	PHI	NL	4-8	101	373	51	87	6	6	0	34	.233	35	105	89	41-48
1887	SS	PHI	NL	2-8	100	374	65	95	14	8	2	56	.254	48	131	103	32-49
1888	SS	PHI	NL	3-8	125	448	51	98	12	4	0	28	.219	33	118	86	39-46
1889	SS	PHI/WA	NL	4/8	103	386	58	89	15	5	0	42	.231	48	114	88	42-53
1890	SS	BOS	PL	1-8	96	354	60	92	17	1	0	45	.260	57	111	96	41-57
1891	SS	BOS	AA	1-8	6	17	1	2	0	0	0	0	.118	2	2	—	—
1894	SS	PHI	NL	4-12	1	0	0	0	0	0	0	0	—	0	0	—	—

MAJOR LEAGUE TOTALS					1010	3871	552	934	141	45	5	396	.241	309	1180	95	9 yrs

Joseph John Sommer　　　　　　　　Born Nov 20, 1858　Covington, KY
Batted right　　　　　　　　　　　　Died Jan 16, 1938　Cincinnati, OH

YR	POS	TEAM	LG	FIN	G	AB	R	H	2B	3B	HR	RBI	AVG	BB	TB	OQ	RANK
1880	LF-CF	CIN	NL	8-8	24	88	10	16	1	0	0	6	.182	0	17	—	—
1882	LF	CIN	AA	1-6	80	354	82	102	12	6	1		.288	24	129	132	7-37
1883	LF	CIN	AA	3-8	97	413	79	115	5	7	3		.278	20	143	110	22-56
1884	3B	BAL	AA	6-12	107	479	96	129	11	10	4		.269	8	172	106	33-59
1885	LF	BAL	AA	8-8	110	471	84	118	23	6	1		.251	24	156	101	29-49
1886	LF-2B	BAL	AA	8-8	139	560	79	117	18	4	1		.209	24	146	72	47-48
1887	LF-2B	BAL	AA	3-8	131	463	88	123	11	5	0		.266	63	144	98	36-49
1888	LF-SS	BAL	AA	5-8	79	297	31	65	10	0	0	35	.219	18	75	79	—
1889	RF	BAL	AA	5-8	106	386	51	85	13	2	1	36	.220	42	105	80	48-51
1890	LF-P	CLE	NL	7-8	9	35	4	8	1	0	0	0	.229	2	9	—	—
1890	LF	BAL	AA	8-8	38	129	13	33	4	2	0		.256	13	41	97	—
MAJOR LEAGUE TOTALS					920	3675	617	911	109	42	11		.248	238	1137	100	7 yrs

Thomas John Esterbrook　　　　　　Born Jun 20, 1857　Staten Island, NY
5'11　167 lbs　Batted right　　　　　Died Apr 30, 1901　Middletown, NY

YR	POS	TEAM	LG	FIN	G	AB	R	H	2B	3B	HR	RBI	AVG	BB	TB	OQ	RANK
1880	1B-CF	BUF	NL	7-8	64	253	20	61	12	1	0	35	.241	0	75	84	46-58
1882	LF	CLE	NL	5-8	45	179	13	44	4	3	0	19	.246	5	54	86	—
1883	3B	NY	AA	4-8	97	407	55	103	9	7	0		.253	15	126	93	37-56
1884	3B	NY	AA	1-12	112	477	110	150	29	11	1		.314	12	204	136	9-59
1885	3B	NY	NL	2-8	88	359	48	92	14	5	2	44	.256	4	122	94	34-46
1886	3B	NY	NL	3-8	123	473	62	125	20	6	3	43	.264	8	166	91	40-48
1887	1B-RF	NY	AA	7-8	26	101	11	17	1	0	0		.168	6	18	46	—
1888	1B	IND	NL	7-8	64	246	21	54	8	0	0	17	.220	2	62	67	—
1888	1B	LOU	AA	7-8	23	93	9	21	6	0	0	7	.226	3	27	—	—
1889	1B-RF	LOU	AA	8-8	11	44	8	14	3	0	0	9	.318	5	17	—	—
1890	1B	NY	NL	6-8	45	197	29	57	14	1	0	29	.289	10	73	100	—
1891	RF-2B	BRO	NL	6-8	3	8	1	3	0	0	0	0	.375	0	3	—	—
MAJOR LEAGUE TOTALS					701	2837	387	741	120	34	6		.261	70	947	100	5 yrs

Harry Duffield Stovey　　　　　　　Born Dec 20, 1856　Philadelphia, PA
5'11　175 lbs　Batted right　　　　　　Died Sep 20, 1937　New Bedford, MA

YR	POS	TEAM	LG	FIN	G	AB	R	H	2B	3B	HR	RBI	AVG	BB	TB	OQ	RANK
1880	CF-1B	WOR	NL	5-8	83	355	76	94	21	14	6	28	.265	12	161	143	8-58
1881	1B-RF	WOR	NL	8-8	75	341	57	92	25	7	2	30	.270	12	137	116	21-56
1882	1B-LF	WOR	NL	8-8	84	360	90	104	13	10	5	26	.289	22	152	134	9-57
1883	1B	PHI	AA	1-8	94	421	110	127	31	6	14		.302	26	212	163	2-56
1884	1B	PHI	AA	7-12	104	448	124	146	22	23	10		.326	26	244	184	1-59
1885	1B-CF	PHI	AA	4-8	112	486	130	153	27	9	13		.315	39	237	164	4-49
1886	1B-CF	PHI	AA	6-8	123	489	115	144	28	11	7		.294	64	215	151	3-48
1887	CF-1B	PHI	AA	5-8	124	497	125	142	31	12	4		.286	56	209	120	16-49
1888	LF-1B	PHI	AA	3-8	130	530	127	152	25	20	9	65	.287	62	244	160	1-47
1889	LF	PHI	AA	3-8	137	556	152	171	38	13	19	119	.308	77	292	157	1-51
1890	RF	BOS	PL	1-8	118	481	142	143	25	12	12	85	.297	81	228	136	7-57
1891	RF	BOS	NL	1-8	134	544	118	152	31	20	16	95	.279	78	271	151	3-52
1892	LF	BO/BA	NL	1/12	112	429	79	101	22	12	4	67	.235	54	159	116	26-72
1893	LF-CF	BA/BR	NL	8/6	56	201	47	48	8	6	1	34	.239	52	71	119	—

MAJOR LEAGUE TOTALS					1486	6138	1492	1769	347	175	122		.288	661	2832	146	13 yrs

Cyrus Edward Swartwood　　　　　　Born Jan 12, 1859　Rockford, IL
Batted left　　　　　　　　　　　　　Died May 15, 1924　Pittsburgh, PA

YR	POS	TEAM	LG	FIN	G	AB	R	H	2B	3B	HR	RBI	AVG	BB	TB	OQ	RANK
1881	RF	BUF	NL	3-8	1	3	0	1	0	0	0	0	.333	1	1	—	—
1882	RF	PIT	AA	4-6	76	325	86	107	18	11	4		.329	21	159	179	2-37
1883	1B-RF	PIT	AA	7-8	94	413	86	147	24	8	3		.356	24	196	166	1-56
1884	RF-1B	PIT	AA	10-12	102	399	74	115	19	6	0		.288	33	146	130	16-59
1885	LF-RF	BRO	AA	5-8	99	399	80	106	8	9	0		.266	36	132	113	18-49
1886	RF	BRO	AA	3-8	122	471	95	132	13	10	3		.280	70	174	135	7-48
1887	RF	BRO	AA	6-8	91	363	72	92	14	8	1		.253	46	125	101	—
1890	RF	TOL	AA	4-8	126	462	106	151	23	11	3		.327	80	205	158	2-42
1892	RF	PIT	NL	6-12	13	42	8	10	1	0	0	4	.238	13	11	—	—

MAJOR LEAGUE TOTALS					724	2877	607	861	120	63	14		.299	324	1149	147	6 yrs

Samuel Washington Wise   Born Aug 18, 1857 Akron, OH
5'10   175 lbs   Batted left   Died Jan 22, 1910   Akron, OH

YR	POS	TEAM	LG	FIN	G	AB	R	H	2B	3B	HR	RBI	AVG	BB	TB	OQ	RANK
1881	3B	DET	NL	4-8	1	4	0	2	0	0	0	0	.500	0	2	—	—
1882	SS	BOS	NL	3-8	78	298	44	66	11	4	4	34	.221	5	97	86	46-57
1883	SS	BOS	NL	1-8	96	406	73	110	25	7	4	58	.271	13	161	109	25-60
1884	SS	BOS	NL	2-8	114	426	60	91	15	9	4	41	.214	25	136	92	41-54
1885	SS-2B	BOS	NL	5-8	107	424	71	120	20	10	4	46	.283	25	172	129	17-46
1886	1B-2B	BOS	NL	5-8	96	387	71	112	19	12	4	72	.289	33	167	132	10-48
1887	SS-RF	BOS	NL	5-8	113	467	103	156	27	17	9	92	.334	36	244	144	5-49
1888	SS	BOS	NL	4-8	105	417	66	100	19	12	4	40	.240	34	155	119	14-46
1889	2B-SS	WAS	NL	8-8	121	472	79	118	15	8	4	62	.250	61	161	101	30-53
1890	2B	BUF	PL	8-8	119	505	95	148	29	11	6	102	.293	46	217	110	29-57
1891	2B	BAL	AA	3-8	103	388	70	96	14	5	1	48	.247	62	123	104	29-48
1893	2B-3B	WAS	NL	12-12	122	521	102	162	27	17	5	77	.311	49	238	118	27-80
MAJOR LEAGUE TOTALS					1175	4715	834	1281	221	112	49	672	.272	389	1873	113	11 yrs

Jeremiah Dennis Denny   Born Mar 16, 1859 New York, NY
5'11   180 lbs   Batted right   Died Aug 16, 1927 Houston, TX

YR	POS	TEAM	LG	FIN	G	AB	R	H	2B	3B	HR	RBI	AVG	BB	TB	OQ	RANK
1881	3B	PRO	NL	2-8	85	320	38	77	16	2	1	24	.241	5	100	84	47-56
1882	3B	PRO	NL	2-8	84	329	54	81	10	9	2	42	.246	4	115	94	40-57
1883	3B	PRO	NL	3-8	98	393	73	108	26	8	8	55	.275	9	174	119	21-60
1884	3B	PRO	NL	1-8	110	439	57	109	22	9	6	59	.248	14	167	104	27-54
1885	3B	PRO	NL	5-8	83	318	40	71	14	4	3	24	.223	12	102	92	36-46
1886	3B	SL	NL	6-8	119	475	58	122	24	6	9	62	.257	14	185	103	28-48
1887	3B	IND	NL	8-8	122	510	86	165	34	12	11	97	.324	13	256	125	14-49
1888	3B-SS	IND	NL	7-8	126	524	92	137	27	7	12	63	.261	9	214	115	19-46
1889	3B	IND	NL	7-8	133	578	96	163	24	0	18	112	.282	27	241	104	26-53
1890	3B	NY	NL	6-8	114	437	50	93	18	7	3	42	.213	28	134	79	44-48
1891	3B-1B	NY/Cl/Ph	NL	3/5/4	59	227	22	56	7	1	0	33	.247	16	65	81	—
1893	SS	LOU	NL	11-12	44	175	22	43	5	4	1	22	.246	9	59	76	—
1894	3B	LOU	NL	12-12	60	221	26	61	11	7	0	32	.276	13	86	80	—
MAJOR LEAGUE TOTALS					1237	4946	714	1286	238	76	74	667	.260	173	1898	102	10 yrs

Hugh Nicol
5'4 145 lbs Batted right

Born Jan 1, 1858 Campsie, Scotland
Died Jun 27, 1921 Lafayette, IN

YR	POS	TEAM	LG	FIN	G	AB	R	H	2B	3B	HR	RBI	AVG	BB	TB	OQ	RANK
1881	RF	CHI	NL	1-8	26	108	13	22	2	0	0	7	.204	4	24	63	—
1882	RF-SS	CHI	NL	1-8	47	186	19	37	9	1	1	16	.199	7	51	76	—
1883	RF-2B	SL	AA	2-8	94	368	73	106	13	3	0		.288	18	125	110	23-56
1884	RF-2B	SL	AA	4-12	110	442	79	115	14	5	0		.260	22	139	101	37-59
1885	RF	SL	AA	1-8	112	425	59	88	11	1	0		.207	34	101	79	46-49
1886	RF-SS	SL	AA	1-8	67	253	44	52	6	3	0		.206	26	64	84	—
1887	RF	CIN	AA	2-8	125	475	122	102	18	2	1		.215	86	127	92	43-49
1888	RF	CIN	AA	4-8	135	548	112	131	10	2	1	35	.239	67	148	102	29-47
1889	RF	CIN	AA	4-8	122	474	82	121	7	8	2	58	.255	54	150	95	40-51
1890	RF	CIN	NL	4-8	50	186	28	39	1	4	0	19	.210	19	48	77	—

| MAJOR LEAGUE TOTALS | | | | | 888 | 3465 | 631 | 813 | 91 | 29 | 5 | | .235 | 337 | 977 | 97 | 6 yrs |

Samuel Clifford Carroll
5'8 163 lbs Batted both

Born Oct 18, 1859 Clay Grove, IA
Died Jun 12, 1923 Portland, OR

YR	POS	TEAM	LG	FIN	G	AB	R	H	2B	3B	HR	RBI	AVG	BB	TB	OQ	RANK
1882	RF	PRO	NL	2-8	10	41	4	5	0	0	0	2	.122	0	5	—	—
1883	LF	PRO	NL	3-8	58	238	37	63	12	3	1	20	.265	4	84	93	—
1884	LF	PRO	NL	1-8	113	452	90	118	16	4	3	54	.261	29	151	103	28-54
1885	LF	PRO	NL	4-8	104	426	62	99	12	3	1	40	.232	29	120	91	37-46
1886	LF	WAS	NL	8-8	111	433	73	99	11	6	2	22	.229	44	128	94	38-48
1887	LF	WAS	NL	7-8	103	420	79	104	17	4	4	37	.248	17	141	80	45-49
1888	RF	PIT	NL	6-8	5	20	1	0	0	0	0	0	.000	0	0	—	—
1890	LF	CHI	NL	2-8	136	582	134	166	16	6	7	65	.285	53	215	109	29-48
1891	RF	CHI	NL	2-8	130	515	87	132	20	8	7	80	.256	50	189	106	30-52
1892	LF	SL	NL	11-12	101	407	82	111	14	8	4	49	.273	47	153	120	—
1893	RF	BOS	NL	1-12	120	438	80	98	7	5	2	54	.224	88	121	91	63-80

| MAJOR LEAGUE TOTALS | | | | | 991 | 3972 | 729 | 995 | 125 | 47 | 31 | 423 | .251 | 361 | 1307 | 96 | 7 yrs |

William F Greenwood   Born 1857   Philadelphia, PA
5'7 180 lbs Batted both   Died May 2, 1902 Philadelphia, PA

YR	POS	TEAM	LG	FIN	G	AB	R	H	2B	3B	HR	RBI	AVG	BB	TB	OQ	RANK
1882	RF-2B	PHI	AA	2-6	7	30	8	9	1	0	0		.300	1	10	—	—
1884	2B	BRO	AA	9-12	92	385	52	83	8	3	3		.216	10	106	79	56-59
1887	2B	BAL	AA	3-8	118	495	114	130	16	6	0		.263	54	158	93	40-49
1888	2B-SS	BAL	AA	5-8	115	409	69	78	13	1	0	29	.191	30	93	74	45-47
1889	2B	COL	AA	6-8	118	414	62	93	7	10	3	49	.225	58	129	96	38-51
1890	2B	ROC	AA	5-8	124	437	76	97	11	6	2		.222	48	126	88	36-42
MAJOR LEAGUE TOTALS					574	2170	381	490	56	26	8		.226	201	622	86	5 yrs

John A Stricker   Born Feb 15, 1860 Philadelphia, PA
5'3 138 lbs Batted right   Died Nov 19, 1937 Philadelphia, PA

YR	POS	TEAM	LG	FIN	G	AB	R	H	2B	3B	HR	RBI	AVG	BB	TB	OQ	RANK
1882	2B	PHI	AA	2-6	72	272	34	59	6	1	0		.217	15	67	84	31-37
1883	2B	PHI	AA	1-8	89	330	67	90	8	0	1		.273	19	101	100	33-56
1884	2B	PHI	AA	7-12	107	399	59	92	16	11	1		.231	19	133	102	35-59
1885	2B	PHI	AA	4-8	106	398	71	93	9	3	1		.234	21	111	86	41-49
1887	2B	CLE	AA	8-8	131	534	122	141	19	4	2		.264	53	174	93	42-49
1888	2B	CLE	AA	6-8	127	493	80	115	13	6	1	33	.233	50	143	101	31-47
1889	2B	CLE	NL	6-8	136	566	83	142	10	4	1	47	.251	58	163	84	46-53
1890	2B	CLE	PL	7-8	127	544	93	133	19	8	2	65	.244	54	174	83	50-57
1891	2B	BOS	AA	1-8	139	514	96	111	15	4	0	46	.216	63	134	80	44-48
1892	2B	SL/BA	NL	11/12	103	367	57	91	6	5	3	48	.248	42	116	102	—
1893	2B-RF	WAS	NL	12-12	59	218	28	40	7	1	0	20	.183	20	49	57	—
MAJOR LEAGUE TOTALS					1196	4635	790	1107	128	47	12		.239	414	1365	90	9 yrs

Michael D Muldoon
5'8   165 lbs

Born 1858   Ireland
Date and place of death unknown

YR	POS	TEAM	LG	FIN	G	AB	R	H	2B	3B	HR	RBI	AVG	BB	TB	OQ	RANK
1882	3B-LF	CLE	NL	5-8	84	341	50	84	17	5	6	45	.246	10	129	106	28-57
1883	3B	CLE	NL	4-8	98	378	54	86	22	3	0	29	.228	10	114	79	52-60
1884	3B	CLE	NL	7-8	110	422	46	101	16	6	2	38	.239	18	135	91	42-54
1885	3B	BAL	AA	8-8	102	410	47	103	20	6	2		.251	20	141	104	26-49
1886	2B-3B	BAL	AA	8-8	101	381	57	76	13	8	0		.199	34	105	85	42-48
MAJOR LEAGUE TOTALS					495	1932	254	450	88	28	10		.233	92	624	93	5 yrs

John Alexander McPhee
5'8   152 lbs   Batted right

Born Nov 1, 1859   Massena, NY
Died Jan 3, 1943   San Diego, CA

YR	POS	TEAM	LG	FIN	G	AB	R	H	2B	3B	HR	RBI	AVG	BB	TB	OQ	RANK
1882	2B	CIN	AA	1-6	78	311	43	71	8	7	1		.228	11	96	97	25-37
1883	2B	CIN	AA	3-8	96	367	61	90	10	10	2		.245	18	126	104	27-56
1884	2B	CIN	AA	5-12	112	450	107	125	8	7	5		.278	27	162	120	20-59
1885	2B	CIN	AA	2-8	110	431	78	114	12	4	0		.265	19	134	95	35-49
1886	2B	CIN	AA	5-8	140	560	139	150	23	12	8		.268	59	221	128	11-48
1887	2B	CIN	AA	2-8	129	540	137	156	20	19	2		.289	55	220	115	19-49
1888	2B	CIN	AA	4-8	111	458	88	110	12	10	4	51	.240	43	154	112	20-47
1889	2B	CIN	AA	4-8	135	540	109	145	25	7	5	57	.269	60	199	108	25-51
1890	2B	CIN	NL	4-8	132	528	125	135	16	22	3	39	.256	82	204	123	15-48
1891	2B	CIN	NL	7-8	138	562	107	144	14	16	6	38	.256	74	208	115	25-52
1892	2B	CIN	NL	5-12	144	573	111	157	19	12	4	60	.274	84	212	127	18-72
1893	2B	CIN	NL	6-12	127	491	101	138	17	11	3	68	.281	94	186	117	28-80
1894	2B	CIN	NL	10-12	126	474	107	144	21	9	5	88	.304	90	198	112	32-77
1895	2B	CIN	NL	8-12	115	432	107	129	24	12	1	75	.299	73	180	120	23-75
1896	2B	CIN	NL	3-12	117	433	81	132	18	7	1	87	.305	51	167	108	35-73
1897	2B	CIN	NL	4-12	81	282	45	85	13	7	1	39	.301	35	115	115	—
1898	2B	CIN	NL	3-12	133	486	72	121	26	9	1	60	.249	66	168	109	39-75
1899	2B	CIN	NL	6-12	111	373	60	104	17	7	1	65	.279	40	138	107	—
MAJOR LEAGUE TOTALS					2135	8291	1678	2250	303	188	53		.271	981	3088	113	16 yrs

William G Gleason   Born Nov 12, 1858   St Louis, MO
5'8   170 lbs   Batted right   Died Jul 21, 1932   St Louis, MO

YR	POS	TEAM	LG	FIN	G	AB	R	H	2B	3B	HR	RBI	AVG	BB	TB	OQ	RANK
1882	SS	SL	AA	5-6	79	347	63	100	11	6	1		.288	6	126	116	11-37
1883	SS	SL	AA	2-8	98	425	81	122	21	9	2		.287	16	167	121	13-56
1884	SS	SL	AA	4-12	110	472	97	127	21	7	1		.269	28	165	115	25-59
1885	SS	SL	AA	1-8	112	472	79	119	9	5	3		.252	29	147	99	31-49
1886	SS	SL	AA	1-8	125	524	97	141	18	5	0		.269	43	169	104	29-48
1887	SS	SL	AA	1-8	135	598	135	172	19	1	0		.288	41	193	88	45-49
1888	SS	PHI	AA	3-8	123	499	55	112	10	2	0	61	.224	12	126	71	47-47
1889	SS	LOU	AA	8-8	16	58	6	14	2	0	0	5	.241	4	16	—	—
MAJOR LEAGUE TOTALS					798	3395	613	907	111	35	7		.267	179	1109	102	7 yrs

Charles Albert Comiskey   Born Aug 15, 1859   Chicago, IL
6'0   180 lbs   Batted right   Died Oct 26, 1931   Eagle River, WI

YR	POS	TEAM	LG	FIN	G	AB	R	H	2B	3B	HR	RBI	AVG	BB	TB	OQ	RANK
1882	1B	SL	AA	5-6	78	329	58	80	9	5	1		.243	4	102	92	28-37
1883	1B	SL	AA	2-8	96	401	87	118	17	9	2		.294	11	159	121	14-56
1884	1B	SL	AA	4-12	108	460	76	110	17	6	2		.239	5	145	88	48-59
1885	1B	SL	AA	1-8	83	340	68	87	15	7	2		.256	14	122	106	23-49
1886	1B	SL	AA	1-8	131	578	95	147	15	9	3		.254	10	189	86	41-48
1887	1B	SL	AA	1-8	125	538	139	180	22	5	4		.335	27	224	113	22-49
1888	1B	SL	AA	1-8	137	576	102	157	22	5	6	83	.273	12	207	104	27-47
1889	1B	SL	AA	2-8	137	587	105	168	28	10	3	102	.286	19	225	96	39-51
1890	1B	CHI	PL	4-8	88	377	53	92	11	3	0	59	.244	14	109	64	—
1891	1B	SL	AA	2-8	141	580	86	152	16	2	3	93	.262	33	181	82	41-48
1892	1B	CIN	NL	5-12	141	551	61	125	14	6	3	71	.227	32	160	80	65-72
1893	1B	CIN	NL	6-12	64	259	38	57	12	1	0	26	.220	11	71	60	—
1894	1B	CIN	NL	10-12	61	220	26	58	8	0	0	33	.264	5	66	56	—
MAJOR LEAGUE TOTALS					1390	5796	994	1531	206	68	29		.264	197	1960	97	10 yrs

Fred J Mann
5'10 178 lbs Batted left

Born Apr 1, 1858 Sutton, VT
Died Apr 6, 1916 Springfield, MA

YR	POS	TEAM	LG	FIN	G	AB	R	H	2B	3B	HR	RBI	AVG	BB	TB	OQ	RANK
1882	3B	WOR	NL	8-8	19	77	12	18	5	0	0	7	.234	2	23	—	—
1882	3B	PHI	AA	2-8	29	121	13	28	7	4	0		.231	4	43	110	—
1883	CF	COL	AA	6-8	96	394	61	98	18	13	1		.249	18	145	111	21-56
1884	CF	COL	AA	2-12	99	366	70	101	12	18	7		.276	25	170	152	7-59
1885	CF	PIT	AA	3-8	99	391	60	99	17	6	0		.253	31	128	108	21-49
1886	CF	PIT	AA	2-8	116	440	85	110	16	14	2		.250	45	160	116	18-48
1887	RF-CF	CL/PH	AA	8/5	119	488	87	143	29	13	2		.293	38	204	113	21-49

| MAJOR LEAGUE TOTALS | | | | | 577 | 2277 | 388 | 597 | 104 | 68 | 12 | | .262 | 163 | 873 | 120 | 5 yrs |

Thomas T Brown
5'10 168 lbs Batted left

Born Sep 21, 1860 Liverpool, England
Died Oct 25, 1927 Washington, DC

YR	POS	TEAM	LG	FIN	G	AB	R	H	2B	3B	HR	RBI	AVG	BB	TB	OQ	RANK
1882	RF	BAL	AA	6-6	45	181	30	55	5	2	1		.304	6	67	126	—
1883	RF	COL	AA	6-8	97	420	69	115	12	7	5		.274	20	156	116	17-56
1884	RF	COL	AA	2-12	107	451	93	123	9	11	5		.273	24	169	121	18-59
1885	RF	PIT	AA	3-8	108	437	81	134	16	12	4		.307	34	186	143	7-49
1886	RF	PIT	AA	2-8	115	460	106	131	11	11	1		.285	56	167	127	12-48
1887	CF-RF	PT/IN	NL	6/8	83	332	50	72	6	4	2	15	.217	19	92	68	—
1888	RF	BOS	NL	4-8	107	420	62	104	10	7	9	49	.248	30	155	117	17-46
1889	LF	BOS	NL	2-8	90	362	93	84	10	5	2	24	.232	59	110	98	34-53
1890	CF	BOS	PL	1-8	128	543	146	150	23	14	4	61	.276	86	213	113	24-57
1891	CF	BOS	AA	1-8	137	589	177	189	30	21	5	71	.321	70	276	142	5-48
1892	CF	LOU	NL	9-12	153	660	105	150	16	8	2	45	.227	47	188	82	64-72
1893	CF	LOU	NL	11-12	122	529	104	127	15	7	5	54	.240	56	171	83	70-80
1894	CF	LOU	NL	12-12	129	536	122	136	22	14	9	57	.254	60	213	88	63-77
1895	CF	SL/WA	NL	11/10	117	484	97	108	19	7	3	47	.223	66	150	82	65-75
1896	CF	WAS	NL	9-12	116	435	87	128	17	6	2	59	.294	58	163	108	37-73
1897	CF	WAS	NL	8-12	116	469	91	137	17	2	5	45	.292	52	173	102	45-69
1898	CF	WAS	NL	11-12	16	55	8	9	1	0	0	2	.164	5	10	—	—

| MAJOR LEAGUE TOTALS | | | | | 1786 | 7363 | 1521 | 1952 | 239 | 138 | 64 | | .265 | 748 | 2659 | 109 | 14 yrs |

William Van Winkle Wolf   Born May 12, 1862 Louisville, KY
5'9 190 lbs Batted right   Died May 16, 1903 Louisville, KY

YR	POS	TEAM	LG	FIN	G	AB	R	H	2B	3B	HR	RBI	AVG	BB	TB	OQ	RANK
1882	RF-SS	LOU	AA	3-6	78	318	46	95	11	8	0		.299	9	122	127	8-37
1883	RF-C	LOU	AA	5-8	98	389	59	102	17	9	1		.262	5	140	101	32-56
1884	RF-C	LOU	AA	3-12	110	486	79	146	24	11	3		.300	4	201	124	17-59
1885	RF	LOU	AA	5-8	112	483	79	141	23	17	1		.292	11	201	123	11-49
1886	RF	LOU	AA	4-8	130	545	93	148	17	12	3		.272	27	198	106	27-48
1887	RF	LOU	AA	4-8	137	569	103	160	27	13	2		.281	34	219	100	32-49
1888	RF-SS	LOU	AA	7-8	128	538	80	154	28	11	0	67	.286	25	204	118	15-47
1889	RF-1B	LOU	AA	8-8	130	546	72	159	20	9	3	57	.291	29	206	100	32-51
1890	RF	LOU	AA	1-8	134	543	100	197	29	11	4		.363	43	260	151	4-42
1891	RF	LOU	AA	7-8	138	537	67	136	17	8	1	82	.253	42	172	88	39-48
1892	RF	SL	NL	11-12	3	14	1	2	0	0	0	1	.143	0	2	—	—
MAJOR LEAGUE TOTALS					1198	4968	779	1440	213	109	18		.290	229	1925	114	10 yrs

Louis Rogers Browning   Born Jun 17, 1861 Louisville, KY
6'0 180 lbs Batted right   Died Sep 10, 1905 Louisville, KY

YR	POS	TEAM	LG	FIN	G	AB	R	H	2B	3B	HR	RBI	AVG	BB	TB	OQ	RANK
1882	2B-SS	LOU	AA	3-6	69	288	67	109	17	3	5		.378	26	147	210	1-37
1883	LF-SS	LOU	AA	5-8	84	358	95	121	15	9	4		.338	23	166	160	3-56
1884	3B-CF	LOU	AA	3-12	103	447	101	150	33	8	4		.336	13	211	155	6-59
1885	CF	LOU	AA	5-8	112	481	98	174	34	10	9		.362	25	255	180	1-49
1886	CF	LOU	AA	4-8	112	467	86	159	29	6	2		.340	30	206	143	5-48
1887	CF	LOU	AA	4-8	134	547	137	220	35	16	4		.402	55	299	174	3-49
1888	CF	LOU	AA	7-8	99	383	58	120	22	8	3	72	.313	37	167	154	4-47
1889	LF	LOU	AA	8-8	83	324	39	83	19	5	2	32	.256	34	118	104	—
1890	LF	CLE	PL	7-8	118	493	112	184	40	8	5	93	.373	75	255	159	2-57
1891	LF	PT/CN	NL	7/8	105	419	64	133	24	4	4	61	.317	51	177	136	6-52
1892	CF	LO/CN	NL	9/5	104	384	57	112	16	5	3	56	.292	52	147	130	—
1893	LF	LOU	NL	11-12	57	220	38	78	11	3	1	37	.355	44	98	148	—
1894	CF	SL/BR	NL	9/5	3	9	2	3	0	0	0	2	.333	1	3	—	—
MAJOR LEAGUE TOTALS					1183	4820	954	1646	295	85	46		.341	466	2249	163	9 yrs

James John Roseman   Born Jul 4, 1856   Brooklyn, NY
5'7   167 lbs   Batted right   Died Jul 7, 1938   Brooklyn, NY

YR	POS	TEAM	LG	FIN	G	AB	R	H	2B	3B	HR	RBI	AVG	BB	TB	OQ	RANK
1882	RF	TRO	NL	7-8	82	331	41	78	21	6	1	29	.236	3	114	91	42-57
1883	RF	NY	AA	4-8	93	398	48	100	13	6	0		.251	11	125	92	40-56
1884	CF	NY	AA	1-12	107	436	97	130	16	11	4		.298	21	180	135	10-59
1885	CF	NY	AA	7-8	101	410	72	114	13	14	4		.278	25	167	128	10-49
1886	LF	NY	AA	7-8	134	559	90	127	19	10	5		.227	24	181	89	39-48
1887	RF	Ph/NY/Br	AA	7/5/6	82	317	48	72	12	2	1		.227	19	91	72	—
1890	CF-1B	SL/LO	AA	3/1	82	310	47	105	26	0	2		.339	30	137	141	—
MAJOR LEAGUE TOTALS					681	2761	443	726	120	49	17		.263	133	995	107	5 yrs

Nathaniel Frederick Pfeffer   Born Mar 17, 1860   Louisville, KY
5'10   184 lbs   Batted right   Died Apr 10, 1932   Chicago, IL

YR	POS	TEAM	LG	FIN	G	AB	R	H	2B	3B	HR	RBI	AVG	BB	TB	OQ	RANK
1882	SS	TRO	NL	7-8	85	330	26	72	7	4	1	43	.218	1	90	69	55-57
1883	2B-SS	CHI	NL	2-8	96	371	41	87	22	7	1	45	.235	8	126	87	46-60
1884	2B	CHI	NL	4-8	112	467	105	135	10	10	25	101	.289	25	240	152	7-54
1885	2B	CHI	NL	1-8	112	469	90	113	12	7	5	73	.241	26	154	101	32-46
1886	2B	CHI	NL	1-8	118	474	88	125	17	8	7	95	.264	36	179	112	19-48
1887	2B	CHI	NL	3-8	123	479	95	133	21	6	16	89	.278	34	214	115	20-49
1888	2B	CHI	NL	2-8	135	517	90	129	22	10	8	57	.250	32	195	117	18-46
1889	2B	CHI	NL	3-8	134	531	85	121	15	7	7	77	.228	53	171	88	41-53
1890	2B	CHI	PL	4-8	124	499	86	128	21	8	5	80	.257	44	180	90	45-57
1891	2B	CHI	NL	2-8	137	498	93	123	12	9	7	77	.247	79	174	115	24-52
1892	2B	LOU	NL	9-12	124	470	78	121	14	9	2	76	.257	67	159	116	28-72
1893	2B	LOU	NL	11-12	125	508	85	129	29	12	3	75	.254	51	191	94	58-80
1894	2B-SS	LOU	NL	12-12	104	409	68	126	12	14	5	59	.308	30	181	96	55-77
1895	SS-2B	LOU	NL	12-12	11	45	8	13	1	0	0	5	.289	5	14	—	—
1896	2B	NY/CH	NL	7/5	98	374	46	90	16	7	2	56	.241	24	126	79	71-73
1897	2B	CHI	NL	9-12	32	114	10	26	0	1	0	11	.228	12	28	69	—
MAJOR LEAGUE TOTALS					1670	6555	1094	1671	231	119	94	1019	.255	527	2422	102	14 yrs

William H Robinson
5'6 170 lbs Batted right

Born Sep 19, 1859 Philadelphia, PA
Died Aug 25, 1894 St Louis, MO

YR	POS	TEAM	LG	FIN	G	AB	R	H	2B	3B	HR	RBI	AVG	BB	TB	OQ	RANK
1882	SS	DET	NL	6-8	11	39	1	7	1	0	0	2	.179	1	8	—	—
1884	3B-SS	BAL	UA	3-8	102	415	101	111	24	4	2		.267	37	149	131	9-33
1885	LF-2B	SL	AA	1-8	78	287	63	75	8	8	0		.261	29	99	119	—
1886	2B	SL	AA	1-8	133	481	89	132	26	9	3		.274	64	185	133	8-48
1887	2B	SL	AA	1-8	125	430	102	131	32	4	1		.305	92	174	143	6-49
1888	2B-SS	SL	AA	1-8	134	455	111	105	17	6	3	53	.231	116	143	147	6-47
1889	2B	SL	AA	2-8	132	452	97	94	17	3	5	70	.208	118	132	115	14-51
1890	2B	PIT	PL	6-8	98	306	59	70	10	3	0	38	.229	101	86	118	—
1891	2B	CN/SL	AA	5/2	98	345	48	61	9	4	1	37	.177	68	81	86	—
1892	3B	WAS	NL	10-12	67	218	26	39	4	3	0	19	.179	38	49	87	—
MAJOR LEAGUE TOTALS					978	3428	697	825	148	44	15		.241	664	1106	134	5 yrs

James Edward O'Neill
6'1 167 lbs Batted right

Born May 25, 1858 Woodstock, ON
Died Dec 31, 1915 Montreal, PQ

YR	POS	TEAM	LG	FIN	G	AB	R	H	2B	3B	HR	RBI	AVG	BB	TB	OQ	RANK
1883	P-RF	NY	NL	6-8	23	76	8	15	3	0	0	5	.197	3	18	—	—
1884	LF-P	SL	AA	4-12	78	297	49	82	13	11	3		.276	12	126	132	—
1885	LF	SL	AA	1-8	52	206	44	72	7	4	3		.350	13	96	161	—
1886	LF	SL	AA	1-8	138	579	106	190	28	14	3		.328	47	255	145	4-48
1887	LF	SL	AA	1-8	124	517	167	225	52	19	14		.435	50	357	224	1-49
1888	LF	SL	AA	1-8	130	529	96	177	24	10	5	98	.335	44	236	157	2-47
1889	LF	SL	AA	2-8	134	534	123	179	33	8	9	110	.335	72	255	151	3-51
1890	LF	CHI	PL	4-8	137	577	112	174	20	16	3	75	.302	65	235	111	27-57
1891	LF	SL	AA	2-8	129	521	112	167	28	4	10	95	.321	62	233	137	9-48
1892	LF	CIN	NL	5-12	109	419	63	105	14	6	2	52	.251	53	137	108	36-72
MAJOR LEAGUE TOTALS					1054	4255	880	1386	222	92	52		.326	421	1948	148	7 yrs

John Francis Coleman
5'9 170 lbs Batted left

Born Mar 6, 1863 Saratoga Springs, NY
Died May 31, 1922 Detroit, MI

YR	POS	TEAM	LG	FIN	G	AB	R	H	2B	3B	HR	RBI	AVG	BB	TB	OQ	RANK
1883	P-LF	PHI	NL	8-8	90	354	33	83	12	8	0	32	.234	15	111	86	48-60
1884	CF-P	PHI	NL	6-8	43	171	16	42	7	2	0	22	.246	8	53	90	—
1884	CF-P	PHI	AA	7-12	28	107	16	22	2	3	2		.206	5	36	99	—
1885	RF	PHI	AA	4-8	96	398	71	119	15	11	3		.299	25	165	135	9-49
1886	RF	PH/PT	AA	6/2	132	535	70	136	20	17	0		.254	35	190	105	28-48
1887	RF	PIT	NL	6-8	115	475	75	139	21	11	2	54	.293	31	188	104	29-49
1888	RF	PIT	NL	6-8	116	438	49	101	11	4	0	26	.231	29	120	88	36-46
1889	P-LF	PHI	AA	3-8	6	19	1	1	0	0	0	1	.053	1	1	—	—
1890	P-RF	PIT	NL	8-8	3	11	1	2	0	0	0	0	.182	3	2	—	—
MAJOR LEAGUE TOTALS					629	2508	332	645	88	56	7		.257	152	866	104	5 yrs

Paul Revere Radford
5'6 148 lbs Batted right

Born Oct 14, 1861 Roxbury, MA
Died Feb 21, 1945 Boston, MA

YR	POS	TEAM	LG	FIN	G	AB	R	H	2B	3B	HR	RBI	AVG	BB	TB	OQ	RANK
1883	RF	BOS	NL	1-8	72	258	46	53	6	3	0	14	.205	9	65	67	—
1884	RF	PRO	NL	1-8	97	355	56	70	11	2	1	29	.197	25	88	75	50-54
1885	RF-SS	PRO	NL	4-8	105	371	55	90	12	5	0	32	.243	33	112	103	31-46
1886	RF-SS	KC	NL	7-8	122	493	78	113	17	5	0	20	.229	58	140	95	34-48
1887	SS-RF	NY	AA	7-8	128	486	127	129	15	5	4		.265	106	166	123	10-49
1888	CF	BRO	AA	2-8	90	308	48	67	9	3	2	29	.218	35	88	101	—
1889	RF	CLE	NL	6-8	136	487	94	116	21	5	1	46	.238	91	150	105	25-53
1890	RF-SS	CLE	PL	7-8	122	466	98	136	24	12	2	62	.292	82	190	123	16-57
1891	SS	BOS	AA	1-8	133	456	102	118	11	5	0	65	.259	96	139	114	22-48
1892	RF-3B	WAS	NL	10-12	137	510	93	130	19	4	1	37	.255	86	160	115	29-72
1893	RF	WAS	NL	12-12	124	464	87	106	18	3	2	34	.228	105	136	99	49-80
1894	SS-2B	WAS	NL	11-12	95	325	61	78	13	5	0	49	.240	65	101	86	—
MAJOR LEAGUE TOTALS					1361	4979	945	1206	176	57	13		.242	791	1535	106	9 yrs

David L Orr   Born Sep 29, 1859   New York, NY
5'11   250 lbs   Batted left   Died Jun 3, 1915   Brooklyn, NY

YR	POS	TEAM	LG	FIN	G	AB	R	H	2B	3B	HR	RBI	AVG	BB	TB	OQ	RANK
1883	LF	NY	NL	6-8	1	3	0	0	0	0	0	0	.000	0	0	—	—
1883	1B	NY	AA	4-8	13	50	6	16	4	3	2		.320	0	32	—	—
1884	1B	NY	AA	1-12	110	458	82	162	32	13	9		.354	5	247	175	2-59
1885	1B	NY	AA	7-8	107	444	76	152	29	21	6		.342	8	241	169	3-49
1886	1B	NY	AA	7-8	136	571	93	193	25	31	7		.338	17	301	157	1-48
1887	1B	NY	AA	7-8	84	345	63	127	25	10	2		.368	22	178	147	—
1888	1B	BRO	AA	2-8	99	394	57	120	20	5	1	59	.305	7	153	116	—
1889	1B	COL	AA	6-8	134	560	70	183	31	12	4	87	.327	9	250	113	17-51
1890	1B	BRO	PL	2-8	107	464	89	173	32	13	6	124	.373	30	249	143	5-57
MAJOR LEAGUE TOTALS					791	3289	536	1126	198	108	37		.342	98	1651	151	5 yrs

William J Kuehne   Born Oct 24, 1858   Leipzig, Germany
185 lbs   Batted right   Died Oct 27, 1921   Sulphur Springs, OH

YR	POS	TEAM	LG	FIN	G	AB	R	H	2B	3B	HR	RBI	AVG	BB	TB	OQ	RANK
1883	3B-2B	COL	AA	6-8	95	374	38	85	8	14	1		.227	2	124	88	44-56
1884	3B	COL	AA	2-12	110	415	48	98	13	16	5		.236	9	158	109	30-59
1885	3B	PIT	AA	3-8	104	411	54	93	9	19	0		.226	15	140	96	34-49
1886	3B-LF	PIT	AA	2-8	117	481	73	98	16	17	1		.204	19	151	83	43-48
1887	SS	PIT	NL	6-8	102	402	68	120	18	15	1	41	.299	14	171	105	28-49
1888	3B-SS	PIT	NL	6-8	138	524	60	123	22	11	3	62	.235	9	176	92	33-46
1889	3B-LF	PIT	NL	5-8	97	390	43	96	20	5	5	57	.246	9	141	82	—
1890	3B	PIT	PL	6-8	126	528	66	126	21	12	5	73	.239	28	186	79	52-57
1891	3B	CO/LO	AA	6/7	109	420	60	100	12	1	3	40	.238	18	123	72	47-48
1892	3B	Lo/SL/Cn	NL	9/X/5	89	339	26	57	6	5	1	40	.168	14	76	57	—
MAJOR LEAGUE TOTALS					1087	4284	536	996	145	115	25		.232	137	1446	91	8 yrs

Sidney Douglas Farrar
5'10 185 lbs

Born Aug 10, 1859 Paris Hill, ME
Died May 7, 1935 New York, NY

YR	POS	TEAM	LG	FIN	G	AB	R	H	2B	3B	HR	RBI	AVG	BB	TB	OQ	RANK
1883	1B	PHI	NL	8-8	99	377	41	88	19	8	0	29	.233	4	123	81	50-60
1884	1B	PHI	NL	6-8	111	428	62	105	16	6	1	45	.245	9	136	86	45-54
1885	1B	PHI	NL	3-8	111	420	49	103	20	3	3	36	.245	28	138	104	29-46
1886	1B	PHI	NL	4-8	118	439	55	109	19	7	5	50	.248	16	157	95	33-48
1887	1B	PHI	NL	2-8	116	443	83	125	20	9	4	72	.282	42	175	109	25-49
1888	1B	PHI	NL	3-8	131	508	53	124	24	7	1	53	.244	31	165	102	25-46
1889	1B	PHI	NL	4-8	130	477	70	128	22	2	3	58	.268	52	163	100	32-53
1890	1B	PHI	PL	5-8	127	481	84	122	17	11	1	69	.254	51	164	89	46-57
MAJOR LEAGUE TOTALS					943	3573	497	904	157	53	18	412	.253	233	1221	96	8 yrs

Joseph H Mulvey
5'11 178 lbs Batted right

Born Oct 27, 1858 Providence, RI
Died Aug 21, 1928 Philadelphia, PA

YR	POS	TEAM	LG	FIN	G	AB	R	H	2B	3B	HR	RBI	AVG	BB	TB	OQ	RANK
1883	SS-3B	PR/PH	NL	3/8	7	28	3	8	2	0	0	5	.286	0	10	—	—
1884	3B	PHI	NL	6-8	100	401	47	92	11	2	2	32	.229	4	113	72	53-54
1885	3B	PHI	NL	3-8	107	443	74	119	25	6	6	64	.269	3	174	109	26-46
1886	3B	PHI	NL	4-8	107	430	71	115	16	10	2	53	.267	15	157	99	30-48
1887	3B	PHI	NL	2-8	111	474	93	136	21	6	2	78	.287	21	175	93	37-49
1888	3B	PHI	NL	3-8	100	398	37	86	12	3	0	39	.216	9	104	72	44-46
1889	3B	PHI	NL	4-8	129	544	77	157	21	9	6	77	.289	23	214	99	33-53
1890	3B	PHI	PL	5-8	120	519	96	149	26	15	6	87	.287	27	223	101	38-57
1891	3B	PHI	AA	4-8	113	453	62	115	9	13	5	66	.254	17	165	88	38-48
1892	3B	PHI	NL	4-12	25	98	9	14	1	1	0	4	.143	6	17	49	—
1893	3B	WAS	NL	12-12	55	226	21	53	9	4	0	19	.235	7	70	66	—
1895	3B	BRO	NL	5-12	13	49	8	15	4	1	0	8	.306	2	21	—	—
MAJOR LEAGUE TOTALS					987	4063	598	1059	157	70	29	532	.261	134	1443	92	8 yrs

John Stewart Corkhill   Born Apr 11, 1858 Parkesburg, PA
5'10   180 lbs   Batted left   Died Apr 4, 1921   Pennshauken, NJ

YR	POS	TEAM	LG	FIN	G	AB	R	H	2B	3B	HR	RBI	AVG	BB	TB	OQ	RANK
1883	RF	CIN	AA	3-8	88	375	53	81	10	8	2		.216	3	113	79	50-56
1884	RF-SS	CIN	AA	5-12	110	452	85	124	13	11	4		.274	6	171	111	27-59
1885	RF	CIN	AA	2-8	112	440	64	111	10	8	1		.252	7	140	88	40-49
1886	RF	CIN	AA	5-8	129	540	81	143	9	7	5		.265	23	181	96	34-48
1887	CF	CIN	AA	2-8	128	541	79	168	19	11	5		.311	14	224	103	30-49
1888	CF	CN/BR	AA	4/2	137	561	85	160	15	12	2	93	.285	19	205	111	21-47
1889	CF	BRO	AA	1-8	138	537	91	134	21	9	8	78	.250	42	197	97	37-51
1890	LF-1B	BRO	NL	1-8	51	204	23	46	4	2	1	21	.225	15	57	77	—
1891	CF	PHI	AA	4-8	83	349	50	73	7	7	0	31	.209	26	94	71	—
1891	CF	CN/PT	NL	7/8	42	149	16	33	1	1	3	20	.221	7	45	76	—
1892	CF	PIT	NL	6-12	68	256	23	47	1	4	0	25	.184	12	56	58	—
MAJOR LEAGUE TOTALS					1086	4404	650	1120	110	80	31		.254	174	1483	98	7 yrs

Thomas Francis Michael McCarthy Born Jul 24, 1863   Boston, MA
5'7   170 lbs   Batted right   Died Aug 5, 1922   Boston, MA

YR	POS	TEAM	LG	FIN	G	AB	R	H	2B	3B	HR	RBI	AVG	BB	TB	OQ	RANK
1884	LF-P	BOS	UA	4-8	53	209	37	45	2	2	0		.215	6	51	74	—
1885	LF	BOS	NL	5-8	40	148	16	27	2	0	0	11	.182	5	29	56	—
1886	RF-P	PHI	NL	4-8	8	27	6	5	2	1	0	3	.185	2	9	—	—
1887	LF-2B	PHI	NL	2-8	18	70	7	13	4	0	0	6	.186	2	17	—	—
1888	RF	SL	AA	1-8	131	511	107	140	20	3	1	68	.274	38	169	110	22-47
1889	RF	SL	AA	2-8	140	604	136	176	24	7	2	63	.291	46	220	102	30-51
1890	RF-3B	SL	AA	3-8	133	548	137	192	28	9	6		.350	66	256	156	3-42
1891	RF-2B	SL	AA	2-8	136	578	127	179	21	6	8	95	.310	50	236	118	18-48
1892	RF	BOS	NL	1-12	152	603	119	146	19	5	4	63	.242	93	187	109	34-72
1893	LF	BOS	NL	1-12	116	462	107	160	28	6	5	111	.346	64	215	136	8-80
1894	LF	BOS	NL	3-12	127	539	118	188	21	8	13	126	.349	59	264	118	26-77
1895	LF	BOS	NL	5-12	117	452	90	131	13	2	2	73	.290	72	154	101	41-75
1896	LF	BRO	NL	9-12	104	377	62	94	8	4	3	47	.249	34	119	81	70-73
MAJOR LEAGUE TOTALS					1275	5128	1069	1496	192	53	44		.292	537	1926	115	9 yrs

Francis John Fennelly　　　　Born Feb 18, 1860　Fall River, MA
5'8　168 lbs　Batted right　　　　Died Aug 4, 1920　Fall River, MA

YR	POS	TEAM	LG	FIN	G	AB	R	H	2B	3B	HR	RBI	AVG	BB	TB	OQ	RANK
1884	SS	WA/CN	AA	12/5	90	379	94	118	22	15	4		.311	31	182	168	4-59
1885	SS	CIN	AA	2-8	112	454	82	124	14	17	10		.273	38	202	144	6-49
1886	SS	CIN	AA	5-8	132	497	113	124	13	17	6		.249	60	189	125	16-48
1887	SS	CIN	AA	2-8	134	526	133	140	15	16	8		.266	82	211	122	11-49
1888	SS	CN/PH	AA	4/3	135	495	77	99	10	9	3	68	.200	72	136	104	26-47
1889	SS	PHI	AA	3-8	138	513	70	132	20	5	1	64	.257	65	165	99	34-51
1890	SS-3B	BRO	AA	8-8	45	178	40	44	8	3	2		.247	30	64	121	—

MAJOR LEAGUE TOTALS					786	3042	609	781	102	82	34		.257	378	1149	127	6 yrs

James Thomas McGuire　　　　Born Nov 18, 1863　Youngstown, OH
6'1　185 lbs　Batted right　　　　Died Oct 31, 1936　Albion, MI

YR	POS	TEAM	LG	FIN	G	AB	R	H	2B	3B	HR	RBI	AVG	BB	TB	OQ	RANK
1884	C	TOL	AA	8-12	45	151	12	28	7	0	1		.185	5	38	72	—
1885	C	DET	NL	6-8	34	121	11	23	4	2	0	9	.190	5	31	73	—
1886	C	PHI	NL	4-8	50	167	25	33	7	1	2	18	.198	19	48	91	—
1887	C	PHI	NL	2-8	41	150	22	46	6	6	2	23	.307	11	70	125	—
1888	C	PH/DE	NL	3/5	15	64	7	17	4	2	0	11	.266	4	25	—	—
1888	C-1B	CLE	AA	6-8	26	94	15	24	1	3	1	13	.255	7	34	116	—
1890	C-1B	ROC	AA	5-8	87	331	46	99	16	4	4		.299	21	135	116	—
1891	C	WAS	AA	8-8	114	413	55	125	22	10	3	66	.303	43	176	125	14-48
1892	C	WAS	NL	10-12	97	315	46	73	14	4	4	43	.232	61	107	124	—
1893	C-1B	WAS	NL	12-12	63	237	29	62	14	3	1	26	.262	26	85	94	—
1894	C	WAS	NL	11-12	105	425	67	130	18	6	6	78	.306	33	178	92	58-77
1895	C	WAS	NL	10-12	132	533	89	179	30	8	10	97	.336	40	255	120	24-75
1896	C	WAS	NL	9-12	108	389	60	125	25	3	2	70	.321	30	162	109	34-73
1897	C	WAS	NL	6-12	93	327	51	112	17	7	4	53	.343	21	155	124	—
1898	C-1B	WAS	NL	11-12	131	489	59	131	18	3	1	57	.268	24	158	87	64-75
1899	C	WA/BR	NL	11/1	105	356	47	104	15	5	1	35	.292	28	132	102	—
1900	C	BRO	NL	1-8	71	241	20	69	15	2	0	34	.286	19	88	101	—
1901	C	BRO	NL	3-8	85	301	28	89	16	4	0	40	.296	18	113	109	—
1902	C	DET	AL	7-8	73	229	27	52	14	1	2	23	.227	24	74	91	—
1903	C	DET	AL	5-8	72	248	15	62	12	1	0	21	.250	19	76	94	—
1904	C	NY	AL	2-8	101	322	17	67	12	2	0	20	.208	27	83	85	—
1905	C	NY	AL	6-8	72	228	9	50	7	2	0	33	.219	18	61	87	—
1906	C	NY	AL	2-8	51	144	11	43	5	0	0	14	.299	12	48	115	—
1907	C	NY/BO	AL	5/7	7	5	1	3	0	0	1	1	.600	0	6	—	—
1908	1B	BO/CL	AL	5/2	2	5	0	1	1	0	0	2	.200	0	2	—	—
1910	C	CLE	AL	5-8	1	3	0	1	0	0	0	0	.333	0	1	—	—
1912	C	DET	AL	6-8	1	2	1	1	0	0	0	0	.500	0	1	—	—

MAJOR LEAGUE TOTALS					1782	6290	770	1749	300	79	45		.278	515	2342	107	5 yrs

James G Fogarty   Born Feb 12, 1864 San Francisco, CA
5'10 180 lbs Batted right   Died May 20, 1891 Philadelphia, PA

YR	POS	TEAM	LG	FIN	G	AB	R	H	2B	3B	HR	RBI	AVG	BB	TB	OQ	RANK
1884	CF-3B	PHI	NL	6-8	97	378	42	80	12	6	1	37	.212	20	107	81	47-54
1885	CF	PHI	NL	3-8	111	427	49	99	13	3	0	39	.232	30	118	90	38-46
1886	RF-2B	PHI	NL	4-8	77	280	54	82	13	5	3	47	.293	42	114	144	—
1887	RF	PHI	NL	2-8	126	495	113	129	26	12	8	50	.261	82	203	125	15-49
1888	RF	PHI	NL	3-8	121	454	72	107	14	6	1	35	.236	53	136	109	22-46
1889	CF	PHI	NL	4-8	128	499	107	129	15	17	3	54	.259	65	187	110	23-53
1890	RF	PHI	PL	5-8	91	347	71	83	17	6	4	58	.239	59	124	103	—
MAJOR LEAGUE TOTALS					751	2880	508	709	110	55	20	320	.246	351	989	103	5 yrs

Charles Louis Zimmer   Born Nov 23, 1860 Marietta, OH
6'0 190 lbs Batted right   Died Aug 22, 1949 Cleveland, OH

YR	POS	TEAM	LG	FIN	G	AB	R	H	2B	3B	HR	RBI	AVG	BB	TB	OQ	RANK
1884	C-RF	DET	NL	8-8	8	29	0	2	1	0	0	0	.069	1	3	—	—
1886	C	NY	AA	7-8	6	19	1	3	0	0	0		.158	1	3	—	—
1887	C-1B	CLE	AA	8-8	14	52	9	12	5	0	0		.231	4	17	—	—
1888	C	CLE	AA	6-8	65	212	27	51	11	4	0	22	.241	18	70	108	—
1889	C	CLE	NL	6-8	84	259	47	67	9	9	1	21	.259	44	97	119	—
1890	C	CLE	NL	7-8	125	444	54	95	16	6	2	57	.214	46	129	84	39-48
1891	C	CLE	NL	5-8	116	440	55	112	21	4	3	69	.255	33	150	95	40-52
1892	C	CLE	NL	2-12	111	413	63	108	29	13	1	64	.262	32	166	116	—
1893	C	CLE	NL	3-12	57	227	27	70	13	7	2	41	.308	16	103	112	—
1894	C	CLE	NL	6-12	90	341	55	97	20	5	4	65	.284	17	139	82	—
1895	C	CLE	NL	2-12	88	315	60	107	21	2	5	56	.340	33	147	124	—
1896	C	CLE	NL	2-12	91	336	46	93	18	3	3	46	.277	31	126	97	—
1897	C	CLE	NL	5-12	80	294	50	93	22	3	0	40	.316	25	121	110	—
1898	C	CLE	NL	5-12	20	63	5	15	2	0	0	4	.238	5	17	—	—
1899	C-1B	CL/LO	NL	12/9	95	335	52	103	13	4	4	43	.307	27	136	113	—
1900	C	PIT	NL	2-8	82	271	27	80	7	10	0	35	.295	17	107	105	—
1901	C	PIT	NL	1-8	69	236	17	52	7	3	0	21	.220	20	65	81	—
1902	C	PIT	NL	1-8	42	142	13	38	4	2	0	17	.268	11	46	105	—
1903	C	PHI	NL	7-8	37	118	9	26	3	1	1	19	.220	9	34	79	—
MAJOR LEAGUE TOTALS					1280	4546	617	1224	222	76	26		.269	390	1676	—	—

George Edward Andrews
5'8 160 lbs Batted right

Born Apr 5, 1859 Painesville, OH
Died Aug 12, 1934 West Palm Beach, FL

YR	POS	TEAM	LG	FIN	G	AB	R	H	2B	3B	HR	RBI	AVG	BB	TB	OQ	RANK
1884	2B	PHI	NL	6-8	109	420	74	93	21	2	0	23	.221	9	118	74	51-54
1885	LF	PHI	NL	3-8	103	421	77	112	15	3	0	23	.266	32	133	106	28-46
1886	CF	PHI	NL	4-8	107	437	93	109	15	4	2	28	.249	31	138	94	37-48
1887	CF	PHI	NL	2-8	104	464	110	151	19	7	4	67	.325	21	196	111	24-49
1888	CF	PHI	NL	3-8	124	528	75	126	14	4	3	44	.239	21	157	89	35-46
1889	CF	PH/IN	NL	4/7	50	212	42	64	12	0	0	29	.302	7	76	91	—
1890	CF	BRO	PL	2-8	94	395	84	100	14	2	3	38	.253	40	127	84	49-57
1891	LF	CIN	AA	5-8	83	356	47	75	7	4	0	26	.211	33	90	72	—

MAJOR LEAGUE TOTALS					774	3233	602	830	117	26	12	278	.257	194	1035	93	6 yrs

John J Clements
5'8 204 lbs Batted left

Born Jul 24, 1864 Philadelphia, PA
Died May 23, 1941 Norristown, PA

YR	POS	TEAM	LG	FIN	G	AB	R	H	2B	3B	HR	RBI	AVG	BB	TB	OQ	RANK
1884	RF-C	PHI	UA	7-8	41	177	37	50	13	2	3		.282	9	76	143	—
1884	C	PHI	NL	6-8	9	30	3	7	0	0	0	0	.233	4	7	—	—
1885	C-CF	PHI	NL	3-8	52	188	14	36	11	3	1	14	.191	2	56	76	—
1886	C-RF	PHI	NL	4-8	54	185	15	38	5	1	0	11	.205	7	45	64	—
1887	C	PHI	NL	2-8	66	246	48	69	13	7	1	47	.280	9	99	98	—
1888	C	PHI	NL	3-8	86	326	26	80	8	4	1	32	.245	10	99	89	—
1889	C	PHI	NL	4-8	78	310	51	88	17	1	4	35	.284	29	119	108	—
1890	C	PHI	NL	3-8	97	381	64	120	23	8	7	74	.315	45	180	145	4-48
1891	C	PHI	NL	4-8	107	423	58	131	29	4	4	75	.310	43	180	130	9-52
1892	C	PHI	NL	4-12	109	402	50	106	25	6	8	76	.264	43	167	126	—
1893	C	PHI	NL	4-12	94	376	64	107	20	3	17	80	.285	39	184	122	22-80
1894	C	PHI	NL	4-12	45	159	26	55	6	5	3	36	.346	24	80	129	—
1895	C	PHI	NL	3-12	88	322	64	127	27	2	13	75	.394	22	197	161	—
1896	C	PHI	NL	8-12	57	184	35	66	5	7	5	45	.359	17	100	148	—
1897	C	PHI	NL	10-12	55	185	18	44	4	2	6	36	.238	12	70	88	—
1898	C	SL	NL	12-12	99	335	39	86	19	5	3	41	.257	21	124	99	—
1899	C	CLE	NL	12-12	4	12	1	3	0	0	0	0	.250	0	3	—	—
1900	C	BOS	NL	4-8	16	42	6	13	1	0	1	10	.310	3	17	—	—

MAJOR LEAGUE TOTALS					1157	4283	619	1226	226	60	77		.286	339	1803	—	—

James Albert Myers　　　　　Born Oct 22, 1863　Danville, IL
5'8　165 lbs　Batted right　　　　Died Dec 24, 1927　Marshall, IL

YR	POS	TEAM	LG	FIN	G	AB	R	H	2B	3B	HR	RBI	AVG	BB	TB	OQ	RANK
1884	2B	MIL	UA	—	12	46	6	15	6	0	0		.326	0	21	—	—
1885	2B	PHI	NL	3-8	93	357	25	73	13	2	1	28	.204	11	93	73	44-46
1886	2B	KC	NL	7-8	118	473	69	131	22	9	4	51	.277	22	183	109	21-48
1887	2B-SS	WAS	NL	7-8	105	362	45	84	9	5	2	36	.232	40	109	86	44-49
1888	2B	WAS	NL	8-8	132	502	46	104	12	7	2	46	.207	37	136	87	38-46
1889	2B	WA/PH	NL	8/4	121	481	76	128	17	2	0	48	.266	58	149	95	36-53
1890	2B	PHI	NL	3-8	117	487	95	135	29	7	2	81	.277	57	184	116	20-48
1891	2B	PHI	NL	4-8	135	514	67	118	27	2	2	69	.230	69	155	96	37-52
MAJOR LEAGUE TOTALS					833	3222	429	788	135	34	13		.245	294	1030	95	7 yrs

William Frederick Ely　　　　Born Jun 7, 1863　Girard, PA
6'1　155 lbs　Batted right　　　　Died Jan 10, 1952　Berkeley, CA

YR	POS	TEAM	LG	FIN	G	AB	R	H	2B	3B	HR	RBI	AVG	BB	TB	OQ	RANK
1884	P	BUF	NL	3-8	1	4	0	0	0	0	0	0	.000	0	0	—	—
1886	P-LF	LOU	AA	4-8	10	32	5	5	0	0	0		.156	2	5	—	—
1890	LF-SS	SYR	AA	6-8	119	496	72	130	16	6	0		.262	31	158	89	35-42
1891	SS	BRO	NL	6-8	31	111	9	17	0	1	0	11	.153	7	19	47	—
1893	SS	SL	NL	10-12	44	178	25	45	1	6	0	16	.253	17	58	83	—
1894	SS	SL	NL	9-12	127	510	85	156	20	12	12	89	.306	30	236	97	53-77
1895	SS	SL	NL	11-12	117	467	68	121	16	2	1	46	.259	19	144	68	75-75
1896	SS	PIT	NL	6-12	128	537	85	153	15	9	3	77	.285	33	195	89	59-73
1897	SS	PIT	NL	8-12	133	516	63	146	20	8	2	74	.283	25	188	87	62-69
1898	SS	PIT	NL	8-12	148	519	49	110	14	5	2	44	.212	24	140	68	74-75
1899	SS	PIT	NL	7-12	138	522	66	145	18	6	3	72	.278	22	184	88	50-61
1900	SS	PIT	NL	2-8	130	475	60	116	6	6	0	51	.244	17	134	68	47-47
1901	SS	PIT	NL	1-8	65	240	18	50	6	3	0	28	.208	6	62	63	—
1901	SS	PHI	AL	4-8	45	171	11	37	6	2	0	16	.216	3	47	61	—
1902	SS	WAS	AL	6-8	105	381	39	100	11	2	1	62	.262	21	118	81	—
MAJOR LEAGUE TOTALS					1341	5159	655	1331	149	68	24		.258	257	1688	82	8 yrs

Frederick Herbert Carroll Born Jul 2, 1864 Sacramento, CA
5'11 185 lbs Batted right Died Nov 7, 1904 San Rafael, CA

YR	POS	TEAM	LG	FIN	G	AB	R	H	2B	3B	HR	RBI	AVG	BB	TB	OQ	RANK
1884	C-LF	COL	AA	2-12	69	252	46	70	13	5	6		.278	13	111	140	—
1885	C-LF	PIT	AA	3-8	71	280	45	75	13	8	0		.268	7	104	107	—
1886	C-LF	PIT	AA	2-8	122	486	92	140	28	11	5		.288	52	205	139	6-48
1887	CF-C	PIT	NL	6-8	102	421	71	138	24	15	6	54	.328	36	210	139	7-49
1888	C-LF	PIT	NL	6-8	97	366	62	91	14	5	2	48	.249	32	121	111	—
1889	C-LF	PIT	NL	5-8	91	318	80	105	21	11	2	51	.330	85	154	181	1-53
1890	C-LF	PIT	PL	6-8	111	416	95	124	20	7	2	71	.298	75	164	122	17-57
1891	RF	PIT	NL	8-8	91	353	55	77	13	4	4	48	.218	48	110	97	—
MAJOR LEAGUE TOTALS					754	2892	546	820	146	66	27		.284	348	1179	—	—

George J Smith Born Apr 21, 1863 Pittsburgh, PA
6'0 175 lbs Batted right Died Dec 1, 1927 Altoona, PA

YR	POS	TEAM	LG	FIN	G	AB	R	H	2B	3B	HR	RBI	AVG	BB	TB	OQ	RANK
1884	SS	ALT	UA	—	25	108	9	34	8	1	0		.315	1	44	130	—
1884	2B-SS	CLE	NL	7-8	72	291	31	74	14	4	4	26	.254	2	108	97	—
1885	SS	BRO	AA	5-8	108	419	63	108	17	11	4		.258	10	159	107	22-49
1886	SS	BRO	AA	3-8	105	426	66	105	17	6	2		.246	19	140	93	37-48
1887	SS	BRO	AA	6-8	103	435	79	128	19	16	4		.294	13	191	107	25-49
1888	SS	BRO	AA	2-8	103	402	47	86	10	7	3	61	.214	22	119	88	—
1889	SS	BRO	AA	1-8	121	446	89	103	22	3	3	53	.231	40	140	86	44-51
1890	SS	BRO	NL	1-8	129	481	76	92	6	5	1	47	.191	42	111	66	47-48
1891	SS	CIN	NL	7-8	138	512	50	103	11	5	3	53	.201	38	133	71	50-52
1892	SS	CIN	NL	5-12	139	506	58	121	13	6	8	63	.239	42	170	98	52-72
1893	SS	CIN	NL	6-12	130	500	63	118	18	6	4	56	.236	38	160	77	78-80
1894	SS	CIN	NL	10-12	127	482	73	127	33	5	3	76	.263	41	179	80	72-77
1895	SS	CIN	NL	8-12	127	503	75	151	23	6	4	74	.300	34	198	95	50-75
1896	SS	CIN	NL	3-12	120	456	65	131	22	9	2	71	.287	28	177	94	53-73
1897	SS	BRO	NL	6-12	112	428	47	86	17	3	0	29	.201	14	109	54	69-69
1898	SS	SL	NL	12-12	51	157	16	25	2	1	1	9	.159	24	32	72	—
MAJOR LEAGUE TOTALS					1710	6552	907	1592	252	94	46		.243	408	2170	86	12 yrs

John Emmett Seery
Batted left

Born Feb 13, 1861 Princeville, IL
Date and place of death unknown

YR	POS	TEAM	LG	FIN	G	AB	R	H	2B	3B	HR	RBI	AVG	BB	TB	OQ	RANK
1884	LF	BA/KC	UA	3/8	106	467	115	146	26	7	2		.313	21	192	142	7-33
1885	LF	SL	NL	8-8	59	216	20	35	7	0	1	14	.162	16	45	67	—
1886	LF	SL	NL	6-8	126	453	73	108	22	6	2	48	.238	57	148	108	22-48
1887	LF	IND	NL	8-8	122	465	104	104	18	15	4	28	.224	71	164	104	29-49
1888	LF	IND	NL	7-8	133	500	87	110	20	10	5	50	.220	64	165	117	16-46
1889	LF	IND	NL	7-8	127	526	123	165	26	12	8	59	.314	67	239	137	8-53
1890	LF	BRO	PL	2-8	104	394	78	88	12	7	1	50	.223	70	117	91	44-57
1891	RF	CIN	AA	5-8	97	372	77	106	15	10	4	36	.285	81	153	144	4-48
1892	RF	LOU	NL	9-12	42	154	18	31	6	1	0	15	.201	24	39	91	—
MAJOR LEAGUE TOTALS					916	3547	695	893	152	68	27		.252	471	1262	120	7 yrs

George Frederick Miller
5'6 Batted right

Born Aug 15, 1864 Brooklyn, NY
Died Apr 6, 1909 Brooklyn, NY

YR	POS	TEAM	LG	FIN	G	AB	R	H	2B	3B	HR	RBI	AVG	BB	TB	OQ	RANK
1884	LF-C	PIT	AA	10-12	89	347	46	78	10	2	0		.225	13	92	80	55-59
1885	C-LF	PIT	AA	3-8	42	166	19	27	3	1	0		.163	4	32	51	—
1886	C-LF	PIT	AA	2-8	83	317	70	80	15	1	2		.252	43	103	115	—
1887	C-CF	PIT	NL	6-8	87	342	58	83	17	4	1	34	.243	35	111	90	40-49
1888	C-LF	PIT	NL	6-8	103	404	50	112	17	5	0	36	.277	18	139	108	23-46
1889	C-RF	PIT	NL	5-8	104	422	77	113	25	3	6	56	.268	31	162	101	31-53
1890	3B-RF	PIT	NL	8-8	138	549	85	150	24	3	4	66	.273	68	192	110	26-48
1891	C-SS	PIT	NL	8-8	135	548	80	156	19	6	4	57	.285	59	199	112	28-52
1892	CF-C	PIT	NL	6-12	149	623	103	158	15	12	2	59	.254	69	203	104	42-72
1893	C	PIT	NL	2-12	41	154	23	28	6	1	0	17	.182	17	36	62	—
1894	3B-C	SL	NL	9-12	127	481	93	163	9	11	8	86	.339	58	218	112	33-77
1895	3B-C	SL	NL	11-12	121	490	81	143	15	4	5	74	.292	25	181	85	61-75
1896	C-2B	LOU	NL	12-12	98	324	54	89	17	4	1	33	.275	27	117	92	—
MAJOR LEAGUE TOTALS					1317	5167	839	1380	192	57	33		.267	467	1785	100	9 yrs

Henry E Larkin   Born Jan 12, 1860 Reading, PA
5'10 175 lbs Batted right   Died Jan 31, 1942 Reading, PA

YR	POS	TEAM	LG	FIN	G	AB	R	H	2B	3B	HR	RBI	AVG	BB	TB	OQ	RANK
1884	CF	PHI	AA	7-12	85	326	59	90	21	9	3		.276	15	138	134	11-59
1885	CF	PHI	AA	4-8	108	453	114	149	37	14	8		.329	26	238	172	2-49
1886	LF	PHI	AA	6-8	139	565	133	180	36	16	2		.319	59	254	152	2-48
1887	LF-1B	PHI	AA	5-8	126	497	105	154	22	12	3		.310	48	209	120	14-49
1888	1B-2B	PHI	AA	3-8	135	546	92	147	28	12	7	101	.269	33	220	126	11-47
1889	1B	PHI	AA	3-8	133	516	105	164	23	12	3	74	.318	83	220	141	5-51
1890	1B	CLE	PL	7-8	125	506	93	168	32	15	5	112	.332	65	245	137	6-57
1891	1B-RF	PHI	AA	4-8	133	526	94	147	27	14	10	93	.279	66	232	129	13-48
1892	1B	WAS	NL	10-12	119	464	76	130	13	7	8	96	.280	39	181	117	22-72
1893	1B	WAS	NL	12-12	81	319	54	101	20	3	4	73	.317	50	139	128	—
MAJOR LEAGUE TOTALS					1184	4718	925	1430	259	114	53		.303	484	2076	136	9 yrs

James B McGarr   Born May 10, 1863 Worcester, MA
Batted right   Died Jun 6, 1904 Worcester, MA

YR	POS	TEAM	LG	FIN	G	AB	R	H	2B	3B	HR	RBI	AVG	BB	TB	OQ	RANK
1884	2B-LF	CHI	UA	5-8	19	70	10	11	2	0	0		.157	0	13	—	—
1886	SS	PHI	AA	6-8	71	267	41	71	9	3	2		.266	9	92	96	—
1887	SS	PHI	AA	5-8	137	536	93	158	23	6	1		.295	23	196	93	41-49
1888	2B	SL	AA	1-8	34	132	17	31	1	0	0	13	.235	6	32	74	—
1889	3B-SS	KC/BA	AA	7/5	28	115	23	32	3	0	0	16	.278	7	35	83	—
1890	3B	BOS	NL	5-8	121	487	68	115	12	7	1	51	.236	34	144	81	43-48
1893	3B	CLE	NL	3-12	63	249	38	77	12	0	0	28	.309	20	89	94	—
1894	3B	CLE	NL	6-12	128	523	94	144	24	6	2	74	.275	28	186	73	74-77
1895	3B	CLE	NL	2-12	112	419	85	111	14	2	2	59	.265	34	135	79	67-75
1896	3B	CLE	NL	2-12	113	455	68	122	16	4	1	53	.268	22	149	77	73-73
MAJOR LEAGUE TOTALS					826	3253	537	872	116	28	9		.268	183	1071	81	5 yrs

Percival Wheritt Werden   Born Jul 21, 1865   St Louis, MO
6'2 220 lbs Batted right   Died Jan 9, 1934   Minneapolis, MN

YR	POS	TEAM	LG	FIN	G	AB	R	H	2B	3B	HR	RBI	AVG	BB	TB	OQ	RANK
1884	P-LF	SL	UA	1-8	18	76	7	18	2	0	0		.237	2	20	—	—
1888	LF	WAS	NL	8-8	3	10	0	3	0	0	0	2	.300	1	3	—	—
1890	1B	TOL	AA	4-8	128	498	113	147	22	20	6		.295	78	227	150	5-42
1891	1B	BAL	AA	3-8	139	552	102	160	20	18	6	104	.290	52	234	120	17-48
1892	1B	SL	NL	11-12	149	598	73	154	22	6	8	84	.258	59	212	109	35-72
1893	1B	SL	NL	10-12	125	500	73	138	22	29	1	94	.276	49	221	110	35-80
1897	1B	LOU	NL	11-12	131	506	76	153	21	14	5	83	.302	40	217	110	33-69
MAJOR LEAGUE TOTALS					693	2740	444	773	109	87	26		.282	281	1134	120	5 yrs

David Luther Foutz   Born Sep 7, 1856   Carroll County, MO
6'2 161 lbs Batted right   Died Mar 5, 1897   Waverly, IN

YR	POS	TEAM	LG	FIN	G	AB	R	H	2B	3B	HR	RBI	AVG	BB	TB	OQ	RANK
1884	P-RF	SL	AA	4-12	33	119	17	27	4	0	0		.227	8	31	87	—
1885	P-1B	SL	AA	1-8	65	238	42	59	6	4	0		.248	11	73	93	—
1886	P-RF	SL	AA	1-8	102	414	66	116	18	9	3		.280	9	161	107	26-48
1887	RF-P	SL	AA	1-8	102	423	79	151	26	13	4		.357	23	215	141	7-49
1888	RF-1B	BRO	AA	2-8	140	563	91	156	20	13	3	99	.277	28	211	116	17-47
1889	1B	BRO	AA	1-8	138	553	118	152	19	8	6	113	.275	64	205	110	22-51
1890	1B-CF	BRO	NL	1-8	129	509	106	154	25	13	5	98	.303	52	220	129	11-48
1891	1B	BRO	NL	6-8	130	521	87	134	26	8	2	73	.257	40	182	98	35-52
1892	LF-P	BRO	NL	3-12	61	220	33	41	5	3	1	26	.186	14	55	69	—
1893	LF-1B	BRO	NL	6-12	130	557	91	137	20	10	7	67	.246	32	198	81	75-80
1894	1B	BRO	NL	5-12	72	293	40	90	12	9	0	51	.307	14	120	85	—
1895	RF-1B	BRO	NL	5-12	31	115	14	34	4	1	0	21	.296	4	40	78	—
1896	1B-CF	BRO	NL	9-12	2	8	0	2	1	0	0	0	.250	1	3	—	—
MAJOR LEAGUE TOTALS					1135	4533	784	1253	186	91	31		.276	300	1714	112	7 yrs

George Burton Pinkney
5'7 160 lbs Batted right

Born Jan 11, 1862 Orange Prairie, IL
Died Nov 10, 1926 Peoria, IL

YR	POS	TEAM	LG	FIN	G	AB	R	H	2B	3B	HR	RBI	AVG	BB	TB	OQ	RANK
1884	2B-SS	CLE	NL	7-8	36	144	18	45	9	0	0	16	.313	10	54	123	—
1885	2B-3B	BRO	AA	5-8	110	447	77	124	16	5	0		.277	27	150	108	20-49
1886	3B	BRO	AA	3-8	141	597	119	156	22	7	0		.261	70	192	111	21-48
1887	3B	BRO	AA	6-8	138	580	133	155	26	6	3		.267	61	202	100	32-49
1888	3B	BRO	AA	2-8	143	575	134	156	18	8	4	52	.271	66	202	127	10-47
1889	3B	BRO	AA	1-8	138	545	103	134	25	7	4	82	.246	59	185	98	36-51
1890	3B	BRO	NL	1-8	126	485	115	150	20	9	7	83	.309	80	209	146	3-48
1891	3B	BRO	NL	6-8	135	501	80	137	19	6	2	71	.273	66	174	112	27-52
1892	3B	SL	NL	11-12	78	290	31	50	3	2	0	25	.172	36	57	69	—
1893	3B	LOU	NL	11-12	118	446	64	105	12	6	1	62	.235	50	132	79	77-80
MAJOR LEAGUE TOTALS					1163	4610	874	1212	170	56	21		.263	525	1557	110	8 yrs

Thomas P Burns
5'8 183 lbs Batted right

Born Sep 6, 1864 Philadelphia, PA
Died Nov 11, 1928 Brooklyn, NY

YR	POS	TEAM	LG	FIN	G	AB	R	H	2B	3B	HR	RBI	AVG	BB	TB	OQ	RANK
1884	SS	WIL	UA	—	2	7	0	1	0	1	0		.143	1	3	—	—
1884	RF-2B	BAL	AA	6-12	35	131	34	39	2	6	6		.298	7	71	175	—
1885	RF-P	BAL	AA	8-8	78	321	47	74	11	6	5		.231	16	112	102	27-49
1887	SS-3B	BAL	AA	3-8	140	551	122	188	33	19	9		.341	63	286	155	4-49
1888	LF-SS	BA/BR	AA	5/2	131	529	94	155	27	15	6	67	.293	38	230	142	7-47
1889	RF-SS	BRO	AA	1-8	131	504	105	153	19	13	5	100	.304	68	213	132	9-51
1890	RF	BRO	NL	1-8	119	472	102	134	22	12	13	128	.284	51	219	135	7-48
1891	RF	BRO	NL	6-8	123	470	75	134	24	13	4	83	.285	53	196	126	12-52
1892	RF	BRO	NL	3-12	141	542	88	171	27	18	4	96	.315	65	246	149	4-72
1893	RF	BRO	NL	6-12	109	415	68	112	22	8	7	60	.270	36	171	101	44-80
1894	RF	BRO	NL	5-12	125	505	106	179	32	14	5	107	.354	44	254	118	29-77
1895	LF	BR/NY	NL	5/9	53	190	28	49	5	4	1	32	.258	22	65	89	—
MAJOR LEAGUE TOTALS					1187	4637	869	1389	224	129	65		.300	464	2066	129	9 yrs

Curtis Benton Welch
5'10 175 lbs Batted right

Born Feb 11, 1862 East Liverpool, OH
Died Aug 29, 1896 East Liverpool, OH

YR	POS	TEAM	LG	FIN	G	AB	R	H	2B	3B	HR	RBI	AVG	BB	TB	OQ	RANK
1884	CF	TOL	AA	8-12	109	425	61	95	24	5	0		.224	10	129	87	49-59
1885	CF	SL	AA	1-8	112	432	84	117	18	8	3		.271	23	160	115	17-49
1886	CF	SL	AA	1-8	138	563	114	158	31	13	2		.281	29	221	115	19-48
1887	CF	SL	AA	1-8	131	544	98	151	32	7	3		.278	25	206	95	39-49
1888	CF	PHI	AA	3-8	136	549	125	155	22	8	1	61	.282	33	196	115	19-47
1889	CF	PHI	AA	3-8	125	516	134	140	39	6	0	39	.271	67	191	113	19-51
1890	CF	PH/BA	AA	7/8	122	464	116	115	25	4	2		.248	58	154	105	27-42
1891	CF-2B	BAL	AA	3-8	132	514	122	138	22	10	3	55	.268	77	189	116	20-48
1892	CF	BA/CN	NL	12/5	88	331	56	75	1	5	2	29	.227	43	92	94	—
1893	CF	LOU	NL	11-12	14	47	5	8	1	0	0	2	.170	16	9	—	—

MAJOR LEAGUE TOTALS   1107   4385   915 1152   215   66   16   .263   381 1547   108   8 yrs

Daniel Richardson
5'8 165 lbs Batted right

Born Jan 25, 1863 Elmira, NY
Died Sep 12, 1926 New York, NY

YR	POS	TEAM	LG	FIN	G	AB	R	H	2B	3B	HR	RBI	AVG	BB	TB	OQ	RANK
1884	RF-SS	NY	NL	4-8	74	277	36	70	8	1	1	27	.253	16	83	91	—
1885	RF-3B	NY	NL	2-8	49	198	26	52	9	3	0	25	.263	10	67	105	—
1886	CF	NY	NL	3-8	68	237	43	55	9	1	1	27	.232	17	69	86	—
1887	2B-3B	NY	NL	4-8	122	450	79	125	19	10	3	62	.278	36	173	103	31-49
1888	2B	NY	NL	1-8	135	561	82	127	16	7	8	61	.226	15	181	90	34-46
1889	2B	NY	NL	1-8	125	497	88	139	22	8	7	100	.280	46	198	110	22-53
1890	SS-2B	NY	PL	6-8	123	528	102	135	12	9	4	80	.256	37	177	81	51-57
1891	2B	NY	NL	3-8	123	516	85	139	18	5	4	51	.269	33	179	96	39-52
1892	SS-2B	WAS	NL	10-12	142	551	48	132	13	4	3	58	.240	25	162	80	66-72
1893	2B	BRO	NL	6-12	54	206	36	46	6	2	0	27	.223	13	56	64	—
1894	SS	LOU	NL	12-12	116	430	51	109	17	2	1	40	.253	35	133	67	75-77

MAJOR LEAGUE TOTALS   1131   4451   676 1129   149   52   32   558   .254   283 1478   90   7 yrs

Richard Frederick Johnston   Born Apr 6, 1863   Kingston, NY
5'8   155 lbs   Batted right   Died Apr 4, 1934   Detroit, MI

YR	POS	TEAM	LG	FIN	G	AB	R	H	2B	3B	HR	RBI	AVG	BB	TB	OQ	RANK
1884	CF	RIC	AA	—	39	146	23	41	5	5	2		.281	2	62	126	—
1885	CF	BOS	NL	5-8	26	111	17	26	6	3	1	23	.234	0	41	96	—
1886	CF	BOS	NL	5-8	109	413	48	99	18	9	1	57	.240	3	138	82	42-48
1887	CF	BOS	NL	5-8	127	507	87	131	13	20	5	77	.258	16	199	92	39-49
1888	CF	BOS	NL	4-8	135	585	102	173	31	18	12	68	.296	15	276	141	8-46
1889	CF	BOS	NL	2-8	132	539	80	123	16	4	5	67	.228	41	162	79	50-53
1890	CF	BO/NY	PL	1/3	79	315	37	75	9	7	1	43	.238	18	101	74	—
1891	CF	CIN	AA	5-8	99	376	59	83	11	2	6	51	.221	38	116	86	40-48
MAJOR LEAGUE TOTALS					746	2992	453	751	109	68	33		.251	133	1095	96	5 yrs

William Mitchell Nash   Born Jun 24, 1865   Richmond, VA
5'8   167 lbs   Batted right   Died Nov 15, 1929   East Orange, NJ

YR	POS	TEAM	LG	FIN	G	AB	R	H	2B	3B	HR	RBI	AVG	BB	TB	OQ	RANK
1884	3B	RIC	AA	—	45	166	31	33	8	8	1		.199	12	60	112	—
1885	3B-2B	BOS	NL	5-8	26	94	9	24	4	0	0	11	.255	2	28	—	—
1886	3B-SS	BOS	NL	5-8	109	417	61	117	11	8	1	45	.281	24	147	104	27-48
1887	3B	BOS	NL	2-8	121	475	100	140	24	12	6	94	.295	60	206	127	13-49
1888	3B-2B	BOS	NL	4-8	135	526	71	149	18	15	4	75	.283	50	209	137	10-46
1889	3B	BOS	NL	2-8	128	481	84	132	20	2	3	76	.274	79	165	113	21-53
1890	3B	BOS	PL	1-8	129	488	103	130	28	6	5	90	.266	88	185	114	23-57
1891	3B	BOS	NL	1-8	140	537	92	148	24	9	5	95	.276	74	205	122	15-52
1892	3B	BOS	NL	1-12	135	526	94	137	25	5	4	95	.260	59	184	111	30-72
1893	3B	BOS	NL	1-12	128	485	115	141	27	6	10	123	.291	85	210	127	17-80
1894	3B	BOS	NL	3-12	132	512	132	148	23	6	8	87	.289	91	207	105	44-77
1895	3B	BOS	NL	5-12	132	508	97	147	23	6	10	108	.289	74	212	114	29-75
1896	3B	PHI	NL	8-12	65	227	29	56	9	1	3	30	.247	34	76	96	—
1897	3B	PHI	NL	10-12	104	337	45	87	20	2	0	39	.258	60	111	103	—
1898	3B	PHI	NL	6-12	20	70	9	17	2	1	0	9	.243	11	21	—	—
MAJOR LEAGUE TOTALS					1549	5849	1072	1606	266	87	60		.275	803	2226	117	10 yrs

Charles Edwin Bassett　　　　　　Born Feb 9, 1863   Central Falls, RI
5'10   150 lbs Batted right　　　　　Died May 28, 1942 Pawtucket, RI

YR	POS	TEAM	LG	FIN	G	AB	R	H	2B	3B	HR	RBI	AVG	BB	TB	OQ	RANK
1884	3B-SS	PRO	NL	1-8	27	79	10	11	2	1	0	6	.139	4	15	—	—
1885	2B-SS	PRO	NL	4-8	82	285	21	41	8	2	0	16	.144	19	53	59	—
1886	SS	KC	NL	7-8	90	342	41	89	19	8	2	32	.260	36	130	119	17-48
1887	2B	IND	NL	8-8	119	452	41	104	14	6	1	47	.230	25	133	73	47-49
1888	2B	IND	NL	7-8	128	481	58	116	20	3	2	60	.241	32	148	99	28-46
1889	2B	IND	NL	7-8	127	477	64	117	12	5	4	68	.245	37	151	84	45-53
1890	2B	NY	NL	6-8	100	410	52	98	13	8	0	54	.239	29	127	84	40-48
1891	3B	NY	NL	3-8	130	524	60	136	19	8	4	68	.260	36	183	96	38-52
1892	3B-2B	NY/LO	NL	8/9	114	443	45	94	7	8	2	51	.212	21	123	74	70-72
MAJOR LEAGUE TOTALS					917	3493	392	806	114	49	15	402	.231	239	1063	90	7 yrs

Joseph J Quinn　　　　　　　　　Born Dec 25, 1864   Sydney, Australia
5'7   158 lbs Batted right　　　　　Died Nov 12, 1940 St Louis, MO

YR	POS	TEAM	LG	FIN	G	AB	R	H	2B	3B	HR	RBI	AVG	BB	TB	OQ	RANK
1884	1B	SL	UA	1-8	103	429	74	116	21	1	0		.270	9	139	101	18-32
1885	CF-3B	SL	NL	8-8	97	343	27	73	8	2	0	15	.213	9	85	69	45-46
1886	CF-2B	SL	NL	6-8	75	271	33	63	11	3	1	21	.232	8	83	80	—
1888	2B	BOS	NL	4-8	38	156	19	47	8	3	4	29	.301	2	73	138	—
1889	SS-2B	BOS	NL	2-8	112	444	57	116	13	5	2	69	.261	25	145	84	47-53
1890	2B	BOS	PL	1-8	130	509	87	153	19	8	7	82	.301	44	209	106	33-57
1891	2B	BOS	NL	1-8	124	508	70	122	8	10	3	63	.240	28	159	82	46-52
1892	2B	BOS	NL	1-12	143	532	63	116	14	1	1	59	.218	35	135	73	71-72
1893	2B	SL	NL	10-12	135	547	68	126	18	6	0	71	.230	33	156	66	80-80
1894	2B	SL	NL	9-12	106	405	59	116	18	1	4	61	.286	24	148	77	73-77
1895	2B	SL	NL	11-12	134	543	84	169	19	9	2	74	.311	36	212	95	48-75
1896	2B-RF	SL/BA	NL	11/1	72	273	41	67	7	2	1	22	.245	15	81	70	—
1897	3B-SS	BAL	NL	2-12	75	285	33	74	11	4	1	45	.260	13	96	78	—
1898	2B-SS	BA/SL	NL	2/12	115	407	40	102	11	5	0	41	.251	25	123	83	—
1899	2B	CLE	NL	12-12	147	615	73	176	24	6	0	72	.286	21	212	86	54-61
1900	2B	SL/CN	NL	5/7	96	346	30	94	7	2	1	36	.272	26	108	86	—
1901	2B	WAS	AL	6-8	66	266	33	67	11	2	2	34	.252	11	88	81	—
MAJOR LEAGUE TOTALS					1768	6879	891	1797	228	70	29		.261	364	2252	84	10 yrs

James Edward McTamany
5'8 190 lbs Batted right

Born Jul 1, 1863 Philadelphia, PA
Died Apr 16, 1916 Lenni, PA

YR	POS	TEAM	LG	FIN	G	AB	R	H	2B	3B	HR	RBI	AVG	BB	TB	OQ	RANK
1885	LF	BRO	AA	5-8	35	131	21	36	7	2	1		.275	9	50	123	—
1886	CF	BRO	AA	3-8	111	418	86	106	23	10	2		.254	54	155	125	14-48
1887	CF	BRO	AA	6-8	134	520	123	134	22	10	1		.258	76	179	106	26-49
1888	CF	KC	AA	8-8	130	516	94	127	12	10	4	41	.246	67	171	121	13-47
1889	CF	COL	AA	6-8	139	529	113	146	21	7	4	52	.276	116	193	133	8-51
1890	CF	COL	AA	2-8	125	466	140	120	27	7	1		.258	112	164	138	9-42
1891	CF	CO/PH	AA	6/4	139	522	116	125	23	12	6	56	.239	101	190	120	16-48
MAJOR LEAGUE TOTALS					813	3102	693	794	135	58	19		.256	535	1102	124	6 yrs

James Edward Ryan
5'9 162 lbs Batted right

Born Feb 11, 1863 Clinton, MA
Died Oct 26, 1923 Chicago, IL

YR	POS	TEAM	LG	FIN	G	AB	R	H	2B	3B	HR	RBI	AVG	BB	TB	OQ	RANK
1885	SS-CF	CHI	NL	1-8	3	13	2	6	1	0	0	2	.462	1	7	—	—
1886	RF	CHI	NL	1-8	84	327	58	100	17	6	4	53	.306	12	141	123	—
1887	CF	CHI	NL	3-8	126	508	117	145	23	10	11	74	.285	53	221	121	17-49
1888	CF	CHI	NL	2-8	129	549	115	182	33	10	16	64	.332	35	283	173	3-46
1889	CF-SS	CHI	NL	3-8	135	576	140	177	31	14	17	72	.307	70	287	145	5-53
1890	CF	CHI	PL	4-8	118	486	99	165	32	5	6	89	.340	60	225	132	11-57
1891	CF	CHI	NL	2-8	118	505	110	140	22	15	9	66	.277	53	219	127	11-52
1892	CF	CHI	NL	7-12	128	505	105	148	21	11	10	65	.293	61	221	141	7-72
1893	CF-SS	CHI	NL	9-12	83	341	82	102	21	7	3	30	.299	59	146	127	16-80
1894	RF	CHI	NL	8-12	108	474	132	171	37	7	3	62	.361	50	231	119	25-77
1895	RF	CHI	NL	4-12	108	438	83	139	22	8	6	49	.317	48	195	117	25-75
1896	RF	CHI	NL	5-12	128	489	83	149	24	10	3	86	.305	46	202	109	33-73
1897	RF	CHI	NL	9-12	136	520	103	156	33	17	5	85	.300	50	238	119	24-69
1898	LF	CHI	NL	4-12	144	572	122	185	32	13	4	79	.323	73	255	144	6-75
1899	LF	CHI	NL	8-12	125	525	91	158	20	10	3	68	.301	43	207	110	31-61
1900	RF	CHI	NL	5-8	105	415	66	115	25	4	5	59	.277	29	163	104	26-47
1902	CF	WAS	AL	6-8	120	484	92	155	32	6	6	44	.320	43	217	129	8-46
1903	CF	WAS	AL	8-8	114	437	42	109	25	4	7	46	.249	17	163	101	34-47
MAJOR LEAGUE TOTALS					2012	8164	1642	2502	451	157	118	1093	.306	803	3621	126	16 yrs

Dennis Patrick Aloysius Lyons   Born Mar 12, 1866 Cincinnati, OH
5'10 185 lbs Batted right   Died Jan 2, 1929   West Covington, KY

YR	POS	TEAM	LG	FIN	G	AB	R	H	2B	3B	HR	RBI	AVG	BB	TB	OQ	RANK
1885	3B	PRO	NL	4-8	4	16	3	2	1	0	0	1	.125	0	3	—	—
1886	3B	PHI	AA	6-8	32	123	22	26	3	1	0		.211	8	31	75	—
1887	3B	PHI	AA	5-8	137	570	128	209	43	14	6		.367	47	298	154	5-49
1888	3B	PHI	AA	3-8	111	456	93	135	22	5	6	83	.296	41	185	139	8-47
1889	3B	PHI	AA	3-8	131	510	135	168	36	4	9	82	.329	79	239	153	2-51
1890	3B	PHI	AA	7-8	88	339	79	120	29	5	7		.354	57	180	187	—
1891	3B	SL	AA	2-8	120	451	124	142	24	3	11	84	.315	88	205	156	2-48
1892	3B	NY	NL	8-12	108	389	71	100	16	7	8	51	.257	59	154	131	—
1893	3B	PIT	NL	2-12	131	490	103	150	19	16	3	105	.306	97	210	133	12-80
1894	3B	PIT	NL	7-12	71	254	51	82	14	4	4	50	.323	42	116	118	—
1895	3B	SL	NL	11-12	33	129	24	38	6	0	2	25	.295	14	50	101	—
1896	3B	PIT	NL	6-12	118	436	77	134	25	6	4	71	.307	67	183	124	19-73
1897	1B	PIT	NL	8-12	37	131	22	27	6	4	2	17	.206	22	47	100	—

| MAJOR LEAGUE TOTALS | | | | | 1121 | 4294 | 932 | 1333 | 244 | 69 | 62 | | .310 | 621 | 1901 | 143 | 6 yrs |

Samuel Luther Thompson   Born Mar 5, 1860 Danville, IL
6'2 207 lbs Batted left   Died Nov 7, 1922 Detroit, MI

YR	POS	TEAM	LG	FIN	G	AB	R	H	2B	3B	HR	RBI	AVG	BB	TB	OQ	RANK
1885	RF	DET	NL	6-8	63	254	58	77	11	9	7	44	.303	16	127	161	—
1886	RF	DET	NL	2-8	122	503	101	156	18	13	8	89	.310	35	224	136	9-48
1887	RF	DET	NL	1-8	127	545	118	203	29	23	11	166	.372	32	311	160	2-49
1888	RF	DET	NL	5-8	56	238	51	67	10	8	6	40	.282	23	111	157	—
1889	RF	PHI	NL	4-8	128	533	103	158	36	4	20	111	.296	36	262	128	14-53
1890	RF	PHI	NL	3-8	132	549	116	172	41	9	4	102	.313	42	243	127	12-48
1891	RF	PHI	NL	4-8	133	554	108	163	23	10	7	90	.294	52	227	121	16-52
1892	RF	PHI	NL	4-12	153	609	109	186	28	11	9	104	.305	59	263	136	10-72
1893	RF	PHI	NL	4-12	131	600	130	222	37	13	11	126	.370	50	318	144	7-80
1894	RF	PHI	NL	4-12	99	437	108	178	29	27	13	141	.407	40	300	169	4-77
1895	RF	PHI	NL	3-12	119	538	131	211	45	21	18	165	.392	31	352	168	2-75
1896	RF	PHI	NL	8-12	119	517	103	154	28	7	12	100	.298	28	232	107	38-73
1897	RF	PHI	NL	10-12	3	13	2	3	0	1	0	3	.231	1	5	—	—
1898	RF	PHI	NL	6-12	14	63	14	22	5	3	1	15	.349	4	36	—	—
1906	RF	DET	AL	6-8	8	31	4	7	0	1	0	3	.226	1	9	—	—

| MAJOR LEAGUE TOTALS | | | | | 1407 | 5984 | 1256 | 1979 | 340 | 160 | 127 | 1299 | .331 | 450 | 3020 | 140 | 10 yrs |

Louis W Bierbauer
5'8 140 lbs Batted left

Born Sep 28, 1865 Erie, PA
Died Jan 31, 1926 Erie, PA

YR	POS	TEAM	LG	FIN	G	AB	R	H	2B	3B	HR	RBI	AVG	BB	TB	OQ	RANK
1886	2B	PHI	AA	6-8	137	522	56	118	17	5	2		.226	21	151	80	45-48
1887	2B	PHI	AA	5-8	126	530	74	144	19	7	1		.272	13	180	80	47-49
1888	2B-3B	PHI	AA	3-8	134	535	83	143	20	9	0	80	.267	25	181	104	25-47
1889	2B	PHI	AA	3-8	130	549	80	167	27	7	7	105	.304	29	229	111	21-51
1890	2B	BRO	PL	1-8	133	589	128	180	31	11	7	99	.306	40	254	107	32-57
1891	2B	PIT	NL	8-8	121	500	60	103	13	6	1	47	.206	28	131	68	52-52
1892	2B	PIT	NL	6-12	152	649	81	153	20	9	8	65	.236	25	215	86	59-72
1893	2B	PIT	NL	2-12	128	528	84	150	19	11	4	94	.284	36	203	93	59-80
1894	2B	PIT	NL	7-12	130	525	86	159	19	13	3	107	.303	26	213	84	68-77
1895	2B	PIT	NL	7-12	117	466	53	120	13	11	0	69	.258	19	155	72	73-75
1896	2B	PIT	NL	6-12	59	258	33	74	10	6	0	39	.287	5	96	82	—
1897	2B	SL	NL	12-12	12	46	1	10	0	0	0	1	.217	0	10	—	—
1898	2B-3B	SL	NL	12-12	4	9	0	0	0	0	0	0	.000	1	0	—	—

| MAJOR LEAGUE TOTALS | | | | | 1383 | 5706 | 819 | 1521 | 208 | 95 | 33 | | .267 | 268 | 2018 | 89 | 10 yrs |

Elmer Ellsworth Smith
5'11 178 lbs Batted left

Born Mar 23, 1868 Pittsburgh, PA
Died Nov 3, 1945 Pittsburgh, PA

YR	POS	TEAM	LG	FIN	G	AB	R	H	2B	3B	HR	RBI	AVG	BB	TB	OQ	RANK
1886	P	CIN	AA	5-8	10	32	7	9	1	1	0		.281	9	12	—	—
1887	P	CIN	AA	2-8	52	186	26	47	10	6	0		.253	11	69	93	—
1888	P	CIN	AA	4-8	40	129	15	29	4	1	0	9	.225	20	35	109	—
1889	P	CIN	AA	4-8	29	83	12	23	3	1	2	17	.277	7	34	—	—
1892	LF-P	PIT	NL	6-12	138	511	86	140	16	14	4	63	.274	82	196	134	13-72
1893	LF	PIT	NL	2-12	128	518	121	179	26	23	7	103	.346	77	272	152	4-80
1894	LF	PIT	NL	7-12	125	489	128	174	33	19	6	72	.356	65	263	134	14-77
1895	LF	PIT	NL	7-12	124	480	88	145	14	12	1	81	.302	55	186	103	40-75
1896	LF	PIT	NL	6-12	122	484	121	175	21	14	7	94	.362	74	245	154	8-73
1897	LF	PIT	NL	8-12	123	467	99	145	19	17	6	54	.310	70	216	134	14-69
1898	LF	CIN	NL	3-12	123	486	79	166	21	10	1	66	.342	69	210	149	5-75
1899	CF	CIN	NL	6-12	87	339	65	101	13	6	1	24	.298	47	129	119	—
1900	RF	CN/NY	NL	7/8	114	423	61	112	13	11	3	52	.265	42	156	103	28-47
1901	RF	PT/BO	NL	1/5	20	61	5	10	2	1	0	3	.164	8	14	—	—

| MAJOR LEAGUE TOTALS | | | | | 1235 | 4688 | 913 | 1455 | 196 | 136 | 38 | | .310 | 636 | 2037 | 133 | 8 yrs |

George Hubbert Collins   Born Apr 15, 1864   Louisville, KY
5'8   160 lbs   Batted right   Died May 21, 1892   Brooklyn, NY

YR	POS	TEAM	LG	FIN	G	AB	R	H	2B	3B	HR	RBI	AVG	BB	TB	OQ	RANK
1886	LF	LOU	AA	4-8	27	101	12	29	3	2	0		.287	5	36	106	—
1887	LF	LOU	AA	4-8	130	559	122	162	22	8	1		.290	39	203	98	35-49
1888	LF-2B	LO/BR	AA	7/2	128	527	133	162	31	12	2	53	.307	50	223	148	5-47
1889	2B	BRO	AA	1-8	138	560	139	149	18	3	2	73	.266	80	179	103	28-51
1890	2B	BRO	NL	1-8	129	510	148	142	32	7	3	69	.278	85	197	129	10-48
1891	2B-LF	BRO	NL	6-8	107	435	82	120	16	5	3	31	.276	59	155	115	22-52
1892	LF	BRO	NL	3-8	21	87	17	26	5	1	0	17	.299	14	33	137	—
MAJOR LEAGUE TOTALS					680	2779	653	790	127	38	11		.284	332	1026	119	5 yrs

Wilbert Robinson   Born Jun 29, 1863   Bolton, MA
5'8   215 lbs   Batted right   Died Aug 8, 1934   Atlanta, GA

YR	POS	TEAM	LG	FIN	G	AB	R	H	2B	3B	HR	RBI	AVG	BB	TB	OQ	RANK
1886	C-1B	PHI	AA	6-8	87	342	57	69	11	3	1		.202	21	89	75	—
1887	C	PHI	AA	5-8	68	264	28	60	6	2	1		.227	14	73	68	—
1888	C	PHI	AA	3-8	66	254	32	62	7	2	1	31	.244	9	76	88	—
1889	C	PHI	AA	3-8	69	264	31	61	13	2	0	28	.231	6	78	68	—
1890	C	PH/BA	AA	7/8	96	377	39	91	14	4	4		.241	19	125	87	—
1891	C	BAL	AA	3-8	93	334	25	72	8	5	2	46	.216	16	96	70	—
1892	C	BAL	NL	12-12	90	330	36	88	14	4	2	57	.267	15	116	96	—
1893	C	BAL	NL	8-12	95	359	49	120	21	3	3	57	.334	26	156	113	—
1894	C	BAL	NL	1-12	109	414	69	146	21	4	1	98	.353	46	178	108	41-77
1895	C	BAL	NL	1-12	77	282	38	74	19	1	0	48	.262	12	95	74	—
1896	C	BAL	NL	1-12	67	245	43	85	9	6	2	38	.347	14	112	118	—
1897	C	BAL	NL	2-12	48	181	25	57	9	0	0	23	.315	8	66	90	—
1898	C	BAL	NL	2-12	79	289	29	80	12	2	0	38	.277	16	96	91	—
1899	C	BAL	NL	4-12	108	356	40	101	15	2	0	47	.284	31	120	95	—
1900	C	SL	NL	5-8	60	210	26	52	5	1	0	28	.248	11	59	72	—
1901	C	BAL	AL	5-8	68	239	32	72	12	3	0	26	.301	10	90	98	—
1902	C	BAL	AL	8-8	91	335	38	98	16	7	1	57	.293	12	131	99	—
MAJOR LEAGUE TOTALS					1371	5075	637	1388	212	51	18		.273	286	1756	—	—

John Anthony Boyle
6'4 190 lbs Batted left

Born Mar 22, 1866 Cincinnati, OH
Died Jan 7, 1913 Cincinnati, OH

YR	POS	TEAM	LG	FIN	G	AB	R	H	2B	3B	HR	RBI	AVG	BB	TB	OQ	RANK
1886	C	CIN	AA	5-8	1	5	0	1	0	0	0		.200	0	1	—	—
1887	C	SL	AA	1-8	88	350	48	66	3	1	2		.189	20	77	55	—
1888	C	SL	AA	1-8	71	257	33	62	8	1	1	23	.241	13	75	89	—
1889	C-3B	SL	AA	2-8	99	347	54	85	11	4	4	42	.245	21	116	86	—
1890	C-3B	CHI	PL	4-8	100	369	56	96	9	5	1	49	.260	44	118	88	—
1891	C-SS	SL	AA	2-8	123	439	78	123	18	8	5	79	.280	47	172	114	23-48
1892	C-1B	NY	NL	8-12	120	436	52	80	8	8	0	32	.183	36	104	70	72-72
1893	1B	PHI	NL	4-12	116	504	105	144	29	9	4	81	.286	41	203	100	47-80
1894	1B	PHI	NL	4-12	114	495	98	149	21	10	4	88	.301	45	202	92	60-77
1895	1B	PHI	NL	3-12	133	565	90	143	17	4	0	67	.253	35	168	69	74-75
1896	C-1B	PHI	NL	8-12	40	145	17	43	4	1	1	28	.297	6	52	85	—
1897	C-1B	PHI	NL	10-12	75	288	37	73	9	1	2	36	.253	19	90	76	—
1898	1B-C	PHI	NL	6-12	6	22	0	2	0	1	0	3	.091	1	4	—	—
MAJOR LEAGUE TOTALS					1086	4222	668	1067	137	53	24		.253	328	1382	89	5 yrs

William Shindle
5'8 155 lbs Batted right

Born Dec 5, 1860 Gloucester, NJ
Died Jun 3, 1936 Lakeland, NJ

YR	POS	TEAM	LG	FIN	G	AB	R	H	2B	3B	HR	RBI	AVG	BB	TB	OQ	RANK
1886	SS	DET	NL	2-8	7	26	4	7	0	0	0	4	.269	0	7	—	—
1887	3B	DET	NL	1-8	22	84	17	24	3	2	0	12	.286	7	31	—	—
1888	3B	BAL	AA	5-8	135	514	61	107	14	8	1	53	.208	20	140	78	43-47
1889	3B	BAL	AA	5-8	138	567	122	178	24	7	3	64	.314	42	225	113	18-51
1890	3B	PHI	PL	5-8	132	584	127	188	21	21	10	90	.322	40	281	121	18-57
1891	3B	PHI	NL	4-8	103	415	68	87	13	1	0	38	.210	33	102	70	51-52
1892	3B	BAL	NL	12-12	143	619	100	156	20	18	3	50	.252	35	221	99	50-72
1893	3B	BAL	NL	8-12	125	521	100	136	22	11	1	75	.261	66	183	96	55-80
1894	3B	BRO	NL	5-12	116	476	94	141	22	9	4	96	.296	29	193	85	66-77
1895	3B	BRO	NL	5-12	116	477	91	133	21	2	3	69	.279	47	167	89	57-75
1896	3B	BRO	NL	9-12	131	516	75	144	24	9	1	61	.279	24	189	86	63-73
1897	3B	BRO	NL	6-12	134	542	83	154	32	6	4	105	.284	35	210	95	51-69
1898	3B	BRO	NL	10-12	120	466	50	105	10	3	1	41	.225	10	124	63	75-75
MAJOR LEAGUE TOTALS					1422	5807	992	1560	226	97	31	758	.269	388	2073	90	11 yrs

Michael Joseph Tiernan
5'11 165 lbs Batted left

Born Jan 21, 1867 Trenton, NJ
Died Nov 9, 1918 New York, NY

YR	POS	TEAM	LG	FIN	G	AB	R	H	2B	3B	HR	RBI	AVG	BB	TB	OQ	RANK
1887	LF	NY	NL	4-8	103	407	82	117	13	12	10	62	.287	32	184	119	19-49
1888	RF	NY	NL	1-8	113	443	75	130	16	8	9	52	.293	42	189	148	7-46
1889	RF	NY	NL	1-8	122	499	147	167	23	14	10	73	.335	96	248	167	3-53
1890	CF	NY	NL	6-8	133	553	132	168	25	21	13	59	.304	68	274	150	2-48
1891	RF	NY	NL	3-8	134	542	111	166	30	12	16	73	.306	69	268	152	2-52
1892	RF	NY	NL	8-12	116	450	79	129	16	10	5	66	.287	57	180	132	14-72
1893	RF	NY	NL	5-12	125	511	114	158	19	12	14	102	.309	72	243	132	13-80
1894	RF	NY	NL	2-12	112	424	84	117	19	13	5	77	.276	54	177	97	52-77
1895	RF	NY	NL	9-12	120	476	127	165	23	21	7	70	.347	66	251	146	9-75
1896	RF	NY	NL	7-12	133	521	132	192	24	16	7	89	.369	77	269	157	7-73
1897	RF	NY	NL	3-12	127	528	123	174	29	10	5	72	.330	61	238	127	21-69
1898	LF-RF	NY	NL	7-12	103	415	90	116	15	11	5	49	.280	43	168	120	—
1899	RF	NY	NL	10-12	35	137	17	35	4	2	0	7	.255	10	43	84	—

MAJOR LEAGUE TOTALS   1476 5906 1313 1834 256 162 106 851 .311 747 2732 139 11 yrs

George Edward Martin **Van Haltren**
5'11 170 lbs Batted left

Born Mar 30, 1866 St Louis, MO
Died Sep 29, 1945 Oakland, CA

YR	POS	TEAM	LG	FIN	G	AB	R	H	2B	3B	HR	RBI	AVG	BB	TB	OQ	RANK
1887	RF-P	CHI	NL	3-8	45	172	30	35	4	0	3	17	.203	15	48	74	—
1888	LF-P	CHI	NL	2-8	81	318	46	90	9	14	4	34	.283	22	139	141	—
1889	LF	CHI	NL	3-8	134	543	126	168	20	10	9	81	.309	82	235	137	10-53
1890	RF-P	BRO	PL	2-8	92	376	84	126	8	9	5	54	.335	41	167	124	14-57
1891	LF-SS	BAL	AA	3-8	139	566	136	180	14	15	9	83	.318	71	251	137	8-48
1892	RF	BA/PT	NL	12/6	148	611	115	179	22	14	7	62	.293	76	250	135	12-72
1893	CF	PIT	NL	2-12	124	529	129	179	14	11	3	79	.338	75	224	126	18-80
1894	CF	NY	NL	2-12	137	519	109	172	22	4	7	104	.331	55	223	103	45-77
1895	CF	NY	NL	9-12	131	521	113	177	23	19	8	103	.340	57	262	133	14-75
1896	CF	NY	NL	7-12	133	562	136	197	18	21	5	74	.351	55	272	134	12-73
1897	CF	NY	NL	3-12	129	564	117	186	22	9	3	64	.330	40	235	110	34-69
1898	CF	NY	NL	7-12	156	654	129	204	28	16	2	68	.312	59	270	125	17-75
1899	CF	NY	NL	10-12	151	604	117	182	21	3	2	58	.301	74	215	110	29-61
1900	CF	NY	NL	8-8	141	571	114	180	30	7	1	51	.315	50	227	115	18-47
1901	CF	NY	NL	7-8	135	543	82	182	23	6	1	47	.335	51	220	132	13-45
1902	CF	NY	NL	8-8	24	88	14	23	1	2	0	7	.261	17	28	132	—
1903	CF	NY	NL	2-8	84	280	42	72	6	1	0	28	.257	28	80	88	—

MAJOR LEAGUE TOTALS   1984 8021 1639 2532 285 161 69 1014 .316 868 3346 125 13 yrs

Edwin John McKean　　　　　Born Jun 6, 1864　Grafton, OH
5'9　160 lbs　Batted right　　　　Died Aug 16, 1919　Cleveland, OH

YR	POS	TEAM	LG	FIN	G	AB	R	H	2B	3B	HR	RBI	AVG	BB	TB	OQ	RANK
1887	SS	CLE	AA	8-8	132	539	97	154	16	13	2		.286	60	202	109	23-49
1888	SS-LF	CLE	AA	6-8	131	548	94	164	21	15	6	68	.299	28	233	135	9-47
1889	SS	CLE	NL	6-8	123	500	88	159	22	8	4	75	.318	42	209	119	17-53
1890	SS	CLE	NL	7-8	136	530	95	157	15	14	7	61	.296	87	221	139	6-48
1891	SS	CLE	NL	5-8	141	603	115	170	13	12	6	69	.282	64	225	113	26-52
1892	SS	CLE	NL	2-12	129	531	76	139	14	10	0	93	.262	49	173	101	47-72
1893	SS	CLE	NL	3-12	125	545	103	169	29	24	4	133	.310	50	258	121	23-80
1894	SS	CLE	NL	6-12	130	554	116	198	30	15	8	128	.357	49	282	120	24-77
1895	SS	CLE	NL	2-12	131	565	131	193	32	17	8	119	.342	45	283	127	21-75
1896	SS	CLE	NL	2-12	133	571	100	193	29	12	7	112	.338	45	267	123	20-73
1897	SS	CLE	NL	5-12	125	523	83	143	21	14	2	78	.273	40	198	94	52-69
1898	SS	CLE	NL	5-12	151	604	89	172	23	1	9	94	.285	56	224	110	37-75
1899	SS-1B	SL	NL	5-12	67	277	40	72	7	3	3	40	.260	20	94	90	—

| MAJOR LEAGUE TOTALS | | | | | 1654 | 6890 | 1227 | 2083 | 272 | 158 | 66 | | .302 | 635 | 2869 | 118 | 12 yrs |

Oliver Wendell Tebeau　　　　Born Dec 5, 1864　St Louis, MO
5'8　163 lbs　Batted right　　　　Died May 15, 1918　St Louis, MO

YR	POS	TEAM	LG	FIN	G	AB	R	H	2B	3B	HR	RBI	AVG	BB	TB	OQ	RANK
1887	3B	CHI	NL	3-8	20	68	8	11	3	0	0	10	.162	4	14	—	—
1889	3B	CLE	NL	6-8	136	521	72	147	20	6	8	76	.282	37	203	104	29-53
1890	3B	CLE	PL	7-8	110	450	86	135	26	6	5	74	.300	34	188	105	35-57
1891	3B	CLE	NL	5-8	61	249	38	65	8	3	1	41	.261	16	82	91	—
1892	3B	CLE	NL	2-12	86	340	47	83	13	3	2	49	.244	23	108	91	—
1893	1B-3B	CLE	NL	3-12	116	486	90	160	32	8	2	102	.329	32	214	112	33-80
1894	1B	CLE	NL	6-12	125	523	82	158	23	7	3	89	.302	35	204	84	67-77
1895	1B-2B	CLE	NL	2-12	63	264	50	84	13	2	2	52	.318	16	107	98	—
1896	1B	CLE	NL	2-12	132	543	56	146	22	6	2	94	.269	21	186	78	72-73
1897	1B-2B	CLE	NL	5-12	109	412	62	110	15	9	0	59	.267	30	143	86	63-69
1898	1B-2B	CLE	NL	5-12	131	477	53	123	11	4	1	63	.258	53	145	95	51-75
1899	1B-SS	SL	NL	5-12	77	281	27	69	10	3	1	26	.246	18	88	81	—
1900	SS	SL	NL	5-8	1	4	0	0	0	0	0	0	.000	0	0	—	—

| MAJOR LEAGUE TOTALS | | | | | 1167 | 4618 | 671 | 1291 | 196 | 57 | 27 | 735 | .280 | 319 | 1682 | 95 | 7 yrs |

Thomas Joseph Tucker   Born Oct 28, 1863   Holyoke, MA
5'11   165 lbs   Batted both   Died Oct 22, 1935   Montague, MA

YR	POS	TEAM	LG	FIN	G	AB	R	H	2B	3B	HR	RBI	AVG	BB	TB	OQ	RANK
1887	1B	BAL	AA	3-8	136	524	114	144	15	9	6		.275	29	195	95	38-49
1888	1B	BAL	AA	5-8	136	520	74	149	17	12	6	61	.287	16	208	120	14-47
1889	1B	BAL	AA	5-8	134	527	103	196	22	11	5	99	.372	42	255	147	4-51
1890	1B	BOS	NL	5-8	132	539	104	159	17	8	1	62	.295	56	195	111	23-48
1891	1B	BOS	NL	1-8	140	548	103	148	16	5	2	69	.270	37	180	92	41-52
1892	1B	BOS	NL	1-12	149	542	85	153	15	7	1	62	.282	45	185	105	41-72
1893	1B	BOS	NL	1-12	121	486	83	138	13	2	7	91	.284	27	176	86	67-80
1894	1B	BOS	NL	3-12	123	500	112	165	24	6	3	100	.330	53	210	101	47-77
1895	1B	BOS	NL	5-12	125	462	87	115	19	6	3	73	.249	61	155	89	57-75
1896	1B	BOS	NL	4-12	122	474	74	144	27	5	2	72	.304	30	187	98	47-73
1897	1B	BO/WA	NL	1/6	97	366	52	122	20	5	5	65	.333	29	167	121	—
1898	1B	BR/SL	NL	10/12	145	535	53	139	16	6	1	54	.260	30	170	86	65-75
1899	1B	CLE	NL	12-12	127	456	40	110	19	3	0	40	.241	24	135	74	59-61

MAJOR LEAGUE TOTALS   1687   6479 1084 1882 240 85 42   .290 479 2418 100 12 yrs

Thomas Peter Daly   Born Feb 7, 1866   Philadelphia, PA
5'7   170 lbs   Batted both   Died Oct 29, 1939   Brooklyn, NY

YR	POS	TEAM	LG	FIN	G	AB	R	H	2B	3B	HR	RBI	AVG	BB	TB	OQ	RANK
1887	C-CF	CHI	NL	3-8	74	256	45	53	10	4	2	17	.207	22	77	78	—
1888	C	CHI	NL	2-8	65	219	34	42	2	6	0	29	.192	10	56	75	—
1889	C-1B	WAS	NL	8-8	71	250	39	75	13	5	1	40	.300	38	101	128	—
1890	C-1B	BRO	NL	1-8	82	292	55	71	9	4	5	43	.243	32	103	103	—
1891	C-1B	BRO	NL	6-8	58	200	29	50	11	5	2	27	.250	21	77	111	—
1892	3B-CF	BRO	NL	3-12	124	446	76	114	15	6	4	51	.256	64	153	117	24-72
1893	2B-3B	BRO	NL	6-12	126	470	94	136	21	14	8	70	.289	76	209	126	19-80
1894	2B	BRO	NL	5-12	123	492	135	168	22	10	8	82	.341	77	234	124	18-77
1895	2B	BRO	NL	5-12	120	455	89	128	17	8	2	68	.281	52	167	96	45-75
1896	2B	BRO	NL	9-12	67	224	43	63	13	6	3	29	.281	33	97	121	—
1898	2B	BRO	NL	10-12	23	73	11	24	3	1	0	11	.329	14	29	—	—
1899	2B	BRO	NL	1-12	141	498	95	156	24	9	5	88	.313	69	213	133	13-61
1900	2B	BRO	NL	1-8	97	343	72	107	17	3	4	55	.312	46	142	129	—
1901	2B	BRO	NL	3-8	133	520	88	164	38	10	3	90	.315	42	231	135	11-45
1902	2B	CHI	AL	4-8	137	489	57	110	22	3	1	54	.225	55	141	85	41-46
1903	2B	CHI	AL	7-8	43	150	20	31	11	0	0	19	.207	20	42	96	—
1903	2B	CIN	NL	4-8	80	307	42	90	14	9	1	38	.293	16	125	110	—

MAJOR LEAGUE TOTALS   1564   5684 1024 1582 262 103 49 811 .278 687 2197 117 7 yrs

Michael Joseph Griffin
5'7   160 lbs   Batted left

Born Mar 20, 1865   Utica, NY
Died Apr 10, 1908   Utica, NY

YR	POS	TEAM	LG	FIN	G	AB	R	H	2B	3B	HR	RBI	AVG	BB	TB	OQ	RANK
1887	CF	BAL	AA	3-8	136	532	142	160	32	13	3		.301	55	227	122	12-49
1888	CF	BAL	AA	5-8	137	542	103	139	21	11	0	46	.256	55	182	116	16-47
1889	CF-SS	BAL	AA	5-8	137	531	152	148	21	14	4	48	.279	91	209	129	11-51
1890	CF	PHI	PL	5-8	115	489	127	140	29	6	6	54	.286	64	199	112	26-57
1891	CF	BRO	NL	6-8	134	521	106	139	36	9	3	65	.267	57	202	115	23-52
1892	CF	BRO	NL	3-12	129	452	103	125	17	11	3	66	.277	68	173	131	15-72
1893	CF	BRO	NL	6-12	95	362	85	103	21	7	6	59	.285	59	156	123	21-80
1894	CF	BRO	NL	5-12	107	402	122	144	28	4	5	75	.358	78	195	136	9-77
1895	CF	BRO	NL	5-12	131	519	140	173	38	7	4	65	.333	93	237	137	12-75
1896	CF	BRO	NL	9-12	122	493	101	152	27	9	4	51	.308	48	209	113	30-73
1897	CF	BRO	NL	6-12	134	534	136	169	25	11	2	56	.316	81	222	125	22-69
1898	CF	BRO	NL	10-12	134	537	88	161	18	6	2	40	.300	60	197	117	28-75

MAJOR LEAGUE TOTALS   1511 5914 1405 1753 313 108 42   .296 809 2408 123 12 yrs

Lafayette Napoleon Cross
5'8   155 lbs   Batted right

Born May 12, 1866 Milwaukee, WI
Died Sep 6, 1927   Toledo, OH

YR	POS	TEAM	LG	FIN	G	AB	R	H	2B	3B	HR	RBI	AVG	BB	TB	OQ	RANK
1887	C-RF	LOU	AA	4-8	54	203	32	54	8	3	0		.266	15	68	90	—
1888	C-RF	LOU	AA	7-8	47	181	20	41	3	0	0	15	.227	2	44	65	—
1889	C	PHI	AA	3-8	55	199	22	44	8	2	0	23	.221	14	56	74	—
1890	C-RF	PHI	PL	5-8	63	245	42	73	7	8	3	47	.298	12	105	101	—
1891	C-RF	PHI	AA	4-8	110	402	66	121	20	14	5	52	.301	38	184	130	12-48
1892	3B-C	PHI	NL	4-12	140	541	84	149	15	10	4	69	.275	39	196	107	37-72
1893	C-3B	PHI	NL	4-12	96	415	81	124	17	6	4	78	.299	26	165	97	52-80
1894	3B-C	PHI	NL	4-12	119	529	123	204	34	9	7	125	.386	29	277	121	20-77
1895	3B	PHI	NL	3-12	125	535	95	145	26	9	2	101	.271	35	195	85	62-75
1896	3B-SS	PHI	NL	8-12	106	406	63	104	23	5	1	73	.256	32	140	85	64-73
1897	3B-2B	PHI	NL	10-12	88	344	37	89	17	5	3	51	.259	10	125	80	—
1898	3B	SL	NL	12-12	151	602	71	191	28	8	3	79	.317	28	244	113	31-75
1899	3B	CL/SL	NL	12/5	141	557	76	166	19	5	5	84	.298	25	210	97	43-61
1900	3B	SL/BR	NL	6/1	133	522	79	153	15	6	4	73	.293	26	192	96	37-47
1901	3B	PHI	AL	4-8	100	424	82	139	28	12	2	73	.328	19	197	123	13-46
1902	3B	PHI	AL	1-8	137	559	90	191	39	8	0	108	.342	27	246	121	16-46
1903	3B	PHI	AL	2-8	137	559	60	163	22	4	2	90	.292	10	199	97	38-47
1904	3B	PHI	AL	5-8	155	607	73	176	31	10	1	71	.290	13	230	111	26-47
1905	3B	PHI	AL	1-8	147	587	69	156	29	5	0	77	.266	26	195	101	31-41
1906	3B	WAS	AL	7-8	130	494	55	130	14	6	1	46	.263	28	159	100	26-40
1907	3B	WAS	AL	8-8	41	161	13	32	8	0	0	10	.199	10	40	77	—

MAJOR LEAGUE TOTALS   2275 9072 1333 2645 411 135 47   .292 464 3467 106 15 yrs

William D O'Brien   Born Sep 1, 1863   Peoria, IL
6'1   186 lbs   Batted right   Died Jun 15, 1893   Peoria, IL

YR	POS	TEAM	LG	FIN	G	AB	R	H	2B	3B	HR	RBI	AVG	BB	TB	OQ	RANK
1887	LF	NY	AA	7-8	127	522	97	157	30	13	5		.301	40	228	118	18-49
1888	LF	BRO	AA	2-8	136	532	105	149	27	6	2	65	.280	30	194	116	18-47
1889	LF	BRO	AA	1-8	136	567	146	170	30	11	5	80	.300	61	237	123	12-51
1890	CF	BRO	NL	1-8	85	350	78	110	28	6	2	63	.314	32	156	132	—
1891	LF	BRO	NL	6-8	103	395	79	100	18	6	5	57	.253	39	145	106	31-52
1892	LF	BRO	NL	3-12	122	490	72	119	14	5	1	56	.243	29	146	84	61-72
MAJOR LEAGUE TOTALS					709	2856	577	805	147	47	20		.282	231	1106	109	5 yrs

John Joseph O'Connor   Born Jun 2, 1869   St Louis, MO
5'10   170 lbs   Batted right   Died Nov 14, 1937   St Louis, MO

YR	POS	TEAM	LG	FIN	G	AB	R	H	2B	3B	HR	RBI	AVG	BB	TB	OQ	RANK
1887	LF-C	CIN	AA	2-8	12	40	4	4	0	0	0		.100	2	4	—	—
1888	CF	CIN	AA	4-8	36	137	14	28	3	1	1	17	.204	6	36	76	—
1889	C-RF	COL	AA	6-8	107	398	69	107	17	7	4	60	.269	33	150	103	29-51
1890	C	COL	AA	2-8	121	457	89	148	14	10	2		.324	38	188	126	10-42
1891	RF-C	COL	AA	6-8	56	229	28	61	12	3	0	37	.266	11	79	88	—
1892	RF-C	CLE	NL	2-12	140	572	71	142	22	5	1	58	.248	25	177	84	63-72
1893	C-CF	CLE	NL	3-12	96	384	72	110	23	1	4	75	.286	29	147	95	56-80
1894	C-CF	CLE	NL	6-12	86	330	67	104	23	7	2	51	.315	15	147	92	—
1895	C-1B	CLE	NL	2-12	89	340	51	99	14	10	0	58	.291	30	133	97	—
1896	C-1B	CLE	NL	2-12	68	256	41	76	11	1	1	43	.297	15	92	89	—
1897	RF-1B	CLE	NL	5-12	103	397	49	115	21	4	2	69	.290	26	150	94	53-69
1898	1B-C	CLE	NL	5-12	131	478	50	119	17	4	1	56	.249	26	147	82	67-75
1899	C-1B	SL	NL	5-12	84	289	33	73	5	6	0	43	.253	15	90	78	—
1900	C	SL/PT	NL	5/2	53	179	19	42	4	1	0	25	.235	5	48	63	—
1901	C	PIT	NL	1-8	61	202	16	39	7	3	0	22	.193	10	52	67	—
1902	C-1B	PIT	NL	1-8	49	170	13	50	1	2	1	28	.294	3	58	97	—
1903	C	NY	AL	4-8	64	212	13	43	4	1	0	12	.203	8	49	62	—
1904	C	SL	AL	6-8	14	47	4	10	1	0	0	2	.213	2	11	—	—
1906	C	SL	AL	5-8	55	174	8	33	0	0	0	11	.190	2	33	48	—
1907	C	SL	AL	6-8	25	89	2	14	2	0	0	4	.157	0	16	—	—
1910	C	SL	AL	8-8	1	0	0	0	0	0	0	0	.000	0	0	—	—
MAJOR LEAGUE TOTALS					1451	5380	713	1417	201	66	19		.263	301	1807	97	6 yrs

William Benjamin Fuller Born Oct 10, 1867 Cincinnati, OH
Batted right   Died Apr 11, 1904 Cincinnati, OH

YR	POS	TEAM	LG	FIN	G	AB	R	H	2B	3B	HR	RBI	AVG	BB	TB	OQ	RANK
1888	SS	WAS	NL	8-8	49	170	11	31	5	2	0	12	.182	10	40	72	—
1889	SS	SL	AA	2-8	140	517	91	117	18	6	0	51	.226	52	147	82	47-51
1890	SS	SL	AA	3-8	130	526	118	146	9	9	1		.278	73	176	113	21-42
1891	SS-2B	SL	AA	2-8	137	586	107	127	15	7	2	63	.217	67	162	82	42-48
1892	SS	NY	NL	8-12	141	508	74	115	11	4	1	48	.226	52	137	86	60-72
1893	SS	NY	NL	5-12	130	474	78	112	14	8	0	51	.236	60	142	82	72-80
1894	SS	NY	NL	2-12	93	368	81	104	14	4	2	46	.283	52	132	90	61-77
1895	SS	NY	NL	9-12	126	458	82	103	11	3	0	32	.225	64	120	74	71-75
1896	SS	NY	NL	7-12	18	72	10	12	0	0	0	7	.167	14	12	—	—

| MAJOR LEAGUE TOTALS | | | | | 964 | 3679 | 652 | 867 | 97 | 43 | 6 | | .236 | 444 | 1068 | 87 | 7 yrs |

Jacob Peter Beckley   Born Aug 4, 1867 Hannibal, MO
5'10 200 lbs Batted left   Died Jun 25, 1918 Kansas City, MO

YR	POS	TEAM	LG	FIN	G	AB	R	H	2B	3B	HR	RBI	AVG	BB	TB	OQ	RANK
1888	1B	PIT	NL	6-8	71	283	35	97	15	3	0	27	.343	7	118	134	—
1889	1B	PIT	NL	5-8	123	522	91	157	24	10	9	97	.301	29	228	114	19-53
1890	1B	PIT	PL	6-8	121	516	109	167	38	22	9	120	.324	42	276	136	9-57
1891	1B	PIT	NL	8-8	133	554	94	162	20	19	4	73	.292	44	232	120	18-52
1892	1B	PIT	NL	6-12	151	614	102	145	21	19	10	96	.236	31	234	101	48-72
1893	1B	PIT	NL	2-12	131	542	108	164	32	19	5	106	.303	54	249	118	26-80
1894	1B	PIT	NL	7-12	131	533	121	183	36	18	7	120	.343	43	276	117	30-77
1895	1B	PIT	NL	7-12	129	530	104	174	31	19	5	110	.328	24	258	114	30-75
1896	1B	PT/NY	NL	6/7	105	399	81	110	15	9	8	70	.276	31	167	102	42-73
1897	1B	NY/CN	NL	3/4	114	433	84	143	19	12	8	87	.330	20	210	120	23-69
1898	1B	CIN	NL	3-12	118	459	86	135	20	12	4	72	.294	28	191	115	30-75
1899	1B	CIN	NL	6-12	134	513	87	171	27	16	3	99	.333	40	239	131	14-61
1900	1B	CIN	NL	7-8	141	558	98	190	26	10	2	94	.341	40	242	124	10-47
1901	1B	CIN	NL	8-8	140	580	78	178	36	13	3	79	.307	28	249	121	20-45
1902	1B	CIN	NL	4-8	129	531	82	175	23	7	5	69	.330	34	227	140	7-46
1903	1B	CIN	NL	4-8	120	459	85	150	29	10	2	81	.327	42	205	136	12-49
1904	1B	SL	NL	5-8	142	551	72	179	22	9	1	67	.325	35	222	132	6-42
1905	1B	SL	NL	6-8	134	514	48	147	20	10	1	57	.286	30	190	109	21-45
1906	1B	SL	NL	7-8	87	320	29	79	16	6	0	44	.247	13	107	95	—
1907	1B	SL	NL	8-8	32	115	6	24	3	0	0	7	.209	1	27	59	—

| MAJOR LEAGUE TOTALS | | | | | 2386 | 9526 | 1600 | 2930 | 473 | 243 | 86 | 1575 | .308 | 616 | 4147 | 121 | 17 yrs |

William B Weaver   Born Mar 23, 1868 Parkersburg, WV
Batted left   Died Jan 23, 1943   Akron, OH

YR	POS	TEAM	LG	FIN	G	AB	R	H	2B	3B	HR	RBI	AVG	BB	TB	OQ	RANK
1888	CF	LOU	AA	7-8	26	112	12	28	1	1	0	8	.250	3	31	80	—
1889	CF	LOU	AA	8-8	124	499	62	145	17	6	0	60	.291	40	174	99	33-51
1890	CF	LOU	AA	1-8	130	557	101	161	27	9	3		.289	29	215	106	26-42
1891	CF	LOU	AA	7-8	135	565	76	160	25	7	1	55	.283	33	202	95	33-48
1892	LF-C	LOU	NL	9-12	138	551	58	140	15	4	0	57	.254	40	163	88	58-72
1893	RF-C	LOU	NL	11-12	106	439	79	128	17	7	2	49	.292	27	165	91	61-80
1894	RF-C	LO/PT	NL	12/7	94	359	35	94	12	4	3	48	.262	13	123	66	—
MAJOR LEAGUE TOTALS					753	3082	423	856	114	38	9		.278	185	1073	96	5 yrs

William J Gleason   Born Oct 26, 1866 Camden, NJ
5'7 158 lbs Batted both   Died Jan 2, 1933   Philadelphia, PA

YR	POS	TEAM	LG	FIN	G	AB	R	H	2B	3B	HR	RBI	AVG	BB	TB	OQ	RANK
1888	P	PHI	NL	3-8	24	83	4	17	2	0	0	5	.205	3	19	—	—
1889	P	PHI	NL	4-8	30	99	11	25	5	0	0	8	.253	8	30	83	—
1890	P	PHI	NL	3-8	63	224	22	47	3	0	0	17	.210	12	50	59	—
1891	P-CF	PHI	NL	4-8	65	214	31	53	5	2	0	17	.248	20	62	87	—
1892	P-RF	SL	NL	11-12	66	233	35	50	4	2	3	25	.215	34	67	98	—
1893	P-RF	SL	NL	10-12	59	199	25	51	6	4	0	20	.256	19	65	84	—
1894	P	SL/BA	NL	9/1	35	114	25	37	5	2	0	18	.325	9	46	92	—
1895	2B-3B	BAL	NL	1-12	112	421	90	130	14	12	0	74	.309	33	168	99	43-75
1896	2B	NY	NL	7-12	133	541	79	162	17	5	4	89	.299	42	201	96	49-73
1897	2B	NY	NL	3-12	131	540	85	172	16	4	1	106	.319	26	199	92	57-69
1898	2B	NY	NL	7-12	150	570	78	126	8	5	0	62	.221	39	144	70	73-75
1899	2B	NY	NL	10-12	146	576	72	152	14	4	0	59	.264	24	174	75	58-61
1900	2B	NY	NL	8-8	111	420	60	104	11	3	1	29	.248	17	124	72	46-47
1901	2B	DET	AL	3-8	135	547	82	150	16	12	3	75	.274	41	199	99	31-46
1902	2B	DET	AL	7-8	118	441	42	109	11	4	1	38	.247	25	131	77	44-46
1903	2B	PHI	NL	7-8	106	412	65	117	19	6	1	49	.284	23	151	100	33-49
1904	2B	PHI	NL	8-8	153	587	61	161	23	6	0	42	.274	37	196	104	29-42
1905	2B	PHI	NL	4-8	155	608	95	150	17	7	1	50	.247	45	184	91	41-45
1906	2B	PHI	NL	4-8	135	494	47	112	17	2	0	34	.227	36	133	85	42-42
1907	2B-SS	PHI	NL	3-8	36	126	11	18	3	0	0	6	.143	7	21	50	—
1908	2B	PHI	NL	4-8	2	1	0	0	0	0	0	0	.000	0	0	—	—
1912	2B	CHI	AL	4-8	1	2	0	1	0	0	0	0	.500	0	1	—	—
MAJOR LEAGUE TOTALS					1966	7452	1020	1944	216	80	15	823	.261	500	2365	88	12 yrs

Walter Robert Wilmot
Batted both

Born Oct 18, 1863 Plover, WI
Died Feb 1, 1929 Chicago, IL

YR	POS	TEAM	LG	FIN	G	AB	R	H	2B	3B	HR	RBI	AVG	BB	TB	OQ	RANK
1888	LF	WAS	NL	8-8	119	473	61	106	16	9	4	43	.224	23	152	95	30-46
1889	LF	WAS	NL	8-8	108	432	88	125	19	19	9	57	.289	51	209	137	9-53
1890	CF	CHI	NL	2-8	139	571	114	159	15	12	13	99	.278	64	237	123	14-48
1891	LF	CHI	NL	2-8	121	498	102	139	14	10	11	71	.279	55	206	124	13-52
1892	LF	CHI	NL	7-12	92	380	47	82	7	7	2	35	.216	40	109	89	—
1893	LF	CHI	NL	9-12	94	392	69	118	14	14	3	61	.301	40	169	113	32-80
1894	LF	CHI	NL	8-12	133	597	134	197	45	12	5	130	.330	35	281	102	46-77
1895	LF	CHI	NL	4-12	108	466	86	132	16	6	8	72	.283	30	184	92	56-75
1897	LF	NY	NL	3-12	11	34	8	9	2	0	1	4	.265	2	14	—	—
1898	RF	NY	NL	7-12	35	138	16	33	4	2	2	22	.239	9	47	91	—
MAJOR LEAGUE TOTALS					960	3981	725	1100	152	91	58	594	.276	349	1608	112	7 yrs

Charles Andrew Farrell
6'1 208 lbs Batted both

Born Aug 31, 1866 Oakdale, MA
Died Feb 15, 1925 Boston, MA

YR	POS	TEAM	LG	FIN	G	AB	R	H	2B	3B	HR	RBI	AVG	BB	TB	OQ	RANK
1888	C-RF	CHI	NL	2-8	64	241	34	56	6	3	3	19	.232	4	77	88	—
1889	C-CF	CHI	NL	3-8	101	407	66	101	19	7	11	75	.248	41	167	110	24-53
1890	C-1B	CHI	PL	4-8	117	451	79	131	21	12	2	84	.290	42	182	104	36-57
1891	3B-C	BOS	AA	1-8	122	473	108	143	19	13	12	110	.302	59	224	141	6-48
1892	3B-LF	PIT	NL	6-12	152	605	96	130	10	13	8	77	.215	46	190	89	57-72
1893	C-3B	WAS	NL	12-12	124	511	84	143	13	13	4	75	.280	47	194	97	53-80
1894	C	NY	NL	2-12	114	401	47	114	20	12	4	66	.284	35	170	92	59-77
1895	C-3B	NY	NL	9-12	90	312	38	90	16	9	1	58	.288	38	127	107	—
1896	C-3B	NY/WA	NL	7/9	95	321	41	93	14	6	2	67	.290	26	125	99	—
1897	C	WAS	NL	6-12	78	261	41	84	9	6	0	53	.322	17	105	104	—
1898	C-1B	WAS	NL	11-12	99	338	47	106	12	6	1	53	.314	34	133	123	—
1899	C	WA/BR	NL	11/1	85	266	42	80	11	7	2	56	.301	37	111	128	—
1900	C	BRO	NL	1-8	76	273	33	75	11	5	0	39	.275	11	96	88	—
1901	C-1B	BRO	NL	3-8	80	284	38	84	10	6	1	31	.296	7	109	102	—
1902	C-1B	BRO	NL	2-8	74	264	14	64	5	2	0	24	.242	12	73	81	—
1903	C	BOS	AL	1-8	17	52	5	21	5	1	0	8	.404	5	28	—	—
1904	C	BOS	AL	1-8	68	198	11	42	9	2	0	15	.212	15	55	88	—
1905	C	BOS	AL	4-8	7	21	2	6	1	0	0	2	.286	1	7	—	—
MAJOR LEAGUE TOTALS					1563	5679	826	1563	211	123	51	912	.275	477	2173	106	6 yrs

William Robert Hamilton   Born Feb 16, 1866   Newark, NJ
5'6   165 lbs   Batted left   Died Dec 16, 1940   Worcester, MA

YR	POS	TEAM	LG	FIN	G	AB	R	H	2B	3B	HR	RBI	AVG	BB	TB	OQ	RANK
1888	RF	KC	AA	8-8	35	129	21	34	4	4	0	11	.264	4	46	104	—
1889	RF	KC	AA	7-8	137	534	144	161	17	12	3	77	.301	87	211	131	10-51
1890	LF	PHI	NL	3-8	123	496	133	161	13	9	2	49	.325	83	198	141	5-48
1891	LF	PHI	NL	4-8	133	527	141	179	23	7	2	60	.340	102	222	158	1-52
1892	LF	PHI	NL	4-12	139	554	132	183	21	7	3	53	.330	81	227	148	5-72
1893	CF	PHI	NL	4-12	82	355	110	135	22	7	5	44	.380	63	186	167	1-80
1894	CF	PHI	NL	4-12	129	544	192	220	25	15	4	87	.404	126	287	164	5-77
1895	CF	PHI	NL	3-12	123	517	166	201	22	6	7	74	.389	96	256	160	4-75
1896	CF	BOS	NL	4-12	131	523	152	191	24	9	3	52	.365	110	242	158	5-73
1897	CF	BOS	NL	1-12	127	507	152	174	17	5	3	61	.343	105	210	143	6-69
1898	CF	BOS	NL	1-12	110	417	110	154	16	5	3	50	.369	87	189	179	1-75
1899	CF	BOS	NL	2-12	84	297	63	92	7	1	1	33	.310	72	104	138	—
1900	CF	BOS	NL	4-8	136	520	103	173	20	5	1	47	.333	107	206	146	4-47
1901	CF	BOS	NL	5-8	102	348	71	100	11	2	3	38	.287	64	124	133	—

MAJOR LEAGUE TOTALS   1591   6268 1690 2158 242 94 40 736 .344 1187 2708 154   11 yrs

Hugh Duffy   Born Nov 26, 1866   Cranston, RI
5'7   168 lbs   Batted right   Died Oct 19, 1954   Boston, MA

YR	POS	TEAM	LG	FIN	G	AB	R	H	2B	3B	HR	RBI	AVG	BB	TB	OQ	RANK
1888	RF	CHI	NL	2-8	71	298	60	84	10	4	7	41	.282	9	123	123	—
1889	RF	CHI	NL	3-8	136	584	144	172	21	7	12	89	.295	46	243	113	20-53
1890	RF	CHI	PL	4-8	138	596	161	191	36	16	7	82	.320	59	280	125	13-57
1891	RF	BOS	AA	1-8	127	536	134	180	20	8	9	110	.336	61	243	140	7-48
1892	CF	BOS	NL	1-12	147	612	125	184	28	12	5	81	.301	60	251	130	16-72
1893	CF	BOS	NL	1-12	131	560	147	203	23	7	6	118	.363	50	258	127	15-80
1894	CF	BOS	NL	3-12	125	539	160	237	51	16	18	145	.440	66	374	188	1-77
1895	CF	BOS	NL	5-12	130	531	110	187	30	6	9	100	.352	63	256	133	14-75
1896	LF	BOS	NL	4-12	131	527	97	158	16	8	5	113	.300	52	205	104	41-73
1897	LF	BOS	NL	1-12	134	550	130	187	25	10	11	129	.340	52	265	132	18-69
1898	LF	BOS	NL	1-12	152	568	97	169	13	3	8	108	.298	59	212	116	29-75
1899	LF	BOS	NL	2-12	147	588	103	164	29	7	5	102	.279	39	222	99	39-61
1900	LF	BOS	NL	4-8	55	181	27	55	5	4	2	31	.304	16	74	116	—
1901	CF	MIL	AL	8-8	79	285	40	86	15	9	2	45	.302	16	125	115	—
1904	LF-CF	PHI	NL	8-8	18	46	10	13	1	1	0	5	.283	13	16	—	—
1905	RF-CF	PHI	NL	4-8	15	40	7	12	2	1	0	3	.300	1	16	—	—
1906	PH	PHI	NL	4-8	1	1	0	0	0	0	0	0	.000	0	0	—	—

MAJOR LEAGUE TOTALS   1737   7042 1552 2282 325 119 106 1302 .324 662 3163 128   11 yrs

William Ellsworth Hoy
5'4 148 lbs Batted left

Born May 23, 1862 Houckstown, OH
Died Dec 15, 1961 Cincinnati, OH

YR	POS	TEAM	LG	FIN	G	AB	R	H	2B	3B	HR	RBI	AVG	BB	TB	OQ	RANK
1888	CF	WAS	NL	8-8	136	503	77	138	10	8	2	29	.274	69	170	131	11-46
1889	CF	WAS	NL	8-8	127	507	98	139	11	6	0	39	.274	75	162	104	27-53
1890	CF	BUF	PL	8-8	122	493	107	147	17	8	1	53	.298	94	183	119	19-57
1891	CF	SL	AA	2-8	141	567	136	165	14	5	5	66	.291	119	204	132	10-48
1892	CF	WAS	NL	10-12	152	593	108	166	19	8	3	75	.280	86	210	124	20-72
1893	CF	WAS	NL	12-12	130	564	106	138	12	6	0	45	.245	66	162	79	76-80
1894	CF	CIN	NL	10-12	126	495	114	148	22	13	5	70	.299	87	211	111	35-77
1895	LF-CF	CIN	NL	8-12	107	429	93	119	21	12	3	55	.277	52	173	104	38-75
1896	CF	CIN	NL	3-12	121	443	120	132	23	7	4	57	.298	65	181	118	22-73
1897	CF	CIN	NL	4-12	128	497	87	145	24	6	2	42	.292	54	187	103	43-69
1898	CF	LOU	NL	9-12	148	582	104	177	15	16	6	66	.304	49	242	122	19-75
1899	CF	LOU	NL	9-12	154	633	116	194	17	13	5	49	.306	61	252	115	25-61
1901	CF	CHI	AL	1-8	132	527	112	155	28	11	2	60	.294	86	211	130	8-46
1902	CF	CIN	NL	4-8	72	279	48	81	15	2	2	20	.290	41	106	142	—
MAJOR LEAGUE TOTALS					1796	7112	1426	2044	248	121	40	726	.287	1004	2654	115	13 yrs

Edward James Delahanty
6'1 170 lbs Batted right

Born Oct 30, 1867 Cleveland, OH
Died Jul 2, 1903 Niagara Falls, NY

YR	POS	TEAM	LG	FIN	G	AB	R	H	2B	3B	HR	RBI	AVG	BB	TB	OQ	RANK
1888	2B-LF	PHI	NL	3-8	74	290	40	66	12	2	1	31	.228	12	85	87	—
1889	LF-2B	PHI	NL	4-8	56	246	37	72	13	3	0	27	.293	14	91	97	—
1890	SS-2B	CLE	PL	7-8	115	517	107	154	26	13	3	64	.298	24	215	98	39-57
1891	CF-1B	PHI	NL	4-8	128	543	92	132	19	9	5	86	.243	33	184	90	42-52
1892	CF	PHI	NL	4-12	123	477	79	146	30	21	6	91	.306	31	236	144	6-72
1893	LF-2B	PHI	NL	4-12	132	595	145	219	35	18	19	146	.368	47	347	155	3-80
1894	LF-1B	PHI	NL	4-12	114	489	147	199	39	18	4	131	.407	60	286	154	6-77
1895	LF	PHI	NL	3-12	116	480	149	194	49	10	11	106	.404	86	296	192	1-75
1896	LF-1B	PHI	NL	8-12	123	499	131	198	44	17	13	126	.397	62	315	187	1-73
1897	LF	PHI	NL	10-12	129	530	109	200	40	15	5	96	.377	60	285	158	1-69
1898	LF	PHI	NL	6-12	144	548	115	183	36	9	4	92	.334	77	249	152	4-75
1899	LF	PHI	NL	3-12	146	581	135	238	55	9	9	137	.410	55	338	185	2-61
1900	1B	PHI	NL	3-8	131	539	82	174	32	10	2	109	.323	41	232	121	13-47
1901	LF-1B	PHI	NL	2-8	139	542	106	192	38	16	8	108	.354	65	286	176	1-45
1902	LF-1B	WAS	AL	6-8	123	473	103	178	43	14	10	93	.376	62	279	189	1-46
1903	LF	WAS	AL	8-8	42	156	22	52	11	1	1	21	.333	12	68	141	—
MAJOR LEAGUE TOTALS					1835	7505	1599	2597	522	185	101	1464	.346	741	3792	154	13 yrs

Clarence Algernon Childs   Born Aug 14, 1867 Calvert County, MO
5'8   185 lbs   Batted left   Died Nov 8, 1912   Baltimore, MD

YR	POS	TEAM	LG	FIN	G	AB	R	H	2B	3B	HR	RBI	AVG	BB	TB	OQ	RANK
1888	2B	PHI	NL	3-8	2	4	0	0	0	0	0	0	.000	0	0	—	—
1890	2B	SYR	AA	6-8	126	493	109	170	33	14	2		.345	72	237	165	1-42
1891	2B	CLE	NL	5-8	141	551	120	155	21	12	2	83	.281	97	206	130	8-52
1892	2B	CLE	NL	2-12	145	558	136	177	14	11	3	53	.317	117	222	159	3-72
1893	2B	CLE	NL	3-12	124	485	145	158	19	10	3	65	.326	120	206	147	5-80
1894	2B	CLE	NL	6-12	118	479	143	169	21	12	2	52	.353	107	220	136	10-77
1895	2B	CLE	NL	2-12	119	462	96	133	15	3	4	90	.288	74	166	105	37-75
1896	2B	CLE	NL	2-12	132	498	106	177	24	9	1	106	.355	100	222	150	9-73
1897	2B	CLE	NL	5-12	114	444	105	150	15	9	1	61	.338	74	186	133	15-69
1898	2B	CLE	NL	5-12	110	413	90	119	9	4	1	31	.288	69	139	120	22-75
1899	2B	SL	NL	5-12	125	464	73	123	11	11	1	48	.265	74	159	110	30-61
1900	2B	CHI	NL	5-8	137	531	67	128	14	5	0	44	.241	57	152	84	43-47
1901	2B	CHI	NL	6-8	63	236	24	61	9	0	0	21	.258	30	70	100	—
MAJOR LEAGUE TOTALS					1456	5618	1214	1720	205	100	20		.306	991	2185	131	11 yrs

William Wilson Hallman   Born Mar 31, 1867 Pittsburgh, PA
5'8   160 lbs   Batted right   Died Sep 11, 1920 Philadelphia, PA

YR	POS	TEAM	LG	FIN	G	AB	R	H	2B	3B	HR	RBI	AVG	BB	TB	OQ	RANK
1888	C-2B	PHI	NL	3-8	18	63	5	13	4	1	0	6	.206	1	19	—	—
1889	SS-2B	PHI	NL	4-8	119	462	67	117	21	8	2	60	.253	36	160	92	40-53
1890	RF-C	PHI	PL	5-8	84	356	59	95	16	7	1	37	.267	33	128	92	—
1891	2B	PHI	AA	4-8	141	587	112	166	21	13	6	69	.283	38	231	105	27-48
1892	2B	PHI	NL	4-12	138	586	106	171	27	10	2	84	.292	32	224	110	32-72
1893	2B	PHI	NL	4-12	132	596	119	183	28	7	5	76	.307	51	240	104	41-80
1894	2B	PHI	NL	4-12	119	505	107	156	19	7	0	66	.309	36	189	83	70-77
1895	2B	PHI	NL	3-12	124	539	94	169	26	5	1	91	.314	34	208	94	52-75
1896	2B	PHI	NL	8-12	120	469	82	150	21	3	2	83	.320	45	183	107	39-73
1897	2B	PH/SL	NL	10/12	110	424	47	99	9	2	0	41	.233	32	112	67	68-69
1898	2B	BRO	NL	10-12	134	509	57	124	10	7	2	63	.244	29	154	81	68-75
1901	SS	CLE	AL	7-8	5	19	2	4	0	0	0	3	.211	2	4	—	—
1901	2B-3B	PHI	NL	2-8	123	445	46	82	13	5	0	38	.184	26	105	63	45-45
1902	3B	PHI	NL	7-8	73	254	14	63	8	4	0	35	.248	14	79	93	—
1903	2B-3B	PHI	NL	7-8	63	198	20	42	11	2	0	17	.212	16	57	79	—
MAJOR LEAGUE TOTALS					1503	6012	937	1634	234	81	21	769	.272	425	2093	91	10 yrs

John Charles Crooks
170 lbs Batted right

Born Nov 9, 1865 St Paul, MN
Died Feb 2, 1918 St Louis, MO

YR	POS	TEAM	LG	FIN	G	AB	R	H	2B	3B	HR	RBI	AVG	BB	TB	OQ	RANK
1889	2B	COL	AA	6-8	12	43	13	14	2	3	0	7	.326	10	22	—	—
1890	2B	COL	AA	2-8	135	485	86	107	5	4	1		.221	96	123	100	30-42
1891	2B	COL	AA	6-8	138	519	110	127	19	13	0	46	.245	103	172	115	21-48
1892	2B-3B	SL	NL	11-12	128	445	82	95	7	4	7	38	.213	136	131	136	9-72
1893	2B	SL	NL	10-12	128	448	93	106	10	9	1	48	.237	121	137	111	34-80
1895	2B	WAS	NL	10-12	117	409	80	114	19	8	6	57	.279	68	167	115	28-75
1896	2B	WA/LO	NL	9/12	64	206	39	53	8	1	5	35	.257	36	78	111	—
1898	2B	SL	NL	12-12	72	225	33	52	4	2	1	20	.231	40	63	101	—
MAJOR LEAGUE TOTALS					794	2780	536	668	74	44	21		.240	610	893	115	5 yrs

John Joseph Doyle
5'9 155 lbs Batted right

Born Oct 25, 1869 Killorglin, Ireland
Died Dec 31, 1958 Holyoke, MA

YR	POS	TEAM	LG	FIN	G	AB	R	H	2B	3B	HR	RBI	AVG	BB	TB	OQ	RANK
1889	C-RF	COL	AA	6-8	11	36	6	10	1	1	0	3	.278	6	13	—	—
1890	C-SS	COL	AA	2-8	77	298	47	80	17	7	2		.268	13	117	103	—
1891	C-RF	CLE	NL	5-8	69	250	43	69	14	4	0	43	.276	26	91	110	—
1892	C-2B	CL/NY	NL	2/8	114	454	78	135	26	2	6	69	.297	24	183	116	27-72
1893	C-CF	NY	NL	5-12	82	318	56	102	17	5	1	51	.321	27	132	109	—
1894	1B	NY	NL	2-12	105	422	90	155	30	8	3	100	.367	35	210	118	28-77
1895	1B-2B	NY	NL	9-12	82	319	52	100	21	3	1	66	.313	24	130	101	—
1896	1B	BAL	NL	1-12	118	487	116	165	29	4	1	101	.339	42	205	115	27-73
1897	1B	BAL	NL	2-12	114	460	91	163	29	4	2	87	.354	29	206	119	24-69
1898	1B-RF	WA/NY	NL	11/7	125	474	68	138	17	5	3	69	.291	19	174	98	48-75
1899	1B	NY	NL	10-12	118	448	55	134	15	7	3	76	.299	33	172	105	35-61
1900	1B	NY	NL	8-8	133	505	69	135	24	1	1	66	.267	34	164	87	41-47
1901	1B	CHI	NL	6-8	75	285	21	66	9	2	0	39	.232	7	79	69	—
1902	1B	NY	NL	8-8	49	186	21	56	13	0	1	19	.301	10	72	121	—
1902	2B-1B	WAS	AL	6-8	78	312	52	77	15	2	1	20	.247	29	99	89	—
1903	1B	BRO	NL	5-8	139	524	84	164	27	6	0	91	.313	54	203	121	17-49
1904	1B	BR/PH	NL	6/8	74	258	22	57	11	3	1	24	.221	25	77	97	—
1905	1B	NY	AL	6-8	1	3	0	0	0	0	0	0	.000	0	0	—	—
MAJOR LEAGUE TOTALS					1564	6039	971	1806	315	64	26		.299	437	2327	110	8 yrs

James Wear Holliday
5'11 151 lbs Batted right

Born Feb 8, 1867 St Louis, MO
Died Feb 15, 1910 Cincinnati, OH

YR	POS	TEAM	LG	FIN	G	AB	R	H	2B	3B	HR	RBI	AVG	BB	TB	OQ	RANK
1889	CF	CIN	AA	4-8	135	563	107	181	28	7	19	104	.321	43	280	139	6-51
1890	CF	CIN	NL	4-8	131	518	93	140	18	14	4	75	.270	49	198	110	25-48
1891	CF	CIN	NL	7-8	111	442	74	141	21	10	9	84	.319	37	209	139	5-52
1892	RF	CIN	NL	5-12	152	602	114	176	23	16	13	91	.292	57	270	137	8-72
1893	CF	CIN	NL	6-12	126	500	108	155	24	10	5	89	.310	73	214	123	20-80
1894	LF	CIN	NL	10-12	121	511	119	190	24	7	13	119	.372	40	267	123	19-77
1895	CF	CIN	NL	8-12	32	127	25	38	9	2	0	20	.299	10	51	98	—
1896	CF	CIN	NL	3-12	29	84	17	27	4	0	0	8	.321	9	31	—	—
1897	LF	CIN	NL	4-12	61	195	50	61	9	4	2	20	.313	27	84	125	—
1898	CF	CIN	NL	3-12	30	106	21	25	2	1	0	7	.236	14	29	90	—
MAJOR LEAGUE TOTALS					928	3648	728	1134	162	71	65	617	.311	359	1633	129	6 yrs

Herman C Long
5'8 160 lbs Batted left

Born Apr 13, 1866 Chicago, IL
Died Sep 17, 1909 Denver, CO

YR	POS	TEAM	LG	FIN	G	AB	R	H	2B	3B	HR	RBI	AVG	BB	TB	OQ	RANK
1889	SS	KC	AA	7-8	136	574	137	158	32	6	3	60	.275	64	211	109	24-51
1890	SS	BOS	NL	5-8	101	431	95	108	15	3	8	52	.251	40	153	101	34-48
1891	SS	BOS	NL	1-8	139	577	129	163	21	11	10	74	.282	80	236	130	10-52
1892	SS	BOS	NL	1-12	151	646	115	181	33	6	6	77	.280	44	244	110	31-72
1893	SS	BOS	NL	1-12	128	552	149	159	22	6	6	58	.288	73	211	107	39-80
1894	SS	BOS	NL	3-12	104	475	137	154	28	11	12	79	.324	35	240	110	37-77
1895	SS	BOS	NL	5-12	124	535	109	169	23	10	9	75	.316	31	239	106	36-75
1896	SS	BOS	NL	4-12	120	501	105	172	26	8	6	100	.343	26	232	117	24-73
1897	SS	BOS	NL	1-12	107	450	89	145	32	7	3	69	.322	23	200	110	32-69
1898	SS	BOS	NL	1-12	144	589	99	156	21	10	6	99	.265	39	215	100	46-75
1899	SS	BOS	NL	2-12	145	578	91	153	30	8	6	100	.265	45	217	99	39-61
1900	SS	BOS	NL	4-8	125	486	80	127	19	4	12	66	.261	44	190	106	23-47
1901	SS	BOS	NL	5-8	138	518	54	112	14	6	3	68	.216	25	147	75	42-45
1902	SS-2B	BOS	NL	3-8	120	439	40	101	11	0	2	44	.230	31	118	84	39-46
1903	SS-2B	NY/DE	AL	4/5	91	319	27	68	15	0	0	31	.213	12	83	69	—
1904	2B	PHI	NL	8-8	1	4	0	1	0	0	0	0	.250	0	1	—	—
MAJOR LEAGUE TOTALS					1874	7674	1456	2127	342	96	92	1052	.277	612	2937	105	14 yrs

James Robert McAleer　　　　　　　Born Jul 10, 1864　Youngstown, OH
6'0　175 lbs　Batted right　　　　　　　Died Apr 29, 1931　Youngstown, OH

YR	POS	TEAM	LG	FIN	G	AB	R	H	2B	3B	HR	RBI	AVG	BB	TB	OQ	RANK
1889	CF	CLE	NL	6-8	110	447	66	105	6	6	1	35	.235	30	126	74	52-53
1890	CF	CLE	PL	7-8	86	341	58	91	8	7	1	42	.267	37	116	91	—
1891	LF	CLE	NL	5-8	136	565	97	134	16	11	1	61	.237	49	175	88	44-52
1892	CF	CLE	NL	2-12	149	571	92	136	26	7	4	70	.238	63	188	103	44-72
1893	CF	CLE	NL	3-12	91	350	63	83	5	1	2	41	.237	35	96	73	—
1894	CF	CLE	NL	6-12	64	253	36	73	15	1	2	40	.289	13	96	78	—
1895	CF	CLE	NL	2-12	131	528	84	143	17	2	0	68	.271	38	164	75	70-75
1896	CF	CLE	NL	2-12	116	455	70	131	16	4	1	54	.288	47	158	95	52-73
1897	CF	CLE	NL	5-12	24	91	6	20	2	0	0	10	.220	7	22	—	—
1898	CF	CLE	NL	5-12	106	366	47	87	3	0	0	48	.238	46	90	83	—
1901	CF	CLE	AL	7-8	3	7	0	1	0	0	0	0	.143	0	1	—	—
1902	RF	SL	AL	2-8	2	3	0	2	0	0	0	0	.667	0	2	—	—
1907	PR	SL	AL	6-8	2	0	0	0	0	0	0	0	—	0	0	—	—
MAJOR LEAGUE TOTALS					1020	3977	619	1006	114	39	12	469	.253	365	1234	87	5 yrs

Walter Scott Brodie　　　　　　　　Born Sep 11, 1868　Warrenton, VA
5'11　180 lbs　Batted left　　　　　　　Died Oct 30, 1935　Baltimore, MD

YR	POS	TEAM	LG	FIN	G	AB	R	H	2B	3B	HR	RBI	AVG	BB	TB	OQ	RANK
1890	RF-CF	BOS	NL	5-8	132	514	77	152	19	9	0	67	.296	66	189	119	18-48
1891	CF	BOS	NL	1-8	133	523	84	136	13	6	2	78	.260	63	167	101	33-52
1892	CF-2B	SL	NL	11-12	154	602	85	152	10	9	4	60	.252	52	192	97	53-72
1893	CF	SL/BA	NL	10/8	132	566	89	184	23	10	2	98	.325	45	233	108	38-80
1894	CF	BAL	NL	1-12	129	573	134	210	25	11	3	113	.366	18	266	101	48-77
1895	CF	BAL	NL	1-12	131	528	85	184	27	10	2	134	.348	26	237	110	34-75
1896	CF	BAL	NL	1-12	132	516	98	153	19	11	2	87	.297	36	200	97	48-73
1897	CF	PIT	NL	8-12	100	370	47	108	7	12	2	53	.292	25	145	98	—
1898	CF	PT/BA	NL	8/2	65	254	27	71	8	2	0	40	.280	11	83	88	—
1899	CF	BAL	NL	4-12	137	531	82	164	26	1	3	87	.309	31	201	102	37-61
1901	CF	BAL	AL	5-8	83	306	41	95	6	6	2	41	.310	25	119	111	—
1902	CF	NY	NL	8-8	109	416	37	117	8	2	3	42	.281	22	138	102	30-46
MAJOR LEAGUE TOTALS					1437	5699	886	1726	191	89	25	900	.303	420	2170	104	9 yrs

William Frederick Clingman   Born Nov 21, 1869 Cincinnati, OH
5'11   150 lbs Batted both   Died May 14, 1958 Cincinnati, OH

YR	POS	TEAM	LG	FIN	G	AB	R	H	2B	3B	HR	RBI	AVG	BB	TB	OQ	RANK
1890	SS-2B	CIN	NL	4-8	7	27	2	7	1	0	0	5	.259	1	8	—	—
1891	2B	CIN	AA	5-8	1	5	0	1	1	0	0		.200	0	2	—	—
1895	3B	PIT	NL	7-12	106	382	69	99	16	4	0	45	.259	41	123	83	64-75
1896	3B	LOU	NL	12-12	121	423	57	99	10	2	2	37	.234	57	119	81	69-73
1897	3B	LOU	NL	11-12	113	395	59	90	14	7	2	47	.228	37	124	80	67-69
1898	3B-SS	LOU	NL	9-12	154	538	65	138	12	6	0	50	.257	51	162	91	59-75
1899	SS	LOU	NL	9-12	109	366	67	96	15	4	2	44	.262	46	125	102	—
1900	SS	CHI	NL	5-8	47	159	15	33	6	0	0	11	.208	17	39	72	—
1901	SS	WAS	AL	6-8	137	480	66	116	10	7	2	55	.242	42	146	84	45-46
1903	2B-SS	CLE	AL	3-8	21	64	10	18	1	1	0	7	.281	11	21	—	—
MAJOR LEAGUE TOTALS					816	2839	410	697	86	31	8		.246	303	869	84	5 yrs

Jesse Cail Burkett   Born Dec 4, 1868   Wheeling, WV
5'8   155 lbs Batted left   Died May 27, 1953 Worcester, MA

YR	POS	TEAM	LG	FIN	G	AB	R	H	2B	3B	HR	RBI	AVG	BB	TB	OQ	RANK
1890	RF-P	NY	NL	6-8	101	401	67	124	23	13	4	60	.309	33	185	133	8-48
1891	RF	CLE	NL	5-8	40	167	29	45	7	4	0	13	.269	23	60	116	—
1892	LF	CLE	NL	2-12	145	608	119	167	15	14	6	66	.275	67	228	119	21-72
1893	LF	CLE	NL	3-12	125	511	145	178	25	15	6	82	.348	98	251	155	2-80
1894	LF	CLE	NL	6-12	125	523	138	187	27	14	8	94	.358	84	266	134	13-77
1895	LF	CLE	NL	2-12	131	550	153	225	22	13	5	83	.409	74	288	160	5-75
1896	LF	CLE	NL	2-12	133	586	160	240	27	16	6	72	.410	49	317	158	6-73
1897	LF	CLE	NL	5-12	127	517	129	198	28	7	2	60	.383	76	246	152	4-69
1898	LF	CLE	NL	5-12	150	624	114	213	18	9	0	42	.341	69	249	132	12-75
1899	LF	SL	NL	5-12	141	558	116	221	21	8	7	71	.396	67	279	165	3-61
1900	LF	SL	NL	6-8	141	559	88	203	11	15	7	68	.363	62	265	149	3-47
1901	LF	SL	NL	4-8	142	601	142	226	20	15	10	75	.376	59	306	171	2-45
1902	LF	SL	AL	2-8	138	553	97	169	29	9	5	52	.306	71	231	129	9-46
1903	LF	SL	AL	6-8	132	515	73	151	20	7	3	40	.293	52	194	124	15-47
1904	LF	SL	AL	6-8	147	575	72	156	15	10	2	27	.271	78	197	129	9-47
1905	LF	BOS	AL	4-8	148	573	78	147	12	13	4	47	.257	67	197	122	12-41
MAJOR LEAGUE TOTALS					2066	8421	1720	2850	320	182	75	952	.338	1029	3759	142	15 yrs

Frank Harry Shugart   Born Dec 10, 1866 Luthersburg, PA
5'8   170 lbs   Batted right   Died Sep 9, 1944   Clearfield, PA

YR	POS	TEAM	LG	FIN	G	AB	R	H	2B	3B	HR	RBI	AVG	BB	TB	OQ	RANK
1890	SS-RF	CHI	PL	4-8	29	106	8	20	5	5	0	15	.189	5	35	69	—
1891	SS	PIT	NL	8-8	75	320	57	88	19	8	3	33	.275	20	132	111	—
1892	SS	PIT	NL	6-12	137	554	94	148	19	14	0	62	.267	47	195	106	38-72
1893	SS-CF	PT/SL	NL	2/10	111	456	78	124	17	7	1	60	.272	41	158	88	64-80
1894	CF	SL	NL	9-12	133	527	103	154	19	18	7	72	.292	38	230	92	57-77
1895	SS-CF	LOU	NL	12-12	113	473	61	125	14	13	4	70	.264	31	177	86	60-75
1897	SS	PHI	NL	10-12	40	163	20	41	8	2	5	25	.252	8	68	94	—
1901	SS	CHI	AL	1-8	107	415	62	104	9	12	2	47	.251	28	143	90	37-46
MAJOR LEAGUE TOTALS					745	3014	483	804	110	79	22	384	.267	218	1138	92	5 yrs

Patrick Joseph Donovan   Born Mar 16, 1865 County Cork, Ireland
5'11   175 lbs   Batted left   Died Dec 25, 1953 Lawrence, MA

YR	POS	TEAM	LG	FIN	G	AB	R	H	2B	3B	HR	RBI	AVG	BB	TB	OQ	RANK
1890	CF	BO/BR	NL	1/5	60	245	34	59	5	1	0	17	.241	13	66	72	—
1891	LF	LO/WA	AA	7/8	122	509	82	155	11	3	2	56	.305	34	178	98	31-48
1892	RF	WA/PT	NL	10/6	130	551	106	153	18	6	2	38	.278	31	189	99	51-72
1893	RF	PIT	NL	2-12	113	499	114	158	5	8	2	56	.317	42	185	98	50-80
1894	RF	PIT	NL	7-12	132	576	145	174	21	10	4	76	.302	33	227	83	69-77
1895	RF	PIT	NL	7-12	125	519	114	160	17	6	1	58	.308	47	192	96	47-75
1896	RF	PIT	NL	6-12	131	573	113	183	20	5	3	59	.319	35	222	99	46-73
1897	RF	PIT	NL	8-12	120	479	82	154	16	7	0	57	.322	25	184	97	49-69
1898	RF	PIT	NL	8-12	147	610	112	184	16	8	1	37	.302	34	219	101	45-75
1899	RF	PIT	NL	7-12	121	531	82	156	11	7	1	55	.294	17	184	86	52-61
1900	RF	SL	NL	6-8	126	503	78	159	11	1	0	61	.316	38	172	99	32-47
1901	RF	SL	NL	4-8	130	531	92	161	23	5	1	73	.303	27	197	106	26-45
1902	RF	SL	NL	6-8	126	502	70	158	12	4	0	35	.315	28	178	115	18-46
1903	RF	SL	NL	8-8	105	410	63	134	15	3	0	39	.327	25	155	111	23-49
1904	RF	WAS	AL	8-8	125	436	30	100	6	0	0	19	.229	24	106	76	—
1906	RF	BRO	NL	5-8	7	21	1	5	0	0	0	0	.238	0	5	—	—
1907	RF	BRO	NL	5-8	1	1	0	0	0	0	0	0	.000	0	0	—	—
MAJOR LEAGUE TOTALS					1821	7496	1318	2253	207	74	17	736	.301	453	2659	99	13 yrs

Jacob Charles Stenzel Born Jun 24, 1867 Cincinnati, OH
5'10 168 lbs Batted right Died Jan 6, 1919 Cincinnati, OH

YR	POS	TEAM	LG	FIN	G	AB	R	H	2B	3B	HR	RBI	AVG	BB	TB	OQ	RANK
1890	RF-C	CHI	NL	2-8	11	41	3	11	1	0	0	3	.268	1	12	—	—
1892	CF-C	PIT	NL	6-12	3	9	0	0	0	0	0	0	.000	1	0	—	—
1893	CF-C	PIT	NL	2-12	60	224	57	81	13	4	4	37	.362	24	114	143	—
1894	CF	PIT	NL	7-12	131	522	148	185	39	20	13	121	.354	75	303	144	7-77
1895	CF	PIT	NL	7-12	129	514	114	192	38	13	7	97	.374	57	277	149	8-75
1896	CF	PIT	NL	6-12	114	479	104	173	26	14	2	82	.361	32	233	129	16-73
1897	CF	BAL	NL	2-12	131	536	113	189	43	7	4	116	.353	36	258	128	20-69
1898	CF	BA/SL	NL	2/12	143	542	97	149	20	13	1	55	.275	53	198	109	40-75
1899	CF	SL/CN	NL	5/6	44	157	26	44	10	0	1	22	.280	20	57	110	—
MAJOR LEAGUE TOTALS					766	3024	662	1024	190	71	32	533	.339	299	1452	132	5 yrs

Thomas William Corcoran Born Jan 4, 1869 New Haven, CT
5'9 164 lbs Batted right Died Jun 25, 1960 Plainfield, CT

YR	POS	TEAM	LG	FIN	G	AB	R	H	2B	3B	HR	RBI	AVG	BB	TB	OQ	RANK
1890	SS	PIT	PL	6-8	123	503	80	117	14	13	1	61	.233	38	160	76	54-57
1891	SS	PHI	AA	4-8	133	511	84	130	11	15	7	71	.254	29	192	95	34-48
1892	SS	BRO	NL	3-12	151	613	77	145	11	6	1	74	.237	34	171	78	67-72
1893	SS	BRO	NL	6-12	115	459	61	126	11	10	2	58	.275	27	163	84	69-80
1894	SS	BRO	NL	5-12	129	576	123	173	21	20	5	92	.300	25	249	88	64-77
1895	SS	BRO	NL	5-12	127	535	81	142	17	10	2	69	.265	23	185	76	68-75
1896	SS	BRO	NL	9-12	132	532	63	154	15	7	3	73	.289	15	192	82	67-73
1897	SS-2B	CIN	NL	4-12	109	445	76	128	30	5	3	57	.288	13	177	90	60-69
1898	SS	CIN	NL	3-12	153	619	80	155	28	15	2	87	.250	26	219	90	61-75
1899	SS-2B	CIN	NL	6-12	137	537	91	149	11	8	0	81	.277	28	176	85	55-61
1900	SS	CIN	NL	7-8	127	523	64	128	21	9	1	54	.245	22	170	79	44-47
1901	SS	CIN	NL	8-8	31	115	14	24	3	3	0	15	.209	11	33	85	—
1902	SS	CIN	NL	4-8	138	538	54	136	18	4	0	54	.253	11	162	82	41-46
1903	SS	CIN	NL	4-8	115	459	61	113	18	7	2	73	.246	12	151	80	48-49
1904	SS	CIN	NL	3-8	150	578	55	133	17	9	2	74	.230	19	174	83	40-42
1905	SS	CIN	NL	5-8	151	605	70	150	21	11	2	85	.248	23	199	89	43-45
1906	SS	CIN	NL	6-8	117	430	29	89	13	1	1	33	.207	19	107	71	—
1907	SS	NY	NL	4-8	62	226	21	60	9	2	0	24	.265	7	73	93	—
MAJOR LEAGUE TOTALS					2200	8804	1184	2252	289	155	34	1135	.256	382	2953	84	15 yrs

Edward D Burke
5'6 161 lbs Batted right

Born Oct 6, 1866 Northumberland, PA
Died Nov 26, 1907 Utica, NY

YR	POS	TEAM	LG	FIN	G	AB	R	H	2B	3B	HR	RBI	AVG	BB	TB	OQ	RANK
1890	CF	PH/PT	NL	3/8	131	554	102	139	21	13	5	57	.251	63	201	107	32-48
1891	CF	MIL	AA	5-8	35	144	31	34	9	0	2	21	.236	12	49	91	—
1892	2B-LF	CN/NY	NL	5/8	104	404	87	100	11	5	6	45	.248	55	139	114	—
1893	LF	NY	NL	5-12	135	537	122	150	23	10	9	80	.279	51	220	103	42-80
1894	LF	NY	NL	2-12	136	566	121	172	23	11	4	77	.304	37	229	87	65-77
1895	LF	NY/CN	NL	9/8	95	395	90	104	14	8	2	37	.263	29	140	83	63-75
1896	LF	CIN	NL	3-12	122	521	120	177	24	9	1	52	.340	41	222	114	28-73
1897	LF	CIN	NL	4-12	95	387	71	103	17	1	1	41	.266	29	125	82	65-69
MAJOR LEAGUE TOTALS					853	3508	744	979	142	57	30	410	.279	317	1325	96	6 yrs

George Stacey Davis
5'9 180 lbs Batted both

Born Aug 23, 1870 Cohoes, NY
Died Oct 17, 1940 Philadelphia, PA

YR	POS	TEAM	LG	FIN	G	AB	R	H	2B	3B	HR	RBI	AVG	BB	TB	OQ	RANK
1890	CF	CLE	NL	7-8	136	526	98	139	22	9	6	73	.264	53	197	109	27-48
1891	CF-3B	CLE	NL	5-8	136	570	115	165	35	12	3	89	.289	53	233	120	17-52
1892	3B-RF	CLE	NL	2-12	144	597	95	144	27	12	5	82	.241	58	210	106	40-72
1893	3B	NY	NL	5-12	133	549	112	195	22	27	11	119	.355	42	304	144	6-80
1894	3B	NY	NL	2-12	122	477	120	168	26	19	8	91	.352	66	256	134	12-77
1895	3B-1B	NY	NL	9-12	110	430	108	146	36	9	5	101	.340	55	215	137	13-75
1896	3B-SS	NY	NL	7-12	124	494	98	158	25	12	6	99	.320	50	225	122	21-73
1897	SS	NY	NL	3-12	130	519	112	183	31	10	10	136	.353	41	264	137	11-69
1898	SS	NY	NL	7-12	121	486	80	149	20	5	2	86	.307	32	185	110	38-75
1899	SS	NY	NL	10-12	108	416	68	140	21	5	1	57	.337	37	174	123	—
1900	SS	NY	NL	8-8	114	426	69	136	20	4	3	61	.319	35	173	116	17-47
1901	SS-3B	NY	NL	7-8	130	491	69	148	26	7	7	65	.301	40	209	128	16-45
1902	SS	CHI	AL	4-8	132	485	76	145	27	7	3	93	.299	65	195	125	11-46
1903	SS	NY	NL	2-8	4	15	2	4	0	0	0	1	.267	1	4	—	—
1904	SS	CHI	AL	3-8	152	563	75	142	27	15	1	69	.252	43	202	115	20-47
1905	SS	CHI	AL	2-8	151	550	74	153	28	3	1	55	.278	60	190	124	9-41
1906	SS	CHI	AL	1-8	133	484	63	134	26	6	0	80	.277	41	172	118	16-40
1907	SS	CHI	AL	3-8	132	466	59	111	16	2	1	52	.238	47	134	101	33-48
1908	2B-SS	CHI	AL	3-8	128	419	41	91	14	1	0	26	.217	41	107	92	—
1909	1B	CHI	AL	4-8	28	68	5	9	1	0	0	2	.132	10	10	—	—
MAJOR LEAGUE TOTALS					2368	9031	1539	2660	450	165	73	1437	.295	870	3659	122	16 yrs

William Michael Joyce   Born Sep 21, 1865   St Louis, MO
5'11   185 lbs   Batted left   Died May 8, 1941   St Louis, MO

YR	POS	TEAM	LG	FIN	G	AB	R	H	2B	3B	HR	RBI	AVG	BB	TB	OQ	RANK
1890	3B	BRO	PL	2-8	133	489	121	123	18	18	1	78	.252	123	180	123	15-57
1891	3B	BOS	AA	1-8	65	243	76	75	9	15	3	51	.309	63	123	182	—
1892	3B	BRO	NL	3-12	97	372	89	91	15	12	6	45	.245	82	148	146	—
1894	3B	WAS	NL	11-12	99	355	103	126	25	14	17	89	.355	87	230	178	2-77
1895	3B	WAS	NL	10-12	126	474	110	148	25	13	17	95	.312	96	250	152	7-75
1896	3B-2B	WA/NY	NL	9/7	130	475	121	158	25	12	13	94	.333	101	246	164	3-73
1897	3B	NY	NL	3-12	109	388	109	118	15	13	3	64	.304	78	168	137	9-69
1898	1B-3B	NY	NL	7-12	145	508	91	131	20	9	10	91	.258	88	199	130	14-75
MAJOR LEAGUE TOTALS					904	3304	820	970	152	106	70	607	.294	718	1544	147	6 yrs

Robert Lincoln Lowe   Born Jul 10, 1868   Pittsburgh, PA
5'10   150 lbs   Batted right   Died Dec 8, 1951   Detroit, MI

YR	POS	TEAM	LG	FIN	G	AB	R	H	2B	3B	HR	RBI	AVG	BB	TB	OQ	RANK
1890	SS-CF	BOS	NL	5-8	52	207	35	58	13	2	2	21	.280	26	81	121	—
1891	LF	BOS	NL	1-8	125	497	92	129	19	5	6	74	.260	53	176	106	32-52
1892	LF-3B	BOS	NL	1-12	124	475	79	115	16	7	3	57	.242	37	154	95	55-72
1893	2B	BOS	NL	1-12	126	526	130	157	19	5	14	89	.298	55	228	113	29-80
1894	2B	BOS	NL	3-12	133	613	158	212	34	11	17	115	.346	50	319	118	27-77
1895	2B	BOS	NL	5-12	99	412	101	122	12	7	7	62	.296	40	169	104	39-75
1896	2B	BOS	NL	4-12	73	305	59	98	11	4	2	48	.321	20	123	103	—
1897	2B	BOS	NL	1-12	123	499	87	154	24	8	5	106	.309	32	209	105	40-69
1898	2B	BOS	NL	1-12	147	559	65	152	11	7	4	94	.272	29	189	91	57-75
1899	2B	BOS	NL	2-12	152	559	81	152	5	9	4	88	.272	35	187	88	51-61
1900	2B	BOS	NL	4-8	127	474	65	132	11	5	3	71	.278	26	162	89	40-47
1901	3B-2B	BOS	NL	5-8	129	491	47	125	11	1	3	47	.255	17	147	79	40-45
1902	2B	CHI	NL	5-8	119	472	41	116	13	3	0	31	.246	11	135	78	43-46
1903	2B-1B	CHI	NL	3-8	32	105	14	28	5	3	0	15	.267	4	39	95	—
1904	PH	PIT	NL	4-8	1	1	0	0	0	0	0	0	.000	0	0	—	—
1904	2B	DET	AL	7-8	140	506	47	105	14	6	0	40	.208	17	131	73	46-47
1905	LF-3B	DET	AL	3-8	58	181	17	35	7	2	0	9	.193	13	46	79	—
1906	SS-2B	DET	AL	6-8	41	145	11	30	3	0	1	12	.207	4	36	67	—
1907	3B-LF	DET	AL	1-8	17	37	2	9	2	0	0	5	.243	4	11	—	—
MAJOR LEAGUE TOTALS					1818	7064	1131	1929	230	85	71	984	.273	473	2542	95	12 yrs

Thomas Jefferson Dowd   Born Apr 20, 1869   Holyoke, MA
5'8 173 lbs Batted right   Died Jul 2, 1933   Holyoke, MA

YR	POS	TEAM	LG	FIN	G	AB	R	H	2B	3B	HR	RBI	AVG	BB	TB	OQ	RANK
1891	2B	BO/WA	AA	1/8	116	475	67	121	9	10	1	44	.255	19	153	80	46-48
1892	2B-RF	WAS	NL	10-12	144	584	94	142	9	10	1	50	.243	34	174	84	62-72
1893	RF	SL	NL	10-12	132	581	114	164	18	7	1	54	.282	49	199	88	65-80
1894	RF	SL	NL	9-12	123	524	92	142	16	8	4	62	.271	54	186	81	71-77
1895	RF-3B	SL	NL	11-12	129	505	95	163	19	17	7	74	.323	30	237	112	32-75
1896	2B-RF	SL	NL	11-12	126	521	93	138	17	11	5	46	.265	42	192	91	58-73
1897	RF-2B	SL/PH	NL	12/10	126	536	93	152	23	5	0	52	.284	25	185	83	64-69
1898	RF	SL	NL	12-12	139	586	70	143	17	7	0	32	.244	30	174	78	70-75
1899	CF	CLE	NL	12-12	147	605	81	168	17	6	2	35	.278	48	203	92	47-61
1901	LF	BOS	AL	2-8	138	594	104	159	18	7	3	52	.268	38	200	89	38-46
MAJOR LEAGUE TOTALS					1320	5511	903	1492	163	88	24	501	.271	369	1903	88	10 yrs

William Frederick Dahlen   Born Jan 5, 1870   Nelliston, NY
5'9 180 lbs Batted right   Died Dec 5, 1950   Brooklyn, NY

YR	POS	TEAM	LG	FIN	G	AB	R	H	2B	3B	HR	RBI	AVG	BB	TB	OQ	RANK
1891	3B-LF	CHI	NL	2-8	135	549	114	143	18	13	9	76	.260	67	214	118	20-52
1892	SS-3B	CHI	NL	7-12	143	581	114	169	23	19	5	58	.291	45	245	125	19-72
1893	SS-CF	CHI	NL	9-12	116	485	113	146	28	15	5	64	.301	58	219	121	24-80
1894	SS-3B	CHI	NL	8-12	121	502	149	179	32	14	15	107	.357	76	284	144	8-77
1895	SS	CHI	NL	4-12	129	516	106	131	19	10	7	62	.254	61	191	94	51-75
1896	SS	CHI	NL	5-12	125	474	137	167	30	19	9	74	.352	64	262	159	4-73
1897	SS	CHI	NL	9-12	75	276	67	80	18	8	6	40	.290	43	132	135	—
1898	SS	CHI	NL	4-12	142	521	96	151	35	8	1	79	.290	58	205	121	21-75
1899	SS	BRO	NL	1-12	121	428	87	121	22	7	4	76	.283	67	169	124	20-61
1900	SS	BRO	NL	1-8	133	483	87	125	16	11	1	69	.259	73	166	108	21-47
1901	SS	BRO	NL	3-8	131	511	69	136	17	9	4	82	.266	30	183	100	30-45
1902	SS	BRO	NL	2-8	138	527	67	139	25	8	2	74	.264	43	186	113	18-46
1903	SS	BRO	NL	5-8	138	474	71	124	17	9	1	64	.262	82	162	118	18-49
1904	SS	NY	NL	1-8	145	523	70	140	26	2	2	80	.268	44	176	109	24-42
1905	SS	NY	NL	1-8	148	520	67	126	20	4	7	81	.242	62	175	109	20-45
1906	SS	NY	NL	2-8	143	471	63	113	18	3	1	49	.240	76	140	115	17-42
1907	SS	NY	NL	4-8	143	464	40	96	20	1	0	34	.207	51	118	89	36-41
1908	SS	BOS	NL	6-8	144	524	50	125	23	2	3	48	.239	35	161	98	30-41
1909	SS	BOS	NL	8-8	69	197	22	46	6	1	2	16	.234	29	60	111	—
1910	PH	BRO	NL	6-8	3	2	0	0	0	0	0	0	.000	0	0	—	—
1911	SS	BRO	NL	7-8	1	3	0	0	0	0	0	0	.000	0	0	—	—
MAJOR LEAGUE TOTALS					2443	9031	1589	2457	413	163	84	1233	.272	1064	3448	116	17 yrs

Joseph James Kelley　　　　　　　　Born Dec 9, 1871　Cambridge, MA
5'11　190 lbs　Batted right　　　　　　Died Aug 14, 1943　Baltimore, MD

YR	POS	TEAM	LG	FIN	G	AB	R	H	2B	3B	HR	RBI	AVG	BB	TB	OQ	RANK
1891	LF	BOS	NL	1-8	12	45	7	11	1	1	0	3	.244	2	14	—	—
1892	CF	PT/BA	NL	6/12	66	238	29	56	7	7	0	32	.235	21	77	96	—
1893	CF	BAL	NL	8-12	125	502	120	153	27	16	9	76	.305	77	239	134	10-80
1894	LF	BAL	NL	1-12	129	507	165	199	48	20	6	111	.393	107	305	172	3-77
1895	LF	BAL	NL	1-12	131	518	148	189	26	19	10	134	.365	77	283	157	6-75
1896	LF	BAL	NL	1-12	131	519	148	189	31	19	8	100	.364	91	282	169	2-73
1897	LF	BAL	NL	2-12	131	505	113	183	31	9	5	118	.362	70	247	148	5-69
1898	CF	BAL	NL	2-12	124	464	71	149	18	15	2	110	.321	56	203	140	8-75
1899	LF	BRO	NL	1-12	143	538	108	175	21	14	6	93	.325	70	242	138	7-61
1900	LF-1B	BRO	NL	1-8	121	454	90	145	23	17	6	91	.319	53	220	143	6-47
1901	1B	BRO	NL	3-8	120	492	77	151	22	12	4	65	.307	40	209	128	15-45
1902	CF-3B	BAL	AL	8-8	60	222	50	69	17	7	1	34	.311	34	103	146	—
1902	CF-2B	CIN	NL	4-8	40	156	24	50	9	2	1	12	.321	15	66	146	—
1903	LF-SS	CIN	NL	4-8	105	383	85	121	22	4	3	45	.316	51	160	137	10-49
1904	1B	CIN	NL	3-8	123	449	75	126	21	13	0	63	.281	49	173	131	8-42
1905	LF	CIN	NL	5-8	90	321	43	89	7	6	1	37	.277	27	111	108	—
1906	LF	CIN	NL	6-8	129	465	43	106	19	11	1	53	.228	44	150	103	25-42
1908	LF-1B	BOS	NL	6-8	73	228	25	59	8	2	2	17	.259	27	77	122	—
MAJOR LEAGUE TOTALS					1853	7006	1421	2220	358	194	65	1194	.317	911	3161	142	12 yrs

John Joseph McGraw　　　　　　　　Born Apr 7, 1873　Truxton, NY
5'7　155 lbs　Batted left　　　　　　　Died Feb 25, 1934　New Rochelle, NY

YR	POS	TEAM	LG	FIN	G	AB	R	H	2B	3B	HR	RBI	AVG	BB	TB	OQ	RANK
1891	SS-RF	BAL	AA	3-8	33	115	17	31	3	5	0	14	.270	12	44	110	—
1892	RF-2B	BAL	NL	12-12	79	286	41	77	13	2	1	26	.269	32	97	110	—
1893	SS	BAL	NL	8-12	127	480	123	154	9	10	5	64	.321	101	198	135	9-80
1894	3B	BAL	NL	1-12	124	512	156	174	18	14	1	92	.340	91	223	120	22-77
1895	3B	BAL	NL	1-12	96	388	110	143	13	6	2	48	.369	60	174	137	11-75
1896	3B	BAL	NL	1-12	23	77	20	25	2	2	0	14	.325	11	31	—	—
1897	3B	BAL	NL	2-12	106	391	90	127	15	3	0	48	.325	99	148	141	7-69
1898	3B	BAL	NL	2-12	143	515	143	176	8	10	0	53	.342	112	204	159	2-75
1899	3B	BAL	NL	4-12	117	399	140	156	13	3	1	33	.391	124	178	200	1-61
1900	3B	SL	NL	6-8	99	334	84	115	10	4	2	33	.344	85	139	166	—
1901	3B	BAL	AL	5-8	73	232	71	81	14	9	0	28	.349	61	113	188	—
1902	3B	BAL	AL	8-8	20	63	14	18	3	2	1	3	.286	17	28	—	—
1902	SS	NY	NL	8-8	35	107	13	25	0	0	0	5	.234	26	25	119	—
1903	2B-LF	NY	NL	2-8	12	11	2	3	0	0	0	1	.273	1	3	—	—
1904	2B-SS	NY	NL	1-8	5	12	0	4	0	0	0	0	.333	3	4	—	—
1905	LF	NY	NL	1-8	3	0	0	0	0	0	0	0	—	0	0	—	—
1906	3B	NY	NL	2-8	4	2	0	0	0	0	0	0	.000	1	0	—	—
MAJOR LEAGUE TOTALS					1099	3924	1024	1309	121	70	13	462	.334	836	1609	149	6 yrs

John Frank Freeman
5'9   169 lbs   Batted left

Born Oct 30, 1871   Catasauqua, PA
Died Jun 25, 1949   Wilkes-Barre, PA

YR	POS	TEAM	LG	FIN	G	AB	R	H	2B	3B	HR	RBI	AVG	BB	TB	OQ	RANK
1891	P	WAS	AA	8-8	5	18	1	4	1	0	0	1	.222	2	5	—	—
1898	RF	WAS	NL	11-12	29	107	19	39	2	3	3	21	.364	7	56	158	—
1899	RF	WAS	NL	11-12	155	588	107	187	19	25	25	122	.318	23	331	142	6-61
1900	RF-1B	BOS	NL	4-8	117	418	58	126	19	13	6	65	.301	25	189	119	14-47
1901	1B	BOS	AL	2-8	129	490	88	166	23	15	12	114	.339	44	255	150	2-46
1902	RF	BOS	AL	3-8	138	564	75	174	38	19	11	121	.309	32	283	132	6-46
1903	RF	BOS	AL	1-8	141	567	74	163	39	20	13	104	.287	30	281	142	6-47
1904	RF	BOS	AL	1-8	157	597	64	167	20	19	7	84	.280	32	246	127	10-47
1905	1B-RF	BOS	AL	4-8	130	455	59	109	20	8	3	49	.240	46	154	113	21-41
1906	RF-1B	BOS	AL	8-8	121	392	42	98	18	9	1	30	.250	28	137	109	—
1907	RF	BOS	AL	7-8	4	12	1	2	0	0	1	2	.167	3	5	—	—
MAJOR LEAGUE TOTALS					1126	4208	588	1235	199	131	82	713	.293	272	1942	132	7 yrs

Hugh Ambrose Jennings
5'8   165 lbs   Batted right

Born Apr 2, 1869   Pittston, PA
Died Feb 1, 1928   Scranton, PA

YR	POS	TEAM	LG	FIN	G	AB	R	H	2B	3B	HR	RBI	AVG	BB	TB	OQ	RANK
1891	SS-1B	LOU	AA	7-8	90	360	53	105	10	8	1	58	.292	17	134	97	—
1892	SS	LOU	NL	9-12	152	594	65	132	16	4	2	61	.222	30	162	74	69-72
1893	SS	LO/BA	NL	11/8	39	143	12	26	3	0	1	15	.182	7	32	49	—
1894	SS	BAL	NL	1-12	128	501	134	168	28	16	4	109	.335	37	240	107	43-77
1895	SS	BAL	NL	1-12	131	529	159	204	41	7	4	125	.386	24	271	130	18-75
1896	SS	BAL	NL	1-12	130	521	125	209	27	9	0	121	.401	19	254	131	14-73
1897	SS	BAL	NL	2-12	117	439	133	156	26	9	2	79	.355	42	206	132	17-69
1898	SS	BAL	NL	2-12	143	534	135	175	25	11	1	87	.328	78	225	144	7-75
1899	1B-SS	BA/BR	NL	4/1	69	224	44	67	3	12	0	42	.299	22	94	119	—
1900	1B	BRO	NL	1-8	115	441	61	120	18	6	1	69	.272	31	153	93	38-47
1901	1B	PHI	NL	2-8	82	302	38	79	21	2	1	39	.262	25	107	104	—
1902	1B	PHI	NL	7-8	78	290	32	79	13	4	1	32	.272	14	103	106	—
1903	RF	BRO	NL	5-8	6	17	2	4	0	0	0	1	.235	1	4	—	—
1907	SS-2B	DET	AL	1-8	1	4	0	1	1	0	0	0	.250	0	2	—	—
1909	1B	DET	AL	1-8	2	4	1	2	0	0	0	2	.500	0	2	—	—
1912	PH	DET	AL	6-8	1	1	0	0	0	0	0	0	.000	0	0	—	—
1918	1B	DET	AL	7-8	1	0	0	0	0	0	0	0	—	0	0	—	—
MAJOR LEAGUE TOTALS					1285	4904	994	1527	232	88	18	840	.311	347	1989	116	7 yrs

Montford Montgomery Cross
6'2 180 lbs Batted right

Born Aug 31, 1869 Philadelphia, PA
Died Jun 21, 1934 Philadelphia, PA

YR	POS	TEAM	LG	FIN	G	AB	R	H	2B	3B	HR	RBI	AVG	BB	TB	OQ	RANK
1892	SS	BAL	NL	12-12	15	50	5	8	0	0	0	2	.160	4	8	—	—
1894	SS	PIT	NL	7-12	13	43	14	19	1	5	2	13	.442	5	36	—	—
1895	SS	PIT	NL	7-12	108	393	67	101	14	13	3	54	.257	38	150	93	55-75
1896	SS	SL	NL	11-12	125	427	66	104	10	6	6	52	.244	58	144	93	54-73
1897	SS	SL	NL	12-12	131	462	59	132	17	11	4	55	.286	62	183	112	31-69
1898	SS	PHI	NL	6-12	149	525	68	135	25	5	1	50	.257	55	173	100	47-75
1899	SS	PHI	NL	3-12	154	557	85	143	25	6	3	65	.257	56	189	95	44-61
1900	SS	PHI	NL	3-8	131	466	59	94	11	3	3	62	.202	51	120	75	45-47
1901	SS	PHI	NL	2-8	139	483	49	95	14	1	1	44	.197	52	114	75	41-45
1902	SS	PHI	AL	1-8	137	497	72	115	22	2	3	59	.231	32	150	78	43-46
1903	SS	PHI	AL	2-8	137	470	44	116	21	2	3	45	.247	49	150	103	30-47
1904	SS	PHI	AL	5-8	153	503	33	95	23	4	1	38	.189	46	129	84	42-47
1905	SS	PHI	AL	1-8	79	252	28	67	17	2	0	24	.266	19	88	113	—
1906	SS	PHI	AL	4-8	134	445	32	89	23	3	1	40	.200	50	121	93	33-40
1907	SS	PHI	AL	2-8	77	248	37	51	9	5	0	18	.206	39	70	110	—
MAJOR LEAGUE TOTALS					1682	5821	718	1364	232	68	31	621	.234	616	1825	91	11 yrs

William Henry Keeler
5'4 140 lbs Batted left

Born Mar 3, 1872 Brooklyn, NY
Died Jan 1, 1923 Brooklyn, NY

YR	POS	TEAM	LG	FIN	G	AB	R	H	2B	3B	HR	RBI	AVG	BB	TB	OQ	RANK
1892	3B	NY	NL	8-12	14	53	7	17	3	0	0	6	.321	3	20	—	—
1893	3B-LF	NY/BR	NL	5/6	27	104	19	33	3	2	2	16	.317	9	46	114	—
1894	RF	BAL	NL	1-12	129	590	165	219	27	22	5	94	.371	40	305	120	23-77
1895	RF	BAL	NL	1-12	131	565	162	213	24	15	4	78	.377	37	279	129	20-75
1896	RF	BAL	NL	1-12	126	544	153	210	22	13	4	82	.386	37	270	137	11-73
1897	RF	BAL	NL	2-12	129	564	145	239	27	19	0	74	.424	35	304	157	2-69
1898	RF	BAL	NL	2-12	129	561	126	216	7	2	1	44	.385	31	230	129	15-75
1899	RF	BRO	NL	1-12	141	570	140	216	12	13	1	61	.379	37	257	134	11-61
1900	RF	BRO	NL	1-8	136	563	106	204	13	12	4	68	.362	30	253	128	9-47
1901	RF	BRO	NL	3-8	136	595	123	202	18	12	2	43	.339	21	250	121	19-45
1902	RF	BRO	NL	2-8	133	559	86	186	20	5	0	38	.333	21	216	121	11-46
1903	RF	NY	AL	4-8	132	512	95	160	14	7	0	32	.313	32	188	115	20-47
1904	RF	NY	AL	2-8	143	543	78	186	14	8	2	40	.343	35	222	142	4-47
1905	RF	NY	AL	6-8	149	560	81	169	14	4	4	38	.302	43	203	123	10-41
1906	RF	NY	AL	2-8	152	592	96	180	9	3	2	33	.304	40	201	113	19-40
1907	RF	NY	AL	5-8	107	423	50	99	5	2	0	17	.234	15	108	76	—
1908	RF	NY	AL	8-8	91	323	38	85	3	1	1	14	.263	31	93	106	—
1909	RF	NY	AL	5-8	99	360	44	95	7	5	1	32	.264	24	115	104	—
1910	CF	NY	NL	2-8	19	10	5	3	0	0	0	0	.300	3	3	—	—
MAJOR LEAGUE TOTALS					2123	8591	1719	2932	242	145	33	810	.341	524	3563	128	13 yrs

Charles Edwin Irwin
5'10   160 lbs   Batted left

Born Feb 15, 1869   Clinton, IL
Died Sep 21, 1925   Chicago, IL

YR	POS	TEAM	LG	FIN	G	AB	R	H	2B	3B	HR	RBI	AVG	BB	TB	OQ	RANK
1893	SS	CHI	NL	9-12	21	82	14	25	6	2	0	13	.305	10	35	—	—
1894	3B-SS	CHI	NL	8-12	128	498	84	144	24	9	8	95	.289	63	210	99	50-77
1895	SS	CHI	NL	4-12	3	10	4	2	0	0	0	0	.200	2	2	—	—
1896	3B	CIN	NL	3-12	127	476	77	141	16	6	1	67	.296	26	172	88	60-73
1897	3B	CIN	NL	4-12	134	505	89	146	26	6	0	74	.289	47	184	97	48-69
1898	3B	CIN	NL	3-12	136	501	77	120	14	5	3	55	.240	31	153	82	66-75
1899	3B	CIN	NL	6-12	90	314	42	73	4	8	1	52	.232	26	96	81	—
1900	3B-SS	CIN	NL	7-8	87	333	59	91	15	6	1	44	.273	14	121	91	—
1901	3B	CN/BR	NL	8/3	132	502	50	114	25	4	0	45	.227	28	147	79	39-45
1902	3B	BRO	NL	2-8	131	458	59	125	14	0	2	43	.273	39	145	106	26-46
MAJOR LEAGUE TOTALS					989	3679	555	981	144	46	16	488	.267	286	1265	92	6 yrs

George Joseph LaChance
6'1   183 lbs   Batted both

Born Feb 15, 1870   Waterbury, CT
Died Aug 18, 1932   Waterville, CT

YR	POS	TEAM	LG	FIN	G	AB	R	H	2B	3B	HR	RBI	AVG	BB	TB	OQ	RANK
1893	C-LF	BRO	NL	6-12	11	35	1	6	1	0	0	6	.171	2	7	—	—
1894	1B-C	BRO	NL	5-12	68	257	48	83	13	8	5	52	.323	16	127	106	—
1895	1B	BRO	NL	5-12	127	536	99	167	22	8	8	108	.312	29	229	100	42-75
1896	1B	BRO	NL	9-12	89	348	60	99	10	13	7	58	.284	23	156	107	—
1897	1B	BRO	NL	6-12	126	520	86	160	28	16	4	90	.308	15	232	103	42-69
1898	1B-SS	BRO	NL	10-12	136	526	62	130	23	7	5	65	.247	31	182	92	56-75
1899	1B	BAL	NL	4-12	125	472	65	145	23	10	1	75	.307	21	191	104	36-61
1901	1B	CLE	AL	7-8	133	548	81	166	22	9	1	75	.303	7	209	92	36-46
1902	1B	BOS	AL	3-8	138	541	60	151	13	4	6	56	.279	18	190	87	39-46
1903	1B	BOS	AL	1-8	141	522	60	134	22	6	1	53	.257	28	171	94	39-47
1904	1B	BOS	AL	1-8	157	573	55	130	19	5	1	47	.227	23	162	82	43-47
1905	1B	BOS	AL	4-8	12	41	1	6	1	0	0	5	.146	6	7	—	—
MAJOR LEAGUE TOTALS					1263	4919	678	1377	197	86	39	690	.280	219	1863	94	8 yrs

William Alexander Lange
6'1 190 lbs Batted right

Both Jun 6, 1871 San Francisco, CA
Died Jul 23, 1950 San Francisco, CA

YR	POS	TEAM	LG	FIN	G	AB	R	H	2B	3B	HR	RBI	AVG	BB	TB	OQ	RANK
1893	2B-CF	CHI	NL	9-12	117	469	92	132	8	7	8	88	.281	52	178	101	45-80
1894	CF	CHI	NL	8-12	111	442	84	145	16	9	6	90	.328	56	197	110	38-77
1895	CF	CHI	NL	4-12	123	478	120	186	27	16	10	98	.389	55	275	162	3-75
1896	CF	CHI	NL	5-12	122	469	114	153	21	16	4	92	.326	65	218	134	13-73
1897	CF	CHI	NL	9-12	118	479	119	163	24	14	5	83	.340	48	230	133	16-69
1898	CF	CHI	NL	4-12	113	442	79	141	16	11	5	69	.319	36	194	130	13-75
1899	CF-1B	CHI	NL	8-12	107	416	81	135	21	7	1	58	.325	38	173	121	—
MAJOR LEAGUE TOTALS					811	3195	689	1055	133	80	39	578	.330	350	1465	128	6 yrs

Duff Gordon Cooley
Batted left

Born Mar 14, 1873 Dallas, TX
Died Aug 9, 1937 Dallas, TX

YR	POS	TEAM	LG	FIN	G	AB	R	H	2B	3B	HR	RBI	AVG	BB	TB	OQ	RANK
1893	RF-C	SL	NL	10-12	29	107	20	37	2	3	0	21	.346	8	45	112	—
1894	RF-3B	SL	NL	9-12	54	206	35	61	3	1	1	21	.296	12	69	72	—
1895	LF	SL	NL	11-12	132	563	106	191	9	20	7	75	.339	36	261	115	27-75
1896	CF	SL/PH	NL	11/8	104	453	92	139	11	7	2	35	.307	25	170	93	55-73
1897	CF	PHI	NL	10-12	133	566	124	186	14	13	4	40	.329	51	238	115	28-69
1898	CF	PHI	NL	6-12	149	629	123	196	24	12	4	55	.312	48	256	120	24-75
1899	1B-CF	PHI	NL	3-12	94	406	75	112	15	8	1	31	.276	29	146	96	—
1900	1B	PIT	NL	2-8	66	249	30	50	8	1	0	22	.201	14	60	60	—
1901	LF-1B	BOS	NL	5-8	63	240	27	62	13	3	0	27	.258	14	81	94	—
1902	LF	BOS	NL	3-8	135	548	73	162	26	8	0	58	.296	34	204	118	15-46
1903	LF	BOS	NL	6-8	138	553	76	160	26	10	1	70	.289	44	209	109	26-49
1904	LF	BOS	NL	7-8	122	467	41	127	18	7	5	70	.272	24	174	111	21-42
1905	CF	DET	AL	3-8	97	377	25	93	11	9	1	32	.247	26	125	104	—
MAJOR LEAGUE TOTALS					1316	5364	847	1576	180	102	26	557	.294	365	2038	112	7 yrs

Henry P Reitz   Born Jun 29, 1867   Chicago, IL
5'7 158 lbs Batted left   Died Nov 10, 1914 Sacramento, CA

YR	POS	TEAM	LG	FIN	G	AB	R	H	2B	3B	HR	RBI	AVG	BB	TB	OQ	RANK
1893	2B	BAL	NL	8-12	130	490	90	140	17	13	1	76	.286	65	186	106	40-80
1894	2B-3B	BAL	NL	1-12	108	446	86	135	22	31	2	105	.303	42	225	111	36-77
1895	2B-3B	BAL	NL	1-12	71	245	45	72	15	5	0	29	.294	18	97	96	—
1896	2B	BAL	NL	1-12	120	464	76	133	15	6	4	106	.287	49	172	100	44-73
1897	2B	BAL	NL	2-12	128	477	76	138	15	6	2	84	.289	50	171	98	47-69
1898	2B	WAS	NL	11-12	132	489	62	148	20	2	2	47	.303	32	178	105	43-75
1899	2B	PIT	NL	7-12	34	130	11	34	4	2	0	15	.262	10	42	87	—

| MAJOR LEAGUE TOTALS | | | | | 723 | 2741 | 446 | 800 | 108 | 65 | 11 | 462 | .292 | 266 | 1071 | 104 | 5 yrs |

Roderick John Wallace   Born Nov 4, 1873   Pittsburgh, PA
5'8 170 lbs Batted right   Died Nov 3, 1960   Torrance, CA

YR	POS	TEAM	LG	FIN	G	AB	R	H	2B	3B	HR	RBI	AVG	BB	TB	OQ	RANK
1894	P	CLE	NL	6-12	4	13	0	2	1	0	0	1	.154	0	3	—	—
1895	P	CLE	NL	2-12	30	98	16	21	2	3	0	10	.214	6	29	65	—
1896	RF-P	CLE	NL	2-12	45	149	19	35	6	3	1	17	.235	11	50	80	—
1897	3B	CLE	NL	5-12	130	516	99	173	33	21	4	112	.335	48	260	135	12-69
1898	3B	CLE	NL	5-12	154	593	81	160	25	13	3	99	.270	63	220	111	36-75
1899	SS-3B	SL	NL	5-12	151	577	91	170	28	14	12	108	.295	54	262	125	17-61
1900	SS	SL	NL	5-8	126	485	70	130	25	9	4	70	.268	40	185	103	29-47
1901	SS	SL	NL	4-8	134	550	69	178	34	15	2	91	.324	20	248	127	18-45
1902	SS	SL	AL	2-8	133	494	71	141	32	9	1	63	.285	45	194	111	26-46
1903	SS	SL	AL	6-8	135	511	63	136	21	7	1	54	.266	28	174	99	37-47
1904	SS	SL	AL	6-8	139	541	57	149	29	4	2	69	.275	42	192	118	17-47
1905	SS	SL	AL	8-8	156	587	67	159	25	9	1	59	.271	45	205	115	18-41
1906	SS	SL	AL	5-8	139	476	64	123	21	7	2	67	.258	58	164	122	11-40
1907	SS	SL	AL	6-8	147	538	56	138	20	7	0	70	.257	54	172	112	16-48
1908	SS	SL	AL	4-8	137	487	59	123	24	4	1	60	.253	52	158	118	15-36
1909	SS-3B	SL	AL	7-8	116	403	36	96	12	2	0	35	.238	38	112	97	—
1910	SS-3B	SL	AL	8-8	138	508	47	131	19	7	0	37	.258	49	164	108	20-36
1911	SS	SL	AL	8-8	125	410	35	95	12	2	0	31	.232	46	111	81	42-44
1912	SS-3B	SL	AL	7-8	100	323	39	78	14	5	0	31	.241	43	102	99	—
1913	SS-3B	SL	AL	8-8	55	147	11	31	5	0	0	21	.211	14	36	75	—
1914	SS	SL	AL	5-8	26	73	3	16	2	1	0	5	.219	5	20	—	—
1915	SS	SL	AL	6-8	9	13	1	3	0	1	0	4	.231	5	5	—	—
1916	3B-SS	SL	AL	5-8	14	18	0	5	0	0	0	1	.278	2	5	—	—
1917	3B-SS	SL	NL	3-8	8	10	0	1	0	0	0	2	.100	0	1	—	—
1918	2B-SS	SL	NL	8-8	32	98	3	15	1	0	0	4	.153	6	16	49	—

| MAJOR LEAGUE TOTALS | | | | | 2383 | 8618 | 1057 | 2309 | 391 | 143 | 34 | 1121 | .268 | 774 | 3088 | 113 | 14 yrs |

Eugene Napoleon DeMontreville   Born Mar 26, 1874 St Paul, MN
5'8 165 lbs Batted right   Died Feb 18, 1935 Memphis, TN

YR	POS	TEAM	LG	FIN	G	AB	R	H	2B	3B	HR	RBI	AVG	BB	TB	OQ	RANK
1894	SS	PIT	NL	7-12	2	8	0	2	0	0	0	0	.250	1	2	—	—
1895	SS	WAS	NL	10-12	12	46	7	10	1	3	0	9	.217	3	17	—	—
1896	SS	WAS	NL	9-12	133	533	94	183	24	5	8	77	.343	29	241	115	26-73
1897	SS-2B	WAS	NL	6-12	133	566	92	193	27	8	3	93	.341	21	245	108	37-69
1898	2B-SS	BAL	NL	2-12	151	567	93	186	19	2	0	86	.328	52	209	117	27-75
1899	SS-2B	CH/BA	NL	8/4	142	550	83	154	19	7	1	76	.280	27	190	88	49-61
1900	2B-SS	BRO	NL	1-8	69	234	34	57	8	1	0	28	.244	10	67	71	—
1901	2B-3B	BOS	NL	5-8	140	577	83	173	14	4	5	72	.300	17	210	99	31-45
1902	2B	BOS	NL	3-8	124	481	51	125	16	5	0	53	.260	12	151	88	37-46
1903	2B	WAS	AL	8-8	12	44	0	12	2	0	0	3	.273	0	14	—	—
1904	2B	SL	AL	6-8	4	9	0	1	0	0	0	0	.111	2	1	—	—

MAJOR LEAGUE TOTALS   922 3615 537 1096 130 35 17 497 .303 174 1347 103 6 yrs

Fred Clifford Clarke   Born Oct 3, 1872   Winterset, IA
5'10 165 lbs Batted left   Died Aug 14, 1960 Winfield, KS

YR	POS	TEAM	LG	FIN	G	AB	R	H	2B	3B	HR	RBI	AVG	BB	TB	OQ	RANK
1894	LF	LOU	NL	12-12	75	310	54	83	11	7	7	48	.268	25	129	87	—
1895	LF	LOU	NL	12-12	132	550	96	191	21	5	4	82	.347	34	234	107	35-75
1896	LF	LOU	NL	12-12	131	517	96	168	15	18	9	79	.325	43	246	124	18-73
1897	LF	LOU	NL	11-12	128	518	120	202	30	13	6	67	.390	45	276	153	3-69
1898	LF	LOU	NL	9-12	149	599	116	184	23	12	3	47	.307	48	240	118	26-75
1899	LF	LOU	NL	9-12	148	602	122	206	23	9	5	70	.342	49	262	126	16-61
1900	LF	PIT	NL	2-8	106	399	84	110	15	12	3	32	.276	51	158	117	15-47
1901	LF	PIT	NL	1-8	129	527	118	171	24	15	6	60	.324	51	243	145	8-45
1902	LF	PIT	NL	1-8	113	459	103	145	27	14	2	53	.316	51	206	156	2-46
1903	LF	PIT	NL	1-8	104	427	88	150	32	15	5	70	.351	41	227	164	3-49
1904	LF	PIT	NL	4-8	72	278	51	85	7	11	0	25	.306	22	114	134	—
1905	LF	PIT	NL	2-8	141	525	95	157	18	15	2	51	.299	55	211	131	9-45
1906	LF	PIT	NL	3-8	118	417	69	129	14	13	1	39	.309	40	172	141	—
1907	LF	PIT	NL	2-8	148	501	97	145	18	13	2	59	.289	68	195	143	3-41
1908	LF	PIT	NL	2-8	151	551	83	146	18	15	2	53	.265	65	200	130	7-41
1909	LF	PIT	NL	1-8	152	550	97	158	16	11	3	68	.287	80	205	137	3-39
1910	LF	PIT	NL	3-8	123	429	57	113	23	9	2	63	.263	53	160	115	18-47
1911	LF	PIT	NL	3-8	110	392	73	127	25	13	5	49	.324	53	193	149	—
1913	LF	PIT	NL	4-8	9	13	0	1	1	0	0	0	.077	0	2	—	—
1914	PH	PIT	NL	7-8	2	2	0	0	0	0	0	0	.000	0	0	—	—
1915	LF	PIT	NL	5-8	1	2	0	1	0	0	0	0	.500	0	1	—	—

MAJOR LEAGUE TOTALS   2242 8568 1619 2672 361 220 67 1015 .312 874 3674 133 14 yrs

Albert Karl Selbach
5'7 190 lbs Batted right

Born Mar 24, 1872 Columbus, OH
Died Feb 17, 1956 Columbus, OH

YR	POS	TEAM	LG	FIN	G	AB	R	H	2B	3B	HR	RBI	AVG	BB	TB	OQ	RANK
1894	LF-SS	WAS	NL	11-12	97	372	69	114	21	17	7	71	.306	51	190	120	21-77
1895	LF	WAS	NL	10-12	129	516	115	166	21	22	6	55	.322	69	249	131	16-75
1896	LF	WAS	NL	9-12	127	487	100	148	17	13	5	100	.304	76	206	124	17-73
1897	LF	WAS	NL	6-12	124	486	113	152	25	16	5	59	.313	80	224	137	10-69
1898	LF	WAS	NL	11-12	132	515	88	156	28	11	3	60	.303	64	215	132	11-75
1899	LF	CIN	NL	6-12	140	521	104	154	27	11	3	87	.296	70	212	124	21-61
1900	LF	NY	NL	8-8	141	523	98	176	29	12	4	68	.337	72	241	146	4-47
1901	LF	NY	NL	7-8	125	502	89	145	29	6	1	56	.289	45	189	115	21-45
1902	LF	BAL	AL	8-8	128	503	86	161	27	9	3	60	.320	58	215	131	7-46
1903	LF	WAS	AL	8-8	140	533	68	134	23	12	3	49	.251	41	190	106	29-47
1904	LF	WA/BO	AL	8/1	146	554	65	146	27	12	0	44	.264	72	197	130	8-47
1905	RF	BOS	AL	4-8	121	418	54	103	16	6	4	47	.246	67	143	131	7-41
1906	RF	BOS	AL	8-8	60	228	15	48	9	2	0	23	.211	18	61	85	—

MAJOR LEAGUE TOTALS 1610 6158 1064 1803 299 149 44 779 .293 783 2532 127 12 yrs

Frederick Tenney
5'9 155 lbs Batted left

Born Nov 26, 1871 Georgetown, MA
Died Jul 3, 1952 Boston, MA

YR	POS	TEAM	LG	FIN	G	AB	R	H	2B	3B	HR	RBI	AVG	BB	TB	OQ	RANK
1894	C-LF	BOS	NL	3-12	27	86	23	34	7	1	2	21	.395	12	49	—	—
1895	LF-C	BOS	NL	5-12	49	173	35	47	9	1	1	21	.272	24	61	97	—
1896	RF-C	BOS	NL	4-12	88	348	64	117	14	3	2	49	.336	36	143	116	—
1897	1B	BOS	NL	1-12	132	566	125	180	24	3	1	85	.318	49	213	102	44-69
1898	1B	BOS	NL	1-12	117	488	106	160	25	5	0	62	.328	33	195	118	25-75
1899	1B	BOS	NL	2-12	150	603	115	209	19	17	1	67	.347	63	265	134	10-61
1900	1B	BOS	NL	4-8	112	437	77	122	13	5	1	56	.279	39	148	96	36-47
1901	1B	BOS	NL	5-8	115	451	66	127	13	1	1	22	.282	37	145	99	32-45
1902	1B	BOS	NL	3-8	134	489	88	154	18	3	2	30	.315	73	184	147	4-46
1903	1B	BOS	NL	6-8	122	447	79	140	22	3	3	41	.313	70	177	137	11-49
1904	1B	BOS	NL	7-8	147	533	76	144	17	9	1	37	.270	57	182	117	16-42
1905	1B	BOS	NL	7-8	149	549	84	158	18	3	0	28	.288	67	182	116	17-45
1906	1B	BOS	NL	8-8	143	544	61	154	12	8	1	28	.283	58	185	119	16-42
1907	1B	BOS	NL	7-8	150	554	83	151	18	8	0	26	.273	82	185	128	9-41
1908	1B	NY	NL	2-8	156	583	101	149	20	1	2	49	.256	72	177	114	20-41
1909	1B	NY	NL	3-8	101	375	43	88	8	2	3	30	.235	52	109	106	—
1911	1B	BOS	NL	8-8	102	369	52	97	13	4	1	36	.263	50	121	101	—

MAJOR LEAGUE TOTALS 1994 7595 1278 2231 270 77 22 688 .294 874 2721 119 12 yrs

John Joseph Anderson　　　　　　Born Dec 14, 1873　Sarpsborg, Norway
6'2　180 lbs　Batted both　　　　　　Died Jul 23, 1949　Worcester, MA

YR	POS	TEAM	LG	FIN	G	AB	R	H	2B	3B	HR	RBI	AVG	BB	TB	OQ	RANK
1894	LF	BRO	NL	5-12	17	63	14	19	1	3	1	19	.302	3	29	—	—
1895	LF	BRO	NL	5-12	102	419	76	120	11	14	9	87	.286	12	186	95	49-75
1896	LF-1B	BRO	NL	9-12	108	430	70	135	23	17	1	55	.314	18	195	108	36-73
1897	LF	BRO	NL	6-12	117	492	93	160	28	12	4	85	.325	17	224	110	35-69
1898	CF-1B	BR/WA	NL	10/11	135	520	82	153	33	22	9	81	.294	29	257	133	10-75
1899	CF-1B	BRO	NL	1-12	117	439	65	118	18	7	4	92	.269	27	162	95	45-61
1901	1B	MIL	AL	8-8	138	576	90	190	46	7	8	99	.330	24	274	126	11-46
1902	1B	SL	AL	2-8	126	524	60	149	29	6	4	85	.284	21	202	97	32-46
1903	1B	SL	AL	6-8	138	550	65	156	34	8	2	78	.284	23	212	110	27-47
1904	CF-1B	NY	AL	2-8	143	558	62	155	27	12	3	82	.278	23	215	116	18-47
1905	RF	NY/WA	AL	6/7	133	499	62	139	24	7	1	52	.279	30	180	114	19-41
1906	LF	WAS	AL	7-8	151	583	62	158	25	4	3	70	.271	19	200	100	25-40
1907	1B-LF	WAS	AL	8-8	87	333	33	96	12	4	0	44	.288	34	116	126	—
1908	RF	CHI	AL	3-8	123	355	36	93	17	1	0	47	.262	30	112	111	—
MAJOR LEAGUE TOTALS					1635	6341	870	1841	328	124	49	976	.290	310	2564	109	11 yrs

James Joseph Collins　　　　　　Born Jan 16, 1870　Buffalo, NY
5'9　178 lbs　Batted right　　　　　　Died Mar 6, 1943　Buffalo, NY

YR	POS	TEAM	LG	FIN	G	AB	R	H	2B	3B	HR	RBI	AVG	BB	TB	OQ	RANK
1895	3B-RF	BO/LO	NL	5/12	107	411	75	112	20	5	7	57	.273	37	163	96	46-75
1896	3B	BOS	NL	4-12	84	304	48	90	10	9	1	46	.296	30	121	106	—
1897	3B	BOS	NL	1-12	134	529	103	183	28	13	6	132	.346	41	255	129	20-69
1898	3B	BOS	NL	1-12	152	597	107	196	35	5	15	111	.328	40	286	139	9-75
1899	3B	BOS	NL	2-12	151	599	98	166	28	11	5	92	.277	40	231	101	38-61
1900	3B	BOS	NL	4-8	142	586	104	178	25	5	6	95	.304	34	231	106	24-47
1901	3B	BOS	AL	2-8	138	564	108	187	42	16	6	94	.332	34	279	135	6-46
1902	3B	BOS	AL	3-8	108	429	71	138	21	10	6	61	.322	24	197	124	13-46
1903	3B	BOS	AL	1-8	130	540	88	160	33	17	5	72	.296	24	242	129	14-47
1904	3B	BOS	AL	1-8	156	631	85	171	33	13	3	67	.271	27	239	114	23-47
1905	3B	BOS	AL	4-8	131	508	66	140	26	5	4	65	.276	37	188	120	14-41
1906	3B	BOS	AL	8-8	37	142	17	39	8	4	1	16	.275	4	58	117	—
1907	3B	BO/PH	AL	7/2	141	523	51	146	30	0	0	45	.279	34	176	111	19-48
1908	3B	PHI	AL	6-8	115	433	34	94	14	3	0	30	.217	20	114	81	—
MAJOR LEAGUE TOTALS					1726	6796	1055	2000	353	116	65	983	.294	426	2780	119	11 yrs

William J McCormick
5'9

Born Dec 25, 1874 Maysville, KY
Died Jan 28, 1956 Cincinnati, OH

YR	POS	TEAM	LG	FIN	G	AB	R	H	2B	3B	HR	RBI	AVG	BB	TB	OQ	RANK
1895	SS-2B	LOU	NL	12-12	3	12	2	3	0	1	0	0	.250	0	5	—	—
1896	3B-SS	CHI	NL	5-12	45	168	22	37	3	1	1	23	.220	14	45	67	—
1897	3B-SS	CHI	NL	8-12	101	419	87	112	8	10	2	55	.267	33	146	88	61-69
1898	3B	CHI	NL	4-12	137	530	76	131	15	9	2	78	.247	47	170	93	53-75
1899	2B	CHI	NL	8-12	102	376	48	97	15	2	2	52	.258	25	122	85	—
1900	SS-3B	CHI	NL	5-8	110	379	35	83	13	5	3	48	.219	38	115	84	—
1901	SS	CHI	NL	6-8	115	427	45	100	15	6	1	32	.234	31	130	86	36-45
1902	3B	SL	AL	2-8	139	504	55	124	14	4	3	51	.246	37	155	83	42-46
1903	2B-3B	SL/WA	AL	6/8	124	426	27	92	16	3	1	39	.216	28	117	80	44-47
1904	2B	WAS	AL	8-8	113	404	36	88	11	1	0	39	.218	27	101	80	—
MAJOR LEAGUE TOTALS					989	3645	433	867	110	42	15	417	.238	280	1106	86	5 yrs

Dennis Lawrence McGann
6'0   190 lbs   Batted both

Born Jul 15, 1871   Shelbyville, KY
Died Dec 13, 1910   Louisville, KY

YR	POS	TEAM	LG	FIN	G	AB	R	H	2B	3B	HR	RBI	AVG	BB	TB	OQ	RANK
1895	SS-3B	LOU	NL	12-12	20	73	9	21	5	2	0	9	.288	8	30	—	—
1896	2B	BOS	NL	4-12	43	171	25	55	6	7	2	30	.322	12	81	120	—
1898	1B	BAL	NL	2-12	145	535	99	161	18	8	5	106	.301	53	210	120	23-75
1899	1B	BR/WA	NL	1/11	139	494	114	148	20	12	7	90	.300	35	213	115	23-61
1900	1B	SL	NL	6-8	121	444	79	132	10	9	4	58	.297	32	172	106	22-47
1901	1B	SL	NL	4-8	103	423	73	115	15	9	6	56	.272	16	166	104	27-45
1902	1B	BAL	AL	8-8	68	250	40	79	10	8	0	42	.316	19	105	119	—
1902	1B	NY	NL	8-8	61	227	25	68	5	7	0	21	.300	12	87	119	—
1903	1B	NY	NL	2-8	129	482	75	130	21	6	3	50	.270	32	172	98	34-49
1904	1B	NY	NL	1-8	141	517	81	148	22	6	6	71	.286	36	200	122	13-42
1905	1B	NY	NL	1-8	136	491	88	147	23	14	5	75	.299	55	213	142	6-45
1906	1B	NY	NL	2-8	134	451	62	107	14	8	0	37	.237	60	137	110	20-42
1907	1B	NY	NL	4-8	81	262	29	78	9	1	2	36	.298	29	95	130	—
1908	1B	BOS	NL	6-8	135	475	52	114	8	5	2	55	.240	38	138	97	32-41
MAJOR LEAGUE TOTALS					1456	5295	851	1503	186	102	42	736	.284	437	2019	113	9 yrs

William L Everett
6'0   185 lbs   Batted left

Born Dec 13, 1868   Fort Wayne, IN
Died Jan 19, 1938   Denver, CO

YR	POS	TEAM	LG	FIN	G	AB	R	H	2B	3B	HR	RBI	AVG	BB	TB	OQ	RANK
1895	3B	CHI	NL	4-12	133	550	129	197	16	10	3	88	.358	33	242	112	33-75
1896	3B-LF	CHI	NL	5-12	132	575	130	184	16	13	2	46	.320	41	232	104	40-73
1897	3B	CHI	NL	9-12	92	379	63	119	14	7	5	39	.314	36	162	115	27-69
1898	1B	CHI	NL	4-12	149	596	102	190	15	6	0	69	.319	53	217	113	33-75
1899	1B	CHI	NL	8-12	136	536	87	166	17	5	1	74	.310	31	196	99	41-61
1900	1B	CHI	NL	5-8	23	91	10	24	4	0	0	17	.264	3	28	—	—
1901	1B	WAS	AL	6-8	33	115	14	22	3	2	0	8	.191	15	29	77	—

MAJOR LEAGUE TOTALS					698	2842	535	902	85	43	11	341	.317	212	1106	109	5 yrs

Harry Davis
5'10   180 lbs   Batted right

Born Jul 19, 1873   Philadelphia, PA
Died Aug 11, 1947   Philadelphia, PA

YR	POS	TEAM	LG	FIN	G	AB	R	H	2B	3B	HR	RBI	AVG	BB	TB	OQ	RANK
1895	1B	NY	NL	9-12	7	24	1	7	0	1	0	6	.292	2	9	—	—
1896	1B-LF	NY/PT	NL	7/6	108	401	67	96	16	16	2	73	.239	44	150	95	51-73
1897	1B-3B	PIT	NL	8-12	111	429	70	131	10	28	2	63	.305	26	203	116	26-69
1898	1B	Pt/Lo/Wa	NL	8/9/0	96	363	49	95	14	15	2	40	.262	19	145	104	—
1899	1B	WAS	NL	11-12	18	64	3	12	2	3	0	8	.188	8	20	—	—
1901	1B	PHI	AL	4-8	117	496	92	152	28	10	8	76	.306	23	224	117	17-46
1902	1B	PHI	AL	1-8	133	561	89	172	43	8	6	92	.307	30	249	117	20-46
1903	1B	PHI	AL	2-8	106	420	77	125	28	7	6	55	.298	24	185	130	12-47
1904	1B	PHI	AL	5-8	102	404	54	125	21	11	10	62	.309	23	198	156	—
1905	1B	PHI	AL	1-8	150	607	93	173	47	6	8	83	.285	43	256	135	4-41
1906	1B	PHI	AL	4-8	145	551	94	161	40	8	12	96	.292	49	253	150	3-40
1907	1B	PHI	AL	2-8	149	582	84	155	37	8	8	87	.266	42	232	128	7-48
1908	1B	PHI	AL	6-8	147	513	65	127	23	9	5	62	.248	61	183	129	10-36
1909	1B	PHI	AL	2-8	149	530	73	142	22	11	4	75	.268	51	198	127	12-33
1910	1B	PHI	AL	1-8	139	492	61	122	19	4	1	41	.248	53	152	106	23-36
1911	1B	PHI	AL	1-8	57	183	27	36	9	1	1	22	.197	24	50	82	—
1912	1B	CLE	AL	5-8	2	5	0	0	0	0	0	0	.000	0	0	—	—
1913	1B	PHI	AL	1-8	7	17	2	6	2	0	0	4	.353	1	8	—	—
1914	1B	PHI	AL	1-8	5	7	0	3	0	0	0	2	.429	1	3	—	—
1915	1B	PHI	AL	8-8	5	3	0	1	0	0	0	4	.333	0	1	—	—
1916	LF	PHI	AL	8-8	1	0	0	0	0	0	0	0	—	1	0	—	—
1917	PH	PHI	AL	8-8	1	1	0	0	0	0	0	0	.000	0	0	—	—

MAJOR LEAGUE TOTALS					1755	6653	1001	1841	361	146	75	951	.277	525	2719	123	11 yrs

Patrick Henry Dolan Born Dec 3, 1872 Cambridge, MA
5'10 160 lbs Batted left Died Mar 29, 1907 Louisville, KY

YR	POS	TEAM	LG	FIN	G	AB	R	H	2B	3B	HR	RBI	AVG	BB	TB	OO	RANK
1892	P	WAS	NL	10-12	5	13	1	3	0	0	0	1	.231	2	3	—	—
1895	P	BOS	NL	5-12	26	83	12	20	4	1	0	7	.241	6	26	—	—
1896	P	BOS	NL	4-12	6	14	4	2	0	0	0	0	.143	0	2	—	—
1900	RF	CHI	NL	5-8	13	48	5	13	1	0	0	2	.271	2	14	—	—
1901	CF	CH/BR	NL	6/3	109	424	62	111	12	3	0	45	.262	24	129	86	37-45
1902	CF	BRO	NL	2-8	141	592	72	166	16	7	1	54	.280	33	199	104	29-46
1903	1B-CF	CHI	AL	7-8	27	104	16	27	5	1	0	7	.260	6	34	95	—
1903	RF	CIN	NL	4-8	93	385	64	111	20	3	0	58	.288	28	137	102	—
1904	RF-1B	CIN	NL	3-8	129	465	88	132	8	10	6	51	.284	39	178	124	12-42
1905	RF-1B	CN/BO	NL	5/7	134	510	51	137	13	8	3	52	.269	34	175	102	30-45
1906	RF	BOS	NL	8-8	152	549	54	136	20	4	0	39	.248	55	164	101	27-42
MAJOR LEAGUE TOTALS					835	3187	429	858	99	37	10	316	.269	229	1061	103	5 yrs

Fielder Allison Jones Born Aug 13, 1871 Shinglehouse, PA
5'11 180 lbs Batted left Died Mar 13, 1934 Portland, OR

YR	POS	TEAM	LG	FIN	G	AB	R	H	2B	3B	HR	RBI	AVG	BB	TB	OO	RANK
1896	RF	BRO	NL	9-12	104	395	82	140	10	8	3	46	.354	48	175	131	15-73
1897	RF	BRO	NL	6-12	135	548	134	172	15	10	1	49	.314	61	210	109	36-69
1898	RF	BRO	NL	10-12	146	596	89	181	15	9	1	69	.304	46	217	108	41-75
1899	CF	BRO	NL	1-12	102	365	75	104	8	2	2	38	.285	54	122	109	—
1900	CF	BRO	NL	1-8	136	552	106	171	26	4	4	54	.310	57	217	117	16-47
1901	RF	CHI	AL	1-8	133	521	120	162	16	3	2	65	.311	84	190	124	12-46
1902	CF	CHI	AL	4-8	135	532	98	171	16	5	0	54	.321	57	197	115	23-46
1903	CF	CHI	AL	7-8	136	530	71	152	18	5	0	45	.287	47	180	110	25-47
1904	CF	CHI	AL	3-8	149	547	72	133	14	5	3	42	.243	53	166	104	31-47
1905	CF	CHI	AL	2-8	153	568	91	139	17	12	2	38	.245	73	186	118	16-41
1906	CF	CHI	AL	1-8	144	496	77	114	22	4	2	34	.230	83	150	118	15-40
1907	CF	CHI	AL	3-8	154	559	72	146	18	1	0	47	.261	67	166	112	15-48
1908	CF	CHI	AL	3-8	149	529	92	134	11	7	1	50	.253	86	162	128	11-36
1914	PH	SL	FL	8-8	5	3	0	1	0	0	0	0	.333	1	1	—	—
1915	RF-CF	SL	FL	2-8	7	6	1	0	0	0	0	0	.000	0	0	—	—
MAJOR LEAGUE TOTALS					1788	6747	1180	1920	206	75	21	631	.285	817	2339	116	12 yrs

Oliver Daniel Pickering   Born Apr 9, 1870 Olney, IL
5'11 170 lbs Batted left   Died Jan 20, 1952 Vincennes, IN

YR	POS	TEAM	LG	FIN	G	AB	R	H	2B	3B	HR	RBI	AVG	BB	TB	OQ	RANK
1896	CF	LOU	NL	12-12	45	165	28	50	6	4	1	22	.303	12	67	103	—
1897	CF	LO/CL	NL	11/5	109	428	67	126	10	4	2	42	.294	36	150	93	55-69
1901	CF	CLE	AL	7-8	137	547	102	169	25	6	0	40	.309	58	206	114	21-46
1902	CF	CLE	AL	5-8	69	293	46	75	5	2	3	26	.256	19	93	84	—
1903	CF	PHI	AL	2-8	137	512	93	144	18	6	1	36	.281	53	177	115	20-47
1904	CF	PHI	AL	5-8	124	455	56	103	10	3	0	30	.226	45	119	92	37-47
1907	RF	SL	AL	6-8	151	576	63	159	15	10	0	60	.276	35	194	109	24-48
1908	RF	WAS	AL	7-8	113	373	45	84	7	4	2	30	.225	28	105	94	—
MAJOR LEAGUE TOTALS					885	3349	500	910	96	39	9	286	.272	286	1111	105	5 yrs

Napoleon Lajoie   Born Sep 5, 1874 Woonsocket, RI
6'1 195 lbs Batted right   Died Feb 7, 1959 Daytona Beach, FL

YR	POS	TEAM	LG	FIN	G	AB	R	H	2B	3B	HR	RBI	AVG	BB	TB	OQ	RANK
1896	1B	PHI	NL	8-12	39	175	36	57	12	7	4	42	.326	1	95	122	—
1897	1B-RF	PHI	NL	10-12	127	545	107	197	40	23	9	127	.361	15	310	141	8-69
1898	2B	PHI	NL	6-12	147	608	113	197	43	11	6	127	.324	21	280	125	16-75
1899	2B	PHI	NL	3-12	77	312	70	118	19	9	6	70	.378	12	173	154	—
1900	2B	PHI	NL	3-8	102	451	95	152	33	12	7	92	.337	10	230	130	8-47
1901	2B	PHI	AL	4-8	131	544	145	232	48	14	14	125	.426	24	350	195	1-46
1902	2B	PH/CL	AL	1/5	87	352	81	133	35	5	7	65	.378	19	199	163	—
1903	2B	CLE	AL	3-8	125	485	90	167	41	11	7	93	.344	24	251	159	2-47
1904	2B-SS	CLE	AL	4-8	140	553	92	208	49	15	6	102	.376	27	305	189	1-47
1905	2B	CLE	AL	5-8	65	249	29	82	12	2	2	41	.329	17	104	142	—
1906	2B	CLE	AL	3-8	152	602	88	214	48	9	0	91	.355	30	280	155	2-40
1907	2B	CLE	AL	4-8	137	509	53	152	30	6	2	63	.299	30	200	128	6-48
1908	2B	CLE	AL	2-8	157	581	77	168	32	6	2	74	.289	47	218	131	9-36
1909	2B	CLE	AL	6-8	128	469	56	152	33	7	1	47	.324	35	202	148	5-33
1910	2B	CLE	AL	5-8	159	591	92	227	51	7	4	76	.384	60	304	191	2-36
1911	1B-2B	CLE	AL	3-8	90	315	36	115	20	1	2	60	.365	26	143	138	—
1912	2B-1B	CLE	AL	5-8	117	448	66	165	34	4	0	90	.368	28	207	139	6-33
1913	2B	CLE	AL	3-8	137	465	66	156	25	2	1	68	.335	33	188	124	9-37
1914	2B-1B	CLE	AL	8-8	121	419	37	108	14	3	0	50	.258	32	128	92	—
1915	2B	PHI	AL	8-8	129	490	40	137	24	5	1	61	.280	11	174	92	35-42
1916	2B	PHI	AL	8-8	113	426	33	105	14	4	2	35	.246	14	133	81	—
MAJOR LEAGUE TOTALS					2480	9589	1502	3242	657	163	83	1599	.338	516	4474	146	14 yrs

Richard Joseph Padden   Born Sep 17, 1870 Martins Ferry, OH
5'10 165 lbs Batted right   Died Oct 31, 1922 Martins Ferry, OH

YR	POS	TEAM	LG	FIN	G	AB	R	H	2B	3B	HR	RBI	AVG	BB	TB	OQ	RANK
1896	2B	PIT	NL	6-12	61	219	33	53	4	8	2	24	.242	14	79	84	—
1897	2B	PIT	NL	8-12	134	517	84	146	16	10	2	58	.282	38	188	92	59-69
1898	2B	PIT	NL	8-12	128	463	61	119	7	6	2	43	.257	35	144	89	63-75
1899	SS-2B	WAS	NL	11-12	134	451	66	125	20	7	2	61	.277	24	165	93	46-61
1901	2B	SL	NL	4-8	123	489	71	125	17	7	2	62	.256	31	162	93	33-45
1902	2B	SL	AL	2-8	117	413	54	109	26	3	1	40	.264	30	144	94	37-46
1903	2B	SL	AL	6-8	29	94	7	19	3	0	0	6	.202	9	22	76	—
1904	2B	SL	AL	6-8	132	453	42	108	19	4	0	36	.238	40	135	100	35-47
1905	2B	SL	AL	8-8	16	58	5	10	1	1	0	4	.172	3	13	—	—

MAJOR LEAGUE TOTALS   874 3157 423 814 113 46 11 334 .258 224 1052 94 6 yrs

James Bentley Seymour   Born Dec 9, 1872 Albany, NY
6'0 200 lbs Batted left   Died Sep 20, 1919 New York, NY

YR	POS	TEAM	LG	FIN	G	AB	R	H	2B	3B	HR	RBI	AVG	BB	TB	OQ	RANK
1896	P	NY	NL	7-12	12	32	2	7	0	0	0	0	.219	0	7	—	—
1897	P-CF	NY	NL	3-12	44	137	13	33	5	1	2	14	.241	4	46	73	—
1898	P-RF	NY	NL	7-12	80	297	41	82	5	2	4	23	.276	9	103	89	—
1899	P-RF	NY	NL	10-12	50	159	25	52	3	2	2	27	.327	4	65	104	—
1900	P-RF	NY	NL	8-8	23	40	9	12	0	0	0	2	.300	3	12	—	—
1901	RF	BAL	AL	5-8	134	547	84	166	19	8	1	77	.303	28	204	99	30-46
1902	RF	BAL	AL	8-8	72	280	38	75	8	8	3	41	.268	18	108	101	—
1902	CF	CIN	NL	4-8	62	244	27	83	8	2	2	37	.340	12	101	134	—
1903	CF	CIN	NL	4-8	135	558	85	191	25	15	7	72	.342	33	267	139	9-49
1904	CF	CIN	NL	3-8	131	531	71	166	26	13	5	58	.313	29	233	137	4-42
1905	CF	CIN	NL	5-8	149	581	95	219	40	21	8	121	.377	51	325	189	1-45
1906	CF	CN/NY	NL	6/2	151	576	70	165	19	5	8	80	.286	42	218	121	14-42
1907	CF	NY	NL	4-8	131	473	46	139	25	8	3	75	.294	36	189	130	7-41
1908	CF	NY	NL	2-8	156	587	60	157	23	2	5	92	.267	30	199	106	24-41
1909	CF	NY	NL	3-8	80	280	37	87	12	5	1	30	.311	25	112	134	—
1910	CF	NY	NL	2-8	79	287	32	76	9	4	1	40	.265	23	96	96	—
1913	CF	BOS	NL	5-8	39	73	2	13	2	0	0	10	.178	7	15	—	—

MAJOR LEAGUE TOTALS   1528 5682 737 1723 229 96 52 799 .303 354 2300 132 7 yrs

Samuel Blair Mertes   Born Aug 6, 1872   San Francisco, CA
5'10   185 lbs   Batted right   Died Mar 11, 1945   San Francisco, CA

YR	POS	TEAM	LG	FIN	G	AB	R	H	2B	3B	HR	RBI	AVG	BB	TB	OQ	RANK
1896	CF	PHI	NL	8-12	37	143	20	34	4	4	0	14	.238	8	46	74	—
1898	RF-SS	CHI	NL	4-12	83	269	45	80	4	8	1	47	.297	34	103	124	—
1899	RF	CHI	NL	8-12	117	426	83	127	13	16	9	81	.298	33	199	125	19-61
1900	RF-1B	CHI	NL	5-8	127	481	72	142	25	4	7	60	.295	42	196	114	19-47
1901	2B	CHI	AL	1-8	137	545	94	151	16	17	5	98	.277	52	216	111	22-46
1902	LF	CHI	AL	4-8	129	497	60	140	23	7	1	79	.282	37	180	100	29-46
1903	LF	NY	NL	2-8	138	517	100	145	32	14	7	104	.280	61	226	131	14-49
1904	LF	NY	NL	1-8	148	532	83	147	28	11	4	78	.276	54	209	130	9-42
1905	LF	NY	NL	1-8	150	551	81	154	27	17	5	108	.279	56	230	131	10-45
1906	LF	NY/SL	NL	2/7	124	444	57	107	16	10	1	52	.241	45	146	108	22-42

MAJOR LEAGUE TOTALS   1190 4405 695 1227 188 108 40 721 .279 422 1751 119   8 yrs

Charles Taylor Hickman   Born Mar 4, 1876   Taylortown, PA
5'11   215 lbs   Batted right   Died Apr 19, 1934   Morgantown, WV

YR	POS	TEAM	LG	FIN	G	AB	R	H	2B	3B	HR	RBI	AVG	BB	TB	OQ	RANK
1897	P	BOS	NL	1-12	2	3	1	2	0	0	1	2	.667	0	5	—	—
1898	LF-P	BOS	NL	1-12	19	58	4	15	2	0	0	7	.259	1	17	—	—
1899	P-CF	BOS	NL	2-12	19	63	15	25	2	7	0	15	.397	2	41	—	—
1900	3B	NY	NL	8-8	127	473	65	148	19	17	9	91	.313	17	228	122	12-47
1901	RF-SS	NY	NL	7-8	112	406	44	113	20	6	4	62	.278	15	157	103	—
1902	1B-LF	BO/CL	AL	3/5	130	534	73	193	36	13	11	110	.361	15	288	145	2-46
1903	1B	CLE	AL	3-8	131	522	64	154	31	11	12	97	.295	17	243	130	13-47
1904	1B-2B	CL/DE	AL	4/7	128	481	52	132	28	16	6	67	.274	24	210	132	7-47
1905	2B-RF	DE/WA	AL	3/7	147	573	69	159	37	12	4	66	.277	21	232	120	13-41
1906	RF-1B	WAS	AL	7-8	120	451	53	128	25	5	9	57	.284	14	190	122	10-40
1907	1B-RF	WA/CH	AL	8/3	81	221	21	61	11	4	1	24	.276	18	83	125	—
1908	RF-1B	CLE	AL	2-8	65	197	16	46	6	1	2	16	.234	9	60	93	—

MAJOR LEAGUE TOTALS   1081 3982 477 1176 217 92 59 614 .295 153 1754 129   6 yrs

Richard Joseph Harley
5'10 165 lbs Batted left

Born Sep 25, 1872 Philadelphia, PA
Died Apr 3, 1952 Philadelphia, PA

YR	POS	TEAM	LG	FIN	G	AB	R	H	2B	3B	HR	RBI	AVG	BB	TB	OQ	RANK
1897	CF	SL	NL	12-12	89	330	43	96	6	4	3	35	.291	36	119	100	—
1898	LF	SL	NL	12-12	142	549	74	135	6	5	0	42	.246	34	151	76	71-75
1899	LF	CLE	NL	12-12	142	567	70	142	15	7	1	50	.250	40	174	81	56-61
1900	LF	CIN	NL	7-8	5	21	2	9	1	0	0	5	.429	1	10	—	—
1901	LF	CIN	NL	8-8	133	535	69	146	13	2	4	27	.273	31	175	93	35-45
1902	LF	DET	AL	7-8	125	491	59	138	9	8	2	44	.281	36	169	95	35-46
1903	RF	CHI	NL	3-8	104	386	72	89	9	1	0	33	.231	45	100	83	45-49
MAJOR LEAGUE TOTALS					740	2879	389	755	59	27	10	236	.262	223	898	86	5 yrs

Roger Philip Bresnahan
5'9 200 lbs Batted right

Born Jun 11, 1879 Toledo, OH
Died Dec 4, 1944 Toledo, OH

YR	POS	TEAM	LG	FIN	G	AB	R	H	2B	3B	HR	RBI	AVG	BB	TB	OQ	RANK
1897	P	WAS	NL	6-12	6	16	1	6	0	0	0	3	.375	1	6	—	—
1900	C	CHI	NL	5-8	2	2	0	0	0	0	0	0	.000	0	0	—	—
1901	C	BAL	AL	5-8	86	295	40	79	9	9	1	32	.268	23	109	100	—
1902	3B-C	BAL	AL	8-8	65	235	30	64	8	6	4	34	.272	21	96	112	—
1902	CF-C	NY	NL	8-8	51	178	16	51	9	3	1	22	.287	16	69	128	—
1903	CF-1B	NY	NL	2-8	113	406	87	142	30	8	4	55	.350	61	200	168	1-49
1904	CF-1B	NY	NL	1-8	109	402	81	114	22	7	5	33	.284	58	165	147	—
1905	C	NY	NL	1-8	104	331	58	100	18	3	0	46	.302	50	124	137	—
1906	C-CF	NY	NL	2-8	124	405	69	114	22	4	0	43	.281	81	144	148	4-42
1907	C	NY	NL	4-8	110	328	57	83	9	7	4	38	.253	61	118	141	—
1908	C	NY	NL	2-8	140	449	70	127	25	3	1	54	.283	83	161	151	3-41
1909	C-2B	SL	NL	7-8	72	234	27	57	4	1	0	23	.244	46	63	116	—
1910	C	SL	NL	7-8	88	234	35	65	15	3	0	27	.278	55	86	142	—
1911	C	SL	NL	5-8	81	227	22	63	17	8	3	41	.278	45	105	147	—
1912	C	SL	NL	6-8	48	108	8	36	7	2	1	15	.333	14	50	139	—
1913	C	CHI	NL	3-8	69	162	20	37	5	2	1	21	.228	21	49	94	—
1914	C-2B	CHI	NL	4-8	101	248	42	69	10	4	0	24	.278	49	87	135	—
1915	C	CHI	NL	4-8	77	221	19	45	8	1	1	19	.204	29	58	90	—
MAJOR LEAGUE TOTALS					1446	4481	682	1252	218	71	26	530	.279	714	1690	—	—

Charles Sylvester Stahl   Born Jan 10, 1873   Avila, IN
5'10   160 lbs   Batted left   Died Mar 28, 1907   West Baden, IN

YR	POS	TEAM	LG	FIN	G	AB	R	H	2B	3B	HR	RBI	AVG	BB	TB	OQ	RANK
1897	RF	BOS	NL	1-12	114	469	112	166	30	13	4	97	.354	38	234	135	13-69
1898	RF	BOS	NL	1-12	125	467	72	144	21	8	3	52	.308	46	190	125	18-75
1899	RF	BOS	NL	2-12	148	576	122	202	23	19	7	53	.351	72	284	153	5-61
1900	LF	BOS	NL	4-8	136	553	88	163	23	16	5	82	.295	34	233	111	20-47
1901	CF	BOS	AL	2-8	131	515	105	156	20	16	6	72	.303	54	226	127	9-46
1902	CF	BOS	AL	3-8	127	508	92	164	22	11	2	58	.323	37	214	119	18-46
1903	CF	BOS	AL	1-8	77	299	60	82	12	6	2	44	.274	28	112	119	—
1904	CF	BOS	AL	1-8	157	587	83	170	27	19	3	67	.290	64	244	145	3-47
1905	CF	BOS	AL	4-8	134	500	61	129	17	4	0	47	.258	50	154	108	24-41
1906	CF	BOS	AL	8-8	155	595	62	170	24	6	4	51	.286	47	218	121	12-40

| MAJOR LEAGUE TOTALS | | | | | 1304 | 5069 | 857 | 1546 | 219 | 118 | 36 | 623 | .305 | 470 | 2109 | 127 | 9 yrs |

John Peter Wagner   Born Feb 24, 1874   Mansfield, PA
5'11   200 lbs   Batted right   Died Dec 6, 1955   Carnegie, PA

YR	POS	TEAM	LG	FIN	G	AB	R	H	2B	3B	HR	RBI	AVG	BB	TB	OQ	RANK
1897	CF-2B	LOU	NL	11-12	61	237	37	80	17	4	2	39	.338	15	111	121	—
1898	1B-3B	LOU	NL	9-12	151	588	80	176	29	3	10	105	.299	31	241	112	34-75
1899	3B-RF	LOU	NL	9-12	147	571	98	192	43	13	7	113	.336	40	282	137	8-61
1900	RF	PIT	NL	2-8	135	527	107	201	45	22	4	100	.381	41	302	171	1-47
1901	SS-RF	PIT	NL	1-8	140	549	101	194	37	11	6	126	.353	53	271	160	5-45
1902	RF-SS	PIT	NL	1-8	136	534	105	176	30	16	3	91	.330	43	247	155	3-46
1903	SS	PIT	NL	1-8	129	512	97	182	30	19	5	101	.355	44	265	159	4-49
1904	SS	PIT	NL	4-8	132	490	97	171	44	14	4	75	.349	59	255	187	1-42
1905	SS	PIT	NL	2-8	147	548	114	199	32	14	6	101	.363	54	277	172	2-45
1906	SS	PIT	NL	3-8	142	516	103	175	38	9	2	71	.339	58	237	165	1-42
1907	SS	PIT	NL	2-8	142	515	98	180	38	14	6	82	.350	46	264	179	1-41
1908	SS	PIT	NL	2-8	151	568	100	201	39	19	10	109	.354	54	308	196	1-41
1909	SS	PIT	NL	1-8	137	495	92	168	39	10	5	100	.339	66	242	177	1-39
1910	SS	PIT	NL	3-8	150	556	90	178	34	8	4	81	.320	59	240	135	5-47
1911	SS-1B	PIT	NL	3-8	130	473	87	158	23	16	9	89	.334	67	240	157	1-45
1912	SS	PIT	NL	2-8	145	558	91	181	35	20	7	102	.324	59	277	140	3-43
1913	SS	PIT	NL	4-8	114	413	51	124	18	4	3	56	.300	26	159	108	—
1914	SS-3B	PIT	NL	7-8	150	552	60	139	15	9	1	50	.252	51	175	97	34-42
1915	SS	PIT	NL	5-8	156	566	68	155	32	17	6	78	.274	39	239	124	9-45
1916	SS-1B	PIT	NL	6-8	123	432	45	124	15	9	1	39	.287	34	160	118	—
1917	1B-3B	PIT	NL	8-8	74	230	15	61	7	1	0	24	.265	24	70	104	—

| MAJOR LEAGUE TOTALS | | | | | 2792 | 10430 | 1736 | 3415 | 640 | 252 | 101 | 1732 | .327 | 963 | 4862 | 154 | 17 yrs |

Edward James Abbaticchio
5'11 170 lbs Batted right

Born Apr 15, 1877 Latrobe, PA
Died Jan 6, 1957 Fort Lauderdale, FL

YR	POS	TEAM	LG	FIN	G	AB	R	H	2B	3B	HR	RBI	AVG	BB	TB	OQ	RANK
1897	2B	PHI	NL	10-12	3	10	0	3	0	0	0	0	.300	1	3	—	—
1898	3B-2B	PHI	NL	6-12	25	92	9	21	4	0	0	14	.228	7	25	—	—
1903	2B-SS	BOS	NL	6-8	136	489	61	111	18	5	1	46	.227	52	142	87	42-49
1904	SS	BOS	NL	7-8	154	579	76	148	18	10	3	54	.256	40	195	104	30-42
1905	SS	BOS	NL	7-8	153	610	70	170	25	12	3	41	.279	35	228	109	22-45
1907	2B	PIT	NL	2-8	147	496	63	130	14	7	2	82	.262	65	164	121	15-41
1908	2B	PIT	NL	2-8	146	500	43	125	16	7	1	61	.250	58	158	115	18-41
1909	SS-2B	PIT	NL	1-8	36	87	13	20	0	0	1	16	.230	19	23	118	—
1910	SS	PT/BO	NL	3/8	55	181	20	44	4	2	0	10	.243	12	52	80	—
MAJOR LEAGUE TOTALS					855	3044	355	772	99	43	11	324	.254	289	990	107	5 yrs

Samuel James Tilden Sheckard
5'9 175 lbs Batted left

Born Nov 23, 1878 Upper Chanceford, PA
Died Jan 15, 1947 Lancaster, PA

YR	POS	TEAM	LG	FIN	G	AB	R	H	2B	3B	HR	RBI	AVG	BB	TB	OQ	RANK
1897	SS-RF	BRO	NL	6-12	13	49	12	14	3	2	3	14	.286	6	30	—	—
1898	LF	BRO	NL	10-12	105	408	51	113	17	9	4	64	.277	37	160	114	—
1899	RF	BAL	NL	4-12	147	536	104	158	18	10	3	75	.295	56	205	111	28-61
1900	LF	BRO	NL	1-8	85	273	74	82	19	10	1	39	.300	42	124	141	—
1901	LF	BRO	NL	3-8	133	554	116	196	29	19	11	104	.354	47	296	168	3-45
1902	CF	BAL	AL	8-8	4	15	3	4	1	0	0	0	.267	1	5	—	—
1902	LF	BRO	NL	2-8	123	486	86	129	20	10	4	37	.265	57	181	128	10-46
1903	LF	BRO	NL	5-8	139	515	99	171	29	9	9	75	.332	75	245	158	5-49
1904	LF	BRO	NL	6-8	143	507	70	121	23	6	1	46	.239	56	159	106	27-42
1905	LF	BRO	NL	8-8	130	480	58	140	20	11	3	41	.292	61	191	135	8-45
1906	LF	CHI	NL	1-8	149	549	90	144	27	10	1	45	.262	67	194	123	13-42
1907	LF	CHI	NL	1-8	143	484	76	129	23	1	1	36	.267	76	157	127	12-41
1908	LF	CHI	NL	1-8	115	403	54	93	18	3	2	22	.231	62	123	119	—
1909	LF	CHI	NL	2-8	148	525	81	134	29	5	1	43	.255	72	176	119	15-39
1910	LF	CHI	NL	1-8	144	507	82	130	27	6	5	51	.256	83	184	121	14-47
1911	LF	CHI	NL	2-8	156	539	121	149	26	11	4	50	.276	147	209	147	4-45
1912	LF	CHI	NL	3-8	146	523	85	128	22	10	3	47	.245	122	179	119	15-43
1913	RF	SL/CN	NL	8/7	99	252	34	49	3	4	0	24	.194	68	60	106	—
MAJOR LEAGUE TOTALS					2122	7605	1296	2084	354	136	56	813	.274	1135	2878	130	12 yrs

Claude Cassius Ritchey   Born Oct 5, 1873   Emlenton, PA
5'6 167 lbs Batted both   Died Nov 8, 1951 Emlenton, PA

YR	POS	TEAM	LG	FIN	G	AB	R	H	2B	3B	HR	RBI	AVG	BB	TB	OQ	RANK
1897	SS-LF	CIN	NL	4-12	101	337	58	95	12	4	0	41	.282	42	115	98	—
1898	SS-2B	LOU	NL	9-12	151	551	65	140	10	4	5	51	.254	46	173	91	58-75
1899	2B	LOU	NL	9-12	147	536	65	161	15	7	4	71	.300	49	202	108	34-61
1900	2B	PIT	NL	2-8	123	476	62	139	17	8	1	67	.292	29	175	98	33-47
1901	2B	PIT	NL	1-8	140	540	66	160	20	4	1	74	.296	47	191	110	25-45
1902	2B	PIT	NL	1-8	115	405	54	112	13	1	2	55	.277	53	133	121	12-46
1903	2B	PIT	NL	1-8	138	506	66	145	28	10	0	59	.287	55	193	117	19-49
1904	2B	PIT	NL	4-8	156	544	79	143	22	12	0	51	.263	59	189	118	15-42
1905	2B	PIT	NL	2-8	153	533	54	136	29	6	0	52	.255	51	177	104	26-45
1906	2B	PIT	NL	3-8	152	484	46	130	21	5	1	62	.269	68	164	125	12-42
1907	2B	BOS	NL	7-8	144	499	45	127	17	4	2	51	.255	50	158	108	26-41
1908	2B	BOS	NL	6-8	121	421	44	115	10	3	2	36	.273	50	137	121	14-41
1909	2B	BOS	NL	8-8	30	87	4	15	1	0	0	3	.172	8	16	—	—
MAJOR LEAGUE TOTALS					1671	5919	708	1618	215	68	18	673	.273	607	2023	111	11 yrs

William Edward Bransfield   Born Jan 7, 1875   Worcester, MA
5'11 207 lbs Batted right   Died May 1, 1947 Worcester, MA

YR	POS	TEAM	LG	FIN	G	AB	R	H	2B	3B	HR	RBI	AVG	BB	TB	OQ	RANK
1898	C-1B	BOS	NL	1-12	5	9	2	2	0	1	0	1	.222	0	4	—	—
1901	1B	PIT	NL	1-8	139	566	92	167	26	16	0	91	.295	29	225	112	23-45
1902	1B	PIT	NL	1-8	102	413	49	126	21	8	0	69	.305	17	163	120	13-46
1903	1B	PIT	NL	1-8	127	505	69	134	23	7	2	57	.265	33	177	96	37-49
1904	1B	PIT	NL	4-8	139	520	47	116	17	9	0	60	.223	22	151	82	41-42
1905	1B	PHI	NL	4-8	151	580	55	150	23	9	3	76	.259	27	200	96	38-45
1906	1B	PHI	NL	4-8	140	524	47	144	28	5	1	60	.275	16	185	101	29-42
1907	1B	PHI	NL	3-8	94	348	25	81	15	2	0	38	.233	14	100	82	—
1908	1B	PHI	NL	4-8	144	527	53	160	25	7	3	71	.304	23	208	125	12-41
1909	1B	PHI	NL	5-8	140	527	47	154	27	6	1	59	.292	18	196	108	24-39
1910	1B	PHI	NL	4-8	123	427	39	102	17	4	3	52	.239	20	136	82	—
1911	1B	PH/CH	NL	4/2	26	53	4	15	3	1	0	3	.283	2	20	—	—
MAJOR LEAGUE TOTALS					1330	4999	529	1351	225	75	13	637	.270	221	1765	105	8 yrs

Edward Green
Batted left

Born Nov 6, 1876 Burlington, NJ
Died Nov 9, 1914 Camden, NJ

YR	POS	TEAM	LG	FIN	G	AB	R	H	2B	3B	HR	RBI	AVG	BB	TB	OQ	RANK
1898	RF	CHI	NL	4-12	47	188	26	59	4	3	4	27	.314	7	81	116	—
1899	RF	CHI	NL	8-12	117	475	90	140	12	11	6	56	.295	35	192	109	32-61
1900	CF	CHI	NL	5-8	103	389	63	116	21	5	5	49	.298	17	162	106	—
1901	CF	CHI	NL	6-8	133	537	82	168	16	12	6	61	.313	40	226	127	17-45
1902	RF	CHI	AL	4-8	129	481	77	150	16	11	0	62	.312	53	188	119	19-46
1903	RF	CHI	AL	7-8	135	499	75	154	26	7	6	62	.309	47	212	138	9-47
1904	RF	CHI	AL	3-8	147	536	83	142	16	10	2	62	.265	63	184	123	14-47
1905	RF	CHI	AL	2-8	112	379	56	92	13	6	0	44	.243	53	117	116	—

| MAJOR LEAGUE TOTALS | | | | | 923 | 3484 | 552 | 1021 | 124 | 65 | 29 | 423 | .293 | 315 | 1362 | 123 | 5 yrs |

Thomas William Leach
5'6 150 lbs Batted right

Born Nov 4, 1877 French Creek, NY
Died Sep 29, 1969 Haines City, FL

YR	POS	TEAM	LG	FIN	G	AB	R	H	2B	3B	HR	RBI	AVG	BB	TB	OQ	RANK
1898	3B-2B	LOU	NL	9-12	3	10	0	1	0	0	0	0	.100	0	1	—	—
1899	3B-SS	LOU	NL	9-12	106	406	75	117	10	6	5	57	.288	37	154	106	—
1900	3B-SS	PIT	NL	2-8	51	160	20	34	1	2	1	16	.213	21	42	81	—
1901	3B	PIT	NL	1-8	98	374	64	114	12	13	2	44	.305	20	158	120	—
1902	3B	PIT	NL	1-8	135	514	97	143	14	22	6	85	.278	45	219	136	8-46
1903	3B	PIT	NL	1-8	127	507	97	151	16	17	7	87	.298	40	222	125	15-49
1904	3B	PIT	NL	4-8	146	579	92	149	15	12	2	56	.257	45	194	106	28-42
1905	CF-3B	PIT	NL	2-8	131	499	71	128	10	14	2	53	.257	37	172	102	29-45
1906	3B-CF	PIT	NL	3-8	133	476	66	136	10	7	1	39	.286	33	163	110	19-42
1907	CF-3B	PIT	NL	2-8	149	547	102	166	19	12	4	43	.303	40	221	132	6-41
1908	3B	PIT	NL	2-8	152	583	93	151	24	16	5	41	.259	54	222	127	11-41
1909	CF-3B	PIT	NL	1-8	151	587	126	153	29	8	6	43	.261	66	216	122	11-39
1910	CF	PIT	NL	3-8	135	529	83	143	24	5	4	52	.270	38	189	100	35-47
1911	CF-SS	PIT	NL	3-8	108	386	60	92	12	6	3	43	.238	46	125	94	—
1912	CF	PT/CH	NL	2/3	110	362	74	93	14	5	2	51	.257	67	123	111	—
1913	CF	CHI	NL	3-8	131	456	99	131	23	10	6	32	.287	77	192	139	4-45
1914	CF-3B	CHI	NL	4-8	153	577	80	152	24	9	7	46	.263	79	215	123	13-42
1915	CF	CIN	NL	7-8	107	335	42	75	7	5	0	17	.224	56	92	104	—
1918	LF-SS	PIT	NL	4-8	30	72	14	14	2	3	0	5	.194	19	22	—	—

| MAJOR LEAGUE TOTALS | | | | | 2156 | 7959 | 1355 | 2143 | 266 | 172 | 63 | 810 | .269 | 820 | 2942 | 120 | 11 yrs |

John Emmett Heidrick   Born Jul 9, 1876   Queenstown, PA
6'0 185 lbs Batted left   Died Jan 20, 1916   Clarion, PA

YR	POS	TEAM	LG	FIN	G	AB	R	H	2B	3B	HR	RBI	AVG	BB	TB	OQ	RANK
1898	CF	CLE	NL	5-12	19	76	10	23	2	2	0	8	.303	3	29	—	—
1899	RF-CF	SL	NL	5-12	146	591	109	194	21	14	2	82	.328	34	249	115	26-61
1900	CF	SL	NL	6-8	85	339	51	102	6	8	2	45	.301	18	130	101	—
1901	CF	SL	NL	4-8	118	502	94	170	24	12	6	67	.339	21	236	136	10-45
1902	CF	SL	AL	2-8	110	447	75	129	19	10	3	56	.289	34	177	109	28-46
1903	CF	SL	AL	6-8	120	461	55	129	20	15	1	42	.280	19	182	111	24-47
1904	CF	SL	AL	6-8	133	538	66	147	14	10	1	36	.273	16	184	101	34-47
1908	CF	SL	AL	4-8	26	93	8	20	2	2	1	6	.215	1	29	—	—
MAJOR LEAGUE TOTALS					757	3047	468	914	108	73	16	342	.300	146	1216	114	5 yrs

Frank Leroy Chance   Born Sep 9, 1877   Fresno, CA
6'0 190 lbs Batted right   Died Sep 15, 1924   Los Angeles, CA

YR	POS	TEAM	LG	FIN	G	AB	R	H	2B	3B	HR	RBI	AVG	BB	TB	OQ	RANK
1898	C-RF	CHI	NL	4-12	53	147	32	41	4	3	1	14	.279	7	54	98	—
1899	C	CHI	NL	8-12	64	192	37	55	6	2	1	22	.286	15	68	98	—
1900	C	CHI	NL	5-8	56	149	26	44	9	3	0	13	.295	15	59	114	—
1901	RF-C	CHI	NL	6-8	69	241	38	67	12	4	0	36	.278	29	87	117	—
1902	1B-C	CHI	NL	5-8	75	240	39	69	9	4	1	31	.288	35	89	139	—
1903	1B	CHI	NL	3-8	125	441	83	144	24	10	2	81	.327	78	194	156	6-49
1904	1B	CHI	NL	2-8	124	451	89	140	16	10	6	49	.310	36	194	141	3-42
1905	1B	CHI	NL	3-8	118	392	92	124	16	12	2	70	.316	78	170	168	3-45
1906	1B	CHI	NL	1-8	136	474	103	151	24	10	3	71	.319	70	204	162	3-42
1907	1B	CHI	NL	1-8	111	382	58	112	19	2	1	49	.293	51	138	135	—
1908	1B	CHI	NL	1-8	129	452	65	123	27	4	2	55	.272	37	164	121	15-41
1909	1B	CHI	NL	2-8	93	324	53	88	16	4	0	46	.272	30	112	113	—
1910	1B	CHI	NL	1-8	88	295	54	88	12	8	0	36	.298	37	116	126	—
1911	1B	CHI	NL	2-8	31	88	23	21	6	3	1	17	.239	25	36	147	—
1912	1B	CHI	NL	3-8	2	5	2	1	0	0	0	0	.200	3	1	—	—
1913	1B	NY	AL	7-8	12	24	3	5	0	0	0	6	.208	8	5	—	—
1914	1B	NY	AL	6-8	1	0	0	0	0	0	0	0	—	0	0	—	—
MAJOR LEAGUE TOTALS					1287	4297	797	1273	200	79	20	596	.296	554	1691	150	5 yrs

Elmer Harrison Flick   Born Jan 11, 1876   Bedford, OH
5'9 168 lbs Batted left   Died Jan 9, 1971   Bedford, OH

YR	POS	TEAM	LG	FIN	G	AB	R	H	2B	3B	HR	RBI	AVG	BB	TB	OQ	RANK
1898	RF	PHI	NL	6-12	134	453	84	137	16	13	8	81	.302	86	203	156	3-75
1899	RF	PHI	NL	3-12	127	485	98	166	22	11	2	98	.342	42	216	130	15-61
1900	RF	PHI	NL	3-8	138	545	106	200	32	16	11	110	.367	56	297	166	2-47
1901	RF	PHI	NL	2-8	138	540	112	180	32	17	8	88	.333	52	270	157	6-45
1902	RF	PH/CL	AL	1/5	121	461	85	137	22	12	2	64	.297	53	189	122	15-46
1903	RF	CLE	AL	3-8	140	523	81	155	23	16	2	51	.296	51	216	133	10-47
1904	RF	CLE	AL	4-8	150	579	97	177	31	17	6	56	.306	51	260	152	2-47
1905	RF	CLE	AL	5-8	132	500	72	154	29	18	4	64	.308	53	231	161	1-41
1906	CF-RF	CLE	AL	3-8	157	624	98	194	33	22	1	62	.311	54	274	148	4-40
1907	RF	CLE	AL	4-8	147	549	78	166	15	18	3	58	.302	64	226	150	4-48
1908	RF	CLE	AL	2-8	9	35	4	8	1	1	0	2	.229	3	11	—	—
1909	RF-CF	CLE	AL	6-8	66	235	28	60	10	2	0	15	.255	22	74	109	—
1910	RF	CLE	AL	5-8	24	68	5	18	2	1	1	7	.265	10	25	—	—

MAJOR LEAGUE TOTALS   1483 5597 948 1752 268 164 48 756 .313 597 2492 148 10 yrs

Harry M Steinfeldt   Born Sep 29, 1877   St Louis, MO
5'9 180 lbs Batted right   Died Aug 17, 1914   Bellevue, KY

YR	POS	TEAM	LG	FIN	G	AB	R	H	2B	3B	HR	RBI	AVG	BB	TB	OQ	RANK
1898	2B-LF	CIN	NL	3-12	88	308	47	91	18	6	0	43	.295	27	121	116	—
1899	3B-2B	CIN	NL	6-12	107	386	62	94	16	8	0	43	.244	40	126	91	—
1900	3B-2B	CIN	NL	7-8	134	510	57	125	29	7	2	66	.245	27	174	85	42-47
1901	3B-2B	CIN	NL	8-8	105	382	40	95	18	7	6	47	.249	28	145	106	—
1902	3B	CIN	NL	4-8	129	479	53	133	20	7	1	49	.278	24	170	107	25-46
1903	3B-SS	CIN	NL	4-8	118	439	71	137	32	12	6	83	.312	47	211	145	8-49
1904	3B	CIN	NL	3-8	99	349	35	85	11	6	1	52	.244	29	111	101	—
1905	3B	CIN	NL	5-8	114	384	49	104	16	9	1	39	.271	30	141	111	—
1906	3B	CHI	NL	1-8	151	539	81	176	27	10	3	83	.327	47	232	147	5-42
1907	3B	CHI	NL	1-8	152	542	52	144	25	5	1	70	.266	37	182	106	27-41
1908	3B	CHI	NL	1-8	150	539	63	130	20	6	1	62	.241	36	165	98	29-41
1909	3B	CHI	NL	2-8	151	528	73	133	27	6	2	59	.252	57	178	112	21-39
1910	3B	CHI	NL	1-8	129	448	70	113	21	1	2	58	.252	36	142	90	39-47
1911	3B	BOS	NL	8-8	19	63	5	16	4	0	1	8	.254	6	23	—	—

MAJOR LEAGUE TOTALS   1646 5896 758 1576 284 90 27 762 .267 471 2121 111 8 yrs

William Frank Isbell   Born Aug 21, 1875 Delevan, NY
5'11 190 lbs Batted left   Died Jul 15, 1941 Wichita, KS

YR	POS	TEAM	LG	FIN	G	AB	R	H	2B	3B	HR	RBI	AVG	BB	TB	OQ	RANK
1898	RF-P	CHI	NL	4-12	45	159	17	37	4	0	0	8	.233	3	41	61	—
1901	1B	CHI	AL	1-8	137	556	93	143	15	8	3	70	.257	36	183	86	43-46
1902	1B	CHI	AL	4-8	137	515	62	130	14	4	4	59	.252	14	164	76	45-46
1903	1B-3B	CHI	AL	7-8	138	546	52	132	25	9	2	59	.242	12	181	86	42-47
1904	1B-2B	CHI	AL	3-8	96	314	27	66	10	3	1	34	.210	16	85	80	—
1905	2B-RF	CHI	AL	2-8	94	341	55	101	21	11	2	45	.296	15	150	135	—
1906	2B	CHI	AL	1-8	143	549	71	153	18	11	0	57	.279	30	193	109	21-40
1907	2B	CHI	AL	3-8	125	486	60	118	19	7	0	41	.243	22	151	93	38-48
1908	1B-2B	CHI	AL	3-8	84	320	31	79	15	3	1	49	.247	19	103	103	—
1909	1B	CHI	AL	4-8	120	433	33	97	17	6	0	33	.224	23	126	88	—
MAJOR LEAGUE TOTALS					1119	4219	501	1056	158	62	13	455	.250	190	1377	90	5 yrs

Tully Frederick Hartsel   Born Jun 26, 1874 Polk, OH
5'5 155 lbs Batted left   Died Oct 14, 1944 Toledo, OH

YR	POS	TEAM	LG	FIN	G	AB	R	H	2B	3B	HR	RBI	AVG	BB	TB	OQ	RANK
1898	RF	LOU	NL	9-12	22	71	11	23	0	0	0	9	.324	11	23	—	—
1899	LF	LOU	NL	9-12	30	75	8	18	1	1	1	7	.240	11	24	—	—
1900	LF	CIN	NL	7-8	18	64	10	21	2	1	2	5	.328	8	31	—	—
1901	LF	CHI	NL	6-8	140	558	111	187	25	16	7	54	.335	74	265	161	4-45
1902	LF	PHI	AL	1-8	137	545	109	154	20	12	5	58	.283	87	213	126	10-46
1903	LF	PHI	AL	2-8	98	373	65	116	19	14	5	26	.311	49	178	162	1-47
1904	LF	PHI	AL	5-8	147	534	79	135	17	12	2	25	.253	75	182	127	11-47
1905	LF	PHI	AL	1-8	150	538	88	148	22	8	0	28	.275	121	186	154	2-41
1906	LF	PHI	AL	4-8	144	533	96	136	21	9	1	30	.255	88	178	130	6-40
1907	LF	PHI	AL	2-8	143	507	93	142	23	6	3	29	.280	106	186	159	1-48
1908	LF	PHI	AL	6-8	129	460	73	112	16	6	4	29	.243	93	152	144	5-36
1909	LF	PHI	AL	2-8	83	267	30	72	4	4	1	18	.270	48	87	137	—
1910	LF	PHI	AL	1-8	90	285	45	63	10	3	0	22	.221	58	79	118	—
1911	LF	PHI	AL	1-8	25	38	8	9	2	0	0	1	.237	8	11	—	—
MAJOR LEAGUE TOTALS					1356	4848	826	1336	182	92	31	341	.276	837	1795	145	8 yrs

James Patrick Casey
5'6...Batted both

Born Mar 15, 1870 Lawrence, MA
Died Dec 31, 1936 Detroit, MI

YR	POS	TEAM	LG	FIN	G	AB	R	H	2B	3B	HR	RBI	AVG	BB	TB	OQ	RANK
1898	3B-SS	WAS	NL	11-12	28	112	13	31	2	0	0	15	.277	3	33	76	—
1899	3B	WA/BR	NL	11/1	143	559	78	145	16	8	1	45	.259	27	180	81	57-61
1900	3B	BRO	NL	1-8	1	3	0	1	0	0	0	1	.333	0	1	—	—
1901	3B	DET	AL	3-8	128	540	105	153	16	9	2	46	.283	32	193	95	33-46
1902	3B	DET	AL	7-8	132	520	69	142	18	7	3	55	.273	44	183	98	31-46
1903	3B	CHI	NL	3-8	112	435	56	126	8	3	1	40	.290	19	143	89	41-49
1904	3B	CHI	NL	2-8	136	548	71	147	20	4	1	43	.268	18	178	93	37-42
1905	3B	CHI	NL	3-8	144	526	66	122	21	10	1	56	.232	41	166	93	39-45
1906	3B	BRO	NL	5-8	149	571	71	133	17	8	0	34	.233	52	166	95	34-42
1907	3B	BRO	NL	5-8	141	527	55	122	19	3	0	19	.231	34	147	86	39-41

| MAJOR LEAGUE TOTALS | | | | | 1114 | 4341 | 584 | 1122 | 137 | 52 | 9 | 354 | .258 | 270 | 1390 | 91 | 8 yrs |

Norman Arthur Elberfeld
5'7 158 lbs Batted right

Born Apr 13, 1875 Pomeroy, OH
Died Jan 13, 1944 Chattanooga, TN

YR	POS	TEAM	LG	FIN	G	AB	R	H	2B	3B	HR	RBI	AVG	BB	TB	OQ	RANK
1898	3B	PHI	NL	6-12	14	38	1	9	4	0	0	7	.237	5	13	—	—
1899	SS-3B	CIN	NL	6-12	41	138	23	36	4	2	0	22	.261	15	44	93	—
1901	SS	DET	AL	3-8	121	432	76	133	21	11	3	76	.308	57	185	132	7-46
1902	SS	DET	AL	7-8	130	488	70	127	17	6	1	64	.260	55	159	97	33-46
1903	SS	DE/NY	AL	5/4	125	481	78	145	23	8	0	64	.301	33	184	119	18-47
1904	SS	NY	AL	2-8	122	445	55	117	13	5	2	46	.263	37	146	110	28-47
1905	SS	NY	AL	6-8	111	390	48	102	18	2	0	53	.262	23	124	100	—
1906	SS	NY	AL	2-8	99	346	59	106	12	4	2	31	.306	30	132	131	—
1907	SS	NY	AL	5-8	120	447	61	121	17	6	0	51	.271	36	150	114	13-48
1908	SS	NY	AL	8-8	19	56	11	11	3	0	0	5	.196	6	14	—	—
1909	SS-3B	NY	AL	5-8	106	379	47	90	9	5	0	26	.237	28	109	94	—
1910	3B	WAS	AL	7-8	127	455	53	114	9	2	2	42	.251	35	133	94	30-36
1911	2B-3B	WAS	AL	7-8	127	404	58	110	19	4	0	47	.272	65	137	112	24-44
1914	SS	BRO	NL	5-8	30	62	7	14	1	0	0	1	.226	2	15	—	—

| MAJOR LEAGUE TOTALS | | | | | 1292 | 4561 | 647 | 1235 | 170 | 55 | 10 | 535 | .271 | 427 | 1545 | 111 | 7 yrs |

James Franklin Slagle
5'7 144 lbs Batted left

Born Jul 11, 1873 Worthville, PA
Died May 10, 1956 Chicago, IL

YR	POS	TEAM	LG	FIN	G	AB	R	H	2B	3B	HR	RBI	AVG	BB	TB	OQ	RANK
1899	CF	WAS	NL	11-12	147	599	92	163	15	8	0	41	.272	55	194	92	48-61
1900	LF	PHI	NL	3-8	141	574	115	165	16	9	0	45	.287	60	199	103	31-47
1901	RF	PH/BO	NL	2/5	114	438	55	106	13	2	1	27	.242	50	126	93	34-45
1902	LF	CHI	NL	5-8	115	454	64	143	11	4	0	28	.315	53	162	132	9-46
1903	LF	CHI	NL	3-8	139	543	104	162	20	6	0	44	.298	81	194	123	16-49
1904	LF	CHI	NL	2-8	120	481	73	125	12	10	1	31	.260	41	160	108	25-42
1905	CF	CHI	NL	3-8	155	568	96	153	19	4	0	37	.269	97	180	121	15-45
1906	CF	CHI	NL	1-8	127	498	71	119	8	6	0	33	.239	63	139	102	26-42
1907	CF	CHI	NL	1-8	136	489	71	126	6	6	0	32	.258	76	144	117	20-41
1908	CF	CHI	NL	1-8	104	352	38	78	4	1	0	26	.222	43	84	92	—
MAJOR LEAGUE TOTALS					1298	4996	779	1340	124	56	2	344	.268	619	1582	110	9 yrs

Roy Allen Thomas
5'11 150 lbs Batted left

Born Mar 24, 1874 Norristown, PA
Died Nov 20, 1959 Norristown, PA

YR	POS	TEAM	LG	FIN	G	AB	R	H	2B	3B	HR	RBI	AVG	BB	TB	OQ	RANK
1899	CF	PHI	NL	3-12	150	547	137	178	12	4	0	47	.325	115	198	137	9-61
1900	CF	PHI	NL	3-8	140	531	132	168	4	3	0	33	.316	115	178	131	7-47
1901	CF	PHI	NL	2-8	129	479	102	148	5	2	1	28	.309	100	160	138	9-45
1902	CF	PHI	NL	7-8	138	500	89	143	4	7	0	24	.286	107	161	144	6-46
1903	CF	PHI	NL	7-8	130	477	88	156	11	2	1	27	.327	107	174	149	7-49
1904	CF	PHI	NL	8-8	139	496	92	144	6	6	3	29	.290	102	171	148	2-42
1905	CF	PHI	NL	4-8	147	562	118	178	11	6	0	31	.317	93	201	139	7-45
1906	CF	PHI	NL	4-8	142	493	81	125	10	7	0	16	.254	107	149	133	8-42
1907	CF	PHI	NL	3-8	121	419	70	102	15	3	1	23	.243	83	126	127	11-41
1908	CF	PH/PT	NL	4/2	108	410	54	103	11	10	1	24	.251	51	137	122	—
1909	LF	BOS	NL	8-8	82	281	36	74	9	1	0	11	.263	47	85	120	—
1910	CF	PHI	NL	4-8	23	71	7	13	0	2	0	4	.183	7	17	—	—
1911	RF	PHI	NL	4-8	21	30	5	5	2	0	0	2	.167	8	7	—	—
MAJOR LEAGUE TOTALS					1470	5296	1011	1537	100	53	7	299	.290	1042	1764	138	9 yrs

Clarence Howeth Beaumont Born Jul 23, 1876 Rochester, WI
5'8 190 lbs Batted left Died Apr 10, 1956 Burlington, WI

YR	POS	TEAM	LG	FIN	G	AB	R	H	2B	3B	HR	RBI	AVG	BB	TB	OQ	RANK
1899	CF	PIT	NL	7-12	111	437	90	154	15	8	3	38	.352	41	194	134	12-61
1900	CF	PIT	NL	2-8	138	567	105	158	14	9	5	50	.279	40	205	97	34-47
1901	CF	PIT	NL	1-8	133	558	120	185	14	5	8	72	.332	44	233	130	14-45
1902	CF	PIT	NL	1-8	130	541	100	193	21	6	0	67	.357	39	226	146	5-46
1903	CF	PIT	NL	1-8	141	613	137	209	30	6	7	68	.341	44	272	132	13-49
1904	CF	PIT	NL	4-8	153	615	97	185	12	12	3	54	.301	34	230	116	17-42
1905	CF	PIT	NL	2-8	103	384	60	126	12	8	3	40	.328	22	163	130	—
1906	CF	PIT	NL	3-8	80	310	48	82	9	3	2	32	.265	19	103	102	—
1907	CF	BOS	NL	7-8	150	580	67	187	19	14	4	62	.322	37	246	138	4-41
1908	CF	BOS	NL	6-8	125	476	66	127	20	6	2	52	.267	42	165	117	17-41
1909	CF	BOS	NL	8-8	123	407	35	107	11	4	0	60	.263	35	126	101	—
1910	CF	CHI	NL	1-8	76	172	30	46	5	1	2	22	.267	28	59	118	—

| MAJOR LEAGUE TOTALS | | | | | 1463 | 5660 | 955 | 1759 | 182 | 82 | 39 | 617 | .311 | 425 | 2222 | 126 | 8 yrs |

Charles Judson Hemphill Born Apr 20, 1876 Greenville, MI
5'9 160 lbs Batted left Died Jun 22, 1953 Detroit, MI

YR	POS	TEAM	LG	FIN	G	AB	R	H	2B	3B	HR	RBI	AVG	BB	TB	OQ	RANK
1899	RF	SL/CL	NL	5/12	66	239	27	65	3	5	3	26	.272	12	87	92	—
1901	RF	BOS	AL	2-8	136	545	71	142	10	10	3	62	.261	39	181	89	39-46
1902	RF	CL/SL	AL	5/2	128	510	81	157	16	11	6	69	.308	49	213	121	16-46
1903	RF	SL	AL	6-8	105	383	36	94	6	3	3	29	.245	23	115	88	—
1904	RF	SL	AL	6-8	114	438	47	112	13	2	2	45	.256	35	135	103	33-47
1906	CF	SL	AL	5-8	154	585	90	169	19	12	4	62	.289	43	224	124	7-40
1907	CF	SL	AL	6-8	153	603	66	156	20	9	0	38	.259	51	194	109	25-48
1908	CF	NY	AL	8-8	142	505	62	150	12	9	0	44	.297	59	180	137	6-36
1909	CF	NY	AL	5-8	73	181	23	44	5	1	0	10	.243	32	51	119	—
1910	CF	NY	AL	2-8	102	351	45	84	9	4	0	21	.239	55	101	111	—
1911	CF	NY	AL	6-8	69	201	32	57	4	2	1	15	.284	37	68	119	—

| MAJOR LEAGUE TOTALS | | | | | 1242 | 4541 | 580 | 1230 | 117 | 68 | 22 | 421 | .271 | 435 | 1549 | 114 | 6 yrs |

James Thomas Williams   Born Dec 20, 1876 St Louis, MO
5'9 175 lbs Batted right   Died Jan 16, 1965 St Petersburg, FL

YR	POS	TEAM	LG	FIN	G	AB	R	H	2B	3B	HR	RBI	AVG	BB	TB	OO	RANK
1899	3B	PIT	NL	7-12	152	617	126	219	28	27	9	116	.355	60	328	157	4-61
1900	3B	PIT	NL	2-8	106	416	73	110	15	11	5	68	.264	32	162	103	30-47
1901	2B	BAL	AL	5-8	130	501	113	159	26	21	7	96	.317	56	248	145	4-46
1902	2B-3B	BAL	AL	8-8	125	498	83	156	27	21	8	83	.313	36	249	136	5-46
1903	2B	NY	AL	4-8	132	502	60	134	30	12	3	82	.267	39	197	118	19-47
1904	2B	NY	AL	2-8	146	559	62	147	31	7	2	74	.263	38	198	113	24-47
1905	2B	NY	AL	6-8	129	470	54	107	20	8	6	62	.228	50	161	114	20-41
1906	2B	NY	AL	2-8	139	501	62	139	25	7	3	77	.277	44	187	124	9-40
1907	2B	NY	AL	5-8	139	504	53	136	17	11	2	63	.270	35	181	117	11-48
1908	2B	SL	AL	4-8	148	539	63	127	20	7	4	53	.236	55	173	113	20-36
1909	2B	SL	AL	7-8	110	374	32	73	3	6	0	22	.195	29	88	77	—
MAJOR LEAGUE TOTALS					1456	5481	781	1507	242	138	49	796	.275	474	2172	124	10 yrs

Frederick Alfred Parent   Born Nov 25, 1875 Biddeford, ME
5'7 154 lbs Batted right   Died Nov 2, 1972 Sanford, ME

YR	POS	TEAM	LG	FIN	G	AB	R	H	2B	3B	HR	RBI	AVG	BB	TB	OO	RANK
1899	2B	SL	NL	5-12	2	8	0	1	0	0	0	1	.125	0	1	—	—
1901	SS	BOS	AL	2-8	138	517	87	158	23	9	4	59	.306	41	211	114	19-46
1902	SS	BOS	AL	3-8	138	567	91	156	31	8	3	62	.275	24	212	94	36-46
1903	SS	BOS	AL	1-8	139	560	83	170	31	17	4	80	.304	13	247	123	17-47
1904	SS	BOS	AL	1-8	155	591	85	172	22	9	6	77	.291	28	230	121	16-47
1905	SS	BOS	AL	4-8	153	602	55	141	16	5	0	33	.234	47	167	91	35-41
1906	SS	BOS	AL	8-8	149	600	67	141	14	10	1	49	.235	31	178	88	38-40
1907	LF-SS	BOS	AL	7-8	114	409	51	113	19	5	1	26	.276	22	145	112	—
1908	SS	CHI	AL	3-8	119	391	28	81	7	5	0	35	.207	50	98	97	—
1909	SS-CF	CHI	AL	4-8	136	472	61	123	10	5	0	30	.261	46	143	107	20-33
1910	CF-2B	CHI	AL	6-8	81	258	23	46	6	1	1	16	.178	29	57	77	—
1911	2B	CHI	AL	4-8	3	9	2	4	1	0	0	3	.444	2	5	—	—
MAJOR LEAGUE TOTALS					1327	4984	633	1306	180	74	20	471	.262	333	1694	105	7 yrs

James Erigena Barrett   Born Mar 28, 1875 Athol, MA
5'9 170 lbs Batted left   Died Oct 24, 1921 Detroit, MI

YR	POS	TEAM	LG	FIN	G	AB	R	H	2B	3B	HR	RBI	AVG	BB	TB	OQ	RANK
1899	RF	CIN	NL	6-12	26	92	30	34	2	4	0	10	.370	18	44	172	—
1900	CF	CIN	NL	7-8	137	545	114	172	11	7	5	42	.316	72	212	124	11-47
1901	CF	DET	AL	3-8	135	542	110	159	16	9	4	65	.293	76	205	120	15-46
1902	CF	DET	AL	7-8	136	509	93	154	19	6	4	44	.303	74	197	125	12-46
1903	CF	DET	AL	5-8	136	517	95	163	13	10	2	31	.315	74	202	143	5-47
1904	CF	DET	AL	7-8	162	624	83	167	10	5	0	31	.268	79	187	115	21-47
1905	CF	DET	AL	3-8	20	67	2	17	1	0	0	3	.254	6	18	—	—
1906	RF	CIN	NL	6-8	5	12	1	0	0	0	0	0	.000	2	0	—	—
1907	LF	BOS	AL	7-8	106	390	52	95	11	6	1	28	.244	38	121	107	—
1908	LF	BOS	AL	5-8	3	8	0	1	0	0	0	1	.125	1	1	—	—

| MAJOR LEAGUE TOTALS | | | | | 866 | 3306 | 580 | 962 | 83 | 47 | 16 | 255 | .291 | 440 | 1187 | 125 | 5 yrs |

William Joseph Bradley   Born Feb 13, 1878 Cleveland, OH
6'0 185 lbs Batted right   Died Mar 11, 1954 Cleveland, OH

YR	POS	TEAM	LG	FIN	G	AB	R	H	2B	3B	HR	RBI	AVG	BB	TB	OQ	RANK
1899	3B-SS	CHI	NL	8-12	35	129	26	40	6	1	2	18	.310	12	54	119	—
1900	3B-1B	CHI	NL	5-8	122	444	63	125	21	8	5	49	.282	27	177	104	27-47
1901	3B	CLE	AL	7-8	133	516	95	151	28	13	1	55	.293	26	208	104	26-46
1902	3B	CLE	AL	5-8	137	550	104	187	39	12	11	77	.340	27	283	140	4-46
1903	3B	CLE	AL	3-8	136	536	101	168	36	22	6	68	.313	25	266	145	4-47
1904	3B	CLE	AL	4-8	154	609	94	183	32	8	5	83	.300	26	246	126	13-47
1905	3B	CLE	AL	5-8	146	541	63	145	34	6	0	51	.268	27	191	108	25-41
1906	3B	CLE	AL	3-8	82	302	32	83	15	2	2	25	.275	18	108	111	—
1907	3B	CLE	AL	4-8	139	498	48	111	20	1	0	34	.223	35	133	86	46-48
1908	3B-SS	CLE	AL	2-8	148	548	70	133	24	7	1	46	.243	29	174	100	28-36
1909	3B	CLE	AL	6-8	95	334	30	62	6	3	0	22	.186	19	74	68	—
1910	3B	CLE	AL	5-8	61	214	12	42	3	0	0	12	.196	10	45	61	—
1914	PH	BRO	FL	5-8	7	6	1	3	1	0	0	3	.500	0	4	—	—
1915	3B	KC	FL	4-8	66	203	15	38	9	1	0	9	.187	9	49	61	—

| MAJOR LEAGUE TOTALS | | | | | 1461 | 5430 | 754 | 1471 | 274 | 84 | 33 | 552 | .271 | 290 | 2012 | 114 | 8 yrs |

William Paul Coughlin   Born Jul 12, 1878   Scranton, PA
5'9   140 lbs   Batted right   Died May 7, 1943   Scranton, PA

YR	POS	TEAM	LG	FIN	G	AB	R	H	2B	3B	HR	RBI	AVG	BB	TB	OQ	RANK
1899	3B	WAS	NL	11-12	6	24	2	3	0	1	0	3	.125	1	5	—	—
1901	3B	WAS	AL	6-8	137	506	75	139	17	13	6	68	.275	25	200	100	29-46
1902	3B-SS	WAS	AL	6-8	123	469	84	141	27	4	6	71	.301	26	194	110	27-46
1903	3B	WAS	AL	8-8	125	473	56	116	18	3	1	31	.245	9	143	78	46-47
1904	3B	WA/DE	AL	8/7	121	471	50	120	21	4	0	34	.255	14	149	91	38-47
1905	3B	DET	AL	3-8	137	489	48	123	20	6	0	44	.252	34	155	101	30-41
1906	3B	DET	AL	6-8	147	498	54	117	15	5	2	60	.235	36	148	94	30-40
1907	3B	DET	AL	1-8	134	519	80	126	10	2	0	46	.243	35	140	88	43-48
1908	3B	DET	AL	1-8	119	405	32	87	5	1	0	23	.215	23	94	75	—
MAJOR LEAGUE TOTALS					1049	3854	481	972	133	39	15	380	.252	203	1228	95	7 yrs

Samuel Earl Crawford   Born Apr 18, 1880   Wahoo, NB
6'0   190 lbs   Batted left   Died Jun 15, 1968   Hollywood, CA

YR	POS	TEAM	LG	FIN	G	AB	R	H	2B	3B	HR	RBI	AVG	BB	TB	OQ	RANK
1899	CF-LF	CIN	NL	6-12	31	127	25	39	3	7	1	20	.307	2	59	112	—
1900	LF	CIN	NL	7-8	101	389	68	101	15	15	7	59	.260	28	167	110	—
1901	RF	CIN	NL	8-8	131	515	91	170	20	16	16	104	.330	37	270	156	7-45
1902	RF	CIN	NL	4-8	140	555	92	185	18	22	3	78	.333	47	256	157	1-46
1903	RF	DET	AL	5-8	137	550	88	184	23	25	4	89	.335	25	269	148	3-47
1904	RF	DET	AL	7-8	150	562	49	143	22	16	2	73	.254	44	203	116	19-47
1905	RF-1B	DET	AL	3-8	154	575	73	171	38	10	6	75	.297	50	247	144	3-41
1906	RF-1B	DET	AL	6-8	145	563	65	166	25	16	2	72	.295	38	229	130	5-40
1907	CF	DET	AL	1-8	144	582	102	188	34	17	4	81	.323	37	268	154	3-48
1908	CF-1B	DET	AL	1-8	152	591	102	184	33	16	7	80	.311	37	270	154	3-36
1909	CF-1B	DET	AL	1-8	156	589	83	185	35	14	6	97	.314	47	266	153	3-33
1910	RF	DET	AL	3-8	154	588	83	170	26	19	5	120	.289	37	249	131	8-36
1911	RF	DET	AL	2-8	146	574	109	217	36	14	7	115	.378	61	302	166	3-44
1912	RF	DET	AL	6-8	149	581	81	189	30	21	4	109	.325	42	273	134	8-33
1913	RF-1B	DET	AL	6-8	153	609	78	193	32	23	9	83	.317	52	298	146	6-37
1914	RF	DET	AL	4-8	157	582	74	183	22	26	8	104	.314	69	281	157	3-41
1915	RF	DET	AL	2-8	156	612	81	183	31	19	5	112	.299	66	267	136	8-42
1916	RF	DET	AL	3-8	100	322	41	92	11	13	0	42	.286	37	129	128	—
1917	1B	DET	AL	4-8	61	104	6	18	4	0	2	12	.173	4	28	68	—
MAJOR LEAGUE TOTALS					2517	9570	1391	2961	458	309	98	1525	.309	760	4331	145	15 yrs

Ralph Orlando Seybold   Born Nov 23, 1870 Washingtonville, OH
5'11 175 lbs Batted right   Died Dec 22, 1921 Greensburg, PA

YR	POS	TEAM	LG	FIN	G	AB	R	H	2B	3B	HR	RBI	AVG	BB	TB	OQ	RANK
1899	RF	CIN	NL	6-12	22	85	13	19	5	1	0	8	.224	6	26	—	—
1901	RF-1B	PHI	AL	4-8	114	449	74	150	24	14	8	90	.334	40	226	145	3-46
1902	RF	PHI	AL	1-8	137	522	91	165	27	12	16	97	.316	43	264	141	3-46
1903	RF-1B	PHI	AL	2-8	137	522	76	156	45	8	8	84	.299	38	241	140	8-47
1904	RF-1B	PHI	AL	5-8	143	510	56	149	26	9	3	64	.292	42	202	133	5-47
1905	RF	PHI	AL	1-8	133	492	64	135	37	4	6	59	.274	42	198	132	6-41
1906	RF	PHI	AL	4-8	116	411	41	130	23	2	5	59	.316	30	172	139	—
1907	RF	PHI	AL	2-8	147	564	58	153	29	4	5	92	.271	40	205	118	10-48
1908	RF	PHI	AL	6-8	48	130	5	28	2	0	0	3	.215	12	30	84	—
MAJOR LEAGUE TOTALS					997	3685	478	1085	218	54	51	556	.294	293	1564	135	6 yrs

Daniel Francis Murphy   Born Aug 11, 1876 Philadelphia, PA
5'9 175 lbs Batted right   Died Nov 22, 1955 Jersey City, NJ

YR	POS	TEAM	LG	FIN	G	AB	R	H	2B	3B	HR	RBI	AVG	BB	TB	OQ	RANK
1900	2B	NY	NL	8-8	22	74	11	20	1	0	0	6	.270	8	21	—	—
1901	2B	NY	NL	7-8	5	20	0	4	0	0	0	0	.200	1	4	—	—
1902	2B	PHI	AL	1-8	76	291	48	91	11	8	1	48	.313	13	121	110	—
1903	2B	PHI	AL	2-8	133	513	66	140	31	11	1	60	.273	13	196	103	31-47
1904	2B	PHI	AL	5-8	150	557	78	160	30	17	7	77	.287	22	245	132	6-47
1905	2B	PHI	AL	1-8	151	537	71	149	34	4	6	71	.277	42	209	127	8-41
1906	2B	PHI	AL	4-8	119	448	48	135	24	7	2	60	.301	21	179	124	8-40
1907	2B	PHI	AL	2-8	124	469	51	127	23	3	2	57	.271	30	162	112	17-48
1908	RF-2B	PHI	AL	6-8	142	525	51	139	28	7	4	66	.265	32	193	119	13-36
1909	RF	PHI	AL	2-8	149	541	61	152	28	14	5	69	.281	35	223	131	9-33
1910	RF	PHI	AL	1-8	151	560	70	168	28	18	4	64	.300	31	244	134	6-36
1911	RF	PHI	AL	1-8	141	508	104	167	27	11	6	66	.329	50	234	136	10-44
1912	RF	PHI	AL	3-8	36	130	27	42	6	2	2	20	.323	16	58	140	—
1913	RF	PHI	AL	1-8	40	59	3	19	5	1	0	6	.322	4	26	—	—
1914	RF	BRO	FL	5-8	52	161	16	49	9	0	4	32	.304	17	70	129	—
1915	RF	BRO	FL	7-8	5	6	0	1	0	0	0	0	.167	0	1	—	—
MAJOR LEAGUE TOTALS					1496	5399	705	1563	285	103	44	702	.289	335	2186	124	9 yrs

Matthew W McIntyre   Born Jun 12, 1880   Stonington, CT
5'11   175 lbs   Batted left   Died Apr 2, 1920   Detroit, MI

YR	POS	TEAM	LG	FIN	G	AB	R	H	2B	3B	HR	RBI	AVG	BB	TB	OO	RANK
1901	LF	PHI	AL	4-8	82	308	38	85	12	4	0	46	.276	30	105	99	—
1904	LF	DET	AL	7-8	152	578	74	146	11	10	2	46	.253	44	183	103	32-47
1905	LF	DET	AL	3-8	131	495	59	130	21	5	0	30	.263	48	161	112	22-41
1906	LF	DET	AL	6-8	133	493	63	128	19	11	0	39	.260	56	169	119	13-40
1907	LF	DET	AL	1-8	20	81	6	23	1	1	0	9	.284	7	26	—	—
1908	LF	DET	AL	1-8	151	569	105	168	24	13	0	28	.295	83	218	153	4-36
1909	LF	DET	AL	1-8	125	476	65	116	18	9	1	34	.244	54	155	115	16-33
1910	LF	DET	AL	3-8	83	305	40	72	15	5	0	25	.236	39	97	111	—
1911	RF	CHI	AL	4-8	146	569	102	184	19	11	1	52	.323	64	228	124	13-44
1912	LF-RF	CHI	AL	4-8	49	84	10	14	0	0	0	10	.167	14	14	—	—
MAJOR LEAGUE TOTALS					1072	3958	562	1066	140	69	4	319	.269	439	1356	121	6 yrs

James Christopher Delahanty   Born Jun 20, 1879   Cleveland, OH
5'10   170 lbs   Batted right   Died Oct 17, 1953   Cleveland, OH

YR	POS	TEAM	LG	FIN	G	AB	R	H	2B	3B	HR	RBI	AVG	BB	TB	OO	RANK
1901	3B	CHI	NL	6-8	17	63	4	12	2	0	0	4	.190	3	14	—	—
1902	RF	NY	NL	8-8	7	26	3	6	1	0	0	3	.231	1	7	—	—
1904	3B-2B	BOS	NL	7-8	142	499	56	142	27	8	3	60	.285	27	194	118	14-42
1905	LF	BOS	NL	7-8	125	461	50	119	11	8	5	55	.258	28	161	101	31-45
1906	3B	CIN	NL	6-8	115	379	63	106	21	4	1	39	.280	45	138	128	—
1907	2B-3B	SL/WA	AL	6/8	141	499	52	139	21	7	2	60	.279	41	180	122	8-48
1908	2B	WAS	AL	7-8	83	287	33	91	11	4	1	30	.317	24	113	143	—
1909	2B	WA/DE	AL	8/1	136	452	47	105	23	6	1	41	.232	40	143	104	23-33
1910	2B	DET	AL	3-8	106	378	67	111	16	2	3	45	.294	43	140	131	—
1911	1B-2B	DET	AL	2-8	144	542	83	184	30	14	3	94	.339	56	251	140	8-44
1912	2B-LF	DET	AL	6-8	79	266	34	76	14	1	0	41	.286	42	92	118	—
1914	2B	BRO	FL	5-8	74	214	28	62	13	5	0	15	.290	25	85	120	—
1915	2B	BRO	FL	7-8	17	25	0	6	1	0	0	2	.240	3	7	—	—
MAJOR LEAGUE TOTALS					1186	4091	520	1159	191	59	19	489	.283	378	1525	117	5 yrs

William Edward Conroy   Born Apr 5, 1877 Camden, NJ
5'9 158 lbs Batted right   Died Dec 6, 1959 Mount Holly, NJ

YR	POS	TEAM	LG	FIN	G	AB	R	H	2B	3B	HR	RBI	AVG	BB	TB	OQ	RANK
1901	SS	MIL	AL	8-8	131	503	74	129	20	6	5	64	.256	36	176	92	35-46
1902	SS	PIT	NL	1-8	99	365	55	89	10	6	1	47	.244	24	114	96	—
1903	3B	NY	AL	4-8	126	503	74	137	23	12	1	45	.272	32	187	110	26-47
1904	3B-SS	NY	AL	2-8	140	489	58	119	18	12	1	52	.243	43	164	110	27-47
1905	3B-LF	NY	AL	6-8	101	385	55	105	19	11	2	25	.273	32	152	129	—
1906	LF-SS	NY	AL	2-8	148	567	67	139	17	10	4	54	.245	47	188	106	22-40
1907	LF-SS	NY	AL	5-8	140	530	58	124	12	11	3	51	.234	30	167	96	35-48
1908	3B	NY	AL	8-8	141	531	44	126	22	3	1	39	.237	14	157	86	35-36
1909	3B	WAS	AL	8-8	139	488	44	119	13	4	1	20	.244	37	143	97	25-33
1910	3B-LF	WAS	AL	7-8	103	351	36	89	11	3	1	27	.254	30	109	101	—
1911	3B-LF	WAS	AL	7-8	106	349	40	81	11	4	2	28	.232	20	106	77	—
MAJOR LEAGUE TOTALS					1374	5061	605	1257	176	82	22	452	.248	345	1663	100	7 yrs

George Edward Browne   Born Jan 12, 1876 Richmond, VA
5'10 160 lbs Batted left   Died Dec 9, 1920 Hyde Park, NY

YR	POS	TEAM	LG	FIN	G	AB	R	H	2B	3B	HR	RBI	AVG	BB	TB	OQ	RANK
1901	LF	PHI	NL	2-8	8	26	2	5	1	0	0	4	.192	1	6	—	—
1902	LF	PHI/NY	NL	7/8	123	497	71	142	16	6	0	40	.286	25	170	105	27-46
1903	RF	NY	NL	2-8	141	591	105	185	20	3	3	45	.313	43	220	110	25-49
1904	RF	NY	NL	1-8	150	596	99	169	16	5	4	39	.284	39	207	110	23-42
1905	RF	NY	NL	1-8	127	536	95	157	16	14	4	43	.293	20	213	112	19-45
1906	RF	NY	NL	2-8	122	477	61	126	10	4	0	38	.264	27	144	93	37-42
1907	RF	NY	NL	4-8	127	458	54	119	11	10	5	37	.260	31	165	112	23-41
1908	RF	BOS	NL	6-8	138	536	61	122	10	6	1	34	.228	36	147	88	37-41
1909	CF	CHI	NL	2-8	12	39	7	8	0	1	0	1	.205	5	10	—	—
1909	LF	WAS	AL	8-8	103	393	40	107	15	5	1	16	.272	17	135	105	—
1910	CF-RF	WA/CH	AL	7/6	37	134	18	31	4	1	0	4	.231	13	37	93	—
1911	RF	BRO	NL	7-8	8	12	1	4	0	0	0	2	.333	1	4	—	—
1912	3B	PHI	NL	5-8	6	5	0	1	0	0	0	0	.200	1	1	—	—
MAJOR LEAGUE TOTALS					1102	4300	614	1176	119	55	18	303	.273	259	1459	104	7 yrs

Albert Sayles Ferris   Born Dec 7, 1877 Providence, RI
5'8 162 lbs Batted right   Died Mar 18, 1938 Detroit, MI

YR	POS	TEAM	LG	FIN	G	AB	R	H	2B	3B	HR	RBI	AVG	BB	TB	OQ	RANK
1901	2B	BOS	AL	2-8	138	523	68	131	16	15	2	63	.250	23	183	86	44-46
1902	2B	BOS	AL	3-8	134	499	57	122	16	14	8	63	.244	21	190	92	38-46
1903	2B	BOS	AL	1-8	141	525	69	132	19	7	9	66	.251	25	192	101	32-47
1904	2B	BOS	AL	1-8	156	563	50	120	23	10	3	63	.213	23	172	87	40-47
1905	2B	BOS	AL	4-8	142	523	51	115	24	16	6	59	.220	23	189	102	29-41
1906	2B	BOS	AL	8-8	130	495	47	121	25	13	2	44	.244	10	178	97	28-40
1907	2B	BOS	AL	7-8	150	561	41	135	25	2	4	60	.241	10	176	87	44-48
1908	3B	SL	AL	4-8	148	555	54	150	26	7	2	74	.270	14	196	106	24-36
1909	3B-2B	SL	AL	7-8	148	556	36	120	18	5	4	58	.216	12	160	78	33-33
MAJOR LEAGUE TOTALS					1287	4800	473	1146	192	89	40	550	.239	161	1636	93	9 yrs

George Florian McBride   Born Nov 20, 1880 Milwaukee, WI
5'11 170 lbs Batted right   Died Jul 2, 1973   Milwaukee, WI

YR	POS	TEAM	LG	FIN	G	AB	R	H	2B	3B	HR	RBI	AVG	BB	TB	OQ	RANK
1901	SS	MIL	AL	8-8	3	12	0	2	0	0	0	0	.167	1	2	—	—
1905	SS-3B	PT/SL	NL	2/6	108	368	31	80	5	2	2	41	.217	20	95	73	—
1906	SS	SL	NL	7-8	90	313	24	53	8	2	0	13	.169	17	65	60	—
1908	SS	WAS	AL	7-8	155	518	47	120	10	6	0	34	.232	41	142	94	30-36
1909	SS	WAS	AL	8-8	156	504	38	118	16	0	0	34	.234	36	134	87	31-33
1910	SS	WAS	AL	7-8	154	514	54	118	19	4	1	55	.230	61	148	101	25-36
1911	SS	WAS	AL	7-8	154	557	58	131	11	4	0	59	.235	52	150	77	44-44
1912	SS	WAS	AL	2-8	152	521	56	118	13	7	1	52	.226	38	148	77	31-33
1913	SS	WAS	AL	2-8	150	499	52	107	18	7	1	52	.214	43	142	82	37-37
1914	SS	WAS	AL	3-8	156	503	49	102	12	4	0	24	.203	43	122	74	41-41
1915	SS	WAS	AL	4-8	146	476	54	97	8	6	1	30	.204	29	120	69	42-42
1916	SS	WAS	AL	7-8	139	466	36	106	15	4	1	36	.227	23	132	77	38-38
1917	SS-3B	WAS	AL	5-8	50	141	6	27	3	0	0	9	.191	10	30	64	—
1918	SS-2B	WAS	AL	3-8	18	53	2	7	0	0	0	1	.132	0	7	—	—
1919	SS	WAS	AL	7-8	15	40	3	8	1	1	0	4	.200	3	11	—	—
1920	SS	WAS	AL	6-8	13	41	6	9	1	0	0	3	.220	2	10	—	—
MAJOR LEAGUE TOTALS					1659	5526	516	1203	140	47	7	447	.218	419	1458	82	9 yrs

David Leonard Brain
5'10 170 lbs Batted right

Born Jan 24, 1879 Hereford, England
Died May 25, 1959 Los Angeles, CA

YR	POS	TEAM	LG	FIN	G	AB	R	H	2B	3B	HR	RBI	AVG	BB	TB	OQ	RANK
1901	2B	CHI	AL	1-8	5	20	2	7	1	0	0	5	.350	1	8	—	—
1903	SS-3B	SL	NL	8-8	119	464	44	107	8	15	1	60	.231	25	148	82	47-49
1904	SS-3B	SL	NL	5-8	127	488	57	130	24	12	7	72	.266	17	199	115	20-42
1905	3B-SS	SL/PT	NL	6/2	129	465	42	115	21	11	4	63	.247	23	170	100	32-45
1906	3B	BOS	NL	8-8	139	525	43	131	19	5	5	45	.250	29	175	99	30-42
1907	3B	BOS	NL	7-8	133	509	60	142	24	9	10	56	.279	29	214	128	10-41
1908	LF-2B	CN/NY	NL	5/2	27	72	6	9	0	0	0	2	.125	10	9	—	—
MAJOR LEAGUE TOTALS					679	2543	254	641	97	52	27	303	.252	134	923	105	5 yrs

Terrence Lamont Turner
5'8 149 lbs Batted right

Born Feb 28, 1881 Sandy Lake, PA
Died Jul 18, 1960 Cleveland, OH

YR	POS	TEAM	LG	FIN	G	AB	R	H	2B	3B	HR	RBI	AVG	BB	TB	OQ	RANK
1901	3B	PIT	NL	1-8	2	7	0	3	0	0	0	1	.429	0	3	—	—
1904	SS	CLE	AL	4-8	111	404	41	95	9	6	1	45	.235	11	119	83	—
1905	SS	CLE	AL	5-8	155	586	49	155	16	14	4	72	.265	14	211	102	28-41
1906	SS	CLE	AL	3-8	147	584	85	170	27	7	2	62	.291	35	217	118	16-40
1907	SS	CLE	AL	4-8	140	524	57	127	20	7	0	46	.242	19	161	90	41-48
1908	RF-SS	CLE	AL	2-8	60	201	21	48	11	1	0	19	.239	15	61	101	—
1909	SS-2B	CLE	AL	6-8	53	208	25	52	7	4	0	16	.250	14	67	103	—
1910	SS-3B	CLE	AL	5-8	150	574	71	132	14	6	0	33	.230	53	158	91	32-36
1911	3B-2B	CLE	AL	3-8	117	417	59	105	16	9	0	28	.252	34	139	91	—
1912	3B	CLE	AL	5-8	103	370	54	114	14	4	0	33	.308	31	136	109	—
1913	3B-2B	CLE	AL	3-8	120	388	60	96	13	4	0	44	.247	55	117	102	—
1914	3B-2B	CLE	AL	8-8	121	428	43	105	14	9	1	33	.245	44	140	102	28-41
1915	2B-3B	CLE	AL	7-8	75	262	35	66	14	1	0	14	.252	29	82	99	—
1916	3B-2B	CLE	AL	6-8	124	428	52	112	15	3	0	38	.262	40	133	97	—
1917	3B-2B	CLE	AL	3-8	69	180	16	37	7	0	0	15	.206	14	44	74	—
1918	3B-2B	CLE	AL	2-8	74	233	24	58	7	2	0	23	.249	22	69	93	—
1919	SS-2B	PHI	AL	8-8	38	127	7	24	3	0	0	6	.189	5	27	51	—
MAJOR LEAGUE TOTALS					1659	5921	699	1499	207	77	8	528	.253	435	1884	101	5 yrs

Thomas Jones
6'1 195 lbs Batted right

Born Jan 22, 1877 Honesdale, PA
Died Jun 21, 1923 Danville, PA

YR	POS	TEAM	LG	FIN	G	AB	R	H	2B	3B	HR	RBI	AVG	BB	TB	OQ	RANK
1902	1B	BAL	AL	8-8	37	159	22	45	8	4	0	14	.283	2	61	91	—
1904	1B-2B	SL	AL	6-8	156	625	53	152	15	10	2	68	.243	15	193	87	41-47
1905	1B	SL	AL	8-8	135	504	44	122	16	2	0	48	.242	30	142	88	36-41
1906	1B	SL	AL	5-8	144	539	51	136	22	6	0	30	.252	24	170	93	32-40
1907	1B	SL	AL	6-8	155	549	53	137	17	3	0	34	.250	34	160	94	37-48
1908	1B	SL	AL	4-8	155	549	43	135	14	2	1	50	.246	30	156	92	33-36
1909	1B	SL/DE	AL	7/1	141	490	43	127	18	3	0	47	.259	23	151	95	27-33
1910	1B	DET	AL	3-8	135	432	32	110	12	4	1	45	.255	35	133	100	28-36
MAJOR LEAGUE TOTALS					1058	3847	341	964	122	34	4	336	.251	193	1166	93	7 yrs

Joseph Bert Tinker
5'9 175 lbs Batted right

Born Jul 27, 1880 Muscotah, KS
Died Jul 27, 1948 Orlando, FL

YR	POS	TEAM	LG	FIN	G	AB	R	H	2B	3B	HR	RBI	AVG	BB	TB	OQ	RANK
1902	SS	CHI	NL	5-8	131	494	55	129	19	5	2	54	.261	26	164	100	32-46
1903	SS-3B	CHI	NL	3-8	124	460	67	134	21	7	2	70	.291	37	175	110	24-49
1904	SS	CHI	NL	2-8	141	488	55	108	12	13	3	41	.221	29	155	92	38-42
1905	SS	CHI	NL	3-8	149	547	70	135	18	8	2	66	.247	34	175	92	40-45
1906	SS	CHI	NL	1-8	148	523	75	122	18	4	1	64	.233	43	151	93	38-42
1907	SS	CHI	NL	1-8	117	402	36	89	11	3	1	36	.221	25	109	83	—
1908	SS	CHI	NL	1-8	157	548	67	146	22	14	6	68	.266	32	214	122	13-41
1909	SS	CHI	NL	2-8	143	516	56	132	26	11	4	57	.256	17	192	102	31-39
1910	SS	CHI	NL	1-8	134	473	48	136	25	9	3	69	.288	24	188	107	28-47
1911	SS	CHI	NL	2-8	144	536	61	149	24	12	4	69	.278	39	209	103	34-45
1912	SS	CHI	NL	3-8	142	550	80	155	24	7	0	75	.282	38	193	92	38-43
1913	SS	CIN	NL	7-8	110	382	47	121	20	13	1	57	.317	20	170	122	—
1914	SS	CHI	FL	2-8	126	438	50	112	21	7	2	46	.256	38	153	97	28-41
1915	SS-2B	CHI	FL	1-8	31	67	7	18	2	1	0	9	.269	13	22	—	—
1916	SS-3B	CHI	NL	5-8	7	10	0	1	0	0	0	1	.100	1	1	—	—
MAJOR LEAGUE TOTALS					1804	6434	774	1687	263	114	31	782	.262	416	2271	101	11 yrs

Homer Vernon Smoot
5'10 180 lbs Batted left

Born Mar 26, 1878 Galestown, MD
Died Mar 25, 1928 Salisbury, MD

YR	POS	TEAM	LG	FIN	G	AB	R	H	2B	3B	HR	RBI	AVG	BB	TB	OQ	RANK
1902	CF	SL	NL	6-8	129	518	58	161	19	4	3	48	.311	23	197	118	17-46
1903	CF	SL	NL	8-8	129	500	67	148	22	8	4	49	.296	32	198	111	22-49
1904	CF	SL	NL	5-8	137	520	58	146	23	6	3	66	.281	37	190	116	19-42
1905	CF	SL	NL	6-8	139	534	73	166	21	16	4	58	.311	33	231	130	11-45
1906	CF	SL/CN	NL	7/6	146	563	52	142	17	11	1	48	.252	24	184	94	36-42

| MAJOR LEAGUE TOTALS | | | | | 680 | 2635 | 308 | 763 | 102 | 45 | 15 | 269 | .290 | 149 | 1000 | 114 | 5 yrs |

John Joseph Evers
5'9 125 lbs Batted left

Born Jul 22, 1883 Troy, NY
Died Mar 28, 1947 Albany, NY

YR	POS	TEAM	LG	FIN	G	AB	R	H	2B	3B	HR	RBI	AVG	BB	TB	OQ	RANK
1902	2B-SS	CHI	NL	5-8	26	90	7	20	0	0	0	2	.222	3	20	—	—
1903	2B	CHI	NL	3-8	124	464	70	136	27	7	0	52	.293	19	177	102	31-49
1904	2B	CHI	NL	2-8	152	532	49	141	14	7	0	47	.265	28	169	96	35-42
1905	2B	CHI	NL	3-8	99	340	44	94	11	2	1	37	.276	27	112	103	—
1906	2B	CHI	NL	1-8	154	533	65	136	17	6	1	51	.255	36	168	98	31-42
1907	2B	CHI	NL	1-8	151	508	66	127	18	4	2	51	.250	38	159	100	31-41
1908	2B	CHI	NL	1-8	126	416	83	125	19	6	0	37	.300	66	156	152	2-41
1909	2B	CHI	NL	2-8	127	463	88	122	19	6	1	24	.263	73	156	127	8-39
1910	2B	CHI	NL	1-8	125	433	87	114	11	7	0	28	.263	108	139	132	7-47
1911	2B-3B	CHI	NL	2-8	46	155	29	35	4	3	0	7	.226	34	45	106	—
1912	2B	CHI	NL	3-8	143	478	73	163	23	11	1	63	.341	74	211	142	2-43
1913	2B	CHI	NL	3-8	136	446	81	127	20	5	3	49	.285	50	166	114	22-45
1914	2B	BOS	NL	1-8	139	491	81	137	20	3	1	40	.279	87	166	127	10-42
1915	2B	BOS	NL	2-8	83	278	38	73	4	1	1	22	.263	50	82	118	—
1916	2B	BOS	NL	3-8	71	241	33	52	4	1	0	15	.216	40	58	97	—
1917	2B	BO/PH	NL	6/2	80	266	25	57	5	1	1	12	.214	43	67	98	—
1922	2B	CHI	AL	5-8	1	3	0	0	0	0	0	1	.000	2	0	—	—
1929	2B	BOS	NL	8-8	1	0	0	0	0	0	0	0	—	0	0	—	—

| MAJOR LEAGUE TOTALS | | | | | 1784 | 6137 | 919 | 1659 | 216 | 70 | 12 | 538 | .270 | 778 | 2051 | 119 | 10 yrs |

Patrick Henry Dougherty   Born Oct 27, 1876   Andover, NY
6'2   190 lbs   Batted left   Died Apr 30, 1940   Bolivar, NY

YR	POS	TEAM	LG	FIN	G	AB	R	H	2B	3B	HR	RBI	AVG	BB	TB	OQ	RANK
1902	LF	BOS	AL	3-8	108	438	77	150	12	6	0	34	.342	42	174	123	14-46
1903	LF	BOS	AL	1-8	139	590	106	195	19	12	4	59	.331	33	250	132	11-47
1904	LF	BO/NY	AL	1/2	155	647	113	181	18	14	6	26	.280	44	245	122	15-47
1905	LF	NY	AL	6-8	116	418	56	110	9	6	3	29	.263	28	140	107	—
1906	LF	NY/CH	AL	2/1	87	305	33	69	11	4	1	31	.226	19	91	90	—
1907	LF	CHI	AL	3-8	148	533	69	144	17	2	1	59	.270	36	168	104	30-48
1908	LF	CHI	AL	3-8	138	482	68	134	11	6	0	45	.278	58	157	126	12-36
1909	LF	CHI	AL	4-8	139	491	71	140	23	13	1	55	.285	51	192	137	8-33
1910	LF	CHI	AL	6-8	127	443	45	110	8	6	1	43	.248	41	133	100	27-36
1911	LF	CHI	AL	4-8	76	211	39	61	10	9	0	32	.289	26	89	125	—

| | | MAJOR LEAGUE TOTALS | | | 1233 | 4558 | 677 | 1294 | 138 | 78 | 17 | 413 | .284 | 378 | 1639 | 121 | 7 yrs |

John Franklin Titus   Born Feb 21, 1876   St Clair, PA
5'9   156 lbs   Batted left   Died Jan 8, 1943   St Clair, PA

YR	POS	TEAM	LG	FIN	G	AB	R	H	2B	3B	HR	RBI	AVG	BB	TB	OQ	RANK
1903	LF-RF	PHI	NL	7-8	72	280	38	80	15	6	2	34	.286	19	113	112	—
1904	LF-RF	PHI	NL	8-8	146	504	60	148	25	5	4	55	.294	46	195	129	10-42
1905	RF	PHI	NL	4-8	147	548	99	169	36	14	2	89	.308	69	239	148	5-45
1906	RF	PHI	NL	4-8	145	484	67	129	22	5	1	57	.267	78	164	130	10-42
1907	RF	PHI	NL	3-8	145	523	72	144	23	12	3	63	.275	47	200	126	13-41
1908	RF	PHI	NL	4-8	149	539	75	154	24	5	2	48	.286	53	194	128	10-41
1909	RF	PHI	NL	5-8	151	540	69	146	22	6	3	46	.270	66	189	122	12-39
1910	RF	PHI	NL	4-8	143	535	91	129	26	5	3	35	.241	93	174	112	21-47
1911	RF	PHI	NL	4-8	76	236	35	67	14	1	8	26	.284	32	107	132	—
1912	RF	PH/BO	NL	5/8	141	502	99	155	32	11	5	70	.309	82	224	138	4-43
1913	RF	BOS	NL	5-8	87	269	33	80	14	2	5	38	.297	35	113	132	—

| | | MAJOR LEAGUE TOTALS | | | 1402 | 4960 | 738 | 1401 | 253 | 72 | 38 | 561 | .282 | 620 | 1912 | 129 | 8 yrs |

Lee Ford Tannehill Born Oct 26, 1880 Dayton, KY
5'11 170 lbs Batted right Died Feb 16, 1938 Live Oak, FL

YR	POS	TEAM	LG	FIN	G	AB	R	H	2B	3B	HR	RBI	AVG	BB	TB	OQ	RANK
1903	SS	CHI	AL	7-8	138	503	48	113	14	3	2	50	.225	25	139	77	47-47
1904	3B	CHI	AL	3-8	153	547	50	125	31	5	0	61	.229	20	166	87	39-47
1905	3B	CHI	AL	2-8	142	480	38	96	17	2	0	39	.200	45	117	83	37-41
1906	3B-SS	CHI	AL	1-8	116	378	26	69	8	3	0	33	.183	31	83	72	—
1907	3B	CHI	AL	3-8	33	108	9	26	2	0	0	11	.241	8	28	87	—
1908	3B	CHI	AL	3-8	141	482	44	104	15	3	0	35	.216	25	125	81	36-36
1909	3B-SS	CHI	AL	4-8	155	531	39	118	21	5	0	47	.222	31	149	86	32-33
1910	SS-1B	CHI	AL	6-8	67	230	17	51	10	0	1	21	.222	11	64	80	—
1911	SS-2B	CHI	AL	4-8	141	516	60	131	17	6	0	49	.254	32	160	82	41-44
1912	3B	CHI	AL	4-8	4	3	0	0	0	0	0	0	.000	1	0	—	—

| MAJOR LEAGUE TOTALS | | | | | 1090 | 3778 | 331 | 833 | 135 | 27 | 3 | 346 | .220 | 229 | 1031 | 83 | 6 yrs |

Garland Stahl Born Apr 13, 1879 Elkhart, IL
6'2 195 lbs Batted right Died Sep 18, 1922 Monrovia, CA

YR	POS	TEAM	LG	FIN	G	AB	R	H	2B	3B	HR	RBI	AVG	BB	TB	OQ	RANK
1903	C	BOS	AL	1-8	40	92	14	22	3	5	2	8	.239	4	41	—	—
1904	1B-CF	WAS	AL	8-8	142	520	54	136	29	12	3	50	.262	21	198	112	25-47
1905	1B	WAS	AL	7-8	141	501	66	125	22	12	5	66	.250	28	186	112	23-41
1906	1B	WAS	AL	7-8	137	482	38	107	9	8	0	51	.222	21	132	79	39-40
1908	1B-LF	NY/BO	AL	8/5	153	536	63	134	27	16	2	65	.250	31	199	117	17-36
1909	1B	BOS	AL	3-8	127	435	62	128	19	12	6	60	.294	43	189	150	4-33
1910	1B	BOS	AL	4-8	144	531	68	144	19	16	10	77	.271	42	225	132	7-36
1912	1B	BOS	AL	1-8	95	326	40	98	21	6	3	60	.301	31	140	125	—
1913	PH	BOS	AL	4-8	2	2	0	0	0	0	0	0	.000	0	0	—	—

| MAJOR LEAGUE TOTALS | | | | | 981 | 3425 | 405 | 894 | 149 | 87 | 31 | 437 | .261 | 221 | 1310 | 117 | 6 yrs |

Harry Homer Gessler
5'10 180 lbs Batted left

Born Dec 23, 1880 Indiana, PA
Died Dec 26, 1924 Indiana, PA

YR	POS	TEAM	LG	FIN	G	AB	R	H	2B	3B	HR	RBI	AVG	BB	TB	OQ	RANK
1903	RF	DET	AL	5-8	29	105	9	25	5	4	0	12	.238	3	38	94	—
1903	RF	BRO	NL	5-8	49	154	20	38	8	3	0	18	.247	17	52	101	—
1904	CF	BRO	NL	6-8	104	341	41	99	18	4	2	28	.290	30	131	127	—
1905	1B	BRO	NL	8-8	126	431	44	125	17	4	3	46	.290	38	159	117	16-45
1906	CF-1B	BR/CH	NL	5/1	43	116	11	29	4	2	0	14	.250	15	37	114	—
1908	RF	BOS	AL	5-8	128	435	55	134	13	14	3	63	.308	51	184	159	2-36
1909	RF	BO/WA	AL	3/8	128	450	67	128	26	2	0	54	.284	43	158	124	14-33
1910	RF	WAS	AL	7-8	145	487	58	126	17	11	2	50	.259	62	171	123	14-36
1911	RF	WAS	AL	7-8	128	450	65	127	19	5	4	78	.282	74	168	122	15-44
MAJOR LEAGUE TOTALS					880	2969	370	831	127	49	14	363	.280	333	1098	129	5 yrs

George Joseph Moriarty
6'0 185 lbs Batted right

Born Jul 7, 1884 Chicago, IL
Died Apr 8, 1964 Miami, FL

YR	POS	TEAM	LG	FIN	G	AB	R	H	2B	3B	HR	RBI	AVG	BB	TB	OQ	RANK
1903	3B	CHI	NL	3-8	1	5	1	0	0	0	0	0	.000	0	0	—	—
1904	3B-CF	CHI	NL	2-8	4	13	0	0	0	0	0	0	.000	1	0	—	—
1906	3B-LF	NY	AL	2-8	65	197	22	46	7	7	0	23	.234	17	67	108	—
1907	3B-1B	NY	AL	5-8	126	437	51	121	16	5	0	43	.277	25	147	108	27-48
1908	1B-3B	NY	AL	8-8	101	348	25	82	12	1	0	27	.236	11	96	82	—
1909	3B-1B	DET	AL	1-8	133	473	43	129	20	4	1	39	.273	24	160	106	22-33
1910	3B	DET	AL	3-8	136	490	53	123	24	3	2	60	.251	33	159	100	26-36
1911	3B	DET	AL	2-8	130	478	51	116	20	4	1	60	.243	27	147	79	43-44
1912	1B-3B	DET	AL	6-8	105	375	38	93	23	1	0	54	.248	26	118	85	—
1913	3B	DET	AL	6-8	105	347	29	83	5	2	0	30	.239	24	92	76	—
1914	3B	DET	AL	4-8	132	465	56	118	19	5	1	40	.254	39	150	98	31-41
1915	3B	DET	AL	2-8	31	38	2	8	1	0	0	0	.211	5	9	—	—
1916	3B-1B	CHI	AL	2-8	7	5	1	1	0	0	0	0	.200	2	1	—	—
MAJOR LEAGUE TOTALS					1076	3671	372	920	147	32	5	376	.251	234	1146	98	5 yrs

George Robert Stone Born Sep 3, 1877 Lost Nation, IA
5'9 175 lbs Batted right Died Jan 3, 1945 Clinton, IA

YR	POS	TEAM	LG	FIN	G	AB	R	H	2B	3B	HR	RBI	AVG	BB	TB	OQ	RANK
1903	PH	BOS	AL	1-8	2	2	0	0	0	0	0	0	.000	0	0	—	—
1905	LF	SL	AL	8-8	154	632	76	187	25	13	7	52	.296	44	259	134	5-41
1906	LF	SL	AL	5-8	154	581	91	208	25	20	6	71	.358	52	291	178	1-40
1907	LF	SL	AL	6-8	155	596	77	191	13	11	4	59	.320	59	238	146	5-48
1908	LF	SL	AL	4-8	148	588	89	165	21	8	5	31	.281	55	217	131	8-36
1909	LF	SL	AL	7-8	83	310	33	89	5	4	1	15	.287	24	105	116	—
1910	LF	SL	AL	8-8	152	562	60	144	17	12	0	40	.256	48	185	106	21-36
MAJOR LEAGUE TOTALS					848	3271	426	984	106	68	23	268	.301	282	1295	139	5 yrs

John Bernard Lobert Born Oct 18, 1881 Wilmington, DE
5'9 170 lbs Batted right Died Sep 14, 1968 Philadelphia, PA

YR	POS	TEAM	LG	FIN	G	AB	R	H	2B	3B	HR	RBI	AVG	BB	TB	OQ	RANK
1903	3B-SS	PIT	NL	1-8	5	13	1	1	1	0	0	0	.077	1	2	—	—
1905	3B	CHI	NL	3-8	14	46	7	9	2	0	0	1	.196	3	11	—	—
1906	3B-SS	CIN	NL	6-8	79	268	39	83	5	5	0	19	.310	19	98	121	—
1907	SS	CIN	NL	6-8	148	537	61	132	9	12	1	41	.246	37	168	98	32-41
1908	3B-SS	CIN	NL	5-8	155	570	71	167	17	18	4	63	.293	46	232	137	6-41
1909	3B	CIN	NL	4-8	122	425	50	90	13	5	4	52	.212	48	125	97	35-39
1910	3B	CIN	NL	5-8	93	314	43	97	6	6	3	40	.309	30	124	121	—
1911	3B	PHI	NL	4-8	147	541	94	154	20	9	9	72	.285	66	219	119	14-45
1912	3B	PHI	NL	5-8	65	257	37	84	12	5	2	33	.327	19	112	119	—
1913	3B	PHI	NL	2-8	150	573	98	172	28	11	7	55	.300	42	243	119	16-45
1914	3B	PHI	NL	6-8	135	505	83	139	24	5	1	52	.275	49	176	109	22-42
1915	3B	NY	NL	8-8	106	386	46	97	18	4	0	38	.251	25	123	94	—
1916	3B	NY	NL	4-8	48	76	6	17	3	2	0	11	.224	5	24	—	—
1917	3B	NY	NL	1-8	50	52	4	10	1	0	1	5	.192	5	14	—	—
MAJOR LEAGUE TOTALS					1317	4563	640	1252	159	82	32	482	.274	395	1671	113	6 yrs

Harry G Lumley   Born Sep 29, 1880   Forest City, PA
5'10   183 lbs   Batted left   Died May 22, 1938 Binghamton, NY

YR	POS	TEAM	LG	FIN	G	AB	R	H	2B	3B	HR	RBI	AVG	BB	TB	OQ	RANK
1904	RF	BRO	NL	6-8	150	577	79	161	23	18	9	78	.279	41	247	132	5-42
1905	RF	BRO	NL	8-8	130	505	50	148	19	10	7	47	.293	36	208	124	14-45
1906	RF	BRO	NL	5-8	133	484	72	157	23	12	9	61	.324	48	231	163	2-42
1907	RF	BRO	NL	5-8	127	454	47	121	23	11	9	66	.267	31	193	130	8-41
1908	RF	BRO	NL	7-8	127	440	36	95	13	12	4	39	.216	29	144	100	27-41
1909	RF	BRO	NL	6-8	55	172	13	43	8	3	0	14	.250	16	57	107	—
1910	RF	BRO	NL	6-8	8	21	3	3	0	0	0	0	.143	3	3	—	—

MAJOR LEAGUE TOTALS   730 2653 300 728 109 66 38 305 .274 204 1083 130   5 yrs

Sherwood Robert Magee   Born Aug 6, 1884   Clarendon, PA
5'11   179 lbs   Batted right   Died Mar 13, 1929 Philadelphia, PA

YR	POS	TEAM	LG	FIN	G	AB	R	H	2B	3B	HR	RBI	AVG	BB	TB	OQ	RANK
1904	RF	PHI	NL	8-8	95	364	51	101	15	12	3	57	.277	14	149	118	—
1905	LF	PHI	NL	4-8	155	603	100	180	24	17	5	98	.299	44	253	128	12-45
1906	LF	PHI	NL	4-8	154	563	77	159	36	8	6	67	.282	52	229	133	9-42
1907	LF	PHI	NL	3-8	140	503	75	165	28	12	4	85	.328	53	229	161	2-41
1908	LF	PHI	NL	4-8	143	508	79	144	30	16	2	57	.283	49	212	143	5-41
1909	LF	PHI	NL	5-8	143	522	60	141	33	14	2	66	.270	43	208	124	9-39
1910	LF	PHI	NL	4-8	154	519	110	172	39	17	6	123	.331	94	263	175	1-47
1911	LF	PHI	NL	4-8	121	445	79	128	32	5	15	94	.288	49	215	134	6-45
1912	LF	PHI	NL	5-8	132	464	79	142	25	9	6	66	.306	55	203	126	12-43
1913	LF	PHI	NL	2-8	138	470	92	144	36	6	11	70	.306	38	225	136	6-45
1914	LF-SS	PHI	NL	6-8	146	544	96	171	39	11	15	103	.314	55	277	158	2-42
1915	CF	BOS	NL	2-8	156	571	72	160	34	12	2	87	.280	54	224	124	9-45
1916	LF	BOS	NL	3-8	122	419	44	101	17	5	3	54	.241	44	137	107	—
1917	LF	BO/CN	NL	6/4	117	383	41	107	16	8	1	52	.279	29	142	116	—
1918	1B-LF	CIN	NL	3-8	115	400	46	119	15	13	2	76	.298	37	166	134	4-40
1919	LF	CIN	NL	1-8	56	163	11	35	6	1	0	21	.215	26	43	98	—

MAJOR LEAGUE TOTALS   2087 7441 1112 2169 425 166 83 1176 .291 736 3175 140 12 yrs

Arthur McArthur Devlin Born Oct 16, 1879 Washington, DC
6'0 175 lbs Batted right Died Sep 18, 1948 Jersey City, NJ

YR	POS	TEAM	LG	FIN	G	AB	R	H	2B	3B	HR	RBI	AVG	BB	TB	OQ	RANK
1904	3B	NY	NL	1-8	130	474	81	133	16	8	1	66	.281	62	168	128	11-42
1905	3B	NY	NL	1-8	153	525	74	129	14	7	2	61	.246	66	163	105	25-45
1906	3B	NY	NL	2-8	148	498	76	149	23	8	2	65	.299	74	194	147	6-42
1907	3B	NY	NL	4-8	143	491	61	136	16	2	1	54	.277	63	159	121	16-41
1908	3B	NY	NL	2-8	157	534	59	135	18	4	2	45	.253	62	167	114	19-41
1909	3B	NY	NL	3-8	143	491	61	130	19	8	0	56	.265	65	165	120	14-39
1910	3B	NY	NL	2-8	147	493	71	128	17	5	2	67	.260	62	161	104	32-47
1911	3B	NY	NL	1-8	95	260	42	71	16	2	0	25	.273	42	91	113	—
1912	1B-SS	BOS	NL	8-8	124	436	59	126	18	8	0	54	.289	51	160	107	25-43
1913	3B	BOS	NL	5-8	73	210	19	48	7	5	0	12	.229	29	65	97	—

| MAJOR LEAGUE TOTALS | | | | | 1313 | 4412 | 603 | 1185 | 164 | 57 | 10 | 505 | .269 | 576 | 1493 | 118 | 8 yrs |

Frank M Schulte Born Sep 17, 1882 Cohocton, NY
5'11 170 lbs Batted left Died Oct 2, 1949 Oakland, CA

YR	POS	TEAM	LG	FIN	G	AB	R	H	2B	3B	HR	RBI	AVG	BB	TB	OQ	RANK
1904	LF	CHI	NL	2-8	20	84	16	24	4	3	2	13	.286	2	40	—	—
1905	LF	CHI	NL	3-8	123	493	67	135	15	14	1	47	.274	32	181	108	23-45
1906	RF	CHI	NL	1-8	146	563	77	158	18	13	7	60	.281	31	223	120	15-42
1907	RF	CHI	NL	1-8	97	342	44	98	14	7	2	32	.287	22	132	122	—
1908	RF	CHI	NL	1-8	102	386	42	91	20	2	1	43	.236	29	118	99	—
1909	RF	CHI	NL	2-8	140	538	57	142	16	11	4	60	.264	24	192	103	30-39
1910	RF	CHI	NL	1-8	151	559	93	168	29	15	10	68	.301	39	257	129	8-47
1911	RF	CHI	NL	2-8	154	577	105	173	30	21	21	107	.300	76	308	153	3-45
1912	RF	CHI	NL	3-8	139	553	90	146	27	11	12	64	.264	53	231	109	22-43
1913	RF	CHI	NL	3-8	132	497	85	138	28	6	9	68	.278	39	205	114	21-45
1914	LF	CHI	NL	5-8	137	465	54	112	22	7	5	61	.241	39	163	101	32-42
1915	LF	CHI	NL	4-8	151	550	66	137	20	6	12	62	.249	49	205	113	20-45
1916	LF	CH/PT	NL	5/6	127	407	43	113	16	4	5	41	.278	37	152	121	—
1917	RF	PT/PH	NL	8/2	94	252	32	54	15	1	1	22	.214	26	74	94	—
1918	RF	WAS	AL	3-8	93	267	35	77	14	3	0	44	.288	47	97	135	—

| MAJOR LEAGUE TOTALS | | | | | 1806 | 6533 | 906 | 1766 | 288 | 124 | 92 | 792 | .270 | 545 | 2578 | 117 | 9 yrs |

George Thomas Stovall　　　　　　Born Nov 23, 1878 Independence, MO
6'2 180 lbs Batted right　　　　　　　Died Nov 5, 1951 Burlington, IA

YR	POS	TEAM	LG	FIN	G	AB	R	H	2B	3B	HR	RBI	AVG	BB	TB	OQ	RANK
1904	1B-2B	CLE	AL	4-8	52	181	18	54	10	1	1	31	.298	2	69	110	—
1905	1B-2B	CLE	AL	5-8	112	423	41	115	31	1	1	47	.272	13	151	104	—
1906	1B-3B	CLE	AL	3-8	116	443	54	121	19	5	0	37	.273	8	150	95	—
1907	1B	CLE	AL	4-8	124	466	38	110	17	6	1	36	.236	18	142	89	42-48
1908	1B	CLE	AL	2-8	138	534	71	156	29	6	2	45	.292	17	203	119	14-36
1909	1B	CLE	AL	6-8	145	565	60	139	17	10	2	49	.246	6	182	87	30-33
1910	1B	CLE	AL	5-8	142	521	49	136	19	4	0	52	.261	14	163	88	35-36
1911	1B	CLE	AL	3-8	126	458	48	124	17	7	0	79	.271	21	155	86	38-44
1912	1B	SL	AL	7-8	116	398	35	101	17	5	0	45	.254	14	128	80	—
1913	1B	SL	AL	8-8	89	303	34	87	14	3	1	24	.287	7	110	94	—
1914	1B	KC	FL	6-8	124	450	51	128	20	5	7	75	.284	23	179	104	26-41
1915	1B	KC	FL	4-8	130	480	48	111	21	3	0	44	.231	29	138	79	39-40

| MAJOR LEAGUE TOTALS | | | | | 1414 | 5222 | 547 | 1382 | 231 | 56 | 15 | 564 | .265 | 172 | 1770 | 93 | 7 yrs |

Miller James Huggins　　　　　　Born Mar 27, 1879 Cincinnati, OH
5'6 140 lbs Batted both　　　　　　　Died Sep 25, 1929 New York, NY

YR	POS	TEAM	LG	FIN	G	AB	R	H	2B	3B	HR	RBI	AVG	BB	TB	OQ	RANK
1904	2B	CIN	NL	3-8	140	491	96	129	12	7	2	30	.263	88	161	131	7-42
1905	2B	CIN	NL	5-8	149	564	117	154	11	8	1	38	.273	103	184	127	13-45
1906	2B	CIN	NL	6-8	146	545	81	159	11	7	0	26	.292	71	184	126	11-42
1907	2B	CIN	NL	6-8	156	561	64	139	12	4	1	31	.248	83	162	112	21-41
1908	2B	CIN	NL	5-8	135	498	65	119	14	5	0	23	.239	58	143	105	26-41
1909	2B-3B	CIN	NL	4-8	57	159	18	34	3	1	0	6	.214	28	39	101	—
1910	2B	SL	NL	7-8	151	547	101	145	15	6	1	36	.265	116	175	123	13-47
1911	2B	SL	NL	5-8	138	509	106	133	19	2	1	24	.261	96	159	109	26-45
1912	2B	SL	NL	6-8	120	431	82	131	15	4	0	29	.304	87	154	126	11-43
1913	2B	SL	NL	8-8	121	382	74	109	12	0	0	27	.285	92	121	131	9-45
1914	2B	SL	NL	3-8	148	509	85	134	17	4	1	24	.263	105	162	126	11-42
1915	2B	SL	NL	6-8	107	353	57	85	5	2	2	24	.241	74	100	119	—
1916	2B	SL	NL	7-8	18	9	2	3	0	0	0	0	.333	2	3	—	—

| MAJOR LEAGUE TOTALS | | | | | 1586 | 5558 | 948 | 1474 | 146 | 50 | 9 | 318 | .265 | 1003 | 1747 | 122 | 10 yrs |

Michael Joseph Doolan
5'10 170 lbs Batted right

Born May 7, 1880 Ashland, PA
Died Nov 1, 1951 Orlando, FL

YR	POS	TEAM	LG	FIN	G	AB	R	H	2B	3B	HR	RBI	AVG	BB	TB	OQ	RANK
1905	SS	PHI	NL	4-8	136	492	53	125	27	11	1	48	.254	24	177	100	33-45
1906	SS	PHI	NL	4-8	154	535	41	123	19	7	1	55	.230	27	159	86	40-42
1907	SS	PHI	NL	3-8	145	509	33	104	19	7	1	47	.204	25	140	79	41-41
1908	SS	PHI	NL	4-8	129	445	29	104	25	4	2	49	.234	17	143	93	—
1909	SS	PHI	NL	5-8	147	493	39	108	12	10	1	35	.219	37	143	88	38-39
1910	SS	PHI	NL	4-8	148	536	58	141	31	6	2	57	.263	35	190	97	36-47
1911	SS	PHI	NL	4-8	146	512	51	122	23	6	1	49	.238	44	160	84	41-45
1912	SS	PHI	NL	5-8	146	532	47	137	26	6	1	62	.258	34	178	84	42-43
1913	SS	PHI	NL	2-8	151	518	32	113	12	6	1	43	.218	29	140	70	45-45
1914	SS	BAL	FL	3-8	145	486	58	119	23	6	1	53	.245	40	157	89	31-41
1915	SS	BA/CH	FL	8/1	143	490	50	98	14	8	2	30	.200	26	134	71	40-40
1916	SS	CH/NY	NL	5/4	46	121	8	27	5	2	1	8	.223	10	39	98	—
1918	2B	BRO	NL	5-8	92	308	14	55	8	2	0	18	.179	22	67	65	—
MAJOR LEAGUE TOTALS					1728	5977	513	1376	244	81	15	554	.230	370	1827	85	10 yrs

Franz Otto Knabe
5'8 175 lbs Batted right

Born Jun 12, 1884 Carrick, PA
Died May 17, 1961 Philadelphia, PA

YR	POS	TEAM	LG	FIN	G	AB	R	H	2B	3B	HR	RBI	AVG	BB	TB	OQ	RANK
1905	3B	PIT	NL	2-8	3	10	0	3	1	0	0	2	.300	3	4	—	—
1907	2B	PHI	NL	3-8	129	444	67	113	16	9	1	34	.255	52	150	118	18-41
1908	2B	PHI	NL	4-8	151	555	63	121	26	8	0	27	.218	49	163	97	31-41
1909	2B	PHI	NL	5-8	113	402	40	94	13	3	0	34	.234	35	113	91	—
1910	2B	PHI	NL	4-8	137	510	73	133	18	6	1	44	.261	47	166	96	38-47
1911	2B	PHI	NL	4-8	142	528	99	125	15	6	1	42	.237	94	155	100	35-45
1912	2B	PHI	NL	5-8	126	426	56	120	11	4	0	46	.282	55	139	99	33-43
1913	2B	PHI	NL	2-8	148	571	70	150	25	7	2	53	.263	45	195	96	37-45
1914	2B	BAL	FL	3-8	147	469	45	106	26	2	2	42	.226	53	142	89	31-41
1915	2B	BAL	FL	8-8	103	320	38	81	16	2	1	25	.253	37	104	102	—
1916	2B	PT/CH	NL	6/5	79	234	21	57	11	1	0	16	.244	15	70	90	—
MAJOR LEAGUE TOTALS					1278	4469	572	1103	178	48	8	365	.247	485	1401	99	7 yrs

Harry Harlan Mowrey　　　　　　　　Born Apr 20, 1884　Browns Mill, PA
5'10　180 lbs　Batted right　　　　　　Died Mar 20, 1947　Chambersburg, PA

YR	POS	TEAM	LG	FIN	G	AB	R	H	2B	3B	HR	RBI	AVG	BB	TB	OQ	RANK
1905	3B	CIN	NL	5-8	7	30	4	8	1	0	0	6	.267	1	9	—	—
1906	3B	CIN	NL	6-8	21	53	3	17	3	0	0	6	.321	5	20	—	—
1907	3B	CIN	NL	6-8	138	448	43	113	16	6	1	44	.252	35	144	103	29-41
1908	3B	CIN	NL	5-8	77	227	17	50	9	1	0	23	.220	12	61	82	—
1909	3B-SS	CN/SL	NL	4/7	50	144	13	29	6	0	0	9	.201	24	35	97	—
1910	3B	SL	NL	7-8	143	489	69	138	24	6	2	70	.282	67	180	120	16-47
1911	3B	SL	NL	5-8	137	471	59	126	29	7	0	61	.268	59	169	106	28-45
1912	3B	SL	NL	6-8	114	408	59	104	13	8	2	50	.255	46	139	95	—
1913	3B	SL	NL	8-8	132	450	61	117	18	4	0	33	.260	53	143	99	36-45
1914	3B	PIT	NL	7-8	79	284	24	72	7	5	1	25	.254	22	92	95	—
1915	3B	PIT	FL	3-8	151	521	56	146	26	6	1	49	.280	66	187	117	17-40
1916	3B	BRO	NL	1-8	144	495	57	121	22	6	0	60	.244	50	155	103	29-36
1917	3B	BRO	NL	7-8	83	271	20	58	9	5	0	25	.214	29	77	93	—

MAJOR LEAGUE TOTALS　　　　　1276 4291 485 1099 183 54 7 461 .256 469 1411 108　6 yrs

John Edwin Hummel　　　　　　　　Born Apr 4, 1883　Bloomsburg, PA
5'11　160 lbs　Batted right　　　　　　Died May 18, 1959　Springfield, MA

YR	POS	TEAM	LG	FIN	G	AB	R	H	2B	3B	HR	RBI	AVG	BB	TB	OQ	RANK
1905	2B	BRO	NL	8-8	30	109	19	29	3	4	0	7	.266	9	40	111	—
1906	2B-LF	BRO	NL	5-8	97	286	20	57	6	4	1	21	.199	36	74	92	—
1907	2B-LF	BRO	NL	5-8	107	342	41	80	12	3	3	31	.234	26	107	98	—
1908	LF-2B	BRO	NL	7-8	154	594	51	143	11	12	4	41	.241	34	190	99	28-41
1909	1B-2B	BRO	NL	6-8	146	542	54	152	15	9	4	52	.280	22	197	106	26-39
1910	2B	BRO	NL	6-8	153	578	67	141	21	13	5	74	.244	57	203	101	34-47
1911	2B	BRO	NL	7-8	137	477	54	129	21	11	5	58	.270	67	187	118	16-45
1912	2B-RF	BRO	NL	7-8	122	411	55	116	21	7	5	54	.282	49	166	114	17-43
1913	RF-SS	BRO	NL	6-8	67	198	20	48	7	7	2	24	.242	13	75	99	—
1914	1B-RF	BRO	NL	5-8	73	208	25	55	8	9	0	20	.264	16	81	112	—
1915	RF-1B	BRO	NL	3-8	53	100	6	23	2	3	0	8	.230	6	31	88	—
1918	LF-1B	NY	AL	4-8	22	61	9	18	1	2	0	4	.295	11	23	—	—

MAJOR LEAGUE TOTALS　　　　　1161 3906 421 991 128 84 29 394 .254 346 1374 108　5 yrs

Albert Henry Bridwell Born Jan 4, 1884 Friendship, OH
5'9 170 lbs Batted left Died Jan 23, 1969 Portsmouth, OH

YR	POS	TEAM	LG	FIN	G	AB	R	H	2B	3B	HR	RBI	AVG	BB	TB	OQ	RANK
1905	3B-RF	CIN	NL	5-8	82	254	17	64	3	1	0	17	.252	19	69	84	—
1906	SS	BOS	NL	8-8	120	459	41	104	9	1	0	22	.227	44	115	86	41-42
1907	SS	BOS	NL	7-8	140	509	49	111	8	2	0	26	.218	61	123	89	35-41
1908	SS	NY	NL	2-8	147	467	53	133	14	1	0	46	.285	52	149	120	16-41
1909	SS	NY	NL	3-8	145	476	59	140	11	5	0	55	.294	67	161	128	7-39
1910	SS	NY	NL	2-8	142	492	74	136	15	7	0	48	.276	73	165	114	20-47
1911	SS	NY/BO	NL	1/8	127	445	57	124	15	1	0	41	.279	66	141	104	32-45
1912	SS	BOS	NL	8-8	31	106	6	25	5	1	0	14	.236	5	32	72	—
1913	SS	CHI	NL	3-8	136	405	35	97	6	6	1	37	.240	74	118	105	29-45
1914	SS	SL	FL	8-8	117	381	46	90	6	5	1	33	.236	71	109	103	—
1915	2B-3B	SL	FL	2-8	65	175	20	40	3	2	0	9	.229	25	47	92	—

| MAJOR LEAGUE TOTALS | | | | | 1252 | 4169 | 457 | 1064 | 95 | 32 | 2 | 348 | .255 | 557 | 1229 | 107 | 7 yrs |

Harold Homer Chase Born Feb 13, 1883 Los Gatos, CA
6'0 175 lbs Batted right Died May 18, 1947 Colusa, CA

YR	POS	TEAM	LG	FIN	G	AB	R	H	2B	3B	HR	RBI	AVG	BB	TB	OQ	RANK
1905	1B	NY	AL	6-8	128	465	60	116	16	6	3	49	.249	15	153	94	33-41
1906	1B	NY	AL	2-8	151	597	84	193	23	10	0	76	.323	13	236	119	14-40
1907	1B	NY	AL	5-8	125	498	72	143	23	3	2	68	.287	19	178	110	22-48
1908	1B	NY	AL	8-8	106	405	50	104	11	3	1	36	.257	15	124	94	—
1909	1B	NY	AL	5-8	118	474	60	134	17	3	4	63	.283	20	169	110	19-33
1910	1B	NY	AL	2-8	130	524	67	152	20	5	3	73	.290	16	191	106	22-36
1911	1B	NY	AL	6-8	133	527	82	166	32	7	3	62	.315	21	221	109	25-44
1912	1B	NY	AL	8-8	131	522	61	143	21	9	4	58	.274	17	194	93	28-33
1913	1B	NY/CH	AL	7/5	141	530	64	141	13	14	2	48	.266	27	188	96	34-37
1914	1B	CHI	AL	6-8	58	206	27	55	10	5	0	20	.267	23	75	117	—
1914	1B	BUF	FL	4-8	75	291	43	101	19	9	3	48	.347	6	147	134	—
1915	1B	BUF	FL	6-8	145	567	85	165	31	10	17	89	.291	20	267	124	14-40
1916	1B-CF	CIN	NL	7-8	142	542	66	184	29	12	4	82	.339	19	249	141	5-36
1917	1B	CIN	NL	4-8	152	602	71	167	28	15	4	86	.277	15	237	108	22-38
1918	1B	CIN	NL	3-8	74	259	30	78	12	6	2	38	.301	13	108	124	—
1919	1B	NY	NL	2-8	110	408	58	116	17	7	5	45	.284	17	162	112	19-41

| MAJOR LEAGUE TOTALS | | | | | 1919 | 7417 | 980 | 2158 | 322 | 124 | 57 | 941 | .291 | 276 | 2899 | 110 | 12 yrs |

William White Hinchman
5'11 190 lbs Batted right

Born Apr 4, 1883 Philadelphia, PA
Died Feb 21, 1963 Columbus, OH

YR	POS	TEAM	LG	FIN	G	AB	R	H	2B	3B	HR	RBI	AVG	BB	TB	OQ	RANK
1905	LF-3B	CIN	NL	5-8	17	51	10	13	4	1	0	10	.255	13	19	—	—
1906	LF-RF	CIN	NL	6-8	18	54	7	11	1	1	0	1	.204	8	14	—	—
1907	LF	CLE	AL	4-8	152	514	62	117	19	9	1	50	.228	47	157	102	32-48
1908	RF-SS	CLE	AL	2-8	137	464	55	107	23	8	6	59	.231	38	164	116	19-36
1909	LF	CLE	AL	6-8	139	457	57	118	20	13	2	53	.258	41	170	123	15-33
1915	RF	PIT	NL	5-8	156	577	72	177	33	14	5	77	.307	48	253	138	4-45
1916	RF-1B	PIT	NL	6-8	152	555	64	175	18	16	4	76	.315	54	237	144	3-36
1917	RF-1B	PIT	NL	8-8	69	244	27	46	5	5	2	29	.189	33	67	94	—
1918	RF	PIT	NL	4-8	50	111	10	26	5	2	0	13	.234	15	35	109	—
1920	PH	PIT	NL	4-8	18	16	0	3	0	0	0	1	.188	1	3	—	—
MAJOR LEAGUE TOTALS					908	3043	364	793	128	69	20	369	.261	298	1119	125	5 yrs

Tyrus Raymond Cobb
6'1 175 lbs Batted left

Born Dec 18, 1886 The Narrows, GA
Died Jul 17, 1961 Atlanta, GA

YR	POS	TEAM	LG	FIN	G	AB	R	H	2B	3B	HR	RBI	AVG	BB	TB	OQ	RANK
1905	CF	DET	AL	3-8	41	150	19	36	6	0	1	15	.240	10	45	95	—
1906	CF	DET	AL	6-8	98	358	45	113	15	5	1	34	.316	19	141	127	—
1907	RF	DET	AL	1-8	150	605	97	212	28	14	5	119	.350	24	283	155	2-48
1908	RF	DET	AL	1-8	150	581	88	188	36	20	4	108	.324	34	276	161	1-36
1909	RF	DET	AL	1-8	156	573	116	216	33	10	9	107	.377	48	296	191	1-33
1910	CF	DET	AL	3-8	140	506	106	194	35	13	8	91	.383	64	279	210	1-36
1911	CF	DET	AL	2-8	146	591	147	248	47	24	8	127	.420	44	367	196	1-44
1912	CF	DET	AL	6-8	140	553	119	227	30	23	7	83	.410	43	324	188	2-33
1913	CF	DET	AL	6-8	122	428	70	167	18	16	4	67	.390	58	229	191	2-37
1914	CF	DET	AL	4-8	98	345	69	127	22	11	2	57	.368	57	177	193	—
1915	CF	DET	AL	2-8	156	563	144	208	31	13	3	99	.369	118	274	193	1-42
1916	CF	DET	AL	3-8	145	542	113	201	31	10	5	68	.371	78	267	180	2-38
1917	CF	DET	AL	4-8	152	588	107	225	44	24	6	102	.383	61	335	198	1-40
1918	CF	DET	AL	7-8	111	421	83	161	19	14	3	64	.382	41	217	177	1-39
1919	CF	DET	AL	4-8	124	497	92	191	36	13	1	70	.384	38	256	157	2-49
1920	CF	DET	AL	7-8	112	428	86	143	28	8	2	63	.334	58	193	132	11-49
1921	CF	DET	AL	6-8	128	507	124	197	37	16	12	101	.389	56	302	163	2-49
1922	CF	DET	AL	3-8	137	526	99	211	42	16	4	99	.401	55	297	164	6-50
1923	CF	DET	AL	2-8	145	556	103	189	40	7	6	88	.340	66	261	132	9-46
1924	CF	DET	AL	3-8	155	625	115	211	38	10	4	78	.338	85	281	127	10-40
1925	CF	DET	AL	4-8	121	415	97	157	31	12	12	102	.378	65	248	169	2-42
1926	CF	DET	AL	6-8	79	233	48	79	18	5	4	62	.339	26	119	137	—
1927	RF	PHI	AL	2-8	134	490	104	175	32	7	5	93	.357	67	236	139	5-43
1928	RF	PHI	AL	2-8	95	353	54	114	27	4	1	40	.323	34	152	115	—
MAJOR LEAGUE TOTALS					3035	11434	2245	4190	724	295	117	1937	.366	1249	5855	170	19 yrs

Frank Breyfogle LaPorte   Born Feb 6, 1880   Urichsville, OH
5'8 175 lbs Batted right   Died Sep 25, 1939 Newcomerstown, OH

YR	POS	TEAM	LG	FIN	G	AB	R	H	2B	3B	HR	RBI	AVG	BB	TB	OQ	RANK
1905	2B	NY	AL	6-8	11	40	4	16	1	0	1	12	.400	1	20	—	—
1906	3B	NY	AL	2-8	123	454	60	120	23	9	2	54	.264	22	167	110	20-40
1907	3B-RF	NY	AL	5-8	130	470	56	127	20	11	0	48	.270	27	169	114	13-48
1908	2B-LF	BO/NY	AL	5/8	101	301	21	75	4	7	1	30	.249	20	96	105	—
1909	2B	NY	AL	5-8	89	309	35	92	19	3	0	31	.298	18	117	123	—
1910	2B-LF	NY	AL	2-8	124	432	43	114	14	6	2	67	.264	33	146	107	—
1911	2B	SL	AL	8-8	136	507	71	159	37	12	2	82	.314	34	226	122	16-44
1912	2B-RF	SL/WA	AL	7/2	120	402	45	125	20	5	1	55	.311	32	158	115	—
1913	3B-2B	WAS	AL	2-8	79	242	25	61	5	4	0	18	.252	17	74	87	—
1914	2B	IND	FL	1-8	133	505	86	157	27	12	4	107	.311	36	220	122	13-41
1915	2B	NWK	FL	5-8	148	550	55	139	28	10	2	56	.253	48	193	102	29-40

| MAJOR LEAGUE TOTALS | | | | | 1194 | 4212 | 501 | 1185 | 198 | 79 | 15 | 560 | .281 | 288 | 1586 | 114 | 5 yrs |

Edward Trowbridge Collins   Born May 2, 1887   Millerton, NY
5'9 175 lbs Batted left   Died Mar 25, 1951 Boston, MA

YR	POS	TEAM	LG	FIN	G	AB	R	H	2B	3B	HR	RBI	AVG	BB	TB	OQ	RANK
1906	SS-2B	PHI	AL	4-8	6	15	2	3	0	0	0	0	.200	0	3	—	—
1907	SS	PHI	AL	2-8	14	20	0	5	0	0	0	2	.250	0	5	—	—
1908	2B-SS	PHI	AL	6-8	102	330	39	90	18	7	1	40	.273	16	125	120	—
1909	2B	PHI	AL	2-8	153	572	104	198	30	10	3	56	.346	62	257	169	2-33
1910	2B	PHI	AL	1-8	153	583	81	188	16	15	3	81	.322	49	243	141	4-36
1911	2B	PHI	AL	1-8	132	493	92	180	22	13	3	73	.365	62	237	156	4-44
1912	2B	PHI	AL	3-8	153	543	137	189	25	11	0	64	.348	101	236	159	5-33
1913	2B	PHI	AL	1-8	148	534	125	184	23	13	3	73	.345	85	242	162	4-37
1914	2B	PHI	AL	1-8	152	526	122	181	23	14	2	85	.344	97	238	174	1-41
1915	2B	CHI	AL	3-8	155	521	118	173	22	10	4	77	.332	119	227	174	2-42
1916	2B	CHI	AL	2-8	155	545	87	168	14	17	0	52	.308	86	216	142	4-38
1917	2B	CHI	AL	1-8	156	564	91	163	18	12	0	67	.289	89	205	133	7-40
1918	2B	CHI	AL	6-8	97	330	51	91	8	2	2	30	.276	73	109	136	7-39
1919	2B	CHI	AL	1-8	140	518	87	165	19	7	4	80	.319	68	210	129	9-49
1920	2B	CHI	AL	2-8	153	601	115	222	37	13	3	75	.369	69	294	144	5-49
1921	2B	CHI	AL	7-8	139	526	79	177	20	10	2	58	.337	66	223	117	17-49
1922	2B	CHI	AL	5-8	154	598	92	194	20	12	1	69	.324	73	241	114	19-50
1923	2B	CHI	AL	7-8	145	505	89	182	22	5	5	67	.360	84	229	143	6-46
1924	2B	CHI	AL	8-8	152	556	108	194	27	7	6	86	.349	89	253	136	6-40
1925	2B	CHI	AL	5-8	118	425	80	147	26	3	3	80	.346	87	188	138	6-42
1926	2B	CHI	AL	5-8	106	375	66	129	32	4	1	62	.344	62	172	139	—
1927	2B	PHI	AL	2-8	95	226	50	76	12	1	1	15	.336	56	93	143	—
1928	2B-SS	PHI	AL	2-8	36	33	3	10	3	0	0	7	.303	4	13	—	—
1929	PH	PHI	AL	1-8	9	7	0	0	0	0	0	0	.000	2	0	—	—
1930	PH	PHI	AL	1-8	3	2	1	1	0	0	0	0	.500	0	1	—	—

| MAJOR LEAGUE TOTALS | | | | | 2826 | 9948 | 1819 | 3310 | 437 | 186 | 47 | 1299 | .333 | 1499 | 4260 | 145 | 17 yrs |

Roy Allen Hartzell   Born Jul 6, 1881   Golden, CO
5'8 155 lbs Batted left   Died Nov 6, 1961   Golden, CO

YR	POS	TEAM	LG	FIN	G	AB	R	H	2B	3B	HR	RBI	AVG	BB	TB	OQ	RANK
1906	3B	SL	AL	5-8	113	404	43	86	7	0	0	24	.213	19	93	68	—
1907	3B-2B	SL	AL	6-8	60	220	20	52	3	5	0	13	.236	11	65	90	—
1908	RF-SS	SL	AL	4-8	115	422	41	112	5	6	2	32	.265	19	135	101	—
1909	RF-SS	SL	AL	7-8	152	595	64	161	12	5	0	32	.271	29	183	97	24-33
1910	3B-SS	SL	AL	8-8	151	542	52	118	13	5	2	30	.218	49	147	88	34-36
1911	3B	NY	AL	6-8	144	527	67	156	17	11	3	91	.296	63	204	118	18-44
1912	3B-RF	NY	AL	8-8	125	416	50	113	10	11	1	38	.272	64	148	117	15-33
1913	2B-RF	NY	AL	7-8	141	490	60	127	18	1	0	38	.259	67	147	102	29-37
1914	LF	NY	AL	6-8	137	481	55	112	15	9	1	32	.233	68	148	105	24-41
1915	LF	NY	AL	5-8	119	387	39	97	11	2	3	60	.251	57	121	107	—
1916	RF-LF	NY	AL	4-8	33	64	12	12	1	0	0	7	.188	9	13	—	—

| MAJOR LEAGUE TOTALS | | | | | 1290 | 4548 | 503 | 1146 | 112 | 55 | 12 | 397 | .252 | 455 | 1404 | 105 | 6 yrs |

John Joseph Murray   Born Mar 4, 1884   Arnot, PA
5'10 190 lbs Batted right   Died Dec 4, 1958   Sayre, PA

YR	POS	TEAM	LG	FIN	G	AB	R	H	2B	3B	HR	RBI	AVG	BB	TB	OQ	RANK
1906	RF-C	SL	NL	7-8	46	144	18	37	9	7	1	16	.257	9	63	129	—
1907	LF	SL	NL	8-8	132	485	46	127	10	10	7	46	.262	24	178	109	24-41
1908	RF	SL	NL	8-8	154	593	64	167	19	15	7	62	.282	37	237	128	9-41
1909	RF	NY	NL	3-8	149	570	74	150	15	12	7	91	.263	45	210	114	20-39
1910	RF	NY	NL	2-8	149	553	78	153	27	8	4	87	.277	52	208	111	23-47
1911	RF	NY	NL	1-8	140	488	70	142	27	15	3	78	.291	43	208	117	17-45
1912	RF	NY	NL	1-8	143	549	83	152	26	20	3	92	.277	27	227	100	31-43
1913	RF	NY	NL	1-8	147	520	70	139	21	3	2	59	.267	34	172	91	41-45
1914	RF	NY	NL	2-8	86	139	19	31	6	3	0	23	.223	9	43	85	—
1915	CF-RF	NY/CH	NL	8/4	96	271	32	71	7	3	3	22	.262	15	93	99	—
1917	RF-CF	NY	NL	1-8	22	22	1	1	1	0	0	3	.045	4	2	—	—

| MAJOR LEAGUE TOTALS | | | | | 1264 | 4334 | 555 | 1170 | 168 | 96 | 37 | 579 | .270 | 299 | 1641 | 110 | 7 yrs |

John William Bates　　　　　　Born Aug 21, 1882　Steubenville, OH
5'7　168 lbs　Batted left　　　　Died Feb 10, 1949　Steubenville, OH

YR	POS	TEAM	LG	FIN	G	AB	R	H	2B	3B	HR	RBI	AVG	BB	TB	OQ	RANK
1906	CF	BOS	NL	8-8	140	504	52	127	21	5	6	54	.252	36	176	107	23-42
1907	RF	BOS	NL	7-8	126	447	52	116	18	12	2	49	.260	39	164	118	17-41
1908	LF	BOS	NL	6-8	127	445	48	115	14	6	1	29	.258	35	144	108	23-41
1909	LF-CF	BO/PH	NL	8/5	140	502	70	146	26	4	2	38	.291	48	186	124	10-39
1910	CF	PHI	NL	4-8	135	498	91	152	26	11	3	61	.305	61	209	133	6-47
1911	CF	CIN	NL	6-8	148	518	89	151	24	13	1	61	.292	103	204	135	5-45
1912	CF	CIN	NL	4-8	81	239	45	69	12	7	1	29	.289	47	98	134	—
1913	RF	CIN	NL	7-8	131	407	63	113	13	7	6	51	.278	67	158	129	10-45
1914	CF	CN/CH	NL	8/4	67	163	31	40	7	5	2	16	.245	29	63	133	—
1914	CF-LF	BAL	FL	3-8	59	190	24	58	6	3	1	29	.305	38	73	140	—

MAJOR LEAGUE TOTALS　1154　3913　565 1087　167　73　25　417　.278　503 1475　122　7 yrs

Jesse Clyde Milan　　　　　　Born Mar 25, 1887　Linden, TN
5'9　168 lbs　Batted left　　　　Died Mar 3, 1953　Orlando, FL

YR	POS	TEAM	LG	FIN	G	AB	R	H	2B	3B	HR	RBI	AVG	BB	TB	OQ	RANK
1907	CF-RF	WAS	AL	8-8	48	183	22	51	3	3	0	9	.279	8	60	102	—
1908	CF	WAS	AL	7-8	130	485	55	116	10	12	1	32	.239	38	153	106	25-36
1909	CF	WAS	AL	8-8	130	400	36	80	12	4	1	15	.200	31	103	83	—
1910	CF	WAS	AL	7-8	142	531	89	148	17	6	0	16	.279	71	177	124	13-36
1911	CF	WAS	AL	7-8	154	616	109	194	24	8	3	35	.315	74	243	123	14-44
1912	CF	WAS	AL	2-8	154	601	105	184	19	11	1	79	.306	63	228	117	16-33
1913	CF	WAS	AL	2-8	154	579	92	174	18	9	3	54	.301	58	219	119	15-37
1914	CF	WAS	AL	3-8	115	437	63	129	19	11	1	39	.295	32	173	120	—
1915	CF	WAS	AL	4-8	153	573	83	165	13	7	2	66	.288	53	198	108	25-42
1916	CF	WAS	AL	7-8	150	565	58	154	14	3	1	45	.273	56	177	101	28-38
1917	CF	WAS	AL	5-8	155	579	60	170	15	4	0	48	.294	58	193	111	21-40
1918	CF	WAS	AL	3-8	128	503	56	146	18	5	0	56	.290	36	174	105	23-39
1919	CF	WAS	AL	7-8	88	321	43	92	12	6	0	37	.287	40	116	111	—
1920	LF	WAS	AL	6-8	126	506	70	163	22	5	3	41	.322	28	204	101	30-49
1921	RF	WAS	AL	4-8	113	406	55	117	19	11	1	40	.288	37	161	97	—
1922	RF-LF	WAS	AL	6-8	42	74	8	17	5	0	0	5	.230	2	22	—	—

MAJOR LEAGUE TOTALS　1982　7359 1004 2100　240 105　17　617　.285　685 2601　112　10 yrs

Henry Zimmerman   Born Feb 9, 1887 New York, NY
5'11 176 lbs Batted right   Died Mar 14, 1969 New York, NY

YR	POS	TEAM	LG	FIN	G	AB	R	H	2B	3B	HR	RBI	AVG	BB	TB	OQ	RANK
1907	2B-SS	CHI	NL	1-8	5	9	0	2	1	0	0	1	.222	0	3	—	—
1908	2B-CF	CHI	NL	1-8	46	113	17	33	4	1	0	9	.292	1	39	99	—
1909	2B-3B	CHI	NL	2-8	65	183	23	50	9	2	0	21	.273	3	63	93	—
1910	2B-SS	CHI	NL	1-8	99	335	35	95	16	6	3	38	.284	20	132	108	—
1911	2B-3B	CHI	NL	2-8	143	535	80	164	22	17	9	85	.307	25	247	118	15-45
1912	3B-1B	CHI	NL	3-8	145	557	95	207	41	14	14	99	.372	38	318	159	1-43
1913	3B	CHI	NL	3-8	127	447	69	140	28	12	9	95	.313	41	219	142	2-45
1914	3B-SS	CHI	NL	4-8	146	564	75	167	36	12	4	87	.296	20	239	116	16-42
1915	2B-3B	CHI	NL	4-8	139	520	65	138	28	11	3	62	.265	21	197	105	28-45
1916	3B-2B	CHI/NY	NL	5/4	147	549	76	157	29	5	6	83	.286	23	214	114	20-36
1917	3B	NY	NL	1-8	150	585	61	174	22	9	5	102	.297	16	229	111	18-38
1918	3B-1B	NY	NL	2-8	121	463	43	126	19	10	1	56	.272	13	168	99	27-40
1919	3B	NY	NL	2-8	123	444	56	113	20	6	4	58	.255	21	157	98	33-41

MAJOR LEAGUE TOTALS   1456 5304 695 1566 275 105 58 796 .295 242 2225 118 9 yrs

George Henry Paskert   Born Aug 28, 1881 Cleveland, OH
5'11 165 lbs Batted right   Died Feb 12, 1959 Cleveland, OH

YR	POS	TEAM	LG	FIN	G	AB	R	H	2B	3B	HR	RBI	AVG	BB	TB	OQ	RANK
1907	CF	CIN	NL	6-8	16	50	10	14	4	0	1	8	.280	2	21	—	—
1908	LF	CIN	NL	5-8	118	395	40	96	14	4	1	36	.243	27	121	98	—
1909	CF-LF	CIN	NL	4-8	104	322	49	81	7	4	0	33	.252	34	96	102	—
1910	CF	CIN	NL	5-8	144	506	63	152	21	5	2	46	.300	70	189	125	12-47
1911	CF	PHI	NL	4-8	153	560	96	153	18	5	4	47	.273	70	193	104	30-45
1912	CF	PHI	NL	5-8	145	540	102	170	37	5	2	43	.315	91	223	133	7-43
1913	CF	PHI	NL	2-8	124	454	83	119	21	9	4	29	.262	65	170	118	19-45
1914	CF	PHI	NL	6-8	132	451	59	119	25	6	3	44	.264	56	165	118	15-42
1915	CF	PHI	NL	1-8	109	328	51	80	17	4	3	39	.244	35	114	110	—
1916	CF	PHI	NL	2-8	149	555	82	155	30	7	8	46	.279	54	223	130	9-36
1917	CF	PHI	NL	2-8	141	546	78	137	27	11	4	43	.251	62	198	119	13-38
1918	CF	CHI	NL	1-8	127	461	69	132	24	4	2	59	.286	53	170	126	10-40
1919	CF	CHI	NL	3-8	88	270	21	53	11	3	2	29	.196	28	76	87	—
1920	CF	CHI	NL	5-8	139	487	57	136	22	10	5	71	.279	64	193	125	11-45
1921	CF-RF	CIN	NL	6-8	27	92	8	16	1	1	0	4	.174	4	19	—	—

MAJOR LEAGUE TOTALS   1716 6017 868 1613 279 78 41 577 .268 715 2171 122 9 yrs

William John Sweeney
5'11 175 lbs Batted right

Born Mar 6, 1886 Covington, KY
Died May 26, 1948 Cambridge, MA

YR	POS	TEAM	LG	FIN	G	AB	R	H	2B	3B	HR	RBI	AVG	BB	TB	OQ	RANK
1907	3B-SS	CHI/BO	NL	1/7	61	201	25	51	2	0	0	19	.254	16	53	89	—
1908	3B	BOS	NL	6-8	127	418	44	102	15	3	0	40	.244	45	123	106	—
1909	3B-SS	BOS	NL	8-8	138	493	44	120	19	3	1	36	.243	37	148	93	37-39
1910	SS-3B	BOS	NL	8-8	150	499	43	133	22	4	5	46	.267	61	178	111	22-47
1911	2B	BOS	NL	8-8	137	523	92	164	33	6	3	63	.314	77	218	132	7-45
1912	2B	BOS	NL	8-8	153	593	84	204	31	13	1	100	.344	68	264	134	5-43
1913	2B	BOS	NL	5-8	139	502	65	129	17	6	0	47	.257	66	158	101	34-45
1914	2B	CHI	NL	4-8	134	463	45	101	14	5	1	38	.218	53	128	89	41-42

MAJOR LEAGUE TOTALS					1039	3692	442	1004	153	40	11	389	.272	423	1270	110	6 yrs

Tristam E Speaker
5'11 193 lbs Batted left

Born Apr 4, 1888 Hubbard, TX
Died Dec 8, 1958 Lake Whitney, TX

YR	POS	TEAM	LG	FIN	G	AB	R	H	2B	3B	HR	RBI	AVG	BB	TB	OQ	RANK
1907	RF	BOS	AL	7-8	7	19	0	3	0	0	0	1	.158	1	3	—	—
1908	CF	BOS	AL	5-8	31	116	12	26	2	2	0	9	.224	4	32	82	—
1909	CF	BOS	AL	3-8	143	544	73	168	26	13	7	77	.309	38	241	147	6-33
1910	CF	BOS	AL	4-8	141	538	92	183	20	14	7	65	.340	52	252	163	3-36
1911	CF	BOS	AL	5-8	141	500	88	167	34	13	8	70	.334	59	251	152	6-44
1912	CF	BOS	AL	1-8	153	580	136	222	53	12	10	90	.383	82	329	192	1-33
1913	CF	BOS	AL	4-8	141	520	94	189	35	22	3	71	.363	65	277	179	3-37
1914	CF	BOS	AL	2-8	158	571	101	193	46	18	4	90	.338	77	287	173	2-41
1915	CF	BOS	AL	1-8	150	547	108	176	25	12	0	69	.322	81	225	144	4-42
1916	CF	CLE	AL	6-8	151	546	102	211	41	8	2	79	.386	82	274	189	1-38
1917	CF	CLE	AL	3-8	142	523	90	184	42	11	2	60	.352	67	254	172	2-40
1918	CF	CLE	AL	2-8	127	471	73	150	33	11	0	61	.318	64	205	150	2-39
1919	CF	CLE	AL	2-8	134	494	83	146	38	12	2	63	.296	73	214	135	6-49
1920	CF	CLE	AL	1-8	150	552	137	214	50	11	8	107	.388	97	310	181	2-49
1921	CF	CLE	AL	2-8	132	506	107	183	52	14	3	75	.362	68	272	149	5-49
1922	CF	CLE	AL	4-8	131	426	85	161	48	8	11	71	.378	77	258	185	2-50
1923	CF	CLE	AL	3-8	150	574	133	218	59	11	17	130	.380	93	350	184	3-46
1924	CF	CLE	AL	6-8	135	486	94	167	36	9	9	65	.344	72	248	144	4-40
1925	CF	CLE	AL	6-8	117	429	79	167	35	5	12	87	.389	70	248	169	1-42
1926	CF	CLE	AL	2-8	150	539	96	164	52	8	7	86	.304	94	253	135	7-41
1927	CF	WAS	AL	3-8	141	523	71	171	43	6	2	73	.327	55	232	118	14-43
1928	CF	PHI	AL	2-8	64	191	28	51	22	2	3	30	.267	10	86	101	—

MAJOR LEAGUE TOTALS					2789	10195	1882	3514	792	222	117	1529	.345	1381	5101	161	19 yrs

Robert Matthew Byrne　　　　　Born Dec 31, 1884　St Louis, MO
5'7　145 lbs　Batted right　　　　　Died Dec 31, 1964　Wayne, PA

YR	POS	TEAM	LG	FIN	G	AB	R	H	2B	3B	HR	RBI	AVG	BB	TB	OQ	RANK
1907	3B	SL	NL	8-8	149	559	55	143	11	5	0	29	.256	35	164	92	33-41
1908	3B	SL	NL	8-8	127	439	27	84	7	1	0	14	.191	23	93	65	41-41
1909	3B	SL/PT	NL	7/1	151	589	92	133	19	8	1	40	.226	78	171	103	29-39
1910	3B	PIT	NL	3-8	148	602	101	178	43	12	2	52	.296	66	251	127	10-47
1911	3B	PIT	NL	3-8	153	598	96	155	24	17	2	52	.259	67	219	104	31-45
1912	3B	PIT	NL	2-8	130	528	99	152	31	11	3	35	.288	54	214	112	19-43
1913	3B	PT/PH	NL	4/2	132	506	63	134	23	0	2	51	.265	34	163	89	43-45
1914	2B-3B	PHI	NL	6-8	126	467	61	127	12	1	0	26	.272	45	141	97	35-42
1915	3B	PHI	NL	1-8	105	387	50	81	6	4	0	21	.209	39	95	80	—
1916	3B	PHI	NL	2-8	48	141	22	33	10	1	0	9	.234	14	45	102	—
1917	3B	PHI	NL	2-8	13	14	1	5	0	0	0	0	.357	1	5	—	—
1917	2B	CHI	AL	1-8	1	1	0	0	0	0	0	0	.000	0	0	—	—
MAJOR LEAGUE TOTALS					1283	4831	667	1225	186	60	10	329	.254	456	1561	99	8 yrs

Edward Joseph Konetchy　　　　Born Sep 3, 1885　La Crosse, WI
6'2　195 lbs　Batted right　　　　　Died May 27, 1947　Fort Worth, TX

YR	POS	TEAM	LG	FIN	G	AB	R	H	2B	3B	HR	RBI	AVG	BB	TB	OQ	RANK
1907	1B	SL	NL	8-8	91	331	34	83	11	8	3	30	.251	26	119	113	—
1908	1B	SL	NL	8-8	154	545	46	135	19	12	5	50	.248	38	193	112	21-41
1909	1B	SL	NL	7-8	152	576	88	165	23	14	4	80	.286	65	228	134	6-39
1910	1B	SL	NL	7-8	144	520	87	157	23	16	3	78	.302	78	221	140	4-47
1911	1B	SL	NL	5-8	158	571	90	165	38	13	6	88	.289	81	247	130	8-45
1912	1B	SL	NL	6-8	143	538	81	169	26	13	8	82	.314	62	245	130	8-43
1913	1B	SL	NL	8-8	140	504	75	139	18	17	8	68	.276	53	215	123	12-45
1914	1B	PIT	NL	7-8	154	563	56	140	23	9	4	51	.249	32	193	94	38-42
1915	1B	PIT	FL	3-8	152	576	79	181	31	18	10	93	.314	41	278	140	2-40
1916	1B	BOS	NL	3-8	158	566	76	147	29	13	3	70	.260	43	211	114	18-36
1917	1B	BOS	NL	6-8	130	474	56	129	19	13	2	54	.272	36	180	117	14-38
1918	1B	BOS	NL	7-8	119	437	33	103	15	5	2	56	.236	32	134	92	33-40
1919	1B	BRO	NL	5-8	132	486	46	145	24	9	1	47	.298	29	190	117	13-41
1920	1B	BRO	NL	1-8	131	497	62	153	22	12	5	63	.308	33	214	123	15-45
1921	1B	BR/PH	NL	5/8	127	465	63	139	23	9	11	82	.299	40	213	118	16-39
MAJOR LEAGUE TOTALS					2085	7649	972	2150	344	181	75	992	.281	689	3081	120	14 yrs

Harry Donald Lord　　　　　Born Mar 8, 1882　Porter, ME
5'10　165 lbs　Batted left　　　Died Aug 9, 1948　Westbrook, ME

YR	POS	TEAM	LG	FIN	G	AB	R	H	2B	3B	HR	RBI	AVG	BB	TB	OQ	RANK
1907	3B	BOS	AL	7-8	10	38	4	6	1	0	0	3	.158	1	7	—	—
1908	3B	BOS	AL	5-8	145	560	61	145	15	6	2	37	.259	22	178	98	29-36
1909	3B	BOS	AL	3-8	136	534	86	166	12	7	0	31	.311	20	192	114	17-33
1910	3B	BO/CH	AL	4/6	121	453	51	121	11	8	1	42	.267	28	151	103	24-36
1911	3B	CHI	AL	4-8	141	561	103	180	18	18	3	61	.321	32	243	118	17-44
1912	3B-LF	CHI	AL	4-8	151	570	81	152	19	12	5	54	.267	52	210	105	24-33
1913	3B	CHI	AL	5-8	150	547	62	144	18	12	1	42	.263	45	189	101	31-37
1914	3B	CHI	AL	6-8	21	69	8	13	1	1	1	3	.188	5	19	—	—
1915	3B	BUF	FL	6-8	97	359	50	97	12	6	1	21	.270	21	124	96	—
MAJOR LEAGUE TOTALS					972	3691	506	1024	107	70	14	294	.277	226	1313	107	6 yrs

Frederick Charles Merkle　　　Born Dec 20, 1888　Watertown, WI
6'1　190 lbs　Batted right　　　Died Mar 2, 1956　Daytona Beach, FL

YR	POS	TEAM	LG	FIN	G	AB	R	H	2B	3B	HR	RBI	AVG	BB	TB	OQ	RANK
1907	1B	NY	NL	4-8	15	47	0	12	1	0	0	5	.255	1	13	—	—
1908	1B-RF	NY	NL	2-8	38	41	6	11	2	1	1	7	.268	4	18	—	—
1909	1B	NY	NL	3-8	79	236	15	45	9	1	0	20	.191	16	56	71	—
1910	1B	NY	NL	2-8	144	506	75	148	35	14	4	70	.292	44	223	127	11-47
1911	1B	NY	NL	1-8	149	541	80	153	24	10	12	84	.283	43	233	114	19-45
1912	1B	NY	NL	1-8	129	479	82	148	22	6	11	84	.309	42	215	122	13-43
1913	1B	NY	NL	1-8	153	563	78	147	30	13	2	69	.261	41	209	101	32-45
1914	1B	NY	NL	2-8	146	512	71	132	25	7	7	63	.258	52	192	114	17-42
1915	1B-CF	NY	NL	8-8	140	505	52	151	25	3	4	62	.299	36	194	119	14-45
1916	1B	NY/BR	NL	4/1	135	470	51	111	20	3	7	46	.236	40	158	104	28-36
1917	1B	BR/CH	NL	7/5	148	557	66	147	31	9	3	57	.264	42	205	113	16-38
1918	1B	CHI	NL	1-8	129	482	55	143	25	5	3	65	.297	35	187	121	14-40
1919	1B	CHI	NL	3-8	133	498	52	133	20	6	3	62	.267	33	174	103	22-41
1920	1B	CHI	NL	5-8	92	330	33	94	20	4	3	38	.285	24	131	112	—
1925	1B	NY	AL	7-8	7	13	4	5	1	0	0	1	.385	1	6	—	—
1926	1B	NY	AL	1-8	1	2	0	0	0	0	0	0	.000	0	0	—	—
MAJOR LEAGUE TOTALS					1638	5782	720	1580	290	82	60	733	.273	454	2214	114	10 yrs

Michael Francis Mitchell   Born Dec 12, 1879 Springfield, OH
6'1   185 lbs   Batted right   Died Jul 16, 1961 Phoenix, AZ

YR	POS	TEAM	LG	FIN	G	AB	R	H	2B	3B	HR	RBI	AVG	BB	TB	OQ	RANK
1907	RF	CIN	NL	6-8	148	558	64	163	17	12	3	47	.292	37	213	122	14-41
1908	RF	CIN	NL	5-8	119	406	41	90	9	6	1	37	.222	46	114	101	—
1909	RF	CIN	NL	4-8	145	523	83	162	17	17	4	86	.310	57	225	147	2-39
1910	RF	CIN	NL	5-8	156	583	79	167	16	18	5	88	.286	59	234	120	15-47
1911	RF	CIN	NL	6-8	142	529	74	154	22	22	2	84	.291	44	226	116	18-45
1912	RF	CIN	NL	4-8	147	552	60	156	14	13	4	78	.283	41	208	99	34-43
1913	LF-CF	CH/PT	NL	3/4	136	478	62	127	19	8	5	51	.266	46	177	107	27-45
1914	RF	PIT	NL	7-8	76	273	31	64	11	5	2	23	.234	16	91	91	—
1914	LF	WAS	AL	3-8	55	193	20	55	5	3	1	20	.285	22	69	118	—

MAJOR LEAGUE TOTALS					1124	4095	514	1138	130	104	27	514	.278	368	1557	119	6 yrs

Lawrence Joseph Doyle   Born Jul 31, 1886 Caseyville, IL
5'10   165 lbs   Batted left   Died Mar 1, 1974 Saranac Lake, NY

YR	POS	TEAM	LG	FIN	G	AB	R	H	2B	3B	HR	RBI	AVG	BB	TB	OQ	RANK
1907	2B	NY	NL	4-8	69	227	16	59	3	0	0	16	.260	20	62	94	—
1908	2B	NY	NL	2-8	104	377	65	116	16	9	0	33	.308	22	150	131	—
1909	2B	NY	NL	3-8	147	570	86	172	27	11	6	49	.302	45	239	134	5-39
1910	2B	NY	NL	2-8	151	575	97	164	21	14	8	69	.285	71	237	128	9-47
1911	2B	NY	NL	1-8	143	526	102	163	25	25	13	77	.310	71	277	154	2-45
1912	2B	NY	NL	1-8	143	558	98	184	33	8	10	90	.330	56	263	134	6-43
1913	2B	NY	NL	1-8	132	482	67	135	25	6	5	73	.280	59	187	119	17-45
1914	2B	NY	NL	2-8	145	539	87	140	19	8	5	63	.260	58	190	110	19-42
1915	2B	NY	NL	8-8	150	591	86	189	40	10	4	70	.320	32	261	134	6-45
1916	2B	NY/CH	NL	4/5	122	479	61	133	29	11	3	54	.278	28	193	120	15-36
1917	2B	CHI	NL	5-8	135	476	48	121	19	5	6	61	.254	48	168	114	15-38
1918	2B	NY	NL	2-8	75	257	38	67	7	4	3	36	.261	37	91	125	—
1919	2B	NY	NL	2-8	113	381	61	110	14	10	7	52	.289	31	165	132	—
1920	2B	NY	NL	2-8	137	471	48	134	21	2	4	50	.285	47	171	110	24-45

MAJOR LEAGUE TOTALS					1766	6509	960	1887	299	123	74	793	.290	625	2654	126	10 yrs

John Joseph Barry   Born Apr 26, 1887 Meriden, CT
5'9 158 lbs Batted right   Died Apr 23, 1961 Shrewsbury, MA

YR	POS	TEAM	LG	FIN	G	AB	R	H	2B	3B	HR	RBI	AVG	BB	TB	OQ	RANK
1908	2B-SS	PHI	AL	6-8	40	135	13	30	4	3	0	8	.222	10	40	97	—
1909	SS	PHI	AL	2-8	124	409	56	88	11	2	1	23	.215	44	106	92	—
1910	SS	PHI	AL	1-8	145	487	64	126	19	5	3	60	.259	52	164	114	18-36
1911	SS	PHI	AL	1-8	127	442	73	117	18	7	1	63	.265	38	152	96	33-44
1912	SS	PHI	AL	3-8	140	483	76	126	19	9	0	55	.261	47	163	98	26-33
1913	SS	PHI	AL	1-8	134	455	62	125	20	6	3	85	.275	44	166	110	22-37
1914	SS	PHI	AL	1-8	140	467	57	113	12	0	0	42	.242	53	125	90	33-41
1915	2B-SS	PHI/BO	AL	8/1	132	442	46	108	19	4	0	41	.244	39	135	91	37-42
1916	2B	BOS	AL	1-8	94	330	28	67	6	1	0	20	.203	17	75	62	—
1917	2B	BOS	AL	2-8	116	388	45	83	9	0	2	30	.214	47	98	86	—
1919	2B	BOS	AL	6-8	31	108	13	26	5	1	0	2	.241	5	33	76	—

| MAJOR LEAGUE TOTALS | | | | | 1223 | 4146 | 533 | 1009 | 142 | 38 | 10 | 429 | .243 | 396 | 1257 | 100 | 6 yrs |

Owen Joseph Bush   Born Oct 8, 1887   Indianapolis, IN
5'6 140 lbs Batted both   Died Mar 28, 1972 Indianapolis, IN

YR	POS	TEAM	LG	FIN	G	AB	R	H	2B	3B	HR	RBI	AVG	BB	TB	OQ	RANK
1908	SS	DET	AL	1-8	20	68	13	20	1	1	0	4	.294	7	23	—	—
1909	SS	DET	AL	1-8	157	532	114	145	18	2	0	33	.273	88	167	130	10-33
1910	SS	DET	AL	3-8	142	496	90	130	13	4	3	34	.262	78	160	124	11-36
1911	SS	DET	AL	2-8	150	561	126	130	18	5	1	36	.232	98	161	98	32-44
1912	SS	DET	AL	6-8	144	511	107	118	14	8	2	38	.231	117	154	115	18-33
1913	SS	DET	AL	6-8	153	597	98	150	19	10	1	40	.251	80	192	106	26-37
1914	SS	DET	AL	4-8	157	596	97	150	18	4	0	32	.252	112	176	116	11-41
1915	SS	DET	AL	2-8	155	561	99	128	12	8	1	44	.228	118	159	112	19-42
1916	SS	DET	AL	3-8	145	550	73	124	5	9	0	34	.225	75	147	93	34-38
1917	SS	DET	AL	4-8	147	581	112	163	18	3	0	24	.281	80	187	116	16-40
1918	SS	DET	AL	7-8	128	500	74	117	10	3	0	22	.234	79	133	99	28-39
1919	SS	DET	AL	4-8	129	509	82	124	11	6	0	26	.244	75	147	94	35-49
1920	SS	DET	AL	7-8	141	506	85	133	18	5	1	33	.263	73	164	95	35-49
1921	SS-2B	DE/WA	AL	6/4	127	486	87	131	7	5	0	29	.270	57	148	81	46-49
1922	3B	WAS	AL	6-8	41	134	17	32	4	1	0	7	.239	21	38	85	—
1923	3B-2B	WAS	AL	4-8	10	22	6	9	0	0	0	0	.409	0	9	—	—

| MAJOR LEAGUE TOTALS | | | | | 1946 | 7210 | 1280 | 1804 | 186 | 74 | 9 | 436 | .250 | 1158 | 2165 | 106 | 13 yrs |

John Owen Wilson   Born Aug 21, 1883 Austin, TX
6'2 185 lbs Batted left   Died Feb 22, 1954 Bertram, TX

YR	POS	TEAM	LG	FIN	G	AB	R	H	2B	3B	HR	RBI	AVG	BB	TB	OQ	RANK
1908	RF	PIT	NL	2-8	144	529	47	120	8	7	3	43	.227	22	151	84	39-41
1909	RF	PIT	NL	1-8	154	569	64	155	22	12	4	59	.272	19	213	105	27-39
1910	RF	PIT	NL	3-8	146	536	59	148	14	13	4	50	.276	21	200	97	37-47
1911	RF	PIT	NL	3-8	148	544	72	163	34	12	12	107	.300	41	257	126	9-45
1912	CF	PIT	NL	2-8	152	583	80	175	19	36	11	95	.300	35	299	128	9-43
1913	RF	PIT	NL	4-8	155	580	71	154	12	14	10	73	.266	32	224	101	33-45
1914	RF	SL	NL	3-8	154	580	64	150	27	12	9	73	.259	32	228	107	25-42
1915	CF	SL	NL	6-8	107	348	33	96	13	6	3	39	.276	19	130	108	—
1916	CF	SL	NL	7-8	120	355	30	85	8	2	3	32	.239	20	106	88	—

MAJOR LEAGUE TOTALS   1280 4624 520 1246 157 114 59 571 .269 241 1808 107 7 yrs

Amos Aaron Strunk   Born Jan 22, 1889 Philadelphia, PA
5'11 175 lbs Batted left   Died Jul 22, 1979 Llanerch, PA

YR	POS	TEAM	LG	FIN	G	AB	R	H	2B	3B	HR	RBI	AVG	BB	TB	OQ	RANK
1908	CF	PHI	AL	6-8	12	34	4	8	1	0	0	0	.235	4	9	—	—
1909	CF	PHI	AL	2-8	11	35	1	4	0	0	0	2	.114	1	4	—	—
1910	CF	PHI	AL	1-8	16	48	9	16	0	1	0	2	.333	3	18	—	—
1911	CF-LF	PHI	AL	1-8	74	215	42	55	7	2	1	21	.256	35	69	106	—
1912	LF	PHI	AL	3-8	122	412	58	119	13	12	3	63	.289	47	165	121	10-33
1913	CF	PHI	AL	1-8	94	292	30	89	11	12	0	46	.305	29	124	131	—
1914	CF	PHI	AL	1-8	122	404	58	111	15	3	2	45	.275	57	138	120	—
1915	CF-1B	PHI	AL	8-8	132	485	76	144	28	16	1	45	.297	56	207	135	9-42
1916	CF	PHI	AL	8-8	150	544	71	172	30	9	3	49	.316	66	229	141	5-38
1917	CF	PHI	AL	8-8	148	540	83	152	26	7	1	45	.281	68	195	123	10-40
1918	CF	BOS	AL	1-8	114	413	50	106	18	9	0	35	.257	36	142	104	25-39
1919	CF	BO/PH	AL	6/8	108	378	42	91	17	7	0	30	.241	36	122	90	—
1920	CF	PH/CH	AL	8/2	111	390	56	105	17	4	1	36	.269	49	133	96	—
1921	CF	CHI	AL	7-8	121	401	68	133	19	10	3	69	.332	38	181	115	—
1922	CF-1B	CHI	AL	5-8	92	311	36	90	11	4	0	33	.289	33	109	94	—
1923	LF-1B	CHI	AL	7-8	54	54	7	17	0	0	0	8	.315	8	17	—	—
1924	LF-RF	CH/PH	AL	8/5	31	43	5	6	0	0	0	1	.140	7	6	—	—

MAJOR LEAGUE TOTALS   1512 4999 696 1418 213 96 15 530 .284 573 1868 125 5 yrs

Robert Henry Bescher　　　　　　Born Feb 25, 1884　London, OH
6'1　200 lbs　Batted both　　　　　　Died Nov 29, 1942　London, OH

YR	POS	TEAM	LG	FIN	G	AB	R	H	2B	3B	HR	RBI	AVG	BB	TB	OQ	RANK
1908	LF	CIN	NL	5-8	32	114	16	31	5	5	0	17	.272	9	46	132	—
1909	LF	CIN	NL	4-8	124	446	73	107	17	6	1	34	.240	56	139	108	23-39
1910	LF	CIN	NL	5-8	150	589	95	147	20	10	4	48	.250	81	199	108	25-47
1911	LF	CIN	NL	6-8	153	599	106	165	32	10	1	45	.275	102	220	119	12-45
1912	LF	CIN	NL	4-8	145	548	120	154	29	11	4	38	.281	83	217	119	16-43
1913	LF	CIN	NL	7-8	141	511	86	132	22	11	1	37	.258	94	179	121	14-45
1914	CF	NY	NL	2-8	135	512	82	138	23	4	6	35	.270	45	187	110	20-42
1915	LF	SL	NL	6-8	130	486	71	128	15	7	4	34	.263	52	169	113	19-45
1916	LF	SL	NL	7-8	151	561	78	132	24	8	6	43	.235	60	190	109	21-36
1917	LF	SL	NL	3-8	42	110	10	17	1	1	1	8	.155	20	23	86	—
1918	RF	CLE	AL	2-8	25	60	12	20	2	1	0	6	.333	17	24	—	—

| MAJOR LEAGUE TOTALS | | | | | 1228 | 4536 | 749 | 1171 | 190 | 74 | 28 | 345 | .258 | 619 | 1593 | 113 | 8 yrs |

John Gladstone Graney　　　　　　Born Jun 10, 1886　St Thomas, ON
5'9　180 lbs　Batted left　　　　　　Died Apr 20, 1978　Louisiana, MO

YR	POS	TEAM	LG	FIN	G	AB	R	H	2B	3B	HR	RBI	AVG	BB	TB	OQ	RANK
1908	P	CLE	AL	2-8	2	0	0	0	0	0	0	0	—	0	0	—	—
1910	RF	CLE	AL	5-8	116	454	62	107	13	9	1	31	.236	37	141	98	29-36
1911	LF	CLE	AL	3-8	146	527	84	142	25	5	1	45	.269	66	180	104	28-44
1912	LF	CLE	AL	5-8	78	264	44	64	13	2	0	20	.242	50	81	109	—
1913	LF	CLE	AL	3-8	148	517	56	138	18	12	3	68	.267	48	189	108	25-37
1914	LF	CLE	AL	8-8	130	460	63	122	17	10	1	39	.265	67	162	122	9-41
1915	LF	CLE	AL	7-8	116	404	42	105	20	7	1	56	.260	59	142	117	11-42
1916	LF	CLE	AL	6-8	155	589	106	142	41	14	5	54	.241	102	226	130	7-38
1917	LF	CLE	AL	3-8	146	535	87	122	29	7	3	35	.228	94	174	118	14-40
1918	LF	CLE	AL	2-8	70	177	27	42	7	4	0	9	.237	28	57	113	—
1919	LF	CLE	AL	2-8	128	461	79	108	22	8	1	30	.234	105	149	117	17-49
1920	LF	CLE	AL	1-8	62	152	31	45	11	1	0	13	.296	27	58	119	—
1921	LF	CLE	AL	2-8	68	107	19	32	3	0	2	18	.299	20	41	115	—
1922	LF	CLE	AL	4-8	37	58	6	9	0	0	0	2	.155	9	9	—	—

| MAJOR LEAGUE TOTALS | | | | | 1402 | 4705 | 706 | 1178 | 219 | 79 | 18 | 420 | .250 | 712 | 1609 | 114 | 8 yrs |

Louis Richard Evans   Born Feb 17, 1885 Cleveland, OH
5'10 175 lbs Batted left   Died Dec 28, 1943 Cleveland, OH

YR	POS	TEAM	LG	FIN	G	AB	R	H	2B	3B	HR	RBI	AVG	BB	TB	OQ	RANK
1908	CF	NY	NL	2-8	2	2	0	1	0	0	0	0	.500	0	1	—	—
1909	RF	SL	NL	7-8	143	498	67	129	17	6	2	56	.259	66	164	117	18-39
1910	RF	SL	NL	7-8	151	506	73	122	21	8	2	73	.241	78	165	108	26-47
1911	RF	SL	NL	5-8	154	547	74	161	24	13	5	71	.294	46	226	114	22-45
1912	RF	SL	NL	6-8	135	491	59	139	23	9	6	72	.283	36	198	104	29-43
1913	RF	SL	NL	8-8	97	245	18	61	15	6	1	31	.249	20	91	101	—
1914	RF-1B	BRO	FL	5-8	145	514	93	179	41	15	12	96	.348	50	286	167	2-41
1915	RF	BR/BA	FL	7/8	151	556	94	171	34	10	4	67	.308	63	237	135	5-40

| MAJOR LEAGUE TOTALS | | | | | 978 | 3359 | 478 | 963 | 175 | 67 | 32 | 466 | .287 | 359 | 1368 | 124 | 6 yrs |

William Lawrence Gardner   Born May 13, 1886 Enosburg Falls, VT
5'8 165 lbs Batted left   Died Mar 11, 1976 St George, VT

YR	POS	TEAM	LG	FIN	G	AB	R	H	2B	3B	HR	RBI	AVG	BB	TB	OQ	RANK
1908	3B	BOS	AL	5-8	3	10	0	3	1	0	0	1	.300	0	4	—	—
1909	3B-SS	BOS	AL	3-8	19	37	7	11	1	2	0	5	.297	4	16	—	—
1910	2B	BOS	AL	4-8	113	413	55	117	12	10	2	36	.283	41	155	126	—
1911	3B-2B	BOS	AL	5-8	138	492	80	140	17	8	4	44	.285	64	185	116	21-44
1912	3B	BOS	AL	1-8	143	517	88	163	24	18	3	86	.315	56	232	136	7-33
1913	3B	BOS	AL	4-8	131	473	64	133	17	10	0	63	.281	47	170	111	20-37
1914	3B	BOS	AL	2-8	155	553	50	143	23	19	3	68	.259	35	213	109	20-41
1915	3B	BOS	AL	1-8	127	430	51	111	14	6	1	55	.258	39	140	98	33-42
1916	3B	BOS	AL	1-8	148	493	47	152	19	7	2	62	.308	48	191	125	9-38
1917	3B	BOS	AL	2-8	146	501	53	133	23	7	1	61	.265	54	173	112	20-40
1918	3B	PHI	AL	8-8	127	463	50	132	22	6	1	52	.285	43	169	114	13-39
1919	3B	CLE	AL	2-8	139	524	67	157	29	7	2	79	.300	39	206	109	25-49
1920	3B	CLE	AL	1-8	154	597	72	185	31	11	3	118	.310	53	247	109	23-49
1921	3B	CLE	AL	2-8	153	586	101	187	32	14	3	120	.319	65	256	114	19-49
1922	3B	CLE	AL	4-8	137	470	74	134	31	3	2	68	.285	49	177	99	36-50
1923	3B	CLE	AL	3-8	52	79	4	20	5	1	0	12	.253	12	27	—	—
1924	3B-2B	CLE	AL	6-8	38	50	3	10	0	0	0	4	.200	5	10	—	—

| MAJOR LEAGUE TOTALS | | | | | 1923 | 6688 | 866 | 1931 | 301 | 129 | 27 | 934 | .289 | 654 | 2571 | 113 | 12 yrs |

Clifford Carlton Cravath
5'10 186 lbs Batted right

Born Mar 23, 1881 Escondido, CA
Died May 23, 1963 Laguna Beach, CA

YR	POS	TEAM	LG	FIN	G	AB	R	H	2B	3B	HR	RBI	AVG	BB	TB	OQ	RANK
1908	LF	BOS	AL	5-8	94	277	43	71	10	11	1	34	.256	38	106	143	—
1909	CF	CH/WA	AL	4/8	23	56	7	9	0	0	1	9	.161	20	12	—	—
1912	RF	PHI	NL	5-8	130	436	63	124	30	9	11	70	.284	47	205	127	10-43
1913	RF	PHI	NL	2-8	147	525	78	179	34	14	19	128	.341	55	298	171	1-45
1914	RF	PHI	NL	6-8	149	499	76	149	27	8	19	100	.299	83	249	168	1-42
1915	RF	PHI	NL	1-8	150	522	89	149	31	7	24	115	.285	86	266	173	1-45
1916	RF	PHI	NL	2-8	137	448	70	127	21	8	11	70	.283	64	197	153	1-36
1917	RF	PHI	NL	2-8	140	503	70	141	29	16	12	83	.280	70	238	159	1-38
1918	RF	PHI	NL	6-8	121	426	43	99	27	5	8	54	.232	54	160	121	15-40
1919	RF	PHI	NL	8-8	83	214	34	73	18	5	12	45	.341	35	137	222	—
1920	LF	PHI	NL	8-8	46	45	2	13	5	0	1	11	.289	9	21	—	—
MAJOR LEAGUE TOTALS					1220	3951	575	1134	232	83	119	719	.287	561	1889	153	7 yrs

John Franklin Baker
5'11 173 lbs Batted left

Born Mar 13, 1886 Trappe, MD
Died Jun 28, 1963 Trappe, MD

YR	POS	TEAM	LG	FIN	G	AB	R	H	2B	3B	HR	RBI	AVG	BB	TB	OQ	RANK
1908	3B	PHI	AL	6-8	9	31	5	9	3	0	0	2	.290	0	12	—	—
1909	3B	PHI	AL	2-8	148	541	73	165	27	19	4	85	.305	26	242	141	7-33
1910	3B	PHI	AL	1-8	146	561	83	159	25	15	2	74	.283	34	220	121	15-36
1911	3B	PHI	AL	1-8	148	592	96	198	42	14	11	115	.334	40	301	141	7-44
1912	3B	PHI	AL	3-8	149	577	116	200	40	21	10	130	.347	50	312	160	4-33
1913	3B	PHI	AL	1-8	149	564	116	190	34	9	12	117	.337	63	278	158	5-37
1914	3B	PHI	AL	1-8	150	570	84	182	23	10	9	89	.319	53	252	141	5-41
1916	3B	NY	AL	4-8	100	360	46	97	23	2	10	52	.269	36	154	128	—
1917	3B	NY	AL	6-8	146	553	57	156	24	2	6	71	.282	48	202	114	19-40
1918	3B	NY	AL	4-8	126	504	65	154	24	5	6	62	.306	38	206	124	10-39
1919	3B	NY	AL	3-8	141	567	70	166	22	1	10	83	.293	44	220	107	26-49
1921	3B	NY	AL	1-8	94	330	46	97	16	2	9	71	.294	26	144	103	—
1922	3B	NY	AL	1-8	69	234	30	65	12	3	7	36	.278	15	104	103	—
MAJOR LEAGUE TOTALS					1575	5984	887	1838	315	103	96	987	.307	473	2647	134	9 yrs

Richard Carleton Hoblitzel   Born Oct 26, 1888   Waverly, WV
6'0   172 lbs Batted right   Died Nov 14, 1962 Parkersburg, WV

YR	POS	TEAM	LG	FIN	G	AB	R	H	2B	3B	HR	RBI	AVG	BB	TB	OQ	RANK
1908	1B	CIN	NL	5-8	32	114	8	29	3	2	0	8	.254	7	36	101	—
1909	1B	CIN	NL	4-8	142	517	59	159	23	11	4	67	.308	44	216	137	4-39
1910	1B	CIN	NL	5-8	155	611	85	170	24	13	4	70	.278	47	232	108	27-47
1911	1B	CIN	NL	6-8	158	622	81	180	19	13	11	91	.289	42	258	109	25-45
1912	1B	CIN	NL	4-8	148	558	73	164	32	12	2	85	.294	48	226	109	23-43
1913	1B	CIN	NL	7-8	137	502	59	143	23	7	3	62	.285	35	189	105	28-45
1914	1B	CIN	NL	8-8	78	248	31	52	8	7	0	26	.210	26	74	90	—
1914	1B	BOS	AL	2-8	69	229	31	73	10	3	0	33	.319	19	89	124	—
1915	1B	BOS	AL	1-8	124	399	54	113	15	12	2	61	.283	38	158	120	—
1916	1B	BOS	AL	1-8	130	417	57	108	17	1	0	39	.259	47	127	100	—
1917	1B	BOS	AL	2-8	120	420	49	108	19	7	1	47	.257	46	144	111	—
1918	1B	BOS	AL	1-8	25	69	4	11	1	0	0	4	.159	8	12	—	—

MAJOR LEAGUE TOTALS   1318 4706 591 1310 194 88 27 593 .278 407 1761 114   5 yrs

Charles Lincoln Herzog   Born Jul 9, 1885   Baltimore, MD
5'11   160 lbs Batted right   Died Sep 4, 1953   Baltimore, MD

YR	POS	TEAM	LG	FIN	G	AB	R	H	2B	3B	HR	RBI	AVG	BB	TB	OQ	RANK
1908	2B-SS	NY	NL	2-8	64	160	38	48	6	2	0	11	.300	36	58	167	—
1909	LF-3B	NY	NL	3-8	42	130	16	24	2	0	0	8	.185	13	26	69	—
1910	3B	BOS	NL	8-8	106	380	51	95	20	3	3	32	.250	30	130	96	—
1911	SS-3B	BO/NY	NL	8/1	148	541	90	157	33	9	6	67	.290	47	226	114	20-45
1912	3B	NY	NL	1-8	140	482	72	127	20	9	2	47	.263	57	171	101	30-43
1913	3B	NY	NL	1-8	96	290	46	83	15	3	3	31	.286	22	113	110	—
1914	SS	CIN	NL	8-8	138	498	54	140	14	8	1	40	.281	42	173	107	28-42
1915	SS	CIN	NL	7-8	155	579	61	153	14	10	1	42	.264	34	190	96	36-45
1916	SS-2B	CN/NY	NL	7/4	156	561	70	148	24	6	1	49	.264	43	187	105	25-36
1917	2B	NY	NL	1-8	114	417	69	98	10	8	2	31	.235	31	130	94	—
1918	2B-1B	BOS	NL	7-8	118	473	57	108	12	6	0	26	.228	29	132	82	38-40
1919	2B	BO/CH	NL	6/3	125	468	42	130	12	9	1	42	.278	23	163	100	27-41
1920	2B-3B	CHI	NL	5-8	91	305	39	59	9	2	0	19	.193	20	72	64	—

MAJOR LEAGUE TOTALS   1493 5284 705 1370 191 75 20 445 .259 427 1771 101   7 yrs

Joseph Jefferson Jackson   Born Jul 16, 1889 Pickens County, SC
6'1 200 lbs Batted left   Died Dec 5, 1951 Greenville, SC

YR	POS	TEAM	LG	FIN	G	AB	R	H	2B	3B	HR	RBI	AVG	BB	TB	OQ	RANK
1908	CF	PHI	AL	6-8	5	23	0	3	0	0	0	3	.130	0	3	—	—
1909	LF-CF	PHI	AL	2-8	5	17	3	3	0	0	0	3	.176	1	3	—	—
1910	CF	CLE	AL	5-8	20	75	15	29	2	5	1	11	.387	8	44	—	—
1911	RF	CLE	AL	3-8	147	571	126	233	45	19	7	83	.408	56	337	190	2-44
1912	RF	CLE	AL	5-8	154	572	121	226	44	26	3	90	.395	54	331	186	3-33
1913	RF	CLE	AL	3-8	148	528	109	197	39	17	7	71	.373	80	291	194	1-37
1914	RF	CLE	AL	8-8	122	453	61	153	22	13	3	53	.338	41	210	150	4-41
1915	RF-1B	CL/CH	AL	7/3	128	461	63	142	20	14	5	81	.308	52	205	141	5-42
1916	LF	CHI	AL	2-8	155	592	91	202	40	21	3	78	.341	46	293	154	3-38
1917	LF	CHI	AL	1-8	146	538	91	162	20	17	5	75	.301	57	231	139	5-40
1918	LF	CHI	AL	6-8	17	65	9	23	2	2	1	20	.354	8	32	—	—
1919	LF	CHI	AL	1-8	139	516	79	181	31	14	7	96	.351	60	261	156	3-49
1920	LF	CHI	AL	2-8	146	570	105	218	42	20	12	121	.382	56	336	167	4-49

| MAJOR LEAGUE TOTALS | | | | | 1332 | 4981 | 873 | 1772 | 307 | 168 | 54 | 785 | .356 | 519 | 2577 | 164 | 9 yrs |

Harry Bartholomew Hooper   Born Aug 24, 1887 Bell Station, CA
5'10 168 lbs Batted left   Died Dec 18, 1974 Santa Cruz, CA

YR	POS	TEAM	LG	FIN	G	AB	R	H	2B	3B	HR	RBI	AVG	BB	TB	OQ	RANK
1909	RF	BOS	AL	3-8	81	255	29	72	3	4	0	12	.282	16	83	107	—
1910	RF	BOS	AL	4-8	155	584	81	156	9	10	2	27	.267	62	191	113	19-36
1911	RF	BOS	AL	5-8	130	524	93	163	20	6	4	45	.311	73	207	127	12-44
1912	RF	BOS	AL	1-8	147	590	98	143	20	12	2	53	.242	66	193	97	27-33
1913	RF	BOS	AL	4-8	148	586	100	169	29	12	4	40	.288	60	234	122	11-37
1914	RF	BOS	AL	2-8	142	530	85	137	23	15	1	41	.258	58	193	115	14-41
1915	RF	BOS	AL	1-8	149	566	90	133	20	13	2	51	.235	89	185	111	22-42
1916	RF	BOS	AL	1-8	151	575	75	156	20	11	1	37	.271	80	201	119	14-38
1917	RF	BOS	AL	2-8	151	559	89	143	21	11	3	45	.256	80	195	120	12-40
1918	RF	BOS	AL	1-8	126	474	81	137	26	13	1	44	.289	75	192	141	4-39
1919	RF	BOS	AL	6-8	128	491	76	131	25	6	3	49	.267	79	177	116	20-49
1920	LF	BOS	AL	5-8	139	536	91	167	30	17	7	53	.312	88	252	138	7-49
1921	RF	CHI	AL	7-8	108	419	74	137	26	5	8	58	.327	55	197	126	12-49
1922	RF	CHI	AL	5-8	152	602	111	183	35	8	11	80	.304	68	267	117	14-50
1923	RF	CHI	AL	7-8	145	576	87	166	32	4	10	65	.288	68	236	110	24-46
1924	RF	CHI	AL	8-8	130	476	107	156	27	8	10	62	.328	65	229	132	7-40
1925	RF	CHI	AL	5-8	127	442	62	117	23	5	6	55	.265	54	168	95	36-42

| MAJOR LEAGUE TOTALS | | | | | 2309 | 8785 | 1429 | 2466 | 389 | 160 | 75 | 817 | .281 | 1136 | 3400 | 119 | 16 yrs |

John Barney Miller   Born Sep 9, 1886   Kearny, NJ
5'11 170 lbs Batted right   Died Sep 5, 1923   Saranac Lake, NY

YR	POS	TEAM	LG	FIN	G	AB	R	H	2B	3B	HR	RBI	AVG	BB	TB	OQ	RANK
1909	2B	PIT	NL	1-8	151	560	71	156	31	13	3	87	.279	39	222	122	13-39
1910	2B	PIT	NL	3-8	120	444	45	101	13	10	1	48	.227	33	137	84	44-47
1911	2B	PIT	NL	3-8	137	470	82	126	17	8	6	78	.268	51	177	107	27-45
1912	1B	PIT	NL	2-8	148	567	74	156	33	12	4	87	.275	37	225	100	32-43
1913	1B	PIT	NL	4-8	154	580	75	158	24	20	7	90	.272	37	243	112	23-45
1914	1B-SS	SL	NL	3-8	155	573	67	166	27	10	4	88	.290	34	225	113	18-42
1915	1B-2B	SL	NL	6-8	150	553	73	146	17	10	2	72	.264	43	189	104	29-45
1916	1B-2B	SL	NL	7-8	143	505	47	120	22	7	1	46	.238	40	159	97	31-36
1917	2B-1B	SL	NL	3-8	148	544	61	135	15	9	2	45	.248	33	174	95	34-38
1919	1B-2B	PHI	NL	8-8	101	346	38	80	10	4	1	24	.231	13	101	78	—
1920	2B-3B	PHI	NL	8-8	98	343	41	87	12	2	1	27	.254	16	106	81	—
1921	3B-1B	PHI	NL	8-8	84	320	37	95	11	3	0	23	.297	15	112	86	—
MAJOR LEAGUE TOTALS					1589	5805	711	1526	232	108	32	715	.263	391	2070	104	9 yrs

Zachary Davis Wheat   Born May 23, 1888 Hamilton, MO
5'10 170 lbs Batted left   Died Mar 11, 1972 Sedalia, MO

YR	POS	TEAM	LG	FIN	G	AB	R	H	2B	3B	HR	RBI	AVG	BB	TB	OQ	RANK
1909	LF	BRO	NL	6-8	26	102	15	31	7	3	0	4	.304	6	44	133	—
1910	LF	BRO	NL	6-8	156	606	78	172	36	15	2	55	.284	47	244	114	19-47
1911	LF	BRO	NL	7-8	140	534	55	153	26	13	5	76	.287	29	220	105	29-45
1912	LF	BRO	NL	7-8	123	453	70	138	28	7	8	65	.305	39	204	121	14-43
1913	LF	BRO	NL	6-8	138	535	64	161	28	10	7	58	.301	25	230	115	20-45
1914	LF	BRO	NL	5-8	145	533	66	170	26	9	9	89	.319	47	241	141	5-42
1915	LF	BRO	NL	3-8	146	528	64	136	15	12	5	66	.258	52	190	113	18-45
1916	LF	BRO	NL	1-8	149	568	76	177	32	13	9	73	.312	43	262	146	2-36
1917	LF	BRO	NL	7-8	109	362	38	113	15	11	1	41	.312	20	153	130	—
1918	LF	BRO	NL	5-8	105	409	39	137	15	3	0	51	.335	16	158	119	19-40
1919	LF	BRO	NL	5-8	137	536	70	159	23	11	5	62	.297	33	219	122	9-41
1920	LF	BRO	NL	1-8	148	583	89	191	26	13	9	73	.328	48	270	138	4-45
1921	LF	BRO	NL	5-8	148	568	91	182	31	10	14	85	.320	44	275	126	9-39
1922	LF	BRO	NL	6-8	152	600	92	201	29	12	16	112	.335	45	302	127	9-39
1923	LF	BRO	NL	6-8	98	349	63	131	13	5	8	65	.375	23	178	138	—
1924	LF	BRO	NL	2-8	141	566	92	212	41	8	14	97	.375	49	311	156	4-38
1925	LF	BRO	NL	6-8	150	616	125	221	42	14	14	103	.359	45	333	137	6-37
1926	LF	BRO	NL	6-8	111	411	68	119	31	2	5	35	.290	21	169	100	—
1927	LF	PHI	AL	2-8	88	247	34	80	12	1	1	38	.324	18	97	99	—
MAJOR LEAGUE TOTALS					2410	9106	1289	2884	476	172	132	1248	.317	650	4100	127	14 yrs

Arthur Fletcher　　　　　　　Born Jan 5, 1885　Collinsville, IL
5'10　170 lbs　Batted right　　　Died Feb 6, 1950　Los Angeles, CA

YR	POS	TEAM	LG	FIN	G	AB	R	H	2B	3B	HR	RBI	AVG	BB	TB	OQ	RANK
1909	SS-3B	NY	NL	3-8	33	98	7	21	0	1	0	6	.214	1	23	—	—
1910	SS-3B	NY	NL	2-8	51	125	12	28	2	1	0	13	.224	4	32	63	—
1911	SS-3B	NY	NL	1-8	112	326	73	104	17	8	1	37	.319	30	140	123	—
1912	SS	NY	NL	1-8	129	419	64	118	17	9	1	57	.282	16	156	89	—
1913	SS	NY	NL	1-8	136	538	76	160	20	9	4	71	.297	24	210	104	30-45
1914	SS	NY	NL	2-8	135	514	62	147	26	8	2	79	.286	22	195	105	30-42
1915	SS	NY	NL	8-8	149	562	59	143	17	7	3	74	.254	6	183	83	44-45
1916	SS	NY	NL	4-8	133	500	53	143	23	8	3	66	.286	13	191	107	23-36
1917	SS	NY	NL	1-8	151	557	70	145	24	5	4	56	.260	23	191	97	32-38
1918	SS	NY	NL	2-8	124	468	51	123	20	2	0	47	.263	18	147	89	34-40
1919	SS	NY	NL	2-8	127	488	54	135	20	5	3	54	.277	9	174	94	37-41
1920	SS	NY/PH	NL	2/8	143	550	57	156	32	9	4	62	.284	16	218	101	31-45
1922	SS	PHI	NL	7-8	110	396	46	111	20	5	7	53	.280	21	162	94	—
MAJOR LEAGUE TOTALS					1533	5541	684	1534	238	77	32	675	.277	203	2022	98	8 yrs

Henry Harrison Myers　　　　Born Apr 27, 1889　East Liverpool, OH
5'9　175 lbs　Batted right　　　Died May 1, 1965　Minerva, OH

YR	POS	TEAM	LG	FIN	G	AB	R	H	2B	3B	HR	RBI	AVG	BB	TB	OQ	RANK
1909	RF	BRO	NL	6-8	6	22	1	5	1	0	0	6	.227	2	6	—	—
1911	CF	BRO	NL	7-8	13	43	2	7	1	0	0	0	.163	2	8	—	—
1914	CF-RF	BRO	NL	5-8	70	227	35	65	3	9	0	17	.286	7	86	102	—
1915	CF	BRO	NL	3-8	153	605	69	150	21	7	2	46	.248	17	191	84	43-45
1916	CF	BRO	NL	1-8	113	412	54	108	12	14	3	36	.262	21	157	110	—
1917	CF-1B	BRO	NL	7-8	120	471	37	126	15	10	1	41	.268	18	164	99	30-38
1918	CF	BRO	NL	5-8	107	407	36	104	9	8	4	40	.256	20	141	98	29-40
1919	CF	BRO	NL	5-8	133	512	62	157	23	14	5	73	.307	23	223	126	7-41
1920	CF	BRO	NL	1-8	154	582	83	177	36	22	4	80	.304	35	269	128	8-45
1921	CF-2B	BRO	NL	5-8	144	549	51	158	14	4	4	68	.288	22	192	84	34-39
1922	CF	BRO	NL	6-8	153	618	82	196	20	9	6	89	.317	13	252	92	32-39
1923	CF	SL	NL	5-8	96	330	29	99	18	2	2	48	.300	12	127	90	—
1924	CF-3B	SL	NL	6-8	43	124	12	26	5	1	1	15	.210	3	36	61	—
1925	CF	SL/CN	NL	4/3	5	8	2	2	1	0	0	0	.250	0	3	—	—
MAJOR LEAGUE TOTALS					1310	4910	555	1380	179	100	32	559	.281	195	1855	102	7 yrs

Ennis Telfair Oakes   Born Dec 17, 1886   Homer, LA
5'8   170 lbs   Batted left   Died Feb 29, 1948   Rocky Springs, LA

YR	POS	TEAM	LG	FIN	G	AB	R	H	2B	3B	HR	RBI	AVG	BB	TB	OO	RANK
1909	CF	CIN	NL	4-8	120	415	55	112	10	5	3	31	.270	40	141	112	—
1910	CF	SL	NL	7-8	131	468	50	118	14	6	0	43	.252	38	144	89	42-47
1911	CF	SL	NL	5-8	154	551	69	145	13	6	2	59	.263	41	176	86	39-45
1912	CF	SL	NL	6-8	136	495	57	139	19	5	3	58	.281	31	177	92	39-43
1913	CF	SL	NL	8-8	147	539	60	158	14	5	0	49	.293	43	182	99	35-45
1914	CF	PIT	FL	7-8	145	571	82	178	18	10	7	75	.312	35	237	115	17-41
1915	CF	PIT	FL	3-8	153	580	55	161	24	5	0	82	.278	37	195	96	35-40
MAJOR LEAGUE TOTALS					986	3619	428	1011	112	42	15	397	.279	265	1252	96	6 yrs

James Philip Austin   Born Dec 8, 1879   Swansea, Wales
5'7   155 lbs   Batted both   Died Mar 6, 1965   Laguna Beach, CA

YR	POS	TEAM	LG	FIN	G	AB	R	H	2B	3B	HR	RBI	AVG	BB	TB	OO	RANK
1909	3B-SS	NY	AL	5-8	136	437	37	101	11	5	1	39	.231	32	125	92	29-33
1910	3B	NY	AL	2-8	133	432	46	94	11	4	2	36	.218	47	119	94	31-36
1911	3B	SL	AL	8-8	148	541	84	141	25	11	2	45	.261	69	194	108	27-44
1912	3B	SL	AL	7-8	149	536	57	135	14	8	2	44	.252	38	171	87	30-33
1913	3B	SL	AL	8-8	142	489	56	130	18	6	2	42	.266	45	166	102	28-37
1914	3B	SL	AL	5-8	130	466	55	111	16	4	0	30	.238	40	135	89	36-41
1915	3B	SL	AL	6-8	141	477	61	127	6	6	1	30	.266	64	148	106	26-42
1916	3B	SL	AL	5-8	129	411	55	85	15	6	1	28	.207	74	115	103	23-38
1917	3B	SL	AL	7-8	127	455	61	109	18	8	0	19	.240	50	143	101	28-40
1918	SS-3B	SL	AL	5-8	110	367	42	97	14	4	0	20	.264	53	119	114	16-39
1919	3B	SL	AL	5-8	106	396	54	94	9	9	1	21	.237	42	124	90	41-49
1920	3B	SL	AL	4-8	83	280	38	76	11	3	1	32	.271	31	96	93	—
1921	SS-2B	SL	AL	3-8	27	66	8	18	2	1	0	2	.273	4	22	—	—
1922	3B-2B	SL	AL	2-8	15	31	6	9	3	1	0	1	.290	3	14	—	—
1923	C	SL	AL	5-8	1	0	0	0	0	0	0	0	—	0	0	—	—
1925	3B	SL	AL	3-8	1	1	0	0	0	0	0	0	.000	0	0	—	—
1926	3B	SL	AL	7-8	1	2	1	1	1	0	0	1	.500	0	2	—	—
1929	3B	SL	AL	4-8	1	1	0	0	0	0	0	0	.000	0	0	—	—
MAJOR LEAGUE TOTALS					1580	5388	661	1328	174	76	13	390	.246	592	1693	99	11 yrs

Frederick William Luderus Born Sep 12, 1885 Milwaukee, WI
5'11 185 lbs Batted left   Died Jan 4, 1961 Milwaukee, WI

YR	POS	TEAM	LG	FIN	G	AB	R	H	2B	3B	HR	RBI	AVG	BB	TB	OQ	RANK
1909	1B	CHI	NL	2-8	11	37	8	11	1	1	1	9	.297	3	17	—	—
1910	1B	CH/PH	NL	1/4	45	122	15	31	6	3	0	17	.254	13	43	105	—
1911	1B	PHI	NL	4-8	146	551	69	166	24	11	16	99	.301	40	260	125	10-45
1912	1B	PHI	NL	5-8	148	572	77	147	31	5	10	69	.257	44	218	97	37-43
1913	1B	PHI	NL	2-8	155	588	67	154	32	7	18	86	.262	34	254	112	23-45
1914	1B	PHI	NL	6-8	121	443	55	110	16	5	12	55	.248	33	172	109	21-42
1915	1B	PHI	NL	1-8	141	499	55	157	36	7	7	62	.315	42	228	145	2-45
1916	1B	PHI	NL	2-8	146	508	52	143	26	3	5	53	.281	41	190	119	16-36
1917	1B	PHI	NL	2-8	154	522	57	136	24	4	5	72	.261	65	183	120	12-38
1918	1B	PHI	NL	6-8	125	468	54	135	23	2	5	67	.288	42	177	122	13-40
1919	1B	PHI	NL	8-8	138	509	60	149	30	6	5	49	.293	54	206	132	6-41
1920	1B	PHI	NL	8-8	16	32	1	5	2	0	0	4	.156	3	7	—	—

MAJOR LEAGUE TOTALS   1346 4851 570 1344 251 54 84 642 .277 414 1955 120 9 yrs

John Phalen McInnis Born Sep 19, 1890 Gloucester, MA
5'9 162 lbs Batted right   Died Feb 16, 1960 Ipswich, MA

YR	POS	TEAM	LG	FIN	G	AB	R	H	2B	3B	HR	RBI	AVG	BB	TB	OQ	RANK
1909	SS	PHI	AL	2-8	19	46	4	11	0	0	1	4	.239	2	14	—	—
1910	SS-2B	PHI	AL	1-8	38	73	10	22	2	4	0	12	.301	7	32	—	—
1911	1B-SS	PHI	AL	1-8	126	468	76	150	20	10	3	77	.321	25	199	115	22-44
1912	1B	PHI	AL	3-8	153	568	83	186	25	13	3	101	.327	49	246	129	9-33
1913	1B	PHI	AL	1-8	148	543	79	176	30	4	4	90	.324	45	226	128	8-37
1914	1B	PHI	AL	1-8	149	576	74	181	12	8	1	95	.314	19	212	105	25-41
1915	1B	PHI	AL	8-8	119	456	44	143	14	4	0	49	.314	14	165	100	31-42
1916	1B	PHI	AL	8-8	140	512	42	151	25	3	1	60	.295	25	185	103	22-38
1917	1B	PHI	AL	8-8	150	567	50	172	19	4	0	44	.303	33	199	107	26-40
1918	1B-3B	BOS	AL	1-8	117	423	40	115	11	5	0	56	.272	19	136	90	33-39
1919	1B	BOS	AL	6-8	120	440	32	134	12	5	1	58	.305	23	159	97	32-49
1920	1B	BOS	AL	5-8	148	559	50	166	21	3	2	71	.297	18	199	83	45-49
1921	1B	BOS	AL	5-8	152	584	72	179	31	10	0	76	.307	21	230	88	41-49
1922	1B	CLE	AL	4-8	142	537	58	164	28	7	1	78	.305	15	209	88	38-50
1923	1B	BOS	NL	7-8	154	607	70	191	23	9	2	95	.315	26	238	95	33-41
1924	1B	BOS	NL	8-8	146	581	57	169	23	7	1	59	.291	15	209	83	35-38
1925	1B	PIT	NL	1-8	59	155	19	57	10	4	0	24	.368	17	75	134	—
1926	1B	PIT	NL	3-8	47	127	12	38	6	1	0	13	.299	7	46	92	—
1927	1B	PHI	NL	8-8	1	0	0	0	0	0	0	0	—	0	0	—	—

MAJOR LEAGUE TOTALS   2128 7822 872 2405 312 101 20 1062 .307 380 2979 101 14 yrs

Burton Edwin Shotton
5'11 175 lbs Batted left

Born Oct 18, 1884 Brownhelm, OH
Died Jul 29, 1962 Lake Wales, FL

YR	POS	TEAM	LG	FIN	G	AB	R	H	2B	3B	HR	RBI	AVG	BB	TB	OO	RANK
1909	CF	SL	AL	7-8	17	61	5	16	0	1	0	0	.262	5	18	—	—
1911	CF	SL	AL	8-8	139	572	84	146	11	8	0	36	.255	51	173	86	39-44
1912	CF	SL	AL	7-8	154	580	87	168	15	8	2	40	.290	86	205	118	12-33
1913	CF	SL	AL	8-8	147	549	105	163	23	8	1	28	.297	99	205	137	7-37
1914	CF	SL	AL	5-8	154	579	82	156	19	9	0	38	.269	64	193	109	19-41
1915	LF	SL	AL	6-8	156	559	93	158	18	11	1	30	.283	118	201	139	7-42
1916	LF	SL	AL	5-8	157	618	97	174	23	6	1	36	.282	111	212	129	8-38
1917	LF	SL	AL	7-8	118	398	47	89	9	1	1	20	.224	62	103	97	—
1918	LF	WAS	AL	3-8	126	505	68	132	16	7	0	21	.261	67	162	110	17-39
1919	LF	SL	NL	7-8	85	270	35	77	13	5	1	20	.285	22	103	118	—
1920	LF	SL	NL	6-8	62	180	28	41	5	0	1	12	.228	18	49	82	—
1921	CF	SL	NL	3-8	38	48	9	12	1	1	1	7	.250	7	18	—	—
1922	CF	SL	NL	3-8	34	30	5	6	1	0	0	2	.200	4	7	—	—
1923	PR	SL	NL	5-8	1	0	1	0	0	0	0	0	—	0	0	—	—
MAJOR LEAGUE TOTALS					1388	4949	746	1338	154	65	9	290	.270	714	1649	118	7 yrs

Jacob Ellsworth Daubert
5'10 160 lbs Batted left

Born Apr 7, 1884 Shamokin, PA
Died Oct 9, 1924 Cincinnati, OH

YR	POS	TEAM	LG	FIN	G	AB	R	H	2B	3B	HR	RBI	AVG	BB	TB	OO	RANK
1910	1B	BRO	NL	6-8	144	552	67	146	15	15	8	50	.264	47	215	110	24-47
1911	1B	BRO	NL	7-8	149	573	89	176	17	8	5	45	.307	51	224	112	24-45
1912	1B	BRO	NL	7-8	145	559	81	172	19	16	3	66	.308	48	232	113	18-43
1913	1B	BRO	NL	6-8	139	508	76	178	17	7	2	52	.350	44	215	132	8-45
1914	1B	BRO	NL	5-8	126	474	89	156	17	7	6	45	.329	30	205	131	9-42
1915	1B	BRO	NL	3-8	150	544	62	164	21	8	2	47	.301	57	207	127	8-45
1916	1B	BRO	NL	1-8	127	478	75	151	16	7	3	33	.316	38	190	131	8 36
1917	1B	BRO	NL	7-8	125	468	59	122	4	4	2	30	.261	51	140	103	29-38
1918	1B	BRO	NL	5-8	108	396	50	122	12	15	2	47	.308	27	170	133	5-40
1919	1B	CIN	NL	1-8	140	537	79	148	10	12	2	44	.276	35	188	104	21-41
1920	1B	CIN	NL	3-8	142	553	97	168	28	13	4	48	.304	47	234	125	12-45
1921	1B	CIN	NL	6-8	136	516	69	158	18	12	2	64	.306	24	206	98	29-39
1922	1B	CIN	NL	2-8	156	610	114	205	15	22	12	66	.336	56	300	128	6-39
1923	1B	CIN	NL	2-8	125	500	63	146	27	10	2	54	.292	40	199	101	28-41
1924	1B	CIN	NL	4-8	102	405	47	114	14	9	1	31	.281	28	149	93	—
MAJOR LEAGUE TOTALS					2014	7673	1117	2326	250	165	56	722	.303	623	3074	118	14 yrs

Arnold Gandil
6'1 190 lbs Batted right

Born Jan 19, 1887 St Paul, MN
Died Dec 13, 1970 Calistoga, CA

YR	POS	TEAM	LG	FIN	G	AB	R	H	2B	3B	HR	RBI	AVG	BB	TB	OQ	RANK
1910	1B	CHI	AL	6-8	77	275	21	53	7	3	2	21	.193	24	72	82	—
1912	1B	WAS	AL	2-8	117	443	59	135	20	15	2	81	.305	27	191	118	11-33
1913	1B	WAS	AL	2-8	148	550	61	175	25	8	1	72	.318	36	219	118	16-37
1914	1B	WAS	AL	3-8	145	526	48	136	24	10	3	75	.259	44	189	107	22-41
1915	1B	WAS	AL	4-8	136	485	53	141	20	15	2	64	.291	29	197	115	13-42
1916	1B	CLE	AL	6-8	146	533	51	138	26	9	0	72	.259	36	182	98	29-38
1917	1B	CHI	AL	1-8	149	553	53	151	9	7	0	57	.273	30	174	92	36-40
1918	1B	CHI	AL	6-8	114	439	49	119	18	4	0	55	.271	27	145	96	30-39
1919	1B	CHI	AL	1-8	115	441	54	128	24	7	1	60	.290	20	169	99	30-49
MAJOR LEAGUE TOTALS					1147	4245	449	1176	173	78	11	557	.277	273	1538	105	8 yrs

Max George Carey
5'11 170 lbs Batted both

Born Jan 11, 1890 Terre Haute, IN
Died May 30, 1976 Miami, FL

YR	POS	TEAM	LG	FIN	G	AB	R	H	2B	3B	HR	RBI	AVG	BB	TB	OQ	RANK
1910	LF	PIT	NL	3-8	2	6	2	3	0	1	0	2	.500	2	5	—	—
1911	CF	PIT	NL	3-8	129	427	77	110	15	10	5	43	.258	44	160	104	33-45
1912	LF	PIT	NL	2-8	150	587	114	177	23	8	5	66	.302	61	231	112	20-43
1913	LF	PIT	NL	4-8	154	620	99	172	23	10	5	49	.277	55	230	107	26-45
1914	LF	PIT	NL	7-8	156	593	76	144	25	17	1	31	.243	59	206	105	31-42
1915	LF	PIT	NL	5-8	140	564	76	143	26	5	3	27	.254	57	188	107	26-45
1916	CF	PIT	NL	6-8	154	599	90	158	23	11	7	42	.264	59	224	120	14-36
1917	CF	PIT	NL	8-8	155	588	82	174	21	12	1	51	.296	58	222	126	9-38
1918	CF	PIT	NL	4-8	126	468	70	128	14	6	3	48	.274	62	163	123	12-40
1919	CF	PIT	NL	4-8	66	244	41	75	10	2	0	9	.307	25	89	123	—
1920	CF	PIT	NL	4-8	130	485	74	140	18	4	1	35	.289	59	169	113	18-45
1921	CF	PIT	NL	2-8	140	521	85	161	34	4	7	56	.309	70	224	125	10-39
1922	CF	PIT	NL	3-8	155	629	140	207	28	12	10	70	.329	80	289	128	7-39
1923	CF	PIT	NL	3-8	153	610	120	188	32	19	6	63	.308	73	276	124	10-41
1924	CF	PIT	NL	3-8	149	599	113	178	30	9	7	55	.297	58	247	111	16-38
1925	CF	PIT	NL	1-8	133	542	109	186	39	13	5	44	.343	66	266	133	8-37
1926	CF	PT/BR	NL	3/6	113	424	64	98	17	6	0	35	.231	38	127	78	—
1927	RF	BRO	NL	6-8	144	538	70	143	30	10	1	54	.266	64	196	101	24-40
1928	CF	BRO	NL	6-8	108	296	41	73	11	0	2	19	.247	47	90	91	—
1929	CF	BRO	NL	6-8	19	23	2	7	0	0	0	1	.304	3	7	—	—
MAJOR LEAGUE TOTALS					2476	9363	1545	2665	419	159	69	800	.285	1040	3609	116	15 yrs

Edward Cunningham Foster   Born Feb 13, 1887   Chicago, IL
5'6   145 lbs   Batted right   Died Jan 15, 1937   Washington, DC

YR	POS	TEAM	LG	FIN	G	AB	R	H	2B	3B	HR	RBI	AVG	BB	TB	OQ	RANK
1910	SS	NY	AL	2-8	30	83	5	11	2	0	0	1	.133	8	13	—	—
1912	3B	WAS	AL	2-8	154	618	98	176	34	9	2	70	.285	53	234	108	22-33
1913	3B	WAS	AL	2-8	106	409	56	101	11	5	1	41	.247	36	125	91	—
1914	3B	WAS	AL	3-8	157	616	82	174	16	10	2	50	.282	60	216	112	16-41
1915	3B-2B	WAS	AL	4-8	154	618	75	170	25	10	0	52	.275	48	215	103	28-42
1916	3B-2B	WAS	AL	7-8	158	606	75	153	18	9	1	44	.252	68	192	102	26-38
1917	3B-2B	WAS	AL	5-8	143	554	66	130	16	8	0	43	.235	46	162	89	37-40
1918	3B	WAS	AL	3-8	129	519	70	147	13	3	0	29	.283	41	166	99	26-39
1919	3B	WAS	AL	7-8	120	478	57	126	12	5	0	26	.264	33	148	84	43-49
1920	3B-2B	BOS	AL	5-8	117	386	48	100	17	6	0	41	.259	42	129	90	—
1921	3B-2B	BOS	AL	5-8	120	412	51	117	18	6	0	35	.284	57	147	98	34-49
1922	3B	BO/SL	AL	8/2	85	253	40	67	7	0	0	15	.265	29	74	81	—
1923	2B-3B	SL	AL	5-8	27	100	9	18	2	0	0	4	.180	7	20	49	—
MAJOR LEAGUE TOTALS					1500	5652	732	1490	191	71	6	451	.264	528	1841	99	8 yrs

John Francis Collins   Born Dec 4, 1885   Charlestown, MA
6'0   185 lbs   Batted right   Died Sep 10, 1955   Newton, MA

YR	POS	TEAM	LG	FIN	G	AB	R	H	2B	3B	HR	RBI	AVG	BB	TB	OQ	RANK
1910	RF-1B	CHI	AL	6-8	97	315	29	62	10	8	1	24	.197	25	91	87	—
1911	1B	CHI	AL	4-8	106	370	48	97	16	12	4	48	.262	20	149	101	—
1912	RF-1B	CHI	AL	4-8	153	579	75	168	34	10	2	81	.290	29	228	104	25-33
1913	RF	CHI	AL	5-8	148	535	53	128	26	9	1	47	.239	32	175	88	36-37
1914	RF	CHI	AL	6-8	154	598	61	164	34	9	3	65	.274	27	225	104	27-41
1915	LF-1B	CHI	AL	3-8	153	576	73	148	24	17	2	85	.257	28	212	98	34-42
1916	RF	CHI	AL	2-8	143	527	74	128	28	12	0	42	.243	59	180	106	20-38
1917	RF	CHI	AL	1-8	82	252	38	59	13	3	1	14	.234	10	81	86	—
1918	CF	CHI	AL	6-8	103	365	30	100	18	11	1	56	.274	17	143	108	20-39
1919	RF-1B	CHI	AL	1-8	63	179	21	50	6	3	1	16	.279	7	65	91	—
1920	1B	CHI	AL	2-8	133	495	70	150	21	10	1	63	.303	23	194	94	36-49
1921	RF	BOS	AL	5-8	141	542	63	155	29	12	4	69	.286	18	220	87	42-49
1922	RF	BOS	AL	8-8	135	472	33	128	24	7	1	52	.271	7	169	75	48-50
1923	RF	BOS	AL	8-8	97	342	41	79	10	5	0	18	.231	11	99	62	—
1924	RF-1B	BOS	AL	7-8	89	240	37	70	17	5	0	28	.292	18	97	97	—
1925	CF	BOS	AL	8-8	2	3	1	1	0	0	0	1	.333	0	1	—	—
MAJOR LEAGUE TOTALS					1799	6390	747	1687	310	133	22	709	.264	331	2329	96	9 yrs

George Edward Lewis Born Apr 18, 1888 San Francisco, CA
5'10 165 lbs Batted left Died Jun 17, 1979 Salem, NH

YR	POS	TEAM	LG	FIN	G	AB	R	H	2B	3B	HR	RBI	AVG	BB	TB	OO	RANK
1910	LF	BOS	AL	4-8	151	541	64	153	29	7	8	68	.283	32	220	124	12-36
1911	LF	BOS	AL	5-8	130	469	64	144	32	4	7	86	.307	25	205	116	20-44
1912	LF	BOS	AL	1-8	154	581	85	165	36	9	6	109	.284	52	237	116	17-33
1913	LF	BOS	AL	4-8	149	551	54	164	31	12	0	90	.298	30	219	111	19-37
1914	LF	BOS	AL	2-8	146	510	53	142	37	9	2	79	.278	57	203	127	7-41
1915	LF	BOS	AL	1-8	152	557	69	162	31	7	2	76	.291	45	213	114	15-42
1916	LF	BOS	AL	1-8	152	563	56	151	29	5	1	56	.268	33	193	98	30-38
1917	LF	BOS	AL	2-8	150	553	55	167	29	9	1	65	.302	29	217	116	18-40
1919	LF	NY	AL	3-8	141	559	67	152	23	4	7	89	.272	17	204	89	42-49
1920	LF	NY	AL	3-8	107	365	34	99	8	1	4	61	.271	24	121	82	—
1921	LF	WAS	AL	4-8	27	102	11	19	4	1	0	14	.186	8	25	56	—

| MAJOR LEAGUE TOTALS | | | | | 1459 | 5351 | 612 | 1518 | 289 | 68 | 38 | 793 | .284 | 352 | 2057 | 112 | 9 yrs |

Roger Thorpe Peckinpaugh Born Feb 5, 1891 Wooster, OH
5'10 165 lbs Batted right Died Nov 17, 1977 Cleveland, OH

YR	POS	TEAM	LG	FIN	G	AB	R	H	2B	3B	HR	RBI	AVG	BB	TB	OO	RANK
1910	SS	CLE	AL	5-8	15	45	1	9	0	0	0	6	.200	1	9	—	—
1912	SS	CLE	AL	5-8	70	236	18	50	4	1	1	22	.212	16	59	67	—
1913	SS	CL/NY	AL	3/7	96	340	36	91	10	7	1	32	.268	24	118	99	—
1914	SS	NY	AL	6-8	157	570	55	127	14	6	3	51	.223	51	162	86	39-41
1915	SS	NY	AL	5-8	142	540	67	119	18	7	5	44	.220	49	166	89	38-42
1916	SS	NY	AL	4-8	145	552	65	141	22	8	4	58	.255	62	191	109	17-38
1917	SS	NY	AL	6-8	148	543	63	141	24	7	0	41	.260	64	179	110	23-40
1918	SS	NY	AL	4-8	122	446	59	103	15	3	0	43	.231	43	124	87	35-39
1919	SS	NY	AL	3-8	122	453	89	138	20	2	7	33	.305	59	183	125	11-49
1920	SS	NY	AL	3-8	139	534	109	144	26	6	8	54	.270	72	206	107	25-49
1921	SS	NY	AL	1-8	149	577	128	166	25	7	8	71	.288	84	229	108	24-49
1922	SS	WAS	AL	6-8	147	520	62	132	14	4	2	48	.254	55	160	81	44-50
1923	SS	WAS	AL	4-8	154	568	73	150	18	4	2	62	.264	64	182	87	42-46
1924	SS	WAS	AL	1-8	155	523	72	142	20	5	2	73	.272	72	178	94	31-40
1925	SS	WAS	AL	1-8	126	422	67	124	16	4	4	64	.294	49	160	98	33-42
1926	SS	WAS	AL	4-8	57	147	19	35	4	1	1	14	.238	28	44	94	—
1927	SS	CHI	AL	5-8	68	217	23	64	6	3	0	23	.295	21	76	91	—

| MAJOR LEAGUE TOTALS | | | | | 2012 | 7233 | 1006 | 1876 | 256 | 75 | 48 | 739 | .259 | 814 | 2426 | 98 | 12 yrs |

Leo Christopher Magee   Born Jun 4, 1889   Cincinnati, OH
5'11   165 lbs   Batted both   Died Mar 14, 1966   Columbus, OH

YR	POS	TEAM	LG	FIN	G	AB	R	H	2B	3B	HR	RBI	AVG	BB	TB	OQ	RANK
1911	2B-SS	SL	NL	5-8	26	69	9	18	1	1	0	8	.261	8	21	—	—
1912	LF-2B	SL	NL	6-8	128	458	60	133	13	8	0	40	.290	39	162	97	36-43
1913	LF-2B	SL	NL	8-8	137	531	54	142	13	7	2	31	.267	34	175	90	42-45
1914	CF-1B	SL	NL	3-8	142	529	59	150	23	4	2	40	.284	42	187	107	27-42
1915	2B	BRO	FL	7-8	121	452	87	146	19	10	4	49	.323	22	197	124	13-40
1916	CF	NY	AL	4-8	131	510	57	131	18	4	3	45	.257	50	166	101	27-38
1917	CF-3B	NY/SL	AL	6/7	87	285	28	57	5	1	0	12	.200	19	64	66	—
1918	2B	CIN	NL	3-8	119	459	61	133	22	13	0	28	.290	28	181	119	18-40
1919	CF-2B	BR/CH	NL	5/3	124	448	52	121	19	6	1	24	.270	23	155	99	28-41
MAJOR LEAGUE TOTALS					1015	3741	467	1031	133	54	12	277	.276	265	1308	105	7 yrs

James Harle Johnston   Born Dec 10, 1889   Cleveland, TN
5'10   160 lbs   Batted right   Died Feb 14, 1967   Chattanooga, TN

YR	POS	TEAM	LG	FIN	G	AB	R	H	2B	3B	HR	RBI	AVG	BB	TB	OQ	RANK
1911	CF	CHI	AL	4-8	1	2	0	0	0	0	0	2	.000	0	0	—	—
1914	CF	CHI	NL	4-8	50	101	9	23	3	2	1	8	.228	4	33	84	—
1916	RF	BRO	NL	1-8	118	425	58	107	13	8	1	26	.252	35	139	103	—
1917	LF-1B	BRO	NL	7-8	103	330	33	89	10	4	0	25	.270	23	107	101	—
1918	RF-1B	BRO	NL	5-8	123	484	54	136	16	8	0	27	.281	33	168	107	25-40
1919	2B-CF	BRO	NL	5-8	117	405	56	114	11	4	1	23	.281	29	136	103	24-41
1920	3B	BRO	NL	1-8	155	635	87	185	17	12	1	52	.291	43	229	103	30-45
1921	3B	BRO	NL	5-8	152	624	104	203	41	14	5	56	.325	45	287	120	15-39
1922	2B-SS	BRO	NL	6-8	138	567	110	181	20	7	4	49	.319	38	227	100	24-39
1923	2B-SS	BRO	NL	6-8	151	625	111	203	29	11	4	60	.325	53	266	114	19-41
1924	SS-3B	BRO	NL	2-8	86	315	51	94	11	2	2	29	.298	27	115	99	—
1925	3B-RF	BRO	NL	6-8	123	431	63	128	13	3	2	43	.297	45	153	93	33-37
1926	CF-3B	BO/NY	NL	7/5	60	126	18	30	1	0	1	10	.238	16	34	80	—
MAJOR LEAGUE TOTALS					1377	5070	754	1493	185	75	22	410	.294	391	1894	106	7 yrs

Clarence William Walker Born Sep 4, 1887 Telford, TN
5'11 165 lbs Batted right Died Sep 20, 1959 Chattanooga, TN

YR	POS	TEAM	LG	FIN	G	AB	R	H	2B	3B	HR	RBI	AVG	BB	TB	OQ	RANK
1911	LF	WAS	AL	7-8	95	356	44	99	6	4	2	39	.278	15	119	85	—
1912	LF	WAS	AL	2-8	39	110	22	30	2	1	0	9	.273	8	34	88	—
1913	LF	SL	AL	8-8	23	85	7	25	4	1	0	11	.294	2	31	—	—
1914	LF	SL	AL	5-8	151	517	67	154	24	16	6	78	.298	51	228	138	6-41
1915	CF	SL	AL	6-8	144	510	53	137	20	7	5	49	.269	36	186	104	27-42
1916	CF	BOS	AL	1-8	128	467	68	124	29	11	3	46	.266	23	184	107	18-38
1917	CF	BOS	AL	2-8	106	337	41	83	18	7	2	37	.246	25	121	104	—
1918	CF	PHI	AL	8-8	114	414	56	122	20	0	11	48	.295	41	175	132	8-39
1919	CF	PHI	AL	8-8	125	456	47	133	30	6	10	64	.292	26	205	117	19-49
1920	LF	PHI	AL	8-8	149	585	79	157	23	7	17	82	.268	41	245	100	32-49
1921	LF	PHI	AL	8-8	142	556	89	169	32	5	23	101	.304	73	280	129	9-49
1922	LF	PHI	AL	7-8	153	565	111	160	31	4	37	99	.283	61	310	134	7-50
1923	LF	PHI	AL	6-8	52	109	12	30	5	2	2	16	.275	14	45	111	—
MAJOR LEAGUE TOTALS					1421	5067	696	1423	244	71	118	679	.281	416	2163	120	8 yrs

Ivan Massie Olson Born Oct 14, 1885 Kansas City, MO
5'10 175 lbs Batted right Died Sep 1, 1965 Inglewood, CA

YR	POS	TEAM	LG	FIN	G	AB	R	H	2B	3B	HR	RBI	AVG	BB	TB	OQ	RANK
1911	SS	CLE	AL	3-8	140	545	89	142	20	8	1	50	.261	34	181	87	36-44
1912	SS-3B	CLE	AL	5-8	125	467	68	118	13	1	0	33	.253	21	133	74	32-33
1913	3B-1B	CLE	AL	3-8	104	370	47	92	13	3	0	32	.249	22	111	83	—
1914	SS-2B	CLE	AL	8-8	89	310	22	75	6	2	1	20	.242	13	88	77	—
1915	2B-3B	CN/BR	NL	7/3	81	233	20	50	5	5	0	17	.215	13	65	78	—
1916	SS	BRO	NL	1-8	108	351	29	89	13	4	1	38	.254	21	113	96	—
1917	SS	BRO	NL	7-8	139	580	64	156	18	5	2	38	.269	14	190	90	37-38
1918	SS	BRO	NL	5-8	126	506	63	121	16	4	1	17	.239	27	148	84	36-40
1919	SS	BRO	NL	5-8	140	590	73	164	14	9	1	38	.278	30	199	98	34-41
1920	SS-2B	BRO	NL	1-8	143	637	71	162	13	11	1	46	.254	20	200	79	43-45
1921	SS-2B	BRO	NL	5-8	151	652	88	174	22	10	3	35	.267	28	225	81	36-39
1922	2B-SS	BRO	NL	6-8	136	551	63	150	26	6	1	47	.272	25	191	79	37-39
1923	2B	BRO	NL	6-8	82	292	33	76	11	1	1	35	.260	14	92	74	—
1924	SS-2B	BRO	NL	2-8	10	27	0	6	1	0	0	0	.222	3	7	—	—
MAJOR LEAGUE TOTALS					1574	6111	730	1575	191	69	13	446	.258	285	1943	84	8 yrs

James Carlisle Smith   Born Apr 6, 1890   Greenville, SC
5'11   165 lbs   Batted right   Died Oct 11, 1966   Atlanta, GA

YR	POS	TEAM	LG	FIN	G	AB	R	H	2B	3B	HR	RBI	AVG	BB	TB	OQ	RANK
1911	3B	BRO	NL	7-8	28	111	10	29	6	1	0	19	.261	5	37	82	—
1912	3B	BRO	NL	7-8	128	486	75	139	28	6	4	57	.286	54	191	111	21-43
1913	3B	BRO	NL	6-8	151	540	70	160	40	10	6	76	.296	45	238	125	11-45
1914	3B	BR/BO	NL	5/1	150	537	69	146	27	9	7	85	.272	58	212	123	14-42
1915	3B	BOS	NL	2-8	157	549	66	145	34	4	2	65	.264	67	193	118	15-45
1916	3B	BOS	NL	3-8	150	509	48	132	16	10	3	60	.259	53	177	114	17-36
1917	3B	BOS	NL	6-8	147	505	60	149	31	6	2	62	.295	53	198	132	7-38
1918	3B	BOS	NL	7-8	119	429	55	128	20	3	2	65	.298	45	160	126	8-40
1919	CF-3B	BOS	NL	6-8	87	241	24	59	6	0	1	25	.245	40	68	108	—
MAJOR LEAGUE TOTALS					1117	3907	477	1087	208	49	27	514	.278	420	1474	121	7 yrs

Stephen Francis O'Neill   Born Jul 6, 1891   Minooka, PA
5'10   165 lbs   Batted right   Died Jan 26, 1962   Cleveland, OH

YR	POS	TEAM	LG	FIN	G	AB	R	H	2B	3B	HR	RBI	AVG	BB	TB	OQ	RANK
1911	C	CLE	AL	3-8	9	27	1	4	1	0	0	1	.148	4	5	—	—
1912	C	CLE	AL	5-8	69	215	17	49	4	0	0	14	.228	12	53	65	—
1913	C	CLE	AL	3-8	80	234	19	69	13	3	0	29	.295	10	88	103	—
1914	C	CLE	AL	8-8	87	269	28	68	12	2	0	20	.253	15	84	89	—
1915	C	CLE	AL	7-8	121	386	32	91	14	2	2	34	.236	26	115	84	—
1916	C	CLE	AL	6-8	130	378	30	89	23	0	0	29	.235	24	112	84	—
1917	C	CLE	AL	3-8	129	370	21	68	10	2	0	29	.184	41	82	74	—
1918	C	CLE	AL	2-8	114	359	34	87	8	7	1	35	.242	48	112	105	23-39
1919	C	CLE	AL	2-8	125	398	46	115	35	7	2	47	.289	48	170	126	10-49
1920	C	CLE	AL	1-8	149	489	63	157	39	5	3	55	.321	69	215	128	12-49
1921	C	CLE	AL	2-8	106	335	39	108	22	1	1	50	.322	57	135	119	—
1922	C	CLE	AL	4-8	133	392	33	122	27	4	2	65	.311	73	163	128	10-50
1923	C	CLE	AL	3-8	113	330	31	82	12	0	0	50	.248	64	94	94	—
1924	C	BOS	AL	7-8	106	307	29	73	15	1	0	38	.238	63	90	94	—
1925	C	NY	AL	7-8	35	91	7	26	5	0	1	13	.286	10	34	94	—
1927	C	SL	AL	7-8	74	191	14	44	7	0	1	22	.230	20	54	73	—
1928	C	SL	AL	3-8	10	24	4	7	1	0	0	6	.292	8	8	—	—
MAJOR LEAGUE TOTALS					1590	4795	448	1259	248	34	13	537	.263	592	1614	—	—

Victor Sylvester Saier Born May 4, 1891 Lansing, MI
5'11 185 lbs Batted left Died May 14, 1967 East Lansing, MI

YR	POS	TEAM	LG	FIN	G	AB	R	H	2B	3B	HR	RBI	AVG	BB	TB	OO	RANK
1911	1B	CHI	NL	2-8	86	259	42	67	15	1	1	37	.259	25	87	94	—
1912	1B	CHI	NL	3-8	122	451	74	130	25	14	2	61	.288	34	189	109	24-43
1913	1B	CHI	NL	3-8	149	519	94	150	15	21	14	92	.289	62	249	142	3-45
1914	1B	CHI	NL	4-8	153	537	87	129	24	8	18	72	.240	94	223	138	6-42
1915	1B	CHI	NL	4-8	144	497	74	131	35	11	11	64	.264	64	221	143	3-45
1916	1B	CHI	NL	5-8	147	498	60	126	25	3	7	50	.253	79	178	130	10-36
1917	1B	CHI	NL	5-8	6	21	5	5	1	0	0	2	.238	2	6	—	—
1919	1B	PIT	NL	4-8	58	166	19	37	3	3	2	17	.223	18	52	99	—
MAJOR LEAGUE TOTALS					865	2948	455	775	143	61	55	395	.263	378	1205	132	5 yrs

Henry Levai Severeid Born Jun 1, 1891 Story City, IA
6'0 175 lbs Batted right Died Dec 17, 1968 San Antonio, TX

YR	POS	TEAM	LG	FIN	G	AB	R	H	2B	3B	HR	RBI	AVG	BB	TB	OO	RANK
1911	C	CIN	NL	6-8	37	56	5	17	6	1	0	10	.304	3	25	—	—
1912	C-1B	CIN	NL	4-8	50	114	10	27	0	3	0	13	.237	8	33	74	—
1913	C-LF	CIN	NL	7-8	8	6	0	0	0	0	0	0	.000	1	0	—	—
1915	C	SL	AL	6-8	80	203	12	45	6	1	1	22	.222	16	56	80	—
1916	C	SL	AL	5-8	100	293	23	80	8	2	0	34	.273	26	92	98	—
1917	C	SL	AL	7-8	143	501	45	133	23	4	1	57	.265	28	167	96	32-40
1918	C	SL	AL	5-8	51	133	8	34	4	0	0	11	.256	18	38	101	—
1919	C	SL	AL	5-8	112	351	16	87	12	2	0	36	.248	21	103	77	—
1920	C	SL	AL	4-8	123	422	46	117	14	5	2	49	.277	33	147	88	—
1921	C	SL	AL	3-8	143	472	66	153	23	7	2	78	.324	42	196	105	27-49
1922	C	SL	AL	2-8	137	517	49	166	32	7	3	78	.321	28	221	104	31-50
1923	C	SL	AL	5-8	122	432	50	133	27	6	3	51	.308	31	181	105	30-46
1924	C	SL	AL	4-8	137	432	37	133	23	2	4	48	.308	36	172	100	28-40
1925	C	SL/WA	AL	3/1	84	219	26	79	17	1	1	35	.361	24	101	125	—
1926	C	WA/NY	AL	4/1	63	161	15	41	9	1	0	17	.255	16	52	83	—
MAJOR LEAGUE TOTALS					1390	4312	408	1245	204	42	17	539	.289	331	1584	102	5 yrs

Frank Stephan Bodie   Born Oct 8, 1887   San Francisco, CA
5'8   195 lbs   Batted right   Died Dec 17, 1961   San Francisco, CA

YR	POS	TEAM	LG	FIN	G	AB	R	H	2B	3B	HR	RBI	AVG	BB	TB	OQ	RANK
1911	CF-2B	CHI	AL	4-8	145	551	75	159	27	13	4	97	.289	49	224	114	23-44
1912	CF	CHI	AL	4-8	138	472	58	139	24	7	5	72	.294	43	192	118	13-33
1913	CF	CHI	AL	5-8	127	406	39	107	14	8	8	48	.264	35	161	114	—
1914	CF	CHI	AL	6-8	107	327	21	75	9	5	3	29	.229	21	103	88	—
1917	LF	PHI	AL	8-8	148	557	51	162	28	11	7	74	.291	53	233	131	8-40
1918	LF	NY	AL	4-8	91	324	36	83	12	6	3	46	.256	27	116	106	—
1919	CF	NY	AL	3-8	134	475	45	132	27	8	6	59	.278	36	193	109	24-49
1920	CF	NY	AL	3-8	129	471	63	139	26	12	7	79	.295	40	210	113	19-49
1921	CF	NY	AL	1-8	31	87	5	15	2	2	0	12	.172	8	21	—	—
MAJOR LEAGUE TOTALS					1050	3670	393	1011	169	72	43	516	.275	312	1453	117	5 yrs

George Joseph Burns   Born Nov 24, 1889   Utica, NY
5'7   160 lbs   Batted right   Died Aug 15, 1966   Gloversville, NY

YR	POS	TEAM	LG	FIN	G	AB	R	H	2B	3B	HR	RBI	AVG	BB	TB	OQ	RANK
1911	CF	NY	NL	1-8	6	17	2	1	0	0	0	0	.059	1	1	—	—
1912	LF	NY	NL	1-8	29	51	11	15	4	0	0	3	.294	8	19	—	—
1913	LF	NY	NL	1-8	150	605	81	173	37	4	2	54	.286	58	224	110	25-45
1914	LF	NY	NL	2-8	154	561	100	170	35	10	3	60	.303	89	234	146	3-42
1915	LF	NY	NL	8-8	155	622	83	169	27	14	3	51	.272	56	233	117	16-45
1916	LF	NY	NL	4-8	155	623	105	174	24	8	5	41	.279	63	229	122	12-36
1917	LF	NY	NL	1-8	152	597	103	180	25	13	5	45	.302	75	246	144	3-38
1918	LF	NY	NL	2-8	119	465	80	135	22	6	4	51	.290	43	181	126	9-40
1919	LF	NY	NL	2-8	139	534	86	162	30	9	2	46	.303	82	216	146	2-41
1920	LF	NY	NL	2-8	154	631	115	181	35	9	6	46	.287	76	252	124	13-45
1921	CF	NY	NL	1-8	149	605	111	181	28	9	4	61	.299	80	239	115	18-39
1922	CF	CIN	NL	2-8	156	631	104	180	20	10	1	53	.285	78	223	97	25-39
1923	RF	CIN	NL	2-8	154	614	99	168	27	13	3	45	.274	101	230	111	22-41
1924	LF-RF	CIN	NL	4-8	93	336	43	86	19	2	2	33	.256	29	115	88	—
1925	LF	PHI	NL	7-8	88	349	65	102	29	1	1	22	.292	33	136	98	—
MAJOR LEAGUE TOTALS					1853	7241	1188	2077	362	108	41	611	.287	872	2778	123	11 yrs

Benjamin Michael Kauff
5'8 157 lbs Batted left

Born Jan 5, 1890 Pomeroy, OH
Died Nov 17, 1961 Columbus, OH

YR	POS	TEAM	LG	FIN	G	AB	R	H	2B	3B	HR	RBI	AVG	BB	TB	OQ	RANK
1912	CF	NY	AL	8-8	5	11	4	3	0	0	0	2	.273	3	3	—	—
1914	RF	IND	FL	1-8	154	571	120	211	44	13	8	95	.370	72	305	174	1-41
1915	CF	BRO	FL	7-8	136	483	92	165	23	11	12	83	.342	85	246	180	1-40
1916	CF	NY	NL	4-8	154	552	71	146	22	15	9	74	.264	68	225	135	6-36
1917	CF	NY	NL	1-8	153	559	89	172	22	4	5	68	.308	59	217	133	6-38
1918	CF	NY	NL	2-8	67	270	41	85	19	4	2	39	.315	16	118	134	—
1919	CF	NY	NL	2-8	135	491	73	136	27	7	10	67	.277	39	207	126	7-41
1920	CF	NY	NL	2-8	55	157	31	43	12	3	3	26	.274	25	70	142	—

| MAJOR LEAGUE TOTALS | | | | | 859 | 3094 | 521 | 961 | 169 | 57 | 49 | 454 | .311 | 367 | 1391 | 150 | 5 yrs |

Fred Williams
6'2 180 lbs Batted left

Born Dec 21, 1887 Wadena, IN
Died Apr 23, 1974 Eagle River, WI

YR	POS	TEAM	LG	FIN	G	AB	R	H	2B	3B	HR	RBI	AVG	BB	TB	OQ	RANK
1912	CF-LF	CHI	NL	3-8	28	62	3	15	1	1	0	1	.242	6	18	—	—
1913	LF	CHI	NL	3-8	49	156	17	35	3	3	4	32	.224	5	56	85	—
1914	LF	CHI	NL	4-8	55	94	12	19	2	2	0	5	.202	13	25	90	—
1915	CF	CHI	NL	4-8	151	518	59	133	22	6	13	64	.257	26	206	110	21-45
1916	CF	CHI	NL	5-8	118	405	55	113	19	9	12	66	.279	51	186	152	—
1917	CF	CHI	NL	5-8	138	468	53	113	22	4	5	42	.241	38	158	103	28-38
1918	CF	PHI	NL	6-8	94	351	49	97	14	1	6	39	.276	27	131	115	21-40
1919	CF	PHI	NL	8-8	109	435	54	121	21	1	9	39	.278	30	171	117	14-41
1920	CF	PHI	NL	8-8	148	590	88	192	36	10	15	72	.325	32	293	139	3-45
1921	CF	PHI	NL	8-8	146	562	67	180	28	6	18	75	.320	30	274	122	13-39
1922	CF	PHI	NL	7-8	151	584	98	180	30	6	26	92	.308	74	300	135	4-39
1923	CF	PHI	NL	8-8	136	535	98	157	22	3	41	114	.293	59	308	146	4-41
1924	CF	PHI	NL	7-8	148	558	101	183	31	11	24	93	.328	67	308	153	5-38
1925	RF	PHI	NL	6-8	107	314	78	104	11	5	13	60	.331	53	164	148	—
1926	RF	PHI	NL	8-8	107	336	63	116	13	4	18	53	.345	38	191	160	—
1927	RF	PHI	NL	8-8	131	492	86	135	18	2	30	98	.274	61	247	133	8-40
1928	RF	PHI	NL	8-8	99	238	31	61	9	0	12	37	.256	54	106	133	—
1929	CF	PHI	NL	5-8	66	65	11	19	2	0	5	21	.292	22	36	—	—
1930	CF	PHI	NL	8-8	21	17	1	8	2	0	0	2	.471	4	10	—	—

| MAJOR LEAGUE TOTALS | | | | | 2002 | 6780 | 1024 | 1981 | 306 | 74 | 251 | 1005 | .292 | 690 | 3188 | 127 | 10 yrs |

George William Cutshaw   Born Jul 27, 1887 Wilmington, IL
5'9 160 lbs Batted right   Died Aug 22, 1973 San Diego, CA

YR	POS	TEAM	LG	FIN	G	AB	R	H	2B	3B	HR	RBI	AVG	BB	TB	OQ	RANK
1912	2B	BRO	NL	7-8	102	357	41	100	14	4	0	28	.280	31	122	93	—
1913	2B	BRO	NL	6-8	147	592	72	158	23	13	7	80	.267	39	228	103	31-45
1914	2B	BRO	NL	5-8	153	583	69	150	22	12	2	78	.257	30	202	95	36-42
1915	2B	BRO	NL	3-8	154	566	68	139	18	9	0	62	.246	34	175	90	40-45
1916	2B	BRO	NL	1-8	154	581	58	151	21	4	2	63	.260	25	186	92	35-36
1917	2B	BRO	NL	7-8	135	487	42	126	17	7	4	49	.259	21	169	98	31-38
1918	2B	PIT	NL	4-8	126	463	56	132	16	10	5	68	.285	27	183	117	20-40
1919	2B	PIT	NL	4-8	139	512	49	124	15	8	3	51	.242	30	164	91	38-41
1920	2B	PIT	NL	4-8	131	488	56	123	16	8	0	47	.252	23	155	83	42-45
1921	2B	PIT	NL	2-8	98	350	46	119	18	4	0	53	.340	11	145	103	—
1922	2B	DET	AL	3-8	132	499	57	133	14	8	2	61	.267	20	169	76	47-50
1923	2B	DET	AL	2-8	45	143	15	32	1	2	0	13	.224	9	37	61	—
MAJOR LEAGUE TOTALS					1516	5621	629	1487	195	89	25	653	.265	300	1935	94	9 yrs

Jacques Frank Fournier   Born Sep 29, 1892 Au Sable, MI
6'0 195 lbs Batted left   Died Sep 5, 1973 Tacoma, WA

YR	POS	TEAM	LG	FIN	G	AB	R	H	2B	3B	HR	RBI	AVG	BB	TB	OQ	RANK
1912	1B	CHI	AL	4-8	35	73	5	14	5	2	0	2	.192	4	23	—	—
1913	1B-LF	CHI	AL	5-8	68	172	20	40	8	5	1	23	.233	21	61	108	—
1914	1B	CHI	AL	6-8	109	379	44	118	14	9	6	44	.311	31	168	137	—
1915	1B-LF	CHI	AL	3-8	126	422	86	136	20	18	5	77	.322	64	207	166	3-42
1916	1B	CHI	AL	2-8	105	313	36	75	13	9	3	44	.240	36	115	113	—
1917	PH	CHI	AL	1-8	1	1	0	0	0	0	0	0	.000	0	0	—	—
1918	1B	NY	AL	4-8	27	100	9	35	6	1	0	12	.350	7	43	137	—
1920	1B	SL	NL	5-8	141	530	77	162	33	14	3	61	.306	42	232	127	9-45
1921	1B	SL	NL	3-8	149	574	103	197	27	9	16	86	.343	56	290	140	3-39
1922	1B	SL	NL	3-8	128	404	64	119	23	9	10	61	.295	40	190	118	—
1923	1B	BRO	NL	6-8	133	515	91	181	30	13	22	102	.351	43	303	156	2-41
1924	1B	BRO	NL	2-8	154	563	93	188	25	4	27	116	.334	83	302	158	3-38
1925	1B	BRO	NL	6-8	145	545	99	191	21	16	22	130	.350	86	310	160	2-37
1926	1B	BRO	NL	6-8	87	243	39	69	9	2	11	48	.284	30	115	128	—
1927	1B	BOS	NL	7-8	122	374	55	106	18	2	10	53	.283	44	158	116	—
MAJOR LEAGUE TOTALS					1530	5208	821	1631	252	113	136	859	.313	587	2517	151	6 yrs

Charles Dillon Stengel Born Jul 30, 1890 Kansas City, MO
5'11 175 lbs Batted left Died Sep 29, 1975 Glendale, CA

YR	POS	TEAM	LG	FIN	G	AB	R	H	2B	3B	HR	RBI	AVG	BB	TB	OQ	RANK
1912	CF	BRO	NL	7-8	17	57	9	18	1	0	1	13	.316	15	22	—	—
1913	CF	BRO	NL	6-8	124	438	60	119	16	8	7	43	.272	56	172	120	15-45
1914	RF	BRO	NL	5-8	126	412	55	130	13	10	4	60	.316	56	175	145	4-42
1915	RF	BRO	NL	3-8	132	459	52	109	20	12	3	50	.237	34	162	103	31-45
1916	RF	BRO	NL	1-8	127	462	66	129	27	8	8	53	.279	33	196	129	11-36
1917	RF	BRO	NL	7-8	150	549	69	141	23	12	6	73	.257	60	206	122	11-38
1918	RF	PIT	NL	4-8	39	122	18	30	4	1	1	12	.246	16	39	111	—
1919	RF	PIT	NL	4-8	89	321	38	94	10	10	4	43	.293	35	136	137	—
1920	RF	PHI	NL	8-8	129	445	53	130	25	6	9	50	.292	38	194	126	10-45
1921	RF	PH/NY	NL	8/1	42	81	11	23	4	1	0	6	.284	7	29	—	—
1922	CF	NY	NL	1-8	84	250	48	92	8	10	7	48	.368	21	141	150	—
1923	CF	NY	NL	1-8	75	218	39	74	11	5	5	43	.339	20	110	136	—
1924	RF	BOS	NL	8-8	131	461	57	129	20	6	5	39	.280	45	176	102	21-38
1925	RF	BOS	NL	5-8	12	13	0	1	0	0	0	2	.077	1	1	—	—

| MAJOR LEAGUE TOTALS | | | | | 1277 | 4288 | 575 | 1219 | 182 | 89 | 60 | 535 | .284 | 437 | 1759 | 121 | 7 yrs |

Robert Hayes Veach Born Jun 29, 1888 Island, KY
5'11 160 lbs Batted left Died Aug 7, 1945 Detroit, MI

YR	POS	TEAM	LG	FIN	G	AB	R	H	2B	3B	HR	RBI	AVG	BB	TB	OQ	RANK
1912	LF	DET	AL	6-8	23	79	8	27	5	1	0	15	.342	5	34	—	—
1913	LF	DET	AL	6-8	137	491	54	132	22	10	0	64	.269	53	174	110	23-37
1914	LF	DET	AL	4-8	149	531	56	146	19	14	1	72	.275	50	196	115	13-41
1915	LF	DET	AL	2-8	152	569	81	178	40	10	3	112	.313	68	247	141	6-42
1916	LF	DET	AL	3-8	150	566	92	173	33	15	3	91	.306	52	245	134	6-38
1917	LF	DET	AL	4-8	154	571	79	182	31	12	8	103	.319	61	261	150	3-40
1918	LF	DET	AL	7-8	127	499	59	139	21	13	3	78	.279	35	195	114	14-39
1919	LF	DET	AL	4-8	139	538	87	191	45	17	3	101	.355	33	279	147	5-49
1920	LF	DET	AL	7-8	154	612	92	188	39	15	11	113	.307	36	290	115	18-49
1921	LF	DET	AL	6-8	150	612	110	207	43	13	16	128	.338	48	324	130	8-49
1922	LF	DET	AL	3-8	155	618	96	202	34	13	9	126	.327	42	289	117	16-50
1923	LF	DET	AL	2-8	114	293	45	94	13	3	2	39	.321	29	119	110	—
1924	LF	BOS	AL	7-8	142	519	77	153	35	9	5	99	.295	47	221	105	25-40
1925	RF-LF	Bo/NY/Wa	AL	8/7/1	75	158	17	51	13	2	0	25	.323	12	68	104	—

| MAJOR LEAGUE TOTALS | | | | | 1821 | 6656 | 953 | 2063 | 393 | 147 | 64 | 1166 | .310 | 571 | 2942 | 125 | 11 yrs |

George Bostic Whitted
5'8 168 lbs Batted right

Born Feb 4, 1890 Durham, NC
Died Oct 16, 1962 Wilmington, NC

YR	POS	TEAM	LG	FIN	G	AB	R	H	2B	3B	HR	RBI	AVG	BB	TB	OQ	RANK
1912	3B	SL	NL	6-8	12	46	7	12	3	0	0	7	.261	3	15	—	—
1913	LF-SS	SL	NL	8-8	123	404	44	89	10	5	0	38	.220	31	109	75	—
1914	CF-3B	SL/BO	NL	3/1	86	249	39	61	12	4	2	32	.245	18	87	99	—
1915	LF-CF	PHI	NL	1-8	128	448	46	126	17	3	1	43	.281	29	152	103	30-45
1916	LF-1B	PHI	NL	2-8	147	526	68	148	20	12	6	68	.281	19	210	114	19-36
1917	LF	PHI	NL	2-8	149	553	69	155	24	9	3	70	.280	30	206	111	20-38
1918	LF	PHI	NL	6-8	24	86	7	21	4	0	0	3	.244	4	25	—	—
1919	LF-1B	PH/PT	NL	8/4	113	420	47	123	21	8	3	53	.293	20	169	116	15-41
1920	3B	PIT	NL	4-8	134	494	53	129	11	12	1	74	.261	35	167	94	37-45
1921	RF	PIT	NL	2-8	108	403	60	114	23	7	7	63	.283	26	172	105	—
1922	PH	BRO	NL	6-8	1	1	0	0	0	0	0	0	.000	0	0	—	—

MAJOR LEAGUE TOTALS 1025 3630 440 978 145 60 23 451 .269 215 1312 108 5 yrs

Henry Knight Groh
5'8 158 lbs Batted right

Born Sep 18, 1889 Rochester, NY
Died Aug 22, 1968 Cincinnati, OH

YR	POS	TEAM	LG	FIN	G	AB	R	H	2B	3B	HR	RBI	AVG	BB	TB	OQ	RANK
1912	2B-SS	NY	NL	1-8	27	48	8	13	2	1	0	3	.271	8	17	—	—
1913	2B	NY/CN	NL	1/7	121	399	51	112	19	5	3	48	.281	38	150	110	—
1914	2B	CIN	NL	8-8	139	455	59	131	18	4	2	32	.288	64	163	124	12-42
1915	3B-2B	CIN	NL	7-8	160	587	72	170	32	9	3	50	.290	50	229	123	11-45
1916	3B-2B	CIN	NL	7-8	149	553	85	149	24	14	2	28	.269	84	207	135	7-36
1917	3B	CIN	NL	4-8	156	599	91	182	39	11	1	53	.304	71	246	142	5-38
1918	3B	CIN	NL	3-8	126	493	86	158	28	3	1	37	.320	54	195	138	3-40
1919	3B	CIN	NL	1-8	122	448	79	139	17	11	5	63	.310	56	193	147	1-41
1920	3B	CIN	NL	3-8	145	550	86	164	28	12	0	49	.298	60	216	122	16-45
1921	3B	CIN	NL	6-8	97	357	54	118	19	6	0	48	.331	36	149	118	—
1922	3B	NY	NL	1-8	115	426	63	113	21	3	3	51	.265	53	149	94	29-39
1923	3B	NY	NL	1-8	123	465	91	135	22	5	4	48	.290	60	179	109	24-41
1924	3B	NY	NL	1-8	145	559	82	157	32	3	2	46	.281	52	201	96	25-38
1925	3B	NY	NL	2-8	25	65	7	15	4	0	0	4	.231	6	19	—	—
1926	3B	NY	NL	5-8	12	35	2	8	2	0	0	3	.229	2	10	—	—
1927	3B	PIT	NL	1-8	14	35	2	10	1	0	0	3	.286	2	11	—	—

MAJOR LEAGUE TOTALS 1676 6074 918 1774 308 87 26 566 .292 696 2334 123 10 yrs

Derrill Burnham Pratt
5'11   175 lbs   Batted right

Born Jan 10, 1888   Walhalla, SC
Died Sep 30, 1977   Texas City, TX

YR	POS	TEAM	LG	FIN	G	AB	R	H	2B	3B	HR	RBI	AVG	BB	TB	OQ	RANK
1912	2B-SS	SL	AL	7-8	152	570	76	172	26	15	5	69	.302	36	243	117	14-33
1913	2B	SL	AL	8-8	155	592	60	175	31	13	2	87	.296	40	238	116	18-37
1914	2B	SL	AL	5-8	158	584	85	165	34	13	5	65	.283	50	240	124	8-41
1915	2B	SL	AL	6-8	159	602	61	175	31	11	3	78	.291	26	237	108	24-42
1916	2B	SL	AL	5-8	158	596	64	159	35	12	5	103	.267	54	233	117	15-38
1917	2B	SL	AL	7-8	123	450	40	111	22	8	1	53	.247	33	152	99	30-40
1918	2B	NY	AL	4-8	126	477	65	131	19	7	2	55	.275	35	170	106	22-39
1919	2B	NY	AL	3-8	140	527	69	154	27	7	4	56	.292	36	207	106	28-49
1920	2B	NY	AL	3-8	154	574	84	180	37	8	4	97	.314	50	245	112	20-49
1921	2B	BOS	AL	5-8	135	521	80	169	36	10	5	102	.324	44	240	114	18-49
1922	2B	BOS	AL	8-8	154	607	73	183	44	7	6	86	.301	53	259	108	28-50
1923	2B-1B	DET	AL	2-8	101	297	43	92	18	3	0	40	.310	25	116	102	—
1924	2B-1B	DET	AL	3-8	121	429	56	130	32	3	1	77	.303	31	171	97	—
MAJOR LEAGUE TOTALS					1836	6826	856	1996	392	117	43	968	.292	513	2751	112	11 yrs

Howard Samuel Shanks
5'11   170 lbs   Batted right

Born Jul 21, 1890   Chicago, IL
Died Jul 30, 1941   Monaca, PA

YR	POS	TEAM	LG	FIN	G	AB	R	H	2B	3B	HR	RBI	AVG	BB	TB	OQ	RANK
1912	LF	WAS	AL	2-8	116	399	52	92	14	7	1	48	.231	40	123	89	—
1913	LF	WAS	AL	2-8	109	390	38	99	11	5	1	37	.254	15	123	82	—
1914	LF	WAS	AL	3-8	143	500	44	112	22	10	4	64	.224	29	166	90	34-41
1915	LF-3B	WAS	AL	4-8	141	492	52	123	19	8	0	47	.250	30	158	89	39-42
1916	LF-3B	WAS	AL	7-8	140	471	51	119	15	7	1	48	.253	41	151	97	31-38
1917	SS-LF	WAS	AL	5-8	126	430	45	87	15	5	0	28	.202	33	112	77	—
1918	LF-2B	WAS	AL	3-8	120	436	42	112	19	4	1	56	.257	31	142	95	31-39
1919	SS-2B	WAS	AL	7-8	135	491	33	122	8	7	1	54	.248	25	147	76	49-49
1920	3B-LF	WAS	AL	6-8	128	444	56	119	16	7	4	37	.268	29	161	88	42-49
1921	3B	WAS	AL	4-8	154	562	81	170	24	18	7	69	.302	57	251	111	22-49
1922	3B-LF	WAS	AL	6-8	84	272	35	77	10	9	1	32	.283	25	108	100	—
1923	3B-2B	BOS	AL	8-8	131	464	38	118	19	5	3	57	.254	19	156	75	44-46
1924	SS-3B	BOS	AL	7-8	72	193	22	50	16	3	0	25	.259	21	72	94	—
1925	3B-2B	NY	AL	7-8	66	155	15	40	3	1	1	18	.258	20	48	82	—
MAJOR LEAGUE TOTALS					1665	5699	604	1440	211	96	25	620	.253	415	1918	90	8 yrs

George Daniel Weaver
5'11 170 lbs Batted right

Born Aug 18, 1890 Pottstown, PA
Died Jan 31, 1956 Chicago, IL

YR	POS	TEAM	LG	FIN	G	AB	R	H	2B	3B	HR	RBI	AVG	BB	TB	OQ	RANK
1912	SS	CHI	AL	4-8	147	523	55	117	21	8	1	43	.224	9	157	68	33-33
1913	SS	CHI	AL	5-8	151	533	51	145	17	8	4	52	.272	15	190	92	35-37
1914	SS	CHI	AL	6-8	136	541	64	133	20	9	2	28	.246	20	177	87	38-41
1915	SS	CHI	AL	3-8	148	563	83	151	18	11	3	49	.268	32	200	98	32-42
1916	3B-SS	CHI	AL	2-8	151	582	78	132	27	6	3	38	.227	30	180	83	36-38
1917	3B-SS	CHI	AL	1-8	118	447	64	127	16	5	3	32	.284	27	162	107	25-40
1918	SS-3B	CHI	AL	6-8	112	420	37	126	12	5	0	29	.300	11	148	97	29-39
1919	3B-SS	CHI	AL	1-8	140	571	89	169	33	9	3	75	.296	11	229	97	31-49
1920	3B-SS	CHI	AL	2-8	151	630	104	210	35	8	2	75	.333	28	267	105	28-49
MAJOR LEAGUE TOTALS					1254	4810	625	1310	199	69	21	421	.272	183	1710	93	9 yrs

Walter James Vincent Maranville
5'5 155 lbs Batted right

Born Nov 11, 1891 Springfield, MA
Died Jan 5, 1954 New York, NY

YR	POS	TEAM	LG	FIN	G	AB	R	H	2B	3B	HR	RBI	AVG	BB	TB	OQ	RANK
1912	SS	BOS	NL	8-8	26	86	8	18	2	0	0	8	.209	9	20	—	—
1913	SS	BOS	NL	5-8	143	571	68	141	13	8	2	48	.247	68	176	95	38-45
1914	SS	BOS	NL	1-8	156	586	74	144	23	6	4	78	.246	45	191	95	37-42
1915	SS	BOS	NL	2-8	149	509	51	124	23	6	2	43	.244	45	165	100	34-45
1916	SS	BOS	NL	3-8	155	604	79	142	16	13	4	38	.235	50	196	100	30-36
1917	SS	BOS	NL	6-8	142	561	69	146	19	13	3	43	.260	40	200	108	23-38
1918	SS	BOS	NL	7-8	11	38	3	12	0	1	0	3	.316	4	14	—	—
1919	SS	BOS	NL	6-8	131	480	44	128	18	10	5	43	.267	36	181	112	17-41
1920	SS	BOS	NL	7-8	134	493	48	131	19	15	1	43	.266	28	183	99	33-45
1921	SS	PIT	NL	2-8	153	612	90	180	25	12	1	70	.294	47	232	99	28-39
1922	SS-2B	PIT	NL	3-8	155	672	115	198	26	15	0	63	.295	61	254	97	26-39
1923	SS	PIT	NL	3-8	141	581	78	161	19	9	1	41	.277	42	201	87	39-41
1924	2B	PIT	NL	3-8	152	594	62	158	33	20	2	71	.266	35	237	96	27-38
1925	SS	CHI	NL	8-8	75	266	37	62	10	3	0	23	.233	29	78	75	—
1926	SS-2B	BRO	NL	6-8	78	234	32	55	8	5	0	24	.235	26	73	85	—
1927	SS	SL	NL	2-8	9	29	0	7	1	0	0	0	.241	2	8	—	—
1928	SS	SL	NL	1-8	112	366	40	88	14	10	1	34	.240	36	125	85	—
1929	SS	BOS	NL	8-8	146	560	87	159	26	10	0	55	.284	47	205	86	43-46
1930	SS	BOS	NL	6-8	142	558	85	157	26	8	2	43	.281	48	205	83	38-44
1931	SS	BOS	NL	7-8	145	562	69	146	22	5	0	33	.260	56	178	87	32-36
1932	2B	BOS	NL	5-8	149	571	67	134	20	4	0	37	.235	46	162	74	37-38
1933	2B	BOS	NL	4-8	143	478	46	104	15	4	0	38	.218	36	127	74	46-48
1935	2B	BOS	NL	8-8	23	67	3	10	2	0	0	5	.149	3	12	—	—
MAJOR LEAGUE TOTALS					2670	10078	1255	2605	380	177	28	884	.258	839	3423	93	16 yrs

Raymond Johnson Chapman　　　　Born Jan 15, 1891　Beaver Dam, KY
5'10　170 lbs　Batted right　　　　　　Died Aug 17, 1920　New York, NY

YR	POS	TEAM	LG	FIN	G	AB	R	H	2B	3B	HR	RBI	AVG	BB	TB	OQ	RANK
1912	SS	CLE	AL	5-8	31	109	29	34	6	3	0	19	.312	10	46	125	—
1913	SS	CLE	AL	3-8	141	508	78	131	19	7	3	39	.258	46	173	101	30-37
1914	SS-2B	CLE	AL	8-8	106	375	59	103	16	10	2	42	.275	48	145	127	—
1915	SS	CLE	AL	7-8	154	570	101	154	14	17	3	67	.270	70	211	118	10-42
1916	SS-3B	CLE	AL	6-8	109	346	50	80	10	5	0	27	.231	50	100	100	—
1917	SS	CLE	AL	3-8	156	563	98	170	28	13	2	36	.302	61	230	134	6-40
1918	SS	CLE	AL	2-8	128	446	84	119	19	8	1	32	.267	84	157	132	9-39
1919	SS	CLE	AL	2-8	115	433	75	130	23	10	3	53	.300	31	182	115	21-49
1920	SS	CLE	AL	1-8	111	435	97	132	27	8	3	49	.303	52	184	117	17-49

MAJOR LEAGUE TOTALS　　　　1051　3785　671　1053　162　81　17　364　.278　452　1428　120　6 yrs

Raymond William Schalk　　　　Born Aug 12, 1892　Harvey, IL
5'9　165 lbs　Batted right　　　　　　Died May 19, 1970　Chicago, IL

YR	POS	TEAM	LG	FIN	G	AB	R	H	2B	3B	HR	RBI	AVG	BB	TB	OQ	RANK
1912	C	CHI	AL	4-8	23	63	7	18	2	0	0	8	.286	3	20	—	—
1913	C	CHI	AL	5-8	129	401	38	98	15	5	1	38	.244	27	126	88	—
1914	C	CHI	AL	6-8	136	392	30	106	13	2	0	36	.270	38	123	101	—
1915	C	CHI	AL	3-8	135	413	46	110	14	4	1	54	.266	62	135	114	16-42
1916	C	CHI	AL	2-8	129	410	36	95	12	9	0	41	.232	41	125	94	—
1917	C	CHI	AL	1-8	140	424	48	96	12	5	2	51	.226	59	124	101	27-40
1918	C	CHI	AL	6-8	108	333	35	73	6	3	0	22	.219	36	85	83	—
1919	C	CHI	AL	1-8	131	394	57	111	9	3	0	34	.282	51	126	102	29-49
1920	C	CHI	AL	2-8	151	485	64	131	25	5	1	61	.270	68	169	100	31-49
1921	C	CHI	AL	7-8	128	416	32	105	24	4	0	47	.252	40	137	80	—
1922	C	CHI	AL	5-8	142	442	57	124	22	3	4	60	.281	67	164	106	30-50
1923	C	CHI	AL	7-8	123	382	42	87	12	2	1	44	.228	39	106	73	—
1924	C	CHI	AL	8-8	57	153	15	30	4	2	1	11	.196	21	41	73	—
1925	C	CHI	AL	5-8	125	343	44	94	18	1	0	52	.274	57	114	96	—
1926	C	CHI	AL	5-8	82	226	26	60	9	1	0	32	.265	27	71	86	—
1927	C	CHI	AL	5-8	16	26	2	6	2	0	0	2	.231	2	8	—	—
1928	C	CHI	AL	5-8	2	1	0	1	0	0	0	1	1.000	0	1	—	—
1929	C	NY	NL	3-8	5	2	0	0	0	0	0	0	.000	0	0	—	—

MAJOR LEAGUE TOTALS　　　　1762　5306　579　1345　199　49　11　594　.253　638　1675　105　5 yrs

Harry Loram Leibold Born Feb 17, 1892 Butler, IN
5'6 157 lbs Batted left Died Feb 4, 1977 Detroit, MI

YR	POS	TEAM	LG	FIN	G	AB	R	H	2B	3B	HR	RBI	AVG	BB	TB	OQ	RANK
1913	CF	CLE	AL	3-8	93	286	37	74	11	6	0	12	.259	21	97	97	—
1914	CF	CLE	AL	8-8	115	402	46	106	13	3	0	32	.264	54	125	109	—
1915	CF	CL/CH	AL	7/3	93	281	38	70	6	4	0	15	.249	39	84	102	—
1916	CF	CHI	AL	2-8	45	82	5	20	1	2	0	13	.244	7	25	—	—
1917	RF	CHI	AL	1-8	125	428	59	101	12	6	0	29	.236	74	125	111	22-40
1918	LF	CHI	AL	6-8	116	440	57	110	14	7	0	31	.250	63	138	109	18-39
1919	RF	CHI	AL	1-8	122	434	81	131	18	2	0	26	.302	72	153	121	15-49
1920	RF	CHI	AL	2-8	108	413	61	91	16	3	1	28	.220	55	116	80	48-49
1921	CF	BOS	AL	5-8	123	467	88	143	26	6	0	31	.306	41	181	97	35-49
1922	CF	BOS	AL	8-8	81	271	42	70	8	1	1	18	.258	41	83	90	—
1923	CF	BO/WA	AL	8/4	107	333	69	98	13	4	1	22	.294	54	122	111	—
1924	CF	WAS	AL	1-8	84	246	41	72	6	4	0	20	.293	42	86	106	—
1925	CF	WAS	AL	1-8	56	84	14	23	1	1	0	7	.274	8	26	—	—

| MAJOR LEAGUE TOTALS | | | | | 1268 | 4167 | 638 | 1109 | 145 | 49 | 3 | 284 | .266 | 571 | 1361 | 104 | 5 yrs |

Walter Clement Pipp Born Feb 17, 1893 Chicago, IL
6'1 180 lbs Batted left Died Jan 11, 1965 Grand Rapids, MI

YR	POS	TEAM	LG	FIN	G	AB	R	H	2B	3B	HR	RBI	AVG	BB	TB	OQ	RANK
1913	1B	DET	AL	6-8	12	31	3	5	0	3	0	5	.161	2	11	—	—
1915	1B	NY	AL	5-8	136	479	59	118	20	13	4	60	.246	66	176	117	12-42
1916	1B	NY	AL	4-8	151	545	70	143	20	14	12	93	.262	54	227	124	11-38
1917	1B	NY	AL	6-8	155	587	82	143	29	12	9	70	.244	60	223	116	17-40
1918	1B	NY	AL	4-8	91	349	48	106	15	9	2	44	.304	22	145	123	—
1919	1B	NY	AL	3-8	138	523	74	144	23	10	7	50	.275	39	208	106	27-49
1920	1B	NY	AL	3-8	153	610	109	171	30	14	11	76	.280	48	262	106	27-49
1921	1B	NY	AL	1-8	153	588	96	174	35	9	8	97	.296	45	251	101	32-49
1922	1B	NY	AL	1-8	152	577	96	190	32	10	9	90	.329	56	269	123	12-50
1923	1B	NY	AL	1-8	144	569	79	173	19	8	6	108	.304	36	226	98	34-46
1924	1B	NY	AL	2-8	153	589	88	174	30	19	9	113	.295	51	269	111	23-40
1925	1B	NY	AL	7-8	62	178	19	41	6	3	3	24	.230	13	62	76	—
1926	1B	CIN	NL	2-8	155	574	72	167	22	15	6	99	.291	49	237	108	22-42
1927	1B	CIN	NL	5-8	122	443	49	115	19	6	2	41	.260	32	152	86	37-40
1928	1B	CIN	NL	5-8	95	272	30	77	11	3	2	26	.283	23	100	93	—

| MAJOR LEAGUE TOTALS | | | | | 1872 | 6914 | 974 | 1941 | 311 | 148 | 90 | 996 | .281 | 596 | 2818 | 109 | 11 yrs |

Ralph Stuart Young
5'5 165 lbs Batted both

Born Sep 19, 1889 Philadelphia, PA
Died Jan 24, 1965 Philadelphia, PA

YR	POS	TEAM	LG	FIN	G	AB	R	H	2B	3B	HR	RBI	AVG	BB	TB	OQ	RANK
1913	SS	NY	AL	7-8	7	15	2	1	0	0	0	0	.067	3	1	—	—
1915	2B	DET	AL	2-8	123	378	44	92	6	5	0	31	.243	53	108	98	—
1916	2B	DET	AL	3-8	153	528	60	139	16	6	1	45	.263	62	170	106	21-38
1917	2B	DET	AL	4-8	141	503	64	116	18	2	1	35	.231	61	141	95	33-40
1918	2B	DET	AL	7-8	91	298	31	56	7	1	0	21	.188	54	65	88	—
1919	2B	DET	AL	4-8	125	456	63	96	13	5	1	25	.211	53	122	79	48-49
1920	2B	DET	AL	7-8	150	594	84	173	21	6	0	33	.291	85	206	104	29-49
1921	2B	DET	AL	6-8	107	401	70	120	8	3	0	29	.299	69	134	102	29-49
1922	2B	PHI	AL	7-8	125	470	62	105	19	2	1	35	.223	55	131	75	49-50
MAJOR LEAGUE TOTALS					1022	3643	480	898	108	30	4	254	.247	495	1078	94	6 yrs

Walter Henry Schang
5'10 180 lbs Batted both

Born Aug 22, 1889 South Wales, NY
Died Mar 6, 1965 St Louis, MO

YR	POS	TEAM	LG	FIN	G	AB	R	H	2B	3B	HR	RBI	AVG	BB	TB	OQ	RANK
1913	C	PHI	AL	1-8	79	207	32	55	16	3	3	30	.266	34	86	137	—
1914	C	PHI	AL	1-8	107	307	44	88	11	8	3	45	.287	32	124	128	—
1915	3B-CF	PHI	AL	8-8	116	359	64	89	9	11	1	44	.248	66	123	122	—
1916	LF-C	PHI	AL	8-8	110	338	41	90	15	8	7	38	.266	38	142	129	—
1917	C-3B	PHI	AL	8-8	118	316	41	90	14	9	3	36	.285	29	131	128	—
1918	C-LF	BOS	AL	1-8	88	225	36	55	7	1	0	20	.244	46	64	116	—
1919	C	BOS	AL	6-8	113	330	43	101	16	3	0	55	.306	71	123	138	—
1920	C-CF	BOS	AL	5-8	122	387	58	118	30	7	4	51	.305	64	174	133	—
1921	C	NY	AL	1-8	134	424	77	134	30	5	6	55	.316	78	192	131	7-49
1922	C	NY	AL	1-8	124	408	46	130	21	7	1	53	.319	53	168	117	—
1923	C	NY	AL	1-8	84	272	39	75	8	2	2	29	.276	27	93	90	—
1924	C	NY	AL	2-8	114	356	46	104	19	7	5	52	.292	48	152	114	—
1925	C	NY	AL	7-8	73	167	17	40	8	1	2	24	.240	17	56	80	—
1926	C	SL	AL	7-8	103	285	36	94	19	5	8	50	.330	32	147	137	—
1927	C	SL	AL	7-8	97	264	40	84	15	2	5	42	.318	41	118	127	—
1928	C	SL	AL	3-8	91	245	41	70	10	5	3	39	.286	68	99	141	—
1929	C	SL	AL	4-8	94	249	43	59	10	5	5	36	.237	74	94	126	—
1930	C	PHI	AL	1-8	45	92	16	16	4	1	1	9	.174	17	25	77	—
1931	C	DET	AL	7-8	30	76	9	14	2	0	0	2	.184	14	16	—	—
MAJOR LEAGUE TOTALS					1842	5307	769	1506	264	90	59	710	.284	849	2127	—	—

Milton Joseph Stock   Born Jul 11, 1893   Chicago, IL
5'8   154 lbs   Batted right   Died Jul 16, 1977   Montrose, AL

YR	POS	TEAM	LG	FIN	G	AB	R	H	2B	3B	HR	RBI	AVG	BB	TB	OQ	RANK
1913	SS	NY	NL	1-8	7	17	2	3	1	0	0	1	.176	2	4	—	—
1914	3B	NY	NL	2-8	115	365	52	96	17	1	3	41	.263	34	124	104	—
1915	3B	PHI	NL	1-8	69	227	37	59	7	3	1	15	.260	22	75	106	—
1916	3B-SS	PHI	NL	2-8	132	509	61	143	25	6	1	43	.281	27	183	108	22-36
1917	3B-SS	PHI	NL	2-8	150	564	76	149	27	6	3	53	.264	51	197	112	17-38
1918	3B	PHI	NL	6-8	123	481	62	132	14	1	1	42	.274	35	151	99	28-40
1919	2B-3B	SL	NL	7-8	135	492	56	151	16	4	0	52	.307	49	175	120	11-41
1920	3B	SL	NL	5-8	155	639	85	204	28	6	0	76	.319	40	244	111	22-45
1921	3B	SL	NL	3-8	149	587	96	180	27	6	3	84	.307	48	228	104	23-39
1922	3B	SL	NL	3-8	151	581	85	177	33	9	5	79	.305	42	243	103	22-39
1923	3B	SL	NL	5-8	151	603	63	174	33	3	2	96	.289	40	219	91	37-41
1924	3B	BRO	NL	2-8	142	561	66	136	14	4	2	52	.242	26	164	69	38-38
1925	2B	BRO	NL	6-8	146	615	98	202	28	9	1	62	.328	38	251	100	27-37
1926	2B	BRO	NL	6-8	3	8	0	0	0	0	0	0	.000	1	0	—	—

MAJOR LEAGUE TOTALS   1628 6249 839 1806 270 58 22 696 .289 455 2258 102 10 yrs

William Harrison Southworth   Born Mar 9, 1893   Harvard, NE
5'9   170 lbs   Batted left   Died Nov 15, 1969   Columbus, OH

YR	POS	TEAM	LG	FIN	G	AB	R	H	2B	3B	HR	RBI	AVG	BB	TB	OQ	RANK
1913	LF	CLE	AL	3-8	1	0	0	0	0	0	0	0	—	0	0	—	—
1915	CF	CLE	AL	7-8	60	177	25	39	2	5	0	8	.220	36	51	110	—
1918	RF	PIT	NL	4-8	64	246	37	84	5	7	2	43	.341	26	109	154	—
1919	LF	PIT	NL	4-8	121	453	56	127	14	14	4	61	.280	32	181	119	12-41
1920	RF	PIT	NL	4-8	146	546	64	155	17	13	2	53	.284	52	204	112	21-45
1921	RF	BOS	NL	4-8	141	569	86	175	25	15	7	79	.308	36	251	111	19-39
1922	RF	BOS	NL	8-8	43	158	27	51	4	4	4	18	.323	18	75	127	—
1923	RF	BOS	NL	7-8	153	611	95	195	29	16	6	78	.319	61	274	121	13-41
1924	CF	NY	NL	1-8	94	281	40	72	13	0	3	36	.256	32	94	92	—
1925	CF	NY	NL	2-8	123	473	79	138	19	5	6	44	.292	51	185	101	26-37
1926	RF	NY/SL	NL	5/1	135	507	99	162	28	7	16	99	.320	33	252	127	9-42
1927	RF	SL	NL	2-8	92	306	52	92	15	5	2	39	.301	23	123	105	—
1929	RF	SL	NL	4-8	19	32	1	6	2	0	0	3	.188	2	8	—	—

MAJOR LEAGUE TOTALS   1192 4359 661 1296 173 91 52 561 .297 402 1807 115 6 yrs

Thomas Herman Griffith
5'10 175 lbs Batted left

Born Oct 26, 1889 Prospect, OH
Died Apr 13, 1967 Cincinnati, OH

YR	POS	TEAM	LG	FIN	G	AB	R	H	2B	3B	HR	RBI	AVG	BB	TB	OQ	RANK
1913	RF	BOS	NL	5-8	37	127	16	32	4	1	1	12	.252	9	41	88	—
1914	RF	BOS	NL	1-8	16	48	3	5	0	0	0	1	.104	2	5	—	—
1915	RF	CIN	NL	7-8	160	583	59	179	31	16	4	85	.307	41	254	134	5-45
1916	RF	CIN	NL	7-8	155	595	50	158	28	7	2	61	.266	36	206	104	26-36
1917	RF	CIN	NL	4-8	115	363	45	98	18	7	1	45	.270	19	133	107	—
1918	RF	CIN	NL	3-8	118	427	47	113	10	4	2	48	.265	39	137	104	26-40
1919	RF	BRO	NL	5-8	125	484	65	136	18	4	6	57	.281	23	180	106	20-41
1920	RF	BRO	NL	1-8	93	334	41	87	9	4	2	30	.260	15	110	86	—
1921	RF	BRO	NL	5-8	129	455	66	142	21	6	12	71	.312	36	211	120	14-39
1922	RF	BRO	NL	6-8	99	329	44	104	17	8	4	49	.316	23	149	112	—
1923	RF	BRO	NL	6-8	131	481	70	141	21	9	8	66	.293	50	204	112	21-41
1924	RF	BRO	NL	2-8	140	482	43	121	19	5	3	67	.251	34	159	82	36-38
1925	RF	BR/CH	NL	6/8	83	239	40	67	12	1	7	27	.280	24	102	105	—

MAJOR LEAGUE TOTALS   1401 4947 589 1383 208 72 52 619 .280 351 1891 109   7 yrs

Edd J Roush
5'11 170 lbs Batted left

Born May 8, 1893 Oakland City, IN
Died Mar 21, 1988 Bradenton, FL

YR	POS	TEAM	LG	FIN	G	AB	R	H	2B	3B	HR	RBI	AVG	BB	TB	OQ	RANK
1913	CF	CHI	AL	5-8	9	10	2	1	0	0	0	0	.100	0	1	—	—
1914	LF	IND	FL	1-8	74	166	26	54	8	4	1	30	.325	6	73	117	—
1915	CF	NWK	FL	5-8	145	551	73	164	20	11	3	60	.298	38	215	113	21-40
1916	CF	NY/CN	NL	4/7	108	341	38	91	7	15	0	20	.267	14	128	107	—
1917	CF	CIN	NL	4-8	136	522	82	178	19	14	4	67	.341	27	237	143	4-38
1918	CF	CIN	NL	3-8	113	435	61	145	18	10	5	62	.333	22	198	141	1-40
1919	CF	CIN	NL	1-8	133	504	73	162	19	13	3	71	.321	42	216	137	4-41
1920	CF	CIN	NL	3-8	149	579	81	196	22	16	4	90	.339	42	262	135	5-45
1921	CF	CIN	NL	6-8	112	418	68	147	27	12	4	71	.352	31	210	136	—
1922	CF	CIN	NL	2-8	49	165	29	58	7	4	1	24	.352	19	76	130	—
1923	CF	CIN	NL	2-8	138	527	88	185	41	18	6	88	.351	46	280	143	5-41
1924	CF	CIN	NL	4-8	121	483	67	168	23	21	3	72	.348	22	242	129	9-38
1925	CF	CIN	NL	3-8	134	540	91	183	28	16	8	83	.339	35	267	121	10-37
1926	CF	CIN	NL	2-8	144	563	95	182	37	10	7	79	.323	38	260	120	13-42
1927	CF	NY	NL	3-8	140	570	83	173	27	4	7	58	.304	26	229	99	28-40
1928	CF	NY	NL	2-8	46	163	20	41	5	3	2	13	.252	14	58	87	—
1929	CF	NY	NL	3-8	115	450	76	146	19	7	8	52	.324	45	203	111	24-46
1931	LF	CIN	NL	8-8	101	376	46	102	12	5	1	41	.271	17	127	81	—

MAJOR LEAGUE TOTALS   1967 7363 1099 2376 339 183 67 981 .323 484 3282 127 11 yrs

Leslie Mann   Born Nov 18, 1893 Lincoln, NE
5'9 172 lbs Batted right   Died Jan 14, 1962 Pasadena, CA

YR	POS	TEAM	LG	FIN	G	AB	R	H	2B	3B	HR	RBI	AVG	BB	TB	OQ	RANK
1913	CF	BOS	NL	5-8	120	407	54	103	24	7	3	51	.253	18	150	93	—
1914	CF	BOS	NL	1-8	126	389	44	96	16	11	4	40	.247	24	146	103	—
1915	LF	CHI	FL	1-8	135	470	75	144	12	19	4	58	.306	36	206	129	9-40
1916	LF	CHI	NL	5-8	127	415	46	113	13	9	2	29	.272	19	150	105	—
1917	LF	CHI	NL	5-8	117	444	63	121	19	10	1	44	.273	27	163	110	21-38
1918	LF	CHI	NL	1-8	129	489	69	141	27	7	2	55	.288	38	188	120	16-40
1919	LF	CH/BO	NL	3/6	120	444	46	109	14	12	4	42	.245	20	159	97	35-41
1920	LF	BOS	NL	7-8	115	424	48	117	7	8	3	32	.276	38	149	104	28-45
1921	CF	SL	NL	3-8	97	256	57	84	12	7	7	30	.328	23	131	137	—
1922	CF-LF	SL	NL	3-8	84	147	42	51	14	1	2	20	.347	16	73	135	—
1923	RF-CF	SL/CN	NL	5/2	46	90	21	33	5	2	5	11	.367	9	57	—	—
1924	RF	BOS	NL	8-8	32	102	13	28	7	4	0	10	.275	8	43	106	—
1925	RF	BOS	NL	5-8	60	184	27	63	11	4	2	20	.342	5	88	110	—
1926	CF-LF	BOS	NL	7-8	50	129	23	39	8	2	1	20	.302	9	54	108	—
1927	RF-LF	BO/NY	NL	7/3	58	133	21	39	7	2	2	16	.293	16	56	118	—
1928	RF-CF	NY	NL	2-8	82	193	29	51	7	1	2	25	.264	18	66	87	—

MAJOR LEAGUE TOTALS   1498 4716 678 1332 203 106 44 503 .282 324 1879 112 5 yrs

Emil Frederick Meusel   Born Jun 9, 1893   Oakland, CA
5'11 178 lbs Batted right   Died Mar 1, 1963   Long Beach, CA

YR	POS	TEAM	LG	FIN	G	AB	R	H	2B	3B	HR	RBI	AVG	BB	TB	OQ	RANK
1914	LF	WAS	AL	3-8	1	2	0	0	0	0	0	0	.000	0	0	—	—
1918	LF	PHI	NL	6-8	124	473	48	132	25	6	4	62	.279	30	181	115	22-40
1919	LF	PHI	NL	8-8	135	521	65	159	26	7	5	59	.305	15	214	115	16-41
1920	LF	PHI	NL	8-8	138	518	75	160	27	8	14	69	.309	32	245	132	7-45
1921	LF	PH/NY	NL	8/1	146	586	96	201	33	13	14	87	.343	33	302	133	5-39
1922	LF	NY	NL	1-8	154	617	100	204	28	17	16	132	.331	35	314	123	11-39
1923	LF	NY	NL	1-8	146	595	102	177	22	14	19	125	.297	38	284	116	17-41
1924	LF	NY	NL	1-8	139	549	75	170	26	9	6	102	.310	33	232	107	17-38
1925	LF	NY	NL	2-8	135	516	82	169	35	8	21	111	.328	26	283	127	9-37
1926	LF	NY	NL	5-8	129	449	51	131	25	10	6	65	.292	16	194	102	31-42
1927	LF	BRO	NL	6-8	42	74	7	18	3	1	1	7	.243	11	26	—	—

MAJOR LEAGUE TOTALS   1289 4900 701 1521 250 93 106 819 .310 269 2275 119 9 yrs

Max John Flack
5'7 148 lbs Batted left

Born Feb 5, 1890 Belleville, IL
Died Jul 31, 1975 Belleville, IL

YR	POS	TEAM	LG	FIN	G	AB	R	H	2B	3B	HR	RBI	AVG	BB	TB	OQ	RANK
1914	LF	CHI	FL	2-8	134	502	66	124	15	3	2	39	.247	51	151	89	33-41
1915	RF	CHI	FL	1-8	141	523	88	164	20	14	3	45	.314	40	221	126	10-40
1916	RF	CHI	NL	5-8	141	465	65	120	14	3	3	20	.258	42	149	104	27-36
1917	RF	CHI	NL	5-8	131	447	65	111	18	7	0	21	.248	51	143	108	24-38
1918	RF	CHI	NL	1-8	123	478	74	123	17	10	4	41	.257	56	172	119	17-40
1919	RF	CHI	NL	3-8	116	469	71	138	20	4	6	35	.294	34	184	120	10-41
1920	RF	CHI	NL	5-8	135	520	85	157	30	6	4	49	.302	52	211	124	14-45
1921	RF	CHI	NL	7-8	133	572	80	172	31	4	6	37	.301	32	229	100	26-39
1922	RF	CH/SL	NL	5/4	83	321	53	90	13	1	2	27	.280	33	111	91	—
1923	RF	SL	NL	5-8	128	505	82	147	16	9	3	28	.291	41	190	97	30-41
1924	RF	SL	NL	6-8	67	209	31	55	11	3	2	21	.263	21	78	99	—
1925	RF	SL	NL	4-8	79	241	23	60	7	8	0	28	.249	21	83	82	—
MAJOR LEAGUE TOTALS					1411	5252	783	1461	212	72	35	391	.278	474	1922	110	9 yrs

George Herman Ruth
6'2 215 lbs Batted left

Born Feb 6, 1895 Baltimore, MD
Died Aug 16, 1948 New York, NY

YR	POS	TEAM	LG	FIN	G	AB	R	H	2B	3B	HR	RBI	AVG	BB	TB	OQ	RANK
1914	P	BOS	AL	2-8	5	10	1	2	1	0	0	2	.200	0	3	—	—
1915	P	BOS	AL	1-8	42	92	16	29	10	1	4	21	.315	9	53	172	—
1916	P	BOS	AL	1-8	67	136	18	37	5	3	3	15	.272	10	57	120	—
1917	P	BOS	AL	2-8	52	123	14	40	6	3	2	12	.325	12	58	153	—
1918	LF-P	BOS	AL	1-8	95	317	50	95	26	11	11	66	.300	57	176	188	—
1919	LF-P	BOS	AL	6-8	130	432	103	139	34	12	29	114	.322	101	284	214	1-49
1920	RF	NY	AL	3-8	142	458	158	172	36	9	54	137	.376	148	388	281	1-49
1921	LF	NY	AL	1-8	152	540	177	204	44	16	59	171	.378	144	457	253	1-49
1922	LF	NY	AL	1-8	110	406	94	128	24	8	35	96	.315	84	273	188	1-50
1923	RF	NY	AL	1-8	152	522	151	205	45	13	41	130	.393	170	399	266	1-46
1924	RF	NY	AL	2-8	153	529	143	200	39	7	46	121	.378	142	391	233	1-40
1925	RF	NY	AL	7-8	98	359	61	104	12	2	25	66	.290	59	195	139	—
1926	RF	NY	AL	1-8	152	495	139	184	30	5	47	146	.372	144	365	239	1-41
1927	RF	NY	AL	1-8	151	540	158	192	29	8	60	164	.356	138	417	230	1-43
1928	RF	NY	AL	1-8	154	536	163	173	29	8	54	142	.323	135	380	209	1-42
1929	RF	NY	AL	2-8	135	499	121	172	26	6	46	154	.345	72	348	183	1-41
1930	RF	NY	AL	3-8	145	518	150	186	28	9	49	153	.359	136	379	215	1-40
1931	RF	NY	AL	2-8	145	534	149	199	31	3	46	163	.373	128	374	220	1-47
1932	RF	NY	AL	1-8	133	457	120	156	13	5	41	137	.341	130	302	205	2-48
1933	RF	NY	AL	2-8	137	459	97	138	21	3	34	103	.301	114	267	175	2-52
1934	RF	NY	AL	2-8	125	365	78	105	17	4	22	84	.288	103	196	164	3-44
1935	LF	BOS	NL	8-8	28	72	13	13	0	0	6	12	.181	20	31	—	—
MAJOR LEAGUE TOTALS					2503	8399	2174	2873	506	136	714	2209	.342	2056	5793	218	15 yrs

William Adolph Wambsganss   Born Mar 19, 1894 Cleveland, OH
5'11 175 lbs Batted right   Died Dec 8, 1985 Lakewood, OH

YR	POS	TEAM	LG	FIN	G	AB	R	H	2B	3B	HR	RBI	AVG	BB	TB	OQ	RANK
1914	SS-2B	CLE	AL	8-8	43	143	12	31	6	2	0	12	.217	8	41	79	—
1915	2B-3B	CLE	AL	7-8	121	375	30	73	4	4	0	21	.195	36	85	70	—
1916	SS-2B	CLE	AL	6-8	136	475	57	117	14	4	0	45	.246	41	139	89	35-38
1917	2B	CLE	AL	3-8	141	499	52	127	17	6	0	43	.255	37	156	94	34-40
1918	2B	CLE	AL	2-8	87	315	34	93	15	2	0	40	.295	21	112	107	—
1919	2B	CLE	AL	2-8	139	526	60	146	17	6	2	60	.278	32	181	92	37-49
1920	2B	CLE	AL	1-8	153	565	83	138	16	11	1	55	.244	54	179	82	46-49
1921	2B	CLE	AL	2-8	107	410	80	117	28	5	2	47	.285	44	161	99	—
1922	2B-SS	CLE	AL	4-8	142	538	89	141	22	6	0	47	.262	60	175	87	40-50
1923	2B	CLE	AL	3-8	101	345	59	100	20	4	1	59	.290	43	131	105	—
1924	2B	BOS	AL	7-8	156	632	93	174	41	5	0	49	.275	54	225	88	37-40
1925	2B	BOS	AL	8-8	111	360	50	83	12	4	1	41	.231	52	106	79	—
1926	SS-2B	PHI	AL	3-8	54	54	11	19	3	0	0	1	.352	8	22	—	—

MAJOR LEAGUE TOTALS					1491	5237	710	1359	215	59	7	520	.259	490	1713	89	6 yrs

Walter Gerber   Born Aug 18, 1891 Columbus, OH
5'10 152 lbs Batted right   Died Jun 19, 1951 Columbus, OH

YR	POS	TEAM	LG	FIN	G	AB	R	H	2B	3B	HR	RBI	AVG	BB	TB	OQ	RANK
1914	SS	PIT	NL	7-8	17	54	5	13	1	1	0	5	.241	2	16	—	—
1915	SS-3B	PIT	NL	5-8	56	144	8	28	2	0	0	7	.194	9	30	62	—
1917	SS-2B	SL	AL	7-8	14	39	2	12	1	1	0	2	.308	3	15	—	—
1918	SS	SL	AL	5-8	56	171	10	41	4	0	0	10	.240	19	45	88	—
1919	SS	SL	AL	5-8	140	462	43	105	14	6	1	37	.227	49	134	84	44-49
1920	SS	SL	AL	4-8	154	584	70	163	26	2	2	60	.279	58	199	91	39-49
1921	SS	SL	AL	3-8	114	436	55	121	12	9	2	48	.278	34	157	86	43-49
1922	SS	SL	AL	2-8	153	604	81	161	22	8	1	51	.267	52	202	84	43-50
1923	SS	SL	AL	5-8	154	605	85	170	26	3	1	62	.281	54	205	88	39-46
1924	SS	SL	AL	4-8	148	496	61	135	20	4	0	55	.272	43	163	82	38-40
1925	SS	SL	AL	3-8	72	246	29	67	13	1	0	19	.272	26	82	84	—
1926	SS	SL	AL	7-8	131	411	37	111	8	0	0	42	.270	40	119	77	—
1927	SS	SL	AL	7-8	142	438	44	98	13	9	0	45	.224	35	129	70	43-43
1928	SS	SL/BO	AL	3/8	110	318	22	69	7	1	0	28	.217	33	78	66	—
1929	SS-2B	BOS	AL	8-8	61	91	6	15	3	1	0	5	.165	8	20	—	—

MAJOR LEAGUE TOTALS					1522	5099	558	1309	172	46	7	476	.257	465	1594	84	7 yrs

Lewis Everett Scott
5'8 148 lbs Batted right

Born Nov 19, 1892 Bluffton, IN
Died Nov 2, 1960 Fort Wayne, IN

YR	POS	TEAM	LG	FIN	G	AB	R	H	2B	3B	HR	RBI	AVG	BB	TB	OQ	RANK
1914	SS	BOS	AL	2-8	144	539	66	129	15	6	2	37	.239	32	162	85	40-41
1915	SS	BOS	AL	1-8	100	359	25	72	11	0	0	28	.201	17	83	61	—
1916	SS	BOS	AL	1-8	123	366	37	85	19	2	0	27	.232	23	108	83	—
1917	SS	BOS	AL	2-8	157	528	40	127	24	7	0	50	.241	20	165	84	40-40
1918	SS	BOS	AL	1-8	126	443	40	98	11	5	0	43	.221	12	119	68	38-39
1919	SS	BOS	AL	6-8	138	507	41	141	19	0	0	38	.278	19	160	80	47-49
1920	SS	BOS	AL	5-8	154	569	41	153	21	12	4	61	.269	21	210	83	44-49
1921	SS	BOS	AL	5-8	154	576	65	151	21	9	1	62	.262	27	193	73	47-49
1922	SS	NY	AL	1-8	154	557	64	150	23	5	3	45	.269	23	192	77	46-50
1923	SS	NY	AL	1-8	152	533	48	131	16	4	6	60	.246	13	173	68	45-46
1924	SS	NY	AL	2-8	153	548	56	137	12	6	4	64	.250	21	173	68	40-40
1925	SS	NY/WA	AL	7/1	55	163	13	41	6	1	0	22	.252	6	49	63	—
1926	SS	CHI	AL	5-8	40	143	15	36	10	1	0	13	.252	9	48	78	—
1926	SS	CIN	NL	2-8	4	6	1	4	0	0	0	1	.667	0	4	—	—

MAJOR LEAGUE TOTALS					1654	5837	552	1455	208	58	20	551	.249	243	1839	76	9 yrs

John Thomas Tobin
5'8 142 lbs Batted left

Born May 4, 1892 St Louis, MO
Died Dec 10, 1969 St Louis, MO

YR	POS	TEAM	LG	FIN	G	AB	R	H	2B	3B	HR	RBI	AVG	BB	TB	OQ	RANK
1914	RF	SL	FL	8-8	139	529	81	143	24	10	7	35	.270	51	208	111	23-41
1915	RF	SL	FL	2-8	158	625	92	184	26	13	6	51	.294	68	254	127	9-40
1916	RF	SL	AL	5-8	77	150	16	32	4	1	0	10	.213	12	38	75	—
1918	CF	SL	AL	5-8	122	480	59	133	19	5	0	36	.277	48	162	108	19-39
1919	LF	SL	AL	5-8	127	486	54	159	22	7	6	57	.327	36	213	124	12-49
1920	RF	SL	AL	4-8	147	593	94	202	34	10	4	62	.341	39	268	118	16-49
1921	RF	SL	AL	3-8	150	671	132	236	31	18	8	59	.352	45	327	121	16-49
1922	RF	SL	AL	2-8	146	625	122	207	34	8	13	66	.331	56	296	123	11-50
1923	RF	SL	AL	5-8	151	637	91	202	32	15	13	73	.317	42	303	117	16-46
1924	RF	SL	AL	4-8	136	569	87	170	30	8	2	48	.299	50	222	98	29-40
1925	RF	SL	AL	3-8	77	193	25	58	11	0	2	27	.301	9	75	87	—
1926	RF	WA/BO	AL	4/8	78	242	31	64	9	1	1	17	.264	16	78	77	—
1927	RF	BOS	AL	8-8	111	374	52	116	18	3	2	40	.310	36	146	102	—

MAJOR LEAGUE TOTALS					1619	6174	936	1906	294	99	64	581	.309	508	2590	116	9 yrs

Walter Henry Holke　　　　　Born Dec 25, 1892　St Louis, MO
6'1　185 lbs　Batted both　　　　Died Oct 12, 1954　St Louis, MO

YR	POS	TEAM	LG	FIN	G	AB	R	H	2B	3B	HR	RBI	AVG	BB	TB	OQ	RANK
1914	1B	NY	NL	2-8	2	6	0	2	0	0	0	0	.333	0	2	—	—
1916	1B	NY	NL	4-8	34	111	16	39	4	2	0	13	.351	6	47	138	—
1917	1B	NY	NL	1-8	153	527	55	146	12	7	2	55	.277	34	178	104	26-38
1918	1B	NY	NL	2-8	88	326	38	82	17	4	1	27	.252	10	110	91	—
1919	1B	BOS	NL	6-8	137	518	48	151	14	6	0	48	.292	21	177	98	32-41
1920	1B	BOS	NL	7-8	144	551	53	162	15	11	3	64	.294	28	208	104	29-45
1921	1B	BOS	NL	4-8	150	579	60	151	15	10	3	63	.261	17	195	76	39-39
1922	1B	BOS	NL	8-8	105	395	35	115	9	4	0	46	.291	14	132	76	—
1923	1B	PHI	NL	8-8	147	562	64	175	31	4	7	70	.311	16	235	97	29-41
1924	1B	PHI	NL	7-8	148	563	60	169	23	6	6	64	.300	25	222	96	26-38
1925	1B	PH/CN	NL	6/3	104	318	35	86	13	4	2	37	.270	20	113	82	—

| MAJOR LEAGUE TOTALS | | | | | 1212 | 4456 | 464 | 1278 | 153 | 58 | 24 | 487 | .287 | 191 | 1619 | 96 | 6 yrs |

Harry Edwin Heilmann　　　　Born Aug 3, 1894　San Francisco, CA
6'1　195 lbs　Batted right　　　　Died Jul 9, 1951　Southfield, MI

YR	POS	TEAM	LG	FIN	G	AB	R	H	2B	3B	HR	RBI	AVG	BB	TB	OQ	RANK
1914	CF-1B	DET	AL	4-8	69	182	25	41	8	1	2	18	.225	22	57	101	—
1916	RF-1B	DET	AL	3-8	136	451	57	127	30	11	2	73	.282	42	185	125	10-38
1917	RF-1B	DET	AL	4-8	150	556	57	156	22	11	5	86	.281	41	215	116	15-40
1918	RF-1B	DET	AL	7-8	79	286	34	79	10	6	5	39	.276	35	116	130	—
1919	1B	DET	AL	4-8	140	537	74	172	30	15	8	93	.320	37	256	131	7-49
1920	1B-RF	DET	AL	7-8	145	543	66	168	28	5	9	89	.309	39	233	109	24-49
1921	RF	DET	AL	6-8	149	602	114	237	43	14	19	139	.394	53	365	162	3-49
1922	RF	DET	AL	3-8	118	455	92	162	27	10	21	92	.356	58	272	165	5-50
1923	RF	DET	AL	2-8	144	524	121	211	44	11	18	115	.403	74	331	191	2-46
1924	RF	DET	AL	3-8	153	570	107	197	45	16	10	114	.346	78	304	147	3-40
1925	RF	DET	AL	4-8	150	573	97	225	40	11	13	134	.393	67	326	157	3-42
1926	RF	DET	AL	6-8	141	502	90	184	41	8	9	103	.367	67	268	153	3-41
1927	RF	DET	AL	4-8	141	505	106	201	50	9	14	120	.398	72	311	182	3-43
1928	RF-1B	DET	AL	6-8	151	558	83	183	38	10	14	107	.328	57	283	134	8-42
1929	RF	DET	AL	6-8	125	453	86	156	41	7	15	120	.344	50	256	147	6-41
1930	RF-1B	CIN	NL	7-8	142	459	79	153	43	6	19	91	.333	64	265	141	9-44
1932	1B	CIN	NL	8-8	15	31	3	8	2	0	0	6	.258	0	10	—	—

| MAJOR LEAGUE TOTALS | | | | | 2148 | 7787 | 1291 | 2660 | 542 | 151 | 183 | 1539 | .342 | 856 | 4053 | 147 | 14 yrs |

George Henry Burns
6'1 180 lbs Batted right

Born Jan 31, 1893 Niles, OH
Died Jan 7, 1978 Kirkland, WA

YR	POS	TEAM	LG	FIN	G	AB	R	H	2B	3B	HR	RBI	AVG	BB	TB	OQ	RANK
1914	1B	DET	AL	4-8	137	478	55	139	22	5	5	57	.291	32	186	115	12-41
1915	1B	DET	AL	2-8	105	392	49	99	18	3	5	50	.253	22	138	95	—
1916	1B	DET	AL	3-8	135	479	60	137	22	6	4	73	.286	22	183	106	19-38
1917	1B	DET	AL	4-8	119	407	42	92	14	10	1	40	.226	15	129	83	—
1918	1B	PHI	AL	8-8	130	505	61	178	22	9	6	70	.352	23	236	141	5-39
1919	1B-RF	PHI	AL	8-8	126	470	63	139	29	9	8	57	.296	19	210	113	23-49
1920	RF-1B	PH/CL	AL	8/1	66	116	8	29	7	1	1	20	.250	10	41	88	—
1921	1B	CLE	AL	2-8	84	244	52	88	21	4	0	49	.361	13	117	118	—
1922	1B	BOS	AL	8-8	147	558	71	171	32	5	12	73	.306	20	249	102	35-50
1923	1B	BOS	AL	8-8	146	551	91	181	47	5	7	82	.328	45	259	122	12-46
1924	1B	CLE	AL	6-8	129	462	64	143	37	5	4	68	.310	29	202	104	26-40
1925	1B	CLE	AL	6-8	127	488	69	164	41	4	6	79	.336	24	231	110	22-42
1926	1B	CLE	AL	2-8	151	603	97	216	64	3	4	114	.358	28	298	123	11-41
1927	1B	CLE	AL	6-8	140	549	84	175	51	2	3	78	.319	42	239	108	19-43
1928	1B	CL/NY	AL	7/1	86	213	30	54	12	1	5	30	.254	17	83	93	—
1929	1B	NY/PH	AL	2/1	38	58	5	13	5	0	1	11	.224	2	21	—	—

MAJOR LEAGUE TOTALS					1866	6573	901	2018	444	72	72	951	.307	363	2822	114	10 yrs

Herold Dominic Ruel
5'9 150 lbs Batted right

Born Feb 20, 1896 St Louis, MO
Died Nov 13, 1963 Palo Alto, CA

YR	POS	TEAM	LG	FIN	G	AB	R	H	2B	3B	HR	RBI	AVG	BB	TB	OQ	RANK
1915	C	SL	AL	6-8	10	14	0	0	0	0	0	1	.000	5	0	—	—
1917	C	NY	AL	6-8	6	17	1	2	0	0	0	1	.118	2	2	—	—
1918	C	NY	AL	4-8	3	6	0	2	0	0	0	0	.333	2	2	—	—
1919	C	NY	AL	3-8	79	233	18	56	6	0	0	31	.240	34	62	88	—
1920	C	NY	AL	3-8	82	261	30	70	14	1	1	15	.268	15	89	82	—
1921	C	BOS	AL	5-8	113	358	41	99	21	1	1	45	.277	41	125	91	—
1922	C	BOS	AL	8-8	116	361	34	92	15	1	0	28	.255	41	109	82	—
1923	C	WAS	AL	4-8	136	449	63	142	24	3	0	54	.316	55	172	109	25-46
1924	C	WAS	AL	1-8	149	501	50	142	20	2	0	57	.283	62	166	91	33-40
1925	C	WAS	AL	1-8	127	393	55	122	9	2	0	54	.310	63	135	102	28-42
1926	C	WAS	AL	4-8	117	368	42	110	22	4	1	53	.299	61	143	115	—
1927	C	WAS	AL	3-8	131	428	61	132	16	5	1	52	.308	63	161	109	17-43
1928	C	WAS	AL	4-8	108	350	31	90	18	2	0	55	.257	44	112	88	—
1929	C	WAS	AL	5-8	69	188	16	46	4	2	0	20	.245	31	54	85	—
1930	C	WAS	AL	2-8	66	198	18	50	3	4	0	26	.253	24	61	80	—
1931	C	BO/DE	AL	6/7	47	133	7	31	6	0	0	9	.233	14	37	73	—
1932	C	DET	AL	5-8	51	136	10	32	4	2	0	18	.235	17	40	78	—
1933	C	SL	AL	8-8	36	63	13	12	2	0	0	8	.190	24	14	—	—
1934	C	CHI	AL	8-8	22	57	4	12	3	0	0	7	.211	8	15	—	—

MAJOR LEAGUE TOTALS					1468	4514	494	1242	187	29	4	534	.275	606	1499	—	—

David James Bancroft　　　　　　　Born Apr 20, 1891　Sioux City, IA
5'9　160 lbs　Batted both　　　　　　　Died Oct 9, 1972　Superior, WI

YR	POS	TEAM	LG	FIN	G	AB	R	H	2B	3B	HR	RBI	AVG	BB	TB	OQ	RANK
1915	SS	PHI	NL	1-8	153	563	85	143	18	2	7	30	.254	77	186	115	17-45
1916	SS	PHI	NL	2-8	142	477	53	101	10	0	3	33	.212	74	120	97	33-36
1917	SS	PHI	NL	2-8	127	478	56	116	22	5	4	43	.243	44	160	105	25-38
1918	SS	PHI	NL	6-8	125	499	69	132	19	4	0	26	.265	54	159	107	24-40
1919	SS	PHI	NL	8-8	92	335	45	91	13	7	0	25	.272	31	118	111	—
1920	SS	PH/NY	NL	8/2	150	613	102	183	36	9	0	36	.299	42	237	111	23-45
1921	SS	NY	NL	1-8	153	606	121	193	26	15	6	67	.318	66	267	123	11-39
1922	SS	NY	NL	1-8	156	651	117	209	41	5	4	60	.321	79	272	116	17-39
1923	SS-2B	NY	NL	1-8	107	444	80	135	33	3	1	31	.304	62	177	116	14-41
1924	SS	BOS	NL	8-8	79	319	49	89	11	1	2	21	.279	37	108	97	—
1925	SS	BOS	NL	5-8	128	479	75	153	29	8	2	49	.319	64	204	118	15-37
1926	SS	BOS	NL	7-8	127	453	70	141	18	6	1	44	.311	64	174	117	15-42
1927	SS	BOS	NL	7-8	111	375	44	91	13	4	1	31	.243	43	115	86	—
1928	SS	BRO	NL	6-8	149	515	47	127	19	5	0	51	.247	59	156	82	40-45
1929	SS	BRO	NL	6-8	104	358	35	99	11	3	1	44	.277	29	119	78	—
1930	SS	NY	NL	3-8	10	17	0	1	1	0	0	0	.059	2	2	—	—

| MAJOR LEAGUE TOTALS | | | | | 1913 | 7182 | 1048 | 2004 | 320 | 77 | 32 | 591 | .279 | 827 | 2574 | 110 | 11 yrs |

Robert Arthur O'Farrell　　　　　　　Born Oct 19, 1896　Waukegan, IL
5'9　180 lbs　Batted right　　　　　　　Died Feb 20, 1988　Waukegan, IL

YR	POS	TEAM	LG	FIN	G	AB	R	H	2B	3B	HR	RBI	AVG	BB	TB	OQ	RANK
1915	C	CHI	NL	4-8	2	3	0	1	0	0	0	0	.333	0	1	—	—
1916	C	CHI	NL	5-8	1	0	0	0	0	0	0	0	—	0	0	—	—
1917	C	CHI	NL	5-8	3	8	1	3	2	0	0	1	.375	1	5	—	—
1918	C	CHI	NL	1-8	52	113	9	32	7	3	1	14	.283	10	48	133	—
1919	C	CHI	NL	3-8	49	125	11	27	4	2	0	9	.216	7	35	78	—
1920	C	CHI	NL	5-8	94	270	29	67	11	4	3	19	.248	34	95	108	—
1921	C	CHI	NL	7-8	96	260	32	65	12	7	4	32	.250	18	103	95	—
1922	C	CHI	NL	5-8	128	392	68	127	18	8	4	60	.324	79	173	139	3-39
1923	C	CHI	NL	4-8	131	452	73	144	25	4	12	84	.319	67	213	136	6-41
1924	C	CHI	NL	5-8	71	183	25	44	6	2	3	28	.240	30	63	103	—
1925	C	CH/SL	NL	8/4	111	339	39	92	13	3	3	35	.271	48	120	97	—
1926	C	SL	NL	1-8	147	492	63	144	30	9	7	68	.293	61	213	121	12-42
1927	C	SL	NL	2-8	61	178	19	47	10	1	0	18	.264	23	59	96	—
1928	C	SL/NY	NL	1/2	91	185	29	37	7	0	2	24	.200	47	50	97	—
1929	C	NY	NL	3-8	91	248	35	76	14	3	4	42	.306	28	108	108	—
1930	C	NY	NL	3-8	94	249	37	75	16	4	4	54	.301	31	111	107	—
1931	C	NY	NL	2-8	85	174	11	39	8	3	1	19	.224	21	56	88	—
1932	C	NY	NL	6-8	50	67	7	16	3	0	0	8	.239	11	19	—	—
1933	C	SL	NL	5-8	55	163	16	39	4	2	2	20	.239	15	53	93	—
1934	C	CN/CH	NL	8/3	66	190	13	45	11	3	1	14	.237	14	65	84	—
1935	C	SL	NL	2-8	14	10	0	0	0	0	0	0	.000	2	0	—	—

| MAJOR LEAGUE TOTALS | | | | | 1492 | 4101 | 517 | 1120 | 201 | 58 | 51 | 549 | .273 | 547 | 1590 | — | — |

George Harold Sisler
5'11 170 lbs Batted left

Born Mar 24, 1893 Manchester, OH
Died Mar 26, 1973 Richmond Heights, MO

YR	POS	TEAM	LG	FIN	G	AB	R	H	2B	3B	HR	RBI	AVG	BB	TB	OQ	RANK
1915	1B-RF	SL	AL	6-8	81	274	28	78	10	2	3	29	.285	7	101	96	—
1916	1B	SL	AL	5-8	151	580	83	177	21	11	4	76	.305	40	232	120	13-38
1917	1B	SL	AL	7-8	135	539	60	190	30	9	2	52	.353	30	244	142	4-40
1918	1B	SL	AL	5-8	114	452	69	154	21	9	2	41	.341	40	199	143	3-39
1919	1B	SL	AL	5-8	132	511	96	180	31	15	10	83	.352	27	271	147	4-49
1920	1B	SL	AL	4-8	154	631	137	257	49	18	19	122	.407	46	399	178	3-49
1921	1B	SL	AL	3-8	138	582	125	216	38	18	12	104	.371	34	326	139	6-49
1922	1B	SL	AL	2-8	142	586	134	246	42	18	8	105	.420	49	348	171	3-50
1924	1B	SL	AL	4-8	151	636	94	194	27	10	9	74	.305	31	268	97	30-40
1925	1B	SL	AL	3-8	150	649	100	224	21	15	12	105	.345	27	311	111	19-42
1926	1B	SL	AL	7-8	150	613	78	178	21	12	7	71	.290	30	244	92	33-41
1927	1B	SL	AL	7-8	149	614	87	201	32	8	5	97	.327	24	264	101	28-43
1928	1B	WAS	AL	4-8	20	49	1	12	1	0	0	2	.245	1	13	—	—
1928	1B	BOS	NL	7-8	118	491	71	167	26	4	4	68	.340	30	213	111	20-45
1929	1B	BOS	NL	8-8	154	629	67	205	40	8	2	79	.326	33	267	96	33-46
1930	1B	BOS	NL	8-8	116	431	54	133	15	7	3	67	.309	23	171	85	—

MAJOR LEAGUE TOTALS 2055 8267 1284 2812 425 164 102 1175 .340 472 3871 127 13 yrs

George Lange Kelly
6'4 190 lbs Batted right

Born Sep 10, 1895 San Francisco, CA
Died Oct 13, 1984 Burlingame, CA

YR	POS	TEAM	LG	FIN	G	AB	R	H	2B	3B	HR	RBI	AVG	BB	TB	OQ	RANK
1915	1B-CF	NY	NL	8-8	17	38	2	6	0	0	1	4	.158	1	9	—	—
1916	1B-RF	NY	NL	4-8	49	76	4	12	2	1	0	3	.158	6	16	—	—
1917	1B-LF	NY/PIT	NL	1/8	19	30	2	2	0	1	0	0	.067	1	4	—	—
1919	1B	NY	NL	2-8	32	107	12	31	6	2	1	14	.290	3	44	113	—
1920	1B	NY	NL	2-8	155	590	69	157	22	11	11	94	.266	41	234	108	26-45
1921	1B	NY	NL	1-8	149	587	95	181	42	9	23	122	.308	40	310	132	6-39
1922	1B	NY	NL	1-8	151	592	96	194	33	8	17	107	.328	30	294	119	15-39
1923	1B	NY	NL	1-8	145	560	82	172	23	5	16	103	.307	47	253	116	15-41
1924	1B	NY	NL	1-8	144	571	91	185	37	9	21	136	.324	38	303	135	7-38
1925	2B-1B	NY	NL	2-8	147	586	87	181	29	3	20	99	.309	35	276	110	20-37
1926	1B-2B	NY	NL	5-8	136	499	70	151	24	4	13	80	.303	36	222	114	16-42
1927	1B-2B	CIN	NL	5-8	61	222	27	60	16	4	5	21	.270	11	99	104	—
1928	1B-LF	CIN	NL	5-8	116	402	46	119	33	7	3	58	.296	28	175	106	—
1929	1B	CIN	NL	7-8	147	577	73	169	45	9	5	103	.293	33	247	93	37-46
1930	1B	CN/CH	NL	7/2	90	354	40	109	16	2	8	54	.308	14	153	89	—
1932	1B	BRO	NL	3-8	64	202	23	49	9	1	4	22	.243	22	72	95	—

MAJOR LEAGUE TOTALS 1622 5993 819 1778 337 76 148 1020 .297 386 2711 116 8 yrs

William Chester Jacobson   Born Aug 16, 1890 Cable, IL
6'3 215 lbs Batted right   Died Jan 16, 1977 Orion, IL

YR	POS	TEAM	LG	FIN	G	AB	R	H	2B	3B	HR	RBI	AVG	BB	TB	OQ	RANK
1915	RF-1B	DE/SL	AL	2/6	71	180	18	38	12	3	1	13	.211	15	59	91	—
1917	RF	SL	AL	7-8	148	529	53	131	23	7	4	55	.248	31	180	96	31-40
1919	CF	SL	AL	5-8	120	455	70	147	31	8	4	51	.323	24	206	122	14-49
1920	CF	SL	AL	4-8	154	609	97	216	34	14	9	122	.355	46	305	134	9-49
1921	CF	SL	AL	3-8	151	599	90	211	38	14	5	90	.352	42	292	122	14-49
1922	CF	SL	AL	2-8	145	555	88	176	22	16	9	102	.317	46	257	117	15-50
1923	CF	SL	AL	5-8	147	592	76	183	29	6	8	81	.309	29	248	100	32-46
1924	CF	SL	AL	4-8	152	579	103	184	41	12	19	97	.318	35	306	124	13-40
1925	CF	SL	AL	3-8	142	540	103	184	30	9	15	76	.341	45	277	126	8-42
1926	RF	SL/BO	AL	7/8	148	576	62	172	51	2	8	90	.299	31	251	102	29-41
1927	LF-CF	Bo/Cl/Ph	AL	8/6/2	94	293	27	72	17	3	1	42	.246	11	98	71	—

MAJOR LEAGUE TOTALS					1472	5507	787	1714	328	94	83	819	.311	355	2479	116	9 yrs

Joseph Ignatius Judge   Born May 25, 1894 Brooklyn, NY
5'8 155 lbs Batted left   Died Mar 11, 1963 Washington, DC

YR	POS	TEAM	LG	FIN	G	AB	R	H	2B	3B	HR	RBI	AVG	BB	TB	OQ	RANK
1915	1B-RF	WAS	AL	4-8	12	41	7	17	2	0	0	9	.415	4	19	—	—
1916	1B	WAS	AL	7-8	103	336	42	74	10	8	0	28	.220	54	100	104	—
1917	1B	WAS	AL	5-8	102	393	62	112	15	15	2	30	.285	50	163	138	—
1918	1B	WAS	AL	3-8	130	502	56	131	23	7	1	46	.261	49	171	106	21-39
1919	1B	WAS	AL	7-8	135	521	83	150	33	12	2	31	.288	81	213	129	8-49
1920	1B	WAS	AL	6-8	126	493	103	164	19	15	5	51	.333	65	228	134	10-49
1921	1B	WAS	AL	4-8	153	622	87	187	26	11	7	72	.301	68	256	105	28-49
1922	1B	WAS	AL	6-8	148	591	84	174	32	15	10	81	.294	50	266	111	22-50
1923	1B	WAS	AL	4-8	113	405	56	127	24	6	2	63	.314	58	169	121	—
1924	1B	WAS	AL	1-8	140	516	71	167	38	9	3	79	.324	53	232	118	18-40
1925	1B	WAS	AL	1-8	112	376	65	118	31	5	8	66	.314	55	183	129	—
1926	1B	WAS	AL	4-8	134	453	70	132	25	11	7	92	.291	53	200	115	17-41
1927	1B	WAS	AL	3-8	137	522	68	161	29	11	2	71	.308	45	218	105	24-43
1928	1B	WAS	AL	4-8	153	542	78	166	31	10	3	93	.306	80	226	120	15-42
1929	1B	WAS	AL	5-8	143	543	83	171	35	8	6	71	.315	73	240	120	18-41
1930	1B	WAS	AL	2-8	126	442	83	144	29	11	10	80	.326	60	225	133	13-40
1931	1B	WAS	AL	3-8	35	74	11	21	3	0	0	9	.284	8	24	—	—
1932	1B	WAS	AL	3-8	82	291	45	75	16	3	3	29	.258	37	106	95	—
1933	1B	BRO	NL	6-8	42	112	7	24	2	1	0	9	.214	7	28	68	—
1933	1B	BOS	AL	7-8	35	108	20	32	8	1	0	22	.296	13	42	107	—
1934	1B	BOS	AL	4-8	10	15	3	5	2	0	0	2	.333	2	7	—	—

MAJOR LEAGUE TOTALS					2171	7898	1184	2352	433	159	71	1034	.298	965	3316	118	11 yrs

Kenneth Roy Williams
6'0 170 lbs Batted left

Born Jun 28, 1890 Grants Pass, OR
Died Jan 22, 1959 Grants Pass, OR

YR	POS	TEAM	LG	FIN	G	AB	R	H	2B	3B	HR	RBI	AVG	BB	TB	OQ	RANK
1915	LF	CIN	NL	7-8	71	219	22	53	10	4	0	16	.242	15	71	95	—
1916	LF	CIN	NL	7-8	10	27	1	3	0	0	0	1	.111	2	3	—	—
1918	PH	SL	AL	5-8	2	1	0	0	0	0	0	1	.000	1	0	—	—
1919	CF	SL	AL	5-8	65	227	32	68	10	5	6	35	.300	26	106	135	—
1920	LF	SL	AL	4-8	141	521	90	160	34	13	10	72	.307	41	250	121	15-49
1921	LF	SL	AL	3-8	146	547	115	190	31	7	24	117	.347	74	307	151	4-49
1922	LF	SL	AL	2-8	153	585	128	194	34	11	39	155	.332	74	367	165	4-50
1923	LF	SL	AL	5-8	147	555	106	198	37	12	29	91	.357	79	346	176	4-46
1924	LF	SL	AL	4-8	114	398	78	129	21	4	18	84	.324	69	212	150	2-40
1925	LF	SL	AL	3-8	102	411	83	136	31	5	25	105	.331	37	252	147	—
1926	LF	SL	AL	7-8	108	347	55	97	15	7	17	74	.280	39	177	126	—
1927	LF	SL	AL	7-8	131	423	70	136	23	6	17	74	.322	57	222	140	4-43
1928	LF	BOS	AL	8-8	133	462	59	140	25	1	8	67	.303	37	191	104	28-42
1929	CF	BOS	AL	8-8	74	139	21	48	14	2	3	21	.345	15	75	141	—

| MAJOR LEAGUE TOTALS | | | | | 1397 | 4862 | 860 | 1552 | 285 | 77 | 196 | 913 | .319 | 566 | 2579 | 144 | 7 yrs |

Edgar Charles Rice
5'9 150 lbs Batted left

Born Feb 20, 1890 Morocco, IN
Died Oct 13, 1974 Rossmor, MD

YR	POS	TEAM	LG	FIN	G	AB	R	H	2B	3B	HR	RBI	AVG	BB	TB	OQ	RANK
1915	P	WAS	AL	4-8	4	8	0	3	0	0	0	0	.375	0	3	—	—
1916	RF	WAS	AL	7-8	58	197	26	59	8	3	1	17	.299	15	76	117	—
1917	RF	WAS	AL	5-8	155	586	77	177	25	7	0	69	.302	50	216	118	13-40
1918	RF	WAS	AL	3-8	7	23	3	8	1	0	0	3	.348	2	9	—	—
1919	RF	WAS	AL	7-8	141	557	80	179	23	9	3	71	.321	42	229	117	18-49
1920	CF	WAS	AL	6-8	153	624	83	211	29	9	3	80	.338	39	267	111	21-49
1921	CF	WAS	AL	4-8	143	561	83	185	39	13	4	79	.330	38	262	113	20-49
1922	CF	WAS	AL	6-8	154	633	91	187	37	13	6	69	.295	48	268	104	33-50
1923	RF	WAS	AL	4-8	148	595	117	188	35	18	3	75	.316	57	268	118	14-46
1924	RF	WAS	AL	1-8	154	646	106	216	39	14	1	76	.334	46	286	111	22-40
1925	RF	WAS	AL	1-8	152	649	111	227	31	13	1	87	.350	37	287	107	25-42
1926	RF	WAS	AL	4-8	152	641	98	216	32	14	3	76	.337	42	285	112	20-41
1927	RF	WAS	AL	3-8	142	603	98	179	33	14	2	65	.297	36	246	96	32-43
1928	RF	WAS	AL	4-8	148	616	95	202	32	15	2	55	.328	49	270	114	19-42
1929	RF	WAS	AL	5-8	150	616	119	199	39	10	1	62	.323	55	261	108	27-41
1930	RF	WAS	AL	2-8	147	593	121	207	35	13	1	73	.349	55	271	117	22-40
1931	RF	WAS	AL	3-8	120	413	81	128	21	8	0	42	.310	35	165	103	—
1932	RF	WAS	AL	3-8	106	288	58	93	16	7	1	34	.323	32	126	116	—
1933	RF	WAS	AL	1-8	73	85	19	25	4	3	1	12	.294	3	38	101	—
1934	RF	CLE	AL	3-8	97	335	48	98	19	1	1	33	.293	28	122	90	—

| MAJOR LEAGUE TOTALS | | | | | 2404 | 9269 | 1514 | 2987 | 498 | 184 | 34 | 1078 | .322 | 709 | 3955 | 111 | 13 yrs |

Oscar Emil Felsch   Born Aug 22, 1891 Milwaukee, WI
5'11 175 lbs Batted right   Died Aug 17, 1964 Milwaukee, WI

YR	POS	TEAM	LG	FIN	G	AB	R	H	2B	3B	HR	RBI	AVG	BB	TB	OQ	RANK
1915	CF	CHI	AL	3-8	121	427	65	106	18	11	3	53	.248	51	155	112	18-42
1916	CF	CHI	AL	2-8	146	546	73	164	24	12	7	70	.300	31	233	123	12-38
1917	CF	CHI	AL	1-8	152	575	75	177	17	10	6	102	.308	33	232	121	11-40
1918	CF	CHI	AL	6-8	53	206	16	52	2	5	1	20	.252	15	67	95	—
1919	CF	CHI	AL	1-8	135	502	68	138	34	11	7	86	.275	40	215	114	22-49
1920	CF	CHI	AL	2-8	142	556	88	188	40	15	14	115	.338	37	300	137	8-49

MAJOR LEAGUE TOTALS   749 2812 385 825 135 64 38 446 .293 207 1202 121 5 yrs

Rogers Hornsby   Born Apr 27, 1896 Winters, TX
5'11 175 lbs Batted right   Died Jan 5, 1963   Chicago, IL

YR	POS	TEAM	LG	FIN	G	AB	R	H	2B	3B	HR	RBI	AVG	BB	TB	OQ	RANK
1915	SS	SL	NL	6-8	18	57	5	14	2	0	0	4	.246	2	16	—	—
1916	3B-SS	SL	NL	7-8	139	495	63	155	17	15	6	65	.313	40	220	144	4-36
1917	SS	SL	NL	3-8	145	523	86	171	24	17	8	66	.327	45	253	158	2-38
1918	SS	SL	NL	8-8	115	416	51	117	19	11	5	60	.281	40	173	132	7-40
1919	3B-SS	SL	NL	7-8	138	512	68	163	15	9	8	71	.318	48	220	140	3-41
1920	2B	SL	NL	5-8	149	589	96	218	44	20	9	94	.370	60	329	179	1-45
1921	2B	SL	NL	3-8	154	592	131	235	44	18	21	126	.397	60	378	187	1-39
1922	2B	SL	NL	3-8	154	623	141	250	46	14	42	152	.401	65	450	202	1-39
1923	2B	SL	NL	5-8	107	424	89	163	32	10	17	83	.384	55	266	185	1-41
1924	2B	SL	NL	6-8	143	536	121	227	43	14	25	94	.424	89	373	229	1-38
1925	2B	SL	NL	4-8	138	504	133	203	41	10	39	143	.403	83	381	221	1-37
1926	2B	SL	NL	1-8	134	527	96	167	34	5	11	93	.317	61	244	130	8-42
1927	2B	NY	NL	3-8	155	568	133	205	32	9	26	125	.361	86	333	178	1-40
1928	2B	BOS	NL	7-8	140	486	99	188	42	7	21	94	.387	107	307	205	1-45
1929	2B	CHI	NL	1-8	156	602	156	229	47	8	39	149	.380	87	409	181	1-46
1930	2B	CHI	NL	2-8	42	104	15	32	5	1	2	18	.308	12	45	104	—
1931	2B-3B	CHI	NL	3-8	100	357	64	118	37	1	16	90	.331	56	205	169	—
1932	RF-3B	CHI	NL	1-8	19	58	10	13	2	0	1	7	.224	10	18	—	—
1933	2B	SL	NL	5-8	46	83	9	27	6	0	2	21	.325	12	39	—	—
1933	PH	SL	AL	8-8	11	9	2	3	1	0	1	2	.333	2	7	—	—
1934	RF-3B	SL	AL	6-8	24	23	2	7	2	0	1	11	.304	7	12	—	—
1935	1B-2B	SL	AL	7-8	10	24	1	5	3	0	0	3	.208	3	8	—	—
1936	1B	SL	AL	7-8	2	5	1	2	0	0	0	2	.400	1	2	—	—
1937	2B	SL	AL	8-8	20	56	7	18	3	0	1	11	.321	7	24	—	—

MAJOR LEAGUE TOTALS   2259 8173 1579 2930 541 169 301 1584 .358 1038 4712 177 14 yrs

Charles Devine Jamieson   Born Feb 7, 1893   Paterson, NJ
5'8 165 lbs Batted left   Died Oct 27, 1969 Paterson, NJ

YR	POS	TEAM	LG	FIN	G	AB	R	H	2B	3B	HR	RBI	AVG	BB	TB	OQ	RANK
1915	LF	WAS	AL	4-8	17	68	9	19	3	2	0	7	.279	6	26	—	—
1916	LF-RF	WAS	AL	7-8	64	145	16	36	4	0	0	13	.248	18	40	94	—
1917	RF	WA/PH	AL	5/8	105	380	45	98	8	2	0	29	.258	43	110	99	—
1918	RF	PHI	AL	8-8	110	416	50	84	11	2	0	11	.202	54	99	82	36-39
1919	P-CF	CLE	AL	2-8	26	17	3	6	2	1	0	2	.353	0	10	—	—
1920	LF	CLE	AL	1-8	108	370	69	118	17	7	1	40	.319	41	152	115	—
1921	LF	CLE	AL	2-8	140	536	94	166	33	10	1	46	.310	67	222	110	23-49
1922	LF	CLE	AL	4-8	145	567	87	183	29	11	3	57	.323	54	243	113	20-50
1923	LF	CLE	AL	3-8	152	644	130	222	36	12	2	51	.345	80	288	129	10-46
1924	LF	CLE	AL	6-8	143	594	98	213	34	8	3	54	.359	47	272	120	17-40
1925	LF	CLE	AL	6-8	138	557	109	165	24	5	4	42	.296	72	211	101	29-42
1926	LF	CLE	AL	2-8	143	555	89	166	33	7	2	45	.299	53	219	102	27-41
1927	LF	CLE	AL	6-8	127	489	73	151	23	6	0	36	.309	64	186	107	22-43
1928	LF	CLE	AL	7-8	112	433	63	133	18	4	1	37	.307	56	162	107	23-42
1929	LF	CLE	AL	3-8	102	364	56	106	22	1	0	26	.291	50	130	99	—
1930	LF	CLE	AL	4-8	103	366	64	110	22	1	1	52	.301	36	137	94	—
1931	LF	CLE	AL	4-8	28	43	7	13	2	1	0	4	.302	5	17	—	—
1932	LF	CLE	AL	4-8	16	16	0	1	1	0	0	0	.063	2	2	—	—
MAJOR LEAGUE TOTALS					1779	6560	1062	1990	322	80	18	552	.303	748	2526	108	9 yrs

Lawton Walter Witt   Born Sep 28, 1895 Orange, MA
5'7 150 lbs Batted left   Died Jul 14, 1988   Alloway, NJ

YR	POS	TEAM	LG	FIN	G	AB	R	H	2B	3B	HR	RBI	AVG	BB	TB	OQ	RANK
1916	SS	PHI	AL	8-8	143	563	64	138	16	15	2	36	.245	55	190	102	25-38
1917	SS	PHI	AL	8-8	128	452	62	114	13	4	0	28	.252	65	135	107	24-40
1919	LF-2B	PHI	AL	8-8	122	460	56	123	15	6	0	33	.267	46	150	95	33-49
1920	RF-2B	PHI	AL	8-8	65	218	29	70	11	3	1	25	.321	27	90	119	—
1921	RF	PHI	AL	8-8	154	629	100	198	31	11	4	45	.315	77	263	111	21-49
1922	CF	NY	AL	1-8	140	528	98	157	11	6	4	40	.297	89	192	111	24-50
1923	CF	NY	AL	1-8	146	596	113	187	18	10	6	56	.314	67	243	112	21-46
1924	CF	NY	AL	2-8	147	600	88	178	26	5	1	36	.297	45	217	89	36-40
1925	CF	NY	AL	7-8	31	40	9	8	2	1	0	0	.200	6	12	—	—
1926	CF	BRO	NL	6-8	63	85	13	22	1	1	0	3	.259	12	25	—	—
MAJOR LEAGUE TOTALS					1139	4171	632	1195	144	62	18	302	.287	489	1517	104	7 yrs

Carson Lee Bigbee   Born Mar 31, 1895   Waterloo, OR
5'9 157 lbs Batted left   Died Oct 17, 1964 Portland, OR

YR	POS	TEAM	LG	FIN	G	AB	R	H	2B	3B	HR	RBI	AVG	BB	TB	OQ	RANK
1916	2B-LF	PIT	NL	6-8	43	164	17	41	3	6	0	3	.250	7	56	96	—
1917	LF-2B	PIT	NL	8-8	133	469	46	112	11	6	0	21	.239	37	135	90	36-38
1918	LF	PIT	NL	4-8	92	310	47	79	11	3	1	19	.255	42	99	113	—
1919	CF	PIT	NL	4-8	125	478	61	132	11	4	2	27	.276	37	157	102	26-41
1920	LF	PIT	NL	4-8	137	550	78	154	19	15	4	32	.280	45	215	112	20-45
1921	LF	PIT	NL	2-8	147	632	100	204	23	17	3	42	.323	41	270	111	20-39
1922	LF	PIT	NL	3-8	150	614	113	215	29	15	5	99	.350	56	289	126	10-39
1923	LF	PIT	NL	3-8	123	499	79	149	18	7	0	54	.299	43	181	96	32-41
1924	LF	PIT	NL	3-8	89	282	42	74	4	1	0	15	.262	26	80	78	—
1925	LF-RF	PIT	NL	1-8	66	126	31	30	7	0	0	8	.238	7	37	66	—
1926	LF	PIT	NL	3-8	42	68	15	15	3	1	2	4	.221	3	26	—	—
MAJOR LEAGUE TOTALS					1147	4192	629	1205	139	75	17	324	.287	344	1545	106	6 yrs

Charles John Grimm   Born Aug 25, 1896   St Louis, MO
5'11 173 lbs Batted left   Died Nov 15, 1983 Scottsdale, AZ

YR	POS	TEAM	LG	FIN	G	AB	R	H	2B	3B	HR	RBI	AVG	BB	TB	OQ	RANK
1916	RF	PHI	AL	8-8	12	22	0	2	0	0	0	0	.091	2	2	—	—
1918	1B	SL	NL	8-8	50	141	11	31	7	0	0	12	.220	6	38	74	—
1919	1B	PIT	NL	4-8	14	44	6	14	1	3	0	6	.318	2	21	—	—
1920	1B	PIT	NL	4-8	148	533	38	121	13	7	2	54	.227	30	154	76	45-45
1921	1B	PIT	NL	2-8	151	562	62	154	21	17	7	71	.274	31	230	98	30-39
1922	1B	PIT	NL	3-8	154	593	64	173	28	13	0	76	.292	43	227	94	31-39
1923	1B	PIT	NL	3-8	152	563	78	194	29	13	7	99	.345	41	270	127	9-41
1924	1B	PIT	NL	3-8	151	542	53	156	25	12	2	63	.288	37	211	98	24-38
1925	1B	CHI	NL	8-8	141	519	73	159	29	5	10	76	.306	38	228	106	22-37
1926	1B	CHI	NL	4-8	147	524	58	145	30	6	8	82	.277	49	211	106	25-42
1927	1B	CHI	NL	4-8	147	543	68	169	29	6	2	74	.311	45	216	107	18-40
1928	1B	CHI	NL	3-8	147	547	67	161	25	5	5	62	.294	39	211	96	30-45
1929	1B	CHI	NL	1-8	120	463	66	138	28	3	10	91	.298	42	202	102	31-46
1930	1B	CHI	NL	2-8	114	429	58	124	27	2	6	66	.289	41	173	92	35-44
1931	1B	CHI	NL	3-8	146	531	65	176	33	11	4	66	.331	53	243	129	12-36
1932	1B	CHI	NL	1-8	149	570	66	175	42	2	7	80	.307	35	242	108	24-38
1933	1B	CHI	NL	3-8	107	384	38	95	15	2	3	37	.247	23	123	86	—
1934	1B	CHI	NL	3-8	75	267	24	79	8	1	5	47	.296	16	104	98	—
1935	1B	CHI	NL	1-8	2	8	0	0	0	0	0	0	.000	0	0	—	—
1936	1B	CHI	NL	2-8	39	132	13	33	4	0	1	16	.250	5	40	70	—
MAJOR LEAGUE TOTALS					2166	7917	908	2299	394	108	79	1078	.290	578	3146	103	13 yrs

Aaron Lee Ward　　　　　　　　　　Born Aug 28, 1896 Booneville, AR
5'10　160 lbs　Batted right　　　　　Died Jan 30, 1961　New Orleans, LA

YR	POS	TEAM	LG	FIN	G	AB	R	H	2B	3B	HR	RBI	AVG	BB	TB	OQ	RANK
1917	SS	NY	AL	6-8	8	26	0	3	0	0	0	1	.115	1	3	—	—
1918	SS-CF	NY	AL	4-8	20	32	2	4	1	0	0	1	.125	2	5	—	—
1919	1B-3B	NY	AL	3-8	27	34	5	7	2	0	0	2	.206	5	9	—	—
1920	3B-SS	NY	AL	3-8	127	496	62	127	18	7	11	54	.256	33	192	91	40-49
1921	2B-3B	NY	AL	1-8	153	556	77	170	30	10	5	75	.306	42	235	101	31-49
1922	2B	NY	AL	1-8	154	558	69	149	19	5	7	68	.267	45	199	88	39-50
1923	2B	NY	AL	1-8	152	567	79	161	26	11	10	82	.284	56	239	108	26-46
1924	2B	NY	AL	2-8	120	400	42	101	13	10	8	66	.253	40	158	95	—
1925	2B	NY	AL	7-8	125	439	41	108	22	3	4	38	.246	49	148	83	40-42
1926	2B-3B	NY	AL	1-8	22	31	5	10	2	0	0	3	.323	2	12	—	—
1927	2B	CHI	AL	5-8	145	463	75	125	25	8	5	56	.270	63	181	104	25-43
1928	3B-SS	CLE	AL	7-8	6	9	0	1	0	0	0	0	.111	1	1	—	—

| MAJOR LEAGUE TOTALS | | | | | 1059 | 3611 | 457 | 966 | 158 | 54 | 50 | 446 | .268 | 339 | 1382 | 96 | 6 yrs |

Joseph Anthony Dugan　　　　　　Born May 12, 1897 Mahanoy City, PA
5'11　160 lbs　Batted right　　　　　Died Jul 7, 1982　Norwood, MA

YR	POS	TEAM	LG	FIN	G	AB	R	H	2B	3B	HR	RBI	AVG	BB	TB	OQ	RANK
1917	SS	PHI	AL	8-8	43	134	9	26	8	0	0	16	.194	3	34	62	—
1918	SS-2B	PHI	AL	8-8	121	411	26	80	11	3	3	34	.195	16	106	66	39-39
1919	SS	PHI	AL	8-8	104	387	25	105	17	2	1	30	.271	11	129	81	—
1920	3B-SS	PHI	AL	8-8	123	491	65	158	40	5	3	60	.322	19	217	106	26-49
1921	3B	PHI	AL	8-8	119	461	54	136	22	6	10	58	.295	28	200	99	33-49
1922	3B-SS	BO/NY	AL	8/1	144	593	89	170	31	4	6	63	.287	22	227	86	42-50
1923	3B	NY	AL	1-8	146	644	111	182	30	7	7	67	.283	25	247	87	41-46
1924	3B	NY	AL	2-8	148	610	105	184	31	7	3	56	.302	31	238	91	34-40
1925	3B	NY	AL	7-8	102	404	50	118	19	4	0	31	.292	19	145	80	—
1926	3B	NY	AL	1-8	123	434	39	125	19	5	1	64	.288	25	157	86	—
1927	3B	NY	AL	1-8	112	387	44	104	24	3	2	43	.269	27	140	85	—
1928	3B	NY	AL	1-8	94	312	33	86	15	0	6	34	.276	16	119	88	—
1929	3B	BOS	NL	8-8	60	125	14	38	10	0	0	15	.304	8	48	88	—
1931	3B	DET	AL	7-8	8	17	1	4	0	0	0	0	.235	0	4	—	—

| MAJOR LEAGUE TOTALS | | | | | 1447 | 5410 | 665 | 1516 | 277 | 46 | 42 | 571 | .280 | 250 | 2011 | 89 | 6 yrs |

Ross Middlebrook Youngs
5'8 162 lbs Batted left

Born Apr 10, 1897 Shiner, TX
Died Oct 22, 1927 San Antonio, TX

YR	POS	TEAM	LG	FIN	G	AB	R	H	2B	3B	HR	RBI	AVG	BB	TB	OO	RANK
1917	CF	NY	NL	1-8	7	26	5	9	2	3	0	1	.346	1	17	—	—
1918	RF	NY	NL	2-8	121	474	70	143	16	8	1	25	.302	44	178	124	11-40
1919	RF	NY	NL	2-8	130	489	73	152	31	7	2	43	.311	51	203	137	5-41
1920	RF	NY	NL	2-8	153	581	92	204	27	14	6	78	.351	75	277	159	2-45
1921	RF	NY	NL	1-8	141	504	90	165	24	16	3	102	.327	71	230	136	4-39
1922	RF	NY	NL	1-8	149	559	105	185	34	10	7	86	.331	55	260	123	12-39
1923	RF	NY	NL	1-8	152	596	121	200	33	12	3	87	.336	73	266	129	7-41
1924	RF	NY	NL	1-8	133	526	112	187	33	12	10	74	.356	77	274	159	2-38
1925	RF	NY	NL	2-8	130	500	82	132	24	6	6	53	.264	66	186	98	30-37
1926	RF	NY	NL	5-8	95	372	62	114	12	5	4	43	.306	37	148	110	—

MAJOR LEAGUE TOTALS					1211	4627	812	1491	236	93	42	592	.322	550	2039	133	8 yrs

James Joseph Dykes
5'9 185 lbs Batted right

Born Nov 10, 1896 Philadelphia, PA
Died Jun 15, 1976 Philadelphia, PA

YR	POS	TEAM	LG	FIN	G	AB	R	H	2B	3B	HR	RBI	AVG	BB	TB	OO	RANK
1918	2B	PHI	AL	8-8	59	186	13	35	3	3	0	13	.188	19	44	74	—
1919	2B	PHI	AL	8-8	17	49	4	9	1	0	0	1	.184	7	10	—	—
1920	2B-3B	PHI	AL	8-8	142	546	81	140	25	4	8	35	.256	55	197	93	37-49
1921	2B	PHI	AL	8-8	155	613	88	168	32	13	16	77	.274	60	274	106	26-49
1922	3B	PHI	AL	7-8	145	501	66	138	23	7	12	68	.275	55	211	107	29-50
1923	2B-SS	PHI	AL	6-8	124	416	50	105	28	1	4	43	.252	35	147	87	—
1924	2B-3B	PHI	AL	5-8	110	410	68	128	26	6	3	50	.312	38	175	109	—
1925	3B-2B	PHI	AL	2-8	122	465	93	150	32	11	5	55	.323	46	219	117	13-42
1926	3B-2B	PHI	AL	3-8	124	429	54	123	32	5	1	44	.287	49	168	103	25-41
1927	1B-3B	PHI	AL	2-8	121	417	61	135	33	6	3	60	.324	44	189	119	—
1928	2B-SS	PHI	AL	2-8	85	242	39	67	11	0	5	30	.277	27	93	101	—
1929	SS-3B	PHI	AL	1-8	119	401	76	131	34	6	13	79	.327	51	216	141	—
1930	3B	PHI	AL	1-8	125	435	69	131	28	4	6	73	.301	74	185	118	21-40
1931	3B-SS	PHI	AL	1-8	101	355	48	97	28	2	3	46	.273	49	138	106	—
1932	3B	PHI	AL	2-8	153	558	71	148	29	5	7	90	.265	77	208	99	34-48
1933	3B	CHI	AL	6-8	151	554	49	144	22	6	1	68	.260	69	181	90	44-52
1934	3B-2B	CHI	AL	8-8	127	456	52	122	17	4	7	82	.268	64	168	99	32-44
1935	3B-1B	CHI	AL	5-8	117	403	45	116	24	2	4	61	.288	59	156	106	27-51
1936	3B	CHI	AL	3-8	127	435	62	116	16	3	7	60	.267	61	159	92	41-52
1937	1B-3B	CHI	AL	3-8	30	85	10	26	5	0	1	23	.306	9	34	—	—
1938	2B	CHI	AL	6-8	26	89	9	27	4	2	2	13	.303	10	41	—	—
1939	3B	CHI	AL	4-8	2	1	0	0	0	0	0	0	.000	0	0	—	—

MAJOR LEAGUE TOTALS					2282	8046	1108	2256	453	90	108	1071	.280	958	3213	103	11 yrs

John Anthony Mostil   Born Jun 1, 1896   Chicago, IL
5'8 168 lbs Batted right   Died Dec 10, 1970 Midlothian, IL

YR	POS	TEAM	LG	FIN	G	AB	R	H	2B	3B	HR	RBI	AVG	BB	TB	OQ	RANK
1918	2B	CHI	AL	6-8	10	33	4	9	2	2	0	4	.273	1	15	—	—
1921	CF	CHI	AL	7-8	100	326	43	98	21	7	3	42	.301	28	142	105	—
1922	CF	CHI	AL	5-8	132	458	74	139	28	14	7	70	.303	38	216	117	16-50
1923	CF	CHI	AL	7-8	153	546	91	159	37	15	3	64	.291	62	235	113	20-46
1924	CF	CHI	AL	8-8	118	385	75	125	22	5	4	49	.325	45	169	118	—
1925	CF	CHI	AL	5-8	153	605	135	181	36	16	2	50	.299	90	255	114	16-42
1926	CF	CHI	AL	5-8	148	600	120	197	41	15	4	42	.328	79	280	130	9-41
1927	CF	CHI	AL	5-8	13	16	3	2	0	0	0	1	.125	0	2	—	—
1928	CF	CHI	AL	5-8	133	503	69	136	19	8	0	51	.270	66	171	95	32-42
1929	CF	CHI	AL	7-8	12	35	4	8	3	0	0	3	.229	6	11	—	—
MAJOR LEAGUE TOTALS					972	3507	618	1054	209	82	23	376	.301	415	1496	114	5 yrs

Frank Francis Frisch   Born Sep 9, 1898   Bronx, NY
5'11 165 lbs Batted both   Died Mar 12, 1973 Wilmington, DE

YR	POS	TEAM	LG	FIN	G	AB	R	H	2B	3B	HR	RBI	AVG	BB	TB	OQ	RANK
1919	2B-3B	NY	NL	2-8	54	190	21	43	3	2	2	24	.226	4	56	74	—
1920	3B	NY	NL	2-8	110	440	57	123	10	10	4	77	.280	20	165	100	—
1921	3B-2B	NY	NL	1-8	153	618	121	211	31	17	8	100	.341	42	300	128	8-39
1922	2B-3B	NY	NL	1-8	132	514	101	168	16	13	5	51	.327	47	225	115	19-39
1923	2B-3B	NY	NL	1-8	151	641	116	223	32	10	12	111	.348	46	311	128	8-41
1924	2B	NY	NL	1-8	145	603	121	198	33	15	7	69	.328	56	282	128	10-38
1925	3B-2B	NY	NL	2-8	120	502	89	166	26	6	11	48	.331	32	237	115	18-37
1926	2B	NY	NL	5-8	135	545	75	171	29	4	5	44	.314	33	223	105	26-42
1927	2B	SL	NL	2-8	153	617	112	208	31	11	10	78	.337	43	291	126	10-40
1928	2B	SL	NL	1-8	141	547	107	164	29	9	10	86	.300	64	241	117	18-45
1929	2B	SL	NL	4-8	138	527	93	176	40	12	5	74	.334	53	255	119	18-46
1930	2B	SL	NL	1-8	133	540	121	187	46	9	10	114	.346	55	281	125	17-44
1931	2B	SL	NL	1-8	131	518	96	161	24	4	4	82	.311	45	205	108	21-36
1932	2B-3B	SL	NL	6-8	115	486	59	142	26	2	3	60	.292	25	181	93	35-38
1933	2B-SS	SL	NL	5-8	147	585	74	177	32	6	4	66	.303	48	233	117	20-48
1934	2B-3B	SL	NL	1-8	140	550	74	168	30	6	3	75	.305	45	219	106	30-48
1935	2B	SL	NL	2-8	103	354	52	104	16	2	1	55	.294	35	127	100	—
1936	2B-3B	SL	NL	2-8	93	303	40	83	10	0	1	26	.274	36	96	93	—
1937	2B	SL	NL	4-8	17	32	3	7	2	0	0	4	.219	1	9	—	—
MAJOR LEAGUE TOTALS					2311	9112	1532	2880	466	138	105	1244	.316	730	3937	116	14 yrs

William Curtis Walker　　　　　　　Born Jul 3, 1896　Beeville, TX
5'9　170 lbs　Batted left　　　　　　　Died Dec 9, 1955　Beeville, TX

YR	POS	TEAM	LG	FIN	G	AB	R	H	2B	3B	HR	RBI	AVG	BB	TB	OO	RANK
1919	PH	NY	AL	3-8	1	1	0	0	0	0	0	0	.000	0	0	—	—
1920	LF	NY	NL	2-8	8	14	0	1	0	0	0	0	.071	1	1	—	—
1921	CF-RF	NY/PH	NL	1/8	85	269	41	81	15	6	3	43	.301	20	117	111	—
1922	RF	PHI	NL	7-8	148	581	102	196	36	11	12	89	.337	56	290	131	5-39
1923	RF	PHI	NL	8-8	140	527	66	148	26	5	5	66	.281	45	199	97	31-41
1924	RF	PH/CN	NL	7/4	133	468	66	140	27	11	5	54	.299	51	204	119	15-38
1925	RF	CIN	NL	3-8	145	509	86	162	22	16	6	71	.318	57	234	120	11-37
1926	RF	CIN	NL	2-8	155	571	83	175	24	20	6	78	.306	60	257	123	10-42
1927	RF	CIN	NL	5-8	146	527	60	154	16	10	6	80	.292	47	208	105	22-40
1928	RF	CIN	NL	5-8	123	427	64	119	15	12	6	73	.279	49	176	108	24-45
1929	RF	CIN	NL	7-8	141	492	76	154	28	15	7	83	.313	85	233	128	14-46
1930	LF	CIN	NL	7-8	134	472	74	145	26	11	8	51	.307	64	217	112	24-44

| MAJOR LEAGUE TOTALS | | | | | 1359 | 4858 | 718 | 1475 | 235 | 117 | 64 | 688 | .304 | 535 | 2136 | 116 | 9 yrs |

Bernard Albert Friberg　　　　　　Born Aug 18, 1899　Manchester, NH
5'11　178 lbs　Batted right　　　　　　Died Dec 8, 1958　Lynn, MA

YR	POS	TEAM	LG	FIN	G	AB	R	H	2B	3B	HR	RBI	AVG	BB	TB	OO	RANK
1919	CF	CHI	NL	3-8	8	20	0	4	1	0	0	1	.200	0	5	—	—
1920	LF-2B	CHI	NL	5-8	50	114	11	24	5	1	0	7	.211	6	31	70	—
1922	RF	CHI	NL	5-8	97	296	51	92	8	2	0	23	.311	37	104	101	—
1923	3B	CHI	NL	4-8	146	547	91	174	27	11	12	88	.318	45	259	122	12-41
1924	3B	CHI	NL	5-8	142	495	67	138	19	3	5	82	.279	66	178	105	20-38
1925	2B-3B	CH/PH	NL	8/6	135	456	53	121	17	4	6	38	.265	53	164	93	34-37
1926	2B	PHI	NL	8-8	144	478	38	128	21	3	1	51	.268	57	158	94	36-42
1927	3B	PHI	NL	8-8	111	335	31	78	8	2	1	28	.233	41	93	80	—
1928	SS	PHI	NL	8-8	52	94	11	19	3	0	1	7	.202	12	25	73	—
1929	SS-LF	PHI	NL	5-8	128	455	74	137	21	10	7	55	.301	49	199	106	28-46
1930	2B-LF	PHI	NL	8-8	105	331	62	113	21	1	4	42	.341	47	148	117	—
1931	2B-3B	PHI	NL	6-8	103	353	33	92	19	5	1	26	.261	33	124	93	—
1932	2B	PHI	NL	4-8	61	154	17	37	8	2	0	14	.240	19	49	90	—
1933	2B-3B	BOS	AL	7-8	17	41	5	13	3	0	0	9	.317	6	16	—	—

| MAJOR LEAGUE TOTALS | | | | | 1299 | 4169 | 544 | 1170 | 181 | 44 | 38 | 471 | .281 | 471 | 1553 | 104 | 5 yrs |

Horace Hills Ford　　　　　　　　Born Jul 23, 1897　New Haven, CT
5'10　165 lbs　Batted right　　　　　Died Jan 29, 1977　Winchester, MA

YR	POS	TEAM	LG	FIN	G	AB	R	H	2B	3B	HR	RBI	AVG	BB	TB	OQ	RANK
1919	SS-3B	BOS	NL	6-8	10	28	4	6	0	1	0	3	.214	2	8	—	—
1920	2B-SS	BOS	NL	7-8	88	257	16	62	12	5	1	30	.241	18	87	92	—
1921	2B-SS	BOS	NL	4-8	152	555	50	155	29	5	2	61	.279	36	200	90	32-39
1922	SS-2B	BOS	NL	8-8	143	515	58	140	23	9	2	60	.272	30	187	85	35-39
1923	2B-SS	BOS	NL	7-8	111	380	27	103	16	7	2	50	.271	31	139	92	—
1924	2B	PHI	NL	7-8	145	530	58	144	27	5	3	53	.272	27	190	86	34-38
1925	SS	BRO	NL	6-8	66	216	32	59	11	0	1	15	.273	26	73	90	—
1926	SS	CIN	NL	2-8	57	197	14	55	6	1	0	18	.279	14	63	83	—
1927	SS-2B	CIN	NL	5-8	115	409	45	112	16	2	1	46	.274	33	135	87	—
1928	SS	CIN	NL	5-8	149	506	49	122	17	4	0	54	.241	47	147	74	44-45
1929	SS-2B	CIN	NL	7-8	148	529	68	146	14	6	3	50	.276	41	181	79	45-46
1930	SS-2B	CIN	NL	7-8	132	424	36	98	16	7	1	34	.231	24	131	62	—
1931	SS	CIN	NL	8-8	84	175	18	40	8	1	0	13	.229	13	50	72	—
1932	2B-SS	SL/BO	NL	6/5	41	97	9	26	5	2	0	6	.268	6	35	89	—
1933	SS	BOS	NL	4-8	5	15	0	1	0	0	0	1	.067	3	1	—	—

MAJOR LEAGUE TOTALS　　　　　　1446　4833　484　1269　200　55　16　494　.263　351　1627　83　5 yrs

Clarence Edward Galloway　　　　Born Aug 4, 1896　Clinton, SC
5'8　160 lbs　Batted right　　　　　Died Nov 7, 1969　Clinton, SC

YR	POS	TEAM	LG	FIN	G	AB	R	H	2B	3B	HR	RBI	AVG	BB	TB	OQ	RANK
1919	SS	PHI	AL	8-8	17	63	2	9	0	0	0	4	.143	1	9	—	—
1920	SS	PHI	AL	8-8	98	298	28	60	9	3	0	18	.201	22	75	61	—
1921	SS-3B	PHI	AL	8-8	131	465	42	123	28	5	3	47	.265	29	170	82	45-49
1922	SS	PHI	AL	7-8	155	571	83	185	26	9	6	69	.324	39	247	109	26-50
1923	SS	PHI	AL	6-8	134	504	64	140	18	9	2	62	.278	37	182	89	38-46
1924	SS	PHI	AL	5-8	129	464	41	128	16	4	2	48	.276	23	158	78	39-40
1925	SS	PHI	AL	2-8	149	481	52	116	11	4	3	71	.241	59	144	78	41-42
1926	SS	PHI	AL	3-8	133	408	37	98	13	6	0	49	.240	31	123	72	—
1927	SS	PHI	AL	2-8	77	181	25	48	10	4	0	22	.265	18	66	91	—
1928	SS-3B	DET	AL	6-8	53	148	17	39	5	2	1	17	.264	15	51	89	—

MAJOR LEAGUE TOTALS　　　　　　1076　3583　391　946　136　46　17　407　.264　274　1225　87　5 yrs

Stanley Raymond Harris   Born Nov 8, 1896   Port Jervis, NY
5'9   156 lbs   Batted right   Died Nov 8, 1977   Bethesda, MD

YR	POS	TEAM	LG	FIN	G	AB	R	H	2B	3B	HR	RBI	AVG	BB	TB	OQ	RANK
1919	2B	WAS	AL	7-8	8	28	0	6	2	0	0	4	.214	1	8	—	—
1920	2B	WAS	AL	6-8	136	506	76	152	26	6	1	68	.300	41	193	99	33-49
1921	2B	WAS	AL	4-8	154	584	82	169	22	8	0	54	.289	54	207	89	40-49
1922	2B	WAS	AL	6-8	154	602	95	162	24	8	2	40	.269	52	208	87	41-50
1923	2B	WAS	AL	4-8	145	532	60	150	21	13	2	70	.282	50	203	98	33-46
1924	2B	WAS	AL	1-8	143	544	88	146	28	9	1	58	.268	56	195	91	35-40
1925	2B	WAS	AL	1-8	144	551	91	158	30	3	1	66	.287	64	197	93	38-42
1926	2B	WAS	AL	4-8	141	537	94	152	39	9	1	63	.283	58	212	102	26-41
1927	2B	WAS	AL	3-8	128	475	98	127	20	3	1	55	.267	66	156	92	36-43
1928	2B	WAS	AL	4-8	99	358	34	73	11	5	0	28	.204	27	94	63	—
1929	2B-SS	DET	AL	6-8	7	11	3	1	0	0	0	0	.091	2	1	—	—
1931	2B	DET	AL	7-8	4	8	1	1	1	0	0	0	.125	1	2	—	—
MAJOR LEAGUE TOTALS					1263	4736	722	1297	224	64	9	506	.274	472	1676	94	8 yrs

Bibb August Falk   Born Jan 27, 1899   Austin, TX
6'0   175 lbs   Batted left   Died Jun 8, 1989   Austin, TX

YR	POS	TEAM	LG	FIN	G	AB	R	H	2B	3B	HR	RBI	AVG	BB	TB	OQ	RANK
1920	RF	CHI	AL	2-8	7	17	1	5	1	1	0	2	.294	0	8	—	—
1921	LF	CHI	AL	7-8	152	585	62	167	31	11	5	82	.285	37	235	92	37-49
1922	LF	CHI	AL	5-8	131	483	58	144	27	1	12	79	.298	27	209	102	34-50
1923	LF	CHI	AL	7-8	87	274	44	84	18	6	5	38	.307	25	129	120	—
1924	LF	CHI	AL	8-8	138	526	77	185	37	8	6	99	.352	47	256	128	9-40
1925	LF	CHI	AL	5-8	154	602	80	181	35	9	4	99	.301	51	246	98	32-42
1926	LF	CHI	AL	5-8	155	566	86	195	43	4	8	108	.345	66	270	132	8-41
1927	LF	CHI	AL	5-8	145	535	76	175	35	6	9	83	.327	52	249	121	13-43
1928	LF	CHI	AL	5-8	98	286	42	83	18	4	1	37	.290	25	112	100	—
1929	RF	CLE	AL	3-8	125	426	65	133	30	7	13	93	.312	42	216	125	15-41
1930	LF-RF	CLE	AL	4-8	82	191	34	62	12	1	4	36	.325	23	88	119	—
1931	RF	CLE	AL	4-8	79	161	30	49	13	1	2	28	.304	17	70	114	—
MAJOR LEAGUE TOTALS					1353	4652	655	1463	300	59	69	784	.314	412	2088	114	7 yrs

Martin Joseph McManus
5'10 160 lbs Batted right

Born Mar 14, 1900 Chicago, IL
Died Feb 18, 1966 St Louis, MO

YR	POS	TEAM	LG	FIN	G	AB	R	H	2B	3B	HR	RBI	AVG	BB	TB	OQ	RANK
1920	3B	SL	AL	4-8	1	3	0	1	0	1	0	1	.333	0	3	—	—
1921	2B-3B	SL	AL	3-8	121	412	49	107	19	8	3	64	.260	27	151	82	—
1922	2B	SL	AL	2-8	154	606	88	189	34	11	11	109	.312	38	278	111	22-50
1923	2B-1B	SL	AL	5-8	154	582	86	180	35	10	15	94	.309	49	280	121	13-46
1924	2B	SL	AL	4-8	123	442	71	147	23	5	5	80	.333	55	195	122	16-40
1925	2B	SL	AL	3-8	154	587	108	169	44	8	13	90	.288	73	268	114	15-42
1926	3B-2B	SL	AL	7-8	149	549	102	156	30	10	9	68	.284	55	233	107	22-41
1927	SS-2B	DET	AL	4-8	108	369	60	99	19	7	9	69	.268	34	159	103	—
1928	3B-1B	DET	AL	6-8	139	500	78	144	37	5	8	73	.288	51	215	110	21-42
1929	3B	DET	AL	6-8	154	599	99	168	32	8	18	90	.280	60	270	109	24-41
1930	3B	DET	AL	5-8	132	484	74	155	40	4	9	89	.320	59	230	122	18-40
1931	3B-2B	DE/BO	AL	7/6	124	424	47	116	21	3	4	62	.274	57	155	101	33-47
1932	2B-3B	BOS	AL	8-8	93	302	39	71	19	4	5	24	.235	36	113	92	—
1933	3B-2B	BOS	AL	7-8	106	366	51	104	30	4	3	36	.284	49	151	113	—
1934	2B-3B	BOS	NL	4-8	119	435	56	120	18	0	8	47	.276	32	162	95	40-48

MAJOR LEAGUE TOTALS 1831 6660 1008 1926 401 88 120 996 .289 675 2863 111 10 yrs

Robert William Meusel
6'3 190 lbs Batted right

Born Jul 19, 1896 San Jose, CA
Died Nov 28, 1977 Downey, CA

YR	POS	TEAM	LG	FIN	G	AB	R	H	2B	3B	HR	RBI	AVG	BB	TB	OQ	RANK
1920	RF-3B	NY	AL	3-8	119	460	75	151	40	7	11	83	.328	20	238	125	13-49
1921	RF	NY	AL	1-8	149	598	104	190	40	16	24	135	.318	34	334	127	10-49
1922	RF	NY	AL	1-8	121	473	61	151	26	11	16	84	.319	40	247	131	9-50
1923	LF	NY	AL	1-8	132	460	59	144	29	10	9	91	.313	31	220	117	15-46
1924	LF	NY	AL	2-8	143	579	93	188	40	11	12	120	.325	32	286	117	19-40
1925	LF-3B	NY	AL	7-8	156	624	101	181	34	12	33	138	.290	54	338	123	11-42
1926	LF	NY	AL	1-8	108	413	73	130	22	3	12	81	.315	37	194	119	—
1927	LF	NY	AL	1-8	135	516	75	174	47	9	8	103	.337	45	263	130	10-43
1928	LF	NY	AL	1-8	131	518	77	154	45	5	11	113	.297	39	242	114	18-42
1929	LF	NY	AL	2-8	100	391	46	102	15	3	10	57	.261	17	153	84	—
1930	CF	CIN	NL	7-8	113	443	62	128	30	8	10	62	.289	26	204	96	33-44

MAJOR LEAGUE TOTALS 1407 5475 826 1693 368 95 156 1067 .309 375 2719 120 9 yrs

Edward William Brown   Born Jul 17, 1891   Milligan, NE
6'3   190 lbs   Batted right   Died Sep 10, 1956   Vallejo, CA

YR	POS	TEAM	LG	FIN	G	AB	R	H	2B	3B	HR	RBI	AVG	BB	TB	OQ	RANK
1920	CF	NY	NL	2-8	3	8	1	1	1	0	0	0	.125	0	2	—	—
1921	CF	NY	NL	1-8	70	128	16	36	6	2	0	12	.281	4	46	83	—
1924	CF	BRO	NL	2-8	114	455	56	140	30	4	5	78	.308	26	193	107	18-38
1925	CF	BRO	NL	6-8	153	618	88	189	39	11	5	99	.306	22	265	96	32-37
1926	LF	BOS	NL	7-8	153	612	71	201	31	8	2	84	.328	23	254	104	28-42
1927	LF	BOS	NL	7-8	155	558	64	171	35	6	2	75	.306	28	224	100	27-40
1928	LF	BOS	NL	7-8	142	523	45	140	28	2	2	59	.268	24	178	78	43-45
MAJOR LEAGUE TOTALS					790	2902	341	878	170	33	16	407	.303	127	1162	97	5 yrs

Harold Joseph Traynor   Born Nov 11, 1899   Framingham, MA
6'0   170 lbs   Batted right   Died Mar 16, 1972   Pittsburgh, PA

YR	POS	TEAM	LG	FIN	G	AB	R	H	2B	3B	HR	RBI	AVG	BB	TB	OQ	RANK
1920	SS	PIT	NL	4-8	17	52	6	11	3	1	0	2	.212	3	16	—	—
1921	3B-SS	PIT	NL	2-8	7	19	0	5	0	0	0	2	.263	1	5	—	—
1922	3B-SS	PIT	NL	3-8	142	571	89	161	17	12	4	81	.282	27	214	86	34-39
1923	3B	PIT	NL	3-8	153	616	108	208	19	19	12	101	.338	34	301	123	11-41
1924	3B	PIT	NL	3-8	142	545	86	160	26	13	5	82	.294	37	227	105	19-38
1925	3B	PIT	NL	1-8	150	591	114	189	39	14	6	106	.320	52	274	116	17-37
1926	3B	PIT	NL	3-8	152	574	83	182	25	17	3	92	.317	38	250	113	17-42
1927	3B	PIT	NL	1-8	149	573	93	196	32	9	5	106	.342	22	261	116	14-40
1928	3B	PIT	NL	4-8	144	569	91	192	38	12	3	124	.337	28	263	114	19-45
1929	3B	PIT	NL	2-8	130	540	94	192	27	12	4	108	.356	30	255	112	23-46
1930	3B	PIT	NL	5-8	130	497	90	182	22	11	9	119	.366	48	253	125	16-44
1931	3B	PIT	NL	5-8	155	615	81	183	37	15	2	103	.298	54	256	111	18-36
1932	3B	PIT	NL	2-8	135	513	74	169	27	10	2	68	.329	32	222	114	17-38
1933	3B	PIT	NL	2-8	154	624	85	190	27	6	1	82	.304	35	232	104	29-48
1934	3B	PIT	NL	5-8	119	444	62	137	22	10	1	61	.309	21	182	102	38-48
1935	3B	PIT	NL	4-8	57	204	24	57	10	3	1	36	.279	10	76	91	—
1937	3B	PIT	NL	3-8	5	12	3	2	0	0	0	0	.167	0	2	—	—
MAJOR LEAGUE TOTALS					1941	7559	1183	2416	371	164	58	1273	.320	472	3289	111	13 yrs

Joseph Wheeler Sewell   Born Oct 9, 1898   Titus, AL
5'6 155 lbs Batted left   Died Mar 6, 1990   Mobile, AL

YR	POS	TEAM	LG	FIN	G	AB	R	H	2B	3B	HR	RBI	AVG	BB	TB	OQ	RANK
1920	SS	CLE	AL	1-8	22	70	14	23	4	1	0	12	.329	9	29	—	—
1921	SS	CLE	AL	2-8	154	572	101	182	36	12	4	93	.318	80	254	121	15-49
1922	SS	CLE	AL	4-8	153	558	80	167	28	7	2	83	.299	73	215	108	27-50
1923	SS	CLE	AL	3-8	153	553	98	195	41	10	3	109	.353	98	265	150	5-46
1924	SS	CLE	AL	6-8	153	594	99	188	45	5	4	106	.316	67	255	114	21-40
1925	SS	CLE	AL	6-8	155	608	78	204	37	7	1	98	.336	64	258	111	18-42
1926	SS	CLE	AL	2-8	154	578	91	187	41	5	4	85	.324	65	250	117	13-41
1927	SS	CLE	AL	6-8	153	569	83	180	48	5	1	92	.316	51	241	108	20-43
1928	SS	CLE	AL	7-8	155	588	79	190	40	2	4	70	.323	58	246	113	20-42
1929	SS-3B	CLE	AL	3-8	152	578	90	182	38	3	7	73	.315	48	247	106	29-41
1930	3B	CLE	AL	4-8	109	353	44	102	17	6	0	48	.289	42	131	96	—
1931	3B	NY	AL	2-8	130	484	102	146	22	1	6	64	.302	61	188	108	28-47
1932	3B	NY	AL	1-8	125	503	95	137	21	3	11	68	.272	56	197	99	36-48
1933	3B	NY	AL	2-8	135	524	87	143	18	1	2	54	.273	71	169	93	40-52
MAJOR LEAGUE TOTALS					1903	7132	1141	2226	436	68	49	1055	.312	843	2945	112	12 yrs

James Luther Sewell   Born Jan 5, 1901   Titus, AL
5'9 160 lbs Batted right   Died May 14, 1987 Akron, OH

YR	POS	TEAM	LG	FIN	G	AB	R	H	2B	3B	HR	RBI	AVG	BB	TB	OQ	RANK
1921	C	CLE	AL	2-8	3	6	0	0	0	0	0	1	.000	0	0	—	—
1922	C	CLE	AL	4-8	41	87	14	23	5	0	0	10	.264	5	28	—	—
1923	C	CLE	AL	3-8	10	10	2	2	0	1	0	1	.200	1	4	—	—
1924	C	CLE	AL	6-8	63	165	27	48	9	1	0	17	.291	22	59	100	—
1925	C	CLE	AL	6-8	74	220	30	51	10	2	0	18	.232	33	65	81	—
1926	C	CLE	AL	2-8	126	433	41	103	16	4	0	46	.238	36	127	72	41-41
1927	C	CLE	AL	6-8	128	470	52	138	27	6	0	53	.294	20	177	86	40-43
1928	C	CLE	AL	7-8	122	411	52	111	16	9	3	52	.270	26	154	88	—
1929	C	CLE	AL	3-8	124	406	41	96	16	3	1	39	.236	29	121	69	—
1930	C	CLE	AL	4-8	76	292	40	75	21	2	1	43	.257	14	103	75	—
1931	C	CLE	AL	4-8	108	375	45	103	30	4	1	53	.275	36	144	97	—
1932	C	CLE	AL	4-8	87	300	36	76	20	2	2	52	.253	38	106	92	—
1933	C	WAS	AL	1-8	141	474	65	125	30	4	2	61	.264	48	169	92	41-52
1934	C	WAS	AL	7-8	72	207	21	49	7	3	2	21	.237	22	68	81	—
1935	C	CHI	AL	5-8	118	421	52	120	19	3	2	67	.285	32	151	86	—
1936	C	CHI	AL	3-8	128	451	59	113	20	5	5	73	.251	54	158	84	48-52
1937	C	CHI	AL	3-8	122	412	51	111	21	6	1	61	.269	46	147	88	—
1938	C	CHI	AL	6-8	65	211	23	45	4	1	0	27	.213	20	51	58	—
1939	C	CLE	AL	3-8	16	20	1	3	1	0	0	1	.150	3	4	—	—
1942	C	SL	AL	3-8	6	12	1	1	0	0	0	0	.083	1	1	—	—
MAJOR LEAGUE TOTALS					1630	5383	653	1393	272	56	20	696	.259	486	1837	—	—

Luzerne Atwell Blue Born Mar 5, 1897 Washington, DC
5'10 165 lbs Batted both Died Jul 28, 1958 Alexandria, VA

YR	POS	TEAM	LG	FIN	G	AB	R	H	2B	3B	HR	RBI	AVG	BB	TB	OQ	RANK
1921	1B	DET	AL	6-8	153	585	103	180	33	11	5	75	.308	103	250	123	13-49
1922	1B	DET	AL	3-8	145	584	131	175	31	9	6	45	.300	82	242	116	18-50
1923	1B	DET	AL	2-8	129	504	100	143	27	7	1	46	.284	96	187	116	17-46
1924	1B	DET	AL	3-8	108	395	81	123	26	7	2	53	.311	64	169	123	—
1925	1B	DET	AL	4-8	150	532	91	163	18	9	3	94	.306	83	208	110	21-42
1926	1B	DET	AL	6-8	128	429	92	123	24	14	1	52	.287	90	178	128	10-41
1927	1B	DET	AL	4-8	112	365	71	95	17	9	1	42	.260	71	133	109	—
1928	1B	SL	AL	3-8	154	549	116	154	32	11	14	80	.281	105	250	133	9-42
1929	1B	SL	AL	4-8	151	573	111	168	40	10	6	61	.293	126	246	131	11-41
1930	1B	SL	AL	6-8	117	425	85	100	27	5	4	42	.235	81	149	98	30-40
1931	1B	CHI	AL	8-8	155	589	119	179	23	15	1	62	.304	127	235	130	12-47
1932	1B	CHI	AL	7-8	112	373	51	93	21	2	0	43	.249	64	118	93	—
1933	1B	BRO	NL	6-8	1	1	0	0	0	0	0	0	.000	0	0	—	—
MAJOR LEAGUE TOTALS					1615	5904	1151	1696	319	109	44	695	.287	1092	2365	121	9 yrs

Hazen Shirley Cuyler Born Aug 30, 1899 Harrisville, MI
5'10 180 lbs Batted right Died Feb 11, 1950 Ann Arbor, MI

YR	POS	TEAM	LG	FIN	G	AB	R	H	2B	3B	HR	RBI	AVG	BB	TB	OQ	RANK
1921	RF	PIT	NL	2-8	1	3	0	0	0	0	0	0	.000	0	0	—	—
1922	PR	PIT	NL	3-8	1	0	0	0	0	0	0	0	—	0	0	—	—
1923	LF	PIT	NL	3-8	11	40	4	10	1	1	0	2	.250	5	13	—	—
1924	LF	PIT	NL	3-8	117	466	94	165	27	16	9	85	.354	30	251	143	6-38
1925	RF	PIT	NL	1-8	153	617	144	220	43	26	18	102	.357	58	369	154	3-37
1926	LF	PIT	NL	3-8	157	614	113	197	31	15	8	92	.321	50	282	122	11-42
1927	LF	PIT	NL	1-8	85	285	60	88	13	7	3	31	.309	37	124	126	—
1928	RF	CHI	NL	3-8	133	499	92	142	25	9	17	79	.285	51	236	119	16-45
1929	RF	CHI	NL	1-8	139	509	111	183	29	7	15	102	.360	66	271	141	9-46
1930	RF	CHI	NL	2-8	156	642	155	228	50	17	13	134	.355	72	351	134	12-44
1931	RF	CHI	NL	3-8	154	613	100	202	37	12	9	88	.330	72	290	136	7-36
1932	RF	CHI	NL	1-8	110	446	58	130	19	9	10	77	.291	29	197	111	23-38
1933	LF-CF	CHI	NL	3-8	70	262	37	83	13	3	5	35	.317	21	117	131	—
1934	CF	CHI	NL	3-8	142	559	80	189	42	8	6	69	.338	31	265	123	18-48
1935	CF	CHI/CN	NL	1/6	107	380	58	98	13	4	6	40	.258	37	137	96	—
1936	CF	CIN	NL	5-8	144	567	96	185	29	11	7	74	.326	47	257	123	13-43
1937	LF	CIN	NL	8-8	117	406	48	110	12	4	0	32	.271	36	130	87	—
1938	RF-CF	BRO	NL	7-8	82	253	45	69	10	8	2	23	.273	34	101	116	—
MAJOR LEAGUE TOTALS					1879	7161	1295	2299	394	157	128	1065	.321	676	3391	131	10 yrs

Earl Homer Sheely Born Feb 12, 1893 Bushnell, IL
6'3 195 lbs Batted right Died Sep 16, 1952 Seattle, WA

YR	POS	TEAM	LG	FIN	G	AB	R	H	2B	3B	HR	RBI	AVG	BB	TB	OQ	RANK
1921	1B	CHI	AL	7-8	154	563	68	171	25	6	11	95	.304	57	241	107	25-49
1922	1B	CHI	AL	5-8	149	526	72	167	37	4	6	80	.317	60	230	118	13-50
1923	1B	CHI	AL	7-8	156	570	74	169	25	3	4	88	.296	79	212	107	28-46
1924	1B	CHI	AL	8-8	146	535	84	171	34	3	3	103	.320	95	220	124	11-40
1925	1B	CHI	AL	5-8	153	600	93	189	43	3	9	111	.315	68	265	113	17-42
1926	1B	CHI	AL	5-8	145	525	77	157	40	2	6	89	.299	75	219	116	16-41
1927	1B	CHI	AL	5-8	45	129	11	27	3	0	2	16	.209	20	36	79	—
1929	1B	PIT	NL	2-8	139	485	63	142	22	4	6	88	.293	75	190	105	29-46
1931	1B	BOS	NL	7-8	147	538	30	147	15	2	1	77	.273	34	169	80	34-36
MAJOR LEAGUE TOTALS					1234	4471	572	1340	244	27	48	747	.300	563	1782	109	8 yrs

Leon Allen Goslin Born Oct 16, 1900 Salem, NJ
5'11 185 lbs Batted left Died May 15, 1971 Bridgeton, NJ

YR	POS	TEAM	LG	FIN	G	AB	R	H	2B	3B	HR	RBI	AVG	BB	TB	OQ	RANK
1921	RF	WAS	AL	4-8	14	50	8	13	1	1	1	6	.260	6	19	—	—
1922	LF	WAS	AL	6-8	101	358	44	116	19	7	3	53	.324	25	158	111	—
1923	LF	WAS	AL	4-8	150	600	86	180	29	18	9	99	.300	40	272	110	23-46
1924	LF	WAS	AL	1-8	154	579	100	199	30	17	12	129	.344	68	299	139	5-40
1925	LF	WAS	AL	1-8	150	601	116	201	34	20	18	113	.334	53	329	133	7-42
1926	LF	WAS	AL	4-8	147	568	105	201	26	15	17	108	.354	63	308	147	4-41
1927	LF	WAS	AL	3-8	148	581	96	194	37	15	13	120	.334	50	300	130	9-43
1928	LF	WAS	AL	4-8	135	456	80	173	36	10	17	102	.379	48	280	171	3-42
1929	LF	WAS	AL	5-8	145	553	82	159	28	7	18	91	.288	66	255	116	20-41
1930	LF	WA/SL	AL	2/6	148	584	115	180	36	12	37	138	.308	67	351	144	6-40
1931	LF	SL	AL	5-8	151	591	114	194	42	10	24	105	.328	80	328	151	6-47
1932	LF	SL	AL	6-8	150	572	88	171	28	9	17	104	.299	92	268	128	8-48
1933	RF	WAS	AL	1-8	132	549	97	163	35	10	10	64	.297	42	248	111	28-52
1934	LF	DET	AL	1-8	151	614	106	187	38	7	13	100	.305	65	278	114	21-44
1935	LF	DET	AL	1-8	147	590	88	172	34	6	9	109	.292	56	245	102	33-51
1936	LF	DET	AL	2-8	147	572	122	180	33	8	24	125	.315	85	301	132	11-52
1937	LF	DET	AL	2-8	79	181	30	43	11	1	4	35	.238	35	68	102	—
1938	LF	WAS	AL	5-8	38	57	6	9	3	0	2	8	.158	8	18	—	—
MAJOR LEAGUE TOTALS					2287	8656	1483	2735	500	173	248	1609	.316	949	4325	131	14 yrs

Edmund John Miller
6'0 185 lbs Batted right

Born Aug 30, 1894 Vinton, IA
Died May 7, 1966 Philadelphia, PA

YR	POS	TEAM	LG	FIN	G	AB	R	H	2B	3B	HR	RBI	AVG	BB	TB	OQ	RANK
1921	LF	WAS	AL	4-8	114	420	57	121	28	8	9	71	.288	25	192	103	—
1922	CF	PHI	AL	7-8	143	535	90	179	29	12	21	90	.335	24	295	131	8-50
1923	LF	PHI	AL	6-8	123	458	68	137	25	4	12	64	.299	27	206	107	27-46
1924	RF	PHI	AL	5-8	113	398	62	136	22	4	6	62	.342	12	184	108	—
1925	RF	PHI	AL	2-8	124	474	78	151	29	10	10	81	.319	19	230	108	24-42
1926	RF	PHI/SL	AL	3/7	132	463	73	149	33	7	6	63	.322	33	214	115	18-41
1927	CF	SL	AL	7-8	143	492	83	160	32	7	5	75	.325	30	221	109	18-43
1928	CF	PHI	AL	2-8	139	510	76	168	34	7	8	85	.329	27	240	115	17-42
1929	RF	PHI	AL	1-8	147	556	84	186	32	16	8	93	.335	40	274	121	16-41
1930	RF	PHI	AL	1-8	154	585	89	177	38	7	9	100	.303	47	256	103	28-40
1931	RF	PHI	AL	1-8	137	534	75	150	43	5	8	77	.281	36	227	101	35-47
1932	RF	PHI	AL	2-8	95	305	40	90	17	4	7	58	.295	20	136	104	—
1933	RF	PHI	AL	3-8	67	120	22	33	7	1	2	17	.275	12	48	102	—
1934	RF	PHI	AL	5-8	81	177	22	43	10	2	1	22	.243	16	60	81	—
1935	RF	BOS	AL	4-8	78	138	18	42	8	1	3	26	.304	10	61	105	—
1936	RF	BOS	AL	6-8	30	47	9	14	2	1	1	6	.298	5	21	—	—

MAJOR LEAGUE TOTALS   1820 6212 946 1936 389 96 116 990 .312 383 2865 112   9 yrs

Travis Calvin Jackson
5'10 160 lbs Batted right

Born Nov 2, 1903 Waldo, AR
Died Jul 27, 1987 Waldo, AR

YR	POS	TEAM	LG	FIN	G	AB	R	H	2B	3B	HR	RBI	AVG	BB	TB	OQ	RANK
1922	SS	NY	NL	1-8	3	8	1	0	0	0	0	0	.000	0	0	—	—
1923	SS-3B	NY	NL	1-8	96	327	45	90	12	7	4	37	.275	22	128	95	—
1924	SS	NY	NL	1-8	151	596	81	180	26	8	11	76	.302	21	255	102	22-38
1925	SS	NY	NL	2-8	112	411	51	117	15	2	9	59	.285	24	163	91	—
1926	SS	NY	NL	5-8	111	385	64	126	24	8	8	51	.327	20	190	125	—
1927	SS	NY	NL	3-8	127	469	67	149	29	4	14	98	.318	32	228	125	11-40
1928	SS	NY	NL	2-8	150	537	73	145	35	6	14	77	.270	56	234	109	23-45
1929	SS	NY	NL	3-8	149	551	92	162	21	12	21	94	.294	64	270	117	20-46
1930	SS	NY	NL	3-8	116	431	70	146	27	8	13	82	.339	32	228	119	19-44
1931	SS	NY	NL	2-8	145	555	65	172	26	10	5	71	.310	36	233	108	20-36
1932	SS	NY	NL	6-8	52	195	23	50	17	1	4	38	.256	13	81	100	—
1933	SS-3B	NY	NL	1-8	53	122	11	30	5	0	0	12	.246	8	35	79	—
1934	SS	NY	NL	2-8	137	523	75	140	26	7	16	101	.268	37	228	106	28-48
1935	3B	NY	NL	3-8	128	511	74	154	20	12	9	80	.301	29	225	110	21-44
1936	3B	NY	NL	1-8	126	465	41	107	8	1	7	53	.230	18	138	67	43-43

MAJOR LEAGUE TOTALS   1656 6086 833 1768 291 86 135 929 .291 412 2636 107   9 yrs

Earl John Adams
5'5 151 lbs Batted right

Born Aug 26, 1894 Zerbe, PA
Died Feb 24, 1989 Pottsville, PA

YR	POS	TEAM	LG	FIN	G	AB	R	H	2B	3B	HR	RBI	AVG	BB	TB	OQ	RANK
1922	2B	CHI	NL	5-8	11	44	5	11	0	1	0	3	.250	4	13	—	—
1923	SS	CHI	NL	4-8	95	311	40	90	12	0	4	35	.289	26	114	95	—
1924	SS-2B	CHI	NL	5-8	117	418	66	117	11	5	1	27	.280	40	141	92	—
1925	2B	CHI	NL	8-8	149	627	95	180	29	8	2	48	.287	44	231	88	35-37
1926	2B-3B	CHI	NL	4-8	154	624	95	193	35	3	0	39	.309	52	234	102	30-42
1927	2B-3B	CHI	NL	4-8	146	647	100	189	17	7	0	49	.292	42	220	88	35-40
1928	2B-SS	PIT	NL	4-8	135	539	91	149	14	6	0	38	.276	64	175	90	37-45
1929	SS-2B	PIT	NL	2-8	74	196	37	51	8	1	0	11	.260	15	61	71	—
1930	3B-2B	SL	NL	1-8	137	570	98	179	36	9	0	55	.314	45	233	93	34-44
1931	3B	SL	NL	1-8	143	608	97	178	46	5	1	40	.293	42	237	100	27-36
1932	3B	SL	NL	6-8	31	127	22	35	3	1	0	13	.276	14	40	91	—
1933	3B	SL/CN	NL	5/8	145	568	60	146	22	1	1	22	.257	45	173	88	42-48
1934	3B-2B	CIN	NL	8-8	87	278	38	70	16	1	0	14	.252	20	88	80	—
MAJOR LEAGUE TOTALS					1424	5557	844	1588	249	48	9	394	.286	453	1960	93	7 yrs

Charles Leo Hartnett
6'1 195 lbs Batted right

Born Dec 20, 1900 Woonsocket, RI
Died Dec 20, 1972 Park Ridge, IL

YR	POS	TEAM	LG	FIN	G	AB	R	H	2B	3B	HR	RBI	AVG	BB	TB	OQ	RANK
1922	C	CHI	NL	5-8	31	72	4	14	1	1	0	4	.194	6	17	—	—
1923	C-1B	CHI	NL	4-8	85	231	28	62	12	2	8	39	.268	25	102	113	—
1924	C	CHI	NL	5-8	111	354	56	106	17	7	16	67	.299	39	185	138	—
1925	C	CHI	NL	8-8	117	398	61	115	28	3	24	67	.289	36	221	130	—
1926	C	CHI	NL	4-8	93	284	35	78	25	3	8	41	.275	32	133	123	—
1927	C	CHI	NL	4-8	127	449	56	132	32	5	10	80	.294	44	204	120	12-40
1928	C	CHI	NL	3-8	120	388	61	117	26	9	14	57	.302	65	203	146	—
1929	C	CHI	NL	1-8	25	22	2	6	2	1	1	9	.273	5	13	—	—
1930	C	CHI	NL	2-8	141	508	84	172	31	3	37	122	.339	55	320	146	8-44
1931	C	CHI	NL	3-8	116	380	53	107	32	1	8	70	.282	52	165	123	—
1932	C	CHI	NL	1-8	121	406	52	110	25	3	12	52	.271	51	177	119	—
1933	C	CHI	NL	3-8	140	490	55	135	21	4	16	88	.276	37	212	119	18-48
1934	C	CHI	NL	3-8	130	438	58	131	21	1	22	90	.299	37	220	129	12-48
1935	C	CHI	NL	1-8	116	413	67	142	32	6	13	91	.344	41	225	152	—
1936	C	CHI	NL	2-8	121	424	49	130	25	6	7	64	.307	30	188	114	—
1937	C	CHI	NL	2-8	110	356	47	126	21	6	12	82	.354	43	195	161	—
1938	C	CHI	NL	1-8	88	299	40	82	19	1	10	59	.274	48	133	132	—
1939	C	CHI	NL	4-8	97	306	36	85	18	2	12	59	.278	37	143	124	—
1940	C	CHI	NL	5-8	37	64	3	17	3	0	1	12	.266	8	23	—	—
1941	C	NY	NL	5-8	64	150	20	45	5	0	5	26	.300	12	65	119	—
MAJOR LEAGUE TOTALS					1990	6432	867	1912	396	64	236	1179	.297	703	3144	—	—

George Farley Grantham
5'10 170 lbs Batted left

Born May 20, 1900 Galena, KS
Died Mar 16, 1954 Kingman, AZ

YR	POS	TEAM	LG	FIN	G	AB	R	H	2B	3B	HR	RBI	AVG	BB	TB	OQ	RANK
1922	3B	CHI	NL	5-8	7	23	3	4	1	1	0	3	.174	1	7	—	—
1923	2B	CHI	NL	4-8	152	570	81	160	36	8	8	70	.281	71	236	112	20-41
1924	2B	CHI	NL	5-8	127	469	85	148	19	6	12	60	.316	55	215	129	8-38
1925	1B	PIT	NL	1-8	114	359	74	117	24	6	8	52	.326	50	177	134	—
1926	1B	PIT	NL	3-8	141	449	66	143	27	13	8	70	.318	60	220	141	3-42
1927	2B-1B	PIT	NL	1-8	151	531	96	162	33	11	8	66	.305	74	241	131	9-40
1928	1B	PIT	NL	4-8	124	440	93	142	24	9	10	85	.323	59	214	135	10-45
1929	2B-LF	PIT	NL	2-8	110	349	85	107	23	10	12	90	.307	93	186	157	—
1930	2B	PIT	NL	5-8	146	552	120	179	34	14	18	99	.324	81	295	132	13-44
1931	1B-2B	PIT	NL	5-8	127	465	91	142	26	6	10	46	.305	71	210	134	8-36
1932	2B	CIN	NL	8-8	126	493	81	144	29	6	6	39	.292	56	203	115	16-38
1933	2B-1B	CIN	NL	8-8	87	260	32	53	14	3	4	28	.204	38	85	101	—
1934	1B-3B	NY	NL	2-8	32	29	5	7	2	0	1	4	.241	8	12	—	—

MAJOR LEAGUE TOTALS 1444 4989 912 1508 292 93 105 712 .302 717 2301 129 8 yrs

James Leroy Bottomley
6'0 180 lbs Batted left

Born Apr 23, 1900 Oglesby, IL
Died Dec 11, 1959 St Louis, MO

YR	POS	TEAM	LG	FIN	G	AB	R	H	2B	3B	HR	RBI	AVG	BB	TB	OQ	RANK
1922	1B	SL	NL	3-8	37	151	29	49	8	5	5	35	.325	6	82	126	—
1923	1B	SL	NL	5-8	134	523	79	194	34	14	8	94	.371	45	280	148	3-41
1924	1B	SL	NL	6-8	137	528	87	167	31	12	14	111	.316	35	264	127	11-38
1925	1B	SL	NL	4-8	153	619	92	227	44	12	21	128	.367	47	358	148	4-37
1926	1B	SL	NL	1-8	154	603	98	180	40	14	19	120	.299	58	305	132	7-42
1927	1B	SL	NL	2-8	152	574	95	174	31	15	19	124	.303	74	292	141	6-40
1928	1B	SL	NL	1-8	149	576	123	187	42	20	31	136	.325	71	362	164	2-45
1929	1B	SL	NL	4-8	146	560	108	176	31	12	29	137	.314	70	318	138	11-46
1930	1B	SL	NL	1-8	131	487	92	148	33	7	15	97	.304	44	240	110	25-44
1931	1B	SL	NL	1-8	108	382	73	133	34	5	9	75	.348	34	204	148	—
1932	1B	SL	NL	6-8	91	311	45	92	16	3	11	48	.296	25	147	121	—
1933	1B	CIN	NL	8-8	145	549	57	137	23	9	13	83	.250	42	217	107	26-48
1934	1B	CIN	NL	8-8	142	556	72	158	31	11	11	78	.284	33	244	107	26-48
1935	1B	CIN	NL	6-8	107	399	44	103	21	1	1	49	.258	18	129	77	—
1936	1B	SL	AL	7-8	140	544	72	162	39	11	12	95	.298	44	259	106	27-52
1937	1B	SL	AL	8-8	65	109	11	26	7	0	1	12	.239	18	36	89	—

MAJOR LEAGUE TOTALS 1991 7471 1177 2313 465 151 219 1422 .310 664 3737 130 11 yrs

Andrew Aird High   Born Nov 21, 1897 Alva, IL
5'6 155 lbs Batted left   Died Feb 22, 1981 Toledo, OH

YR	POS	TEAM	LG	FIN	G	AB	R	H	2B	3B	HR	RBI	AVG	BB	TB	OQ	RANK
1922	3B-SS	BRO	NL	6-8	153	579	82	164	27	10	6	65	.283	59	229	101	23-39
1923	3B-SS	BRO	NL	6-8	123	426	51	115	23	9	3	37	.270	47	165	102	27-41
1924	2B-SS	BRO	NL	2-8	144	582	98	191	26	13	6	61	.328	57	261	125	14-38
1925	3B-2B	BR/BO	NL	6/5	104	334	42	86	15	2	4	34	.257	38	117	89	—
1926	3B-2B	BOS	NL	7-8	130	476	55	141	17	10	2	66	.296	39	184	102	29-42
1927	3B	BOS	NL	7-8	113	384	59	116	15	9	4	46	.302	26	161	107	—
1928	3B-2B	SL	NL	1-8	111	368	58	105	14	3	6	37	.285	37	143	101	—
1929	3B-2B	SL	NL	4-8	146	603	95	178	32	4	10	63	.295	38	248	92	38-46
1930	3B	SL	NL	1-8	72	215	34	60	12	2	2	29	.279	23	82	89	—
1931	3B-2B	SL	NL	1-8	63	131	20	35	6	1	0	19	.267	24	43	108	—
1932	3B-2B	CIN	NL	8-8	84	191	16	36	4	2	0	12	.188	23	44	67	—
1933	3B	CIN	NL	8-8	24	43	4	9	2	0	1	6	.209	5	14	—	—
1934	3B	PHI	NL	7-8	47	68	4	14	2	0	0	7	.206	9	16	—	—

| MAJOR LEAGUE TOTALS | | | | | 1314 | 4400 | 618 | 1250 | 195 | 65 | 44 | 482 | .284 | 425 | 1707 | 104 | 5 yrs |

Oswald Louis Bluege   Born Oct 24, 1900 Chicago, IL
5'11 162 lbs Batted right   Died Oct 14, 1985 Edina, MN

YR	POS	TEAM	LG	FIN	G	AB	R	H	2B	3B	HR	RBI	AVG	BB	TB	OQ	RANK
1922	3B-SS	WAS	AL	6-8	19	61	5	12	1	0	0	2	.197	7	13	—	—
1923	3B	WAS	AL	4-8	109	379	48	93	15	7	2	42	.245	48	128	91	—
1924	3B	WAS	AL	1-8	117	402	59	113	15	4	2	49	.281	39	142	90	—
1925	3B	WAS	AL	1-8	145	522	77	150	27	4	4	79	.287	59	197	96	34-42
1926	3B	WAS	AL	4-8	139	487	69	132	19	8	3	65	.271	70	176	101	31-41
1927	3B	WAS	AL	3-8	146	503	71	138	21	10	1	66	.274	57	182	95	33-43
1928	3B	WAS	AL	4-8	146	518	78	154	33	7	2	75	.297	46	207	103	31-42
1929	3B-2B	WAS	AL	5-8	64	220	35	65	6	0	5	31	.295	19	86	96	—
1930	3B	WAS	AL	2-8	134	476	64	138	27	7	3	69	.290	51	188	98	31-40
1931	3B	WAS	AL	3-8	152	570	82	155	25	7	8	98	.272	50	218	95	39-47
1932	3B	WAS	AL	3-8	149	507	64	131	22	4	5	64	.258	84	176	99	35-48
1933	3B	WAS	AL	1-8	140	501	63	131	14	0	6	71	.261	55	163	87	46-52
1934	3B-SS	WAS	AL	7-8	99	285	39	70	9	2	0	11	.246	23	83	70	—
1935	SS-3B	WAS	AL	6-8	100	320	44	84	14	3	0	34	.263	37	104	85	—
1936	2B-SS	WAS	AL	4-8	90	319	43	92	12	1	1	55	.288	38	109	87	—
1937	SS	WAS	AL	6-8	42	127	12	36	4	2	1	13	.283	13	47	90	—
1938	2B-SS	WAS	AL	5-8	58	184	25	48	12	1	0	21	.261	21	62	83	—
1939	1B-2B	WAS	AL	6-8	18	59	5	9	0	0	0	3	.153	7	9	—	—

| MAJOR LEAGUE TOTALS | | | | | 1867 | 6440 | 883 | 1751 | 276 | 67 | 43 | 848 | .272 | 724 | 2290 | 97 | 8 yrs |

Lewis Robert Wilson   Born Apr 26, 1900 Ellwood City, PA
5'6 190 lbs Batted right   Died Nov 23, 1948 Baltimore, MD

YR	POS	TEAM	LG	FIN	G	AB	R	H	2B	3B	HR	RBI	AVG	BB	TB	OO	RANK
1923	CF	NY	NL	1-8	3	10	0	2	0	0	0	0	.200	0	2	—	—
1924	CF	NY	NL	1-8	107	383	62	113	19	12	10	57	.295	44	186	131	—
1925	CF	NY	NL	2-8	62	180	28	43	7	4	6	30	.239	21	76	101	—
1926	CF	CHI	NL	4-8	142	529	97	170	36	8	21	109	.321	69	285	152	1-42
1927	CF	CHI	NL	4-8	146	551	119	175	30	12	30	129	.318	71	319	160	3-40
1928	CF	CHI	NL	3-8	145	520	89	163	32	9	31	120	.313	77	306	158	3-45
1929	CF	CHI	NL	1-8	150	574	135	198	30	5	39	159	.345	78	355	157	5-46
1930	CF	CHI	NL	2-8	155	585	146	208	35	6	56	190	.356	105	423	183	1-44
1931	CF	CHI	NL	3-8	112	395	66	103	22	4	13	61	.261	63	172	124	—
1932	RF	BRO	NL	3-8	135	481	77	143	37	5	23	123	.297	51	259	142	7-38
1933	LF	BRO	NL	6-8	117	360	41	96	13	2	9	54	.267	52	140	123	—
1934	LF	BR/PH	NL	6/7	74	192	24	47	5	0	6	30	.245	43	70	120	—

| MAJOR LEAGUE TOTALS | | | | | 1348 | 4760 | 884 | 1461 | 266 | 67 | 244 | 1062 | .307 | 674 | 2593 | 159 | 6 yrs |

William Edward Kamm   Born Feb 2, 1900 San Francisco, CA
5'10 170 lbs Batted right   Died Dec 21, 1988 Belmont, CA

YR	POS	TEAM	LG	FIN	G	AB	R	H	2B	3B	HR	RBI	AVG	BB	TB	OO	RANK
1923	3B	CHI	AL	7-8	149	544	57	159	39	9	6	87	.292	62	234	114	19-46
1924	3B	CHI	AL	8-8	147	528	58	134	28	6	6	93	.254	64	192	94	32-40
1925	3B	CHI	AL	5-8	152	509	82	142	32	4	6	83	.279	90	200	110	20-42
1926	3B	CHI	AL	5-8	143	480	63	141	24	10	0	62	.294	77	185	113	19-41
1927	3B	CHI	AL	5-8	148	540	85	146	32	13	0	59	.270	70	204	100	29-43
1928	3B	CHI	AL	5-8	155	552	70	170	30	12	1	84	.308	73	227	116	16-42
1929	3B	CHI	AL	7-8	147	523	72	140	33	6	3	63	.268	75	194	100	33-41
1930	3B	CHI	AL	7-8	112	331	49	89	21	6	3	47	.269	51	131	104	—
1931	3B	CH/CL	AL	8/4	132	469	77	136	35	5	0	75	.290	71	181	111	27-47
1932	3B	CLE	AL	4-8	148	524	76	150	34	9	3	83	.286	75	211	109	23-48
1933	3B	CLE	AL	4-8	133	447	59	126	17	2	1	47	.282	54	150	94	38-52
1934	3B	CLE	AL	3-8	121	386	52	104	23	3	0	42	.269	62	133	98	—
1935	3B	CLE	AL	3-8	6	18	2	6	0	0	0	1	.333	0	6	—	—

| MAJOR LEAGUE TOTALS | | | | | 1693 | 5851 | 802 | 1643 | 348 | 85 | 29 | 826 | .281 | 824 | 2248 | 106 | 10 yrs |

John Henry Sand
5'8 160 lbs Batted right

Born Jul 3, 1897 San Francisco, CA
Died Nov 3, 1958 San Francisco, CA

YR	POS	TEAM	LG	FIN	G	AB	R	H	2B	3B	HR	RBI	AVG	BB	TB	OQ	RANK
1923	SS	PHI	NL	8-8	132	470	85	107	16	5	4	32	.228	82	145	94	34-41
1924	SS	PHI	NL	7-8	137	539	79	132	21	6	6	40	.245	52	183	88	32-38
1925	SS	PHI	NL	6-8	148	496	69	138	30	7	3	55	.278	64	191	102	24-37
1926	SS	PHI	NL	8-8	149	567	99	154	30	5	4	37	.272	66	206	101	32-42
1927	SS-3B	PHI	NL	8-8	141	535	87	160	22	8	1	49	.299	58	201	106	20-40
1928	SS	PHI	NL	8-8	141	426	38	90	26	1	0	38	.211	60	118	78	42-45
MAJOR LEAGUE TOTALS					848	3033	457	781	145	32	18	251	.258	382	1044	95	6 yrs

James Wilson
6'1 200 lbs Batted right

Born Jul 23, 1900 Philadelphia, PA
Died May 31, 1947 Bradenton, FL

YR	POS	TEAM	LG	FIN	G	AB	R	H	2B	3B	HR	RBI	AVG	BB	TB	OQ	RANK
1923	C	PHI	NL	8-8	85	252	27	66	9	0	1	25	.262	4	78	66	—
1924	C	PHI	NL	7-8	95	280	32	78	16	3	6	39	.279	17	118	102	—
1925	C	PHI	NL	6-8	108	335	42	110	19	3	3	54	.328	32	144	112	—
1926	C	PHI	NL	8-8	90	279	40	85	10	2	4	32	.305	25	111	108	—
1927	C	PHI	NL	8-8	128	443	50	122	15	2	2	45	.275	34	147	87	36-40
1928	C	PH/SL	NL	8/1	141	481	56	127	30	3	2	63	.264	54	169	93	35-45
1929	C	SL	NL	4-8	120	394	59	128	27	8	4	71	.325	43	183	116	—
1930	C	SL	NL	1-8	107	362	54	115	25	7	1	58	.318	28	157	98	—
1931	C	SL	NL	1-8	115	383	45	105	20	2	0	51	.274	28	129	87	—
1932	C	SL	NL	6-8	92	274	36	68	16	2	2	28	.248	15	94	82	—
1933	C	SL	NL	5-8	113	369	34	94	17	0	1	45	.255	23	114	85	—
1934	C	PHI	NL	7-8	91	277	25	81	11	0	3	35	.292	14	101	90	—
1935	C	PHI	NL	7-8	93	290	38	81	20	0	1	37	.279	19	104	91	—
1936	C	PHI	NL	8-8	85	230	25	64	12	0	1	27	.278	12	79	85	—
1937	C	PHI	NL	7-8	39	87	15	24	3	0	1	8	.276	6	30	—	—
1938	C	PHI	NL	8-8	3	2	0	0	0	0	0	0	.000	0	0	—	—
1939	C	CIN	NL	1-8	4	3	0	1	0	0	0	0	.333	0	1	—	—
1940	C	CIN	NL	1-8	16	37	2	9	2	0	0	3	.243	2	11	—	—
MAJOR LEAGUE TOTALS					1525	4778	580	1358	252	32	32	621	.284	356	1770	—	—

Taylor Lee Douthit   Born Apr 22, 1901   Little Rock, AR
5'11   175 lbs   Batted right   Died May 28, 1986 Fremont, CA

YR	POS	TEAM	LG	FIN	G	AB	R	H	2B	3B	HR	RBI	AVG	BB	TB	OQ	RANK
1923	RF-LF	SL	NL	5-8	9	27	3	5	0	2	0	0	.185	0	9	—	—
1924	CF-RF	SL	NL	6-8	53	173	24	48	13	1	0	13	.277	16	63	97	—
1925	CF	SL	NL	4-8	30	73	13	20	3	1	1	8	.274	2	28	—	—
1926	CF	SL	NL	1-8	139	530	96	163	20	4	3	52	.308	55	200	107	23-42
1927	CF	SL	NL	2-8	130	488	81	128	29	6	5	50	.262	52	184	101	26-40
1928	CF	SL	NL	1-8	154	648	111	191	35	3	3	43	.295	84	241	105	25-45
1929	CF	SL	NL	4-8	150	613	128	206	42	7	9	62	.336	79	289	123	15-46
1930	CF	SL	NL	1-8	154	664	109	201	41	10	7	93	.303	60	283	97	32-44
1931	CF	SL/CN	NL	1/8	131	507	63	142	20	3	1	45	.280	53	171	95	30-36
1932	CF	CIN	NL	8-8	96	333	28	81	12	1	0	25	.243	31	95	77	—
1933	CF	CN/CH	NL	8/3	28	71	9	16	5	0	0	5	.225	11	21	—	—
MAJOR LEAGUE TOTALS					1074	4127	665	1201	220	38	29	396	.291	443	1584	105	6 yrs

William Harold Terry   Born Oct 30, 1898   Atlanta, GA
6'1   200 lbs   Batted left   Died Jan 9, 1989   Jacksonville, FL

YR	POS	TEAM	LG	FIN	G	AB	R	H	2B	3B	HR	RBI	AVG	BB	TB	OQ	RANK
1923	1B	NY	NL	1-8	3	7	1	1	0	0	0	0	.143	2	1	—	—
1924	1B	NY	NL	1-8	77	163	26	39	7	2	5	24	.239	17	65	101	—
1925	1B	NY	NL	2-8	133	489	75	156	31	6	11	70	.319	42	232	118	14-37
1926	1B-RF	NY	NL	5-8	98	225	26	65	12	5	5	43	.289	22	102	119	—
1927	1B	NY	NL	3-8	150	580	101	189	32	13	20	121	.326	46	307	139	7-40
1928	1B	NY	NL	2-8	149	568	100	185	36	11	17	101	.326	64	294	138	9-45
1929	1B	NY	NL	3-8	150	607	103	226	39	5	14	117	.372	48	317	131	12-46
1930	1B	NY	NL	3-8	154	633	139	254	39	15	23	129	.401	57	392	155	5-44
1931	1B	NY	NL	2-8	153	611	121	213	43	20	9	112	.349	47	323	144	4-36
1932	1B	NY	NL	6-8	154	643	124	225	42	11	28	117	.350	32	373	150	5-38
1933	1B	NY	NL	1-8	123	475	68	153	20	5	6	58	.322	40	201	127	12-48
1934	1B	NY	NL	2-8	153	602	109	213	30	6	8	83	.354	60	279	134	8-48
1935	1B	NY	NL	3-8	145	596	91	203	32	8	6	64	.341	41	269	122	14-44
1936	1B	NY	NL	1-8	79	229	36	71	10	5	2	39	.310	19	97	113	—
MAJOR LEAGUE TOTALS					1721	6428	1120	2193	373	112	154	1078	.341	537	3252	136	10 yrs

Harry Francis Rice　　　　　　Born Nov 22, 1901　Ware Station, IL
5'9　185 lbs　Batted left　　　　　　Died Jan 1, 1971　Portland, OR

YR	POS	TEAM	LG	FIN	G	AB	R	H	2B	3B	HR	RBI	AVG	BB	TB	OQ	RANK
1923	PH	SL	AL	5-8	4	3	0	0	0	0	0	0	.000	0	0	—	—
1924	3B	SL	AL	4-8	54	93	19	26	7	0	0	15	.280	7	33	86	—
1925	RF	SL	AL	3-8	103	354	87	127	25	8	11	47	.359	54	201	157	—
1926	CF	SL	AL	7-8	148	578	86	181	27	10	9	59	.313	63	255	117	14-41
1927	RF	SL	AL	7-8	137	520	90	149	26	9	7	68	.287	50	214	103	26-43
1928	CF	DET	AL	6-8	131	510	87	154	21	12	6	81	.302	44	217	108	22-42
1929	CF	DET	AL	6-8	130	536	97	163	33	7	6	69	.304	61	228	110	22-41
1930	CF	DE/NY	AL	5/3	137	474	78	142	23	5	9	98	.300	50	202	105	27-40
1931	RF-CF	WAS	AL	3-8	47	162	32	43	5	6	0	15	.265	12	60	89	—
1933	RF	CIN	NL	8-8	143	510	44	133	19	6	0	54	.261	35	164	90	40-48
MAJOR LEAGUE TOTALS					1034	3740	620	1118	186	63	48	506	.299	376	1574	106	6 yrs

Henry Louis Gehrig　　　　　　Born Jun 19, 1903　New York, NY
6'0　200 lbs　Batted left　　　　　　Died Jun 2, 1941　Riverdale, NY

YR	POS	TEAM	LG	FIN	G	AB	R	H	2B	3B	HR	RBI	AVG	BB	TB	OQ	RANK
1923	1B	NY	AL	1-8	13	26	6	11	4	1	1	9	.423	2	20	—	—
1924	1B-RF	NY	AL	2-8	10	12	2	6	1	0	0	5	.500	1	7	—	—
1925	1B	NY	AL	7-8	126	437	73	129	23	10	20	68	.295	46	232	126	10-42
1926	1B	NY	AL	1-8	155	572	135	179	47	20	16	107	.313	105	314	155	2-41
1927	1B	NY	AL	1-8	155	584	149	218	52	18	47	175	.373	109	447	219	2-43
1928	1B	NY	AL	1-8	154	562	139	210	47	13	27	142	.374	95	364	192	2-42
1929	1B	NY	AL	2-8	154	553	127	166	32	10	35	126	.300	122	323	164	3-41
1930	1B	NY	AL	3-8	154	581	143	220	42	17	41	174	.379	101	419	200	2-40
1931	1B	NY	AL	2-8	155	619	163	211	31	15	46	184	.341	117	410	190	2-47
1932	1B	NY	AL	1-8	156	596	138	208	42	9	34	151	.349	108	370	176	3-48
1933	1B	NY	AL	2-8	152	593	138	198	41	12	32	139	.334	92	359	169	3-52
1934	1B	NY	AL	2-8	154	579	128	210	40	6	49	165	.363	109	409	200	1-44
1935	1B	NY	AL	2-8	149	535	125	176	26	10	30	119	.329	132	312	175	2-51
1936	1B	NY	AL	1-8	155	579	167	205	37	7	49	152	.354	130	403	190	1-52
1937	1B	NY	AL	1-8	157	569	138	200	37	9	37	159	.351	127	366	183	1-47
1938	1B	NY	AL	1-8	157	576	115	170	32	6	29	114	.295	107	301	136	12-52
1939	1B	NY	AL	1-8	8	28	2	4	0	0	0	1	.143	5	4	—	—
MAJOR LEAGUE TOTALS					2164	8001	1888	2721	534	163	493	1990	.340	1508	5060	177	14 yrs

Frederick Leach
5'11 183 lbs Batted left

Born Nov 23, 1897 Springfield, MO
Died Dec 10, 1981 Hagerman, ID

YR	POS	TEAM	LG	FIN	G	AB	R	H	2B	3B	HR	RBI	AVG	BB	TB	OQ	RANK
1923	LF-CF	PHI	NL	8-8	52	104	5	27	4	0	1	16	.260	3	34	72	—
1924	LF	PHI	NL	7-8	8	28	6	13	2	1	2	7	.464	2	23	—	—
1925	CF	PHI	NL	7-8	65	292	47	91	15	4	5	28	.312	5	129	95	—
1926	CF	PHI	NL	8-8	129	492	73	162	29	7	11	71	.329	16	238	118	14-42
1927	CF	PHI	NL	8-8	140	536	69	164	30	4	12	83	.306	21	238	107	19-40
1928	LF-1B	PHI	NL	8-8	145	588	83	179	36	11	13	96	.304	30	276	110	21-45
1929	LF	NY	NL	3-8	113	411	74	119	22	6	8	47	.290	17	177	90	—
1930	LF	NY	NL	3-8	126	544	90	178	19	13	13	71	.327	22	262	102	30-44
1931	LF	NY	NL	2-8	129	515	75	159	30	5	6	61	.309	29	217	107	23-36
1932	LF	BOS	NL	5-8	84	223	21	55	9	2	1	29	.247	18	71	82	—
MAJOR LEAGUE TOTALS					991	3733	543	1147	196	53	72	509	.307	163	1665	109	5 yrs

Henry Emmett Manush
6'1 200 lbs Batted left

Born Jul 20, 1901 Tuscumbia, AL
Died May 12, 1971 Sarasota, FL

YR	POS	TEAM	LG	FIN	G	AB	R	H	2B	3B	HR	RBI	AVG	BB	TB	OQ	RANK
1923	LF	DET	AL	2-8	109	308	59	103	20	5	4	54	.334	20	145	119	—
1924	LF	DET	AL	3-8	120	422	83	122	24	8	9	68	.289	27	189	104	—
1925	LF-CF	DET	AL	4-8	99	278	46	84	14	3	5	47	.302	24	119	103	—
1926	CF	DET	AL	6-8	136	498	95	188	35	8	14	86	.378	31	281	147	5-41
1927	CF	DET	AL	4-8	151	593	102	177	31	18	6	90	.298	47	262	107	21-43
1928	LF	SL	AL	3-8	154	638	104	241	47	20	13	108	.378	39	367	151	5-42
1929	LF	SL	AL	4-8	142	574	85	204	45	10	6	81	.355	43	287	127	14-41
1930	LF	SL/WA	AL	6/2	137	554	100	194	49	12	9	94	.350	31	294	125	17-40
1931	LF	WAS	AL	3-8	146	616	110	189	41	11	6	70	.307	36	270	105	29-47
1932	LF	WAS	AL	3-8	149	625	121	214	41	14	14	116	.342	36	325	126	10-48
1933	LF	WAS	AL	1-8	153	658	115	221	32	17	5	95	.336	36	302	114	26-52
1934	LF	WAS	AL	7-8	137	556	88	194	42	11	11	89	.349	36	291	129	12-44
1935	LF	WAS	AL	6-8	119	479	68	131	26	9	4	56	.273	35	187	90	44-51
1936	LF	BOS	AL	6-8	82	313	43	91	15	5	0	45	.291	17	116	80	—
1937	RF	BRO	NL	6-8	132	466	57	155	25	7	4	73	.333	40	206	123	10-40
1938	RF	BR/PT	NL	7/2	32	64	11	16	4	2	0	10	.250	7	24	—	—
1939	RF	PIT	NL	6-8	10	12	0	0	0	0	0	1	.000	1	0	—	—
MAJOR LEAGUE TOTALS					2008	7654	1287	2524	491	160	110	1183	.330	506	3665	122	11 yrs

Philip Julius Todt   Born Aug 9, 1901 St Louis, MO
6'0 175 lbs Batted left   Died Nov 15, 1973 St Louis, MO

YR	POS	TEAM	LG	FIN	G	AB	R	H	2B	3B	HR	RBI	AVG	BB	TB	OQ	RANK
1924	1B	BOS	AL	7-8	52	103	17	27	8	2	1	14	.262	6	42	91	—
1925	1B	BOS	AL	8-8	141	544	62	151	29	13	11	75	.278	44	239	100	30-42
1926	1B	BOS	AL	8-8	154	599	56	153	19	12	7	69	.255	40	217	84	37-41
1927	1B	BOS	AL	8-8	140	516	55	122	22	6	6	52	.236	28	174	74	42-43
1928	1B	BOS	AL	8-8	144	539	61	136	31	8	12	73	.252	26	219	90	38-42
1929	1B	BOS	AL	8-8	153	534	49	140	38	10	4	64	.262	31	210	87	37-41
1930	1B	BOS	AL	8-8	111	383	49	103	22	5	11	62	.269	24	168	95	—
1931	1B	PHI	AL	1-8	62	197	23	48	14	2	5	44	.244	8	81	88	—
MAJOR LEAGUE TOTALS					957	3415	372	880	183	58	57	453	.258	207	1350	87	5 yrs

Aloysius Harry Simmons   Born May 22, 1902 Milwaukee, WI
5'11 190 lbs Batted right   Died May 26, 1956 Milwaukee, WI

YR	POS	TEAM	LG	FIN	G	AB	R	H	2B	3B	HR	RBI	AVG	BB	TB	OQ	RANK
1924	CF	PHI	AL	5-8	152	594	69	183	31	9	8	102	.308	30	256	100	27-40
1925	CF	PHI	AL	2-8	153	654	122	253	43	12	24	129	.387	35	392	149	5-42
1926	CF	PHI	AL	3-8	147	583	90	199	53	10	19	109	.341	48	329	143	6-41
1927	CF	PHI	AL	2-8	106	406	86	159	36	11	15	108	.392	31	262	171	—
1928	LF	PHI	AL	2-8	119	464	78	163	33	9	15	107	.351	31	259	142	6-42
1929	LF	PHI	AL	1-8	143	581	114	212	41	9	34	157	.365	31	373	156	4-41
1930	LF	PHI	AL	1-8	138	554	152	211	41	16	36	165	.381	39	392	174	3-40
1931	LF	PHI	AL	1-8	128	513	105	200	37	13	22	128	.390	47	329	176	3-47
1932	LF	PHI	AL	2-8	154	670	144	216	28	9	35	151	.322	47	367	130	7-48
1933	LF	CHI	AL	6-8	146	605	85	200	29	10	14	119	.331	39	291	120	19-52
1934	LF	CHI	AL	8-8	138	558	102	192	36	7	18	104	.344	53	296	136	10-44
1935	CF	CHI	AL	5-8	128	525	68	140	22	7	16	79	.267	33	224	95	41-51
1936	CF	DET	AL	2-8	143	568	96	186	38	6	13	112	.327	49	275	113	24-52
1937	LF	WAS	AL	6-8	103	419	60	117	21	10	8	84	.279	27	182	95	—
1938	LF	WAS	AL	5-8	125	470	79	142	23	6	21	95	.302	38	240	115	18-52
1939	LF	BO/CN	NL	7/1	102	351	39	96	17	5	7	44	.274	24	144	101	—
1940	LF	PHI	AL	8-8	37	81	7	25	4	0	1	19	.309	4	32	—	—
1941	LF	PHI	AL	8-8	9	24	1	3	1	0	0	1	.125	1	4	—	—
1943	LF	BOS	AL	7-8	40	133	9	27	5	0	1	12	.203	8	35	69	—
1944	LF	PHI	AL	5-8	4	6	1	3	0	0	0	2	.500	0	3	—	—
MAJOR LEAGUE TOTALS					2215	8759	1507	2927	539	149	307	1827	.334	615	4685	135	13 yrs

Max Frederick Bishop
5'8 165 lbs Batted left

Born Sep 5, 1899 Waynesboro, PA
Died Feb 24, 1962 Waynesboro, PA

YR	POS	TEAM	LG	FIN	G	AB	R	H	2B	3B	HR	RBI	AVG	BB	TB	OQ	RANK
1924	2B	PHI	AL	5-8	91	294	52	75	13	2	2	21	.255	54	98	100	—
1925	2B	PHI	AL	2-8	105	368	66	103	18	4	4	27	.280	87	141	120	—
1926	2B	PHI	AL	3-8	122	400	77	106	20	2	0	33	.265	116	130	122	12-41
1927	2B	PHI	AL	2-8	117	372	80	103	15	1	0	22	.277	105	120	121	12-43
1928	2B	PHI	AL	2-8	126	472	104	149	27	5	6	50	.316	97	204	137	7-42
1929	2B	PHI	AL	1-8	129	475	102	110	19	6	3	36	.232	128	150	108	26-41
1930	2B	PHI	AL	1-8	130	441	117	111	27	6	10	38	.252	128	180	129	15-40
1931	2B	PHI	AL	1-8	130	497	115	146	30	4	5	37	.294	112	199	130	11-47
1932	2B	PHI	AL	2-8	114	409	89	104	24	2	5	37	.254	110	147	121	14-48
1933	2B	PHI	AL	3-8	117	391	80	115	27	1	4	42	.294	106	156	140	5-52
1934	2B-1B	BOS	AL	4-8	97	253	65	66	13	1	1	22	.261	82	84	126	—
1935	2B-1B	BOS	AL	4-8	60	122	19	28	3	1	1	14	.230	28	36	97	—

MAJOR LEAGUE TOTALS   1338 4494 966 1216 236 35 41 379 .271 1153 1645 126   8 yrs

Charles Leonard Gehringer
5'11 180 lbs Batted left

Born May 11, 1903 Fowlerville, MI
Died Jan 21, 1993 Bloomfield Hills, MI

YR	POS	TEAM	LG	FIN	G	AB	R	H	2B	3B	HR	RBI	AVG	BB	TB	OQ	RANK
1924	2B	DET	AL	3-8	5	13	2	6	0	0	0	1	.462	0	6	—	—
1925	2B	DET	AL	4-8	8	18	3	3	0	0	0	0	.167	2	3	—	—
1926	2B	DET	AL	6-8	123	459	62	127	19	17	1	48	.277	30	183	94	32-41
1927	2B	DET	AL	4-8	133	508	110	161	29	11	4	61	.317	52	224	115	15-43
1928	2B	DET	AL	6-8	154	603	108	193	29	16	6	74	.320	69	272	123	14-42
1929	2B	DET	AL	6-8	155	634	131	215	45	19	13	106	.339	64	337	136	10-41
1930	2B	DET	AL	5-8	154	610	144	201	47	15	16	98	.330	69	326	134	12-40
1931	2B	DET	AL	7-8	101	383	67	119	24	5	4	53	.311	29	165	108	—
1932	2B	DET	AL	5-8	152	618	112	184	44	11	19	107	.298	68	307	124	12-48
1933	2B	DET	AL	5-8	155	628	103	204	42	6	12	105	.325	68	294	126	10-52
1934	2B	DET	AL	1-8	154	601	134	214	50	7	11	127	.356	99	311	151	6-44
1935	2B	DET	AL	1-8	150	610	123	201	32	8	19	108	.330	79	306	133	7-51
1936	2B	DET	AL	2-8	154	641	144	227	60	12	15	116	.354	83	356	142	7-52
1937	2B	DET	AL	2-8	144	564	133	209	40	1	14	96	.371	90	293	148	5-47
1938	2B	DET	AL	4-8	152	568	133	174	32	5	20	107	.306	113	276	134	14-52
1939	2B	DET	AL	5-8	118	406	86	132	29	6	16	86	.325	68	221	147	9-42
1940	2B	DET	AL	1-8	139	515	108	161	33	3	10	81	.313	101	230	133	8-49
1941	2B	DET	AL	4-8	127	436	65	96	19	4	3	46	.220	95	132	98	36-48
1942	2B	DET	AL	5-8	45	45	6	12	0	0	1	7	.267	7	15	—	—

MAJOR LEAGUE TOTALS   2323 8860 1774 2839 574 146 184 1427 .320 1186 4257 129 15 yrs

Hugh Melville Critz
5'8 147 lbs Batted right

Born Sep 17, 1900 Starkville, MS
Died Jan 10, 1980 Greenwood, MS

YR	POS	TEAM	LG	FIN	G	AB	R	H	2B	3B	HR	RBI	AVG	BB	TB	OO	RANK
1924	2B	CIN	NL	4-8	102	413	67	133	15	14	3	35	.322	19	185	112	—
1925	2B	CIN	NL	3-8	144	541	74	150	14	8	2	51	.277	34	186	81	37-37
1926	2B	CIN	NL	2-8	155	607	96	164	24	14	3	79	.270	39	225	92	37-42
1927	2B	CIN	NL	5-8	113	396	50	110	10	8	4	49	.278	16	148	88	—
1928	2B	CIN	NL	5-8	153	641	95	190	21	11	5	52	.296	37	248	93	33-45
1929	2B	CIN	NL	7-8	107	425	55	105	17	9	1	50	.247	27	143	72	—
1930	2B	CN/NY	NL	7/3	152	662	108	172	20	13	4	61	.260	30	230	70	42-44
1931	2B	NY	NL	2-8	66	238	33	69	7	2	4	17	.290	8	92	91	—
1932	2B	NY	NL	6-8	151	659	90	182	32	7	2	50	.276	34	234	87	36-38
1933	2B	NY	NL	1-8	133	558	68	137	18	5	2	33	.246	23	171	78	45-48
1934	2B	NY	NL	2-8	137	571	77	138	17	1	6	40	.242	19	175	69	48-48
1935	2B	NY	NL	3-8	65	219	19	41	0	3	2	14	.187	3	53	49	—

| MAJOR LEAGUE TOTALS | | | | | 1478 | 5930 | 832 | 1591 | 195 | 95 | 38 | 531 | .268 | 289 | 2090 | 81 | 7 yrs |

Frederick Charles Lindstrom
5'11 170 lbs Batted right

Born Nov 21, 1905 Chicago, IL
Died Oct 4, 1981 Chicago, IL

YR	POS	TEAM	LG	FIN	G	AB	R	H	2B	3B	HR	RBI	AVG	BB	TB	OO	RANK
1924	2B-3B	NY	NL	1-8	52	79	19	20	3	1	0	4	.253	6	25	—	—
1925	3B	NY	NL	2-8	104	356	43	102	15	12	4	33	.287	22	153	99	—
1926	3B	NY	NL	5-8	140	543	90	164	19	9	9	76	.302	39	228	108	21-42
1927	3B-LF	NY	NL	3-8	138	562	107	172	36	8	7	58	.306	40	245	112	15-40
1928	3B	NY	NL	2-8	153	646	99	231	39	9	14	107	.358	25	330	126	14-45
1929	3B	NY	NL	3-8	130	549	99	175	23	6	15	91	.319	30	255	104	30-46
1930	3B	NY	NL	3-8	148	609	127	231	39	7	22	106	.379	48	350	138	10-44
1931	RF	NY	NL	2-8	78	303	38	91	12	6	5	36	.300	26	130	114	—
1932	CF-3B	NY	NL	6-8	144	595	83	161	26	5	15	92	.271	27	242	96	32-38
1933	CF	PIT	NL	2-8	138	538	70	167	39	10	5	55	.310	33	241	125	13-48
1934	LF	PIT	NL	5-8	97	383	59	111	24	4	4	49	.290	23	155	100	—
1935	CF-3B	CHI	NL	1-8	90	342	49	94	22	4	3	62	.275	10	133	89	—
1936	LF-CF	BRO	NL	7-8	26	106	12	28	4	0	0	10	.264	5	32	73	—

| MAJOR LEAGUE TOTALS | | | | | 1438 | 5611 | 895 | 1747 | 301 | 81 | 103 | 779 | .311 | 334 | 2519 | 116 | 7 yrs |

Earle Bryan Combs
6'0 185 lbs Batted left

Born May 14, 1899 Pebworth, KY
Died Jul 21, 1976 Richmond, KY

YR	POS	TEAM	LG	FIN	G	AB	R	H	2B	3B	HR	RBI	AVG	BB	TB	OQ	RANK
1924	LF-CF	NY	AL	2-8	24	35	10	14	5	0	0	2	.400	4	19	—	—
1925	CF	NY	AL	7-8	150	593	117	203	36	13	3	61	.342	65	274	121	12-42
1926	CF	NY	AL	1-8	145	606	113	181	31	12	8	56	.299	47	260	105	23-41
1927	CF	NY	AL	1-8	152	648	137	231	36	23	6	64	.356	62	331	136	7-43
1928	CF	NY	AL	1-8	149	626	118	194	33	21	7	56	.310	77	290	125	12-42
1929	CF	NY	AL	2-8	142	586	119	202	33	15	3	65	.345	69	274	127	13-41
1930	CF	NY	AL	3-8	137	532	129	183	30	22	7	82	.344	74	278	140	7-40
1931	CF	NY	AL	2-8	138	563	120	179	31	13	5	58	.318	68	251	122	16-47
1932	CF	NY	AL	1-8	144	591	143	190	32	10	9	65	.321	81	269	125	11-48
1933	CF	NY	AL	2-8	122	417	86	125	22	16	5	64	.300	47	194	122	15-52
1934	CF	NY	AL	2-8	63	251	47	80	13	5	2	25	.319	40	109	124	—
1935	LF-CF	NY	AL	2-8	89	298	47	84	7	4	3	35	.282	36	108	95	—

MAJOR LEAGUE TOTALS   1455   5746 1186 1866 309 154 58 633 .325 670 2657 125   9 yrs

Charles James Hafey
6'0 185 lbs Batted right

Born Feb 12, 1903 Berkeley, CA
Died Jul 2, 1973 Calistoga, CA

YR	POS	TEAM	LG	FIN	G	AB	R	H	2B	3B	HR	RBI	AVG	BB	TB	OQ	RANK
1924	LF-CF	SL	NL	6-8	24	91	10	23	5	2	2	22	.253	4	38	—	—
1925	RF	SL	NL	4-8	93	358	36	108	25	2	5	57	.302	10	152	93	—
1926	LF-RF	SL	NL	1-8	78	225	30	61	19	2	4	38	.271	11	96	100	—
1927	LF	SL	NL	2-8	103	346	62	114	26	5	18	63	.329	36	204	159	—
1928	LF	SL	NL	1-8	138	520	101	175	46	6	27	111	.337	40	314	151	5-45
1929	LF	SL	NL	4-8	134	517	101	175	47	9	29	125	.338	45	327	148	8-46
1930	LF	SL	NL	1-8	120	446	108	150	39	12	26	107	.336	46	291	149	7-44
1931	LF	SL	NL	1-8	122	450	94	157	35	8	16	95	.349	39	256	155	2-36
1932	LF	CIN	NL	8-8	83	253	34	87	19	3	2	36	.344	22	118	130	—
1933	CF	CIN	NL	8-8	144	568	77	172	34	6	7	62	.303	40	239	120	17-48
1934	CF	CIN	NL	8-8	140	535	75	157	29	6	18	67	.293	52	252	124	16-48
1935	CF	CIN	NL	6-8	15	59	10	20	6	1	1	9	.339	4	31	—	—
1937	CF	CIN	NL	8-8	89	257	39	67	11	5	9	41	.261	23	115	113	—

MAJOR LEAGUE TOTALS   1283   4625 777 1466 341 67 164 833 .317 372 2433 141   6 yrs

Forest Glenn Wright Born Feb 6, 1901 Archie, MO
5'11 170 lbs Batted right Died Apr 6, 1984 Olathe, KS

YR	POS	TEAM	LG	FIN	G	AB	R	H	2B	3B	HR	RBI	AVG	BB	TB	OQ	RANK
1924	SS	PIT	NL	3-8	153	616	80	177	28	18	7	111	.287	27	262	101	23-38
1925	SS	PIT	NL	1-8	153	614	97	189	32	10	18	121	.308	31	295	110	21-37
1926	SS	PIT	NL	3-8	119	458	73	141	15	15	8	77	.308	19	210	111	20-42
1927	SS	PIT	NL	1-8	143	570	78	160	26	4	9	105	.281	39	221	98	30-40
1928	SS	PIT	NL	4-8	108	407	63	126	20	8	8	66	.310	21	186	109	—
1929	SS	BRO	NL	6-8	24	25	4	5	0	0	1	6	.200	3	8	—	—
1930	SS	BRO	NL	4-8	135	532	83	171	28	12	22	126	.321	32	289	116	22-44
1931	SS	BRO	NL	4-8	77	268	36	76	9	4	9	32	.284	14	120	108	—
1932	SS	BRO	NL	3-8	127	446	50	122	31	5	11	60	.274	12	196	99	—
1933	SS-1B	BRO	NL	6-8	71	192	19	49	13	0	1	18	.255	11	65	90	—
1935	2B	CHI	AL	5-8	9	25	1	3	1	0	0	1	.120	0	4	—	—
MAJOR LEAGUE TOTALS					1119	4153	584	1219	203	76	94	723	.294	209	1856	107	5 yrs

Leo Ernest Durocher Born Jul 27, 1905 West Springfield, MA
5'10 160 lbs Batted right Died Oct 7, 1991 Palm Springs, CA

YR	POS	TEAM	LG	FIN	G	AB	R	H	2B	3B	HR	RBI	AVG	BB	TB	OQ	RANK
1925	PH	NY	AL	7-8	2	1	1	0	0	0	0	0	.000	0	0	—	—
1928	2B-SS	NY	AL	1-8	102	296	46	80	8	6	0	31	.270	22	100	83	—
1929	SS-2B	NY	AL	2-8	106	341	53	84	4	5	0	32	.246	34	98	73	—
1930	SS-2B	CIN	NL	7-8	119	354	31	86	15	3	3	32	.243	20	116	66	—
1931	SS	CIN	NL	8-8	121	361	26	82	11	5	1	29	.227	18	106	69	—
1932	SS	CIN	NL	8-8	143	457	43	99	22	5	1	33	.217	36	134	73	38-38
1933	SS	CN/SL	NL	8/5	139	446	51	113	19	4	3	44	.253	30	149	91	39-48
1934	SS	SL	NL	1-8	146	500	62	130	26	5	3	70	.260	33	175	86	44-48
1935	SS	SL	NL	2-8	143	513	62	136	23	5	8	78	.265	29	193	91	39-44
1936	SS	SL	NL	2-8	136	510	57	146	22	3	1	58	.286	29	177	87	39-43
1937	SS	SL	NL	4-8	135	477	46	97	11	3	1	47	.203	38	117	63	40-40
1938	SS	BRO	NL	7-8	141	479	41	105	18	5	1	56	.219	47	136	77	45-46
1939	SS	BRO	NL	3-8	116	390	42	108	21	6	1	34	.277	27	144	93	—
1940	SS	BRO	NL	2-8	62	160	10	37	9	1	1	14	.231	12	51	81	—
1941	SS	BRO	NL	1-8	18	42	2	12	1	0	0	6	.286	1	13	—	—
1943	SS	BRO	NL	3-8	6	18	1	4	0	0	0	1	.222	1	4	—	—
1945	2B	BRO	NL	3-8	2	5	1	1	0	0	0	2	.200	0	1	—	—
MAJOR LEAGUE TOTALS					1637	5350	575	1320	210	56	24	567	.247	377	1714	81	7 yrs

Gordon Stanley Cochrane Born Apr 6, 1903 Bridgewater, MA
5'10 180 lbs Batted left Died Jun 28, 1962 Lake Forest, IL

YR	POS	TEAM	LG	FIN	G	AB	R	H	2B	3B	HR	RBI	AVG	BB	TB	OQ	RANK
1925	C	PHI	AL	2-8	134	420	69	139	21	5	6	55	.331	44	188	115	14-42
1926	C	PHI	AL	3-8	120	370	50	101	8	9	8	47	.273	56	151	112	—
1927	C	PHI	AL	2-8	126	432	80	146	20	6	12	80	.338⁻	50	214	133	8-43
1928	C	PHI	AL	2-8	131	468	92	137	26	12	10	57	.293	76	217	131	10-42
1929	C	PHI	AL	1-8	135	514	113	170	37	8	7	95	.331	69	244	129	12-41
1930	C	PHI	AL	1-8	130	487	110	174	42	5	10	85	.357	55	256	138	8-40
1931	C	PHI	AL	1-8	122	459	87	160	31	6	17	89	.349	56	254	152	5-47
1932	C	PHI	AL	2-8	139	518	118	152	35	4	23	112	.293	100	264	142	5-48
1933	C	PHI	AL	3-8	130	429	104	138	30	4	15	60	.322	106	221	166	4-52
1934	C	DET	AL	1-8	129	437	74	140	32	1	2	76	.320	78	180	124	16-44
1935	C	DET	AL	1-8	115	411	93	131	33	3	5	47	.319	96	185	142	4-51
1936	C	DET	AL	2-8	44	126	24	34	8	0	2	17	.270	46	48	136	—
1937	C	DET	AL	2-8	27	98	27	30	10	1	2	12	.306	25	48	147	—

MAJOR LEAGUE TOTALS   1482 5169 1041 1652 333 64 119 832 .320 857 2470 137 10 yrs

James Emory Foxx Born Oct 22, 1907 Sudlersville, MD
6'0 195 lbs Batted right Died Jul 21, 1967 Miami, FL

YR	POS	TEAM	LG	FIN	G	AB	R	H	2B	3B	HR	RBI	AVG	BB	TB	OQ	RANK
1925	C	PHI	AL	2-8	10	9	2	6	1	0	0	0	.667	0	7	—	—
1926	C-RF	PHI	AL	3-8	26	32	8	10	2	1	0	5	.313	1	14	—	—
1927	1B	PHI	AL	2-8	61	130	23	42	6	5	3	20	.323	14	67	133	—
1928	3B-1B	PHI	AL	2-8	118	400	85	131	29	10	13	79	.328	60	219	153	4-42
1929	1B	PHI	AL	1-8	149	517	123	183	23	9	33	118	.354	103	323	181	2-41
1930	1B	PHI	AL	1-8	153	562	127	188	33	13	37	156	.335	93	358	167	4-40
1931	1B-3B	PHI	AL	1-8	139	515	93	150	32	10	30	120	.291	73	292	147	8-47
1932	1B	PHI	AL	2-8	154	585	151	213	33	9	58	169	.364	116	438	213	1-48
1933	1B	PHI	AL	3-8	149	573	125	204	37	9	48	163	.356	96	403	200	1-52
1934	1B	PHI	AL	5-8	150	539	120	180	28	6	44	130	.334	111	352	184	2-44
1935	1B-C	PHI	AL	8-8	147	535	118	185	33	7	36	115	.346	114	340	184	1-51
1936	1B-LF	BOS	AL	6-8	155	585	130	198	32	8	41	143	.338	105	369	164	2-52
1937	1B	BOS	AL	5-8	150	569	111	162	24	6	36	127	.285	99	306	136	9-47
1938	1B	BOS	AL	2-8	149	565	139	197	33	9	50	175	.349	119	398	190	1-52
1939	1B	BOS	AL	2-8	124	467	130	168	31	10	35	105	.360	89	324	193	1-42
1940	1B-C	BOS	AL	4-8	144	515	106	153	30	4	36	119	.297	101	299	157	4-49
1941	1B	BOS	AL	2-8	135	487	87	146	27	8	19	105	.300	93	246	146	6-48
1942	1B	BOS	AL	2-8	30	100	18	27	4	0	5	14	.270	18	46	142	—
1942	1B	CHI	NL	6-8	70	205	25	42	8	0	3	19	.205	22	59	85	—
1944	3B-C	CHI	NL	4-8	15	20	0	1	1	0	0	2	.050	2	2	—	—
1945	1B-3B	PHI	NL	8-8	89	224	30	60	11	1	7	38	.268	23	94	114	—

MAJOR LEAGUE TOTALS   2317 8134 1751 2646 458 125 534 1922 .325 1452 4956 173 14 yrs

Charles Solomon Myer   Born Mar 16, 1904 Ellisville, MS
5'10 163 lbs Batted left   Died Oct 31, 1974 Baton Rouge, LA

YR	POS	TEAM	LG	FIN	G	AB	R	H	2B	3B	HR	RBI	AVG	BB	TB	OQ	RANK
1925	SS	WAS	AL	1-8	4	8	1	2	0	0	0	0	.250	0	2	—	—
1926	SS	WAS	AL	4-8	132	434	66	132	18	6	1	62	.304	45	165	101	30-41
1927	SS-3B	WA/BO	AL	3/8	148	520	66	146	23	11	2	54	.281	56	197	98	31-43
1928	3B	BOS	AL	8-8	147	536	78	168	26	6	1	44	.313	53	209	105	27-42
1929	2B-3B	WAS	AL	5-8	141	563	80	169	29	10	3	82	.300	63	227	105	30-41
1930	2B	WAS	AL	2-8	138	541	97	164	18	8	2	61	.303	58	204	96	32-40
1931	2B	WAS	AL	3-8	139	591	114	173	33	11	4	56	.293	58	240	105	30-47
1932	2B	WAS	AL	3-8	143	577	120	161	38	16	5	52	.279	69	246	108	24-48
1933	2B	WAS	AL	1-8	131	530	95	160	29	15	4	61	.302	60	231	116	24-52
1934	2B	WAS	AL	7-8	139	524	103	160	33	8	3	57	.305	102	218	125	14-44
1935	2B	WAS	AL	6-8	151	616	115	215	36	11	5	100	.349	96	288	136	6-51
1936	2B	WAS	AL	4-8	51	156	31	42	5	2	0	15	.269	42	51	109	—
1937	2B	WAS	AL	6-8	125	430	54	126	16	10	1	65	.293	78	165	109	24-47
1938	2B	WAS	AL	5-8	127	437	79	147	22	8	6	71	.336	93	203	138	9-52
1939	2B	WAS	AL	6-8	83	258	33	78	10	3	1	32	.302	40	97	106	—
1940	2B	WAS	AL	7-8	71	210	28	61	14	4	0	29	.290	34	83	112	—
1941	2B	WAS	AL	6-8	53	107	14	27	3	1	0	9	.252	18	32	92	—

MAJOR LEAGUE TOTALS   1923 7038 1174 2131 353 130 38 850 .303 965 2858 112 12 yrs

William George Rogell   Born Nov 24, 1904 Springfield, IL
5'10 163 lbs Batted both

YR	POS	TEAM	LG	FIN	G	AB	R	H	2B	3B	HR	RBI	AVG	BB	TB	OQ	RANK
1925	2B-SS	BOS	AL	8-8	58	169	12	33	5	1	0	17	.195	11	40	52	—
1927	3B	BOS	AL	8-8	82	207	35	55	14	6	2	28	.266	24	87	105	—
1928	SS-2B	BOS	AL	8-8	102	296	33	69	10	4	0	29	.233	22	87	71	—
1930	SS-3B	DET	AL	5-8	54	144	20	24	4	2	0	9	.167	15	32	54	—
1931	SS	DET	AL	7-8	48	185	21	56	12	3	2	24	.303	24	80	118	—
1932	SS	DET	AL	5-8	144	554	88	150	29	6	9	61	.271	50	218	95	39-48
1933	SS	DET	AL	5-8	155	587	67	173	42	11	0	57	.295	79	237	113	27-52
1934	SS	DET	AL	1-8	154	592	114	175	32	8	3	100	.296	74	232	105	28-44
1935	SS	DET	AL	1-8	150	560	88	154	23	11	6	71	.275	80	217	104	30-51
1936	SS	DET	AL	2-8	146	585	85	160	27	5	6	68	.274	73	215	91	43-52
1937	SS	DET	AL	2-8	146	536	85	148	30	7	8	64	.276	83	216	105	32-47
1938	SS	DET	AL	4-8	136	501	76	130	22	8	3	55	.259	86	177	96	42-52
1939	SS-3B	DET	AL	5-8	74	174	24	40	6	3	2	23	.230	26	58	88	—
1940	SS-3B	CHI	NL	5-8	33	59	7	8	0	0	1	3	.136	2	11	—	—

MAJOR LEAGUE TOTALS   1482 5149 755 1375 256 75 42 609 .267 649 1907 101 7 yrs

George William Haas   Born Oct 15, 1903   Montclair, NJ
6'1   175 lbs   Batted left   Died Jun 30, 1974   New Orleans, LA

YR	POS	TEAM	LG	FIN	G	AB	R	H	2B	3B	HR	RBI	AVG	BB	TB	OQ	RANK
1925	RF	PIT	NL	1-8	4	3	1	0	0	0	0	0	.000	0	0	—	—
1928	CF	PHI	AL	2-8	91	332	41	93	21	4	6	39	.280	23	140	101	—
1929	CF	PHI	AL	1-8	139	578	115	181	41	9	16	82	.313	34	288	115	21-41
1930	CF	PHI	AL	1-8	132	532	91	159	33	7	2	68	.299	43	212	95	33-40
1931	CF	PHI	AL	1-8	102	440	82	142	29	7	8	56	.323	30	209	118	19-47
1932	CF	PHI	AL	2-8	143	558	91	170	28	5	6	65	.305	62	226	106	27-48
1933	CF	CHI	AL	6-8	146	585	97	168	33	4	1	51	.287	65	212	98	34-52
1934	CF	CHI	AL	8-8	106	351	54	94	16	3	2	22	.268	47	122	94	—
1935	RF	CHI	AL	5-8	92	327	44	95	22	1	2	40	.291	37	125	99	—
1936	RF	CHI	AL	3-8	119	408	75	116	26	2	0	46	.284	64	146	96	39-52
1937	1B	CHI	AL	3-8	54	111	8	23	3	3	0	15	.207	16	32	75	—
1938	RF-1B	PHI	AL	8-8	40	78	7	16	2	0	0	12	.205	12	18	—	—
MAJOR LEAGUE TOTALS					1168	4303	706	1257	254	45	43	496	.292	433	1730	105	6 yrs

Floyd Caves Herman   Born Jun 26, 1903   Buffalo, NY
6'4   190 lbs   Batted left   Died Nov 27, 1987   Glendale, CA

YR	POS	TEAM	LG	FIN	G	AB	R	H	2B	3B	HR	RBI	AVG	BB	TB	OQ	RANK
1926	1B-RF	BRO	NL	6-8	137	496	64	158	35	11	11	81	.319	44	248	133	6-42
1927	1B	BRO	NL	6-8	130	412	65	112	26	9	14	73	.272	39	198	122	—
1928	RF	BRO	NL	6-8	134	486	64	165	37	6	12	91	.340	38	250	132	12-45
1929	RF	BRO	NL	6-8	146	569	105	217	42	13	21	113	.381	55	348	156	6-46
1930	RF	BRO	NL	4-8	153	614	143	241	48	11	35	130	.393	66	416	169	2-44
1931	RF	BRO	NL	4-8	151	610	93	191	43	16	18	97	.313	50	320	136	6-36
1932	RF	CIN	NL	8-8	148	577	87	188	38	19	16	87	.326	60	312	148	6-38
1933	RF	CHI	NL	3-8	137	508	77	147	36	12	16	93	.289	50	255	143	4-48
1934	RF	CHI	NL	3-8	125	467	65	142	34	5	14	84	.304	35	228	124	14-48
1935	LF-1B	PT/CN	NL	4/6	118	430	52	136	31	6	10	65	.316	38	209	130	10-44
1936	LF	CIN	NL	5-8	119	380	59	106	25	2	13	71	.279	39	174	120	—
1937	LF	DET	AL	2-8	17	20	2	6	3	0	0	3	.300	1	9	—	—
1945	RF	BRO	NL	3-8	37	34	6	9	1	0	1	9	.265	5	13	—	—
MAJOR LEAGUE TOTALS					1552	5603	882	1818	399	110	181	997	.324	520	2980	141	9 yrs

Ethan Nathan Allen
6'1 180 lbs Batted right

Born Jan 1, 1904 Cincinnati, OH
Died Sep 15, 1993 Brookings, OR

YR	POS	TEAM	LG	FIN	G	AB	R	H	2B	3B	HR	RBI	AVG	BB	TB	OQ	RANK
1926	LF	CIN	NL	2-8	18	13	3	4	1	0	0	0	.308	0	5	—	—
1927	CF	CIN	NL	5-8	111	359	54	106	26	4	2	20	.295	14	146	97	—
1928	CF	CIN	NL	5-8	129	485	55	148	30	7	1	62	.305	27	195	97	29-45
1929	CF	CIN	NL	7-8	143	538	69	157	27	11	6	64	.292	20	224	87	40-46
1930	CF	CN/NY	NL	7/3	97	284	58	83	10	2	10	38	.292	17	127	94	—
1931	CF-RF	NY	NL	2-8	94	298	58	98	18	2	5	43	.329	15	135	116	—
1932	CF-LF	NY	NL	6-8	54	103	13	18	6	2	1	7	.175	1	31	58	—
1933	CF-RF	SL	NL	5-8	91	261	25	63	7	3	0	36	.241	13	76	76	—
1934	LF	PHI	NL	7-8	145	581	87	192	42	4	10	85	.330	33	272	120	20-48
1935	CF	PHI	NL	7-8	156	645	90	198	46	1	8	63	.307	43	270	108	22-44
1936	LF	PH/CH	NL	8/2	121	498	68	147	21	7	4	48	.295	17	194	93	32-43
1937	CF-RF	SL	AL	8-8	103	320	39	101	18	1	0	31	.316	21	121	89	—
1938	CF-LF	SL	AL	7-8	19	33	4	10	3	1	0	4	.303	2	15	—	—
MAJOR LEAGUE TOTALS					1281	4418	623	1325	255	45	47	501	.300	223	1811	101	5 yrs

Paul Glee Waner
5'8 153 lbs Batted left

Born Apr 16, 1903 Harrah, OK
Died Aug 29, 1965 Sarasota, FL

YR	POS	TEAM	LG	FIN	G	AB	R	H	2B	3B	HR	RBI	AVG	BB	TB	OQ	RANK
1926	RF	PIT	NL	3-8	144	536	101	180	35	22	8	79	.336	66	283	151	2-42
1927	RF-1B	PIT	NL	1-8	155	623	114	237	42	18	9	131	.380	60	342	160	2-40
1928	RF-1B	PIT	NL	4-8	152	602	142	223	50	19	6	86	.370	77	329	158	4-45
1929	RF	PIT	NL	2-8	151	596	131	200	43	15	15	100	.336	89	318	140	10-46
1930	RF	PIT	NL	5-8	145	589	117	217	32	18	8	77	.368	57	309	129	15-44
1931	RF	PIT	NL	5-8	150	559	88	180	35	10	6	70	.322	73	253	133	11-36
1932	RF	PIT	NL	2-8	154	630	107	215	62	10	8	82	.341	56	321	140	8-38
1933	RF	PIT	NL	2-8	154	618	101	191	38	16	7	70	.309	60	282	136	8-48
1934	RF	PIT	NL	5-8	146	599	122	217	32	16	14	90	.362	68	323	157	3-48
1935	RF	PIT	NL	4-8	139	549	98	176	29	12	11	78	.321	61	262	134	8-44
1936	RF	PIT	NL	4-8	148	585	107	218	53	9	5	94	.373	74	304	159	3-43
1937	RF	PIT	NL	3-8	154	619	94	219	30	9	2	74	.354	63	273	131	8-40
1938	RF	PIT	NL	2-8	148	625	77	175	31	6	6	69	.280	47	236	99	32-46
1939	RF	PIT	NL	6-8	125	461	62	151	30	6	3	45	.328	35	202	117	21-33
1940	RF	PIT	NL	4-8	89	238	32	69	16	1	1	32	.290	23	90	106	—
1941	RF	BR/BO	NL	1/7	106	329	45	88	10	2	2	50	.267	55	108	109	—
1942	RF	BOS	NL	7-8	114	333	43	86	17	1	1	39	.258	62	108	117	—
1943	RF	BRO	NL	3-8	82	225	29	70	16	0	1	26	.311	35	89	134	—
1944	RF	BRO	NL	7-8	83	136	16	39	4	1	0	16	.287	27	45	120	—
1944	PH	NY	AL	3-8	9	7	1	1	0	0	0	1	.143	2	1	—	—
1945	PH	NY	AL	4-8	1	0	0	0	0	0	0	0	—	1	0	—	—
MAJOR LEAGUE TOTALS					2549	9459	1627	3152	605	191	113	1309	.333	1091	4478	139	14 yrs

Anthony Michael Lazzeri
5'11 170 lbs Batted right

Born Dec 6, 1903 San Francisco, CA
Died Aug 6, 1946 San Francisco, CA

YR	POS	TEAM	LG	FIN	G	AB	R	H	2B	3B	HR	RBI	AVG	BB	TB	OQ	RANK
1926	2B	NY	AL	1-8	155	589	79	162	28	14	18	114	.275	54	272	111	21-41
1927	2B-SS	NY	AL	1-8	153	570	92	176	29	8	18	102	.309	69	275	126	11-43
1928	2B	NY	AL	1-8	116	404	62	134	30	11	10	82	.332	43	216	141	—
1929	2B	NY	AL	2-8	147	545	101	193	37	11	18	106	.354	68	306	151	5-41
1930	2B-3B	NY	AL	3-8	143	571	109	173	34	15	9	121	.303	60	264	113	25-40
1931	2B-3B	NY	AL	2-8	135	484	67	129	27	7	8	83	.267	79	194	113	24-47
1932	2B	NY	AL	1-8	142	510	79	153	28	16	15	113	.300	82	258	136	6-48
1933	2B	NY	AL	2-8	139	523	94	154	22	12	18	104	.294	73	254	131	7-52
1934	2B-3B	NY	AL	2-8	123	438	59	117	24	6	14	67	.267	71	195	118	18-44
1935	2B	NY	AL	2-8	130	477	72	130	18	6	13	83	.273	63	199	107	26-51
1936	2B	NY	AL	1-8	150	537	82	154	29	6	14	109	.287	97	237	116	23-52
1937	2B	NY	AL	1-8	126	446	56	109	21	3	14	70	.244	71	178	101	33-47
1938	SS-3B	CHI	NL	1-8	54	120	21	32	5	0	5	23	.267	22	52	133	—
1939	3B-2B	BR/NY	NL	3/5	27	83	13	24	2	0	4	14	.289	17	38	143	—

| MAJOR LEAGUE TOTALS | | | | | 1740 | 6297 | 986 | 1840 | 334 | 115 | 178 | 1191 | .292 | 869 | 2938 | 120 | 11 yrs |

Joseph Edward Cronin
5'11 180 lbs Batted right

Born Oct 12, 1906 San Francisco, CA
Died Sep 7, 1984 Osterville, MA

YR	POS	TEAM	LG	FIN	G	AB	R	H	2B	3B	HR	RBI	AVG	BB	TB	OQ	RANK
1926	2B-SS	PIT	NL	3-8	38	83	9	22	2	2	0	11	.265	6	28	—	—
1927	2B-SS	PIT	NL	1-8	12	22	2	5	1	0	0	3	.227	2	6	—	—
1928	SS	WAS	AL	4-8	63	227	23	55	10	4	0	25	.242	22	73	81	—
1929	SS	WAS	AL	5-8	145	494	72	139	29	8	8	61	.281	85	208	117	19-41
1930	SS	WAS	AL	2-8	154	587	127	203	41	9	13	126	.346	72	301	135	10-40
1931	SS	WAS	AL	3-8	156	611	103	187	44	13	12	126	.306	81	293	130	13-47
1932	SS	WAS	AL	3-8	143	557	95	177	43	18	6	116	.318	66	274	128	9-48
1933	SS	WAS	AL	1-8	152	602	89	186	45	11	5	118	.309	87	268	126	11-52
1934	SS	WAS	AL	7-8	127	504	68	143	30	9	7	101	.284	53	212	105	27-44
1935	SS	BOS	AL	4-8	144	556	70	164	37	14	9	95	.295	63	256	115	20-51
1936	SS-3B	BOS	AL	6-8	81	295	36	83	22	4	2	43	.281	32	119	95	—
1937	SS	BOS	AL	5-8	148	570	102	175	40	4	18	110	.307	84	277	125	12-47
1938	SS	BOS	AL	2-8	143	530	98	172	51	5	17	94	.325	91	284	142	7-52
1939	SS	BOS	AL	2-8	143	520	97	160	33	3	19	107	.308	87	256	133	11-42
1940	SS	BOS	AL	4-8	149	548	104	156	35	6	24	111	.285	83	275	130	11-49
1941	SS-3B	BOS	AL	2-8	143	518	98	161	38	8	16	95	.311	82	263	142	7-48
1942	3B-1B	BOS	AL	2-8	45	79	7	24	3	0	4	24	.304	15	39	—	—
1943	3B	BOS	AL	7-8	59	77	8	24	4	0	5	29	.312	11	43	—	—
1944	1B	BOS	AL	4-8	76	191	24	46	7	0	5	28	.241	34	68	117	—
1945	3B	BOS	AL	7-8	3	8	1	3	0	0	0	1	.375	3	3	—	—

| MAJOR LEAGUE TOTALS | | | | | 2124 | 7579 | 1233 | 2285 | 515 | 118 | 170 | 1424 | .301 | 1059 | 3546 | 127 | 12 yrs |

Oscar Donald Melillo Born Aug 4, 1899 Chicago, IL
5'8 150 lbs Batted right Died Nov 14, 1963 Chicago, IL

YR	POS	TEAM	LG	FIN	G	AB	R	H	2B	3B	HR	RBI	AVG	BB	TB	OQ	RANK
1926	2B-3B	SL	AL	7-8	99	385	54	98	18	5	1	30	.255	32	129	82	—
1927	2B	SL	AL	7-8	107	356	45	80	18	2	0	26	.225	25	102	66	—
1928	2B-3B	SL	AL	3-8	51	132	9	25	2	0	0	9	.189	9	27	50	—
1929	2B	SL	AL	4-8	141	494	57	146	17	10	5	67	.296	29	198	93	36-41
1930	2B	SL	AL	6-8	149	574	62	147	30	10	5	59	.256	23	212	76	40-40
1931	2B	SL	AL	5-8	151	617	88	189	34	11	2	75	.306	37	251	99	37-47
1932	2B	SL	AL	6-8	154	612	71	148	19	11	3	66	.242	36	198	72	48-48
1933	2B	SL	AL	8-8	132	496	50	145	23	6	3	79	.292	29	189	92	42-52
1934	2B	SL	AL	6-8	144	552	54	133	19	3	2	55	.241	28	164	65	44-44
1935	2B	SL/BO	AL	7/4	125	462	53	117	16	2	1	44	.253	46	140	76	51-51
1936	2B	BOS	AL	6-8	98	327	39	74	12	4	0	32	.226	28	94	64	—
1937	2B	BOS	AL	5-8	26	56	8	14	2	0	0	6	.250	5	16	—	—

MAJOR LEAGUE TOTALS					1377	5063	590	1316	210	64	22	548	.260	327	1720	82	7 yrs

Melvin Thomas Ott Born Mar 2, 1909 Gretna, LA
5'9 170 lbs Batted left Died Nov 21, 1958 New Orleans, LA

YR	POS	TEAM	LG	FIN	G	AB	R	H	2B	3B	HR	RBI	AVG	BB	TB	OQ	RANK
1926	LF	NY	NL	5-8	35	60	7	23	2	0	0	4	.383	1	25	—	—
1927	CF	NY	NL	3-8	82	163	23	46	7	3	1	19	.282	13	62	99	—
1928	RF	NY	NL	2-8	124	435	69	140	26	4	18	77	.322	52	228	140	8-45
1929	RF	NY	NL	3-8	150	545	138	179	37	2	42	151	.328	113	346	171	2-46
1930	RF	NY	NL	3-8	148	521	122	182	34	5	25	119	.349	103	301	156	4-44
1931	CF-RF	NY	NL	2-8	138	497	104	145	23	8	29	115	.292	80	271	154	3-36
1932	RF	NY	NL	6-8	154	566	119	180	30	8	38	123	.318	100	340	176	1-38
1933	RF	NY	NL	1-8	152	580	98	164	36	1	23	103	.283	75	271	141	5-48
1934	RF	NY	NL	2-8	153	582	119	190	29	10	35	135	.326	85	344	168	1-48
1935	RF-3B	NY	NL	3-8	152	593	113	191	33	6	31	114	.322	82	329	158	2-44
1936	RF	NY	NL	1-8	150	534	120	175	28	6	33	135	.328	111	314	183	1-43
1937	RF-3B	NY	NL	1-8	151	545	99	160	28	2	31	95	.294	102	285	156	4-40
1938	3B-RF	NY	NL	3-8	150	527	116	164	23	6	36	116	.311	118	307	185	1-46
1939	RF-3B	NY	NL	5-8	125	396	85	122	23	2	27	80	.308	100	230	184	2-33
1940	RF-3B	NY	NL	6-8	151	536	89	155	27	3	19	79	.289	100	245	144	4-44
1941	RF	NY	NL	5-8	148	525	89	150	29	0	27	90	.286	100	260	155	4-45
1942	RF	NY	NL	3-8	152	549	118	162	21	0	30	93	.295	109	273	168	1-40
1943	RF	NY	NL	8-8	125	380	65	89	12	2	18	47	.234	95	159	146	3-44
1944	RF	NY	NL	5-8	120	399	91	115	16	4	26	82	.288	90	217	175	2-42
1945	RF	NY	NL	5-8	135	451	73	139	23	0	21	79	.308	71	225	152	3-41
1946	RF	NY	NL	8-8	31	68	2	5	1	0	1	4	.074	8	9	—	—
1947	PH	NY	NL	4-8	4	4	0	0	0	0	0	0	.000	0	0	—	—

MAJOR LEAGUE TOTALS					2730	9456	1859	2876	488	72	511	1860	.304	1708	5041	162	18 yrs

Carl Nettles Reynolds
6'0 194 lbs Batted right

Born Feb 1, 1903 LaRue, TX
Died May 29, 1978 Houston, TX

YR	POS	TEAM	LG	FIN	G	AB	R	H	2B	3B	HR	RBI	AVG	BB	TB	OO	RANK
1927	LF	CHI	AL	5-8	14	42	5	9	3	0	1	7	.214	5	15	—	—
1928	RF-LF	CHI	AL	5-8	84	291	51	94	21	11	2	36	.323	17	143	120	—
1929	RF	CHI	AL	7-8	131	517	81	164	24	12	11	67	.317	20	245	107	28-41
1930	LF	CHI	AL	7-8	138	563	103	202	25	18	22	104	.359	20	329	134	11-40
1931	RF	CHI	AL	8-8	118	462	71	134	24	14	6	77	.290	24	204	102	32-47
1932	RF	WAS	AL	3-8	102	406	53	124	28	7	9	63	.305	14	193	105	—
1933	LF	SL	AL	8-8	135	475	81	136	26	14	8	71	.286	50	214	115	25-52
1934	CF	BOS	AL	4-8	113	413	61	125	26	9	4	86	.303	27	181	103	—
1935	RF	BOS	AL	4-8	78	244	33	66	13	4	6	35	.270	24	105	103	—
1936	RF	WAS	AL	4-8	89	293	41	81	18	2	4	41	.276	21	115	86	—
1937	LF	CHI	NL	2-8	7	11	0	3	1	0	0	1	.273	2	4	—	—
1938	CF	CHI	NL	1-8	125	497	59	150	28	10	3	67	.302	22	207	104	23-46
1939	CF-RF	CHI	NL	4-8	88	281	33	69	10	6	4	44	.246	16	103	86	—

| MAJOR LEAGUE TOTALS | | | | | 1222 | 4495 | 672 | 1357 | 247 | 107 | 80 | 699 | .302 | 262 | 2058 | 112 | 5 yrs |

Samuel Filmore West
5'11 165 lbs Batted left

Born Oct 5, 1904 Longview, TX
Died Nov 23, 1985 Lubbock, TX

YR	POS	TEAM	LG	FIN	G	AB	R	H	2B	3B	HR	RBI	AVG	BB	TB	OO	RANK
1927	CF-LF	WAS	AL	3-8	38	67	9	16	4	1	0	6	.239	8	22	—	—
1928	CF-LF	WAS	AL	4-8	125	378	59	114	30	7	3	40	.302	20	167	104	—
1929	CF	WAS	AL	5-8	142	510	60	136	16	8	3	75	.267	45	177	84	39-41
1930	CF	WAS	AL	2-8	120	411	75	135	22	10	6	67	.328	37	195	117	—
1931	CF	WAS	AL	3-8	132	526	77	175	43	13	3	91	.333	30	253	118	18-47
1932	CF	WAS	AL	3-8	146	554	88	159	27	12	6	83	.287	48	228	100	33-48
1933	CF	SL	AL	8-8	133	517	93	155	25	12	11	48	.300	59	237	121	17-52
1934	CF	SL	AL	6-8	122	482	90	157	22	10	9	55	.326	62	226	126	13-44
1935	CF	SL	AL	7-8	138	527	93	158	37	4	10	70	.300	75	233	118	16-51
1936	CF	SL	AL	7-8	152	533	78	148	26	4	7	70	.278	94	203	103	33-52
1937	CF	SL	AL	8-8	122	457	68	150	37	4	7	58	.328	46	216	117	19-47
1938	CF	SL/WA	AL	7/5	136	509	68	155	27	7	6	74	.305	47	214	100	38-52
1939	CF-1B	WAS	AL	6-8	115	390	52	110	20	8	3	52	.282	67	155	111	—
1940	1B-RF	WAS	AL	7-8	57	99	7	25	6	1	1	18	.253	16	36	100	—
1941	LF	WAS	AL	7-8	26	37	3	10	0	0	0	6	.270	11	10	—	—
1942	CF-LF	CHI	AL	6-8	49	151	14	35	5	0	0	25	.232	31	40	99	—

| MAJOR LEAGUE TOTALS | | | | | 1753 | 6148 | 934 | 1838 | 347 | 101 | 75 | 838 | .299 | 696 | 2612 | 110 | 9 yrs |

Elwood George English   Born Mar 2, 1907   Fredonia, OH
5'10   155 lbs   Batted right

YR	POS	TEAM	LG	FIN	G	AB	R	H	2B	3B	HR	RBI	AVG	BB	TB	OQ	RANK
1927	SS	CHI	NL	4-8	87	334	46	97	14	4	1	28	.290	16	122	90	—
1928	SS	CHI	NL	3-8	116	475	68	142	22	4	2	34	.299	30	178	92	36-45
1929	SS	CHI	NL	1-8	144	608	131	168	29	3	1	52	.276	68	206	85	44-46
1930	3B-SS	CHI	NL	2-8	156	638	152	214	36	17	14	59	.335	100	326	132	14-44
1931	SS-3B	CHI	NL	3-8	156	634	117	202	38	8	2	53	.319	68	262	118	14-36
1932	3B-SS	CHI	NL	1-8	127	522	70	142	23	7	3	47	.272	55	188	99	30-38
1933	3B	CHI	NL	3-8	105	398	54	104	19	2	3	41	.261	53	136	109	—
1934	SS-3B	CHI	NL	3-8	109	421	65	117	26	5	3	31	.278	48	162	106	31-48
1935	3B-SS	CHI	NL	1-8	34	84	11	17	2	0	2	8	.202	20	25	104	—
1936	SS-3B	CHI	NL	2-8	64	182	33	45	9	0	0	20	.247	40	54	106	—
1937	SS	BRO	NL	6-8	129	378	45	90	16	2	1	42	.238	65	113	96	—
1938	3B	BRO	NL	7-8	34	72	9	18	2	0	0	7	.250	8	20	—	—
MAJOR LEAGUE TOTALS					1261	4746	801	1356	236	52	32	422	.286	571	1792	105	6 yrs

Lloyd James Waner   Born Mar 16, 1906   Harrah, OK
5'9   150 lbs   Batted left   Died Jul 22, 1982   Oklahoma City, OK

YR	POS	TEAM	LG	FIN	G	AB	R	H	2B	3B	HR	RBI	AVG	BB	TB	OQ	RANK
1927	CF	PIT	NL	1-8	150	629	133	223	17	6	2	27	.355	37	258	112	16-40
1928	CF	PIT	NL	4-8	152	659	121	221	22	14	5	61	.335	40	286	110	22-45
1929	CF	PIT	NL	2-8	151	662	134	234	28	20	5	74	.353	37	317	113	21-46
1930	CF	PIT	NL	5-8	68	260	32	94	8	3	1	36	.362	5	111	91	—
1931	CF	PIT	NL	5-8	154	681	90	214	25	13	4	57	.314	39	277	104	24-36
1932	CF	PIT	NL	2-8	134	565	90	188	27	11	2	38	.333	31	243	112	18-38
1933	LF	PIT	NL	2-8	121	500	59	138	14	5	0	26	.276	22	162	86	43-48
1934	CF	PIT	NL	5-8	140	611	95	173	27	6	1	48	.283	38	215	89	42-48
1935	CF	PIT	NL	4-8	122	537	83	166	22	14	0	46	.309	22	216	99	29-44
1936	CF	PIT	NL	4-8	106	414	67	133	13	8	1	31	.321	31	165	108	—
1937	CF	PIT	NL	3-8	129	537	80	177	23	4	1	45	.330	34	211	106	25-40
1938	CF	PIT	NL	2-8	147	619	79	194	25	7	5	57	.313	28	248	103	25-46
1939	CF	PIT	NL	6-8	112	379	49	108	15	3	0	24	.285	17	129	82	—
1940	CF	PIT	NL	4-8	72	166	30	43	3	0	0	3	.259	5	46	66	—
1941	RF-CF	Pt/Bo/Cn	NL	4/7/6	77	219	26	64	5	1	0	11	.292	12	71	87	—
1942	CF	PHI	NL	8-8	101	287	23	75	7	3	0	10	.261	16	88	84	—
1944	CF	BR/PT	NL	7/2	34	28	5	9	0	0	0	3	.321	5	9	—	—
1945	LF	PIT	NL	4-8	23	19	5	5	0	0	0	1	.263	1	5	—	—
MAJOR LEAGUE TOTALS					1993	7772	1201	2459	281	118	27	598	.316	420	3057	103	10 yrs

Fred William Schulte   Born Jan 13, 1901   Belvidere, IL
6'1   183 lbs   Batted right   Died May 20, 1983 Belvidere, IL

YR	POS	TEAM	LG	FIN	G	AB	R	H	2B	3B	HR	RBI	AVG	BB	TB	OQ	RANK
1927	CF	SL	AL	7-8	60	189	32	60	16	5	3	34	.317	20	95	129	—
1928	CF	SL	AL	3-8	146	556	90	159	44	6	7	85	.286	51	236	107	25-42
1929	CF	SL	AL	4-8	121	446	63	137	24	5	3	71	.307	59	180	110	23-41
1930	CF	SL	AL	6-8	113	392	59	109	23	5	5	62	.278	41	157	97	—
1931	CF	SL	AL	5-8	134	553	100	168	32	7	9	65	.304	56	241	113	23-47
1932	CF	SL	AL	6-8	146	565	106	166	35	6	9	73	.294	71	240	111	20-48
1933	CF	WAS	AL	1-8	144	550	98	162	30	7	5	87	.295	61	221	107	31-52
1934	CF	WAS	AL	7-8	136	524	72	156	32	6	3	73	.298	53	209	101	30-44
1935	RF-CF	WAS	AL	6-8	76	226	33	60	6	4	2	23	.265	26	80	91	—
1936	CF	PIT	NL	4-8	74	238	28	62	7	3	1	17	.261	20	78	86	—
1937	CF	PIT	NL	3-8	29	20	5	2	0	0	0	3	.100	4	2	—	—

| | | MAJOR LEAGUE TOTALS | | | 1179 | 4259 | 686 | 1241 | 249 | 54 | 47 | 593 | .291 | 462 | 1739 | 108 | 6 yrs |

Richard William Bartell   Born Nov 22, 1907   Chicago, IL
5'9   160 lbs   Batted right

YR	POS	TEAM	LG	FIN	G	AB	R	H	2B	3B	HR	RBI	AVG	BB	TB	OQ	RANK
1927	SS	PIT	NL	1-8	1	2	0	0	0	0	0	0	.000	2	0	—	—
1928	2B-SS	PIT	NL	4-8	72	233	27	71	8	4	1	36	.305	21	90	101	—
1929	SS-2B	PIT	NL	2-8	143	610	101	184	40	13	2	57	.302	40	256	95	36-46
1930	SS	PIT	NL	5-8	129	475	69	152	32	13	4	75	.320	39	222	106	27-44
1931	SS	PHI	NL	6-8	135	554	88	160	43	7	0	34	.289	27	217	96	29-36
1932	SS	PHI	NL	4-8	154	614	118	189	48	7	1	53	.308	64	254	116	14-38
1933	SS	PHI	NL	7-8	152	587	78	159	25	5	1	37	.271	56	197	100	31-48
1934	SS	PHI	NL	7-8	146	604	102	187	30	4	0	37	.310	64	225	106	27-48
1935	SS	NY	NL	3-8	137	539	60	141	28	4	14	53	.262	37	219	100	28-44
1936	SS	NY	NL	1-8	145	510	71	152	31	3	8	42	.298	40	213	109	19-43
1937	SS	NY	NL	1-8	128	516	91	158	38	2	14	62	.306	40	242	123	12-40
1938	SS	NY	NL	3-8	127	481	67	126	26	1	9	49	.262	55	181	105	21-46
1939	SS	CHI	NL	4-8	105	336	37	80	24	2	3	34	.238	42	117	95	—
1940	SS	DET	AL	1-8	139	528	76	123	24	3	7	53	.233	76	174	88	40-49
1941	SS	DET	AL	5-8	5	12	0	2	1	0	0	1	.167	2	3	—	—
1941	3B-SS	NY	NL	5-8	104	373	44	113	20	0	5	35	.303	52	148	124	—
1942	3B-SS	NY	NL	3-8	90	316	53	77	10	3	5	24	.244	44	108	108	—
1943	3B-SS	NY	NL	8-8	99	337	48	91	14	0	5	28	.270	47	120	114	—
1946	3B-2B	NY	NL	8-8	5	2	0	0	0	0	0	0	.000	0	0	—	—

| | | MAJOR LEAGUE TOTALS | | | 2016 | 7629 | 1130 | 2165 | 442 | 71 | 79 | 710 | .284 | 748 | 2986 | 104 | 11 yrs |

Ralph Kress   Born Jan 2, 1907   Columbia, CA
5'11 165 lbs Batted right   Died Nov 29, 1962 Los Angeles, CA

YR	POS	TEAM	LG	FIN	G	AB	R	H	2B	3B	HR	RBI	AVG	BB	TB	OQ	RANK
1927	SS	SL	AL	7-8	7	23	3	7	2	1	1	3	.304	3	14	—	—
1928	SS	SL	AL	3-8	150	560	78	153	26	10	3	81	.273	48	208	93	35-42
1929	SS	SL	AL	4-8	147	557	82	170	38	4	9	107	.305	52	243	108	25-41
1930	SS-3B	SL	AL	6-8	154	614	94	192	43	8	16	112	.313	50	299	115	23-40
1931	3B-RF	SL	AL	5-8	150	605	87	188	46	8	16	114	.311	46	298	121	17-47
1932	RF-SS	SL/CH	AL	6/7	149	567	85	156	42	5	11	66	.275	51	241	102	31-48
1933	1B	CHI	AL	6-8	129	467	47	116	20	5	10	78	.248	37	176	90	45-52
1934	1B-LF	CH/WA	AL	8/7	64	185	21	43	4	3	4	25	.232	20	65	85	—
1935	SS	WAS	AL	6-8	84	252	32	75	13	4	2	42	.298	25	102	102	—
1936	SS-2B	WAS	AL	4-8	109	391	51	111	20	6	8	51	.284	39	167	98	—
1938	SS	SL	AL	7-8	150	566	74	171	33	3	7	79	.302	69	231	103	33-52
1939	SS-2B	SL/DE	AL	8/5	64	200	24	50	8	0	1	30	.250	23	61	78	—
1940	3B-SS	DET	AL	1-8	33	99	13	22	3	1	1	11	.222	10	30	74	—
1946	P	NY	NL	8-8	1	1	0	0	0	0	0	0	.000	1	0	—	—

MAJOR LEAGUE TOTALS 1391 5087 691 1454 298 58 89 799 .286 474 2135 105 7 yrs

John Thomas Stone   Born Oct 10, 1905 Lynchburg, TN
6'1 178 lbs Batted left   Died Nov 30, 1955 Shelbyville, TN

YR	POS	TEAM	LG	FIN	G	AB	R	H	2B	3B	HR	RBI	AVG	BB	TB	OQ	RANK
1928	LF	DET	AL	6-8	26	113	20	40	10	3	2	21	.354	5	62	135	—
1929	LF	DET	AL	6-8	51	150	23	39	11	2	2	15	.260	11	60	91	—
1930	LF	DET	AL	5-8	126	422	60	132	29	11	3	56	.313	32	192	107	—
1931	LF	DET	AL	7-8	147	584	86	191	28	11	10	76	.327	56	271	122	15-47
1932	LF	DET	AL	5-8	145	582	106	173	35	12	17	108	.297	58	283	119	15-48
1933	RF	DET	AL	5-8	148	574	86	161	33	11	11	80	.280	54	249	108	29-52
1934	RF	WAS	AL	7-8	113	419	77	132	28	7	7	67	.315	52	195	123	17-44
1935	RF	WAS	AL	6-8	125	455	78	143	27	18	1	78	.314	39	209	113	22-51
1936	LF	WAS	AL	4-8	123	437	95	149	22	11	15	90	.341	60	238	138	8-52
1937	RF	WAS	AL	6-8	139	542	84	179	33	15	6	88	.330	66	260	123	14-47
1938	RF	WAS	AL	5-8	56	213	24	52	12	4	3	28	.244	30	81	93	—

MAJOR LEAGUE TOTALS 1199 4491 739 1391 268 105 77 707 .310 463 2100 121 7 yrs

Charles Herbert Klein
6'0 185 lbs Batted left

Born Oct 7, 1904 Indianapolis, IN
Died Mar 28, 1958 Indianapolis, IN

YR	POS	TEAM	LG	FIN	G	AB	R	H	2B	3B	HR	RBI	AVG	BB	TB	OQ	RANK
1928	RF	PHI	NL	8-8	64	253	41	91	14	4	11	34	.360	14	146	146	—
1929	RF	PHI	NL	5-8	149	616	126	219	45	6	43	145	.356	54	405	157	4-46
1930	RF	PHI	NL	8-8	156	648	158	250	59	8	40	170	.386	54	445	164	3-44
1931	LF	PHI	NL	6-8	148	594	121	200	34	10	31	121	.337	59	347	159	1-36
1932	RF	PHI	NL	4-8	154	650	152	226	50	15	38	137	.348	60	420	175	2-38
1933	RF	PHI	NL	7-8	152	606	101	223	44	7	28	120	.368	56	365	187	1-48
1934	LF	CHI	NL	3-8	115	435	78	131	27	2	20	80	.301	47	222	136	7-48
1935	RF	CHI	NL	1-8	119	434	71	127	14	4	21	73	.293	41	212	128	12-44
1936	RF	CH/PH	NL	2/8	146	601	102	184	35	7	25	104	.306	49	308	132	8-43
1937	RF	PHI	NL	7-8	115	406	74	132	20	2	15	57	.325	39	201	136	—
1938	RF	PHI	NL	8-8	129	458	53	113	22	2	8	61	.247	38	163	92	40-46
1939	LF	PH/PT	NL	8/6	110	317	45	90	18	5	12	56	.284	36	154	128	—
1940	RF	PHI	NL	8-8	116	354	39	77	16	2	7	37	.218	44	118	93	—
1941	RF	PHI	NL	8-8	50	73	6	9	0	0	1	3	.123	10	12	—	—
1942	PH	PHI	NL	8-8	14	14	0	1	0	0	0	0	.071	0	1	—	—
1943	LF	PHI	NL	7-8	12	20	0	2	0	0	0	3	.100	0	2	—	—
1944	RF	PHI	NL	8-8	4	7	1	1	0	0	0	0	.143	0	1	—	—

| MAJOR LEAGUE TOTALS | | | | | 1753 | 6486 | 1168 | 2076 | 398 | 74 | 300 | 1201 | .320 | 601 | 3522 | 148 | 9 yrs |

Virgil Lawrence Davis
6'1 197 lbs Batted right

Born Dec 20, 1904 Birmingham, AL
Died Aug 14, 1984 Birmingham, AL

YR	POS	TEAM	LG	FIN	G	AB	R	H	2B	3B	HR	RBI	AVG	BB	TB	OQ	RANK
1928	C	SL/PH	NL	1/8	69	168	17	47	2	0	3	19	.280	16	58	90	—
1929	C	PHI	NL	5-8	98	263	31	90	18	0	7	48	.342	19	129	116	—
1930	C	PHI	NL	8-8	106	329	41	103	16	1	14	65	.313	17	163	104	—
1931	C	PHI	NL	6-8	120	393	30	128	32	1	4	51	.326	36	174	122	—
1932	C	PHI	NL	4-8	125	402	44	135	23	5	14	70	.336	40	210	145	—
1933	C	PHI	NL	7-8	141	495	51	173	28	3	9	65	.349	32	234	140	7-48
1934	C	SL	NL	1-8	107	347	45	104	22	4	9	65	.300	34	161	123	—
1935	C	SL	NL	2-8	102	315	28	100	24	2	1	60	.317	33	131	118	—
1936	C	SL	NL	2-8	112	363	24	99	26	2	4	59	.273	35	141	103	—
1937	C	CIN	NL	8-8	76	209	19	56	10	1	3	33	.268	23	77	102	—
1938	C	CN/PH	NL	4/8	82	251	14	59	8	0	2	24	.235	19	73	76	—
1939	C	PHI	NL	8-8	87	202	10	62	8	1	0	23	.307	24	72	105	—
1940	C	PIT	NL	4-8	99	285	23	93	14	1	5	39	.326	35	124	131	—
1941	C	PIT	NL	4-8	57	107	3	27	4	1	0	6	.252	11	33	89	—
1944	C	PIT	NL	2-8	54	93	6	28	7	0	2	14	.301	10	41	127	—
1945	C	PIT	NL	4-8	23	33	2	8	2	0	0	6	.242	2	10	—	—

| MAJOR LEAGUE TOTALS | | | | | 1458 | 4255 | 388 | 1312 | 244 | 22 | 77 | 647 | .308 | 386 | 1831 | — | — |

Frank O'Donnell Hurst   Born Aug 12, 1905 Maysville, KY
6'0 215 lbs Batted left   Died Dec 6, 1952 Los Angeles, CA

YR	POS	TEAM	LG	FIN	G	AB	R	H	2B	3B	HR	RBI	AVG	BB	TB	OQ	RANK
1928	1B	PHI	NL	8-8	107	396	73	113	23	4	19	64	.285	68	201	140	7-45
1929	1B	PHI	NL	5-8	154	589	100	179	29	4	31	125	.304	80	309	129	13-46
1930	1B	PHI	NL	8-8	119	391	78	128	19	3	17	78	.327	46	204	124	—
1931	1B	PHI	NL	6-8	137	489	63	149	37	5	11	91	.305	64	229	133	10-36
1932	1B	PHI	NL	4-8	150	579	109	196	41	4	24	143	.339	65	317	154	4-38
1933	1B	PHI	NL	7-8	147	550	58	147	27	8	8	76	.267	48	214	110	22-48
1934	1B	PH/CH	NL	7/3	91	281	29	64	14	0	5	33	.228	20	93	80	—

| MAJOR LEAGUE TOTALS | | | | | 905 | 3275 | 510 | 976 | 190 | 28 | 115 | 610 | .298 | 391 | 1567 | 133 | 5 yrs |

Ralston Burdett Hemsley   Born Jun 24, 1907 Syracuse, OH
5'10 170 lbs Batted right   Died Jul 31, 1972 Washington, DC

YR	POS	TEAM	LG	FIN	G	AB	R	H	2B	3B	HR	RBI	AVG	BB	TB	OQ	RANK
1928	C	PIT	NL	4-8	50	133	14	36	2	3	0	18	.271	4	44	73	—
1929	C	PIT	NL	2-8	88	235	31	68	13	7	0	37	.289	11	95	87	—
1930	C	PIT	NL	5-8	104	324	45	82	19	6	2	45	.253	22	119	76	—
1931	C	PT/CH	NL	5/3	76	239	31	69	20	4	3	32	.289	20	106	114	—
1932	C	CHI	NL	1-8	60	151	27	36	10	3	4	20	.238	10	64	99	—
1933	C	CIN	NL	8-8	49	116	9	22	8	0	0	7	.190	6	30	65	—
1933	C	SL	AL	8-8	32	95	7	23	2	1	1	15	.242	11	30	84	—
1934	C	SL	AL	6-8	123	431	47	133	31	7	2	52	.309	29	184	102	—
1935	C	SL	AL	7-8	144	504	57	146	32	7	0	48	.290	44	192	93	43-51
1936	C	SL	AL	7-8	116	377	43	99	24	2	2	39	.263	46	133	86	—
1937	C	SL	AL	8-8	100	334	30	74	12	3	3	28	.222	25	101	66	—
1938	C	CLE	AL	3-8	66	203	27	60	11	3	2	28	.296	23	83	100	—
1939	C	CLE	AL	3-8	107	395	58	104	17	4	2	36	.263	26	135	77	—
1940	C	CLE	AL	2-8	119	416	46	111	20	5	4	42	.267	22	153	82	—
1941	C	CLE	AL	4-8	98	288	29	69	10	5	2	24	.240	18	95	76	—
1942	C	CIN	NL	4-8	36	115	7	13	1	2	0	7	.113	4	18	37	—
1942	C	NY	AL	1-8	31	85	12	25	3	1	0	15	.294	5	30	—	—
1943	C	NY	AL	1-8	62	180	12	43	6	3	2	24	.239	13	61	91	—
1944	C	NY	AL	3-8	81	284	23	76	12	5	2	26	.268	9	104	90	—
1946	C	PHI	NL	5-8	49	139	7	31	4	1	0	11	.223	9	37	69	—
1947	C	PHI	NL	7-8	2	3	0	1	0	0	0	1	.333	0	1	—	—

| MAJOR LEAGUE TOTALS | | | | | 1593 | 5047 | 562 | 1321 | 257 | 72 | 31 | 555 | .262 | 357 | 1815 | — | — |

Arthur Carter Whitney   Born Jan 2, 1905   San Antonio, TX
5'10 165 lbs Batted right   Died Sep 1, 1987   Center, TX

YR	POS	TEAM	LG	FIN	G	AB	R	H	2B	3B	HR	RBI	AVG	BB	TB	OQ	RANK
1928	3B	PHI	NL	8-8	151	585	73	176	35	4	10	103	.301	36	249	103	27-45
1929	3B	PHI	NL	5-8	154	612	89	200	43	14	8	115	.327	61	295	118	19-46
1930	3B	PHI	NL	8-8	149	606	87	207	41	5	8	117	.342	40	282	106	28-44
1931	3B	PHI	NL	6-8	130	501	64	144	36	5	9	74	.287	30	217	107	22-36
1932	3B	PHI	NL	4-8	154	624	93	186	33	11	13	124	.298	35	280	111	22-38
1933	3B-2B	PH/BO	NL	7/4	131	503	54	126	21	2	11	68	.250	33	184	98	34-48
1934	3B-2B	BOS	NL	4-8	146	563	58	146	26	2	12	79	.259	25	212	87	43-48
1935	3B-2B	BOS	NL	8-8	126	458	41	125	23	4	4	60	.273	24	168	89	41-44
1936	3B	BO/PH	NL	6/8	124	451	45	128	17	3	6	64	.284	39	169	99	28-43
1937	3B	PHI	NL	7-8	138	487	56	166	19	4	8	79	.341	43	217	126	9-40
1938	3B	PHI	NL	8-8	102	300	27	83	9	1	3	38	.277	27	103	95	—
1939	1B-2B	PHI	NL	8-8	34	75	9	14	0	1	1	6	.187	7	19	—	—

| MAJOR LEAGUE TOTALS | | | | | 1539 | 5765 | 696 | 1701 | 303 | 56 | 93 | 927 | .295 | 400 | 2395 | 104 | 10 yrs |

William Malcolm Dickey   Born Jun 6, 1907   Bastrop, LA
6'1 185 lbs Batted left   Died Nov 12, 1993 Little Rock, AR

YR	POS	TEAM	LG	FIN	G	AB	R	H	2B	3B	HR	RBI	AVG	BB	TB	OQ	RANK
1928	C	NY	AL	1-8	10	15	1	3	1	1	0	2	.200	0	6	—	—
1929	C	NY	AL	2-8	130	447	60	145	30	6	10	65	.324	14	217	109	—
1930	C	NY	AL	3-8	109	366	55	124	25	7	5	65	.339	21	178	114	—
1931	C	NY	AL	2-8	130	477	65	156	17	10	6	78	.327	39	211	114	21-47
1932	C	NY	AL	1-8	108	423	66	131	20	4	15	84	.310	34	204	117	—
1933	C	NY	AL	2-8	130	478	58	152	24	8	14	97	.318	47	234	127	8-52
1934	C	NY	AL	2-8	104	395	56	127	24	4	12	72	.322	38	195	124	—
1935	C	NY	AL	2-8	120	448	54	125	26	6	14	81	.279	35	205	105	28-51
1936	C	NY	AL	1-8	112	423	99	153	26	8	22	107	.362	46	261	152	4-52
1937	C	NY	AL	1-8	140	530	87	176	35	2	29	133	.332	73	302	145	6-47
1938	C	NY	AL	1-8	132	454	84	142	27	4	27	115	.313	75	258	145	5-52
1939	C	NY	AL	1-8	128	480	98	145	23	3	24	105	.302	77	246	135	10-42
1940	C	NY	AL	3-8	106	372	45	92	11	1	9	54	.247	48	132	92	—
1941	C	NY	AL	1-8	109	348	35	99	15	5	7	71	.284	45	145	112	—
1942	C	NY	AL	1-8	82	268	28	79	13	1	2	38	.295	26	100	108	—
1943	C	NY	AL	1-8	85	242	29	85	18	2	4	33	.351	41	119	172	—
1946	C	NY	AL	3-8	54	134	10	35	8	0	2	10	.261	19	49	109	—

| MAJOR LEAGUE TOTALS | | | | | 1789 | 6300 | 930 | 1969 | 343 | 72 | 202 | 1210 | .313 | 678 | 3062 | 132 | 7 yrs |

John Francis Moore   Born Mar 23, 1902 Waterville, CT
5'10 175 lbs Batted left   Died Apr 4, 1991 Bradenton, FL

YR	POS	TEAM	LG	FIN	G	AB	R	H	2B	3B	HR	RBI	AVG	BB	TB	OQ	RANK
1928	PH	CHI	NL	3-8	4	4	0	0	0	0	0	0	.000	0	0	—	—
1929	LF	CHI	NL	1-8	37	63	13	18	1	0	2	8	.286	4	25	—	—
1931	CF	CHI	NL	3-8	39	104	19	25	3	1	2	16	.240	7	36	84	—
1932	CF	CHI	NL	1-8	119	443	59	135	24	5	13	64	.305	22	208	115	15-38
1933	LF	CIN	NL	8-8	135	514	60	135	19	5	1	44	.263	29	167	88	41-48
1934	RF	CN/PH	NL	8/7	132	500	73	165	35	7	11	98	.330	43	247	133	10-48
1935	RF	PHI	NL	7-8	153	600	84	194	33	3	19	93	.323	45	290	128	11-44
1936	LF	PHI	NL	8-8	124	472	85	155	24	3	16	68	.328	26	233	126	12-43
1937	LF	PHI	NL	7-8	96	307	46	98	16	2	9	59	.319	18	145	121	—
1945	PH	CHI	NL	1-8	7	6	0	1	0	0	0	2	.167	1	1	—	—
MAJOR LEAGUE TOTALS					846	3013	439	926	155	26	73	452	.307	195	1352	118	5 yrs

Alfonso Ramon Lopez   Born Aug 20, 1908 Tampa, FL
5'11 165 lbs Batted right

YR	POS	TEAM	LG	FIN	G	AB	R	H	2B	3B	HR	RBI	AVG	BB	TB	OQ	RANK
1928	C	BRO	NL	6-8	3	12	0	0	0	0	0	0	.000	0	0	—	—
1930	C	BRO	NL	4-8	128	421	60	130	20	4	6	57	.309	33	176	94	—
1931	C	BRO	NL	4-8	111	360	38	97	13	4	0	40	.269	28	118	86	—
1932	C	BRO	NL	3-8	126	404	44	111	18	6	1	43	.275	34	144	94	—
1933	C	BRO	NL	6-8	126	372	39	112	11	4	3	41	.301	21	140	105	—
1934	C	BRO	NL	6-8	140	439	58	120	23	2	7	54	.273	49	168	104	34-48
1935	C	BRO	NL	5-8	128	379	50	95	12	4	3	39	.251	35	124	87	—
1936	C	BOS	NL	6-8	128	426	46	103	12	5	7	50	.242	41	146	89	—
1937	C	BOS	NL	5-8	105	334	31	68	11	1	3	38	.204	35	90	73	—
1938	C	BOS	NL	5-8	71	236	19	63	6	1	1	14	.267	11	74	78	—
1939	C	BOS	NL	7-8	131	412	32	104	22	1	8	49	.252	40	152	95	—
1940	C	BO/PT	NL	7/4	95	293	35	80	9	3	3	41	.273	19	104	92	—
1941	C	PIT	NL	4-8	114	317	33	84	9	1	5	43	.265	31	110	98	—
1942	C	PIT	NL	5-8	103	289	17	74	8	2	1	26	.256	34	89	97	—
1943	C	PIT	NL	4-8	118	372	40	98	9	4	1	39	.263	44	118	99	—
1944	C	PIT	NL	2-8	115	331	27	76	12	1	1	34	.230	34	93	81	—
1945	C	PIT	NL	4-8	91	243	22	53	8	0	0	18	.218	35	61	81	—
1946	C	PIT	NL	7-8	56	150	13	46	2	0	1	12	.307	23	51	115	—
1947	C	CLE	AL	4-8	61	126	9	33	1	0	0	14	.262	9	34	72	—
MAJOR LEAGUE TOTALS					1950	5916	613	1547	206	43	51	652	.261	556	1992	—	—

Lynford Hobart Lary   Born Jan 28, 1906 Armona, CA
6'0   165 lbs   Batted right   Died Jan 9, 1973 Downey, CA

YR	POS	TEAM	LG	FIN	G	AB	R	H	2B	3B	HR	RBI	AVG	BB	TB	OQ	RANK
1929	3B-SS	NY	AL	2-8	80	236	48	73	9	2	5	26	.309	24	101	109	—
1930	SS	NY	AL	3-8	117	464	93	134	20	8	3	52	.289	45	179	94	35-40
1931	SS	NY	AL	3-8	155	610	100	171	35	9	10	107	.280	88	254	114	20-47
1932	SS	NY	AL	1-8	91	280	56	65	14	4	3	39	.232	52	96	98	—
1933	3B-SS	NY	AL	2-8	52	127	25	28	3	3	0	13	.220	28	37	97	—
1934	SS	NY/BO	AL	2/4	130	419	58	101	20	4	2	54	.241	67	135	90	41-44
1935	SS	WA/SL	AL	6/7	132	474	86	127	29	7	2	42	.268	76	176	103	31-51
1936	SS	SL	AL	7-8	155	619	112	179	30	6	2	52	.289	117	227	104	31-52
1937	SS	CLE	AL	4-8	156	644	110	187	46	7	8	77	.290	88	271	108	29-47
1938	SS	CLE	AL	3-8	141	568	94	152	36	4	3	51	.268	88	205	95	43-52
1939	SS	CLE	AL	3-8	3	2	0	0	0	0	0	0	.000	0	0	—	—
1939	SS-3B	BR/SL	NL	3/2	63	106	18	19	4	1	0	10	.179	28	25	93	—
1940	SS	SL	AL	6-8	27	54	5	3	1	1	0	3	.056	4	6	—	—

MAJOR LEAGUE TOTALS   1302 4603 805 1239 247 56 38 526 .269 705 1712 101   7 yrs

Richard Benjamin Ferrell   Born Oct 12, 1905   Durham, NC
5'10   160 lbs   Batted right

YR	POS	TEAM	LG	FIN	G	AB	R	H	2B	3B	HR	RBI	AVG	BB	TB	OQ	RANK
1929	C	SL	AL	4-8	64	144	21	33	6	1	0	20	.229	32	41	94	—
1930	C	SL	AL	6-8	101	314	43	84	18	4	1	41	.268	46	113	96	—
1931	C	SL	AL	5-8	117	386	47	118	30	4	3	57	.306	56	165	121	—
1932	C	SL	AL	6-8	126	438	67	138	30	5	2	65	.315	66	184	119	16-48
1933	C	SL/BO	AL	8/7	140	493	58	143	21	4	4	77	.290	70	184	107	32-52
1934	C	BOS	AL	4-8	132	437	50	130	29	4	1	48	.297	66	170	110	23-44
1935	C	BOS	AL	4-8	133	458	54	138	34	4	3	61	.301	65	189	113	23-51
1936	C	BOS	AL	6-8	121	410	59	128	27	5	8	55	.312	65	189	120	17-52
1937	C	BO/WA	AL	5/6	104	344	39	84	8	0	2	36	.244	65	98	86	—
1938	C	WAS	AL	5-8	135	411	55	120	24	5	1	58	.292	75	157	108	26-52
1939	C	WAS	AL	6-8	87	274	32	77	13	1	0	31	.281	41	92	94	—
1940	C	WAS	AL	7-8	103	326	35	89	18	2	0	28	.273	47	111	95	—
1941	C	WA/SL	AL	6/6	121	387	38	99	19	3	2	36	.256	67	130	101	—
1942	C	SL	AL	3-8	99	273	20	61	6	1	0	26	.223	33	69	78	—
1943	C	SL	AL	6-8	74	209	12	50	7	0	0	20	.239	34	57	97	—
1944	C	WAS	AL	8-8	99	339	14	94	11	1	0	25	.277	46	107	104	—
1945	C	WAS	AL	2-8	91	286	33	76	12	1	1	38	.266	43	93	108	—
1947	C	WAS	AL	7-8	37	99	10	30	11	0	0	12	.303	14	41	124	—

MAJOR LEAGUE TOTALS   1884 6028 687 1692 324 45 28 734 .281 931 2190 113   6 yrs

Donald Eric McNair   Born Apr 12, 1909 Meridian, MS
5'8 160 lbs Batted right   Died Mar 11, 1949 Meridian, MS

YR	POS	TEAM	LG	FIN	G	AB	R	H	2B	3B	HR	RBI	AVG	BB	TB	OQ	RANK
1929	SS	PHI	AL	1-8	4	8	2	4	1	0	0	3	.500	0	5	—	—
1930	SS-3B	PHI	AL	1-8	78	237	27	63	12	2	0	34	.266	9	79	70	—
1931	3B-2B	PHI	AL	1-8	79	280	41	76	10	1	5	33	.271	11	103	82	—
1932	SS	PHI	AL	2-8	135	554	87	158	47	3	18	95	.285	28	265	106	28-48
1933	SS-2B	PHI	AL	3-8	89	310	57	81	15	4	7	48	.261	15	125	90	—
1934	SS	PHI	AL	5-8	151	599	80	168	20	4	17	82	.280	35	247	93	38-44
1935	SS	PHI	AL	8-8	137	526	55	142	22	2	4	57	.270	35	180	79	50-51
1936	SS-2B	BOS	AL	6-8	128	494	68	141	36	2	4	74	.285	27	193	83	49-52
1937	2B	BOS	AL	5-8	126	455	60	133	29	4	12	76	.292	30	206	100	35-47
1938	SS-2B	BOS	AL	2-8	46	96	9	15	1	1	0	7	.156	3	18	—	—
1939	3B-2B	CHI	AL	4-8	129	479	62	155	18	5	7	82	.324	38	204	104	28-42
1940	2B	CHI	AL	4-8	66	251	26	57	13	1	7	31	.227	12	93	77	—
1941	3B-SS	DET	AL	4-8	23	59	5	11	1	0	0	3	.186	4	12	—	—
1942	SS	DE/PH	AL	5/8	60	171	13	36	4	0	1	8	.211	14	43	68	—

| MAJOR LEAGUE TOTALS | | | | | 1251 | 4519 | 592 | 1240 | 229 | 29 | 82 | 633 | .274 | 261 | 1773 | 94 | 6 yrs |

Roger Maxwell Cramer   Born Jul 22, 1905 Beach Haven, NJ
6'2 185 lbs Batted left   Died Sep 9, 1990 Manahawkin, NJ

YR	POS	TEAM	LG	FIN	G	AB	R	H	2B	3B	HR	RBI	AVG	BB	TB	OQ	RANK
1929	LF	PHI	AL	1-8	2	6	0	0	0	0	0	0	.000	0	0	—	—
1930	LF	PHI	AL	1-8	30	82	12	19	1	1	0	6	.232	2	22	—	—
1931	CF	PHI	AL	1-8	65	223	37	58	8	2	2	20	.260	11	76	77	—
1932	RF	PHI	AL	2-8	92	384	73	129	27	6	3	46	.336	17	177	109	—
1933	CF	PHI	AL	3-8	152	661	109	195	27	8	8	75	.295	36	262	94	37-52
1934	CF	PHI	AL	5-8	153	649	99	202	29	9	6	46	.311	40	267	98	34-44
1935	CF	PHI	AL	8-8	149	644	96	214	37	4	3	70	.332	37	268	101	34-51
1936	CF	BOS	AL	6-8	154	643	99	188	31	7	0	41	.292	49	233	83	50-52
1937	CF	BOS	AL	5-8	133	560	90	171	22	11	0	51	.305	35	215	88	42-47
1938	CF	BOS	AL	2-8	148	658	116	198	36	8	0	71	.301	51	250	89	47-52
1939	CF	BOS	AL	2-8	137	589	110	183	30	6	0	56	.311	36	225	90	39-42
1940	CF	BOS	AL	4-8	150	661	94	200	27	12	1	51	.303	36	254	90	39-49
1941	CF	WAS	AL	7-8	154	660	93	180	25	6	2	66	.273	37	223	80	44-48
1942	CF	DET	AL	5-8	151	630	71	166	26	4	0	43	.263	43	200	85	43-45
1943	CF	DET	AL	5-8	140	606	79	182	18	4	1	43	.300	31	211	97	34-45
1944	CF	DET	AL	2-8	143	578	69	169	20	9	2	42	.292	37	213	101	28-46
1945	CF	DET	AL	1-8	141	541	62	149	22	8	6	58	.275	36	205	103	25-39
1946	CF	DET	AL	2-8	68	204	26	60	8	2	1	26	.294	15	75	99	—
1947	CF	DET	AL	2-8	73	157	21	42	2	2	2	30	.268	20	54	100	—
1948	CF	DET	AL	5-8	4	4	1	0	0	0	0	1	.000	3	0	—	—

| MAJOR LEAGUE TOTALS | | | | | 2239 | 9140 | 1357 | 2705 | 396 | 109 | 37 | 842 | .296 | 572 | 3430 | 92 | 13 yrs |

Roy Cleland Johnson　　　　　Born　Feb 23, 1903　Pryor, OK
5'9　175 lbs　Batted left　　　　Died　Sep 10, 1973　Tacoma, WA

YR	POS	TEAM	LG	FIN	G	AB	R	H	2B	3B	HR	RBI	AVG	BB	TB	OQ	RANK
1929	LF	DET	AL	6-8	148	640	128	201	45	14	10	69	.314	67	304	120	17-41
1930	RF	DET	AL	5-8	125	462	84	127	30	13	2	35	.275	40	189	95	34-40
1931	RF	DET	AL	7-8	151	621	107	173	37	19	8	55	.279	72	272	113	25-47
1932	RF	DE/BO	AL	5/8	143	544	103	153	38	6	14	69	.281	64	245	113	19-48
1933	RF	BOS	AL	7-8	133	483	88	151	30	7	10	95	.313	55	225	125	12-52
1934	LF	BOS	AL	4-8	143	569	85	182	43	10	7	119	.320	54	266	118	19-44
1935	LF	BOS	AL	4-8	145	553	70	174	33	9	3	66	.315	74	234	115	21-51
1936	LF	NY	AL	1-8	63	147	21	39	8	2	1	19	.265	21	54	93	—
1937	LF	NY	AL	1-8	12	51	5	15	3	0	0	6	.294	3	18	—	—
1937	LF	BOS	NL	5-8	85	260	24	72	8	3	3	22	.277	38	95	110	—
1938	LF	BOS	NL	5-8	7	29	2	5	0	0	0	1	.172	1	5	—	—

MAJOR LEAGUE TOTALS　　　　1155　4359　717 1292 275 83 58 556 .296 489 1907 114　7 yrs

Howard Earl Averill　　　　　Born　May 21, 1902　Snohomish, WA
5'9　172 lbs　Batted left　　　　Died　Aug 16, 1983　Everett, WA

YR	POS	TEAM	LG	FIN	G	AB	R	H	2B	3B	HR	RBI	AVG	BB	TB	OQ	RANK
1929	CF	CLE	AL	3-8	151	597	110	198	43	13	18	96	.332	63	321	137	9-41
1930	CF	CLE	AL	4-8	139	534	102	181	33	8	19	119	.339	56	287	135	9-40
1931	CF	CLE	AL	4-8	155	627	140	209	36	10	32	143	.333	68	361	151	7-47
1932	CF	CLE	AL	4-8	153	631	116	198	37	14	32	124	.314	75	359	143	4-48
1933	CF	CLE	AL	4-8	151	599	83	180	39	16	11	92	.301	54	284	119	20-52
1934	CF	CLE	AL	3-8	154	598	128	187	48	6	31	113	.313	99	340	152	5-44
1935	CF	CLE	AL	3-8	140	563	109	162	34	13	19	79	.288	70	279	123	11-51
1936	CF	CLE	AL	5-8	152	614	136	232	39	15	28	126	.378	65	385	157	3-52
1937	CF	CLE	AL	4-8	156	609	121	182	33	11	21	92	.299	88	300	124	13-47
1938	CF	CLE	AL	3-8	134	482	101	159	27	15	14	93	.330	81	258	142	6-52
1939	LF	CL/DE	AL	3/5	111	364	66	96	28	6	11	65	.264	49	169	114	—
1940	CF-LF	DET	AL	1-8	64	118	10	33	4	1	2	20	.280	5	45	84	—
1941	CF	BOS	NL	7-8	8	17	2	2	0	0	0	2	.118	1	2	—	—

MAJOR LEAGUE TOTALS　　　　1668　6353 1224 2019 401 128 238 1164 .318 774 3390 138　10 yrs

Bruce Douglas Campbell Born Oct 20, 1909 Chicago, IL
6'1 185 lbs Batted left

YR	POS	TEAM	LG	FIN	G	AB	R	H	2B	3B	HR	RBI	AVG	BB	TB	OQ	RANK
1930	LF	CHI	AL	7-8	5	10	4	5	1	1	0	5	.500	1	8	—	—
1931	LF	CHI	AL	8-8	4	17	4	7	2	0	2	5	.412	0	15	—	—
1932	RF	CH/SL	AL	7/6	146	611	86	173	36	11	14	87	.283	40	273	102	30-48
1933	RF	SL	AL	8-8	148	567	87	157	38	8	16	106	.277	69	259	118	22-52
1934	RF	SL	AL	6-8	138	481	62	134	25	6	9	74	.279	51	198	102	29-44
1935	RF	CLE	AL	3-8	80	308	56	100	26	3	7	54	.325	31	153	126	—
1936	RF	CLE	AL	5-8	76	172	35	64	15	2	6	30	.372	19	101	148	—
1937	RF	CLE	AL	4-8	134	448	82	135	42	11	4	61	.301	67	211	121	17-47
1938	RF	CLE	AL	3-8	133	511	90	148	27	12	12	72	.290	53	235	107	27-52
1939	RF	CLE	AL	3-8	130	450	84	129	23	13	8	72	.287	67	202	117	19-42
1940	RF	DET	AL	1-8	103	297	56	84	15	5	8	44	.283	45	133	119	—
1941	RF	DET	AL	4-8	141	512	72	141	28	10	15	93	.275	68	234	120	18-48
1942	RF	WAS	AL	7-8	122	378	41	105	17	5	5	63	.278	37	147	109	—

MAJOR LEAGUE TOTALS					1360	4762	759	1382	295	87	106	766	.290	548	2169	112	7 yrs

Joseph Franklin Vosmik Born Apr 4, 1910 Cleveland, OH
6'0 185 lbs Batted right   Died Jan 27, 1962 Cleveland, OH

YR	POS	TEAM	LG	FIN	G	AB	R	H	2B	3B	HR	RBI	AVG	BB	TB	OQ	RANK
1930	CF	CLE	AL	4-8	9	26	1	6	2	0	0	4	.231	1	8	—	—
1931	LF	CLE	AL	4-8	149	591	80	189	36	14	7	117	.320	38	274	114	22-47
1932	LF	CLE	AL	4-8	153	621	106	194	39	12	10	97	.312	58	287	116	18-48
1933	LF	CLE	AL	4-8	119	438	53	115	20	10	4	56	.263	42	167	96	36-52
1934	LF	CLE	AL	3-8	104	405	71	138	33	2	6	78	.341	35	193	122	—
1935	LF	CLE	AL	3-8	152	620	93	216	47	20	10	110	.348	59	333	138	5-51
1936	LF	CLE	AL	5-8	138	506	76	145	29	7	7	94	.287	79	209	107	26-52
1937	LF	SL	AL	8-8	144	594	81	193	47	9	4	93	.325	49	270	109	27-47
1938	LF	BOS	AL	2-8	146	621	121	201	37	6	9	86	.324	59	277	108	24-52
1939	LF	BOS	AL	2-8	145	554	89	153	29	6	7	84	.276	66	215	98	32-42
1940	RF	BRO	NL	2-8	116	404	45	114	14	6	1	42	.282	22	143	90	—
1941	RF	BRO	NL	1-8	25	56	0	11	0	0	0	4	.196	4	11	—	—
1944	RF	WAS	AL	8-8	14	36	2	7	2	0	0	9	.194	2	9	—	—

MAJOR LEAGUE TOTALS					1414	5472	818	1682	335	92	65	874	.307	514	2396	111	8 yrs

John Irving Burns   Born Aug 31, 1907 Cambridge, MA
5'10   175 lbs   Batted left   Died Apr 18, 1975 Brighton, MA

YR	POS	TEAM	LG	FIN	G	AB	R	H	2B	3B	HR	RBI	AVG	BB	TB	OQ	RANK
1930	1B	SL	AL	6-8	8	30	5	9	3	0	0	2	.300	5	12	—	—
1931	1B	SL	AL	5-8	144	570	75	148	27	7	4	70	.260	42	201	85	43-47
1932	1B	SL	AL	6-8	150	617	111	188	33	8	11	70	.305	61	270	110	21-48
1933	1B	SL	AL	8-8	144	556	89	160	43	4	7	71	.288	56	232	107	30-52
1934	1B	SL	AL	6-8	154	612	86	157	28	8	13	73	.257	62	240	95	36-44
1935	1B	SL	AL	7-8	143	549	77	157	28	1	5	67	.286	68	202	98	37-51
1936	1B	SL/DE	AL	7/2	147	572	98	161	37	3	4	64	.281	82	216	97	38-52

MAJOR LEAGUE TOTALS   890 3506 541 980 199 31 44 417 .280 376 1373   99   6 yrs

Joseph Anthony Kuhel   Born Jun 25, 1906   Cleveland, OH
6'0   180 lbs   Batted left   Died Feb 26, 1984   Kansas City, KS

YR	POS	TEAM	LG	FIN	G	AB	R	H	2B	3B	HR	RBI	AVG	BB	TB	OQ	RANK
1930	1B	WAS	AL	2-8	18	63	9	18	3	3	0	17	.286	5	27	—	—
1931	1B	WAS	AL	3-8	139	524	70	141	34	8	8	85	.269	47	215	100	36-47
1932	1B	WAS	AL	3-8	101	347	52	101	21	5	4	52	.291	32	144	102	—
1933	1B	WAS	AL	1-8	153	602	89	194	34	10	11	107	.322	59	281	123	14-52
1934	1B	WAS	AL	7-8	63	263	49	76	12	3	3	25	.289	30	103	101	—
1935	1B	WAS	AL	6-8	151	633	99	165	25	9	2	74	.261	78	214	89	45-51
1936	1B	WAS	AL	4-8	149	588	107	189	42	8	16	118	.321	64	295	120	18-52
1937	1B	WAS	AL	6-8	136	547	73	155	24	11	6	61	.283	63	219	98	38-47
1938	1B	CHI	AL	6-8	117	412	67	110	27	4	8	51	.267	72	169	108	25-52
1939	1B	CHI	AL	4-8	139	546	107	164	24	9	15	56	.300	64	251	115	22-42
1940	1B	CHI	AL	4-8	155	603	111	169	28	8	27	94	.280	87	294	125	16-49
1941	1B	CHI	AL	3-8	153	600	99	150	39	5	12	63	.250	70	235	100	34-48
1942	1B	CHI	AL	6-8	115	413	60	103	14	4	4	52	.249	60	137	103	30-45
1943	1B	CHI	AL	4-8	153	531	55	113	21	1	5	46	.213	76	151	92	36-45
1944	1B	WAS	AL	8-8	139	518	90	144	26	7	4	51	.278	68	196	117	18-46
1945	1B	WAS	AL	2-8	142	533	73	152	29	13	2	75	.285	79	213	128	8-39
1946	1B	WA/CH	AL	4/5	78	258	26	68	9	3	4	22	.264	26	95	101	—
1947	PH	CHI	AL	6-8	3	3	0	0	0	0	0	0	.000	0	0	—	—

MAJOR LEAGUE TOTALS   2104 7984 1236 2212 412 111 131 1049 .277 980 3239 109 13 yrs

August Richard Suhr Born Jan 3, 1906 San Francisco, CA
6'0 180 lbs Batted left

YR	POS	TEAM	LG	FIN	G	AB	R	H	2B	3B	HR	RBI	AVG	BB	TB	OQ	RANK
1930	1B	PIT	NL	5-8	151	542	93	155	26	14	17	107	.286	80	260	115	23-44
1931	1B	PIT	NL	5-8	87	270	26	57	13	4	4	32	.211	38	90	93	—
1932	1B	PIT	NL	2-8	154	581	78	153	31	16	5	81	.263	63	231	106	25-38
1933	1B	PIT	NL	2-8	154	566	72	151	31	11	10	75	.267	72	234	125	14-48
1934	1B	PIT	NL	5-8	151	573	67	162	36	13	13	103	.283	66	263	123	17-48
1935	1B	PIT	NL	4-8	153	529	68	144	33	12	10	81	.272	70	231	121	15-44
1936	1B	PIT	NL	4-8	156	583	111	182	33	12	11	118	.312	95	272	141	6-43
1937	1B	PIT	NL	3-8	151	575	69	160	28	14	5	97	.278	83	231	118	15-40
1938	1B	PIT	NL	2-8	145	530	82	156	35	14	3	64	.294	87	228	133	10-46
1939	1B	PT/PH	NL	6/8	123	402	44	122	22	4	4	55	.303	59	164	122	14-33
1940	1B	PHI	NL	8-8	10	25	4	4	0	0	2	5	.160	5	10	—	—
MAJOR LEAGUE TOTALS					1435	5176	714	1446	288	114	84	818	.279	718	2214	123	9 yrs

Henry Benjamin Greenberg Born Jan 1, 1911 New York, NY
6'3 210 lbs Batted right Died Sep 4, 1986 Beverly Hills, CA

YR	POS	TEAM	LG	FIN	G	AB	R	H	2B	3B	HR	RBI	AVG	BB	TB	OQ	RANK
1930	PH	DET	AL	5-8	1	1	0	0	0	0	0	0	.000	0	0	—	—
1933	1B	DET	AL	5-8	117	449	59	135	33	3	12	87	.301	46	210	120	18-52
1934	1B	DET	AL	1-8	153	593	118	201	63	7	26	139	.339	63	356	152	4-44
1935	1B	DET	AL	1-8	152	619	121	203	46	16	36	170	.328	87	389	162	3-51
1936	1B	DET	AL	2-8	12	46	10	16	6	2	1	16	.348	9	29	—	—
1937	1B	DET	AL	2-8	154	594	137	200	49	14	40	183	.337	102	397	173	2-47
1938	1B	DET	AL	4-8	155	556	144	175	23	4	58	146	.315	119	380	178	2-52
1939	1B	DET	AL	5-8	138	500	112	156	42	7	33	112	.312	91	311	163	4-42
1940	LF	DET	AL	1-8	148	573	129	195	50	8	41	150	.340	93	384	180	1-49
1941	LF	DET	AL	5-8	19	67	12	18	5	1	2	12	.269	16	31	—	—
1945	LF	DET	AL	1-8	78	270	47	84	20	2	13	60	.311	42	147	170	—
1946	1B	DET	AL	2-8	142	523	91	145	29	5	44	127	.277	80	316	167	2-35
1947	1B	PIT	NL	7-8	125	402	71	100	13	2	25	74	.249	104	192	145	5-44
MAJOR LEAGUE TOTALS					1394	5193	1051	1628	379	71	331	1276	.313	852	3142	160	9 yrs

Joseph Gregg Moore Born Dec 25, 1908 Gause, TX
5'11 155 lbs Batted left

YR	POS	TEAM	LG	FIN	G	AB	R	H	2B	3B	HR	RBI	AVG	BB	TB	OQ	RANK
1930	CF	NY	NL	3-8	3	5	1	1	0	0	0	0	.200	0	1	—	—
1931	LF	NY	NL	2-8	4	8	0	2	1	0	0	3	.250	0	3	—	—
1932	LF	NY	NL	6-8	86	361	53	110	15	2	2	27	.305	20	135	96	—
1933	LF	NY	NL	1-8	132	524	56	153	16	5	0	42	.292	21	179	92	38-48
1934	LF	NY	NL	2-8	139	580	106	192	37	4	15	61	.331	31	282	124	15-48
1935	LF	NY	NL	3-8	155	681	108	201	28	9	15	71	.295	53	292	111	20-44
1936	LF	NY	NL	1-8	152	649	110	205	29	9	7	63	.316	37	273	108	21-43
1937	LF	NY	NL	1-8	142	580	89	180	37	10	6	57	.310	46	255	117	16-40
1938	LF	NY	NL	3-8	125	506	76	153	23	6	11	56	.302	22	221	109	18-46
1939	LF	NY	NL	5-8	138	562	80	151	23	2	10	47	.269	45	208	94	30-33
1940	LF	NY	NL	6-8	138	543	83	150	33	4	6	46	.276	43	209	102	31-44
1941	LF	NY	NL	5-8	121	428	47	117	16	2	7	40	.273	30	158	98	—
MAJOR LEAGUE TOTALS					1335	5427	809	1615	258	53	79	513	.298	348	2216	107	8 yrs

William Benjamin Chapman Born Dec 25, 1908 Nashville, TN
6'0 190 lbs Batted right Died Jul 7, 1993 Hoover, AL

YR	POS	TEAM	LG	FIN	G	AB	R	H	2B	3B	HR	RBI	AVG	BB	TB	OQ	RANK
1930	3B-2B	NY	AL	3-8	138	513	74	162	31	10	10	81	.316	43	243	113	24-40
1931	LF	NY	AL	2-8	149	600	120	189	28	11	17	122	.315	75	290	130	10-47
1932	LF	NY	AL	1-8	151	581	101	174	41	15	10	107	.299	71	275	122	13-48
1933	LF	NY	AL	2-8	147	565	112	176	36	4	9	98	.312	72	247	121	16-52
1934	CF	NY	AL	2-8	149	588	82	181	21	13	5	86	.308	67	243	109	26-44
1935	CF	NY	AL	2-8	140	553	118	160	38	8	8	74	.289	61	238	108	25-51
1936	CF	NY/WA	AL	1/4	133	540	110	170	50	10	5	81	.315	84	255	122	14-52
1937	RF	WA/BO	AL	6/5	148	553	99	164	30	12	7	69	.297	83	239	113	22-47
1938	RF	BOS	AL	2-8	127	480	92	163	40	8	6	80	.340	65	237	129	15-52
1939	CF	CLE	AL	3-8	149	545	101	158	31	9	6	82	.290	87	225	113	23-42
1940	LF	CLE	AL	2-8	143	548	82	157	40	6	4	50	.286	78	221	109	29-49
1941	LF-CF	WA/CH	AL	6/3	85	300	35	71	15	1	3	29	.237	29	97	81	—
1944	P	BRO	NL	7-8	20	38	11	14	4	0	0	11	.368	5	18	—	—
1945	P-CF	BR/PH	NL	3/8	37	73	6	19	2	0	0	7	.260	4	21	—	—
1946	P	PHI	NL	5-8	1	1	1	0	0	0	0	0	.000	0	0	—	—
MAJOR LEAGUE TOTALS					1717	6478	1144	1958	407	107	90	977	.302	824	2849	117	11 yrs

Walter Antone Berger
6'2 198 lbs Batted right

Born Oct 10, 1905 Chicago, IL
Died Nov 30, 1988 Redondo Beach, CA

YR	POS	TEAM	LG	FIN	G	AB	R	H	2B	3B	HR	RBI	AVG	BB	TB	OQ	RANK
1930	LF	BOS	NL	6-8	151	555	98	172	27	14	38	119	.310	54	341	135	11-44
1931	CF	BOS	NL	7-8	156	617	94	199	44	8	19	84	.323	55	316	137	5-36
1932	CF	BOS	NL	5-8	145	602	90	185	34	6	17	73	.307	33	282	117	12-38
1933	CF	BOS	NL	4-8	137	528	84	165	37	8	27	106	.313	41	299	159	2-48
1934	CF	BOS	NL	4-8	150	615	92	183	35	8	34	121	.298	49	336	137	6-48
1935	CF	BOS	NL	8-8	150	589	91	174	39	4	34	130	.295	50	323	139	5-44
1936	CF	BOS	NL	6-8	138	534	88	154	23	3	25	91	.288	53	258	126	11-43
1937	CF-LF	BO/NY	NL	5/1	89	312	54	89	20	3	17	65	.285	29	166	136	—
1938	LF	NY/CN	NL	3/4	115	439	79	131	23	4	16	60	.298	31	210	124	11-46
1939	LF	CIN	NL	1-8	97	329	36	85	15	1	14	44	.258	36	144	113	—
1940	RF-LF	CN/PH	NL	1/8	22	43	3	13	2	0	1	5	.302	4	18	—	—

| MAJOR LEAGUE TOTALS | | | | | 1350 | 5163 | 809 | 1550 | 299 | 59 | 242 | 898 | .300 | 435 | 2693 | 134 | 8 yrs |

Anthony Francis Cuccinello
5'7 160 lbs Batted right

Born Nov 8, 1907 Long Island City, NY

YR	POS	TEAM	LG	FIN	G	AB	R	H	2B	3B	HR	RBI	AVG	BB	TB	OQ	RANK
1930	3B-2B	CIN	NL	7-8	125	443	64	138	22	5	10	78	.312	47	200	106	26-44
1931	2B	CIN	NL	8-8	154	575	67	181	39	11	2	93	.315	54	248	118	13-36
1932	2B	BRO	NL	3-8	154	597	76	168	32	6	12	77	.281	46	248	106	26-38
1933	2B-3B	BRO	NL	6-8	134	485	58	122	31	4	9	65	.252	44	188	108	24-48
1934	2B-3B	BRO	NL	6-8	140	528	59	138	32	2	14	94	.261	49	216	104	35-48
1935	2B-3B	BRO	NL	5-8	102	360	49	105	20	3	8	53	.292	40	155	118	—
1936	2B	BOS	NL	6-8	150	565	68	174	26	3	7	86	.308	58	227	113	16-43
1937	2B	BOS	NL	5-8	152	575	77	156	36	4	11	80	.271	61	233	109	22-40
1938	2B	BOS	NL	5-8	147	555	62	147	25	2	9	76	.265	52	203	99	35-46
1939	2B	BOS	NL	7-8	81	310	42	95	17	1	2	40	.306	26	120	104	—
1940	3B-2B	BO/NY	NL	7/6	122	433	40	98	18	2	5	55	.226	24	135	75	—
1942	3B-2B	BOS	NL	7-8	40	104	8	21	3	0	1	8	.202	9	27	74	—
1943	3B-2B	BOS	NL	6-8	13	19	0	0	0	0	0	2	.000	3	0	—	—
1943	3B	CHI	AL	4-8	34	103	5	28	5	0	2	11	.272	13	39	117	—
1944	3B-2B	CHI	AL	7-8	38	130	5	34	3	0	0	17	.262	8	37	78	—
1945	3B	CHI	AL	6-8	118	402	50	124	25	3	2	49	.308	45	161	124	—

| MAJOR LEAGUE TOTALS | | | | | 1704 | 6184 | 730 | 1729 | 334 | 46 | 94 | 884 | .280 | 579 | 2437 | 108 | 8 yrs |

George Archibald Watkins
6'0 175 lbs Batted left

Born Jun 4, 1900 Freestone County, TX
Died Jun 1, 1970 Houston, TX

YR	POS	TEAM	LG	FIN	G	AB	R	H	2B	3B	HR	RBI	AVG	BB	TB	OQ	RANK
1930	RF-1B	SL	NL	1-8	119	391	85	146	32	7	17	87	.373	24	243	143	—
1931	RF	SL	NL	1-8	131	503	93	145	30	13	13	51	.288	31	240	117	15-36
1932	RF	SL	NL	6-8	127	458	67	143	35	3	9	63	.312	45	211	126	9-38
1933	RF	SL	NL	5-8	138	525	66	146	24	5	5	62	.278	39	195	105	28-48
1934	CF	NY	NL	2-8	105	296	38	73	18	3	6	33	.247	24	115	96	—
1935	LF	PHI	NL	7-8	150	600	80	162	25	5	17	76	.270	40	248	102	25-44
1936	LF	PH/BR	NL	8/7	124	434	61	110	28	6	6	48	.253	43	168	100	27-43
MAJOR LEAGUE TOTALS					894	3207	490	925	192	42	73	420	.288	246	1420	110	5 yrs

Lucius Benjamin Appling
5'10 183 lbs Batted right

Born Apr 2, 1909 High Point, NC
Died Jan 3, 1991 Cumming, GA

YR	POS	TEAM	LG	FIN	G	AB	R	H	2B	3B	HR	RBI	AVG	BB	TB	OQ	RANK
1930	SS	CHI	AL	7-8	6	26	2	8	2	0	0	2	.308	0	10	—	—
1931	SS	CHI	AL	8-8	96	297	36	69	13	4	1	28	.232	29	93	79	—
1932	SS-2B	CHI	AL	7-8	139	489	66	134	20	10	3	63	.274	40	183	90	40-48
1933	SS	CHI	AL	6-8	151	612	90	197	36	10	6	85	.322	56	271	116	23-52
1934	SS	CHI	AL	8-8	118	452	75	137	28	6	2	61	.303	59	183	109	25-44
1935	SS	CHI	AL	5-8	153	525	94	161	28	6	1	71	.307	122	204	127	9-51
1936	SS	CHI	AL	3-8	138	526	111	204	31	7	6	128	.388	85	267	146	5-52
1937	SS	CHI	AL	3-8	154	574	98	182	42	8	4	77	.317	86	252	118	18-47
1938	SS	CHI	AL	6-8	81	294	41	89	14	0	0	44	.303	42	103	96	—
1939	SS	CHI	AL	4-8	148	516	82	162	16	6	0	56	.314	105	190	116	20-42
1940	SS	CHI	AL	4-8	150	566	96	197	27	13	0	79	.348	69	250	123	17-49
1941	SS	CHI	AL	3-8	154	592	93	186	26	8	1	57	.314	82	231	113	27-48
1942	SS	CHI	AL	6-8	142	543	78	142	26	4	3	53	.262	63	185	100	32-45
1943	SS	CHI	AL	4-8	155	585	63	192	33	2	3	80	.328	90	238	141	5-45
1945	SS	CHI	AL	6-8	18	57	12	21	2	2	1	10	.368	12	30	—	—
1946	SS	CHI	AL	5-8	149	582	59	180	27	5	1	55	.309	71	220	115	18-35
1947	SS	CHI	AL	6-8	139	503	67	154	29	0	8	49	.306	64	207	121	11-43
1948	3B-SS	CHI	AL	8-8	139	497	63	156	16	2	0	47	.314	94	176	115	18-45
1949	SS	CHI	AL	6-8	142	492	82	148	21	5	5	58	.301	121	194	131	7-41
1950	SS-1B	CHI	AL	6-8	50	128	11	30	3	4	0	13	.234	12	41	74	—
MAJOR LEAGUE TOTALS					2422	8856	1319	2749	440	102	45	1116	.310	1302	3528	119	15 yrs

William Murray Werber   Born Jun 20, 1908   Berwyn, MD
5'10 170 lbs Batted right

YR	POS	TEAM	LG	FIN	G	AB	R	H	2B	3B	HR	RBI	AVG	BB	TB	OQ	RANK
1930	SS-3B	NY	AL	3-8	4	14	5	4	0	0	0	2	.286	3	4	—	—
1933	SS-3B	NY/BO	AL	2/7	111	427	64	110	30	6	3	39	.258	33	161	90	43-52
1934	3B	BOS	AL	4-8	152	623	129	200	41	10	11	67	.321	77	294	125	15-44
1935	3B	BOS	AL	4-8	124	462	84	118	30	3	14	61	.255	69	196	109	24-51
1936	3B-LF	BOS	AL	6-8	145	535	89	147	29	6	10	67	.275	89	218	106	28-52
1937	3B	PHI	AL	7-8	128	493	85	144	31	4	7	70	.292	74	204	109	26-47
1938	3B	PHI	AL	8-8	134	499	92	129	22	7	11	69	.259	93	198	107	28-52
1939	3B	CIN	NL	1-8	147	599	115	173	35	5	5	57	.289	91	233	116	22-33
1940	3B	CIN	NL	1-8	143	584	105	162	35	5	12	48	.277	68	243	117	20-44
1941	3B	CIN	NL	3-8	109	418	56	100	9	2	4	46	.239	53	125	91	38-45
1942	3B	NY	NL	3-8	98	370	51	76	9	2	1	13	.205	51	92	83	—
MAJOR LEAGUE TOTALS					1295	5024	875	1363	271	50	78	539	.271	701	1968	108	9 yrs

Michael Franklin Higgins   Born May 27, 1909 Red Oak, TX
6'1 185 lbs Batted right   Died Mar 21, 1969 Dallas, TX

YR	POS	TEAM	LG	FIN	G	AB	R	H	2B	3B	HR	RBI	AVG	BB	TB	OQ	RANK
1930	3B	PHI	AL	1-8	14	24	1	6	2	0	0	0	.250	4	8	—	—
1933	3B	PHI	AL	3-8	152	567	85	178	35	11	13	99	.314	61	274	127	9-52
1934	3B	PHI	AL	5-8	144	543	89	179	37	6	16	90	.330	56	276	130	11-44
1935	3B	PHI	AL	8-8	133	524	69	155	32	4	23	94	.296	42	264	118	17-51
1936	3B	PHI	AL	8-8	146	550	89	159	32	2	12	80	.289	67	231	102	34-52
1937	3B	BOS	AL	5-8	153	570	88	172	33	5	9	106	.302	76	242	109	25-47
1938	3B	BOS	AL	2-8	139	524	77	159	29	5	5	106	.303	71	213	105	31-52
1939	3B	DET	AL	5-8	132	489	57	135	23	2	8	76	.276	56	186	96	35-42
1940	3B	DET	AL	1-8	131	480	70	130	24	3	13	76	.271	61	199	106	30-49
1941	3B	DET	AL	4-8	147	540	79	161	28	3	11	73	.298	67	228	114	26-48
1942	3B	DET	AL	5-8	143	499	65	133	34	2	11	79	.267	72	204	122	16-45
1943	3B	DET	AL	5-8	138	523	62	145	20	1	10	84	.277	57	197	114	18-45
1944	3B	DET	AL	2-8	148	543	79	161	32	4	7	76	.297	81	222	132	12-46
1946	3B	DE/BO	AL	2/1	82	260	20	68	14	2	2	36	.262	29	92	100	—
MAJOR LEAGUE TOTALS					1802	6636	930	1941	375	50	140	1075	.292	800	2836	115	12 yrs

Marvin James Owen　　　　　　　　Born　Mar 22, 1906　Agnew, CA
6'1　175 lbs　Batted right　　　　　　　Died　Jun 22, 1991　Mountain View, CA

YR	POS	TEAM	LG	FIN	G	AB	R	H	2B	3B	HR	RBI	AVG	BB	TB	OQ	RANK
1931	SS-3B	DET	AL	7-8	105	377	35	84	11	6	3	39	.223	29	116	73	—
1933	3B	DET	AL	5-8	138	550	77	144	24	9	2	65	.262	44	192	86	49-52
1934	3B	DET	AL	1-8	154	565	79	179	34	9	8	96	.317	59	255	116	20-44
1935	3B	DET	AL	1-8	134	483	52	127	24	5	2	71	.263	43	167	84	49-51
1936	3B	DET	AL	2-8	154	583	72	172	20	4	9	105	.295	53	227	91	42-52
1937	3B	DET	AL	2-8	107	396	48	114	22	5	1	45	.288	41	149	92	—
1938	3B	CHI	AL	6-8	141	577	84	162	23	6	6	55	.281	45	215	85	50-52
1939	3B	CHI	AL	4-8	58	194	22	46	9	0	0	15	.237	16	55	67	—
1940	3B-1B	BOS	AL	4-8	20	57	4	12	0	0	0	6	.211	8	12	—	—
MAJOR LEAGUE TOTALS					1011	3782	473	1040	167	44	31	497	.275	338	1388	92	5 yrs

William Frederick Jurges　　　　　　Born　May 9, 1908　Bronx, NY
5'11　175 lbs　Batted right

YR	POS	TEAM	LG	FIN	G	AB	R	H	2B	3B	HR	RBI	AVG	BB	TB	OQ	RANK
1931	3B-2B	CHI	NL	3-8	88	293	34	59	15	5	0	23	.201	25	84	72	—
1932	SS	CHI	NL	1-8	115	396	40	100	24	4	2	52	.253	19	138	82	—
1933	SS	CHI	NL	3-8	143	487	49	131	17	6	5	50	.269	26	175	96	36-48
1934	SS	CHI	NL	3-8	100	358	43	88	15	2	8	33	.246	19	131	85	—
1935	SS	CHI	NL	1-8	146	519	69	125	33	1	1	59	.241	42	163	80	43-44
1936	SS	CHI	NL	2-8	118	429	51	120	25	1	1	42	.280	23	150	86	—
1937	SS	CHI	NL	2-8	129	450	53	134	18	10	1	65	.298	42	175	107	24-40
1938	SS	CHI	NL	1-8	137	465	53	114	18	3	1	47	.245	58	141	90	42-46
1939	SS	NY	NL	5-8	138	543	84	155	21	11	6	63	.285	47	216	104	25-33
1940	SS	NY	NL	6-8	63	214	23	54	3	3	2	36	.252	25	69	93	—
1941	SS	NY	NL	5-8	134	471	50	138	25	2	5	61	.293	47	182	111	22-45
1942	SS	NY	NL	3-8	127	464	45	119	7	1	2	30	.256	43	134	87	35-40
1943	SS-3B	NY	NL	8-8	136	481	46	110	8	2	4	29	.229	53	134	85	39-44
1944	3B-SS	NY	NL	5-8	85	246	28	52	2	1	1	23	.211	23	59	69	—
1945	3B-SS	NY	NL	5-8	61	176	22	57	3	1	3	24	.324	24	71	127	—
1946	SS	CHI	NL	3-8	82	221	26	49	9	2	0	17	.222	43	62	99	—
1947	SS	CHI	NL	6-8	14	40	5	8	2	0	1	2	.200	9	13	—	—
MAJOR LEAGUE TOTALS					1816	6253	721	1613	245	55	43	656	.258	568	2097	95	8 yrs

Robert Abial Rolfe
5'11 170 lbs Batted left

Born Oct 17, 1908 Pennacook, NH
Died Jul 8, 1969 Guilford, NH

YR	POS	TEAM	LG	FIN	G	AB	R	H	2B	3B	HR	RBI	AVG	BB	TB	OQ	RANK
1931	SS	NY	AL	2-8	1	0	0	0	0	0	0	0	—	0	0	—	—
1934	SS-3B	NY	AL	2-8	89	279	54	80	13	2	0	18	.287	26	97	88	—
1935	3B-SS	NY	AL	2-8	149	639	108	192	33	9	5	67	.300	57	258	100	35-51
1936	3B	NY	AL	1-8	135	568	116	181	39	15	10	70	.319	68	280	120	19-52
1937	3B	NY	AL	1-8	154	648	143	179	34	10	4	62	.276	90	245	98	39-47
1938	3B	NY	AL	1-8	151	631	132	196	36	8	10	80	.311	74	278	110	22-52
1939	3B	NY	AL	1-8	152	648	139	213	46	10	14	80	.329	81	321	129	12-42
1940	3B	NY	AL	3-8	139	588	102	147	26	6	10	53	.250	50	215	86	45-49
1941	3B	NY	AL	1-8	136	561	106	148	22	5	8	42	.264	57	204	93	39-48
1942	3B	NY	AL	1-8	69	265	42	58	8	2	8	25	.219	23	94	91	—
MAJOR LEAGUE TOTALS					1175	4827	942	1394	257	67	69	497	.289	526	1992	105	7 yrs

William Jennings Bryan Herman
5'11 180 lbs Batted right

Born Jul 7, 1909 New Albany, IN
Died Sep 5, 1992 West Palm Beach, FL

YR	POS	TEAM	LG	FIN	G	AB	R	H	2B	3B	HR	RBI	AVG	BB	TB	OQ	RANK
1931	2B	CHI	NL	3-8	25	98	14	32	7	0	0	16	.327	13	39	122	—
1932	2B	CHI	NL	1-8	154	656	102	206	42	7	1	51	.314	40	265	105	27-38
1933	2B	CHI	NL	3-8	153	619	82	173	35	2	0	44	.279	45	212	98	32-48
1934	2B	CHI	NL	3-8	113	456	79	138	21	6	3	42	.303	34	180	103	36-48
1935	2B	CHI	NL	1-8	154	666	113	227	57	6	7	83	.341	42	317	127	13-44
1936	2B	CHI	NL	2-8	153	632	101	211	57	7	5	93	.334	59	297	131	9-43
1937	2B	CHI	NL	2-8	138	564	106	189	35	11	8	65	.335	56	270	135	5-40
1938	2B	CHI	NL	1-8	152	624	86	173	34	7	1	56	.277	59	224	99	33-46
1939	2B	CHI	NL	4-8	156	623	111	191	34	18	7	70	.307	66	282	123	13-33
1940	2B	CHI	NL	5-8	135	558	77	163	24	4	5	57	.292	47	210	103	29-44
1941	2B	CH/BR	NL	6/1	144	572	81	163	30	5	3	41	.285	67	212	110	23-45
1942	2B	BRO	NL	2-8	155	571	76	146	34	2	2	65	.256	72	190	105	23-40
1943	2B-3B	BRO	NL	3-8	153	585	76	193	41	2	2	100	.330	66	244	133	9-44
1946	2B-3B	BR/BO	NL	2/4	122	436	56	130	31	5	3	50	.298	69	180	132	7-35
1947	2B-3B	PIT	NL	7-8	15	47	3	10	4	0	0	6	.213	2	14	—	—
MAJOR LEAGUE TOTALS					1922	7707	1163	2345	486	82	47	839	.304	737	3136	116	13 yrs

William Michael Urbanski   Born Jun 5, 1903   Linoleumville, NY
5'8 165 lbs Batted right   Died Jul 12, 1973   Perth Amboy, NJ

YR	POS	TEAM	LG	FIN	G	AB	R	H	2B	3B	HR	RBI	AVG	BB	TB	OQ	RANK
1931	3B-SS	BOS	NL	7-8	82	303	22	72	13	4	0	17	.238	10	93	69	—
1932	SS	BOS	NL	5-8	136	563	80	153	25	8	8	46	.272	28	218	93	34-38
1933	SS	BOS	NL	4-8	144	566	65	142	21	4	0	35	.251	33	171	82	44-48
1934	SS	BOS	NL	4-8	146	605	104	177	30	6	7	53	.293	56	240	106	29-48
1935	SS	BOS	NL	8-8	132	514	53	118	17	0	4	30	.230	40	147	73	44-44
1936	SS-3B	BOS	NL	6-8	122	494	55	129	17	5	0	26	.261	31	156	79	42-43
1937	PH	BOS	NL	5-8	1	1	0	0	0	0	0	0	.000	0	0	—	—
MAJOR LEAGUE TOTALS					763	3046	379	791	123	27	19	207	.260	198	1025	87	5 yrs

Fred Walker   Born Sep 24, 1910   Villa Rica, GA
6'1 175 lbs Batted left   Died May 17, 1982 Birmingham, AL

YR	POS	TEAM	LG	FIN	G	AB	R	H	2B	3B	HR	RBI	AVG	BB	TB	OQ	RANK
1931	LF-RF	NY	AL	2-8	2	10	1	3	2	0	0	1	.300	0	5	—	—
1933	CF-LF	NY	AL	2-8	98	328	68	90	15	7	15	51	.274	26	164	118	—
1934	LF	NY	AL	2-8	17	17	2	2	0	0	0	0	.118	1	2	—	—
1935	LF	NY	AL	2-8	8	13	1	2	1	0	0	1	.154	0	3	—	—
1936	CF	NY/CH	AL	1/3	32	90	15	26	2	2	1	16	.289	15	35	104	—
1937	RF	CHI	AL	3-8	154	593	105	179	28	16	9	95	.302	78	266	114	21-47
1938	LF	DET	AL	4-8	127	454	84	140	27	6	6	43	.308	65	197	113	20-52
1939	LF	DET	AL	5-8	43	154	30	47	4	5	4	19	.305	15	73	115	—
1939	CF	BRO	NL	3-8	61	225	27	63	6	4	2	38	.280	20	83	97	—
1940	CF	BRO	NL	2-8	143	556	75	171	37	8	6	66	.308	42	242	117	19-44
1941	RF	BRO	NL	1-8	148	531	88	165	32	8	9	71	.311	70	240	137	10-45
1942	RF	BRO	NL	2-8	118	393	57	114	28	1	6	54	.290	47	162	128	—
1943	RF	BRO	NL	3-8	138	540	83	163	32	6	5	71	.302	49	222	121	13-44
1944	RF	BRO	NL	7-8	147	535	77	191	37	8	13	91	.357	72	283	167	3-42
1945	RF	BRO	NL	3-8	154	607	102	182	42	9	8	124	.300	75	266	128	9-41
1946	RF	BRO	NL	2-8	150	576	80	184	29	9	9	116	.319	67	258	134	5-35
1947	RF	BRO	NL	1-8	148	529	77	162	31	3	9	94	.306	97	226	130	13-44
1948	RF	PIT	NL	4-8	129	408	39	129	19	3	2	54	.316	52	160	115	—
1949	RF	PIT	NL	6-8	88	181	26	51	4	1	1	18	.282	26	60	99	—
MAJOR LEAGUE TOTALS					1905	6740	1037	2064	376	96	105	1023	.306	817	2947	129	9 yrs

Arvel Odell Hale
5'10 175 lbs Batted right

Born Aug 10, 1908 Hosston, LA
Died Jun 9, 1980 El Dorado, AR

YR	POS	TEAM	LG	FIN	G	AB	R	H	2B	3B	HR	RBI	AVG	BB	TB	OQ	RANK
1931	3B-2B	CLE	AL	4-8	25	92	14	26	2	4	1	5	.283	8	39	105	—
1933	2B-3B	CLE	AL	4-8	98	351	49	97	19	8	10	64	.276	30	162	112	—
1934	2B	CLE	AL	3-8	143	563	82	170	44	6	13	101	.302	48	265	113	22-44
1935	3B	CLE	AL	3-8	150	589	80	179	37	11	16	101	.304	52	286	117	18-51
1936	3B	CLE	AL	5-8	153	620	126	196	50	13	14	87	.316	64	314	119	22-52
1937	3B-2B	CLE	AL	4-8	154	561	74	150	32	4	6	82	.267	56	208	88	43-47
1938	2B	CLE	AL	3-8	130	496	69	138	32	2	8	69	.278	44	198	92	46-52
1939	2B	CLE	AL	3-8	108	253	36	79	16	2	4	48	.312	25	111	109	—
1940	3B	CLE	AL	2-8	48	50	3	11	3	1	0	6	.220	5	16	—	—
1941	3B-2B	BOS	AL	2-8	12	24	5	5	2	0	1	1	.208	3	10	—	—
1941	2B	NY	NL	5-8	41	102	13	20	3	0	0	9	.196	18	23	81	—
MAJOR LEAGUE TOTALS					1062	3701	551	1071	240	51	73	573	.289	353	1632	106	5 yrs

Gerald Holmes Walker
5'11 188 lbs Batted right

Born Mar 19, 1908 Gulfport, MS
Died Mar 20, 1981 Whitfield, MS

YR	POS	TEAM	LG	FIN	G	AB	R	H	2B	3B	HR	RBI	AVG	BB	TB	OQ	RANK
1931	CF	DET	AL	7-8	59	189	20	56	17	2	1	28	.296	14	80	104	—
1932	CF	DET	AL	5-8	127	480	71	155	32	6	8	78	.323	13	223	104	29-48
1933	LF	DET	AL	5-8	127	483	68	135	29	7	9	64	.280	15	205	93	39-52
1934	CF	DET	AL	1-8	98	347	54	104	19	2	6	39	.300	19	145	96	—
1935	CF	DET	AL	1-8	98	362	52	109	22	6	7	53	.301	15	164	100	—
1936	RF	DET	AL	2-8	134	550	105	194	55	5	12	93	.353	23	295	119	20-52
1937	LF	DET	AL	2-8	151	635	105	213	42	4	18	113	.335	41	317	116	20-47
1938	LF	CHI	AL	6-8	120	442	69	135	23	6	16	87	.305	38	218	113	21-52
1939	LF	CHI	AL	4-8	149	598	95	174	30	11	13	111	.291	28	265	97	34-42
1940	LF	WAS	AL	7-8	140	595	87	175	29	7	13	96	.294	24	257	95	35-49
1941	LF	CLE	AL	4-8	121	445	56	126	26	11	6	48	.283	18	192	97	—
1942	CF	CIN	NL	4-8	119	422	40	97	20	2	5	50	.230	31	136	88	—
1943	CF	CIN	NL	2-8	114	429	48	105	23	2	3	54	.245	12	141	79	—
1944	RF	CIN	NL	3-8	121	478	56	133	21	3	5	62	.278	23	175	93	31-42
1945	RF	CIN	NL	7-8	106	316	28	80	11	2	2	21	.253	16	101	79	—
MAJOR LEAGUE TOTALS					1784	6771	954	1991	399	76	124	997	.294	330	2914	104	8 yrs

James Anthony Collins
5'9 165 lbs Batted both

Born Mar 30, 1904 Altoona, PA
Died Apr 15, 1970 New Haven, CT

YR	POS	TEAM	LG	FIN	G	AB	R	H	2B	3B	HR	RBI	AVG	BB	TB	OO	RANK
1931	1B	SL	NL	1-8	89	279	34	84	20	10	4	59	.301	18	136	122	—
1932	1B-RF	SL	NL	6-8	149	549	82	153	28	8	21	91	.279	38	260	116	13-38
1933	1B	SL	NL	5-8	132	493	66	153	26	7	10	68	.310	38	223	130	11-48
1934	1B	SL	NL	1-8	154	600	116	200	40	12	35	128	.333	57	369	164	2-48
1935	1B	SL	NL	2-8	150	578	109	181	36	10	23	122	.313	65	306	145	4-44
1936	1B	SL	NL	2-8	103	277	48	81	15	3	13	48	.292	48	141	149	—
1937	1B	CHI	NL	2-8	115	456	77	125	16	5	16	71	.274	32	199	109	23-40
1938	1B	CHI	NL	1-8	143	490	78	131	22	8	13	61	.267	54	208	115	15-46
1941	1B	PIT	NL	4-8	49	62	5	13	2	2	0	11	.210	6	19	—	—
MAJOR LEAGUE TOTALS					1084	3784	615	1121	205	65	135	659	.296	356	1861	130	6 yrs

Ernesto Natali Lombardi
6'3 230 lbs Batted right

Born Apr 6, 1908 Oakland, CA
Died Sep 26, 1977 Santa Cruz, CA

YR	POS	TEAM	LG	FIN	G	AB	R	H	2B	3B	HR	RBI	AVG	BB	TB	OO	RANK
1931	C	BRO	NL	4-8	73	182	20	54	7	1	4	23	.297	12	75	105	—
1932	C	CIN	NL	8-8	118	413	43	125	22	9	11	68	.303	41	198	128	—
1933	C	CIN	NL	8-8	107	350	30	99	21	1	4	47	.283	16	134	102	—
1934	C	CIN	NL	8-8	132	417	42	127	19	4	9	62	.305	16	181	104	—
1935	C	CIN	NL	6-8	120	332	36	114	23	3	12	64	.343	16	179	138	—
1936	C	CIN	NL	5-8	121	387	42	129	23	2	12	68	.333	19	192	126	—
1937	C	CIN	NL	8-8	120	368	41	123	22	1	9	59	.334	14	174	119	—
1938	C	CIN	NL	4-8	129	489	60	167	30	1	19	95	.342	40	256	145	5-46
1939	C	CIN	NL	1-8	130	450	43	129	26	2	20	85	.287	35	219	121	16-33
1940	C	CIN	NL	1-8	109	376	50	120	22	0	14	74	.319	31	184	133	—
1941	C	CIN	NL	3-8	117	398	33	105	12	1	10	60	.264	36	149	102	—
1942	C	BOS	NL	7-8	105	309	32	102	14	0	11	46	.330	37	149	153	—
1943	C	NY	NL	8-8	104	295	19	90	7	0	10	51	.305	16	127	117	—
1944	C	NY	NL	5-8	117	373	37	95	13	0	10	58	.255	33	138	100	—
1945	C	NY	NL	5-8	115	368	46	113	7	1	19	70	.307	43	179	139	—
1946	C	NY	NL	8-8	88	238	19	69	4	1	12	39	.290	18	111	123	—
1947	C	NY	NL	4-8	48	110	8	31	5	0	4	21	.282	7	48	103	—
MAJOR LEAGUE TOTALS					1853	5855	601	1792	277	27	190	990	.306	430	2693	—	—

Michael Andreas Kreevich Born Jun 10, 1980 Mount Olive, IL
5'7 168 lbs Batted right

YR	POS	TEAM	LG	FIN	G	AB	R	H	2B	3B	HR	RBI	AVG	BB	TB	OQ	RANK
1931	RF	CHI	NL	3-8	5	12	0	2	0	0	0	0	.167	0	2	—	—
1935	3B	CHI	AL	5-8	6	23	3	10	2	0	0	2	.435	1	12	—	—
1936	CF	CHI	AL	3-8	137	550	99	169	32	11	5	69	.307	61	238	105	30-52
1937	CF	CHI	AL	3-8	144	583	94	176	29	16	12	73	.302	43	273	106	31-47
1938	CF	CHI	AL	6-8	129	489	73	145	26	12	6	73	.297	55	213	106	29-52
1939	CF	CHI	AL	4-8	145	541	85	175	30	8	5	77	.323	59	236	113	24-42
1940	CF	CHI	AL	4-8	144	582	86	154	27	10	8	55	.265	34	225	86	44-49
1941	CF	CHI	AL	3-8	121	436	44	101	16	8	0	37	.232	35	133	74	46-48
1942	CF	PHI	AL	8-8	116	444	57	113	19	1	1	30	.255	47	137	90	41-45
1943	CF	SL	AL	6-8	60	161	24	41	6	0	0	10	.255	26	47	103	—
1944	LF	SL	AL	1-8	105	402	55	121	15	6	5	44	.301	27	163	112	—
1945	CF	SL/WA	AL	3/2	129	453	56	114	19	3	3	44	.252	58	148	102	26-39

MAJOR LEAGUE TOTALS   1241 4676 676 1321 221 75 45 514 .283 446 1827 98 8 yrs

Joseph Michael Medwick Born Nov 24, 1911 Carteret, NJ
5'10 187 lbs Batted right Died Mar 21, 1975 St Petersburg, FL

YR	POS	TEAM	LG	FIN	G	AB	R	H	2B	3B	HR	RBI	AVG	BB	TB	OQ	RANK
1932	CF-LF	SL	NL	6-8	26	106	13	37	12	1	2	12	.349	2	57	132	—
1933	LF	SL	NL	5-8	148	595	92	182	40	10	18	98	.306	26	296	132	10-48
1934	LF	SL	NL	1-8	149	620	110	198	40	18	18	106	.319	21	328	127	13-48
1935	LF	SL	NL	2-8	154	634	132	224	46	13	23	126	.353	30	365	149	3-44
1936	LF	SL	NL	2-8	155	636	115	223	64	13	18	138	.351	34	367	150	5-43
1937	LF	SL	NL	4-8	156	633	111	237	56	10	31	154	.374	41	406	176	2-40
1938	LF	SL	NL	6-8	146	590	100	190	47	8	21	122	.322	42	316	141	6-46
1939	LF	SL	NL	2-8	150	606	98	201	48	8	14	117	.332	45	307	133	5-33
1940	LF	SL/BR	NL	3/2	143	581	83	175	30	12	17	86	.301	32	280	122	17-44
1941	LF	BRO	NL	1-8	133	538	100	171	33	10	18	88	.318	38	278	139	9-45
1942	LF	BRO	NL	2-8	142	553	69	166	37	4	4	96	.300	32	223	112	17-40
1943	LF	BR/NY	NL	3/8	126	497	54	138	30	3	5	70	.278	19	189	97	33-44
1944	LF	NY	NL	5-8	128	490	64	165	24	3	7	85	.337	38	216	127	15-42
1945	LF-1B	NY/BO	NL	5/6	92	310	31	90	17	0	3	37	.290	14	116	94	—
1946	LF	BRO	NL	2-8	41	77	7	24	4	0	2	18	.312	6	34	—	—
1947	RF-LF	SL	NL	2-8	75	150	19	46	12	0	4	28	.307	16	70	123	—
1948	PH	SL	NL	2-8	20	19	0	4	0	0	0	2	.211	1	4	—	—

MAJOR LEAGUE TOTALS   1984 7635 1198 2471 540 113 205 1383 .324 437 3852 134 12 yrs

Joseph Franklin Demaree   Born Jun 10, 1910   Winters, CA
5'11   185 lbs   Batted right   Died Aug 30, 1958   Los Angeles, CA

YR	POS	TEAM	LG	FIN	G	AB	R	H	2B	3B	HR	RBI	AVG	BB	TB	OQ	RANK
1932	CF-RF	CHI	NL	1-8	23	56	4	14	3	0	0	6	.250	2	17	—	—
1933	CF	CHI	NL	3-8	134	515	68	140	24	6	6	51	.272	22	194	98	33-48
1935	CF	CHI	NL	1-8	107	385	60	125	19	4	2	66	.325	26	158	110	—
1936	RF	CHI	NL	2-8	154	605	93	212	34	3	16	96	.350	49	300	137	7-43
1937	RF	CHI	NL	2-8	154	615	104	199	36	6	17	115	.324	57	298	133	6-40
1938	RF	CHI	NL	1-8	129	476	63	130	15	7	8	62	.273	45	183	104	24-46
1939	CF	NY	NL	5-8	150	560	68	170	27	2	11	79	.304	66	234	118	20-33
1940	CF	NY	NL	6-8	121	460	68	139	18	6	7	61	.302	45	190	116	21-44
1941	CF-RF	NY/BO	NL	5/7	64	148	23	32	5	2	2	16	.216	16	47	88	—
1942	LF-RF	BOS	NL	7-8	64	187	18	42	5	0	3	24	.225	17	56	86	—
1943	LF-RF	SL	NL	1-8	39	86	5	25	2	0	0	9	.291	8	27	—	—
1944	LF	SL	AL	1-8	16	51	4	13	2	0	0	6	.255	6	15	—	—
MAJOR LEAGUE TOTALS					1155	4144	578	1241	190	36	72	591	.299	359	1719	118	6 yrs

Stanley Camfield Hack   Born Dec 6, 1909   Sacramento, CA
6'0   170 lbs   Batted left   Died Dec 15, 1979   Dixon, IL

YR	POS	TEAM	LG	FIN	G	AB	R	H	2B	3B	HR	RBI	AVG	BB	TB	OQ	RANK
1932	3B	CHI	NL	1-8	72	178	32	42	5	6	2	19	.236	17	65	93	—
1933	3B	CHI	NL	3-8	20	60	10	21	3	1	1	2	.350	8	29	—	—
1934	3B	CHI	NL	3-8	111	402	54	116	16	6	1	21	.289	45	147	103	—
1935	3B	CHI	NL	1-8	124	427	75	133	23	9	4	64	.311	65	186	132	9-44
1936	3B	CHI	NL	2-8	149	561	102	167	27	4	6	78	.298	89	220	121	14-43
1937	3B	CHI	NL	2-8	154	582	106	173	27	6	2	63	.297	83	218	114	19-40
1938	3B	CHI	NL	1-8	152	609	109	195	34	11	4	67	.320	94	263	136	9-46
1939	3B	CHI	NL	4-8	156	641	112	191	28	6	8	56	.298	65	255	109	24-33
1940	3B	CHI	NL	5-8	149	603	101	191	38	6	8	40	.317	75	265	131	10-44
1941	3B	CHI	NL	6-8	151	586	111	186	33	5	7	45	.317	99	250	141	8-45
1942	3B	CHI	NL	6-8	140	553	91	166	36	3	6	39	.300	94	226	141	8-40
1943	3B	CHI	NL	5-8	144	533	78	154	24	4	3	35	.289	82	195	123	12-44
1944	3B-1B	CHI	NL	4-8	98	383	65	108	16	1	3	32	.282	53	135	111	—
1945	3B	CHI	NL	1-8	150	597	110	193	29	7	2	43	.323	99	242	135	6-41
1946	3B	CHI	NL	3-8	92	323	55	92	13	4	0	26	.285	83	113	137	—
1947	3B	CHI	NL	6-8	76	240	28	65	11	2	0	12	.271	41	80	102	—
MAJOR LEAGUE TOTALS					1938	7278	1239	2193	363	81	57	642	.301	1092	2889	128	10 yrs

Richard Walther Siebert
6'0 170 lbs Batted left

Born Feb 19, 1912 Fall River, MA
Died Dec 9, 1978 Minneapolis, MN

YR	POS	TEAM	LG	FIN	G	AB	R	H	2B	3B	HR	RBI	AVG	BB	TB	OQ	RANK
1932	1B	BRO	NL	3-8	6	7	1	2	0	0	0	0	.286	2	2	—	—
1936	RF	BRO	NL	7-8	2	2	0	0	0	0	0	0	.000	0	0	—	—
1937	1B	SL	NL	4-8	22	38	3	7	2	0	0	2	.184	4	9	—	—
1938	1B	SL	NL	6-8	1	1	0	1	0	0	0	0	.000	0	1	—	—
1938	1B	PHI	AL	8-8	48	194	24	55	8	3	0	28	.284	10	69	77	—
1939	1B	PHI	AL	7-8	101	402	58	118	28	3	6	47	.294	21	170	94	—
1940	1B	PHI	AL	8-8	154	595	69	170	31	6	5	77	.286	33	228	87	42-49
1941	1B	PHI	AL	8-8	123	467	63	156	28	8	5	79	.334	37	215	119	21-48
1942	1B	PHI	AL	8-8	153	612	57	159	25	7	2	74	.260	24	204	81	44-45
1943	1B	PHI	AL	8-8	146	558	50	140	26	7	1	72	.251	33	183	87	38-45
1944	1B-LF	PHI	AL	5-8	132	468	52	143	27	5	6	52	.306	62	198	133	10-46
1945	1B	PHI	AL	8-8	147	573	62	153	29	1	7	51	.267	50	205	102	27-39
MAJOR LEAGUE TOTALS					1035	3917	439	1104	204	40	32	482	.282	276	1484	102	6 yrs

Frank Peter Joseph Crosetti
5'10 165 lbs Batted right

Born Oct 4, 1910 San Francisco, CA

YR	POS	TEAM	LG	FIN	G	AB	R	H	2B	3B	HR	RBI	AVG	BB	TB	OQ	RANK
1932	SS-3B	NY	AL	1-8	116	398	47	96	20	9	5	57	.241	51	149	95	—
1933	SS	NY	AL	2-8	136	451	71	114	20	5	9	60	.253	55	171	99	33-52
1934	SS-3B	NY	AL	2-8	138	554	85	147	22	10	11	67	.265	61	222	99	31-44
1935	SS	NY	AL	2-8	87	305	49	78	17	6	8	50	.256	41	131	108	—
1936	SS	NY	AL	1-8	151	632	137	182	35	7	15	78	.288	90	276	109	25-52
1937	SS	NY	AL	1-8	149	611	127	143	29	5	11	49	.234	86	215	88	41-47
1938	SS	NY	AL	1-8	157	631	113	166	35	3	9	55	.263	106	234	99	39-52
1939	SS	NY	AL	1-8	152	656	109	153	25	5	10	56	.233	65	218	79	42-42
1940	SS	NY	AL	3-8	145	546	84	106	23	4	4	31	.194	72	149	72	49-49
1941	SS-3B	NY	AL	1-8	50	148	13	33	2	2	1	22	.223	18	42	77	—
1942	3B-SS	NY	AL	1-8	74	285	50	69	5	5	4	23	.242	31	96	95	—
1943	SS	NY	AL	1-8	95	348	36	81	8	1	2	20	.233	36	97	84	—
1944	SS	NY	AL	3-8	55	197	20	47	4	2	5	30	.239	11	70	90	—
1945	SS	NY	AL	4-8	130	441	57	105	12	0	4	48	.238	59	129	94	32-39
1946	SS	NY	AL	3-8	28	59	4	17	3	0	0	3	.288	8	20	—	—
1947	SS-2B	NY	AL	1-8	3	1	0	0	0	0	0	0	.000	0	0	—	—
1948	2B-SS	NY	AL	3-8	17	14	4	4	0	1	0	0	.286	2	6	—	—
MAJOR LEAGUE TOTALS					1683	6277	1006	1541	260	65	98	649	.245	792	2225	92	8 yrs

Joseph Floyd Vaughan
5'10 175 lbs Batted left

Born Mar 9, 1912 Clifty, AR
Died Aug 30, 1952 Eagleville, CA

YR	POS	TEAM	LG	FIN	G	AB	R	H	2B	3B	HR	RBI	AVG	BB	TB	OQ	RANK
1932	SS	PIT	NL	2-8	129	497	71	158	15	10	4	61	.318	39	205	111	21-38
1933	SS	PIT	NL	2-8	152	573	85	180	29	19	9	97	.314	64	274	146	3-48
1934	SS	PIT	NL	5-8	149	558	115	186	41	11	12	94	.333	94	285	157	4-48
1935	SS	PIT	NL	4-8	137	499	108	192	34	10	19	99	.385	97	303	202	1-44
1936	SS	PIT	NL	4-8	156	568	122	190	30	11	9	78	.335	118	269	158	4-43
1937	SS	PIT	NL	3-8	126	469	71	151	17	17	5	72	.322	54	217	133	7-40
1938	SS	PIT	NL	2-8	148	541	88	174	35	5	7	68	.322	104	240	148	4-46
1939	SS	PIT	NL	6-8	152	595	94	182	30	11	6	62	.306	70	252	119	19-33
1940	SS	PIT	NL	4-8	156	594	113	178	40	15	7	95	.300	88	269	136	7-44
1941	SS	PIT	NL	4-8	106	374	69	118	20	7	6	38	.316	50	170	139	—
1942	3B	BRO	NL	2-8	128	495	82	137	18	4	2	49	.277	51	169	105	24-40
1943	SS-3B	BRO	NL	3-8	149	610	112	186	39	6	5	66	.305	60	252	123	11-44
1947	LF-3B	BRO	NL	1-8	64	126	24	41	5	2	2	25	.325	27	56	145	—
1948	LF-3B	BRO	NL	3-8	65	123	19	30	3	0	3	22	.244	21	42	103	—
MAJOR LEAGUE TOTALS					1817	6622	1173	2103	356	128	96	926	.318	937	3003	140	11 yrs

Adolph Louis Camilli
5'10 185 lbs Batted left

Born Apr 23, 1907 San Francisco, CA

YR	POS	TEAM	LG	FIN	G	AB	R	H	2B	3B	HR	RBI	AVG	BB	TB	OQ	RANK
1933	1B	CHI	NL	3-8	16	58	8	13	2	1	2	7	.224	4	23	—	—
1934	1B	CH/PH	NL	3/7	134	498	69	133	28	3	16	87	.267	53	215	113	21-48
1935	1B	PHI	NL	7-8	156	602	88	157	23	5	25	83	.261	65	265	115	18-44
1936	1B	PHI	NL	8-8	151	530	106	167	29	13	28	102	.315	116	306	179	2-43
1937	1B	PHI	NL	7-8	131	475	101	161	23	7	27	80	.339	90	279	183	1-40
1938	1B	BRO	NL	7-8	146	509	106	128	25	11	24	100	.251	119	247	152	3-46
1939	1B	BRO	NL	3-8	157	565	105	164	30	12	26	104	.290	110	296	155	3-33
1940	1B	BRO	NL	2-8	142	512	92	147	29	13	23	96	.287	89	271	157	2-44
1941	1B	BRO	NL	1-8	149	529	92	151	29	6	34	120	.285	104	294	170	1-45
1942	1B	BRO	NL	2-8	150	524	89	132	23	7	26	109	.252	97	247	150	5-40
1943	1B	BRO	NL	3-8	95	353	56	87	15	6	6	43	.246	65	132	124	—
1945	1B	BOS	AL	7-8	63	198	24	42	5	2	2	19	.212	35	57	99	—
MAJOR LEAGUE TOTALS					1490	5353	936	1482	261	86	239	950	.277	947	2632	153	9 yrs

Linus Reinhard Frey Born Aug 23, 1910 St Louis, MO
5'10 160 lbs Batted left

YR	POS	TEAM	LG	FIN	G	AB	R	H	2B	3B	HR	RBI	AVG	BB	TB	OQ	RANK
1933	SS	BRO	NL	6-8	34	135	25	43	5	3	0	12	.319	13	54	124	—
1934	SS-3B	BRO	NL	6-8	125	490	77	139	24	5	8	57	.284	52	197	109	22-48
1935	SS	BRO	NL	5-8	131	515	88	135	35	11	11	77	.262	66	225	119	16-44
1936	SS-2B	BRO	NL	7-8	148	524	63	146	29	4	4	60	.279	71	195	109	20-43
1937	SS-2B	CHI	NL	2-8	78	198	33	55	9	3	1	22	.278	33	73	115	—
1938	2B	CIN	NL	4-8	124	501	76	133	26	6	4	36	.265	49	183	100	31-46
1939	2B	CIN	NL	1-8	125	484	95	141	27	9	11	55	.291	72	219	130	8-33
1940	2B	CIN	NL	1-8	150	563	102	150	23	6	8	54	.266	80	209	111	23-44
1941	2B	CIN	NL	3-8	146	543	78	138	29	5	6	59	.254	72	195	107	26-45
1942	2B	CIN	NL	4-8	141	523	66	139	23	6	2	39	.266	87	180	118	15-40
1943	2B	CIN	NL	2-8	144	586	78	154	20	8	2	43	.263	76	196	106	28-44
1946	2B-RF	CIN	NL	6-8	111	333	46	82	10	3	3	24	.246	63	107	110	—
1947	2B	CHI	NL	6-8	24	43	4	9	0	0	0	3	.209	4	9	—	—
1947	2B	NY	AL	1-8	24	28	10	5	2	0	0	2	.179	10	7	—	—
1948	PR	NY	AL	3-8	1	0	1	0	0	0	0	0	—	0	0	—	—
1948	2B	NY	NL	5-8	29	51	6	13	1	0	1	6	.255	4	17	—	—

MAJOR LEAGUE TOTALS   1535 5517 848 1482 263 69 61 549 .269 752 2066 112 9 yrs

Harold Arthur Trosky Born Nov 11, 1912 Norway, IA
6'2 207 lbs Batted left   Died Jun 18, 1979 Cedar Rapids, IA

YR	POS	TEAM	LG	FIN	G	AB	R	H	2B	3B	HR	RBI	AVG	BB	TB	OQ	RANK
1933	1B	CLE	AL	4-8	11	44	6	13	1	2	1	8	.295	2	21	—	—
1934	1B	CLE	AL	3-8	154	625	117	206	45	9	35	142	.330	58	374	147	7-44
1935	1B	CLE	AL	3-8	154	632	84	171	33	7	26	113	.271	46	296	105	29-51
1936	1B	CLE	AL	5-8	151	629	124	216	45	9	42	162	.343	36	405	143	6-52
1937	1B	CLE	AL	4-8	153	601	104	179	36	9	32	128	.298	65	329	128	10-47
1938	1B	CLE	AL	3-8	150	554	106	185	40	9	19	110	.334	67	300	135	13-52
1939	1B	CLE	AL	3-8	122	448	89	150	31	4	25	104	.335	52	264	148	7-42
1940	1B	CLE	AL	2-8	140	522	85	154	39	4	25	93	.295	79	276	137	7-49
1941	1B	CLE	AL	4-8	89	310	43	91	17	0	11	51	.294	44	141	124	—
1944	1B	CHI	AL	7-8	135	497	55	120	32	2	10	70	.241	62	186	109	22-46
1946	1B	CHI	AL	5-8	88	299	22	76	12	3	2	31	.254	34	100	96	—

MAJOR LEAGUE TOTALS   1347 5161 835 1561 331 58 228 1012 .302 545 2692 132 8 yrs

Ervin Fox   Born Mar 8, 1909   Evansville, IN
5'11 165 lbs Batted right   Died Jul 5, 1966   Detroit, MI

YR	POS	TEAM	LG	FIN	G	AB	R	H	2B	3B	HR	RBI	AVG	BB	TB	OQ	RANK
1933	CF	DET	AL	5-8	128	535	82	154	26	13	7	57	.288	23	227	97	35-52
1934	RF	DET	AL	1-8	128	516	101	147	31	2	2	45	.285	49	188	91	39-44
1935	RF	DET	AL	1-8	131	517	116	166	38	8	15	73	.321	45	265	125	10-51
1936	RF	DET	AL	2-8	73	220	46	67	12	1	4	26	.305	34	93	111	—
1937	RF	DET	AL	2-8	148	628	116	208	39	8	12	82	.331	41	299	111	23-47
1938	RF	DET	AL	4-8	155	634	91	186	35	10	7	96	.293	31	262	89	48-52
1939	RF	DET	AL	5-8	141	519	69	153	24	6	7	66	.295	35	210	93	37-42
1940	RF	DET	AL	1-8	93	350	49	101	17	4	5	48	.289	21	141	93	—
1941	RF	BOS	AL	2-8	73	268	38	81	12	7	0	31	.302	21	107	101	—
1942	RF	BOS	AL	2-8	77	256	42	67	15	5	3	42	.262	20	101	103	—
1943	RF	BOS	AL	7-8	127	489	54	141	24	4	2	44	.288	34	179	104	27-45
1944	RF	BOS	AL	4-8	121	496	70	156	37	6	1	64	.315	27	208	115	19-46
1945	RF	BOS	AL	7-8	66	208	21	51	4	1	0	20	.245	11	57	72	—

MAJOR LEAGUE TOTALS   1461 5636 895 1678 314 75 65 694 .298 392 2337 103 8 yrs

Cecil Howell Travis   Born Aug 8, 1913   Riverdale, GA
6'1 185 lbs Batted left

YR	POS	TEAM	LG	FIN	G	AB	R	H	2B	3B	HR	RBI	AVG	BB	TB	OQ	RANK
1933	3B	WAS	AL	1-8	18	43	7	13	1	0	0	2	.302	2	14	—	—
1934	3B	WAS	AL	7-8	109	392	48	125	22	4	1	53	.319	24	158	97	—
1935	3B-LF	WAS	AL	6-8	138	534	85	170	27	8	0	61	.318	41	213	99	36-51
1936	SS-RF	WAS	AL	4-8	138	517	77	164	34	10	2	92	.317	39	224	99	36-52
1937	SS	WAS	AL	6-8	135	526	72	181	27	7	3	66	.344	39	231	107	30-47
1938	SS	WAS	AL	5-8	146	567	96	190	30	5	5	67	.335	58	245	109	23-52
1939	SS	WAS	AL	6-8	130	476	55	139	20	9	5	63	.292	34	192	94	36-42
1940	3B-SS	WAS	AL	7-8	136	528	60	170	37	11	2	76	.322	48	235	113	24-49
1941	SS-3B	WAS	AL	6-8	152	608	106	218	39	19	7	101	.359	52	316	139	8-48
1945	3B	WAS	AL	2-8	15	54	4	13	2	1	0	10	.241	4	17	—	—
1946	SS-3B	WAS	AL	4-8	137	465	45	117	22	3	1	56	.252	45	148	88	30-35
1947	3B-SS	WAS	AL	7-8	74	204	10	44	4	1	1	10	.216	16	53	67	—

MAJOR LEAGUE TOTALS   1328 4914 665 1544 265 78 27 657 .314 402 2046 106 8 yrs

Robert Lee Johnson   Born Nov 26, 1906 Pryor, OK
6'0 180 lbs Batted right   Died Jul 6, 1982   Tacoma, WA

YR	POS	TEAM	LG	FIN	G	AB	R	H	2B	3B	HR	RBI	AVG	BB	TB	OQ	RANK
1933	LF	PHI	AL	3-8	142	535	103	155	44	4	21	93	.290	85	270	138	6-52
1934	LF	PHI	AL	5-8	141	547	111	168	26	6	34	92	.307	58	308	138	8-44
1935	LF	PHI	AL	8-8	147	582	103	174	29	5	28	109	.299	78	297	130	8-51
1936	LF	PHI	AL	8-8	153	566	91	165	29	14	25	121	.292	88	297	128	12-52
1937	LF	PHI	AL	7-8	138	477	91	146	32	6	25	108	.306	98	265	150	4-47
1938	CF	PHI	AL	8-8	152	563	114	176	27	9	30	113	.313	87	311	139	8-52
1939	LF	PHI	AL	7-8	150	544	115	184	30	9	23	114	.338	99	301	155	5-42
1940	LF	PHI	AL	8-8	138	512	93	137	25	4	31	103	.268	83	263	131	9-49
1941	LF	PHI	AL	8-8	149	552	98	152	30	8	22	107	.275	95	264	132	11-48
1942	LF	PHI	AL	8-8	149	550	78	160	35	7	13	80	.291	82	248	137	9-45
1943	LF	WAS	AL	2-8	117	438	65	116	22	8	7	63	.265	64	175	126	12-45
1944	LF	BOS	AL	4-8	144	525	106	170	40	8	17	106	.324	95	277	174	1-46
1945	LF	BOS	AL	7-8	143	529	71	148	27	7	12	74	.280	63	225	126	10-39

MAJOR LEAGUE TOTALS   1863 6920 1239 2051 396 95 288 1283 .296 1075 3501 139 13 yrs

Frank Witman Hayes   Born Oct 13, 1914 Jamesburg, NJ
6'0 185 lbs Batted right   Died Jun 22, 1955 Point Pleasant, NJ

YR	POS	TEAM	LG	FIN	G	AB	R	H	2B	3B	HR	RBI	AVG	BB	TB	OQ	RANK
1933	C	PHI	AL	3-8	3	5	0	0	0	0	0	0	.000	0	0	—	—
1934	C	PHI	AL	5-8	92	248	24	56	10	0	6	30	.226	20	84	77	—
1936	C	PHI	AL	8-8	144	505	39	137	25	2	10	67	.271	46	196	88	46-52
1937	C	PHI	AL	7-8	60	188	24	49	11	1	10	38	.261	29	92	119	—
1938	C	PHI	AL	8-8	99	316	56	92	19	3	11	55	.291	54	150	123	—
1939	C	PHI	AL	7-8	124	431	66	122	28	5	20	83	.283	40	220	117	18-42
1940	C	PHI	AL	8-8	136	465	73	143	23	4	16	70	.308	61	222	125	15-49
1941	C	PHI	AL	8-8	126	439	66	123	27	4	12	63	.280	62	194	119	22-48
1942	C	PH/SL	AL	8/3	77	222	22	55	10	0	2	22	.248	37	71	105	—
1943	C	SL	AL	6-8	88	250	16	47	7	0	5	30	.188	37	69	88	—
1944	C	PHI	AL	5-8	155	581	62	144	18	6	13	78	.248	57	213	103	27-46
1945	C	PH/CL	AL	8/5	151	495	51	116	17	7	9	57	.234	71	174	108	22-39
1946	C	CL/CH	AL	6/5	104	335	26	78	18	0	5	34	.233	50	111	100	—
1947	C	BOS	AL	3-8	5	13	0	2	0	0	0	1	.154	0	2	—	—

MAJOR LEAGUE TOTALS   1364 4493 525 1164 213 32 119 628 .259 564 1798 110   6 yrs

Harlond Benton Clift   Born Aug 12, 1912 El Reno, OK
5'11 180 lbs Batted right   Died Apr 27, 1992 Yakima, WA

YR	POS	TEAM	LG	FIN	G	AB	R	H	2B	3B	HR	RBI	AVG	BB	TB	OQ	RANK
1934	3B	SL	AL	6-8	147	572	104	149	30	10	14	56	.260	84	241	109	24-44
1935	3B	SL	AL	7-8	137	475	101	140	26	4	11	69	.295	83	207	123	12-51
1936	3B	SL	AL	7-8	152	576	145	174	40	11	20	73	.302	115	296	136	9-52
1937	3B	SL	AL	8-8	155	571	103	175	36	7	29	118	.306	98	312	142	8-47
1938	3B	SL	AL	7-8	149	534	119	155	25	7	34	118	.290	118	296	148	4-52
1939	3B	SL	AL	8-8	151	526	90	142	25	2	15	84	.270	111	216	119	17-42
1940	3B	SL	AL	6-8	150	523	92	143	29	5	20	87	.273	104	242	130	12-49
1941	3B	SL	AL	6-8	154	584	108	149	33	9	17	84	.255	113	251	123	15-48
1942	3B	SL	AL	3-8	143	541	108	148	39	4	7	55	.274	106	216	132	11-45
1943	3B	SL/WA	AL	6/2	113	409	47	97	11	3	3	29	.237	59	123	99	31-45
1944	3B	WAS	AL	8-8	12	44	4	7	3	0	0	3	.159	3	10	—	—
1945	3B	WAS	AL	2-8	119	375	49	79	12	0	8	53	.211	76	115	108	—

MAJOR LEAGUE TOTALS   1582 5730 1070 1558 309 62 178 829 .272 1070 2525 126 10 yrs

Elburt Preston Fletcher   Born Mar 18, 1916 Milton, MA
6'0 180 lbs Batted left

YR	POS	TEAM	LG	FIN	G	AB	R	H	2B	3B	HR	RBI	AVG	BB	TB	OQ	RANK
1934	1B	BOS	NL	4-8	8	4	4	2	0	0	0	0	.500	0	2	—	—
1935	1B	BOS	NL	8-8	39	148	12	35	7	1	1	9	.236	7	47	74	—
1937	1B	BOS	NL	5-8	148	539	56	133	22	4	1	38	.247	56	166	85	36-40
1938	1B	BOS	NL	5-8	147	529	71	144	24	7	6	48	.272	60	200	107	19-46
1939	1B	BO/PT	NL	7/6	137	476	63	138	25	4	12	77	.290	67	207	124	12-33
1940	1B	PIT	NL	4-8	147	510	94	139	22	7	16	104	.273	119	223	146	3-44
1941	1B	PIT	NL	4-8	151	521	95	150	29	13	11	74	.288	118	238	155	5-45
1942	1B	PIT	NL	5-8	145	506	86	146	22	5	7	57	.289	105	199	144	7-40
1943	1B	PIT	NL	4-8	154	544	91	154	24	5	9	70	.283	95	215	133	7-44
1946	1B	PIT	NL	7-8	148	532	72	136	25	8	4	66	.256	111	189	123	14-35
1947	1B	PIT	NL	7-8	69	157	22	38	9	1	1	22	.242	29	52	101	—
1949	1B	BOS	NL	4-8	122	413	57	108	19	3	11	51	.262	84	166	123	15-38

MAJOR LEAGUE TOTALS   1415 4879 723 1323 228 58 79 616 .271 851 1904 127 9 yrs

Harry Arthur Lavagetto
6'0 170 lbs Batted right

Born Dec 1, 1912 Oakland, CA
Died Aug 10, 1990 Orinda, CA

YR	POS	TEAM	LG	FIN	G	AB	R	H	2B	3B	HR	RBI	AVG	BB	TB	OQ	RANK
1934	2B	PIT	NL	5-8	87	304	41	67	16	3	3	46	.220	32	98	84	—
1935	2B-3B	PIT	NL	4-8	78	231	27	67	9	4	0	19	.290	18	84	96	—
1936	2B-3B	PIT	NL	4-8	60	197	21	48	15	2	2	26	.244	15	73	91	—
1937	2B-3B	BRO	NL	6-8	149	503	64	142	26	6	8	70	.282	74	204	120	13-40
1938	3B	BRO	NL	7-8	137	487	68	133	34	6	6	79	.273	68	197	118	13-46
1939	3B	BRO	NL	3-8	153	587	93	176	28	5	10	87	.300	78	244	120	18-33
1940	3B	BRO	NL	2-8	118	448	56	115	21	3	4	43	.257	70	154	107	26-44
1941	3B	BRO	NL	1-8	132	441	75	122	24	7	1	78	.277	80	163	123	18-45
1946	3B	BRO	NL	2-8	88	242	36	57	9	1	3	27	.236	38	77	101	—
1947	3B	BRO	NL	1-8	41	69	6	18	1	0	3	11	.261	12	28	—	—

MAJOR LEAGUE TOTALS 1043 3509 487 945 183 37 40 486 .269 485 1322 118 5 yrs

Frank Andrew McCormick
6'4 205 lbs Batted right

Born Jun 9, 1911 New York, NY
Died Nov 21, 1982 Manhassett, NY

YR	POS	TEAM	LG	FIN	G	AB	R	H	2B	3B	HR	RBI	AVG	BB	TB	OQ	RANK
1934	1B	CIN	NL	8-8	12	16	1	5	2	1	0	5	.313	0	9	—	—
1937	1B-2B	CIN	NL	8-8	24	83	5	27	5	0	0	9	.325	2	32	—	—
1938	1B	CIN	NL	4-8	151	640	89	209	40	4	5	106	.327	18	272	106	20-46
1939	1B	CIN	NL	1-8	156	630	99	209	41	4	18	128	.332	40	312	128	9-33
1940	1B	CIN	NL	1-8	155	618	93	191	44	3	19	127	.309	52	298	130	11-44
1941	1B	CIN	NL	3-8	154	603	77	162	31	5	17	97	.269	40	254	108	25-45
1942	1B	CIN	NL	4-8	145	564	58	156	24	0	13	89	.277	45	219	110	20-40
1943	1B	CIN	NL	2-8	126	472	56	143	28	0	8	56	.303	29	195	114	19-44
1944	1B	CIN	NL	3-8	153	581	85	177	37	3	20	102	.305	57	280	135	10-42
1945	1B	CIN	NL	7-8	152	580	68	160	33	0	10	81	.276	56	223	106	26-41
1946	1B	PHI	NL	5-8	135	504	46	143	20	2	11	66	.284	36	200	106	23-35
1947	1B	PH/BO	NL	7/3	96	252	31	84	20	2	3	51	.333	14	117	116	—
1948	1B	BOS	NL	1-8	75	180	14	45	9	2	4	34	.250	10	70	90	—

MAJOR LEAGUE TOTALS 1534 5723 722 1711 334 26 128 951 .299 399 2481 116 9 yrs

Henry John Bonura   Born Sep 20, 1908   New Orleans, LA
6'0   210 lbs   Batted right   Died Mar 9, 1987   New Orleans, LA

YR	POS	TEAM	LG	FIN	G	AB	R	H	2B	3B	HR	RBI	AVG	BB	TB	OQ	RANK
1934	1B	CHI	AL	8-8	127	510	86	154	35	4	27	110	.302	64	278	137	9-44
1935	1B	CHI	AL	5-8	138	550	107	162	34	4	21	92	.295	57	267	118	15-51
1936	1B	CHI	AL	3-8	148	587	120	194	39	7	12	138	.330	94	283	128	13-52
1937	1B	CHI	AL	3-8	116	447	79	154	41	2	19	100	.345	49	256	142	7-47
1938	1B	WAS	AL	5-8	137	540	72	156	27	3	22	114	.289	44	255	106	30-52
1939	1B	NY	NL	5-8	123	455	75	146	26	6	11	85	.321	46	217	130	7-33
1940	1B	WAS	AL	7-8	79	311	41	85	16	3	3	45	.273	40	116	98	—
1940	1B	CHI	NL	5-8	49	182	20	48	14	0	4	20	.264	10	74	100	—
MAJOR LEAGUE TOTALS					917	3582	600	1099	232	29	119	704	.307	404	1746	127	6 yrs

Philip Joseph Cavarretta   Born Jul 19, 1916   Chicago, IL
5'11   175 lbs   Batted left

YR	POS	TEAM	LG	FIN	G	AB	R	H	2B	3B	HR	RBI	AVG	BB	TB	OQ	RANK
1934	1B	CHI	NL	3-8	7	21	5	8	0	1	1	6	.381	2	13	—	—
1935	1B	CHI	NL	1-8	146	589	85	162	28	12	8	82	.275	39	238	100	26-44
1936	1B	CHI	NL	2-8	124	458	55	125	18	1	9	56	.273	17	172	88	38-43
1937	CF-1B	CHI	NL	2-8	106	329	43	94	18	7	5	56	.286	32	141	114	—
1938	RF-1B	CHI	NL	1-8	92	268	29	64	11	4	1	28	.239	14	86	77	—
1939	1B	CHI	NL	4-8	22	55	4	15	3	1	0	0	.273	4	20	—	—
1940	1B	CHI	NL	5-8	65	193	34	54	11	4	2	22	.280	31	79	126	—
1941	CF-1B	CHI	NL	6-8	107	346	46	99	18	4	6	40	.286	53	143	128	—
1942	CF-1B	CHI	NL	6-8	136	482	59	130	28	4	3	54	.270	71	175	119	14-40
1943	1B	CHI	NL	5-8	143	530	93	154	27	9	8	73	.291	75	223	133	8-44
1944	1B	CHI	NL	4-8	152	614	106	197	35	15	5	82	.321	67	277	134	11-42
1945	1B	CHI	NL	1-8	132	498	94	177	34	10	6	97	.355	81	249	164	2-41
1946	RF-1B	CHI	NL	3-8	139	510	89	150	28	10	8	78	.294	88	222	139	3-35
1947	LF-1B	CHI	NL	6-8	127	459	56	144	22	5	2	63	.314	58	182	113	20-44
1948	1B-LF	CHI	NL	8-8	111	334	41	93	16	5	3	40	.278	35	128	103	—
1949	1B-RF	CHI	NL	8-8	105	360	46	106	22	4	8	49	.294	45	160	121	—
1950	1B	CHI	NL	7-8	82	256	49	70	11	1	10	31	.273	40	113	120	—
1951	1B	CHI	NL	8-8	89	206	24	64	7	1	6	28	.311	27	91	125	—
1952	1B	CHI	NL	5-8	41	63	7	15	1	1	1	8	.238	9	21	—	—
1953	PH	CHI	NL	7-8	27	21	3	6	3	0	0	3	.286	6	9	—	—
1954	1B-RF	CHI	AL	3-8	71	158	21	50	6	0	3	24	.316	26	65	129	—
1955	1B	CHI	AL	3-8	6	4	1	0	0	0	0	0	.000	0	0	—	—
MAJOR LEAGUE TOTALS					2030	6754	990	1977	347	99	95	920	.293	820	2807	124	8 yrs

Raymond Allen Radcliff
5'10 170 lbs Batted left

Born Jan 19, 1906 Kiowa, OK
Died May 23, 1962 Enid, OK

YR	POS	TEAM	LG	FIN	G	AB	R	H	2B	3B	HR	RBI	AVG	BB	TB	OQ	RANK
1934	RF	CHI	AL	8-8	14	56	7	15	2	1	0	5	.268	0	19	—	—
1935	LF	CHI	AL	5-8	146	623	95	178	28	8	10	68	.286	53	252	97	38-51
1936	LF	CHI	AL	3-8	138	618	120	207	31	7	8	82	.335	44	276	104	32-52
1937	LF	CHI	AL	3-8	144	584	105	190	38	10	4	79	.325	53	260	109	28-47
1938	LF-1B	CHI	AL	6-8	129	503	64	166	23	6	5	81	.330	36	216	101	35-52
1939	RF-1B	CHI	AL	4-8	113	397	49	105	25	2	2	53	.264	26	140	79	—
1940	LF	SL	AL	6-8	150	584	83	200	33	9	7	81	.342	47	272	118	20-49
1941	LF	SL/DE	AL	6/4	115	450	59	140	16	7	5	54	.311	29	185	101	33-48
1942	RF	DET	AL	5-8	62	144	13	36	5	0	1	20	.250	9	44	79	—
1943	RF	DET	AL	5-8	70	115	3	30	4	0	0	10	.261	13	34	94	—

| MAJOR LEAGUE TOTALS | | | | | 1081 | 4074 | 598 | 1267 | 205 | 50 | 42 | 533 | .311 | 310 | 1698 | 105 | 6 yrs |

August John Galan
6'0 175 lbs Batted both

Born May 25, 1912 Berkeley, CA

YR	POS	TEAM	LG	FIN	G	AB	R	H	2B	3B	HR	RBI	AVG	BB	TB	OQ	RANK
1934	2B	CHI	NL	3-8	66	192	31	50	6	2	5	22	.260	16	75	98	—
1935	LF	CHI	NL	1-8	154	646	133	203	41	11	12	79	.314	87	302	136	7-44
1936	CF-LF	CHI	NL	2-8	145	575	74	152	26	4	8	81	.264	67	210	101	26-43
1937	LF	CHI	NL	2-8	147	611	104	154	24	10	18	78	.252	79	252	113	21-40
1938	LF	CHI	NL	1-8	110	395	52	113	16	9	6	69	.286	49	165	120	—
1939	LF	CHI	NL	4-8	148	549	104	167	36	8	6	71	.304	75	237	125	10-33
1940	LF	CHI	NL	5-8	68	209	33	48	14	2	3	22	.230	37	75	110	—
1941	LF	CH/BR	NL	6/1	82	147	21	32	6	0	1	17	.218	25	41	93	—
1942	CF	BRO	NL	2-8	69	209	24	55	16	0	0	22	.263	24	71	105	—
1943	CF	BRO	NL	3-8	139	495	83	142	26	3	9	67	.287	103	201	144	4-44
1944	LF	BRO	NL	7-8	151	547	96	174	43	9	12	93	.318	101	271	162	4-42
1945	1B-LF	BRO	NL	3-8	152	576	114	177	36	7	9	92	.307	114	254	147	4-41
1946	LF-3B	BRO	NL	2-8	99	274	53	85	22	5	3	38	.310	68	126	166	—
1947	LF	CIN	NL	5-8	124	392	60	123	18	2	6	61	.314	94	163	141	7-44
1948	RF	CIN	NL	7-8	54	77	18	22	3	2	2	16	.286	26	35	168	—
1949	1B	NY	NL	5-8	22	17	0	1	1	0	0	2	.059	5	2	—	—
1949	LF	PHI	AL	5-8	12	26	4	8	2	0	0	0	.308	9	10	—	—

| MAJOR LEAGUE TOTALS | | | | | 1742 | 5937 | 1004 | 1706 | 336 | 74 | 100 | 830 | .287 | 979 | 2490 | 134 | 8 yrs |

Preston Rudolph York   Born Aug 17, 1913 Ragland, AL
6'1   209 lbs   Batted right   Died Feb 5, 1970   Rome, GA

YR	POS	TEAM	LG	FIN	G	AB	R	H	2B	3B	HR	RBI	AVG	BB	TB	OQ	RANK
1934	C	DET	AL	1-8	3	6	0	1	0	0	0	0	.167	1	1	—	—
1937	C-3B	DET	AL	2-8	104	375	72	115	18	3	35	103	.307	41	244	150	—
1938	C-LF	DET	AL	4-8	135	463	85	138	27	2	33	127	.298	92	268	150	3-52
1939	C-1B	DET	AL	5-8	102	329	66	101	16	1	20	68	.307	41	179	135	—
1940	1B	DET	AL	1-8	155	588	105	186	46	6	33	134	.316	89	343	153	5-49
1941	1B	DET	AL	4-8	155	590	91	153	29	3	27	111	.259	92	269	121	16-48
1942	1B	DET	AL	5-8	153	577	81	150	26	4	21	90	.260	73	247	121	18-45
1943	1B	DET	AL	5-8	155	571	90	155	22	11	34	118	.271	84	301	157	2-45
1944	1B	DET	AL	2-8	151	583	77	161	27	7	18	98	.276	68	256	128	14-46
1945	1B	DET	AL	1-8	155	595	71	157	25	5	18	87	.264	60	246	117	17-39
1946	1B	BOS	AL	1-8	154	579	78	160	30	6	17	119	.276	86	253	129	10-35
1947	1B	BO/CH	AL	3/6	150	584	56	136	25	4	21	91	.233	58	232	101	31-43
1948	1B	PHI	AL	4-8	31	51	4	8	0	0	0	6	.157	7	8	—	—
MAJOR LEAGUE TOTALS					1603	5891	876	1621	291	52	277	1152	.275	792	2847	131	9 yrs

Terry Bluford Moore   Born May 27, 1912 Vernon, AL
5'11   195 lbs   Batted right

YR	POS	TEAM	LG	FIN	G	AB	R	H	2B	3B	HR	RBI	AVG	BB	TB	OQ	RANK
1935	CF	SL	NL	2-8	119	456	63	131	34	3	6	53	.287	15	189	97	34-44
1936	CF	SL	NL	2-8	143	590	85	156	39	4	5	47	.264	37	218	91	35-43
1937	CF	SL	NL	4-8	115	461	76	123	17	3	5	43	.267	32	161	89	32-40
1938	CF	SL	NL	6-8	94	312	49	85	21	3	4	21	.272	46	124	118	—
1939	CF	SL	NL	2-8	130	417	65	123	25	2	17	77	.295	43	203	128	—
1940	CF	SL	NL	3-8	136	537	92	163	33	4	17	64	.304	42	255	126	14-44
1941	CF	SL	NL	2-8	122	493	86	145	26	4	6	68	.294	52	197	116	20-45
1942	CF	SL	NL	1-8	130	489	80	141	26	3	6	49	.288	56	191	121	12-40
1946	CF	SL	NL	1-8	91	278	32	73	14	1	3	28	.263	18	98	92	—
1947	CF	SL	NL	2-8	127	460	61	130	17	1	7	45	.283	38	170	93	40-44
1948	CF	SL	NL	2-8	91	207	30	48	11	0	4	18	.232	27	71	93	—
MAJOR LEAGUE TOTALS					1298	4700	719	1318	263	28	80	513	.280	406	1877	105	7 yrs

Ival Richard Goodman Born Jul 23, 1908 Northview, MO
5'11 170 lbs Batted left Died Nov 25, 1984 Cincinnati, OH

YR	POS	TEAM	LG	FIN	G	AB	R	H	2B	3B	HR	RBI	AVG	BB	TB	OQ	RANK
1935	RF	CIN	NL	6-8	148	592	86	159	23	18	12	72	.269	35	254	103	24-44
1936	RF	CIN	NL	5-8	136	489	81	139	15	14	17	71	.284	38	233	119	15-43
1937	RF	CIN	NL	8-8	147	549	86	150	25	12	12	55	.273	55	235	113	20-40
1938	RF	CIN	NL	4-8	145	568	103	166	27	10	30	92	.292	53	303	140	7-46
1939	RF	CIN	NL	1-8	124	470	85	152	37	16	7	84	.323	54	242	142	4-33
1940	RF	CIN	NL	1-8	136	519	78	134	20	6	12	63	.258	60	202	108	24-44
1941	RF	CIN	NL	3-8	42	149	14	40	5	2	1	12	.268	16	52	101	—
1942	RF	CIN	NL	4-8	87	226	21	55	18	1	0	15	.243	24	75	99	—
1943	LF	CHI	NL	5-8	80	225	31	72	10	5	3	45	.320	24	101	137	—
1944	LF	CHI	NL	4-8	62	141	24	37	8	1	1	16	.262	23	50	114	—

MAJOR LEAGUE TOTALS | | | | | 1107 | 3928 | 609 | 1104 | 188 | 85 | 95 | 525 | .281 | 382 | 1747 | 121 | 6 yrs

Wallace Moses Born Oct 8, 1910 Uvalda, GA
5'10 160 lbs Batted left Died Oct 10, 1990 Vidalia, GA

YR	POS	TEAM	LG	FIN	G	AB	R	H	2B	3B	HR	RBI	AVG	BB	TB	OQ	RANK
1935	RF	PHI	AL	8-8	85	345	60	112	21	3	5	35	.325	25	154	109	—
1936	CF	PHI	AL	8-8	146	585	98	202	35	11	7	66	.345	62	280	119	21-52
1937	RF	PHI	AL	7-8	154	649	113	208	48	13	25	86	.320	54	357	127	11-47
1938	RF	PHI	AL	8-8	142	589	86	181	29	8	8	49	.307	58	250	102	34-52
1939	RF	PHI	AL	7-8	115	437	68	134	28	7	3	33	.307	44	185	106	27-42
1940	RF	PHI	AL	8-8	142	537	91	166	41	9	9	50	.309	75	252	125	14-49
1941	RF	PHI	AL	8-8	116	438	78	132	31	4	4	35	.301	62	183	118	23-48
1942	RF	CHI	AL	6-8	146	577	73	156	28	4	7	49	.270	74	213	110	26-45
1943	RF	CHI	AL	4-8	150	599	82	147	22	12	3	48	.245	55	202	96	35-45
1944	RF	CHI	AL	7-8	136	535	82	150	26	9	3	34	.280	52	203	110	21-46
1945	RF	CHI	AL	6-8	140	569	79	168	35	15	2	50	.295	69	239	128	7-39
1946	RF	CHI/BO	AL	5/1	104	343	43	82	20	4	6	33	.239	31	128	97	—
1947	RF	BOS	AL	3-8	90	255	32	70	18	2	2	27	.275	27	98	105	—
1948	RF	BOS	AL	2-8	78	189	26	49	12	1	2	29	.259	21	69	93	—
1949	RF	PHI	AL	5-8	110	308	49	85	19	3	1	25	.276	51	113	105	—
1950	RF	PHI	AL	8-8	88	265	47	70	16	5	2	21	.264	40	102	100	—
1951	RF	PHI	AL	6-8	70	136	17	26	6	0	0	9	.191	21	32	72	—

MAJOR LEAGUE TOTALS | | | | | 2012 | 7356 | 1124 | 2138 | 435 | 110 | 89 | 679 | .291 | 821 | 3060 | 114 | 10 yrs

John Kelly Lewis   Born Aug 10, 1916 Gastonia, NC
6'1   175 lbs   Batted left

YR	POS	TEAM	LG	FIN	G	AB	R	H	2B	3B	HR	RBI	AVG	BB	TB	OQ	RANK
1935	3B	WAS	AL	6-8	8	28	0	3	0	0	0	2	.107	0	3	—	—
1936	3B	WAS	AL	4-8	143	601	100	175	21	13	6	67	.291	47	240	90	44-52
1937	3B	WAS	AL	6-8	156	668	107	210	32	6	10	79	.314	52	284	100	34-47
1938	3B	WAS	AL	5-8	151	656	122	194	35	9	12	91	.296	58	283	100	37-52
1939	3B	WAS	AL	6-8	140	536	87	171	23	16	10	75	.319	72	256	126	14-42
1940	RF-3B	WAS	AL	7-8	148	600	101	190	38	10	6	63	.317	74	266	118	21-49
1941	RF-3B	WAS	AL	6-8	149	569	97	169	29	11	9	72	.297	82	247	121	17-48
1945	RF	WAS	AL	2-8	69	258	42	86	14	7	2	37	.333	37	120	153	—
1946	RF	WAS	AL	4-8	150	582	82	170	28	13	7	45	.292	59	245	117	17-35
1947	RF	WAS	AL	7-8	140	506	67	132	15	4	6	48	.261	51	173	93	36-43
1949	RF	WAS	AL	8-8	95	257	25	63	14	4	3	28	.245	41	94	100	—
MAJOR LEAGUE TOTALS					1349	5261	830	1563	249	93	71	607	.297	573	2211	108	8 yrs

Ellsworth Tenney Dahlgren   Born Jun 15, 1912   San Francisco, CA
6'0   190 lbs   Batted right

YR	POS	TEAM	LG	FIN	G	AB	R	H	2B	3B	HR	RBI	AVG	BB	TB	OQ	RANK
1935	1B	BOS	AL	4-8	149	525	77	138	27	7	9	63	.263	56	206	96	39-51
1936	1B	BOS	AL	6-8	16	57	6	16	3	1	1	7	.281	7	24	—	—
1937	PH	NY	AL	1-8	1	1	0	0	0	0	0	0	.000	0	0	—	—
1938	3B-1B	NY	AL	1-8	27	43	8	8	1	0	0	1	.186	1	9	—	—
1939	1B	NY	AL	1-8	144	531	71	125	18	6	15	89	.235	57	200	88	40-42
1940	1B	NY	AL	3-8	155	568	51	150	24	4	12	73	.264	46	218	90	38-49
1941	1B	BO/CH	NL	7/6	143	525	70	140	28	2	23	89	.267	59	241	126	16-45
1942	1B	CH/BR	NL	6/2	34	75	6	13	1	0	0	6	.173	8	14	—	—
1942	PH	SL	AL	3-8	2	2	0	0	0	0	0	0	.000	0	0	—	—
1943	1B-3B	PHI	NL	7-8	136	508	55	146	19	2	5	56	.287	50	184	108	23-44
1944	1B	PIT	NL	2-8	158	599	67	173	28	7	12	101	.289	47	251	113	20-42
1945	1B	PIT	NL	4-8	144	531	57	133	24	8	5	75	.250	51	188	96	32-41
1946	1B	SL	AL	7-8	28	80	2	14	1	0	0	9	.175	8	15	—	—
MAJOR LEAGUE TOTALS					1137	4045	470	1056	174	37	82	569	.261	390	1550	103	7 yrs

George Hartley McQuinn
5'11 165 lbs Batted left

Born May 29, 1910 Arlington, VA
Died Dec 24, 1978 Alexandria, VA

YR	POS	TEAM	LG	FIN	G	AB	R	H	2B	3B	HR	RBI	AVG	BB	TB	OQ	RANK
1936	1B	CIN	NL	5-8	38	134	5	27	3	4	0	13	.201	10	38	69	—
1938	1B	SL	AL	7-8	148	602	100	195	42	7	12	82	.324	58	287	115	17-52
1939	1B	SL	AL	8-8	154	617	101	195	37	13	20	94	.316	65	318	127	13-42
1940	1B	SL	AL	6-8	151	594	78	166	39	10	16	84	.279	57	273	110	28-49
1941	1B	SL	AL	6-8	130	495	93	147	28	4	18	80	.297	74	237	131	12-48
1942	1B	SL	AL	3-8	145	554	86	145	32	5	12	78	.262	60	223	112	24-45
1943	1B	SL	AL	6-8	125	449	53	109	19	2	12	74	.243	56	168	112	19-45
1944	1B	SL	AL	1-8	146	516	83	129	26	3	11	72	.250	85	194	120	17-46
1945	1B	SL	AL	3-8	139	483	69	134	31	3	7	61	.277	65	192	123	13-39
1946	1B	PHI	AL	8-8	136	484	47	109	23	6	3	35	.225	64	153	92	27-35
1947	1B	NY	AL	1-8	144	517	84	157	24	3	13	80	.304	78	226	132	7-43
1948	1B	NY	AL	3-8	94	302	33	75	11	4	11	41	.248	40	127	107	—

MAJOR LEAGUE TOTALS   1550 5747 832 1588 315 64 135 794 .276 712 2436 117 10 yrs

John Robert Mize
6'2 215 lbs Batted left

Born Jan 7, 1913 Demorest, GA
Died Jun 2, 1993 Demorest, GA

YR	POS	TEAM	LG	FIN	G	AB	R	H	2B	3B	HR	RBI	AVG	BB	TB	OQ	RANK
1936	1B	SL	NL	2-8	126	414	76	136	30	8	19	93	.329	50	239	160	—
1937	1B	SL	NL	4-8	145	560	103	204	40	7	25	113	.364	56	333	170	3-40
1938	1B	SL	NL	6-8	149	531	85	179	34	16	27	102	.337	74	326	179	2-46
1939	1B	SL	NL	2-8	153	564	104	197	44	14	28	108	.349	92	353	185	1-33
1940	1B	SL	NL	3-8	155	579	111	182	31	13	43	137	.314	82	368	180	1-44
1941	1B	SL	NL	2-8	126	473	67	150	39	8	16	100	.317	70	253	162	2-45
1942	1B	NY	NL	3-8	142	541	97	165	25	7	26	110	.305	60	282	155	3-40
1946	1B	NY	NL	8-8	101	377	70	127	18	3	22	70	.337	62	217	181	—
1947	1B	NY	NL	4-8	154	586	137	177	26	2	51	138	.302	74	360	157	2-44
1948	1B	NY	NL	5-8	152	560	110	162	26	4	40	125	.289	94	316	156	2-37
1949	1B	NY	NL	5-8	106	388	59	102	15	0	18	62	.263	50	171	116	—
1949	1B	NY	AL	1-8	13	23	4	6	1	0	1	2	.261	4	10	—	—
1950	1B	NY	AL	1-8	90	274	43	76	12	0	25	72	.277	29	163	133	—
1951	1B	NY	AL	1-8	113	332	37	86	14	1	10	49	.259	36	132	101	—
1952	1B	NY	AL	1-8	78	137	9	36	9	0	4	29	.263	11	57	106	—
1953	1B	NY	AL	1-8	81	104	6	26	3	0	4	27	.250	12	41	102	—

MAJOR LEAGUE TOTALS   1884 6443 1118 2011 367 83 359 1337 .312 856 3621 168 8 yrs

John Aloysius Hassett　　　　Born Sep 5, 1911　New York, NY
5'11　180 lbs　Batted left

YR	POS	TEAM	LG	FIN	G	AB	R	H	2B	3B	HR	RBI	AVG	BB	TB	OQ	RANK
1936	1B	BRO	NL	7-8	156	635	79	197	29	11	3	82	.310	35	257	103	24-43
1937	1B	BRO	NL	6-8	137	556	71	169	31	6	1	53	.304	20	215	94	29-40
1938	LF	BRO	NL	7-8	115	335	49	98	11	6	0	40	.293	32	121	102	—
1939	1B-RF	BOS	NL	7-8	147	590	72	182	15	3	2	60	.308	29	209	89	33-33
1940	1B	BOS	NL	7-8	124	458	59	107	19	4	0	27	.234	25	134	72	44-44
1941	1B	BOS	NL	7-8	118	405	59	120	9	4	1	33	.296	36	140	100	—
1942	1B	NY	AL	1-8	132	538	80	153	16	6	5	48	.284	32	196	96	33-44
MAJOR LEAGUE TOTALS					929	3517	469	1026	130	40	12	343	.292	209	1272	91	5 yrs

Edwin David Joost　　　　Born Jun 5, 1916　San Francisco, CA
6'0　175 lbs　Batted right

YR	POS	TEAM	LG	FIN	G	AB	R	H	2B	3B	HR	RBI	AVG	BB	TB	OQ	RANK
1936	SS-2B	CIN	NL	5-8	13	26	1	4	1	0	0	1	.154	2	5	—	—
1937	2B	CIN	NL	8-8	6	12	0	1	0	0	0	0	.083	0	1	—	—
1939	2B-SS	CIN	NL	1-8	42	143	23	36	6	3	0	14	.252	12	48	86	—
1940	SS	CIN	NL	1-8	88	278	24	60	7	2	1	24	.216	32	74	77	—
1941	SS	CIN	NL	3-8	152	537	67	136	25	4	4	40	.253	69	181	101	32-45
1942	SS-2B	CIN	NL	4-8	142	562	65	126	30	3	6	41	.224	62	180	95	29-40
1943	3B-2B	BOS	NL	6-8	124	421	34	78	16	3	2	20	.185	68	106	85	38-44
1945	2B-3B	BOS	NL	6-8	35	141	16	35	7	1	0	9	.248	13	44	86	—
1947	SS	PHI	AL	5-8	151	540	76	111	22	3	13	64	.206	114	178	106	23-43
1948	SS	PHI	AL	4-8	135	509	99	127	22	2	16	55	.250	119	201	122	14-45
1949	SS	PHI	AL	5-8	144	525	128	138	25	3	23	81	.263	149	238	143	3-41
1950	SS	PHI	AL	8-8	131	476	79	111	12	3	18	58	.233	103	183	108	26-41
1951	SS	PHI	AL	6-8	140	553	107	160	28	5	19	78	.289	106	255	137	6-39
1952	SS	PHI	AL	4-8	146	540	94	132	26	3	20	75	.244	122	224	134	8-38
1953	SS	PHI	AL	7-8	51	177	39	44	6	0	6	15	.249	45	68	128	—
1954	SS-3B	PHI	AL	8-8	19	47	7	17	3	0	1	9	.362	10	23	—	—
1955	SS-2B	BOS	AL	4-8	55	119	15	23	2	0	5	17	.193	17	40	89	—
MAJOR LEAGUE TOTALS					1574	5606	874	1339	238	35	134	601	.239	1043	2049	115	9 yrs

John Geoffrey Heath
5'11 200 lbs Batted left

Born Apr 1, 1915 Fort William, ON
Died Dec 9, 1975 Seattle, WA

YR	POS	TEAM	LG	FIN	G	AB	R	H	2B	3B	HR	RBI	AVG	BB	TB	OQ	RANK
1936	LF	CLE	AL	5-8	12	41	6	14	3	3	1	8	.341	3	26	—	—
1937	RF	CLE	AL	4-8	20	61	8	14	1	4	0	8	.230	0	23	—	—
1938	LF	CLE	AL	3-8	126	502	104	172	31	18	21	112	.343	33	302	138	10-52
1939	LF	CLE	AL	3-8	121	431	64	126	31	7	14	69	.292	41	213	116	21-42
1940	LF	CLE	AL	2-8	100	356	55	78	16	3	14	50	.219	40	142	93	—
1941	RF	CLE	AL	4-8	151	585	89	199	32	20	24	123	.340	50	343	150	5-48
1942	LF	CLE	AL	4-8	147	568	82	158	37	13	10	76	.278	62	251	123	15-45
1943	LF	CLE	AL	3-8	118	424	58	116	22	6	18	79	.274	63	204	147	3-45
1944	LF	CLE	AL	5-8	60	151	20	50	5	2	5	33	.331	18	74	151	—
1945	LF	CLE	AL	5-8	102	370	60	113	16	7	15	61	.305	56	188	159	—
1946	LF	WA/SL	AL	4/7	134	482	69	134	32	7	16	84	.278	73	228	138	6-35
1947	LF	SL	AL	8-8	141	491	81	123	20	7	27	85	.251	88	238	138	5-43
1948	LF	BOS	NL	1-8	115	364	64	116	26	5	20	76	.319	51	212	161	—
1949	LF	BOS	NL	4-8	36	111	17	34	7	0	9	23	.306	15	68	162	—

MAJOR LEAGUE TOTALS 1383 4937 777 1447 279 102 194 887 .293 593 2512 136 7 yrs

Edward Robert Miller
5'9 180 lbs Batted right

Born Nov 26, 1916 Pittsburgh, PA

YR	POS	TEAM	LG	FIN	G	AB	R	H	2B	3B	HR	RBI	AVG	BB	TB	OQ	RANK
1936	SS-2B	CIN	NL	5-8	5	10	0	1	0	0	0	0	.100	1	1	—	—
1937	SS	CIN	NL	8-8	36	60	3	9	3	1	0	5	.150	3	14	—	—
1939	SS	BOS	NL	7-8	77	296	32	79	12	2	4	31	.267	16	107	87	—
1940	SS	BOS	NL	7-8	151	569	78	157	33	3	14	79	.276	41	238	107	25-44
1941	SS	BOS	NL	7-8	154	585	54	140	27	3	6	68	.239	35	191	82	43-45
1942	SS	BOS	NL	7-8	142	534	47	130	28	2	6	47	.243	22	180	85	38-40
1943	SS	CIN	NL	2-8	154	576	49	129	26	4	2	71	.224	33	169	76	43-44
1944	SS	CIN	NL	3-8	155	536	48	112	21	5	4	55	.209	41	155	75	41-42
1945	SS	CIN	NL	7-8	115	421	46	100	27	2	13	49	.238	18	170	94	—
1946	SS	CIN	NL	6-8	91	299	30	58	10	0	6	36	.194	25	86	75	—
1947	SS	CIN	NL	5-8	151	545	69	146	38	4	19	87	.268	49	249	111	22-44
1948	SS	PHI	NL	6-8	130	468	45	115	20	1	14	61	.246	19	179	85	33-37
1949	2B	PHI	NL	3-8	85	266	21	55	10	1	6	29	.207	29	85	81	—
1950	SS	SL	NL	5-8	64	172	17	39	8	0	3	22	.227	19	56	82	—

MAJOR LEAGUE TOTALS 1510 5337 539 1270 263 28 97 640 .238 351 1880 89 7 yrs

Donald Joseph Gutteridge   Born Jun 19, 1912   Pittsburg, KS
5'10   165 lbs   Batted right

YR	POS	TEAM	LG	FIN	G	AB	R	H	2B	3B	HR	RBI	AVG	BB	TB	OQ	RANK
1936	3B	SL	NL	2-8	23	91	13	29	3	4	3	16	.319	1	49	—	—
1937	3B	SL	NL	4-8	119	447	66	121	26	10	7	61	.271	25	188	102	27-40
1938	3B-SS	SL	NL	6-8	142	552	61	141	21	15	9	64	.255	29	219	95	39-46
1939	3B	SL	NL	2-8	148	524	71	141	27	4	7	54	.269	27	197	89	32-33
1940	3B	SL	NL	3-8	69	108	19	29	5	0	3	14	.269	5	43	97	—
1942	2B	SL	AL	3-8	147	616	90	157	27	11	1	50	.255	59	209	94	36-45
1943	2B	SL	AL	6-8	132	538	77	147	35	6	1	36	.273	50	197	107	24-45
1944	2B	SL	AL	1-8	148	603	89	148	27	11	3	36	.245	51	206	94	34-46
1945	2B	SL	AL	3-8	143	543	72	129	24	3	2	49	.238	43	165	84	36-39
1946	2B-3B	BOS	AL	1-8	22	47	8	11	3	0	1	6	.234	2	17	—	—
1947	2B-3B	BOS	AL	3-8	54	131	20	22	2	0	2	5	.168	17	30	67	—
1948	PH	PIT	NL	4-8	4	2	0	0	0	0	0	0	.000	0	0	—	—

MAJOR LEAGUE TOTALS   1151 4202 586 1075 200 64 39 391 .256 309 1520 95   7 yrs

William Beck Nicholson   Born Dec 11, 1914   Chestertown, MD
6'0   205 lbs   Batted left

YR	POS	TEAM	LG	FIN	G	AB	R	H	2B	3B	HR	RBI	AVG	BB	TB	OQ	RANK
1936	RF	PHI	AL	8-8	11	12	2	0	0	0	0	0	.000	0	0	—	—
1939	RF	CHI	NL	4-8	58	220	37	65	12	5	5	38	.295	20	102	120	—
1940	RF	CHI	NL	5-8	135	491	78	146	27	7	25	98	.297	50	262	143	5-44
1941	RF	CHI	NL	6-8	147	532	74	135	26	1	26	98	.254	82	241	132	11-45
1942	RF	CHI	NL	6-8	152	588	83	173	22	11	21	78	.294	76	280	146	6-40
1943	RF	CHI	NL	5-8	154	608	95	188	30	9	29	128	.309	71	323	157	2-44
1944	RF	CHI	NL	4-8	156	582	116	167	35	8	33	122	.287	93	317	160	5-42
1945	RF	CHI	NL	1-8	151	559	82	136	28	4	13	88	.243	92	211	114	22-41
1946	RF	CHI	NL	3-8	105	296	36	65	13	2	8	41	.220	44	106	105	—
1947	RF	CHI	NL	6-8	148	487	69	119	28	1	26	75	.244	87	227	126	14-44
1948	RF	CHI	NL	8-8	143	494	68	129	24	5	19	67	.261	81	220	125	10-37
1949	RF	PHI	NL	3-8	98	299	42	70	8	3	11	40	.234	45	117	106	—
1950	RF	PHI	NL	1-8	41	58	3	13	2	1	3	10	.224	8	26	—	—
1951	RF	PHI	NL	5-8	85	170	23	41	9	2	8	30	.241	25	78	120	—
1952	RF	PHI	NL	4-8	55	88	17	24	3	0	6	19	.273	14	45	146	—
1953	RF	PHI	NL	3-8	38	62	12	13	5	1	2	16	.210	12	26	—	—

MAJOR LEAGUE TOTALS   1677 5546 837 1484 272 60 235 948 .268 800 2581 138   8 yrs

Joseph Paul DiMaggio   Born Nov 25, 1914 Martinez, CA
6'2 193 lbs Batted right

YR	POS	TEAM	LG	FIN	G	AB	R	H	2B	3B	HR	RBI	AVG	BB	TB	OQ	RANK
1936	LF-CF	NY	AL	1-8	138	637	132	206	44	15	29	125	.323	24	367	121	16-52
1937	CF	NY	AL	1-8	151	621	151	215	35	15	46	167	.346	64	418	162	3-47
1938	CF	NY	AL	1-8	145	599	129	194	32	13	32	140	.324	59	348	136	10-52
1939	CF	NY	AL	1-8	120	462	108	176	32	6	30	126	.381	52	310	177	2-42
1940	CF	NY	AL	3-8	132	508	93	179	28	9	31	133	.352	61	318	164	3-49
1941	CF	NY	AL	1-8	139	541	122	193	43	11	30	125	.357	76	348	179	2-48
1942	CF	NY	AL	1-8	154	610	123	186	29	13	21	114	.305	68	304	142	7-45
1946	CF	NY	AL	3-8	132	503	81	146	20	8	25	95	.290	59	257	141	5-35
1947	CF	NY	AL	1-8	141	534	97	168	31	10	20	97	.315	64	279	146	2-43
1948	CF	NY	AL	3-8	153	594	110	190	26	11	39	155	.320	67	355	152	3-45
1949	CF	NY	AL	1-8	76	272	58	94	14	6	14	67	.346	55	162	175	—
1950	CF	NY	AL	1-8	139	525	114	158	33	10	32	122	.301	80	307	145	2-41
1951	CF	NY	AL	1-8	116	415	72	109	22	4	12	71	.263	61	175	115	15-39
MAJOR LEAGUE TOTALS					1736	6821	1390	2214	389	131	361	1537	.325	790	3948	148	12 yrs

Vincent Paul DiMaggio   Born Sep 6, 1912   Martinez, CA
5'11 183 lbs Batted right   Died Oct 3, 1986   North Hollywood, CA

YR	POS	TEAM	LG	FIN	G	AB	R	H	2B	3B	HR	RBI	AVG	BB	TB	OQ	RANK
1937	CF	BOS	NL	5-8	132	493	56	126	18	4	13	69	.256	39	191	98	28-40
1938	CF	BOS	NL	5-8	150	540	71	123	28	3	14	61	.228	65	199	100	30-46
1939	LF	CIN	NL	1-8	8	14	1	1	1	0	0	2	.071	2	2	—	—
1940	CF	CN/PT	NL	1/4	112	360	61	104	26	0	19	54	.289	38	187	140	—
1941	CF	PIT	NL	4-8	151	528	73	141	27	5	21	100	.267	68	241	129	12-45
1942	CF	PIT	NL	5-8	143	496	57	118	22	3	15	75	.238	52	191	110	21-40
1943	CF	PIT	NL	4-8	157	580	64	144	41	2	15	88	.248	70	234	117	16-44
1944	CF	PIT	NL	2-8	109	342	41	82	20	4	9	50	.240	33	137	106	—
1945	CF	PHI	NL	8-8	127	452	64	116	25	3	19	84	.257	43	204	117	19-41
1946	CF	PH/NY	NL	5/8	21	44	3	4	1	0	0	1	.091	2	5	—	—
MAJOR LEAGUE TOTALS					1110	3849	491	959	209	24	125	584	.249	412	1591	112	6 yrs

James Henry Bloodworth Born Jul 26, 1917   Tallahassee, FL
5'11 180 lbs Batted right

YR	POS	TEAM	LG	FIN	G	AB	R	H	2B	3B	HR	RBI	AVG	BB	TB	OQ	RANK
1937	2B	WAS	AL	6-8	15	50	3	11	2	1	0	8	.220	5	15	—	—
1939	2B	WAS	AL	6-8	83	318	34	92	24	1	4	40	.289	10	130	86	—
1940	2B-1B	WAS	AL	7-8	119	469	47	115	17	8	11	70	.245	16	181	79	46-49
1941	2B	WAS	AL	6-8	142	506	59	124	24	3	7	66	.245	41	175	83	42-48
1942	2B	DET	AL	5-8	137	533	62	129	23	1	13	57	.242	35	193	91	39-45
1943	2B	DET	AL	5-8	129	474	41	114	23	4	6	52	.241	29	163	90	37-45
1946	2B	DET	AL	2-8	76	249	26	61	8	1	5	36	.245	12	86	83	—
1947	2B	PIT	NL	7-8	88	316	27	79	9	0	7	48	.250	16	109	78	—
1949	2B-1B	CIN	NL	7-8	134	452	40	118	27	1	9	59	.261	27	174	90	33-38
1950	2B-1B	CN/PH	NL	6/1	58	110	7	25	3	0	0	14	.227	8	28	62	—
1951	2B-1B	PHI	NL	5-8	21	42	2	6	0	0	0	1	.143	3	6	—	—
MAJOR LEAGUE TOTALS					1002	3519	348	874	160	20	62	451	.248	202	1260	87	5 yrs

Kenneth Frederick Keltner Born Oct 31, 1916   Milwaukee, WI
6'0 190 lbs Batted right Died Dec 12, 1991   New Berlin, WI

YR	POS	TEAM	LG	FIN	G	AB	R	H	2B	3B	HR	RBI	AVG	BB	TB	OQ	RANK
1937	3B	CLE	AL	4-8	1	1	0	0	0	0	0	1	.000	0	0	—	—
1938	3B	CLE	AL	3-8	149	576	86	159	31	9	26	113	.276	33	286	104	32-52
1939	3B	CLE	AL	3-8	154	587	84	191	35	11	13	97	.325	51	287	119	16-42
1940	3B	CLE	AL	2-8	149	543	67	138	24	10	15	77	.254	51	227	98	33-49
1941	3B	CLE	AL	4-8	149	581	83	156	31	13	23	84	.269	51	282	115	24-48
1942	3B	CLE	AL	4-8	152	624	72	179	34	4	6	78	.287	20	239	94	37-45
1943	3B	CLE	AL	3-8	110	427	47	111	31	3	4	39	.260	36	160	105	26-45
1944	3B	CLE	AL	5-8	149	573	74	169	41	9	13	91	.295	53	267	132	13-46
1946	3B	CLE	AL	6-8	116	398	47	96	17	1	13	45	.241	30	154	97	—
1947	3B	CLE	AL	4-8	151	541	49	139	29	3	11	76	.257	59	207	103	27-43
1948	3B	CLE	AL	1-8	153	558	91	166	24	4	31	119	.297	89	291	141	5-45
1949	3B	CLE	AL	3-8	80	246	35	57	9	2	8	30	.232	38	94	100	—
1950	3B	BOS	AL	3-8	13	28	2	9	2	0	0	2	.321	3	11	—	—
MAJOR LEAGUE TOTALS					1526	5683	737	1570	308	69	163	852	.276	514	2505	112	9 yrs

James Roberson Brown Born Apr 25, 1910 Jamesville, NC
5'8 165 lbs Batted both Died Dec 29, 1977 Bath, NC

YR	POS	TEAM	LG	FIN	G	AB	R	H	2B	3B	HR	RBI	AVG	BB	TB	OQ	RANK
1937	2B-SS	SL	NL	4-8	138	525	86	145	20	9	2	53	.276	27	189	88	34-40
1938	2B-SS	SL	NL	6-8	108	382	50	115	12	6	0	38	.301	27	139	98	—
1939	SS-2B	SL	NL	2-8	147	645	88	192	31	8	3	51	.298	32	248	94	29-33
1940	2B-3B	SL	NL	3-8	107	454	56	127	17	4	0	30	.280	24	152	85	37-44
1941	3B	SL	NL	2-8	132	549	81	168	28	9	3	56	.306	45	223	114	21-45
1942	2B-3B	SL	NL	1-8	145	606	75	155	28	4	1	71	.256	52	194	93	33-40
1943	2B-3B	SL	NL	1-8	34	110	6	20	4	2	0	8	.182	6	28	63	—
1946	SS-2B	PIT	NL	7-8	79	241	23	58	6	0	0	12	.241	18	64	72	—
MAJOR LEAGUE TOTALS					890	3512	465	980	146	42	9	319	.279	231	1237	95	5 yrs

Robert Pershing Doerr Born Apr 7, 1918 Los Angeles, CA
5'11 175 lbs Batted right

YR	POS	TEAM	LG	FIN	G	AB	R	H	2B	3B	HR	RBI	AVG	BB	TB	OQ	RANK
1937	2B	BOS	AL	5-8	55	147	22	33	5	1	2	14	.224	18	46	77	—
1938	2B	BOS	AL	2-8	145	509	70	147	26	7	5	80	.289	59	202	98	41-52
1939	2B	BOS	AL	2-8	127	525	75	167	28	2	12	73	.318	38	235	107	26-42
1940	2B	BOS	AL	4-8	151	595	87	173	37	10	22	105	.291	57	296	119	19-49
1941	2B	BOS	AL	2-8	132	500	74	141	28	4	16	93	.282	43	225	110	31-48
1942	2B	BOS	AL	2-8	144	545	71	158	35	5	15	102	.290	67	248	132	12-45
1943	2B	BOS	AL	7-8	155	604	78	163	32	3	16	75	.270	62	249	119	16-45
1944	2B	BOS	AL	4-8	125	468	95	152	30	10	15	81	.325	58	247	160	2-46
1946	2B	BOS	AL	1-8	151	583	95	158	34	9	18	116	.271	66	264	123	13-35
1947	2B	BOS	AL	3-8	146	561	79	145	23	10	17	95	.258	59	239	112	20-43
1948	2B	BOS	AL	2-8	140	527	94	150	23	6	27	111	.285	83	266	134	7-45
1949	2B	BOS	AL	2-8	139	541	91	167	30	9	18	109	.309	75	269	132	5-41
1950	2B	BOS	AL	3-8	149	586	103	172	29	11	27	120	.294	67	304	123	12-41
1951	2B	BOS	AL	3-8	106	402	60	116	21	2	13	73	.289	57	180	123	—
MAJOR LEAGUE TOTALS					1865	7093	1094	2042	381	89	223	1247	.288	809	3270	122	12 yrs

George Washington Case   Born Nov 11, 1915 Trenton, NJ
6'0 183 lbs Batted right   Died Jan 23, 1989 Trenton, NJ

YR	POS	TEAM	LG	FIN	G	AB	R	H	2B	3B	HR	RBI	AVG	BB	TB	OQ	RANK
1937	RF-LF	WAS	AL	6-8	22	90	14	26	6	2	0	11	.289	3	36	—	—
1938	RF	WAS	AL	5-8	107	433	69	132	27	3	2	40	.305	39	171	95	44-52
1939	RF	WAS	AL	6-8	128	530	103	160	20	7	2	35	.302	56	200	97	33-42
1940	CF	WAS	AL	7-8	154	656	109	192	29	5	5	56	.293	52	246	91	37-49
1941	LF	WAS	AL	6-8	153	649	95	176	32	8	2	53	.271	51	230	87	40-48
1942	LF	WAS	AL	7-8	125	513	101	164	26	2	5	43	.320	44	209	117	20-45
1943	RF	WAS	AL	2-8	141	613	102	180	36	5	1	52	.294	41	229	106	25-45
1944	LF	WAS	AL	8-8	119	464	63	116	14	2	2	32	.250	49	140	90	35-46
1945	LF	WAS	AL	2-8	123	504	72	148	19	5	1	31	.294	49	180	108	23-39
1946	LF	CLE	AL	6-8	118	484	46	109	23	4	1	22	.225	34	143	75	35-35
1947	LF-RF	WAS	AL	7-8	36	80	11	12	1	0	0	2	.150	8	13	—	—
MAJOR LEAGUE TOTALS					1226	5016	785	1415	233	43	21	377	.282	426	1797	96	9 yrs

Thomas David Henrich   Born Feb 20, 1913 Massillon, OH
6'0 180 lbs Batted left

YR	POS	TEAM	LG	FIN	G	AB	R	H	2B	3B	HR	RBI	AVG	BB	TB	OQ	RANK
1937	RF-LF	NY	AL	1-8	67	206	39	66	14	5	8	42	.320	35	114	146	—
1938	RF	NY	AL	1-8	131	471	109	127	24	7	22	91	.270	92	231	127	16-52
1939	RF-CF	NY	AL	1-8	99	347	64	96	18	4	9	57	.277	51	149	111	—
1940	RF-CF	NY	AL	3-8	90	293	57	90	28	5	10	53	.307	48	158	145	—
1941	RF	NY	AL	1-8	144	538	106	149	27	5	31	85	.277	81	279	136	10-48
1942	RF	NY	AL	1-8	127	483	77	129	30	5	13	67	.267	58	208	121	17-45
1946	RF-1B	NY	AL	3-8	150	565	92	142	25	4	19	83	.251	87	232	120	15-35
1947	RF	NY	AL	1-8	142	550	109	158	35	13	16	98	.287	71	267	134	6-43
1948	RF-1B	NY	AL	3-8	146	588	138	181	42	14	25	100	.308	76	326	143	4-45
1949	RF-1B	NY	AL	1-8	115	411	90	118	20	3	24	85	.287	86	216	148	2-41
1950	1B	NY	AL	1-8	73	151	20	41	6	8	6	34	.272	27	81	135	—
MAJOR LEAGUE TOTALS					1284	4603	901	1297	269	73	183	795	.282	712	2261	133	7 yrs

Nicholas Raymond Thomas Etten   Born Sep 19, 1913   Spring Grove, IL
6'2 198 lbs Batted left   Died Oct 18, 1990   Hinsdale, IL

YR	POS	TEAM	LG	FIN	G	AB	R	H	2B	3B	HR	RBI	AVG	BB	TB	OQ	RANK
1938	1B	PHI	AL	8-8	22	81	6	21	6	2	0	11	.259	9	31	—	—
1939	1B	PHI	AL	7-8	43	155	20	39	11	2	3	29	.252	16	63	95	—
1941	1B	PHI	NL	8-8	151	540	78	168	27	4	14	79	.311	82	245	142	7-45
1942	1B	PHI	NL	8-8	139	459	37	121	21	3	8	41	.264	67	172	120	13-40
1943	1B	NY	AL	1-8	154	583	78	158	35	5	14	107	.271	76	245	128	10-45
1944	1B	NY	AL	3-8	154	573	88	168	25	4	22	91	.293	97	267	149	3-46
1945	1B	NY	AL	4-8	152	565	77	161	24	4	18	111	.285	90	247	139	5-39
1946	1B	NY	AL	3-8	108	323	37	75	14	1	9	49	.232	38	118	100	—
1947	1B	PHI	NL	7-8	14	41	5	10	4	0	1	8	.244	5	17	—	—
MAJOR LEAGUE TOTALS					937	3320	426	921	167	25	89	526	.277	480	1405	136	5 yrs

Joseph Lowell Gordon   Born Feb 18, 1915   Los Angeles, CA
5'10 180 lbs Batted right   Died Apr 14, 1978   Sacramento, CA

YR	POS	TEAM	LG	FIN	G	AB	R	H	2B	3B	HR	RBI	AVG	BB	TB	OQ	RANK
1938	2B	NY	AL	1-8	127	458	83	117	24	7	25	97	.255	56	230	114	19-52
1939	2B	NY	AL	1-8	151	567	92	161	32	5	28	111	.284	75	287	125	15-42
1940	2B	NY	AL	3-8	155	616	112	173	32	10	30	103	.281	52	315	118	22-49
1941	2B-1B	NY	AL	1-8	156	588	104	162	26	7	24	87	.276	72	274	119	19-48
1942	2B	NY	AL	1-8	147	538	88	173	29	4	18	103	.322	79	264	152	4-45
1943	2B	NY	AL	1-8	152	543	82	135	28	5	17	69	.249	98	224	134	7-45
1946	2B	NY	AL	3-8	112	376	35	79	15	0	11	47	.210	49	127	94	—
1947	2B	CLE	AL	4-8	155	562	89	153	27	6	29	93	.272	62	279	130	8-43
1948	2B	CLE	AL	1-8	144	550	96	154	21	4	32	124	.280	77	279	130	8-45
1949	2B	CLE	AL	3-8	148	541	74	136	18	3	20	84	.251	83	220	107	24-41
1950	2B	CLE	AL	4-8	119	368	59	87	12	1	19	57	.236	56	158	105	—
MAJOR LEAGUE TOTALS					1566	5707	914	1530	264	52	253	975	.268	759	2657	125	9 yrs

Roy Joseph Cullenbine   Born Oct 18, 1915 Nashville, TN
6'1   190 lbs   Batted both   Died May 28, 1991 Mount Clemens, MI

YR	POS	TEAM	LG	FIN	G	AB	R	H	2B	3B	HR	RBI	AVG	BB	TB	OQ	RANK
1938	LF	DET	AL	4-8	25	67	12	19	1	3	0	9	.284	12	26	—	—
1939	LF-RF	DET	AL	5-8	75	179	31	43	9	2	6	23	.240	34	74	111	—
1940	RF	BRO	NL	2-8	22	61	8	11	1	0	1	9	.180	23	15	—	—
1940	RF-LF	SL	AL	6-8	86	257	41	59	11	2	7	31	.230	50	95	104	—
1941	LF-1B	SL	AL	6-8	149	501	82	159	29	9	9	98	.317	121	233	152	4-48
1942	LF-3B	SL/Wa/NY	AL	3/7/1	123	427	61	118	33	1	6	66	.276	92	171	137	8-45
1943	RF	CLE	AL	3-8	138	488	66	141	24	4	8	56	.289	96	197	143	4-45
1944	RF	CLE	AL	5-8	154	571	98	162	34	5	16	80	.284	87	254	139	7-46
1945	RF	CL/DE	AL	5/1	154	536	83	146	28	5	18	93	.272	113	238	151	1-39
1946	RF-1B	DET	AL	2-8	113	328	63	110	21	0	15	56	.335	88	176	193	—
1947	1B	DET	AL	2-8	142	464	82	104	18	1	24	78	.224	137	196	144	3-43
MAJOR LEAGUE TOTALS					1181	3879	627	1072	209	32	110	599	.276	853	1675	144	6 yrs

Samuel Blake Chapman   Born Apr 11, 1916 Tiburon, CA
6'0   180 lbs   Batted right

YR	POS	TEAM	LG	FIN	G	AB	R	H	2B	3B	HR	RBI	AVG	BB	TB	OQ	RANK
1938	LF	PHI	AL	8-8	114	406	60	105	17	7	17	63	.259	55	187	109	—
1939	CF-1B	PHI	AL	7-8	140	498	74	134	24	6	15	64	.269	51	215	102	30-42
1940	CF	PHI	AL	8-8	134	508	88	140	26	3	23	75	.276	46	241	111	26-49
1941	CF	PHI	AL	8-8	143	552	97	178	29	9	25	106	.322	47	300	136	9-48
1945	CF	PHI	AL	8-8	9	30	3	6	2	0	0	1	.200	2	8	—	—
1946	LF	PHI	AL	8-8	146	545	77	142	22	5	20	67	.261	54	234	114	20-35
1947	CF	PHI	AL	5-8	149	551	84	139	18	5	14	83	.252	65	209	104	25-43
1948	CF	PHI	AL	4-8	123	445	58	115	18	6	13	70	.258	55	184	105	29-45
1949	CF	PHI	AL	5-8	154	589	89	164	24	4	24	108	.278	80	268	118	16-41
1950	CF	PHI	AL	8-8	144	553	93	139	20	6	23	95	.251	68	240	102	32-41
1951	CF-LF	PH/CL	AL	6/2	112	311	31	67	10	1	6	41	.215	39	97	83	—
MAJOR LEAGUE TOTALS					1368	4988	754	1329	210	52	180	773	.266	562	2183	112	8 yrs

James Reubin Tabor
6'2 175 lbs Batted right

Born Nov 5, 1916 New Hope, AL
Died Aug 22, 1953 Sacramento, CA

YR	POS	TEAM	LG	FIN	G	AB	R	H	2B	3B	HR	RBI	AVG	BB	TB	OQ	RANK
1938	3B-SS	BOS	AL	2-8	19	57	8	18	3	2	1	8	.316	1	28	—	—
1939	3B	BOS	AL	2-8	149	577	76	167	33	8	14	95	.289	40	258	102	31-42
1940	3B	BOS	AL	4-8	120	459	73	131	28	6	21	81	.285	42	234	120	18-49
1941	3B	BOS	AL	2-8	126	498	65	139	29	3	16	101	.279	36	222	106	32-48
1942	3B	BOS	AL	2-8	139	508	56	128	18	2	12	75	.252	37	186	95	35-45
1943	3B	BOS	AL	7-8	137	537	57	130	26	3	13	85	.242	43	201	102	28-45
1944	3B	BOS	AL	4-8	116	438	58	125	25	3	13	72	.285	31	195	120	16-46
1946	3B	PHI	NL	5-8	124	463	53	124	15	2	10	50	.268	36	173	100	25-35
1947	3B	PHI	NL	7-8	75	251	27	59	14	0	4	31	.235	20	85	81	—

MAJOR LEAGUE TOTALS | | | | | 1005 | 3788 | 473 | 1021 | 191 | 29 | 104 | 598 | .270 | 286 | 1582 | 106 | 7 yrs

Louis Boudreau
5'11 185 lbs Batted right

Born Jul 17, 1917 Harvey, IL

YR	POS	TEAM	LG	FIN	G	AB	R	H	2B	3B	HR	RBI	AVG	BB	TB	OQ	RANK
1938	3B	CLE	AL	3-8	1	1	0	0	0	0	0	0	.000	1	0	—	—
1939	SS	CLE	AL	3-8	53	225	42	58	15	4	0	19	.258	28	81	91	—
1940	SS	CLE	AL	2-8	155	627	97	185	46	10	9	101	.295	73	278	113	23-49
1941	SS	CLE	AL	4-8	148	579	95	149	45	8	10	56	.257	85	240	111	29-48
1942	SS	CLE	AL	4-8	147	506	57	143	18	10	2	58	.283	75	187	117	22-45
1943	SS	CLE	AL	3-8	152	539	69	154	32	7	3	67	.286	90	209	131	9-45
1944	SS	CLE	AL	5-8	150	584	91	191	45	5	3	67	.327	73	255	139	6-46
1945	SS	CLE	AL	5-8	97	345	50	106	24	1	3	48	.307	35	141	123	—
1946	SS	CLE	AL	6-8	140	515	51	151	30	6	6	62	.293	40	211	110	21-35
1947	SS	CLE	AL	4-8	150	538	79	165	45	3	4	67	.307	67	228	123	10-43
1948	SS	CLE	AL	1-8	152	560	116	199	34	6	18	106	.355	98	299	160	2-45
1949	SS-3B	CLE	AL	3-8	134	475	53	135	20	3	4	60	.284	70	173	103	28-41
1950	SS	CLE	AL	4-8	81	260	23	70	13	2	1	29	.269	31	90	88	—
1951	SS-3B	BOS	AL	3-8	82	273	37	73	18	1	5	47	.267	30	108	103	—
1952	SS-3B	BOS	AL	6-8	4	2	1	0	0	0	0	2	.000	0	0	—	—

MAJOR LEAGUE TOTALS | | | | | 1646 | 6029 | 861 | 1779 | 385 | 66 | 68 | 789 | .295 | 796 | 2500 | 123 | 9 yrs

Enos Bradsher Slaughter
Born Apr 27, 1916   Roxboro, NC
5'9   180 lbs   Batted left

YR	POS	TEAM	LG	FIN	G	AB	R	H	2B	3B	HR	RBI	AVG	BB	TB	OQ	RANK
1938	RF	SL	NL	6-8	112	395	59	109	20	10	8	58	.276	32	173	113	—
1939	RF	SL	NL	2-8	149	604	95	193	52	5	12	86	.320	44	291	125	11-33
1940	RF	SL	NL	3-8	140	516	96	158	25	13	17	73	.306	50	260	137	6-44
1941	RF	SL	NL	2-8	113	425	71	132	22	9	13	76	.311	53	211	146	6-45
1942	RF	SL	NL	1-8	152	591	100	188	31	17	13	98	.318	88	292	161	2-40
1946	RF	SL	NL	1-8	156	609	100	183	30	8	18	130	.300	69	283	134	6-35
1947	LF-RF	SL	NL	2-8	147	551	100	162	31	13	10	86	.294	59	249	117	17-44
1948	RF	SL	NL	2-8	146	549	91	176	27	11	11	90	.321	81	258	138	6-37
1949	LF	SL	NL	2-8	151	568	92	191	34	13	13	96	.336	79	290	147	4-38
1950	RF	SL	NL	5-8	148	556	82	161	26	7	10	101	.290	66	231	109	22-42
1951	RF	SL	NL	3-8	123	409	48	115	17	8	4	64	.281	67	160	116	19-44
1952	RF	SL	NL	3-8	140	510	73	153	17	12	11	101	.300	70	227	131	9-39
1953	RF	SL	NL	3-8	143	492	64	143	34	9	6	89	.291	80	213	121	14-44
1954	RF	NY	AL	2-8	69	125	19	31	4	2	1	19	.248	28	42	114	—
1955	RF	NY/KC	AL	1/6	118	276	50	87	12	4	5	35	.315	41	122	129	—
1956	RF-LF	KC/NY	AL	8/1	115	306	52	86	18	5	2	27	.281	34	120	101	—
1957	LF	NY	AL	1-8	96	209	24	53	7	1	5	34	.254	40	77	115	—
1958	RF-LF	NY	AL	1-8	77	138	21	42	4	1	4	19	.304	21	60	131	—
1959	RF-LF	NY	AL	3-8	74	99	10	17	2	0	6	21	.172	13	37	94	—
1959	LF	MIL	NL	2-8	11	18	0	3	0	0	0	1	.167	3	3	—	—
MAJOR LEAGUE TOTALS					2380	7946	1247	2383	413	148	169	1304	.300	1018	3599	132	12 yrs

William Barney McCosky
Born Apr 11, 1918   Coal Run, PA
6'1   184 lbs   Batted left

YR	POS	TEAM	LG	FIN	G	AB	R	H	2B	3B	HR	RBI	AVG	BB	TB	OQ	RANK
1939	CF	DET	AL	5-8	147	611	120	190	33	14	4	58	.311	70	263	110	25-42
1940	CF	DET	AL	1-8	143	589	123	200	39	19	4	57	.340	67	289	130	10-49
1941	CF	DET	AL	4-8	127	494	80	160	25	8	3	55	.324	61	210	119	20-48
1942	LF	DET	AL	5-8	154	600	75	176	28	11	7	50	.293	68	247	120	19-45
1946	CF	DE/PH	AL	2/8	117	399	44	127	22	4	2	45	.318	60	163	130	—
1947	LF	PHI	AL	5-8	137	546	77	179	22	7	1	52	.328	57	218	117	15-43
1948	LF	PHI	AL	4-8	135	515	95	168	21	5	0	46	.326	68	199	112	23-45
1950	LF	PHI	AL	8-8	66	179	19	43	10	1	0	11	.240	22	55	78	—
1951	RF-LF	PH/CL	AL	6/2	43	88	12	21	5	0	1	3	.239	11	29	—	—
1951	LF-CF	CIN	NL	6-8	25	50	2	16	2	1	1	11	.320	4	23	—	—
1952	LF-RF	CLE	AL	2-8	54	80	14	17	4	1	1	6	.213	8	26	—	—
1953	PH	CLE	AL	2-8	22	21	3	4	3	0	0	3	.190	1	7	—	—
MAJOR LEAGUE TOTALS					1170	4172	664	1301	214	71	24	397	.312	497	1729	118	6 yrs

Theodore Samuel Williams   Born Aug 30, 1918 San Diego, CA
6'3   205 lbs   Batted left

YR	POS	TEAM	LG	FIN	G	AB	R	H	2B	3B	HR	RBI	AVG	BB	TB	OQ	RANK
1939	RF	BOS	AL	2-8	149	565	131	185	44	11	31	145	.327	107	344	166	3-42
1940	LF	BOS	AL	4-8	144	561	134	193	43	14	23	113	.344	96	333	166	2-49
1941	LF	BOS	AL	2-8	143	456	135	185	33	3	37	120	.406	145	335	260	1-48
1942	LF	BOS	AL	2-8	150	522	141	186	34	5	36	137	.356	145	338	232	1-45
1946	LF	BOS	AL	1-8	150	514	142	176	37	8	38	123	.342	156	343	235	1-35
1947	LF	BOS	AL	3-8	156	528	125	181	40	9	32	114	.343	162	335	223	1-43
1948	LF	BOS	AL	2-8	137	509	124	188	44	3	25	127	.369	126	313	199	1-45
1949	LF	BOS	AL	2-8	155	566	150	194	39	3	43	159	.343	162	368	204	1-41
1950	LF	BOS	AL	3-8	89	334	82	106	24	1	28	97	.317	82	216	180	—
1951	LF	BOS	AL	3-8	148	531	109	169	28	4	30	126	.318	144	295	180	1-39
1952	LF	BOS	AL	6-8	6	10	2	4	0	1	1	3	.400	2	9	—	—
1953	LF	BOS	AL	4-8	37	91	17	37	6	0	13	34	.407	19	82	282	—
1954	LF	BOS	AL	4-8	117	386	93	133	23	1	29	89	.345	136	245	231	1-34
1955	LF	BOS	AL	4-8	98	320	77	114	21	3	28	83	.356	91	225	229	—
1956	LF	BOS	AL	4-8	136	400	71	138	28	2	24	82	.345	102	242	189	2-40
1957	LF	BOS	AL	3-8	132	420	96	163	28	1	38	87	.388	119	307	255	1-35
1958	LF	BOS	AL	3-8	129	411	81	135	23	2	26	85	.328	98	240	190	1-39
1959	LF	BOS	AL	5-8	103	272	32	69	15	0	10	43	.254	52	114	126	—
1960	LF	BOS	AL	7-8	113	310	56	98	15	0	29	72	.316	75	200	196	—

MAJOR LEAGUE TOTALS   2292 7706 1798 2654 525 71 521 1839 .344 2019 4884 210 13 yrs

Charles Ernest Keller   Born Sep 12, 1916 Middletown, MD
5'10   185 lbs   Batted left   Died May 23, 1990 Frederick, MD

YR	POS	TEAM	LG	FIN	G	AB	R	H	2B	3B	HR	RBI	AVG	BB	TB	OQ	RANK
1939	RF	NY	AL	1-8	111	398	87	133	21	6	11	83	.334	81	199	148	8-42
1940	RF	NY	AL	3-8	138	500	102	143	18	15	21	93	.286	106	254	144	6-49
1941	LF	NY	AL	1-8	140	507	102	151	24	10	33	122	.298	102	294	164	3-48
1942	LF	NY	AL	1-8	152	544	106	159	24	9	26	108	.292	114	279	165	2-44
1943	LF	NY	AL	1-8	141	512	97	139	15	11	31	86	.271	106	269	170	1-45
1945	LF	NY	AL	4-8	44	163	26	49	7	4	10	34	.301	31	94	183	—
1946	LF	NY	AL	3-8	150	538	98	148	29	10	30	101	.275	113	287	163	3-35
1947	LF	NY	AL	1-8	45	151	36	36	6	1	13	36	.238	41	83	168	—
1948	LF	NY	AL	3-8	83	247	41	66	15	2	6	44	.267	41	103	116	—
1949	LF	NY	AL	1-8	60	116	17	29	4	1	3	16	.250	25	44	114	—
1950	RF-LF	DET	AL	2-8	50	51	7	16	1	3	2	16	.314	13	29	—	—
1951	RF-LF	DET	AL	5-8	54	62	6	16	2	0	3	21	.258	11	27	—	—
1952	LF	NY	AL	1-8	2	1	0	0	0	0	0	0	.000	0	0	—	—

MAJOR LEAGUE TOTALS   1170 3790 725 1085 166 72 189 760 .286 784 1962 159 6 yrs

Frank William Gustine   Born Feb 20, 1920 Hoopeston, IL
6'0 175 lbs Batted right   Died Apr 1, 1991 Davenport, IA

YR	POS	TEAM	LG	FIN	G	AB	R	H	2B	3B	HR	RBI	AVG	BB	TB	OQ	RANK
1939	3B	PIT	NL	6-8	22	70	5	13	3	0	0	3	.186	9	16	—	—
1940	2B	PIT	NL	4-8	133	524	59	147	32	7	1	55	.281	35	196	97	34-44
1941	2B-3B	PIT	NL	4-8	121	463	46	125	24	7	1	46	.270	28	166	93	37-45
1942	2B	PIT	NL	5-8	115	388	34	89	11	4	2	35	.229	29	114	81	—
1943	SS-2B	PIT	NL	4-8	112	414	40	120	21	3	0	43	.290	32	147	102	—
1944	SS	PIT	NL	2-8	127	405	42	93	18	3	2	42	.230	33	123	81	—
1945	SS-2B	PIT	NL	4-8	128	478	67	134	27	5	2	66	.280	37	177	99	30-41
1946	2B-SS	PIT	NL	7-8	131	495	60	128	23	6	8	52	.259	40	187	100	24-35
1947	3B	PIT	NL	7-8	156	616	102	183	30	6	9	67	.297	63	252	108	26-44
1948	3B	PIT	NL	4-8	131	449	68	120	19	2	9	42	.267	42	170	98	27-37
1949	3B-2B	CHI	NL	8-8	76	261	29	59	13	4	4	27	.226	18	92	82	—
1950	3B	SL	AL	7-8	9	19	1	3	1	0	0	2	.158	3	4	—	—

| MAJOR LEAGUE TOTALS | | | | | 1261 | 4582 | 553 | 1214 | 222 | 47 | 38 | 480 | .265 | 369 | 1644 | 99 | 6 yrs |

James Barton Vernon   Born Apr 22, 1918 Marcus Hook, PA
6'2 170 lbs Batted left

YR	POS	TEAM	LG	FIN	G	AB	R	H	2B	3B	HR	RBI	AVG	BB	TB	OQ	RANK
1939	1B	WAS	AL	6-8	76	276	23	71	15	4	1	30	.257	24	97	82	—
1940	1B	WAS	AL	7-8	5	19	0	3	0	0	0	0	.158	0	3	—	—
1941	1B	WAS	AL	6-8	138	531	73	159	27	11	9	93	.299	43	235	110	30-48
1942	1B	WAS	AL	7-8	151	621	76	168	34	6	9	86	.271	59	241	107	27-45
1943	1B	WAS	AL	2-8	145	553	89	148	29	8	7	70	.268	67	214	117	17-45
1946	1B	WAS	AL	4-8	148	587	88	207	51	8	8	85	.353	49	298	145	4-35
1947	1B	WAS	AL	7-8	154	600	77	159	29	12	7	85	.265	49	233	100	34-43
1948	1B	WAS	AL	7-8	150	558	78	135	27	7	3	48	.242	54	185	82	44-45
1949	1B	CLE	AL	3-8	153	584	72	170	27	4	18	83	.291	58	259	110	22-41
1950	1B	CL/WA	AL	4/5	118	417	55	117	17	3	9	75	.281	62	167	105	30-41
1951	1B	WAS	AL	7-8	141	546	69	160	30	7	9	87	.293	53	231	109	22-39
1952	1B	WAS	AL	5-8	154	569	71	143	33	9	10	80	.251	89	224	116	22-38
1953	1B	WAS	AL	5-8	152	608	101	205	43	11	15	115	.337	63	315	141	5-43
1954	1B	WAS	AL	6-8	151	597	90	173	33	14	20	97	.290	61	294	129	3-34
1955	1B	WAS	AL	8-8	150	538	74	162	23	8	14	85	.301	74	243	126	7-39
1956	1B	BOS	AL	4-8	119	403	67	125	28	4	15	84	.310	57	206	136	—
1957	1B	BOS	AL	3-8	102	270	36	65	18	1	7	38	.241	41	106	110	—
1958	1B	CLE	AL	4-8	119	355	49	104	22	3	8	55	.293	44	156	124	—
1959	1B-LF	MIL	NL	2-8	74	91	8	20	4	0	3	14	.220	7	33	—	—
1960	PH	PIT	NL	1-8	9	8	0	1	0	0	0	1	.125	1	1	—	—

| MAJOR LEAGUE TOTALS | | | | | 2409 | 8731 | 1196 | 2495 | 490 | 120 | 172 | 1311 | .286 | 955 | 3741 | 115 | 13 yrs |

Robert Irving Elliott Born Nov 26, 1916 San Francisco, CA
6'0 185 lbs Batted right Died May 4, 1966 San Diego, CA

YR	POS	TEAM	LG	FIN	G	AB	R	H	2B	3B	HR	RBI	AVG	BB	TB	OQ	RANK
1939	CF	PIT	NL	6-8	32	129	18	43	10	3	3	19	.333	9	68	137	—
1940	RF	PIT	NL	4-8	148	551	88	161	34	11	5	64	.292	45	232	113	32-44
1941	RF	PIT	NL	4-8	141	527	74	144	24	10	3	76	.273	64	197	110	24-45
1942	3B	PIT	NL	5-8	143	560	75	166	26	7	9	89	.296	52	233	123	11-40
1943	3B	PIT	NL	4-8	156	581	82	183	30	12	7	101	.315	56	258	132	10-44
1944	3B	PIT	NL	2-8	143	538	85	160	28	16	10	108	.297	75	250	139	9-42
1945	3B-RF	PIT	NL	4-8	144	541	80	157	36	6	8	108	.290	64	229	122	15-41
1946	RF-3B	PIT	NL	7-8	140	486	50	128	25	3	5	68	.263	64	174	108	21-35
1947	3B	BOS	NL	3-8	150	555	93	176	35	5	22	113	.317	87	287	146	4-44
1948	3B	BOS	NL	1-8	151	540	99	153	24	5	23	100	.283	131	256	152	3-37
1949	3B	BOS	NL	4-8	139	482	77	135	29	5	17	76	.280	90	225	136	7-38
1950	3B	BOS	NL	4-8	142	531	94	162	28	5	24	107	.305	68	272	134	12-42
1951	3B	BOS	NL	4-8	136	480	73	137	29	2	15	70	.285	65	215	123	13-44
1952	LF-3B	NY	NL	2-8	98	272	33	62	6	2	10	35	.228	36	102	104	—
1953	3B	SL/CH	AL	8/3	115	368	43	94	18	2	9	61	.255	61	143	112	—

| MAJOR LEAGUE TOTALS | | | | | 1978 | 7141 | 1064 | 2061 | 382 | 94 | 170 | 1195 | .289 | 967 | 3141 | 128 | 12 yrs |

John Leonard Hopp Born Jul 18, 1916 Hastings, NE
5'10 170 lbs Batted left

YR	POS	TEAM	LG	FIN	G	AB	R	H	2B	3B	HR	RBI	AVG	BB	TB	OQ	RANK
1939	1B	SL	NL	2-8	6	4	1	2	1	0	0	2	.500	1	3	—	—
1940	CF-1B	SL	NL	3-8	80	152	24	41	7	4	1	14	.270	9	59	97	—
1941	LF-1B	SL	NL	2-8	134	445	83	135	25	11	4	50	.303	50	194	127	14-45
1942	1B	SL	NL	1-8	95	314	41	81	16	7	3	37	.258	36	120	114	—
1943	LF-1B	SL	NL	1-8	91	241	33	54	10	2	2	25	.224	24	74	88	—
1944	CF	SL	NL	1-8	139	527	106	177	35	9	11	72	.336	58	263	149	6-42
1945	RF-1B	SL	NL	2-8	124	446	67	129	22	8	3	44	.289	49	176	113	23-41
1946	1B-CF	BOS	NL	4-8	129	445	71	148	23	8	3	48	.333	34	196	125	10-35
1947	CF	BOS	NL	3-8	134	430	74	124	20	2	2	32	.288	58	154	103	30-44
1948	CF-1B	PIT	NL	4-8	120	392	64	109	15	12	1	31	.278	40	151	102	—
1949	1B-RF	PT/BR	NL	6/1	113	385	55	118	14	5	5	39	.306	37	157	109	—
1950	1B	PIT	NL	8-8	106	318	51	108	24	5	8	47	.340	43	166	145	—
1950	1B-LF	NY	AL	1-8	19	27	9	9	2	1	1	8	.333	8	16	—	—
1951	1B	NY	AL	1-8	46	63	10	13	1	0	2	4	.206	9	20	—	—
1952	1B	NY/DE	AL	1/8	57	71	9	14	1	0	0	5	.197	8	15	—	—

| MAJOR LEAGUE TOTALS | | | | | 1393 | 4260 | 698 | 1262 | 216 | 74 | 46 | 458 | .296 | 464 | 1764 | 123 | 5 yrs |

Walter Franklin Judnich Born Jan 24, 1917 San Francisco, CA
6'1 205 lbs Batted left Died Jul 12, 1971 Glendale, CA

YR	POS	TEAM	LG	FIN	G	AB	R	H	2B	3B	HR	RBI	AVG	BB	TB	OQ	RANK
1940	CF	SL	AL	6-8	137	519	97	157	27	7	24	89	.303	54	270	127	13-49
1941	CF	SL	AL	6-8	146	546	90	155	40	6	14	83	.284	80	249	124	14-48
1942	CF	SL	AL	3-8	132	457	78	143	22	6	17	82	.313	74	228	155	3-45
1946	CF	SL	AL	7-8	142	511	60	134	23	4	15	72	.262	60	210	114	19-35
1947	1B-CF	SL	AL	8-8	144	500	58	129	24	3	18	64	.258	60	213	115	18-43
1948	CF-1B	CLE	AL	1-8	79	218	36	56	13	3	2	29	.257	56	81	123	—
1949	CF	PIT	NL	6-8	10	35	5	8	1	0	0	1	.229	1	9	—	—
MAJOR LEAGUE TOTALS					790	2786	424	782	150	29	90	420	.281	385	1260	127	5 yrs

Elmer William Valo Born Mar 5, 1921 Ribnik, Czechoslovakia
5'11 190 lbs Batted left

YR	POS	TEAM	LG	FIN	G	AB	R	H	2B	3B	HR	RBI	AVG	BB	TB	OQ	RANK
1940	LF	PHI	AL	8-8	6	23	6	8	0	0	0	0	.348	3	8	—	—
1941	LF	PHI	AL	8-8	15	50	13	21	0	1	2	6	.420	4	29	—	—
1942	RF	PHI	AL	8-8	133	459	64	115	13	10	2	40	.251	70	154	105	28-45
1943	RF	PHI	AL	8-8	77	249	31	55	6	2	3	18	.221	35	74	95	—
1946	RF	PHI	AL	8-8	108	348	59	107	21	6	1	31	.307	60	143	134	—
1947	RF	PHI	AL	5-8	112	370	60	111	12	6	5	36	.300	64	150	129	—
1948	RF	PHI	AL	4-8	113	383	72	117	17	4	3	46	.305	81	151	127	10-45
1949	LF	PHI	AL	5-8	150	547	86	155	27	12	5	85	.283	119	221	124	11-41
1950	RF	PHI	AL	8-8	129	446	62	125	16	5	10	46	.280	82	181	113	24-41
1951	RF	PHI	AL	6-8	123	444	75	134	27	8	7	55	.302	75	198	131	8-39
1952	RF	PHI	AL	4-8	129	388	69	109	26	4	5	47	.281	101	158	146	5-38
1953	RF-LF	PHI	AL	7-8	50	85	15	19	3	0	0	9	.224	22	22	101	—
1954	LF-RF	PHI	AL	8-8	95	224	28	48	11	6	1	33	.214	51	74	109	—
1955	LF-RF	KC	AL	6-8	112	283	50	103	17	4	3	37	.364	52	137	157	—
1956	LF	KC	AL	8-8	9	9	1	2	0	0	0	2	.222	1	2	—	—
1956	RF	PHI	NL	5-8	98	291	40	84	13	3	5	37	.289	48	118	120	—
1957	LF-RF	BRO	NL	3-8	81	161	14	44	10	1	4	26	.273	25	68	120	—
1958	LF-RF	LA	NL	7-8	65	101	9	25	2	1	1	14	.248	12	32	85	—
1959	RF	CLE	AL	2-8	34	24	3	7	0	0	0	5	.292	7	7	—	—
1960	RF	NY/WA	AL	1/5	84	69	7	18	3	0	0	16	.261	19	21	—	—
1961	LF	MIN	AL	7-10	33	32	0	5	2	0	0	4	.156	3	7	—	—
1961	RF	PHI	NL	8-8	50	43	4	8	2	0	1	8	.186	8	13	—	—
MAJOR LEAGUE TOTALS					1806	5029	768	1420	228	73	58	601	.282	942	1968	124	6 yrs

Stanley Orville Spence　　　　　Born Mar 20, 1915　South Portsmouth, KY
5'10　180 lbs　Batted left　　　　　　Died Jan 9, 1983　Kinston, NC

YR	POS	TEAM	LG	FIN	G	AB	R	H	2B	3B	HR	RBI	AVG	BB	TB	OO	RANK
1940	RF	BOS	AL	4-8	51	68	5	19	2	1	2	13	.279	4	29	—	—
1941	LF-RF	BOS	AL	2-8	86	203	22	47	10	3	2	28	.232	18	69	82	—
1942	CF	WAS	AL	7-8	149	629	94	203	27	15	4	79	.323	62	272	127	13-45
1943	CF	WAS	AL	2-8	149	570	72	152	23	10	12	88	.267	84	231	128	11-45
1944	CF	WAS	AL	8-8	153	592	83	187	31	8	18	100	.316	69	288	146	4-46
1946	CF	WAS	AL	4-8	152	578	83	169	50	10	16	87	.292	62	287	136	8-35
1947	CF	WAS	AL	7-8	147	506	62	141	22	6	16	73	.279	81	223	130	9-43
1948	RF-1B	BOS	AL	2-8	114	391	71	92	17	4	12	61	.235	82	153	114	19-45
1949	CF	BO/SL	AL	2/7	111	334	49	80	14	3	13	46	.240	58	139	111	—
MAJOR LEAGUE TOTALS					1112	3871	541	1090	196	60	95	575	.282	520	1691	130	6 yrs

Dominic Paul DiMaggio　　　　　Born Feb 12, 1917　San Francisco, CA
5'9　168 lbs　Batted right

YR	POS	TEAM	LG	FIN	G	AB	R	H	2B	3B	HR	RBI	AVG	BB	TB	OO	RANK
1940	RF	BOS	AL	4-8	108	418	81	126	32	6	8	46	.301	41	194	115	—
1941	CF	BOS	AL	2-8	144	584	117	165	37	6	8	58	.283	90	238	115	25-48
1942	CF	BOS	AL	2-8	151	622	110	178	36	8	14	48	.286	70	272	124	14-45
1946	CF	BOS	AL	1-8	142	534	85	169	24	7	7	73	.316	66	228	128	11-35
1947	CF	BOS	AL	3-8	136	513	75	145	21	5	8	71	.283	74	200	116	17-43
1948	CF	BOS	AL	2-8	155	648	127	185	40	4	9	87	.285	101	260	113	20-45
1949	CF	BOS	AL	2-8	145	605	126	186	34	5	8	60	.307	96	254	120	14-41
1950	CF	BOS	AL	3-8	141	588	131	193	30	11	7	70	.328	82	266	121	16-41
1951	CF	BOS	AL	3-8	146	639	113	189	34	4	12	72	.296	73	267	112	17-39
1952	CF	BOS	AL	6-8	128	486	81	143	20	1	6	33	.294	57	183	110	26-38
1953	PH	BOS	AL	4-8	3	3	0	1	0	0	0	0	.333	0	1	—	—
MAJOR LEAGUE TOTALS					1399	5640	1046	1680	308	57	87	618	.298	750	2363	118	9 yrs

Donald Martin Kolloway   Born Aug 4, 1918   Posen, IL
6'3   200 lbs   Batted right

YR	POS	TEAM	LG	FIN	G	AB	R	H	2B	3B	HR	RBI	AVG	BB	TB	OQ	RANK
1940	2B	CHI	AL	4-8	10	40	5	9	1	0	0	3	.225	0	10	—	—
1941	2B	CHI	AL	3-8	71	280	33	76	8	3	3	24	.271	6	99	76	—
1942	2B-1B	CHI	AL	6-8	147	601	72	164	40	4	3	60	.273	30	221	93	38-45
1943	2B	CHI	AL	4-8	85	348	29	75	14	4	1	33	.216	9	100	68	—
1946	2B-3B	CHI	AL	5-8	123	482	45	135	23	4	3	53	.280	9	175	84	32-35
1947	2B	CHI	AL	6-8	124	485	49	135	25	4	2	35	.278	17	174	85	40-43
1948	2B-3B	CHI	AL	8-8	119	417	60	114	14	4	6	38	.273	18	154	82	—
1949	2B-1B	CH/DE	AL	6/4	130	487	71	142	19	3	2	47	.292	49	173	92	37-41
1950	1B	DET	AL	2-8	125	467	55	135	20	4	6	62	.289	29	181	87	38-41
1951	1B	DET	AL	5-8	78	212	28	54	7	0	1	17	.255	15	64	74	—
1952	1B-2B	DET	AL	8-8	65	173	19	42	9	0	2	21	.243	7	57	77	—
1953	3B	PHI	AL	7-8	2	1	0	0	0	0	0	0	.000	0	0	—	—
MAJOR LEAGUE TOTALS					1079	3993	466	1081	180	30	29	393	.271	189	1408	88	5 yrs

Harold Henry Reese   Born Jul 23, 1918   Ekron, KY
5'10   160 lbs   Batted right

YR	POS	TEAM	LG	FIN	G	AB	R	H	2B	3B	HR	RBI	AVG	BB	TB	OQ	RANK
1940	SS	BRO	NL	2-8	84	312	58	85	8	4	5	28	.272	45	116	113	—
1941	SS	BRO	NL	1-8	152	595	76	136	23	5	2	46	.229	68	175	86	41-45
1942	SS	BRO	NL	2-8	151	564	87	144	24	5	3	53	.255	82	187	109	22-40
1946	SS	BRO	NL	2-8	152	542	79	154	16	10	5	60	.284	87	205	122	15-35
1947	SS	BRO	NL	1-8	142	476	81	135	24	4	12	73	.284	104	203	133	12-44
1948	SS	BRO	NL	3-8	151	566	96	155	31	4	9	75	.274	79	221	111	19-37
1949	SS	BRO	NL	1-8	155	617	132	172	27	3	16	73	.279	116	253	124	14-38
1950	SS	BRO	NL	2-8	141	531	97	138	21	5	11	52	.260	91	202	108	24-42
1951	SS	BRO	NL	2-8	154	616	94	176	20	8	10	84	.286	81	242	111	23-44
1952	SS	BRO	NL	1-8	149	559	94	152	18	8	6	58	.272	86	204	113	19-39
1953	SS	BRO	NL	1-8	140	524	108	142	25	7	13	61	.271	82	220	114	21-44
1954	SS	BRO	NL	2-8	141	554	98	171	35	8	10	69	.309	90	252	128	9-48
1955	SS	BRO	NL	1-8	145	553	99	156	29	4	10	61	.282	78	223	110	22-43
1956	SS	BRO	NL	1-8	147	572	85	147	19	2	9	46	.257	56	197	89	37-43
1957	3B-SS	BRO	NL	3-8	103	330	33	74	3	1	1	29	.224	39	82	71	—
1958	SS-3B	LA	NL	7-8	59	147	21	33	7	2	4	17	.224	26	56	106	—
MAJOR LEAGUE TOTALS					2166	8058	1338	2170	330	80	126	885	.269	1210	3038	112	13 yrs

Martin Whitford Marion   Born Dec 1, 1917   Richburg, SC
6'2   170 lbs   Batted right

YR	POS	TEAM	LG	FIN	G	AB	R	H	2B	3B	HR	RBI	AVG	BB	TB	OO	RANK
1940	SS	SL	NL	3-8	125	435	44	121	18	1	3	46	.278	21	150	87	—
1941	SS	SL	NL	2-8	155	547	50	138	22	3	3	58	.252	42	175	86	40-45
1942	SS	SL	NL	1-8	147	485	66	134	38	5	0	54	.276	48	182	112	18-40
1943	SS	SL	NL	1-8	129	418	38	117	15	3	1	52	.280	32	141	96	—
1944	SS	SL	NL	1-8	144	506	50	135	26	2	6	63	.267	43	183	99	27-42
1945	SS	SL	NL	2-8	123	430	63	119	27	5	1	59	.277	39	159	102	28-41
1946	SS	SL	NL	1-8	146	498	51	116	29	4	3	46	.233	59	162	94	30-35
1947	SS	SL	NL	2-8	149	540	57	147	19	6	4	74	.272	49	190	90	42-44
1948	SS	SL	NL	2-8	144	567	70	143	26	4	4	43	.252	37	189	81	35-37
1949	SS	SL	NL	2-8	134	515	61	140	31	2	5	70	.272	37	190	91	32-38
1950	SS	SL	NL	5-8	106	372	36	92	10	2	4	40	.247	44	118	84	—
1952	SS	SL	AL	7-8	67	186	16	46	11	0	2	19	.247	19	63	92	—
1953	3B	SL	AL	8-8	3	7	0	0	0	0	0	0	.000	0	0	—	—
MAJOR LEAGUE TOTALS					1572	5506	602	1448	272	37	36	624	.263	470	1902	94	8 yrs

Philip Francis Rizzuto   Born Sep 25, 1917   Brooklyn, NY
5'6   150 lbs   Batted right

YR	POS	TEAM	LG	FIN	G	AB	R	H	2B	3B	HR	RBI	AVG	BB	TB	OO	RANK
1941	SS	NY	AL	1-8	133	515	65	158	20	9	3	46	.307	27	205	96	37-48
1942	SS	NY	AL	1-8	144	553	79	157	24	7	4	68	.284	44	207	102	31-45
1946	SS	NY	AL	3-8	126	471	53	121	17	1	2	38	.257	34	146	82	33-35
1947	SS	NY	AL	1-8	153	549	78	150	26	9	2	60	.273	57	200	100	33-43
1948	SS	NY	AL	3-8	128	464	65	117	13	2	6	50	.252	60	152	89	40-45
1949	SS	NY	AL	1-8	153	614	110	169	22	7	5	65	.275	72	220	94	36-41
1950	SS	NY	AL	1-8	155	617	125	200	36	7	7	66	.324	92	271	120	19-41
1951	SS	NY	AL	1-8	144	540	87	148	21	6	2	43	.274	58	187	93	31-39
1952	SS	NY	AL	1-8	152	578	89	147	24	10	2	43	.254	67	197	97	33-38
1953	SS	NY	AL	1-8	134	413	54	112	21	3	2	54	.271	71	145	108	24-43
1954	SS	NY	AL	2-8	127	307	47	60	11	0	2	15	.195	41	77	73	—
1955	SS	NY	AL	1-8	81	143	19	37	4	1	1	9	.259	22	46	96	—
1956	SS	NY	AL	1-8	31	52	6	12	0	0	0	6	.231	6	12	—	—
MAJOR LEAGUE TOTALS					1661	5816	877	1588	239	62	38	563	.273	651	2065	98	10 yrs

George John Kurowski   Born Apr 19, 1918 Reading, PA
5'11   193 lbs Batted right

YR	POS	TEAM	LG	FIN	G	AB	R	H	2B	3B	HR	RBI	AVG	BB	TB	OO	RANK
1941	3B	SL	NL	2-8	5	9	1	3	2	0	0	2	.333	0	5	—	—
1942	3B	SL	NL	1-8	115	366	51	93	17	3	9	42	.254	33	143	110	—
1943	3B	SL	NL	1-8	139	522	69	150	24	8	13	70	.287	31	229	117	15-44
1944	3B	SL	NL	1-8	149	555	95	150	25	7	20	87	.270	58	249	123	17-42
1945	3B	SL	NL	2-8	133	511	84	165	27	3	21	102	.323	45	261	141	5-41
1946	3B	SL	NL	1-8	142	519	76	156	32	5	14	89	.301	72	240	139	4-35
1947	3B	SL	NL	2-8	146	513	108	159	27	6	27	104	.310	87	279	153	3-44
1948	3B	SL	NL	2-8	77	220	34	47	8	0	2	33	.214	42	61	90	—
1949	3B	SL	NL	2-8	10	14	0	2	0	0	0	0	.143	1	2	—	—
MAJOR LEAGUE TOTALS					916	3229	518	925	162	32	106	529	.286	369	1469	135	5 yrs

Stanley Frank Musial   Born Nov 21, 1920 Donora, PA
6'0   175 lbs Batted left

YR	POS	TEAM	LG	FIN	G	AB	R	H	2B	3B	HR	RBI	AVG	BB	TB	OO	RANI
1941	RF	SL	NL	2-8	12	47	8	20	4	0	1	7	.426	2	27	—	—
1942	LF	SL	NL	1-8	140	467	87	147	32	10	10	72	.315	62	229	155	4-4(
1943	RF	SL	NL	1-8	157	617	108	220	48	20	13	81	.357	72	347	177	1-4:
1944	RF	SL	NL	1-8	146	568	112	197	51	14	12	94	.347	90	312	176	1-4:
1946	1B-LF	SL	NL	1-8	156	624	124	228	50	20	16	103	.365	73	366	179	1-35
1947	1B	SL	NL	2-8	149	587	113	183	30	13	19	95	.312	80	296	138	9-44
1948	LF	SL	NL	2-8	155	611	135	230	46	18	39	131	.376	79	429	202	1-37
1949	RF	SL	NL	2-8	157	612	128	207	41	13	36	123	.338	107	382	181	2-38
1950	LF-1B	SL	NL	5-8	146	555	105	192	41	7	28	109	.346	87	331	167	1-42
1951	LF-1B	SL	NL	3-8	152	578	124	205	30	12	32	108	.355	98	355	183	2-44
1952	CF-1B	SL	NL	3-8	154	578	105	194	42	6	21	91	.336	96	311	167	1-39
1953	LF	SL	NL	3-8	157	593	127	200	53	9	30	113	.337	105	361	171	1-44
1954	RF	SL	NL	6-8	153	591	120	195	41	9	35	126	.330	103	359	167	4-48
1955	1B-RF	SL	NL	7-8	154	562	97	179	30	5	33	108	.319	80	318	151	5-43
1956	1B-RF	SL	NL	4-8	156	594	87	184	33	6	27	109	.310	75	310	141	5-43
1957	1B	SL	NL	2-8	134	502	82	176	38	3	29	102	.351	66	307	173	1-44
1958	1B	SL	NL	5-8	135	472	64	159	35	2	17	62	.337	72	249	151	2-34
1959	1B	SL	NL	7-8	115	341	37	87	13	2	14	44	.255	60	146	122	—
1960	LF-1B	SL	NL	3-8	116	331	49	91	17	1	17	63	.275	41	161	130	—
1961	LF	SL	NL	5-8	123	372	46	107	22	4	15	70	.288	52	182	130	—
1962	LF	SL	NL	6-10	135	433	57	143	18	1	19	82	.330	64	220	148	4-51
1963	LF	SL	NL	2-10	124	337	34	86	10	2	12	58	.255	35	136	115	—
MAJOR LEAGUE TOTALS					3026	10972	1949	3630	725	177	475	1951	.331	1599	6134	166	17 yrs

Gerald Edward Priddy　　　　　Born Nov 9, 1919　Los Angeles, CA
5'11　180 lbs　Batted right　　　　Died Mar 3, 1980　North Hollywood, CA

YR	POS	TEAM	LG	FIN	G	AB	R	H	2B	3B	HR	RBI	AVG	BB	TB	OQ	RANK
1941	2B-3B	NY	AL	1-8	56	174	18	37	7	0	1	26	.213	18	47	70	—
1942	3B-1B	NY	AL	1-8	59	189	23	53	9	2	2	28	.280	31	72	122	—
1943	2B-SS	WAS	AL	2-8	149	560	68	152	31	3	4	62	.271	67	201	111	20-45
1946	2B	WAS	AL	4-8	138	511	54	130	22	8	6	58	.254	57	186	101	24-35
1947	2B	WAS	AL	7-8	147	505	42	108	20	3	3	49	.214	62	143	80	43-43
1948	2B	SL	AL	6-8	151	560	96	166	40	9	8	79	.296	86	248	123	13-45
1949	2B	SL	AL	7-8	145	544	83	158	26	4	11	63	.290	80	225	113	21-41
1950	2B	DET	AL	2-8	157	618	104	171	26	6	13	75	.277	95	248	106	29-41
1951	2B	DET	AL	5-8	154	584	73	152	22	6	8	57	.260	69	210	96	28-39
1952	2B	DET	AL	8-8	75	279	37	79	23	3	4	20	.283	42	120	128	—
1953	2B-1B	DET	AL	6-8	65	196	14	46	6	2	1	24	.235	17	59	76	—
MAJOR LEAGUE TOTALS					1296	4720	612	1252	232	46	61	541	.265	624	1759	104	7 yrs

David Earl Philley　　　　　　Born May 16, 1920　Paris, TX
6'0　188 lbs　Batted both

YR	POS	TEAM	LG	FIN	G	AB	R	H	2B	3B	HR	RBI	AVG	BB	TB	OQ	RANK
1941	LF	CHI	AL	3-8	7	9	4	2	1	0	0	0	.222	3	3	—	—
1946	LF	CHI	AL	5-8	17	68	10	24	2	3	0	17	.353	4	32	—	—
1947	CF	CHI	AL	6-8	143	551	55	142	25	11	2	45	.258	35	195	88	39-43
1948	CF	CHI	AL	8-8	137	488	51	140	28	3	5	42	.287	50	189	100	31-45
1949	RF	CHI	AL	6-8	146	598	84	171	20	8	0	44	.286	54	207	88	39-41
1950	CF	CHI	AL	6-8	156	619	69	150	21	5	14	80	.242	52	223	81	39-41
1951	CF	CH/PH	AL	4/6	132	493	71	129	20	7	7	61	.262	65	184	102	26-39
1952	CF	PHI	AL	4-8	151	586	80	154	25	4	7	71	.263	59	208	97	32-38
1953	RF	PHI	AL	7-8	157	620	80	188	30	9	9	59	.303	51	263	110	23-43
1954	RF	CLE	AL	1-8	133	452	48	102	13	3	12	60	.226	57	157	94	28-34
1955	LF	CL/BA	AL	2/7	126	415	65	124	17	5	8	50	.299	46	175	113	—
1956	RF-1B	BA/CH	AL	6/3	118	396	57	98	18	4	5	64	.247	46	139	89	—
1957	RF-1B	CH/DE	AL	2/4	87	244	24	72	12	1	2	25	.295	11	92	92	—
1958	RF-1B	PHI	NL	8-8	91	207	30	64	11	4	3	31	.309	15	92	110	—
1959	RF-1B	PHI	NL	8-8	99	254	32	74	18	2	7	37	.291	18	117	112	—
1960	LF	PH/SF	NL	8/5	53	76	7	15	2	0	1	11	.197	9	20	—	—
1960	LF	BAL	AL	2-8	14	34	6	9	2	1	1	5	.265	4	16	—	—
1961	LF	BAL	AL	3-10	99	144	13	36	9	2	1	23	.250	10	52	85	—
1962	RF	BOS	AL	8-10	38	42	3	6	2	0	0	4	.143	5	8	—	—
MAJOR LEAGUE TOTALS					1904	6296	789	1700	276	72	84	729	.270	594	2372	95	8 yrs

Sidney Gordon
5'10 185 lbs Batted right

Born Aug 13, 1917 Brooklyn, NY
Died Jun 17, 1975 New York, NY

YR	POS	TEAM	LG	FIN	G	AB	R	H	2B	3B	HR	RBI	AVG	BB	TB	OQ	RANK
1941	CF	NY	NL	5-8	9	31	4	8	1	1	0	4	.258	6	11	—	—
1942	3B	NY	NL	3-8	6	19	4	6	0	1	0	2	.316	3	8	—	—
1943	3B-1B	NY	NL	8-8	131	474	50	119	9	11	9	63	.251	43	177	104	29-44
1946	LF-3B	NY	NL	8-8	135	450	64	132	15	4	5	45	.293	60	170	117	17-35
1947	LF	NY	NL	4-8	130	437	57	119	19	8	13	57	.272	50	193	113	19-44
1948	3B-LF	NY	NL	5-8	142	521	100	156	26	4	30	107	.299	74	280	147	5-37
1949	3B-RF	NY	NL	5-8	141	489	87	139	26	2	26	90	.284	95	247	146	5-38
1950	LF	BOS	NL	4-8	134	481	78	146	33	4	27	103	.304	78	268	150	4-42
1951	LF-3B	BOS	NL	4-8	150	550	96	158	28	1	29	109	.287	80	275	136	8-44
1952	LF	BOS	NL	7-8	144	522	69	151	22	2	25	75	.289	77	252	140	7-39
1953	LF	MIL	NL	2-8	140	464	67	127	22	4	19	75	.274	71	214	122	13-44
1954	RF-3B	PIT	NL	8-8	131	363	38	111	12	0	12	49	.306	67	159	129	—
1955	3B-LF	PT/NY	NL	8/3	82	191	21	43	7	1	7	26	.225	27	73	99	—
MAJOR LEAGUE TOTALS					1475	4992	735	1415	220	43	202	805	.283	731	2327	131	9 yrs

Henry John Sauer
6'3 198 lbs Batted right

Born Mar 17, 1917 Pittsburgh, PA

YR	POS	TEAM	LG	FIN	G	AB	R	H	2B	3B	HR	RBI	AVG	BB	TB	OQ	RANK
1941	LF	CIN	NL	3-8	9	33	4	10	4	0	0	5	.303	1	14	—	—
1942	1B	CIN	NL	4-8	7	20	4	5	0	0	2	4	.250	2	11	—	—
1945	LF	CIN	NL	7-8	31	116	18	34	1	0	5	20	.293	6	50	109	—
1948	LF	CIN	NL	7-8	145	530	78	138	22	1	35	97	.260	60	267	127	9-37
1949	LF	CN/CH	NL	7/8	138	509	81	140	23	1	31	99	.275	55	258	127	10-38
1950	LF-1B	CHI	NL	7-8	145	540	85	148	32	2	32	103	.274	60	280	126	15-42
1951	LF	CHI	NL	8-8	141	525	77	138	19	4	30	89	.263	45	255	117	18-44
1952	LF	CHI	NL	5-8	151	567	89	153	31	3	37	121	.270	77	301	144	5-39
1953	RF	CHI	NL	7-8	108	395	61	104	16	5	19	60	.263	50	187	117	—
1954	RF	CHI	NL	7-8	142	520	98	150	18	1	41	103	.288	70	293	141	7-48
1955	LF	CHI	NL	6-8	79	261	29	55	8	1	12	28	.211	26	101	90	—
1956	LF	SL	NL	4-8	75	151	11	45	4	0	5	24	.298	25	64	126	—
1957	LF	NY	NL	6-8	127	378	46	98	14	1	26	76	.259	49	192	130	—
1958	LF	SF	NL	3-8	88	236	27	59	8	0	12	46	.250	35	103	115	—
1959	LF	SF	NL	3-8	13	15	1	1	0	0	1	1	.067	0	4	—	—
MAJOR LEAGUE TOTALS					1399	4796	709	1278	200	19	288	876	.266	561	2380	130	6 yrs

Edward Stephen Waitkus Born Sep 4, 1919 Cambridge, MA
6'0 170 lbs Batted left Died Sep 15, 1972 Jamaica Plain, MA

YR	POS	TEAM	LG	FIN	G	AB	R	H	2B	3B	HR	RBI	AVG	BB	TB	OQ	RANK
1941	1B	CHI	NL	6-8	12	28	1	5	0	0	0	0	.179	0	5	—	—
1946	1B	CHI	NL	3-8	113	441	50	134	24	5	4	55	.304	23	180	107	—
1947	1B	CHI	NL	6-8	130	514	60	150	28	6	2	35	.292	32	196	93	41-44
1948	1B-LF	CHI	NL	8-8	139	562	87	166	27	10	7	44	.295	43	234	106	22-37
1949	1B	PHI	NL	3-8	54	209	41	64	16	3	1	28	.306	33	89	126	—
1950	1B	PHI	NL	1-8	154	641	102	182	32	5	2	44	.284	55	230	90	36-42
1951	1B	PHI	NL	5-8	145	610	65	157	27	4	1	46	.257	53	195	82	44-44
1952	1B	PHI	NL	4-8	146	499	51	144	29	4	2	49	.289	64	187	112	20-39
1953	1B	PHI	NL	3-8	81	247	24	72	9	2	1	16	.291	13	88	83	—
1954	1B	BAL	AL	7-8	95	311	35	88	17	4	2	33	.283	28	119	101	—
1955	1B	BAL	AL	7-8	38	85	2	22	1	1	0	9	.259	11	25	—	—
1955	1B	PHI	NL	4-8	33	107	10	30	5	0	2	14	.280	17	41	110	—

MAJOR LEAGUE TOTALS   1140 4254 528 1214 215 44 24 373 .285 372 1589 97 5 yrs

James Edward Hegan Born Aug 3, 1920 Lynn, MA
6'2 195 lbs Batted right Died Jun 17, 1984 Swampscott, MA

YR	POS	TEAM	LG	FIN	G	AB	R	H	2B	3B	HR	RBI	AVG	BB	TB	OQ	RANK
1941	C	CLE	AL	4-8	16	47	4	15	2	0	1	5	.319	4	20	—	—
1942	C	CLE	AL	4-8	68	170	10	33	5	0	0	11	.194	11	38	58	—
1946	C	CLE	AL	6-8	88	271	29	64	11	5	0	17	.236	17	85	78	—
1947	C	CLE	AL	4-8	135	378	38	94	14	5	4	42	.249	41	130	94	—
1948	C	CLE	AL	1-8	144	472	60	117	21	6	14	61	.248	48	192	98	33-45
1949	C	CLE	AL	3-8	152	468	54	105	19	5	8	55	.224	49	158	82	40-41
1950	C	CLE	AL	4-8	131	415	53	91	16	5	14	58	.219	42	159	85	—
1951	C	CLE	AL	2-8	133	416	60	99	17	5	6	43	.238	38	144	85	—
1952	C	CLE	AL	2-8	112	333	39	75	17	2	4	41	.225	29	108	84	—
1953	C	CLE	AL	2-8	112	299	37	65	10	1	9	37	.217	25	104	83	—
1954	C	CLE	AL	1-8	139	423	56	99	12	7	11	40	.234	34	158	91	—
1955	C	CLE	AL	2-8	116	304	30	67	5	2	9	40	.220	34	103	86	—
1956	C	CLE	AL	2-8	122	315	42	70	15	2	6	34	.222	49	107	92	—
1957	C	CLE	AL	6-8	58	148	14	32	7	0	4	15	.216	16	51	89	—
1958	C	DET	AL	5-8	45	130	14	25	6	0	1	7	.192	10	34	65	—
1958	C	PHI	NL	8-8	25	59	5	13	6	0	0	6	.220	4	19	—	—
1959	C	PH/SF	NL	8/3	46	81	1	14	2	0	0	8	.173	4	16	—	—
1960	C	CHI	NL	7-8	24	43	4	9	2	1	1	5	.209	1	16	—	—

MAJOR LEAGUE TOTALS   1666 4772 550 1087 187 46 92 525 .228 456 1642 — —

Peter Suder   Born Apr 16, 1916 Aliquippa, PA
6'0 175 lbs Batted right

YR	POS	TEAM	LG	FIN	G	AB	R	H	2B	3B	HR	RBI	AVG	BB	TB	OQ	RANK
1941	3B	PHI	AL	8-8	139	531	45	130	20	9	4	52	.245	19	180	73	47-48
1942	SS-3B	PHI	AL	8-8	128	476	46	122	20	4	4	54	.256	24	162	85	42-45
1943	2B-3B	PHI	AL	8-8	131	475	30	105	14	5	3	41	.221	14	138	70	44-45
1946	SS-3B	PHI	AL	8-8	128	455	38	128	20	3	2	50	.281	18	160	86	31-35
1947	2B	PHI	AL	5-8	145	528	45	127	28	4	5	60	.241	35	178	83	41-43
1948	2B	PHI	AL	4-8	148	519	64	125	23	5	7	60	.241	60	179	88	41-45
1949	2B-3B	PHI	AL	5-8	118	445	44	119	24	6	10	75	.267	23	185	92	38-41
1950	2B-3B	PHI	AL	8-8	77	248	34	61	10	0	8	35	.246	23	95	87	—
1951	2B-SS	PHI	AL	6-8	123	440	46	108	18	1	1	42	.245	30	131	72	39-39
1952	2B-SS	PHI	AL	4-8	74	228	22	55	7	2	1	20	.241	16	69	77	—
1953	3B-2B	PHI	AL	7-8	115	454	44	130	11	3	4	35	.286	17	159	82	41-43
1954	2B-3B	PHI	AL	8-8	69	205	8	41	11	1	0	16	.200	7	54	57	—
1955	2B	KC	AL	6-8	26	81	3	17	4	1	0	1	.210	2	23	—	—
MAJOR LEAGUE TOTALS					1421	5085	469	1268	210	44	49	541	.249	288	1713	81	9 yrs

Vernon Decatur Stephens   Born Oct 23, 1920 McAlister, NM
5'10 185 lbs Batted right   Died Nov 3, 1968 Long Beach, CA

YR	POS	TEAM	LG	FIN	G	AB	R	H	2B	3B	HR	RBI	AVG	BB	TB	OQ	RANK
1941	SS	SL	AL	6-8	3	2	0	1	0	0	0	0	.500	0	1	—	—
1942	SS	SL	AL	3-8	145	575	84	169	26	6	14	92	.294	41	249	115	23-45
1943	SS	SL	AL	6-8	137	512	75	148	27	3	22	91	.289	54	247	140	6-45
1944	SS	SL	AL	1-8	145	559	91	164	32	1	20	109	.293	62	258	135	9-46
1945	SS	SL	AL	3-8	149	571	90	165	27	3	24	89	.289	55	270	134	6-39
1946	SS	SL	AL	7-8	115	450	67	138	19	4	14	64	.307	35	207	123	14-35
1947	SS	SL	AL	8-8	150	562	74	157	18	4	15	83	.279	70	228	115	19-43
1948	SS	BOS	AL	2-8	155	635	114	171	25	8	29	137	.269	77	299	118	15-45
1949	SS	BOS	AL	2-8	155	610	113	177	31	2	39	159	.290	101	329	142	4-41
1950	SS	BOS	AL	3-8	149	628	125	185	34	6	30	144	.295	65	321	120	18-41
1951	3B	BOS	AL	3-8	109	377	62	113	21	2	17	78	.300	38	189	128	—
1952	SS-3B	BOS	AL	6-8	92	295	35	75	13	2	7	44	.254	39	113	109	—
1953	3B	CH/SL	AL	3/8	90	294	30	77	14	0	5	31	.262	31	106	95	—
1954	3B	BAL	AL	7-8	101	365	31	104	17	1	8	46	.285	17	147	96	—
1955	3B	BA/CH	AL	7/3	25	62	10	15	3	0	3	7	.242	7	27	—	—
MAJOR LEAGUE TOTALS					1720	6497	1001	1859	307	42	247	1174	.286	692	2991	127	9 yrs

Cornelius Joseph Ryan Born Feb 27, 1920 New Orleans, LA
5'11 175 lbs Batted right

YR	POS	TEAM	LG	FIN	G	AB	R	H	2B	3B	HR	RBI	AVG	BB	TB	OQ	RANK
1942	2B	NY	NL	3-8	11	27	4	5	0	0	0	2	.185	4	5	—	—
1943	2B-3B	BOS	NL	6-8	132	457	52	97	10	2	1	24	.212	58	114	80	42-44
1944	2B-3B	BOS	NL	6-8	88	332	56	98	18	5	4	25	.295	36	138	121	—
1946	2B-3B	BOS	NL	4-8	143	502	55	121	28	8	1	48	.241	55	168	95	29-35
1947	2B	BOS	NL	3-8	150	544	60	144	33	5	5	69	.265	71	202	101	34-44
1948	2B	BOS	NL	1-8	51	122	14	26	3	0	0	10	.213	21	29	79	—
1949	3B-SS	BOS	NL	4-8	85	208	28	52	13	1	6	20	.250	21	85	102	—
1950	2B	BO/CN	NL	4/6	126	439	57	109	20	5	6	49	.248	64	157	97	32-42
1951	2B	CIN	NL	6-8	136	473	75	112	17	4	16	53	.237	79	185	110	24-44
1952	2B	PHI	NL	4-8	154	577	81	139	24	6	12	49	.241	69	211	101	31-39
1953	2B	PHI	NL	3-8	90	247	47	73	14	6	5	26	.296	30	114	119	—
1953	3B	CHI	AL	3-8	17	54	6	12	1	0	0	6	.222	9	13	—	—
1954	PH	CIN	NL	5-8	1	0	0	0	0	0	0	0	—	1	0	—	—
MAJOR LEAGUE TOTALS					1184	3982	535	988	181	42	56	381	.248	518	1421	97	6 yrs

John Michael Pesky Born Sep 27, 1919 Portland, OR
5'9 168 lbs Batted left

YR	POS	TEAM	LG	FIN	G	AB	R	H	2B	3B	HR	RBI	AVG	BB	TB	OQ	RANK
1942	SS	BOS	AL	2-8	147	620	105	205	29	9	2	51	.331	42	258	117	21-45
1946	SS	BOS	AL	1-8	153	621	115	208	43	4	2	55	.335	65	265	127	12-35
1947	SS-3B	BOS	AL	3-8	155	638	106	207	27	8	0	39	.324	72	250	117	16-43
1948	3B	BOS	AL	2-8	143	565	124	159	26	6	3	55	.281	99	206	109	28-45
1949	3B	BOS	AL	2-8	148	604	111	185	27	7	2	69	.306	100	232	114	20-41
1950	3B	BOS	AL	3-8	127	490	112	153	22	6	1	49	.312	104	190	120	17-41
1951	SS	BOS	AL	3-8	131	480	93	150	20	6	3	41	.313	84	191	124	12-39
1952	SS-3B	BO/DE	AL	6/8	94	244	36	55	6	0	1	11	.225	56	64	100	—
1953	2B	DET	AL	6-8	103	308	43	90	22	1	2	24	.292	27	120	102	—
1954	2B	DE/WA	AL	5/6	69	175	22	43	4	3	1	10	.246	13	56	80	—
MAJOR LEAGUE TOTALS					1270	4745	867	1455	226	50	17	404	.307	662	1832	118	7 yrs

James William Russell   Born Oct 1, 1918 Fayette City, PA
6'1   181 lbs Batted both   Died Nov 24, 1987 Pittsburgh, PA

YR	POS	TEAM	LG	FIN	G	AB	R	H	2B	3B	HR	RBI	AVG	BB	TB	OO	RANK
1942	CF	PIT	NL	5-8	5	14	2	1	0	0	0	0	.071	1	1	—	—
1943	LF	PIT	NL	4-8	146	533	79	138	19	11	4	44	.259	77	191	114	20-44
1944	LF	PIT	NL	2-8	152	580	109	181	34	14	8	66	.312	79	267	141	7-42
1945	LF	PIT	NL	4-8	146	510	88	145	24	8	12	77	.284	71	221	128	10-41
1946	CF	PIT	NL	7-8	146	516	68	143	29	6	8	50	.277	67	208	119	16-35
1947	CF	PIT	NL	7-8	128	478	68	121	21	8	8	51	.253	63	182	102	32-44
1948	CF	BOS	NL	1-8	89	322	44	85	18	1	9	54	.264	46	132	114	—
1949	LF	BOS	NL	4-8	130	415	57	96	22	1	8	54	.231	64	144	98	25-38
1950	LF	BRO	NL	2-8	77	214	37	49	8	2	10	32	.229	31	91	107	—
1951	LF	BRO	NL	2-8	16	13	2	0	0	0	0	0	.000	4	0	—	—

MAJOR LEAGUE TOTALS   1035 3595 554 959 175 51 67 428 .267 503 1437 117   6 yrs

Harry Lee Lowrey   Born Aug 27, 1918 Culver City, CA
5'8   170 lbs Batted right   Died Jul 2, 1986   Inglewood, CA

YR	POS	TEAM	LG	FIN	G	AB	R	H	2B	3B	HR	RBI	AVG	BB	TB	OO	RANK
1942	CF	CHI	NL	6-8	27	58	4	11	0	0	1	4	.190	4	14	—	—
1943	CF-SS	CHI	NL	5-8	130	480	59	140	25	12	1	63	.292	35	192	112	22-44
1945	LF	CHI	NL	1-8	143	523	72	148	22	7	7	89	.283	48	205	108	25-41
1946	CF-3B	CHI	NL	3-8	144	540	75	139	24	5	4	54	.257	56	185	97	26-35
1947	3B-LF	CHI	NL	6-8	115	448	56	126	17	5	5	37	.281	38	168	95	37-44
1948	LF	CHI	NL	8-8	129	435	47	128	12	3	2	54	.294	34	152	92	31-37
1949	LF	CH/CN	NL	8/7	127	420	66	115	21	2	4	35	.274	46	152	97	26-38
1950	CF	CN/SL	NL	6/5	108	320	44	75	14	0	2	15	.234	42	95	81	—
1951	CF	SL	NL	3-8	114	370	52	112	19	5	5	40	.303	35	156	111	—
1952	LF	SL	NL	3-8	132	374	48	107	18	2	1	48	.286	34	132	98	—
1953	LF	SL	NL	3-8	104	182	26	49	9	2	5	27	.269	15	77	100	—
1954	RF-LF	SL	NL	6-8	74	61	6	7	1	2	0	5	.115	9	12	—	—
1955	RF-CF	PHI	NL	4-8	54	106	9	20	4	0	0	8	.189	7	24	52	—

MAJOR LEAGUE TOTALS   1401 4317 564 1177 186 45 37 479 .273 403 1564 100   6 yrs

John Barney Wyrostek
6'2 180 lbs Batted left

Born Jul 12, 1919 Fairmont City, IL
Died Dec 12, 1986 St Louis, MO

YR	POS	TEAM	LG	FIN	G	AB	R	H	2B	3B	HR	RBI	AVG	BB	TB	OQ	RANK
1942	LF	PIT	NL	5-8	9	35	0	4	0	1	0	3	.114	3	6	—	—
1943	RF	PIT	NL	4-8	51	79	7	12	3	0	0	1	.152	3	15	—	—
1946	CF	PHI	NL	5-8	145	545	73	153	30	4	6	45	.281	70	209	115	19-35
1947	RF	PHI	NL	7-8	128	454	68	124	24	7	5	51	.273	61	177	107	27-44
1948	CF	CIN	NL	7-8	136	512	74	140	24	9	17	76	.273	52	233	116	17-37
1949	RF	CIN	NL	7-8	134	474	54	118	20	4	9	46	.249	58	173	97	27-38
1950	RF	CIN	NL	6-8	131	509	70	145	34	5	8	76	.285	52	213	106	29-42
1951	RF	CIN	NL	7-8	142	537	52	167	31	3	2	61	.311	54	210	108	27-44
1952	RF	CN/PH	NL	6/4	128	427	57	113	17	6	2	47	.265	62	148	106	24-39
1953	RF	PHI	NL	3-8	125	409	42	111	14	2	6	47	.271	38	147	89	—
1954	RF-1B	PHI	NL	4-8	92	259	28	62	12	4	3	28	.239	29	91	87	—
MAJOR LEAGUE TOTALS					1221	4240	525	1149	209	45	58	481	.271	482	1622	108	7 yrs

Willard Warren Marshall
6'1 205 lbs Batted left

Born Feb 8, 1921 Richmond, VA

YR	POS	TEAM	LG	FIN	G	AB	R	H	2B	3B	HR	RBI	AVG	BB	TB	OQ	RANK
1942	CF	NY	NL	3-8	116	401	41	103	9	2	11	59	.257	26	149	100	—
1946	CF	NY	NL	8-8	131	510	63	144	18	3	13	48	.282	33	207	106	22-35
1947	RF	NY	NL	4-8	155	587	102	171	19	6	36	107	.291	67	310	134	11-44
1948	RF	NY	NL	5-8	143	537	72	146	21	8	14	86	.272	64	225	112	18-37
1949	RF	NY	NL	5-8	141	499	81	153	19	3	12	70	.307	78	214	127	12-38
1950	RF	BOS	NL	4-8	105	298	38	70	10	2	5	40	.235	36	99	86	—
1951	RF	BOS	NL	4-8	136	469	65	132	24	7	11	62	.281	48	203	112	21-44
1952	RF	BO/CN	NL	7/6	128	463	57	121	27	2	10	57	.261	41	182	103	28-39
1953	RF	CIN	NL	6-8	122	357	51	95	14	6	17	62	.266	41	172	117	—
1954	RF	CHI	AL	3-8	47	71	7	18	2	0	1	7	.254	11	23	—	—
1955	RF	CHI	AL	3-8	22	41	6	7	0	0	0	6	.171	13	7	—	—
MAJOR LEAGUE TOTALS					1246	4233	583	1160	163	39	130	604	.274	458	1791	116	6 yrs

Thomas Francis Holmes   Born Mar 29, 1917 Brooklyn, NY
5'10 180 lbs Batted left

YR	POS	TEAM	LG	FIN	G	AB	R	H	2B	3B	HR	RBI	AVG	BB	TB	OQ	RANK
1942	CF	BOS	NL	7-8	141	558	56	155	24	4	4	41	.278	64	199	111	19-40
1943	CF	BOS	NL	6-8	152	629	75	170	33	10	5	41	.270	58	238	108	24-44
1944	CF	BOS	NL	6-8	155	631	93	195	42	6	13	73	.309	61	288	130	12-42
1945	RF	BOS	NL	6-8	154	636	125	224	47	6	28	117	.352	70	367	169	1-41
1946	RF	BOS	NL	4-8	149	568	80	176	35	6	6	79	.310	58	241	123	13-35
1947	RF	BOS	NL	3-8	150	618	90	191	33	3	9	53	.309	44	257	104	28-44
1948	RF	BOS	NL	1-8	139	585	85	190	35	7	6	61	.325	46	257	116	16-37
1949	RF	BOS	NL	4-8	117	380	47	101	20	4	8	59	.266	39	153	103	—
1950	RF	BOS	NL	4-8	105	322	44	96	20	1	9	51	.298	33	145	115	—
1951	LF	BOS	NL	4-8	27	29	1	5	2	0	0	5	.172	3	7	—	—
1952	RF	BRO	NL	1-8	31	36	2	4	1	0	0	1	.111	4	5	—	—

| MAJOR LEAGUE TOTALS | | | | | 1320 | 4992 | 698 | 1507 | 292 | 47 | 88 | 581 | .302 | 480 | 2157 | 123 | 7 yrs |

William Edward Robinson   Born Dec 15, 1920 Paris, TX
6'2 210 lbs Batted left

YR	POS	TEAM	LG	FIN	G	AB	R	H	2B	3B	HR	RBI	AVG	BB	TB	OQ	RANK
1942	1B	CLE	AL	4-8	8	8	1	1	0	0	0	2	.125	1	1	—	—
1946	1B	CLE	AL	6-8	8	30	6	12	1	0	3	4	.400	2	22	—	—
1947	1B	CLE	AL	4-8	95	318	52	78	10	1	14	52	.245	30	132	105	—
1948	1B	CLE	AL	1-8	134	493	53	125	18	5	16	83	.254	36	201	93	36-45
1949	1B	WAS	AL	8-8	143	527	66	155	27	3	18	78	.294	67	242	119	15-41
1950	1B	WA/CH	AL	5/6	155	553	83	163	15	4	21	86	.295	85	249	118	20-41
1951	1B	CHI	AL	4-8	151	564	85	159	23	5	29	117	.282	77	279	131	9-39
1952	1B	CHI	AL	3-8	155	594	79	176	33	1	22	104	.296	70	277	131	11-38
1953	1B	PHI	AL	7-8	156	615	64	152	28	4	22	102	.247	63	254	103	28-43
1954	1B	NY	AL	2-8	85	142	11	37	9	0	3	27	.261	19	55	108	—
1955	1B	NY	AL	1-8	88	173	25	36	1	0	16	42	.208	36	85	132	—
1956	1B	NY/KC	AL	1/8	101	226	20	46	6	1	7	23	.204	31	75	85	—
1957	1B	De/Cl/Ba	AL	4/6/5	36	39	1	6	1	0	1	3	.154	4	10	—	—

| MAJOR LEAGUE TOTALS | | | | | 1315 | 4282 | 546 | 1146 | 172 | 24 | 172 | 723 | .268 | 521 | 1882 | 116 | 6 yrs |

George Henry Stirnweiss
5'8 175 lbs Batted right

Born Oct 26, 1918 New York, NY
Died Sep 15, 1958 Newark Bay, NJ

YR	POS	TEAM	LG	FIN	G	AB	R	H	2B	3B	HR	RBI	AVG	BB	TB	OQ	RANK
1943	SS	NY	AL	1-8	83	274	34	60	8	4	1	25	.219	47	79	100	—
1944	2B	NY	AL	3-8	154	643	125	205	35	16	8	43	.319	73	296	140	5-46
1945	2B	NY	AL	4-8	152	632	107	195	32	22	10	64	.309	78	301	145	3-39
1946	3B-2B	NY	AL	3-8	129	487	75	122	19	7	0	37	.251	66	155	96	26-35
1947	2B	NY	AL	1-8	148	571	102	146	18	8	5	41	.256	89	195	104	24-43
1948	2B	NY	AL	3-8	141	515	90	130	20	7	3	32	.252	86	173	98	34-45
1949	2B	NY	AL	1-8	70	157	29	41	8	2	0	11	.261	29	53	101	—
1950	2B-3B	NY/SL	AL	1/7	100	328	32	71	16	2	1	24	.216	51	94	78	—
1951	2B	CLE	AL	2-8	50	88	10	19	1	0	1	4	.216	22	23	97	—
1952	3B	CLE	AL	2-8	1	0	0	0	0	0	0	0	—	0	0	—	—

MAJOR LEAGUE TOTALS — 1028 3695 604 989 157 68 29 281 .268 541 1369 117 5 yrs

Gilbert Raymond Hodges
6'1 200 lbs Batted right

Born Apr 4, 1924 Princeton, IN
Died Apr 2, 1972 West Palm Beach, FL

YR	POS	TEAM	LG	FIN	G	AB	R	H	2B	3B	HR	RBI	AVG	BB	TB	OQ	RANK
1943	3B	BRO	NL	3-8	1	2	0	0	0	0	0	0	.000	1	0	—	—
1947	C	BRO	NL	1-8	28	77	9	12	3	1	1	7	.156	14	20	—	—
1948	1B-C	BRO	NL	3-8	134	481	48	120	18	5	11	70	.249	43	181	94	29-37
1949	1B	BRO	NL	1-8	156	596	94	170	23	4	23	115	.285	66	270	118	19-38
1950	1B	BRO	NL	2-8	153	561	98	159	26	2	32	113	.283	73	285	130	13-42
1951	1B	BRO	NL	2-8	158	582	118	156	25	3	40	103	.268	93	307	141	7-44
1952	1B	BRO	NL	1-8	153	508	87	129	27	1	32	102	.254	107	254	151	3-39
1953	1B-LF	BRO	NL	1-8	141	520	101	157	22	7	31	122	.302	75	286	143	5-44
1954	1B	BRO	NL	2-8	154	579	106	176	23	5	42	130	.304	74	335	146	6-48
1955	1B-LF	BRO	NL	1-8	150	546	75	158	24	5	27	102	.289	80	273	133	10-43
1956	1B-LF	BRO	NL	1-8	153	550	86	146	29	4	32	87	.265	76	279	132	11-43
1957	1B	BRO	NL	3-8	150	579	94	173	28	7	27	98	.299	63	296	134	10-44
1958	1B-3B	LA	NL	7-8	141	475	68	123	15	1	22	64	.259	52	206	108	20-34
1959	1B	LA	NL	1-8	124	413	57	114	19	2	25	80	.276	58	212	135	9-38
1960	1B-3B	LA	NL	4-8	101	197	22	39	8	1	8	30	.198	26	73	97	—
1961	1B	LA	NL	2-8	109	215	25	52	4	0	8	31	.242	24	80	94	—
1962	1B	NY	NL	10-10	54	127	15	32	1	0	9	17	.252	15	60	120	—
1963	1B	NY	NL	10-10	11	22	2	5	0	0	0	3	.227	3	5	—	—

MAJOR LEAGUE TOTALS — 2071 7030 1105 1921 295 48 370 1274 .273 943 3422 130 12 yrs

John Joseph Kerr   Born Nov 6, 1922   Astoria, NY
6'2   175 lbs   Batted right

YR	POS	TEAM	LG	FIN	G	AB	R	H	2B	3B	HR	RBI	AVG	BB	TB	OQ	RANK
1943	SS	NY	NL	8-8	27	98	14	28	3	0	2	12	.286	8	37	108	—
1944	SS	NY	NL	5-8	150	548	68	146	31	4	9	63	.266	37	212	100	26-42
1945	SS	NY	NL	5-8	149	546	53	136	20	3	4	40	.249	41	174	84	38-41
1946	SS-3B	NY	NL	8-8	145	497	50	124	20	3	6	40	.249	53	168	96	28-35
1947	SS	NY	NL	4-8	138	547	73	157	23	5	7	49	.287	36	211	94	39-44
1948	SS	NY	NL	5-8	144	496	41	119	16	4	0	46	.240	56	143	80	36-37
1949	SS	NY	NL	5-8	90	220	16	46	4	0	0	19	.209	21	50	61	—
1950	SS	BOS	NL	4-8	155	507	45	115	24	6	2	46	.227	50	157	77	41-42
1951	SS	BOS	NL	4-8	69	172	18	32	4	0	1	18	.186	22	39	66	—
MAJOR LEAGUE TOTALS					1067	3631	378	903	145	25	31	333	.249	324	1191	89	6 yrs

Eugene Richard Woodling   Born Aug 16, 1922   Akron, OH
5'9   195 lbs   Batted left

YR	POS	TEAM	LG	FIN	G	AB	R	H	2B	3B	HR	RBI	AVG	BB	TB	OQ	RANK
1943	RF	CLE	AL	3-8	8	25	5	8	2	1	1	5	.320	1	15	—	—
1946	CF	CLE	AL	6-8	61	133	8	25	1	4	0	9	.188	16	34	74	—
1947	CF	PIT	NL	7-8	22	79	7	21	2	2	0	10	.266	7	27	—	—
1949	LF	NY	AL	1-8	112	296	60	80	13	7	5	44	.270	52	122	116	—
1950	LF	NY	AL	1-8	122	449	81	127	20	10	6	60	.283	70	185	109	25-41
1951	LF	NY	AL	1-8	120	420	65	118	15	8	15	71	.281	62	194	126	11-39
1952	LF	NY	AL	1-8	122	408	58	126	19	6	12	63	.309	59	193	141	7-38
1953	LF	NY	AL	1-8	125	395	64	121	26	4	10	58	.306	82	185	147	2-43
1954	LF	NY	AL	2-8	97	304	33	76	12	5	3	40	.250	53	107	108	—
1955	LF	BA/CL	AL	7/2	126	404	55	104	21	3	8	53	.257	60	155	107	25-39
1956	LF	CLE	AL	2-8	100	317	56	83	17	0	8	38	.262	69	124	119	—
1957	LF	CLE	AL	6-8	133	430	74	138	25	2	19	78	.321	64	224	151	4-35
1958	LF	BAL	AL	6-8	133	413	57	114	16	1	15	65	.276	66	177	126	11-39
1959	LF	BAL	AL	6-8	140	440	63	132	22	2	14	77	.300	78	200	139	6-35
1960	LF	BAL	AL	2-8	140	435	68	123	18	3	11	62	.283	84	180	128	8-44
1961	RF-LF	WAS	AL	9-10	110	342	39	107	16	4	10	57	.313	50	161	133	—
1962	RF	WAS	AL	10-10	44	107	19	30	4	0	5	16	.280	24	49	142	—
1962	LF-RF	NY	NL	10-10	81	190	18	52	8	1	5	24	.274	24	77	111	—
MAJOR LEAGUE TOTALS					1796	5587	830	1585	257	63	147	830	.284	921	2409	130	9 yrs

Edward Raymond Stanky Born Sep 3, 1916 Philadelphia, PA
5'8 170 lbs Batted right

YR	POS	TEAM	LG	FIN	G	AB	R	H	2B	3B	HR	RBI	AVG	BB	TB	OQ	RANK
1943	2B	CHI	NL	5-8	142	510	92	125	15	1	0	47	.245	92	142	102	30-44
1944	2B-SS	CH/BR	NL	4/7	102	286	36	78	9	3	0	16	.273	46	93	108	—
1945	2B	BRO	NL	3-8	153	555	128	143	29	5	1	39	.258	148	185	129	7-41
1946	2B	BRO	NL	2-8	144	483	98	132	24	7	0	36	.273	137	170	142	2-35
1947	2B	BRO	NL	1-8	146	559	97	141	24	5	3	53	.252	103	184	102	31-44
1948	2B	BOS	NL	1-8	67	247	49	79	14	2	2	29	.320	61	103	148	—
1949	2B	BOS	NL	4-8	138	506	90	144	24	5	1	42	.285	113	181	122	16-38
1950	2B	NY	NL	3-8	152	527	115	158	25	5	8	51	.300	144	217	142	5-42
1951	2B	NY	NL	1-8	145	515	88	127	17	2	14	43	.247	127	190	123	12-44
1952	2B	SL	NL	3-8	53	83	13	19	4	0	0	7	.229	19	23	104	—
1953	2B	SL	NL	3-8	17	30	5	8	0	0	0	1	.267	6	8	—	—
MAJOR LEAGUE TOTALS					1259	4301	811	1154	185	35	29	364	.268	996	1496	123	7 yrs

Andrew Pafko Born Feb 25, 1921 Boyceville, WI
6'0 190 lbs Batted right

YR	POS	TEAM	LG	FIN	G	AB	R	H	2B	3B	HR	RBI	AVG	BB	TB	OQ	RANK
1943	CF	CHI	NL	5-8	13	58	7	22	3	0	0	10	.379	2	25	—	—
1944	CF	CHI	NL	4-8	128	469	47	126	16	2	6	62	.269	28	164	91	34-42
1945	CF	CHI	NL	1-8	144	534	64	159	24	12	12	110	.298	45	243	123	13-41
1946	CF	CHI	NL	3-8	65	234	18	66	6	4	3	39	.282	27	89	112	—
1947	CF	CHI	NL	6-8	129	513	68	155	25	7	13	66	.302	31	233	109	24-44
1948	3B	CHI	NL	8-8	142	548	82	171	30	2	26	101	.312	50	283	134	7-37
1949	CF-3B	CHI	NL	8-8	144	519	79	146	29	2	18	69	.281	63	233	119	18-38
1950	CF	CHI	NL	7-8	146	514	95	156	24	8	36	92	.304	69	304	151	3-42
1951	LF	CH/BR	NL	8/2	133	455	68	116	16	3	30	93	.255	52	228	124	10-44
1952	LF	BRO	NL	1-8	150	551	76	158	17	5	19	85	.287	64	242	123	13-39
1953	RF	MIL	NL	2-8	140	516	70	153	23	4	17	72	.297	37	235	108	26-44
1954	RF	MIL	NL	3-8	138	510	61	146	22	4	14	69	.286	37	218	101	33-48
1955	LF-3B	MIL	NL	2-8	86	252	29	67	3	5	5	34	.266	7	95	80	—
1956	LF	MIL	NL	2-8	45	93	15	24	5	0	2	9	.258	10	35	98	—
1957	LF	MIL	NL	1-8	83	220	31	61	6	1	8	27	.277	10	93	98	—
1958	LF	MIL	NL	1-8	95	164	17	39	7	1	3	23	.238	15	57	85	—
1959	LF	MIL	NL	2-8	71	142	17	31	8	2	1	15	.218	14	46	81	—
MAJOR LEAGUE TOTALS					1852	6292	844	1796	264	62	213	976	.285	561	2823	118	10 yrs

Casimir Eugene Michaels   Born Mar 4, 1926   Detroit, MI
5'11 175 lbs Batted right   Died Nov 12, 1982 Grosse Pointe, MI

YR	POS	TEAM	LG	FIN	G	AB	R	H	2B	3B	HR	RBI	AVG	BB	TB	OQ	RANK
1943	3B	CHI	AL	4-8	2	7	0	0	0	0	0	0	.000	0	0	—	—
1944	SS-3B	CHI	AL	7-8	27	68	4	12	4	1	0	5	.176	2	18	—	—
1945	SS	CHI	AL	6-8	129	445	47	109	8	5	2	54	.245	37	133	85	35-39
1946	2B-3B	CHI	AL	5-8	91	291	37	75	8	0	1	22	.258	29	86	85	—
1947	2B-3B	CHI	AL	6-8	110	355	31	97	15	4	3	34	.273	39	129	102	—
1948	SS-2B	CHI	AL	8-8	145	484	47	120	12	6	5	56	.248	69	159	91	38-45
1949	2B	CHI	AL	6-8	154	561	73	173	27	9	6	83	.308	101	236	125	10-41
1950	2B	CHI/WA	AL	6/5	142	526	69	140	14	7	8	66	.266	68	192	93	37-41
1951	2B	WAS	AL	7-8	138	485	59	125	20	4	4	45	.258	61	165	93	30-39
1952	2B-3B	Wa/SL/Ph	AL	5/7/4	132	452	53	114	16	8	5	50	.252	53	161	100	31-38
1953	2B	PHI	AL	7-8	117	411	53	103	10	0	12	42	.251	51	149	98	—
1954	3B	CHI	AL	3-8	101	282	35	74	13	2	7	44	.262	56	112	124	—

| MAJOR LEAGUE TOTALS | | | | | 1288 | 4367 | 508 | 1142 | 147 | 46 | 53 | 501 | .262 | 566 | 1540 | 98 | 6 yrs |

George Clyde Kell   Born Aug 23, 1922 Swifton, AR
5'9 175 lbs Batted right

YR	POS	TEAM	LG	FIN	G	AB	R	H	2B	3B	HR	RBI	AVG	BB	TB	OQ	RANK
1943	3B	PHI	AL	8-8	1	5	1	1	0	1	0	1	.200	0	3	—	—
1944	3B	PHI	AL	6-8	139	514	51	138	15	3	0	44	.268	22	159	80	44-46
1945	3B	PHI	AL	8-8	147	567	50	154	30	3	4	56	.272	27	202	93	34-39
1946	3B	PH/DE	AL	8/2	131	521	70	168	25	10	4	52	.322	40	225	119	16-35
1947	3B	DET	AL	2-8	152	588	75	188	29	5	5	93	.320	61	242	118	13-43
1948	3B	DET	AL	5-8	92	368	47	112	24	3	2	44	.304	33	148	103	—
1949	3B	DET	AL	4-8	134	522	97	179	38	9	3	59	.343	71	244	132	6-41
1950	3B	DET	AL	2-8	157	641	114	218	56	6	8	101	.340	66	310	122	15-41
1951	3B	DET	AL	5-8	147	598	92	191	36	3	2	59	.319	61	239	110	20-39
1952	3B	DE/BO	AL	8/6	114	428	52	133	23	2	7	57	.311	46	181	121	16-38
1953	3B	BOS	AL	4-8	134	460	68	141	41	2	12	73	.307	52	222	130	11-43
1954	3B-1B	BO/CH	AL	4/3	97	326	40	90	13	0	5	58	.276	33	118	98	—
1955	3B-1B	CHI	AL	3-8	128	429	44	134	24	1	8	81	.312	51	184	119	14-39
1956	3B	CH/BA	AL	3/6	123	425	52	115	22	2	9	48	.271	33	168	93	—
1957	3B-1B	BAL	AL	5-8	99	310	28	92	9	0	9	44	.297	25	128	108	—

| MAJOR LEAGUE TOTALS | | | | | 1795 | 6702 | 881 | 2054 | 385 | 50 | 78 | 870 | .306 | 621 | 2773 | 114 | 10 yrs |

Granville Wilbur Hamner Born Apr 26, 1927 Richmond, VA
5'10 163 lbs Batted right Died Sep 12, 1993 Philadelphia, PA

YR	POS	TEAM	LG	FIN	G	AB	R	H	2B	3B	HR	RBI	AVG	BB	TB	OQ	RANK
1944	SS	PHI	NL	8-8	21	77	6	19	1	0	0	5	.247	3	20	—	—
1945	SS	PHI	NL	8-8	14	41	3	7	2	0	0	6	.171	1	9	—	—
1946	SS	PHI	NL	5-8	2	7	0	1	0	0	0	0	.143	0	1	—	—
1947	SS	PHI	NL	7-8	2	7	1	2	0	0	0	0	.286	1	2	—	—
1948	2B-SS	PHI	NL	6-8	129	446	42	116	21	5	3	48	.260	22	156	82	34-37
1949	SS	PHI	NL	3-8	154	662	83	174	32	5	6	53	.263	25	234	80	36-38
1950	SS	PHI	NL	1-8	157	637	78	172	27	5	11	82	.270	39	242	88	37-42
1951	SS	PHI	NL	5-8	150	589	61	150	23	7	9	72	.255	29	214	83	43-44
1952	SS	PHI	NL	4-8	151	596	74	164	30	5	17	87	.275	27	255	103	27-39
1953	2B-SS	PHI	NL	3-8	154	609	90	168	30	8	21	92	.276	32	277	101	33-44
1954	2B	PHI	NL	4-8	152	596	83	178	39	11	13	89	.299	53	278	114	16-48
1955	2B-SS	PHI	NL	4-8	104	405	57	104	12	4	5	43	.257	41	139	87	—
1956	SS	PHI	NL	5-8	122	401	42	90	24	3	4	42	.224	30	132	78	—
1957	2B	PHI	NL	5-8	133	502	59	114	19	5	10	62	.227	34	173	81	42-44
1958	3B-2B	PHI	NL	8-8	35	133	18	40	7	3	2	18	.301	8	59	106	—
1959	SS	PHI	NL	8-8	21	64	10	19	4	0	2	6	.297	5	29	—	—
1959	SS-2B	CLE	AL	2-8	27	67	4	11	1	1	1	3	.164	1	17	—	—
1962	P	KC	AL	9-10	3	0	0	0	0	0	0	0	—	0	0	—	—

MAJOR LEAGUE TOTALS | | | | | 1531 | 5839 | 711 | 1529 | 272 | 62 | 104 | 708 | .262 | 351 | 2237 | 92 | 8 yrs

Edward Frederick Joseph Yost Born Oct 13, 1926 Brooklyn, NY
5'10 170 lbs Batted right

YR	POS	TEAM	LG	FIN	G	AB	R	H	2B	3B	HR	RBI	AVG	BB	TB	OQ	RANK
1944	3B-SS	WAS	AL	8-8	7	14	3	2	0	0	0	0	.143	1	2	—	—
1946	3B	WAS	AL	4-8	8	25	2	2	1	0	0	1	.080	5	3	—	—
1947	3B	WAS	AL	7-8	115	428	52	102	17	3	0	14	.238	45	125	81	42-43
1948	3B	WAS	AL	7-8	145	555	74	138	32	11	2	50	.249	82	198	97	35-45
1949	3B	WAS	AL	8-8	124	435	57	110	19	7	9	45	.253	91	170	115	18-41
1950	3B	WAS	AL	5-8	155	573	114	169	26	2	11	58	.295	141	232	127	8-41
1951	3B	WAS	AL	7-8	154	568	109	161	36	4	12	65	.283	126	241	134	7-39
1952	3B	WAS	AL	5-8	157	587	92	137	32	3	12	49	.233	129	211	119	19-38
1953	3B	WAS	AL	5-8	152	577	107	157	30	7	9	45	.272	123	228	126	12-43
1954	3B	WAS	AL	6-8	155	539	101	138	26	4	11	47	.256	131	205	129	12-34
1955	3B	WAS	AL	8-8	122	375	64	91	17	5	7	48	.243	95	139	123	9-33
1956	3B	WAS	AL	7-8	152	515	94	119	17	2	11	53	.231	151	173	118	17-40
1957	3B	WAS	AL	8-8	110	414	47	104	13	5	9	38	.251	73	154	112	21-35
1958	3B	WAS	AL	8-8	134	406	55	91	16	0	8	37	.224	81	131	105	24-39
1959	3B	DET	AL	4-8	148	521	115	145	19	0	21	61	.278	135	227	148	2-35
1960	3B	DET	AL	6-8	143	497	78	129	23	2	14	47	.260	125	198	132	5-44
1961	3B	LA	AL	8-10	76	213	29	43	4	0	3	15	.202	50	56	92	—
1962	3B-1B	LA	AL	3-10	52	104	22	25	9	1	0	10	.240	30	36	125	—

MAJOR LEAGUE TOTALS | | | | | 2109 | 7346 | 1215 | 1863 | 337 | 56 | 139 | 683 | .254 | 1614 | 2729 | 119 | 14 yrs

Carroll Walter Lockman Born Jul 25, 1926 Lowell, NC
6'1 175 lbs Batted left

YR	POS	TEAM	LG	FIN	G	AB	R	H	2B	3B	HR	RBI	AVG	BB	TB	OQ	RANK
1945	CF	NY	NL	5-8	32	129	16	44	9	0	3	18	.341	13	62	141	—
1947	PH	NY	NL	4-8	2	2	0	1	0	0	0	1	.500	0	1	—	—
1948	CF	NY	NL	5-8	146	584	117	167	24	10	18	59	.286	68	265	121	11-37
1949	LF	NY	NL	5-8	151	617	97	186	32	7	11	65	.301	62	265	114	20-38
1950	LF	NY	NL	3-8	129	532	72	157	28	5	6	52	.295	42	213	99	31-42
1951	1B-LF	NY	NL	1-8	153	614	85	173	27	7	12	73	.282	50	250	102	34-44
1952	1B	NY	NL	2-8	154	606	99	176	17	4	13	58	.290	67	240	113	18-39
1953	1B-LF	NY	NL	5-8	150	607	85	179	22	4	9	61	.295	52	236	97	34-44
1954	1B	NY	NL	1-8	148	570	73	143	17	3	16	60	.251	59	214	92	40-48
1955	LF-1B	NY	NL	3-8	147	576	76	157	19	0	15	49	.273	39	221	91	37-43
1956	LF-CF	NY/SL	NL	6/4	118	362	27	94	7	3	1	20	.260	34	110	81	—
1957	1B-LF	NY	NL	6-8	133	456	51	113	9	4	7	30	.248	39	151	84	39-44
1958	LF-2B	SF	NL	3-8	92	122	15	29	5	0	2	7	.238	13	40	84	—
1959	1B-2B	BAL	AL	6-8	38	69	7	15	1	1	0	2	.217	8	18	—	—
1959	1B-2B	CIN	NL	5-8	52	84	10	22	5	1	0	7	.262	4	29	—	—
1960	1B	CIN	NL	6-8	21	10	6	2	0	0	1	1	.200	2	5	—	—
MAJOR LEAGUE TOTALS					1666	5940	836	1658	222	49	114	563	.279	552	2320	101	9 yrs

Albert Fred Schoendienst Born Feb 2, 1923 Germantown, IL
6'0 170 lbs Batted both

YR	POS	TEAM	LG	FIN	G	AB	R	H	2B	3B	HR	RBI	AVG	BB	TB	OQ	RANK
1945	LF	SL	NL	2-8	137	565	89	157	22	6	1	47	.278	21	194	84	37-41
1946	2B	SL	NL	1-8	142	606	94	170	28	5	0	34	.281	37	208	91	32-35
1947	2B	SL	NL	2-8	151	659	91	167	25	9	3	48	.253	48	219	80	43-44
1948	2B	SL	NL	2-8	119	408	64	111	21	4	4	36	.272	28	152	92	—
1949	2B-SS	SL	NL	2-8	151	640	102	190	25	2	3	54	.297	51	228	93	29-38
1950	2B	SL	NL	5-8	153	642	81	177	43	9	7	63	.276	33	259	91	34-42
1951	2B	SL	NL	3-8	135	553	88	160	32	7	6	54	.289	35	224	99	35-44
1952	2B	SL	NL	3-8	152	620	91	188	40	7	7	67	.303	42	263	112	21-39
1953	2B	SL	NL	3-8	146	564	107	193	35	5	15	79	.342	60	283	133	11-44
1954	2B	SL	NL	6-8	148	610	98	192	38	8	5	79	.315	54	261	108	22-48
1955	2B	SL	NL	7-8	145	553	68	148	21	3	11	51	.268	54	208	94	31-43
1956	2B	SL/NY	NL	4/6	132	487	61	147	21	3	2	29	.302	41	180	97	32-43
1957	2B	NY/ML	NL	6/1	150	648	91	200	31	8	15	65	.309	33	292	110	19-44
1958	2B	MIL	NL	1-8	106	427	47	112	23	1	1	24	.262	31	140	80	—
1959	2B	MIL	NL	2-8	5	3	0	0	0	0	0	0	.000	0	0	—	—
1960	2B	MIL	NL	2-8	68	226	21	58	9	1	1	19	.257	17	72	82	—
1961	2B	SL	NL	5-8	72	120	9	36	9	0	1	12	.300	12	48	105	—
1962	2B-3B	SL	NL	6-10	98	143	21	43	4	0	2	12	.301	9	53	94	—
1963	PH	SL	NL	2-10	6	5	0	0	0	0	0	0	.000	0	0	—	—
MAJOR LEAGUE TOTALS					2216	8479	1223	2449	427	78	84	773	.289	606	3284	99	12 yrs

Robert Brown Thomson Born Oct 25, 1923 Glasgow, Scotland
6'2 180 lbs Batted right

YR	POS	TEAM	LG	FIN	G	AB	R	H	2B	3B	HR	RBI	AVG	BB	TB	OQ	RANK
1946	3B	NY	NL	8-8	18	54	8	17	4	1	2	9	.315	4	29	—	—
1947	CF	NY	NL	4-8	138	545	105	154	26	5	29	85	.283	40	277	120	16-44
1948	LF	NY	NL	5-8	138	471	75	117	20	2	16	63	.248	30	189	94	30-37
1949	CF	NY	NL	5-8	156	641	99	198	35	9	27	109	.309	44	332	127	9-38
1950	CF	NY	NL	3-8	149	563	79	142	22	7	25	85	.252	55	253	106	25-42
1951	LF-3B	NY	NL	1-8	148	518	89	152	27	8	32	101	.293	73	291	150	5-44
1952	3B-CF	NY	NL	2-8	153	608	89	164	29	14	24	108	.270	52	293	123	14-39
1953	CF	NY	NL	5-8	154	608	80	175	22	6	26	106	.288	43	287	110	23-44
1954	LF	MIL	NL	3-8	43	99	7	23	3	0	2	15	.232	12	32	83	—
1955	LF	MIL	NL	2-8	101	343	40	88	12	3	12	56	.257	34	142	101	—
1956	LF	MIL	NL	2-8	142	451	59	106	10	4	20	74	.235	43	184	99	30-43
1957	LF-RF	ML/NY	NL	1/6	122	363	39	87	12	7	12	61	.240	27	149	96	—
1958	CF	CHI	NL	5-8	152	547	67	155	27	5	21	82	.283	56	255	117	17-34
1959	LF	CHI	NL	5-8	122	374	55	97	15	2	11	52	.259	35	149	100	—
1960	CF-LF	BO/BA	AL	7/2	43	120	12	30	3	1	5	20	.250	11	50	102	—

MAJOR LEAGUE TOTALS 1779 6305 903 1705 267 74 264 1026 .270 559 2912 116 9 yrs

Alvin Ralph Dark Born Jan 7, 1922 Comanche, OK
5'11 185 lbs Batted right

YR	POS	TEAM	LG	FIN	G	AB	R	H	2B	3B	HR	RBI	AVG	BB	TB	OQ	RANK
1946	SS	BOS	NL	4-8	15	13	0	3	3	0	0	1	.231	0	6	—	—
1948	SS	BOS	NL	1-8	137	543	85	175	39	6	3	48	.322	24	235	107	21-37
1949	SS	BOS	NL	4-8	130	529	74	146	23	5	3	53	.276	31	188	86	34-38
1950	SS	NY	NL	3-8	154	587	79	164	36	5	16	67	.279	39	258	102	28-42
1951	SS	NY	NL	1-8	156	646	114	196	41	7	14	69	.303	42	293	112	22-44
1952	SS	NY	NL	2-8	151	589	92	177	29	3	14	73	.301	47	254	115	17-39
1953	SS-2B	NY	NL	5-8	155	647	126	194	41	6	23	88	.300	28	316	109	24-44
1954	SS	NY	NL	1-8	154	644	98	189	26	6	20	70	.293	27	287	99	34-48
1955	SS	NY	NL	3-8	115	475	77	134	20	3	9	45	.282	22	187	89	37-43
1956	SS	NY/SL	NL	6/4	148	619	73	170	26	7	6	54	.275	29	228	86	40-43
1957	SS	SL	NL	2-8	140	583	80	169	25	8	4	64	.290	29	222	92	34-44
1958	3B	SL/CH	NL	5/5	132	528	61	156	16	4	4	48	.295	31	192	88	31-34
1959	3B	CHI	NL	5-8	136	477	60	126	22	9	6	45	.264	55	184	102	25-38
1960	3B-LF	PH/ML	NL	8/2	105	339	45	90	11	3	4	32	.265	26	119	90	—

MAJOR LEAGUE TOTALS 1828 7219 1064 2089 358 72 126 757 .289 430 2969 99 12 yrs

Grady Edgebert Hatton
5'8   170 lbs   Batted left

Born Oct 7, 1922   Beaumont, TX

YR	POS	TEAM	LG	FIN	G	AB	R	H	2B	3B	HR	RBI	AVG	BB	TB	OO	RANK
1946	3B	CIN	NL	6-8	116	436	56	118	18	3	14	69	.271	66	184	127	9-35
1947	3B	CIN	NL	5-8	146	524	91	147	24	8	16	77	.281	81	235	124	15-44
1948	3B	CIN	NL	7-8	133	458	58	110	17	2	9	44	.240	72	158	100	25-37
1949	3B	CIN	NL	7-8	137	537	71	141	38	5	11	69	.263	62	222	107	22-38
1950	3B	CIN	NL	6-8	130	438	67	114	17	1	11	54	.260	70	166	106	28-42
1951	3B	CIN	NL	6-8	96	331	41	84	9	3	4	37	.254	33	111	88	—
1952	2B	CIN	NL	6-8	128	433	48	92	14	1	9	57	.212	66	135	93	37-39
1953	2B-1B	CIN	NL	6-8	83	159	22	37	3	1	7	22	.233	29	63	108	—
1954	PH	CIN	NL	5-8	1	1	0	0	0	0	0	0	.000	0	0	—	—
1954	3B	CH/BO	AL	3/4	112	332	43	90	13	3	5	36	.271	63	124	119	—
1955	3B	BOS	AL	4-8	126	380	48	93	11	4	4	49	.245	76	124	104	—
1956	2B-3B	BO/BA	AL	4/6	32	66	4	11	1	0	1	5	.167	13	15	—	—
1956	2B	SL	NL	4-8	44	73	10	18	1	2	0	7	.247	13	23	—	—
1960	2B	CHI	NL	7-8	28	38	3	13	0	0	0	7	.342	2	13	—	—
MAJOR LEAGUE TOTALS					1312	4206	562	1068	166	33	91	533	.254	646	1573	110	6 yrs

John Sherman Lollar
6'1   185 lbs   Batted right

Born Aug 23, 1924 Durham, AR
Died Sep 24, 1977 Springfield, MO

YR	POS	TEAM	LG	FIN	G	AB	R	H	2B	3B	HR	RBI	AVG	BB	TB	OO	RANK
1946	C	CLE	AL	6-8	28	62	7	15	6	0	1	9	.242	5	24	—	—
1947	C	NY	AL	1-8	11	32	4	7	0	1	1	6	.219	1	12	—	—
1948	C	NY	AL	3-8	22	38	0	8	0	0	0	4	.211	1	8	—	—
1949	C	SL	AL	7-8	109	284	28	74	9	1	8	49	.261	32	109	96	—
1950	C	SL	AL	7-8	126	396	55	111	22	3	13	65	.280	64	178	117	—
1951	C	SL	AL	8-8	98	310	44	78	21	0	8	44	.252	43	123	106	—
1952	C	CHI	AL	3-8	132	375	35	90	15	0	13	50	.240	54	144	109	—
1953	C	CHI	AL	3-8	113	334	46	96	19	0	8	54	.287	47	139	118	—
1954	C	CHI	AL	3-8	107	316	31	77	13	0	7	34	.244	37	111	95	—
1955	C	CHI	AL	3-8	138	426	67	111	13	1	16	61	.261	68	174	115	17-39
1956	C	CHI	AL	3-8	136	450	55	132	28	2	11	75	.293	53	197	113	21-40
1957	C	CHI	AL	2-8	101	351	33	90	11	2	11	70	.256	35	138	102	—
1958	C	CHI	AL	2-8	127	421	53	115	16	0	20	84	.273	57	191	126	12-39
1959	C-1B	CHI	AL	1-8	140	505	63	134	22	3	22	84	.265	55	228	118	17-35
1960	C	CHI	AL	3-8	129	421	43	106	23	0	7	46	.252	42	150	92	35-44
1961	C	CHI	AL	4-10	116	337	38	95	10	1	7	41	.282	37	128	101	—
1962	C	CHI	AL	5-10	84	220	17	59	12	0	2	26	.268	32	77	102	—
1963	C	CHI	AL	2-10	35	73	4	17	4	0	0	6	.233	8	21	—	—
MAJOR LEAGUE TOTALS					1752	5351	623	1415	244	14	155	808	.264	671	2152	113	5 yrs

Loren Dale Mitchell   Born Aug 23, 1921 Colony, OK
6'1   195 lbs   Batted left   Died Jan 5, 1987   Tulsa, OK

YR	POS	TEAM	LG	FIN	G	AB	R	H	2B	3B	HR	RBI	AVG	BB	TB	OQ	RANK
1946	CF	CLE	AL	6-8	11	44	7	19	3	0	0	5	.432	1	22	—	—
1947	LF	CLE	AL	4-8	123	493	69	156	16	10	1	34	.316	23	195	101	32-43
1948	LF	CLE	AL	1-8	141	608	82	204	30	8	4	56	.336	45	262	110	27-45
1949	LF	CLE	AL	3-8	149	640	81	203	16	23	3	56	.317	43	274	104	26-41
1950	LF	CLE	AL	4-8	130	506	81	156	27	5	3	49	.308	67	202	106	28-41
1951	LF	CLE	AL	2-8	134	510	83	148	21	7	11	62	.290	53	216	110	19-39
1952	LF	CLE	AL	2-8	134	511	61	165	26	3	5	58	.323	52	212	120	17-38
1953	LF	CLE	AL	2-8	134	500	76	150	26	4	13	60	.300	42	223	114	19-43
1954	LF	CLE	AL	1-8	53	60	6	17	1	0	1	6	.283	9	21	—	—
1955	1B	CLE	AL	2-8	61	58	4	15	2	1	0	10	.259	4	19	—	—
1956	LF	CLE	AL	2-8	38	30	2	4	0	0	0	6	.133	7	4	—	—
1956	LF	BRO	NL	1-8	19	24	3	7	1	0	0	1	.292	0	8	—	—

MAJOR LEAGUE TOTALS   1127 3984 555 1244 169 61 41 403 .312 346 1658 109   7 yrs

Lawrence Peter Berra   Born May 12, 1925 St Louis, MO
5'7   185 lbs   Batted left

YR	POS	TEAM	LG	FIN	G	AB	R	H	2B	3B	HR	RBI	AVG	BB	TB	OQ	RANK
1946	C	NY	AL	3-8	7	22	3	8	1	0	2	4	.364	1	15	—	—
1947	C-LF	NY	AL	1-8	83	293	41	82	15	3	11	54	.280	13	136	110	—
1948	C-LF	NY	AL	3-8	125	469	70	143	24	10	14	98	.305	25	229	113	21-45
1949	C	NY	AL	1-8	116	415	59	115	20	2	20	91	.277	22	199	106	—
1950	C	NY	AL	1-8	151	597	116	192	30	6	28	124	.322	55	318	127	9-41
1951	C	NY	AL	1-8	141	547	92	161	19	4	27	88	.294	44	269	121	13-39
1952	C	NY	AL	1-8	142	534	97	146	17	1	30	98	.273	66	255	130	12-38
1953	C	NY	AL	1-8	137	503	80	149	23	5	27	108	.296	50	263	133	8-43
1954	C	NY	AL	2-8	151	584	88	179	28	6	22	125	.307	56	285	129	10-34
1955	C	NY	AL	1-8	147	541	84	147	20	3	27	108	.272	60	254	119	13-39
1956	C	NY	AL	1-8	140	521	93	155	29	2	30	105	.298	65	278	135	9-40
1957	C	NY	AL	1-8	134	482	74	121	14	2	24	82	.251	57	211	114	19-35
1958	C-LF	NY	AL	1-8	122	433	60	115	17	3	22	90	.266	35	204	117	17-39
1959	C	NY	AL	3-8	131	472	64	134	25	1	19	69	.284	43	218	119	16-35
1960	C-LF	NY	AL	1-8	120	359	46	99	14	1	15	62	.276	38	160	115	—
1961	LF-C	NY	AL	1-10	119	395	62	107	11	0	22	61	.271	35	184	113	—
1962	C-LF	NY	AL	1-10	86	232	25	52	8	0	10	35	.224	24	90	95	—
1963	C	NY	AL	1-10	64	147	20	43	6	0	8	28	.293	15	73	135	—
1965	C	NY	NL	10-10	4	9	1	2	0	0	0	0	.222	0	2	—	—

MAJOR LEAGUE TOTALS   2120 7555 1175 2150 321 49 358 1430 .285 704 3643 123   11 yrs

Delmer Ennis   Born Jun 8, 1925   Philadelphia, PA
6'0   195 lbs   Batted right

YR	POS	TEAM	LG	FIN	G	AB	R	H	2B	3B	HR	RBI	AVG	BB	TB	OO	RANK
1946	LF	PHI	NL	5-8	141	540	70	169	30	6	17	73	.313	39	262	131	8-35
1947	LF	PHI	NL	7-8	139	541	71	149	25	6	12	81	.275	37	222	98	35-44
1948	RF	PHI	NL	6-8	152	589	86	171	40	4	30	95	.290	47	309	129	8-37
1949	LF	PHI	NL	3-8	154	610	92	184	39	11	25	110	.302	59	320	133	8-38
1950	RF	PHI	NL	1-8	153	595	92	185	34	8	31	126	.311	56	328	136	10-42
1951	RF	PHI	NL	5-8	144	532	76	142	20	5	15	73	.267	68	217	110	25-44
1952	LF	PHI	NL	4-8	151	592	90	171	30	10	20	107	.289	47	281	123	12-39
1953	LF	PHI	NL	3-8	152	578	79	165	22	3	29	125	.285	57	280	117	17-44
1954	LF	PHI	NL	4-8	145	556	73	145	23	2	25	119	.261	50	247	104	26-48
1955	LF	PHI	NL	4-8	146	564	82	167	24	7	29	120	.296	46	292	124	16-43
1956	LF	PHI	NL	5-8	153	630	80	164	23	3	26	95	.260	33	271	98	31-43
1957	RF	SL	NL	2-8	136	490	61	140	24	3	24	105	.286	37	242	120	14-44
1958	LF	SL	NL	5-8	106	329	22	86	18	1	3	47	.261	15	115	79	—
1959	LF	CIN	NL	5-8	5	12	1	4	0	0	0	1	.333	2	4	—	—
1959	LF	CHI	AL	1-8	26	96	10	21	6	0	2	7	.219	4	33	76	—

MAJOR LEAGUE TOTALS					1903	7254	985	2063	358	69	288	1284	.284	597	3423	119	12 yrs

Carl Anthony Furillo   Born Mar 8, 1922   Stony Creek Mills, PA
6'0   190 lbs   Batted right   Died Jan 21, 1989   Stony Creek Mills, PA

YR	POS	TEAM	LG	FIN	G	AB	R	H	2B	3B	HR	RBI	AVG	BB	TB	OO	RANK
1946	CF	BRO	NL	2-8	117	335	29	95	18	6	3	35	.284	31	134	111	—
1947	CF	BRO	NL	1-8	124	437	61	129	24	7	8	88	.295	34	191	108	25-44
1948	CF	BRO	NL	3-8	108	364	55	108	20	4	4	44	.297	43	148	113	—
1949	RF	BRO	NL	1-8	142	549	95	177	27	10	18	106	.322	37	278	127	11-38
1950	RF	BRO	NL	2-8	153	620	99	189	30	6	18	106	.305	41	285	110	21-42
1951	RF	BRO	NL	2-8	158	667	93	197	32	4	16	91	.295	43	285	105	32-44
1952	RF	BRO	NL	1-8	134	425	52	105	18	1	8	59	.247	31	149	89	—
1953	RF	BRO	NL	1-8	132	479	82	165	38	6	21	92	.344	34	278	143	6-44
1954	RF	BRO	NL	2-8	150	547	56	161	23	1	19	96	.294	49	243	108	21-48
1955	RF	BRO	NL	1-8	140	523	83	164	24	3	26	95	.314	43	272	128	13-43
1956	RF	BRO	NL	1-8	149	523	66	151	30	0	21	83	.289	57	244	121	15-43
1957	RF	BRO	NL	3-8	119	395	61	121	17	4	12	66	.306	29	182	116	—
1958	RF	LA	NL	7-8	122	411	54	119	19	3	18	83	.290	35	198	118	—
1959	RF	LA	NL	1-8	50	93	8	27	4	0	0	13	.290	7	31	86	—
1960	RF	LA	NL	4-8	8	10	1	2	0	1	0	1	.200	0	4	—	—

MAJOR LEAGUE TOTALS					1806	6378	895	1910	324	56	192	1058	.299	514	2922	119	8 yrs

Ralph McPherran Kiner Born Oct 27, 1922 Santa Rita, NM
6'2 195 lbs Batted right

YR	POS	TEAM	LG	FIN	G	AB	R	H	2B	3B	HR	RBI	AVG	BB	TB	OQ	RANK
1946	LF	PIT	NL	7-8	144	502	63	124	17	3	23	81	.247	74	216	124	12-35
1947	LF	PIT	NL	7-8	152	565	118	177	23	4	51	127	.313	98	361	175	1-44
1948	LF	PIT	NL	4-8	156	555	104	147	19	5	40	123	.265	112	296	152	3-37
1949	LF	PIT	NL	6-8	152	549	116	170	19	5	54	127	.310	117	361	189	1-38
1950	LF	PIT	NL	8-8	150	547	112	149	21	6	47	118	.272	122	323	163	2-42
1951	LF-1B	PIT	NL	8-8	151	531	124	164	31	6	42	109	.309	137	333	193	1-44
1952	LF	PIT	NL	8-8	149	516	90	126	17	2	37	87	.244	110	258	149	4-39
1953	LF	PT/CH	NL	8/7	158	562	100	157	20	3	35	116	.279	100	288	138	10-44
1954	LF	CHI	NL	7-8	147	557	88	159	36	5	22	73	.285	76	271	125	12-48
1955	LF	CLE	AL	2-8	113	321	56	78	13	0	18	54	.243	65	145	129	—

MAJOR LEAGUE TOTALS 1472 5205 971 1451 216 39 369 1015 .279 1011 2852 156 9 yrs

Edwin Donald Snider Born Sep 19, 1926 Los Angeles, CA
6'0 179 lbs Batted left

YR	POS	TEAM	LG	FIN	G	AB	R	H	2B	3B	HR	RBI	AVG	BB	TB	OQ	RANK
1947	CF-RF	BRO	NL	1-8	40	83	6	20	3	1	0	5	.241	3	25	—	—
1948	CF	BRO	NL	3-8	53	160	22	39	6	6	5	21	.244	12	72	105	—
1949	CF	BRO	NL	1-8	146	552	100	161	28	7	23	92	.292	56	272	126	13-38
1950	CF	BRO	NL	2-8	152	620	109	199	31	10	31	107	.321	58	343	138	8-42
1951	CF	BRO	NL	2-8	150	606	96	168	26	6	29	101	.277	62	293	122	14-44
1952	CF	BRO	NL	1-8	144	534	80	162	25	7	21	92	.303	55	264	136	8-39
1953	CF	BRO	NL	1-8	153	590	132	198	38	4	42	126	.336	82	370	166	2-44
1954	CF	BRO	NL	2-8	149	584	120	199	39	10	40	130	.341	84	378	172	1-48
1955	CF	BRO	NL	1-8	148	538	126	166	34	6	42	136	.309	104	338	173	1-43
1956	CF	BRO	NL	1-8	151	542	112	158	33	2	43	101	.292	99	324	165	1-43
1957	CF	BRO	NL	3-8	139	508	91	139	25	7	40	92	.274	77	298	153	4-44
1958	CF	LA	NL	7-8	106	327	45	102	12	3	15	58	.312	32	165	129	—
1959	RF-CF	LA	NL	1-8	126	370	59	114	11	2	23	88	.308	58	198	150	—
1960	CF-RF	LA	NL	4-8	101	235	38	57	13	5	14	36	.243	46	122	146	—
1961	RF-CF	LA	NL	2-8	85	233	35	69	8	3	16	56	.296	29	131	144	—
1962	RF-LF	LA	NL	2-10	80	158	28	44	11	3	5	30	.278	36	76	149	—
1963	RF	NY	NL	10-10	129	354	44	86	8	3	14	45	.243	56	142	125	—
1964	RF-LF	SF	NL	4-10	91	167	16	35	7	0	4	17	.210	22	54	95	—

MAJOR LEAGUE TOTALS 2143 7161 1259 2116 358 85 407 1333 .295 971 3865 150 9 yrs

Theodore Bernard Kluszewski Born Sep 10, 1924 Argo, IL
6'2 225 lbs Batted left   Died Mar 29, 1988 Cincinnati, OH

YR	POS	TEAM	LG	FIN	G	AB	R	H	2B	3B	HR	RBI	AVG	BB	TB	OQ	RANK
1947	1B	CIN	NL	5-8	9	10	1	1	0	0	0	2	.100	1	1	—	—
1948	1B	CIN	NL	7-8	113	379	49	104	23	4	12	57	.274	18	171	104	—
1949	1B	CIN	NL	7-8	136	531	63	164	26	2	8	68	.309	19	218	97	28-38
1950	1B	CIN	NL	6-8	134	538	76	165	37	0	25	111	.307	33	277	121	17-42
1951	1B	CIN	NL	6-8	154	607	74	157	35	2	13	77	.259	35	235	90	39-44
1952	1B	CIN	NL	6-8	135	497	62	159	24	11	16	86	.320	47	253	140	6-39
1953	1B	CIN	NL	6-8	149	570	97	180	25	0	40	108	.316	55	325	140	9-44
1954	1B	CIN	NL	5-8	149	573	104	187	28	3	49	141	.326	78	368	166	5-48
1955	1B	CIN	NL	5-8	153	612	116	192	25	0	47	113	.314	66	358	147	6-43
1956	1B	CIN	NL	3-8	138	517	91	156	14	1	35	102	.302	49	277	135	9-43
1957	1B	CIN	NL	4-8	69	127	12	34	7	0	6	21	.268	5	59	104	—
1958	1B	PIT	NL	2-8	100	301	29	88	13	4	4	37	.292	26	121	102	—
1959	1B	PIT	NL	4-8	60	122	11	32	10	1	2	17	.262	5	50	92	—
1959	1B	CHI	AL	1-8	31	101	11	30	2	1	2	10	.297	9	40	106	—
1960	1B	CHI	AL	3-8	81	181	20	53	9	0	5	39	.293	22	77	117	—
1961	1B	LA	AL	8-10	107	263	32	64	12	0	15	39	.243	24	121	108	—

| MAJOR LEAGUE TOTALS | | | | | 1718 | 5929 | 848 | 1766 | 290 | 29 | 279 | 1028 | .298 | 492 | 2951 | 130 | 8 yrs |

Clifford Earl Torgeson Born Jan 1, 1924 Snohomish, WA
6'3 180 lbs Batted left   Died Nov 8, 1990 Everett, WA

YR	POS	TEAM	LG	FIN	G	AB	R	H	2B	3B	HR	RBI	AVG	BB	TB	OQ	RANK
1947	1B	BOS	NL	3-8	128	399	73	112	20	6	16	78	.281	82	192	141	8-44
1948	1B	BOS	NL	1-8	134	438	70	111	23	5	10	67	.253	81	174	118	15-37
1949	1B	BOS	NL	4-8	25	100	17	26	5	1	4	19	.260	13	45	118	—
1950	1B	BOS	NL	4-8	156	576	120	167	30	3	23	87	.290	119	272	139	7-42
1951	1B	BOS	NL	4-8	155	581	99	153	21	4	24	92	.263	102	254	125	9-44
1952	1B	BOS	NL	7-8	122	382	49	88	17	0	5	34	.230	81	120	108	—
1953	1B	PHI	NL	3-8	111	379	58	104	25	8	11	64	.274	53	178	121	—
1954	1B	PHI	NL	4-8	135	490	63	133	22	6	5	54	.271	75	182	103	27-48
1955	1B	PHI	NL	4-8	47	150	29	40	5	3	1	17	.267	32	54	114	—
1955	1B	DET	AL	5-8	89	300	58	85	10	1	9	50	.283	61	124	129	—
1956	1B	DET	AL	5-8	117	318	61	84	9	3	12	42	.264	78	135	131	—
1957	1B	DE/CH	AL	4/2	116	301	58	86	13	3	8	51	.286	61	129	136	—
1958	1B	CHI	AL	2-8	96	188	37	50	8	0	10	30	.266	48	88	153	—
1959	1B	CHI	AL	1-8	127	277	40	61	5	3	9	45	.220	62	99	115	—
1960	1B	CHI	AL	3-8	68	57	12	15	2	0	2	9	.263	21	23	—	—
1961	1B	CH/NY	AL	4/1	42	33	4	3	0	0	0	1	.091	11	3	—	—

| MAJOR LEAGUE TOTALS | | | | | 1668 | 4969 | 848 | 1318 | 215 | 46 | 149 | 740 | .265 | 980 | 2072 | 125 | 5 yrs |

Ferris Roy Fain
5'11 180 lbs Batted left

Born May 29, 1921 San Antonio, TX

YR	POS	TEAM	LG	FIN	G	AB	R	H	2B	3B	HR	RBI	AVG	BB	TB	OQ	RANK
1947	1B	PHI	AL	5-8	136	461	70	134	28	6	7	71	.291	95	195	138	4-43
1948	1B	PHI	AL	4-8	145	520	81	146	27	6	7	88	.281	113	206	124	11-45
1949	1B	PHI	AL	5-8	150	525	81	138	21	5	3	78	.263	136	178	116	17-41
1950	1B	PHI	AL	8-8	151	522	83	147	25	4	10	83	.282	133	210	126	11-41
1951	1B	PHI	AL	6-8	117	425	63	146	30	3	6	57	.344	80	200	149	3-39
1952	1B	PHI	AL	4-8	145	538	82	176	43	3	2	59	.327	105	231	146	6-38
1953	1B	CHI	AL	3-8	128	446	73	114	18	2	6	52	.256	108	154	119	16-43
1954	1B	CHI	AL	3-8	65	235	30	71	10	1	5	51	.302	40	98	129	—
1955	1B	DE/CL	AL	5/2	114	258	32	67	11	0	2	31	.260	94	84	139	—

| MAJOR LEAGUE TOTALS | | | | | 1151 | 3930 | 595 | 1139 | 213 | 30 | 48 | 570 | .290 | 904 | 1556 | 131 | 7 yrs |

Jacob Nelson Fox
5'10 160 lbs Batted left

Born Dec 25, 1927 St Thomas, PA
Died Dec 1, 1975 Baltimore, MD

YR	POS	TEAM	LG	FIN	G	AB	R	H	2B	3B	HR	RBI	AVG	BB	TB	OQ	RANK
1947	2B	PHI	AL	5-8	7	3	2	0	0	0	0	0	.000	1	0	—	—
1948	2B	PHI	AL	4-8	3	13	0	2	0	0	0	0	.154	1	2	—	—
1949	2B	PHI	AL	5-8	88	247	42	63	6	2	0	21	.255	32	73	82	—
1950	2B	CHI	AL	6-8	130	457	45	113	12	7	0	30	.247	35	139	70	40-41
1951	2B	CHI	AL	4-8	147	604	93	189	32	12	4	55	.313	43	257	107	23-39
1952	2B	CHI	AL	3-8	152	648	76	192	25	10	0	39	.296	34	237	94	35-38
1953	2B	CHI	AL	3-8	154	624	92	178	31	8	3	72	.285	49	234	96	33-43
1954	2B	CHI	AL	3-8	155	631	111	201	24	8	2	47	.319	51	247	106	19-34
1955	2B	CHI	AL	3-8	154	636	100	198	28	7	6	59	.311	38	258	101	29-39
1956	2B	CHI	AL	3-8	154	649	109	192	20	10	4	52	.296	44	244	91	31-40
1957	2B	CHI	AL	2-8	155	619	110	196	27	8	6	61	.317	75	257	121	12-35
1958	2B	CHI	AL	2-8	155	623	82	187	21	6	0	49	.300	47	220	95	33-39
1959	2B	CHI	AL	1-8	156	624	84	191	34	6	2	70	.306	71	243	112	22-35
1960	2B	CHI	AL	3-8	150	605	85	175	24	10	2	59	.289	50	225	97	30-44
1961	2B	CHI	AL	4-10	159	606	67	152	11	5	2	51	.251	59	179	78	48-49
1962	2B	CHI	AL	5-10	157	621	79	166	27	7	2	54	.267	38	213	83	51-54
1963	2B	CHI	AL	2-10	137	539	54	140	19	0	2	42	.260	24	165	76	51-51
1964	2B	HOU	NL	9-10	133	442	45	117	12	6	0	28	.265	27	141	85	—
1965	3B-1B	HOU	NL	9-10	21	41	3	11	2	0	0	1	.268	0	13	—	—

| MAJOR LEAGUE TOTALS | | | | | 2367 | 9232 | 1279 | 2663 | 355 | 112 | 35 | 790 | .288 | 719 | 3347 | 95 | 14 yrs |

Sabath Anthony Mele
6'1   183 lbs   Batted right

Born Jan 21, 1923   Astoria, NY

YR	POS	TEAM	LG	FIN	G	AB	R	H	2B	3B	HR	RBI	AVG	BB	TB	OQ	RANK
1947	RF	BOS	AL	3-8	123	453	71	137	14	8	12	73	.302	37	203	118	12-43
1948	RF	BOS	AL	2-8	66	180	25	42	12	1	2	25	.233	13	62	79	—
1949	RF-1B	BO/WA	AL	2/8	96	310	22	73	13	3	3	32	.235	24	101	76	—
1950	RF-1B	WAS	AL	5-8	126	435	57	119	21	6	12	86	.274	51	188	104	31-41
1951	RF-1B	WAS	AL	7-8	143	558	58	153	36	7	5	94	.274	32	218	92	32-39
1952	RF	WA/CH	AL	5/3	132	451	48	117	21	2	16	69	.259	49	190	113	24-38
1953	RF	CHI	AL	3-8	140	481	64	132	26	8	12	82	.274	58	210	116	18-43
1954	LF-RF	BA/BO	AL	7/4	114	362	39	97	15	4	12	55	.268	30	156	108	—
1955	LF	BOS	AL	4-8	14	31	1	4	2	0	0	1	.129	0	6	—	—
1955	LF	CIN	NL	5-8	35	62	4	13	1	0	2	7	.210	5	20	—	—
1956	LF-RF	CLE	AL	2-8	57	114	17	29	7	0	4	20	.254	12	48	102	—
MAJOR LEAGUE TOTALS					1046	3437	406	916	168	39	80	544	.267	311	1402	109	5 yrs

William Dale Goodman
5'11   165 lbs   Batted left

Born Mar 22, 1926   Concord, NC
Died Oct 1, 1984   Sarasota, FL

YR	POS	TEAM	LG	FIN	G	AB	R	H	2B	3B	HR	RBI	AVG	BB	TB	OQ	RANK
1947	RF	BOS	AL	3-8	12	11	1	2	0	0	0	1	.182	1	2	—	—
1948	1B	BOS	AL	2-8	127	445	65	138	27	2	1	66	.310	74	172	116	16-45
1949	1B	BOS	AL	2-8	122	443	54	132	23	3	0	56	.298	58	161	101	30-41
1950	LF-3B	BOS	AL	3-8	110	424	91	150	25	3	4	68	.354	52	193	123	13-41
1951	1B-2B	BOS	AL	3-8	141	546	92	162	34	4	0	50	.297	79	204	110	21-39
1952	2B-1B	BOS	AL	6-8	138	513	79	157	27	3	4	56	.306	48	202	111	25-38
1953	2B-1B	BOS	AL	4-8	128	514	73	161	33	5	2	41	.313	57	210	114	20-43
1954	2B-1B	BOS	AL	4-8	127	489	71	148	25	4	1	36	.303	51	184	106	20-34
1955	2B	BOS	AL	4-8	149	599	100	176	31	2	0	52	.294	99	211	110	22-39
1956	2B	BOS	AL	4-8	105	399	61	117	22	8	2	38	.293	40	161	103	—
1957	3B	BO/BA	AL	3/5	91	279	37	82	11	3	3	33	.294	23	108	102	—
1958	3B	CHI	AL	2-8	116	425	41	127	15	5	0	40	.299	37	152	98	—
1959	3B	CHI	AL	1-8	104	268	21	67	14	1	1	28	.250	19	86	80	—
1960	3B-2B	CHI	AL	3-8	30	77	5	18	4	0	0	6	.234	12	22	—	—
1961	3B	CHI	AL	4-10	41	51	4	13	4	0	1	10	.255	7	20	—	—
1962	2B-3B	HOU	NL	8-10	82	161	12	41	4	1	0	10	.255	12	47	75	—
MAJOR LEAGUE TOTALS					1623	5644	807	1691	299	44	19	591	.300	669	2135	111	8 yrs

Albert Leonard Rosen   Born Feb 29, 1924   Spartanburg, SC
5'10   180 lbs   Batted right

YR	POS	TEAM	LG	FIN	G	AB	R	H	2B	3B	HR	RBI	AVG	BB	TB	OQ	RANK
1947	3B	CLE	AL	4-8	7	9	1	1	0	0	0	0	.111	0	1	—	—
1948	3B	CLE	AL	1-8	5	5	0	1	0	0	0	0	.200	0	1	—	—
1949	3B	CLE	AL	3-8	23	44	3	7	2	0	0	5	.159	7	9	—	—
1950	3B	CLE	AL	4-8	155	554	100	159	23	4	37	116	.287	100	301	140	3-41
1951	3B	CLE	AL	2-8	154	573	82	152	30	1	24	102	.265	85	256	120	14-39
1952	3B	CLE	AL	2-8	148	567	101	171	32	5	28	105	.302	75	297	148	3-38
1953	3B	CLE	AL	2-8	155	599	115	201	27	5	43	145	.336	85	367	171	1-43
1954	3B-1B	CLE	AL	1-8	137	466	76	140	20	2	24	102	.300	85	236	151	4-34
1955	3B-1B	CLE	AL	2-8	139	492	61	120	13	1	21	81	.244	92	198	117	15-39
1956	3B	CLE	AL	2-8	121	416	64	111	18	2	15	61	.267	58	178	112	22-40
MAJOR LEAGUE TOTALS					1044	3725	603	1063	165	20	192	717	.285	587	1844	137	7 yrs

Victor Woodrow Wertz   Born Feb 9, 1925   York, PA
6'0   186 lbs   Batted left   Died Jul 7, 1983   Detroit, MI

YR	POS	TEAM	LG	FIN	G	AB	R	H	2B	3B	HR	RBI	AVG	BB	TB	OQ	RANK
1947	LF	DET	AL	2-8	102	333	60	96	22	4	6	44	.288	47	144	126	—
1948	LF	DET	AL	5-8	119	391	49	97	19	9	7	67	.248	48	155	100	—
1949	RF	DET	AL	4-8	155	608	96	185	26	6	20	133	.304	80	283	123	12-41
1950	RF	DET	AL	2-8	149	559	99	172	37	4	27	123	.308	91	298	138	5-41
1951	RF	DET	AL	5-8	138	501	86	143	24	4	27	94	.285	78	256	139	5-39
1952	RF	DE/SL	AL	8/7	122	415	68	115	20	3	23	70	.277	69	210	146	4-38
1953	RF	SL	AL	8-8	128	440	61	118	18	6	19	70	.268	72	205	130	10-43
1954	1B-RF	BA/CL	AL	7/1	123	389	38	100	15	2	15	61	.257	45	164	111	—
1955	1B-RF	CLE	AL	2-8	74	257	30	65	11	2	14	55	.253	32	122	120	—
1956	1B	CLE	AL	2-8	136	481	65	127	22	0	32	106	.264	75	245	130	12-40
1957	1B	CLE	AL	6-8	144	515	84	145	21	0	28	105	.282	78	250	136	5-35
1958	1B	CLE	AL	4-8	25	43	5	12	1	0	3	12	.279	5	22	—	—
1959	1B	BOS	AL	5-8	94	247	38	68	13	0	7	49	.275	22	102	107	—
1960	1B	BOS	AL	7-8	131	443	45	125	22	0	19	103	.282	37	204	114	17-44
1961	1B	BO/DE	AL	6/2	107	323	33	84	16	2	11	61	.260	38	137	108	—
1962	1B	DET	AL	4-10	74	105	7	34	2	0	5	18	.324	5	51	118	—
1963	1B	DE/MN	AL	5/3	41	49	3	6	0	0	3	7	.122	6	15	—	—
MAJOR LEAGUE TOTALS					1862	6099	867	1692	289	42	266	1178	.277	828	2863	132	8 yrs

Jack Roosevelt Robinson   Born Jan 31, 1919   Cairo, GA
5'11   195 lbs   Batted right   Died Oct 24, 1972   Stamford, CT

YR	POS	TEAM	LG	FIN	G	AB	R	H	2B	3B	HR	RBI	AVG	BB	TB	OQ	RANK
1947	1B	BRO	NL	1-8	151	590	125	175	31	5	12	48	.297	74	252	116	18-44
1948	2B-1B	BRO	NL	3-8	147	574	108	170	38	8	12	85	.296	57	260	119	14-37
1949	2B	BRO	NL	1-8	156	593	122	203	38	12	16	124	.342	86	313	153	3-38
1950	2B	BRO	NL	2-8	144	518	99	170	39	4	14	81	.328	80	259	142	6-42
1951	2B	BRO	NL	2-8	153	548	106	185	33	7	19	88	.338	79	289	153	4-44
1952	2B	BRO	NL	1-8	149	510	104	157	17	3	19	75	.308	106	237	154	2-39
1953	LF-3B	BRO	NL	1-8	136	484	109	159	34	7	12	95	.329	74	243	140	8-44
1954	LF-3B	BRO	NL	2-8	124	386	62	120	22	4	15	59	.311	63	195	139	—
1955	3B	BRO	NL	1-8	105	317	51	81	6	2	8	36	.256	61	115	109	—
1956	3B-2B	BRO	NL	1-8	117	357	61	98	15	2	10	43	.275	60	147	120	—

MAJOR LEAGUE TOTALS   1382 4877 947 1518 273 54 137 734 .311 740 2310 140   7 yrs

Willie Edward Jones   Born Aug 16, 1925 Dillon, SC
6'1   188 lbs   Batted right   Died Oct 18, 1983 Cincinnati, OH

YR	POS	TEAM	LG	FIN	G	AB	R	H	2B	3B	HR	RBI	AVG	BB	TB	OQ	RANK
1947	3B	PHI	NL	7-8	18	62	5	14	0	1	0	10	.226	7	16	—	—
1948	3B	PHI	NL	6-8	17	60	9	20	2	0	2	9	.333	3	28	—	—
1949	3B	PHI	NL	3-8	149	532	71	130	35	1	19	77	.244	65	224	108	21-38
1950	3B	PHI	NL	1-8	157	610	100	163	28	6	25	88	.267	61	278	110	20-42
1951	3B	PHI	NL	5-8	148	564	79	161	28	5	22	81	.285	60	265	121	15-44
1952	3B	PHI	NL	4-8	147	541	60	135	12	3	18	72	.250	53	207	101	30-39
1953	3B	PHI	NL	3-8	149	481	61	108	16	2	19	70	.225	85	185	104	29-44
1954	3B	PHI	NL	4-8	142	535	64	145	28	3	12	56	.271	61	215	102	29-48
1955	3B	PHI	NL	4-8	146	516	65	133	20	3	16	81	.258	77	207	108	23-43
1956	3B	PHI	NL	5-8	149	520	88	144	20	4	17	78	.277	92	223	126	13-43
1957	3B	PHI	NL	5-8	133	440	58	96	19	2	9	47	.218	61	146	91	35-44
1958	3B	PHI	NL	8-8	118	398	52	108	15	1	14	60	.271	49	167	110	—
1959	3B	PH/CN	NL	8/5	119	393	56	101	21	2	14	55	.257	47	168	110	—
1959	3B	CLE	AL	2-8	11	18	1	4	1	0	0	1	.222	1	5	—	—
1960	3B	CIN	NL	6-8	79	149	16	40	7	0	3	27	.268	31	56	124	—
1961	3B	CIN	NL	1-8	9	7	1	0	0	0	0	0	.000	2	0	—	—

MAJOR LEAGUE TOTALS   1691 5826 786 1502 252 33 190 812 .258 755 2390 108   9 yrs

Lawrence Eugene Doby　　　　　Born Dec 13, 1924　Camden, SC
6'1　180 lbs　Batted left

YR	POS	TEAM	LG	FIN	G	AB	R	H	2B	3B	HR	RBI	AVG	BB	TB	OQ	RANK
1947	2B-SS	CLE	AL	4-8	29	32	3	5	1	0	0	2	.156	1	6	—	—
1948	RF	CLE	AL	1-8	121	439	83	132	23	9	14	66	.301	54	215	127	9-45
1949	CF	CLE	AL	3-8	147	547	106	153	25	3	24	85	.280	91	256	126	9-41
1950	CF	CLE	AL	4-8	142	503	110	164	25	5	25	102	.326	98	274	151	1-41
1951	CF	CLE	AL	2-8	134	447	84	132	27	5	20	69	.295	101	229	156	2-39
1952	CF	CLE	AL	2-8	140	519	104	143	26	8	32	104	.276	90	281	155	1-38
1953	CF	CLE	AL	2-8	149	513	92	135	18	5	29	102	.263	96	250	138	7-43
1954	CF	CLE	AL	1-8	153	577	94	157	18	4	32	126	.272	85	279	133	6-34
1955	CF	CLE	AL	2-8	131	491	91	143	17	5	26	75	.291	61	248	133	4-39
1956	CF	CHI	AL	3-8	140	504	89	135	22	3	24	102	.268	102	235	132	11-40
1957	CF	CHI	AL	2-8	119	416	57	120	27	2	14	79	.288	56	193	129	9-35
1958	CF	CLE	AL	4-8	89	247	41	70	10	1	13	45	.283	26	121	129	—
1959	RF-LF	DE/CH	AL	4/1	39	113	6	26	4	2	0	13	.230	10	34	78	—
MAJOR LEAGUE TOTALS					1533	5348	960	1515	243	52	253	970	.283	871	2621	138	10 yrs

Rich Ashburn　　　　　Born Mar 19, 1927　Tilden, NE
5'10　170 lbs　Batted left

YR	POS	TEAM	LG	FIN	G	AB	R	H	2B	3B	HR	RBI	AVG	BB	TB	OQ	RANK
1948	CF	PHI	NL	6-8	117	463	78	154	17	4	2	40	.333	60	185	120	12-37
1949	CF	PHI	NL	3-8	154	662	84	188	18	11	1	37	.284	58	231	91	30-38
1950	CF	PHI	NL	1-8	151	594	84	180	25	14	2	41	.303	63	239	106	27-42
1951	CF	PHI	NL	5-8	154	643	92	221	31	5	4	63	.344	50	274	116	20-44
1952	CF	PHI	NL	4-8	154	613	93	173	31	6	1	42	.282	75	219	106	25-39
1953	CF	PHI	NL	3-8	156	622	110	205	25	9	2	57	.330	61	254	109	25-44
1954	CF	PHI	NL	4-8	153	559	111	175	16	8	1	41	.313	125	210	125	11-48
1955	CF	PHI	NL	4-8	140	533	91	180	32	9	3	42	.338	105	239	142	8-43
1956	CF	PHI	NL	5-8	154	628	94	190	26	8	3	50	.303	79	241	110	24-43
1957	CF	PHI	NL	5-8	156	626	93	186	26	8	0	33	.297	94	228	111	18-44
1958	CF	PHI	NL	8-8	152	615	98	215	24	13	2	33	.350	97	271	135	5-34
1959	CF	PHI	NL	8-8	153	564	86	150	16	2	1	20	.266	79	173	91	33-38
1960	CF	CHI	NL	7-8	151	547	99	159	16	5	0	40	.291	116	185	120	11-38
1961	CF	CHI	NL	7-8	109	307	49	79	7	4	0	19	.257	55	94	97	—
1962	RF	NY	NL	10-10	135	389	60	119	7	3	7	28	.306	81	153	131	—
MAJOR LEAGUE TOTALS					2189	8365	1322	2574	317	109	29	586	.308	1198	3196	114	13 yrs

Roy Campanella   Born Nov 19, 1921 Philadelphia, PA
5'9 190 lbs Batted right   Died Jun 26, 1993 Woodland Hills, CA

YR	POS	TEAM	LG	FIN	G	AB	R	H	2B	3B	HR	RBI	AVG	BB	TB	OQ	RANK
1948	C	BRO	NL	3-8	83	279	32	72	11	3	9	45	.258	36	116	111	—
1949	C	BRO	NL	1-8	130	436	65	125	22	2	22	82	.287	67	217	137	6-38
1950	C	BRO	NL	2-8	126	437	70	123	19	3	31	89	.281	55	241	137	9-42
1951	C	BRO	NL	2-8	143	505	90	164	33	1	33	108	.325	53	298	155	3-44
1952	C	BRO	NL	1-8	128	468	73	126	18	1	22	97	.269	57	212	124	11-39
1953	C	BRO	NL	1-8	144	519	103	162	26	3	41	142	.312	67	317	155	4-44
1954	C	BRO	NL	2-8	111	397	43	82	14	3	19	51	.207	42	159	92	—
1955	C	BRO	NL	1-8	123	446	81	142	20	1	32	107	.318	56	260	151	4-43
1956	C	BRO	NL	1-8	124	388	39	85	6	1	20	73	.219	66	153	108	—
1957	C	BRO	NL	3-8	103	330	31	80	9	0	13	62	.242	34	128	98	—

MAJOR LEAGUE TOTALS   1215 4205 627 1161 178 18 242 856 .276 533 2101 143   6 yrs

Raymond Otis Boone   Born Jul 27, 1923   San Diego, CA
6'0 172 lbs Batted right

YR	POS	TEAM	LG	FIN	G	AB	R	H	2B	3B	HR	RBI	AVG	BB	TB	OQ	RANK
1948	SS	CLE	AL	1-8	6	5	0	2	1	0	0	1	.400	0	3	—	—
1949	SS	CLE	AL	3-8	86	258	39	65	4	4	4	26	.252	38	89	94	—
1950	SS	CLE	AL	4-8	109	365	53	110	14	6	7	58	.301	56	157	115	—
1951	SS	CLE	AL	2-8	151	544	65	127	14	1	12	51	.233	48	179	81	37-39
1952	SS	CLE	AL	2-8	103	316	57	83	8	2	7	45	.263	53	116	114	—
1953	3B-SS	CL/DE	AL	2/6	135	497	94	147	17	8	26	114	.296	72	258	142	4-43
1954	3B	DET	AL	5-8	148	543	76	160	19	7	20	85	.295	71	253	130	9-34
1955	3B	DET	AL	5-8	135	500	61	142	22	7	20	116	.284	50	238	120	10-39
1956	3B	DET	AL	5-8	131	481	77	148	14	6	25	81	.308	77	249	141	6-40
1957	1B	DET	AL	4-8	129	462	48	126	25	3	12	65	.273	57	193	114	18-35
1958	1B	DE/CH	AL	5/2	116	360	41	87	16	2	13	61	.242	32	146	101	—
1959	1B	CH/KC	AL	1/7	70	153	22	41	6	0	3	17	.268	34	56	124	—
1959	1B	MIL	NL	2-8	13	15	3	3	0	0	1	2	.200	4	6	—	—
1960	1B	MIL	NL	2-8	7	12	3	3	1	0	0	4	.250	5	4	—	—
1960	1B	BOS	AL	7-8	34	78	6	16	1	0	1	11	.205	11	20	—	—

MAJOR LEAGUE TOTALS   1373 4589 645 1260 162 46 151 737 .275 608 1967 121   6 yrs

Donald Frederick Mueller Born Apr 14, 1927 St Louis, MO
6'0 185 lbs Batted left

YR	POS	TEAM	LG	FIN	G	AB	R	H	2B	3B	HR	RBI	AVG	BB	TB	OQ	RANK
1948	LF	NY	NL	5-8	36	81	12	29	4	1	1	9	.358	0	38	—	—
1949	RF	NY	NL	5-8	51	56	5	13	4	0	0	1	.232	5	17	—	—
1950	RF	NY	NL	3-8	132	525	60	153	15	6	7	84	.291	10	201	82	40-42
1951	RF	NY	NL	1-8	122	469	58	130	10	7	16	69	.277	19	202	98	37-44
1952	RF	NY	NL	2-8	126	456	61	128	14	7	12	49	.281	34	192	109	22-39
1953	RF	NY	NL	5-8	131	480	56	160	12	2	6	60	.333	19	194	96	35-44
1954	RF	NY	NL	1-8	153	619	90	212	35	8	4	71	.342	22	275	105	24-48
1955	RF	NY	NL	3-8	147	605	67	185	21	4	8	83	.306	19	238	89	39-43
1956	RF	NY	NL	6-8	138	453	38	122	12	1	5	41	.269	15	151	75	43-43
1957	RF	NY	NL	6-8	135	450	45	116	7	1	6	37	.258	13	143	71	44-44
1958	RF	CHI	AL	2-8	70	166	7	42	5	0	0	16	.253	11	47	73	—
1959	PH	CHI	AL	1-8	4	4	0	2	0	0	0	0	.500	0	2	—	—

| MAJOR LEAGUE TOTALS | | | | | 1245 | 4364 | 499 | 1292 | 139 | 37 | 65 | 520 | .296 | 167 | 1700 | 91 | 8 yrs |

Henry Albert Bauer Born Jul 31, 1922 East St Louis, MO
6'0 192 lbs Batted right

YR	POS	TEAM	LG	FIN	G	AB	R	H	2B	3B	HR	RBI	AVG	BB	TB	OQ	RANK
1948	LF-RF	NY	AL	3-8	19	50	6	9	1	1	1	9	.180	6	15	—	—
1949	RF	NY	AL	1-8	103	301	56	82	6	6	10	45	.272	37	130	109	—
1950	RF	NY	AL	1-8	113	415	72	133	16	2	13	70	.320	35	192	111	—
1951	RF	NY	AL	1-8	118	348	53	103	19	3	10	54	.296	42	158	121	—
1952	RF	NY	AL	1-8	141	553	86	162	31	6	17	74	.293	50	256	123	14-38
1953	RF	NY	AL	1-8	133	437	77	133	20	6	10	57	.304	59	195	126	13-43
1954	RF	NY	AL	2-8	114	377	73	111	16	5	12	54	.294	40	173	123	—
1955	RF	NY	AL	1-8	139	492	97	137	20	5	20	53	.278	56	227	119	12-39
1956	RF	NY	AL	1-8	147	539	96	130	18	7	26	84	.241	59	240	105	27-40
1957	RF	NY	AL	1-8	137	479	70	124	22	9	18	65	.259	42	218	112	20-35
1958	RF	NY	AL	1-8	128	452	62	121	22	6	12	50	.268	32	191	105	23-39
1959	RF	NY	AL	3-8	114	341	44	81	20	0	9	39	.238	33	128	95	—
1960	RF	KC	AL	8-8	95	255	30	70	15	0	3	31	.275	21	94	94	—
1961	RF-LF	KC	AL	9-10	43	106	11	28	3	1	3	18	.264	9	42	97	—

| MAJOR LEAGUE TOTALS | | | | | 1544 | 5145 | 833 | 1424 | 229 | 57 | 164 | 703 | .277 | 521 | 2259 | 115 | 6 yrs |

Roberto Francisco Avila
5'10   175 lbs Batted right

Born Apr 2, 1924   Veracruz, Mexico

YR	POS	TEAM	LG	FIN	G	AB	R	H	2B	3B	HR	RBI	AVG	BB	TB	OQ	RANK
1949	2B	CLE	AL	3-8	31	14	3	3	0	0	0	3	.214	1	3	—	—
1950	2B	CLE	AL	4-8	80	201	39	60	10	2	1	21	.299	29	77	103	—
1951	2B	CLE	AL	2-8	141	542	76	165	21	3	10	58	.304	60	222	111	18-39
1952	2B	CLE	AL	2-8	150	597	102	179	26	11	7	45	.300	67	248	119	20-38
1953	2B	CLE	AL	2-8	141	559	85	160	22	3	8	55	.286	58	212	102	30-43
1954	2B	CLE	AL	1-8	143	555	112	189	27	2	15	67	.341	59	265	136	5-34
1955	2B	CLE	AL	2-8	141	537	83	146	22	4	13	61	.272	82	215	114	18-39
1956	2B	CLE	AL	2-8	138	513	74	115	14	2,	10	54	.224	70	163	84	33-40
1957	2B-3B	CLE	AL	6-8	129	463	60	124	19	3	5	48	.268	46	164	95	29-35
1958	2B-3B	CLE	AL	4-8	113	375	54	95	21	3	5	30	.253	55	137	107	—
1959	2B-RF	BA/BO	AL	6/5	42	92	8	19	0	0	3	6	.207	10	28	80	—
1959	2B	MIL	NL	2-8	51	172	29	41	3	2	3	19	.238	24	57	93	—

| MAJOR LEAGUE TOTALS | | | | | 1300 | 4620 | 725 | 1296 | 185 | 35 | 80 | 467 | .281 | 561 | 1791 | 109 | 7 yrs |

Roy Edward Sievers
6'1   195 lbs Batted right

Born Nov 18, 1926 St Louis, MO

YR	POS	TEAM	LG	FIN	G	AB	R	H	2B	3B	HR	RBI	AVG	BB	TB	OQ	RANK
1949	LF	SL	AL	7-8	140	471	84	144	28	1	16	91	.306	70	222	128	8-41
1950	CF-3B	SL	AL	7-8	113	370	46	88	20	4	10	57	.238	34	146	88	—
1951	CF-LF	SL	AL	8-8	31	89	10	20	2	1	1	11	.225	9	27	—	—
1952	1B	SL	AL	7-8	11	30	3	6	3	0	0	5	.200	1	9	—	—
1953	1B	SL	AL	8-8	92	285	37	77	15	0	8	35	.270	32	116	107	—
1954	LF	WAS	AL	6-8	145	514	75	119	26	6	24	102	.232	80	229	120	16-34
1955	LF-1B	WAS	AL	8-8	144	509	74	138	20	8	25	106	.271	73	249	130	6-39
1956	LF-1B	WAS	AL	7-8	152	550	92	139	27	2	29	95	.253	100	257	125	13-40
1957	LF-1B	WAS	AL	8-8	152	572	99	172	23	5	42	114	.301	76	331	156	3-35
1958	LF-1B	WAS	AL	8-8	148	550	85	162	18	1	39	108	.295	53	299	141	6-39
1959	1B-LF	WAS	AL	8-8	115	385	55	93	19	0	21	49	.242	53	175	120	—
1960	1B	CHI	AL	3-8	127	444	87	131	22	0	28	93	.295	74	237	150	3-44
1961	1B	CHI	AL	4-10	141	492	76	145	26	6	27	92	.295	61	264	139	7-49
1962	1B	PHI	NL	7-10	144	477	61	125	19	5	21	80	.262	56	217	118	23-51
1963	1B	PHI	NL	4-10	138	450	46	108	19	2	19	82	.240	43	188	114	23-50
1964	1B	PHI	NL	2-10	49	120	7	22	3	1	4	16	.183	13	39	87	—
1964	1B	WAS	AL	9-10	33	58	5	10	1	0	4	11	.172	9	23	—	—
1965	1B	WAS	AL	8-10	12	21	3	4	1	0	0	0	.190	4	5	—	—

| MAJOR LEAGUE TOTALS | | | | | 1887 | 6387 | 945 | 1703 | 292 | 42 | 318 | 1147 | .267 | 841 | 3033 | 132 | 10 yrs |

Gus Edward Zernial Born Jun 27, 1923 Beaumont, TX
6'2 210 lbs Batted right

YR	POS	TEAM	LG	FIN	G	AB	R	H	2B	3B	HR	RBI	AVG	BB	TB	OQ	RANK
1949	LF	CHI	AL	6-8	73	198	29	63	17	2	5	38	.318	15	99	121	—
1950	LF	CHI	AL	6-8	143	543	75	152	16	4	29	93	.280	38	263	106	27-41
1951	LF	CH/PH	AL	4/6	143	571	92	153	30	5	33	129	.268	63	292	126	10-39
1952	LF	PHI	AL	4-8	145	549	76	144	15	1	29	100	.262	70	248	124	13-38
1953	LF	PHI	AL	7-8	147	556	85	158	21	3	42	108	.284	57	311	140	6-43
1954	LF	PHI	AL	8-8	97	336	42	84	8	2	14	62	.250	30	138	102	—
1955	LF	KC	AL	6-8	120	413	62	105	9	3	30	84	.254	30	210	116	—
1956	LF	KC	AL	8-8	109	272	36	61	12	0	16	44	.224	33	121	105	—
1957	LF	KC	AL	7-8	131	437	56	103	20	1	27	69	.236	34	206	110	22-35
1958	LF	DET	AL	5-8	66	124	8	40	7	1	5	23	.323	6	64	129	—
1959	1B	DET	AL	4-8	60	132	11	30	4	0	7	26	.227	7	55	94	—

MAJOR LEAGUE TOTALS 1234 4131 572 1093 159 22 237 776 .265 383 2007 121 5 yrs

Saturnino Orestes Armas Minoso Born Nov 29, 1922 Havana, Cuba
5'10 175 lbs Batted right

YR	POS	TEAM	LG	FIN	G	AB	R	H	2B	3B	HR	RBI	AVG	BB	TB	OQ	RANK
1949	RF	CLE	AL	3-8	9	16	2	3	0	0	1	1	.188	2	6	—	—
1951	LF-3B	CL/CH	AL	2/4	146	530	112	173	34	14	10	76	.326	72	265	140	4-39
1952	LF	CHI	AL	3-8	147	569	96	160	24	9	13	61	.281	71	241	120	18-38
1953	LF	CHI	AL	3-8	151	556	104	174	24	8	15	104	.313	74	259	132	9-43
1954	LF	CHI	AL	3-8	153	568	119	182	29	18	19	116	.320	77	304	152	3-34
1955	LF	CHI	AL	3-8	139	517	79	149	26	7	10	70	.288	76	219	120	11-39
1956	LF	CHI	AL	3-8	151	545	106	172	29	11	21	88	.316	86	286	144	5-40
1957	LF	CHI	AL	2-8	153	568	96	176	36	5	12	103	.310	79	258	132	7-35
1958	LF	CLE	AL	4-8	149	556	94	168	25	2	24	80	.302	59	269	131	10-39
1959	LF	CLE	AL	2-8	148	570	92	172	32	0	21	92	.302	54	267	124	13-35
1960	LF	CHI	AL	3-8	154	591	89	184	32	4	20	105	.311	52	284	125	10-44
1961	LF	CHI	AL	4-10	152	540	91	151	28	3	14	82	.280	67	227	112	25-49
1962	LF	SL	NL	6-10	39	97	14	19	5	0	1	10	.196	7	27	66	—
1963	LF	WAS	AL	10-10	109	315	38	72	12	2	4	30	.229	33	100	87	—
1964	LF	CHI	AL	2-10	30	31	4	7	0	0	1	5	.226	5	10	—	—
1976	DH	CHI	AL	6-6	3	8	0	1	0	0	0	0	.125	0	1	—	—
1980	PH	CHI	AL	5-7	2	2	0	0	0	0	0	0	.000	0	0	—	—

MAJOR LEAGUE TOTALS 1835 6579 1136 1963 336 83 186 1023 .298 814 3023 130 11 yrs

Walter Charles Post　　　　　Born Jul 9, 1929　St Wendelin, OH
6'1　190 lbs　Batted right　　　　Died Jan 6, 1982　St Henry, OH

YR	POS	TEAM	LG	FIN	G	AB	R	H	2B	3B	HR	RBI	AVG	BB	TB	OQ	RANK
1949	RF-CF	CIN	NL	7-8	6	8	1	2	0	0	0	1	.250	0	2	—	—
1951	CF	CIN	NL	6-8	15	41	6	9	3	0	1	7	.220	3	15	—	—
1952	LF	CIN	NL	6-8	19	58	5	9	1	0	2	7	.155	4	16	—	—
1953	RF-CF	CIN	NL	6-8	11	33	3	8	1	0	1	4	.242	4	12	—	—
1954	RF	CIN	NL	5-8	130	451	46	115	21	3	18	83	.255	26	196	95	37-48
1955	RF	CIN	NL	5-8	154	601	116	186	33	3	40	109	.309	60	345	142	7-43
1956	RF	CIN	NL	3-8	143	539	94	134	25	3	36	83	.249	37	273	115	20-43
1957	RF	CIN	NL	4-8	134	467	68	114	26	2	20	74	.244	33	204	101	27-44
1958	RF	PHI	NL	8-8	110	379	51	107	21	3	12	62	.282	32	170	109	—
1959	RF	PHI	NL	8-8	132	468	62	119	17	6	22	94	.254	36	214	107	21-38
1960	LF	PH/CN	NL	8/6	111	333	47	94	20	1	19	50	.282	37	173	136	—
1961	LF	CIN	NL	1-8	99	282	44	83	16	3	20	57	.294	22	165	139	—
1962	LF	CIN	NL	3-10	109	285	43	75	10	3	17	62	.263	32	142	126	—
1963	LF	CIN	NL	5-10	5	7	1	0	0	0	0	0	.000	0	0	—	—
1963	RF	MIN	AL	3-10	21	47	6	9	0	1	2	6	.191	2	17	—	—
1964	RF	CLE	AL	6-10	5	8	1	0	0	0	0	0	.000	3	0	—	—
MAJOR LEAGUE TOTALS					1204	4007	594	1064	194	28	210	699	.266	331	1944	112	5 yrs

Delmar Wesley Crandall　　　　Born Mar 5, 1930　Ontario, CA
6'1　180 lbs　Batted right

YR	POS	TEAM	LG	FIN	G	AB	R	H	2B	3B	HR	RBI	AVG	BB	TB	OQ	RANK
1949	C	BOS	NL	4-8	67	228	21	60	10	1	4	34	.263	9	84	83	—
1950	C	BOS	NL	4-8	79	255	21	56	11	0	4	37	.220	13	79	67	—
1953	C	MIL	NL	2-8	116	382	55	104	13	1	15	51	.272	33	164	102	—
1954	C	MIL	NL	3-8	138	463	60	112	18	2	21	64	.242	40	197	97	36-48
1955	C	MIL	NL	2-8	133	440	61	104	15	2	26	62	.236	40	201	105	25-43
1956	C	MIL	NL	2-8	112	311	37	74	14	2	16	48	.238	35	140	111	—
1957	C	MIL	NL	1-8	118	383	45	97	11	2	15	46	.253	30	157	99	—
1958	C	MIL	NL	1-8	131	427	50	116	23	1	18	63	.272	48	195	115	18-34
1959	C	MIL	NL	2-8	150	518	65	133	19	2	21	72	.257	46	219	103	24-38
1960	C	MIL	NL	2-8	142	537	81	158	14	1	19	77	.294	34	231	108	24-38
1961	C	MIL	NL	4-8	15	30	3	6	3	0	0	1	.200	1	9	—	—
1962	C	MIL	NL	5-10	107	350	35	104	12	3	8	45	.297	27	146	107	—
1963	C	MIL	NL	6-10	86	259	18	52	4	0	3	28	.201	18	65	68	—
1964	C	SF	NL	4-10	69	195	12	45	8	1	3	11	.231	22	64	94	—
1965	C	PIT	NL	3-10	60	140	11	30	2	0	2	10	.214	14	38	77	—
1966	C	CLE	AL	5-10	50	108	10	25	2	0	4	8	.231	14	39	106	—
MAJOR LEAGUE TOTALS					1573	5026	585	1276	179	18	179	657	.254	424	2028	106	5 yrs

Daniel Francis O'Connell Born Jan 21, 1927 Paterson, NJ
5'11 168 lbs Batted right Died Oct 2, 1969 Clifton, NJ

YR	POS	TEAM	LG	FIN	G	AB	R	H	2B	3B	HR	RBI	AVG	BB	TB	OQ	RANK
1950	SS-3B	PIT	NL	8-8	79	315	39	92	16	1	8	32	.292	24	134	103	—
1953	3B-2B	PIT	NL	8-8	149	588	88	173	26	8	7	55	.294	57	236	102	32-44
1954	2B-3B	MIL	NL	3-8	146	541	61	151	28	4	2	37	.279	38	193	85	43-48
1955	2B	MIL	NL	2-8	124	453	47	102	15	4	6	40	.225	28	143	71	43-43
1956	2B	MIL	NL	2-8	139	498	71	119	17	9	2	42	.239	76	160	93	34-43
1957	2B-3B	MIL/NY	NL	1/6	143	547	86	140	27	4	8	36	.256	52	199	93	33-44
1958	2B	SF	NL	3-8	107	306	44	71	12	2	3	23	.232	51	96	92	—
1959	3B-2B	SF	NL	3-8	34	58	6	11	3	0	0	0	.190	5	14	—	—
1961	3B-2B	WAS	AL	9-10	138	493	61	128	30	1	1	37	.260	77	163	97	32-49
1962	3B-2B	WAS	AL	10-10	84	236	24	62	7	2	2	18	.263	23	79	88	—
MAJOR LEAGUE TOTALS					1143	4035	527	1049	181	35	39	320	.260	431	1417	90	6 yrs

Joseph Wilbur Adcock Born Oct 30, 1927 Coushatta, LA
6'4 210 lbs Batted right

YR	POS	TEAM	LG	FIN	G	AB	R	H	2B	3B	HR	RBI	AVG	BB	TB	OQ	RANK
1950	LF-1B	CIN	NL	6-8	102	372	46	109	16	1	8	55	.293	24	151	97	—
1951	LF	CIN	NL	6-8	113	395	40	96	16	4	10	47	.243	24	150	88	—
1952	LF-1B	CIN	NL	6-8	117	378	43	105	22	4	13	52	.278	23	174	114	—
1953	1B	MIL	NL	2-8	157	590	71	168	33	6	18	80	.285	42	267	105	27-44
1954	1B	MIL	NL	3-8	133	500	73	154	27	5	23	87	.308	44	260	126	10-48
1955	1B	MIL	NL	2-8	84	288	40	76	14	0	15	45	.264	31	135	114	—
1956	1B	MIL	NL	2-8	137	454	76	132	23	1	38	103	.291	32	271	141	4-43
1957	1B	MIL	NL	1-8	65	209	31	60	13	2	12	38	.287	20	113	135	—
1958	1B-LF	MIL	NL	1-8	105	320	40	88	15	1	19	54	.275	21	162	116	—
1959	1B-LF	MIL	NL	2-8	115	404	53	118	19	2	25	76	.292	32	216	130	—
1960	1B	MIL	NL	2-8	138	514	55	153	21	4	25	91	.298	46	257	130	8-38
1961	1B	MIL	NL	4-8	152	562	77	160	20	0	35	108	.285	59	285	126	12-37
1962	1B	MIL	NL	5-10	121	391	48	97	12	1	29	78	.248	50	198	128	—
1963	1B	CLE	AL	5-10	97	283	28	71	7	1	13	49	.251	30	119	112	—
1964	1B	LA	AL	5-10	118	366	39	98	13	0	21	64	.268	48	174	131	—
1965	1B	CAL	AL	7-10	122	349	30	84	14	0	14	47	.241	37	140	108	—
1966	1B	CAL	AL	6-10	83	231	33	63	10	3	18	48	.273	31	133	161	—
MAJOR LEAGUE TOTALS					1959	6606	823	1832	295	35	336	1122	.277	594	3205	126	5 yrs

Alfonso Carrasquel

Born Jan 23, 1928 Caracas, Venezuela

6'0 170 lbs Batted right

YR	POS	TEAM	LG	FIN	G	AB	R	H	2B	3B	HR	RBI	AVG	BB	TB	OQ	RANK
1950	SS	CHI	AL	6-8	141	524	72	148	21	5	4	46	.282	66	191	94	36-41
1951	SS	CHI	AL	4-8	147	538	41	142	22	4	2	58	.264	46	178	84	34-39
1952	SS	CHI	AL	3-8	100	359	36	89	7	4	1	42	.248	33	107	82	—
1953	SS	CHI	AL	3-8	149	552	72	154	30	4	2	47	.279	38	198	89	38-43
1954	SS	CHI	AL	3-8	155	620	106	158	28	3	12	62	.255	85	228	104	22-34
1955	SS	CHI	AL	3-8	145	523	83	134	11	2	11	52	.256	61	182	93	36-39
1956	SS	CLE	AL	2-8	141	474	60	115	15	1	7	48	.243	52	153	82	37-40
1957	SS	CLE	AL	6-8	125	392	37	108	14	1	8	57	.276	41	148	102	—
1958	SS-3B	CL/KC	AL	4/7	108	316	33	74	11	1	4	34	.234	35	99	86	—
1959	SS-2B	BAL	AL	6-8	114	346	28	77	13	0	4	28	.223	34	102	78	—

MAJOR LEAGUE TOTALS   1325 4644 568 1199 172 25 55 474 .258 491 1586 91 6 yrs

James Anthony Piersall

Born Nov 14, 1929 Waterbury, CT

6'0 175 lbs Batted right

YR	POS	TEAM	LG	FIN	G	AB	R	H	2B	3B	HR	RBI	AVG	BB	TB	OQ	RANK
1950	CF	BOS	AL	3-8	6	7	4	2	0	0	0	0	.286	4	2	—	—
1952	SS-RF	BOS	AL	6-8	56	161	28	43	8	0	1	16	.267	28	54	109	—
1953	RF	BOS	AL	4-8	151	585	76	159	21	9	3	52	.272	41	207	88	39-43
1954	RF	BOS	AL	4-8	133	474	77	135	24	2	8	38	.285	36	187	101	24-34
1955	CF	BOS	AL	4-8	149	515	68	146	25	5	13	62	.283	67	220	116	16-39
1956	CF	BOS	AL	4-8	155	601	91	176	40	6	14	87	.293	58	270	111	24-40
1957	CF	BOS	AL	3-8	151	609	103	159	27	5	19	63	.261	62	253	108	24-35
1958	CF	BOS	AL	3-8	130	417	55	99	13	5	8	48	.237	42	146	92	—
1959	CF	CLE	AL	2-8	100	317	42	78	13	2	4	30	.246	25	107	85	—
1960	CF	CLE	AL	4-8	138	486	70	137	12	4	18	66	.282	24	211	102	27-44
1961	CF	CLE	AL	5-10	121	484	81	156	26	7	6	40	.322	43	214	116	22-49
1962	CF	WAS	AL	10-10	135	471	38	115	20	4	4	31	.244	39	155	82	52-54
1963	CF-RF	WA/LA	AL	10/9	49	146	13	39	2	0	1	9	.267	11	44	82	—
1963	CF	NY	NL	10-10	40	124	13	24	4	1	1	10	.194	10	33	73	—
1964	LF-CF	LA	AL	5-10	87	255	28	80	11	0	2	13	.314	16	97	102	—
1965	LF-CF	CAL	AL	7-10	53	112	10	30	5	2	2	12	.268	5	45	99	—
1966	RF-LF	CAL	AL	6-10	75	123	14	26	5	0	0	14	.211	13	31	75	—
1967	LF	CAL	AL	5-10	5	3	0	0	0	0	0	0	.000	0	0	—	—

MAJOR LEAGUE TOTALS   1734 5890 811 1604 256 52 104 591 .272 524 2276 103 8 yrs

James Robert Lemon   Born Mar 23, 1928 Covington, VA
6'4 200 lbs Batted right

YR	POS	TEAM	LG	FIN	G	AB	R	H	2B	3B	HR	RBI	AVG	BB	TB	OQ	RANK
1950	LF	CLE	AL	4-8	12	34	4	6	1	0	1	1	.176	3	10	—	—
1953	LF-1B	CLE	AL	2-8	16	46	5	8	1	0	1	5	.174	3	12	—	—
1954	RF	WAS	AL	6-8	37	128	12	30	2	3	2	13	.234	9	44	83	—
1955	RF	WAS	AL	8-8	10	25	3	5	2	0	1	3	.200	3	10	—	—
1956	RF	WAS	AL	7-8	146	538	77	146	21	11	27	96	.271	65	270	123	15-40
1957	RF	WAS	AL	8-8	137	518	58	147	23	6	17	64	.284	49	233	117	17-35
1958	RF	WAS	AL	8-8	142	501	65	123	15	9	26	75	.246	50	234	117	18-39
1959	LF	WAS	AL	8-8	147	531	73	148	18	3	33	100	.279	46	271	128	10-35
1960	LF	WAS	AL	5-8	148	528	81	142	10	1	38	100	.269	67	268	131	6-44
1961	LF	MIN	AL	7-10	129	423	57	109	26	1	14	52	.258	44	179	105	—
1962	RF-LF	MIN	AL	2-10	12	17	1	3	0	0	1	5	.176	3	6	—	—
1963	1B-LF	MN/CH	AL	3/2	43	97	4	18	0	1	1	9	.186	13	23	73	—
1963	LF	PHI	NL	4-10	31	59	6	16	2	0	2	6	.271	8	24	—	—

| MAJOR LEAGUE TOTALS | | | | | 1010 | 3445 | 446 | 901 | 121 | 35 | 164 | 529 | .262 | 363 | 1584 | 123 | 5 yrs |

James Franklin Busby   Born Jan 8, 1927   Kenedy, TX
6'1 175 lbs Batted right

YR	POS	TEAM	LG	FIN	G	AB	R	H	2B	3B	HR	RBI	AVG	BB	TB	OQ	RANK
1950	CF	CHI	AL	6-8	18	48	5	10	0	0	0	4	.208	1	10	—	—
1951	CF	CHI	AL	4-8	143	477	59	135	15	2	5	68	.283	40	169	91	33-39
1952	CF	CH/WA	AL	3/5	145	551	63	130	24	4	2	47	.236	24	168	72	38-38
1953	CF	WAS	AL	5-8	150	586	68	183	28	7	6	82	.312	38	243	105	26-43
1954	CF	WAS	AL	6-8	155	628	83	187	22	7	7	80	.298	43	244	100	26-34
1955	CF	WA/CH	AL	8/3	146	528	61	126	19	6	7	41	.239	38	178	80	37-39
1956	CF	CLE	AL	2-8	135	494	72	116	17	3	12	50	.235	43	175	83	35-40
1957	CF	CL/BA	AL	6/5	116	362	40	86	12	2	5	23	.238	24	117	78	—
1958	CF	BAL	AL	6-8	113	215	32	51	7	2	3	19	.237	24	71	90	—
1959	CF	BOS	AL	5-8	61	102	16	23	8	0	1	5	.225	5	34	76	—
1960	CF	BO/BA	AL	7/2	80	159	25	41	7	1	0	12	.258	20	50	89	—
1961	CF	BAL	AL	3-10	75	89	15	23	3	1	0	6	.258	8	28	—	—
1962	CF	HOU	NL	8-10	15	11	2	2	0	0	0	1	.182	2	2	—	—

| MAJOR LEAGUE TOTALS | | | | | 1352 | 4250 | 541 | 1113 | 162 | 35 | 48 | 438 | .262 | 310 | 1489 | 89 | 6 yrs |

Jack Eugene Jensen
5'11 190 lbs Batted right

Born Mar 9, 1927 San Francisco, CA
Died Jul 14, 1982 Charlottesville, VA

YR	POS	TEAM	LG	FIN	G	AB	R	H	2B	3B	HR	RBI	AVG	BB	TB	OQ	RANK
1950	LF	NY	AL	1-8	45	70	13	12	2	2	1	5	.171	7	21	—	—
1951	CF	NY	AL	1-8	56	168	30	50	8	1	8	25	.298	18	84	128	—
1952	RF	NY/WA	AL	1/5	151	589	83	165	30	6	10	82	.280	67	237	113	23-38
1953	RF	WAS	AL	5-8	147	552	87	147	32	8	10	84	.266	73	225	111	22-43
1954	CF	BOS	AL	4-8	152	580	92	160	25	7	25	117	.276	79	274	129	11-34
1955	RF	BOS	AL	4-8	152	574	95	158	27	6	26	116	.275	89	275	131	5-39
1956	RF	BOS	AL	4-8	151	578	80	182	23	11	20	97	.315	89	287	137	7-40
1957	RF	BOS	AL	3-8	145	544	82	153	29	2	23	103	.281	75	255	130	8-35
1958	RF	BOS	AL	3-8	154	548	83	157	31	0	35	122	.286	99	293	156	4-39
1959	RF	BOS	AL	5-8	148	535	101	148	31	0	28	112	.277	88	263	140	4-35
1961	RF	BOS	AL	6-10	137	498	64	131	21	2	13	66	.263	66	195	105	29-49
MAJOR LEAGUE TOTALS					1438	5236	810	1463	259	45	199	929	.279	750	2409	128	9 yrs

David Russell Bell
6'1 190 lbs Batted left

Born Nov 15, 1928 Louisville, KY

YR	POS	TEAM	LG	FIN	G	AB	R	H	2B	3B	HR	RBI	AVG	BB	TB	OQ	RANK
1950	RF	PIT	NL	8-8	111	422	62	119	22	11	8	53	.282	28	187	103	—
1951	RF	PIT	NL	7-8	149	600	80	167	27	12	16	89	.278	42	266	107	29-44
1952	RF	PIT	NL	8-8	131	468	53	117	21	5	16	59	.250	36	196	104	26-39
1953	CF	CIN	NL	6-8	151	610	102	183	37	5	30	105	.300	48	320	124	12-44
1954	CF	CIN	NL	5-8	153	619	104	185	38	7	17	101	.299	48	288	111	18-48
1955	CF	CIN	NL	5-8	154	610	88	188	30	6	27	104	.308	54	311	126	15-43
1956	CF	CIN	NL	3-8	150	603	82	176	31	4	29	84	.292	50	302	124	14-43
1957	CF	CIN	NL	4-8	121	510	65	149	20	3	13	61	.292	30	214	102	25-44
1958	CF	CIN	NL	4-8	112	385	42	97	16	2	10	46	.252	36	147	94	—
1959	RF	CIN	NL	5-8	148	580	59	170	27	2	19	115	.293	29	258	105	22-38
1960	RF	CIN	NL	6-8	143	515	65	135	19	5	12	62	.262	29	200	93	33-38
1961	LF-RF	CIN	NL	1-8	103	235	27	60	10	1	3	33	.255	18	81	84	—
1962	LF-RF	NY/ML	NL	10/5	109	315	36	76	13	3	6	30	.241	22	113	86	—
1963	PH	MIL	NL	6-10	3	3	0	1	0	0	0	0	.333	0	1	—	—
1964	PH	MIL	NL	5-10	3	3	0	0	0	0	0	0	.000	0	0	—	—
MAJOR LEAGUE TOTALS					1741	6478	865	1823	311	66	206	942	.281	470	2884	111	9 yrs

James Edward Runnels
6'0 170 lbs Batted left

Born Jan 28, 1928 Lufkin, TX
Died May 20, 1991 Palestine, TX

YR	POS	TEAM	LG	FIN	G	AB	R	H	2B	3B	HR	RBI	AVG	BB	TB	OQ	RANK
1951	SS	WAS	AL	7-8	78	273	31	76	12	2	0	25	.278	31	92	93	—
1952	SS	WAS	AL	5-8	152	555	70	158	18	3	1	64	.285	72	185	102	28-38
1953	SS	WAS	AL	5-8	137	486	64	125	15	5	2	50	.257	64	156	92	36-43
1954	SS-2B	WAS	AL	6-8	139	488	75	131	17	15	3	56	.268	78	187	114	18-34
1955	2B	WAS	AL	8-8	134	503	66	143	16	4	2	49	.284	55	173	95	34-39
1956	1B-2B	WAS	AL	7-8	147	578	72	179	29	9	8	76	.310	58	250	111	23-40
1957	1B-3B	WAS	AL	8-8	134	473	53	109	18	4	2	35	.230	55	141	83	35-35
1958	2B-1B	BOS	AL	3-8	147	568	103	183	32	5	8	59	.322	87	249	136	7-39
1959	2B-1B	BOS	AL	5-8	147	560	95	176	33	6	6	57	.314	95	239	134	8-35
1960	2B-1B	BOS	AL	7-8	143	528	80	169	29	2	2	35	.320	71	208	117	14-44
1961	1B	BOS	AL	6-10	143	360	49	114	20	3	3	38	.317	46	149	117	—
1962	1B	BOS	AL	8-10	152	562	80	183	33	5	10	60	.326	79	256	133	7-54
1963	1B-2B	HOU	NL	9-10	124	388	35	98	9	1	2	23	.253	45	115	93	—
1964	1B	HOU	NL	9-10	22	51	3	10	1	0	0	3	.196	8	11	—	—

MAJOR LEAGUE TOTALS					1799	6373	876	1854	282	64	49	630	.291	844	2411	112	10 yrs

Frank Joseph Thomas
6'3 200 lbs Batted right

Born Jun 11, 1929 Pittsburgh, PA

YR	POS	TEAM	LG	FIN	G	AB	R	H	2B	3B	HR	RBI	AVG	BB	TB	OQ	RANK
1951	CF	PIT	NL	7-8	39	148	21	39	9	2	2	16	.264	9	58	93	—
1952	CF	PIT	NL	8-8	6	21	1	2	0	0	0	0	.095	1	2	—	—
1953	LF	PIT	NL	8-8	128	455	68	116	22	1	30	102	.255	50	230	119	15-44
1954	CF-LF	PIT	NL	8-8	153	577	81	172	32	7	23	94	.298	51	287	120	13-48
1955	LF	PIT	NL	8-8	142	510	72	125	16	2	25	72	.245	60	220	106	24-43
1956	3B-LF	PIT	NL	7-8	157	588	69	166	24	3	25	80	.282	36	271	109	25-43
1957	1B-LF	PIT	NL	7-8	151	594	72	172	30	1	23	89	.290	44	273	113	17-44
1958	3B	PIT	NL	2-8	149	562	89	158	26	4	35	109	.281	42	297	124	11-34
1959	3B-LF	CIN	NL	5-8	108	374	41	84	18	2	12	47	.225	27	142	87	—
1960	1B-LF	CHI	NL	7-8	135	479	54	114	12	1	21	64	.238	28	191	93	34-38
1961	LF-1B	CH/ML	NL	7/4	139	473	65	133	15	3	27	73	.281	31	235	116	19-37
1962	LF	NY	NL	10-10	156	571	69	152	23	3	34	94	.266	48	283	120	18-51
1963	LF-1B	NY	NL	10-10	126	420	34	109	9	1	15	60	.260	33	165	108	—
1964	1B-LF	NY/PH	NL	10/2	99	340	39	92	17	1	10	45	.271	15	141	103	—
1965	1B-LF	Ph/Ho/Ml	NL	6/9/5	73	168	17	37	9	0	4	17	.220	9	58	83	—
1966	PH	CHI	NL	10-10	5	5	0	0	0	0	0	0	.000	0	0	—	—

MAJOR LEAGUE TOTALS					1766	6285	792	1671	262	31	286	962	.266	484	2853	113	9 yrs

Gilbert James McDougald   Born May 19, 1928 San Francisco, CA
6'0   175 lbs   Batted right

YR	POS	TEAM	LG	FIN	G	AB	R	H	2B	3B	HR	RBI	AVG	BB	TB	OQ	RANK
1951	3B-2B	NY	AL	1-8	131	402	72	123	23	4	14	63	.306	56	196	134	—
1952	3B-2B	NY	AL	1-8	152	555	65	146	16	5	11	78	.263	57	205	101	20-38
1953	3B-2B	NY	AL	1-8	141	541	82	154	27	7	10	83	.285	60	225	111	21-43
1954	2B-3B	NY	AL	2-8	126	394	66	102	22	2	12	48	.259	62	164	119	—
1955	2B-3B	NY	AL	1-8	141	533	79	152	10	8	13	53	.285	65	217	111	21-39
1956	SS-2B	NY	AL	1-8	120	438	79	136	13	3	13	56	.311	68	194	125	14-40
1957	SS-2B	NY	AL	1-8	141	539	87	156	25	9	13	62	.289	59	238	119	14-35
1958	2B-SS	NY	AL	1-8	138	503	69	126	19	1	14	65	.250	59	189	102	30-39
1959	2B-SS	NY	AL	3-8	127	434	44	109	16	8	4	34	.251	35	153	89	32-35
1960	3B-2B	NY	AL	1-8	119	337	54	87	16	4	8	34	.258	38	135	104	—

MAJOR LEAGUE TOTALS   1336   4676   697 1291   187   51 112   576   .276   559 1916   108   7 yrs

Mickey Charles Mantle   Born Oct 20, 1931   Spavinaw, OK
5'11   195 lbs   Batted both

YR	POS	TEAM	LG	FIN	G	AB	R	H	2B	3B	HR	RBI	AVG	BB	TB	OQ	RANK
1951	RF	NY	AL	1-8	96	341	61	91	11	5	13	65	.267	43	151	115	—
1952	CF	NY	AL	1-8	142	549	94	171	37	7	23	87	.311	75	291	152	2-38
1953	CF	NY	AL	1-8	127	461	105	136	24	3	21	92	.295	79	229	143	3-43
1954	CF	NY	AL	2-8	146	543	129	163	17	12	27	102	.300	102	285	156	2-34
1955	CF	NY	AL	1-8	147	517	121	158	25	11	37	99	.306	113	316	179	1-39
1956	CF	NY	AL	1-8	150	533	132	188	22	5	52	130	.353	112	376	204	1-40
1957	CF	NY	AL	1-8	144	474	121	173	28	6	34	94	.365	146	315	235	2-35
1958	CF	NY	AL	1-8	150	519	127	158	21	1	42	97	.304	129	307	188	2-39
1959	CF	NY	AL	3-8	144	541	104	154	23	4	31	75	.285	93	278	148	3-35
1960	CF	NY	AL	1-8	153	527	119	145	17	6	40	94	.275	111	294	160	1-44
1961	CF	NY	AL	1-10	153	514	132	163	16	6	54	128	.317	126	353	202	2-49
1962	CF	NY	AL	1-10	123	377	96	121	15	1	30	89	.321	122	228	205	1-54
1963	CF	NY	AL	1-10	65	172	40	54	8	0	15	35	.314	40	107	199	—
1964	CF	NY	AL	1-10	143	465	92	141	25	2	35	111	.303	99	275	182	1-52
1965	LF	NY	AL	6-10	122	361	44	92	12	1	19	46	.255	73	163	142	—
1966	CF	NY	AL	10-10	108	333	40	96	12	1	23	56	.288	57	179	165	—
1967	1B	NY	AL	9-10	144	440	63	108	17	0	22	55	.245	107	191	155	5-48
1968	1B	NY	AL	5-10	144	435	57	103	14	1	18	54	.237	106	173	150	6-45

MAJOR LEAGUE TOTALS   2401   8102 1677 2415   344   72 536 1509   .298 1733 4511   176   14 yrs

Dee Virgil Fondy   Born Oct 31, 1924 Slaton, TX
6'3 195 lbs Batted left

YR	POS	TEAM	LG	FIN	G	AB	R	H	2B	3B	HR	RBI	AVG	BB	TB	OQ	RANK
1951	1B	CHI	NL	8-8	49	170	23	46	7	2	3	20	.271	11	66	94	—
1952	1B	CHI	NL	5-8	145	554	69	166	21	9	10	67	.300	28	235	107	23-39
1953	1B	CHI	NL	7-8	150	595	79	184	24	11	18	78	.309	44	284	115	19-44
1954	1B	CHI	NL	7-8	141	568	77	162	30	4	9	49	.285	35	227	93	38-48
1955	1B	CHI	NL	6-8	150	574	69	152	23	8	17	65	.265	35	242	96	29-43
1956	1B	CHI	NL	8-8	137	543	52	146	22	9	9	46	.269	20	213	88	39-43
1957	1B	CH/PT	NL	7/7	106	374	45	117	16	3	2	37	.313	25	145	100	—
1958	1B-RF	CIN	NL	4-8	89	124	23	27	1	1	1	11	.218	5	33	58	—

MAJOR LEAGUE TOTALS   967 3502 437 1000 144 47 69 373 .286 203 1445 100 5 yrs

Willie Howard Mays   Born May 6, 1931 Westfield, AL
5'10 170 lbs Batted right

YR	POS	TEAM	LG	FIN	G	AB	R	H	2B	3B	HR	RBI	AVG	BB	TB	OQ	RANK
1951	CF	NY	NL	1-8	121	464	59	127	22	5	20	68	.274	57	219	123	11-44
1952	CF	NY	NL	2-8	34	127	17	30	2	4	4	23	.236	16	52	111	—
1954	CF	NY	NL	1-8	151	565	119	195	33	13	41	110	.345	66	377	172	2-48
1955	CF	NY	NL	3-8	152	580	123	185	18	13	51	127	.319	79	382	170	2-43
1956	CF	NY	NL	6-8	152	578	101	171	27	8	36	84	.296	68	322	144	2-43
1957	CF	NY	NL	6-8	152	585	112	195	26	20	35	97	.333	76	366	171	2-44
1958	CF	SF	NL	3-8	152	600	121	208	33	11	29	96	.347	78	350	161	1-34
1959	CF	SF	NL	3-8	151	575	125	180	43	5	34	104	.313	65	335	152	5-38
1960	CF	SF	NL	5-8	153	595	107	190	29	12	29	103	.319	61	330	149	3-38
1961	CF	SF	NL	3-8	154	572	129	176	32	3	40	123	.308	81	334	155	2-37
1962	CF	SF	NL	1-10	162	621	130	189	36	5	49	141	.304	78	382	161	3-51
1963	CF	SF	NL	3-10	157	596	115	187	32	7	38	103	.314	66	347	171	2-50
1964	CF	SF	NL	4-10	157	578	121	171	21	9	47	111	.296	82	351	175	1-42
1965	CF	SF	NL	2-10	157	558	118	177	21	3	52	112	.317	76	360	187	1-52
1966	CF	SF	NL	2-10	152	552	99	159	29	4	37	103	.288	70	307	154	6-55
1967	CF	SF	NL	2-10	141	486	83	128	22	2	22	70	.263	51	220	127	19-54
1968	CF	SF	NL	2-10	148	498	84	144	20	5	23	79	.289	67	243	158	4-45
1969	CF	SF	NL	2-6	117	403	64	114	17	3	13	58	.283	49	176	125	—
1970	CF	SF	NL	3-6	139	478	94	139	15	2	28	83	.291	79	242	142	12-56
1971	CF-1B	SF	NL	1-6	136	417	82	113	24	5	18	61	.271	112	201	168	3-58
1972	CF-1B	SF/NY	NL	5/3	88	244	35	61	11	1	8	22	.250	60	98	141	—
1973	CF-1B	NY	NL	1-6	66	209	24	44	10	0	6	25	.211	27	72	94	—

MAJOR LEAGUE TOTALS   2992 10881 2062 3283 523 140 660 1903 .302 1464 6066 158 18 yrs

John Logan   Born Mar 23, 1927 Endicott, NY
5'11   175 lbs   Batted right

YR	POS	TEAM	LG	FIN	G	AB	R	H	2B	3B	HR	RBI	AVG	BB	TB	OQ	RANK
1951	SS	BOS	NL	4-8	62	169	14	37	7	1	0	16	.219	18	46	73	—
1952	SS	BOS	NL	7-8	117	456	56	129	21	3	4	42	.283	31	168	96	36-39
1953	SS	MIL	NL	2-8	150	611	100	167	27	8	11	73	.273	41	243	92	38-44
1954	SS	MIL	NL	3-8	154	560	66	154	17	7	8	66	.275	51	209	92	39-48
1955	SS	MIL	NL	2-8	154	595	95	177	37	5	13	83	.297	58	263	112	19-43
1956	SS	MIL	NL	2-8	148	545	69	153	27	5	15	46	.281	46	235	107	26-43
1957	SS	MIL	NL	1-8	129	494	59	135	19	7	10	49	.273	31	198	96	31-44
1958	SS	MIL	NL	1-8	145	530	54	120	20	0	11	53	.226	40	173	77	32-34
1959	SS	MIL	NL	2-8	138	470	59	137	17	0	13	50	.291	57	193	113	16-38
1960	SS	MIL	NL	2-8	136	482	52	118	14	4	7	42	.245	43	161	87	36-38
1961	SS-3B	ML/PT	NL	4/6	45	71	5	14	5	0	0	6	.197	5	19	—	—
1962	3B	PIT	NL	4-10	44	80	7	24	3	0	1	12	.300	7	30	—	—
1963	SS	PIT	NL	8-10	81	181	15	42	2	1	0	9	.232	23	46	84	—
MAJOR LEAGUE TOTALS					1503	5244	651	1407	216	41	93	547	.268	451	1984	97	9 yrs

Roy David McMillan   Born Jul 17, 1930   Bonham, TX
5'11   170 lbs   Batted right

YR	POS	TEAM	LG	FIN	G	AB	R	H	2B	3B	HR	RBI	AVG	BB	TB	OQ	RANK
1951	SS-3B	CIN	NL	6-8	85	199	21	42	4	0	1	8	.211	17	49	63	—
1952	SS	CIN	NL	6-8	154	540	60	132	32	2	7	57	.244	45	189	91	38-39
1953	SS	CIN	NL	6-8	155	557	51	130	15	4	5	43	.233	43	168	71	43-44
1954	SS	CIN	NL	5-8	154	588	86	147	21	2	4	42	.250	47	184	75	46-48
1955	SS	CIN	NL	5-8	151	470	50	126	21	2	1	37	.268	66	154	93	36-43
1956	SS	CIN	NL	3-8	150	479	51	126	16	7	3	62	.263	76	165	102	27-43
1957	SS	CIN	NL	4-8	151	448	50	122	25	5	1	55	.272	66	160	105	23-44
1958	SS	CIN	NL	4-8	145	393	48	90	18	3	1	25	.229	47	117	80	—
1959	SS	CIN	NL	5-8	79	246	38	65	14	2	9	24	.264	27	110	113	—
1960	SS	CIN	NL	6-8	124	399	42	94	12	2	10	42	.236	35	140	89	—
1961	SS	MIL	NL	4-8	154	505	42	111	16	0	7	48	.220	61	148	78	36-37
1962	SS	MIL	NL	5-10	137	468	66	115	13	0	12	41	.246	60	164	96	41-51
1963	SS	MIL	NL	6-10	100	320	35	80	10	1	4	29	.250	17	104	85	—
1964	SS	ML/NY	NL	5/10	121	392	31	84	8	2	1	27	.214	14	99	60	—
1965	SS	NY	NL	10-10	157	528	44	128	19	2	1	42	.242	24	154	73	51-52
1966	SS	NY	NL	9-10	76	220	24	47	9	1	1	12	.214	20	61	75	—
MAJOR LEAGUE TOTALS					2093	6752	739	1639	253	35	68	594	.243	665	2166	87	9 yrs

Daryl Dean Spencer   Born Jul 13, 1929   Wichita, KS
6'2   185 lbs   Batted right

YR	POS	TEAM	LG	FIN	G	AB	R	H	2B	3B	HR	RBI	AVG	BB	TB	OQ	RANK
1952	SS-3B	NY	NL	2-8	7	17	0	5	0	1	0	3	.294	1	7	—	—
1953	SS-3B	NY	NL	5-8	118	408	55	85	18	5	20	56	.208	42	173	96	—
1956	2B-SS	NY	NL	6-8	146	489	46	108	13	2	14	42	.221	35	167	79	42-43
1957	SS-2B	NY	NL	6-8	148	534	65	133	31	2	11	50	.249	50	201	95	32-44
1958	SS-2B	SF	NL	3-8	148	539	71	138	20	5	17	74	.256	73	219	107	21-34
1959	2B	SF	NL	3-8	152	555	59	147	20	1	12	62	.265	58	205	97	30-38
1960	SS-2B	SL	NL	3-8	148	507	70	131	20	3	16	58	.258	81	205	118	16-38
1961	3B-SS	SL/LA	NL	5/2	97	319	46	79	11	0	12	48	.248	43	126	104	—
1962	3B-SS	LA	NL	2-10	77	157	24	37	5	1	2	12	.236	32	50	103	—
1963	3B	LA/CN	NL	1/5	57	164	21	38	7	0	1	23	.232	34	48	110	—
MAJOR LEAGUE TOTALS					1098	3689	457	901	145	20	105	428	.244	449	1401	99	5 yrs

Richard Morrow Groat   Born Nov 4, 1930   Wilkinsburg, PA
5'11   180 lbs   Batted right

YR	POS	TEAM	LG	FIN	G	AB	R	H	2B	3B	HR	RBI	AVG	BB	TB	OQ	RANK
1952	SS	PIT	NL	8-8	95	384	38	109	6	1	1	29	.284	19	120	80	—
1955	SS	PIT	NL	8-8	151	521	45	139	28	2	4	51	.267	38	183	84	40-43
1956	SS	PIT	NL	7-8	142	520	40	142	19	3	0	37	.273	35	167	80	41-43
1957	SS	PIT	NL	7-8	125	501	58	158	30	5	7	54	.315	27	219	108	21-44
1958	SS	PIT	NL	2-8	151	584	67	175	36	9	3	66	.300	23	238	94	29-34
1959	SS	PIT	NL	4-8	147	593	74	163	22	7	5	51	.275	32	214	86	35-38
1960	SS	PIT	NL	1-8	138	573	85	186	26	4	2	50	.325	39	226	106	26-38
1961	SS	PIT	NL	6-8	148	596	71	164	25	6	6	55	.275	40	219	89	31-37
1962	SS	PIT	NL	4-10	161	678	76	199	34	3	2	61	.294	31	245	87	49-51
1963	SS	SL	NL	2-10	158	631	85	201	43	11	6	73	.319	56	284	134	12-50
1964	SS	SL	NL	1-10	161	636	70	186	35	6	1	70	.292	44	236	102	32-42
1965	SS	SL	NL	7-10	153	587	55	149	26	5	0	52	.254	56	185	90	43-52
1966	SS-3B	PHI	NL	4-10	155	584	58	152	21	4	2	53	.260	40	187	84	51-55
1967	SS	PH/SF	NL	5/2	44	96	7	15	1	1	0	5	.156	10	18	58	—
MAJOR LEAGUE TOTALS					1929	7484	829	2138	352	67	39	707	.286	490	2741	95	12 yrs

Manuel Joseph Rivera Born Jul 22, 1922 New York, NY
6'0 196 lbs Batted left

YR	POS	TEAM	LG	FIN	G	AB	R	H	2B	3B	HR	RBI	AVG	BB	TB	OQ	RANK
1952	CF	SL/CH	AL	7/3	150	537	72	136	20	9	7	48	.253	50	195	96	34-38
1953	CF	CHI	AL	3-8	156	567	79	147	26	16	11	78	.259	53	238	105	27-43
1954	RF	CHI	AL	3-8	145	490	62	140	16	8	13	61	.286	49	211	114	17-34
1955	RF	CHI	AL	3-8	147	454	71	120	24	4	10	52	.264	62	182	109	23-39
1956	RF	CHI	AL	3-8	139	491	76	125	23	5	12	66	.255	49	194	96	29-40
1957	RF-1B	CHI	AL	2-8	125	402	51	103	21	6	14	52	.256	40	178	112	—
1958	RF	CHI	AL	2-8	116	276	37	62	8	4	9	35	.225	24	105	94	—
1959	RF	CHI	AL	1-8	80	177	18	39	9	4	4	19	.220	11	68	88	—
1960	RF-LF	CHI	AL	3-8	48	17	17	5	0	0	1	1	.294	3	8	—	—
1961	RF	CH/KC	AL	4/9	65	141	20	34	8	0	2	10	.241	24	48	100	—

MAJOR LEAGUE TOTALS | | | | | 1171 | 3552 | 503 | 911 | 155 | 56 | 83 | 422 | .256 | 365 | 1427 | 104 | 5 yrs

Edwin Lee Mathews Born Oct 31, 1931 Texarkana, TX
6'1 190 lbs Batted left

YR	POS	TEAM	LG	FIN	G	AB	R	H	2B	3B	HR	RBI	AVG	BB	TB	OQ	RANK
1952	3B	BOS	NL	7-8	145	528	80	128	23	5	25	58	.242	59	236	117	16-39
1953	3B	MIL	NL	2-8	157	579	110	175	31	8	47	135	.302	99	363	165	3-44
1954	3B	MIL	NL	3-8	138	476	96	138	21	4	40	103	.290	113	287	170	3-48
1955	3B	MIL	NL	2-8	141	499	108	144	23	5	41	101	.289	109	300	168	3-43
1956	3B	MIL	NL	2-8	151	552	103	150	21	2	37	95	.272	91	286	141	6-43
1957	3B	MIL	NL	1-8	148	572	109	167	28	9	32	94	.292	90	309	149	5-44
1958	3B	MIL	NL	1-8	149	546	97	137	18	1	31	77	.251	85	250	121	15-34
1959	3B	MIL	NL	2-8	148	594	118	182	16	8	46	114	.306	80	352	157	2-38
1960	3B	MIL	NL	2-8	153	548	108	152	19	7	39	124	.277	111	302	161	2-38
1961	3B	MIL	NL	4-8	152	572	103	175	23	6	32	91	.306	93	306	148	5-37
1962	3B	MIL	NL	5-10	152	536	106	142	25	6	29	90	.265	101	266	141	6-51
1963	3B-LF	MIL	NL	6-10	158	547	82	144	27	4	23	84	.263	124	248	156	3-50
1964	3B	MIL	NL	5-10	141	502	83	117	19	1	23	74	.233	85	207	125	17-42
1965	3B	MIL	NL	5-10	156	546	77	137	23	0	32	95	.251	73	256	131	14-52
1966	3B	ATL	NL	5-10	134	452	72	113	21	4	16	53	.250	63	190	120	22-55
1967	1B-3B	HOU	NL	9-10	101	328	39	78	13	2	10	38	.238	48	125	116	—
1967	3B-1B	DET	AL	2-10	36	108	14	25	3	0	6	19	.231	15	46	127	—
1968	3B-1B	DET	AL	1-10	31	52	4	11	0	0	3	8	.212	5	20	—	—

MAJOR LEAGUE TOTALS | | | | | 2391 | 8537 | 1509 | 2315 | 354 | 72 | 512 | 1453 | .271 | 1444 | 4349 | 145 | 15 yrs

William Robert Tuttle   Born Jul 4, 1929   Elwood, IL
6'0 190 lbs Batted right

YR	POS	TEAM	LG	FIN	G	AB	R	H	2B	3B	HR	RBI	AVG	BB	TB	OQ	RANK
1952	CF-LF	DET	AL	8-8	7	25	2	6	0	0	0	2	.240	0	6	—	—
1954	CF	DET	AL	5-8	147	530	64	141	20	11	7	58	.266	62	204	105	21-34
1955	CF	DET	AL	5-8	154	603	102	168	23	4	14	78	.279	76	241	109	24-39
1956	CF	DET	AL	5-8	140	546	61	138	22	4	9	65	.253	38	195	82	36-40
1957	CF	DET	AL	4-8	133	451	49	113	12	4	5	47	.251	44	148	87	33-35
1958	CF	KC	AL	7-8	148	511	77	118	14	9	11	51	.231	74	183	102	32-39
1959	CF	KC	AL	7-8	126	463	74	139	19	6	7	43	.300	48	191	114	20-35
1960	CF	KC	AL	8-8	151	559	75	143	21	3	8	40	.256	66	194	94	33-44
1961	CF-3B	KC/MN	AL	9/7	138	454	53	113	14	5	5	46	.249	52	152	89	45-49
1962	CF-RF	MIN	AL	2-10	110	123	21	26	4	1	1	13	.211	19	35	84	—
1963	CF	MIN	AL	3-10	16	3	0	0	0	0	0	0	.000	1	0	—	—
MAJOR LEAGUE TOTALS					1270	4268	578	1105	149	47	67	443	.259	480	1549	98	8 yrs

Harvey Edward Kuenn   Born Dec 4, 1930   West Allis, WI
6'2 187 lbs Batted right   Died Feb 28, 1988   Peoria, AZ

YR	POS	TEAM	LG	FIN	G	AB	R	H	2B	3B	HR	RBI	AVG	BB	TB	OQ	RANK
1952	SS	DET	AL	8-8	19	80	2	26	2	2	0	8	.325	2	32	—	—
1953	SS	DET	AL	6-8	155	679	94	209	33	7	2	48	.308	50	262	100	31-43
1954	SS	DET	AL	5-8	155	656	81	201	28	6	5	48	.306	29	256	96	27-34
1955	SS	DET	AL	5-8	145	620	101	190	38	5	8	62	.306	40	262	105	26-39
1956	SS	DET	AL	5-8	146	591	96	196	32	7	12	88	.332	55	278	121	16-40
1957	SS-3B	DET	AL	4-8	151	624	74	173	30	6	9	44	.277	47	242	98	28-35
1958	CF	DET	AL	5-8	139	561	73	179	39	3	8	54	.319	51	248	122	13-39
1959	RF	DET	AL	4-8	139	561	99	198	42	7	9	71	.353	48	281	140	5-35
1960	RF	CLE	AL	4-8	126	474	65	146	24	0	9	54	.308	55	197	116	15-44
1961	LF-3B	SF	NL	3-8	131	471	60	125	22	4	5	46	.265	47	170	93	27-37
1962	LF-3B	SF	NL	1-10	130	487	73	148	23	5	10	68	.304	49	211	116	24-51
1963	LF-3B	SF	NL	3-10	120	417	61	121	13	2	6	31	.290	44	156	114	—
1964	LF-1B	SF	NL	4-10	111	351	42	92	16	2	4	22	.262	35	124	101	—
1965	LF-1B	SF/CH	NL	2/8	77	179	15	40	5	0	0	12	.223	32	45	91	—
1966	LF-1B	CH/PH	NL	10/4	89	162	15	48	9	0	0	15	.296	10	57	94	—
MAJOR LEAGUE TOTALS					1833	6913	951	2092	356	56	87	671	.303	594	2821	111	10 yrs

John Ellis Temple Born Aug 8, 1928 Lexington, NC
5'11 175 lbs Batted right

YR	POS	TEAM	LG	FIN	G	AB	R	H	2B	3B	HR	RBI	AVG	BB	TB	OQ	RANK
1952	2B	CIN	NL	6-8	30	97	8	19	3	0	1	5	.196	5	25	61	—
1953	2B	CIN	NL	6-8	63	110	14	29	4	0	1	9	.264	7	36	76	—
1954	2B	CIN	NL	5-8	146	505	60	155	14	8	0	44	.307	62	185	101	31-48
1955	2B	CIN	NL	5-8	150	588	94	165	20	3	0	50	.281	80	191	93	35-43
1956	2B	CIN	NL	3-8	154	632	88	180	18	3	2	41	.285	58	210	89	38-43
1957	2B	CIN	NL	4-8	145	557	85	158	24	4	0	37	.284	94	190	108	22-44
1958	2B	CIN	NL	4-8	141	542	82	166	31	6	3	47	.306	91	218	121	14-34
1959	2B	CIN	NL	5-8	149	598	102	186	35	6	8	67	.311	72	257	120	13-38
1960	2B-3B	CLE	AL	4-8	98	381	50	102	13	1	2	19	.268	32	123	84	—
1961	2B	CLE	AL	5-10	129	518	73	143	22	3	3	30	.276	61	180	95	36-49
1962	2B	BAL	AL	7-10	78	270	28	71	8	1	1	17	.263	36	84	91	—
1962	2B	HOU	NL	8-10	31	95	14	25	4	0	0	12	.263	7	29	78	—
1963	2B-3B	HOU	NL	9-10	100	322	22	85	12	1	1	17	.264	41	102	102	—
1964	PH	CIN	NL	2-10	6	3	0	0	0	0	0	0	.000	2	0	—	—

MAJOR LEAGUE TOTALS 1420 5218 720 1484 208 36 22 395 .284 648 1830 104 7 yrs

James William Gilliam Born Oct 17, 1928 Nashville, TN
5'10 175 lbs Batted both Died Oct 8, 1978 Inglewood, CA

YR	POS	TEAM	LG	FIN	G	AB	R	H	2B	3B	HR	RBI	AVG	BB	TB	OQ	RANK
1953	2B	BRO	NL	1-8	151	605	125	168	31	17	6	63	.278	100	251	116	18-44
1954	2B	BRO	NL	2-8	146	607	107	171	28	8	13	52	.282	76	254	109	20-48
1955	2B-LF	BRO	NL	1-8	147	538	110	134	20	8	7	40	.249	70	191	94	32-43
1956	2B-LF	BRO	NL	1-8	153	594	102	178	23	8	6	43	.300	95	235	119	19-43
1957	2B	BRO	NL	3-8	149	617	89	154	26	4	2	37	.250	64	194	84	37-44
1958	LF-3B	LA	NL	7-8	147	555	81	145	25	5	2	43	.261	78	186	95	28-34
1959	3B	LA	NL	1-8	145	553	91	156	18	4	3	34	.282	96	191	108	20-38
1960	3B-2B	LA	NL	4-8	151	557	96	138	20	2	5	40	.248	96	177	101	28-38
1961	3B-2B	LA	NL	2-8	144	439	74	107	26	3	4	32	.244	79	151	102	24-37
1962	2B-3B	LA	NL	2-10	160	588	83	159	24	1	4	43	.270	93	197	102	31-51
1963	2B-3B	LA	NL	1-10	148	525	77	148	27	4	6	49	.282	60	201	117	20-50
1964	3B-2B	LA	NL	6-10	116	334	44	76	8	3	2	27	.228	42	96	88	—
1965	3B-LF	LA	NL	1-10	111	372	54	104	19	4	4	39	.280	53	143	119	—
1966	3B	LA	NL	1-10	88	235	30	51	9	0	1	16	.217	34	63	85	—

MAJOR LEAGUE TOTALS 1956 7119 1163 1889 304 71 65 558 .265 1036 2530 104 11 yrs

William Haron Bruton Born Dec 22, 1925 Panola, AL
6'0 169 lbs Batted left

YR	POS	TEAM	LG	FIN	G	AB	R	H	2B	3B	HR	RBI	AVG	BB	TB	OQ	RANK
1953	CF	MIL	NL	2-8	151	613	82	153	18	14	1	41	.250	44	202	77	41-44
1954	CF	MIL	NL	3-8	142	567	89	161	20	7	4	30	.284	40	207	87	42-48
1955	CF	MIL	NL	2-8	149	636	106	175	30	12	9	47	.275	43	256	95	30-43
1956	CF	MIL	NL	2-8	147	525	73	143	23	15	8	56	.272	26	220	97	33-43
1957	CF	MIL	NL	1-8	79	306	41	85	16	9	5	30	.278	19	134	105	—
1958	CF	MIL	NL	1-8	100	325	47	91	11	3	3	28	.280	27	117	91	—
1959	CF	MIL	NL	2-8	133	478	72	138	22	6	6	41	.289	35	190	99	27-38
1960	CF	MIL	NL	2-8	151	629	112	180	27	13	12	54	.286	41	269	107	25-38
1961	CF	DET	AL	2-10	160	596	99	153	15	5	17	63	.257	61	229	97	35-49
1962	CF	DET	AL	4-10	147	561	90	156	27	5	16	74	.278	55	241	110	29-54
1963	CF	DET	AL	5-10	145	524	84	134	21	8	8	48	.256	59	195	104	34-51
1964	CF	DET	AL	4-10	106	296	42	82	11	5	5	33	.277	32	118	111	—

MAJOR LEAGUE TOTALS					1610	6056	937	1651	241	102	94	545	.273	482	2378	97	9 yrs

Ernest Banks Born Jan 31, 1931 Dallas, TX
6'1 180 lbs Batted right

YR	POS	TEAM	LG	FIN	G	AB	R	H	2B	3B	HR	RBI	AVG	BB	TB	OQ	RANK
1953	SS	CHI	NL	7-8	10	35	3	11	1	1	2	6	.314	4	20	—	—
1954	SS	CHI	NL	7-8	154	593	70	163	19	7	19	79	.275	40	253	98	35-48
1955	SS	CHI	NL	6-8	154	596	98	176	29	9	44	117	.295	45	355	139	9-43
1956	SS	CHI	NL	8-8	139	538	82	160	25	8	28	85	.297	52	285	134	10-43
1957	SS-3B	CHI	NL	7-8	156	594	113	169	34	6	43	102	.285	70	344	147	6-44
1958	SS	CHI	NL	5-8	154	617	119	193	23	11	47	129	.313	52	379	150	3-34
1959	SS	CHI	NL	5-8	155	589	97	179	25	6	45	143	.304	64	351	152	6-38
1960	SS	CHI	NL	7-8	156	597	94	162	32	7	41	117	.271	71	331	143	6-38
1961	SS-LF	CHI	NL	7-8	138	511	75	142	22	4	29	80	.278	54	259	125	14-37
1962	1B	CHI	NL	9-10	154	610	87	164	20	6	37	104	.269	30	307	115	25-51
1963	1B	CHI	NL	7-10	130	432	41	98	20	1	18	64	.227	39	174	108	—
1964	1B	CHI	NL	8-10	157	591	67	156	29	6	23	95	.264	36	266	114	23-42
1965	1B	CHI	NL	8-10	163	612	79	162	25	3	28	106	.265	55	277	121	24-52
1966	1B	CHI	NL	10-10	141	511	52	139	23	7	15	75	.272	29	221	108	31-55
1967	1B	CHI	NL	3-10	151	573	68	158	26	4	23	95	.276	27	261	116	26-54
1968	1B	CHI	NL	3-10	150	552	71	136	27	0	32	83	.246	27	259	124	16-45
1969	1B	CHI	NL	2-6	155	565	60	143	19	2	23	106	.253	42	235	105	37-62
1970	1B	CHI	NL	2-6	72	222	25	56	6	2	12	44	.252	20	102	110	—
1971	1B	CHI	NL	3-6	39	83	4	16	2	0	3	6	.193	6	27	—	—

MAJOR LEAGUE TOTALS					2528	9421	1305	2583	407	90	512	1636	.274	763	4706	126	15 yrs

Alphonse Eugene Smith   Born Feb 7, 1928   Kirkwood, MO
6'0 189 lbs Batted right

YR	POS	TEAM	LG	FIN	G	AB	R	H	2B	3B	HR	RBI	AVG	BB	TB	OQ	RANK
1953	RF	CLE	AL	2-8	47	150	28	36	9	0	3	14	.240	20	54	98	—
1954	LF-3B	CLE	AL	1-8	131	481	101	135	29	6	11	50	.281	88	209	132	7-34
1955	RF-3B	CLE	AL	2-8	154	607	123	186	27	4	22	77	.306	93	287	135	3-39
1956	LF-3B	CLE	AL	2-8	141	526	87	144	26	5	16	71	.274	84	228	118	18-40
1957	3B-LF	CLE	AL	6-8	135	507	78	125	23	5	11	49	.247	79	191	109	23-35
1958	LF	CHI	AL	2-8	139	480	61	121	23	5	12	58	.252	48	190	103	28-39
1959	LF	CHI	AL	1-8	129	472	65	112	16	4	17	55	.237	46	187	100	28-35
1960	RF	CHI	AL	3-8	142	536	80	169	31	3	12	72	.315	50	242	120	13-44
1961	3B-RF	CHI	AL	4-10	147	532	88	148	29	4	28	93	.278	56	269	125	13-49
1962	3B-RF	CHI	AL	5-10	142	511	62	149	23	8	16	82	.292	57	236	121	15-54
1963	RF	BAL	AL	4-10	120	368	45	100	17	1	10	39	.272	32	149	108	—
1964	RF-3B	CL/BO	AL	6/8	90	187	25	33	5	1	6	16	.176	21	58	81	—
MAJOR LEAGUE TOTALS					1517	5357	843	1458	258	46	164	676	.272	674	2300	118	9 yrs

Albert William Kaline   Born Dec 19, 1934   Baltimore, MD
6'1 175 lbs Batted right

YR	POS	TEAM	LG	FIN	G	AB	R	H	2B	3B	HR	RBI	AVG	BB	TB	OQ	RANK
1953	CF	DET	AL	6-8	30	28	9	7	0	0	1	2	.250	1	10	—	—
1954	RF	DET	AL	5-8	138	504	42	139	18	3	4	43	.276	22	175	83	33-34
1955	RF	DET	AL	5-8	152	588	121	200	24	8	27	102	.340	82	321	155	2-39
1956	RF	DET	AL	5-8	153	617	96	194	32	10	27	128	.314	70	327	135	8-40
1957	RF	DET	AL	4-8	149	577	83	170	29	4	23	90	.295	43	276	120	13-35
1958	RF	DET	AL	5-8	146	543	84	170	34	7	16	85	.313	54	266	133	8-39
1959	CF	DET	AL	4-8	136	511	86	167	19	2	27	94	.327	72	271	154	1-35
1960	CF	DET	AL	6-8	147	551	77	153	29	4	15	68	.278	65	235	114	19-44
1961	RF	DET	AL	2-10	153	586	116	190	41	7	19	82	.324	66	302	138	8-49
1962	RF	DET	AL	4-10	100	398	78	121	16	6	29	94	.304	47	236	153	—
1963	RF	DET	AL	5-10	145	551	89	172	24	3	27	101	.312	54	283	142	5-51
1964	RF	DET	AL	4-10	146	525	77	154	31	5	17	68	.293	75	246	137	9-52
1965	RF	DET	AL	4-10	125	399	72	112	18	2	18	72	.281	72	188	147	—
1966	CF	DET	AL	3-10	142	479	85	138	29	1	29	88	.288	81	256	163	3-44
1967	RF	DET	AL	2-10	131	458	94	141	28	2	25	78	.308	83	248	180	4-48
1968	RF-1B	DET	AL	1-10	102	327	49	94	14	1	10	53	.287	55	140	150	—
1969	RF	DET	AL	2-6	131	456	74	124	17	0	21	69	.272	54	204	123	19-59
1970	RF-1B	DET	AL	4-6	131	467	64	130	24	4	16	71	.278	77	210	133	10-59
1971	RF	DET	AL	2-6	133	405	69	119	19	2	15	54	.294	82	187	153	3-57
1972	RF-1B	DET	AL	1-6	106	278	46	87	11	2	10	32	.313	28	132	146	—
1973	RF-1B	DET	AL	3-6	91	310	40	79	13	0	10	45	.255	29	122	101	—
1974	DH	DET	AL	6-6	147	558	71	146	28	2	13	64	.262	65	217	109	31-67
MAJOR LEAGUE TOTALS					2834	10116	1622	3007	498	75	399	1583	.297	1277	4852	136	16 yrs

Wallace Wade Moon   Born Apr 3, 1930   Bay, AR
6'0   169 lbs   Batted left

YR	POS	TEAM	LG	FIN	G	AB	R	H	2B	3B	HR	RBI	AVG	BB	TB	OQ	RANK
1954	CF	SL	NL	6-8	151	635	106	193	29	9	12	76	.304	71	276	113	17-48
1955	RF-1B	SL	NL	7-8	152	593	86	175	24	8	19	76	.295	47	272	111	20-43
1956	RF-1B	SL	NL	4-8	149	540	86	161	22	11	16	68	.298	80	253	132	12-43
1957	LF	SL	NL	2-8	142	516	86	152	28	5	24	73	.295	62	262	134	8-44
1958	RF-LF	SL	NL	5-8	108	290	36	69	10	3	7	38	.238	47	106	102	—
1959	LF	LA	NL	1-8	145	543	93	164	26	11	19	74	.302	81	269	138	7-38
1960	LF	LA	NL	4-8	138	469	74	140	21	6	13	69	.299	67	212	131	7-38
1961	LF	LA	NL	2-8	134	463	79	152	25	3	17	88	.328	89	234	153	3-37
1962	LF-1B	LA	NL	2-10	95	244	36	59	9	1	4	31	.242	30	82	92	—
1963	RF-LF	LA	NL	1-10	122	343	41	90	13	2	8	48	.262	45	131	118	—
1964	RF-LF	LA	NL	6-10	68	118	8	26	2	1	2	9	.220	12	36	86	—
1965	RF-LF	LA	NL	1-10	53	89	6	18	3	0	1	11	.202	13	24	85	—

MAJOR LEAGUE TOTALS   1457 4843 737 1399 212 60 142 661 .289 644 2157 130 7 yrs

Henry Louis Aaron   Born Feb 5, 1934   Mobile, AL
6'0   180 lbs   Batted right

YR	POS	TEAM	LG	FIN	G	AB	R	H	2B	3B	HR	RBI	AVG	BB	TB	OQ	RANK
1954	LF	MIL	NL	3-8	122	468	58	131	27	6	13	69	.280	28	209	101	32-48
1955	RF-2B	MIL	NL	2-8	153	602	105	189	37	9	27	106	.314	49	325	132	11-43
1956	RF	MIL	NL	2-8	153	609	106	200	34	14	26	92	.328	37	340	138	7-43
1957	RF	MIL	NL	1-8	151	615	118	198	27	6	44	132	.322	57	369	154	3-44
1958	RF	MIL	NL	1-8	153	601	109	196	34	4	30	95	.326	59	328	141	4-34
1959	RF	MIL	NL	2-8	154	629	116	223	46	7	39	123	.355	51	400	167	1-38
1960	RF	MIL	NL	2-8	153	590	102	172	20	11	40	126	.292	60	334	146	5-38
1961	CF	MIL	NL	4-8	155	603	115	197	39	10	34	120	.327	56	358	151	4-37
1962	CF	MIL	NL	5-10	156	592	127	191	28	6	45	128	.323	66	366	163	2-51
1963	RF	MIL	NL	6-10	161	631	121	201	29	4	44	130	.319	78	370	176	1-50
1964	RF	MIL	NL	5-10	145	570	103	187	30	2	24	95	.328	62	293	152	6-42
1965	RF	MIL	NL	5-10	150	570	109	181	40	1	32	89	.318	60	319	159	2-52
1966	RF	ATL	NL	5-10	158	603	117	168	23	1	44	127	.279	76	325	148	7-55
1967	RF	ATL	NL	7-10	155	600	113	184	37	3	39	109	.307	63	344	164	2-54
1968	RF	ATL	NL	5-10	160	606	84	174	33	4	29	86	.287	64	302	153	5-45
1969	RF	ATL	NL	1-6	147	547	100	164	30	3	44	97	.300	87	332	176	3-62
1970	RF	ATL	NL	5-6	150	516	103	154	26	1	38	118	.298	74	296	153	7-56
1971	1B-RF	ATL	NL	3-6	139	495	95	162	22	3	47	118	.327	71	331	197	1-58
1972	1B-RF	ATL	NL	4-6	129	449	75	119	10	0	34	77	.265	92	231	160	3-57
1973	RF	ATL	NL	5-6	120	392	84	118	12	1	40	96	.301	68	252	184	—
1974	RF	ATL	NL	3-6	112	340	47	91	16	0	20	69	.268	39	167	131	—
1975	DH	MIL	AL	5-6	137	465	45	109	16	2	12	60	.234	70	165	102	40-66
1976	DH	MIL	AL	5-6	85	271	22	62	8	0	10	35	.229	35	100	106	—

MAJOR LEAGUE TOTALS   3298 12364 2174 3771 624 98 755 2297 .305 1402 6856 152 20 yrs

Robert Ralph Skinner   Born Oct 3, 1931   La Jolla, CA
6'4   190 lbs   Batted left

YR	POS	TEAM	LG	FIN	G	AB	R	H	2B	3B	HR	RBI	AVG	BB	TB	OQ	RANK
1954	1B	PIT	NL	8-8	132	470	67	117	15	9	8	46	.249	47	174	90	41-48
1956	LF-1B	PIT	NL	7-8	113	233	29	47	8	3	5	29	.202	26	76	82	—
1957	LF	PIT	NL	7-8	126	387	58	118	12	6	13	45	.305	38	181	123	—
1958	LF	PIT	NL	2-8	144	529	93	170	33	9	13	70	.321	58	260	130	7-34
1959	LF	PIT	NL	4-8	143	547	78	153	18	4	13	61	.280	67	218	108	19-38
1960	LF	PIT	NL	1-8	145	571	83	156	33	6	15	86	.273	59	246	114	19-38
1961	LF	PIT	NL	6-8	119	381	61	102	20	3	3	42	.268	51	137	100	—
1962	LF	PIT	NL	4-10	144	510	87	154	29	7	20	75	.302	76	257	142	5-51
1963	LF	PT/CN	NL	8/5	106	316	43	82	15	7	3	25	.259	34	120	111	—
1964	RF-LF	CN/SL	NL	2/1	80	177	16	45	8	0	4	21	.254	15	65	100	—
1965	RF-LF	SL	NL	7-10	80	152	25	47	5	4	5	26	.309	12	75	135	—
1966	PH	SL	NL	6-10	49	45	2	7	1	0	1	5	.156	2	11	—	—
MAJOR LEAGUE TOTALS					1381	4318	642	1198	197	58	103	531	.277	485	1820	117	5 yrs

Harmon Clayton Killebrew   Born Jun 29, 1936   Payette, ID
6'0   195 lbs   Batted right

YR	POS	TEAM	LG	FIN	G	AB	R	H	2B	3B	HR	RBI	AVG	BB	TB	OQ	RANK
1954	2B	WAS	AL	6-8	9	13	1	4	1	0	0	3	.308	2	5	—	—
1955	3B-2B	WAS	AL	8-8	38	80	12	16	1	0	4	7	.200	9	29	—	—
1956	3B-2B	WAS	AL	7-8	44	99	10	22	2	0	5	13	.222	10	39	92	—
1957	3B-2B	WAS	AL	8-8	9	31	4	9	2	0	2	5	.290	2	17	—	—
1958	3B	WAS	AL	8-8	13	31	2	6	0	0	0	2	.194	0	6	—	—
1959	3B	WAS	AL	8-8	153	546	98	132	20	2	42	105	.242	90	282	139	7-35
1960	1B-3B	WAS	AL	5-8	124	442	84	122	19	1	31	80	.276	71	236	145	4-44
1961	1B-3B	MIN	AL	7-10	150	541	94	156	20	7	46	122	.288	107	328	167	4-49
1962	LF	MIN	AL	2-10	155	552	85	134	21	1	48	126	.243	106	301	146	3-54
1963	LF	MIN	AL	3-10	142	515	88	133	18	0	45	96	.258	72	286	150	3-51
1964	LF	MIN	AL	7-10	158	577	95	156	11	1	49	111	.270	93	316	153	4-52
1965	1B-3B	MIN	AL	1-10	113	401	78	108	16	1	25	75	.269	72	201	151	—
1966	3B-1B	MIN	AL	2-10	162	569	89	160	27	1	39	110	.281	103	306	165	2-44
1967	1B	MIN	AL	2-10	163	547	105	147	24	1	44	113	.269	131	305	188	2-48
1968	1B-3B	MIN	AL	7-10	100	295	40	62	7	2	17	40	.210	70	124	149	—
1969	3B-1B	MIN	AL	1-6	162	555	106	153	20	2	49	140	.276	145	324	185	1-59
1970	3B-1B	MIN	AL	1-6	157	527	96	143	20	1	41	113	.271	128	288	168	3-59
1971	1B-3B	MIN	AL	5-6	147	500	61	127	19	1	28	119	.254	114	232	150	5-57
1972	1B	MIN	AL	3-6	139	433	53	100	13	2	26	74	.231	94	195	151	6-56
1973	1B-DH	MIN	AL	3-6	69	248	29	60	9	1	5	32	.242	41	86	104	—
1974	DH-1B	MIN	AL	3-6	122	333	28	74	7	0	13	54	.222	45	120	102	—
1975	DH	KC	AL	2-6	106	312	25	62	13	0	14	44	.199	54	117	106	—
MAJOR LEAGUE TOTALS					2435	8147	1283	2086	290	24	573	1584	.256	1559	4143	159	12 yrs

Victor Pellot Power Born Nov 1, 1931 Arecibo, PR
6'0 186 lbs Batted right

YR	POS	TEAM	LG	FIN	G	AB	R	H	2B	3B	HR	RBI	AVG	BB	TB	OQ	RANK
1954	LF-1B	PHI	AL	8-8	127	462	36	118	17	5	8	38	.255	19	169	84	31-34
1955	1B	KC	AL	6-8	147	596	91	190	34	10	19	76	.319	35	301	124	8-39
1956	1B-2B	KC	AL	8-8	127	530	77	164	21	5	14	63	.309	24	237	103	28-40
1957	1B	KC	AL	7-8	129	467	48	121	15	1	14	42	.259	19	180	88	31-35
1958	1B-3B	KC/CL	AL	7/4	145	590	98	184	37	10	16	80	.312	20	289	118	16-39
1959	1B-2B	CLE	AL	2-8	147	595	102	172	31	6	10	60	.289	40	245	104	26-35
1960	1B	CLE	AL	4-8	147	580	69	167	26	3	10	84	.288	24	229	92	34-44
1961	1B	CLE	AL	5-10	147	563	64	151	34	4	5	63	.268	38	208	88	46-49
1962	1B	MIN	AL	2-10	144	611	80	177	28	2	16	63	.290	22	257	97	46-54
1963	1B-2B	MIN	AL	3-10	138	541	65	146	28	2	10	52	.270	22	208	93	41-51
1964	1B-3B	MN/LA	AL	6/5	87	266	23	65	8	0	3	14	.244	9	82	72	—
1964	1B	PHI	NL	2-10	18	48	1	10	4	0	0	3	.208	2	14	—	—
1965	1B	CAL	AL	7-10	124	197	11	51	7	1	1	20	.259	5	63	76	—

MAJOR LEAGUE TOTALS   1627 6046 765 1716 290 49 126 658 .284 279 2482 99 10 yrs

Williams Joseph Skowron Born Dec 18, 1930 Chicago, IL
5'11 195 lbs Batted right

YR	POS	TEAM	LG	FIN	G	AB	R	H	2B	3B	HR	RBI	AVG	BB	TB	OQ	RANK
1954	1B	NY	AL	2-8	87	215	37	73	12	9	7	41	.340	19	124	155	—
1955	1B	NY	AL	1-8	108	288	46	92	17	3	12	61	.319	21	151	131	—
1956	1B	NY	AL	1-8	134	464	78	143	21	6	23	90	.308	50	245	132	10-40
1957	1B	NY	AL	1-8	122	457	54	139	15	5	17	88	.304	31	215	119	15-35
1958	1B	NY	AL	1-8	126	465	61	127	22	3	14	73	.273	28	197	103	27-39
1959	1B	NY	AL	3-8	74	282	39	84	13	5	15	59	.298	20	152	134	—
1960	1B	NY	AL	1-8	146	538	63	166	34	3	26	91	.309	38	284	131	7-44
1961	1B	NY	AL	1-10	150	561	76	150	23	4	28	89	.267	35	265	108	27-49
1962	1B	NY	AL	1-10	140	478	63	129	16	6	23	80	.270	36	226	113	22-54
1963	1B	LA	NL	1-10	89	237	19	48	8	0	4	19	.203	13	68	72	—
1964	1B	WA/CH	AL	9/2	146	535	47	151	21	3	17	79	.282	30	229	106	31-52
1965	1B	CHI	AL	2-10	146	559	63	153	24	3	18	78	.274	32	237	108	25-46
1966	1B	CHI	AL	4-10	120	337	27	84	15	2	6	29	.249	26	121	96	—
1967	1B	CH/CA	AL	4/5	70	131	8	27	2	1	1	11	.206	4	34	63	—

MAJOR LEAGUE TOTALS   1658 5547 681 1566 243 53 211 888 .282 383 2548 115 8 yrs

Frank Elmore Bolling　　　　　Born Nov 16, 1931　Mobile, AL
6'1　175 lbs　Batted right

YR	POS	TEAM	LG	FIN	G	AB	R	H	2B	3B	HR	RBI	AVG	BB	TB	OQ	RANK
1954	2B	DET	AL	5-8	117	368	46	87	15	2	6	38	.236	36	124	87	—
1956	2B	DET	AL	5-8	102	366	53	103	21	7	7	45	.281	42	159	110	—
1957	2B	DET	AL	4-8	146	576	72	149	27	6	15	40	.259	57	233	104	25-35
1958	2B	DET	AL	5-8	154	610	91	164	25	4	14	75	.269	54	239	102	31-39
1959	2B	DET	AL	4-8	127	459	56	122	18	3	13	55	.266	45	185	105	25-35
1960	2B	DET	AL	6-8	139	536	64	136	20	4	9	59	.254	40	191	87	38-44
1961	2B	MIL	NL	4-8	148	585	86	153	16	4	15	56	.262	57	222	95	26-37
1962	2B	MIL	NL	5-10	122	406	45	110	17	4	9	43	.271	35	162	101	—
1963	2B	MIL	NL	6-10	142	542	73	132	18	2	5	43	.244	41	169	86	46-50
1964	2B	MIL	NL	5-10	120	352	35	70	11	1	5	34	.199	21	98	69	—
1965	2B	MIL	NL	5-10	148	535	55	141	26	3	7	50	.264	24	194	90	41-52
1966	2B	ATL	NL	5-10	75	227	16	48	7	0	1	18	.211	10	58	61	—

| MAJOR LEAGUE TOTALS | | | | | 1540 | 5562 | 692 | 1415 | 221 | 40 | 106 | 556 | .254 | 462 | 2034 | 96 | 7 yrs |

Elston Gene Howard　　　　　Born Feb 23, 1929　St Louis, MO
6'2　196 lbs　Batted right　　　　　Died Dec 14, 1980　New York, NY

YR	POS	TEAM	LG	FIN	G	AB	R	H	2B	3B	HR	RBI	AVG	BB	TB	OQ	RANK
1955	LF-C	NY	AL	1-8	97	279	33	81	8	7	10	43	.290	20	133	116	—
1956	LF-C	NY	AL	1-8	98	290	35	76	8	3	5	34	.262	21	105	85	—
1957	LF-C	NY	AL	1-8	110	356	33	90	13	4	8	44	.253	16	135	87	—
1958	C-LF	NY	AL	1-8	103	376	45	118	19	5	11	66	.314	22	180	122	—
1959	1B-C	NY	AL	3-8	125	443	59	121	24	6	18	73	.273	20	211	110	—
1960	C	NY	AL	1-8	107	323	29	79	11	3	6	39	.245	28	114	88	—
1961	C	NY	AL	1-10	129	446	64	155	17	5	21	77	.348	28	245	139	—
1962	C	NY	AL	1-10	136	494	63	138	23	5	21	91	.279	31	234	112	26-54
1963	C	NY	AL	1-10	135	487	75	140	21	6	28	85	.287	35	257	134	8-51
1964	C	NY	AL	1-10	150	550	63	172	27	3	15	84	.313	48	250	124	19-52
1965	C	NY	AL	6-10	110	391	38	91	15	1	9	45	.233	24	135	86	—
1966	C-1B	NY	AL	10-10	126	410	38	105	19	2	6	35	.256	37	146	99	—
1967	C	NY/BO	AL	9/1	108	315	22	56	9	0	4	28	.178	21	77	65	—
1968	C	BOS	AL	4-10	71	203	22	49	4	0	5	18	.241	22	68	104	—

| MAJOR LEAGUE TOTALS | | | | | 1605 | 5363 | 619 | 1471 | 218 | 50 | 167 | 762 | .274 | 373 | 2290 | — | — |

Don Lee Blasingame   Born Mar 16, 1932 Corinth, MS
5'10   160 lbs Batted left

YR	POS	TEAM	LG	FIN	G	AB	R	H	2B	3B	HR	RBI	AVG	BB	TB	OQ	RANK
1955	2B-SS	SL	NL	7-8	5	16	4	6	1	0	0	0	.375	6	7	—	—
1956	2B-SS	SL	NL	4-8	150	587	94	153	22	7	0	27	.261	72	189	90	36-43
1957	2B	SL	NL	2-8	154	650	108	176	25	7	8	58	.271	71	239	99	28-44
1958	2B	SL	NL	5-8	143	547	71	150	19	10	2	36	.274	57	195	94	30-34
1959	2B	SL	NL	7-8	150	615	90	178	26	7	1	24	.289	67	221	99	28-38
1960	2B	SF	NL	5-8	136	523	72	123	12	8	2	31	.235	49	157	80	37-38
1961	2B	SF/CN	NL	3/1	126	451	60	100	18	4	1	21	.222	41	129	71	37-37
1962	2B	CIN	NL	3-10	141	494	77	139	9	7	2	35	.281	63	168	99	39-51
1963	2B	CIN	NL	5-10	18	31	4	5	2	0	0	0	.161	7	7	—	—
1963	2B	WAS	AL	10-10	69	254	29	65	10	2	2	12	.256	24	85	92	—
1964	2B	WAS	AL	9-10	143	506	56	135	17	2	1	34	.267	40	159	85	45-52
1965	2B	WAS	AL	8-10	129	403	47	90	8	8	1	18	.223	35	117	79	—
1966	2B	WA/KC	AL	8/7	80	219	19	46	9	0	1	12	.210	20	58	75	—
MAJOR LEAGUE TOTALS					1444	5296	731	1366	178	62	21	308	.258	552	1731	90	8 yrs

Robert Clinton Richardson   Born Aug 19, 1935 Sumter, SC
5'9   170 lbs Batted right

YR	POS	TEAM	LG	FIN	G	AB	R	H	2B	3B	HR	RBI	AVG	BB	TB	OQ	RANK
1955	2B-SS	NY	AL	1-8	11	26	2	4	0	0	0	3	.154	2	4	—	—
1956	2B	NY	AL	1-8	5	7	1	1	0	0	0	0	.143	0	1	—	—
1957	2B	NY	AL	1-8	97	305	36	78	11	1	0	19	.256	9	91	68	—
1958	2B-3B	NY	AL	1-8	73	182	18	45	6	2	0	14	.247	8	55	71	—
1959	2B-SS	NY	AL	3-8	134	469	53	141	18	6	2	33	.301	26	177	95	29-35
1960	2B	NY	AL	1-8	150	460	45	116	12	3	1	26	.252	35	137	75	43-44
1961	2B	NY	AL	1-10	162	662	80	173	17	5	3	49	.261	30	209	72	49-49
1962	2B	NY	AL	1-10	161	692	99	209	38	5	8	59	.302	37	281	99	41-54
1963	2B	NY	AL	1-10	151	630	72	167	20	6	3	48	.265	25	208	80	49-51
1964	2B	NY	AL	1-10	159	679	90	181	25	4	4	50	.267	28	226	81	49-52
1965	2B	NY	AL	6-10	160	664	76	164	28	2	6	47	.247	37	214	81	46-46
1966	2B	NY	AL	10-10	149	610	71	153	21	3	7	42	.251	25	201	82	43-44
MAJOR LEAGUE TOTALS					1412	5386	643	1432	196	37	34	390	.266	262	1804	83	8 yrs

Frank James Malzone
Born Feb 28, 1930 Bronx, NY
5'10 180 lbs Batted right

YR	POS	TEAM	LG	FIN	G	AB	R	H	2B	3B	HR	RBI	AVG	BB	TB	OQ	RANK
1955	3B	BOS	AL	4-8	6	20	2	7	1	0	0	1	.350	1	8	—	—
1956	3B	BOS	AL	4-8	27	103	15	17	3	1	2	11	.165	9	28	62	—
1957	3B	BOS	AL	3-8	153	634	82	185	31	5	15	103	.292	31	271	103	26-35
1958	3B	BOS	AL	3-8	155	627	76	185	30	2	15	87	.295	33	264	104	25-39
1959	3B	BOS	AL	5-8	154	604	90	169	34	2	19	92	.280	42	264	108	24-35
1960	3B	BOS	AL	7-8	152	595	60	161	30	2	14	79	.271	36	237	95	31-44
1961	3B	BOS	AL	6-10	151	590	74	157	21	4	14	87	.266	44	228	93	37-49
1962	3B	BOS	AL	8-10	156	619	74	175	20	3	21	95	.283	35	264	101	40-54
1963	3B	BOS	AL	7-10	151	580	66	169	25	2	15	71	.291	31	243	107	31-51
1964	3B	BOS	AL	8-10	148	537	62	142	19	0	13	56	.264	37	200	95	40-52
1965	3B	BOS	AL	9-10	106	364	40	87	20	0	3	34	.239	28	116	84	—
1966	3B	CAL	AL	6-10	82	155	6	32	5	0	2	12	.206	10	43	71	—

MAJOR LEAGUE TOTALS					1441	5428	647	1486	239	21	133	728	.274	337	2166	101	8 yrs

Brooks Calbert Robinson
Born May 18, 1937 Little Rock, AR
6'1 180 lbs Batted right

YR	POS	TEAM	LG	FIN	G	AB	R	H	2B	3B	HR	RBI	AVG	BB	TB	OQ	RANK
1955	3B	BAL	AL	7-8	6	22	0	2	0	0	0	1	.091	0	2	—	—
1956	3B	BAL	AL	6-8	15	44	5	10	4	0	1	1	.227	1	17	—	—
1957	3B	BAL	AL	5-8	50	117	13	28	6	1	2	14	.239	7	42	85	—
1958	3B-2B	BAL	AL	6-8	145	463	31	110	16	3	3	32	.238	31	141	76	38-39
1959	3B	BAL	AL	6-8	88	313	29	89	15	2	4	24	.284	17	120	94	—
1960	3B	BAL	AL	2-8	152	595	74	175	27	9	14	88	.294	35	262	107	25-44
1961	3B	BAL	AL	3-10	163	668	89	192	38	7	7	61	.287	47	265	97	34-49
1962	3B	BAL	AL	7-10	162	634	77	192	29	9	23	86	.303	42	308	119	17-54
1963	3B	BAL	AL	4-10	161	589	67	148	26	4	11	67	.251	46	215	95	39-51
1964	3B	BAL	AL	3-10	163	612	82	194	35	3	28	118	.317	51	319	140	7-52
1965	3B	BAL	AL	3-10	144	559	81	166	25	2	18	80	.297	47	249	122	15-46
1966	3B	BAL	AL	1-10	157	620	91	167	35	2	23	100	.269	56	275	121	18-44
1967	3B	BAL	AL	6-10	158	610	88	164	25	5	22	77	.269	54	265	123	16-48
1968	3B	BAL	AL	2-10	162	608	65	154	36	6	17	75	.253	44	253	117	20-45
1969	3B	BAL	AL	1-6	156	598	73	140	21	3	23	84	.234	56	236	101	41-59
1970	3B	BAL	AL	1-6	158	608	84	168	31	4	18	94	.276	53	261	111	35-59
1971	3B	BAL	AL	1-6	156	589	67	160	21	1	20	92	.272	63	243	116	29-57
1972	3B	BAL	AL	3-6	153	556	48	139	23	2	8	64	.250	43	190	98	40-56
1973	3B	BAL	AL	1-6	155	549	53	141	17	2	9	72	.257	55	189	92	46-60
1974	3B	BAL	AL	1-6	153	553	46	159	27	0	7	59	.288	56	207	107	39-67
1975	3B	BAL	AL	2-6	144	482	50	97	15	1	6	53	.201	44	132	71	65-66
1976	3B	BAL	AL	2-6	71	218	16	46	8	2	3	11	.211	8	67	71	—
1977	3B	BAL	AL	2-7	24	47	3	7	2	0	1	4	.149	4	12	—	—

MAJOR LEAGUE TOTALS					2896	10654	1232	2848	482	68	268	1357	.267	860	4270	107	17 yrs

Cletis Leroy Boyer   Born Feb 9, 1937   Cassville, MO
6'0   165 lbs   Batted right

YR	POS	TEAM	LG	FIN	G	AB	R	H	2B	3B	HR	RBI	AVG	BB	TB	OQ	RANK
1955	SS-3B	KC	AL	6-8	47	79	3	19	1	0	0	6	.241	3	20	—	—
1956	2B-3B	KC	AL	8-8	67	129	15	28	3	1	1	4	.217	11	36	67	—
1957	2B-3B	KC	AL	7-8	10	0	0	0	0	0	0	0	—	0	0	—	—
1959	SS-3B	NY	AL	3-8	47	114	4	20	2	0	0	3	.175	6	22	46	—
1960	3B-SS	NY	AL	1-8	124	393	54	95	20	1	14	46	.242	23	159	92	—
1961	3B	NY	AL	1-10	148	504	61	113	19	5	11	55	.224	63	175	90	42-49
1962	3B	NY	AL	1-10	158	566	85	154	24	1	18	68	.272	51	234	104	35-54
1963	3B	NY	AL	1-10	152	557	59	140	20	3	12	54	.251	33	202	90	44-51
1964	3B-SS	NY	AL	1-10	147	510	43	111	10	5	8	52	.218	36	155	76	51-52
1965	3B	NY	AL	6-10	148	514	69	129	23	6	18	58	.251	39	218	108	23-46
1966	3B-SS	NY	AL	10-10	144	500	59	120	22	4	14	57	.240	46	192	103	27-44
1967	3B	ATL	NL	7-10	154	572	63	140	18	3	26	96	.245	39	242	109	33-54
1968	3B	ATL	NL	5-10	71	273	19	62	7	2	4	17	.227	16	85	86	—
1969	3B	ATL	NL	1-6	144	496	57	124	16	1	14	57	.250	55	184	103	40-62
1970	3B	ATL	NL	5-6	134	475	44	117	14	1	16	62	.246	41	181	93	45-56
1971	3B	ATL	NL	3-6	30	98	10	24	1	0	6	19	.245	8	43	112	—

MAJOR LEAGUE TOTALS   1725 5780 645 1396 200 33 162 654 .242 470 2148 97 9 yrs

Kenton Lloyd Boyer   Born May 20, 1931 Liberty, MO
6'1   190 lbs   Batted right   Died Sep 7, 1982   St Louis, MO

YR	POS	TEAM	LG	FIN	G	AB	R	H	2B	3B	HR	RBI	AVG	BB	TB	OQ	RANK
1955	3B-SS	SL	NL	7-8	147	530	78	140	27	2	18	62	.264	37	225	98	27-43
1956	3B	SL	NL	4-8	150	595	91	182	30	2	26	98	.306	38	294	121	16-43
1957	CF-3B	SL	NL	2-8	142	544	79	144	18	3	19	62	.265	44	225	102	26-44
1958	3B	SL	NL	5-8	150	570	101	175	21	9	23	90	.307	49	283	124	9-34
1959	3B	SL	NL	7-8	149	563	86	174	18	5	28	94	.309	67	286	136	8-38
1960	3B	SL	NL	3-8	151	552	95	168	26	10	32	97	.304	56	310	148	4-38
1961	3B	SL	NL	5-8	153	589	109	194	26	11	24	95	.329	68	314	143	7-37
1962	3B	SL	NL	6-10	160	611	92	178	27	5	24	98	.291	75	287	127	12-51
1963	3B	SL	NL	2-10	159	617	86	176	28	2	24	111	.285	70	280	134	11-50
1964	3B	SL	NL	1-10	162	628	100	185	30	10	24	119	.295	70	307	140	11-42
1965	3B	SL	NL	7-10	144	535	71	139	18	2	13	75	.260	57	200	106	33-52
1966	3B	NY	NL	9-10	136	496	62	132	28	2	14	61	.266	30	206	104	36-55
1967	3B-1B	NY	NL	10-10	56	166	17	39	7	2	3	13	.235	26	59	112	—
1967	3B-1B	CHI	AL	4-10	57	180	17	47	5	1	4	21	.261	7	66	95	—
1968	3B-1B	CHI	AL	8-10	10	24	0	3	0	0	0	0	.125	1	3	—	—
1968	3B-1B	LA	NL	7-10	83	221	20	60	7	2	6	41	.271	16	89	118	—
1969	1B	LA	NL	4-6	25	34	0	7	2	0	0	4	.206	2	9	—	—

MAJOR LEAGUE TOTALS   2034 7455 1104 2143 318 68 282 1141 .287 713 3443 124 12 yrs

Roberto Clemente
5'11   175 lbs   Batted right

Born Aug 18, 1934 Carolina, PR
Died Dec 31, 1972 San Juan, PR

YR	POS	TEAM	LG	FIN	G	AB	R	H	2B	3B	HR	RBI	AVG	BB	TB	OQ	RANK
1955	RF	PIT	NL	8-8	124	474	48	121	23	11	5	47	.255	18	181	82	41-43
1956	RF	PIT	NL	7-8	147	543	66	169	30	7	7	60	.311	13	234	99	29-43
1957	RF	PIT	NL	8-8	111	451	42	114	17	7	4	30	.253	23	157	81	41-44
1958	RF	PIT	NL	2-8	140	519	69	150	24	10	6	50	.289	31	212	97	24-34
1959	RF	PIT	NL	4-8	105	432	60	128	17	7	4	50	.296	15	171	92	—
1960	RF	PIT	NL	1-8	144	570	89	179	22	6	16	94	.314	39	261	119	14-38
1961	RF	PIT	NL	6-8	146	572	100	201	30	10	23	89	.351	35	320	141	8-37
1962	RF	PIT	NL	4-10	144	538	95	168	28	9	10	74	.312	35	244	114	26-51
1963	RF	PIT	NL	8-10	152	600	77	192	23	8	17	76	.320	31	282	130	14-50
1964	RF	PIT	NL	6-10	155	622	95	211	40	7	12	87	.339	51	301	141	9-42
1965	RF	PIT	NL	3-10	152	589	91	194	21	14	10	65	.329	43	273	131	15-52
1966	RF	PIT	NL	3-10	154	638	105	202	31	11	29	119	.317	46	342	143	8-55
1967	RF	PIT	NL	6-10	147	585	103	209	26	10	23	110	.357	41	324	163	3-54
1968	RF	PIT	NL	6-10	132	502	74	146	18	12	18	57	.291	51	242	149	7-45
1969	RF	PIT	NL	3-6	138	507	87	175	20	12	19	91	.345	56	276	161	6-62
1970	RF	PIT	NL	1-6	108	412	65	145	22	10	14	60	.352	38	229	149	—
1971	RF	PIT	NL	1-6	132	522	82	178	29	8	13	86	.341	26	262	137	13-58
1972	RF	PIT	NL	1-6	102	378	68	118	19	7	10	60	.312	29	181	132	—

MAJOR LEAGUE TOTALS   2433   9454 1416 3000 440 166 240 1305 .317 621 4492 126 15 yrs

William Charles Virdon
6'0   175 lbs   Batted left

Born Jun 9, 1931   Hazel Park, MI

YR	POS	TEAM	LG	FIN	G	AB	R	H	2B	3B	HR	RBI	AVG	BB	TB	OQ	RANK
1955	CF	SL	NL	7-8	144	534	58	150	18	6	17	68	.281	36	231	101	26-43
1956	CF	SL/PT	NL	4/7	157	580	77	185	23	10	10	46	.319	38	258	112	21-43
1957	CF	PIT	NL	7-8	144	561	59	141	28	11	8	50	.251	33	215	89	36-44
1958	CF	PIT	NL	2-8	144	604	75	161	24	11	9	46	.267	52	234	95	26-34
1959	CF	PIT	NL	4-8	144	519	67	132	24	2	8	41	.254	55	184	93	32-38
1960	CF	PIT	NL	1-8	120	409	60	108	16	9	8	40	.264	40	166	106	—
1961	CF	PIT	NL	6-8	146	599	81	156	22	8	9	58	.260	49	221	90	28-37
1962	CF	PIT	NL	4-10	156	663	82	164	27	10	6	47	.247	36	229	80	51-51
1963	CF	PIT	NL	8-10	142	554	58	149	22	6	8	53	.269	43	207	104	32-50
1964	CF	PIT	NL	6-10	145	473	59	115	11	3	3	27	.243	30	141	79	42-42
1965	CF	PIT	NL	3-10	135	481	58	134	22	5	4	24	.279	30	178	98	37-52
1968	RF	PIT	NL	6-10	6	3	1	1	0	0	1	2	.333	0	4	—	—

MAJOR LEAGUE TOTALS   1583   5980 735 1596 237 81 91 502 .267 442 2268 94 10 yrs

Rocco Domenico Colavito　　　　　Born Aug 10, 1933 Bronx, NY
6'3　190 lbs　Batted right

YR	POS	TEAM	LG	FIN	G	AB	R	H	2B	3B	HR	RBI	AVG	BB	TB	OQ	RANK
1955	RF	CLE	AL	2-8	5	9	3	4	2	0	0	0	.444	0	6	—	—
1956	RF	CLE	AL	2-8	101	322	55	89	11	4	21	65	.276	49	171	136	—
1957	RF	CLE	AL	3-8	134	461	66	116	26	0	25	84	.252	71	217	128	10-35
1958	RF	CLE	AL	4-8	143	489	80	148	26	3	41	113	.303	84	303	176	3-39
1959	RF	CLE	AL	2-8	154	588	90	151	24	0	42	111	.257	71	301	131	9-35
1960	RF	DET	AL	6-8	145	555	67	138	18	1	35	87	.249	53	263	114	18-44
1961	LF	DET	AL	2-10	163	583	129	169	30	2	45	140	.290	113	338	161	5-49
1962	LF	DET	AL	4-10	161	601	90	164	30	2	37	112	.273	96	309	139	5-54
1963	LF	DET	AL	6-10	160	597	91	162	29	2	22	91	.271	84	261	127	13-51
1964	RF	KC	AL	10-10	160	588	89	161	31	2	34	102	.274	83	298	141	6-52
1965	RF	CLE	AL	5-10	162	592	92	170	25	2	26	108	.287	93	277	142	4-46
1966	RF	CLE	AL	5-10	151	533	68	127	13	0	30	72	.238	76	230	125	16-44
1967	RF	CL/CH	AL	8/4	123	381	30	88	13	1	8	50	.231	49	127	104	—
1968	LF-RF	LA	NL	7-10	40	113	8	23	3	0	3	11	.204	15	35	100	—
1968	RF-LF	NY	AL	5-10	39	91	13	20	2	2	5	13	.220	14	41	139	—

MAJOR LEAGUE TOTALS　　　　1841　6503　971 1730　283　21 374 1159　.266　951 3177　138　10 yrs

Curtis Charles Flood　　　　　Born Jan 18, 1938　Houston, TX
5'9　165 lbs　Batted right

YR	POS	TEAM	LG	FIN	G	AB	R	H	2B	3B	HR	RBI	AVG	BB	TB	OQ	RANK
1956	PR-PH	CIN	NL	3-8	5	1	0	0	0	0	0	0	.000	0	0	—	—
1957	3B-2B	CIN	NL	4-8	3	3	2	1	0	0	1	1	.333	0	4	—	—
1958	CF	SL	NL	5-8	121	422	50	110	17	2	10	41	.261	31	161	91	—
1959	CF	SL	NL	7-8	121	208	24	53	7	3	7	26	.255	16	87	100	—
1960	CF	SL	NL	3-8	140	396	37	94	20	1	8	38	.237	35	140	90	—
1961	CF	SL	NL	5-8	132	335	53	108	15	5	2	21	.322	35	139	113	—
1962	CF	SL	NL	6-10	151	635	99	188	30	5	12	70	.296	42	264	104	30-51
1963	CF	SL	NL	2-10	158	662	112	200	34	9	5	63	.302	42	267	113	24-50
1964	CF	SL	NL	1-10	162	679	97	211	25	3	5	46	.311	43	257	105	29-42
1965	CF	SL	NL	7-10	156	617	90	191	30	3	11	83	.310	51	260	119	25-52
1966	CF	SL	NL	6-10	160	626	64	167	21	5	10	78	.267	26	228	89	47-55
1967	CF	SL	NL	1-10	134	514	68	172	24	1	5	50	.335	37	213	122	22-54
1968	CF	SL	NL	1-10	150	618	71	186	17	4	5	60	.301	33	226	108	27-45
1969	CF	SL	NL	4-6	153	606	80	173	31	3	4	57	.285	48	222	100	43-62
1971	CF	WAS	AL	5-6	13	35	4	7	0	0	0	2	.200	5	7	—	—

MAJOR LEAGUE TOTALS　　　　1759　6357　851 1861　271　44　85　636　.293　444 2475　108　8 yrs

Jerry Dean Lumpe

Born Jun 2, 1933   Lincoln, MO

6'2   185 lbs   Batted left

YR	POS	TEAM	LG	FIN	G	AB	R	H	2B	3B	HR	RBI	AVG	BB	TB	OQ	RANK
1956	SS	NY	AL	1-8	20	62	12	16	3	0	0	4	.258	5	19	—	—
1957	3B-SS	NY	AL	1-8	40	103	15	35	6	2	0	11	.340	9	45	122	—
1958	3B	NY	AL	1-8	81	232	34	59	8	4	3	32	.254	23	84	96	—
1959	2B-SS	NY/KC	AL	3/7	126	448	49	108	11	5	3	30	.241	47	138	84	35-35
1960	2B-SS	KC	AL	8-8	146	574	69	156	19	3	8	53	.272	48	205	91	36-44
1961	2B	KC	AL	9-10	148	569	81	167	29	9	3	54	.293	48	223	100	31-49
1962	2B	KC	AL	9-10	156	641	89	193	34	10	10	83	.301	44	277	108	31-54
1963	2B	KC	AL	8-10	157	595	75	161	26	7	5	59	.271	58	216	101	35-51
1964	2B	DET	AL	4-10	158	624	75	160	21	6	6	46	.256	50	211	89	44-52
1965	2B	DET	AL	4-10	145	502	72	129	15	3	4	39	.257	56	162	95	37-46
1966	2B	DET	AL	3-10	113	385	30	89	14	3	1	26	.231	24	112	76	—
1967	2B	DET	AL	2-10	81	177	19	41	4	0	4	17	.232	16	57	93	—

MAJOR LEAGUE TOTALS   1371   4912 620 1314 190 52 47 454 .268 428 1749 95 7 yrs

William Stanley Mazeroski

Born Sep 5, 1936   Wheeling, WV

5'11   183 lbs   Batted right

YR	POS	TEAM	LG	FIN	G	AB	R	H	2B	3B	HR	RBI	AVG	BB	TB	OQ	RANK
1956	2B	PIT	NL	7-8	81	255	30	62	8	1	3	14	.243	18	81	77	—
1957	2B	PIT	NL	7-8	148	526	59	149	27	7	8	54	.283	27	214	97	29-44
1958	2B	PIT	NL	2-8	152	567	69	156	24	6	19	68	.275	25	249	98	23-34
1959	2B	PIT	NL	4-8	135	493	50	119	15	6	7	59	.241	29	167	79	37-38
1960	2B	PIT	NL	1-8	151	538	58	147	21	5	11	64	.273	40	211	99	29-38
1961	2B	PIT	NL	6-8	152	558	71	148	21	2	13	59	.265	26	212	86	32-37
1962	2B	PIT	NL	4-10	159	572	55	155	24	9	14	81	.271	37	239	100	35-51
1963	2B	PIT	NL	8-10	142	534	43	131	22	3	8	52	.245	32	183	90	45-50
1964	2B	PIT	NL	6-10	162	601	66	161	22	8	10	64	.268	29	229	96	34-42
1965	2B	PIT	NL	3-10	130	494	52	134	17	1	6	54	.271	18	171	86	47-52
1966	2B	PIT	NL	3-10	162	621	56	163	22	7	16	82	.262	31	247	97	40-55
1967	2B	PIT	NL	6-10	163	639	62	167	25	3	9	77	.261	30	225	90	47-54
1968	2B	PIT	NL	6-10	143	506	36	127	18	2	3	42	.251	38	158	93	39-45
1969	2B	PIT	NL	3-6	67	227	13	52	7	1	3	25	.229	22	70	85	—
1970	2B	PIT	NL	1-6	112	367	29	84	14	0	7	39	.229	27	119	77	—
1971	2B	PIT	NL	1-6	70	193	17	49	3	1	1	16	.254	15	57	82	—
1972	2B	PIT	NL	1-6	34	64	3	12	4	0	0	3	.188	3	16	—	—

MAJOR LEAGUE TOTALS   2163   7755 769 2016 294 62 138 853 .260 447 2848 93 12 yrs

John George Brandt   Born Apr 28, 1934 Omaha, NE
5'11 165 lbs Batted right

YR	POS	TEAM	LG	FIN	G	AB	R	H	2B	3B	HR	RBI	AVG	BB	TB	OQ	RANK
1956	LF	SL/NY	NL	4/6	125	393	54	117	19	8	12	50	.298	21	188	113	—
1958	LF-RF	SF	NL	3-8	18	52	7	13	1	0	0	3	.250	6	14	—	—
1959	LF-3B	SF	NL	3-8	137	429	63	116	16	5	12	57	.270	35	178	102	26-38
1960	CF	BAL	AL	2-8	145	511	73	130	24	6	15	65	.254	47	211	102	26-44
1961	CF	BAL	AL	3-10	139	516	93	153	18	5	16	72	.297	62	229	119	19-49
1962	CF	BAL	AL	7-10	143	505	76	129	29	5	19	75	.255	55	225	112	25-54
1963	CF	BAL	AL	4-10	142	451	49	112	15	5	15	61	.248	34	182	102	—
1964	CF	BAL	AL	3-10	137	523	66	127	25	1	13	47	.243	45	193	95	39-52
1965	LF-CF	BAL	AL	3-10	96	243	35	59	17	0	8	24	.243	21	100	107	—
1966	CF-LF	PHI	NL	4-10	82	164	16	41	6	1	1	15	.250	17	52	90	—
1967	1B-LF	PH/HO	NL	5/9	57	108	8	23	5	1	1	16	.213	8	33	81	—
MAJOR LEAGUE TOTALS					1221	3895	540	1020	175	37	112	485	.262	351	1605	106	5 yrs

Luis Ernesto Aparico   Born Apr 29, 1934 Maracaibo, Venezuela
5'9 160 lbs Batted right

YR	POS	TEAM	LG	FIN	G	AB	R	H	2B	3B	HR	RBI	AVG	BB	TB	OQ	RANK
1956	SS	CHI	AL	3-8	152	533	69	142	19	6	3	56	.266	34	182	80	38-40
1957	SS	CHI	AL	2-8	143	575	82	148	22	6	3	41	.257	52	191	87	32-35
1958	SS	CHI	AL	2-8	145	557	76	148	20	9	2	40	.266	35	192	86	35-39
1959	SS	CHI	AL	1-8	152	612	98	157	18	5	6	51	.257	53	203	87	33-35
1960	SS	CHI	AL	3-8	153	600	86	166	20	7	2	61	.277	43	206	87	39-44
1961	SS	CHI	AL	4-10	156	625	90	170	24	4	6	45	.272	38	220	84	47-49
1962	SS	CHI	AL	5-10	153	581	72	140	23	5	7	40	.241	32	194	77	54-54
1963	SS	BAL	AL	4-10	146	601	73	150	18	8	5	45	.250	36	199	83	47-51
1964	SS	BAL	AL	3-10	146	578	93	154	20	3	10	37	.266	49	210	97	37-52
1965	SS	BAL	AL	3-10	144	564	67	127	20	10	8	40	.225	46	191	88	43-46
1966	SS	BAL	AL	1-10	151	659	97	182	25	8	6	41	.276	33	241	95	37-44
1967	SS	BAL	AL	6-10	134	546	55	127	22	5	4	31	.233	29	171	82	47-48
1968	SS	CHI	AL	8-10	155	622	55	164	24	4	4	36	.264	33	208	94	39-45
1969	SS	CHI	AL	5-6	156	599	77	168	24	5	5	51	.280	66	217	104	40-59
1970	SS	CHI	AL	6-6	146	552	86	173	29	3	5	43	.313	53	223	113	32-59
1971	SS	BOS	AL	3-6	125	491	56	114	23	0	4	45	.232	35	149	79	56-57
1972	SS	BOS	AL	2-6	110	436	47	112	26	3	3	39	.257	26	153	96	—
1973	SS	BOS	AL	2-6	132	499	56	135	17	1	0	49	.271	43	154	83	53-60
MAJOR LEAGUE TOTALS					2599	10230	1335	2677	394	92	83	791	.262	736	3504	89	17 yrs

William De Kova White

Born Jan 28, 1934   Lakewood, FL

6'0   185 lbs   Batted left

YR	POS	TEAM	LG	FIN	G	AB	R	H	2B	3B	HR	RBI	AVG	BB	TB	OQ	RANK
1956	1B	NY	NL	6-8	138	508	63	130	23	7	22	59	.256	47	233	111	23-43
1958	1B-RF	SF	NL	3-8	26	29	5	7	1	0	1	4	.241	7	11	—	—
1959	LF-1B	SL	NL	7-8	138	517	77	156	33	9	12	72	.302	34	243	115	15-38
1960	1B-CF	SL	NL	3-8	144	554	81	157	27	10	16	79	.283	42	252	115	18-38
1961	1B	SL	NL	5-8	153	591	89	169	28	11	20	90	.286	64	279	120	17-37
1962	1B-RF	SL	NL	6-10	159	614	93	199	31	3	20	102	.324	58	296	129	11-51
1963	1B	SL	NL	2-10	162	658	106	200	26	8	27	109	.304	59	323	141	7-50
1964	1B	SL	NL	1-10	160	631	92	191	37	4	21	102	.303	52	299	131	14-42
1965	1B	SL	NL	7-10	148	543	82	157	26	3	24	73	.289	63	261	137	11-52
1966	1B	PHI	NL	4-10	159	577	85	159	23	6	22	103	.276	68	260	126	15-55
1967	1B	PHI	NL	5-10	110	308	29	77	6	2	8	33	.250	52	111	118	—
1968	1B	PHI	NL	7-10	127	385	34	92	16	2	9	40	.239	39	139	110	—
1969	1B	SL	NL	4-6	49	57	7	12	1	0	0	4	.211	11	13	—	—
MAJOR LEAGUE TOTALS					1673	5972	843	1706	278	65	202	870	.286	596	2720	125	9 yrs

Robert Thomas Aspromonte

Born Jun 19, 1938   Brooklyn, NY

6'2   170 lbs   Batted right

YR	POS	TEAM	LG	FIN	G	AB	R	H	2B	3B	HR	RBI	AVG	BB	TB	OQ	RANK
1956	PH	BRO	NL	1-8	1	1	0	0	0	0	0	0	.000	0	0	—	—
1960	SS-3B	LA	NL	4-8	21	55	1	10	1	0	1	6	.182	0	14	—	—
1961	3B-SS	LA	NL	2-8	47	58	7	14	3	0	0	2	.241	4	17	—	—
1962	3B	HOU	NL	8-10	149	534	59	142	18	4	11	59	.266	46	201	95	42-51
1963	3B	HOU	NL	9-10	136	468	42	100	9	5	8	49	.214	40	143	84	48-50
1964	3B	HOU	NL	9-10	157	553	51	155	20	3	12	69	.280	35	217	104	31-42
1965	3B	HOU	NL	9-10	152	578	53	152	15	2	5	52	.263	38	186	86	46-52
1966	3B	HOU	NL	8-10	152	560	55	141	16	3	8	52	.252	35	187	85	49-55
1967	3B	HOU	NL	9-10	137	486	51	143	24	5	6	58	.294	45	195	117	26-54
1968	3B-LF	HOU	NL	10-10	124	409	25	92	9	2	1	46	.225	35	108	81	—
1969	LF-3B	ATL	NL	1-6	82	198	16	50	8	1	3	24	.253	13	69	89	—
1970	3B	ATL	NL	5-6	62	127	5	27	3	0	0	7	.213	13	30	64	—
1971	3B	NY	NL	3-6	104	342	21	77	9	1	5	33	.225	29	103	81	—
MAJOR LEAGUE TOTALS					1324	4369	386	1103	135	26	60	457	.252	333	1470	95	6 yrs

Norman Leroy Siebern   Born Jul 26, 1933   St Louis, MO
6'2   200 lbs   Batted left

YR	POS	TEAM	LG	FIN	G	AB	R	H	2B	3B	HR	RBI	AVG	BB	TB	OQ	RANK
1956	LF	NY	AL	1-8	54	162	27	33	1	4	4	21	.204	19	54	82	—
1958	LF	NY	AL	1-8	134	460	79	138	19	5	14	55	.300	66	209	133	9-39
1959	LF	NY	AL	3-8	120	380	52	103	17	0	11	53	.271	41	153	108	—
1960	LF-1B	KC	AL	8-8	144	520	69	145	31	6	19	69	.279	72	245	127	9-44
1961	1B-LF	KC	AL	9-10	153	560	68	166	36	5	18	98	.296	82	266	131	9-49
1962	1B	KC	AL	9-10	162	600	114	185	25	6	25	117	.308	110	297	147	2-54
1963	1B-LF	KC	AL	8-10	152	556	80	151	25	2	16	83	.272	79	228	121	18-51
1964	1B	BAL	AL	3-10	150	478	92	117	24	2	12	56	.245	106	181	126	17-52
1965	1B	BAL	AL	3-10	106	297	44	76	13	4	8	32	.256	50	121	126	—
1966	1B	CAL	AL	6-10	125	336	29	83	14	1	5	41	.247	63	114	116	—
1967	1B	SF	NL	2-10	46	58	6	9	1	1	0	4	.155	14	12	—	—
1967	1B	BOS	AL	1-10	33	44	2	9	0	2	0	7	.205	6	13	—	—
1968	1B-RF	BOS	AL	4-10	27	30	0	2	0	0	0	0	.067	0	2	—	—

MAJOR LEAGUE TOTALS   1406   4481 662 1217 206 38 132 636 .272 708 1895 131   6 yrs

John Patsy Francona   Born Nov 4, 1933   Aliquippa, PA
5'11   190 lbs   Batted left

YR	POS	TEAM	LG	FIN	G	AB	R	H	2B	3B	HR	RBI	AVG	BB	TB	OQ	RANK
1956	RF-1B	BAL	AL	6-8	139	445	62	115	16	4	9	57	.258	51	166	95	30-40
1957	RF-LF	BAL	AL	5-8	97	279	35	65	8	3	7	38	.233	29	100	93	—
1958	RF-LF	CH/DE	AL	2/5	86	197	21	50	8	2	1	20	.254	29	65	99	—
1959	CF-1B	CLE	AL	2-8	122	399	68	145	17	2	20	79	.363	35	226	158	—
1960	LF	CLE	AL	4-8	147	544	84	159	36	2	17	79	.292	67	250	124	11-44
1961	LF	CLE	AL	5-10	155	592	87	178	30	8	16	85	.301	56	272	117	20-49
1962	1B	CLE	AL	6-10	158	621	82	169	28	5	14	70	.272	47	249	98	43-54
1963	LF	CLE	AL	5-10	142	500	57	114	29	0	10	41	.228	47	173	91	43-51
1964	RF-1B	CLE	AL	6-10	111	270	35	67	13	2	8	24	.248	44	108	118	—
1965	RF-1B	SL	NL	7-10	81	174	15	45	6	2	5	19	.259	17	70	110	—
1966	1B-LF	SL	NL	6-10	83	156	14	33	4	1	4	17	.212	7	51	76	—
1967	1B	PH/AT	NL	5/7	109	327	35	78	6	1	6	28	.239	27	104	88	—
1968	LF-1B	ATL	NL	5-10	122	346	32	99	13	1	2	47	.286	51	120	125	—
1969	LF-1B	ATL	NL	1-6	51	88	5	26	1	0	2	22	.295	13	33	119	—
1969	1B	OAK	AL	2-6	32	85	12	29	6	1	3	20	.341	12	46	—	—
1970	1B	OA/ML	AL	2/4	84	98	6	23	3	0	1	10	.235	12	29	85	—

MAJOR LEAGUE TOTALS   1719   5121 650 1395 224 34 125 656 .272 544 2062 105   5 yrs

Charles Lenard Neal   Born Jan 30, 1931   Longview, TX
5'10 165 lbs Batted right

YR	POS	TEAM	LG	FIN	G	AB	R	H	2B	3B	HR	RBI	AVG	BB	TB	OQ	RANK
1956	2B	BRO	NL	1-8	62	136	22	39	5	1	2	14	.287	14	52	102	—
1957	SS-3B	BRO	NL	3-8	128	448	62	121	13	7	12	62	.270	53	184	110	20-44
1958	2B	LA	NL	7-8	140	473	87	120	9	6	22	65	.254	61	207	112	19-34
1959	2B	LA	NL	1-8	151	616	103	177	30	11	19	83	.287	43	286	112	17-38
1960	2B	LA	NL	4-8	139	477	60	122	23	2	8	40	.256	48	173	96	32-38
1961	2B	LA	NL	2-8	108	341	40	80	6	1	10	48	.235	30	118	84	—
1962	2B-SS	NY	NL	10-10	136	508	59	132	14	9	11	58	.260	56	197	102	33-51
1963	3B	NY/CN	NL	10/5	106	317	28	67	13	1	3	21	.211	32	91	83	—
MAJOR LEAGUE TOTALS					970	3316	461	858	113	38	87	391	.259	337	1308	106	5 yrs

Frank Robinson   Born Aug 31, 1935 Beaumont, TX
6'1 183 lbs Batted right

YR	POS	TEAM	LG	FIN	G	AB	R	H	2B	3B	HR	RBI	AVG	BB	TB	OQ	RANK
1956	LF	CIN	NL	3-8	152	572	122	166	27	6	38	83	.290	64	319	141	3-43
1957	LF-1B	CIN	NL	4-8	150	611	97	197	29	5	29	75	.322	44	323	134	9-44
1958	LF	CIN	NL	4-8	148	554	90	149	25	6	31	83	.269	62	279	124	8-34
1959	1B-LF	CIN	NL	5-8	146	540	106	168	31	4	36	125	.311	69	315	155	3-38
1960	1B-LF	CIN	NL	6-8	139	464	86	138	33	6	31	83	.297	82	276	170	1-38
1961	RF	CIN	NL	1-8	153	545	117	176	32	7	37	124	.323	71	333	162	1-37
1962	RF	CIN	NL	3-10	162	609	134	208	51	2	39	136	.342	76	380	172	1-51
1963	LF	CIN	NL	5-10	140	482	79	125	19	3	21	91	.259	81	213	139	9-50
1964	RF	CIN	NL	2-10	156	568	103	174	38	6	29	96	.306	79	311	163	3-42
1965	RF	CIN	NL	4-10	156	582	109	172	33	5	33	113	.296	70	314	153	5-52
1966	RF	BAL	AL	1-10	155	576	122	182	34	2	49	122	.316	87	367	190	1-44
1967	RF	BAL	AL	6-10	129	479	83	149	23	7	30	94	.311	71	276	181	3-48
1968	RF	BAL	AL	2-10	130	421	69	113	27	1	15	52	.268	73	187	151	5-45
1969	RF-1B	BAL	AL	1-6	148	539	111	166	19	5	32	100	.308	88	291	161	6-59
1970	RF	BAL	AL	1-6	132	471	88	144	24	1	25	78	.306	69	245	149	5-59
1971	RF-1B	BAL	AL	1-6	133	455	82	128	16	2	28	99	.281	72	232	151	4-57
1972	RF	LA	NL	3-6	103	342	41	86	6	1	19	59	.251	55	151	132	—
1973	DH-LF	CAL	AL	4-6	147	534	85	142	29	0	30	97	.266	82	261	135	7-60
1974	DH	CA/CL	AL	6/4	144	477	81	117	27	3	22	68	.245	85	216	134	6-67
1975	DH	CLE	AL	4-6	49	118	19	28	5	0	9	24	.237	29	60	153	—
1976	DH	CLE	AL	4-6	36	67	5	15	0	0	3	10	.224	11	24	—	—
MAJOR LEAGUE TOTALS					2808	10006	1829	2943	528	72	586	1812	.294	1420	5373	154	18 yrs

James Henry Landis Born Mar 9, 1934 Fresno, CA
6'1 180 lbs Batted right

YR	POS	TEAM	LG	FIN	G	AB	R	H	2B	3B	HR	RBI	AVG	BB	TB	OQ	RANK
1957	RF	CHI	AL	2-8	96	274	38	58	11	3	2	16	.212	45	81	90	—
1958	CF	CHI	AL	2-8	142	523	72	145	23	7	15	64	.277	52	227	115	19-39
1959	CF	CHI	AL	1-8	149	515	78	140	26	7	5	60	.272	78	195	112	21-35
1960	CF	CHI	AL	3-8	148	494	89	125	25	6	10	49	.253	80	192	111	21-44
1961	CF	CHI	AL	4-10	140	534	87	151	18	8	22	85	.283	65	251	122	17-49
1962	CF	CHI	AL	5-10	149	534	82	122	21	6	15	61	.228	80	200	102	38-54
1963	CF	CHI	AL	2-10	133	396	56	89	6	6	13	45	.225	47	146	100	—
1964	CF	CHI	AL	2-10	106	298	30	62	8	4	1	18	.208	36	81	78	—
1965	CF	KC	AL	10-10	118	364	46	87	15	1	3	36	.239	57	113	100	—
1966	CF-LF	CLE	AL	5-10	85	158	23	35	5	1	3	14	.222	20	51	95	—
1967	LF-RF	HOU	NL	9-10	50	143	19	36	11	1	1	14	.252	20	52	113	—
1967	RF-LF	DE/BO	AL	2/1	30	55	5	11	0	0	3	5	.200	8	20	—	—
MAJOR LEAGUE TOTALS					1346	4288	625	1061	169	50	93	467	.247	588	1609	112	5 yrs

Roger Eugene Maris Born Sep 10, 1934 Hibbing, MN
6'0 197 lbs Batted left Died Dec 14, 1985 Houston, TX

YR	POS	TEAM	LG	FIN	G	AB	R	H	2B	3B	HR	RBI	AVG	BB	TB	OQ	RANK
1957	CF	CLE	AL	6-8	116	358	61	84	9	5	14	51	.235	60	145	115	—
1958	RF-CF	CL/KC	AL	4/7	150	583	87	140	19	4	28	80	.240	45	251	104	26-39
1959	RF	KC	AL	7-8	122	433	69	118	21	7	16	72	.273	58	201	127	12-35
1960	RF	NY	AL	1-8	136	499	98	141	18	7	39	112	.283	70	290	152	2-44
1961	RF	NY	AL	1-10	161	590	132	159	16	4	61	142	.269	94	366	158	6-49
1962	RF	NY	AL	1-10	157	590	92	151	34	1	33	100	.256	87	286	128	11-54
1963	RF	NY	AL	1-10	90	312	53	84	14	1	23	53	.269	35	169	143	—
1964	RF	NY	AL	1-10	141	513	86	144	12	2	26	71	.281	62	238	128	14-52
1965	RF	NY	AL	6-10	46	155	22	37	7	0	8	27	.239	29	68	133	—
1966	RF	NY	AL	10-10	119	348	37	81	9	2	13	43	.233	36	133	105	—
1967	RF	SL	NL	1-10	125	410	64	107	18	7	9	55	.261	52	166	120	—
1968	RF	SL	NL	1-10	100	310	25	79	18	2	5	45	.255	24	116	109	—
MAJOR LEAGUE TOTALS					1463	5101	826	1325	195	42	275	851	.260	652	2429	133	6 yrs

Anthony Christopher Kubek   Born Oct 12, 1936   Milwaukee, WI
6'3   190 lbs   Batted left

YR	POS	TEAM	LG	FIN	G	AB	R	H	2B	3B	HR	RBI	AVG	BB	TB	OQ	RANK
1957	LF-SS	NY	AL	1-8	127	431	56	128	21	3	3	39	.297	24	164	95	—
1958	SS	NY	AL	1-8	138	559	66	148	21	1	2	48	.265	25	177	76	37-39
1959	SS-RF	NY	AL	3-8	132	512	67	143	25	7	6	51	.279	24	200	94	30-35
1960	SS-LF	NY	AL	1-8	147	568	77	155	25	3	14	62	.273	31	228	95	32-44
1961	SS	NY	AL	1-10	153	617	84	170	38	6	8	46	.276	27	244	90	43-49
1962	SS-LF	NY	AL	1-10	45	169	28	53	6	1	4	17	.314	12	73	110	—
1963	SS	NY	AL	1-10	135	557	72	143	21	3	7	44	.257	28	191	85	46-51
1964	SS	NY	AL	1-10	106	415	46	95	16	3	8	31	.229	26	141	82	—
1965	SS	NY	AL	6-10	109	339	26	74	5	3	5	35	.218	20	100	74	—

| MAJOR LEAGUE TOTALS | | | | | 1092 | 4167 | 522 | 1109 | 178 | 30 | 57 | 373 | .266 | 217 | 1518 | 88 | 5 yrs |

John Junior Roseboro   Born May 13, 1933 Ashland, OH
5'11   190 lbs   Batted left

YR	POS	TEAM	LG	FIN	G	AB	R	H	2B	3B	HR	RBI	AVG	BB	TB	OQ	RANK
1957	C-1B	BRO	NL	3-8	35	69	6	10	2	0	2	6	.145	10	18	—	—
1958	C	LA	NL	7-8	114	384	52	104	11	9	14	43	.271	36	175	111	—
1959	C	LA	NL	1-8	118	397	39	92	14	7	10	38	.232	52	150	99	—
1960	C	LA	NL	4-8	103	287	22	61	15	3	8	42	.213	44	106	103	—
1961	C	LA	NL	2-8	128	394	59	99	16	6	18	59	.251	56	181	119	—
1962	C	LA	NL	2-10	128	389	45	97	16	7	7	55	.249	50	148	103	—
1963	C	LA	NL	1-10	135	470	50	111	13	7	9	49	.236	36	165	95	39-50
1964	C	LA	NL	6-10	134	414	42	119	24	1	3	45	.287	44	154	110	—
1965	C	LA	NL	1-10	136	437	42	102	10	0	8	57	.233	34	136	83	—
1966	C	LA	NL	1-10	142	445	47	123	23	2	9	53	.276	44	177	110	29-55
1967	C	LA	NL	8-10	116	334	37	91	18	2	4	24	.272	38	125	112	—
1968	C	MIN	AL	7-10	135	380	31	82	12	0	8	39	.216	46	118	98	—
1969	C	MIN	AL	1-6	115	361	33	95	12	0	3	32	.263	39	116	92	—
1970	C	WAS	AL	6-6	46	86	7	20	4	0	1	6	.233	18	27	106	—

| MAJOR LEAGUE TOTALS | | | | | 1585 | 4847 | 512 | 1206 | 190 | 44 | 104 | 548 | .249 | 547 | 1796 | — | — |

Ronald Lavern Hansen   Born Apr 5, 1938   Oxford, NE
6'3 190 lbs Batted right

YR	POS	TEAM	LG	FIN	G	AB	R	H	2B	3B	HR	RBI	AVG	BB	TB	OQ	RANK
1958	SS	BAL	AL	6-8	12	19	1	0	0	0	0	1	.000	0	0	—	—
1959	SS	BAL	AL	6-8	2	4	0	0	0	0	0	0	.000	1	0	—	—
1960	SS	BAL	AL	2-8	153	530	72	135	22	5	22	86	.255	69	233	115	16-44
1961	SS	BAL	AL	3-10	155	533	51	132	13	2	12	51	.248	66	185	93	39-49
1962	SS	BAL	AL	7-10	71	196	12	34	7	0	3	17	.173	30	50	74	—
1963	SS	CHI	AL	2-10	144	482	55	109	17	2	13	67	.226	78	169	106	32-51
1964	SS	CHI	AL	2-10	158	575	85	150	25	3	20	68	.261	73	241	117	25-52
1965	SS	CHI	AL	2-10	162	587	61	138	23	4	11	66	.235	60	202	95	38-46
1966	SS	CHI	AL	4-10	23	74	3	13	1	0	0	4	.176	15	14	—	—
1967	SS	CHI	AL	4-10	157	498	35	116	20	0	8	51	.233	64	160	101	34-48
1968	SS-3B	WA/CH	AL	10/8	126	362	35	71	15	0	9	32	.196	46	113	98	—
1969	2B-1B	CHI	AL	5-6	85	185	15	48	6	1	2	22	.259	18	62	92	—
1970	SS-3B	NY	AL	2-6	59	91	13	27	4	0	4	14	.297	19	43	151	—
1971	3B-2B	NY	AL	4-6	61	145	6	30	3	0	2	20	.207	9	39	68	—
1972	SS-3B	KC	AL	4-6	16	30	2	4	0	0	0	2	.133	3	4	—	—

| MAJOR LEAGUE TOTALS | | | | | 1384 | 4311 | 446 | 1007 | 156 | 17 | 106 | 501 | .234 | 551 | 1515 | 105 | 6 yrs |

Frank Oliver Howard   Born Aug 8, 1936   Columbus, OH
6'7 255 lbs Batted right

YR	POS	TEAM	LG	FIN	G	AB	R	H	2B	3B	HR	RBI	AVG	BB	TB	OQ	RANK
1958	RF-LF	LA	NL	7-8	8	29	3	7	1	0	1	2	.241	1	11	—	—
1959	LF-RF	LA	NL	1-8	9	21	2	3	0	1	1	6	.143	2	8	—	—
1960	RF	LA	NL	4-8	117	448	54	120	15	2	23	77	.268	32	208	113	20-38
1961	RF	LA	NL	2-8	92	267	36	79	10	2	15	45	.296	21	138	125	—
1962	RF	LA	NL	2-10	141	493	80	146	25	6	31	119	.296	39	276	138	8-51
1963	RF	LA	NL	1-10	123	417	58	114	16	1	28	64	.273	33	216	139	—
1964	RF	LA	NL	6-10	134	433	60	98	13	2	24	69	.226	51	187	117	—
1965	LF	WAS	AL	8-10	149	516	53	149	22	6	21	84	.289	55	246	133	9-46
1966	LF	WAS	AL	8-10	146	493	52	137	19	4	18	71	.278	53	218	126	14-44
1967	LF	WAS	AL	6-10	149	519	71	133	20	2	36	89	.256	60	265	145	7-48
1968	LF-1B	WAS	AL	10-10	158	598	79	164	28	3	44	106	.274	54	330	158	4-45
1969	LF-1B	WAS	AL	4-6	161	592	111	175	17	2	48	111	.296	102	340	168	4-59
1970	LF-1B	WAS	AL	6-6	161	566	90	160	15	1	44	126	.283	132	309	169	2-59
1971	LF-1B	WAS	AL	5-6	153	549	60	153	25	2	26	83	.279	77	260	138	12-57
1972	1B-LF	TX/DE	AL	6/1	109	320	29	78	10	0	10	38	.244	46	118	118	—
1973	DH	DET	AL	3-6	85	227	26	58	9	1	12	29	.256	24	105	117	—

| MAJOR LEAGUE TOTALS | | | | | 1895 | 6488 | 864 | 1774 | 245 | 35 | 382 | 1119 | .273 | 782 | 3235 | 143 | 9 yrs |

William Robert Allison   Born Jul 11, 1934   Raytown, MO
6'3   205 lbs   Batted right

YR	POS	TEAM	LG	FIN	G	AB	R	H	2B	3B	HR	RBI	AVG	BB	TB	OQ	RANK
1958	CF	WAS	AL	8-8	11	35	1	7	1	0	0	0	.200	2	8	—	—
1959	CF	WAS	AL	8-8	150	570	83	149	18	9	30	85	.261	60	275	123	14-35
1960	RF	WAS	AL	5-8	144	501	79	126	30	3	15	69	.251	92	207	120	12-44
1961	RF-1B	MIN	AL	7-10	159	556	83	136	21	3	29	105	.245	103	250	124	14-49
1962	RF	MIN	AL	2-10	149	519	102	138	24	8	29	102	.266	84	265	138	6-54
1963	RF	MIN	AL	3-10	148	527	99	143	25	4	35	91	.271	90	281	154	1-51
1964	1B-CF	MIN	AL	6-10	149	492	90	141	27	4	32	86	.287	92	272	164	3-52
1965	LF	MIN	AL	1-10	135	438	71	102	14	5	23	78	.233	73	195	130	11-46
1966	LF-RF	MIN	AL	2-10	70	168	34	37	6	1	8	19	.220	30	69	125	—
1967	LF	MIN	AL	2-10	153	496	73	128	21	6	24	75	.258	74	233	144	8-48
1968	LF-1B	MIN	AL	7-10	145	469	63	116	16	8	22	52	.247	52	214	135	10-45
1969	LF	MIN	AL	1-6	81	189	18	43	8	2	8	27	.228	29	79	117	—
1970	LF-1B	MIN	AL	1-6	47	72	15	15	5	0	1	7	.208	14	23	—	—

MAJOR LEAGUE TOTALS   1541   5032   811   1281   216   53   256   796   .255   795   2371   137   9 yrs

Felipe Rojas Alou   Born May 12, 1935 Haina, DR
6'0   195 lbs   Batted right

YR	POS	TEAM	LG	FIN	G	AB	R	H	2B	3B	HR	RBI	AVG	BB	TB	OQ	RANK
1958	LF-RF	SF	NL	3-8	75	182	21	46	9	2	4	16	.253	19	71	97	—
1959	RF-CF	SF	NL	3-8	95	247	38	68	13	2	10	33	.275	17	115	110	—
1960	LF-RF	SF	NL	5-8	106	322	48	85	17	3	8	44	.264	16	132	97	—
1961	RF	SF	NL	3-8	132	415	59	120	19	0	18	52	.289	26	193	110	—
1962	RF	SF	NL	1-10	154	561	96	177	30	3	25	98	.316	33	288	127	13-51
1963	RF	SF	NL	3-10	157	565	75	159	31	9	20	82	.281	27	268	123	18-50
1964	LF-1B	MIL	NL	5-10	121	415	60	105	26	3	9	51	.253	30	164	103	—
1965	LF-1B	MIL	NL	5-10	143	555	80	165	29	2	23	78	.297	31	267	125	22-52
1966	1B-LF	ATL	NL	5-10	154	666	122	218	32	6	31	74	.327	24	355	136	11-55
1967	1B-CF	ATL	NL	7-10	140	574	76	157	26	3	15	43	.274	32	234	107	35-54
1968	CF	ATL	NL	5-10	160	662	72	210	37	5	11	57	.317	48	290	135	10-45
1969	CF	ATL	NL	1-6	123	476	54	134	13	1	5	32	.282	23	164	88	55-62
1970	LF	OAK	AL	2-6	154	575	70	156	25	3	8	55	.271	32	211	90	54-59
1971	RF-1B	OA/NY	AL	1/4	133	469	52	135	21	6	8	69	.288	32	192	109	33-57
1972	1B-RF	NY	AL	4-6	120	324	33	90	18	1	6	37	.278	22	128	112	—
1973	1B-RF	NY	AL	4-6	93	280	25	66	12	0	4	27	.236	9	90	71	—
1973	LF	MON	NL	4-6	19	48	4	10	1	0	1	4	.208	2	14	—	—
1974	RF	MIL	AL	5-6	3	3	0	0	0	0	0	0	.000	0	0	—	—

MAJOR LEAGUE TOTALS   2082   7339   985   2101   359   49   206   852   .286   423   3176   116   9 yrs

John Wesley Callison   Born Mar 12, 1939
5'10 175 lbs Batted left

YR	POS	TEAM	LG	FIN	G	AB	R	H	2B	3B	HR	RBI	AVG	BB	TB	OQ	RANK
1958	LF	CHI	AL	2-8	18	64	10	19	4	2	1	12	.297	6	30	—	—
1959	LF	CHI	AL	1-8	49	104	12	18	3	0	3	12	.173	13	30	77	—
1960	LF	PHI	NL	8-8	99	288	36	75	11	5	9	30	.260	45	123	122	—
1961	LF	PHI	NL	8-8	138	455	74	121	20	11	9	47	.266	69	190	114	20-37
1962	RF	PHI	NL	7-10	157	603	107	181	26	10	23	83	.300	54	296	126	15-51
1963	RF	PHI	NL	4-10	157	626	96	178	36	11	26	78	.284	50	314	137	10-50
1964	RF	PHI	NL	2-10	162	654	101	179	30	10	31	104	.274	36	322	124	19-42
1965	RF	PHI	NL	6-10	160	619	93	162	25	16	32	101	.262	57	315	133	12-52
1966	RF	PHI	NL	4-10	155	612	93	169	40	7	11	55	.276	56	256	113	27-55
1967	RF	PHI	NL	5-10	149	556	62	145	30	5	14	64	.261	55	227	115	30-54
1968	RF	PHI	NL	7-10	121	398	46	97	18	4	14	40	.244	42	165	124	—
1969	RF	PHI	NL	5-6	134	495	66	131	29	5	16	64	.265	49	218	118	28-62
1970	RF	CHI	NL	2-6	147	477	65	126	23	2	19	68	.264	60	210	115	32-56
1971	RF	CHI	NL	3-6	103	290	27	61	12	1	8	38	.210	36	99	96	—
1972	RF	NY	AL	4-6	92	275	28	71	10	0	9	34	.258	18	108	108	—
1973	RF-DH	NY	AL	4-6	45	136	10	24	4	0	1	10	.176	4	31	48	—

MAJOR LEAGUE TOTALS 1886 6652 926 1757 321 89 226 840 .264 650 2934 122   9 yrs

Vada Edward Pinson   Born Aug 11, 1936 Memphis, TN
5'11 170 lbs Batted left

YR	POS	TEAM	LG	FIN	G	AB	R	H	2B	3B	HR	RBI	AVG	BB	TB	OQ	RANK
1958	RF	CIN	NL	4-8	27	96	20	26	7	0	1	8	.271	11	36	99	—
1959	CF	CIN	NL	5-8	154	648	131	205	47	9	20	84	.316	55	330	130	10-38
1960	CF	CIN	NL	6-8	154	652	107	187	37	12	20	61	.287	47	308	118	15-38
1961	CF	CIN	NL	1-8	154	607	101	208	34	8	16	87	.343	39	306	128	11-37
1962	CF	CIN	NL	3-10	155	619	107	181	31	7	23	100	.292	45	295	118	20-51
1963	CF	CIN	NL	5-10	162	652	96	204	37	14	22	106	.313	36	335	140	8-50
1964	CF	CIN	NL	2-10	156	625	99	166	23	11	23	84	.266	42	280	115	22-42
1965	CF	CIN	NL	4-10	159	669	97	204	34	10	22	94	.305	43	324	129	18-52
1966	CF	CIN	NL	7-10	156	618	70	178	35	6	16	76	.288	33	273	112	28-55
1967	CF	CIN	NL	4-10	158	650	90	187	28	13	18	66	.288	26	295	116	28-54
1968	CF	CIN	NL	4-10	130	499	60	135	29	6	5	48	.271	32	191	111	26-45
1969	RF	SL	NL	4-6	132	495	58	126	22	6	10	70	.255	35	190	98	47-62
1970	RF	CLE	AL	5-6	148	574	74	164	28	6	24	82	.286	28	276	115	31-59
1971	RF	CLE	AL	6-6	146	566	60	149	23	4	11	35	.263	21	213	91	50-57
1972	LF	CAL	AL	5-6	136	484	56	133	24	2	7	49	.275	30	182	105	34-56
1973	LF	CAL	AL	4-6	124	466	56	121	14	6	8	57	.260	20	171	85	51-60
1974	LF	KC	AL	5-6	115	406	46	112	18	2	6	41	.276	21	152	94	—
1975	RF	KC	AL	2-6	103	319	38	71	14	5	4	22	.223	10	107	73	—

MAJOR LEAGUE TOTALS 2469 9645 1366 2757 485 127 256 1170 .286 574 4264 114   15 yrs

James Houston Davenport   Born Aug 17, 1933 Siluria, AL
5'11   170 lbs   Batted right

YR	POS	TEAM	LG	FIN	G	AB	R	H	2B	3B	HR	RBI	AVG	BB	TB	OQ	RANK
1958	3B	SF	NL	3-8	134	434	70	111	22	3	12	41	.256	33	175	95	27-34
1959	3B	SF	NL	3-8	123	469	65	121	16	3	6	38	.258	28	161	81	36-38
1960	3B	SF	NL	5-8	112	363	43	91	15	3	6	38	.251	26	130	89	—
1961	3B	SF	NL	3-8	137	436	64	121	28	4	12	65	.278	45	193	112	22-37
1962	3B	SF	NL	1-10	144	485	83	144	25	5	14	58	.297	45	221	118	19-51
1963	3B-2B	SF	NL	3-10	147	460	40	116	19	3	4	36	.252	32	153	91	44-50
1964	SS-3B	SF	NL	4-10	116	297	24	70	10	6	2	26	.236	29	98	92	—
1965	3B-SS	SF	NL	2-10	106	271	29	68	14	3	4	31	.251	21	100	97	—
1966	SS-3B	SF	NL	2-10	111	305	42	76	6	2	9	30	.249	22	113	95	—
1967	3B-SS	SF	NL	2-10	124	295	42	81	10	3	5	30	.275	39	112	118	—
1968	3B-SS	SF	NL	2-10	113	272	27	61	1	1	1	17	.224	26	67	80	—
1969	3B	SF	NL	2-6	112	303	20	73	10	1	2	42	.241	29	91	84	—
1970	3B	SF	NL	3-6	22	37	3	9	1	0	0	4	.243	7	10	—	—
MAJOR LEAGUE TOTALS					1501	4427	552	1142	177	37	77	456	.258	382	1624	99	5 yrs

Orlando Manuel Cepeda   Born Sep 17, 1937 Ponce, PR
6'2   210 lbs   Batted right

YR	POS	TEAM	LG	FIN	G	AB	R	H	2B	3B	HR	RBI	AVG	BB	TB	OQ	RANK
1958	1B	SF	NL	3-8	148	603	88	188	38	4	25	96	.312	29	309	120	16-34
1959	1B-LF	SF	NL	3-8	151	605	92	192	35	4	27	105	.317	33	316	127	11-38
1960	LF-1B	SF	NL	5-8	151	569	81	169	36	3	24	96	.297	34	283	123	10-38
1961	1B-LF	SF	NL	3-8	152	585	105	182	28	4	46	142	.311	39	356	145	6-37
1962	1B	SF	NL	1-10	162	625	105	191	26	1	35	114	.306	37	324	126	14-51
1963	1B	SF	NL	3-10	156	579	100	183	33	4	34	97	.316	37	326	155	4-50
1964	1B	SF	NL	4-10	142	529	75	161	27	2	31	97	.304	43	285	147	8-42
1965	1B	SF	NL	2-10	33	34	1	6	1	0	1	5	.176	3	10	—	—
1966	1B	SF/SL	NL	2/6	142	501	70	151	26	0	20	73	.301	38	237	126	14-55
1967	1B	SL	NL	1-10	151	563	91	183	37	0	25	111	.325	62	295	157	6-54
1968	1B	SL	NL	1-10	157	600	71	149	26	2	16	73	.248	43	227	108	28-45
1969	1B	ATL	NL	1-6	154	573	74	147	28	2	22	88	.257	55	245	113	33-62
1970	1B	ATL	NL	5-6	148	567	87	173	33	0	34	111	.305	47	308	135	14-56
1971	1B	ATL	NL	3-6	71	250	31	69	10	1	14	44	.276	22	123	131	—
1972	1B	ATL	NL	4-6	28	84	6	25	3	0	4	9	.298	7	40	—	—
1972	PH	OAK	AL	1-6	3	3	0	0	0	0	0	0	.000	0	0	—	—
1973	DH	BOS	AL	2-6	142	550	51	159	25	0	20	86	.289	50	244	116	18-60
1974	DH	KC	AL	5-6	33	107	3	23	5	0	1	18	.215	9	31	76	—
MAJOR LEAGUE TOTALS					2124	7927	1131	2351	417	27	379	1365	.297	588	3959	131	13 yrs

Leon Lamar Wagner Born May 13, 1934 Chattanooga, TN
6'1 195 lbs Batted left

YR	POS	TEAM	LG	FIN	G	AB	R	H	2B	3B	HR	RBI	AVG	BB	TB	OQ	RANK
1958	LF	SF	NL	3-8	74	221	31	70	9	0	13	35	.317	18	118	133	—
1959	LF	SF	NL	3-8	87	129	20	29	4	3	5	22	.225	25	54	118	—
1960	LF	SL	NL	3-8	39	98	12	21	2	0	4	11	.214	17	35	104	—
1961	LF	LA	AL	8-10	133	453	74	127	19	2	28	79	.280	48	234	128	11-49
1962	LF	LA	AL	3-10	160	612	96	164	21	5	37	107	.268	50	306	119	16-54
1963	LF	LA	AL	9-10	149	550	73	160	11	1	26	90	.291	49	251	123	17-51
1964	LF	CLE	AL	6-10	163	641	94	162	19	2	31	100	.253	56	278	110	29-52
1965	LF	CLE	AL	5-10	144	517	91	152	18	1	28	79	.294	60	256	141	5-46
1966	LF	CLE	AL	5-10	150	549	70	153	20	0	23	66	.279	46	242	120	19-44
1967	LF	CLE	AL	8-10	135	433	56	105	15	1	15	54	.242	37	167	107	—
1968	LF	CL/CH	AL	3/8	107	211	19	55	12	0	1	24	.261	27	70	111	—
1969	RF	SF	NL	2-6	11	12	0	4	0	0	0	2	.333	2	4	—	—

MAJOR LEAGUE TOTALS 1352 4426 636 1202 150 15 211 669 .272 435 2015 124 6 yrs

Antonio Nemesio Taylor Born Dec 19, 1935 Central Alara, Cuba
5'9 170 lbs Batted right

YR	POS	TEAM	LG	FIN	G	AB	R	H	2B	3B	HR	RBI	AVG	BB	TB	OQ	RANK
1958	2B	CHI	NL	5-8	140	497	63	117	15	3	6	27	.235	40	156	76	33-34
1959	2B	CHI	NL	5-8	150	624	96	175	30	8	8	38	.280	45	245	97	29-38
1960	2B	CH/PH	NL	7/8	146	581	80	165	25	7	5	44	.284	41	219	97	31-38
1961	2B	PHI	NL	8-8	106	400	47	100	17	3	2	26	.250	29	129	78	—
1962	2B	PHI	NL	7-10	152	625	87	162	21	5	7	43	.259	68	214	92	43-51
1963	2B	PHI	NL	4-10	157	640	102	180	20	10	5	49	.281	42	235	102	33-50
1964	2B	PHI	NL	2-10	154	570	62	143	13	6	4	46	.251	46	180	87	41-42
1965	2B	PHI	NL	6-10	106	323	41	74	14	3	3	27	.229	22	103	82	—
1966	2B-3B	PHI	NL	4-10	125	434	47	105	14	8	5	40	.242	31	150	88	—
1967	1B-3B	PHI	NL	5-10	132	462	55	110	16	6	2	34	.238	42	144	88	48-54
1968	3B	PHI	NL	7-10	145	547	59	137	20	2	3	38	.250	39	170	92	40-45
1969	3B-2B	PHI	NL	5-6	138	557	68	146	24	5	3	30	.262	42	189	90	53-62
1970	2B-3B	PHI	NL	5-6	124	439	74	132	26	9	9	55	.301	50	203	123	24-56
1971	2B-3B	PHI	NL	6-6	36	107	9	25	2	1	1	5	.234	9	32	82	—
1971	2B	DET	AL	2-6	55	181	27	52	10	2	3	19	.287	12	75	109	—
1972	2B-3B	DET	AL	1-6	78	228	33	69	12	4	1	20	.303	14	92	116	—
1973	2B	DET	AL	3-6	84	275	35	63	9	3	5	24	.229	17	93	80	—
1974	1B-3B	PHI	NL	3-6	62	64	5	21	4	0	2	13	.328	6	31	—	—
1975	3B-1B	PHI	NL	2-6	79	103	13	25	5	1	1	17	.243	17	35	105	—
1976	2B-3B	PHI	NL	1-6	26	23	2	6	1	0	0	3	.261	1	7	—	—

MAJOR LEAGUE TOTALS 2195 7680 1005 2007 298 86 75 598 .261 613 2702 94 10 yrs

Richard Lee Stuart   Born Nov 7, 1932   San Francisco, CA
6'4   212 lbs   Batted right

YR	POS	TEAM	LG	FIN	G	AB	R	H	2B	3B	HR	RBI	AVG	BB	TB	OQ	RANK
1958	1B	PIT	NL	2-8	67	254	38	68	12	5	16	48	.268	11	138	118	—
1959	1B	PIT	NL	4-8	118	397	64	118	15	2	27	78	.297	42	218	140	—
1960	1B	PIT	NL	1-8	122	438	48	114	17	5	23	83	.260	39	210	119	13-38
1961	1B	PIT	NL	6-8	138	532	83	160	28	8	35	117	.301	34	309	136	9-37
1962	1B	PIT	NL	4-10	114	394	52	90	11	4	16	64	.228	32	157	94	—
1963	1B	BOS	AL	7-10	157	612	81	160	25	4	42	118	.261	44	319	128	11-51
1964	1B	BOS	AL	8-10	156	603	73	168	27	1	33	114	.279	37	296	121	21-52
1965	1B	PHI	NL	6-10	149	538	53	126	19	1	28	95	.234	39	231	107	32-52
1966	1B	NY/LA	NL	9/1	69	178	11	43	1	0	7	22	.242	20	65	101	—
1969	1B	CAL	AL	3-6	22	51	3	8	2	0	1	4	.157	3	13	—	—

| MAJOR LEAGUE TOTALS | | | | | 1112 | 3997 | 506 | 1055 | 157 | 30 | 228 | 743 | .264 | 301 | 1956 | 122 | 5 yrs |

Ronald Ray Fairly   Born Jul 12, 1938   Macon, GA
5'10   175 lbs   Batted left

YR	POS	TEAM	LG	FIN	G	AB	R	H	2B	3B	HR	RBI	AVG	BB	TB	OQ	RANK
1958	CF-LF	LA	NL	7-8	15	53	6	15	1	0	2	8	.283	6	22	—	—
1959	RF-CF	LA	NL	1-8	118	244	27	58	12	1	4	23	.238	31	84	93	—
1960	RF-LF	LA	NL	4-8	14	37	6	4	0	3	1	3	.108	7	13	—	—
1961	RF-1B	LA	NL	2-8	111	245	42	79	15	2	10	48	.322	48	128	157	—
1962	1B-RF	LA	NL	2-10	147	460	80	128	15	7	14	71	.278	75	199	125	16-51
1963	1B-CF	LA	NL	1-10	152	490	62	133	21	0	12	77	.271	58	190	117	19-50
1964	1B	LA	NL	6-10	150	454	62	116	19	5	10	74	.256	65	175	117	21-42
1965	RF	LA	NL	1-10	158	555	73	152	28	1	9	70	.274	76	209	116	27-52
1966	RF-1B	LA	NL	1-10	117	351	53	101	20	0	14	61	.288	52	163	138	—
1967	RF-1B	LA	NL	8-10	153	486	45	107	19	0	10	55	.220	54	156	93	46-54
1968	RF-1B	LA	NL	7-10	141	441	32	103	15	1	4	43	.234	41	132	92	—
1969	1B-CF	LA/MO	NL	4/6	100	317	38	87	16	6	12	47	.274	37	151	131	—
1970	1B	MON	NL	6-6	119	385	54	111	19	0	15	61	.288	72	175	135	—
1971	1B	MON	NL	5-6	146	447	58	115	23	0	13	71	.257	81	177	127	20-58
1972	LF-1B	MON	NL	5-6	140	446	51	124	15	1	17	68	.278	46	192	121	22-58
1973	LF	MON	NL	4-6	142	413	70	123	13	1	17	49	.298	86	189	149	7-61
1974	1B-LF	MON	NL	4-6	101	282	35	69	9	1	12	43	.245	57	116	129	—
1975	1B-RF	SL	NL	3-6	107	229	32	69	13	2	7	37	.301	45	107	150	—
1976	1B	SL	NL	5-6	73	110	13	29	4	0	0	21	.264	23	33	113	—
1976	1B	OAK	AL	2-6	15	46	9	11	1	0	3	10	.239	9	21	—	—
1977	DH-1B	TOR	AL	7-7	132	458	60	128	24	2	19	64	.279	58	213	121	21-81
1978	1B	CAL	AL	2-7	91	235	23	51	5	0	10	40	.217	25	86	93	—

| MAJOR LEAGUE TOTALS | | | | | 2442 | 7184 | 931 | 1913 | 307 | 33 | 215 | 1044 | .266 | 1052 | 2931 | 121 | 9 yrs |

Norman Dalton Cash
6'0 185 lbs Batted left

Born Nov 10, 1934 Justiceburg, TX
Died Oct 12, 1986 Beaver Island, MI

YR	POS	TEAM	LG	FIN	G	AB	R	H	2B	3B	HR	RBI	AVG	BB	TB	OQ	RANK
1958	RF	CHI	AL	2-8	13	8	2	2	0	0	0	0	.250	0	2	—	—
1959	1B	CHI	AL	1-8	58	104	16	25	0	1	4	16	.240	18	39	111	—
1960	1B	DET	AL	6-8	121	353	64	101	16	3	18	63	.286	65	177	145	—
1961	1B	DET	AL	2-10	159	535	119	193	22	8	41	132	.361	124	354	207	1-49
1962	1B	DET	AL	4-10	148	507	94	123	16	2	39	89	.243	104	260	142	4-54
1963	1B	DET	AL	5-10	147	493	67	133	19	1	26	79	.270	89	232	142	4-51
1964	1B	DET	AL	4-10	144	479	63	123	15	5	23	83	.257	70	217	127	15-52
1965	1B	DET	AL	4-10	142	467	79	124	23	1	30	82	.266	77	239	150	2-46
1966	1B	DET	AL	3-10	160	603	98	168	18	3	32	93	.279	66	288	135	8-44
1967	1B	DET	AL	2-10	152	488	64	118	16	5	22	72	.242	81	210	136	12-48
1968	1B	DET	AL	1-10	127	411	50	108	15	1	25	63	.263	39	200	141	—
1969	1B	DET	AL	2-6	142	483	81	135	15	4	22	74	.280	63	224	131	16-59
1970	1B	DET	AL	4-6	130	370	58	96	18	2	15	53	.259	72	163	133	—
1971	1B	DET	AL	2-6	135	452	72	128	10	3	32	91	.283	59	240	150	6-57
1972	1B	DET	AL	1-6	137	440	51	114	16	0	22	61	.259	50	196	132	15-56
1973	1B	DET	AL	3-6	121	363	51	95	19	0	19	40	.262	47	171	125	—
1974	1B	DET	AL	6-6	53	149	17	34	3	2	7	12	.228	19	62	112	—

MAJOR LEAGUE TOTALS					2089	6705	1046	1820	241	41	377	1103	.271	1043	3274	145	10 yrs

Billy Leo Williams
6'1 175 lbs Batted left

Born Jun 15, 1938 Whistler, AL

YR	POS	TEAM	LG	FIN	G	AB	R	H	2B	3B	HR	RBI	AVG	BB	TB	OQ	RANK
1959	LF	CHI	NL	5-8	18	33	0	5	0	1	0	2	.152	1	7	—	—
1960	LF	CHI	NL	7-8	12	47	4	13	0	2	2	7	.277	5	23	—	—
1961	LF	CHI	NL	7-8	146	529	75	147	20	7	25	86	.278	45	256	116	18-37
1962	LF	CHI	NL	9-10	159	618	94	184	22	8	22	91	.298	70	288	125	17-51
1963	LF	CHI	NL	7-10	161	612	87	175	36	9	25	95	.286	68	304	144	6-50
1964	LF	CHI	NL	8-10	162	645	100	201	39	2	33	98	.312	59	343	149	7-42
1965	LF	CHI	NL	8-10	164	645	115	203	39	6	34	108	.315	65	356	156	4-52
1966	LF	CHI	NL	10-10	162	648	100	179	23	5	29	91	.276	69	299	126	16-55
1967	LF	CHI	NL	3-10	162	634	92	176	21	12	28	84	.278	68	305	136	13-54
1968	LF	CHI	NL	3-10	163	642	91	185	30	8	30	98	.288	48	321	146	8-45
1969	LF	CHI	NL	2-6	163	642	103	188	33	10	21	95	.293	59	304	129	16-62
1970	LF	CHI	NL	2-6	161	636	137	205	34	4	42	129	.322	72	373	154	6-56
1971	LF	CHI	NL	3-6	157	594	86	179	27	5	28	93	.301	77	300	148	5-58
1972	LF	CHI	NL	2-6	150	574	95	191	34	6	37	122	.333	62	348	175	1-58
1973	LF-1B	CHI	NL	5-6	156	576	72	166	22	2	20	86	.288	76	252	126	18-61
1974	1B-LF	CHI	NL	6-6	117	404	55	113	22	0	16	68	.280	67	183	136	—
1975	DH	OAK	AL	1-6	155	520	68	127	20	1	23	81	.244	76	218	115	23-66
1976	DH	OAK	AL	2-6	120	351	36	74	12	0	11	41	.211	58	119	105	—

MAJOR LEAGUE TOTALS					2488	9350	1410	2711	434	88	426	1475	.290	1045	4599	139	14 yrs

Zoilo Casanova Versalles   Born Dec 18, 1939   Veldado, Cuba
5'10   146 lbs   Batted right

YR	POS	TEAM	LG	FIN	G	AB	R	H	2B	3B	HR	RBI	AVG	BB	TB	OQ	RANK
1959	SS	WAS	AL	8-8	29	59	4	9	0	0	1	1	.153	4	12	—	—
1960	SS	WAS	AL	5-8	15	45	2	6	2	2	0	4	.133	2	12	—	—
1961	SS	MIN	AL	7-10	129	510	65	143	25	5	7	53	.280	25	199	90	41-49
1962	SS	MIN	AL	2-10	160	568	69	137	18	3	17	67	.241	37	212	87	49-54
1963	SS	MIN	AL	3-10	159	621	74	162	31	13	10	54	.261	33	249	98	37-51
1964	SS	MIN	AL	6-10	160	659	94	171	33	10	20	64	.259	42	284	106	32-52
1965	SS	MIN	AL	1-10	160	666	126	182	45	12	19	77	.273	41	308	117	18-46
1966	SS	MIN	AL	2-10	137	543	73	135	20	6	7	36	.249	40	188	92	40-44
1967	SS	MIN	AL	2-10	160	581	63	116	16	7	6	50	.200	33	164	73	48-48
1968	SS	LA	NL	7-10	122	403	29	79	16	3	2	24	.196	26	107	74	—
1969	2B-3B	CL/WA	AL	6/4	103	292	30	69	13	2	1	19	.236	24	89	80	—
1971	3B-SS	ATL	NL	3-6	66	194	21	37	11	0	5	22	.191	11	63	77	—
MAJOR LEAGUE TOTALS					1400	5141	650	1246	230	63	95	471	.242	318	1887	95	7 yrs

James Timothy McCarver   Born Oct 16, 1941   Memphis, TN
6'0   183 lbs   Batted left

YR	POS	TEAM	LG	FIN	G	AB	R	H	2B	3B	HR	RBI	AVG	BB	TB	OQ	RANK
1959	C	SL	NL	7-8	8	24	3	4	1	0	0	0	.167	2	5	—	—
1960	C	SL	NL	3-8	10	10	3	2	0	0	0	0	.200	0	2	—	—
1961	C	SL	NL	5-8	22	67	5	16	2	1	1	6	.239	0	23	—	—
1963	C	SL	NL	2-10	127	405	39	117	12	7	4	51	.289	27	155	107	—
1964	C	SL	NL	1-10	143	465	53	134	19	3	9	52	.288	40	186	112	24-42
1965	C	SL	NL	7-10	113	409	48	113	17	2	11	48	.276	31	167	109	—
1966	C	SL	NL	6-10	150	543	50	149	19	13	12	68	.274	36	230	108	30-55
1967	C	SL	NL	1-10	138	471	68	139	26	3	14	69	.295	54	213	135	14-54
1968	C	SL	NL	1-10	128	434	35	110	15	6	5	48	.253	26	152	99	—
1969	C	SL	NL	4-6	138	515	46	134	27	3	7	51	.260	49	188	100	44-62
1970	C	PHI	NL	5-6	44	164	16	47	11	1	4	14	.287	14	72	110	—
1971	C	PHI	NL	6-6	134	474	51	132	20	5	8	46	.278	43	186	109	36-58
1972	C-LF	PH/MO	NL	6/5	122	391	33	96	13	1	7	34	.246	36	132	93	—
1973	1B	SL	NL	2-6	130	331	30	88	16	4	3	49	.266	38	121	103	—
1974	C	SL	NL	2-6	74	106	13	23	0	1	0	11	.217	22	25	90	—
1974	C-DH	BOS	AL	3-6	11	28	3	7	1	0	0	1	.250	4	8	—	—
1975	C	BOS	AL	1-6	12	21	1	8	2	1	0	3	.381	1	12	—	—
1975	C	PHI	NL	2-6	47	59	6	15	2	0	1	7	.254	14	20	—	—
1976	C	PHI	NL	1-6	90	155	26	43	11	2	3	29	.277	35	67	149	—
1977	C	PHI	NL	1-6	93	169	28	54	13	2	6	30	.320	28	89	152	—
1978	C-1B	PHI	NL	1-6	90	146	18	36	9	1	1	14	.247	28	50	113	—
1979	C	PHI	NL	4-6	79	137	13	33	5	1	1	12	.241	19	43	92	—
1980	1B	PHI	NL	1-6	6	5	2	1	1	0	0	2	.200	1	2	—	—
MAJOR LEAGUE TOTALS					1909	5529	590	1501	242	57	97	645	.271	548	2148	113	5 yrs

Maurice Morning Wills   Born Oct 2, 1932   Washington, DC
5'11 170 lbs Batted both

YR	POS	TEAM	LG	FIN	G	AB	R	H	2B	3B	HR	RBI	AVG	BB	TB	OQ	RANK
1959	SS	LA	NL	1-8	83	242	27	63	5	2	0	7	.260	13	72	71	—
1960	SS	LA	NL	4-8	148	516	75	152	15	2	0	27	.295	35	171	88	35-38
1961	SS	LA	NL	2-8	148	613	105	173	12	10	1	31	.282	59	208	90	30-37
1962	SS	LA	NL	2-10	165	695	130	208	13	10	6	48	.299	51	259	97	40-51
1963	SS-3B	LA	NL	1-10	134	527	83	159	19	3	0	34	.302	44	184	105	31-50
1964	SS	LA	NL	6-10	158	630	81	173	15	5	2	34	.275	41	204	88	40-42
1965	SS	LA	NL	1-10	158	650	92	186	14	7	0	33	.286	40	214	89	44-52
1966	SS	LA	NL	1-10	143	594	60	162	14	2	1	39	.273	34	183	81	53-55
1967	3B	PIT	NL	6-10	149	616	92	186	12	9	3	45	.302	31	225	100	39-54
1968	3B	PIT	NL	6-10	153	627	76	174	12	6	0	31	.278	45	198	97	34-45
1969	SS	MO/LA	NL	6/4	151	623	80	171	10	8	4	47	.274	59	209	95	50-62
1970	SS	LA	NL	2-6	132	522	77	141	19	3	0	34	.270	50	166	85	49-56
1971	SS	LA	NL	2-6	149	601	73	169	14	3	3	44	.281	40	198	90	48-58
1972	SS-3B	LA	NL	3-6	71	132	16	17	3	1	0	4	.129	10	22	45	—
MAJOR LEAGUE TOTALS					1942	7588	1067	2134	177	71	20	458	.281	552	2513	92	12 yrs

Willie Lee McCovey   Born Jan 10, 1938   Mobile, AL
6'4 198 lbs Batted left

YR	POS	TEAM	LG	FIN	G	AB	R	H	2B	3B	HR	RBI	AVG	BB	TB	OQ	RANK
1959	1B	SF	NL	3-8	52	192	32	68	9	5	13	38	.354	22	126	179	—
1960	1B	SF	NL	5-8	101	260	37	62	15	3	13	51	.238	45	122	130	—
1961	1B	SF	NL	3-8	106	328	59	89	12	3	18	50	.271	37	161	122	—
1962	LF-1B	SF	NL	1-10	91	229	41	67	6	1	20	54	.293	29	135	153	—
1963	LF-1B	SF	NL	3-10	152	564	103	158	19	5	44	102	.280	50	319	154	5-50
1964	LF-1B	SF	NL	4-10	130	364	55	80	14	1	18	54	.220	61	150	122	—
1965	1B	SF	NL	2-10	160	540	93	149	17	4	39	92	.276	88	291	158	3-52
1966	1B	SF	NL	2-10	150	502	85	148	26	6	36	96	.295	76	294	168	2-55
1967	1B	SF	NL	2-10	135	456	73	126	17	4	31	91	.276	71	244	160	5-54
1968	1B	SF	NL	2-10	148	523	81	153	16	4	36	105	.293	72	285	174	1-45
1969	1B	SF	NL	2-6	149	491	101	157	26	2	45	126	.320	121	322	213	1-62
1970	1B	SF	NL	3-6	152	495	98	143	39	2	39	126	.289	137	303	187	1-56
1971	1B	SF	NL	1-6	105	329	45	91	13	0	18	70	.277	64	158	152	—
1972	1B	SF	NL	5-6	81	263	30	56	8	0	14	35	.213	38	106	114	—
1973	1B	SF	NL	3-6	130	383	52	102	14	3	29	75	.266	105	209	176	2-60
1974	1B	SD	NL	6-6	128	344	53	87	19	1	22	63	.253	96	174	167	—
1975	1B	SD	NL	4-6	122	413	43	104	17	0	23	68	.252	57	190	126	—
1976	1B	SD	NL	5-6	71	202	20	41	9	0	7	36	.203	21	71	93	—
1976	DH	OAK	AL	2-6	11	24	0	5	0	0	0	0	.208	3	5	—	—
1977	1B	SF	NL	4-6	141	478	54	134	21	0	28	86	.280	67	239	133	11-68
1978	1B	SF	NL	3-6	108	351	32	80	19	2	12	64	.228	36	139	103	—
1979	1B	SF	NL	4-6	117	353	34	88	9	0	15	57	.249	36	142	104	—
1980	1B	SF	NL	5-6	48	113	8	23	8	0	1	16	.204	13	34	83	—
MAJOR LEAGUE TOTALS					2588	8197	1229	2211	353	46	521	1555	.270	1345	4219	169	9 yrs

Herman Thomas Davis

Born Mar 21, 1939 Brooklyn, NY

6'2 195 lbs Batted right

YR	POS	TEAM	LG	FIN	G	AB	R	H	2B	3B	HR	RBI	AVG	BB	TB	OQ	RANK
1959	PH	LA	NL	1-8	1	1	0	0	0	0	0	0	.000	0	0	—	—
1960	CF	LA	NL	4-8	110	352	43	97	18	1	11	44	.276	13	150	99	—
1961	RF-3B	LA	NL	2-8	132	460	60	128	13	2	15	58	.278	32	190	99	25-37
1962	LF-3B	LA	NL	2-10	163	665	120	230	27	9	27	153	.346	33	356	135	9-51
1963	LF-3B	LA	NL	1-10	146	556	69	181	19	3	16	88	.326	29	254	128	16-50
1964	LF	LA	NL	6-10	152	592	70	163	20	5	14	86	.275	29	235	101	33-42
1965	LF	LA	NL	1-10	17	60	3	15	1	1	0	9	.250	2	18	—	—
1966	LF	LA	NL	1-10	100	313	27	98	11	1	3	27	.313	16	120	102	—
1967	LF	NY	NL	10-10	154	577	72	174	32	0	16	73	.302	31	254	118	25-54
1968	LF	CHI	AL	8-10	132	456	30	122	5	3	8	50	.268	16	157	93	—
1969	LF	SEA	AL	6-6	123	454	52	123	29	1	6	80	.271	30	172	97	—
1969	LF	HOU	NL	5-6	24	79	2	19	3	0	1	9	.241	8	25	—	—
1970	LF	HO/CH	NL	4/2	68	255	28	71	14	2	5	38	.278	8	104	91	—
1970	LF-1B	OAK	AL	2-6	66	200	17	58	9	1	1	27	.290	8	72	88	—
1971	1B-LF	OAK	AL	1-6	79	219	26	71	8	1	3	42	.324	15	90	115	—
1972	1B-LF	CHI	NL	2-6	15	26	3	7	1	0	0	6	.269	2	8	—	—
1972	LF-1B	BAL	AL	3-6	26	82	9	21	3	0	0	6	.256	6	24	—	—
1973	DH	BAL	AL	1-6	137	552	53	169	20	3	7	89	.306	30	216	99	38-60
1974	DH	BAL	AL	1-6	158	626	67	181	20	1	11	84	.289	34	236	97	47-67
1975	DH	BAL	AL	2-6	116	460	43	130	14	1	6	57	.283	23	164	88	53-66
1976	DH	CA/KC	AL	4/1	80	238	17	63	5	0	3	26	.265	16	77	87	—

MAJOR LEAGUE TOTALS					1999	7223	811	2121	272	35	153	1052	.294	381	2922	108	8 yrs

Donald Ray Mincher

Born Jun 24, 1938 Huntsville, AL

6'3 205 lbs Batted left

YR	POS	TEAM	LG	FIN	G	AB	R	H	2B	3B	HR	RBI	AVG	BB	TB	OQ	RANK
1960	1B	WAS	AL	5-8	27	79	10	19	4	1	2	5	.241	11	31	—	—
1961	1B	MIN	AL	7-10	35	101	18	19	5	1	5	11	.188	22	41	114	—
1962	1B	MIN	AL	2-10	86	121	20	29	1	1	9	29	.240	34	59	152	—
1963	1B	MIN	AL	3-10	82	225	41	58	8	0	17	42	.258	30	117	141	—
1964	1B	MIN	AL	6-10	120	287	45	68	12	4	23	56	.237	27	157	133	—
1965	1B	MIN	AL	1-10	128	346	43	87	17	3	22	65	.251	49	176	141	—
1966	1B	MIN	AL	2-10	139	431	53	108	30	0	14	62	.251	58	180	122	17-44
1967	1B	CAL	AL	5-10	147	487	81	133	23	3	25	76	.273	69	237	149	6-48
1968	1B	CAL	AL	8-10	120	399	35	94	12	1	13	48	.236	43	147	111	—
1969	1B	SEA	AL	6-6	140	427	53	105	14	0	25	78	.246	78	194	134	14-59
1970	1B	OAK	AL	2-6	140	463	62	114	18	0	27	74	.246	56	213	120	25-59
1971	1B	OA/WA	AL	1/5	128	415	44	116	21	2	12	53	.280	73	177	135	14-57
1972	1B	TX/OA	AL	6/1	108	245	25	53	11	0	6	44	.216	56	82	125	—

MAJOR LEAGUE TOTALS					1400	4026	530	1003	176	16	200	643	.249	606	1811	132	5 yrs

William Henry Davis　　　Born Apr 15, 1940　Mineral Springs, AR
5'11　180 lbs　Batted left

YR	POS	TEAM	LG	FIN	G	AB	R	H	2B	3B	HR	RBI	AVG	BB	TB	OQ	RANK
1960	CF	LA	NL	4-8	22	88	12	28	6	1	2	10	.318	4	42	—	—
1961	CF	LA	NL	2-8	128	339	56	86	19	6	12	45	.254	27	153	105	—
1962	CF	LA	NL	2-10	157	600	103	171	18	10	21	85	.285	42	272	111	27-51
1963	CF	LA	NL	1-10	156	515	60	126	19	8	9	60	.245	25	188	93	41-50
1964	CF	LA	NL	6-10	157	613	91	180	23	7	12	77	.294	22	253	104	30-42
1965	CF	LA	NL	1-10	142	558	52	133	24	3	10	57	.238	14	193	80	48-52
1966	CF	LA	NL	1-10	153	624	74	177	31	6	11	61	.284	15	253	96	42-55
1967	CF	LA	NL	8-10	143	569	65	146	27	9	6	41	.257	29	209	94	43-54
1968	CF	LA	NL	7-10	160	643	86	161	24	10	7	31	.250	31	226	96	37-45
1969	CF	LA	NL	4-6	129	498	66	155	23	8	11	59	.311	33	227	122	22-62
1970	CF	LA	NL	2-6	146	593	92	181	23	16	8	93	.305	29	260	105	41-56
1971	CF	LA	NL	2-6	158	641	84	198	33	10	10	74	.309	23	281	112	29-58
1972	CF	LA	NL	3-6	149	615	81	178	22	7	19	79	.289	27	271	112	34-58
1973	CF	LA	NL	2-6	152	599	82	171	29	9	16	77	.285	29	266	109	40-61
1974	CF	MON	NL	4-6	153	611	86	180	27	9	12	89	.295	27	261	106	46-65
1975	CF	TEX	AL	3-6	42	169	16	42	8	2	5	17	.249	4	69	89	—
1975	CF	SL	NL	3-6	98	350	41	102	19	6	6	50	.291	14	151	105	—
1976	CF	SD	NL	5-6	141	493	61	132	18	10	5	46	.268	19	185	92	42-57
1979	RF-DH	CAL	AL	1-6	43	56	9	14	2	1	0	2	.250	4	18	—	—
MAJOR LEAGUE TOTALS					2429	9174	1217	2561	395	138	182	1053	.279	418	3778	102	14 yrs

Manuel Julian Javier　　　Born Aug 9, 1936　San Francisco de Mac., DR
6'1　175 lbs　Batted right

YR	POS	TEAM	LG	FIN	G	AB	R	H	2B	3B	HR	RBI	AVG	BB	TB	OQ	RANK
1960	2B	SL	NL	3-8	119	451	55	107	19	8	4	21	.237	21	154	79	38-38
1961	2B	SL	NL	5-8	113	445	58	124	14	3	2	41	.279	30	150	83	33-37
1962	2B	SL	NL	6-10	155	598	97	157	25	5	7	39	.263	47	213	89	46-51
1963	2B	SL	NL	2-10	161	609	82	160	27	9	9	46	.263	24	232	96	37-50
1964	2B	SL	NL	1-10	155	535	66	129	19	5	12	65	.241	30	194	91	38-42
1965	2B	SL	NL	7-10	77	229	34	52	6	4	2	23	.227	8	72	74	—
1966	2B	SL	NL	6-10	147	460	52	105	13	5	7	31	.228	26	149	79	54-55
1967	2B	SL	NL	1-10	140	520	68	146	16	3	14	64	.281	25	210	105	36-54
1968	2B	SL	NL	1-10	139	519	54	135	25	4	4	52	.260	24	180	96	38-45
1969	2B	SL	NL	4-6	143	493	59	139	28	2	10	42	.282	40	201	109	35-62
1970	2B	SL	NL	4-6	139	513	62	129	16	3	2	42	.251	24	157	70	54-56
1971	2B	SL	NL	2-6	90	259	32	67	6	4	3	28	.259	9	90	84	—
1972	3B-2B	CIN	NL	1-6	44	91	3	19	2	0	2	12	.209	6	27	—	—
MAJOR LEAGUE TOTALS					1622	5722	722	1469	216	55	78	506	.257	314	2029	90	10 yrs

Leonardo Lazaro Cardenas

Born Dec 17, 1938   Matanzas, Cuba

5'11   150 lbs   Batted right

YR	POS	TEAM	LG	FIN	G	AB	R	H	2B	3B	HR	RBI	AVG	BB	TB	OQ	RANK
1960	SS	CIN	NL	6-8	48	142	13	33	2	4	1	12	.232	6	46	74	—
1961	SS	CIN	NL	1-8	74	198	23	61	18	1	5	24	.308	15	96	120	—
1962	SS	CIN	NL	3-10	153	589	77	173	31	4	10	60	.294	39	242	102	32-51
1963	SS	CIN	NL	5-10	158	565	42	133	22	4	7	48	.235	23	184	81	49-50
1964	SS	CIN	NL	2-10	163	597	61	150	32	2	9	69	.251	41	213	93	36-42
1965	SS	CIN	NL	4-10	156	557	65	160	25	11	11	57	.287	60	240	124	23-52
1966	SS	CIN	NL	7-10	160	568	59	145	25	4	20	81	.255	45	238	107	32-55
1967	SS	CIN	NL	4-10	108	379	30	97	14	3	2	21	.256	34	123	93	—
1968	SS	CIN	NL	4-10	137	452	45	106	13	2	7	41	.235	36	144	94	—
1969	SS	MIN	AL	1-6	160	578	67	162	24	4	10	70	.280	66	224	110	32-59
1970	SS	MIN	AL	1-6	160	588	67	145	34	4	11	65	.247	42	220	92	52-59
1971	SS	MIN	AL	5-6	153	554	59	146	25	4	18	75	.264	51	233	113	32-57
1972	SS	CAL	AL	5-6	150	551	25	123	11	2	6	42	.223	35	156	78	54-56
1973	SS	CLE	AL	6-6	72	195	9	42	4	0	0	12	.215	13	46	59	—
1974	3B-SS	TEX	AL	2-6	34	92	5	25	3	0	0	7	.272	2	28	—	—
1975	3B-SS	TEX	AL	3-6	55	102	15	24	2	0	1	5	.235	14	29	85	—
MAJOR LEAGUE TOTALS					1941	6707	662	1725	285	49	118	689	.257	522	2462	100	9 yrs

Mateo Rojas Alou

Born Dec 22, 1938   Haina, DR

5'9   160 lbs   Batted left

YR	POS	TEAM	LG	FIN	G	AB	R	H	2B	3B	HR	RBI	AVG	BB	TB	OQ	RANK
1960	LF	SF	NL	5-8	4	3	1	1	0	0	0	0	.333	0	1	—	—
1961	RF-LF	SF	NL	3-8	81	200	38	62	7	2	6	24	.310	15	91	113	—
1962	LF-RF	SF	NL	1-10	78	195	28	57	8	1	3	14	.292	14	76	99	—
1963	LF-RF	SF	NL	3-10	63	76	4	11	1	0	0	2	.145	2	12	—	—
1964	LF-RF	SF	NL	4-10	110	250	28	66	4	2	1	14	.264	11	77	79	—
1965	LF	SF	NL	2-10	117	324	37	75	12	2	2	18	.231	17	97	75	—
1966	CF	PIT	NL	3-10	141	535	86	183	18	9	2	27	.342	24	225	113	26-55
1967	CF	PIT	NL	6-10	139	550	87	186	21	7	2	28	.338	24	227	116	29-54
1968	CF	PIT	NL	6-10	146	558	59	185	28	4	0	52	.332	27	221	120	20-45
1969	CF	PIT	NL	3-6	162	698	105	231	41	6	1	48	.331	42	287	113	32-62
1970	CF	PIT	NL	1-6	155	677	97	201	21	8	1	47	.297	30	241	85	48-56
1971	RF-1B	SL	NL	2-6	149	609	85	192	28	6	7	74	.315	34	253	112	30-58
1972	1B-RF	SL	NL	4-6	108	404	46	127	17	2	3	31	.314	24	157	107	—
1972	RF	OAK	AL	1-6	32	121	11	34	5	0	1	16	.281	11	42	106	—
1973	RF-1B	NY	AL	4-6	123	497	59	147	22	1	2	28	.296	30	177	91	47-60
1973	1B	SL	NL	2-6	11	11	1	3	0	0	0	1	.273	1	3	—	—
1974	LF	SD	NL	6-6	48	81	8	16	3	0	0	3	.198	5	19	—	—
MAJOR LEAGUE TOTALS					1667	5789	780	1777	236	50	31	427	.307	311	2206	107	7 yrs

Ronald Edward Santo Born Feb 25, 1940 Seattle, WA
6'0 190 lbs Batted right

YR	POS	TEAM	LG	FIN	G	AB	R	H	2B	3B	HR	RBI	AVG	BB	TB	OQ	RANK
1960	3B	CHI	NL	7-8	95	347	44	87	24	2	9	44	.251	31	142	103	—
1961	3B	CHI	NL	7-8	154	578	84	164	32	6	23	83	.284	73	277	125	15-37
1962	3B	CHI	NL	9-10	162	604	44	137	20	4	17	83	.227	65	216	91	44-51
1963	3B	CHI	NL	7-10	162	630	79	187	29	6	25	99	.297	42	303	132	13-50
1964	3B	CHI	NL	8-10	161	592	94	185	33	13	30	114	.313	86	334	170	2-42
1965	3B	CHI	NL	8-10	164	608	88	173	30	4	33	101	.285	88	310	150	6-52
1966	3B	CHI	NL	10-10	155	561	93	175	21	8	30	94	.312	95	302	165	3-55
1967	3B	CHI	NL	3-10	161	586	107	176	23	4	31	98	.300	96	300	162	4-54
1968	3B	CHI	NL	3-10	162	577	86	142	17	3	26	98	.246	96	243	141	9-45
1969	3B	CHI	NL	2-6	160	575	97	166	18	4	29	123	.289	96	279	147	10-62
1970	3B	CHI	NL	2-6	154	555	83	148	30	4	26	114	.267	92	264	131	18-56
1971	3B	CHI	NL	3-6	154	555	77	148	22	1	21	88	.267	79	235	126	21-58
1972	3B	CHI	NL	2-6	133	464	68	140	25	5	17	74	.302	69	226	149	6-58
1973	3B	CHI	NL	5-6	149	536	65	143	29	2	20	77	.267	63	236	120	26-61
1974	DH-2B	CHI	AL	4-6	117	375	29	83	12	1	5	41	.221	37	112	81	—

MAJOR LEAGUE TOTALS   2243 8143 1138 2254 365 67 342 1331 .277 1108 3779 139 13 yrs

Joseph Paul Torre Born Jul 18, 1940 Brooklyn, NY
6'2 212 lbs Batted right

YR	POS	TEAM	LG	FIN	G	AB	R	H	2B	3B	HR	RBI	AVG	BB	TB	OQ	RANK
1960	PH	MIL	NL	2-8	2	2	0	1	0	0	0	0	.500	0	1	—	—
1961	C	MIL	NL	4-8	113	406	40	113	21	4	10	42	.278	28	172	101	—
1962	C	MIL	NL	5-10	80	220	23	62	8	1	5	26	.282	24	87	107	—
1963	C-1B	MIL	NL	6-10	142	501	57	147	19	4	14	71	.293	42	216	123	17-50
1964	C-1B	MIL	NL	5-10	154	601	87	193	36	5	20	109	.321	36	299	135	12-42
1965	C-1B	MIL	NL	5-10	148	523	68	152	21	1	27	80	.291	61	256	140	8-52
1966	C-1B	ATL	NL	5-10	148	546	83	172	20	3	36	101	.315	60	306	157	5-55
1967	C-1B	ATL	NL	7-10	135	477	67	132	18	1	20	68	.277	49	212	127	20-54
1968	C-1B	ATL	NL	5-10	115	424	45	115	11	2	10	55	.271	34	160	113	—
1969	1B-C	SL	NL	4-6	159	602	72	174	29	6	18	101	.289	66	269	126	17-62
1970	C-3B	SL	NL	4-6	161	624	89	203	27	9	21	100	.325	70	311	135	13-56
1971	3B	SL	NL	2-6	161	634	97	230	34	8	24	137	.363	63	352	168	4-58
1972	3B-1B	SL	NL	4-6	149	544	71	157	26	6	11	81	.289	54	228	119	27-58
1973	1B-3B	SL	NL	2-6	141	519	67	149	17	2	13	69	.287	65	209	117	33-61
1974	1B-3B	SL	NL	2-6	147	529	59	149	28	1	11	70	.282	69	212	117	26-65
1975	3B-1B	NY	NL	3-6	114	361	33	89	16	3	6	35	.247	35	129	95	—
1976	1B	NY	NL	3-6	114	310	36	95	10	3	5	31	.306	21	126	112	—
1977	1B	NY	NL	6-6	26	51	2	9	3	0	1	9	.176	2	15	—	—

MAJOR LEAGUE TOTALS   2209 7874 996 2342 344 59 252 1185 .297 779 3560 133 11 yrs

Richard John McAuliffe   Born Nov 29, 1939 Hartford, CT
5'11   176 lbs   Batted left

YR	POS	TEAM	LG	FIN	G	AB	R	H	2B	3B	HR	RBI	AVG	BB	TB	OQ	RANK
1960	SS	DET	AL	6-8	8	27	2	7	0	1	0	1	.259	2	9	—	—
1961	SS-3B	DET	AL	2-10	80	285	36	73	12	4	6	33	.256	24	111	94	—
1962	2B-3B	DET	AL	4-10	139	471	50	124	20	5	12	63	.263	64	190	110	28-54
1963	SS-2B	DET	AL	5-10	150	568	77	149	18	6	13	61	.262	64	218	108	28-51
1964	SS	DET	AL	4-10	162	557	85	134	18	7	24	66	.241	77	238	118	23-52
1965	SS	DET	AL	4-10	113	404	61	105	13	6	15	54	.260	49	175	122	—
1966	SS-3B	DET	AL	3-10	124	430	83	118	16	8	23	56	.274	66	219	151	5-44
1967	2B-SS	DET	AL	2-10	153	557	92	133	16	7	22	65	.239	105	229	136	11-48
1968	2B	DET	AL	1-10	151	570	95	142	24	10	16	56	.249	82	234	132	12-45
1969	2B	DET	AL	2-6	74	271	49	71	10	5	11	33	.262	47	124	135	—
1970	2B-SS	DET	AL	4-6	146	530	73	124	21	1	12	50	.234	101	183	109	39-59
1971	2B	DET	AL	2-6	128	477	67	99	16	6	18	57	.208	53	181	100	43-57
1972	2B	DET	AL	1-6	122	408	47	98	16	3	8	30	.240	59	144	114	28-56
1973	2B	DET	AL	3-6	106	343	39	94	18	1	12	47	.274	49	150	123	—
1974	2B-3B	BOS	AL	3-6	100	272	32	57	13	1	5	24	.210	39	87	94	—
1975	3B	BOS	AL	1-6	7	15	0	2	0	0	0	1	.133	1	2	—	—
MAJOR LEAGUE TOTALS					1763	6185	888	1530	231	71	197	697	.247	882	2494	120	9 yrs

Deron Roger Johnson   Born Jul 17, 1938   San Diego, CA
6'2   200 lbs   Batted right   Died Apr 23, 1992 Poway, Ca

YR	POS	TEAM	LG	FIN	G	AB	R	H	2B	3B	HR	RBI	AVG	BB	TB	OQ	RANK
1960	3B	NY	AL	1-8	6	4	0	2	1	0	0	0	.500	0	3	—	—
1961	RF-3B	NY/KC	AL	1/9	96	302	32	63	11	3	8	44	.209	16	104	74	—
1962	1B-3B	KC	AL	9-10	17	19	1	2	1	0	0	0	.105	3	3	—	—
1964	1B	CIN	NL	2-10	140	477	63	130	24	4	21	79	.273	37	225	124	18-42
1965	3B	CIN	NL	4-10	159	616	92	177	30	7	32	130	.287	52	317	137	10-52
1966	LF-1B	CIN	NL	7-10	142	505	75	130	25	3	24	81	.257	39	233	116	23-55
1967	1B-3B	CIN	NL	4-10	108	361	39	81	18	1	13	53	.224	22	140	97	—
1968	1B-3B	ATL	NL	5-10	127	342	29	71	11	1	8	33	.208	35	108	95	—
1969	LF-3B	PHI	NL	5-6	138	475	51	121	19	4	17	80	.255	60	199	118	29-62
1970	1B	PHI	NL	5-6	159	574	66	147	28	3	27	93	.256	72	262	117	29-56
1971	1B-3B	PHI	NL	6-6	158	582	74	154	29	0	34	95	.265	72	285	136	14-58
1972	1B	PHI	NL	6-6	96	230	19	49	4	1	9	31	.213	26	82	98	—
1973	1B	PHI	NL	6-6	12	36	3	6	2	0	1	5	.167	5	11	—	—
1973	DH-1B	OAK	AL	1-6	131	464	61	114	14	2	19	81	.246	59	189	109	22-60
1974	DH-1B	Oa/Ml/Bo	AL	1/5/3	110	351	30	60	4	2	13	43	.171	32	107	76	—
1975	DH-1B	CH/BO	AL	5/1	151	565	68	135	25	1	19	75	.239	50	219	97	48-66
1976	DH-1B	BOS	AL	3-6	15	38	3	5	1	1	0	0	.132	5	8	—	—
MAJOR LEAGUE TOTALS					1765	5941	706	1447	247	33	245	923	.244	585	2495	119	8 yrs

Edwin Albert Brinkman
6'0 170 lbs Batted right

Born Dec 8, 1941 Cincinnati, OH

YR	POS	TEAM	LG	FIN	G	AB	R	H	2B	3B	HR	RBI	AVG	BB	TB	OQ	RANK
1961	3B	WAS	AL	9-10	4	11	0	1	0	0	0	0	.091	1	1	—	—
1962	SS-3B	WAS	AL	10-10	54	133	8	22	7	1	0	4	.165	11	31	57	—
1963	SS	WAS	AL	10-10	145	514	44	117	20	3	7	45	.228	31	164	78	50-51
1964	SS	WAS	AL	9-10	132	447	54	100	20	3	8	34	.224	26	150	80	—
1965	SS	WAS	AL	8-10	154	444	35	82	13	2	5	35	.185	38	114	68	—
1966	SS	WAS	AL	8-10	158	582	42	133	18	9	7	48	.229	29	190	81	44-44
1967	SS	WAS	AL	6-10	109	320	21	60	9	2	1	18	.188	24	76	66	—
1968	SS	WAS	AL	10-10	77	193	12	36	3	0	0	6	.187	19	39	66	—
1969	SS	WAS	AL	4-6	151	576	71	153	18	5	2	43	.266	50	187	89	53-59
1970	SS	WAS	AL	6-6	158	625	63	164	17	2	1	40	.262	60	188	84	55-59
1971	SS	DET	AL	2-6	159	527	40	120	18	2	1	37	.228	44	145	75	57-57
1972	SS	DET	AL	1-6	156	516	42	105	19	1	6	49	.203	38	144	77	56-56
1973	SS	DET	AL	3-6	162	515	55	122	16	4	7	40	.237	34	167	79	56-60
1974	SS	DET	AL	6-6	153	502	55	111	15	3	14	54	.221	29	174	83	60-67
1975	SS	SL	NL	3-6	28	75	6	18	4	0	1	6	.240	7	25	—	—
1975	SS	TX/NY	AL	3/3	45	65	2	11	4	1	0	2	.169	3	17	—	—
MAJOR LEAGUE TOTALS					1845	6045	550	1355	201	38	60	461	.224	444	1812	81	8 yrs

William Ashley Freehan
6'3 203 lbs Batted right

Born Nov 29, 1941 Detroit, MI

YR	POS	TEAM	LG	FIN	G	AB	R	H	2B	3B	HR	RBI	AVG	BB	TB	OQ	RANK
1961	C	DET	AL	2-10	4	10	1	4	0	0	0	4	.400	1	4	—	—
1963	C-1B	DET	AL	5-10	100	300	37	73	12	2	9	36	.243	39	116	109	—
1964	C	DET	AL	4-10	144	520	69	156	14	8	18	80	.300	36	240	120	22-52
1965	C	DET	AL	4-10	130	431	45	101	15	0	10	43	.234	39	146	91	—
1966	C	DET	AL	3-10	136	492	47	115	22	0	12	46	.234	40	173	93	39-44
1967	C	DET	AL	2-10	155	517	66	146	23	1	20	74	.282	73	231	141	10-48
1968	C-1B	DET	AL	1-10	155	540	73	142	24	2	25	84	.263	65	245	139	8-45
1969	C-1B	DET	AL	2-6	143	489	61	128	16	3	16	49	.262	53	198	110	33-59
1970	C	DET	AL	4-6	117	395	44	95	17	3	16	52	.241	52	166	113	—
1971	C	DET	AL	2-6	148	516	57	143	26	4	21	71	.277	54	240	128	21-57
1972	C	DET	AL	1-6	111	374	51	98	18	2	10	56	.262	48	150	125	—
1973	C	DET	AL	3-6	110	380	33	89	10	1	6	29	.234	40	119	84	—
1974	1B-C	DET	AL	6-6	130	445	58	132	17	5	18	60	.297	42	213	130	8-67
1975	C	DET	AL	6-6	120	427	42	105	17	3	14	47	.246	32	170	97	—
1976	C	DET	AL	5-6	71	237	22	64	10	1	5	27	.270	12	91	98	—
MAJOR LEAGUE TOTALS					1774	6073	706	1591	241	35	200	758	.262	626	2502	123	7 yrs

Thomas Michael Tresh   Born Sep 20, 1937 Detroit, MI
6'1 180 lbs Batted both

YR	POS	TEAM	LG	FIN	G	AB	R	H	2B	3B	HR	RBI	AVG	BB	TB	OQ	RANK
1961	SS	NY	AL	1-10	9	8	1	2	0	0	0	0	.250	0	2	—	—
1962	SS-LF	NY	AL	1-10	157	622	94	178	26	5	20	93	.286	67	274	115	21-54
1963	CF	NY	AL	1-10	145	520	91	140	28	5	25	71	.269	83	253	141	6-51
1964	LF	NY	AL	1-10	153	533	75	131	25	5	16	73	.246	73	214	113	28-52
1965	CF	NY	AL	6-10	156	602	94	168	29	6	26	74	.279	59	287	129	12-46
1966	LF-3B	NY	AL	10-10	151	537	76	125	12	4	27	68	.233	86	226	125	15-44
1967	LF	NY	AL	9-10	130	448	45	98	23	3	14	53	.219	50	169	108	27-48
1968	SS-LF	NY	AL	5-10	152	507	60	99	18	3	11	52	.195	76	156	102	33-45
1969	SS	NY/DE	AL	5/2	139	474	59	100	18	3	14	46	.211	56	166	94	51-59
MAJOR LEAGUE TOTALS					1192	4251	595	1041	179	34	153	530	.245	550	1747	116	8 yrs

James Louis Fregosi   Born Apr 4, 1942 San Francisco, CA
6'1 190 lbs Batted right

YR	POS	TEAM	LG	FIN	G	AB	R	H	2B	3B	HR	RBI	AVG	BB	TB	OQ	RANK
1961	SS	LA	AL	8-10	11	27	7	6	0	0	0	3	.222	1	6	—	—
1962	SS	LA	AL	3-10	58	175	15	51	3	4	3	23	.291	18	71	108	—
1963	SS	LA	AL	9-10	154	592	83	170	29	12	9	50	.287	36	250	108	27-51
1964	SS	LA	AL	5-10	147	505	86	140	22	9	18	72	.277	72	234	132	10-52
1965	SS	CAL	AL	7-10	161	602	66	167	19	7	15	64	.277	54	245	112	21-46
1966	SS	CAL	AL	6-10	162	611	78	154	32	7	13	67	.252	67	239	111	23-44
1967	SS	CAL	AL	5-10	151	590	75	171	23	6	9	56	.290	49	233	116	21-48
1968	SS	CAL	AL	8-10	159	614	77	150	21	13	9	49	.244	60	224	109	25-45
1969	SS	CAL	AL	3-6	161	580	78	151	22	6	12	47	.260	93	221	116	26-59
1970	SS	CAL	AL	3-6	158	601	95	167	33	5	22	82	.278	69	276	124	18-59
1971	SS-1B	CAL	AL	4-6	107	347	31	81	15	1	5	33	.233	39	113	93	—
1972	3B	NY	NL	3-6	101	340	31	79	15	4	5	32	.232	38	117	97	—
1973	3B-SS	NY	NL	1-6	45	124	7	29	4	1	0	11	.234	20	35	91	—
1973	3B-1B	TEX	AL	6-6	45	157	25	42	6	2	6	16	.268	12	70	110	—
1974	1B-3B	TEX	AL	2-6	78	230	31	60	5	0	12	34	.261	22	101	116	—
1975	1B-DH	TEX	AL	3-6	77	191	25	50	5	0	7	33	.262	20	76	105	—
1976	1B-DH	TEX	AL	5-6	58	133	17	31	7	0	2	12	.233	23	44	108	—
1977	3B-DH	TEX	AL	2-7	13	28	4	7	1	0	1	5	.250	3	11	—	—
1977	1B	PIT	NL	2-6	36	56	10	16	1	1	3	16	.286	13	28	—	—
1978	3B-1B	PIT	NL	2-6	20	20	3	4	1	0	0	1	.200	6	5	—	—
MAJOR LEAGUE TOTALS					1902	6523	844	1726	264	78	151	706	.265	715	2599	116	8 yrs

Donn Alvin Clendenon   Born Jul 15, 1935   Neosho, MO
6'4   209 lbs   Batted right

YR	POS	TEAM	LG	FIN	G	AB	R	H	2B	3B	HR	RBI	AVG	BB	TB	OQ	RANK
1961	RF	PIT	NL	6-8	9	35	7	11	1	1	0	2	.314	5	14	—	—
1962	1B-LF	PIT	NL	4-10	80	222	39	67	8	5	7	28	.302	26	106	129	—
1963	1B	PIT	NL	8-10	154	563	65	155	28	7	15	57	.275	39	242	116	22-50
1964	1B	PIT	NL	6-10	133	457	53	129	23	8	12	64	.282	26	204	115	—
1965	1B	PIT	NL	3-10	162	612	89	184	32	14	14	96	.301	48	286	127	20-52
1966	1B	PIT	NL	3-10	155	571	80	171	22	10	28	98	.299	52	297	140	9-55
1967	1B	PIT	NL	6-10	131	478	46	119	15	2	13	56	.249	34	177	98	41-54
1968	1B	PIT	NL	6-10	158	584	63	150	20	6	17	87	.257	47	233	116	21-45
1969	1B-LF	MO/NY	NL	6/1	110	331	45	82	11	1	16	51	.248	25	143	109	—
1970	1B	NY	NL	3-6	121	396	65	114	18	3	22	97	.288	39	204	129	—
1971	1B	NY	NL	3-6	88	263	29	65	10	0	11	37	.247	21	108	106	—
1972	1B	SL	NL	4-6	61	136	13	26	4	0	4	9	.191	17	42	88	—

MAJOR LEAGUE TOTALS   1362 4648 594 1273 192 57 159 682 .274 379 2056 119   5 yrs

John Wesley Powell   Born Aug 17, 1941 Lakeland, FL
6'4   230 lbs   Batted left

YR	POS	TEAM	LG	FIN	G	AB	R	H	2B	3B	HR	RBI	AVG	BB	TB	OQ	RANK
1961	LF	BAL	AL	3-10	4	13	0	1	0	0	0	1	.077	0	1	—	—
1962	LF	BAL	AL	7-10	124	400	44	97	13	2	15	53	.243	38	159	98	—
1963	LF-1B	BAL	AL	4-10	140	491	67	130	22	2	25	82	.265	49	231	124	14-51
1964	LF	BAL	AL	3-10	134	424	74	123	17	0	39	99	.290	76	257	175	2-52
1965	1B-LF	BAL	AL	3-10	144	472	54	117	20	2	17	72	.248	71	192	120	17-46
1966	1B	BAL	AL	1-10	140	491	78	141	18	0	34	109	.287	67	261	155	4-44
1967	1B	BAL	AL	6-10	125	415	53	97	14	1	13	55	.234	55	152	112	—
1968	1B	BAL	AL	2-10	154	550	60	137	21	1	22	85	.249	73	226	130	14-45
1969	1B	BAL	AL	1-6	152	533	83	162	25	0	37	121	.304	72	298	158	7-59
1970	1B	BAL	AL	1-6	154	526	82	156	28	0	35	114	.297	104	289	165	4-59
1971	1B	BAL	AL	1-6	128	418	59	107	19	0	22	92	.256	82	192	143	10-57
1972	1B	BAL	AL	3-6	140	465	53	117	20	1	21	81	.252	65	202	134	13-56
1973	1B	BAL	AL	1-6	114	370	52	98	13	1	11	54	.265	85	146	131	—
1974	1B	BAL	AL	1-6	110	344	37	91	13	1	12	45	.265	52	142	123	—
1975	1B	CLE	AL	4-6	134	435	64	129	18	0	27	86	.297	59	228	145	4-66
1976	1B	CLE	AL	4-6	95	293	29	63	9	0	9	33	.215	41	99	100	—
1977	1B	LA	NL	1-6	50	41	0	10	0	0	0	5	.244	12	10	—	—

MAJOR LEAGUE TOTALS   2042 6681 889 1776 270 11 339 1187 .266 1001 3085 145 10 yrs

James Leroy Thomas   Born Feb 5, 1936   Peoria, IL
6'2   195 lbs   Batted left

YR	POS	TEAM	LG	FIN	G	AB	R	H	2B	3B	HR	RBI	AVG	BB	TB	OQ	RANK
1961	RF-1B	NY/LA	AL	1/8	132	452	77	129	11	5	24	70	.285	47	222	123	16-49
1962	1B-RF	LA	AL	3-10	160	583	88	169	21	2	26	104	.290	55	272	119	18-54
1963	1B-RF	LA	AL	9-10	149	528	52	116	12	6	9	55	.220	53	167	85	45-51
1964	RF	LA/BO	AL	5/8	154	573	58	150	27	3	15	66	.262	52	228	105	33-52
1965	1B-RF	BOS	AL	9-10	151	521	74	141	27	4	22	75	.271	72	242	134	8-46
1966	1B-LF	AT/CH	NL	5/10	114	275	26	61	5	1	7	24	.222	24	89	85	—
1967	RF-1B	CHI	NL	3-10	77	191	16	42	4	1	2	23	.220	15	54	78	—
1968	RF	HOU	NL	10-10	90	201	14	39	4	0	1	11	.194	14	46	67	—
MAJOR LEAGUE TOTALS					1027	3324	405	847	111	22	106	428	.255	332	1320	113	5 yrs

Carl Michael Yastrzemski   Born Aug 22, 1939   Southampton, NY
5'11   175 lbs   Batted left

YR	POS	TEAM	LG	FIN	G	AB	R	H	2B	3B	HR	RBI	AVG	BB	TB	OQ	RANK
1961	LF	BOS	AL	6-10	148	583	71	155	31	6	11	80	.266	50	231	97	33-49
1962	LF	BOS	AL	8-10	160	646	99	191	43	6	19	94	.296	66	303	122	13-54
1963	LF	BOS	AL	7-10	151	570	91	183	40	3	14	68	.321	95	271	151	2-51
1964	LF	BOS	AL	8-10	151	567	77	164	29	9	15	67	.289	75	256	130	12-52
1965	LF	BOS	AL	9-10	133	494	78	154	45	3	20	72	.312	70	265	160	1-46
1966	LF	BOS	AL	9-10	160	594	81	165	39	2	16	80	.278	84	256	131	9-44
1967	LF	BOS	AL	1-10	161	579	112	189	31	4	44	121	.326	91	360	199	1-48
1968	LF	BOS	AL	4-10	157	539	90	162	32	2	23	74	.301	119	267	183	1-45
1969	LF-1B	BOS	AL	3-6	162	603	96	154	28	2	40	111	.255	101	306	143	10-59
1970	1B-LF	BOS	AL	3-6	161	566	125	186	29	0	40	102	.329	128	335	189	1-59
1971	LF	BOS	AL	3-6	148	508	75	129	21	2	15	70	.254	106	199	130	20-57
1972	LF-1B	BOS	AL	2-6	125	455	70	120	18	2	12	68	.264	67	178	128	17-56
1973	1B-3B	BOS	AL	2-6	152	540	82	160	25	4	19	95	.296	105	250	144	4-60
1974	1B-LF	BOS	AL	3-6	148	515	93	155	25	2	15	79	.301	104	229	148	4-67
1975	1B	BOS	AL	1-6	149	543	91	146	30	1	14	60	.269	87	220	119	21-66
1976	1B-LF	BOS	AL	3-6	155	546	71	146	23	2	21	102	.267	80	236	130	11-64
1977	LF	BOS	AL	3-7	150	558	99	165	27	3	28	102	.296	73	282	133	12-81
1978	LF-1B	BOS	AL	2-7	144	523	70	145	21	2	17	81	.277	76	221	121	25-83
1979	DH-1B	BOS	AL	3-7	147	518	69	140	28	1	21	87	.270	62	233	113	30-75
1980	DH-LF	BOS	AL	4-7	105	364	49	100	21	1	15	50	.275	44	168	119	—
1981	DH-1B	BOS	AL	5-7	91	338	36	83	14	1	7	53	.246	49	120	106	41-71
1982	DH-1B	BOS	AL	3-7	131	459	53	126	22	1	16	72	.275	59	198	114	30-77
1983	DH	BOS	AL	6-7	119	380	38	101	24	0	10	56	.266	54	155	112	—
MAJOR LEAGUE TOTALS					3308	11988	1816	3419	646	59	452	1844	.285	1845	5539	138	21 yrs

Norman Michael Hershberger   Born Oct 9, 1939   Massillon, OH
5'10   175 lbs   Batted right

YR	POS	TEAM	LG	FIN	G	AB	R	H	2B	3B	HR	RBI	AVG	BB	TB	OO	RANK
1961	CF-RF	CHI	AL	4-10	15	55	9	17	3	0	0	5	.309	2	20	—	—
1962	RF	CHI	AL	5-10	148	427	54	112	14	2	4	46	.262	37	142	85	—
1963	RF-CF	CHI	AL	2-10	135	476	64	133	26	2	3	45	.279	39	172	98	36-51
1964	RF	CHI	AL	2-10	141	452	55	104	15	3	2	31	.230	48	131	81	48-52
1965	RF	KC	AL	10-10	150	494	43	114	15	5	5	48	.231	37	154	82	45-46
1966	RF	KC	AL	7-10	146	538	55	136	27	7	2	57	.253	47	183	95	38-44
1967	RF	KC	AL	10-10	142	480	55	122	25	1	1	49	.254	38	152	92	44-48
1968	LF	OAK	AL	6-10	99	246	23	67	9	2	5	32	.272	21	95	116	—
1969	RF-LF	OAK	AL	2-6	51	129	11	26	2	0	1	10	.202	10	31	63	—
1970	RF	MIL	AL	4-6	49	98	7	23	5	0	1	6	.235	10	31	85	—
1971	CF	CHI	AL	3-6	74	177	22	46	9	0	2	15	.260	30	61	113	—

MAJOR LEAGUE TOTALS   1150 3572 398 900 150 22 26 344 .252 319 1172 90 5 yrs

Louis Clark Brock   Born Jun 16, 1939   El Dorado, AR
5'11   170 lbs   Batted left

YR	POS	TEAM	LG	FIN	G	AB	R	H	2B	3B	HR	RBI	AVG	BB	TB	OO	RANK
1961	CF	CHI	NL	7-8	4	11	1	1	0	0	0	0	.091	1	1	—	—
1962	CF	CHI	NL	9-10	123	434	73	114	24	7	9	35	.263	35	179	101	—
1963	RF	CHI	NL	7-10	148	547	79	141	19	11	9	37	.258	31	209	100	35-50
1964	LF	CHI/SL	NL	8/1	155	634	111	200	30	11	14	58	.315	40	294	127	16-42
1965	LF	SL	NL	7-10	155	631	107	182	35	8	16	69	.288	45	281	119	26-52
1966	LF	SL	NL	6-10	156	643	94	183	24	12	15	46	.285	31	276	107	33-55
1967	LF	SL	NL	1-10	159	689	113	206	32	12	21	76	.299	24	325	121	23-54
1968	LF	SL	NL	1-10	159	660	92	184	46	14	6	51	.279	46	276	122	18-45
1969	LF	SL	NL	4-6	157	655	97	195	33	10	12	47	.298	50	284	117	30-62
1970	LF	SL	NL	4-6	155	664	114	202	29	5	13	57	.304	60	280	110	35-56
1971	LF	SL	NL	2-6	157	640	126	200	37	7	7	61	.313	76	272	129	16-58
1972	LF	SL	NL	4-6	153	621	81	193	26	8	3	42	.311	47	244	111	35-58
1973	LF	SL	NL	2-6	160	650	110	193	29	8	7	63	.297	71	259	114	36-61
1974	LF	SL	NL	2-6	153	635	105	194	25	7	3	48	.306	61	242	109	41-65
1975	LF	SL	NL	3-6	136	528	78	163	27	6	3	47	.309	38	211	108	39-65
1976	LF	SL	NL	5-6	133	498	73	150	24	5	4	67	.301	35	196	108	32-57
1977	LF	SL	NL	3-6	141	489	69	133	22	6	2	46	.272	30	173	85	63-68
1978	LF	SL	NL	5-6	92	298	31	66	9	0	0	12	.221	17	75	63	—
1979	LF	SL	NL	3-6	120	405	56	123	15	4	5	38	.304	23	161	101	—

MAJOR LEAGUE TOTALS   2616 10332 1610 3023 486 141 149 900 .293 761 4238 112 15 yrs

Tommie Lee Agee   Born Aug 9, 1942 Magnolia, AL
5'11 195 lbs Batted right

YR	POS	TEAM	LG	FIN	G	AB	R	H	2B	3B	HR	RBI	AVG	BB	TB	OQ	RANK
1962	LF-CF	CLE	AL	6-10	5	14	0	3	0	0	0	2	.214	0	3	—	—
1963	RF-LF	CLE	AL	5-10	13	27	3	4	1	0	1	3	.148	2	8	—	—
1964	RF-CF	CLE	AL	6-10	13	12	0	2	0	0	0	0	.167	0	2	—	—
1965	RF-CF	CHI	AL	2-10	10	19	2	3	1	0	0	3	.158	2	4	—	—
1966	CF	CHI	AL	4-10	160	629	98	172	27	8	22	86	.273	41	281	117	21-44
1967	CF	CHI	AL	4-10	158	529	73	124	26	2	14	52	.234	44	196	102	33-48
1968	CF	NY	NL	9-10	132	368	30	80	12	3	5	17	.217	15	113	80	—
1969	CF	NY	NL	1-6	149	565	97	153	23	4	26	76	.271	59	262	125	18-62
1970	CF	NY	NL	3-6	153	636	107	182	30	7	24	75	.286	55	298	116	31-56
1971	CF	NY	NL	3-6	113	425	58	121	19	0	14	50	.285	50	182	124	—
1972	CF	NY	NL	3-6	114	422	52	96	23	0	13	47	.227	53	158	106	36-58
1973	CF-LF	HO/SL	NL	4/2	109	266	38	59	8	3	11	22	.222	21	106	97	—

MAJOR LEAGUE TOTALS   1129 3912 558 999 170 27 130 433 .255 342 1613 113   5 yrs

Robert Sherwood Bailey   Born Oct 13, 1942 Long Beach, CA
6'1 180 lbs Batted right

YR	POS	TEAM	LG	FIN	G	AB	R	H	2B	3B	HR	RBI	AVG	BB	TB	OQ	RANK
1962	3B	PIT	NL	4-10	14	42	6	7	2	1	0	6	.167	6	11	—	—
1963	3B	PIT	NL	8-10	154	570	60	130	15	3	12	45	.228	58	187	94	40-50
1964	3B-LF	PIT	NL	6-10	143	530	73	149	26	3	11	51	.281	44	214	111	25-42
1965	3B-LF	PIT	NL	3-10	159	626	87	160	28	3	11	49	.256	70	227	104	35-52
1966	3B-LF	PIT	NL	3-10	126	380	51	106	19	3	13	46	.279	47	170	127	—
1967	3B-LF	LA	NL	8-10	116	322	21	73	8	2	4	28	.227	40	97	92	—
1968	3B	LA	NL	7-10	105	322	24	73	9	3	8	39	.227	38	112	109	—
1969	1B-LF	MON	NL	6-6	111	358	46	95	16	6	9	53	.265	40	150	116	—
1970	3B-LF	MON	NL	6-6	131	352	77	101	19	3	28	84	.287	72	210	168	—
1971	3B-LF	MON	NL	5-6	157	545	65	137	21	4	14	83	.251	97	208	122	24-58
1972	3B	MON	NL	5-6	143	489	55	114	10	4	16	57	.233	59	180	104	38-58
1973	3B	MON	NL	4-6	151	513	77	140	25	4	26	86	.273	88	251	143	10-61
1974	LF-3B	MON	NL	4-6	152	507	69	142	20	2	20	73	.280	100	226	142	6-65
1975	LF	MON	NL	5-6	106	227	23	62	5	0	5	30	.273	46	82	122	—
1976	LF-3B	CIN	NL	1-6	69	124	17	37	6	1	6	23	.298	16	63	148	—
1977	1B	CIN	NL	2-6	49	79	9	20	2	1	2	11	.253	12	30	—	—
1977	PH	BOS	AL	2-7	2	2	0	0	0	0	0	0	.000	0	0	—	—
1978	DH	BOS	AL	2-7	43	94	12	18	3	0	4	9	.191	19	33	105	—

MAJOR LEAGUE TOTALS   1931 6082 772 1564 234 43 189 773 .257 852 2451 117   7 yrs

Roy Maxwell Alvis Born Feb 2, 1938 Jasper, TX
5'11 185 lbs Batted right

YR	POS	TEAM	LG	FIN	G	AB	R	H	2B	3B	HR	RBI	AVG	BB	TB	OQ	RANK
1962	3B	CLE	AL	6-10	12	51	1	11	2	0	0	3	.216	2	13	—	—
1963	3B	CLE	AL	5-10	158	602	81	165	32	7	22	67	.274	36	277	114	24-51
1964	3B	CLE	AL	6-10	107	381	51	96	14	3	18	53	.252	29	170	110	—
1965	3B	CLE	AL	5-10	159	604	88	149	24	2	21	61	.247	47	240	102	31-46
1966	3B	CLE	AL	5-10	157	596	67	146	22	3	17	55	.245	50	225	101	29-44
1967	3B	CLE	AL	8-10	161	637	66	163	23	4	21	70	.256	38	257	107	28-48
1968	3B	CLE	AL	3-10	131	452	38	101	17	3	8	37	.223	41	148	96	37-45
1969	3B	CLE	AL	6-6	66	191	13	43	6	0	1	15	.225	14	52	71	—
1970	3B	MIL	AL	5-6	62	115	16	21	2	0	3	12	.183	5	32	61	—

| MAJOR LEAGUE TOTALS | | | | | 1013 | 3629 | 421 | 895 | 142 | 22 | 111 | 373 | .247 | 262 | 1414 | 104 | 5 yrs |

Wilver Dornel Stargell Born Mar 6, 1940 Earlsboro, OK
6'2 188 lbs Batted left

YR	POS	TEAM	LG	FIN	G	AB	R	H	2B	3B	HR	RBI	AVG	BB	TB	OQ	RANK
1962	RF	PIT	NL	4-10	10	31	1	9	3	1	0	4	.290	3	14	—	—
1963	LF-1B	PIT	NL	8-10	108	304	34	74	11	6	11	47	.243	19	130	109	—
1964	LF-1B	PIT	NL	6-10	117	421	53	115	19	7	21	78	.273	17	211	123	—
1965	LF	PIT	NL	3-10	144	533	68	145	25	8	27	107	.272	39	267	129	19-52
1966	LF-1B	PIT	NL	3-10	140	485	84	153	30	0	33	102	.315	48	282	160	4-55
1967	LF-1B	PIT	NL	6-10	134	462	54	125	18	6	20	73	.271	67	215	140	11-54
1968	LF-1B	PIT	NL	6-10	128	435	57	103	15	1	24	67	.237	47	192	130	—
1969	LF-1B	PIT	NL	3-6	145	522	89	160	31	6	29	92	.307	61	290	156	8-62
1970	LF	PIT	NL	1-6	136	474	70	125	18	3	31	85	.264	44	242	122	25-56
1971	LF	PIT	NL	1-6	141	511	104	151	26	0	48	125	.295	83	321	183	2-58
1972	1B-LF	PIT	NL	1-6	138	495	75	145	28	2	33	112	.293	65	276	159	4-58
1973	LF	PIT	NL	3-6	148	522	106	156	43	3	44	119	.299	80	337	179	1-61
1974	LF	PIT	NL	1-6	140	508	90	153	37	4	25	96	.301	87	273	161	3-65
1975	1B	PIT	NL	1-6	124	461	71	136	32	2	22	90	.295	58	238	144	4-65
1976	1B	PIT	NL	2-6	117	428	54	110	20	3	20	65	.257	50	196	126	—
1977	1B	PIT	NL	2-6	63	186	29	51	12	0	13	35	.274	31	102	147	—
1978	1B	PIT	NL	2-6	122	390	60	115	18	2	28	97	.295	50	221	157	—
1979	1B	PIT	NL	1-6	126	424	60	119	19	0	32	82	.281	47	234	142	—
1980	1B	PIT	NL	3-6	67	202	28	53	10	1	11	38	.262	26	98	133	—
1981	1B	PIT	NL	4-6	38	60	2	17	4	0	0	9	.283	5	21	—	—
1982	1B	PIT	NL	4-6	74	73	6	17	4	0	3	17	.233	10	30	—	—

| MAJOR LEAGUE TOTALS | | | | | 2360 | 7927 | 1195 | 2232 | 423 | 55 | 475 | 1540 | .282 | 937 | 4190 | 153 | 10 yrs |

Denis John Menke　　　　　　Born Jul 21, 1940　　Algona, IA
6'0　185 lbs　Batted right

YR	POS	TEAM	LG	FIN	G	AB	R	H	2B	3B	HR	RBI	AVG	BB	TB	OQ	RANK
1962	2B-3B	MIL	NL	5-10	50	146	12	28	3	1	2	16	.192	16	39	71	—
1963	SS-3B	MIL	NL	6-10	146	518	58	121	16	4	11	50	.234	37	178	92	43-50
1964	SS-2B	MIL	NL	5-10	151	505	79	143	29	5	20	65	.283	68	242	141	10-42
1965	SS-1B	MIL	NL	5-10	71	181	16	44	13	1	4	18	.243	18	71	106	—
1966	SS-3B	ATL	NL	5-10	138	454	55	114	20	4	15	60	.251	71	187	122	18-55
1967	SS	ATL	NL	7-10	129	418	37	95	14	3	7	39	.227	65	136	104	—
1968	2B-SS	HOU	NL	10-10	150	542	56	135	23	6	6	56	.249	64	188	112	25-45
1969	SS-2B	HOU	NL	5-6	154	553	72	149	25	5	10	90	.269	87	214	120	26-62
1970	SS-2B	HOU	NL	4-6	154	562	82	171	26	6	13	92	.304	82	248	126	23-56
1971	1B-3B	HOU	NL	4-6	146	475	57	117	26	3	1	43	.246	59	152	96	45-58
1972	3B	CIN	NL	1-6	140	447	41	104	19	2	9	50	.233	58	154	101	42-58
1973	3B	CIN	NL	1-6	139	241	38	46	10	0	3	26	.191	69	65	108	—
1974	1B-3B	HOU	NL	4-6	30	29	2	3	1	0	0	1	.103	4	4	—	—
MAJOR LEAGUE TOTALS					1598	5071	605	1270	225	40	101	606	.250	698	1878	114	8 yrs

Kenneth Lee McMullen　　　　　　Born Jun 1, 1942　　Oxnard, CA
6'3　190 lbs　Batted right

YR	POS	TEAM	LG	FIN	G	AB	R	H	2B	3B	HR	RBI	AVG	BB	TB	OQ	RANK
1962	LF	LA	NL	2-10	6	11	0	3	0	0	0	0	.273	0	3	—	—
1963	3B	LA	NL	1-10	79	233	16	55	9	0	5	28	.236	20	79	94	—
1964	1B-3B	LA	NL	6-10	24	67	3	14	0	0	1	2	.209	3	17	—	—
1965	3B	WAS	AL	8-10	150	555	75	146	18	6	18	54	.263	47	230	110	22-46
1966	3B	WAS	AL	8-10	147	524	48	122	19	4	13	54	.233	44	188	95	35-44
1967	3B	WAS	AL	6-10	146	563	73	138	22	2	16	67	.245	46	212	105	30-48
1968	3B	WAS	AL	10-10	151	557	66	138	11	2	20	62	.248	63	213	118	19-45
1969	3B	WAS	AL	4-6	158	562	83	153	25	2	19	87	.272	70	239	120	23-59
1970	3B	WA/CA	AL	6/3	139	481	55	110	11	3	14	64	.229	64	169	98	48-59
1971	3B	CAL	AL	4-6	160	593	63	148	19	2	21	68	.250	53	234	105	38-57
1972	3B	CAL	AL	5-6	137	472	36	127	18	1	9	34	.269	48	174	112	29-56
1973	3B	LA	NL	2-6	42	85	6	21	5	0	5	18	.247	6	41	—	—
1974	3B	LA	NL	1-6	44	60	5	15	1	0	3	12	.250	2	25	—	—
1975	3B	LA	NL	2-6	39	46	4	11	1	1	2	14	.239	7	20	—	—
1976	3B-1B	OAK	AL	2-6	98	186	20	41	6	2	5	23	.220	22	66	100	—
1977	DH-1B	MIL	AL	6-7	63	136	15	31	7	1	5	19	.228	15	55	98	—
MAJOR LEAGUE TOTALS					1583	5131	568	1273	172	26	156	606	.248	510	1965	108	8 yrs

Tommy Harper
5'9   165 lbs   Batted right

Born Oct 14, 1940   Oak Grove, LA

YR	POS	TEAM	LG	FIN	G	AB	R	H	2B	3B	HR	RBI	AVG	BB	TB	OQ	RANK
1962	3B	CIN	NL	3-10	6	23	1	4	0	0	0	1	.174	2	4	—	—
1963	RF	CIN	NL	5-10	129	408	67	106	12	3	10	37	.260	44	154	111	—
1964	LF	CIN	NL	2-10	102	317	42	77	5	2	4	22	.243	39	98	94	—
1965	LF	CIN	NL	4-10	159	646	126	166	28	3	18	64	.257	78	254	113	28-52
1966	RF	CIN	NL	7-10	149	553	85	154	22	5	5	31	.278	57	201	104	37-55
1967	RF	CIN	NL	4-10	103	365	55	82	17	3	7	22	.225	43	126	100	—
1968	RF	CLE	AL	3-10	130	235	26	51	15	2	6	26	.217	26	88	111	—
1969	3B-2B	SEA	AL	6-6	148	537	78	126	10	2	9	41	.235	95	167	101	42-59
1970	3B-2B	MIL	AL	4-6	154	604	104	179	35	4	31	82	.296	77	315	143	6-59
1971	LF-3B	MIL	AL	6-6	152	585	79	151	26	3	14	52	.258	65	225	108	34-57
1972	CF	BOS	AL	2-6	144	556	92	141	29	2	14	49	.254	67	216	119	21-56
1973	LF	BOS	AL	2-6	147	566	92	159	23	3	17	71	.281	61	239	113	21-60
1974	LF-DH	BOS	AL	3-6	118	443	66	105	15	3	5	24	.237	46	141	88	56-67
1975	DH-1B	CA/OA	AL	6/1	123	354	51	90	14	1	5	38	.254	43	121	96	—
1976	DH	BAL	AL	2-6	46	77	8	18	5	0	1	7	.234	10	26	—	—

| MAJOR LEAGUE TOTALS | | | | | 1810 | 6269 | 972 | 1609 | 256 | 36 | 146 | 567 | .257 | 753 | 2375 | 111 | 8 yrs |

Pedro Oliva
6'1   175 lbs   Batted left

Born Jul 20, 1940   Pinar del Rio, Cuba

YR	POS	TEAM	LG	FIN	G	AB	R	H	2B	3B	HR	RBI	AVG	BB	TB	OQ	RANK
1962	RF	MIN	AL	2-10	9	9	3	4	1	0	0	3	.444	3	5	—	—
1963	PH	MIN	AL	3-10	7	7	0	3	0	0	0	1	.429	0	3	—	—
1964	RF	MIN	AL	6-10	161	672	109	217	43	9	32	94	.323	34	374	142	5-52
1965	RF	MIN	AL	1-10	149	576	107	185	40	5	16	98	.321	55	283	140	6-46
1966	RF	MIN	AL	2-10	159	622	99	191	32	7	25	87	.307	42	312	136	7-44
1967	RF	MIN	AL	2-10	146	557	76	161	34	6	17	83	.289	44	258	132	13-48
1968	RF	MIN	AL	7-10	128	470	54	136	24	5	18	68	.289	45	224	144	7-45
1969	RF	MIN	AL	1-6	153	637	97	197	39	4	24	101	.309	45	316	130	17-59
1970	RF	MIN	AL	1-6	157	628	96	204	36	7	23	107	.325	38	323	132	11-59
1971	RF	MIN	AL	5-6	126	487	73	164	30	3	22	81	.337	25	266	146	8-57
1972	RF	MIN	AL	3-6	10	28	1	9	1	0	0	1	.321	2	10	—	—
1973	DH	MIN	AL	3-6	146	571	63	166	20	0	16	92	.291	45	234	106	25-60
1974	DH	MIN	AL	3-6	127	459	43	131	16	2	13	57	.285	27	190	106	—
1975	DH	MIN	AL	4-6	131	455	46	123	10	0	13	58	.270	41	172	99	44-66
1976	DH	MIN	AL	3-6	67	123	3	26	3	0	1	16	.211	2	32	58	—

| MAJOR LEAGUE TOTALS | | | | | 1676 | 6301 | 870 | 1917 | 329 | 48 | 220 | 947 | .304 | 448 | 3002 | 131 | 10 yrs |

Joseph Anthony Pepitone   Born Oct 9, 1940   Brooklyn, NY
6'2   185 lbs   Batted left

YR	POS	TEAM	LG	FIN	G	AB	R	H	2B	3B	HR	RBI	AVG	BB	TB	OQ	RANK
1962	RF-1B	NY	AL	1-10	63	138	14	33	3	2	7	17	.239	3	61	92	—
1963	1B-RF	NY	AL	1-10	157	580	79	157	16	3	27	89	.271	23	260	107	30-51
1964	1B-CF	NY	AL	1-10	160	613	71	154	12	3	28	100	.251	24	256	96	38-52
1965	1B-RF	NY	AL	6-10	143	531	51	131	18	3	18	62	.247	43	209	102	32-46
1966	1B-CF	NY	AL	10-10	152	585	85	149	21	4	31	83	.255	29	271	114	22-44
1967	CF	NY	AL	9-10	133	501	45	126	18	3	13	64	.251	34	189	103	31-48
1968	CF-1B	NY	AL	5-10	108	380	41	93	9	3	15	56	.245	37	153	118	—
1969	1B	NY	AL	5-6	135	513	49	124	16	3	27	70	.242	30	227	105	39-59
1970	CF-1B	HO/CH	NL	4/2	131	492	82	127	18	7	26	79	.258	33	237	111	34-56
1971	1B-CF	CHI	NL	3-6	115	427	50	131	19	4	16	61	.307	24	206	127	—
1972	1B	CHI	NL	2-6	66	214	23	56	5	0	8	21	.262	13	85	101	—
1973	1B	CH/AT	NL	5/5	34	123	16	34	3	0	3	19	.276	9	46	97	—

MAJOR LEAGUE TOTALS   1397 5097 606 1315 158 35 219 721 .258 302 2200 105   7 yrs

Octavio Victor Rojas   Born Mar 6, 1939   Havana, Cuba
5'10   160 lbs   Batted right

YR	POS	TEAM	LG	FIN	G	AB	R	H	2B	3B	HR	RBI	AVG	BB	TB	OQ	RANK
1962	2B	CIN	NL	3-10	39	86	9	19	2	0	0	6	.221	9	21	—	—
1963	2B	PHI	NL	4-10	64	77	18	17	0	1	1	2	.221	3	22	—	—
1964	CF-2B	PHI	NL	2-10	109	340	58	99	19	5	2	31	.291	22	134	106	—
1965	2B-CF	PHI	NL	6-10	142	521	78	158	25	3	3	42	.303	42	198	108	31-52
1966	2B-CF	PHI	NL	4-10	156	626	77	168	18	1	6	55	.268	35	206	84	50-55
1967	2B	PHI	NL	5-10	147	528	60	137	21	2	4	45	.259	30	174	87	50-54
1968	2B	PHI	NL	7-10	152	621	53	144	19	0	9	48	.232	16	190	78	44-45
1969	2B	PHI	NL	5-6	110	391	35	89	11	1	4	30	.228	23	114	73	—
1970	2B	SL	NL	4-6	23	47	2	5	0	0	0	2	.106	3	5	—	—
1970	2B	KC	AL	4-6	98	384	36	100	13	3	2	28	.260	20	125	79	—
1971	2B	KC	AL	2-6	115	414	56	124	22	2	6	59	.300	39	168	116	—
1972	2B	KC	AL	4-6	137	487	49	127	25	0	3	53	.261	41	161	98	39-56
1973	2B	KC	AL	2-6	139	551	78	152	29	3	6	69	.276	37	205	93	44-60
1974	2B	KC	AL	5-6	144	542	52	147	17	1	6	60	.271	30	184	87	58-67
1975	2B	KC	AL	2-6	120	406	34	103	18	2	2	37	.254	30	131	82	—
1976	2B-DH	KC	AL	1-6	63	132	11	32	6	0	0	16	.242	8	38	75	—
1977	3B-2B	KC	AL	1-7	64	156	8	39	9	1	0	10	.250	8	50	73	—

MAJOR LEAGUE TOTALS   1822 6309 714 1660 254 25 54 593 .263 396 2126   91   7 yrs

Americo Peter Petrocelli Born Jun 27, 1943 Brooklyn, NY
6'0 175 lbs Batted right

YR	POS	TEAM	LG	FIN	G	AB	R	H	2B	3B	HR	RBI	AVG	BB	TB	OQ	RANK
1963	SS	BOS	AL	7-10	1	4	0	1	1	0	0	1	.250	0	2	—	—
1965	SS	BOS	AL	9-10	103	323	38	75	15	2	13	33	.232	36	133	111	—
1966	SS	BOS	AL	9-10	139	522	58	124	20	1	18	59	.238	41	200	100	31-44
1967	SS	BOS	AL	1-10	142	491	53	127	24	2	17	66	.259	49	206	121	18-48
1968	SS	BOS	AL	4-10	123	406	41	95	17	2	12	46	.234	31	152	105	—
1969	SS	BOS	AL	3-6	154	535	92	159	32	2	40	97	.297	98	315	174	3-59
1970	SS-3B	BOS	AL	3-6	157	583	82	152	31	3	29	103	.261	67	276	124	17-59
1971	3B	BOS	AL	3-6	158	553	82	139	24	4	28	89	.251	91	255	135	15-57
1972	3B	BOS	AL	2-6	147	521	62	125	15	2	15	75	.240	78	189	118	23-56
1973	3B	BOS	AL	2-6	100	356	44	87	13	1	13	45	.244	47	141	108	—
1974	3B	BOS	AL	3-6	129	454	53	121	23	1	15	76	.267	48	191	115	23-67
1975	3B	BOS	AL	1-6	115	402	31	96	15	1	7	59	.239	41	134	88	—
1976	3B	BOS	AL	3-6	85	240	17	51	7	1	3	24	.213	34	69	89	—
MAJOR LEAGUE TOTALS					1553	5390	653	1352	237	22	210	773	.251	661	2263	127	7 yrs

Willie Watterson Horton Born Oct 18, 1942 Arno, VA
5'11 209 lbs Batted right

YR	POS	TEAM	LG	FIN	G	AB	R	H	2B	3B	HR	RBI	AVG	BB	TB	OQ	RANK
1963	LF	DET	AL	5-10	15	43	6	14	2	1	1	4	.326	0	21	—	—
1964	LF	DET	AL	4-10	25	80	6	13	1	3	1	10	.163	11	23	—	—
1965	LF	DET	AL	4-10	143	512	69	140	20	2	29	104	.273	48	251	131	10-46
1966	LF	DET	AL	3-10	146	526	72	138	22	6	27	100	.262	44	253	126	13-44
1967	LF	DET	AL	2-10	122	401	47	110	20	3	19	67	.274	36	193	136	—
1968	LF	DET	AL	1-10	143	512	68	146	20	2	36	85	.285	49	278	160	2-45
1969	LF	DET	AL	2-6	141	508	66	133	17	1	28	91	.262	52	236	122	20-59
1970	LF	DET	AL	4-6	96	371	53	113	18	2	17	69	.305	28	186	129	—
1971	LF	DET	AL	2-6	119	450	64	130	25	1	22	72	.289	37	223	132	19-57
1972	LF	DET	AL	1-6	108	333	44	77	9	5	11	36	.231	27	129	106	—
1973	LF	DET	AL	3-6	111	411	42	130	19	3	17	53	.316	23	206	125	—
1974	LF	DET	AL	6-6	72	238	32	71	8	1	15	47	.298	21	126	141	—
1975	DH	DET	AL	6-6	159	615	62	169	13	1	25	92	.275	44	259	105	33-66
1976	DH	DET	AL	5-6	114	401	40	105	17	0	14	56	.262	49	164	118	—
1977	DH	DE/TX	AL	4/2	140	523	55	151	23	3	15	75	.289	42	225	106	47-81
1978	DH	Cl/Oa/To	AL	6/6/7	115	393	38	99	21	0	11	60	.252	28	153	95	—
1979	DH	SEA	AL	6-7	162	646	77	180	19	5	29	106	.279	42	296	105	38-75
1980	DH	SEA	AL	7-7	97	335	32	74	10	1	8	36	.221	39	110	85	—
MAJOR LEAGUE TOTALS					2028	7298	873	1993	284	40	325	1163	.273	620	3332	123	8 yrs

Richard Anthony Allen   Born Mar 8, 1942 Wampum, PA
5'11   187 lbs   Batted right

YR	POS	TEAM	LG	FIN	G	AB	R	H	2B	3B	HR	RBI	AVG	BB	TB	OQ	RANK
1963	LF-3B	PHI	NL	4-10	10	24	6	7	2	1	0	2	.292	0	11	—	—
1964	3B	PHI	NL	2-10	162	632	125	201	38	13	29	91	.318	67	352	160	4-42
1965	3B	PHI	NL	6-10	161	619	93	187	31	14	20	85	.302	74	306	144	7-52
1966	3B-LF	PHI	NL	4-10	141	524	112	166	25	10	40	110	.317	68	331	179	1-55
1967	3B	PHI	NL	5-10	122	463	89	142	31	10	23	77	.307	75	262	176	1-54
1968	LF	PHI	NL	7-10	152	521	87	137	17	9	33	90	.263	74	271	162	2-45
1969	1B	PHI	NL	5-6	118	438	79	126	23	3	32	89	.288	64	251	162	5-62
1970	1B-3B	SL	NL	4-6	122	459	88	128	17	5	34	101	.279	71	257	148	8-56
1971	3B-LF	LA	NL	2-6	155	549	82	162	24	1	23	90	.295	93	257	147	6-58
1972	1B	CHI	AL	2-6	148	506	90	156	28	5	37	113	.308	99	305	201	1-56
1973	1B	CHI	AL	5-6	72	250	39	79	20	3	16	41	.316	33	153	167	—
1974	1B	CHI	AL	4-6	128	462	84	139	23	1	32	88	.301	57	260	157	1-67
1975	1B	PHI	NL	2-6	119	416	54	97	21	3	12	62	.233	58	160	108	—
1976	1B	PHI	NL	1-6	85	298	52	80	16	1	15	49	.268	37	143	135	—
1977	1B	OAK	AL	7-7	54	171	19	41	4	0	5	31	.240	24	60	95	—
MAJOR LEAGUE TOTALS					1749	6332	1099	1848	320	79	351	1119	.292	894	3379	164	10 yrs

James Sherman Wynn   Born Mar 12, 1942 Hamilton, OH
5'10   160 lbs   Batted right

YR	POS	TEAM	LG	FIN	G	AB	R	H	2B	3B	HR	RBI	AVG	BB	TB	OQ	RANK
1963	LF-SS	HOU	NL	9-10	70	250	31	61	10	5	4	27	.244	30	93	110	—
1964	CF-LF	HOU	NL	9-10	67	219	19	49	7	0	5	18	.224	24	71	92	—
1965	CF	HOU	NL	9-10	157	564	90	155	30	7	22	73	.275	84	265	139	9-52
1966	CF	HOU	NL	8-10	105	418	62	107	21	1	18	62	.256	41	184	116	—
1967	CF	HOU	NL	9-10	158	594	102	148	29	3	37	107	.249	74	294	138	12-54
1968	LF-CF	HOU	NL	10-10	156	542	85	146	23	5	26	67	.269	90	257	158	3-45
1969	CF	HOU	NL	5-6	149	495	113	133	17	1	33	87	.269	148	251	177	2-62
1970	LF-CF	HOU	NL	4-6	157	554	82	156	32	2	27	88	.282	106	273	142	11-56
1971	RF	HOU	NL	4-6	123	404	38	82	16	0	7	45	.203	56	119	89	—
1972	RF	HOU	NL	2-6	145	542	117	148	29	3	24	90	.273	103	255	149	7-58
1973	RF	HOU	NL	4-6	139	481	90	106	14	5	20	55	.220	91	190	118	30-61
1974	CF	LA	NL	1-6	150	535	104	145	17	4	32	108	.271	108	266	152	5-65
1975	CF	LA	NL	2-6	130	412	80	102	16	0	18	58	.248	110	172	144	5-65
1976	LF	ATL	NL	6-6	148	449	75	93	19	1	17	66	.207	127	165	134	11-57
1977	RF-DH	NY/ML	AL	1/6	66	194	17	34	5	2	1	13	.175	32	46	72	—
MAJOR LEAGUE TOTALS					1920	6653	1105	1665	285	39	291	964	.250	1224	2901	145	10 yrs

Donald Ralph Wert   Born Jul 29, 1938   Strasburg, PA
5'10   162 lbs   Batted right

YR	POS	TEAM	LG	FIN	G	AB	R	H	2B	3B	HR	RBI	AVG	BB	TB	OQ	RANK
1963	3B-2B	DET	AL	5-10	78	251	31	65	6	2	7	25	.259	24	96	103	—
1964	3B	DET	AL	4-10	148	525	63	135	18	5	9	55	.257	50	190	97	35-52
1965	3B	DET	AL	4-10	162	609	81	159	22	2	12	54	.261	73	221	106	27-46
1966	3B	DET	AL	3-10	150	559	56	150	20	2	11	70	.268	64	207	110	24-44
1967	3B	DET	AL	2-10	142	534	60	137	23	2	6	40	.257	44	182	98	39-48
1968	3B	DET	AL	1-10	150	536	44	107	15	1	12	37	.200	37	160	82	42-45
1969	3B	DET	AL	2-6	132	423	46	95	11	1	14	50	.225	49	150	96	—
1970	3B	DET	AL	4-6	128	363	34	79	13	0	6	33	.218	44	110	84	—
1971	3B-SS	WAS	AL	5-6	20	40	2	2	1	0	0	2	.050	4	3	—	—

MAJOR LEAGUE TOTALS   1110 3840 417 929 129 15 77 366 .242 389 1319 99   5 yrs

Daniel Joseph Staub   Born Apr 1, 1944   New Orleans, LA
6'2   190 lbs   Batted left

YR	POS	TEAM	LG	FIN	G	AB	R	H	2B	3B	HR	RBI	AVG	BB	TB	OQ	RANK
1963	1B-RF	HOU	NL	9-10	150	513	43	115	17	4	6	45	.224	59	158	92	42-50
1964	1B-RF	HOU	NL	9-10	89	292	26	63	10	2	8	35	.216	21	101	88	—
1965	RF	HOU	NL	9-10	131	410	43	105	20	1	14	63	.256	52	169	118	—
1966	RF	HOU	NL	8-10	153	554	60	155	28	3	13	81	.280	58	228	115	24-55
1967	RF	HOU	NL	9-10	149	546	71	182	44	1	10	74	.333	60	258	146	8-54
1968	1B	HOU	NL	10-10	161	591	54	172	37	1	6	72	.291	73	229	130	14-45
1969	RF	MON	NL	6-6	158	549	89	166	26	5	29	79	.302	110	289	168	4-62
1970	RF	MON	NL	6-6	160	569	98	156	23	7	30	94	.274	112	283	143	9-56
1971	RF	MON	NL	5-6	162	599	94	186	34	6	19	97	.311	74	289	143	7-58
1972	RF	NY	NL	3-6	66	239	32	70	11	0	9	38	.293	31	108	135	—
1973	RF	NY	NL	1-6	152	585	77	163	36	1	15	76	.279	74	246	119	27-61
1974	RF	NY	NL	5-6	151	561	65	145	22	2	19	78	.258	77	228	116	28-65
1975	RF	NY	NL	3-6	155	574	93	162	30	4	19	105	.282	77	257	128	21-65
1976	RF-DH	DET	AL	5-6	161	589	73	176	28	3	15	96	.299	83	255	134	6-64
1977	DH	DET	AL	4-7	158	623	84	173	34	3	22	101	.278	59	279	110	32-81
1978	DH	DET	AL	5-7	162	642	75	175	30	1	24	121	.273	76	279	117	31-83
1979	DH	DET	AL	5-7	68	246	32	58	12	1	9	40	.236	32	99	101	—
1979	1B	MON	NL	2-6	38	86	9	23	3	0	3	14	.267	14	35	120	—
1980	DH-1B	TEX	AL	4-7	109	340	42	102	23	2	9	55	.300	39	156	122	—
1981	1B	NY	NL	5-6	70	161	9	51	9	0	5	21	.317	22	75	143	—
1982	RF-1B	NY	NL	6-6	112	219	11	53	9	0	3	27	.242	24	71	92	—
1983	LF-1B	NY	NL	6-6	104	115	5	34	6	0	3	28	.296	14	49	122	—
1984	1B	NY	NL	2-6	78	72	2	19	4	0	1	18	.264	4	26	—	—
1985	RF	NY	NL	2-6	54	45	2	12	3	0	1	8	.267	10	18	—	—

MAJOR LEAGUE TOTALS   2951 9720 1189 2716 499 47 292 1466 .279 1255 4185 128 13 yrs

Donald Alvin Buford   Born Feb 2, 1937   Linden, TX
5'7   160 lbs Batted both

YR	POS	TEAM	LG	FIN	G	AB	R	H	2B	3B	HR	RBI	AVG	BB	TB	OQ	RANK
1963	3B-2B	CHI	AL	2-10	12	42	9	12	1	2	0	5	.286	5	17	—	—
1964	2B-3B	CHI	AL	2-10	135	442	62	116	14	6	4	30	.262	46	154	97	36-52
1965	2B-3B	CHI	AL	2-10	155	586	93	166	22	5	10	47	.283	67	228	114	20-46
1966	3B-2B	CHI	AL	4-10	163	607	85	148	26	7	8	52	.244	69	212	101	28-44
1967	3B-2B	CHI	AL	4-10	156	535	61	129	10	9	4	32	.241	65	169	99	37-48
1968	LF-2B	BAL	AL	2-10	130	426	65	120	13	4	15	46	.282	57	186	142	—
1969	LF	BAL	AL	1-6	144	554	99	161	31	3	11	64	.291	96	231	132	15-59
1970	LF	BAL	AL	1-6	144	504	99	137	15	2	17	66	.272	109	207	134	9-59
1971	LF	BAL	AL	1-6	122	449	99	130	19	4	19	54	.290	89	214	154	2-57
1972	LF	BAL	AL	3-6	125	408	46	84	6	2	5	22	.206	69	109	96	43-56

MAJOR LEAGUE TOTALS   1286 4553 718 1203 157 44 93 418 .264 672 1727 116 8 yrs

Peter Edward Rose   Born Apr 14, 1941   Cincinnati, OH
5'11   192 lbs Batted both

YR	POS	TEAM	LG	FIN	G	AB	R	H	2B	3B	HR	RBI	AVG	BB	TB	OQ	RANK
1963	2B	CIN	NL	5-10	157	623	101	170	25	9	6	41	.273	55	231	107	29-50
1964	2B	CIN	NL	2-10	136	516	64	139	13	2	4	34	.269	36	168	89	39-42
1965	2B	CIN	NL	4-10	162	670	117	209	35	11	11	81	.312	69	299	130	16-52
1966	2B-3B	CIN	NL	7-10	156	654	97	205	38	5	16	70	.313	37	301	121	21-55
1967	LF-2B	CIN	NL	4-10	148	585	86	176	32	8	12	76	.301	56	260	129	16-54
1968	RF	CIN	NL	4-10	149	626	94	210	42	6	10	49	.335	56	294	152	6-45
1969	RF	CIN	NL	3-6	156	627	120	218	33	11	16	82	.348	88	321	161	6-62
1970	RF	CIN	NL	1-6	159	649	120	205	37	9	15	52	.316	73	305	127	21-56
1971	RF	CIN	NL	4-6	160	632	86	192	27	4	13	44	.304	68	266	124	22-58
1972	LF	CIN	NL	1-6	154	645	107	198	31	11	6	57	.307	73	269	125	18-58
1973	LF	CIN	NL	1-6	160	680	115	230	36	8	5	64	.338	65	297	127	17-61
1974	LF	CIN	NL	2-6	163	652	110	185	45	7	3	51	.284	106	253	122	21-65
1975	3B-LF	CIN	NL	1-6	162	662	112	210	47	4	7	74	.317	89	286	131	17-65
1976	3B	CIN	NL	1-6	162	665	130	215	42	6	10	63	.323	86	299	140	6-57
1977	3B	CIN	NL	2-6	162	655	95	204	38	7	9	64	.311	66	283	116	31-68
1978	3B	CIN	NL	2-6	159	655	103	198	51	3	7	52	.302	62	276	118	26-63
1979	1B	PHI	NL	4-6	163	628	90	208	40	5	4	59	.331	95	270	134	12-62
1980	1B	PHI	NL	1-6	162	655	95	185	42	1	1	64	.282	66	232	101	43-59
1981	1B	PHI	NL	2-6	107	431	73	140	18	5	0	33	.325	46	168	120	24-69
1982	1B	PHI	NL	2-6	162	634	80	172	25	4	3	54	.271	66	214	97	53-66
1983	1B-RF	PHI	NL	1-6	151	493	52	121	14	3	0	45	.245	52	141	82	61-64
1984	1B-LF	MO/CN	NL	5/5	121	374	43	107	15	2	0	34	.286	40	126	100	—
1985	1B	CIN	NL	2-6	119	405	60	107	12	2	2	46	.264	86	129	115	26-65
1986	1B	CIN	NL	2-6	72	237	15	52	8	2	0	25	.219	30	64	79	—

MAJOR LEAGUE TOTALS   3562 14053 2165 4256 746 135 160 1314 .303 1566 5752 121 22 yrs

Ronald Kenneth Hunt   Born Feb 23, 1941 St Louis, MO
6'0 186 lbs Batted right

YR	POS	TEAM	LG	FIN	G	AB	R	H	2B	3B	HR	RBI	AVG	BB	TB	OQ	RANK
1963	2B	NY	NL	10-10	143	533	64	145	28	4	10	42	.272	40	211	109	26-50
1964	2B	NY	NL	10-10	127	475	59	144	19	6	6	42	.303	29	193	110	26-42
1965	2B-3B	NY	NL	10-10	57	196	21	47	12	1	1	10	.240	14	64	85	—
1966	2B	NY	NL	9-10	132	479	63	138	19	2	3	33	.288	41	170	99	39-55
1967	2B	LA	NL	8-10	110	388	44	102	17	3	3	33	.263	39	134	101	—
1968	2B	SF	NL	2-10	148	529	79	132	19	0	2	28	.250	78	157	107	29-45
1969	2B	SF	NL	2-6	128	478	72	125	23	3	3	41	.262	51	163	97	49-62
1970	2B-3B	SF	NL	3-6	117	367	70	103	17	1	6	41	.281	44	140	104	—
1971	2B-3B	MON	NL	5-6	152	520	89	145	20	3	5	38	.279	58	186	106	38-58
1972	2B	MON	NL	5-6	129	443	56	112	20	0	0	18	.253	51	132	91	46-58
1973	2B-3B	MON	NL	4-6	113	401	61	124	14	0	0	18	.309	52	138	108	—
1974	3B-2B	MO/SL	NL	4/2	127	426	67	112	15	0	0	26	.263	58	127	93	55-65

| MAJOR LEAGUE TOTALS | | | | | 1483 | 5235 | 745 | 1429 | 223 | 23 | 39 | 370 | .273 | 555 | 1815 | 102 | 8 yrs |

Joe Leonard Morgan   Born Sep 19, 1943 Bonham, TX
5'7 160 lbs Batted left

YR	POS	TEAM	LG	FIN	G	AB	R	H	2B	3B	HR	RBI	AVG	BB	TB	OQ	RANK
1963	2B	HOU	NL	9-10	8	25	5	6	0	1	0	3	.240	5	8	—	—
1964	2B	HOU	NL	9-10	10	37	4	7	0	0	0	0	.189	6	7	—	—
1965	2B	HOU	NL	9-10	157	601	100	163	22	12	14	40	.271	97	251	130	17-52
1966	2B	HOU	NL	8-10	122	425	60	121	14	8	5	42	.285	89	166	135	12-55
1967	2B	HOU	NL	9-10	133	494	73	136	27	11	6	42	.275	81	203	133	15-54
1968	2B	HOU	NL	10-10	10	20	6	5	0	1	0	0	.250	7	7	—	—
1969	2B	HOU	NL	5-6	147	535	94	126	18	5	15	43	.236	110	199	122	24-62
1970	2B	HOU	NL	4-6	144	548	102	147	28	9	8	52	.268	102	217	119	27-56
1971	2B	HOU	NL	4-6	160	583	87	149	27	11	13	56	.256	88	237	122	23-58
1972	2B	CIN	NL	1-6	149	552	122	161	23	4	16	73	.292	115	240	149	8-58
1973	2B	CIN	NL	1-6	157	576	116	167	35	2	26	82	.290	111	284	152	5-61
1974	2B	CIN	NL	2-6	149	512	107	150	31	3	22	67	.293	120	253	163	1-65
1975	2B	CIN	NL	1-6	146	498	107	163	27	6	17	94	.327	132	253	181	1-65
1976	2B	CIN	NL	1-6	141	472	113	151	30	5	27	111	.320	114	272	196	1-57
1977	2B	CIN	NL	2-6	153	521	113	150	21	6	22	78	.288	117	249	148	5-68
1978	2B	CIN	NL	2-6	132	441	68	104	27	0	13	75	.236	79	170	118	27-63
1979	2B	CIN	NL	1-6	127	436	70	109	26	1	9	32	.250	93	164	121	21-62
1980	2B	HOU	NL	1-6	141	461	66	112	17	5	11	49	.243	93	172	121	19-59
1981	2B	SF	NL	4-6	90	308	47	74	16	1	8	31	.240	66	116	127	16-69
1982	2B	SF	NL	3-6	134	463	68	134	19	4	14	61	.289	85	203	140	10-66
1983	2B	PHI	NL	1-6	123	404	72	93	20	1	16	59	.230	89	163	127	12-64
1984	2B	OAK	AL	4-7	116	365	50	89	21	0	6	43	.244	66	128	106	—

| MAJOR LEAGUE TOTALS | | | | | 2649 | 9277 | 1650 | 2517 | 449 | 96 | 268 | 1133 | .271 | 1865 | 3962 | 139 | 18 yrs |

James Ray Hart   Born Oct 30, 1941   Hookerton, NC
5'11   185 lbs   Batted right

YR	POS	TEAM	LG	FIN	G	AB	R	H	2B	3B	HR	RBI	AVG	BB	TB	OQ	RANK
1963	3B	SF	NL	3-10	7	20	1	4	1	0	0	2	.200	3	5	—	—
1964	3B	SF	NL	4-10	153	566	71	162	15	6	31	81	.286	47	282	134	13-42
1965	3B	SF	NL	2-10	160	591	91	177	30	6	23	96	.299	47	288	132	13-52
1966	3B-LF	SF	NL	2-10	156	578	88	165	23	4	33	93	.285	48	295	133	13-55
1967	3B-LF	SF	NL	2-10	158	578	98	167	26	7	29	99	.289	77	294	151	7-54
1968	3B-LF	SF	NL	2-10	136	480	67	124	14	3	23	78	.258	46	213	131	13-45
1969	LF	SF	NL	2-6	95	236	27	60	9	0	3	26	.254	28	78	97	—
1970	3B-LF	SF	NL	3-6	76	255	30	72	12	1	8	37	.282	30	110	114	—
1971	3B-LF	SF	NL	1-6	31	39	5	10	0	0	2	5	.256	6	16	—	—
1972	3B	SF	NL	5-6	24	79	10	24	5	0	5	8	.304	6	44	—	—
1973	3B	SF	NL	3-6	5	3	0	0	0	0	0	1	.000	3	0	—	—
1973	DH	NY	AL	4-6	114	339	29	86	13	2	13	52	.254	36	142	108	—
1974	DH	NY	AL	2-6	10	19	1	1	0	0	0	0	.053	3	1	—	—

MAJOR LEAGUE TOTALS   1125 3783 518 1052 148 29 170 578 .278 380 1768 136   5 yrs

Jose Rosario Domec Cardenal   Born Oct 7, 1943   Matanzas, Cuba
5'10   150 lbs   Batted right

YR	POS	TEAM	LG	FIN	G	AB	R	H	2B	3B	HR	RBI	AVG	BB	TB	OQ	RANK
1963	CF-RF	SF	NL	3-10	9	5	1	1	0	0	0	2	.200	1	1	—	—
1964	LF-RF	SF	NL	4-10	20	15	3	0	0	0	0	0	.000	2	0	—	—
1965	CF	CAL	AL	7-10	134	512	58	128	23	2	11	57	.250	27	188	91	40-46
1966	CF	CAL	AL	6-10	154	561	67	155	15	3	16	48	.276	34	224	105	26-44
1967	CF	CAL	AL	5-10	108	381	40	90	13	5	6	27	.236	15	131	87	—
1968	CF	CLE	AL	3-10	157	583	78	150	21	7	7	44	.257	39	206	101	34-45
1969	CF	CLE	AL	6-6	146	557	75	143	26	3	11	45	.257	49	208	98	45-59
1970	CF	SL	NL	4-6	148	552	73	162	32	6	10	74	.293	45	236	108	38-56
1971	CF	SL	NL	2-6	89	301	37	73	12	4	7	48	.243	29	114	102	—
1971	LF	MIL	AL	6-6	53	198	20	51	10	0	3	32	.258	13	70	92	—
1972	RF	CHI	NL	2-6	143	533	96	155	24	6	17	70	.291	55	242	129	16-58
1973	RF	CHI	NL	5-6	145	522	80	158	33	2	11	68	.303	58	228	124	22-61
1974	RF	CHI	NL	6-6	143	542	75	159	35	3	13	72	.293	56	239	122	20-65
1975	RF	CHI	NL	5-6	154	574	85	182	30	2	9	68	.317	77	243	129	19-65
1976	LF	CHI	NL	4-6	136	521	64	156	25	2	8	47	.299	32	209	108	33-57
1977	LF	CHI	NL	4-6	100	226	33	54	12	1	3	18	.239	28	77	91	—
1978	1B-LF	PHI	NL	1-6	87	201	27	50	12	0	4	33	.249	23	74	102	—
1979	RF-LF	PH/NY	NL	4/6	40	85	12	21	7	0	2	13	.247	14	34	—	—
1980	RF-1B	NY	NL	5-6	26	42	4	7	1	0	0	4	.167	6	8	—	—
1980	RF-LF	KC	AL	1-7	25	53	8	18	2	0	0	5	.340	5	20	—	—

MAJOR LEAGUE TOTALS   2017 6964 936 1913 333 46 138 775 .275 608 2752 112 10 yrs

Cleon Joseph Jones Born Aug 4, 1942 Plateau, AL
6'0 185 lbs Batted right

YR	POS	TEAM	LG	FIN	G	AB	R	H	2B	3B	HR	RBI	AVG	BB	TB	OQ	RANK
1963	CF	NY	NL	10-10	6	15	1	2	0	0	0	1	.133	0	2	—	—
1965	CF	NY	NL	10-10	30	74	2	11	1	0	1	9	.149	2	15	—	—
1966	CF	NY	NL	9-10	139	495	74	136	16	4	8	57	.275	30	184	96	43-55
1967	CF	NY	NL	10-10	129	411	46	101	10	5	5	30	.246	19	136	84	—
1968	LF	NY	NL	9-10	147	509	63	151	29	4	14	55	.297	31	230	132	12-45
1969	LF-1B	NY	NL	1-6	137	483	92	164	25	4	12	75	.340	64	233	150	9-62
1970	LF	NY	NL	3-6	134	506	71	140	25	8	10	63	.277	57	211	109	37-56
1971	LF	NY	NL	3-6	136	505	63	161	24	6	14	69	.319	53	239	138	9-58
1972	LF-1B	NY	NL	3-6	106	375	39	92	15	1	5	52	.245	30	124	89	—
1973	LF	NY	NL	1-6	92	339	48	88	13	0	11	48	.260	28	134	102	—
1974	LF	NY	NL	5-6	124	461	62	130	23	1	13	60	.282	38	194	111	37-65
1975	LF	NY	NL	3-6	21	50	2	12	1	0	0	2	.240	3	13	—	—
1976	LF-DH	CHI	AL	6-6	12	40	2	8	1	0	0	3	.200	5	9	—	—

MAJOR LEAGUE TOTALS 1213 4263 565 1196 183 33 93 524 .281 360 1724 123 6 yrs

Ricardo Adolfo Jacobo Carty Born Sep 1, 1939 San Pedro de Macoris, DR
6'3 200 lbs Batted right

YR	POS	TEAM	LG	FIN	G	AB	R	H	2B	3B	HR	RBI	AVG	BB	TB	OQ	RANK
1963	PH	MIL	NL	6-10	2	2	0	0	0	0	0	0	.000	0	0	—	—
1964	LF	MIL	NL	5-10	133	455	72	150	28	4	22	88	.330	43	252	159	5-42
1965	LF	MIL	NL	5-10	83	271	37	84	18	1	10	35	.310	17	134	132	—
1966	LF-C	ATL	NL	5-10	151	521	73	170	25	2	15	76	.326	60	244	139	10-55
1967	LF	ATL	NL	7-10	134	444	41	113	16	2	15	64	.255	49	178	115	31-54
1969	LF	ATL	NL	1-6	104	304	47	104	15	0	16	58	.342	32	167	160	—
1970	LF	ATL	NL	5-6	136	478	84	175	23	3	25	101	.366	77	279	176	2-56
1972	LF	ATL	NL	4-6	86	271	31	75	12	2	6	29	.277	44	109	128	—
1973	LF-DH	TX/OA	AL	6/1	93	314	25	73	13	0	4	34	.232	38	98	87	—
1973	LF	CHI	NL	5-6	22	70	4	15	0	0	1	8	.214	6	18	—	—
1974	DH-1B	CLE	AL	4-6	33	91	6	33	5	0	1	16	.363	5	41	—	—
1975	DH-1B	CLE	AL	4-6	118	383	57	118	19	1	18	64	.308	45	193	139	—
1976	DH	CLE	AL	4-6	152	552	67	171	34	0	13	83	.310	67	244	134	7-64
1977	DH	CLE	AL	5-7	127	461	50	129	23	1	15	80	.280	56	199	113	28-81
1978	DH	TO/OA	AL	7/6	145	528	70	149	21	1	31	99	.282	57	265	131	14-83
1979	DH	TOR	AL	7-7	132	461	48	118	26	0	12	55	.256	46	180	95	53-75

MAJOR LEAGUE TOTALS 1651 5606 712 1677 278 17 204 890 .299 642 2601 133 8 yrs

Robert Frank Knoop   Born Oct 18, 1938   Sioux City, IA
6'1   170 lbs   Batted right

YR	POS	TEAM	LG	FIN	G	AB	R	H	2B	3B	HR	RBI	AVG	BB	TB	OO	RANK
1964	2B	LA	AL	5-10	162	486	42	105	8	1	7	38	.216	46	136	76	52-52
1965	2B	CAL	AL	7-10	142	465	47	125	24	4	7	43	.269	31	178	100	35-46
1966	2B	CAL	AL	6-10	161	590	54	137	18	11	17	72	.232	43	228	99	32-44
1967	2B	CAL	AL	5-10	159	511	51	125	18	5	9	38	.245	44	180	100	36-48
1968	2B	CAL	AL	8-10	152	494	48	123	20	4	3	39	.249	35	160	94	40-45
1969	2B	CA/CH	AL	3/5	131	416	39	93	15	1	7	47	.224	48	131	88	—
1970	2B	CHI	AL	6-6	130	402	34	92	13	2	5	36	.229	34	124	79	—
1971	2B	KC	AL	2-6	72	161	14	33	8	1	1	11	.205	15	46	77	—
1972	2B	KC	AL	4-6	44	97	8	23	5	0	0	7	.237	9	28	87	—

MAJOR LEAGUE TOTALS   1153 3622 337 856 129 29 56 331 .236 305 1211 94   5 yrs

Dagoberto Campaneris   Born Mar 9, 1942   Pueblo Nuevo, Cuba
5'10   160 lbs   Batted right

YR	POS	TEAM	LG	FIN	G	AB	R	H	2B	3B	HR	RBI	AVG	BB	TB	OO	RANK
1964	SS-LF	KC	AL	10-10	67	269	27	69	14	3	4	22	.257	15	101	92	—
1965	SS-LF	KC	AL	10-10	144	578	67	156	23	12	6	42	.270	41	221	101	34-46
1966	SS	KC	AL	7-10	142	573	82	153	29	10	5	42	.267	25	217	95	36-44
1967	SS	KC	AL	10-10	147	601	85	149	29	6	3	32	.248	36	199	90	45-48
1968	SS	OAK	AL	6-10	159	642	87	177	25	9	4	38	.276	50	232	108	26-45
1969	SS	OAK	AL	2-6	135	547	71	142	15	2	2	25	.260	30	167	77	56-59
1970	SS	OAK	AL	2-6	147	603	97	168	28	4	22	64	.279	36	270	109	37-59
1971	SS	OAK	AL	1-6	134	569	80	143	18	4	5	47	.251	29	184	81	54-57
1972	SS	OAK	AL	1-6	149	625	85	150	25	2	8	32	.240	32	203	86	50-56
1973	SS	OAK	AL	1-6	151	601	89	150	17	6	4	46	.250	50	191	82	54-60
1974	SS	OAK	AL	1-6	134	527	77	153	18	8	2	41	.290	47	193	103	44-67
1975	SS	OAK	AL	1-6	137	509	69	135	15	3	4	46	.265	50	168	90	51-66
1976	SS	OAK	AL	2-6	149	536	67	137	14	1	1	52	.256	63	156	90	54-64
1977	SS	TEX	AL	2-7	150	552	77	140	19	7	5	46	.254	47	188	84	77-81
1978	SS	TEX	AL	2-7	98	269	30	50	5	3	1	17	.186	20	64	59	—
1979	SS	TX/CA	AL	3/1	93	248	29	57	4	4	0	15	.230	20	69	67	—
1980	SS	CAL	AL	6-7	77	210	32	53	8	1	2	18	.252	14	69	79	—
1981	3B	CAL	AL	5-7	55	82	11	21	2	1	1	10	.256	5	28	—	—
1983	2B-3B	NY	AL	3-7	60	143	19	46	5	0	0	11	.322	8	51	91	—

MAJOR LEAGUE TOTALS   2328 8684 1181 2249 313 86 79 646 .259 618 2971 92 13 yrs

Alexander Johnson
6'0   205 lbs   Batted right

Born Dec 7, 1942   Helena, AR

YR	POS	TEAM	LG	FIN	G	AB	R	H	2B	3B	HR	RBI	AVG	BB	TB	OQ	RANK
1964	LF	PHI	NL	2-10	43	109	18	33	7	1	4	18	.303	6	54	130	—
1965	LF	PHI	NL	6-10	97	262	27	77	9	3	8	28	.294	15	116	116	—
1966	LF	SL	NL	6-10	25	86	7	16	0	1	2	6	.186	5	24	—	—
1967	RF	SL	NL	1-10	81	175	20	39	9	2	1	12	.223	9	55	79	—
1968	LF	CIN	NL	4-10	149	603	79	188	32	6	2	58	.312	26	238	115	23-45
1969	LF	CIN	NL	3-6	139	523	86	165	18	4	17	88	.315	25	242	120	25-62
1970	LF	CAL	AL	3-6	156	614	85	202	26	6	14	86	.329	35	282	120	26-59
1971	LF	CAL	AL	4-6	65	242	19	63	8	0	2	21	.260	15	77	83	—
1972	LF	CLE	AL	5-6	108	356	31	85	10	1	8	37	.239	22	121	92	—
1973	DH-LF	TEX	AL	6-6	158	624	62	179	26	3	8	68	.287	32	235	92	45-60
1974	LF-DH	TX/NY	AL	2/2	124	481	60	138	15	3	5	43	.287	28	174	94	49-67
1975	DH-LF	NY	AL	3-6	52	119	15	31	5	1	1	15	.261	7	41	84	—
1976	LF-DH	DET	AL	5-6	125	429	41	115	15	2	6	45	.268	19	152	89	—
MAJOR LEAGUE TOTALS					1322	4623	550	1331	180	33	78	525	.288	244	1811	108	5 yrs

Donald Eulon Kessinger
6'1   170 lbs   Batted both

Born Jul 17, 1942   Forrest City, AR

YR	POS	TEAM	LG	FIN	G	AB	R	H	2B	3B	HR	RBI	AVG	BB	TB	OQ	RANK
1964	SS	CHI	NL	8-10	4	12	1	2	0	0	0	0	.167	0	2	—	—
1965	SS	CHI	NL	8-10	106	309	19	62	4	3	0	14	.201	20	72	61	—
1966	SS	CHI	NL	10-10	150	533	50	146	8	2	1	43	.274	26	161	78	55-55
1967	SS	CHI	NL	3-10	145	580	61	134	10	7	0	42	.231	33	158	72	53-54
1968	SS	CHI	NL	3-10	160	655	63	157	14	7	1	32	.240	38	188	82	43-45
1969	SS	CHI	NL	2-6	158	664	109	181	38	6	4	53	.273	61	243	101	42-62
1970	SS	CHI	NL	2-6	154	631	100	168	21	14	1	39	.266	66	220	92	46-56
1971	SS	CHI	NL	3-6	155	617	77	159	18	6	2	38	.258	52	195	88	50-58
1972	SS	CHI	NL	2-6	149	577	77	158	20	6	1	39	.274	67	193	102	41-58
1973	SS	CHI	NL	5-6	160	577	52	151	22	3	0	43	.262	57	179	87	56-61
1974	SS	CHI	NL	6-6	153	599	83	155	20	7	1	42	.259	62	192	91	57-65
1975	SS	CHI	NL	5-6	154	601	77	146	26	10	0	46	.243	68	192	90	54-65
1976	SS-2B	SL	NL	5-6	145	502	55	120	22	6	1	40	.239	61	157	93	41-57
1977	SS-2B	SL	NL	3-6	59	134	14	32	4	0	0	7	.239	14	36	73	—
1977	SS-2B	CHI	AL	3-7	39	119	12	28	3	2	0	11	.235	13	35	78	—
1978	SS	CHI	AL	5-7	131	431	35	110	18	1	1	31	.255	36	133	81	—
1979	SS	CHI	AL	5-7	56	110	14	22	6	0	1	7	.200	10	31	67	—
MAJOR LEAGUE TOTALS					2078	7651	899	1931	254	80	14	527	.252	684	2387	89	11 yrs

Tommy Vann Helms   Born May 5, 1941 Charlotte, NC
5'10 165 lbs Batted right

YR	POS	TEAM	LG	FIN	G	AB	R	H	2B	3B	HR	RBI	AVG	BB	TB	OQ	RANK
1964	PH	CIN	NL	2-10	2	1	0	0	0	0	0	0	.000	0	0	—	—
1965	SS	CIN	NL	4-10	21	42	4	16	2	2	0	6	.381	3	22	—	—
1966	3B-2B	CIN	NL	7-10	138	542	72	154	23	1	9	49	.284	24	206	95	44-55
1967	2B-SS	CIN	NL	4-10	137	497	40	136	27	4	2	35	.274	24	177	93	44-54
1968	2B	CIN	NL	4-10	127	507	35	146	28	2	2	47	.288	12	184	98	33-45
1969	2B	CIN	NL	3-6	126	480	38	129	18	1	1	40	.269	18	152	78	61-62
1970	2B	CIN	NL	1-6	150	575	42	136	21	1	1	45	.237	21	162	62	56-56
1971	2B	CIN	NL	4-6	150	547	40	141	26	1	3	52	.258	26	178	82	55-58
1972	2B	HOU	NL	2-6	139	518	45	134	20	5	5	60	.259	24	179	87	50-58
1973	2B	HOU	NL	4-6	146	543	44	156	28	2	4	61	.287	32	200	94	51-61
1974	2B	HOU	NL	4-6	137	452	32	126	21	1	5	50	.279	23	164	91	—
1975	2B	HOU	NL	6-6	64	135	7	28	2	0	0	14	.207	10	30	59	—
1976	3B-2B	PIT	NL	2-6	62	87	10	24	5	1	1	13	.276	10	34	—	—
1977	PH	PIT	NL	2-6	15	12	0	0	0	0	0	0	.000	0	0	—	—
1977	DH	BOS	AL	2-7	21	59	5	16	2	0	1	5	.271	4	21	—	—

MAJOR LEAGUE TOTALS   1435 4997 414 1342 223 21 34 477 .269 231 1709 86 8 yrs

Santos Alomar Sr   Born Oct 19, 1943 Salinas, PR
5'9 140 lbs Batted both

YR	POS	TEAM	LG	FIN	G	AB	R	H	2B	3B	HR	RBI	AVG	BB	TB	OQ	RANK
1964	SS	MIL	NL	5-10	19	53	3	13	1	0	0	6	.245	0	14	—	—
1965	SS-2B	MIL	NL	5-10	67	108	16	26	1	1	0	8	.241	4	29	66	—
1966	2B-SS	ATL	NL	5-10	31	44	4	4	1	0	0	2	.091	1	5	—	—
1967	SS-3B	NY	NL	10-10	15	22	1	0	0	0	0	0	.000	0	0	—	—
1967	SS-2B	CHI	AL	4-10	12	15	4	3	0	0	0	0	.200	2	3	—	—
1968	2B-3B	CHI	AL	8-10	133	363	41	92	8	2	0	12	.253	20	104	82	—
1969	2B	CH/CA	AL	5/3	156	617	68	153	12	2	1	34	.248	40	172	72	59-59
1970	2B	CAL	AL	3-6	162	672	82	169	18	2	2	36	.251	49	197	76	56-59
1971	2B-SS	CAL	AL	4-6	162	689	77	179	24	3	4	42	.260	41	221	83	52-57
1972	2B	CAL	AL	5-6	155	610	65	146	20	3	1	25	.239	47	175	83	51-56
1973	2B-SS	CAL	AL	4-6	136	470	45	112	7	1	0	28	.238	34	121	67	59-60
1974	2B-SS	CA/NY	AL	6/2	122	333	47	87	8	1	1	28	.261	16	100	75	—
1975	2B	NY	AL	3-6	151	489	61	117	18	4	2	39	.239	26	149	73	63-66
1976	2B-SS	NY	AL	1-6	67	163	20	39	4	0	1	10	.239	13	46	78	—
1977	2B-SS	TEX	AL	2-7	69	83	21	22	3	0	1	11	.265	8	28	—	—
1978	1B-2B	TEX	AL	2-7	24	29	3	6	1	0	0	1	.207	1	7	—	—

MAJOR LEAGUE TOTALS   1481 4760 558 1168 126 19 13 282 .245 302 1371 76 6 yrs

Maurice Wesley Parker   Born Nov 13, 1939 Evanston, IL
6'1   180 lbs Batted both

YR	POS	TEAM	LG	FIN	G	AB	R	H	2B	3B	HR	RBI	AVG	BB	TB	OQ	RANK
1964	RF-1B	LA	NL	6-10	124	214	29	55	7	1	3	10	.257	14	73	90	—
1965	1B	LA	NL	1-10	154	542	80	129	24	7	8	51	.238	75	191	105	34-52
1966	1B	LA	NL	1-10	156	475	67	120	17	5	12	51	.253	69	183	114	25-55
1967	1B-CF	LA	NL	8-10	139	413	56	102	16	5	5	31	.247	65	143	112	—
1968	1B-LF	LA	NL	7-10	135	468	42	112	22	2	3	27	.239	49	147	99	32-45
1969	1B	LA	NL	4-6	132	471	76	131	23	4	13	68	.278	56	201	122	23-62
1970	1B	LA	NL	2-6	161	614	84	196	47	4	10	111	.319	79	281	129	20-56
1971	1B-RF	LA	NL	2-6	157	533	69	146	24	1	6	62	.274	63	190	107	37-58
1972	1B	LA	NL	3-6	130	427	45	119	14	3	4	59	.279	62	151	113	32-58

MAJOR LEAGUE TOTALS   1288 4157 548 1110 194 32 64 470 .267 532 1560 113 7 yrs

Atanasio Perez   Born May 14, 1942 Camaguey, Cuba
6'2   175 lbs Batted right

YR	POS	TEAM	LG	FIN	G	AB	R	H	2B	3B	HR	RBI	AVG	BB	TB	OQ	RANK
1964	1B	CIN	NL	2-10	12	25	1	2	1	0	0	1	.080	3	3	—	—
1965	1B	CIN	NL	4-10	104	281	40	73	14	4	12	47	.260	21	131	119	—
1966	1B	CIN	NL	7-10	99	257	25	68	10	4	4	39	.265	14	98	95	—
1967	3B-1B	CIN	NL	4-10	156	600	78	174	28	7	26	102	.290	33	294	129	17-54
1968	3B	CIN	NL	4-10	160	625	93	176	25	7	18	92	.282	51	269	129	15-45
1969	3B	CIN	NL	3-6	160	629	103	185	31	2	37	122	.294	63	331	143	11-62
1970	3B	CIN	NL	1-6	158	587	107	186	28	6	40	129	.317	83	346	160	4-56
1971	3B-1B	CIN	NL	4-6	158	609	72	164	22	3	25	91	.269	51	267	117	26-58
1972	1B	CIN	NL	1-6	136	515	64	146	33	7	21	90	.283	55	256	138	13-58
1973	1B	CIN	NL	1-6	151	564	73	177	33	3	27	101	.314	74	297	151	6-61
1974	1B	CIN	NL	2-6	158	596	81	158	28	2	28	101	.265	61	274	121	22-65
1975	1B	CIN	NL	1-6	137	511	74	144	28	3	20	109	.282	54	238	126	23-65
1976	1B	CIN	NL	1-6	139	527	77	137	32	6	19	91	.260	50	238	121	26-57
1977	1B	MON	NL	5-6	154	559	71	158	32	6	19	91	.283	63	259	120	26-68
1978	1B	MON	NL	4-6	148	544	63	158	38	3	14	78	.290	38	244	117	28-63
1979	1B	MON	NL	2-6	132	489	58	132	29	4	13	73	.270	38	208	106	38-62
1980	1B	BOS	AL	4-7	151	585	73	161	31	3	25	105	.275	41	273	110	38-69
1981	1B-DH	BOS	AL	5-7	84	306	35	77	11	3	9	39	.252	27	121	103	46-71
1982	DH	BOS	AL	3-7	69	196	18	51	14	2	6	31	.260	19	87	108	—
1983	1B	PHI	NL	1-6	91	253	18	61	11	2	6	43	.241	28	94	100	—
1984	1B	CIN	NL	5-6	71	137	9	33	6	1	2	15	.241	11	47	90	—
1985	1B	CIN	NL	2-6	72	183	25	60	8	0	6	33	.328	22	86	140	—
1986	1B	CIN	NL	2-6	77	200	14	51	12	1	2	29	.255	25	71	100	—

MAJOR LEAGUE TOTALS   2777 9778 1272 2732 505 79 379 1652 .279 925 4532 126 15 yrs

Danny Anderson Cater   Born Feb 25, 1940 Austin, TX
6'0 170 lbs Batted right

YR	POS	TEAM	LG	FIN	G	AB	R	H	2B	3B	HR	RBI	AVG	BB	TB	OQ	RANK
1964	LF-1B	PHI	NL	2-10	60	152	13	45	9	1	1	13	.296	7	59	101	—
1965	LF	CHI	AL	2-10	142	514	74	139	18	4	14	55	.270	33	207	104	28-46
1966	1B-3B	CH/KC	AL	4/7	137	485	50	135	17	4	7	56	.278	28	181	99	33-44
1967	3B-LF	KC	AL	10-10	142	529	55	143	17	4	4	46	.270	34	180	96	41-48
1968	1B-LF	OAK	AL	6-10	147	504	53	146	28	3	6	62	.290	35	198	116	21-45
1969	1B-LF	OAK	AL	2-6	152	584	64	153	24	2	10	76	.262	28	211	88	54-59
1970	1B-3B	NY	AL	2-6	155	582	64	175	26	5	6	76	.301	34	229	100	44-59
1971	1B-3B	NY	AL	4-6	121	428	39	118	16	5	4	50	.276	19	156	92	—
1972	1B	BOS	AL	2-6	92	317	32	75	17	1	8	39	.237	15	118	96	—
1973	1B-3B	BOS	AL	2-6	63	195	30	61	12	0	1	24	.313	10	76	99	—
1974	1B-DH	BOS	AL	3-6	56	126	14	31	5	0	5	20	.246	10	51	103	—
1975	1B	SL	NL	3-6	22	35	3	8	2	0	0	2	.229	1	10	—	—

| MAJOR LEAGUE TOTALS | | | | | 1289 | 4451 | 491 | 1229 | 191 | 29 | 66 | 519 | .276 | 254 | 1676 | 101 | 6 yrs |

Louis Victor Piniella   Born Aug 28, 1943
6'0 182 lbs Batted right

YR	POS	TEAM	LG	FIN	G	AB	R	H	2B	3B	HR	RBI	AVG	BB	TB	OQ	RANK
1964	PH	BAL	AL	3-10	4	1	0	0	0	0	0	0	.000	0	0	—	—
1968	LF	CLE	AL	3-10	6	5	1	0	0	0	0	1	.000	0	0	—	—
1969	LF	KC	AL	4-6	135	493	43	139	21	6	11	68	.282	33	205	106	37-59
1970	LF	KC	AL	4-6	144	542	54	163	24	5	11	88	.301	35	230	109	40-59
1971	LF	KC	AL	2-6	126	448	43	125	21	5	3	51	.279	21	165	93	—
1972	LF	KC	AL	4-6	151	574	65	179	33	4	11	72	.312	34	253	127	18-56
1973	LF	KC	AL	2-6	144	513	53	128	28	1	9	69	.250	30	185	86	50-60
1974	LF	NY	AL	2-6	140	518	71	158	26	0	9	70	.305	32	211	108	35-67
1975	RF-DH	NY	AL	3-6	74	199	7	39	4	1	0	22	.196	16	45	59	—
1976	RF-DH	NY	AL	1-6	100	327	36	92	16	6	3	38	.281	18	129	103	—
1977	RF-DH	NY	AL	1-7	103	339	47	112	19	3	12	45	.330	20	173	125	—
1978	LF-DH	NY	AL	1-7	130	472	67	148	34	5	6	69	.314	34	210	116	33-83
1979	LF-DH	NY	AL	4-7	130	461	49	137	22	2	11	69	.297	17	196	95	—
1980	LF	NY	AL	1-7	116	321	39	92	18	0	2	27	.287	29	116	94	—
1981	RF-DH	NY	AL	3-7	60	159	16	44	9	0	5	18	.277	13	68	112	—
1982	DH-RF	NY	AL	5-7	102	261	33	80	17	1	6	37	.307	18	117	111	—
1983	RF-LF	NY	AL	3-7	53	148	19	43	9	1	2	16	.291	11	60	101	—
1984	LF-RF	NY	AL	3-7	29	86	8	26	4	1	1	6	.302	7	35	—	—

| MAJOR LEAGUE TOTALS | | | | | 1747 | 5867 | 651 | 1705 | 305 | 41 | 102 | 766 | .291 | 368 | 2398 | 109 | 6 yrs |

James Thomas Northrup   Born Nov 24, 1939   Breckenridge, MI

6'3   190 lbs   Batted left

YR	POS	TEAM	LG	FIN	G	AB	R	H	2B	3B	HR	RBI	AVG	BB	TB	OQ	RANK
1964	CF-RF	DET	AL	4-10	5	12	1	1	1	0	0	0	.083	0	2	—	—
1965	RF-LF	DET	AL	4-10	80	219	20	45	12	3	2	16	.205	12	69	76	—
1966	RF	DET	AL	3-10	123	419	53	111	24	6	16	58	.265	33	195	122	—
1967	CF	DET	AL	2-10	144	495	63	134	18	6	10	61	.271	43	194	113	22-48
1968	RF-CF	DET	AL	1-10	154	580	76	153	29	7	21	90	.264	50	259	130	15-45
1969	CF	DET	AL	2-6	148	543	79	160	31	5	25	66	.295	52	276	135	12-59
1970	LF	DET	AL	4-6	139	504	71	132	21	3	24	80	.262	58	231	121	23-59
1971	CF-1B	DET	AL	2-6	136	459	72	124	27	2	16	71	.270	60	203	127	22-57
1972	RF	DET	AL	1-6	134	426	40	111	15	2	8	42	.261	38	154	106	—
1973	RF	DET	AL	3-6	119	404	55	124	14	7	12	44	.307	38	188	124	—
1974	RF	DE/BA	AL	6/1	105	383	43	93	12	1	12	45	.243	38	143	100	—
1974	LF-RF	MON	NL	4-6	21	54	3	13	1	0	2	8	.241	5	20	—	—
1975	CF	BAL	AL	2-6	84	194	27	53	13	0	5	29	.273	22	81	113	—

MAJOR LEAGUE TOTALS					1392	4692	603	1254	218	42	153	610	.267	449	2015	125	5 yrs

Paul L D Blair   Born Feb 1, 1944   Cushing, OK

6'0   168 lbs   Batted right

YR	POS	TEAM	LG	FIN	G	AB	R	H	2B	3B	HR	RBI	AVG	BB	TB	OQ	RANK
1964	CF	BAL	AL	3-10	8	1	0	0	0	0	0	0	.000	0	0	—	—
1965	CF	BAL	AL	3-10	119	364	49	85	19	2	5	25	.234	32	123	90	—
1966	CF	BAL	AL	1-10	133	303	35	84	20	2	6	33	.277	15	126	106	—
1967	CF	BAL	AL	6-10	151	552	72	162	27	12	11	64	.293	50	246	131	14-48
1968	CF	BAL	AL	2-10	141	421	48	89	22	1	7	38	.211	37	134	92	—
1969	CF	BAL	AL	1-6	150	625	102	178	32	5	26	76	.285	40	298	120	22-59
1970	CF	BAL	AL	1-6	133	480	79	128	24	2	18	65	.267	56	210	118	28-59
1971	CF	BAL	AL	1-6	141	516	75	135	24	8	10	44	.262	32	205	101	42-57
1972	CF	BAL	AL	3-6	142	477	47	111	20	8	8	49	.233	25	171	94	46-56
1973	CF	BAL	AL	1-6	146	500	73	140	25	3	10	64	.280	43	201	104	30-60
1974	CF	BAL	AL	1-6	151	552	77	144	27	4	17	62	.261	43	230	107	38-67
1975	CF	BAL	AL	2-6	140	440	51	96	13	4	5	31	.218	25	132	70	—
1976	CF	BAL	AL	2-6	145	375	29	74	16	0	3	16	.197	22	99	66	—
1977	CF-RF	NY	AL	1-7	83	164	20	43	4	3	4	25	.262	9	65	90	—
1978	CF-RF	NY	AL	1-7	75	125	10	22	5	0	2	13	.176	9	33	63	—
1979	CF-RF	NY	AL	4-7	2	5	0	1	0	0	0	0	.200	0	1	—	—
1979	CF-LF	CIN	NL	1-6	75	140	7	21	4	1	2	15	.150	11	33	57	—
1980	RF-LF	NY	AL	1-7	12	2	2	0	0	0	0	0	.000	0	0	—	—

MAJOR LEAGUE TOTALS					1947	6042	776	1513	282	55	134	620	.250	449	2307	111	7 yrs

Curtis LeRoy Blefary   Born Jul 5, 1943   Brooklyn, NY
6'2 195 lbs Batted left

YR	POS	TEAM	LG	FIN	G	AB	R	H	2B	3B	HR	RBI	AVG	BB	TB	OQ	RANK
1965	LF	BAL	AL	3-10	144	462	72	120	23	4	22	70	.260	88	217	145	3-46
1966	LF-1B	BAL	AL	1-10	131	419	73	107	14	3	23	64	.255	73	196	142	6-44
1967	LF-1B	BAL	AL	6-10	155	554	69	134	19	5	22	81	.242	73	229	124	15-48
1968	LF-C	BAL	AL	2-10	137	451	50	90	8	1	15	39	.200	65	145	104	32-45
1969	1B	HOU	NL	5-6	155	542	66	137	26	7	12	67	.253	77	213	115	31-62
1970	RF	NY	AL	2-6	99	269	34	57	6	0	9	37	.212	43	90	98	—
1971	RF-C	NY/OA	AL	4/1	71	137	19	29	3	0	6	14	.212	18	50	102	—
1972	1B-2B	OAK	AL	1-6	8	11	1	5	2	0	0	1	.455	0	7	—	—
1972	C-1B	SD	NL	6-6	74	102	10	20	3	0	3	9	.196	19	32	102	—
MAJOR LEAGUE TOTALS					974	2947	394	699	104	20	112	382	.237	456	1179	126	5 yrs

Bobby Ray Murcer   Born May 20, 1946 Oklahoma City, OK
5'11 160 lbs Batted left

YR	POS	TEAM	LG	FIN	G	AB	R	H	2B	3B	HR	RBI	AVG	BB	TB	OQ	RANK
1965	SS	NY	AL	6-10	11	37	2	9	0	1	1	4	.243	5	14	—	—
1966	SS	NY	AL	10-10	21	69	3	12	1	1	0	5	.174	4	15	—	—
1969	RF-3B	NY	AL	5-6	152	564	82	146	24	4	26	82	.259	50	256	116	25-59
1970	CF	NY	AL	2-6	159	581	95	146	23	3	23	78	.251	87	244	118	27-59
1971	CF	NY	AL	4-6	146	529	94	175	25	6	25	94	.331	91	287	173	1-57
1972	CF	NY	AL	4-6	153	585	102	171	30	7	33	96	.292	63	314	159	4-56
1973	CF	NY	AL	4-6	160	616	83	187	29	2	22	95	.304	50	286	120	15-60
1974	RF	NY	AL	2-6	156	606	69	166	25	4	10	88	.274	57	229	104	42-67
1975	RF	SF	NL	3-6	147	526	80	157	29	4	11	91	.298	91	227	136	12-65
1976	RF	SF	NL	4-6	147	533	73	138	20	2	23	90	.259	84	231	130	14-57
1977	RF	CHI	NL	4-6	154	554	90	147	18	3	27	89	.265	80	252	122	23-68
1978	RF	CHI	NL	3-6	146	499	66	140	22	6	9	64	.281	80	201	125	19-63
1979	RF	CHI	NL	5-6	58	190	22	49	4	1	7	22	.258	36	76	123	—
1979	CF	NY	AL	4-7	74	264	42	72	12	0	8	33	.273	25	108	100	—
1980	LF-DH	NY	AL	1-7	100	297	41	80	9	1	13	57	.269	34	130	112	—
1981	DH	NY	AL	3-7	50	117	14	31	6	0	6	24	.265	12	55	124	—
1982	DH	NY	AL	5-7	65	141	12	32	6	0	7	30	.227	12	59	96	—
1983	DH	NY	AL	3-7	9	22	2	4	2	0	1	1	.182	1	9	—	—
MAJOR LEAGUE TOTALS					1908	6730	972	1862	285	45	252	1043	.277	862	2993	130	10 yrs

Horace Meredith Clarke   Born Jun 2, 1940   Frederiksted, VI
5'9   170 lbs   Batted both

YR	POS	TEAM	LG	FIN	G	AB	R	H	2B	3B	HR	RBI	AVG	BB	TB	OQ	RANK
1965	3B-2B	NY	AL	6-10	51	108	13	28	1	0	1	9	.259	6	32	77	—
1966	SS-2B	NY	AL	10-10	96	312	37	83	10	4	6	28	.266	27	119	105	—
1967	2B	NY	AL	9-10	143	588	74	160	17	0	3	29	.272	42	186	92	43-48
1968	2B	NY	AL	5-10	148	579	52	133	6	1	2	26	.230	23	147	68	45-45
1969	2B	NY	AL	5-6	156	641	82	183	26	7	4	48	.285	53	235	100	43-59
1970	2B	NY	AL	2-6	158	686	81	172	24	2	4	46	.251	35	212	75	58-59
1971	2B	NY	AL	4-6	159	625	76	156	23	7	2	41	.250	64	199	91	51-57
1972	2B	NY	AL	4-6	147	547	65	132	20	2	3	37	.241	56	165	93	47-56
1973	2B	NY	AL	4-6	148	590	60	155	21	0	2	35	.263	47	182	81	55-60
1974	2B	NY	AL	2-6	24	47	3	11	1	0	0	1	.234	4	12	—	—
1974	2B	SD	NL	6-6	42	90	5	17	1	0	0	4	.189	8	18	—	—

| MAJOR LEAGUE TOTALS | | | | | 1272 | 4813 | 548 | 1230 | 150 | 23 | 27 | 304 | .256 | 365 | 1507 | 86 | 7 yrs |

Roy Hilton White   Born Dec 27, 1943   Los Angeles, CA
5'10   160 lbs   Batted both

YR	POS	TEAM	LG	FIN	G	AB	R	H	2B	3B	HR	RBI	AVG	BB	TB	OQ	RANK
1965	RF	NY	AL	6-10	14	42	7	14	2	0	0	3	.333	4	16	—	—
1966	LF	NY	AL	10-10	115	316	39	71	13	2	7	20	.225	37	109	99	—
1967	RF-3B	NY	AL	9-10	70	214	22	48	8	0	2	18	.224	19	62	84	—
1968	LF	NY	AL	5-10	159	577	89	154	20	7	17	62	.267	73	239	132	13-45
1969	LF	NY	AL	5-6	130	448	55	130	30	5	7	74	.290	81	191	135	13-59
1970	LF	NY	AL	2-6	162	609	109	180	30	6	22	94	.296	95	288	139	8-59
1971	LF	NY	AL	4-6	147	524	86	153	22	7	19	84	.292	86	246	145	9-57
1972	LF	NY	AL	4-6	155	556	76	150	29	0	10	54	.270	99	209	132	14-56
1973	LF	NY	AL	4-6	162	639	88	157	22	3	18	60	.246	78	239	101	33-60
1974	LF-DH	NY	AL	2-6	136	473	68	130	19	8	7	43	.275	67	186	118	21-67
1975	LF	NY	AL	3-6	148	556	81	161	32	5	12	59	.290	72	239	121	18-66
1976	LF	NY	AL	1-6	156	626	104	179	29	3	14	65	.286	83	256	124	13-64
1977	LF	NY	AL	1-7	143	519	72	139	25	2	14	52	.268	75	210	110	33-81
1978	LF-DH	NY	AL	1-7	103	346	44	93	13	3	8	43	.269	42	136	108	—
1979	DH-LF	NY	AL	4-7	81	205	24	44	6	0	3	27	.215	23	59	74	—

| MAJOR LEAGUE TOTALS | | | | | 1881 | 6650 | 964 | 1803 | 300 | 51 | 160 | 758 | .271 | 934 | 2685 | 126 | 10 yrs |

Rigoberto Fuentes   Born Jan 4, 1944   Havana, Cuba
5'11   175 lbs   Batted both

YR	POS	TEAM	LG	FIN	G	AB	R	H	2B	3B	HR	RBI	AVG	BB	TB	OQ	RANK
1965	SS-2B	SF	NL	2-10	26	72	12	15	1	0	0	1	.208	5	16	—	—
1966	SS-2B	SF	NL	2-10	133	541	63	141	21	3	9	40	.261	9	195	82	52-55
1967	2B	SF	NL	2-10	133	344	27	72	12	1	5	29	.209	27	101	79	—
1969	3B-SS	SF	NL	2-6	67	183	28	54	4	3	1	14	.295	15	67	102	—
1970	2B-SS	SF	NL	3-6	123	435	49	116	13	7	2	32	.267	36	149	87	—
1971	2B	SF	NL	1-6	152	630	63	172	28	6	4	52	.273	18	224	86	52-58
1972	2B	SF	NL	5-6	152	572	64	151	33	6	7	53	.264	39	217	100	44-58
1973	2B	SF	NL	3-6	160	656	78	182	25	5	6	63	.277	45	235	93	54-61
1974	2B	SF	NL	5-6	108	390	33	97	15	2	0	22	.249	22	116	75	—
1975	2B	SD	NL	4-6	146	565	57	158	21	3	4	43	.280	25	197	86	58-65
1976	2B	SD	NL	5-6	135	520	48	137	18	0	2	36	.263	18	161	76	57-57
1977	2B	DET	AL	4-7	151	615	83	190	19	10	5	51	.309	38	244	98	59-81
1978	2B	OAK	AL	6-7	13	43	5	6	1	0	0	2	.140	1	7	—	—
MAJOR LEAGUE TOTALS					1499	5566	610	1491	211	46	45	438	.268	298	1929	89	7 yrs

David Allen Johnson   Born Jan 30, 1943   Orlando, FL
6'1   170 lbs   Batted right

YR	POS	TEAM	LG	FIN	G	AB	R	H	2B	3B	HR	RBI	AVG	BB	TB	OQ	RANK
1965	3B-2B	BAL	AL	3-10	20	47	5	8	3	0	0	1	.170	5	11	—	—
1966	2B	BAL	AL	1-10	131	501	47	129	20	3	7	56	.257	31	176	92	41-44
1967	2B	BAL	AL	6-10	148	510	62	126	30	3	10	64	.247	59	192	113	23-48
1968	2B-SS	BAL	AL	2-10	145	504	50	122	24	4	9	56	.242	44	181	105	28-45
1969	2B	BAL	AL	1-6	142	511	52	143	34	1	7	57	.280	57	200	110	31-59
1970	2B	BAL	AL	1-6	149	530	68	149	27	1	10	53	.281	66	208	112	34-59
1971	2B	BAL	AL	1-6	142	510	67	144	26	1	18	72	.282	51	226	123	25-57
1972	2B	BAL	AL	3-6	118	376	31	83	22	3	5	32	.221	52	126	106	—
1973	2B	ATL	NL	5-6	157	559	84	151	25	0	43	99	.270	81	305	149	8-61
1974	1B-2B	ATL	NL	3-6	136	454	56	114	18	0	15	62	.251	75	177	117	25-65
1975	PH	ATL	NL	5-6	1	1	0	1	1	0	0	1	1.000	0	2	—	—
1977	1B-2B	PHI	NL	1-6	78	156	23	50	9	1	8	36	.321	23	85	152	—
1978	3B-2B	PH/CH	NL	1/3	68	138	19	32	3	1	4	20	.232	15	49	96	—
MAJOR LEAGUE TOTALS					1435	4797	564	1252	242	18	136	609	.261	559	1938	115	8 yrs

Glenn Alfred Beckert
Born Oct 12, 1940 Pittsburgh, PA
6'1 190 lbs Batted right

YR	POS	TEAM	LG	FIN	G	AB	R	H	2B	3B	HR	RBI	AVG	BB	TB	OQ	RANK
1965	2B	CHI	NL	8-10	154	614	73	147	21	3	3	30	.239	28	183	74	49-52
1966	2B	CHI	NL	10-10	153	656	73	188	23	7	1	59	.287	26	228	87	48-55
1967	2B	CHI	NL	3-10	146	597	91	167	32	3	5	40	.280	30	220	97	42-54
1968	2B	CHI	NL	3-10	155	643	98	189	28	4	4	37	.294	31	237	106	30-45
1969	2B	CHI	NL	2-6	131	543	69	158	22	1	1	37	.291	24	185	87	56-62
1970	2B	CHI	NL	2-6	143	591	99	170	15	6	3	36	.288	32	206	84	50-56
1971	2B	CHI	NL	3-6	131	530	80	181	18	5	2	42	.342	24	215	112	31-58
1972	2B	CHI	NL	2-6	120	474	51	128	22	2	3	43	.270	23	163	88	48-58
1973	2B	CHI	NL	5-6	114	372	38	95	13	0	0	29	.255	30	108	78	—
1974	2B	SD	NL	6-6	64	172	11	44	1	0	0	7	.256	11	45	69	—
1975	3B	SD	NL	4-6	9	16	2	6	1	0	0	0	.375	1	7	—	—

| MAJOR LEAGUE TOTALS | | | | | 1320 | 5208 | 685 | 1473 | 196 | 31 | 22 | 360 | .283 | 260 | 1797 | 92 | 8 yrs |

Mark Henry Belanger
Born Jun 8, 1944 Pittsfield, MA
6'1 170 lbs Batted right

YR	POS	TEAM	LG	FIN	G	AB	R	H	2B	3B	HR	RBI	AVG	BB	TB	OQ	RANK
1965	SS	BAL	AL	3-10	11	3	1	1	0	0	0	0	.333	0	1	—	—
1966	SS	BAL	AL	1-10	8	19	2	3	1	0	0	0	.158	0	4	—	—
1967	SS-2B	BAL	AL	6-10	69	184	19	32	5	0	1	10	.174	12	40	59	—
1968	SS	BAL	AL	2-10	145	472	40	98	13	0	2	21	.208	40	117	75	44-45
1969	SS	BAL	AL	1-6	150	530	76	152	17	4	2	50	.287	53	183	99	44-59
1970	SS	BAL	AL	1-6	145	459	53	100	6	5	1	36	.218	52	119	74	59-59
1971	SS	BAL	AL	1-6	150	500	67	133	19	4	0	35	.266	73	160	103	40-57
1972	SS	BAL	AL	3-6	113	285	36	53	9	1	2	16	.186	18	70	66	—
1973	SS	BAL	AL	1-6	154	470	60	106	15	1	0	27	.226	49	123	73	58-60
1974	SS	BAL	AL	1-6	155	493	54	111	14	4	5	36	.225	51	148	83	59-67
1975	SS	BAL	AL	2-6	152	442	44	100	11	1	3	27	.226	36	122	71	64-66
1976	SS	BAL	AL	2-6	153	522	66	141	22	2	1	40	.270	51	170	95	51-64
1977	SS	BAL	AL	2-7	144	402	39	83	13	4	2	30	.206	43	110	71	—
1978	SS	BAL	AL	4-7	135	348	39	74	13	0	0	16	.213	40	87	71	—
1979	SS	BAL	AL	1-7	101	198	28	33	6	2	0	9	.167	29	43	63	—
1980	SS	BAL	AL	2-7	113	268	37	61	7	3	0	22	.228	12	74	62	—
1981	SS	BAL	AL	2-7	64	139	9	23	3	2	1	10	.165	12	33	62	—
1982	SS	LA	NL	2-6	54	50	6	12	1	0	0	4	.240	5	13	—	—

| MAJOR LEAGUE TOTALS | | | | | 2016 | 5784 | 676 | 1316 | 175 | 33 | 20 | 389 | .228 | 576 | 1617 | 84 | 8 yrs |

Cesar Leonardo Tovar　　　　　　Born Jul 3, 1940　　Caracas, Venezuela
5'9　155 lbs　Batted right

YR	POS	TEAM	LG	FIN	G	AB	R	H	2B	3B	HR	RBI	AVG	BB	TB	OQ	RANK
1965	2B-3B	MIN	AL	1-10	18	25	3	5	1	0	0	2	.200	2	6	—	—
1966	2B-SS	MIN	AL	2-10	134	465	57	121	19	5	2	41	.260	44	156	96	34-44
1967	CF-3B	MIN	AL	2-10	164	649	98	173	32	7	6	47	.267	46	237	103	32-48
1968	CF-3B	MIN	AL	7-10	157	613	89	167	31	6	6	47	.272	34	228	105	30-45
1969	CF-2B	MIN	AL	1-6	158	535	99	154	25	5	11	52	.288	37	222	108	35-59
1970	CF	MIN	AL	1-6	161	650	120	195	36	13	10	54	.300	52	287	116	30-59
1971	LF	MIN	AL	5-6	157	657	94	204	29	3	1	45	.311	45	242	103	41-57
1972	RF	MIN	AL	3-6	141	548	86	145	20	6	2	31	.265	39	183	96	42-56
1973	3B-RF	PHI	NL	6-6	97	328	49	88	18	4	1	21	.268	29	117	96	—
1974	LF	TEX	AL	2-6	138	562	78	164	24	6	4	58	.292	47	212	104	41-67
1975	DH-LF	TX/OA	AL	3/1	121	453	58	116	17	0	3	31	.256	30	142	79	—
1976	LF-DH	OA/NY	AL	2/1	42	84	3	14	1	0	0	6	.167	8	15	—	—

MAJOR LEAGUE TOTALS　　　　1488　5569 834 1546 253 55 46 435 .278 413 2047 104　8 yrs

Kenneth Joseph Henderson　　　Born Jun 15, 1946　　Carroll, IA
6'2　180 lbs　Batted both

YR	POS	TEAM	LG	FIN	G	AB	R	H	2B	3B	HR	RBI	AVG	BB	TB	OQ	RANK
1965	CF-RF	SF	NL	2-10	63	73	10	14	1	1	0	7	.192	9	17	—	—
1966	CF-RF	SF	NL	2-10	11	29	4	9	1	1	1	1	.310	2	15	—	—
1967	CF-RF	SF	NL	2-10	65	179	15	34	3	0	4	14	.190	19	49	79	—
1968	LF	SF	NL	2-10	3	3	1	1	0	0	0	0	.333	2	1	—	—
1969	LF	SF	NL	2-6	113	374	42	84	14	4	6	44	.225	42	124	92	—
1970	LF	SF	NL	3-6	148	554	104	163	35	3	17	88	.294	87	255	131	19-56
1971	LF	SF	NL	1-6	141	504	80	133	26	6	15	65	.264	84	216	132	15-58
1972	LF	SF	NL	5-6	130	439	60	113	21	2	18	51	.257	38	192	116	29-58
1973	LF-DH	CHI	AL	5-6	73	262	32	68	13	0	6	32	.260	27	99	100	—
1974	CF	CHI	AL	4-6	162	602	76	176	35	5	20	95	.292	66	281	130	9-67
1975	LF	CHI	AL	5-6	140	513	65	129	20	3	9	53	.251	74	182	103	36-66
1976	RF	ATL	NL	6-6	133	435	52	114	19	0	13	61	.262	62	172	119	27-57
1977	RF-CF	TEX	AL	2-7	75	244	23	63	14	0	5	23	.258	18	92	89	—
1978	CF-RF	NY/CN	NL	6/2	71	166	12	29	8	1	4	23	.175	27	51	91	—
1979	LF-RF	CN/CH	NL	1/5	72	94	12	22	3	0	2	10	.234	15	31	99	—
1980	LF-RF	CHI	NL	6-6	44	82	7	16	3	0	2	9	.195	17	25	—	—

MAJOR LEAGUE TOTALS　　　　1444　4553 595 1168 216 26 122 576 .257 589 1802 122　6 yrs

Lee Andrew May Born Mar 23, 1943 Birmingham, AL
6'3 195 lbs Batted right

YR	POS	TEAM	LG	FIN	G	AB	R	H	2B	3B	HR	RBI	AVG	BB	TB	OQ	RANK
1965	PH	CIN	NL	4-10	5	4	1	0	0	0	0	0	.000	0	0	—	—
1966	1B	CIN	NL	7-10	25	75	14	25	5	1	2	10	.333	0	38	—	—
1967	1B-LF	CIN	NL	4-10	127	438	54	116	29	2	12	57	.265	19	185	106	—
1968	1B-RF	CIN	NL	4-10	146	559	78	162	32	1	22	80	.290	34	262	135	11-45
1969	1B	CIN	NL	3-6	158	607	85	169	32	3	38	110	.278	45	321	134	13-62
1970	1B	CIN	NL	1-6	153	605	78	153	34	2	34	94	.253	38	293	109	36-56
1971	1B	CIN	NL	4-6	147	553	85	154	17	3	39	98	.278	42	294	137	11-58
1972	1B	HOU	NL	2-6	148	592	87	168	31	2	29	98	.284	52	290	132	15-58
1973	1B	HOU	NL	4-6	148	545	65	147	24	3	28	105	.270	34	261	117	32-61
1974	1B	HOU	NL	4-6	152	556	59	149	26	0	24	85	.268	17	247	103	49-65
1975	1B	BAL	AL	2-6	146	580	67	152	28	3	20	99	.262	36	246	102	41-66
1976	1B-DH	BAL	AL	2-6	148	530	61	137	17	4	25	109	.258	41	237	116	25-64
1977	1B-DH	BAL	AL	2-7	150	585	75	148	16	2	27	99	.253	38	249	97	60-81
1978	DH	BAL	AL	4-7	148	556	56	137	16	1	25	80	.246	31	230	96	59-83
1979	DH	BAL	AL	1-7	124	456	59	116	15	0	19	69	.254	28	188	92	58-75
1980	DH	BAL	AL	2-7	78	222	20	54	10	2	7	31	.243	15	89	92	—
1981	1B-DH	KC	AL	4-7	26	55	3	16	3	0	0	8	.291	3	19	—	—
1982	1B	KC	AL	2-7	42	91	12	28	5	2	3	12	.308	14	46	141	—

MAJOR LEAGUE TOTALS · 2071 · 7609 · 959 · 2031 · 340 · 31 · 354 · 1244 · .267 · 487 · 3495 · 114 · 12 yrs

Nathan Colbert Born Apr 9, 1946 St Louis, MO
6'2 190 lbs Batted right

YR	POS	TEAM	LG	FIN	G	AB	R	H	2B	3B	HR	RBI	AVG	BB	TB	OQ	RANK
1966	PR-PH	HOU	NL	8-10	19	7	3	0	0	0	0	0	.000	0	0	—	—
1968	CF-1B	HOU	NL	10-10	20	53	5	8	1	0	0	4	.151	1	9	—	—
1969	1B	SD	NL	6-6	139	483	64	123	20	9	24	66	.255	45	233	124	19-62
1970	1B	SD	NL	6-6	156	572	84	148	17	6	38	86	.259	56	291	122	26-56
1971	1B	SD	NL	6-6	156	565	81	149	25	3	27	84	.264	63	261	127	18-58
1972	1B	SD	NL	6-6	151	563	87	141	27	2	38	111	.250	70	286	138	12-58
1973	1B	SD	NL	6-6	145	529	73	143	25	2	22	80	.270	54	238	119	28-61
1974	1B-LF	SD	NL	6-6	119	368	53	76	16	0	14	54	.207	62	134	106	—
1975	1B	DET	AL	6-6	45	156	16	23	4	2	4	18	.147	17	43	70	—
1975	1B	MON	NL	5-6	38	81	10	14	4	1	4	11	.173	5	32	—	—
1976	LF-1B	MON	NL	6-6	14	40	5	8	2	0	2	6	.200	9	16	—	—
1976	DH	OAK	AL	2-6	2	5	0	0	0	0	0	0	.000	1	0	—	—

MAJOR LEAGUE TOTALS · 1004 · 3422 · 481 · 833 · 141 · 25 · 173 · 520 · .243 · 383 · 1543 · 126 · 5 yrs

Felix Bernardo Millan   Born Aug 21, 1943 Yabucoa, PR
5'11   172 lbs Batted right

YR	POS	TEAM	LG	FIN	G	AB	R	H	2B	3B	HR	RBI	AVG	BB	TB	OQ	RANK
1966	2B	ATL	NL	5-10	37	91	20	25	6	0	0	5	.275	2	31	—	—
1967	2B	ATL	NL	7-10	41	136	13	32	3	3	2	6	.235	4	47	82	—
1968	2B	ATL	NL	5-10	149	570	49	165	22	2	1	33	.289	22	194	96	36-45
1969	2B	ATL	NL	1-6	162	652	98	174	23	5	6	57	.267	34	225	87	57-62
1970	2B	ATL	NL	5-6	142	590	100	183	25	5	2	37	.310	35	224	95	43-56
1971	2B	ATL	NL	3-6	143	577	65	167	20	8	2	45	.289	37	209	98	42-58
1972	2B	ATL	NL	4-6	125	498	46	128	19	3	1	38	.257	23	156	79	55-58
1973	2B	NY	NL	1-6	153	638	82	185	23	4	3	37	.290	35	225	90	55-61
1974	2B	NY	NL	5-6	136	518	50	139	15	2	1	33	.268	31	161	80	64-65
1975	2B	NY	NL	3-6	162	676	81	191	37	2	1	56	.283	36	235	88	57-65
1976	2B	NY	NL	3-6	139	531	55	150	25	2	1	35	.282	41	182	96	39-57
1977	2B	NY	NL	6-6	91	314	40	78	11	2	2	21	.248	18	99	74	—

MAJOR LEAGUE TOTALS					1480	5791	699	1617	229	38	22	403	.279	318	1988	90	9 yrs

Robert James Monday   Born Nov 20, 1945 Batesville, AR
6'3   193 lbs Batted left

YR	POS	TEAM	LG	FIN	G	AB	R	H	2B	3B	HR	RBI	AVG	BB	TB	OQ	RANK
1966	CF	KC	AL	7-10	17	41	4	4	1	1	0	2	.098	6	7	—	—
1967	CF	KC	AL	10-10	124	406	52	102	14	6	14	58	.251	42	170	120	—
1968	CF	OAK	AL	6-10	148	482	56	132	24	7	8	49	.274	72	194	136	9-45
1969	CF	OAK	AL	2-6	122	399	57	108	17	4	12	54	.271	72	169	131	—
1970	CF	OAK	AL	2-6	112	376	63	109	19	7	10	37	.290	58	172	134	—
1971	CF	OAK	AL	1-6	116	355	53	87	9	3	18	56	.245	49	156	124	—
1972	CF	CHI	NL	2-6	138	434	68	108	22	5	11	42	.249	78	173	126	17-58
1973	CF	CHI	NL	5-6	149	554	93	148	24	5	26	56	.267	92	260	137	15-61
1974	CF	CHI	NL	6-6	142	538	84	158	19	7	20	58	.294	70	251	134	10-65
1975	CF	CHI	NL	5-6	136	491	89	131	29	4	17	60	.267	83	219	132	16-65
1976	CF-1B	CHI	NL	4-6	137	534	107	145	20	5	32	77	.272	60	271	139	7-57
1977	CF	LA	NL	1-6	118	392	47	90	13	1	15	48	.230	60	150	104	—
1978	CF	LA	NL	1-6	119	342	54	87	14	1	19	57	.254	49	160	131	—
1979	CF	LA	NL	3-6	12	33	2	10	0	0	0	2	.303	5	10	—	—
1980	CF-RF	LA	NL	2-6	96	194	35	52	7	1	10	25	.268	28	91	134	—
1981	RF	LA	NL	2-6	66	130	24	41	1	2	11	25	.315	24	79	188	—
1982	RF-LF	LA	NL	2-6	104	210	37	54	6	4	11	42	.257	39	101	144	—
1983	RF-LF	LA	NL	1-6	99	178	21	44	7	1	6	20	.247	29	71	117	—
1984	1B	LA	NL	4-6	31	47	4	9	2	0	1	7	.191	8	14	—	—

MAJOR LEAGUE TOTALS					1986	6136	950	1619	248	64	241	775	.264	924	2718	134	6 yrs

Michael Jay Andrews   Born Jul 9, 1943   Los Angeles, CA
6'3 195 lbs Batted right

YR	POS	TEAM	LG	FIN	G	AB	R	H	2B	3B	HR	RBI	AVG	BB	TB	OQ	RANK
1966	2B	BOS	AL	9-10	5	18	1	3	0	0	0	0	.167	0	3	—	—
1967	2B	BOS	AL	1-10	142	494	79	130	20	0	8	40	.263	62	174	112	25-48
1968	2B	BOS	AL	4-10	147	536	77	145	22	1	7	45	.271	81	190	124	17-45
1969	2B	BOS	AL	3-6	121	464	79	136	26	2	15	59	.293	71	211	136	11-59
1970	2B	BOS	AL	3-6	151	589	91	149	28	1	17	65	.253	81	230	110	36-59
1971	2B-1B	CHI	AL	3-6	109	330	45	93	16	0	12	47	.282	67	145	145	—
1972	2B	CHI	AL	2-6	148	505	58	111	18	0	7	50	.220	70	150	97	41-56
1973	DH-2B	CH/OA	AL	5/1	70	180	11	36	10	0	0	10	.200	26	46	77	—

MAJOR LEAGUE TOTALS   893 3116 441 803 140 4 66 316 .258 458 1149 116   5 yrs

Robert Jose Watson   Born Apr 10, 1946 Los Angeles, CA
6'0 201 lbs Batted right

YR	POS	TEAM	LG	FIN	G	AB	R	H	2B	3B	HR	RBI	AVG	BB	TB	OQ	RANK
1966	PH	HOU	NL	8-10	1	1	0	0	0	0	0	0	.000	0	0	—	—
1967	1B	HOU	NL	9-10	6	14	1	3	0	0	1	2	.214	0	6	—	—
1968	LF	HOU	NL	10-10	45	140	13	32	7	0	2	8	.229	13	45	97	—
1969	LF-1B	HOU	NL	5-6	20	40	3	11	3	0	0	3	.275	6	14	—	—
1970	1B	HOU	NL	4-6	97	327	48	89	19	2	11	61	.272	24	145	106	—
1971	LF-1B	HOU	NL	4-6	129	468	49	135	17	3	9	67	.288	41	185	111	32-58
1972	LF	HOU	NL	2-6	147	548	74	171	27	4	16	86	.312	53	254	133	14-58
1973	LF-1B	HOU	NL	4-6	158	573	97	179	24	3	16	94	.312	85	257	137	14-61
1974	LF-1B	HOU	NL	4-6	150	524	69	156	19	4	11	67	.298	60	216	119	24-65
1975	1B	HOU	NL	6-6	132	485	67	157	27	1	18	85	.324	40	240	135	14-65
1976	1B	HOU	NL	3-6	157	585	76	183	31	3	16	102	.313	62	268	134	10-57
1977	1B	HOU	NL	3-6	151	554	77	160	38	6	22	110	.289	57	276	126	19-68
1978	1B	HOU	NL	5-6	139	461	51	133	25	4	14	79	.289	51	208	126	17-63
1979	1B	HOU	NL	2-6	49	163	15	39	4	0	3	18	.239	16	52	85	—
1979	1B-DH	BOS	AL	3-7	84	312	48	105	19	4	13	53	.337	29	171	140	—
1980	1B-DH	NY	AL	1-7	130	469	62	144	25	3	13	68	.307	48	214	120	20-69
1981	1B-DH	NY	AL	3-7	59	156	15	33	3	3	6	12	.212	24	60	109	—
1982	1B-DH	NY	AL	5-7	7	17	3	4	3	0	0	3	.235	3	7	—	—
1982	1B	ATL	NL	1-6	57	114	16	28	3	1	5	22	.246	14	48	116	—
1983	1B	ATL	NL	2-6	65	149	14	46	9	0	6	37	.309	18	73	139	—
1984	1B	ATL	NL	2-6	49	85	4	18	4	0	2	12	.212	9	28	—	—

MAJOR LEAGUE TOTALS   1832 6185 802 1826 307 41 184 989 .295 653 2767 127   9 yrs

Guillermo Montanez Born Apr 1, 1948 Catano, PR
6'0 170 lbs Batted left

YR	POS	TEAM	LG	FIN	G	AB	R	H	2B	3B	HR	RBI	AVG	BB	TB	OQ	RANK
1966	1B	CAL	AL	6-10	8	2	2	0	0	0	0	0	.000	0	0	—	—
1970	RF-1B	PHI	NL	5-6	18	25	3	6	0	0	0	3	.240	1	6	—	—
1971	CF	PHI	NL	6-6	158	599	78	153	27	6	30	99	.255	67	282	128	17-58
1972	CF	PHI	NL	6-6	147	531	60	131	39	3	13	64	.247	58	215	112	33-58
1973	1B-RF	PHI	NL	6-6	146	552	69	145	16	5	11	65	.263	46	204	97	48-61
1974	1B	PHI	NL	3-6	143	527	55	160	33	1	7	79	.304	32	216	107	45-65
1975	1B	PH/SF	NL	2/3	156	602	61	182	34	2	10	101	.302	49	250	112	34-65
1976	1B	SF/AT	NL	4/6	163	650	74	206	29	2	11	84	.317	36	272	113	28-57
1977	1B	ATL	NL	6-6	136	544	70	156	31	1	20	68	.287	35	249	109	40-68
1978	1B	NY	NL	6-6	159	609	66	156	32	0	17	96	.256	60	239	105	39-63
1979	1B	NY	NL	6-6	109	410	36	96	19	0	5	47	.234	25	130	76	—
1979	1B-DH	TEX	AL	3-7	38	144	19	46	6	0	8	24	.319	8	76	124	—
1980	1B	SD/MO	NL	6/2	142	500	40	136	12	4	6	64	.272	39	174	93	46-59
1981	1B	MO/PT	NL	2/4	55	100	8	21	0	1	1	6	.210	5	26	64	—
1982	1B	PT/PH	NL	4/2	54	48	4	10	1	0	0	2	.208	4	11	—	—
MAJOR LEAGUE TOTALS					1632	5843	645	1604	279	25	139	802	.275	465	2350	108	9 yrs

Salvatore Leonard Bando Born Feb 13, 1944 Cleveland, OH
6'0 195 lbs Batted right

YR	POS	TEAM	LG	FIN	G	AB	R	H	2B	3B	HR	RBI	AVG	BB	TB	OQ	RANK
1966	3B	KC	AL	7-10	11	24	1	7	1	1	0	1	.292	1	10	—	—
1967	3B	KC	AL	10-10	47	130	11	25	3	2	0	6	.192	16	32	79	—
1968	3B	OAK	AL	6-10	162	605	67	152	25	5	9	67	.251	51	214	105	31-45
1969	3B	OAK	AL	2-6	162	609	106	171	25	3	31	113	.281	111	295	147	8-59
1970	3B	OAK	AL	2-6	155	502	93	132	20	2	20	75	.263	118	216	140	7-59
1971	3B	OAK	AL	1-6	153	538	75	146	23	1	24	94	.271	86	243	136	13-57
1972	3B	OAK	AL	1-6	152	535	64	126	20	3	15	77	.236	78	197	117	25-56
1973	3B	OAK	AL	1-6	162	592	97	170	32	3	29	98	.287	82	295	137	5-60
1974	3B	OAK	AL	1-6	146	498	84	121	21	2	22	103	.243	86	212	126	13-67
1975	3B	OAK	AL	1-6	160	562	64	129	24	1	15	78	.230	87	200	102	39-66
1976	3B	OAK	AL	2-6	158	550	75	132	18	2	27	84	.240	76	235	122	16-64
1977	3B	MIL	AL	6-7	159	580	65	145	27	3	17	82	.250	75	229	103	52-81
1978	3B	MIL	AL	3-7	152	540	85	154	20	6	17	78	.285	72	237	123	22-83
1979	3B-DH	MIL	AL	2-7	130	476	57	117	14	3	9	43	.246	57	164	89	62-75
1980	3B-DH	MIL	AL	3-7	78	254	28	50	12	1	5	31	.197	29	79	79	—
1981	3B-1B	MIL	AL	1-7	32	65	10	13	4	0	2	9	.200	6	23	—	—
MAJOR LEAGUE TOTALS					2019	7060	982	1790	289	38	242	1039	.254	1031	2881	121	12 yrs

George Charles Scott Born Mar 23, 1944 Greenville, MS
6'2 200 lbs Batted right

YR	POS	TEAM	LG	FIN	G	AB	R	H	2B	3B	HR	RBI	AVG	BB	TB	OQ	RANK
1966	1B	BOS	AL	9-10	162	601	73	147	18	7	27	90	.245	65	260	118	20-44
1967	1B	BOS	AL	1-10	159	565	74	171	21	7	19	82	.303	63	263	143	9-48
1968	1B	BOS	AL	4-10	124	350	23	60	14	0	3	25	.171	26	83	67	—
1969	3B-1B	BOS	AL	3-6	152	549	63	139	14	5	16	52	.253	61	211	105	38-59
1970	3B-1B	BOS	AL	3-6	127	480	50	142	24	5	16	63	.296	44	224	123	20-59
1971	1B	BOS	AL	3-6	146	537	72	141	16	4	24	78	.263	41	237	114	30-57
1972	1B-3B	MIL	AL	6-6	152	578	71	154	24	4	20	88	.266	43	246	119	22-56
1973	1B	MIL	AL	5-6	158	604	98	185	30	4	24	107	.306	61	295	131	10-60
1974	1B	MIL	AL	5-6	158	604	74	170	36	2	17	82	.281	59	261	118	22-67
1975	1B	MIL	AL	5-6	158	617	86	176	26	4	36	109	.285	51	318	129	9-66
1976	1B	MIL	AL	6-6	156	606	73	166	21	5	18	77	.274	53	251	113	30-64
1977	1B	BOS	AL	2-7	157	584	103	157	26	5	33	95	.269	57	292	120	23-81
1978	1B	BOS	AL	2-7	120	412	51	96	16	4	12	54	.233	44	156	97	—
1979	1B-DH	Bo/KC/NY	AL	3/2/4	105	346	46	88	20	4	6	49	.254	31	134	93	—

MAJOR LEAGUE TOTALS 2034 7433 957 1992 306 60 271 1051 .268 699 3231 121 11 yrs

Carl Reginald Smith Born Apr 2, 1945 Shreveport, LA
6'0 180 lbs Batted both

YR	POS	TEAM	LG	FIN	G	AB	R	H	2B	3B	HR	RBI	AVG	BB	TB	OQ	RANK
1966	CF	BOS	AL	9-10	6	26	1	4	1	0	0	0	.154	0	5	—	—
1967	CF	BOS	AL	1-10	158	565	78	139	24	6	15	61	.246	57	220	112	24-48
1968	CF	BOS	AL	4-10	155	558	78	148	37	5	15	69	.265	64	240	133	11-45
1969	CF	BOS	AL	3-6	143	543	87	168	29	7	25	93	.309	54	286	144	9-59
1970	CF	BOS	AL	3-6	147	580	109	176	32	7	22	74	.303	51	288	130	12-59
1971	RF	BOS	AL	3-6	159	618	85	175	33	2	30	96	.283	63	302	134	18-57
1972	RF	BOS	AL	2-6	131	467	75	126	25	4	21	74	.270	68	222	148	8-56
1973	RF	BOS	AL	2-6	115	423	79	128	23	2	21	69	.303	68	218	149	2-60
1974	RF	SL	NL	2-6	143	517	79	160	26	9	23	100	.309	71	273	153	4-65
1975	RF-1B	SL	NL	3-6	135	477	67	144	26	3	19	76	.302	63	233	140	8-65
1976	RF-1B	SL/LA	NL	5/2	112	395	55	100	15	5	18	49	.253	32	179	117	—
1977	RF	LA	NL	1-6	148	488	104	150	27	4	32	87	.307	104	281	170	1-68
1978	RF	LA	NL	1-6	128	447	82	132	27	2	29	93	.295	70	250	162	3-63
1979	RF	LA	NL	3-6	68	234	41	64	13	1	10	32	.274	31	109	127	—
1980	RF	LA	NL	2-6	92	311	47	100	13	0	15	55	.322	41	158	150	—
1981	1B	LA	NL	2-6	41	35	5	7	1	0	1	8	.200	7	11	—	—
1982	1B	SF	NL	2-6	106	349	51	99	11	0	18	56	.284	46	164	135	—

MAJOR LEAGUE TOTALS 1987 7033 1123 2020 363 57 314 1092 .287 890 3439 143 11 yrs

Manuel De Jesus Sanguillen   Born Mar 21, 1944 Colon, Panama
6'0 193 lbs Batted right

YR	POS	TEAM	LG	FIN	G	AB	R	H	2B	3B	HR	RBI	AVG	BB	TB	OQ	RANK
1967	C	PIT	NL	6-10	30	96	6	26	4	0	0	8	.271	4	30	81	—
1969	C	PIT	NL	3-6	129	459	62	139	21	6	5	57	.303	12	187	100	—
1970	C	PIT	NL	1-6	128	486	63	158	19	9	7	61	.325	17	216	106	40-56
1971	C	PIT	NL	1-6	138	533	60	170	26	5	7	81	.319	19	227	111	33-58
1972	C	PIT	NL	1-6	136	520	55	155	18	8	7	71	.298	21	210	104	39-58
1973	C-RF	PIT	NL	3-6	149	589	64	166	26	7	12	65	.282	17	242	96	49-61
1974	C	PIT	NL	1-6	151	596	77	171	21	4	7	68	.287	21	221	90	59-65
1975	C	PIT	NL	1-6	133	481	60	158	24	4	9	58	.328	48	217	129	18-65
1976	C	PIT	NL	2-6	114	389	52	113	16	6	2	36	.290	28	147	104	—
1977	C-DH	OAK	AL	7-7	152	571	42	157	17	5	6	58	.275	22	202	80	79-81
1978	1B-C	PIT	NL	2-6	85	220	15	58	5	1	3	16	.264	9	74	82	—
1979	C-1B	PIT	NL	1-6	56	74	8	17	5	2	0	4	.230	2	26	—	—
1980	1B	PIT	NL	3-6	47	48	2	12	3	0	0	2	.250	3	15	—	—
MAJOR LEAGUE TOTALS					1448	5062	566	1500	205	57	65	585	.296	223	2014	102	7 yrs

Reginald Martinez Jackson   Born May 18, 1946 Wyncote, PA
6'0 195 lbs Batted left

YR	POS	TEAM	LG	FIN	G	AB	R	H	2B	3B	HR	RBI	AVG	BB	TB	OQ	RANK
1967	LF-RF	KC	AL	10-10	35	118	13	21	4	4	1	6	.178	10	36	82	—
1968	RF	OAK	AL	6-10	154	553	82	138	13	6	29	74	.250	50	250	129	16-45
1969	RF	OAK	AL	2-6	152	549	123	151	36	3	47	118	.275	114	334	178	2-59
1970	RF	OAK	AL	2-6	149	426	57	101	21	2	23	66	.237	75	195	129	13-59
1971	RF	OAK	AL	1-6	150	567	87	157	29	3	32	80	.277	63	288	139	11-57
1972	RF	OAK	AL	1-6	135	499	72	132	25	2	25	75	.265	59	236	140	9-56
1973	RF	OAK	AL	1-6	151	539	99	158	28	2	32	117	.293	76	286	146	3-60
1974	RF-DH	OAK	AL	1-6	148	506	90	146	25	1	29	93	.289	86	260	154	2-67
1975	RF	OAK	AL	1-6	157	593	91	150	39	3	36	104	.253	67	303	129	10-66
1976	RF	BAL	AL	2-6	134	498	84	138	27	2	27	91	.277	54	250	138	4-64
1977	RF-DH	NY	AL	1-7	146	525	93	150	39	2	32	110	.286	74	289	142	5-81
1978	RF-DH	NY	AL	1-7	139	511	82	140	13	5	27	97	.274	58	244	125	19-83
1979	RF	NY	AL	4-7	131	465	78	138	24	2	29	89	.297	65	253	141	7-75
1980	RF-DH	NY	AL	1-7	143	514	94	154	22	4	41	111	.300	83	307	161	2-69
1981	RF-DH	NY	AL	3-7	94	334	33	79	17	1	15	54	.237	46	143	118	23-71
1982	RF	CAL	AL	1-7	153	530	92	146	17	1	39	101	.275	85	282	142	4-77
1983	DH-RF	CAL	AL	5-7	116	397	43	77	14	1	14	49	.194	52	135	87	—
1984	DH	CAL	AL	2-7	143	525	67	117	17	2	25	81	.223	55	213	99	50-68
1985	RF-DH	CAL	AL	2-7	143	460	64	116	27	0	27	85	.252	78	224	129	10-75
1986	DH	CAL	AL	1-7	132	419	65	101	12	2	18	58	.241	92	171	120	21-78
1987	DH-RF	OAK	AL	3-7	115	336	42	74	14	1	15	43	.220	33	135	90	—
MAJOR LEAGUE TOTALS					2820	9864	1551	2584	463	49	563	1702	.262	1375	4834	137	18 yrs

Johnny Lee Bench   Born Dec 7, 1947   Oklahoma City, OK
6'1   197 lbs   Batted right

YR	POS	TEAM	LG	FIN	G	AB	R	H	2B	3B	HR	RBI	AVG	BB	TB	OQ	RANK
1967	C	CIN	NL	4-10	26	86	7	14	3	1	1	6	.163	5	22	—	—
1968	C	CIN	NL	4-10	154	564	67	155	40	2	15	82	.275	31	244	121	19-45
1969	C	CIN	NL	3-6	148	532	83	156	23	1	26	90	.293	49	259	132	14-62
1970	C-LF	CIN	NL	1-6	158	605	97	177	35	4	45	148	.293	54	355	143	10-56
1971	C	CIN	NL	4-6	149	562	80	134	19	2	27	61	.238	49	238	109	35-58
1972	C-RF	CIN	NL	1-6	147	538	87	145	22	2	40	125	.270	100	291	163	2-58
1973	C-RF	CIN	NL	1-6	152	557	83	141	17	3	25	104	.253	83	239	122	24-61
1974	C-3B	CIN	NL	2-6	160	621	108	174	38	2	33	129	.280	80	315	140	7-65
1975	C-LF	CIN	NL	1-6	142	530	83	150	39	1	28	110	.283	65	275	141	7-65
1976	C	CIN	NL	1-6	135	465	62	109	24	1	16	74	.234	81	183	121	25-57
1977	C	CIN	NL	2-6	142	494	67	136	34	2	31	109	.275	58	267	136	9-68
1978	C	CIN	NL	2-6	120	393	52	102	17	1	23	73	.260	50	190	132	—
1979	C	CIN	NL	1-6	130	464	73	128	19	0	22	80	.276	67	213	129	16-62
1980	C	CIN	NL	3-6	114	360	52	90	12	0	24	68	.250	41	174	127	—
1981	1B-C	CIN	NL	1-6	52	178	14	55	8	0	8	25	.309	17	87	138	—
1982	3B	CIN	NL	6-6	119	399	44	103	16	0	13	38	.258	37	158	106	—
1983	3B-1B	CIN	NL	6-6	110	310	32	79	15	2	12	54	.255	24	134	108	—

MAJOR LEAGUE TOTALS   2158   7658 1091 2048 381 24 389 1376 .267 891 3644 132 11 yrs

Joseph Oden Rudi   Born Sep 7, 1946   Modesto, CA
6'2   200 lbs   Batted right

YR	POS	TEAM	LG	FIN	G	AB	R	H	2B	3B	HR	RBI	AVG	BB	TB	OQ	RANK
1967	1B-LF	KC	AL	10-10	19	43	4	8	2	0	0	1	.186	3	10	—	—
1968	LF	OAK	AL	6-10	68	181	10	32	5	1	1	12	.177	12	42	65	—
1969	LF-1B	OAK	AL	2-6	35	122	10	23	3	1	2	6	.189	5	34	62	—
1970	LF-1B	OAK	AL	2-6	106	350	40	108	23	2	11	42	.309	16	168	118	—
1971	LF	OAK	AL	1-6	127	513	62	137	23	4	10	52	.267	28	198	97	48-57
1972	LF	OAK	AL	1-6	147	593	94	181	32	9	19	75	.305	37	288	138	11-56
1973	LF	OAK	AL	1-6	120	437	53	118	25	1	12	66	.270	30	181	102	—
1974	LF-1B	OAK	AL	1-6	158	593	73	174	39	4	22	99	.293	34	287	122	17-67
1975	1B-LF	OAK	AL	1-6	126	468	66	130	26	6	21	75	.278	40	231	124	17-66
1976	LF	OAK	AL	2-6	130	500	54	135	32	3	13	94	.270	41	212	114	28-64
1977	LF	CAL	AL	5-7	64	242	48	64	13	2	13	53	.264	22	120	117	—
1978	LF	CAL	AL	2-7	133	497	58	127	27	1	17	79	.256	28	207	98	54-83
1979	LF	CAL	AL	1-7	90	330	35	80	11	3	11	61	.242	24	130	89	—
1980	LF	CAL	AL	6-7	104	372	42	88	17	1	16	53	.237	17	155	90	—
1981	DH-1B	BOS	AL	5-7	49	122	14	22	3	0	6	24	.180	8	43	81	—
1982	1B-RF	OAK	AL	5-7	71	193	21	41	6	1	5	18	.212	24	64	86	—

MAJOR LEAGUE TOTALS   1547   5556 684 1468 287 39 179 810 .264 369 2370 116 6 yrs

Douglas Lee Rader
6'2　208 lbs　Batted right

Born Jul 30, 1944　Chicago, IL

YR	POS	TEAM	LG	FIN	G	AB	R	H	2B	3B	HR	RBI	AVG	BB	TB	OQ	RANK
1967	1B-3B	HOU	NL	9-10	47	162	24	54	10	4	2	26	.333	7	78	132	—
1968	3B	HOU	NL	10-10	98	333	42	89	16	4	6	43	.267	31	131	120	—
1969	3B	HOU	NL	5-6	155	569	62	140	25	3	11	83	.246	62	204	100	45-62
1970	3B	HOU	NL	4-6	156	576	90	145	25	3	25	87	.252	57	251	107	39-56
1971	3B	HOU	NL	4-6	135	484	51	118	21	4	12	56	.244	40	183	99	41-58
1972	3B	HOU	NL	2-6	152	553	70	131	24	7	22	90	.237	57	235	113	31-58
1973	3B	HOU	NL	4-6	154	574	79	146	26	0	21	89	.254	46	235	103	41-61
1974	3B	HOU	NL	4-6	152	533	61	137	27	3	17	78	.257	60	221	113	34-65
1975	3B	HOU	NL	6-6	129	448	41	100	23	2	12	48	.223	42	163	93	53-65
1976	3B	SD	NL	5-6	139	471	45	121	22	4	9	55	.257	55	178	109	31-57
1977	3B	SD	NL	5-6	52	170	19	46	8	3	5	27	.271	33	75	130	—
1977	3B-DH	TOR	AL	7-7	96	313	47	75	18	2	13	40	.240	38	136	108	—

| MAJOR LEAGUE TOTALS | | | | | 1465 | 5186 | 631 | 1302 | 245 | 39 | 155 | 722 | .251 | 528 | 2090 | 105 | 8 yrs |

Graig Nettles
6'0　180 lbs　Batted left

Born Aug 20, 1944　San Diego, CA

YR	POS	TEAM	LG	FIN	G	AB	R	H	2B	3B	HR	RBI	AVG	BB	TB	OQ	RANK
1967	PH	MIN	AL	2-10	3	3	0	1	1	0	0	0	.333	0	2	—	—
1968	RF-3B	MIN	AL	7-10	22	76	13	17	2	1	5	8	.224	7	36	—	—
1969	LF-3B	MIN	AL	1-6	96	225	27	50	9	2	7	26	.222	32	84	105	—
1970	3B	CLE	AL	5-6	157	549	81	129	13	1	26	62	.235	81	222	112	33-59
1971	3B	CLE	AL	6-6	158	598	78	156	18	1	28	86	.261	82	260	125	24-57
1972	3B	CLE	AL	5-6	150	557	65	141	28	0	17	70	.253	57	220	116	26-56
1973	3B	NY	AL	4-6	160	552	65	129	18	0	22	81	.234	78	213	106	27-60
1974	3B	NY	AL	2-6	155	566	74	139	21	1	22	75	.246	59	228	107	37-67
1975	3B	NY	AL	3-6	157	581	71	155	24	4	21	91	.267	51	250	109	27-66
1976	3B	NY	AL	1-6	158	583	88	148	29	2	32	93	.254	62	277	128	12-64
1977	3B	NY	AL	1-7	158	589	99	150	23	4	37	107	.255	68	292	121	22-81
1978	3B	NY	AL	1-7	159	587	81	162	23	2	27	93	.276	59	270	119	27-83
1979	3B	NY	AL	4-7	145	521	71	132	15	1	20	73	.253	59	209	100	49-75
1980	3B	NY	AL	1-7	89	324	52	79	14	0	16	45	.244	42	141	111	—
1981	3B	NY	AL	3-7	103	349	46	85	7	1	15	46	.244	47	139	112	31-71
1982	3B	NY	AL	5-7	122	405	47	94	11	2	18	55	.232	51	163	102	—
1983	3B	NY	AL	3-7	129	462	56	123	17	3	20	75	.266	51	206	113	31-70
1984	3B	SD	NL	1-6	124	395	56	90	11	1	20	65	.228	58	163	117	—
1985	3B	SD	NL	3-6	137	440	66	115	23	1	15	61	.261	72	185	126	17-65
1986	3B	SD	NL	4-6	126	354	36	77	9	0	16	55	.218	41	134	98	—
1987	3B	ATL	NL	5-6	112	177	16	37	8	1	5	33	.209	22	62	88	—
1988	3B	MON	NL	3-6	80	93	5	16	4	0	1	14	.172	9	23	69	—

| MAJOR LEAGUE TOTALS | | | | | 2700 | 8986 | 1193 | 2225 | 328 | 28 | 390 | 1314 | .248 | 1088 | 3779 | 115 | 13 yrs |

Aurelio Rodriguez   Born Dec 28, 1947 Cananea, Mexico
5'10 180 lbs Batted right

YR	POS	TEAM	LG	FIN	G	AB	R	H	2B	3B	HR	RBI	AVG	BB	TB	OQ	RANK
1967	3B	CAL	AL	5-10	29	130	14	31	3	1	1	8	.238	2	39	71	—
1968	3B	CAL	AL	8-10	76	223	14	54	10	1	1	16	.242	17	69	91	—
1969	3B	CAL	AL	3-6	159	561	47	130	17	2	7	49	.232	32	172	75	57-59
1970	3B	CA/WA	AL	3/6	159	610	70	152	33	7	19	83	.249	40	256	100	43-59
1971	3B	DET	AL	2-6	154	604	68	153	30	7	15	39	.253	27	242	97	49-57
1972	3B	DET	AL	1-6	153	601	65	142	23	5	13	56	.236	28	214	92	48-56
1973	3B	DET	AL	3-6	160	555	46	123	27	3	9	58	.222	31	183	76	57-60
1974	3B	DET	AL	6-6	159	571	54	127	23	5	5	49	.222	26	175	72	67-67
1975	3B	DET	AL	6-6	151	507	47	124	20	6	13	60	.245	30	195	91	50-66
1976	3B	DET	AL	5-6	128	480	40	115	13	2	8	50	.240	19	156	79	62-64
1977	3B	DET	AL	4-7	96	306	30	67	14	1	10	32	.219	16	113	79	—
1978	3B	DET	AL	5-7	134	385	40	102	25	2	7	43	.265	19	152	93	—
1979	3B	DET	AL	5-7	106	343	27	87	18	0	5	36	.254	11	120	74	—
1980	3B	SD	NL	6-6	89	175	7	35	7	2	2	13	.200	6	52	66	—
1980	3B-2B	NY	AL	1-7	52	164	14	36	6	1	3	14	.220	7	53	70	—
1981	3B-2B	NY	AL	3-7	27	52	4	18	2	0	2	8	.346	2	26	—	—
1982	3B	CHI	AL	3-7	118	257	24	62	15	1	3	31	.241	11	88	75	—
1983	3B	BA/CH	AL	1/1	67	87	1	12	1	0	1	3	.138	0	16	—	—
MAJOR LEAGUE TOTALS					2017	6611	612	1570	287	46	124	648	.237	324	2321	85	8 yrs

Amos Joseph Otis   Born Apr 26, 1947 Mobile, AL
5'11 165 lbs Batted right

YR	POS	TEAM	LG	FIN	G	AB	R	H	2B	3B	HR	RBI	AVG	BB	TB	OQ	RANK
1967	CF	NY	NL	10-10	19	59	6	13	2	0	0	1	.220	5	15	—	—
1969	CF	NY	NL	1-6	48	93	6	14	3	1	0	4	.151	6	19	—	—
1970	CF	KC	AL	4-6	159	620	91	176	36	9	11	58	.284	68	263	116	29-59
1971	CF	KC	AL	2-6	147	555	80	167	26	4	15	79	.301	40	246	119	27-57
1972	CF	KC	AL	4-6	143	540	75	158	28	2	11	54	.293	50	223	125	19-56
1973	CF	KC	AL	2-6	148	583	89	175	21	4	26	93	.300	63	282	130	11-60
1974	CF	KC	AL	5-6	146	552	87	157	31	9	12	73	.284	58	242	121	18-67
1975	CF	KC	AL	2-6	132	470	87	116	26	6	9	46	.247	66	181	108	31-66
1976	CF	KC	AL	1-6	153	592	93	165	40	2	18	86	.279	55	263	122	15-64
1977	CF	KC	AL	1-7	142	478	85	120	20	8	17	78	.251	71	207	114	26-81
1978	CF	KC	AL	1-7	141	486	74	145	30	7	22	96	.298	66	255	145	3-83
1979	CF	KC	AL	2-7	151	577	100	170	28	2	18	90	.295	68	256	115	24-75
1980	CF	KC	AL	1-7	107	394	56	99	16	3	10	53	.251	39	151	96	—
1981	CF	KC	AL	4-7	99	372	49	100	22	3	9	57	.269	31	155	109	35-71
1982	CF	KC	AL	2-7	125	475	73	136	25	3	11	88	.286	37	200	104	47-77
1983	RF	KC	AL	2-7	98	356	35	93	16	3	4	41	.261	27	127	87	—
1984	LF	PIT	NL	6-6	40	97	6	16	4	0	0	10	.165	7	20	54	—
MAJOR LEAGUE TOTALS					1998	7299	1092	2020	374	66	193	1007	.277	757	3105	119	12 yrs

Rodney Cline Carew   Born Oct 1, 1945   Gatun, Canal Zone
6'0 170 lbs Batted left

YR	POS	TEAM	LG	FIN	G	AB	R	H	2B	3B	HR	RBI	AVG	BB	TB	OQ	RANK
1967	2B	MIN	AL	3-10	137	514	66	150	22	7	8	51	.292	37	210	117	20-48
1968	2B	MIN	AL	7-10	127	461	46	126	27	2	1	42	.273	26	160	99	35-45
1969	2B	MIN	AL	1-6	123	458	79	152	30	4	8	56	.332	37	214	130	18-59
1970	2B	MIN	AL	1-6	51	191	27	70	12	3	4	28	.366	11	100	143	—
1971	2B	MIN	AL	5-6	147	577	88	177	16	10	2	48	.307	45	219	107	35-57
1972	2B	MIN	AL	3-6	142	535	61	170	21	6	0	51	.318	43	203	118	24-56
1973	2B	MIN	AL	3-6	149	580	98	203	30	11	6	62	.350	62	273	137	6-60
1974	2B	MIN	AL	3-6	153	599	86	218	30	5	3	55	.364	74	267	143	5-67
1975	2B-1B	MIN	AL	4-6	143	535	89	192	24	4	14	80	.359	64	266	148	3-66
1976	1B	MIN	AL	3-6	156	605	97	200	29	12	9	90	.331	67	280	140	3-64
1977	1B	MIN	AL	4-7	155	616	128	239	38	16	14	100	.388	69	351	164	1-81
1978	1B	MIN	AL	4-7	152	564	85	188	26	10	5	70	.333	78	249	134	9-83
1979	1B	CAL	AL	1-7	110	409	78	130	15	3	3	44	.318	73	160	121	—
1980	1B-DH	CAL	AL	6-7	144	540	74	179	34	7	3	59	.331	59	236	121	18-69
1981	1B	CAL	AL	5-7	93	364	57	111	17	1	2	21	.305	45	136	114	27-71
1982	1B	CAL	AL	1-7	138	523	88	167	25	5	3	44	.319	67	211	116	28-77
1983	1B-DH	CAL	AL	5-7	129	472	66	160	24	2	2	44	.339	57	194	120	21-70
1984	1B	CAL	AL	2-7	93	329	42	97	8	1	3	31	.295	40	116	101	—
1985	1B	CAL	AL	2-7	127	443	69	124	17	3	2	39	.280	64	153	100	53-75

| MAJOR LEAGUE TOTALS | | | | | 2469 | 9315 | 1424 | 3053 | 445 | 112 | 92 | 1015 | .328 | 1018 | 3998 | 126 | 16 yrs |

Donald Wayne Money   Born Jun 7, 1947   Washington, DC
6'1 170 lbs Batted right

YR	POS	TEAM	LG	FIN	G	AB	R	H	2B	3B	HR	RBI	AVG	BB	TB	OQ	RANK
1968	SS	PHI	NL	7-10	4	13	1	3	2	0	0	2	.231	2	5	—	—
1969	SS	PHI	NL	5-6	127	450	41	103	22	2	6	42	.229	43	147	88	54-62
1970	3B	PHI	NL	5-6	120	447	66	132	25	4	14	66	.295	43	207	119	28-56
1971	3B-LF	PHI	NL	6-6	121	439	40	98	22	8	7	38	.223	31	157	90	—
1972	3B	PHI	NL	6-6	152	536	54	119	16	2	15	52	.222	41	184	88	47-58
1973	3B-SS	MIL	AL	5-6	145	556	75	158	28	2	11	61	.284	53	223	107	24-60
1974	3B	MIL	AL	5-6	159	629	85	178	32	3	15	65	.283	62	261	114	24-67
1975	3B	MIL	AL	5-6	109	405	58	112	16	1	15	43	.277	31	175	108	—
1976	3B	MIL	AL	6-6	117	439	51	117	18	4	12	62	.267	47	179	115	26-64
1977	2B-LF	MIL	AL	6-7	152	570	86	159	28	3	25	83	.279	57	268	116	24-81
1978	1B-2B	MIL	AL	3-7	137	518	88	152	30	2	14	54	.293	48	228	116	32-83
1979	DH-3B	MIL	AL	2-7	92	350	52	83	20	1	6	38	.237	40	123	88	—
1980	3B-DH	MIL	AL	3-7	86	289	39	74	17	1	17	46	.256	40	144	127	—
1981	3B	MIL	AL	1-7	60	185	17	40	7	0	2	14	.216	19	53	79	—
1982	DH-3B	MIL	AL	1-7	96	275	40	78	14	3	16	55	.284	32	146	134	—
1983	DH-3B	MIL	AL	5-7	43	114	5	17	5	0	1	8	.149	11	25	55	—

| MAJOR LEAGUE TOTALS | | | | | 1720 | 6215 | 798 | 1623 | 302 | 36 | 176 | 729 | .261 | 600 | 2525 | 108 | 8 yrs |

Delbert Bernard Unser   Born Dec 9, 1944 Decatur, IL
6'1 180 lbs Batted left

YR	POS	TEAM	LG	FIN	G	AB	R	H	2B	3B	HR	RBI	AVG	BB	TB	OQ	RANK
1968	CF	WAS	AL	10-10	156	635	66	146	13	7	1	30	.230	46	176	81	43-45
1969	CF	WAS	AL	4-6	153	581	69	166	19	8	7	57	.286	58	222	107	36-59
1970	CF	WAS	AL	6-6	119	322	37	83	5	1	5	30	.258	30	105	88	—
1971	RF	WAS	AL	5-6	153	581	63	148	19	6	9	41	.255	59	206	99	44-57
1972	CF	CLE	AL	5-6	132	383	29	91	12	0	1	17	.238	28	106	80	—
1973	CF	PHI	NL	6-6	136	440	64	127	20	4	11	52	.289	47	188	118	29-61
1974	CF	PHI	NL	3-6	142	454	72	120	18	5	11	61	.264	50	181	110	39-65
1975	CF	NY	NL	3-6	147	531	65	156	18	2	10	53	.294	37	208	103	42-65
1976	CF	NY/MO	NL	3/6	146	496	57	113	19	4	12	40	.228	29	176	87	46-57
1977	CF-1B	MON	NL	5-6	113	289	33	79	14	1	12	40	.273	33	131	117	—
1978	1B-RF	MON	NL	4-6	130	179	16	35	5	0	2	15	.196	24	46	78	—
1979	LF-1B	PHI	NL	4-6	95	141	26	42	8	0	6	29	.298	14	68	128	—
1980	1B-CF	PHI	NL	1-6	96	110	15	29	6	4	0	10	.264	10	43	104	—
1981	1B-CF	PHI	NL	3-6	62	59	5	9	3	0	0	6	.153	13	12	—	—
1982	1B-RF	PHI	NL	2-6	19	14	0	0	0	0	0	0	.000	3	0	—	—

| MAJOR LEAGUE TOTALS | | | | | 1799 | 5215 | 617 | 1344 | 179 | 42 | 87 | 481 | .258 | 481 | 1868 | 101 | 7 yrs |

Larry Eugene Hisle   Born May 5, 1947 Portsmouth, OH
6'2 193 lbs Batted right

YR	POS	TEAM	LG	FIN	G	AB	R	H	2B	3B	HR	RBI	AVG	BB	TB	OQ	RANK
1968	CF	PHI	NL	7-10	7	11	1	4	1	0	0	1	.364	1	5	—	—
1969	CF	PHI	NL	5-6	145	482	75	128	23	5	20	56	.266	48	221	122	21-62
1970	CF	PHI	NL	5-6	126	405	52	83	22	4	10	44	.205	53	143	91	—
1971	LF-CF	PHI	NL	6-6	36	76	7	15	3	0	0	3	.197	6	18	—	—
1973	LF	MIN	AL	3-6	143	545	88	148	25	6	15	64	.272	64	230	114	20-60
1974	LF	MIN	AL	3-6	143	510	68	146	20	7	19	79	.286	48	237	125	15-67
1975	LF-DH	MIN	AL	4-6	80	255	37	80	9	2	11	51	.314	27	126	135	—
1976	LF	MIN	AL	3-6	155	581	81	158	19	5	14	96	.272	56	229	110	33-64
1977	CF	MIN	AL	4-7	141	546	95	165	36	3	28	119	.302	56	291	134	11-81
1978	LF-DH	MIL	AL	3-7	142	520	96	151	24	0	34	115	.290	67	277	143	4-83
1979	DH-LF	MIL	AL	2-7	26	96	18	27	7	0	3	14	.281	11	43	113	—
1980	DH	MIL	AL	3-7	17	60	16	17	0	0	6	16	.283	14	35	—	—
1981	DH	MIL	AL	1-7	27	87	11	20	4	0	4	11	.230	6	36	—	—
1982	DH	MIL	AL	1-7	9	31	7	4	0	0	2	5	.129	5	10	—	—

| MAJOR LEAGUE TOTALS | | | | | 1197 | 4205 | 652 | 1146 | 193 | 32 | 166 | 674 | .273 | 462 | 1901 | 125 | 6 yrs |

Bobby Lee Bonds
6'1 190 lbs Batted right

Born Mar 15, 1946 Riverside, CA

YR	POS	TEAM	LG	FIN	G	AB	R	H	2B	3B	HR	RBI	AVG	BB	TB	OQ	RANK
1968	RF	SF	NL	2-10	81	307	55	78	10	5	9	35	.254	38	125	129	—
1969	RF	SF	NL	2-6	158	622	120	161	25	6	32	90	.259	81	294	131	15-62
1970	RF	SF	NL	3-6	157	663	134	200	36	10	26	78	.302	77	334	133	17-56
1971	RF	SF	NL	1-6	155	619	110	178	32	4	33	102	.288	62	317	140	8-58
1972	RF	SF	NL	5-6	153	626	118	162	29	5	26	80	.259	60	279	120	26-58
1973	RF	SF	NL	3-6	160	643	131	182	34	4	39	96	.283	87	341	146	9-61
1974	RF	SF	NL	5-6	150	567	97	145	22	8	21	71	.256	95	246	128	12-65
1975	RF	NY	AL	3-6	145	529	93	143	26	3	32	85	.270	89	271	144	6-66
1976	CF	CAL	AL	4-6	99	378	48	100	10	3	10	54	.265	41	146	110	—
1977	RF-DH	CAL	AL	5-7	158	592	103	156	23	9	37	115	.264	74	308	129	14-81
1978	RF-DH	CH/TX	AL	5/2	156	565	93	151	19	4	31	90	.267	79	271	130	15-83
1979	RF-DH	CLE	AL	6-7	146	538	93	148	24	1	25	85	.275	74	249	120	20-75
1980	LF	SL	NL	4-6	86	231	37	47	5	3	5	24	.203	33	73	92	—
1981	CF	CHI	NL	6-6	45	163	26	35	7	1	6	19	.215	24	62	109	—

MAJOR LEAGUE TOTALS | | | | | 1849 | 7043 | 1258 | 1886 | 302 | 66 | 332 | 1024 | .268 | 914 | 3316 | 132 | 10 yrs

Richard Joseph Hebner
6'1 195 lbs Batted left

Born Nov 26, 1947 Boston, MA

YR	POS	TEAM	LG	FIN	G	AB	R	H	2B	3B	HR	RBI	AVG	BB	TB	OQ	RANK
1968	PH	PIT	NL	6-10	2	1	0	0	0	0	0	0	.000	0	0	—	—
1969	3B	PIT	NL	3-6	129	459	72	138	23	4	8	47	.301	53	193	123	20-62
1970	3B	PIT	NL	1-6	120	420	60	122	24	8	11	46	.290	42	195	119	—
1971	3B	PIT	NL	1-6	112	388	50	105	17	8	17	67	.271	32	189	127	—
1972	3B	PIT	NL	1-6	124	427	63	128	24	4	19	72	.300	52	217	147	9-58
1973	3B	PIT	NL	3-6	144	509	73	138	28	1	25	74	.271	56	243	127	16-61
1974	3B	PIT	NL	1-6	146	550	97	160	21	6	18	68	.291	60	247	125	15-65
1975	3B	PIT	NL	1-6	128	472	65	116	16	4	15	57	.246	43	185	101	44-65
1976	3B	PIT	NL	2-6	132	434	60	108	21	3	8	51	.249	47	159	103	—
1977	1B-3B	PHI	NL	1-6	118	397	67	113	17	4	18	62	.285	61	192	133	—
1978	1B-3B	PHI	NL	1-6	137	435	61	123	22	3	17	71	.283	53	202	130	16-63
1979	3B	NY	NL	6-6	136	473	54	127	25	2	10	79	.268	59	186	109	34-62
1980	1B-3B	DET	AL	5-7	104	341	48	99	10	7	12	82	.290	38	159	121	—
1981	1B-DH	DET	AL	4-7	78	226	19	51	8	2	5	28	.226	27	78	96	—
1982	1B-DH	DET	AL	4-7	68	179	25	49	6	0	8	18	.274	25	79	119	—
1982	RF-1B	PIT	NL	4-6	25	70	6	21	2	0	2	12	.300	5	29	—	—
1983	3B	PIT	NL	2-6	78	162	23	43	4	1	5	26	.265	17	64	107	—
1984	3B	CHI	NL	1-6	44	81	12	27	3	0	2	8	.333	10	36	—	—
1985	1B	CHI	NL	4-6	83	120	10	26	2	0	3	22	.217	7	37	74	—

MAJOR LEAGUE TOTALS | | | | | 1908 | 6144 | 865 | 1694 | 273 | 57 | 203 | 890 | .276 | 687 | 2690 | 123 | 7 yrs

Frederick Joseph Patek Born Oct 9, 1944 Seguin, TX
5'5 148 lbs Batted right

YR	POS	TEAM	LG	FIN	G	AB	R	H	2B	3B	HR	RBI	AVG	BB	TB	OO	RANK
1968	SS	PIT	NL	6-10	61	208	31	53	4	2	2	18	.255	12	67	92	—
1969	SS	PIT	NL	3-6	147	460	48	110	9	1	5	32	.239	53	136	87	58-62
1970	SS	PIT	NL	1-6	84	237	42	58	10	5	1	19	.245	29	81	92	—
1971	SS	KC	AL	2-6	147	591	86	158	21	11	6	36	.267	44	219	98	46-57
1972	SS	KC	AL	4-6	136	518	59	110	25	4	0	32	.212	47	143	81	52-56
1973	SS	KC	AL	2-6	135	501	82	117	19	5	5	45	.234	54	161	86	49-60
1974	SS	KC	AL	5-6	149	537	72	121	18	6	3	38	.225	77	160	91	52-67
1975	SS	KC	AL	2-6	136	483	58	110	14	5	5	45	.228	42	149	79	61-66
1976	SS	KC	AL	1-6	144	432	58	104	19	3	1	43	.241	50	132	91	—
1977	SS	KC	AL	1-7	154	497	72	130	26	6	5	60	.262	41	183	90	69-81
1978	SS	KC	AL	1-7	138	440	54	109	23	1	2	46	.248	42	140	85	—
1979	SS	KC	AL	2-7	106	306	30	77	17	0	1	37	.252	16	97	71	—
1980	SS	CAL	AL	6-7	86	273	41	72	10	5	5	34	.264	15	107	90	—
1981	2B-3B	CAL	AL	5-7	27	47	3	11	1	1	0	5	.234	1	14	—	—

MAJOR LEAGUE TOTALS 1650 5530 736 1340 216 55 41 490 .242 523 1789 87 7 yrs

Albert Oliver Born Oct 14, 1946 Portsmouth, OH
6'0 195 lbs Batted left

YR	POS	TEAM	LG	FIN	G	AB	R	H	2B	3B	HR	RBI	AVG	BB	TB	OO	RANK
1968	RF	PIT	NL	6-10	4	8	1	1	0	0	0	0	.125	0	1	—	—
1969	1B-LF	PIT	NL	3-6	129	463	55	132	19	2	17	70	.285	21	206	110	—
1970	RF-1B	PIT	NL	1-6	151	551	63	149	33	5	12	83	.270	35	228	98	42-56
1971	CF-1B	PIT	NL	1-6	143	529	69	149	31	7	14	64	.282	27	236	113	28-58
1972	CF	PIT	NL	1-6	140	565	88	176	27	4	12	89	.312	34	247	118	28-58
1973	CF-1B	PIT	NL	3-6	158	654	90	191	38	7	20	99	.292	22	303	111	39-61
1974	CF-1B	PIT	NL	1-6	147	617	96	198	38	12	11	85	.321	33	293	123	17-65
1975	CF	PIT	NL	1-6	155	628	90	176	39	8	18	84	.280	25	285	108	37-65
1976	CF	PIT	NL	2-6	121	443	62	143	22	5	12	61	.323	26	211	129	—
1977	LF	PIT	NL	2-6	154	568	75	175	29	6	19	82	.308	40	273	119	28-68
1978	LF-DH	TEX	AL	2-7	133	525	65	170	35	5	14	89	.324	31	257	125	20-83
1979	CF-LF	TEX	AL	3-7	136	492	69	159	28	4	12	76	.323	34	231	115	25-75
1980	LF	TEX	AL	4-7	163	656	96	209	43	3	19	117	.319	39	315	118	23-69
1981	DH	TEX	AL	2-7	102	421	53	130	29	1	4	55	.309	24	173	108	37-71
1982	1B	MON	NL	3-6	160	617	90	204	43	2	22	109	.331	61	317	147	7-66
1983	1B	MON	NL	3-6	157	614	70	184	38	3	8	84	.300	44	252	108	38-64
1984	1B	SF/PH	NL	6/4	119	432	36	130	26	2	0	48	.301	27	160	100	—
1985	LF	LA	NL	1-6	35	79	1	20	5	0	0	8	.253	5	25	—	—
1985	DH	TOR	AL	1-7	61	187	20	47	6	1	5	23	.251	7	70	81	—

MAJOR LEAGUE TOTALS 2368 9049 1189 2743 529 77 219 1326 .303 535 4083 116 13 yrs

Ralph Allen Garr   Born Dec 12, 1945 Monroe, LA
5'11   185 lbs Batted left

YR	POS	TEAM	LG	FIN	G	AB	R	H	2B	3B	HR	RBI	AVG	BB	TB	OQ	RANK
1968	PH	ATL	NL	5-10	11	7	3	2	0	0	0	0	.286	1	2	—	—
1969	LF	ATL	NL	1-6	22	27	6	6	1	0	0	2	.222	2	7	—	—
1970	RF-CF	ATL	NL	5-6	37	96	18	27	3	0	0	8	.281	5	30	76	—
1971	LF	ATL	NL	3-6	154	639	101	219	24	6	9	44	.343	30	282	121	25-58
1972	LF	ATL	NL	4-6	134	554	87	180	22	0	12	53	.325	25	238	115	30-58
1973	LF	ATL	NL	5-6	148	668	94	200	32	6	11	55	.299	22	277	101	44-61
1974	LF	ATL	NL	3-6	143	606	87	214	24	17	11	54	.353	28	305	135	9-65
1975	LF	ATL	NL	5-6	151	625	74	174	26	11	6	31	.278	44	240	99	47-65
1976	LF	CHI	AL	6-6	136	527	63	158	22	6	4	36	.300	17	204	98	50-64
1977	RF	CHI	AL	3-7	134	543	78	163	29	7	10	54	.300	27	236	102	57-81
1978	LF	CHI	AL	5-7	118	443	67	122	18	9	3	29	.275	24	167	92	—
1979	LF-DH	CHI/CA	AL	5/1	108	331	34	89	10	2	9	39	.269	17	130	88	—
1980	DH-RF	CAL	AL	6-7	21	42	5	8	1	0	0	3	.190	4	9	—	—

MAJOR LEAGUE TOTALS   1317 5108 717 1562 212 64 75 408 .306 246 2127 110   7 yrs

Johnnie B Baker   Born Jun 15, 1949   Riverside, CA
6'2   183 lbs Batted right

YR	POS	TEAM	LG	FIN	G	AB	R	H	2B	3B	HR	RBI	AVG	BB	TB	OQ	RANK
1968	CF	ATL	NL	5-10	6	5	0	2	0	0	0	0	.400	0	2	—	—
1969	CF	ATL	NL	1-6	3	7	0	0	0	0	0	0	.000	0	0	—	—
1970	LF-CF	ATL	NL	5-6	13	24	3	7	0	0	0	4	.292	2	7	—	—
1971	RF-CF	ATL	NL	3-6	29	62	2	14	2	0	0	4	.226	1	16	—	—
1972	CF	ATL	NL	4-6	127	446	62	143	27	2	17	76	.321	45	225	146	10-58
1973	CF	ATL	NL	5-6	159	604	101	174	29	4	21	99	.288	67	274	125	20-61
1974	RF	ATL	NL	3-6	149	574	80	147	35	0	20	69	.256	71	242	116	28-65
1975	RF	ATL	NL	5-6	142	494	63	129	18	2	19	72	.261	67	208	119	30-65
1976	CF	LA	NL	2-6	112	384	36	93	13	0	4	39	.242	31	118	84	—
1977	LF	LA	NL	1-6	153	533	86	155	26	1	30	86	.291	58	273	131	14-68
1978	LF	LA	NL	1-6	149	522	62	137	24	1	11	66	.262	47	196	101	45-63
1979	LF	LA	NL	3-6	151	554	86	152	29	1	23	88	.274	56	252	118	23-62
1980	LF	LA	NL	2-6	153	579	80	170	26	4	29	97	.294	43	291	130	10-59
1981	LF	LA	NL	2-6	103	400	48	128	17	3	9	49	.320	29	178	124	19-69
1982	LF	LA	NL	2-6	147	570	80	171	19	1	23	88	.300	56	261	127	15-66
1983	LF	LA	NL	1-6	149	531	71	138	25	1	15	73	.260	72	210	113	32-64
1984	RF-LF	SF	NL	6-6	100	243	31	71	7	2	3	32	.292	40	91	123	—
1985	1B-LF	OAK	AL	4-7	111	343	48	92	15	1	14	52	.268	50	151	118	—
1986	LF-DH	OAK	AL	3-7	83	242	25	58	8	0	4	19	.240	27	78	83	—

MAJOR LEAGUE TOTALS   2039 7117 964 1981 320 23 242 1013 .278 762 3073 123 11 yrs

William Edwin Melton Born Jul 7, 1945 Gulfport, MS
6'2 200 lbs Batted right

YR	POS	TEAM	LG	FIN	G	AB	R	H	2B	3B	HR	RBI	AVG	BB	TB	OQ	RANK
1968	3B	CHI	AL	8-10	34	109	5	29	8	0	2	16	.266	10	43	119	—
1969	3B	CHI	AL	5-6	157	556	67	142	26	2	23	87	.255	56	241	113	29-59
1970	RF-3B	CHI	AL	6-6	141	514	74	135	15	1	33	96	.263	56	251	126	15-59
1971	3B	CHI	AL	3-6	150	543	72	146	18	2	33	86	.269	61	267	134	17-57
1972	3B	CHI	AL	2-6	57	208	22	51	5	0	7	30	.245	23	77	111	—
1973	3B	CHI	AL	5-6	152	560	83	155	29	1	20	87	.277	75	246	122	14-60
1974	3B	CHI	AL	4-6	136	495	63	120	17	0	21	63	.242	59	200	110	27-67
1975	3B	CHI	AL	5-6	149	512	62	123	16	0	15	70	.240	78	184	104	35-66
1976	DH-1B	CAL	AL	4-6	118	341	31	71	17	3	6	42	.208	44	112	95	—
1977	1B-DH	CLE	AL	5-7	50	133	17	32	11	0	0	14	.241	17	43	87	—

MAJOR LEAGUE TOTALS   1144 3971 496 1004 162 9 160 591 .253 479 1664 118 6 yrs

Ted Lyle Simmons Born Aug 9, 1949 Highland Park, MI
5'11 193 lbs Batted both

YR	POS	TEAM	LG	FIN	G	AB	R	H	2B	3B	HR	RBI	AVG	BB	TB	OQ	RANK
1968	C	SL	NL	1-10	2	3	0	1	0	0	0	0	.333	1	1	—	—
1969	C	SL	NL	4-6	5	14	0	3	0	1	0	3	.214	1	5	—	—
1970	C	SL	NL	4-6	82	284	29	69	8	2	3	24	.243	37	90	88	—
1971	C	SL	NL	2-6	133	510	64	155	32	4	7	77	.304	36	216	116	27-58
1972	C	SL	NL	4-6	152	594	70	180	36	6	16	96	.303	29	276	121	23-58
1973	C	SL	NL	2-6	161	619	62	192	36	2	13	91	.310	61	271	123	23-61
1974	C	SL	NL	2-6	152	599	66	163	33	6	20	103	.272	47	268	114	30-65
1975	C	SL	NL	3-6	157	581	80	193	32	3	18	100	.332	63	285	141	6-65
1976	C-1B	SL	NL	5-6	150	546	60	159	35	3	5	75	.291	73	215	122	23-57
1977	C	SL	NL	3-6	150	516	82	164	25	3	21	95	.318	79	258	143	6-68
1978	C-LF	SL	NL	5-6	152	516	71	148	40	5	22	80	.287	77	264	148	5-63
1979	C	SL	NL	3-6	123	448	68	127	22	0	26	87	.283	61	227	139	10-62
1980	C	SL	NL	4-6	145	495	84	150	33	2	21	98	.303	59	250	143	4-59
1981	C-DH	MIL	AL	1-7	100	380	45	82	13	3	14	61	.216	23	143	89	64-71
1982	C-DH	MIL	AL	1-7	137	539	73	145	29	0	23	97	.269	32	243	103	50-77
1983	C-DH	MIL	AL	5-7	153	600	76	185	39	3	13	108	.308	41	269	111	32-70
1984	DH-1B	MIL	AL	7-7	132	497	44	110	23	2	4	52	.221	30	149	70	66-68
1985	DH-1B	MIL	AL	6-7	143	528	60	144	28	2	12	76	.273	57	212	103	46-75
1986	1B-C	ATL	NL	6-6	76	127	14	32	5	0	4	25	.252	12	49	100	—
1987	1B-C	ATL	NL	5-6	73	177	20	49	8	0	4	30	.277	21	69	103	—
1988	1B-C	ATL	NL	6-6	78	107	6	21	6	0	2	11	.196	15	33	93	—

MAJOR LEAGUE TOTALS   2456 8680 1074 2472 483 47 248 1389 .285 855 3793 119 15 yrs

Carlos May   Born May 17, 1948 Birmingham, AL
5'11   200 lbs   Batted left

YR	POS	TEAM	LG	FIN	G	AB	R	H	2B	3B	HR	RBI	AVG	BB	TB	OQ	RANK
1968	LF	CHI	AL	8-10	17	67	4	12	1	0	0	1	.179	3	13	—	—
1969	LF	CHI	AL	5-6	100	367	62	103	18	2	18	62	.281	58	179	142	—
1970	LF	CHI	AL	6-6	150	555	83	158	28	4	12	68	.285	79	230	121	22-59
1971	1B	CHI	AL	3-6	141	500	64	147	21	7	7	70	.294	62	203	122	26-57
1972	LF	CHI	AL	2-6	148	523	83	161	26	3	12	68	.308	79	229	149	7-56
1973	DH-LF	CHI	AL	5-6	149	553	62	148	20	0	20	96	.268	53	228	107	23-60
1974	LF	CHI	AL	4-6	149	551	66	137	19	2	8	58	.249	46	184	89	54-67
1975	1B-LF	CHI	AL	5-6	128	454	55	123	19	2	8	53	.271	67	170	110	27-66
1976	DH-LF	CHI/NY	AL	6/1	107	351	45	91	13	2	3	43	.259	43	117	101	—
1977	DH	NY/CA	AL	1/5	76	199	21	47	7	1	2	17	.236	22	62	81	—

MAJOR LEAGUE TOTALS   1165 4120 545 1127 172 23 90 536 .274 512 1615 116   6 yrs

Harold Abraham McRae   Born Jul 10, 1945   Avon Park, FL
5'11   180 lbs   Batted right

YR	POS	TEAM	LG	FIN	G	AB	R	H	2B	3B	HR	RBI	AVG	BB	TB	OQ	RANK
1968	2B	CIN	NL	4-10	17	51	1	10	1	0	0	2	.196	4	11	—	—
1970	LF-3B	CIN	NL	1-6	70	165	18	41	6	1	8	23	.248	15	73	106	—
1971	LF	CIN	NL	4-6	99	337	39	89	24	2	9	34	.264	11	144	102	—
1972	RF-3B	CIN	NL	1-6	61	97	9	27	4	0	5	26	.278	2	46	—	—
1973	RF-DH	KC	AL	2-6	106	338	36	79	18	3	9	50	.234	34	130	97	—
1974	DH-LF	KC	AL	5-6	148	539	71	167	36	4	15	88	.310	54	256	133	7-67
1975	LF-DH	KC	AL	2-6	126	480	58	147	38	6	5	71	.306	47	212	120	19-66
1976	DH-LF	KC	AL	1-6	149	527	75	175	34	5	8	73	.332	64	243	143	1-64
1977	DH-LF	KC	AL	1-7	162	641	104	191	54	11	21	92	.298	59	330	127	16-81
1978	DH	KC	AL	1-7	156	623	90	170	39	5	16	72	.273	51	267	108	42-83
1979	DH	KC	AL	2-7	101	393	55	113	32	4	10	74	.288	38	183	114	—
1980	DH	KC	AL	1-7	124	489	73	145	39	5	14	83	.297	29	236	114	28-69
1981	DH	KC	AL	4-7	101	389	38	106	23	2	7	36	.272	34	154	106	40-71
1982	DH	KC	AL	2-7	159	613	91	189	46	8	27	133	.308	55	332	135	7-77
1983	DH	KC	AL	2-7	157	589	84	183	41	6	12	82	.311	50	272	118	24-70
1984	DH	KC	AL	1-7	106	317	30	96	13	4	3	42	.303	34	126	109	—
1985	DH	KC	AL	1-7	112	320	41	83	19	0	14	70	.259	44	144	117	—
1986	DH	KC	AL	3-7	112	278	22	70	14	0	7	37	.252	18	105	86	—
1987	DH	KC	AL	2-7	18	32	5	10	3	0	1	9	.313	5	16	—	—

MAJOR LEAGUE TOTALS   2084 7218 940 2091 484 66 191 1097 .290 648 3280 123   9 yrs

John Claiborn Mayberry Born Feb 18, 1949 Detroit, MI
6'3 215 lbs Batted left

YR	POS	TEAM	LG	FIN	G	AB	R	H	2B	3B	HR	RBI	AVG	BB	TB	OQ	RANK
1968	1B	HOU	NL	10-10	4	9	0	0	0	0	0	0	.000	0	0	—	—
1969	PH	HOU	NL	5-6	5	4	0	0	0	0	0	0	.000	1	0	—	—
1970	1B	HOU	NL	4-6	50	148	23	32	3	2	5	14	.216	21	54	97	—
1971	1B	HOU	NL	4-6	46	137	16	25	0	1	7	14	.182	13	48	89	—
1972	1B	KC	AL	4-6	149	503	65	150	24	3	25	100	.298	78	255	165	2-56
1973	1B	KC	AL	2-6	152	510	87	142	20	2	26	100	.278	122	244	153	1-60
1974	1B-DH	KC	AL	5-6	126	427	63	100	13	1	22	69	.234	77	181	126	14-67
1975	1B-DH	KC	AL	2-6	156	554	95	161	38	1	34	106	.291	119	303	166	1-66
1976	1B	KC	AL	1-6	161	594	76	138	22	2	13	95	.232	82	203	102	45-64
1977	1B	KC	AL	1-7	153	543	73	125	22	1	23	82	.230	83	218	106	46-81
1978	1B	TOR	AL	7-7	152	515	51	129	15	2	22	70	.250	60	214	109	39-83
1979	1B	TOR	AL	7-7	137	464	61	127	22	1	21	74	.274	69	214	122	19-75
1980	1B	TOR	AL	7-7	149	501	62	124	19	2	30	82	.248	77	237	124	16-69
1981	1B-DH	TOR	AL	7-7	94	290	34	72	6	1	17	43	.248	44	131	128	17-71
1982	1B-DH	TO/NY	AL	6/5	86	248	27	54	7	0	10	30	.218	35	91	96	—

MAJOR LEAGUE TOTALS 1620 5447 733 1379 211 19 255 879 .253 881 2393 130 10 yrs

George Arthur Foster Born Dec 1, 1948 Tuscaloosa, AL
6'1 180 lbs Batted right

YR	POS	TEAM	LG	FIN	G	AB	R	H	2B	3B	HR	RBI	AVG	BB	TB	OQ	RANK
1969	LF	SF	NL	2-6	9	5	1	2	0	0	0	1	.400	0	2	—	—
1970	LF	SF	NL	3-6	9	19	2	6	1	1	1	4	.316	2	12	—	—
1971	CF	SF/CN	NL	1/4	140	473	50	114	23	4	13	58	.241	29	184	97	44-58
1972	RF	CIN	NL	1-6	59	145	15	29	4	1	2	12	.200	5	41	65	—
1973	CF	CIN	NL	1-6	17	39	6	11	3	0	4	9	.282	4	26	—	—
1974	CF	CIN	NL	2-6	106	276	31	73	18	0	7	41	.264	30	112	111	—
1975	LF	CIN	NL	1-6	134	463	71	139	24	4	23	78	.300	40	240	136	11-65
1976	LF	CIN	NL	1-6	144	562	86	172	21	9	29	121	.306	52	298	147	4-57
1977	LF	CIN	NL	2-6	158	615	124	197	31	2	52	149	.320	61	388	161	2-68
1978	LF	CIN	NL	2-6	158	604	97	170	26	7	40	120	.281	70	330	147	6-63
1979	LF	CIN	NL	1-6	121	440	68	133	18	3	30	98	.302	59	247	154	3-62
1980	LF	CIN	NL	3-6	144	528	79	144	21	5	25	93	.273	75	250	135	7-59
1981	LF	CIN	NL	1-6	108	414	64	122	23	2	22	90	.295	51	215	148	4-69
1982	LF	NY	NL	6-6	151	550	64	136	23	2	13	70	.247	50	202	98	48-66
1983	LF	NY	NL	6-6	157	601	74	145	19	2	28	90	.241	38	252	100	45-64
1984	LF	NY	NL	2-6	146	553	67	149	22	1	24	86	.269	30	245	110	30-53
1985	LF	NY	NL	2-6	129	452	57	119	24	1	21	77	.263	46	208	121	22-65
1986	LF	NY	NL	1-6	72	233	28	53	6	1	13	38	.227	21	100	105	—
1986	LF-DH	CHI	AL	5-7	15	51	2	11	0	2	1	4	.216	3	18	—	—

MAJOR LEAGUE TOTALS 1977 7023 986 1925 307 47 348 1239 .274 666 3370 130 12 yrs

Fury Gene Tenace   Born Oct 10, 1946   Russellton, PA
6'0   190 lbs   Batted right

YR	POS	TEAM	LG	FIN	G	AB	R	H	2B	3B	HR	RBI	AVG	BB	TB	OQ	RANK
1969	C	OAK	AL	2-6	16	38	1	6	0	0	1	2	.158	1	9	—	—
1970	C	OAK	AL	2-6	38	105	19	32	6	0	7	20	.305	23	59	175	—
1971	C	OAK	AL	1-6	65	179	26	49	7	0	7	25	.274	29	77	132	—
1972	C-RF	OAK	AL	1-6	82	227	22	51	5	3	5	32	.225	24	77	100	—
1973	1B-C	OAK	AL	1-6	160	510	83	132	18	2	24	84	.259	101	226	133	8-60
1974	1B-C	OAK	AL	1-6	158	484	71	102	17	1	26	73	.211	110	199	129	11-67
1975	C-1B	OAK	AL	1-6	158	498	83	127	17	0	29	87	.255	106	231	140	8-66
1976	1B-C	OAK	AL	2-6	128	417	64	104	19	1	22	66	.249	81	191	142	2-64
1977	C-1B	SD	NL	5-6	147	437	66	102	24	4	15	61	.233	125	179	136	10-68
1978	1B-C	SD	NL	4-6	142	401	60	90	18	4	16	61	.224	101	164	136	10-63
1979	C-1B	SD	NL	5-6	151	463	61	122	16	4	20	67	.263	105	206	141	8-62
1980	C-1B	SD	NL	6-6	133	316	46	70	11	1	17	50	.222	92	134	147	—
1981	C-1B	SL	NL	1-6	58	129	26	30	7	0	5	22	.233	38	52	148	—
1982	C-1B	SL	NL	1-5	66	124	18	32	9	0	7	18	.258	36	62	171	—
1983	1B	PIT	NL	2-6	53	62	7	11	5	0	0	6	.177	12	16	—	—

MAJOR LEAGUE TOTALS   1555   4390 653 1060 179 20 201 674 .241 984 1882 137   7 yrs

Steven Patrick Garvey   Born Dec 22, 1948   Tampa, FL
5'10   192 lbs   Batted right

YR	POS	TEAM	LG	FIN	G	AB	R	H	2B	3B	HR	RBI	AVG	BB	TB	OQ	RANK
1969	PH	LA	NL	4-6	3	3	0	1	0	0	0	0	.333	0	1	—	—
1970	3B	LA	NL	2-6	34	93	8	25	5	0	1	6	.269	6	33	—	—
1971	3B	LA	NL	2-6	81	225	27	51	12	1	7	26	.227	21	86	100	—
1972	3B	LA	NL	3-6	96	294	36	79	14	2	9	30	.269	19	124	109	—
1973	1B	LA	NL	2-6	114	349	37	106	17	3	8	50	.304	11	153	106	—
1974	1B	LA	NL	1-6	156	642	95	200	32	3	21	111	.312	31	301	119	23-65
1975	1B	LA	NL	2-6	160	659	85	210	38	6	18	95	.319	33	314	122	27-65
1976	1B	LA	NL	2-6	162	631	85	200	37	4	13	80	.317	50	284	127	19-57
1977	1B	LA	NL	1-6	162	646	91	192	25	3	33	115	.297	38	322	119	29-68
1978	1B	LA	NL	1-6	162	639	89	202	36	9	21	113	.316	40	319	131	13-63
1979	1B	LA	NL	3-6	162	648	92	204	32	1	28	110	.315	37	322	125	18-62
1980	1B	LA	NL	2-6	163	658	78	200	27	1	26	106	.304	36	307	119	22-59
1981	1B	LA	NL	2-6	110	431	63	122	23	1	10	64	.283	25	177	106	39-69
1982	1B	LA	NL	2-6	162	625	66	176	35	1	16	86	.282	20	261	100	46-66
1983	1B	SD	NL	4-6	100	388	76	114	22	0	14	59	.294	29	178	119	—
1984	1B	SD	NL	1-6	161	617	72	175	27	2	8	86	.284	24	230	93	45-53
1985	1B	SD	NL	3-6	162	654	80	184	34	6	17	81	.281	35	281	107	33-65
1986	1B	SD	NL	4-6	155	557	58	142	22	0	21	81	.255	23	227	94	41-49
1987	1B	SD	NL	6-6	27	76	5	16	2	0	1	9	.211	1	21	—	—

MAJOR LEAGUE TOTALS   2332   8835 1143 2599 440 43 272 1308 .294 479 3941 114   12 yrs

Colbert Dale Harrah   Born Oct 26, 1948   Sissonville, WV
6'0 175 lbs Batted right

YR	POS	TEAM	LG	FIN	G	AB	R	H	2B	3B	HR	RBI	AVG	BB	TB	OQ	RANK
1969	SS	WAS	AL	4-6	8	1	4	0	0	0	0	0	.000	0	0	—	—
1971	SS	WAS	AL	5-6	127	383	45	88	11	3	2	22	.230	40	111	83	—
1972	SS	TEX	AL	6-6	116	374	47	97	14	3	1	31	.259	34	120	97	—
1973	SS-3B	TEX	AL	6-6	118	461	64	120	16	1	10	50	.260	46	168	97	40-60
1974	SS	TEX	AL	2-6	161	573	79	149	23	2	21	74	.260	50	239	109	33-67
1975	SS-3B	TEX	AL	3-6	151	522	81	153	24	1	20	93	.293	98	239	141	7-66
1976	SS	TEX	AL	4-6	155	584	64	152	21	1	15	67	.260	91	220	118	21-64
1977	3B	TEX	AL	2-7	159	539	90	142	25	5	27	87	.263	109	258	136	9-81
1978	3B-SS	TEX	AL	2-7	139	450	56	103	17	3	12	59	.229	83	162	109	40-83
1979	3B-SS	CLE	AL	6-7	149	527	99	147	25	1	20	77	.279	89	234	123	17-75
1980	3B	CLE	AL	6-7	160	561	100	150	22	4	11	72	.267	98	213	112	33-69
1981	3B	CLE	AL	6-7	103	361	64	105	12	4	5	44	.291	57	140	123	22-71
1982	3B	CLE	AL	6-7	162	602	100	183	29	4	25	78	.304	84	295	134	10-77
1983	3B	CLE	AL	7-7	138	526	81	140	23	1	9	53	.266	75	192	103	42-70
1984	3B	NY	AL	3-7	88	253	40	55	9	4	1	26	.217	42	75	89	—
1985	2B	TEX	AL	7-7	126	396	65	107	18	1	9	44	.270	113	154	136	7-75
1986	2B	TEX	AL	2-7	95	289	36	63	18	2	7	41	.218	44	106	97	—
MAJOR LEAGUE TOTALS					2155	7402	1115	1954	307	40	195	918	.264	1153	2926	120	12 yrs

William Ellis Russell   Born Oct 21, 1948   Pittsburg, KS
6'0 175 lbs Batted right

YR	POS	TEAM	LG	FIN	G	AB	R	H	2B	3B	HR	RBI	AVG	BB	TB	OQ	RANK
1969	RF	LA	NL	4-6	98	212	35	48	6	2	5	15	.226	22	73	93	—
1970	RF-CF	LA	NL	2-6	81	278	30	72	11	9	0	28	.259	16	101	85	—
1971	2B-RF	LA	NL	2-6	91	211	29	48	7	4	2	15	.227	11	69	80	—
1972	SS	LA	NL	3-6	129	434	47	118	19	5	4	34	.272	34	159	100	43-58
1973	SS	LA	NL	2-6	162	615	55	163	26	3	4	56	.265	34	207	84	57-61
1974	SS	LA	NL	1-6	160	553	61	149	18	6	5	65	.269	53	194	97	53-65
1975	SS	LA	NL	2-6	84	252	24	52	9	2	0	14	.206	23	65	69	—
1976	SS	LA	NL	2-6	149	554	53	152	17	3	5	65	.274	21	190	86	49-57
1977	SS	LA	NL	1-6	153	634	84	176	28	6	4	51	.278	24	228	82	64-68
1978	SS	LA	NL	1-6	155	625	72	179	32	4	3	46	.286	30	228	92	53-63
1979	SS	LA	NL	3-6	153	627	72	170	26	4	7	56	.271	24	225	84	56-62
1980	SS	LA	NL	2-6	130	466	38	123	23	2	3	34	.264	18	159	82	—
1981	SS	LA	NL	2-6	82	262	20	61	9	2	0	22	.233	19	74	75	—
1982	SS	LA	NL	2-6	153	497	64	136	20	2	3	46	.274	63	169	103	43-66
1983	SS	LA	NL	1-6	131	451	47	111	13	1	1	30	.246	33	129	75	—
1984	SS-CF	LA	NL	4-6	89	262	25	70	12	1	0	19	.267	25	84	91	—
1985	SS-LF	LA	NL	1-6	76	169	19	44	6	1	0	13	.260	18	52	89	—
1986	LF-SS	LA	NL	5-6	105	216	21	54	11	0	0	18	.250	15	65	77	—
MAJOR LEAGUE TOTALS					2181	7318	796	1926	293	57	46	627	.263	483	2471	91	8 yrs

David Cash   Born Jun 11, 1948   Utica, NY
5'11   170 lbs   Batted right

YR	POS	TEAM	LG	FIN	G	AB	R	H	2B	3B	HR	RBI	AVG	BB	TB	OQ	RANK
1969	2B	PIT	NL	3-6	18	61	8	17	3	1	0	4	.279	9	22	—	—
1970	2B	PIT	NL	1-6	64	210	30	66	7	6	1	28	.314	17	88	109	—
1971	2B-3B	PIT	NL	1-6	123	478	79	138	17	4	2	34	.289	46	169	103	40-58
1972	2B	PIT	NL	1-6	99	425	58	120	22	4	3	30	.282	22	159	97	—
1973	2B-3B	PIT	NL	3-6	116	436	59	118	21	2	2	31	.271	38	149	93	—
1974	2B	PHI	NL	3-6	162	687	89	206	26	11	2	58	.300	46	260	101	51-65
1975	2B	PHI	NL	2-6	162	699	111	213	40	3	4	57	.305	56	271	106	40-65
1976	2B	PHI	NL	1-6	160	666	92	189	14	12	1	56	.284	54	230	97	37-57
1977	2B	MON	NL	5-6	153	650	91	188	42	7	0	43	.289	52	244	96	52-68
1978	2B	MON	NL	4-6	159	658	66	166	26	3	3	43	.252	37	207	79	62-63
1979	2B	MON	NL	2-6	76	187	24	60	11	1	2	19	.321	12	79	111	—
1980	2B	SD	NL	6-6	130	397	25	90	14	2	1	23	.227	35	111	76	—

MAJOR LEAGUE TOTALS   1422 5554 732 1571 243 56 21 426 .283 424 1989 97   6 yrs

William Joseph Buckner   Born Dec 14, 1949   Vallejo, CA
6'0   185 lbs   Batted left

YR	POS	TEAM	LG	FIN	G	AB	R	H	2B	3B	HR	RBI	AVG	BB	TB	OQ	RANK
1969	PH	LA	NL	4-6	1	1	0	0	0	0	0	0	.000	0	0	—	—
1970	LF	LA	NL	2-6	28	68	6	13	3	1	0	4	.191	3	18	—	—
1971	RF-1B	LA	NL	2-6	108	358	37	99	15	1	5	41	.277	11	131	89	—
1972	RF-1B	LA	NL	3-6	105	383	47	122	14	3	5	37	.319	17	157	109	—
1973	1B-LF	LA	NL	2-6	140	575	68	158	20	0	8	46	.275	17	202	83	58-61
1974	LF	LA	NL	1-6	145	580	83	182	30	3	7	58	.314	30	239	107	44-65
1975	LF	LA	NL	2-6	92	288	30	70	11	2	6	31	.243	17	103	87	—
1976	LF	LA	NL	2-6	154	642	76	193	28	4	7	60	.301	26	250	100	36-57
1977	1B	CHI	NL	4-6	122	426	40	121	27	0	11	60	.284	21	181	99	—
1978	1B	CHI	NL	3-6	117	446	47	144	26	1	5	74	.323	18	187	108	—
1979	1B	CHI	NL	5-6	149	591	72	168	34	7	14	66	.284	30	258	105	40-62
1980	1B-LF	CHI	NL	6-6	145	578	69	187	41	3	10	68	.324	30	264	120	20-59
1981	1B	CHI	NL	6-6	106	421	45	131	35	3	10	75	.311	26	202	128	13-69
1982	1B	CHI	NL	5-6	161	657	93	201	34	5	15	105	.306	36	290	115	28-66
1983	1B	CHI	NL	5-6	153	626	79	175	38	6	16	66	.280	25	273	104	41-64
1984	1B	CHI	NL	1-6	21	43	3	9	0	0	0	2	.209	1	9	—	—
1984	1B	BOS	AL	4-7	114	439	51	122	21	2	11	67	.278	24	180	97	—
1985	1B	BOS	AL	5-7	162	673	89	201	46	3	16	110	.299	30	301	103	45-75
1986	1B	BOS	AL	1-7	153	629	73	168	39	2	18	102	.267	40	265	96	61-78
1987	1B-DH	BO/CA	AL	5/6	132	469	39	134	18	2	5	74	.286	22	171	81	77-79
1988	DH-1B	CA/KC	AL	4/3	108	285	19	71	14	0	3	43	.249	17	94	79	—
1989	DH-1B	KC	AL	2-7	79	176	7	38	4	1	1	16	.216	6	47	59	—
1990	1B	BOS	AL	1-7	22	43	4	8	0	0	1	3	.186	3	11	—	—

MAJOR LEAGUE TOTALS   2517 9397 1077 2715 498 49 174 1208 .289 450 3833 104 11 yrs

Theodore Crawford Sizemore Born Apr 15, 1945 Gadsden, AL
5'10 165 lbs Batted right

YR	POS	TEAM	LG	FIN	G	AB	R	H	2B	3B	HR	RBI	AVG	BB	TB	OQ	RANK
1969	2B-SS	LA	NL	4-6	159	590	69	160	20	5	4	46	.271	45	202	92	51-62
1970	2B	LA	NL	2-6	96	340	40	104	10	1	1	34	.306	34	119	97	—
1971	2B-SS	SL	NL	2-6	135	478	53	126	14	5	3	42	.264	42	159	93	46-58
1972	2B	SL	NL	4-6	120	439	53	116	17	4	2	38	.264	37	147	93	45-58
1973	2B	SL	NL	2-6	142	521	69	147	22	1	1	54	.282	68	174	102	42-61
1974	2B	SL	NL	2-6	129	504	68	126	17	0	2	47	.250	70	149	92	56-65
1975	2B	SL	NL	3-6	153	562	56	135	23	1	3	49	.240	45	169	79	62-65
1976	2B	LA	NL	2-6	84	266	18	64	8	1	0	18	.241	15	74	72	—
1977	2B	PHI	NL	1-6	152	519	64	146	20	3	4	47	.281	52	184	95	53-68
1978	2B	PHI	NL	1-6	108	351	38	77	12	0	0	25	.219	25	89	66	—
1979	2B	CHI	NL	5-6	98	330	36	82	17	0	2	24	.248	32	105	85	—
1979	2B	BOS	AL	3-7	26	88	12	23	7	0	1	6	.261	4	33	—	—
1980	2B	BOS	AL	4-7	9	23	1	5	1	0	0	0	.217	0	6	—	—
MAJOR LEAGUE TOTALS					1411	5011	577	1311	188	21	23	430	.262	469	1610	92	7 yrs

Darrell Wayne Evans Born May 26, 1947 Pasadena, CA
6'2 200 lbs Batted left

YR	POS	TEAM	LG	FIN	G	AB	R	H	2B	3B	HR	RBI	AVG	BB	TB	OQ	RANK
1969	3B	ATL	NL	1-6	12	26	3	6	0	0	0	1	.231	1	6	—	—
1970	3B	ATL	NL	5-6	12	44	4	14	1	1	0	9	.318	7	17	—	—
1971	3B	ATL	NL	3-6	89	260	42	63	11	1	12	38	.242	39	112	125	—
1972	3B	ATL	NL	4-6	125	418	67	106	12	0	19	71	.254	90	175	139	11-58
1973	3B-1B	ATL	NL	5-6	161	595	114	167	25	8	41	104	.281	124	331	167	3-61
1974	3B	ATL	NL	3-6	160	571	99	137	21	3	25	79	.240	126	239	133	11-65
1975	3B	ATL	NL	5-6	156	567	82	138	22	2	22	73	.243	105	230	123	26-65
1976	1B	AT/SF	NL	6/4	136	396	53	81	9	1	11	46	.205	72	125	102	—
1977	LF-1B	SF	NL	4-6	144	461	64	117	18	3	17	72	.254	69	192	113	36-68
1978	3B	SF	NL	3-6	159	547	82	133	24	2	20	78	.243	105	221	126	18-63
1979	3B	SF	NL	4-6	160	562	68	142	23	2	17	70	.253	91	220	114	29-62
1980	3B	SF	NL	5-6	154	556	69	147	23	0	20	78	.264	83	230	122	18-59
1981	3B-1B	SF	NL	4-6	102	357	51	92	13	4	12	48	.258	54	149	125	17-69
1982	3B-1B	SF	NL	3-6	141	465	64	119	20	4	16	61	.256	77	195	126	18-66
1983	1B-3B	SF	NL	5-6	142	523	94	145	29	3	30	82	.277	84	270	147	3-64
1984	DH-1B	DET	AL	1-7	131	401	60	93	11	1	16	63	.232	77	154	113	—
1985	1B-DH	DET	AL	3-7	151	505	81	125	17	0	40	94	.248	85	262	134	8-75
1986	1B-DH	DET	AL	3-7	151	507	78	122	15	0	29	85	.241	91	224	119	22-78
1987	1B-DH	DET	AL	1-7	150	499	90	128	20	0	34	99	.257	100	250	132	11-79
1988	DH-1B	DET	AL	2-7	144	437	48	91	9	0	22	64	.208	84	166	111	33-74
1989	1B-3B	ATL	NL	6-6	107	276	31	57	6	1	11	39	.207	41	98	104	—
MAJOR LEAGUE TOTALS					2687	8973	1344	2223	329	36	414	1354	.248	1605	3866	129	15 yrs

Thurman Lee Munson   Born Jun 7, 1947   Akron, OH
5'11   190 lbs   Batted right   Died Aug 2, 1979   Canton, OH

YR	POS	TEAM	LG	FIN	G	AB	R	H	2B	3B	HR	RBI	AVG	BB	TB	OQ	RANK
1969	C	NY	AL	5-6	26	86	6	22	1	2	1	9	.256	10	30	—	—
1970	C	NY	AL	2-6	132	453	59	137	25	4	6	53	.302	57	188	121	24-59
1971	C	NY	AL	4-6	125	451	71	113	15	4	10	42	.251	52	166	105	37-57
1972	C	NY	AL	4-6	140	511	54	143	16	3	7	46	.280	47	186	110	31-56
1973	C	NY	AL	4-6	147	519	80	156	29	4	20	74	.301	48	253	128	12-60
1974	C	NY	AL	2-6	144	517	64	135	19	2	13	60	.261	44	197	101	45-67
1975	C-DH	NY	AL	3-6	157	597	83	190	24	3	12	102	.318	45	256	114	24-66
1976	C-DH	NY	AL	1-6	152	616	79	186	27	1	17	105	.302	29	266	112	31-64
1977	C	NY	AL	1-7	149	595	85	183	28	5	18	100	.308	39	275	112	30-81
1978	C	NY	AL	1-7	154	617	73	183	27	1	6	71	.297	35	230	94	66-83
1979	C	NY	AL	4-7	97	382	42	110	18	3	3	39	.288	32	143	93	—
MAJOR LEAGUE TOTALS					1423	5344	696	1558	229	32	113	701	.292	438	2190	111	9 yrs

Carlton Ernest Fisk   Born Dec 26, 1947   Bellows Falls, VT
6'3   200 lbs   Batted right

YR	POS	TEAM	LG	FIN	G	AB	R	H	2B	3B	HR	RBI	AVG	BB	TB	OQ	RANK
1969	C	BOS	AL	3-6	2	5	0	0	0	0	0	0	.000	0	0	—	—
1971	C	BOS	AL	3-6	14	48	7	15	2	1	2	6	.313	1	25	—	—
1972	C	BOS	AL	2-6	131	457	74	134	28	9	22	61	.293	52	246	161	3-56
1973	C	BOS	AL	2-6	135	508	65	125	21	0	26	71	.246	37	224	105	29-60
1974	C	BOS	AL	3-6	52	187	36	56	12	1	11	26	.299	24	103	155	—
1975	C	BOS	AL	1-6	79	263	47	87	14	4	10	52	.331	27	139	146	—
1976	C	BOS	AL	3-6	134	487	76	124	17	5	17	58	.255	56	202	117	24-64
1977	C	BOS	AL	2-7	152	536	106	169	26	3	26	102	.315	75	279	142	7-81
1978	C	BOS	AL	2-7	157	571	94	162	39	5	20	88	.284	71	271	129	17-83
1979	DH-C	BOS	AL	3-7	91	320	49	87	23	2	10	42	.272	10	144	96	—
1980	C	BOS	AL	4-7	131	478	73	138	25	3	18	62	.289	36	223	113	31-69
1981	C	CHI	AL	3-7	96	338	44	89	12	0	7	45	.263	38	122	103	47-71
1982	C	CHI	AL	3-7	135	476	66	127	17	3	14	65	.267	46	192	101	51-77
1983	C	CHI	AL	1-7	138	488	85	141	26	4	26	86	.289	46	253	129	11-70
1984	C	CHI	AL	5-7	102	359	54	83	20	1	21	43	.231	26	168	106	—
1985	C-DH	CHI	AL	3-7	153	543	85	129	23	1	37	107	.238	52	265	113	28-75
1986	C-LF	CHI	AL	5-7	125	457	42	101	11	0	14	63	.221	22	154	72	—
1987	C	CHI	AL	5-7	135	454	68	116	22	1	23	71	.256	39	209	103	51-79
1988	C	CHI	AL	5-7	76	253	37	70	8	1	19	50	.277	37	137	146	—
1989	C-DH	CHI	AL	7-7	103	375	47	110	25	2	13	68	.293	36	178	125	—
1990	C-DH	CHI	AL	2-7	137	452	65	129	21	0	18	65	.285	61	204	125	12-69
1991	C-DH	CHI	AL	2-7	134	460	42	111	25	0	18	74	.241	32	190	95	57-72
1992	C	CHI	AL	3-7	62	188	12	43	4	1	3	21	.229	23	58	85	—
1993	C	CHI	AL	1-7	25	53	2	10	0	0	1	4	.189	2	13	—	—
MAJOR LEAGUE TOTALS					2499	8756	1276	2356	421	47	376	1330	.269	849	3999	118	13 yrs

Julio Ruben Morales   Born Feb 18, 1949   Yabucoa, PR
5'10   155 lbs   Batted right

YR	POS	TEAM	LG	FIN	G	AB	R	H	2B	3B	HR	RBI	AVG	BB	TB	OQ	RANK
1969	LF-CF	SD	NL	6-6	19	41	5	8	2	0	1	6	.195	5	13	—	—
1970	LF	SD	NL	6-6	28	58	6	9	0	1	1	4	.155	3	14	—	—
1971	LF	SD	NL	6-6	12	17	1	2	0	0	0	1	.118	2	2	—	—
1972	CF	SD	NL	6-6	115	347	38	83	15	7	4	18	.239	35	124	99	—
1973	LF	SD	NL	6-6	122	388	47	109	23	2	9	34	.281	27	163	107	—
1974	LF	CHI	NL	6-6	151	534	70	146	21	7	15	82	.273	46	226	111	36-65
1975	LF	CHI	NL	5-6	153	578	62	156	21	0	12	91	.270	50	213	98	48-65
1976	RF	CHI	NL	4-6	140	537	66	147	17	0	16	67	.274	41	212	106	35-57
1977	CF	CHI	NL	4-6	136	490	56	142	34	5	11	69	.290	43	219	113	38-68
1978	RF	SL	NL	5-6	130	457	44	109	19	8	4	46	.239	33	156	87	59-63
1979	RF	DET	AL	5-7	129	440	50	93	23	1	14	56	.211	30	160	79	—
1980	CF	NY	NL	5-6	94	193	19	49	7	1	3	30	.254	13	67	89	—
1981	LF	CHI	NL	6-6	84	245	27	70	6	2	1	25	.286	22	83	98	—
1982	CF	CHI	NL	5-6	65	116	14	33	2	2	4	30	.284	9	51	116	—
1983	LF-CF	CHI	NL	5-6	63	87	11	17	9	0	0	11	.195	7	26	—	—

MAJOR LEAGUE TOTALS   1441 4528 516 1173 199 36 95 570 .259 366 1729 103   5 yrs

Jeffrey Alan Burroughs   Born Mar 7, 1951   Long Beach, CA
6'1   200 lbs   Batted right

YR	POS	TEAM	LG	FIN	G	AB	R	H	2B	3B	HR	RBI	AVG	BB	TB	OQ	RANK
1970	RF	WAS	AL	6-6	6	12	1	2	0	0	0	1	.167	2	2	—	—
1971	LF-RF	WAS	AL	5-6	59	181	20	42	9	0	5	25	.232	22	66	103	—
1972	LF	TEX	AL	6-6	22	65	4	12	1	0	1	3	.185	5	16	—	—
1973	RF	TEX	AL	6-6	151	526	71	147	17	1	30	85	.279	67	256	131	9-60
1974	RF	TEX	AL	2-6	152	554	84	167	33	2	25	118	.301	91	279	153	3-67
1975	RF	TEX	AL	3-6	152	585	81	132	20	0	29	94	.226	79	239	108	29-66
1976	RF	TEX	AL	4-6	158	604	71	143	22	2	18	86	.237	69	223	104	41-64
1977	LF	ATL	NL	6-6	154	579	91	157	19	1	41	114	.271	86	301	137	8-68
1978	LF	ATL	NL	6-6	153	488	72	147	30	6	23	77	.301	117	258	175	1-63
1979	RF	ATL	NL	6-6	116	397	49	89	14	1	11	47	.224	73	138	106	—
1980	RF	ATL	NL	4-6	99	278	35	73	14	0	13	51	.263	35	126	125	—
1981	LF	SEA	AL	6-7	89	319	32	81	13	1	10	41	.254	41	126	112	32-71
1982	DH-LF	OAK	AL	5-7	113	285	42	79	13	2	16	48	.277	45	144	136	—
1983	DH	OAK	AL	4-7	121	401	43	108	15	1	10	56	.269	47	155	103	—
1984	DH	OAK	AL	4-7	58	71	5	15	1	0	2	8	.211	18	22	—	—
1985	DH	TOR	AL	1-7	86	191	19	49	9	3	6	28	.257	34	82	120	—

MAJOR LEAGUE TOTALS   1689 5536 720 1443 230 20 240 882 .261 831 2433 131   7 yrs

Timothy John Foli   Born Dec 8, 1950   Culver City, CA
6'0 179 lbs Batted right

YR	POS	TEAM	LG	FIN	G	AB	R	H	2B	3B	HR	RBI	AVG	BB	TB	OQ	RANK
1970	SS-3B	NY	NL	3-6	5	11	0	4	0	0	0	1	.364	0	4	—	—
1971	2B-3B	NY	NL	3-6	97	288	32	65	12	2	0	24	.226	18	81	72	—
1972	SS	MON	NL	5-6	149	540	45	130	12	2	2	35	.241	25	152	71	56-57
1973	SS	MON	NL	4-6	126	458	37	110	11	0	2	36	.240	28	127	70	61-61
1974	SS	MON	NL	4-6	121	441	41	112	10	3	0	39	.254	28	128	75	—
1975	SS	MON	NL	5-6	152	572	64	136	25	2	1	29	.238	36	168	74	65-65
1976	SS	MON	NL	6-6	149	546	41	144	36	1	6	54	.264	16	200	88	46-57
1977	SS	MO/SF	NL	5/4	117	425	32	94	22	4	4	30	.221	11	136	66	—
1978	SS	NY	NL	6-6	113	413	37	106	21	1	1	27	.257	14	132	76	—
1979	SS	NY/PT	NL	6/1	136	532	70	153	23	1	1	65	.288	28	181	85	55-62
1980	SS	PIT	NL	3-6	127	495	61	131	22	0	3	38	.265	19	162	79	59-59
1981	SS	PIT	NL	4-6	86	316	32	78	12	2	0	20	.247	17	94	76	66-69
1982	SS	CAL	AL	1-7	150	480	46	121	14	2	3	56	.252	14	148	67	77-77
1983	SS-3B	CAL	AL	5-7	88	330	29	83	10	0	2	29	.252	5	99	63	—
1984	SS-2B	NY	AL	3-7	61	163	8	41	11	0	0	16	.252	2	52	67	—
1985	SS	PIT	NL	6-6	19	37	1	7	0	0	0	2	.189	4	7	—	—

| MAJOR LEAGUE TOTALS | | | | | 1696 | 6047 | 576 | 1515 | 241 | 20 | 25 | 501 | .251 | 265 | 1871 | 76 | 8 yrs |

Lawrence Robert Bowa   Born Dec 6, 1945   Sacramento, CA
5'10 155 lbs Batted both

YR	POS	TEAM	LG	FIN	G	AB	R	H	2B	3B	HR	RBI	AVG	BB	TB	OQ	RANK
1970	SS	PHI	NL	5-6	145	547	50	137	17	6	0	34	.250	21	166	68	55-56
1971	SS	PHI	NL	6-6	159	650	74	162	18	5	0	25	.249	36	190	76	57-58
1972	SS	PHI	NL	6-6	152	579	67	145	11	13	1	31	.250	32	185	82	53-58
1973	SS	PHI	NL	6-6	122	446	42	94	11	3	0	23	.211	24	111	60	—
1974	SS	PHI	NL	3-6	162	669	97	184	19	10	1	36	.275	23	226	81	63-65
1975	SS	PHI	NL	2-6	136	583	79	178	18	9	2	38	.305	24	220	95	51-65
1976	SS	PHI	NL	1-6	156	624	71	155	15	9	0	49	.248	32	188	77	56-57
1977	SS	PHI	NL	1-6	154	624	93	175	19	3	4	41	.280	32	212	81	65-68
1978	SS	PHI	NL	1-6	156	654	78	192	31	5	3	43	.294	24	242	92	54-63
1979	SS	PHI	NL	4-6	147	539	74	130	17	11	0	31	.241	61	169	87	53-62
1980	SS	PHI	NL	1-6	147	540	57	144	16	4	2	39	.267	24	174	80	58-59
1981	SS	PHI	NL	3-6	103	360	34	102	14	3	0	31	.283	26	122	93	58-69
1982	SS	CHI	NL	5-6	142	499	50	123	15	7	0	29	.246	39	152	82	64-66
1983	SS	CHI	NL	5-6	147	499	73	133	20	5	2	43	.267	35	169	88	58-64
1984	SS	CHI	NL	1-6	133	391	33	87	14	2	0	17	.223	28	105	71	—
1985	SS	CH/NY	NL	4/2	86	214	15	50	7	4	0	15	.234	13	65	76	—

| MAJOR LEAGUE TOTALS | | | | | 2247 | 8418 | 987 | 2191 | 262 | 99 | 15 | 525 | .260 | 474 | 2696 | 83 | 13 yrs |

Roger Henry Metzger   Born Oct 10, 1947   Fredericksburg, TX
6'0   165 lbs   Batted both

YR	POS	TEAM	LG	FIN	G	AB	R	H	2B	3B	HR	RBI	AVG	BB	TB	OQ	RANK
1970	SS	CHI	NL	2-6	1	2	0	0	0	0	0	0	.000	0	0	—	—
1971	SS	HOU	NL	4-6	150	562	64	132	14	11	0	26	.235	44	168	80	56-58
1972	SS	HOU	NL	2-6	153	641	84	142	12	3	2	38	.222	60	166	74	56-58
1973	SS	HOU	NL	4-6	154	580	67	145	11	14	1	35	.250	39	187	82	59-61
1974	SS	HOU	NL	4-6	143	572	66	145	18	10	0	30	.253	37	183	82	62-65
1975	SS	HOU	NL	6-6	127	450	54	102	7	9	2	26	.227	41	133	79	63-65
1976	SS	HOU	NL	3-6	152	481	37	101	13	8	0	29	.210	52	130	78	55-57
1977	SS	HOU	NL	3-6	97	269	24	50	9	6	0	16	.186	32	71	70	—
1978	SS	HO/SF	NL	5/3	120	358	28	88	10	2	0	23	.246	24	102	74	—
1979	SS-2B	SF	NL	4-6	94	259	24	65	7	8	0	31	.251	23	88	88	—
1980	SS	SF	NL	5-6	28	27	5	2	0	0	0	0	.074	3	2	—	—

MAJOR LEAGUE TOTALS   1219   4201   453   972   101   71   5   254   .231   355   1230   79   6 yrs

David Ismael Concepcion   Born Jun 17, 1948   Aragua, Venezuela
6'2   155 lbs   Batted right

YR	POS	TEAM	LG	FIN	G	AB	R	H	2B	3B	HR	RBI	AVG	BB	TB	OQ	RANK
1970	SS	CIN	NL	1-6	101	265	38	69	6	3	1	19	.260	23	84	82	—
1971	SS	CIN	NL	4-6	130	327	24	67	4	4	1	20	.205	18	82	63	—
1972	SS	CIN	NL	1-6	119	378	40	79	13	2	2	29	.209	32	102	73	—
1973	SS	CIN	NL	1-6	89	328	39	94	18	3	8	46	.287	21	142	110	—
1974	SS	CIN	NL	2-6	160	594	70	167	25	1	14	82	.281	44	236	104	47-65
1975	SS	CIN	NL	1-6	140	507	62	139	23	1	5	49	.274	39	179	93	52-65
1976	SS	CIN	NL	1-6	152	576	74	162	28	7	9	69	.281	49	231	110	29-57
1977	SS	CIN	NL	2-6	156	572	59	155	26	3	8	64	.271	46	211	92	57-68
1978	SS	CIN	NL	2-6	153	565	75	170	33	4	6	67	.301	51	229	113	35-63
1979	SS	CIN	NL	1-6	149	590	91	166	25	3	16	84	.281	64	245	113	31-62
1980	SS	CIN	NL	3-6	156	622	72	162	31	8	5	77	.260	37	224	90	51-59
1981	SS	CIN	NL	1-6	106	421	57	129	28	0	5	67	.306	37	172	116	26-69
1982	SS	CIN	NL	6-6	147	572	48	164	25	4	5	53	.287	45	212	101	45-66
1983	SS	CIN	NL	6-6	143	528	54	123	22	0	1	47	.233	56	148	79	63-64
1984	SS-3B	CIN	NL	5-6	154	531	46	130	26	1	4	58	.245	52	170	89	46-53
1985	SS	CIN	NL	2-6	155	560	59	141	19	2	7	48	.252	50	185	89	57-65
1986	SS-1B	CIN	NL	2-6	90	311	42	81	13	2	3	30	.260	26	107	90	—
1987	2B-1B	CIN	NL	2-6	104	279	32	89	15	0	1	33	.319	28	107	105	—
1988	2B-1B	CIN	NL	2-6	84	197	11	39	9	0	0	8	.198	18	48	70	—

MAJOR LEAGUE TOTALS   2488   8723   993   2326   389   48   101   950   .267   736   3114   99   12 yrs

Kenneth Wayne Singleton   Born Jun 10, 1947   New York, NY
6'4   210 lbs   Batted both

YR	POS	TEAM	LG	FIN	G	AB	R	H	2B	3B	HR	RBI	AVG	BB	TB	OQ	RANK
1970	RF-LF	NY	NL	3-6	69	198	22	52	8	0	5	26	.263	30	75	107	—
1971	RF	NY	NL	3-6	115	298	34	73	5	0	13	46	.245	61	117	129	—
1972	RF	MON	NL	5-6	142	507	77	139	23	2	14	50	.274	70	208	124	20-58
1973	RF	MON	NL	4-6	162	560	100	169	26	2	23	103	.302	123	268	157	4-61
1974	RF	MON	NL	4-6	148	511	68	141	20	2	9	74	.276	93	192	122	19-65
1975	RF	BAL	AL	2-6	155	586	88	176	37	4	15	55	.300	118	266	145	5-66
1976	LF-DH	BAL	AL	2-6	154	544	62	151	25	2	13	70	.278	79	219	124	14-64
1977	RF	BAL	AL	2-7	152	536	90	176	24	0	24	99	.328	107	272	155	2-81
1978	RF	BAL	AL	4-7	149	502	67	147	21	2	20	81	.293	98	232	143	5-83
1979	RF-DH	BAL	AL	1-7	159	570	93	168	29	1	35	111	.295	109	304	149	3-75
1980	RF	BAL	AL	2-7	156	583	85	177	28	3	24	104	.304	92	283	137	6-69
1981	RF-DH	BAL	AL	2-7	103	363	48	101	16	1	13	49	.278	61	158	133	12-71
1982	DH	BAL	AL	2-7	156	561	71	141	27	2	14	77	.251	86	214	106	43-77
1983	DH	BAL	AL	1-7	151	507	52	140	21	3	18	84	.276	99	221	130	9-70
1984	DH	BAL	AL	5-7	111	363	28	78	7	1	6	36	.215	37	105	75	—

MAJOR LEAGUE TOTALS   2082 7189 985 2029 317 25 246 1065 .282 1263 3134 135 12 yrs

Cesar Cedeno   Born Feb 25, 1951   Santo Domingo, DR
6'2   175 lbs   Batted right

YR	POS	TEAM	LG	FIN	G	AB	R	H	2B	3B	HR	RBI	AVG	BB	TB	OQ	RANK
1970	CF	HOU	NL	4-6	90	355	46	110	21	4	7	42	.310	15	160	107	—
1971	CF	HOU	NL	4-6	161	611	85	161	40	6	10	81	.264	25	243	97	43-58
1972	CF	HOU	NL	2-6	139	559	103	179	39	8	22	82	.320	56	300	153	5-58
1973	CF	HOU	NL	4-6	139	525	86	168	35	2	25	70	.320	41	282	143	11-61
1974	CF	HOU	NL	4-6	160	610	95	164	29	5	26	102	.269	64	281	123	18-65
1975	CF	HOU	NL	6-6	131	500	93	144	31	3	13	63	.288	62	220	125	24-65
1976	CF	HOU	NL	3-6	150	575	89	171	26	5	18	83	.297	55	261	128	17-57
1977	CF	HOU	NL	3-6	141	530	92	148	36	8	14	71	.279	47	242	113	37-68
1978	CF	HOU	NL	5-6	50	192	31	54	8	2	7	23	.281	15	87	118	—
1979	1B-CF	HOU	NL	2-6	132	470	57	123	27	4	6	54	.262	64	176	107	37-62
1980	CF	HOU	NL	1-6	137	499	71	154	32	8	10	73	.309	66	232	138	5-59
1981	1B-CF	HOU	NL	3-6	82	306	42	83	19	0	5	34	.271	24	117	103	45-69
1982	CF	CIN	NL	6-6	138	492	52	142	35	1	8	57	.289	41	203	112	30-66
1983	RF-1B	CIN	NL	6-6	98	332	40	77	16	0	9	39	.232	33	120	94	—
1984	LF-1B	CIN	NL	5-6	110	380	59	105	24	2	10	47	.276	25	163	110	—
1985	1B-LF	CN/SL	NL	2/1	111	296	38	86	16	1	9	49	.291	24	131	117	—
1986	LF	LA	NL	5-6	37	78	5	18	2	1	0	6	.231	7	22	—	—

MAJOR LEAGUE TOTALS   2006 7310 1084 2087 436 60 199 976 .285 664 3240 122 11 yrs

John Milton Rivers

Born Oct 31, 1948   Miami, FL

5'10   165 lbs   Batted left

YR	POS	TEAM	LG	FIN	G	AB	R	H	2B	3B	HR	RBI	AVG	BB	TB	OQ	RANK
1970	RF	CAL	AL	3-6	17	25	6	8	2	0	0	3	.320	3	10	—	—
1971	CF-RF	CAL	AL	4-6	78	268	31	71	12	2	1	12	.265	19	90	90	—
1972	CF-RF	CAL	AL	5-6	58	159	18	34	6	2	0	7	.214	8	44	73	—
1973	CF	CAL	AL	4-6	30	129	26	45	6	4	0	16	.349	8	59	123	—
1974	CF	CAL	AL	6-6	118	466	69	133	19	11	3	31	.285	39	183	107	40-67
1975	CF	CAL	AL	6-6	155	616	70	175	17	13	1	53	.284	43	221	92	49-66
1976	CF	NY	AL	1-6	137	590	95	184	31	8	8	67	.312	13	255	108	35-64
1977	CF	NY	AL	1-7	138	565	79	184	18	5	12	69	.326	18	248	103	53-81
1978	CF	NY	AL	1-7	141	559	78	148	25	8	11	48	.265	29	222	94	65-83
1979	CF	NY/TX	AL	4/3	132	533	72	156	27	8	9	50	.293	22	226	95	54-75
1980	CF	TEX	AL	4-7	147	630	96	210	32	6	7	60	.333	20	275	104	41-69
1981	CF	TEX	AL	2-7	99	399	62	114	21	2	3	26	.286	24	148	96	55-71
1982	DH	TEX	AL	6-7	19	68	6	16	1	1	1	4	.235	0	22	—	—
1983	DH-LF	TEX	AL	3-7	96	309	37	88	17	0	1	20	.285	11	108	80	—
1984	DH-LF	TEX	AL	7-7	102	313	40	94	13	1	4	33	.300	9	121	89	—

| MAJOR LEAGUE TOTALS | | | | | 1467 | 5629 | 785 | 1660 | 247 | 71 | 61 | 499 | .295 | 266 | 2232 | 100 | 8 yrs |

Jose Cruz

Born Aug 8, 1947   Arroyo, PR

6'0   170 lbs   Batted left

YR	POS	TEAM	LG	FIN	G	AB	R	H	2B	3B	HR	RBI	AVG	BB	TB	OQ	RANK
1970	RF	SL	NL	4-6	6	17	2	6	1	0	0	1	.353	4	7	—	—
1971	CF	SL	NL	2-6	83	292	46	80	13	2	9	27	.274	49	124	133	—
1972	CF	SL	NL	4-6	117	332	33	78	14	4	2	23	.235	36	106	91	—
1973	CF	SL	NL	2-6	132	406	51	92	22	5	10	57	.227	51	154	103	—
1974	RF-LF	SL	NL	2-6	107	161	24	42	4	3	5	20	.261	20	67	116	—
1975	RF	HOU	NL	6-6	120	315	44	81	15	2	9	49	.257	52	127	121	—
1976	RF	HOU	NL	3-6	133	439	49	133	21	5	4	61	.303	53	176	122	22-57
1977	RF	HOU	NL	3-6	157	579	87	173	31	10	17	87	.299	69	275	127	17-68
1978	RF	HOU	NL	5-6	153	565	79	178	34	9	10	83	.315	57	260	131	14-63
1979	LF	HOU	NL	2-6	157	558	73	161	33	7	9	72	.289	72	235	119	22-62
1980	LF	HOU	NL	1-6	160	612	79	185	29	7	11	91	.302	60	261	120	21-59
1981	LF	HOU	NL	3-6	107	409	53	109	16	5	13	55	.267	35	174	113	31-69
1982	LF	HOU	NL	5-6	155	570	62	157	27	2	9	68	.275	60	215	107	38-66
1983	LF	HOU	NL	3-6	160	594	85	189	28	8	14	92	.318	65	275	132	10-64
1984	LF	HOU	NL	2-6	160	600	96	187	28	13	12	95	.312	73	277	136	8-53
1985	LF	HOU	NL	3-6	141	544	69	163	34	4	9	79	.300	43	232	115	25-65
1986	LF	HOU	NL	1-6	141	479	48	133	22	4	10	72	.278	55	193	112	27-49
1987	LF	HOU	NL	3-6	126	365	47	88	17	4	11	38	.241	36	146	97	—
1988	DH-LF	NY	AL	5-7	38	80	9	16	2	0	1	7	.200	8	21	—	—

| MAJOR LEAGUE TOTALS | | | | | 2353 | 7917 | 1036 | 2251 | 391 | 94 | 165 | 1077 | .284 | 898 | 3325 | 121 | 11 yrs |

Don Edward Baylor   Born Jun 28, 1949   Austin, TX
6'1 190 lbs Batted right

YR	POS	TEAM	LG	FIN	G	AB	R	H	2B	3B	HR	RBI	AVG	BB	TB	OQ	RANK
1970	RF-CF	BAL	AL	1-6	8	17	4	4	0	0	0	4	.235	2	4	—	—
1971	RF	BAL	AL	1-6	1	2	0	0	0	0	0	1	.000	2	0	—	—
1972	RF-LF	BAL	AL	3-6	102	320	33	81	13	3	11	38	.253	29	133	118	—
1973	LF	BAL	AL	1-6	118	405	64	116	20	4	11	51	.286	35	177	113	—
1974	LF	BAL	AL	1-6	137	489	66	133	22	1	10	59	.272	43	187	103	43-67
1975	LF	BAL	AL	2-6	145	524	79	148	21	6	25	76	.282	53	256	127	13-66
1976	RF-1B	OAK	AL	2-6	157	595	85	147	25	1	15	68	.247	58	219	101	46-64
1977	LF-DH	CAL	AL	5-7	154	561	87	141	27	0	25	75	.251	62	243	107	44-81
1978	DH-LF	CAL	AL	2-7	158	591	103	151	26	0	34	99	.255	56	279	117	30-83
1979	LF-DH	CAL	AL	1-7	162	628	120	186	33	3	36	139	.296	71	333	132	11-75
1980	LF-DH	CAL	AL	6-7	90	340	39	85	12	2	5	51	.250	24	116	82	—
1981	DH	CAL	AL	5-7	103	377	52	90	18	1	17	66	.239	42	161	113	30-71
1982	DH	CAL	AL	1-7	157	608	80	160	24	1	24	93	.263	57	258	104	46-77
1983	DH	NY	AL	3-7	144	534	82	162	33	3	21	85	.303	40	264	122	19-70
1984	DH	NY	AL	3-7	134	493	84	129	29	1	27	89	.262	38	241	115	26-68
1985	DH	NY	AL	2-7	142	477	70	110	24	1	23	91	.231	52	205	103	47-75
1986	DH	BOS	AL	1-7	160	585	93	139	23	1	31	94	.238	62	257	104	44-78
1987	DH	BO/MN	AL	5/1	128	388	67	95	9	0	16	63	.245	45	152	94	—
1988	DH	OAK	AL	1-7	92	264	28	58	7	0	7	34	.220	34	86	89	—

| MAJOR LEAGUE TOTALS | | | | | 2292 | 8198 | 1236 | 2135 | 366 | 28 | 338 | 1276 | .260 | 805 | 3571 | 112 | 12 yrs |

Gregory Michael Luzinski   Born Nov 22, 1950 Chicago, IL
6'1 200 lbs Batted right

YR	POS	TEAM	LG	FIN	G	AB	R	H	2B	3B	HR	RBI	AVG	BB	TB	OQ	RANK
1970	1B	PHI	NL	5-6	8	12	0	2	0	0	0	0	.167	3	2	—	—
1971	1B	PHI	NL	6-6	28	100	13	30	8	0	3	15	.300	12	47	138	—
1972	LF	PHI	NL	6-6	150	563	66	158	33	5	18	68	.281	42	255	120	25-58
1973	LF	PHI	NL	6-6	161	610	76	174	26	4	29	97	.285	51	295	125	19-61
1974	LF	PHI	NL	3-6	85	302	29	82	14	1	7	48	.272	29	119	107	—
1975	LF	PHI	NL	2-6	161	596	85	179	35	3	34	120	.300	89	322	156	2-65
1976	LF	PHI	NL	1-6	149	533	74	162	28	1	21	95	.304	50	255	134	9-57
1977	LF	PHI	NL	1-6	149	554	99	171	35	3	39	130	.309	80	329	160	3-68
1978	LF	PHI	NL	1-6	155	540	85	143	32	2	35	101	.265	100	284	154	4-63
1979	LF	PHI	NL	4-6	137	452	47	114	23	1	18	81	.252	56	193	114	30-62
1980	LF	PHI	NL	1-6	106	368	44	84	19	1	19	56	.228	60	162	125	—
1981	DH	CHI	AL	3-7	104	378	55	100	15	1	21	62	.265	58	180	137	8-71
1982	DH	CHI	AL	3-7	159	583	87	170	37	1	18	102	.292	89	263	126	17-77
1983	DH	CHI	AL	1-7	144	502	73	128	26	1	32	95	.255	70	252	129	12-70
1984	DH	CHI	AL	5-7	125	412	47	98	13	0	13	58	.238	56	150	99	—

| MAJOR LEAGUE TOTALS | | | | | 1821 | 6505 | 880 | 1795 | 344 | 24 | 307 | 1128 | .276 | 845 | 3108 | 136 | 10 yrs |

Robert Anthony Grich Born Jan 15, 1949 Muskegon, MI
6'2 180 lbs Batted right

YR	POS	TEAM	LG	FIN	G	AB	R	H	2B	3B	HR	RBI	AVG	BB	TB	OQ	RANK
1970	SS-2B	BAL	AL	1-6	30	95	11	20	1	3	0	8	.211	9	27	75	—
1971	SS-2B	BAL	AL	1-6	7	30	7	9	0	0	1	6	.300	5	12	—	—
1972	SS-2B	BAL	AL	3-6	133	460	66	128	21	3	12	50	.278	53	191	128	16-56
1973	2B	BAL	AL	1-6	162	581	82	146	29	7	12	50	.251	107	225	117	17-60
1974	2B	BAL	AL	1-6	160	582	92	153	29	6	19	82	.263	90	251	127	12-67
1975	2B	BAL	AL	2-6	150	524	81	136	26	4	13	57	.260	107	209	126	15-66
1976	2B	BAL	AL	2-6	144	518	93	138	31	4	13	54	.266	86	216	130	9-64
1977	2B	CAL	AL	5-7	52	181	24	44	6	0	7	23	.243	37	71	116	—
1978	2B	CAL	AL	2-7	144	487	68	122	16	2	6	42	.251	75	160	99	51-83
1979	2B	CAL	AL	1-7	153	534	78	157	30	5	30	101	.294	59	287	133	10-75
1980	2B	CAL	AL	6-7	150	498	60	135	22	2	14	62	.271	84	203	118	24-69
1981	2B	CAL	AL	5-7	100	352	56	107	14	2	22	61	.304	40	191	150	2-71
1982	2B	CAL	AL	1-7	145	506	74	132	28	5	19	65	.261	82	227	122	20-77
1983	2B	CAL	AL	5-7	120	387	65	113	17	0	16	62	.292	76	178	138	—
1984	2B-1B	CAL	AL	2-7	116	363	60	93	15	1	18	58	.256	57	164	123	—
1985	2B-1B	CAL	AL	2-7	144	479	74	116	17	3	13	53	.242	81	178	105	42-75
1986	2B-1B	CAL	AL	1-7	98	313	42	84	18	0	9	30	.268	39	129	107	—

MAJOR LEAGUE TOTALS | | | | | 2008 | 6890 | 1033 | 1833 | 320 | 47 | 224 | 864 | .266 | 1087 | 2919 | 123 | 11 yrs

Leonard Shenoff Randle Born Feb 12, 1949 Long Beach, CA
5'10 169 lbs Batted both

YR	POS	TEAM	LG	FIN	G	AB	R	H	2B	3B	HR	RBI	AVG	BB	TB	OQ	RANK
1971	2B	WAS	AL	5-6	75	215	27	47	11	0	2	13	.219	24	64	85	—
1972	2B	TEX	AL	6-6	74	249	23	48	13	0	2	21	.193	13	67	69	—
1973	2B-CF	TEX	AL	6-6	10	29	3	6	1	1	1	1	.207	0	12	—	—
1974	3B-2B	TEX	AL	2-6	151	520	65	157	17	4	1	49	.302	29	185	94	48-67
1975	2B-CF	TEX	AL	3-6	156	601	85	166	24	7	4	57	.276	57	216	97	46-66
1976	2B-LF	TEX	AL	4-6	142	539	53	121	11	6	1	51	.224	46	147	76	64-64
1977	3B-2B	NY	NL	6-6	136	513	78	156	22	7	5	27	.304	65	207	114	35-68
1978	3B	NY	NL	6-6	132	437	53	102	16	8	2	35	.233	64	140	97	49-63
1979	CF-DH	NY	AL	4-7	20	39	2	7	0	0	0	3	.179	3	7	—	—
1980	3B-2B	CHI	NL	6-6	130	489	67	135	19	6	5	39	.276	50	181	104	38-59
1981	3B-2B	SEA	AL	6-7	82	273	22	63	9	1	4	25	.231	17	86	78	—
1982	DH-3B	SEA	AL	4-7	30	46	10	8	2	0	0	1	.174	4	10	—	—

MAJOR LEAGUE TOTALS | | | | | 1138 | 3950 | 488 | 1016 | 145 | 40 | 27 | 322 | .257 | 372 | 1322 | 97 | 6 yrs

Richard Walter Zisk   Born Feb 6, 1949   Brooklyn, NY
6'1   200 lbs   Batted right

YR	POS	TEAM	LG	FIN	G	AB	R	H	2B	3B	HR	RBI	AVG	BB	TB	OQ	RANK
1971	LF-RF	PIT	NL	1-6	7	15	2	3	1	0	1	2	.200	4	7	—	—
1972	LF	PIT	NL	1-6	17	37	4	7	3	0	0	4	.189	7	10	—	—
1973	RF	PIT	NL	3-6	103	333	44	108	23	7	10	54	.324	21	175	137	—
1974	RF	PIT	NL	1-6	149	536	75	168	30	3	17	100	.313	65	255	138	8-65
1975	LF	PIT	NL	1-6	147	504	69	146	27	3	20	75	.290	68	239	135	13-65
1976	LF	PIT	NL	2-6	155	581	91	168	35	2	21	89	.289	52	270	127	18-57
1977	LF-DH	CHI	AL	3-7	141	531	78	154	17	6	30	101	.290	55	273	128	15-81
1978	LF-DH	TEX	AL	2-7	140	511	68	134	19	1	22	85	.262	58	221	114	35-83
1979	RF	TEX	AL	3-7	144	503	69	132	21	1	18	64	.262	57	209	104	40-75
1980	DH-RF	TEX	AL	4-7	135	448	48	130	17	1	19	77	.290	39	206	114	—
1981	DH	SEA	AL	6-7	94	357	42	111	12	1	16	43	.311	28	173	130	15-71
1982	DH	SEA	AL	4-7	131	503	61	147	28	1	21	62	.292	49	240	120	24-77
1983	DH	SEA	AL	7-7	90	285	30	69	12	0	12	36	.242	30	117	102	—

| MAJOR LEAGUE TOTALS | | | | | 1453 | 5144 | 681 | 1477 | 245 | 26 | 207 | 792 | .287 | 533 | 2395 | 125 | 8 yrs |

Darrell Ray Porter   Born Jan 17, 1952
6'0   193 lbs   Batted left

YR	POS	TEAM	LG	FIN	G	AB	R	H	2B	3B	HR	RBI	AVG	BB	TB	OQ	RANK
1971	C	MIL	AL	6-6	22	70	4	15	2	0	2	9	.214	9	23	—	—
1972	C	MIL	AL	6-6	18	56	2	7	1	0	1	2	.125	5	11	—	—
1973	C-DH	MIL	AL	5-6	117	350	50	89	19	2	16	67	.254	57	160	128	—
1974	C	MIL	AL	5-6	131	432	59	104	15	4	12	56	.241	50	163	104	—
1975	C	MIL	AL	5-6	130	409	66	95	12	5	18	60	.232	89	171	128	11-66
1976	C	MIL	AL	6-6	119	389	43	81	14	1	5	32	.208	51	112	87	—
1977	C	KC	AL	1-7	130	425	61	117	21	3	16	60	.275	53	192	117	—
1978	C	KC	AL	1-7	150	520	77	138	27	6	18	78	.265	75	231	123	21-83
1979	C	KC	AL	2-7	157	533	101	155	23	10	20	112	.291	121	258	145	5-75
1980	C-DH	KC	AL	1-7	118	418	51	104	14	2	7	51	.249	69	143	100	50-69
1981	C	SL	NL	1-6	61	174	22	39	10	2	6	31	.224	39	71	133	—
1982	C	SL	NL	1-6	120	373	46	86	18	5	12	48	.231	66	150	121	—
1983	C	SL	NL	4-6	145	443	57	116	24	3	15	66	.262	68	191	125	17-64
1984	C	SL	NL	3-6	127	422	56	98	16	3	11	68	.232	60	153	106	—
1985	C	SL	NL	1-6	84	240	30	53	12	2	10	36	.221	41	99	119	—
1986	C-DH	TEX	AL	2-7	68	155	21	41	6	0	12	29	.265	22	83	134	—
1987	DH	TEX	AL	6-7	85	130	19	31	3	0	7	21	.238	30	55	120	—

| MAJOR LEAGUE TOTALS | | | | | 1782 | 5539 | 765 | 1369 | 237 | 48 | 188 | 826 | .247 | 905 | 2266 | 124 | 5 yrs |

Benjamin Ambrosio Oglivie

Born Feb 11, 1949 Colon, Panama

6'2 160 lbs Batted left

YR	POS	TEAM	LG	FIN	G	AB	R	H	2B	3B	HR	RBI	AVG	BB	TB	OQ	RANK
1971	LF	BOS	AL	3-6	14	38	2	10	3	0	0	4	.263	0	13	—	—
1972	LF-RF	BOS	AL	2-6	94	253	27	61	10	2	8	30	.241	18	99	106	—
1973	RF-DH	BOS	AL	2-6	58	147	16	32	9	1	2	9	.218	9	49	78	—
1974	LF-1B	DET	AL	6-6	92	252	28	68	11	3	4	29	.270	16	138	100	—
1975	LF	DET	AL	6-6	100	332	45	95	14	1	9	36	.286	11	150	121	—
1976	RF-LF	DET	AL	5-6	115	305	36	87	12	3	15	47	.285	11	150	121	—
1977	RF	DET	AL	4-7	132	450	63	118	24	2	21	61	.262	40	209	110	33-81
1978	LF-DH	MIL	AL	3-7	128	469	71	142	29	4	18	72	.303	52	233	134	8-83
1979	LF	MIL	AL	2-7	139	514	88	145	30	4	29	81	.282	48	270	125	16-75
1980	LF	MIL	AL	3-7	156	592	94	180	26	2	41	118	.304	54	333	140	3-69
1981	LF	MIL	AL	1-7	107	400	53	97	15	2	14	72	.243	37	158	103	47-71
1982	LF	MIL	AL	1-7	159	602	92	147	22	1	34	102	.244	70	273	112	38-77
1983	LF	MIL	AL	5-7	125	411	49	115	19	3	13	66	.280	60	179	120	—
1984	LF	MIL	AL	7-7	131	461	49	121	16	2	12	60	.262	44	177	98	51-68
1985	RF	MIL	AL	6-7	101	341	40	99	17	2	10	61	.290	37	150	114	—
1986	LF-DH	MIL	AL	6-7	103	346	31	98	20	1	5	53	.283	30	135	97	—

| MAJOR LEAGUE TOTALS | | | | | 1754 | 5913 | 784 | 1615 | 277 | 33 | 235 | 901 | .273 | 560 | 2663 | 117 | 7 yrs |

Cecil Celester Cooper

Born Dec 20, 1949 Brenham, TX

6'2 165 lbs Batted left

YR	POS	TEAM	LG	FIN	G	AB	R	H	2B	3B	HR	RBI	AVG	BB	TB	OQ	RANK
1971	1B	BOS	AL	3-6	14	42	9	13	4	1	0	3	.310	5	19	—	—
1972	1B	BOS	AL	2-6	12	17	0	4	1	0	0	2	.235	2	5	—	—
1973	1B	BOS	AL	2-6	30	101	12	24	2	0	3	11	.238	7	35	84	—
1974	1B-DH	BOS	AL	3-6	121	414	55	114	24	1	8	43	.275	32	164	104	—
1975	DH-1B	BOS	AL	1-6	106	305	49	95	17	6	14	44	.311	19	166	136	—
1976	1B-DH	BOS	AL	3-6	123	451	66	127	22	6	15	78	.282	16	206	112	—
1977	1B	MIL	AL	6-7	160	643	86	193	31	7	20	78	.300	28	298	106	45-81
1978	1B-DH	MIL	AL	3-7	107	407	60	127	23	2	13	54	.312	32	193	124	—
1979	1B-DH	MIL	AL	2-7	150	590	83	182	44	1	24	106	.308	56	300	126	15-75
1980	1B	MIL	AL	3-7	153	622	96	219	33	4	25	122	.352	39	335	138	5-69
1981	1B	MIL	AL	1-7	106	416	70	133	35	1	12	60	.320	28	206	132	13-71
1982	1B	MIL	AL	1-7	155	654	104	205	38	3	32	121	.313	32	345	124	18-77
1983	1B	MIL	AL	5-7	160	661	106	203	37	3	30	126	.307	37	336	121	20-70
1984	1B-DH	MIL	AL	7-7	148	603	63	166	28	3	11	67	.275	27	233	89	58-68
1985	1B-DH	MIL	AL	6-7	154	631	82	185	39	8	16	99	.293	30	288	105	43-75
1986	1B-DH	MIL	AL	6-7	134	542	46	140	24	1	12	75	.258	41	202	88	69-78
1987	DH	MIL	AL	3-7	63	250	25	62	13	0	6	36	.248	17	93	82	—

| MAJOR LEAGUE TOTALS | | | | | 1896 | 7349 | 1012 | 2192 | 415 | 47 | 241 | 1125 | .298 | 448 | 3424 | 114 | 9 yrs |

Carroll Christopher Chambliss Born Dec 26, 1948 Dayton, OH
6'1 195 lbs Batted left

YR	POS	TEAM	LG	FIN	G	AB	R	H	2B	3B	HR	RBI	AVG	BB	TB	OQ	RANK
1971	1B	CLE	AL	6-6	111	415	49	114	20	4	9	48	.275	40	169	112	—
1972	1B	CLE	AL	5-6	121	466	51	136	27	2	6	44	.292	26	185	112	30-56
1973	1B	CLE	AL	6-6	155	572	70	156	30	2	11	53	.273	58	223	104	31-60
1974	1B	CL/NY	AL	4/2	127	467	46	119	20	3	6	50	.255	28	163	88	57-67
1975	1B	NY	AL	3-6	150	562	66	171	38	4	9	72	.304	29	244	108	30-66
1976	1B	NY	AL	1-6	156	641	79	188	32	6	17	96	.293	27	283	112	32-64
1977	1B	NY	AL	1-7	157	600	90	172	32	6	17	90	.287	45	267	107	41-81
1978	1B	NY	AL	1-7	162	625	81	171	26	3	12	90	.274	41	239	95	63-83
1979	1B-DH	NY	AL	4-7	149	554	61	155	27	3	18	63	.280	34	242	100	47-75
1980	1B	ATL	NL	4-6	158	602	83	170	37	2	18	72	.282	49	265	116	25-59
1981	1B	ATL	NL	5-6	107	404	44	110	25	2	8	51	.272	44	163	114	29-69
1982	1B	ATL	NL	1-6	157	534	57	144	25	2	20	86	.270	57	233	119	21-66
1983	1B	ATL	NL	2-6	131	447	59	125	24	3	20	78	.280	63	215	136	6-64
1984	1B	ATL	NL	2-6	135	389	47	100	14	0	9	44	.257	58	141	111	—
1985	1B	ATL	NL	5-6	101	170	16	40	7	0	3	21	.235	18	56	90	—
1986	1B	ATL	NL	6-6	97	122	13	38	8	0	2	14	.311	15	52	124	—
1988	PH	NY	AL	5-7	1	1	0	0	0	0	0	0	.000	0	0	—	—
MAJOR LEAGUE TOTALS					2175	7571	912	2109	392	42	185	972	.279	632	3140	109	12 yrs

David Arthur Kingman Born Dec 21, 1948 Pendleton, OR
6'6 210 lbs Batted right

YR	POS	TEAM	LG	FIN	G	AB	R	H	2B	3B	HR	RBI	AVG	BB	TB	OQ	RANK
1971	1B-LF	SF	NL	1-6	41	115	17	32	10	2	6	24	.278	9	64	144	—
1972	3B-1B	SF	NL	5-6	135	472	65	106	17	4	29	83	.225	51	218	120	24-58
1973	3B-1B	SF	NL	3-6	112	305	54	62	10	1	24	55	.203	41	146	121	—
1974	1B-3B	SF	NL	5-6	121	350	41	78	18	2	18	55	.223	37	154	111	—
1975	LF-1B	NY	NL	3-6	134	502	65	116	22	1	36	88	.231	34	248	115	33-65
1976	LF-1B	NY	NL	3-6	123	474	70	113	14	1	37	86	.238	28	240	121	24-57
1977	LF-1B	NY/SD	NL	6/5	114	379	38	84	16	0	20	67	.222	25	160	94	—
1977	1B-DH	CA/NY	AL	4/1	18	60	9	13	4	0	6	11	.217	3	35	—	—
1978	LF	CHI	NL	3-6	119	395	65	105	17	4	28	79	.266	39	214	139	—
1979	LF	CHI	NL	5-6	145	532	97	153	19	5	48	115	.288	45	326	151	5-62
1980	LF	CHI	NL	6-6	81	255	31	71	8	0	18	57	.278	21	133	133	—
1981	1B-LF	NY	NL	5-6	100	353	40	78	11	3	22	59	.221	55	161	128	14-69
1982	1B	NY	NL	6-6	149	535	80	109	9	1	37	99	.204	59	231	109	34-66
1983	1B	NY	NL	6-6	100	248	25	49	7	0	13	29	.198	22	95	92	—
1984	DH	OAK	AL	4-7	147	549	68	147	23	1	35	118	.268	44	277	120	21-68
1985	DH	OAK	AL	4-7	158	592	66	141	16	0	30	91	.238	62	247	101	51-75
1986	DH	OAK	AL	3-7	144	561	70	118	19	0	35	94	.210	33	242	90	65-78
MAJOR LEAGUE TOTALS					1941	6677	901	1575	240	25	442	1210	.236	608	3191	117	9 yrs

Franklin Cristostomo Taveras   Born Dec 24, 1949 Las Matas, DR
6'0 155 lbs Batted right

YR	POS	TEAM	LG	FIN	G	AB	R	H	2B	3B	HR	RBI	AVG	BB	TB	OQ	RANK
1971	PR	PIT	NL	1-6	1	0	0	0	0	0	0	0	—	0	0	—	—
1972	SS	PIT	NL	1-6	4	3	0	0	0	0	0	0	.000	1	0	—	—
1974	SS	PIT	NL	1-6	126	333	33	82	4	2	0	26	.246	25	90	73	—
1975	SS	PIT	NL	1-6	134	378	44	80	9	4	0	23	.212	37	97	71	—
1976	SS	PIT	NL	2-6	144	519	76	134	8	6	0	24	.258	44	154	84	51-57
1977	SS	PIT	NL	2-6	147	544	72	137	20	10	1	29	.252	38	180	80	67-68
1978	SS	PIT	NL	2-6	157	654	81	182	31	9	0	38	.278	29	231	88	58-63
1979	SS	PT/NY	NL	1/6	164	680	93	178	29	9	1	34	.262	33	228	80	58-62
1980	SS	NY	NL	5-6	141	562	65	157	27	0	0	25	.279	23	184	81	56-59
1981	SS	NY	NL	5-6	84	283	30	65	11	3	0	11	.230	12	82	70	—
1982	SS-2B	MON	NL	3-6	48	87	9	14	5	1	0	4	.161	7	21	—	—

MAJOR LEAGUE TOTALS   1150 4043 503 1029 144 44   2 214 .255 249 1267 83   5 yrs

Chris Edward Speier   Born Jun 28, 1950 Alameda, CA
6'1 175 lbs Batted right

YR	POS	TEAM	LG	FIN	G	AB	R	H	2B	3B	HR	RBI	AVG	BB	TB	OQ	RANK
1971	SS	SF	NL	1-6	157	601	74	141	17	6	8	46	.235	56	194	89	49-58
1972	SS	SF	NL	5-6	150	562	74	151	25	2	15	71	.269	82	225	122	21-58
1973	SS	SF	NL	3-6	153	542	58	135	17	4	11	71	.249	66	193	100	45-61
1974	SS	SF	NL	5-6	141	501	55	125	19	5	9	53	.250	62	181	102	50-65
1975	SS	SF	NL	3-6	141	487	60	132	30	5	10	69	.271	70	202	121	28-65
1976	SS	SF	NL	4-6	145	495	51	112	18	4	3	40	.226	60	147	88	44-57
1977	SS	SF/MO	NL	4/5	145	548	59	128	31	6	5	38	.234	67	186	90	59-68
1978	SS	MON	NL	4-6	150	501	47	126	18	3	5	51	.251	60	165	96	51-63
1979	SS	MON	NL	2-6	113	344	31	78	13	1	7	26	.227	43	114	91	—
1980	SS	MON	NL	2-6	128	388	35	103	14	4	1	32	.265	52	128	101	—
1981	SS	MON	NL	2-6	96	307	33	69	10	2	2	25	.225	38	89	87	60-69
1982	SS	MON	NL	3-6	156	530	41	136	26	4	7	60	.257	47	191	97	54-66
1983	SS-3B	MON	NL	3-6	88	261	31	67	12	2	2	22	.257	29	89	96	—
1984	SS	MO/SL	NL	5/3	63	158	10	27	7	1	3	9	.171	10	45	68	—
1984	SS	MIN	AL	2-7	12	33	2	7	0	0	0	1	.212	3	7	—	—
1985	SS-3B	CHI	NL	4-6	106	218	16	53	11	0	4	24	.243	17	76	90	—
1986	3B-SS	CHI	NL	5-6	95	155	21	44	8	0	6	23	.284	15	70	119	—
1987	2B-3B	SF	NL	1-6	111	317	39	79	13	0	11	39	.249	42	125	103	—
1988	2B-3B	SF	NL	4-6	82	171	26	37	9	1	3	18	.216	23	57	100	—
1989	SS-3B	SF	NL	1-6	28	37	7	9	4	0	0	2	.243	5	13	—	—

MAJOR LEAGUE TOTALS   2260 7156 770 1759 302 50 112 720 .246 847 2497 99 10 yrs

William Alex North   Born May 15, 1948 Seattle, WA
5'11   185 lbs   Batted both

YR	POS	TEAM	LG	FIN	G	AB	R	H	2B	3B	HR	RBI	AVG	BB	TB	OQ	RANK
1971	RF	CHI	NL	3-6	8	16	3	6	0	0	0	0	.375	4	6	—	—
1972	CF-RF	CHI	NL	2-6	66	127	22	23	2	3	0	4	.181	13	31	69	—
1973	CF	OAK	AL	1-6	146	554	98	158	10	5	5	34	.285	78	193	105	28-60
1974	CF	OAK	AL	1-6	149	543	79	141	20	5	4	33	.260	69	183	100	46-67
1975	CF	OAK	AL	1-6	140	524	74	143	17	5	1	43	.273	81	173	103	36-66
1976	CF	OAK	AL	2-6	154	590	91	163	20	5	2	31	.276	73	199	104	39-64
1977	CF	OAK	AL	7-7	56	184	32	48	3	3	1	9	.261	32	60	99	—
1978	CF	OAK	AL	6-7	24	52	5	11	4	0	0	5	.212	9	15	—	—
1978	CF	LA	NL	1-6	110	304	54	71	10	0	0	10	.234	65	81	100	—
1979	CF	SF	NL	4-6	142	460	87	119	15	4	5	30	.259	96	157	115	27-62
1980	CF	SF	NL	5-6	128	415	73	104	12	1	1	19	.251	81	121	104	39-59
1981	CF	SF	NL	4-6	46	131	22	29	7	0	1	12	.221	26	39	104	—

| MAJOR LEAGUE TOTALS | | | | | 1169 | 3900 | 640 | 1016 | 120 | 31 | 20 | 230 | .261 | 627 | 1258 | 105 | 6 yrs |

George Andrew Hendrick   Born Oct 18, 1949   Los Angeles, CA
6'3   195 lbs   Batted right

YR	POS	TEAM	LG	FIN	G	AB	R	H	2B	3B	HR	RBI	AVG	BB	TB	OQ	RANK
1971	LF-CF	OAK	AL	1-6	42	114	8	27	4	1	0	8	.237	3	33	67	—
1972	CF-RF	OAK	AL	1-6	58	121	10	22	1	1	4	15	.182	3	37	71	—
1973	CF	CLE	AL	6-6	113	440	64	118	18	0	21	61	.268	25	199	107	—
1974	CF	CLE	AL	4-6	139	495	65	138	23	1	19	67	.279	33	220	113	25-67
1975	RF	CLE	AL	4-6	145	561	82	145	21	2	24	86	.258	40	242	105	34-66
1976	CF	CLE	AL	4-6	149	551	72	146	20	3	25	81	.265	51	247	121	20-64
1977	CF	SD	NL	5-6	152	541	75	168	25	2	23	81	.311	61	266	131	13-68
1978	CF	SD/SL	NL	4/5	138	493	64	137	31	1	20	75	.278	40	230	121	24-63
1979	RF	SL	NL	3-6	140	493	67	148	27	1	16	75	.300	49	225	123	19-62
1980	RF	SL	NL	4-6	150	572	73	173	33	2	25	109	.302	32	285	127	16-59
1981	CF	SL	NL	1-6	101	394	67	112	19	3	18	61	.284	41	191	134	9-69
1982	RF	SL	NL	1-6	136	515	65	145	20	5	19	104	.282	37	232	117	25-66
1983	1B-RF	SL	NL	4-6	144	529	73	168	33	3	18	97	.318	51	261	136	5-64
1984	RF	SL	NL	3-6	120	441	57	122	28	1	9	69	.277	32	179	106	—
1985	RF	PIT	NL	6-6	69	256	23	59	15	0	2	25	.230	18	80	79	—
1985	RF	CAL	AL	2-7	16	41	5	5	1	0	2	6	.122	4	12	—	—
1986	RF	CAL	AL	1-7	102	283	45	77	13	1	14	47	.272	26	134	113	—
1987	LF-1B	CAL	AL	6-7	65	162	14	39	10	0	5	25	.241	14	64	89	—
1988	LF-1B	CAL	AL	4-7	69	127	12	31	1	0	3	19	.244	7	41	77	—

| MAJOR LEAGUE TOTALS | | | | | 2048 | 7129 | 941 | 1980 | 343 | 27 | 267 | 1111 | .278 | 567 | 3178 | 123 | 10 yrs |

Ronald Charles Cey Born Feb 15, 1948 Tacoma, WA
5'10 185 lbs Batted right

YR	POS	TEAM	LG	FIN	G	AB	R	H	2B	3B	HR	RBI	AVG	BB	TB	OQ	RANK
1971	PH	LA	NL	2-6	2	2	0	0	0	0	0	0	.000	0	0	—	—
1972	3B	LA	NL	3-6	11	37	3	10	1	0	1	3	.270	7	14	—	—
1973	3B	LA	NL	2-6	152	507	60	124	18	4	15	80	.245	74	195	111	38-61
1974	3B	LA	NL	1-6	159	577	88	151	20	2	18	97	.262	76	229	113	32-65
1975	3B	LA	NL	2-6	158	566	72	160	29	2	25	101	.283	78	268	134	15-65
1976	3B	LA	NL	2-6	145	502	69	139	18	3	23	80	.277	89	232	144	5-57
1977	3B	LA	NL	1-6	153	564	77	136	22	3	30	110	.241	93	254	121	25-68
1978	3B	LA	NL	1-6	159	555	84	150	32	0	23	84	.270	96	251	137	9-63
1979	3B	LA	NL	3-6	150	487	77	137	20	1	28	81	.281	86	243	145	6-62
1980	3B	LA	NL	2-6	157	551	81	140	25	0	28	77	.254	69	249	123	17-59
1981	3B	LA	NL	2-6	85	312	42	90	15	2	13	50	.288	40	148	138	7-69
1982	3B	LA	NL	2-6	150	556	62	141	23	1	24	79	.254	57	238	114	29-66
1983	3B	CHI	NL	5-6	159	581	73	160	33	1	24	90	.275	62	267	123	19-64
1984	3B	CHI	NL	1-6	146	505	71	121	27	0	25	97	.240	61	223	119	19-53
1985	3B	CHI	NL	4-6	145	500	64	116	18	2	22	63	.232	58	204	108	31-65
1986	3B	CHI	NL	5-6	97	256	42	70	21	0	13	36	.273	44	130	146	—
1987	DH-1B	OAK	AL	3-7	45	104	12	23	6	0	4	11	.221	22	41	109	—

| MAJOR LEAGUE TOTALS | | | | | 2073 | 7162 | 977 | 1868 | 328 | 21 | 316 | 1139 | .261 | 1012 | 3186 | 125 | 13 yrs |

David Earl Lopes Born May 3, 1945 East Providence, RI
5'9 170 lbs Batted right

YR	POS	TEAM	LG	FIN	G	AB	R	H	2B	3B	HR	RBI	AVG	BB	TB	OQ	RANK
1972	2B	LA	NL	3-6	11	42	6	9	4	0	0	1	.214	7	13	—	—
1973	2B	LA	NL	2-6	142	535	77	147	13	5	6	37	.275	62	188	101	43-61
1974	2B	LA	NL	1-6	145	530	95	141	26	3	10	35	.266	66	203	110	40-65
1975	2B-CF	LA	NL	2-6	155	618	108	162	24	6	8	41	.262	91	222	108	36-65
1976	2B-CF	LA	NL	2-6	117	427	72	103	17	7	4	20	.241	56	146	102	—
1977	2B	LA	NL	1-6	134	502	85	142	19	5	11	53	.283	73	204	115	33-68
1978	2B	LA	NL	1-6	151	587	93	163	25	4	17	58	.278	71	247	120	25-63
1979	2B	LA	NL	3-6	153	582	109	154	20	6	28	73	.265	97	270	132	15-62
1980	2B	LA	NL	2-6	141	553	79	139	15	3	10	49	.251	58	190	96	44-59
1981	2B	LA	NL	2-6	58	214	35	44	2	0	5	17	.206	22	61	79	—
1982	2B	OAK	AL	5-7	128	450	58	109	19	3	11	42	.242	40	167	90	64-77
1983	2B	OAK	AL	4-7	147	494	64	137	13	4	17	67	.277	51	209	109	36-70
1984	RF-2B	OAK	AL	4-7	72	230	32	59	11	1	9	36	.257	31	99	114	—
1984	RF-2B	CHI	NL	1-6	16	17	5	4	1	0	0	0	.235	6	5	—	—
1985	LF-CF	CHI	NL	4-6	99	275	52	78	11	0	11	44	.284	46	122	136	—
1986	LF-3B	CHI/HO	NL	5/1	96	255	49	70	10	3	7	35	.275	43	107	126	—
1987	LF	HOU	NL	3-6	47	43	4	10	2	0	1	6	.233	13	15	—	—

| MAJOR LEAGUE TOTALS | | | | | 1812 | 6354 | 1023 | 1671 | 232 | 50 | 155 | 614 | .263 | 833 | 2468 | 109 | 9 yrs |

Garry Lee Maddox

Born Sep 1, 1949   Cincinnati, OH

6'3 175 lbs Batted right

YR	POS	TEAM	LG	FIN	G	AB	R	H	2B	3B	HR	RBI	AVG	BB	TB	OQ	RANK
1972	CF	SF	NL	5-6	125	458	62	122	26	7	12	58	.266	14	198	103	40-58
1973	CF	SF	NL	3-6	144	587	81	187	30	10	11	76	.319	24	270	116	34-61
1974	CF	SF	NL	5-6	135	538	74	153	31	3	8	50	.284	29	214	100	52-65
1975	CF	SF/PH	NL	3/2	116	426	54	116	26	8	5	50	.272	42	173	109	—
1976	CF	PHI	NL	1-6	146	531	75	175	37	6	6	68	.330	42	242	130	13-57
1977	CF	PHI	NL	1-6	139	571	85	167	27	10	14	74	.292	24	256	104	46-68
1978	CF	PHI	NL	1-6	155	598	62	172	34	3	11	68	.288	39	245	106	38-63
1979	CF	PHI	NL	4-6	148	548	70	154	28	6	13	61	.281	17	233	98	45-62
1980	CF	PHI	NL	1-6	143	549	59	142	31	3	11	73	.259	18	212	90	52-59
1981	CF	PHI	NL	3-6	94	323	37	85	7	1	5	40	.263	17	109	86	61-69
1982	CF	PHI	NL	2-6	119	412	39	117	27	2	8	61	.284	12	172	100	—
1983	CF	PHI	NL	1-6	97	324	27	89	14	2	4	32	.275	17	119	91	—
1984	CF	PHI	NL	4-6	77	241	29	68	11	0	5	19	.282	13	94	100	—
1985	CF	PHI	NL	5-6	105	218	22	52	8	1	4	23	.239	13	74	83	—
1986	CF	PHI	NL	2-6	6	7	1	3	0	0	0	1	.429	2	3	—	—

MAJOR LEAGUE TOTALS   1749 6331 777 1802 337 62 117 754 .285 323 2614 104 9 yrs

Robert Raymond Boone

Born Nov 19, 1947 San Diego, CA

6'2 195 lbs Batted right

YR	POS	TEAM	LG	FIN	G	AB	R	H	2B	3B	HR	RBI	AVG	BB	TB	OQ	RANK
1972	C	PHI	NL	6-6	16	51	4	14	1	0	1	4	.275	5	18	—	—
1973	C	PHI	NL	6-6	145	521	42	136	20	2	10	61	.261	41	190	94	50-61
1974	C	PHI	NL	3-6	146	488	41	118	24	3	3	52	.242	35	157	82	61-65
1975	C	PHI	NL	2-6	97	289	28	71	14	2	2	20	.246	32	95	92	—
1976	C	PHI	NL	1-6	121	361	40	98	18	2	4	54	.271	45	132	110	—
1977	C	PHI	NL	1-6	132	440	55	125	26	4	11	66	.284	42	192	111	—
1978	C	PHI	NL	1-6	132	435	48	123	18	4	12	62	.283	46	185	118	—
1979	C	PHI	NL	4-6	119	398	38	114	21	3	9	58	.286	49	168	118	—
1980	C	PHI	NL	1-6	141	480	34	110	23	1	9	55	.229	48	162	91	50-59
1981	C	PHI	NL	3-6	76	227	19	48	7	0	4	24	.211	22	67	81	—
1982	C	CAL	AL	1-7	143	472	42	121	17	0	7	58	.256	39	159	84	71-77
1983	C	CAL	AL	5-7	142	468	46	120	18	0	9	52	.256	24	165	81	64-70
1984	C	CAL	AL	2-7	139	450	33	91	16	1	3	32	.202	25	118	60	—
1985	C	CAL	AL	2-7	150	460	37	114	17	0	5	55	.248	37	146	78	71-75
1986	C	CAL	AL	1-7	144	442	48	98	12	2	7	49	.222	43	135	75	—
1987	C	CAL	AL	6-7	128	389	42	94	18	0	3	33	.242	35	121	74	—
1988	C	CAL	AL	4-7	122	352	38	104	17	0	5	39	.295	29	136	102	—
1989	C	KC	AL	2-7	131	405	33	111	13	2	1	43	.274	49	131	95	—
1990	C	KC	AL	6-7	40	117	11	28	3	0	0	9	.239	17	31	82	—

MAJOR LEAGUE TOTALS   2264 7245 679 1838 303 26 105 826 .254 663 2508 85 6 yrs

Kenneth John Reitz   Born Jun 24, 1951   San Francisco, CA
6'0 180 lbs Batted right

YR	POS	TEAM	LG	FIN	G	AB	R	H	2B	3B	HR	RBI	AVG	BB	TB	OQ	RANK
1972	3B	SL	NL	4-6	21	78	5	28	4	0	0	10	.359	2	32	—	—
1973	3B	SL	NL	2-6	147	426	40	100	20	2	6	42	.235	9	142	73	—
1974	3B	SL	NL	2-6	154	579	48	157	28	2	7	54	.271	23	210	87	60-65
1975	3B	SL	NL	3-6	161	592	43	159	25	1	5	63	.269	22	201	81	61-65
1976	3B	SF	NL	4-6	155	577	40	154	21	1	5	66	.267	24	192	83	52-57
1977	3B	SL	NL	3-6	157	587	58	153	36	1	17	79	.261	19	242	90	60-68
1978	3B	SL	NL	5-6	150	540	41	133	26	2	10	75	.246	23	193	85	60-63
1979	3B	SL	NL	3-6	159	605	42	162	41	2	8	73	.268	25	231	89	51-62
1980	3B	SL	NL	4-6	151	523	39	141	33	0	8	58	.270	22	198	92	47-59
1981	3B	CHI	NL	6-6	82	260	10	56	9	1	2	28	.215	15	73	70	—
1982	3B	PIT	NL	4-6	7	10	0	0	0	0	0	0	.000	0	0	—	—

MAJOR LEAGUE TOTALS   1344   4777   366   1243   243   12   68   548   .260   184   1714   87   7 yrs

Michael Jack Schmidt   Born Sep 27, 1949   Dayton, OH
6'2 195 lbs Batted right

YR	POS	TEAM	LG	FIN	G	AB	R	H	2B	3B	HR	RBI	AVG	BB	TB	OQ	RANK
1972	3B	PHI	NL	6-6	13	34	2	7	0	0	1	3	.206	5	10	—	—
1973	3B	PHI	NL	6-6	132	367	43	72	11	0	18	52	.196	62	137	106	—
1974	3B	PHI	NL	3-6	162	568	108	160	28	7	36	116	.282	106	310	162	2-65
1975	3B	PHI	NL	2-6	158	562	93	140	34	3	38	95	.249	101	294	148	3-65
1976	3B	PHI	NL	1-6	160	584	112	153	31	4	38	107	.262	100	306	154	2-57
1977	3B	PHI	NL	1-6	154	544	114	149	27	11	38	101	.274	104	312	157	4-68
1978	3B	PHI	NL	1-6	145	513	93	129	27	2	21	78	.251	91	223	130	15-63
1979	3B	PHI	NL	4-6	160	541	109	137	25	4	45	114	.253	120	305	163	1-62
1980	3B	PHI	NL	1-6	150	548	104	157	25	8	48	121	.286	89	342	176	1-59
1981	3B	PHI	NL	3-6	102	354	78	112	19	2	31	91	.316	73	228	202	1-69
1982	3B	PHI	NL	2-6	148	514	108	144	26	3	35	87	.280	107	281	168	1-66
1983	3B	PHI	NL	1-6	154	534	104	136	16	4	40	109	.255	128	280	161	1-64
1984	3B	PHI	NL	4-6	151	528	93	146	23	3	36	106	.277	92	283	158	1-53
1985	1B-3B	PHI	NL	5-6	158	549	89	152	31	5	33	93	.277	87	292	152	4-65
1986	3B-1B	PHI	NL	2-6	160	552	97	160	29	1	37	119	.290	89	302	155	1-49
1987	3B	PHI	NL	4-6	147	522	88	153	28	0	35	113	.293	83	286	147	8-58
1988	3B-1B	PHI	NL	6-6	108	390	52	97	21	2	12	62	.249	49	158	118	—
1989	3B	PHI	NL	6-6	42	148	19	30	7	0	6	28	.203	21	55	105	—

MAJOR LEAGUE TOTALS   2404   8352   1506   2234   408   59   548   1595   .267   1507   4404   160   14 yrs

Alonza Benjamin Bumbry   Born Apr 21, 1947 Fredericksburg, VA
5'8 170 lbs Batted left

YR	POS	TEAM	LG	FIN	G	AB	R	H	2B	3B	HR	RBI	AVG	BB	TB	OQ	RANK
1972	RF	BAL	AL	3-6	9	11	5	4	0	1	0	0	.364	0	6	—	—
1973	LF-RF	BAL	AL	1-6	110	356	73	120	15	11	7	34	.337	34	178	138	—
1974	LF	BAL	AL	1-6	94	270	35	63	10	3	1	19	.233	21	82	80	—
1975	DH-LF	BAL	AL	2-6	114	349	47	94	19	4	2	32	.269	32	127	96	—
1976	LF-CF	BAL	AL	2-6	133	450	71	113	15	7	9	36	.251	43	169	103	44-64
1977	CF	BAL	AL	2-7	133	518	74	164	31	3	4	41	.317	45	213	107	42-81
1978	CF	BAL	AL	4-7	33	114	21	27	5	2	2	6	.237	17	42	104	—
1979	CF	BAL	AL	1-7	148	569	80	162	29	1	7	49	.285	43	214	91	59-75
1980	CF	BAL	AL	2-7	160	645	118	205	29	9	9	53	.318	78	279	121	19-69
1981	CF	BAL	AL	2-7	101	392	61	107	18	2	1	27	.273	51	132	102	49-71
1982	CF	BAL	AL	2-7	150	562	77	147	20	4	5	40	.262	44	190	84	72-77
1983	CF	BAL	AL	1-7	124	378	63	104	14	4	3	31	.275	31	135	90	—
1984	CF	BAL	AL	5-7	119	344	47	93	12	1	3	24	.270	25	116	85	—
1985	LF	SD	NL	3-6	68	95	6	19	3	0	1	10	.200	7	25	67	—

| MAJOR LEAGUE TOTALS | | | | | 1496 | 5053 | 778 | 1422 | 220 | 52 | 54 | 402 | .281 | 471 | 1908 | 101 | 6 yrs |

Dwight Michael Evans   Born Nov 3, 1951 Santa Monica, CA
6'2 180 lbs Batted right

YR	POS	TEAM	LG	FIN	G	AB	R	H	2B	3B	HR	RBI	AVG	BB	TB	OQ	RANK
1972	LF	BOS	AL	2-6	18	57	2	15	3	1	1	6	.263	7	23	—	—
1973	RF	BOS	AL	2-6	119	282	46	63	13	1	10	32	.223	40	108	104	—
1974	RF	BOS	AL	3-6	133	463	60	130	19	8	10	70	.281	38	195	112	26-67
1975	RF	BOS	AL	1-6	128	412	61	113	24	6	13	56	.274	47	188	121	—
1976	RF	BOS	AL	3-6	146	501	61	121	34	5	17	62	.242	57	216	118	23-64
1977	RF-DH	BOS	AL	2-7	73	230	39	66	9	2	14	36	.287	28	121	134	—
1978	RF	BOS	AL	2-7	147	497	75	123	24	2	24	63	.247	65	223	118	28-83
1979	RF	BOS	AL	3-7	152	489	69	134	24	1	21	58	.274	69	223	119	21-75
1980	RF	BOS	AL	4-7	148	463	72	123	37	5	18	60	.266	64	224	126	14-69
1981	RF	BOS	AL	5-7	108	412	84	122	19	4	22	71	.296	85	215	165	1-71
1982	RF	BOS	AL	3-7	162	609	122	178	37	7	32	98	.292	112	325	150	1-77
1983	RF-DH	BOS	AL	6-7	126	470	74	112	19	4	22	58	.238	70	205	115	27-70
1984	RF	BOS	AL	4-7	162	630	121	186	37	8	32	104	.295	96	335	146	2-68
1985	RF	BOS	AL	5-7	159	617	110	162	29	1	29	78	.263	114	280	127	11-75
1986	RF	BOS	AL	1-7	152	529	86	137	33	2	26	97	.259	97	252	130	6-78
1987	1B-RF	BOS	AL	5-7	154	541	109	165	37	2	34	123	.305	106	308	154	3-79
1988	RF-1B	BOS	AL	1-7	149	559	96	164	31	7	21	111	.293	76	272	135	13-74
1989	RF-DH	BOS	AL	3-7	146	520	82	148	27	3	20	100	.285	99	241	141	4-67
1990	DH	BOS	AL	1-7	123	445	66	111	18	3	13	63	.249	67	174	110	35-69
1991	RF-DH	BAL	AL	6-7	101	270	35	73	9	1	6	38	.270	54	102	119	—

| MAJOR LEAGUE TOTALS | | | | | 2606 | 8996 | 1470 | 2446 | 483 | 73 | 385 | 1384 | .272 | 1391 | 4230 | 131 | 15 yrs |

Jorge Orta Born Nov 26, 1950 Mazatlan, Mexico
5'10 170 lbs Batted left

YR	POS	TEAM	LG	FIN	G	AB	R	H	2B	3B	HR	RBI	AVG	BB	TB	OQ	RANK
1972	SS-2B	CHI	AL	2-6	51	124	20	25	3	1	3	11	.202	6	39	79	—
1973	2B	CHI	AL	5-6	128	425	46	113	9	10	6	40	.266	37	160	97	—
1974	2B	CHI	AL	4-6	139	525	73	166	31	2	10	67	.316	40	231	121	19-67
1975	2B	CHI	AL	5-6	140	542	64	165	26	10	11	83	.304	48	244	120	20-66
1976	RF-3B	CHI	AL	6-6	158	636	74	174	29	8	14	72	.274	38	261	106	37-64
1977	2B	CHI	AL	3-7	144	564	71	159	27	8	11	84	.282	46	235	102	55-81
1978	2B	CHI	AL	5-7	117	420	45	115	19	2	13	53	.274	42	177	110	—
1979	DH-2B	CHI	AL	5-7	113	325	49	85	18	3	11	46	.262	44	142	112	—
1980	RF	CLE	AL	6-7	129	481	78	140	18	3	10	64	.291	71	194	115	27-69
1981	RF	CLE	AL	6-7	88	338	50	92	14	3	5	34	.272	21	127	96	56-71
1982	RF	LA	NL	2-6	86	115	13	25	5	0	2	8	.217	12	36	86	—
1983	DH-RF	TOR	AL	4-7	103	245	30	58	6	3	10	38	.237	19	100	95	—
1984	DH-LF	KC	AL	1-7	122	403	50	120	23	7	9	50	.298	28	184	113	—
1985	DH	KC	AL	1-7	110	300	32	80	21	1	4	45	.267	22	115	92	—
1986	DH	KC	AL	3-7	106	336	35	93	14	2	9	46	.277	23	138	97	—
1987	DH	KC	AL	2-7	21	50	3	9	4	0	2	4	.180	3	19	—	—
MAJOR LEAGUE TOTALS					1755	5829	733	1619	267	63	130	745	.278	500	2402	110	6 yrs

Gary Nathaniel Matthews Born Jul 5, 1950 San Fernando, CA
6'2 185 lbs Batted right

YR	POS	TEAM	LG	FIN	G	AB	R	H	2B	3B	HR	RBI	AVG	BB	TB	OQ	RANK
1972	LF-RF	SF	NL	5-6	20	62	11	18	1	1	4	14	.290	7	33	—	—
1973	LF	SF	NL	3-6	148	540	74	162	22	10	12	58	.300	58	240	124	21-61
1974	LF	SF	NL	5-6	154	561	87	161	27	6	16	82	.287	70	248	126	14-65
1975	LF	SF	NL	3-6	116	425	67	119	22	3	12	58	.280	65	183	128	22-65
1976	LF	SF	NL	4-6	156	587	79	164	28	4	20	84	.279	75	260	129	15-57
1977	RF	ATL	NL	6-6	148	555	89	157	25	5	17	64	.283	67	243	116	30-68
1978	RF	ATL	NL	6-6	129	474	75	135	20	5	18	62	.285	61	219	132	12-63
1979	LF	ATL	NL	6-6	156	631	97	192	34	5	27	90	.304	60	317	133	14-62
1980	LF	ATL	NL	4-6	155	571	79	159	17	3	19	75	.278	42	239	109	30-59
1981	LF	PHI	NL	3-6	101	359	62	108	21	3	9	67	.301	59	162	143	6-69
1982	LF	PHI	NL	2-6	162	616	89	173	31	1	19	83	.281	66	263	119	22-66
1983	LF	PHI	NL	1-6	132	446	66	115	18	2	10	50	.258	69	167	112	34-64
1984	LF	CHI	NL	1-6	147	491	101	143	21	2	14	82	.291	103	210	145	5-53
1985	LF	CHI	NL	4-6	97	298	45	70	12	0	13	40	.235	59	121	125	—
1986	LF	CHI	NL	5-6	123	370	49	96	16	1	21	46	.259	60	177	135	—
1987	LF	CHI	NL	6-6	44	42	3	11	3	0	0	8	.262	4	14	—	—
1987	DH	SEA	AL	4-7	45	119	10	28	1	0	3	15	.235	15	38	81	—
MAJOR LEAGUE TOTALS					2033	7147	1083	2011	319	51	234	978	.281	940	3134	126	12 yrs

Enos Milton Cabell   Born Oct 8, 1949   Fort Riley, KS
6'4 170 lbs Batted right

YR	POS	TEAM	LG	FIN	G	AB	R	H	2B	3B	HR	RBI	AVG	BB	TB	OQ	RANK
1972	1B	BAL	AL	3-6	3	5	0	0	0	0	0	1	.000	0	0	—	—
1973	1B	BAL	AL	1-6	32	47	12	10	2	0	1	3	.213	3	15	—	—
1974	1B-RF	BAL	AL	1-6	80	174	24	42	4	2	3	17	.241	7	59	80	—
1975	LF-1B	HOU	NL	6-6	117	348	43	92	17	6	2	43	.264	18	127	89	—
1976	3B	HOU	NL	3-6	144	586	85	160	13	7	2	43	.273	29	193	85	50-57
1977	3B	HOU	NL	3-6	150	625	101	176	36	7	16	68	.282	27	274	100	48-68
1978	3B	HOU	NL	5-6	162	660	92	195	31	8	7	71	.295	22	263	98	47-63
1979	3B-1B	HOU	NL	2-6	155	603	60	164	30	5	6	67	.272	21	222	86	54-62
1980	3B	HOU	NL	1-6	152	604	69	167	23	8	2	55	.276	26	212	87	54-59
1981	1B-3B	SF	NL	4-6	96	396	41	101	20	1	2	36	.255	10	129	77	65-69
1982	1B-3B	DET	AL	4-7	125	464	45	121	17	3	2	37	.261	15	150	71	—
1983	1B	DET	AL	2-7	121	392	62	122	23	5	5	46	.311	16	170	103	—
1984	1B	HOU	NL	2-6	127	436	52	135	17	3	8	44	.310	21	182	109	—
1985	1B-3B	HO/LA	NL	3/1	117	335	40	91	19	1	2	36	.272	30	118	97	—
1986	1B-RF	LA	NL	5-6	107	277	27	71	11	0	2	29	.256	14	88	77	—

| MAJOR LEAGUE TOTALS | | | | | 1688 | 5952 | 753 | 1647 | 263 | 56 | 60 | 596 | .277 | 259 | 2202 | 89 | 6 yrs |

David Gus Bell   Born Aug 27, 1951 Pittsburgh, PA
6'1 180 lbs Batted right

YR	POS	TEAM	LG	FIN	G	AB	R	H	2B	3B	HR	RBI	AVG	BB	TB	OQ	RANK
1972	RF	CLE	AL	5-6	132	466	49	119	21	1	9	36	.255	34	169	102	36-56
1973	3B	CLE	AL	6-6	156	631	86	169	23	7	14	59	.268	49	248	99	36-60
1974	3B	CLE	AL	4-6	116	423	51	111	15	1	7	46	.262	35	149	94	—
1975	3B	CLE	AL	4-6	153	553	66	150	20	4	10	59	.271	51	208	99	43-66
1976	3B	CLE	AL	4-6	159	604	75	170	26	2	7	60	.281	44	221	100	48-64
1977	3B	CLE	AL	5-7	129	479	64	140	23	4	11	64	.292	45	204	108	40-81
1978	3B	CLE	AL	6-7	142	556	71	157	27	8	6	62	.282	39	218	99	50-83
1979	3B-SS	TEX	AL	3-7	162	670	89	200	42	3	18	101	.299	30	302	102	45-75
1980	3B	TEX	AL	4-7	129	490	76	161	24	4	17	83	.329	40	244	128	10-69
1981	3B	TEX	AL	2-7	97	360	44	106	16	1	10	64	.294	42	154	123	21-71
1982	3B	TEX	AL	6-7	148	537	62	159	27	2	13	67	.296	70	229	117	26-77
1983	3B	TEX	AL	3-7	156	618	75	171	35	3	14	66	.277	50	254	101	44-70
1984	3B	TEX	AL	7-7	148	553	88	174	36	5	11	83	.315	63	253	125	17-68
1985	3B	TEX	AL	7-7	84	313	33	74	13	3	4	32	.236	33	105	85	—
1985	3B	CIN	NL	2-6	67	247	28	54	15	2	6	36	.219	34	91	103	—
1986	3B	CIN	NL	2-6	155	568	89	158	29	3	20	75	.278	73	253	124	15-49
1987	3B	CIN	NL	2-6	143	522	74	148	19	2	17	70	.284	71	222	115	25-59
1988	3B-1B	CN/HO	NL	2/5	95	323	27	78	10	1	7	40	.241	26	111	93	—
1989	DH-3B	TEX	AL	4-7	34	82	4	15	4	0	0	3	.183	7	19	—	—

| MAJOR LEAGUE TOTALS | | | | | 2405 | 8995 | 1151 | 2514 | 425 | 56 | 201 | 1106 | .279 | 836 | 3654 | 110 | 14 yrs |

Michael Anthony Easler Born Nov 29, 1950 Cleveland, OH
6'0 190 lbs Batted left

YR	POS	TEAM	LG	FIN	G	AB	R	H	2B	3B	HR	RBI	AVG	BB	TB	OQ	RANK
1973	LF-RF	HOU	NL	4-6	6	7	1	0	0	0	0	0	.000	2	0	—	—
1974	PH	HOU	NL	4-6	15	15	0	1	0	0	0	0	.067	0	1	—	—
1975	PH	HOU	NL	6-6	5	5	0	0	0	0	0	0	.000	0	0	—	—
1976	DH	CAL	AL	4-6	21	54	6	13	1	1	0	4	.241	2	16	—	—
1977	RF-LF	PIT	NL	2-6	10	18	3	8	2	0	1	5	.444	0	13	—	—
1979	LF-RF	PIT	NL	1-6	55	54	8	15	1	1	2	11	.278	8	24	—	—
1980	LF	PIT	NL	3-6	132	393	66	133	27	3	21	74	.338	43	229	167	—
1981	LF	PIT	NL	4-6	95	339	43	97	18	5	7	42	.286	24	146	114	30-69
1982	LF	PIT	NL	4-6	142	475	52	131	27	2	15	58	.276	40	207	115	27-66
1983	LF	PIT	NL	2-6	115	381	44	117	17	2	10	54	.307	22	168	113	—
1984	DH-1B	BOS	AL	4-7	156	601	87	188	31	5	27	91	.313	58	310	134	9-68
1985	DH-LF	BOS	AL	5-7	155	568	71	149	29	4	16	74	.262	53	234	101	52-75
1986	DH	NY	AL	2-7	146	490	64	148	26	2	14	78	.302	49	220	115	28-78
1987	LF	PHI	NL	4-6	33	110	7	31	4	0	1	10	.282	6	38	82	—
1987	DH-LF	NY	AL	4-7	65	167	13	47	6	0	4	21	.281	14	65	92	—
MAJOR LEAGUE TOTALS					1151	3677	465	1078	189	25	118	522	.293	321	1671	116	5 yrs

Douglas Vernon DeCinces Born Aug 29, 1950 Burbank, CA
6'2 190 lbs Batted right

YR	POS	TEAM	LG	FIN	G	AB	R	H	2B	3B	HR	RBI	AVG	BB	TB	OQ	RANK
1973	3B-2B	BAL	AL	1-6	10	18	2	2	0	0	0	3	.111	1	2	—	—
1974	3B	BAL	AL	1-6	1	1	0	0	0	0	0	0	.000	1	0	—	—
1975	3B-SS	BAL	AL	2-6	61	167	20	42	6	3	4	23	.251	13	66	98	—
1976	3B-2B	BAL	AL	2-6	129	440	36	103	17	2	11	42	.234	29	157	90	—
1977	3B	BAL	AL	2-7	150	522	63	135	28	3	19	69	.259	64	226	110	35-81
1978	3B	BAL	AL	4-7	142	511	72	146	37	1	28	80	.286	46	269	133	11-83
1979	3B	BAL	AL	1-7	120	422	67	97	27	1	16	61	.230	54	174	102	—
1980	3B	BAL	AL	2-7	145	489	64	122	23	2	16	64	.249	49	197	100	52-69
1981	3B	BAL	AL	2-7	100	346	49	91	23	2	13	55	.263	41	157	124	20-71
1982	3B	CAL	AL	1-7	153	575	94	173	42	5	30	97	.301	66	315	140	5-77
1983	3B-DH	CAL	AL	5-7	95	370	49	104	19	3	18	65	.281	32	183	121	—
1984	3B	CAL	AL	2-7	146	547	77	147	23	3	20	82	.269	53	236	109	34-68
1985	3B	CAL	AL	2-7	120	427	50	104	22	1	20	78	.244	47	188	107	—
1986	3B	CAL	AL	1-7	140	512	69	131	20	3	26	96	.256	52	235	110	34-78
1987	3B	CAL	AL	6-7	133	453	65	106	23	0	16	63	.234	70	177	100	55-79
1987	3B	SL	NL	1-6	4	9	1	2	2	0	0	1	.222	0	4	—	—
MAJOR LEAGUE TOTALS					1649	5809	778	1505	312	29	237	879	.259	618	2586	116	8 yrs

David Lee Chalk   Born Aug 30, 1950 Del Rio, TX
5'10   175 lbs   Batted right

YR	POS	TEAM	LG	FIN	G	AB	R	H	2B	3B	HR	RBI	AVG	BB	TB	OQ	RANK
1973	SS	CAL	AL	4-6	24	69	14	16	2	0	0	6	.232	9	18	—	—
1974	SS-3B	CAL	AL	6-6	133	465	44	117	9	3	5	31	.252	30	147	81	61-67
1975	3B	CAL	AL	6-6	149	513	59	140	24	2	3	56	.273	66	177	100	42-66
1976	SS-3B	CAL	AL	4-6	142	438	39	95	14	1	0	33	.217	49	111	76	63-64
1977	3B	CAL	AL	5-7	149	519	58	144	27	2	3	45	.277	52	184	93	66-81
1978	SS-2B	CAL	AL	2-7	135	470	42	119	12	0	1	34	.253	38	134	75	83-83
1979	2B-SS	TX/OA	AL	3/7	75	220	15	49	6	0	2	13	.223	29	61	76	—
1980	3B-2B	KC	AL	1-7	69	167	19	42	10	1	1	20	.251	18	57	89	—
1981	3B-2B	KC	AL	4-7	27	49	2	11	3	0	0	5	.224	4	14	—	—

MAJOR LEAGUE TOTALS   903 2910 292 733 107 9 15 243 .252 295 903 85   5 yrs

George Howard Brett   Born May 15, 1953 Glen Dale, WV
6'0   185 lbs   Batted left

YR	POS	TEAM	LG	FIN	G	AB	R	H	2B	3B	HR	RBI	AVG	BB	TB	OQ	RANK
1973	3B	KC	AL	2-6	13	40	2	5	2	0	0	0	.125	0	7	—	—
1974	3B	KC	AL	5-6	133	457	49	129	21	5	2	47	.282	21	166	91	—
1975	3B	KC	AL	2-6	159	634	84	195	35	13	11	89	.308	46	289	118	22-66
1976	3B	KC	AL	1-6	159	645	94	215	34	14	7	67	.333	49	298	132	8-64
1977	3B	KC	AL	1-7	139	564	105	176	32	13	22	88	.312	55	300	135	10-81
1978	3B	KC	AL	1-7	128	510	79	150	45	8	9	62	.294	39	238	118	29-83
1979	3B	KC	AL	2-7	154	645	119	212	42	20	23	107	.329	51	363	138	8-75
1980	3B	KC	AL	1-7	117	449	87	175	33	9	24	118	.390	58	298	193	1-69
1981	3B	KC	AL	4-7	89	347	42	109	27	7	6	43	.314	27	168	131	14-71
1982	3B	KC	AL	2-7	144	552	101	166	32	9	21	82	.301	71	279	134	9-77
1983	3B-1B	KC	AL	2-7	123	464	90	144	38	2	25	93	.310	57	261	148	2-70
1984	3B	KC	AL	1-7	104	377	42	107	21	3	13	69	.284	38	173	117	—
1985	3B	KC	AL	1-7	155	550	108	184	38	5	30	112	.335	103	322	171	1-75
1986	3B	KC	AL	3-7	124	441	70	128	28	4	16	73	.290	80	212	136	4-78
1987	1B-DH	KC	AL	2-7	115	427	71	124	18	2	22	78	.290	72	212	131	12-79
1988	1B-DH	KC	AL	3-7	157	589	90	180	42	3	24	103	.306	82	300	143	8-74
1989	1B-DH	KC	AL	2-7	124	457	67	129	26	3	12	80	.282	59	197	121	17-67
1990	1B-DH	KC	AL	6-7	142	544	82	179	45	7	14	87	.329	56	280	140	5-69
1991	DH-1B	KC	AL	6-7	131	505	77	129	40	2	10	61	.255	58	203	104	44-72
1992	DH	KC	AL	5-7	152	592	55	169	35	5	7	61	.285	35	235	97	55-73
1993	DH	KC	AL	3-7	145	560	69	149	31	3	19	75	.266	39	243	98	46-73

MAJOR LEAGUE TOTALS   2707 10349 1583 3154 665 137 317 1595 .305 1096 5044 133   18 yrs

Philip Mason Garner Born Apr 30, 1949 Jefferson City, TN
5'10 175 lbs Batted right

YR	POS	TEAM	LG	FIN	G	AB	R	H	2B	3B	HR	RBI	AVG	BB	TB	OQ	RANK
1973	3B	OAK	AL	1-6	9	5	0	0	0	0	0	0	.000	0	0	—	—
1974	SS-2B	OAK	AL	1-6	30	28	4	5	1	0	0	1	.179	1	6	—	—
1975	2B	OAK	AL	1-6	160	488	46	120	21	5	6	54	.246	30	169	83	58-66
1976	2B	OAK	AL	2-6	159	555	54	145	29	12	8	74	.261	36	222	103	43-64
1977	3B-2B	PIT	NL	2-6	153	585	99	152	35	10	17	77	.260	55	258	108	42-68
1978	3B-2B	PIT	NL	2-6	154	528	66	138	25	9	10	66	.261	66	211	113	23-63
1979	2B-3B	PIT	NL	1-6	150	549	76	161	32	8	11	59	.293	55	242	118	25-62
1980	2B	PIT	NL	3-6	151	548	62	142	27	6	5	58	.259	46	196	95	45-59
1981	2B	PT/HO	NL	4/3	87	294	35	73	9	3	1	26	.248	36	91	93	57-69
1982	2B-3B	HOU	NL	5-6	155	588	65	161	33	8	13	83	.274	40	249	109	35-66
1983	3B	HOU	NL	3-6	154	567	76	135	24	2	14	79	.238	63	205	97	48-64
1984	3B-2B	HOU	NL	2-6	128	374	60	104	17	6	4	45	.278	43	145	112	—
1985	3B-2B	HOU	NL	3-6	135	463	65	124	23	10	6	51	.268	34	185	103	42-65
1986	3B	HOU	NL	1-6	107	313	43	83	14	3	9	41	.265	30	130	108	—
1987	3B-2B	HO/LA	NL	3/4	113	238	29	49	9	0	5	23	.206	28	73	79	—
1988	3B	SF	NL	4-6	15	13	0	2	0	0	0	1	.154	1	2	—	—
MAJOR LEAGUE TOTALS					1860	6136	780	1594	299	82	109	738	.260	564	2384	102	10 yrs

Frank White Born Sep 4, 1950 Greenville, MS
5'11 165 lbs Batted right

YR	POS	TEAM	LG	FIN	G	AB	R	H	2B	3B	HR	RBI	AVG	BB	TB	OQ	RANK
1973	SS-2B	KC	AL	2-6	51	139	20	31	6	1	0	5	.223	8	39	67	—
1974	2B-SS	KC	AL	5-6	99	204	19	45	6	3	1	18	.221	5	60	65	—
1975	2B-SS	KC	AL	2-6	111	304	43	76	10	2	7	36	.250	20	111	89	—
1976	2B-SS	KC	AL	1-6	152	446	39	102	17	6	2	46	.229	19	137	74	—
1977	2B	KC	AL	1-7	152	474	59	116	21	5	5	50	.245	25	162	77	80-81
1978	2B	KC	AL	1-7	143	461	66	127	24	6	7	50	.275	26	184	97	55-83
1979	2B	KC	AL	2-7	127	467	73	124	26	4	10	48	.266	25	188	90	61-75
1980	2B	KC	AL	1-7	154	560	70	148	23	4	7	60	.264	19	200	79	68-69
1981	2B	KC	AL	4-7	94	364	35	91	17	1	9	38	.250	19	137	91	61-71
1982	2B	KC	AL	2-7	145	524	71	156	45	6	11	56	.298	16	246	105	44-77
1983	2B	KC	AL	2-7	146	549	52	143	35	6	11	77	.260	20	223	89	59-70
1984	2B	KC	AL	1-7	129	479	58	130	22	5	17	56	.271	27	213	103	40-68
1985	2B	KC	AL	1-7	149	563	62	140	25	1	22	69	.249	28	233	91	65-75
1986	2B	KC	AL	3-7	151	566	76	154	37	3	22	84	.272	43	263	108	39-78
1987	2B	KC	AL	2-7	154	563	67	138	32	2	17	78	.245	51	225	91	67-79
1988	2B	KC	AL	3-7	150	537	48	126	25	1	8	58	.235	21	177	74	71-74
1989	2B	KC	AL	2-7	135	418	34	107	22	1	2	36	.256	30	137	83	—
1990	2B	KC	AL	6-7	82	241	20	52	14	1	2	21	.216	10	74	68	—
MAJOR LEAGUE TOTALS					2324	7859	912	2006	407	58	160	886	.255	412	3009	91	12 yrs

Andre Thornton
6'3   200 lbs   Batted right

Born Aug 13, 1949 Tuskegee, AL

YR	POS	TEAM	LG	FIN	G	AB	R	H	2B	3B	HR	RBI	AVG	BB	TB	OQ	RANK
1973	1B	CHI	NL	5-6	17	35	3	7	3	0	0	2	.200	7	10	—	—
1974	1B	CHI	NL	6-6	107	303	41	79	16	4	10	46	.261	48	133	128	—
1975	1B	CHI	NL	5-6	120	372	70	109	21	4	18	60	.293	88	192	168	—
1976	1B-RF	CHI/MO	NL	4/6	96	268	28	52	11	2	11	38	.194	48	100	112	—
1977	1B	CLE	AL	5-7	131	433	77	114	20	5	28	70	.263	70	228	137	8-81
1978	1B	CLE	AL	6-7	145	508	97	133	22	4	33	105	.262	93	262	146	2-83
1979	1B	CLE	AL	6-7	143	515	89	120	31	1	26	93	.233	90	231	118	23-75
1981	DH-1B	CLE	AL	6-7	69	226	22	54	12	0	6	30	.239	23	84	99	—
1982	DH	CLE	AL	6-7	161	589	90	161	26	1	32	116	.273	109	285	136	6-77
1983	DH-1B	CLE	AL	7-7	141	508	78	143	27	1	17	77	.281	87	223	127	16-70
1984	DH	CLE	AL	6-7	155	587	91	159	26	0	33	99	.271	91	284	132	12-68
1985	DH	CLE	AL	7-7	124	461	49	109	13	0	22	88	.236	47	188	98	54-75
1986	DH	CLE	AL	5-7	120	401	49	92	14	0	17	66	.229	65	157	105	—
1987	DH	CLE	AL	7-7	36	85	8	10	2	0	0	5	.118	10	12	—	—
MAJOR LEAGUE TOTALS					1565	5291	792	1342	244	22	253	895	.254	876	2389	128	7 yrs

Brian Jay Downing
5'10   170 lbs   Batted right

Born Oct 9, 1950   Los Angeles, CA

YR	POS	TEAM	LG	FIN	G	AB	R	H	2B	3B	HR	RBI	AVG	BB	TB	OQ	RANK
1973	LF-C	CHI	AL	5-6	34	73	5	13	1	0	2	4	.178	10	20	—	—
1974	C-RF	CHI	AL	4-6	108	293	41	66	12	1	10	39	.225	51	110	113	—
1975	C	CHI	AL	5-6	138	420	58	101	12	1	7	41	.240	76	136	103	38-66
1976	C-DH	CHI	AL	6-6	104	317	38	81	14	0	3	30	.256	40	104	100	—
1977	C	CHI	AL	3-7	69	169	28	48	4	2	4	25	.284	34	68	124	—
1978	C	CAL	AL	2-7	133	412	42	105	15	0	7	46	.255	52	141	97	—
1979	C-DH	CAL	AL	1-7	148	509	87	166	27	3	12	75	.326	77	235	132	12-75
1980	C-DH	CAL	AL	6-7	30	93	5	27	6	0	2	25	.290	12	39	115	—
1981	LF-C	CAL	AL	5-7	93	317	47	79	14	0	9	41	.249	46	120	111	33-71
1982	LF	CAL	AL	1-7	158	623	109	175	37	2	28	84	.281	86	300	128	13-77
1983	LF-DH	CAL	AL	5-7	113	403	68	99	15	1	19	53	.246	62	173	115	—
1984	LF-DH	CAL	AL	2-7	156	539	65	148	28	2	23	91	.275	70	249	123	19-68
1985	LF-DH	CAL	AL	2-7	150	520	80	137	23	1	20	85	.263	78	222	115	21-75
1986	LF	CAL	AL	1-7	152	513	90	137	27	4	20	95	.267	90	232	125	14-78
1987	DH-LF	CAL	AL	6-7	155	567	110	154	29	3	29	77	.272	106	276	129	13-79
1988	DH	CAL	AL	4-7	135	484	80	117	18	2	25	64	.242	81	214	123	22-74
1989	DH	CAL	AL	3-7	142	544	59	154	25	2	14	59	.283	56	225	111	28-67
1990	DH	CAL	AL	4-7	96	330	47	90	18	2	14	51	.273	50	154	129	—
1991	DH	TEX	AL	3-7	123	407	76	113	17	2	17	49	.278	58	185	124	—
1992	DH	TEX	AL	4-7	107	320	53	89	18	0	10	39	.278	62	137	131	—
MAJOR LEAGUE TOTALS					2344	7853	1188	2099	360	28	275	1073	.267	1197	3340	120	10 yrs

Daniel Driessen   Born Jul 29, 1951   Hilton Head, SC
5'11   187 lbs   Batted left

YR	POS	TEAM	LG	FIN	G	AB	R	H	2B	3B	HR	RBI	AVG	BB	TB	OQ	RANK
1973	3B-1B	CIN	NL	1-6	102	366	49	110	15	2	4	47	.301	24	141	102	—
1974	3B-1B	CIN	NL	2-6	150	470	63	132	23	6	7	56	.281	48	188	111	38-65
1975	1B-LF	CIN	NL	1-6	88	210	38	59	8	1	7	38	.281	35	90	131	—
1976	1B-LF	CIN	NL	1-6	98	219	32	54	11	1	7	44	.247	43	88	130	—
1977	1B	CIN	NL	2-6	151	536	75	161	31	4	17	91	.300	64	251	126	20-68
1978	1B	CIN	NL	2-6	153	524	68	131	23	3	16	70	.250	75	208	115	31-63
1979	1B	CIN	NL	1-6	150	515	72	129	24	3	18	75	.250	62	213	110	33-62
1980	1B	CIN	NL	3-6	154	524	81	139	36	1	14	74	.265	93	219	129	11-59
1981	1B	CIN	NL	1-6	82	233	35	55	14	0	7	33	.236	40	90	119	—
1982	1B	CIN	NL	6-6	149	516	64	139	25	1	17	57	.269	82	217	127	16-66
1983	1B	CIN	NL	6-6	122	386	57	107	17	1	12	57	.277	75	162	133	—
1984	1B	CN/MO	NL	5/5	132	387	47	104	24	0	16	60	.269	54	176	131	—
1985	1B	MO/SF	NL	3/6	145	493	53	120	26	0	9	47	.243	50	173	95	48-65
1986	1B	SF/HO	NL	3/1	32	40	7	10	3	0	1	3	.250	9	16	—	—
1987	1B	SL	NL	1-6	24	60	5	14	2	0	1	11	.233	7	19	—	—

MAJOR LEAGUE TOTALS   1732   5479   746 1464   282   23 153   763   .267   761 2251   116   7 yrs

George Kenneth Griffey Sr   Born Apr 10, 1950   Donora, PA
5'11   190 lbs   Batted left

YR	POS	TEAM	LG	FIN	G	AB	R	H	2B	3B	HR	RBI	AVG	BB	TB	OQ	RANK
1973	RF	CIN	NL	1-6	25	86	19	33	5	1	3	14	.384	6	49	—	—
1974	RF	CIN	NL	2-6	88	227	24	57	9	5	2	19	.251	27	82	102	—
1975	RF	CIN	NL	1-6	132	463	95	141	15	9	4	46	.305	67	186	124	25-65
1976	RF	CIN	NL	1-6	148	562	111	189	28	9	6	74	.336	62	253	138	8-57
1977	RF	CIN	NL	2-6	154	585	117	186	35	8	12	57	.318	69	273	128	15-68
1978	RF	CIN	NL	2-6	158	614	90	177	33	8	10	63	.288	54	256	113	34-63
1979	RF	CIN	NL	1-6	95	380	62	120	27	4	8	32	.316	36	179	128	—
1980	RF	CIN	NL	3-6	146	544	89	160	28	10	13	85	.294	62	247	128	12-59
1981	CF	CIN	NL	1-6	101	396	65	123	21	6	2	34	.311	39	162	120	22-69
1982	RF	NY	AL	5-7	127	484	70	134	23	2	12	54	.277	39	197	100	53-77
1983	1B-CF	NY	AL	3-7	118	458	60	140	21	3	11	46	.306	34	200	110	34-70
1984	CF-1B	NY	AL	3-7	120	399	44	109	20	1	7	56	.273	29	152	94	—
1985	LF	NY	AL	2-7	127	438	68	120	28	4	10	69	.274	41	186	105	—
1986	LF	NY	AL	2-7	59	198	33	60	7	0	9	26	.303	15	94	115	—
1986	LF	ATL	NL	6-6	80	292	36	90	15	3	12	32	.308	20	147	129	—
1987	LF	ATL	NL	5-6	122	399	65	114	24	1	14	64	.286	46	182	118	—
1988	LF-1B	AT/CN	NL	6/2	94	243	26	62	6	0	4	23	.255	19	80	91	—
1989	LF	CIN	NL	5-6	106	236	26	62	8	3	8	30	.263	29	100	121	—
1990	1B-LF	CIN	NL	1-6	46	63	6	13	2	0	1	8	.206	2	18	—	—
1990	LF	SEA	AL	5-7	21	77	13	29	2	0	3	18	.377	10	40	—	—
1991	LF	SEA	AL	5-7	30	85	10	24	7	0	1	9	.282	13	34	—	—

MAJOR LEAGUE TOTALS   2097   7229 1129 2143   364   77 152   859   .296   719 3117   120   8 yrs

James Gorman Thomas   Born Dec 12, 1950   Charleston, SC
6'2   210 lbs   Batted right

YR	POS	TEAM	LG	FIN	G	AB	R	H	2B	3B	HR	RBI	AVG	BB	TB	OQ	RANK
1973	RF	MIL	AL	5-6	59	155	16	29	7	1	2	11	.187	14	44	71	—
1974	RF	MIL	AL	5-6	17	46	10	12	4	0	2	11	.261	8	22	—	—
1975	RF	MIL	AL	5-6	121	240	34	43	12	2	10	28	.179	31	89	94	—
1976	LF	MIL	AL	6-6	99	227	27	45	9	2	8	36	.198	31	82	102	—
1978	CF	MIL	AL	3-7	137	452	70	111	24	1	32	86	.246	73	233	138	7-83
1979	CF	MIL	AL	2-7	156	557	97	136	29	0	45	123	.244	98	300	137	9-75
1980	CF	MIL	AL	3-7	162	628	78	150	26	3	38	105	.239	58	296	110	37-69
1981	CF	MIL	AL	1-7	103	363	54	94	22	0	21	65	.259	50	179	136	9-71
1982	CF	MIL	AL	1-7	158	567	96	139	29	1	39	112	.245	84	287	128	12-77
1983	CF	ML/CL	AL	5/7	152	535	72	112	23	1	22	69	.209	80	203	100	47-70
1984	LF	SEA	AL	5-7	35	108	6	17	3	0	1	13	.157	28	23	84	—
1985	DH	SEA	AL	6-7	135	484	76	104	16	1	32	87	.215	84	218	117	20-75
1986	DH	SE/ML	AL	7/6	101	315	45	59	8	1	16	36	.187	58	117	100	—
MAJOR LEAGUE TOTALS					1435	4677	681	1051	212	13	268	782	.225	697	2093	124	7 yrs

David Gene Parker   Born Jun 9, 1951   Calhoun, MS
6'5   230 lbs   Batted left

YR	POS	TEAM	LG	FIN	G	AB	R	H	2B	3B	HR	RBI	AVG	BB	TB	OQ	RANK
1973	RF-CF	PIT	NL	3-6	54	139	17	40	9	1	4	14	.288	2	63	103	—
1974	RF-CF	PIT	NL	1-6	73	220	27	62	10	3	4	29	.282	10	90	100	—
1975	RF	PIT	NL	1-6	148	558	75	172	35	10	25	101	.308	38	302	139	9-65
1976	RF	PIT	NL	2-6	138	537	82	168	28	10	13	90	.313	30	255	126	20-57
1977	RF	PIT	NL	2-6	159	637	107	215	44	8	21	88	.338	58	338	140	7-68
1978	RF	PIT	NL	2-6	148	581	102	194	32	12	30	117	.334	57	340	164	2-63
1979	RF	PIT	NL	1-6	158	622	109	193	45	7	25	94	.310	67	327	142	7-62
1980	RF	PIT	NL	3-6	139	518	71	153	31	1	17	79	.295	25	237	115	28-59
1981	RF	PIT	NL	4-6	67	240	29	62	14	3	9	48	.258	9	109	108	—
1982	RF	PIT	NL	4-6	73	244	41	66	19	3	6	29	.270	22	109	118	—
1983	RF	PIT	NL	2-6	144	552	68	154	29	4	12	69	.279	28	227	101	44-64
1984	RF	CIN	NL	5-6	156	607	73	173	28	0	16	94	.285	41	249	108	32-53
1985	RF	CIN	NL	2-6	160	635	88	198	42	4	34	125	.312	52	350	146	5-65
1986	RF	CIN	NL	2-6	162	637	89	174	31	3	31	116	.273	56	304	121	18-49
1987	RF	CIN	NL	2-6	153	589	77	149	28	0	26	97	.253	44	255	100	46-59
1988	DH	OAK	AL	1-7	101	377	43	97	18	1	12	55	.257	32	153	101	—
1989	DH	OAK	AL	1-7	144	553	56	146	27	0	22	97	.264	38	239	105	39-67
1990	DH	MIL	AL	6-7	157	610	71	176	30	3	21	92	.289	41	275	111	31-69
1991	DH	CA/TO	AL	7/1	132	502	47	120	26	2	11	59	.239	33	183	85	67-72
MAJOR LEAGUE TOTALS					2466	9358	1272	2712	526	75	339	1493	.290	683	4405	122	14 yrs

Russell Earl Dent

Born Nov 25, 1951 Savannah, GA

5'9 170 lbs Batted right

YR	POS	TEAM	LG	FIN	G	AB	R	H	2B	3B	HR	RBI	AVG	BB	TB	OQ	RANK
1973	SS	CHI	AL	5-6	40	117	17	29	2	0	0	10	.248	10	31	72	—
1974	SS	CHI	AL	4-6	154	496	55	136	15	3	5	45	.274	28	172	89	54-67
1975	SS	CHI	AL	5-6	157	602	52	159	29	4	3	58	.264	36	205	84	56-66
1976	SS	CHI	AL	6-6	158	562	44	138	18	4	2	52	.246	43	170	82	60-64
1977	SS	NY	AL	1-7	158	477	54	118	18	4	8	49	.247	39	168	85	74-81
1978	SS	NY	AL	1-7	123	379	40	92	11	1	5	40	.243	23	120	77	—
1979	SS	NY	AL	4-7	141	431	47	99	14	2	2	32	.230	37	123	70	—
1980	SS	NY	AL	1-7	141	489	57	128	26	2	5	52	.262	48	173	91	59-69
1981	SS	NY	AL	3-7	73	227	20	54	11	0	7	27	.238	19	86	97	—
1982	SS	NY/TX	AL	5/6	105	306	27	59	10	1	1	23	.193	21	74	57	—
1983	SS	TEX	AL	3-7	131	417	36	99	15	2	2	34	.237	23	124	69	—
1984	SS-3B	KC	AL	1-7	11	9	2	3	0	0	0	1	.333	1	3	—	—

MAJOR LEAGUE TOTALS 1392 4512 451 1114 169 23 40 423 .247 328 1449 86 5 yrs

David Mark Winfield

Born Oct 3, 1951 St Paul, MN

6'6 220 lbs Batted right

YR	POS	TEAM	LG	FIN	G	AB	R	H	2B	3B	HR	RBI	AVG	BB	TB	OQ	RANK
1973	LF	SD	NL	6-6	56	141	9	39	4	1	3	12	.277	12	54	102	—
1974	RF	SD	NL	6-6	145	498	57	132	18	4	20	75	.265	40	218	112	35-65
1975	RF	SD	NL	4-6	143	509	74	136	20	2	15	76	.267	69	205	116	32-65
1976	LF	SD	NL	5-6	137	492	81	139	26	4	13	69	.283	65	212	128	16-57
1977	LF	SD	NL	5-6	157	615	104	169	29	7	25	92	.275	58	287	116	32-68
1978	LF	SD	NL	4-6	158	587	88	181	30	5	24	97	.308	55	293	137	8-63
1979	LF	SD	NL	5-6	159	597	97	184	27	10	34	118	.308	85	333	156	2-62
1980	RF	SD	NL	6-6	162	558	89	154	25	6	20	87	.276	79	251	130	9-59
1981	LF	NY	AL	3-7	105	388	52	114	25	1	13	68	.294	43	180	130	16-71
1982	LF	NY	AL	5-7	140	539	84	151	24	8	37	106	.280	45	302	132	11-77
1983	LF	NY	AL	3-7	152	598	99	169	26	8	32	116	.283	58	307	127	15-70
1984	RF	NY	AL	3-7	141	567	106	193	34	4	19	100	.340	53	292	139	5-68
1985	RF	NY	AL	2-7	155	633	105	174	34	6	26	114	.275	52	298	112	29-75
1986	RF	NY	AL	2-7	154	565	90	148	31	5	24	104	.262	77	261	118	23-78
1987	RF	NY	AL	4-7	156	575	83	158	22	1	27	97	.275	76	263	114	31-79
1988	RF	NY	AL	5-7	149	559	96	180	37	2	25	107	.322	69	296	147	5-74
1990	RF	NY/CA	AL	7/4	132	475	70	127	21	2	21	78	.267	52	215	117	22-69
1991	RF	CAL	AL	7-7	150	568	75	149	27	4	28	86	.262	56	268	116	29-72
1992	DH-RF	TOR	AL	1-7	156	583	92	169	33	3	26	108	.290	82	286	136	7-73
1993	DH-RF	MIN	AL	5-7	143	547	72	148	27	2	21	76	.271	45	242	103	38-73

MAJOR LEAGUE TOTALS 2850 10594 1623 3014 520 85 453 1786 .285 1171 5063 126 19 yrs

Jesus Manuel Marcano Trillo   Born Dec 25, 1950   Caripito, Venezuela
6'1   150 lbs   Batted right

YR	POS	TEAM	LG	FIN	G	AB	R	H	2B	3B	HR	RBI	AVG	BB	TB	OQ	RANK
1973	2B	OAK	AL	1-6	17	12	0	3	2	0	0	3	.250	0	5	—	—
1974	2B	OAK	AL	1-6	21	33	3	5	0	0	0	2	.152	2	5	—	—
1975	2B	CHI	NL	5-6	154	545	55	135	12	2	7	70	.248	45	172	83	59-65
1976	2B	CHI	NL	4-6	158	582	42	139	24	3	4	59	.239	53	181	86	48-57
1977	2B	CHI	NL	4-6	152	504	51	141	18	5	7	57	.280	44	190	96	50-68
1978	2B	CHI	NL	3-6	152	552	53	144	17	5	4	55	.261	50	183	91	55-63
1979	2B	PHI	NL	4-6	118	431	40	112	22	1	6	42	.260	20	154	84	—
1980	2B	PHI	NL	1-6	141	531	68	155	25	9	7	43	.292	32	219	107	34-59
1981	2B	PHI	NL	3-6	94	349	37	100	14	3	6	36	.287	26	138	107	38-69
1982	2B	PHI	NL	2-6	149	549	52	149	24	1	0	39	.271	33	175	83	63-66
1983	2B	CLE	AL	7-7	88	320	33	87	13	1	1	29	.272	21	105	81	—
1983	2B	MON	NL	3-6	31	121	16	32	8	0	2	16	.264	10	46	99	—
1984	2B	SF	NL	6-6	98	401	45	102	21	1	4	36	.254	25	137	87	—
1985	2B	SF	NL	6-6	125	451	36	101	16	2	3	25	.224	40	130	77	64-65
1986	3B-1B	CHI	NL	5-6	81	152	22	45	10	0	1	19	.296	16	58	108	—
1987	1B-3B	CHI	NL	6-6	108	214	27	63	8	0	8	26	.294	25	95	117	—
1988	1B-3B	CHI	NL	4-6	76	164	15	41	5	0	1	14	.250	8	49	77	—
1989	2B-1B	CIN	NL	5-6	17	39	3	8	0	0	0	0	.205	2	8	—	—
MAJOR LEAGUE TOTALS					1780	5950	598	1562	239	33	61	571	.263	452	2050	91	8 yrs

Bill Madlock   Born Jan 2, 1951   Memphis, TN
5'11   180 lbs   Batted right

YR	POS	TEAM	LG	FIN	G	AB	R	H	2B	3B	HR	RBI	AVG	BB	TB	OQ	RANK
1973	3B	TEX	AL	6-6	21	77	16	27	5	3	1	5	.351	7	41	—	—
1974	3B	CHI	NL	6-6	128	453	65	142	21	5	9	54	.313	42	200	123	16-65
1975	3B	CHI	NL	5-6	130	514	77	182	29	7	7	64	.354	42	246	137	10-65
1976	3B	CHI	NL	4-6	142	514	68	174	36	1	15	84	.339	56	257	150	3-57
1977	3B	SF	NL	4-6	140	533	70	161	28	1	12	46	.302	43	227	109	41-68
1978	2B	SF	NL	3-6	122	447	76	138	26	3	15	44	.309	48	215	136	11-63
1979	3B-2B	SF/PT	NL	4/1	154	560	85	167	26	5	14	85	.298	52	245	117	26-62
1980	3B	PIT	NL	3-6	137	494	62	137	22	4	10	53	.277	45	197	108	32-59
1981	3B	PIT	NL	4-6	82	279	35	95	23	1	6	45	.341	34	138	152	2-69
1982	3B	PIT	NL	4-6	154	568	92	181	33	3	19	95	.319	48	277	135	12-66
1983	3B	PIT	NL	2-6	130	473	68	153	21	0	12	68	.323	49	210	127	13-64
1984	3B	PIT	NL	6-6	103	403	38	102	16	0	4	44	.253	26	130	83	—
1985	3B	PT/LA	NL	6/1	144	513	69	141	27	1	12	56	.275	49	206	109	30-65
1986	3B	LA	NL	5-6	111	379	38	106	17	0	10	60	.280	30	153	104	—
1987	3B	LA	NL	4-6	21	61	5	11	1	0	3	7	.180	6	21	—	—
1987	DH-1B	DET	AL	1-7	87	326	56	91	17	0	14	50	.279	28	150	106	—
MAJOR LEAGUE TOTALS					1806	6594	920	2008	348	34	163	860	.305	605	2913	128	11 yrs

Charles Ray Knight   Born Dec 28, 1952   Albany, GA
6'1   185 lbs   Batted right

YR	POS	TEAM	LG	FIN	G	AB	R	H	2B	3B	HR	RBI	AVG	BB	TB	OQ	RANK
1974	3B	CIN	NL	2-6	14	11	1	2	1	0	0	2	.182	1	3	—	—
1977	3B-2B	CIN	NL	2-6	80	92	8	24	5	1	1	13	.261	9	34	94	—
1978	3B	CIN	NL	2-6	83	65	7	13	3	0	1	4	.200	3	19	—	—
1979	3B	CIN	NL	1-6	150	551	64	175	37	4	10	79	.318	38	250	118	24-62
1980	3B	CIN	NL	3-6	162	618	71	163	39	7	14	78	.264	36	258	103	41-59
1981	3B	CIN	NL	1-6	106	386	43	100	23	1	6	34	.259	33	143	100	46-69
1982	1B-3B	HOU	NL	5-6	158	609	72	179	36	6	6	70	.294	48	245	109	33-66
1983	1B	HOU	NL	3-6	145	507	43	154	36	4	9	70	.304	42	225	119	21-64
1984	3B-1B	HO/NY	NL	2/2	115	371	28	88	14	0	3	35	.237	21	111	75	—
1985	3B	NY	NL	2-6	90	271	22	59	12	0	6	36	.218	13	89	76	—
1986	3B	NY	NL	1-6	137	486	51	145	24	2	11	76	.298	40	206	112	24-49
1987	3B	BAL	AL	6-7	150	563	46	144	24	0	14	65	.256	39	210	83	74-79
1988	1B-DH	DET	AL	2-7	105	299	34	65	12	2	3	33	.217	20	90	72	—
MAJOR LEAGUE TOTALS					1495	4829	490	1311	266	27	84	595	.271	343	1883	106	7 yrs

Jerry Wayne Mumphrey   Born Sep 9, 1952   Tyler, TX
6'2   185 lbs   Batted both

YR	POS	TEAM	LG	FIN	G	AB	R	H	2B	3B	HR	RBI	AVG	BB	TB	OQ	RANK
1974	LF	SL	NL	2-6	5	2	2	0	0	0	0	0	.000	0	0	—	—
1975	RF	SL	NL	3-6	11	16	2	6	2	0	0	1	.375	4	8	—	—
1976	CF	SL	NL	5-6	112	384	51	99	15	5	1	26	.258	37	127	94	—
1977	CF	SL	NL	3-6	145	463	73	133	20	10	2	38	.287	47	179	102	47-68
1978	LF	SL	NL	5-6	125	367	41	96	13	4	2	37	.262	30	123	90	—
1979	LF	SL	NL	3-6	124	339	53	100	10	3	3	32	.295	26	125	98	—
1980	CF	SD	NL	6-6	160	564	61	168	24	3	4	59	.298	49	210	104	37-59
1981	CF	NY	AL	3-7	80	319	44	98	11	5	6	32	.307	24	137	116	24-71
1982	CF	NY	AL	5-7	123	477	76	143	24	10	9	68	.300	50	214	117	27-77
1983	CF	NY	AL	3-7	83	267	41	70	11	4	7	36	.262	28	110	105	—
1983	CF	HOU	NL	3-6	44	143	17	48	10	2	1	17	.336	22	65	144	—
1984	CF	HOU	NL	2-6	151	524	66	152	20	3	9	83	.290	56	205	113	25-53
1985	RF	HOU	NL	3-6	130	444	52	123	25	2	8	61	.277	37	176	106	—
1986	CF	CHI	NL	5-6	111	309	37	94	11	2	5	32	.304	26	124	109	—
1987	LF	CHI	NL	6-6	118	309	41	103	19	2	13	44	.333	35	165	143	—
1988	LF	CHI	NL	4-6	63	66	3	9	2	0	0	9	.136	7	11	—	—
MAJOR LEAGUE TOTALS					1585	4993	660	1442	217	55	70	575	.289	478	1979	110	5 yrs

Warren Livingston Cromartie

Born Sep 29, 1953 Miami Beach, FL

6'0 180 lbs Batted left

YR	POS	TEAM	LG	FIN	G	AB	R	H	2B	3B	HR	RBI	AVG	BB	TB	OQ	RANK
1974	LF	MON	NL	4-6	8	17	2	3	0	0	0	0	.176	3	3	—	—
1976	RF-LF	MON	NL	6-6	33	81	8	17	1	0	0	2	.210	1	18	—	—
1977	LF	MON	NL	5-6	155	620	64	175	41	7	5	50	.282	33	245	93	56-68
1978	LF	MON	NL	4-6	159	607	77	180	32	6	10	56	.297	33	254	107	37-63
1979	LF	MON	NL	2-6	158	659	84	181	46	5	8	46	.275	38	261	97	48-62
1980	1B	MON	NL	2-6	162	597	74	172	33	5	14	70	.288	51	257	116	26-59
1981	1B-RF	MON	NL	2-6	99	358	41	109	19	2	6	42	.304	39	150	123	21-69
1982	RF	MON	NL	3-6	144	497	59	126	24	3	14	62	.254	69	198	116	26-66
1983	RF	MON	NL	3-6	120	360	37	100	26	2	3	43	.278	43	139	110	—
1991	1B-LF	KC	AL	6-7	69	131	13	41	7	2	1	20	.313	15	55	116	—
MAJOR LEAGUE TOTALS					1107	3927	459	1104	229	32	61	391	.281	325	1580	109	6 yrs

Gary Edmund Carter

Born Apr 8, 1954 Culver City, CA

6'2 205 lbs Batted right

YR	POS	TEAM	LG	FIN	G	AB	R	H	2B	3B	HR	RBI	AVG	BB	TB	OQ	RANK
1974	C-RF	MON	NL	4-6	9	27	5	11	0	1	1	6	.407	1	16	—	—
1975	LF-C	MON	NL	5-6	144	503	58	136	20	1	17	68	.270	72	209	121	29-65
1976	C-RF	MON	NL	6-6	91	311	31	68	8	1	6	38	.219	30	96	85	—
1977	C	MON	NL	5-6	154	522	86	148	29	2	31	84	.284	58	274	133	12-68
1978	C	MON	NL	4-6	157	533	76	136	27	1	20	72	.255	62	225	115	30-63
1979	C	MON	NL	2-6	141	505	74	143	26	5	22	75	.283	40	245	122	20-62
1980	C	MON	NL	2-6	154	549	76	145	25	5	29	101	.264	58	267	128	13-59
1981	C	MON	NL	2-6	100	374	48	94	20	2	16	68	.251	35	166	117	25-69
1982	C	MON	NL	3-6	154	557	91	163	32	1	29	97	.293	78	284	148	6-66
1983	C	MON	NL	3-6	145	541	63	146	37	3	17	79	.270	51	240	116	24-64
1984	C-1B	MON	NL	5-6	159	596	75	175	32	1	27	106	.294	64	290	135	9-53
1985	C	NY	NL	2-6	149	555	83	156	17	1	32	100	.281	69	271	135	9-65
1986	C	NY	NL	1-6	132	490	81	125	14	2	24	105	.255	62	215	118	21-49
1987	C	NY	NL	2-6	139	523	55	123	18	2	20	83	.235	42	205	91	54-59
1988	C	NY	NL	1-6	130	455	39	110	16	2	11	46	.242	34	163	95	50-58
1989	C	NY	NL	2-6	50	153	14	28	8	0	2	15	.183	12	42	71	—
1990	C	SF	NL	3-6	92	244	24	62	10	0	9	27	.254	25	99	106	—
1991	C	LA	NL	2-6	101	248	22	61	14	0	6	26	.246	22	93	98	—
1992	C	MON	NL	2-6	95	285	24	62	18	1	5	29	.218	33	97	95	—
MAJOR LEAGUE TOTALS					2296	7971	1025	2092	371	31	324	1225	.262	848	3497	121	13 yrs

Larry Alton Parrish　　　　　Born Nov 10, 1953 Winter Haven, FL
6'3 190 lbs Batted right

YR	POS	TEAM	LG	FIN	G	AB	R	H	2B	3B	HR	RBI	AVG	BB	TB	OQ	RANK
1974	3B	MON	NL	4-6	25	69	9	14	5	0	0	4	.203	6	19	—	—
1975	3B	MON	NL	5-6	145	532	50	146	32	5	10	65	.274	28	218	100	45-65
1976	3B	MON	NL	6-6	154	543	65	126	28	5	11	61	.232	41	197	93	40-57
1977	3B	MON	NL	5-6	123	402	50	99	19	2	11	46	.246	37	155	95	—
1978	3B	MON	NL	4-6	144	520	68	144	39	4	15	70	.277	32	236	114	32-63
1979	3B	MON	NL	2-6	153	544	83	167	39	2	30	82	.307	41	300	140	9-62
1980	3B	MON	NL	2-6	126	452	55	115	27	3	15	72	.254	36	193	108	31-59
1981	3B	MON	NL	2-6	97	349	41	85	19	3	8	44	.244	28	134	100	47-69
1982	RF	TEX	AL	6-7	128	440	59	116	15	0	17	62	.264	30	182	97	—
1983	RF	TEX	AL	3-7	145	555	76	151	26	4	26	88	.272	46	263	114	28-70
1984	RF-DH	TEX	AL	7-7	156	613	72	175	42	1	22	101	.285	42	285	112	30-68
1985	RF-DH	TEX	AL	7-7	94	346	44	86	11	1	17	51	.249	33	150	104	—
1986	DH-3B	TEX	AL	2-7	129	464	67	128	22	1	28	94	.276	52	236	125	12-78
1987	DH-3B	TEX	AL	6-7	152	557	79	149	22	1	32	100	.268	49	269	109	38-79
1988	DH-1B	TX/BO	AL	6/1	120	406	32	88	14	1	14	52	.217	28	146	84	—

MAJOR LEAGUE TOTALS　　　1891　6792　850　1789　360　33　256　992　.263　529　2983　112　10 yrs

James Edward Rice　　　　　Born Mar 8, 1953 Anderson, SC
6'2 200 lbs Batted right

YR	POS	TEAM	LG	FIN	G	AB	R	H	2B	3B	HR	RBI	AVG	BB	TB	OQ	RANK
1974	DH-LF	BOS	AL	3-6	24	67	6	18	2	1	1	13	.269	4	25	—	—
1975	LF-DH	BOS	AL	1-6	144	564	92	174	29	4	22	102	.309	36	277	124	16-66
1976	LF-DH	BOS	AL	3-6	153	581	75	164	25	8	25	85	.282	28	280	121	17-64
1977	DH-LF	BOS	AL	2-7	160	644	104	206	29	15	39	114	.320	53	382	146	3-81
1978	LF-DH	BOS	AL	2-7	163	677	121	213	25	15	46	139	.315	58	406	154	1-83
1979	LF-DH	BOS	AL	3-7	158	619	117	201	39	6	39	130	.325	57	369	147	4-75
1980	LF-DH	BOS	AL	4-7	124	504	81	148	22	6	24	86	.294	30	254	119	20-69
1981	LF	BOS	AL	5-7	108	451	51	128	18	1	17	62	.284	34	199	115	25-71
1982	LF	BOS	AL	3-7	145	573	86	177	24	5	24	97	.309	55	283	127	15-77
1983	LF	BOS	AL	6-7	155	626	90	191	34	1	39	126	.305	52	344	136	4-70
1984	LF	BOS	AL	4-7	159	657	98	184	25	7	28	122	.280	44	307	112	31-68
1985	LF	BOS	AL	5-7	140	546	85	159	20	3	27	103	.291	51	266	120	16-75
1986	LF	BOS	AL	1-7	157	618	98	200	39	2	20	110	.324	62	303	127	9-78
1987	LF-DH	BOS	AL	5-7	108	404	66	112	14	0	13	62	.277	45	165	101	—
1988	DH-LF	BOS	AL	1-7	135	485	57	128	18	3	15	72	.264	48	197	105	42-74
1989	DH	BOS	AL	3-7	56	209	22	49	10	2	3	28	.234	13	72	82	—

MAJOR LEAGUE TOTALS　　　2089　8225　1249　2452　373　79　382　1451　.298　670　4129　127　13 yrs

Ivan DeJesus   Born Jan 9, 1953   Santurce, PR
5'11   175 lbs   Batted right

YR	POS	TEAM	LG	FIN	G	AB	R	H	2B	3B	HR	RBI	AVG	BB	TB	OQ	RANK
1974	SS	LA	NL	1-6	3	3	1	1	0	0	0	0	.333	0	1	—	—
1975	SS	LA	NL	2-6	63	87	10	16	2	1	0	2	.184	11	20	—	—
1976	SS	LA	NL	2-6	22	41	4	7	2	1	0	2	.171	4	11	—	—
1977	SS	CHI	NL	4-6	155	624	91	166	31	7	3	40	.266	56	220	90	58-68
1978	SS	CHI	NL	3-6	160	619	104	172	24	7	3	35	.278	74	219	104	42-63
1979	SS	CHI	NL	5-6	160	636	92	180	26	10	5	52	.283	59	241	102	44-62
1980	SS	CHI	NL	6-6	157	618	78	160	26	3	3	33	.259	60	201	91	49-59
1981	SS	CHI	NL	6-6	106	403	49	78	8	4	0	13	.194	46	94	70	68-69
1982	SS	PHI	NL	2-6	161	536	53	128	21	5	3	59	.239	54	168	87	61-66
1983	SS	PHI	NL	1-6	158	497	60	126	15	7	4	45	.254	53	167	93	53-64
1984	SS	PHI	NL	4-6	144	435	40	112	15	3	0	35	.257	43	133	88	—
1985	3B-SS	SL	NL	1-6	59	72	11	16	5	0	0	7	.222	4	21	—	—
1986	SS	NY	AL	2-7	7	4	1	0	0	0	0	0	.000	1	0	—	—
1987	SS	SF	NL	1-6	9	10	0	2	0	0	0	1	.200	0	2	—	—
1988	SS	DET	AL	2-7	7	17	1	3	0	0	0	0	.176	1	3	—	—

MAJOR LEAGUE TOTALS   1371   4602 595 1167 175 48 21 324 .254 466 1501   91   7 yrs

Richard Paul Burleson   Born Apr 29, 1951 Lynwood, CA
5'10   165 lbs   Batted right

YR	POS	TEAM	LG	FIN	G	AB	R	H	2B	3B	HR	RBI	AVG	BB	TB	OQ	RANK
1974	SS-2B	BOS	AL	3-6	114	384	36	109	22	0	4	44	.284	21	143	95	—
1975	SS	BOS	AL	1-6	158	580	66	146	25	1	6	62	.252	45	191	84	56-66
1976	SS	BOS	AL	3-6	152	540	75	157	27	1	7	42	.291	60	207	114	27-64
1977	SS	BOS	AL	2-7	154	663	80	194	36	7	3	52	.293	47	253	94	63-81
1978	SS	BOS	AL	2-7	145	626	75	155	32	5	5	49	.248	40	212	82	77-83
1979	SS	BOS	AL	3-7	153	627	93	174	32	5	5	60	.278	35	231	85	68-75
1980	SS	BOS	AL	4-7	155	644	89	179	29	2	8	51	.278	62	236	95	56-69
1981	SS	CAL	AL	5-7	109	430	53	126	17	1	5	33	.293	42	160	106	40-71
1982	SS	CAL	AL	1-7	11	45	4	7	1	0	0	2	.156	6	8	—	—
1983	SS	CAL	AL	5-7	33	119	22	34	7	0	0	11	.286	12	41	93	—
1984	PH	CAL	AL	2-7	7	4	2	0	0	0	0	0	.000	0	0	—	—
1986	DH-SS	CAL	AL	1-7	93	271	35	77	14	0	5	29	.284	33	106	104	—
1987	2B	BAL	AL	6-7	62	206	26	43	14	1	2	14	.209	17	65	70	—

MAJOR LEAGUE TOTALS   1346   5139 656 1401 256 23 50 449 .273 420 1853   94   7 yrs

Alfred Edward Cowens   Born Oct 25, 1951   Los Angeles, CA
6'1   197 lbs   Batted right

YR	POS	TEAM	LG	FIN	G	AB	R	H	2B	3B	HR	RBI	AVG	BB	TB	OQ	RANK
1974	RF-CF	KC	AL	5-6	110	269	28	65	7	1	1	25	.242	23	77	78	—
1975	RF	KC	AL	2-6	120	328	44	91	13	8	4	42	.277	28	132	104	—
1976	RF	KC	AL	1-6	152	581	71	154	23	6	3	59	.265	26	198	86	56-64
1977	RF	KC	AL	1-7	162	606	98	189	32	14	23	112	.312	41	318	127	17-81
1978	RF	KC	AL	1-7	132	485	63	133	24	8	5	63	.274	31	188	96	60-83
1979	RF	KC	AL	2-7	136	516	69	152	18	7	9	73	.295	40	211	100	48-75
1980	RF	CA/DE	AL	6/5	142	522	69	140	20	3	6	59	.268	49	184	91	60-69
1981	CF	DET	AL	4-7	85	253	27	66	11	4	1	18	.261	22	88	94	—
1982	RF	SEA	AL	4-7	146	560	72	151	39	8	20	78	.270	46	266	113	36-77
1983	RF-DH	SEA	AL	7-7	110	356	39	73	19	2	7	35	.205	23	117	74	—
1984	RF	SEA	AL	5-7	139	524	60	145	34	2	15	78	.277	27	228	101	46-68
1985	RF	SEA	AL	6-7	122	452	59	120	32	5	14	69	.265	30	204	104	—
1986	RF	SEA	AL	7-7	28	82	5	15	4	0	0	6	.183	3	19	—	—

MAJOR LEAGUE TOTALS					1584	5534	704	1494	276	68	108	717	.270	389	2230	102	7 yrs

Frederic Michael Lynn   Born Feb 3, 1952   Chicago, IL
6'1   185 lbs   Batted left

YR	POS	TEAM	LG	FIN	G	AB	R	H	2B	3B	HR	RBI	AVG	BB	TB	OQ	RANK
1974	LF-CF	BOS	AL	3-6	15	43	5	18	2	2	2	10	.419	6	30	—	—
1975	CF	BOS	AL	1-6	145	528	103	175	47	7	21	105	.331	62	299	158	2-66
1976	CF	BOS	AL	3-6	132	507	76	159	32	8	10	65	.314	48	237	134	5-64
1977	CF	BOS	AL	2-7	129	497	81	129	29	5	18	76	.260	51	222	109	37-81
1978	CF	BOS	AL	2-7	150	541	75	161	33	3	22	82	.298	75	266	138	6-83
1979	CF	BOS	AL	3-7	147	531	116	177	42	1	39	122	.333	82	338	172	1-75
1980	CF	BOS	AL	4-7	110	415	67	125	32	3	12	61	.301	58	199	132	—
1981	CF	CAL	AL	5-7	76	256	28	56	8	1	5	31	.219	38	81	95	—
1982	CF	CAL	AL	1-7	138	472	89	141	38	1	21	86	.299	58	244	135	8-77
1983	CF	CAL	AL	5-7	117	437	56	119	20	3	22	74	.272	55	211	125	17-70
1984	RF	CAL	AL	2-7	142	517	84	140	28	4	23	79	.271	77	245	128	13-68
1985	CF	BAL	AL	4-7	124	448	59	118	12	1	23	68	.263	53	201	113	27-75
1986	CF	BAL	AL	7-7	112	397	67	114	13	1	23	67	.287	53	198	129	—
1987	CF	BAL	AL	6-7	111	396	49	100	24	0	23	60	.253	39	193	110	—
1988	CF-LF	BA/DE	AL	7/2	114	391	46	96	14	1	25	56	.246	33	187	114	—
1989	LF-DH	DET	AL	7-7	117	353	44	85	11	1	11	46	.241	47	131	103	—
1990	LF-CF	SD	NL	4-6	90	196	18	47	3	1	6	23	.240	22	70	96	—

MAJOR LEAGUE TOTALS					1969	6925	1063	1960	388	43	306	1111	.283	857	3352	135	9 yrs

Dudley Michael Hargrove   Born Oct 26, 1949   Perryton, TX
6'0   195 lbs   Batted left

YR	POS	TEAM	LG	FIN	G	AB	R	H	2B	3B	HR	RBI	AVG	BB	TB	OQ	RANK
1974	1B-DH	TEX	AL	2-6	131	415	57	134	18	6	4	66	.323	49	176	128	—
1975	LF-1B	TEX	AL	3-6	145	519	82	157	22	2	11	62	.303	79	216	126	14-66
1976	1B	TEX	AL	4-6	151	541	80	155	30	1	7	58	.287	97	208	130	10-64
1977	1B	TEX	AL	2-7	153	525	98	160	28	4	18	69	.305	103	250	142	6-81
1978	1B	TEX	AL	2-7	146	494	63	124	24	1	7	40	.251	107	171	116	34-83
1979	1B	SD	NL	5-6	52	125	15	24	5	0	0	8	.192	25	29	83	—
1979	LF-1B	CLE	AL	6-7	100	338	60	110	21	4	10	56	.325	63	169	147	—
1980	1B	CLE	AL	6-7	160	589	86	179	22	2	11	85	.304	111	238	126	12-69
1981	1B	CLE	AL	6-7	94	322	43	102	21	0	2	49	.317	60	129	137	7-71
1982	1B	CLE	AL	6-7	160	591	67	160	26	1	4	65	.271	101	200	103	49-77
1983	1B	CLE	AL	7-7	134	469	57	134	21	4	3	57	.286	78	172	111	33-70
1984	1B	CLE	AL	6-7	133	352	44	94	14	2	2	44	.267	53	118	100	—
1985	1B	CLE	AL	7-7	107	284	31	81	14	1	1	27	.285	39	100	101	—

| MAJOR LEAGUE TOTALS | | | | | 1666 | 5564 | 783 | 1614 | 266 | 28 | 80 | 686 | .290 | 965 | 2176 | 124 | 8 yrs |

Keith Hernandez   Born Oct 20, 1953   San Francisco, CA
6'0   180 lbs   Batted left

YR	POS	TEAM	LG	FIN	G	AB	R	H	2B	3B	HR	RBI	AVG	BB	TB	OQ	RANK
1974	1B	SL	NL	2-6	14	34	3	10	1	2	0	2	.294	7	15	—	—
1975	1B	SL	NL	3-6	64	188	20	47	8	2	3	20	.250	17	68	95	—
1976	1B	SL	NL	5-6	129	374	54	108	21	5	7	46	.289	49	160	128	—
1977	1B	SL	NL	3-6	161	560	90	163	41	4	15	91	.291	79	257	126	18-68
1978	1B	SL	NL	5-6	159	542	90	138	32	4	11	64	.255	82	211	116	29-63
1979	1B	SL	NL	3-6	161	610	116	210	48	11	11	105	.344	80	313	152	4-62
1980	1B	SL	NL	4-6	159	595	111	191	39	8	16	99	.321	86	294	150	3-59
1981	1B	SL	NL	1-6	103	376	65	115	27	4	8	48	.306	61	174	146	5-69
1982	1B	SL	NL	1-6	160	579	79	173	33	6	7	94	.299	100	239	134	13-66
1983	1B	SL/NY	NL	4/6	150	538	77	160	23	7	12	63	.297	88	233	133	8-64
1984	1B	NY	NL	2-6	154	550	83	171	31	0	15	94	.311	97	247	146	3-53
1985	1B	NY	NL	2-6	158	593	87	183	34	4	10	91	.309	77	255	129	14-65
1986	1B	NY	NL	1-6	149	551	94	171	34	1	13	83	.310	94	246	139	3-49
1987	1B	NY	NL	2-6	154	587	87	170	28	2	18	89	.290	81	256	119	19-59
1988	1B	NY	NL	1-6	95	348	43	96	16	0	11	55	.276	31	145	116	—
1989	1B	NY	NL	2-6	75	215	18	50	8	0	4	19	.233	27	70	96	—
1990	1B	CLE	AL	4-7	43	130	7	26	2	0	1	8	.200	14	31	66	—

| MAJOR LEAGUE TOTALS | | | | | 2088 | 7370 | 1124 | 2182 | 426 | 60 | 162 | 1071 | .296 | 1070 | 3214 | 135 | 11 yrs |

Ronald LeFlore   Born Jun 16, 1948   Detroit, MI
6'0   200 lbs   Batted right

YR	POS	TEAM	LG	FIN	G	AB	R	H	2B	3B	HR	RBI	AVG	BB	TB	OQ	RANK
1974	CF	DET	AL	6-6	59	254	37	66	8	1	2	13	.260	13	82	81	—
1975	CF	DET	AL	6-6	136	550	66	142	13	6	8	37	.258	33	191	85	55-66
1976	CF	DET	AL	5-6	135	544	93	172	23	8	4	39	.316	51	223	121	19-64
1977	CF	DET	AL	4-7	154	652	100	212	30	10	16	57	.325	37	310	116	25-81
1978	CF	DET	AL	5-7	155	666	126	198	30	3	12	62	.297	65	270	110	38-83
1979	CF-DH	DET	AL	5-7	148	600	110	180	22	10	9	57	.300	52	249	104	40-75
1980	LF	MON	NL	2-6	139	521	95	134	21	11	4	39	.257	62	189	104	40-59
1981	LF	CHI	AL	3-7	82	337	46	83	10	4	0	24	.246	28	101	81	69-71
1982	CF	CHI	AL	3-7	91	334	58	96	15	4	4	25	.287	22	131	95	—

MAJOR LEAGUE TOTALS   1099 4458 731 1283 172 57 59 353 .288 363 1746 103   7 yrs

Robin R Yount   Born Sep 16, 1955   Danville, IL
6'0   165 lbs   Batted right

YR	POS	TEAM	LG	FIN	G	AB	R	H	2B	3B	HR	RBI	AVG	BB	TB	OQ	RANK
1974	SS	MIL	AL	5-6	107	344	48	86	14	5	3	26	.250	12	119	81	—
1975	SS	MIL	AL	5-6	147	558	67	149	28	2	8	52	.267	33	205	90	52-66
1976	SS	MIL	AL	6-6	161	638	59	161	19	3	2	54	.252	38	192	79	61-64
1977	SS	MIL	AL	6-7	154	605	66	174	34	4	4	49	.288	41	228	92	67-81
1978	SS	MIL	AL	3-7	127	502	66	147	23	9	9	71	.293	24	215	104	49-83
1979	SS	MIL	AL	2-7	149	577	72	154	26	5	8	51	.267	35	214	85	66-75
1980	SS	MIL	AL	3-7	143	611	121	179	49	10	23	87	.293	26	317	118	22-69
1981	SS	MIL	AL	1-7	96	377	50	103	15	5	10	49	.273	22	158	105	43-71
1982	SS	MIL	AL	1-7	156	635	129	210	46	12	29	114	.331	54	367	147	2-77
1983	SS	MIL	AL	5-7	149	578	102	178	42	10	17	80	.308	72	291	136	5-70
1984	SS-DH	MIL	AL	7-7	160	624	105	186	27	7	16	80	.298	67	275	117	23-68
1985	LF	MIL	AL	6-7	122	466	76	129	26	3	15	68	.277	49	206	111	32-75
1986	CF	MIL	AL	6-7	140	522	82	163	31	7	9	46	.312	62	235	120	20-78
1987	CF	MIL	AL	3-7	158	635	99	198	25	9	21	103	.312	76	304	122	22-79
1988	CF	MIL	AL	4-7	162	621	92	190	38	11	13	91	.306	63	289	125	20-74
1989	CF-DH	MIL	AL	4-7	160	614	101	195	38	9	21	103	.318	63	314	139	5-67
1990	CF	MIL	AL	6-7	158	587	98	145	17	5	17	77	.247	78	223	104	42-69
1991	CF-DH	MIL	AL	4-7	130	503	66	131	20	4	10	77	.260	54	189	98	54-72
1992	CF	MIL	AL	2-7	150	557	71	147	40	3	8	77	.264	53	217	101	50-73
1993	CF	MIL	AL	7-7	127	454	62	117	25	3	8	51	.258	44	172	92	58-73

MAJOR LEAGUE TOTALS   2856 11008 1632 3142 583 126 251 1406 .285 966 4730 110   19 yrs

Bruce Anton Bochte   Born Nov 12, 1950 Pasadena, CA
6'3 195 lbs Batted left

YR	POS	TEAM	LG	FIN	G	AB	R	H	2B	3B	HR	RBI	AVG	BB	TB	OQ	RANK
1974	LF-1B	CAL	AL	6-6	57	196	24	53	4	1	5	26	.270	18	74	103	—
1975	1B	CAL	AL	6-6	107	375	41	107	19	3	3	48	.285	45	141	107	—
1976	LF-1B	CAL	AL	4-6	146	466	53	120	17	1	2	49	.258	64	145	99	49-64
1977	LF-1B	CA/CL	AL	5/5	137	492	64	148	23	1	7	51	.301	47	194	103	51-81
1978	RF-DH	SEA	AL	7-7	140	486	58	128	25	3	11	51	.263	60	192	108	41-83
1979	1B	SEA	AL	6-7	150	554	81	175	38	6	16	100	.316	67	273	130	13-75
1980	1B	SEA	AL	7-7	148	520	62	156	34	4	13	78	.300	72	237	126	13-69
1981	1B-LF	SEA	AL	6-7	99	335	39	87	16	0	6	30	.260	47	121	108	36-71
1982	LF-1B	SEA	AL	4-7	144	509	58	151	21	0	12	70	.297	67	208	114	34-77
1984	1B	OAK	AL	4-7	148	469	58	124	23	0	5	52	.264	52	162	93	53-68
1985	1B	OAK	AL	4-7	137	424	48	125	17	1	14	60	.295	49	186	116	—
1986	1B	OAK	AL	3-7	125	407	57	104	13	1	6	43	.256	65	137	97	—
MAJOR LEAGUE TOTALS					1538	5233	643	1478	250	21	100	658	.282	653	2070	110	8 yrs

Claudell Washington   Born Aug 31, 1954 Los Angeles, CA
6'0 190 lbs Batted left

YR	POS	TEAM	LG	FIN	G	AB	R	H	2B	3B	HR	RBI	AVG	BB	TB	OQ	RANK
1974	DH-LF	OAK	AL	1-6	73	221	16	63	10	5	0	19	.285	13	83	97	—
1975	LF	OAK	AL	1-6	148	590	86	182	24	7	10	77	.308	32	250	107	32-66
1976	RF	OAK	AL	2-6	134	490	65	126	20	6	5	53	.257	30	173	91	53-64
1977	RF	TEX	AL	2-7	129	521	63	148	31	2	12	68	.284	25	219	96	61-81
1978	RF	TX/CH	AL	2/5	98	356	34	90	16	5	6	33	.253	13	134	85	—
1979	RF	CHI	AL	5-7	131	471	79	132	33	5	13	66	.280	28	214	103	42-75
1980	RF	CHI	AL	5-7	32	90	15	26	4	2	1	12	.289	5	37	—	—
1980	RF	NY	NL	5-6	79	284	38	78	16	4	10	42	.275	20	132	118	—
1981	RF	ATL	NL	5-6	85	320	37	93	22	3	5	37	.291	15	136	108	36-69
1982	RF	ATL	NL	1-6	150	563	94	150	24	6	16	80	.266	50	234	110	32-66
1983	RF	ATL	NL	2-6	134	496	75	138	24	8	9	44	.278	35	205	105	40-64
1984	RF	ATL	NL	2-6	120	416	62	119	21	2	17	61	.286	59	195	138	—
1985	RF	ATL	NL	5-6	122	398	62	110	14	6	15	43	.276	40	181	122	—
1986	RF	ATL	NL	6-6	40	137	17	37	11	0	5	14	.270	14	63	120	—
1986	CF-LF	NY	AL	2-7	54	135	19	32	5	0	6	16	.237	7	55	88	—
1987	CF-DH	NY	AL	4-7	102	312	42	87	17	0	9	44	.279	27	131	98	—
1988	CF	NY	AL	5-7	126	455	62	140	22	3	11	64	.308	24	201	109	36-74
1989	RF	CAL	AL	3-7	110	418	53	114	18	4	13	42	.273	27	179	105	—
1990	LF-RF	CA/NY	AL	4/7	45	114	7	19	2	1	1	9	.167	4	26	48	—
MAJOR LEAGUE TOTALS					1912	6787	926	1884	334	69	164	824	.278	468	2848	104	8 yrs

Larry Darnell Herndon Born Nov 3, 1953 Sunflower, MS
6'3 190 lbs Batted right

YR	POS	TEAM	LG	FIN	G	AB	R	H	2B	3B	HR	RBI	AVG	BB	TB	OQ	RANK
1974	CF	SL	NL	2-6	12	1	3	1	0	0	0	0	1.000	0	1	—	—
1976	CF	SF	NL	4-6	115	337	42	97	11	3	2	23	.288	23	120	97	—
1977	CF	SF	NL	4-6	49	109	13	26	4	3	1	5	.239	5	39	79	—
1978	CF	SF	NL	3-6	151	471	52	122	15	9	1	32	.259	35	158	88	57-63
1979	LF	SF	NL	4-6	132	354	35	91	14	5	7	36	.257	29	136	97	—
1980	LF	SF	NL	5-6	139	493	54	127	17	11	8	49	.258	19	190	91	48-59
1981	LF	SF	NL	4-6	96	364	48	105	15	8	5	41	.288	20	151	107	37-69
1982	LF	DET	AL	4-7	157	614	92	179	21	13	23	88	.292	38	295	113	35-77
1983	LF-DH	DET	AL	2-7	153	603	88	182	28	9	20	92	.302	46	288	118	23-70
1984	LF	DET	AL	1-7	125	407	52	114	18	5	7	43	.280	32	163	100	—
1985	LF	DET	AL	3-7	137	442	45	108	12	7	12	37	.244	33	170	89	—
1986	LF-DH	DET	AL	3-7	106	283	33	70	13	1	8	37	.247	27	109	93	—
1987	LF-DH	DET	AL	1-7	89	225	32	73	13	2	9	47	.324	23	117	129	—
1988	DH-LF	DET	AL	2-7	76	174	16	39	5	0	4	20	.224	23	56	90	—
MAJOR LEAGUE TOTALS					1537	4877	605	1334	186	76	107	550	.274	353	1993	103	5 yrs

James Howard Sundberg Born May 18, 1951 Galesburg, IL
6'0 190 lbs Batted right

YR	POS	TEAM	LG	FIN	G	AB	R	H	2B	3B	HR	RBI	AVG	BB	TB	OQ	RANK
1974	C	TEX	AL	2-6	132	368	45	91	13	3	3	36	.247	62	119	104	—
1975	C	TEX	AL	3-6	155	472	45	94	9	0	6	36	.199	51	121	70	66-66
1976	C	TEX	AL	4-6	140	448	33	102	24	2	3	34	.228	37	139	83	—
1977	C	TEX	AL	2-7	149	453	61	132	20	3	6	65	.291	53	176	105	48-81
1978	C	TEX	AL	2-7	149	518	54	144	23	6	6	58	.278	64	197	107	43-83
1979	C	TEX	AL	3-7	150	495	50	136	23	4	5	64	.275	51	182	94	56-75
1980	C	TEX	AL	4-7	151	505	59	138	24	1	10	63	.273	64	194	104	40-69
1981	C	TEX	AL	2-7	102	339	42	94	17	2	3	28	.277	50	124	113	28-71
1982	C	TEX	AL	6-7	139	470	37	118	22	5	10	47	.251	49	180	96	56-77
1983	C	TEX	AL	3-7	131	378	30	76	14	0	2	28	.201	35	96	65	—
1984	C	MIL	AL	7-7	110	348	43	91	19	4	7	43	.261	38	139	104	—
1985	C	KC	AL	1-7	115	367	38	90	12	4	10	35	.245	33	140	92	—
1986	C	KC	AL	3-7	140	429	41	91	9	1	12	42	.212	57	138	84	74-78
1987	C	CHI	NL	6-6	61	139	9	28	2	0	4	15	.201	19	42	81	—
1988	C	CHI	NL	4-6	24	54	8	13	1	0	2	9	.241	8	20	—	—
1988	C	TEX	AL	6-7	38	91	13	26	4	0	4	13	.286	5	42	—	—
1989	C	TEX	AL	4-7	76	147	13	29	7	1	2	8	.197	23	44	88	—
MAJOR LEAGUE TOTALS					1962	6021	621	1493	243	36	95	624	.248	699	2093	97	8 yrs

Roy Frederick Smalley Jr
6'1 185 lbs Batted both

Born Oct 25, 1952 Los Angeles, CA

YR	POS	TEAM	LG	FIN	G	AB	R	H	2B	3B	HR	RBI	AVG	BB	TB	OQ	RANK
1975	SS-2B	TEX	AL	3-6	78	250	22	57	8	0	3	33	.228	30	74	83	—
1976	SS-2B	TX/MN	AL	4/3	144	513	61	133	18	3	3	44	.259	76	166	104	40-64
1977	SS	MIN	AL	4-7	150	584	93	135	21	5	6	56	.231	74	184	85	75-81
1978	SS	MIN	AL	4-7	158	586	80	160	31	3	19	77	.273	85	254	122	23-83
1979	SS	MIN	AL	4-7	162	621	94	168	28	3	24	95	.271	80	274	113	29-75
1980	SS	MIN	AL	3-7	133	486	64	135	24	1	12	63	.278	65	197	111	35-69
1981	SS-DH	MIN	AL	7-7	56	167	24	44	7	1	7	22	.263	31	74	136	—
1982	SS-3B	MN/NY	AL	7/5	146	499	57	127	15	2	20	67	.255	71	206	110	40-77
1983	SS-3B	NY	AL	3-7	130	451	70	124	24	1	18	62	.275	58	204	120	22-70
1984	3B-SS	NY/CH	AL	3/5	114	344	32	73	12	1	11	39	.212	37	120	87	—
1985	DH-SS	MIN	AL	4-7	129	388	57	100	20	0	12	45	.258	60	156	110	—
1986	DH-SS	MIN	AL	6-7	143	459	59	113	20	4	20	57	.246	68	201	113	31-78
1987	DH-3B	MIN	AL	1-7	110	309	32	85	16	1	8	34	.275	36	127	102	—

MAJOR LEAGUE TOTALS | | | | | 1653 | 5657 | 745 | 1454 | 244 | 25 | 163 | 694 | .257 | 771 | 2237 | 110 | 8 yrs

Omar Renan Moreno
6'2 180 lbs Batted left

Born Oct 24, 1952 Puerto Armuelles, Panama

YR	POS	TEAM	LG	FIN	G	AB	R	H	2B	3B	HR	RBI	AVG	BB	TB	OQ	RANK
1975	LF	PIT	NL	1-6	6	6	1	1	0	0	0	0	.167	1	1	—	—
1976	CF	PIT	NL	2-6	48	122	24	33	4	1	2	12	.270	16	45	112	—
1977	CF	PIT	NL	2-6	150	492	69	118	19	9	7	34	.240	38	176	86	62-68
1978	CF	PIT	NL	2-6	155	515	95	121	15	7	2	33	.235	81	156	96	50-63
1979	CF	PIT	NL	1-6	162	695	110	196	21	12	8	69	.282	51	265	98	46-62
1980	CF	PIT	NL	3-6	162	676	87	168	20	13	2	36	.249	57	220	87	53-59
1981	CF	PIT	NL	4-6	103	434	62	120	18	8	1	35	.276	26	157	95	53-69
1982	CF	PIT	NL	4-6	158	645	82	158	18	9	3	44	.245	44	203	81	65-66
1983	CF	HOU	NL	3-6	97	405	48	98	12	11	0	25	.242	22	132	79	—
1983	CF	NY	AL	3-7	48	152	17	38	9	1	1	17	.250	8	52	79	—
1984	CF	NY	AL	3-7	117	355	37	92	12	6	4	38	.259	18	128	83	—
1985	CF-RF	NY/KC	AL	2/1	58	136	21	30	5	4	3	16	.221	4	52	78	—
1986	RF	ATL	NL	6-6	118	359	46	84	18	6	4	27	.234	21	126	83	—

MAJOR LEAGUE TOTALS | | | | | 1382 | 4992 | 699 | 1257 | 171 | 87 | 37 | 386 | .252 | 387 | 1713 | 91 | 6 yrs

Richard Eugene Manning Born Sep 2, 1954 Niagara Falls, NY
6'1 180 lbs Batted left

YR	POS	TEAM	LG	FIN	G	AB	R	H	2B	3B	HR	RBI	AVG	BB	TB	OQ	RANK
1975	CF	CLE	AL	4-6	120	480	69	137	16	5	3	35	.285	44	172	97	45-66
1976	RF	CLE	AL	4-6	138	552	73	161	24	7	6	43	.292	41	217	108	36-64
1977	CF	CLE	AL	5-7	68	252	33	57	7	3	5	18	.226	21	85	80	—
1978	CF	CLE	AL	6-7	148	566	65	149	27	3	3	50	.263	38	191	84	74-83
1979	CF	CLE	AL	6-7	144	560	67	145	12	2	3	51	.259	55	170	78	72-75
1980	CF	CLE	AL	6-7	140	471	55	110	17	4	3	52	.234	63	144	85	64-69
1981	CF	CLE	AL	6-7	103	360	47	88	15	3	4	33	.244	40	121	94	58-71
1982	CF	CLE	AL	6-7	152	562	71	152	18	2	8	44	.270	54	198	91	63-77
1983	CF	CL/ML	AL	7/5	158	569	60	140	20	4	4	43	.246	38	180	76	70-70
1984	CF	MIL	AL	7-7	119	341	53	85	10	5	7	31	.249	34	126	94	—
1985	CF	MIL	AL	6-7	79	216	19	47	9	1	2	18	.218	14	64	68	—
1986	LF-CF	MIL	AL	6-7	89	205	31	52	7	3	8	27	.254	17	89	101	—
1987	RF-LF	MIL	AL	3-7	97	114	21	26	7	1	0	13	.228	12	35	75	—
MAJOR LEAGUE TOTALS					1555	5248	664	1349	189	43	56	458	.257	471	1792	89	8 yrs

Chester Earl Lemon Born Feb 12, 1955 Jackson, MS
6'0 190 lbs Batted right

YR	POS	TEAM	LG	FIN	G	AB	R	H	2B	3B	HR	RBI	AVG	BB	TB	OQ	RANK
1975	3B-DH	CHI	AL	5-6	9	35	2	9	2	0	0	1	.257	2	11	—	—
1976	CF	CHI	AL	6-6	132	451	46	111	15	5	4	38	.246	28	148	85	—
1977	CF	CHI	AL	3-7	150	553	99	151	38	4	19	67	.273	52	254	112	31-81
1978	CF	CHI	AL	5-7	105	357	51	107	24	6	13	55	.300	39	182	136	—
1979	CF	CHI	AL	5-7	148	556	79	177	44	2	17	86	.318	56	276	127	14-75
1980	CF	CHI	AL	5-7	147	514	76	150	32	6	11	51	.292	71	227	122	17-69
1981	CF	CHI	AL	3-7	94	328	50	99	23	6	9	50	.302	33	161	135	10-71
1982	RF	DET	AL	4-7	125	436	75	116	20	1	19	52	.266	56	195	116	28-77
1983	CF	DET	AL	2-7	145	491	78	125	21	5	24	69	.255	54	228	115	26-70
1984	CF	DET	AL	1-7	141	509	77	146	34	6	20	76	.287	51	252	126	16-68
1985	CF	DET	AL	3-7	145	517	69	137	28	4	18	68	.265	45	227	105	40-75
1986	CF	DET	AL	3-7	126	403	45	101	21	3	12	53	.251	39	164	98	—
1987	CF	DET	AL	1-7	146	470	75	130	30	3	20	75	.277	70	226	122	21-79
1988	RF-DH	DET	AL	2-7	144	512	67	135	29	4	17	64	.264	59	223	115	27-74
1989	RF	DET	AL	7-7	127	414	45	98	19	2	7	47	.237	46	142	92	—
1990	RF	DET	AL	3-7	104	322	39	83	16	4	5	32	.258	48	122	108	—
MAJOR LEAGUE TOTALS					1988	6868	973	1875	396	61	215	884	.273	749	3038	120	10 yrs

Darnell Glenn Ford   Born May 19, 1952 Los Angeles, CA
6'1 185 lbs Batted right

YR	POS	TEAM	LG	FIN	G	AB	R	H	2B	3B	HR	RBI	AVG	BB	TB	OQ	RANK
1975	CF	MIN	AL	4-6	130	440	72	123	21	1	15	59	.280	30	191	108	—
1976	RF	MIN	AL	3-6	145	514	87	137	24	7	20	86	.267	36	235	118	22-64
1977	RF	MIN	AL	4-7	144	453	66	121	25	7	11	60	.267	41	193	104	50-81
1978	RF	MIN	AL	4-7	151	592	78	162	36	10	11	82	.274	48	251	107	45-83
1979	RF	CAL	AL	1-7	142	569	100	165	26	5	21	101	.290	40	264	109	34-75
1980	RF-DH	CAL	AL	6-7	65	226	22	63	11	0	7	26	.279	19	95	104	—
1981	RF	CAL	AL	5-7	97	375	53	104	14	1	15	48	.277	23	165	111	34-71
1982	RF	BAL	AL	2-7	123	421	46	99	21	3	10	43	.235	23	156	82	—
1983	RF	BAL	AL	1-7	103	407	63	114	30	4	9	55	.280	29	179	106	—
1984	RF-DH	BAL	AL	5-7	25	91	7	21	4	0	1	5	.231	7	28	—	—
1985	DH	BAL	AL	4-7	28	75	4	14	2	0	1	1	.187	7	19	—	—

MAJOR LEAGUE TOTALS   1153   4163   598 1123   214   38 121   566   .270   303 1776   110   5 yrs

Jack Anthony Clark   Born Nov 10, 1955 New Brighton, PA
6'2 175 lbs Batted right

YR	POS	TEAM	LG	FIN	G	AB	R	H	2B	3B	HR	RBI	AVG	BB	TB	OQ	RANK
1975	CF-3B	SF	NL	3-6	8	17	3	4	0	0	0	2	.235	1	4	—	—
1976	CF	SF	NL	4-6	26	102	14	23	6	2	2	10	.225	8	39	97	—
1977	RF	SF	NL	4-6	136	413	64	104	17	4	13	51	.252	49	168	105	—
1978	RF	SF	NL	3-6	156	592	90	181	46	8	25	98	.306	50	318	143	7-63
1979	RF	SF	NL	4-6	143	527	84	144	25	2	26	86	.273	63	251	127	17-62
1980	RF	SF	NL	5-6	127	437	77	124	20	8	22	82	.284	74	226	153	2-59
1981	RF	SF	NL	4-6	99	385	60	103	19	2	17	53	.268	45	177	128	12-69
1982	RF	SF	NL	3-6	157	563	90	154	30	3	27	103	.274	90	271	142	9-66
1983	RF	SF	NL	5-6	135	492	82	132	25	0	20	66	.268	74	217	127	14-64
1984	RF	SF	NL	6-6	57	203	33	65	9	1	11	44	.320	43	109	177	—
1985	1B	SL	NL	1-6	126	442	71	124	26	3	22	87	.281	83	222	152	3-65
1986	1B	SL	NL	3-6	65	232	34	55	12	2	9	23	.237	45	98	126	—
1987	1B	SL	NL	1-6	131	419	93	120	23	1	35	106	.286	136	250	190	1-59
1988	DH-RF	NY	AL	5-7	150	496	81	120	14	0	27	93	.242	113	215	134	14-74
1989	1B	SD	NL	2-6	142	455	76	110	19	1	26	94	.242	132	209	162	4-59
1990	1B	SD	NL	4-6	115	334	59	89	12	1	25	62	.266	104	178	179	—
1991	DH	BOS	AL	2-7	140	481	75	120	18	1	28	87	.249	96	224	133	13-72
1992	DH-1B	BOS	AL	7-7	81	257	32	54	11	0	5	33	.210	56	80	102	—

MAJOR LEAGUE TOTALS   1994   6847 1118 1826   332   39 340 1180   .267 1262 3256   144   11 yrs

Gerald Peter Remy Born Nov 8, 1952 Fall River, MA
5'9 165 lbs Batted left

YR	POS	TEAM	LG	FIN	G	AB	R	H	2B	3B	HR	RBI	AVG	BB	TB	OQ	RANK
1975	2B	CAL	AL	6-6	147	569	82	147	17	5	1	46	.258	45	177	81	59-66
1976	2B	CAL	AL	4-6	143	502	64	132	14	3	0	28	.263	38	152	84	58-64
1977	2B	CAL	AL	5-7	154	575	74	145	19	10	4	44	.252	59	196	87	73-81
1978	2B	BOS	AL	2-7	148	583	87	162	24	6	2	44	.278	40	204	89	69-83
1979	2B	BOS	AL	3-7	80	306	49	91	11	2	0	29	.297	26	106	89	—
1980	2B	BOS	AL	4-7	63	230	24	72	7	2	0	9	.313	10	83	88	—
1981	2B	BOS	AL	5-7	88	358	55	110	9	1	0	31	.307	36	121	101	50-71
1982	2B	BOS	AL	3-7	155	636	89	178	22	3	0	47	.280	55	206	84	70-77
1983	2B	BOS	AL	6-7	146	592	73	163	16	5	0	43	.275	40	189	80	67-70
1984	2B	BOS	AL	4-7	30	104	8	26	1	1	0	8	.250	7	29	69	—
MAJOR LEAGUE TOTALS					1154	4455	605	1226	140	38	7	329	.275	356	1463	87	7 yrs

Willie Larry Randolph Born Jul 6, 1954 Holly Hill, SC
5'11 165 lbs Batted right

YR	POS	TEAM	LG	FIN	G	AB	R	H	2B	3B	HR	RBI	AVG	BB	TB	OQ	RANK
1975	2B	PIT	NL	1-6	30	61	9	10	1	0	0	3	.164	7	11	—	—
1976	2B	NY	AL	1-6	125	430	59	115	15	4	1	40	.267	58	141	104	42-64
1977	2B	NY	AL	1-7	147	551	91	151	28	11	4	40	.274	64	213	102	56-81
1978	2B	NY	AL	1-7	134	499	87	139	18	6	3	42	.279	82	178	111	36-83
1979	2B	NY	AL	4-7	153	574	98	155	15	13	5	61	.270	95	211	106	37-75
1980	2B	NY	AL	1-7	138	513	99	151	23	7	7	46	.294	119	209	135	7-69
1981	2B	NY	AL	3-7	93	357	59	83	14	3	2	24	.232	57	109	97	53-71
1982	2B	NY	AL	5-7	144	553	85	155	21	4	3	36	.280	75	193	100	54-77
1983	2B	NY	AL	3-7	104	420	73	117	21	1	2	38	.279	53	146	98	—
1984	2B	NY	AL	3-7	142	564	86	162	24	2	2	31	.287	86	196	105	38-68
1985	2B	NY	AL	2-7	143	497	75	137	21	2	5	40	.276	85	177	107	39-75
1986	2B	NY	AL	2-7	141	492	76	136	15	2	5	50	.276	94	170	108	40-78
1987	2B	NY	AL	4-7	120	449	96	137	24	2	7	67	.305	82	186	120	24-79
1988	2B	NY	AL	5-7	110	404	43	93	20	1	2	34	.230	55	121	87	—
1989	2B	LA	NL	4-6	145	549	62	155	18	0	2	36	.282	71	179	104	32-59
1990	2B	LA	NL	2-6	26	96	15	26	4	0	1	9	.271	13	33	102	—
1990	2B	OAK	AL	1-7	93	292	37	75	9	3	1	21	.257	32	93	88	—
1991	2B	MIL	AL	4-7	124	431	60	141	14	3	0	54	.327	75	161	122	22-72
1992	2B	NY	NL	5-6	90	286	29	72	11	1	2	15	.252	40	91	100	—
MAJOR LEAGUE TOTALS					2202	8018	1239	2210	316	65	54	687	.276	1243	2818	109	13 yrs

Harold Delano Wynegar   Born Mar 14, 1956 York, PA
6'1   190 lbs   Batted both

YR	POS	TEAM	LG	FIN	G	AB	R	H	2B	3B	HR	RBI	AVG	BB	TB	OQ	RANK
1976	C-DH	MIN	AL	3-6	149	534	58	139	21	2	10	69	.260	79	194	113	29-64
1977	C	MIN	AL	4-7	144	532	76	139	22	3	10	79	.261	68	197	99	58-81
1978	C	MIN	AL	4-7	135	454	36	104	22	1	4	45	.229	47	140	82	78-83
1979	C	MIN	AL	4-7	149	504	74	136	20	0	7	57	.270	74	177	99	52-75
1980	C	MIN	AL	3-7	146	486	61	124	18	3	5	57	.255	63	163	93	58-69
1981	C-DH	MIN	AL	7-7	47	150	11	37	5	0	0	10	.247	17	42	83	—
1982	C	MN/NY	AL	7/5	87	277	36	74	12	1	4	28	.267	50	100	109	—
1983	C	NY	AL	3-7	94	301	40	89	18	2	6	42	.296	52	129	127	—
1984	C	NY	AL	3-7	129	442	48	118	13	1	6	45	.267	65	151	100	47-68
1985	C	NY	AL	2-7	102	309	27	69	15	0	5	32	.223	64	99	100	—
1986	C	NY	AL	2-7	61	194	19	40	4	1	7	29	.206	30	67	92	—
1987	C	CAL	AL	6-7	31	92	4	19	2	0	0	5	.207	9	21	57	—
1988	C	CAL	AL	4-7	27	55	8	14	4	1	1	8	.255	8	23	—	—
MAJOR LEAGUE TOTALS					1301	4330	498	1102	176	15	65	506	.255	626	1503	98	6 yrs

Garry Lewis Templeton   Born Mar 24, 1956 Lockney, TX
5'11   175 lbs   Batted both

YR	POS	TEAM	LG	FIN	G	AB	R	H	2B	3B	HR	RBI	AVG	BB	TB	OQ	RANK
1976	SS	SL	NL	5-6	53	213	32	62	8	2	1	17	.291	7	77	91	—
1977	SS	SL	NL	3-6	153	621	94	200	19	18	8	79	.322	15	279	104	45-68
1978	SS	SL	NL	5-6	155	647	82	181	31	13	2	47	.280	22	244	91	56-63
1979	SS	SL	NL	3-6	154	672	105	211	32	19	9	62	.314	18	308	109	35-62
1980	SS	SL	NL	4-6	118	504	83	161	19	9	4	43	.319	18	210	106	36-59
1981	SS	SL	NL	1-6	80	333	47	96	16	8	1	33	.288	14	131	100	48-69
1982	SS	SD	NL	4-6	141	563	76	139	25	8	6	64	.247	26	198	85	62-66
1983	SS	SD	NL	4-6	126	460	39	121	20	2	3	40	.263	21	154	81	—
1984	SS	SD	NL	1-6	148	493	40	127	19	3	2	35	.258	39	158	87	50-53
1985	SS	SD	NL	3-6	148	546	63	154	30	2	6	55	.282	41	206	100	46-65
1986	SS	SD	NL	4-6	147	510	42	126	21	2	2	44	.247	35	157	78	46-49
1987	SS	SD	NL	6-6	148	510	42	113	13	5	5	48	.222	42	151	71	59-59
1988	SS	SD	NL	3-6	110	362	35	90	15	7	3	36	.249	20	128	91	—
1989	SS	SD	NL	2-6	142	506	43	129	26	3	6	40	.255	23	179	88	53-59
1990	SS	SD	NL	4-6	144	505	45	125	25	3	9	59	.248	24	183	85	59-63
1991	SS-1B	SD/NY	NL	3/5	112	276	25	61	10	2	3	26	.221	10	84	70	—
MAJOR LEAGUE TOTALS					2079	7721	893	2096	329	106	70	728	.271	375	2847	92	12 yrs

Antonio Rafael Armas Born Jul 2, 1953 Anzoatequi, Venezuela
5'11 182 lbs Batted right

YR	POS	TEAM	LG	FIN	G	AB	R	H	2B	3B	HR	RBI	AVG	BB	TB	OQ	RANK
1976	CF-LF	PIT	NL	2-6	4	6	0	2	0	0	0	1	.333	0	2	—	—
1977	CF	OAK	AL	7-7	118	363	26	87	8	2	13	53	.240	20	138	84	—
1978	RF	OAK	AL	6-7	91	239	17	51	6	1	2	13	.213	10	65	61	—
1979	RF	OAK	AL	7-7	80	278	29	69	9	3	11	34	.248	16	117	92	—
1980	RF	OAK	AL	2-7	158	628	87	175	18	8	35	109	.279	29	314	112	32-69
1981	RF	OAK	AL	1-7	109	440	51	115	24	3	22	76	.261	19	211	113	29-71
1982	RF	OAK	AL	5-7	138	536	58	125	19	2	28	89	.233	33	232	96	57-77
1983	CF-DH	BOS	AL	6-7	145	574	77	125	23	2	36	107	.218	29	260	96	53-70
1984	CF-DH	BOS	AL	4-7	157	639	107	171	29	5	43	123	.268	32	339	119	22-68
1985	CF-DH	BOS	AL	5-7	103	385	50	102	17	5	23	64	.265	18	198	112	—
1986	CF	BOS	AL	1-7	121	425	40	112	21	4	11	58	.264	24	174	92	—
1987	RF	CAL	AL	6-7	28	81	8	16	3	1	3	9	.198	1	30	—	—
1988	LF	CAL	AL	4-7	120	368	42	100	20	2	13	49	.272	22	163	106	—
1989	RF	CAL	AL	3-7	60	202	22	52	7	1	11	30	.257	7	94	104	—

MAJOR LEAGUE TOTALS 1432 5164 614 1302 204 39 251 815 .252 260 2337 107 5 yrs

Alfredo Claudino Griffin Born Oct 6, 1957 Santo Domingo, DR
5'11 160 lbs Batted both

YR	POS	TEAM	LG	FIN	G	AB	R	H	2B	3B	HR	RBI	AVG	BB	TB	OQ	RANK
1976	SS	CLE	AL	4-6	12	4	0	1	0	0	0	0	.250	0	1	—	—
1977	SS	CLE	AL	5-7	14	41	5	6	1	0	0	3	.146	3	7	—	—
1978	SS	CLE	AL	6-7	5	4	1	2	1	0	0	0	.500	2	3	—	—
1979	SS	TOR	AL	7-7	153	624	81	179	22	10	2	31	.287	40	227	87	64-75
1980	SS	TOR	AL	7-7	155	653	63	166	26	15	2	41	.254	24	228	77	69-69
1981	SS	TOR	AL	7-7	101	388	30	81	19	6	0	21	.209	17	112	67	71-71
1982	SS	TOR	AL	6-7	162	539	57	130	20	8	1	48	.241	22	169	69	76-77
1983	SS	TOR	AL	4-7	162	528	62	132	22	9	4	47	.250	27	184	80	69-70
1984	SS-2B	TOR	AL	2-7	140	419	53	101	8	2	4	30	.241	4	125	61	—
1985	SS	OAK	AL	4-7	162	614	75	166	18	7	2	64	.270	20	204	74	74-75
1986	SS	OAK	AL	3-7	162	594	74	169	23	6	4	51	.285	35	216	86	72-78
1987	SS	OAK	AL	3-7	144	494	69	130	23	5	3	60	.263	28	172	77	78-79
1988	SS	LA	NL	1-6	95	316	39	63	8	3	1	27	.199	24	80	69	—
1989	SS	LA	NL	4-6	136	506	49	125	27	2	0	29	.247	29	156	80	55-59
1990	SS	LA	NL	2-6	141	461	38	97	11	3	1	35	.210	29	117	62	63-63
1991	SS	LA	NL	2-6	109	350	27	85	6	2	0	27	.243	22	95	71	—
1992	SS-2B	TOR	AL	1-7	63	150	21	35	7	0	0	10	.233	9	42	68	—
1993	SS-2B	TOR	AL	1-7	46	95	15	20	3	0	0	3	.211	3	23	—	—

MAJOR LEAGUE TOTALS 1962 6780 759 1688 245 78 24 527 .249 338 2161 76 10 yrs

Richard Fremont Dauer   Born Jul 27, 1952   San Bernardino, CA
6'0 180 lbs Batted right

YR	POS	TEAM	LG	FIN	G	AB	R	H	2B	3B	HR	RBI	AVG	BB	TB	OQ	RANK
1976	2B	BAL	AL	2-6	11	39	0	4	0	0	0	3	.103	1	4	—	—
1977	2B	BAL	AL	2-7	96	304	38	74	15	1	5	25	.243	20	106	81	—
1978	2B-3B	BAL	AL	4-7	133	459	57	121	23	0	6	46	.264	26	162	86	72-83
1979	2B-3B	BAL	AL	1-7	142	479	63	123	20	0	9	61	.257	36	170	84	69-75
1980	2B-3B	BAL	AL	2-7	152	557	71	158	32	0	2	63	.284	46	196	90	62-69
1981	2B	BAL	AL	2-7	96	369	41	97	27	0	4	38	.263	27	136	96	57-71
1982	2B-3B	BAL	AL	2-7	158	558	75	156	24	2	8	57	.280	50	208	95	59-77
1983	2B-3B	BAL	AL	1-7	140	459	49	108	19	0	5	41	.235	47	142	80	66-70
1984	2B	BAL	AL	5-7	127	397	29	101	26	0	2	24	.254	24	133	80	—
1985	2B-3B	BAL	AL	4-7	85	208	25	42	7	0	2	14	.202	20	55	66	—

| MAJOR LEAGUE TOTALS | | | | | 1140 | 3829 | 448 | 984 | 193 | 3 | 43 | 372 | .257 | 297 | 1312 | 89 | 6 yrs |

James Elmer Gantner   Born Jan 5, 1953   Fond Du Lac, WI
6'0 180 lbs Batted left

YR	POS	TEAM	LG	FIN	G	AB	R	H	2B	3B	HR	RBI	AVG	BB	TB	OQ	RANK
1976	3B	MIL	AL	6-6	26	69	6	17	1	0	0	7	.246	6	18	—	—
1977	3B	MIL	AL	6-7	14	47	4	14	1	0	1	2	.298	2	18	—	—
1978	2B-3B	MIL	AL	3-7	43	97	14	21	1	0	1	8	.216	5	25	61	—
1979	3B-2B	MIL	AL	2-7	70	208	29	59	10	3	2	22	.284	16	81	94	—
1980	3B-2B	MIL	AL	3-7	132	415	47	117	21	3	4	40	.282	30	156	93	—
1981	2B	MIL	AL	1-7	107	352	35	94	14	1	2	33	.267	29	116	90	63-71
1982	2B	MIL	AL	1-7	132	447	48	132	17	2	4	43	.295	26	165	90	—
1983	2B	MIL	AL	5-7	161	603	85	170	23	8	11	74	.282	38	242	97	52-70
1984	2B	MIL	AL	7-7	153	613	61	173	27	1	3	56	.282	30	211	82	62-68
1985	2B-3B	MIL	AL	6-7	143	523	63	133	15	4	5	44	.254	33	171	77	73-75
1986	2B	MIL	AL	6-7	139	497	58	136	25	1	7	38	.274	26	184	85	73-78
1987	2B-3B	MIL	AL	3-7	81	265	37	72	14	0	4	30	.272	19	98	85	—
1988	2B	MIL	AL	3-7	155	539	67	149	28	2	0	47	.276	34	181	84	63-74
1989	2B	MIL	AL	4-7	116	409	51	112	18	3	0	34	.274	21	136	82	—
1990	2B-3B	MIL	AL	6-7	88	323	36	85	8	5	0	25	.263	29	103	84	—
1991	3B-2B	MIL	AL	4-7	140	526	63	149	27	4	2	47	.283	27	190	86	64-72
1992	2B-3B	MIL	AL	2-7	101	256	22	63	12	1	1	18	.246	12	80	73	—

| MAJOR LEAGUE TOTALS | | | | | 1801 | 6189 | 726 | 1696 | 262 | 38 | 47 | 568 | .274 | 383 | 2175 | 86 | 7 yrs |

Lee Louis Mazzilli   Born Mar 25, 1955 New York, NY
6'1 180 lbs Batted both

YR	POS	TEAM	LG	FIN	G	AB	R	H	2B	3B	HR	RBI	AVG	BB	TB	OQ	RANK
1976	CF	NY	NL	3-6	24	77	9	15	2	0	2	7	.195	14	23	—	—
1977	CF	NY	NL	6-6	159	537	66	134	24	3	6	46	.250	72	182	94	54-68
1978	CF	NY	NL	6-6	148	542	78	148	28	5	16	61	.273	69	234	123	22-63
1979	CF	NY	NL	6-6	158	597	78	181	34	4	15	79	.303	93	268	134	13-62
1980	1B-CF	NY	NL	5-6	152	578	82	162	31	4	16	76	.280	82	249	127	15-59
1981	LF	NY	NL	5-6	95	324	36	74	14	5	6	34	.228	46	116	105	40-69
1982	DH-CF	TX/NY	AL	6/5	95	323	43	81	10	0	10	34	.251	43	121	100	—
1983	CF	PIT	NL	2-6	109	246	37	59	9	0	5	24	.240	49	83	111	—
1984	LF	PIT	NL	6-6	111	266	37	63	11	1	4	21	.237	40	88	102	—
1985	1B	PIT	NL	6-6	92	117	20	33	8	0	1	9	.282	29	44	138	—
1986	LF-1B	PT/NY	NL	6/1	100	151	28	37	5	1	3	15	.245	38	53	124	—
1987	RF-1B	NY	NL	2-6	88	124	26	38	8	1	3	24	.306	21	57	133	—
1988	LF-1B	NY	NL	1-6	68	116	9	17	2	0	0	12	.147	12	19	52	—
1989	RF-1B	NY	NL	2-6	48	60	10	11	2	0	2	7	.183	17	19	—	—
1989	DH	TOR	AL	1-7	28	66	12	15	3	0	4	11	.227	17	30	—	—
MAJOR LEAGUE TOTALS					1475	4124	571	1068	191	24	93	460	.259	642	1586	117	5 yrs

Willie James Wilson   Born Jul 9, 1955   Montgomery, AL
6'3 190 lbs Batted both

YR	POS	TEAM	LG	FIN	G	AB	R	H	2B	3B	HR	RBI	AVG	BB	TB	OQ	RANK
1976	CF	KC	AL	1-6	12	6	0	1	0	0	0	0	.167	0	1	—	—
1977	CF	KC	AL	1-7	13	34	10	11	2	0	0	1	.324	1	13	—	—
1978	LF-CF	KC	AL	1-7	127	198	43	43	8	2	0	16	.217	16	55	70	—
1979	LF	KC	AL	2-7	154	588	113	185	18	13	6	49	.315	28	247	99	50-75
1980	LF	KC	AL	1-7	161	705	133	230	28	15	3	49	.326	28	297	102	47-69
1981	LF	KC	AL	4-7	102	439	54	133	10	7	1	32	.303	18	160	93	60-71
1982	LF	KC	AL	2-7	136	585	87	194	19	15	3	46	.332	26	252	105	45-77
1983	CF	KC	AL	2-7	137	576	90	159	22	8	2	33	.276	33	203	84	61-70
1984	CF	KC	AL	1-7	128	541	81	163	24	9	2	44	.301	39	211	99	48-68
1985	CF	KC	AL	1-7	141	605	87	168	25	21	4	43	.278	29	247	93	59-75
1986	CF	KC	AL	3-7	156	631	77	170	20	7	9	44	.269	31	231	83	75-78
1987	CF	KC	AL	2-7	146	610	97	170	18	15	4	30	.279	32	230	83	73-79
1988	CF	KC	AL	3-7	147	591	81	155	17	11	1	37	.262	22	197	77	69-74
1989	CF	KC	AL	2-7	112	383	58	97	17	7	3	43	.253	27	137	89	—
1990	LF-CF	KC	AL	6-7	115	307	49	89	13	3	2	42	.290	30	114	101	—
1991	LF-RF	OAK	AL	4-7	113	294	38	70	14	4	0	28	.238	18	92	74	—
1992	CF	OAK	AL	1-7	132	396	38	107	15	5	0	37	.270	35	132	88	—
1993	CF	CHI	NL	4-7	105	221	29	57	11	3	1	11	.258	11	77	81	—
MAJOR LEAGUE TOTALS					2137	7710	1165	2202	281	145	41	585	.286	424	2896	92	10 yrs

Jason Dolph Thompson Born Jul 6, 1954 Hollywood, CA
6'4 200 lbs Batted left

YR	POS	TEAM	LG	FIN	G	AB	R	H	2B	3B	HR	RBI	AVG	BB	TB	OQ	RANK
1976	1B	DET	AL	5-6	123	412	45	90	12	1	17	54	.218	68	155	114	—
1977	1B	DET	AL	4-7	158	585	87	158	24	5	31	105	.270	73	285	123	18-81
1978	1B	DET	AL	5-7	153	589	79	169	25	3	26	96	.287	74	278	129	16-83
1979	1B	DET	AL	5-7	145	492	58	121	16	1	20	79	.246	70	199	105	39-75
1980	1B-DH	DE/CA	AL	5/6	138	438	69	126	19	0	21	90	.288	83	208	139	4-69
1981	1B	PIT	NL	4-6	86	223	36	54	13	0	15	42	.242	59	112	165	—
1982	1B	PIT	NL	4-6	156	550	87	156	32	0	31	101	.284	101	281	156	2-66
1983	1B	PIT	NL	2-6	152	517	70	134	20	1	18	76	.259	99	210	127	15-64
1984	1B	PIT	NL	6-6	154	543	61	138	22	0	17	74	.254	87	211	119	20-53
1985	1B	PIT	NL	6-6	123	402	42	97	17	1	12	61	.241	84	152	123	21-65
1986	1B	MON	NL	4-6	30	51	6	10	4	0	0	4	.196	18	14	—	—

MAJOR LEAGUE TOTALS					1418	4802	640	1253	204	12	208	782	.261	816	2105	128	8 yrs

Andre Fernando Dawson Born Jul 10, 1954 Miami, FL
6'3 180 lbs Batted right

YR	POS	TEAM	LG	FIN	G	AB	R	H	2B	3B	HR	RBI	AVG	BB	TB	OQ	RANK
1976	CF	MON	NL	6-6	24	85	9	20	4	1	0	7	.235	5	26	—	—
1977	CF	MON	NL	5-6	139	525	64	148	26	9	19	65	.282	34	249	112	39-68
1978	CF	MON	NL	4-6	157	609	84	154	24	8	25	72	.253	30	269	105	40-63
1979	CF	MON	NL	2-6	155	639	90	176	24	12	25	92	.275	27	299	109	36-62
1980	CF	MON	NL	2-6	151	577	96	178	41	7	17	87	.308	44	284	131	8-59
1981	CF	MON	NL	2-6	103	394	71	119	21	3	24	64	.302	35	218	150	3-69
1982	CF	MON	NL	3-6	148	608	107	183	37	7	23	83	.301	34	303	127	17-66
1983	CF	MON	NL	3-6	159	633	104	189	36	10	32	113	.299	38	341	134	7-64
1984	RF	MON	NL	5-6	138	533	73	132	23	6	17	86	.248	41	218	104	36-53
1985	RF	MON	NL	3-6	139	529	65	135	27	2	23	91	.255	29	235	107	34-65
1986	RF	MON	NL	4-6	130	496	65	141	32	2	20	78	.284	37	237	120	20-49
1987	RF	CHI	NL	6-6	153	621	90	178	24	2	49	137	.287	32	353	128	14-59
1988	RF	CHI	NL	4-6	157	591	78	179	31	8	24	79	.303	37	298	136	10-58
1989	RF	CHI	NL	1-6	118	416	62	105	18	6	21	77	.252	35	198	123	—
1990	RF	CHI	NL	4-6	147	529	72	164	28	5	27	100	.310	42	283	139	10-63
1991	RF	CHI	NL	4-6	149	563	69	153	21	4	31	104	.272	22	275	116	28-52
1992	RF	CHI	NL	4-6	143	542	60	150	27	2	22	90	.277	30	247	115	26-49
1993	DH-RF	BOS	AL	5-7	121	461	44	126	29	1	13	67	.273	17	196	91	—

MAJOR LEAGUE TOTALS					2431	9351	1303	2630	473	95	412	1492	.281	569	4529	122	15 yrs

Ruppert Sanderson Jones   Born Mar 12, 1955 Dallas, TX
5'10 170 lbs Batted left

YR	POS	TEAM	LG	FIN	G	AB	R	H	2B	3B	HR	RBI	AVG	BB	TB	OQ	RANK
1976	RF-DH	KC	AL	1-6	28	51	9	11	1	1	1	7	.216	3	17	—	—
1977	CF	SEA	AL	6-7	160	597	85	157	26	8	24	76	.263	55	271	109	39-81
1978	CF	SEA	AL	7-7	129	472	48	111	24	3	6	46	.235	55	159	91	68-83
1979	CF	SEA	AL	6-7	162	622	109	166	29	9	21	78	.267	85	276	115	26-75
1980	CF	NY	AL	1-7	83	328	38	73	11	3	9	42	.223	34	117	88	—
1981	CF	SD	NL	6-6	105	397	53	99	34	1	4	39	.249	43	147	104	42-69
1982	CF	SD	NL	4-6	116	424	69	120	20	2	12	61	.283	62	180	128	14-66
1983	CF	SD	NL	4-6	133	335	42	78	12	3	12	49	.233	35	132	102	—
1984	LF-CF	DET	AL	1-7	79	215	26	61	12	1	12	37	.284	21	111	129	—
1985	RF-DH	CAL	AL	2-7	125	389	66	90	17	2	21	67	.231	57	174	114	—
1986	RF	CAL	AL	1-7	126	393	73	90	21	3	17	49	.229	64	168	111	—
1987	LF-RF	CAL	AL	6-7	85	192	25	47	8	2	8	28	.245	20	83	99	—

| MAJOR LEAGUE TOTALS | | | | | 1331 | 4415 | 643 | 1103 | 215 | 38 | 147 | 579 | .250 | 534 | 1835 | 109 | 5 yrs |

Dale Bryan Murphy   Born Mar 12, 1956 Portland, OR
6'4 210 lbs Batted right

YR	POS	TEAM	LG	FIN	G	AB	R	H	2B	3B	HR	RBI	AVG	BB	TB	OQ	RANK
1976	C	ATL	NL	6-6	19	65	3	17	6	0	0	9	.262	7	23	—	—
1977	C	ATL	NL	6-6	18	76	5	24	8	1	2	14	.316	0	40	—	—
1978	1B-C	ATL	NL	6-6	151	530	66	120	14	3	23	79	.226	42	209	98	48-63
1979	1B-C	ATL	NL	6-6	104	384	53	106	7	2	21	57	.276	38	180	121	—
1980	CF	ATL	NL	4-6	156	569	98	160	27	2	33	89	.281	59	290	136	6-59
1981	CF	ATL	NL	5-6	104	369	43	91	12	1	13	50	.247	44	144	110	34-69
1982	CF	ATL	NL	1-6	162	598	113	168	23	2	36	109	.281	93	303	148	5-66
1983	CF	ATL	NL	2-6	162	589	131	178	24	4	36	121	.302	90	318	156	2-64
1984	CF	ATL	NL	2-6	162	607	94	176	32	8	36	100	.290	79	332	154	2-53
1985	CF	ATL	NL	5-6	162	616	118	185	32	2	37	111	.300	90	332	156	2-65
1986	CF	ATL	NL	6-6	160	614	89	163	29	7	29	83	.265	75	293	127	10-49
1987	RF	ATL	NL	5-6	159	566	115	167	27	1	44	105	.295	115	328	163	2-59
1988	RF	ATL	NL	6-6	156	592	77	134	35	4	24	77	.226	74	249	118	22-58
1989	CF	ATL	NL	6-6	154	574	60	131	16	0	20	84	.228	65	207	100	41-59
1990	RF	AT/PH	NL	6/4	154	563	60	138	23	1	24	83	.245	61	235	108	38-63
1991	RF	PHI	NL	3-6	153	544	66	137	33	1	18	81	.252	48	226	108	35-52
1992	RF	PHI	NL	6-6	18	62	5	10	1	0	2	7	.161	1	17	—	—
1993	RF	PH/CO	NL	1/6	26	42	1	6	1	0	0	7	.143	5	7	—	—

| MAJOR LEAGUE TOTALS | | | | | 2180 | 7960 | 1197 | 2111 | 350 | 39 | 398 | 1266 | .265 | 986 | 3733 | 129 | 13 yrs |

Steven F Kemp
6'0 195 lbs Batted left

Born Aug 7, 1954 San Angelo, TX

YR	POS	TEAM	LG	FIN	G	AB	R	H	2B	3B	HR	RBI	AVG	BB	TB	OQ	RANK
1977	LF	DET	AL	4-7	151	552	75	142	29	4	18	88	.257	71	233	109	38-81
1978	LF	DET	AL	5-7	159	582	75	161	18	4	15	79	.277	97	232	120	26-83
1979	LF	DET	AL	5-7	134	490	88	156	26	3	26	105	.318	68	266	145	6-75
1980	LF-DH	DET	AL	5-7	135	508	88	149	23	3	21	101	.293	69	241	128	9-69
1981	LF-DH	DET	AL	4-7	105	372	52	103	18	4	9	49	.277	70	156	134	11-71
1982	LF	CHI	AL	3-7	160	580	91	166	23	1	19	98	.286	89	248	121	23-77
1983	RF	NY	AL	3-7	109	373	53	90	17	3	12	49	.241	41	149	100	—
1984	LF-DH	NY	AL	3-7	94	313	37	91	12	1	7	41	.291	40	126	112	—
1985	LF	PIT	NL	6-6	92	236	19	59	13	2	2	21	.250	25	82	96	—
1986	LF	PIT	NL	6-6	13	16	1	3	0	0	1	1	.188	4	6	—	—
1988	DH-LF	TEX	AL	6-7	16	36	2	8	0	0	0	2	.222	2	8	—	—

MAJOR LEAGUE TOTALS   1168 4058 581 1128 179 25 130 634 .278 576 1747 126   6 yrs

Lance Michael Parrish
6'3 210 lbs Batted right

Born Jun 15, 1956 Clairton, PA

YR	POS	TEAM	LG	FIN	G	AB	R	H	2B	3B	HR	RBI	AVG	BB	TB	OQ	RANK
1977	C	DET	AL	4-7	12	46	10	9	2	0	3	7	.196	5	20	—	—
1978	C	DET	AL	5-7	85	288	37	63	11	3	14	41	.219	11	122	91	—
1979	C	DET	AL	5-7	143	493	65	136	26	3	19	65	.276	49	225	111	33-75
1980	C-DH	DET	AL	5-7	144	553	79	158	34	6	24	82	.286	31	276	115	26-69
1981	C	DET	AL	4-7	96	348	39	85	18	2	10	46	.244	34	137	104	45-71
1982	C	DET	AL	4-7	133	486	75	138	19	2	32	87	.284	40	257	126	16-77
1983	C-DH	DET	AL	2-7	155	605	80	163	42	3	27	114	.269	44	292	113	30-70
1984	C-DH	DET	AL	1-7	147	578	75	137	16	2	33	98	.237	41	256	101	45-68
1985	C-DH	DET	AL	3-7	140	549	64	150	27	1	28	98	.273	41	263	112	30-75
1986	C	DET	AL	3-7	91	327	53	84	6	1	22	62	.257	38	158	117	—
1987	C	PHI	NL	4-6	130	466	42	114	21	0	17	67	.245	47	186	97	46-58
1988	C	PHI	NL	6-6	123	424	44	91	17	2	15	60	.215	47	157	102	—
1989	C	CAL	AL	3-7	124	433	48	103	12	1	17	50	.238	42	168	98	—
1990	C	CAL	AL	4-7	133	470	54	126	14	0	24	70	.268	46	212	114	26-69
1991	C	CAL	AL	7-7	119	402	38	87	12	0	19	51	.216	35	156	91	—
1992	C-1B	CA/SE	AL	5/7	93	275	26	64	13	1	12	32	.233	24	115	101	—
1993	C	CLE	AL	6-7	10	20	2	4	1	0	1	2	.200	4	8	—	—

MAJOR LEAGUE TOTALS   1878 6763 831 1712 291 27 317 1032 .253 579 3008 111   9 yrs

Louis Rodman Whitaker　　　　Born May 12, 1957 Brooklyn, NY
5'11　160 lbs　Batted left

YR	POS	TEAM	LG	FIN	G	AB	R	H	2B	3B	HR	RBI	AVG	BB	TB	OQ	RANK
1977	2B	DET	AL	4-7	11	32	5	8	1	0	0	2	.250	4	9	—	—
1978	2B	DET	AL	5-7	139	484	71	138	12	7	3	58	.285	61	173	104	47-83
1979	2B	DET	AL	5-7	127	423	75	121	14	8	3	42	.286	78	160	114	28-75
1980	2B	DET	AL	5-7	145	477	68	111	19	1	1	45	.233	73	135	84	66-69
1981	2B	DET	AL	4-7	109	335	48	88	14	4	5	36	.263	40	125	107	39-71
1982	2B	DET	AL	4-7	152	560	76	160	22	8	15	65	.286	48	243	108	41-77
1983	2B	DET	AL	2-7	161	643	94	206	40	6	12	72	.320	67	294	123	18-70
1984	2B	DET	AL	1-7	143	558	90	161	25	1	13	56	.289	62	227	109	32-68
1985	2B	DET	AL	3-7	152	609	102	170	29	8	21	73	.279	80	278	120	17-75
1986	2B	DET	AL	3-7	144	584	95	157	26	6	20	73	.269	63	255	108	37-78
1987	2B	DET	AL	1-7	149	604	110	160	38	6	16	59	.265	71	258	104	48-79
1988	2B	DET	AL	2-7	115	403	54	111	18	2	12	55	.275	66	169	123	—
1989	2B	DET	AL	7-7	148	509	77	128	21	1	28	85	.251	89	235	131	11-67
1990	2B	DET	AL	3-7	132	472	75	112	22	2	18	60	.237	74	192	112	27-69
1991	2B	DET	AL	2-7	138	470	94	131	26	2	23	78	.279	90	230	141	6-72
1992	2B	DET	AL	6-7	130	453	77	126	26	0	19	71	.278	81	209	135	8-73
1993	2B	DET	AL	3-7	119	383	72	111	32	1	9	67	.290	78	172	132	—

MAJOR LEAGUE TOTALS　　2214　7999 1283 2199 385 63 218 997 .275 1125 3364 114 14 yrs

Alan Stuart Trammell　　　　Born Feb 21, 1958　Garden Grove, CA
6'0　165 lbs　Batted right

YR	POS	TEAM	LG	FIN	G	AB	R	H	2B	3B	HR	RBI	AVG	BB	TB	OQ	RANK
1977	SS	DET	AL	4-7	19	43	6	8	0	0	0	0	.186	4	8	—	—
1978	SS	DET	AL	5-7	139	448	49	120	14	6	2	34	.268	45	152	92	67-83
1979	SS	DET	AL	5-7	142	460	68	127	11	4	6	50	.276	43	164	90	60-75
1980	SS	DET	AL	5-7	146	560	107	168	21	5	9	65	.300	69	226	112	34-69
1981	SS	DET	AL	4-7	105	392	52	101	15	3	2	31	.258	49	128	97	52-71
1982	SS	DET	AL	4-7	157	489	66	126	34	3	9	57	.258	52	193	100	52-77
1983	SS	DET	AL	2-7	142	505	83	161	31	2	14	66	.319	57	238	128	13-70
1984	SS-DH	DET	AL	1-7	139	555	85	174	34	5	14	69	.314	60	260	126	14-68
1985	SS	DET	AL	3-7	149	605	79	156	21	7	13	57	.258	50	230	92	62-75
1986	SS	DET	AL	3-7	151	574	107	159	33	7	21	75	.277	59	269	115	27-78
1987	SS	DET	AL	1-7	151	597	109	205	34	3	28	105	.343	60	329	139	6-79
1988	SS	DET	AL	2-7	128	466	73	145	24	1	15	69	.311	46	216	125	21-74
1989	SS	DET	AL	7-7	121	449	54	109	20	3	5	43	.243	45	150	89	58-67
1990	SS	DET	AL	3-7	146	559	71	170	37	1	14	89	.304	68	251	125	13-69
1991	SS	DET	AL	2-7	101	375	57	93	20	0	9	55	.248	37	140	94	—
1992	SS	DET	AL	6-7	29	102	11	28	7	1	1	11	.275	15	40	113	—
1993	SS-3B	DET	AL	3-7	112	401	72	132	25	3	12	60	.329	38	199	126	—

MAJOR LEAGUE TOTALS　　2077　7580 1149 2182 381 54 174 936 .288 797 3193 110 13 yrs

Eugene Richards   Born Sep 29, 1953   Monticello, SC
6'0   175 lbs   Batted left

YR	POS	TEAM	LG	FIN	G	AB	R	H	2B	3B	HR	RBI	AVG	BB	TB	OQ	RANK
1977	RF-1B	SD	NL	5-6	146	525	79	152	16	11	5	32	.290	60	205	106	44-68
1978	CF-1B	SD	NL	4-6	154	555	90	171	26	12	4	45	.308	64	233	123	21-63
1979	CF	SD	NL	5-6	150	545	77	152	17	9	4	41	.279	47	199	97	47-62
1980	LF	SD	NL	6-6	158	642	91	193	26	8	4	41	.301	61	247	109	29-59
1981	RF	SD	NL	6-6	104	393	47	113	14	12	3	42	.288	53	160	124	20-69
1982	LF-1B	SD	NL	4-6	132	521	63	149	13	8	3	28	.286	36	187	96	56-66
1983	LF	SD	NL	4-6	95	233	37	64	11	3	3	22	.275	17	90	100	—
1984	LF-RF	SF	NL	6-6	87	135	18	34	4	0	0	4	.252	18	38	89	—

| MAJOR LEAGUE TOTALS | | | | | 1026 | 3549 | 502 | 1028 | 127 | 63 | 26 | 255 | .290 | 356 | 1359 | 109 | 6 yrs |

Kenneth Ray Oberkfell   Born May 4, 1956   Highland, IL
6'0   175 lbs   Batted left

YR	POS	TEAM	LG	FIN	G	AB	R	H	2B	3B	HR	RBI	AVG	BB	TB	OQ	RANK
1977	2B	SL	NL	3-6	9	9	0	1	0	0	0	1	.111	0	1	—	—
1978	2B-3B	SL	NL	5-6	24	50	7	6	1	0	0	0	.120	3	7	—	—
1979	2B-3B	SL	NL	3-6	135	369	53	111	19	5	1	35	.301	57	143	120	—
1980	2B-3B	SL	NL	4-6	116	422	58	128	27	6	3	46	.303	51	176	123	—
1981	3B	SL	NL	1-6	102	376	43	110	12	6	2	45	.293	37	140	108	35-69
1982	3B	SL	NL	1-6	137	470	55	136	22	5	2	34	.289	40	174	103	44-66
1983	3B-2B	SL	NL	4-6	151	488	62	143	26	5	3	38	.293	61	188	114	30-64
1984	3B	SL/AT	NL	3/2	100	324	38	87	19	2	1	21	.269	31	113	98	—
1985	3B-2B	ATL	NL	5-6	134	412	30	112	19	4	3	35	.272	51	148	105	—
1986	3B-2B	ATL	NL	6-6	151	503	62	136	24	3	5	48	.270	83	181	112	25-49
1987	3B	ATL	NL	5-6	135	508	59	142	29	2	3	48	.280	48	184	93	51-59
1988	3B	AT/PT	NL	6/2	140	476	49	129	22	4	3	42	.271	37	168	99	46-58
1989	3B-1B	PT/SF	NL	5/1	97	156	19	42	6	1	2	17	.269	10	56	95	—
1990	3B-2B	HOU	NL	4-6	77	150	10	31	6	1	1	12	.207	15	42	75	—
1991	1B-3B	HOU	NL	6-6	53	70	7	16	4	0	0	14	.229	14	20	—	—
1992	2B-DH	CAL	AL	5-7	41	91	6	24	1	0	0	10	.264	8	25	—	—

| MAJOR LEAGUE TOTALS | | | | | 1602 | 4874 | 558 | 1354 | 237 | 44 | 29 | 446 | .278 | 546 | 1766 | 105 | 6 yrs |

Elliott Taylor Wills   Born Jul 27, 1952   Washington, DC
5'9   172 lbs   Batted both

YR	POS	TEAM	LG	FIN	G	AB	R	H	2B	3B	HR	RBI	AVG	BB	TB	OQ	RANK
1977	2B	TEX	AL	2-7	152	541	87	155	28	6	9	62	.287	65	222	109	36-81
1978	2B	TEX	AL	2-7	157	539	78	135	17	4	9	57	.250	63	187	95	62-83
1979	2B	TEX	AL	3-7	146	543	90	148	21	3	5	46	.273	53	190	89	63-75
1980	2B	TEX	AL	4-7	146	578	102	152	31	5	5	58	.263	51	208	90	61-69
1981	2B	TEX	AL	2-7	102	410	51	103	13	2	2	41	.251	32	126	82	68-71
1982	2B	CHI	NL	5-6	128	419	64	114	18	4	6	38	.272	46	158	107	—
MAJOR LEAGUE TOTALS					831	3030	472	807	128	24	36	302	.266	310	1091	93	5 yrs

Eddie Clarence Murray   Born Feb 24, 1956   Los Angeles, CA
6'2   190 lbs   Batted both

YR	POS	TEAM	LG	FIN	G	AB	R	H	2B	3B	HR	RBI	AVG	BB	TB	OQ	RANK
1977	DH-1B	BAL	AL	2-7	160	611	81	173	29	2	27	88	.283	48	287	113	29-81
1978	1B	BAL	AL	4-7	161	610	85	174	32	3	27	95	.285	70	293	128	18-83
1979	1B	BAL	AL	1-7	159	606	90	179	30	2	25	99	.295	72	288	122	18-75
1980	1B	BAL	AL	2-7	158	621	100	186	36	2	32	116	.300	54	322	128	8-69
1981	1B	BAL	AL	2-7	99	378	57	111	21	2	22	78	.294	40	202	144	3-71
1982	1B	BAL	AL	2-7	151	550	87	174	30	1	32	110	.316	70	302	147	3-77
1983	1B	BAL	AL	1-7	156	582	115	178	30	3	33	111	.306	86	313	147	3-70
1984	1B	BAL	AL	5-7	162	588	97	180	26	3	29	110	.306	107	299	150	1-68
1985	1B	BAL	AL	4-7	156	583	111	173	37	1	31	124	.297	84	305	140	5-75
1986	1B-DH	BAL	AL	7-7	137	495	61	151	25	1	17	84	.305	78	229	130	5-78
1987	1B	BAL	AL	6-7	160	618	89	171	28	3	30	91	.277	73	295	115	30-79
1988	1B-DH	BAL	AL	7-7	161	603	75	171	27	2	28	84	.284	75	286	128	16-74
1989	1B	LA	NL	4-6	160	594	66	147	29	1	20	88	.247	87	238	119	18-59
1990	1B	LA	NL	2-6	155	558	96	184	22	3	26	95	.330	82	290	155	2-63
1991	1B	LA	NL	2-6	153	576	69	150	23	1	19	96	.260	55	232	108	34-52
1992	1B	NY	NL	5-6	156	551	64	144	37	2	16	93	.261	66	233	120	22-49
1993	1B	NY	NL	7-7	154	610	77	174	28	1	27	100	.285	40	285	112	35-77
MAJOR LEAGUE TOTALS					2598	9734	1420	2820	490	33	441	1662	.290	1187	4699	130	17 yrs

Kenneth Francis Landreaux   Born Dec 22, 1954 Los Angeles, CA
5'10 165 lbs Batted left

YR	POS	TEAM	LG	FIN	G	AB	R	H	2B	3B	HR	RBI	AVG	BB	TB	OQ	RANK
1977	CF	CAL	AL	5-7	23	76	6	19	5	1	0	5	.250	5	26	—	—
1978	RF-LF	CAL	AL	2-7	93	260	37	58	7	5	5	23	.223	20	90	84	—
1979	CF	MIN	AL	4-7	151	564	81	172	27	5	15	83	.305	37	254	107	36-75
1980	CF	MIN	AL	3-7	129	484	56	136	23	11	7	62	.281	39	202	103	44-69
1981	CF	LA	NL	2-6	99	390	48	98	16	4	7	41	.251	25	143	93	56-69
1982	CF	LA	NL	2-6	129	461	71	131	23	7	7	50	.284	39	189	111	31-66
1983	CF	LA	NL	1-6	141	481	63	135	25	3	17	66	.281	34	217	114	28-64
1984	CF	LA	NL	4-6	134	438	39	110	11	5	11	47	.251	29	164	95	—
1985	CF	LA	NL	1-6	147	482	70	129	26	2	12	50	.268	33	195	103	43-65
1986	CF	LA	NL	5-6	103	283	34	74	13	2	4	29	.261	22	103	93	—
1987	RF-LF	LA	NL	4-6	115	182	17	37	4	0	6	23	.203	16	59	76	—

MAJOR LEAGUE TOTALS   1264 4101 522 1099 180 45 91 479 .268 299 1642 105   6 yrs

Jeffrey Leonard   Born Sep 22, 1955 Philadelphia, PA
6'2 200 lbs Batted right

YR	POS	TEAM	LG	FIN	G	AB	R	H	2B	3B	HR	RBI	AVG	BB	TB	OQ	RANK
1977	LF-RF	LA	NL	1-6	11	10	1	3	0	1	0	2	.300	1	5	—	—
1978	LF	HOU	NL	5-6	8	26	2	10	2	0	0	4	.385	1	12	—	—
1979	RF	HOU	NL	2-6	134	411	47	119	15	5	0	47	.290	46	144	101	—
1980	RF-1B	HOU	NL	1-6	88	216	29	46	7	5	3	20	.213	19	72	85	—
1981	CF-1B	HO/SF	NL	3/4	44	145	21	42	12	4	4	29	.290	12	74	136	—
1982	LF	SF	NL	3-6	80	278	32	72	16	1	9	49	.259	19	117	106	—
1983	LF	SF	NL	5-6	139	516	74	144	17	7	21	87	.279	35	238	115	27-64
1984	LF	SF	NL	6-6	136	514	76	155	27	2	21	86	.302	47	249	133	12-53
1985	LF	SF	NL	6-6	133	507	49	122	20	3	17	62	.241	21	199	91	53-65
1986	LF	SF	NL	3-6	89	341	48	95	11	3	6	42	.279	20	130	95	—
1987	LF	SF	NL	1-6	131	503	70	141	29	4	19	63	.280	21	235	104	42-59
1988	LF	SF	NL	4-6	44	160	12	41	8	1	2	20	.256	9	57	93	—
1988	LF	MIL	AL	3-7	94	374	45	88	19	0	8	44	.235	16	131	79	—
1989	DH-LF	SEA	AL	6-7	150	566	69	144	20	1	24	93	.254	38	238	101	47-67
1990	LF-DH	SEA	AL	5-7	134	478	39	120	20	0	10	75	.251	37	170	88	58-69

MAJOR LEAGUE TOTALS   1415 5045 614 1342 223 37 144 723 .266 342 2071 105   6 yrs

Terry Stephen Puhl　　　　Born Jul 8, 1956　　Melville, SK
6'2　195 lbs　Batted left

YR	POS	TEAM	LG	FIN	G	AB	R	H	2B	3B	HR	RBI	AVG	BB	TB	OQ	RANK
1977	LF-CF	HOU	NL	3-6	60	229	40	69	13	5	0	10	.301	30	92	114	—
1978	LF	HOU	NL	5-6	149	585	87	169	25	6	3	35	.289	48	215	101	44-63
1979	CF	HOU	NL	2-6	157	600	87	172	22	4	8	49	.287	58	226	103	43-62
1980	RF	HOU	NL	1-6	141	535	75	151	24	5	13	55	.282	60	224	118	23-59
1981	RF	HOU	NL	3-6	96	350	43	88	19	4	3	28	.251	31	124	96	52-69
1982	RF	HOU	NL	5-6	145	507	64	133	17	9	8	50	.262	51	192	104	42-66
1983	RF	HOU	NL	3-6	137	465	66	136	25	7	8	44	.292	36	199	112	33-64
1984	RF	HOU	NL	2-6	132	449	66	135	19	7	9	55	.301	59	195	130	14-53
1985	RF	HOU	NL	3-6	57	194	34	55	14	3	2	23	.284	18	81	113	—
1986	RF	HOU	NL	1-6	81	172	17	42	10	0	3	14	.244	15	61	91	—
1987	LF-RF	HOU	NL	3-6	90	122	9	28	5	0	2	15	.230	11	39	78	—
1988	LF-RF	HOU	NL	5-6	113	234	42	71	7	2	3	19	.303	35	91	129	—
1989	RF	HOU	NL	3-6	121	354	41	96	25	4	0	27	.271	45	129	110	—
1990	LF-CF	HOU	NL	4-6	37	41	5	12	1	0	0	8	.293	5	13	—	—
1991	DH-LF	KC	AL	6-7	15	18	0	4	0	0	0	3	.222	3	4	—	—
MAJOR LEAGUE TOTALS					1531	4855	676	1361	226	56	62	435	.280	505	1885	109	7 yrs

Dwayne Keith Murphy　　　　Born Mar 18, 1955　Merced, CA
6'1　185 lbs　Batted left

YR	POS	TEAM	LG	FIN	G	AB	R	H	2B	3B	HR	RBI	AVG	BB	TB	OQ	RANK
1978	LF-CF	OAK	AL	6-7	60	52	15	10	2	0	0	5	.192	7	12	—	—
1979	CF	OAK	AL	7-7	121	388	57	99	10	4	11	40	.255	84	150	117	—
1980	CF	OAK	AL	2-7	159	573	86	157	18	2	13	68	.274	102	218	114	29-69
1981	CF	OAK	AL	1-7	107	390	58	98	10	3	15	60	.251	73	159	127	18-71
1982	CF	OAK	AL	5-7	151	543	84	129	15	1	27	94	.238	94	227	115	30-77
1983	CF	OAK	AL	4-7	130	471	55	107	17	2	17	75	.227	62	179	99	49-70
1984	CF	OAK	AL	4-7	153	559	93	143	18	2	33	88	.256	74	264	122	20-68
1985	CF	OAK	AL	4-7	152	523	77	122	21	3	20	59	.233	84	209	108	38-75
1986	CF	OAK	AL	3-7	98	329	50	83	11	3	9	39	.252	56	127	108	—
1987	CF	OAK	AL	3-7	82	219	39	51	7	0	8	35	.233	58	82	117	—
1988	CF-RF	DET	AL	2-7	49	144	14	36	5	0	4	19	.250	24	53	109	—
1989	LF-RF	PHI	NL	6-6	98	156	20	34	5	0	9	27	.218	29	66	127	—
MAJOR LEAGUE TOTALS					1360	4347	648	1069	139	20	166	609	.246	747	1746	114	6 yrs

Damaso Domingo Garcia   Born Feb 7, 1955   Moca, DR
6'1   165 lbs   Batted right

YR	POS	TEAM	LG	FIN	G	AB	R	H	2B	3B	HR	RBI	AVG	BB	TB	OQ	RANK
1978	2B-SS	NY	AL	1-7	18	41	5	8	0	0	0	1	.195	2	8	—	—
1979	SS	NY	AL	4-7	11	38	3	10	1	0	0	4	.263	0	11	—	—
1980	2B	TOR	AL	7-7	140	543	50	151	30	7	4	46	.278	12	207	83	67-69
1981	2B	TOR	AL	7-7	64	250	24	63	8	1	1	13	.252	9	76	73	—
1982	2B	TOR	AL	6-7	147	597	89	185	32	3	5	42	.310	21	238	93	60-77
1983	2B	TOR	AL	4-7	131	525	84	161	23	6	3	38	.307	24	205	94	55-70
1984	2B	TOR	AL	2-7	152	633	79	180	32	5	5	46	.284	16	237	84	60-68
1985	2B	TOR	AL	1-7	146	600	70	169	25	4	8	65	.282	15	226	82	70-75
1986	2B	TOR	AL	4-7	122	424	57	119	22	0	6	46	.281	13	159	82	—
1988	2B	ATL	NL	6-6	21	60	3	7	1	0	1	4	.117	3	11	—	—
1989	2B	MON	NL	4-6	80	203	26	55	9	1	3	18	.271	15	75	100	—

MAJOR LEAGUE TOTALS   1032   3914   490 1108   183   27   36   323   .283   130 1453   87   5 yrs

Paul Leo Molitor   Born Aug 22, 1956   St Paul, MN
6'0   185 lbs   Batted right

YR	POS	TEAM	LG	FIN	G	AB	R	H	2B	3B	HR	RBI	AVG	BB	TB	OQ	RANK
1978	2B-SS	MIL	AL	3-7	125	521	73	142	26	4	6	45	.273	19	194	86	71-83
1979	2B	MIL	AL	2-7	140	584	88	188	27	16	9	62	.322	48	274	118	22-75
1980	2B-SS	MIL	AL	3-7	111	450	81	137	29	2	9	37	.304	48	197	116	25-69
1981	CF-DH	MIL	AL	1-7	64	251	45	67	11	0	2	19	.267	25	84	94	—
1982	3B	MIL	AL	1-7	160	666	136	201	26	8	19	71	.302	69	300	118	25-77
1983	3B	MIL	AL	5-7	152	608	95	164	28	6	15	47	.270	59	249	104	41-70
1984	3B-DH	MIL	AL	7-7	13	46	3	10	1	0	0	6	.217	2	11	—	—
1985	3B	MIL	AL	6-7	140	576	93	171	28	3	10	48	.297	54	235	105	41-75
1986	3B	MIL	AL	6-7	105	437	62	123	24	6	9	55	.281	40	186	105	—
1987	DH-3B	MIL	AL	3-7	118	465	114	164	41	5	16	75	.353	69	263	154	2-79
1988	3B-DH	MIL	AL	3-7	154	609	115	190	34	6	13	60	.312	71	275	126	19-74
1989	3B-DH	MIL	AL	4-7	155	615	84	194	35	4	11	56	.315	64	270	123	16-67
1990	2B-1B	MIL	AL	6-7	103	418	64	119	27	6	12	45	.285	37	194	118	—
1991	DH-1B	MIL	AL	4-7	158	665	133	216	32	13	17	75	.325	77	325	134	11-72
1992	DH-1B	MIL	AL	2-7	158	609	89	195	36	7	12	89	.320	73	281	131	10-73
1993	DH-1B	TOR	AL	1-7	160	636	121	211	37	5	22	111	.332	77	324	135	11-73

MAJOR LEAGUE TOTALS   2016   8156 1396 2492   442   91 182   901   .306   832 3662   121   12 yrs

Glenn Dee Hubbard Born Sep 25, 1957 Hahn AFB, West Germany
5'9 150 lbs Batted right

YR	POS	TEAM	LG	FIN	G	AB	R	H	2B	3B	HR	RBI	AVG	BB	TB	OQ	RANK
1978	2B	ATL	NL	6-6	44	163	15	42	4	0	2	13	.258	10	52	82	—
1979	2B	ATL	NL	6-6	97	325	34	75	12	0	3	29	.231	27	96	76	—
1980	2B	ATL	NL	4-6	117	431	55	107	21	3	9	43	.248	49	161	103	—
1981	2B	ATL	NL	5-6	99	361	39	85	13	5	6	33	.235	33	126	94	55-69
1982	2B	ATL	NL	1-6	145	532	75	132	25	1	9	59	.248	59	186	98	47-66
1983	2B	ATL	NL	2-6	148	517	65	136	24	6	12	70	.263	55	208	108	37-64
1984	2B	ATL	NL	2-6	120	397	53	93	27	2	9	43	.234	55	151	109	—
1985	2B	ATL	NL	5-6	142	439	51	102	21	0	5	39	.232	56	138	92	52-65
1986	2B	ATL	NL	6-6	143	408	42	94	16	1	4	36	.230	66	124	94	—
1987	2B	ATL	NL	5-6	141	443	69	117	33	2	5	38	.264	77	169	111	32-59
1988	2B	OAK	AL	1-7	105	294	35	75	12	2	3	33	.255	33	100	93	—
1989	2B	OAK	AL	1-7	53	131	12	26	6	0	3	12	.198	19	41	88	—

| MAJOR LEAGUE TOTALS | | | | | 1354 | 4441 | 545 | 1084 | 214 | 22 | 70 | 448 | .244 | 539 | 1552 | 101 | 5 yrs |

Ronald John Oester Born May 5, 1956 Cincinnati, OH
6'2 185 lbs Batted both

YR	POS	TEAM	LG	FIN	G	AB	R	H	2B	3B	HR	RBI	AVG	BB	TB	OQ	RANK
1978	SS	CIN	NL	2-6	6	8	1	3	0	0	0	1	.375	0	3	—	—
1979	SS	CIN	NL	1-6	6	3	0	0	0	0	0	0	.000	0	0	—	—
1980	2B-SS	CIN	NL	3-6	100	303	40	84	16	2	2	20	.277	26	110	99	—
1981	2B	CIN	NL	1-6	105	354	45	96	16	7	5	42	.271	42	141	115	28-69
1982	2B-SS	CIN	NL	6-6	151	549	63	143	19	4	9	47	.260	35	197	92	60-66
1983	2B	CIN	NL	6-6	157	549	63	145	23	5	11	58	.264	49	211	101	42-64
1984	2B	CIN	NL	5-6	150	553	54	134	26	3	3	38	.242	41	175	83	51-53
1985	2B	CIN	NL	2-6	152	526	59	155	26	3	1	34	.295	51	190	103	41-65
1986	2B	CIN	NL	2-6	153	523	52	135	23	2	8	44	.258	52	186	95	39-49
1987	2B	CIN	NL	2-6	69	237	28	60	9	6	2	23	.253	22	87	91	—
1988	2B	CIN	NL	2-6	54	150	20	42	7	0	0	10	.280	9	49	90	—
1989	2B	CIN	NL	5-6	109	305	23	75	15	0	1	14	.246	32	93	89	—
1990	2B	CIN	NL	1-6	64	154	10	46	10	1	0	13	.299	10	58	98	—

| MAJOR LEAGUE TOTALS | | | | | 1276 | 4214 | 458 | 1118 | 190 | 33 | 42 | 344 | .265 | 369 | 1500 | 98 | 6 yrs |

James Robert Horner
6'1 195 lbs Batted right

Born Aug 6, 1957 Junction City, KS

YR	POS	TEAM	LG	FIN	G	AB	R	H	2B	3B	HR	RBI	AVG	BB	TB	OQ	RANK
1978	3B	ATL	NL	6-6	89	323	50	86	17	1	23	63	.266	24	174	133	—
1979	3B-1B	ATL	NL	6-6	121	487	66	153	15	1	33	98	.314	22	269	135	11-62
1980	3B	ATL	NL	4-6	124	463	81	124	14	1	35	89	.268	27	245	128	14-59
1981	3B	ATL	NL	5-6	79	300	42	83	10	0	15	42	.277	32	138	127	15-69
1982	3B	ATL	NL	1-6	140	499	85	130	24	0	32	97	.261	66	250	137	11-66
1983	3B	ATL	NL	2-6	104	386	75	117	25	1	20	68	.303	50	204	148	—
1984	3B	ATL	NL	2-6	32	113	15	31	8	0	3	19	.274	14	48	122	—
1985	1B-3B	ATL	NL	5-6	130	483	61	129	25	3	27	89	.267	50	241	131	12-65
1986	1B	ATL	NL	6-6	141	517	70	141	22	0	27	87	.273	52	244	123	16-49
1988	1B	SL	NL	5-6	60	206	15	53	9	1	3	33	.257	32	73	114	—
MAJOR LEAGUE TOTALS					1020	3777	560	1047	169	8	218	685	.277	369	1886	130	6 yrs

Carney Ray Lansford
6'2 195 lbs Batted right

Born Feb 7, 1957 San Jose, CA

YR	POS	TEAM	LG	FIN	G	AB	R	H	2B	3B	HR	RBI	AVG	BB	TB	OQ	RANK
1978	3B	CAL	AL	2-7	121	453	63	133	23	2	8	52	.294	31	184	103	—
1979	3B	CAL	AL	1-7	157	654	114	188	30	5	19	79	.287	39	285	101	46-75
1980	3B	CAL	AL	6-7	151	602	87	157	27	3	15	80	.261	50	235	95	57-69
1981	3B-DH	BOS	AL	5-7	102	399	61	134	23	3	4	52	.336	34	175	126	19-71
1982	3B-DH	BOS	AL	3-7	128	482	65	145	28	4	11	63	.301	46	214	114	32-77
1983	3B	OAK	AL	4-7	80	299	43	92	16	2	10	45	.308	22	142	118	—
1984	3B	OAK	AL	4-7	151	597	70	179	31	5	14	74	.300	40	262	109	35-68
1985	3B	OAK	AL	4-7	98	401	51	111	18	2	13	46	.277	18	172	96	—
1986	3B-1B	OAK	AL	3-7	151	591	80	168	16	4	19	72	.284	39	249	99	55-78
1987	3B-1B	OAK	AL	3-7	151	554	89	160	27	4	19	76	.289	60	252	111	36-79
1988	3B	OAK	AL	1-7	150	556	80	155	20	2	7	57	.279	35	200	90	58-74
1989	3B	OAK	AL	1-7	148	551	81	185	28	2	2	52	.336	51	223	116	22-67
1990	3B	OAK	AL	1-7	134	507	58	136	15	1	3	50	.268	45	162	85	64-69
1991	3B	OAK	AL	4-7	5	16	0	1	0	0	0	1	.063	0	1	—	—
1992	3B-1B	OAK	AL	1-7	135	496	65	130	30	1	7	75	.262	43	183	94	61-73
MAJOR LEAGUE TOTALS					1862	7158	1007	2074	332	40	151	874	.290	553	2939	104	11 yrs

Bobby Keith Moreland
6'0 190 lbs Batted right

Born May 2, 1954 Dallas, TX

YR	POS	TEAM	LG	FIN	G	AB	R	H	2B	3B	HR	RBI	AVG	BB	TB	OQ	RANK
1978	C	PHI	NL	1-6	1	2	0	0	0	0	0	0	.000	0	0	—	—
1979	C	PHI	NL	4-6	14	48	3	18	3	2	0	8	.375	3	25	—	—
1980	C	PHI	NL	1-6	62	159	13	50	8	0	4	29	.314	8	70	114	—
1981	C-3B	PHI	NL	3-6	61	196	16	50	7	0	6	37	.255	15	75	100	—
1982	LF-C	CHI	NL	5-6	138	476	50	124	17	2	15	68	.261	46	190	108	37-66
1983	RF	CHI	NL	5-6	154	533	76	161	30	3	16	70	.302	68	245	132	9-64
1984	RF-1B	CHI	NL	1-6	140	495	59	138	17	3	16	80	.279	34	209	110	31-53
1985	RF	CHI	NL	4-6	161	587	74	180	30	3	14	106	.307	68	258	127	16-65
1986	RF-3B	CHI	NL	5-6	156	586	72	159	30	0	12	79	.271	53	225	101	35-49
1987	3B	CHI	NL	6-6	153	563	63	150	29	1	27	88	.266	39	262	107	38-59
1988	1B-LF	SD	NL	3-6	143	511	40	131	23	0	5	64	.256	40	169	92	53-58
1989	DH-1B	DE/BA	AL	7/2	123	425	45	118	20	0	6	45	.278	31	156	94	—

MAJOR LEAGUE TOTALS 1306 4581 511 1279 214 14 121 674 .279 405 1884 111 7 yrs

Terrence Edward Kennedy
6'3 220 lbs Batted left

Born Jun 4, 1956 Euclid, OH

YR	POS	TEAM	LG	FIN	G	AB	R	H	2B	3B	HR	RBI	AVG	BB	TB	OQ	RANK
1978	C	SL	NL	5-6	10	29	0	5	0	0	0	2	.172	4	5	—	—
1979	C	SL	NL	3-6	33	109	11	31	7	0	2	17	.284	6	44	99	—
1980	C-LF	SL	NL	4-6	84	248	28	63	12	3	4	34	.254	28	93	104	—
1981	C	SD	NL	6-6	101	382	32	115	24	1	2	41	.301	22	147	103	44-69
1982	C	SD	NL	4-6	153	562	75	166	42	1	21	97	.295	26	273	121	20-66
1983	C	SD	NL	4-6	149	549	47	156	27	2	17	98	.284	51	238	116	26-64
1984	C	SD	NL	1-6	148	530	54	127	16	1	14	57	.240	33	187	88	49-53
1985	C	SD	NL	3-6	143	532	54	139	27	1	10	74	.261	31	198	93	51-65
1986	C	SD	NL	4-6	141	432	46	114	22	1	12	57	.264	37	174	103	—
1987	C	BAL	AL	6-7	143	512	51	128	13	1	18	62	.250	35	197	84	72-79
1988	C	BAL	AL	7-7	85	265	20	60	10	0	3	16	.226	15	79	70	—
1989	C	SF	NL	1-6	125	355	19	85	15	0	5	34	.239	35	115	91	—
1990	C	SF	NL	3-6	107	303	25	84	22	0	2	26	.277	31	112	102	—
1991	C	SF	NL	4-6	69	171	12	40	7	1	3	13	.234	11	58	84	—

MAJOR LEAGUE TOTALS 1491 4979 474 1313 244 12 113 628 .264 365 1920 101 6 yrs

Willie Clay Upshaw
6'0 185 lbs Batted left

Born Apr 27, 1957 Blanco, TX

YR	POS	TEAM	LG	FIN	G	AB	R	H	2B	3B	HR	RBI	AVG	BB	TB	OQ	RANK
1978	LF-DH	TOR	AL	7-7	95	224	26	53	8	2	1	17	.237	21	68	80	—
1980	1B-DH	TOR	AL	7-7	34	61	10	13	3	1	1	5	.213	6	21	—	—
1981	DH-1B	TOR	AL	7-7	61	111	15	19	3	1	4	10	.171	11	36	81	—
1982	1B	TOR	AL	6-7	160	580	77	155	25	7	21	75	.267	52	257	108	42-77
1983	1B	TOR	AL	4-7	160	579	99	177	26	7	27	104	.306	61	298	133	6-70
1984	1B	TOR	AL	2-7	152	569	79	158	31	9	19	84	.278	55	264	117	24-68
1985	1B	TOR	AL	1-7	148	501	79	138	31	5	15	65	.275	48	224	110	35-75
1986	1B	TOR	AL	4-7	155	573	85	144	28	6	9	60	.251	78	211	98	59-78
1987	1B	TOR	AL	2-7	150	512	68	125	22	4	15	58	.244	58	200	93	63-79
1988	1B	CLE	AL	6-7	149	493	58	121	22	3	11	50	.245	62	182	100	49-74
MAJOR LEAGUE TOTALS					1264	4203	596	1103	199	45	123	528	.262	452	1761	109	7 yrs

Pedro Guerrero
5'11 176 lbs Batted right

Born Jun 29, 1956 San Pedro de Macoris, DR

YR	POS	TEAM	LG	FIN	G	AB	R	H	2B	3B	HR	RBI	AVG	BB	TB	OQ	RANK
1978	1B	LA	NL	1-6	5	8	3	5	0	1	0	1	.625	0	7	—	—
1979	RF-1B	LA	NL	3-6	25	62	7	15	2	0	2	9	.242	1	23	—	—
1980	CF-2B	LA	NL	2-6	75	183	27	59	9	1	7	31	.322	12	91	133	—
1981	RF-3B	LA	NL	2-6	98	347	46	104	17	2	12	48	.300	34	161	130	10-69
1982	RF-3B	LA	NL	2-6	150	575	87	175	27	5	32	100	.304	65	308	150	4-66
1983	3B	LA	NL	1-6	160	584	87	174	28	6	32	103	.298	72	310	147	4-64
1984	3B-RF	LA	NL	4-6	144	535	85	162	29	4	16	72	.303	49	247	128	15-53
1985	LF-3B	LA	NL	1-6	137	487	99	156	22	2	33	87	.320	83	281	175	1-65
1986	LF-1B	LA	NL	5-6	31	61	7	15	3	0	5	10	.246	2	33	—	—
1987	LF-1B	LA	NL	4-6	152	545	89	184	25	2	27	89	.338	74	294	150	7-59
1988	1B-3B	LA/SL	NL	1/5	103	364	40	104	14	2	10	65	.286	46	152	127	—
1989	1B	SL	NL	3-6	162	570	60	177	42	1	17	117	.311	79	272	146	8-59
1990	1B	SL	NL	6-6	136	498	42	140	31	1	13	80	.281	44	212	111	34-63
1991	1B	SL	NL	2-6	115	427	41	116	12	1	8	70	.272	37	154	98	—
1992	1B-LF	SL	NL	3-6	43	146	10	32	6	1	1	16	.219	11	43	77	—
MAJOR LEAGUE TOTALS					1536	5392	730	1618	267	29	215	898	.300	609	2588	142	8 yrs

Osborne Earl Smith Born Dec 26, 1954 Mobile, AL
5'11 150 lbs Batted both

YR	POS	TEAM	LG	FIN	G	AB	R	H	2B	3B	HR	RBI	AVG	BB	TB	OQ	RANK
1978	SS	SD	NL	4-6	159	590	69	152	17	6	1	46	.258	47	184	84	61-63
1979	SS	SD	NL	5-6	156	587	77	124	18	6	0	27	.211	37	154	64	62-62
1980	SS	SD	NL	6-6	158	609	67	140	18	5	0	35	.230	71	168	81	57-59
1981	SS	SD	NL	6-6	110	450	53	100	11	2	0	21	.222	41	115	73	67-69
1982	SS	SL	NL	1-6	140	488	58	121	24	1	2	43	.248	68	153	97	55-66
1983	SS	SL	NL	4-6	159	552	69	134	30	6	3	50	.243	64	185	94	52-64
1984	SS	SL	NL	3-6	124	412	53	106	20	5	1	44	.257	56	139	103	—
1985	SS	SL	NL	1-6	158	537	70	148	22	3	6	54	.276	65	194	106	36-65
1986	SS	SL	NL	3-6	153	514	67	144	19	4	0	54	.280	79	171	105	31-49
1987	SS	SL	NL	1-6	158	600	104	182	40	4	0	75	.303	89	230	112	31-59
1988	SS	SL	NL	5-6	153	575	80	155	27	1	3	51	.270	74	193	106	35-58
1989	SS	SL	NL	3-6	155	593	82	162	30	8	2	50	.273	55	214	102	38-59
1990	SS	SL	NL	6-6	143	512	61	130	21	1	1	50	.254	61	156	88	56-63
1991	SS	SL	NL	2-6	150	550	96	157	30	3	3	50	.285	83	202	116	26-52
1992	SS	SL	NL	3-6	132	518	73	153	20	2	0	31	.295	59	177	106	34-49
1993	SS	SL	NL	3-7	141	545	75	157	22	6	1	53	.288	43	194	92	68-77

MAJOR LEAGUE TOTALS 2349 8632 1154 2265 369 63 23 734 .262 992 2829 95 15 yrs

Lonnie Smith Born Dec 22, 1955 Chicago, IL
5'9 170 lbs Batted right

YR	POS	TEAM	LG	FIN	G	AB	R	H	2B	3B	HR	RBI	AVG	BB	TB	OQ	RANK
1978	LF	PHI	NL	1-6	17	4	6	0	0	0	0	0	.000	4	0	—	—
1979	CF-RF	PHI	NL	4-6	17	30	4	5	2	0	0	3	.167	1	7	—	—
1980	LF-RF	PHI	NL	1-6	100	298	69	101	14	4	3	20	.339	26	132	128	—
1981	CF-RF	PHI	NL	3-6	62	176	40	57	14	3	2	11	.324	18	83	138	—
1982	LF	SL	NL	1-6	156	592	120	182	35	8	8	69	.307	64	257	126	19-66
1983	LF	SL	NL	4-6	130	492	83	158	31	5	8	45	.321	41	223	124	18-64
1984	LF	SL	NL	3-6	145	504	77	126	20	4	6	49	.250	70	172	103	38-53
1985	LF	SL	NL	1-6	28	96	15	25	2	2	0	7	.260	15	31	103	—
1985	LF	KC	AL	1-7	120	448	77	115	23	4	6	41	.257	41	164	91	66-75
1986	LF	KC	AL	3-7	134	508	80	146	25	7	8	44	.287	46	209	102	47-78
1987	LF-DH	KC	AL	2-7	48	167	26	42	7	1	3	8	.251	24	60	94	—
1988	LF	ATL	NL	6-6	43	114	14	27	3	0	3	9	.237	10	39	94	—
1989	LF	ATL	NL	6-6	134	482	89	152	34	4	21	79	.315	76	257	165	2-59
1990	LF	ATL	NL	6-6	135	466	72	142	27	9	9	42	.305	58	214	131	12-63
1991	LF	ATL	NL	1-6	122	353	58	97	19	1	7	44	.275	50	139	118	—
1992	LF	ATL	NL	1-6	84	158	23	39	8	2	6	33	.247	17	69	118	—
1993	LF	PIT	NL	5-7	94	199	35	57	5	4	6	24	.286	43	88	139	—
1993	DH-LF	BAL	AL	3-7	9	24	8	5	1	0	2	3	.208	8	12	—	—

MAJOR LEAGUE TOTALS 1578 5111 896 1476 270 58 98 531 .289 612 2156 120 7 yrs

Antonio Bernazard   Born Aug 24, 1956 Caguas, PR
5'9   150 lbs Batted both

YR	POS	TEAM	LG	FIN	G	AB	R	H	2B	3B	HR	RBI	AVG	BB	TB	OQ	RANK
1979	2B	MON	NL	2-6	22	40	11	12	2	0	1	8	.300	15	17	—	—
1980	2B-SS	MON	NL	2-6	82	183	26	41	7	1	5	18	.224	17	65	92	—
1981	2B	CHI	AL	3-7	106	384	53	106	14	4	6	34	.276	54	146	115	26-71
1982	2B	CHI	AL	3-7	137	540	90	138	25	9	11	56	.256	67	214	104	48-77
1983	2B	CHI/SE	AL	1/7	139	533	65	141	34	3	8	56	.265	55	205	99	48-70
1984	2B	CLE	AL	6-7	140	439	44	97	15	4	2	38	.221	43	126	74	—
1985	2B	CLE	AL	7-7	153	500	73	137	26	3	11	59	.274	69	202	110	36-75
1986	2B	CLE	AL	5-7	146	562	88	169	28	4	17	73	.301	53	256	114	29-78
1987	2B	CL/OA	AL	7/3	140	507	73	127	26	2	14	49	.250	55	199	93	61-79
1991	2B-DH	DET	AL	2-7	6	12	0	2	0	0	0	0	.167	0	2	—	—
MAJOR LEAGUE TOTALS					1071	3700	523	970	177	30	75	391	.262	428	1432	106	6 yrs

Thomas Mitchell Herr   Born Apr 4, 1956 Lancaster, PA
6'0   175 lbs Batted both

YR	POS	TEAM	LG	FIN	G	AB	R	H	2B	3B	HR	RBI	AVG	BB	TB	OQ	RANK
1979	2B	SL	NL	3-6	14	10	4	2	0	0	0	1	.200	2	2	—	—
1980	2B-SS	SL	NL	4-6	76	222	29	55	12	5	0	15	.248	16	77	89	—
1981	2B	SL	NL	1-6	103	411	50	110	14	9	0	46	.268	39	142	98	49-69
1982	2B	SL	NL	1-6	135	493	83	131	19	4	0	36	.266	57	158	95	57-66
1983	2B	SL	NL	4-6	89	313	43	101	14	4	2	31	.323	43	129	128	—
1984	2B	SL	NL	3-6	145	558	67	154	23	2	4	49	.276	49	193	96	44-53
1985	2B	SL	NL	1-6	159	596	97	180	38	3	8	110	.302	80	248	125	18-65
1986	2B	SL	NL	3-6	152	559	48	141	30	4	2	61	.252	73	185	96	38-49
1987	2B	SL	NL	1-6	141	510	73	134	29	0	2	83	.263	68	169	93	52-59
1988	2B	SL	NL	5-6	15	50	4	13	0	0	1	3	.260	11	16	—	—
1988	2B	MIN	AL	2-7	86	304	42	80	16	0	1	21	.263	40	99	95	—
1989	2B	PHI	NL	6-6	151	561	65	161	25	6	2	37	.287	54	204	106	31-59
1990	2B	PH/NY	NL	4/2	146	547	48	143	26	3	5	60	.261	50	190	93	55-63
1991	2B	NY/SF	NL	5/4	102	215	23	45	8	1	1	21	.209	45	58	97	—
MAJOR LEAGUE TOTALS					1514	5349	676	1450	254	41	28	574	.271	627	1870	100	8 yrs

Gary Lamell Ward Born Dec 6, 1953 Los Angeles, CA
6'2 195 lbs Batted right

YR	POS	TEAM	LG	FIN	G	AB	R	H	2B	3B	HR	RBI	AVG	BB	TB	OQ	RANK
1979	RF-DH	MIN	AL	4-7	10	14	2	4	0	0	0	1	.286	3	4	—	—
1980	LF	MIN	AL	3-7	13	41	11	19	6	2	1	10	.463	3	32	—	—
1981	LF	MIN	AL	7-7	85	295	42	78	7	6	3	29	.264	28	106	99	—
1982	LF	MIN	AL	7-7	152	570	85	165	33	7	28	91	.289	37	296	122	21-77
1983	LF	MIN	AL	5-7	157	623	76	173	34	5	19	88	.278	44	274	106	40-70
1984	RF	TEX	AL	7-7	155	602	97	171	21	7	21	79	.284	55	269	113	29-68
1985	LF	TEX	AL	7-7	154	593	77	170	28	7	15	70	.287	39	257	103	48-75
1986	LF	TEX	AL	2-7	105	380	54	120	15	2	5	51	.316	31	154	104	—
1987	LF-DH	NY	AL	4-7	146	529	65	131	22	1	16	78	.248	33	203	83	75-79
1988	CF-1B	NY	AL	5-7	91	231	26	52	8	0	4	24	.225	24	72	82	—
1989	LF-DH	NY/DE	AL	5/7	113	292	27	74	11	2	9	30	.253	24	116	99	—
1990	LF-DH	DET	AL	3-7	106	309	32	79	11	2	9	46	.256	30	121	100	—
MAJOR LEAGUE TOTALS					1287	4479	594	1236	196	41	130	597	.276	351	1904	105	5 yrs

Kirk Harold Gibson Born May 28, 1957 Pontiac, MI
6'3 215 lbs Batted left

YR	POS	TEAM	LG	FIN	G	AB	R	H	2B	3B	HR	RBI	AVG	BB	TB	OQ	RANK
1979	LF	DET	AL	5-7	12	38	3	9	3	0	1	4	.237	1	15	—	—
1980	CF	DET	AL	5-7	51	175	23	46	2	1	9	16	.263	10	77	100	—
1981	RF	DET	AL	4-7	83	290	41	95	11	3	9	40	.328	18	139	128	—
1982	CF	DET	AL	4-7	69	266	34	74	16	2	8	35	.278	25	118	110	—
1983	DH-LF	DET	AL	2-7	128	401	60	91	12	9	15	51	.227	53	166	105	—
1984	RF	DET	AL	1-7	149	531	92	150	23	10	27	91	.282	63	274	133	11-68
1985	RF	DET	AL	3-7	154	581	96	167	37	5	29	97	.287	71	301	132	9-75
1986	RF	DET	AL	3-7	119	441	84	118	11	2	28	86	.268	68	217	128	7-78
1987	LF	DET	AL	1-7	128	487	95	135	25	3	24	79	.277	71	238	123	19-79
1988	LF	LA	NL	1-6	150	542	106	157	28	1	25	76	.290	73	262	145	5-58
1989	LF	LA	NL	4-6	71	253	35	54	8	2	9	28	.213	35	93	105	—
1990	CF	LA	NL	2-6	89	315	59	82	20	0	8	38	.260	39	126	110	—
1991	LF-DH	KC	AL	6-7	132	462	81	109	17	6	16	55	.236	69	186	108	37-72
1992	RF	PIT	NL	1-6	16	56	6	11	0	0	2	5	.196	3	17	—	—
1993	DH-CF	DET	AL	3-7	116	403	62	105	18	6	13	62	.261	44	174	105	—
MAJOR LEAGUE TOTALS					1467	5241	877	1403	231	50	223	763	.268	643	2403	128	6 yrs

Rickey Henley Henderson   Born Dec 25, 1958   Chicago, IL
5'10   180 lbs   Batted right

YR	POS	TEAM	LG	FIN	G	AB	R	H	2B	3B	HR	RBI	AVG	BB	TB	OQ	RANK
1979	LF	OAK	AL	7-7	89	351	49	96	13	3	1	26	.274	34	118	86	—
1980	LF	OAK	AL	2-7	158	591	111	179	22	4	9	53	.303	117	236	127	11-69
1981	LF	OAK	AL	1-7	108	423	89	135	18	7	6	35	.319	64	185	138	6-71
1982	LF	OAK	AL	5-7	149	536	119	143	24	4	10	51	.267	116	205	121	22-77
1983	LF	OAK	AL	4-7	145	513	105	150	25	7	9	48	.292	103	216	131	8-70
1984	LF	OAK	AL	4-7	142	502	113	147	27	4	16	58	.293	86	230	134	10-68
1985	CF	NY	AL	2-7	143	547	146	172	28	5	24	72	.314	99	282	149	2-75
1986	CF	NY	AL	2-7	153	608	130	160	31	5	28	74	.263	89	285	122	17-78
1987	CF-DH	NY	AL	4-7	95	358	78	104	17	3	17	37	.291	80	178	142	—
1988	LF	NY	AL	5-7	140	554	118	169	30	2	6	50	.305	82	221	121	23-74
1989	LF	NY/OA	AL	5/1	150	541	113	148	26	3	12	57	.274	126	216	134	8-67
1990	LF-DH	OAK	AL	1-7	136	489	119	159	33	3	28	61	.325	97	282	175	1-69
1991	LF-DH	OAK	AL	4-7	134	470	105	126	17	1	18	57	.268	98	199	129	16-72
1992	LF	OAK	AL	1-7	117	396	77	112	18	3	15	46	.283	95	181	148	5-73
1993	LF-DH	OA/TO	AL	7/1	134	481	114	139	22	2	21	59	.289	120	228	146	5-73

MAJOR LEAGUE TOTALS					1993	7360	1586	2139	351	56	220	784	.291	1406	3262	137	13 yrs

Timothy Raines   Born Sep 16, 1959   Sanford, FL
5'8   160 lbs   Batted both

YR	POS	TEAM	LG	FIN	G	AB	R	H	2B	3B	HR	RBI	AVG	BB	TB	OQ	RANK
1979	PR	MON	NL	2-6	6	0	3	0	0	0	0	0	—	0	0	—	—
1980	2B	MON	NL	2-6	15	20	5	1	0	0	0	0	.050	6	1	—	—
1981	LF	MON	NL	2-6	88	313	61	95	13	7	5	37	.304	45	137	136	8-69
1982	LF-2B	MON	NL	3-6	156	647	90	179	32	8	4	43	.277	75	239	108	36-66
1983	LF	MON	NL	3-6	156	615	133	183	32	8	11	71	.298	97	264	131	11-64
1984	CF	MON	NL	5-6	160	622	106	192	38	9	8	60	.309	87	272	134	10-53
1985	LF	MON	NL	3-6	150	575	115	184	30	13	11	41	.320	81	273	144	6-65
1986	LF	MON	NL	4-6	151	580	91	194	35	10	9	62	.334	78	276	143	2-49
1987	LF	MON	NL	3-6	139	530	123	175	34	8	18	68	.330	90	279	153	5-59
1988	LF	MON	NL	3-6	109	429	66	116	19	7	12	48	.270	53	185	127	—
1989	LF	MON	NL	4-6	145	517	76	148	29	6	9	60	.286	93	216	137	11-59
1990	LF	MON	NL	3-6	130	457	65	131	11	5	9	62	.287	70	179	119	27-63
1991	LF	CHI	AL	2-7	155	609	102	163	20	6	5	50	.268	83	210	98	53-72
1992	LF	CHI	AL	3-7	144	551	102	162	22	9	7	54	.294	81	223	119	23-73
1993	LF	CHI	AL	1-7	115	415	75	127	16	4	16	54	.306	64	199	131	—

MAJOR LEAGUE TOTALS					1819	6880	1213	2050	331	100	124	710	.298	1003	2953	129	11 yrs

Rafael Emilio Ramirez   Born Feb 18, 1958   San Pedro de Macoris, DR
6'0   170 lbs   Batted right

YR	POS	TEAM	LG	FIN	G	AB	R	H	2B	3B	HR	RBI	AVG	BB	TB	OQ	RANK
1980	SS	ATL	NL	4-6	50	165	17	44	6	1	2	11	.267	2	58	79	—
1981	SS	ATL	NL	5-6	95	307	30	67	16	2	2	20	.218	24	93	79	63-69
1982	SS	ATL	NL	1-6	157	609	74	169	24	4	10	52	.278	36	231	97	52-66
1983	SS	ATL	NL	2-6	152	622	82	185	13	5	7	58	.297	36	229	95	50-64
1984	SS	ATL	NL	2-6	145	591	51	157	22	4	2	48	.266	26	193	81	53-53
1985	SS	ATL	NL	5-6	138	568	54	141	25	4	5	58	.248	20	189	78	63-65
1986	SS-3B	ATL	NL	6-6	134	496	57	119	21	1	8	33	.240	21	166	77	47-49
1987	SS-3B	ATL	NL	5-6	56	179	22	47	12	0	1	21	.263	8	62	78	—
1988	SS	HOU	NL	5-6	155	566	51	156	30	5	6	59	.276	18	214	94	51-58
1989	SS	HOU	NL	3-6	151	537	46	132	20	2	6	54	.246	29	174	82	54-59
1990	SS	HOU	NL	4-6	132	445	44	116	19	3	2	37	.261	24	147	81	—
1991	SS-2B	HOU	NL	6-6	101	233	17	55	10	0	1	20	.236	13	68	73	—
1992	SS	HOU	NL	4-6	73	176	17	44	6	0	1	13	.250	7	53	74	—

MAJOR LEAGUE TOTALS   1539 5494 562 1432 224 31 53 484 .261 264 1877 85   8 yrs

Harold Douglass Baines   Born Mar 15, 1959   Easton, MD
6'2   175 lbs   Batted left

YR	POS	TEAM	LG	FIN	G	AB	R	H	2B	3B	HR	RBI	AVG	BB	TB	OQ	RANK
1980	RF	CHI	AL	5-7	141	491	55	125	23	6	13	49	.255	19	199	89	63-69
1981	RF	CHI	AL	3-7	82	280	42	80	11	7	10	41	.286	12	135	117	—
1982	RF	CHI	AL	3-7	161	608	89	165	29	8	25	105	.271	49	285	112	37-77
1983	RF	CHI	AL	1-7	156	596	76	167	33	2	20	99	.280	49	264	109	35-70
1984	RF	CHI	AL	5-7	147	569	72	173	28	10	29	94	.304	54	308	137	7-68
1985	RF	CHI	AL	3-7	160	640	86	198	29	3	22	113	.309	42	299	113	25-75
1986	RF	CHI	AL	5-7	145	570	72	169	29	2	21	88	.296	38	265	110	32-78
1987	DH	CHI	AL	5-7	132	505	59	148	26	4	20	93	.293	46	242	113	33-79
1988	DH	CHI	AL	5-7	158	599	55	166	39	1	13	81	.277	67	246	111	32-74
1989	DH-RF	CH/TX	AL	7/4	146	505	73	156	29	1	16	72	.309	73	235	136	6-67
1990	DH	TX/OA	AL	3/1	135	415	52	118	15	1	16	65	.284	67	183	128	—
1991	DH	OAK	AL	4-7	141	488	76	144	25	1	20	90	.295	72	231	132	14-72
1992	DH-RF	OAK	AL	1-7	140	478	58	121	18	0	16	76	.253	59	187	105	39-73
1993	DH	BAL	AL	3-7	118	416	64	130	22	0	20	78	.313	57	212	135	—

MAJOR LEAGUE TOTALS   1962 7160 929 2060 356 46 261 1144 .288 704 3291 115 11 yrs

Hubert Brooks

Born Sep 24, 1956 Los Angeles, CA

6'0 178 lbs Batted right

YR	POS	TEAM	LG	FIN	G	AB	R	H	2B	3B	HR	RBI	AVG	BB	TB	OQ	RANK
1980	3B	NY	NL	5-6	24	81	8	25	2	1	1	10	.309	5	32	—	—
1981	3B	NY	NL	5-6	98	358	34	110	21	2	4	38	.307	23	147	111	32-69
1982	3B	NY	NL	6-6	126	457	40	114	21	2	2	40	.249	28	145	81	—
1983	3B	NY	NL	6-6	150	586	53	147	18	4	5	58	.251	24	188	76	64-64
1984	3B-SS	NY	NL	2-6	153	561	61	159	23	2	16	73	.283	48	234	113	26-53
1985	SS	MON	NL	3-6	156	605	67	163	34	7	13	100	.269	34	250	102	45-65
1986	SS	MON	NL	4-6	80	306	50	104	18	5	14	58	.340	25	174	153	—
1987	SS	MON	NL	3-6	112	430	57	113	22	3	14	72	.263	24	183	96	—
1988	RF	MON	NL	3-6	151	588	61	164	35	2	20	90	.279	35	263	117	23-58
1989	RF	MON	NL	4-6	148	542	56	145	30	1	14	70	.268	39	219	106	29-59
1990	RF	LA	NL	2-6	153	568	74	151	28	1	20	91	.266	33	241	102	41-63
1991	RF	NY	NL	5-6	103	357	48	85	11	1	16	50	.238	44	146	112	—
1992	DH	CAL	AL	5-7	82	306	28	66	13	0	8	36	.216	12	103	73	—
1993	RF-DH	KC	AL	3-7	75	168	14	48	12	0	1	24	.286	11	63	89	—

MAJOR LEAGUE TOTALS 1611 5913 651 1594 288 31 148 810 .270 385 2388 104 7 yrs

William Hayward Wilson

Born Feb 9, 1956 Bamberg, SC

5'10 170 lbs Batted both

YR	POS	TEAM	LG	FIN	G	AB	R	H	2B	3B	HR	RBI	AVG	BB	TB	OQ	RANK
1980	CF	NY	NL	5-6	27	105	16	26	5	3	0	4	.248	12	37	99	—
1981	CF	NY	NL	5-6	92	328	49	89	8	8	3	14	.271	20	122	97	50-69
1982	CF	NY	NL	6-6	159	639	90	178	25	9	5	55	.279	32	236	93	59-66
1983	CF	NY	NL	6-6	152	638	91	176	25	6	7	51	.276	18	234	86	60-64
1984	CF	NY	NL	2-6	154	587	88	162	28	10	10	54	.276	26	240	101	41-53
1985	CF	NY	NL	2-6	93	337	56	93	16	8	6	26	.276	28	143	111	—
1986	CF	NY	NL	1-6	123	381	61	110	17	5	9	45	.289	32	164	113	—
1987	CF	NY	NL	2-6	124	385	58	115	19	7	9	34	.299	35	175	114	—
1988	CF	NY	NL	1-6	112	378	61	112	17	5	8	41	.296	27	163	119	—
1989	CF	NY	NL	2-6	80	249	22	51	10	1	3	18	.205	10	72	68	—
1989	RF-CF	TOR	AL	1-7	54	238	32	71	9	1	2	17	.298	3	88	84	—
1990	CF	TOR	AL	2-7	147	588	81	156	36	4	3	51	.265	31	209	85	65-69
1991	LF-RF	TOR	AL	1-7	86	241	26	58	12	4	2	28	.241	8	84	75	—

MAJOR LEAGUE TOTALS 1403 5094 731 1397 227 71 67 438 .274 282 1967 92 5 yrs

Timothy Charles Wallach Born Sep 14, 1957 Huntington Park, CA
6'3 220 lbs Batted right

YR	POS	TEAM	LG	FIN	G	AB	R	H	2B	3B	HR	RBI	AVG	BB	TB	OQ	RANK
1980	RF-1B	MON	NL	2-6	5	11	1	2	0	0	1	2	.182	1	5	—	—
1981	RF-1B	MON	NL	2-6	71	212	19	50	9	1	4	13	.236	15	73	88	—
1982	3B	MON	NL	3-6	158	596	89	160	31	3	28	97	.268	36	281	117	24-66
1983	3B	MON	NL	3-6	156	581	54	156	33	3	19	70	.269	55	252	114	29-64
1984	3B	MON	NL	5-6	160	582	55	143	25	4	18	72	.246	50	230	103	39-53
1985	3B	MON	NL	3-6	155	569	70	148	36	3	22	81	.260	38	256	111	28-65
1986	3B	MON	NL	4-6	134	480	50	112	22	1	18	71	.233	44	190	99	37-49
1987	3B	MON	NL	3-6	153	593	89	177	42	4	26	123	.298	37	305	121	17-59
1988	3B	MON	NL	3-6	159	592	52	152	32	5	12	69	.257	38	230	102	40-58
1989	3B	MON	NL	4-6	154	573	76	159	42	0	13	77	.277	58	240	118	20-59
1990	3B	MON	NL	3-6	161	626	69	185	37	5	21	98	.296	42	295	119	26-63
1991	3B	MON	NL	6-6	151	577	60	130	22	1	13	73	.225	50	193	87	50-52
1992	3B-1B	MON	NL	2-6	150	537	53	120	29	1	9	59	.223	50	178	89	48-49
1993	3B	LA	NL	4-7	133	477	42	106	19	1	12	62	.222	32	163	79	76-77
MAJOR LEAGUE TOTALS					1900	7006	779	1800	379	32	216	967	.257	546	2891	105	12 yrs

Lloyd Anthony Moseby Born Nov 5, 1959 Portland, AR
6'3 200 lbs Batted left

YR	POS	TEAM	LG	FIN	G	AB	R	H	2B	3B	HR	RBI	AVG	BB	TB	OQ	RANK
1980	RF	TOR	AL	7-7	114	389	44	89	24	1	9	46	.229	25	142	83	—
1981	CF	TOR	AL	7-7	100	378	36	88	16	2	9	43	.233	24	135	87	66-71
1982	CF	TOR	AL	6-7	147	487	51	115	20	9	9	52	.236	33	180	85	69-77
1983	CF	TOR	AL	4-7	151	539	104	170	31	7	18	81	.315	51	269	129	10-70
1984	CF	TOR	AL	2-7	158	592	97	166	28	15	18	92	.280	78	278	126	15-68
1985	CF	TOR	AL	1-7	152	584	92	151	30	7	18	70	.259	76	249	110	34-75
1986	CF	TOR	AL	4-7	152	589	89	149	24	5	21	86	.253	64	246	103	46-78
1987	CF	TOR	AL	2-7	155	592	106	167	27	4	26	96	.282	70	280	115	29-79
1988	CF	TOR	AL	3-7	128	472	77	113	17	7	10	42	.239	70	174	104	44-74
1989	CF-DH	TOR	AL	1-7	135	502	72	111	25	3	11	43	.221	56	175	91	56-67
1990	CF	DET	AL	3-7	122	431	64	107	16	5	14	51	.248	48	175	105	—
1991	LF	DET	AL	2-7	74	260	37	68	15	1	6	35	.262	21	103	97	—
MAJOR LEAGUE TOTALS					1588	5815	869	1494	273	66	169	737	.257	616	2406	106	9 yrs

Michael Lorri Scioscia   Born Nov 27, 1958 Upper Darby, PA
6'2   200 lbs   Batted left

YR	POS	TEAM	LG	FIN	G	AB	R	H	2B	3B	HR	RBI	AVG	BB	TB	OQ	RANK
1980	C	LA	NL	2-6	54	134	8	34	5	1	1	8	.254	12	44	89	—
1981	C	LA	NL	2-6	93	290	27	80	10	0	2	29	.276	36	96	102	—
1982	C	LA	NL	2-6	129	365	31	80	11	1	5	38	.219	44	108	86	—
1983	C	LA	NL	1-6	12	35	3	11	3	0	1	7	.314	5	17	—	—
1984	C	LA	NL	4-6	114	341	29	93	18	0	5	38	.273	52	126	116	—
1985	C	LA	NL	1-6	141	429	47	127	26	3	7	53	.296	77	180	135	10-65
1986	C	LA	NL	5-6	122	374	36	94	18	1	5	26	.251	62	129	106	—
1987	C	LA	NL	4-6	142	461	44	122	26	1	6	38	.265	55	168	97	50-59
1988	C	LA	NL	1-6	130	408	29	105	18	0	3	35	.257	38	132	94	—
1989	C	LA	NL	4-6	133	408	40	102	16	0	10	44	.250	52	148	107	—
1990	C	LA	NL	2-6	135	435	46	115	25	0	12	66	.264	55	176	112	33-63
1991	C	LA	NL	2-6	119	345	39	91	16	2	8	40	.264	47	135	115	—
1992	C	LA	NL	6-6	117	348	19	77	6	3	3	24	.221	32	98	78	—

MAJOR LEAGUE TOTALS   1441 4373 398 1131 198 12 68 446 .259 567 1557 —   —

Antonio Francisco Pena   Born Jun 4, 1957   Monte Cristi, DR
6'0   175 lbs   Batted right

YR	POS	TEAM	LG	FIN	G	AB	R	H	2B	3B	HR	RBI	AVG	BB	TB	OQ	RANK
1980	C	PIT	NL	3-6	8	21	1	9	1	1	0	1	.429	0	12	—	—
1981	C	PIT	NL	4-6	66	210	16	63	9	1	2	17	.300	8	80	97	—
1982	C	PIT	NL	4-6	138	497	53	147	28	4	11	63	.296	17	216	107	39-66
1983	C	PIT	NL	2-6	151	542	51	163	22	3	15	70	.301	31	236	111	35-64
1984	C	PIT	NL	6-6	147	546	77	156	27	2	15	78	.286	36	232	111	28-53
1985	C	PIT	NL	6-6	147	546	53	136	27	2	10	59	.249	29	197	88	58-65
1986	C	PIT	NL	6-6	144	510	56	147	26	2	10	52	.288	53	207	112	28-49
1987	C	SL	NL	1-6	116	384	40	82	13	4	5	44	.214	36	118	75	—
1988	C	SL	NL	5-6	149	505	55	133	23	1	10	51	.263	33	188	99	44-58
1989	C	SL	NL	3-6	141	424	36	110	17	2	4	37	.259	35	143	93	—
1990	C	BOS	AL	1-7	143	491	62	129	19	1	7	56	.263	43	171	90	55-69
1991	C	BOS	AL	2-7	141	464	45	107	23	2	5	48	.231	37	149	78	70-72
1992	C	BOS	AL	7-7	133	410	39	99	21	1	1	38	.241	24	125	73	—
1993	C	BOS	AL	5-7	126	304	20	55	11	0	4	19	.181	25	78	59	—

MAJOR LEAGUE TOTALS   1750 5854 604 1536 267 26 99 633 .262 407 2152 100 8 yrs

Leon Durham   Born Jul 31, 1957   Cincinnati, OH
6'1   185 lbs   Batted left

YR	POS	TEAM	LG	FIN	G	AB	R	H	2B	3B	HR	RBI	AVG	BB	TB	OQ	RANK
1980	LF	SL	NL	4-6	96	303	42	82	15	4	8	42	.271	18	129	106	—
1981	RF	CHI	NL	6-6	87	328	42	95	14	6	10	35	.290	27	151	124	18-69
1982	CF	CHI	NL	5-6	148	539	84	168	33	7	22	90	.312	66	281	150	3-66
1983	LF	CHI	NL	5-6	100	337	58	87	18	8	12	55	.258	66	157	140	—
1984	1B	CHI	NL	1-6	137	473	86	132	30	4	23	96	.279	69	239	145	4-53
1985	1B	CHI	NL	4-6	153	542	58	153	32	2	21	75	.282	64	252	129	13-65
1986	1B	CHI	NL	5-6	141	484	66	127	18	7	20	65	.262	67	219	125	11-49
1987	1B	CHI	NL	6-6	131	439	70	120	22	1	27	63	.273	51	225	127	15-59
1988	1B	CH/CN	NL	4/2	45	124	14	27	9	1	4	8	.218	14	50	110	—
1989	1B	SL	NL	3-6	29	18	2	1	1	0	0	1	.056	2	2	—	—
MAJOR LEAGUE TOTALS					1067	3587	522	992	192	40	147	530	.277	444	1705	133	6 yrs

Calvin Edwin Ripken Jr   Born Aug 24, 1960 Havre de Grace, MD
6'4   200 lbs   Batted right

YR	POS	TEAM	LG	FIN	G	AB	R	H	2B	3B	HR	RBI	AVG	BB	TB	OQ	RANK
1981	SS-3B	BAL	AL	2-7	23	39	1	5	0	0	0	0	.128	1	5	—	—
1982	SS-3B	BAL	AL	2-7	160	598	90	158	32	5	28	93	.264	46	284	111	39-77
1983	SS	BAL	AL	1-7	162	663	121	211	47	2	27	102	.318	58	343	132	7-70
1984	SS	BAL	AL	5-7	162	641	103	195	37	7	27	86	.304	71	327	134	8-68
1985	SS	BAL	AL	4-7	161	642	116	181	32	5	26	110	.282	67	301	117	19-75
1986	SS	BAL	AL	7-7	162	627	98	177	35	1	25	81	.282	70	289	116	26-78
1987	SS	BAL	AL	6-7	162	624	97	157	28	3	27	98	.252	81	272	106	45-79
1988	SS	BAL	AL	7-7	161	575	87	152	25	1	23	81	.264	102	248	127	18-74
1989	SS	BAL	AL	2-7	162	646	80	166	30	0	21	93	.257	57	259	102	45-67
1990	SS	BAL	AL	5-7	161	600	78	150	28	4	21	84	.250	82	249	112	28-69
1991	SS	BAL	AL	6-7	162	650	99	210	46	5	34	114	.323	53	368	143	4-72
1992	SS	BAL	AL	3-7	162	637	73	160	29	1	14	72	.251	64	233	95	60-73
1993	SS	BAL	AL	3-7	162	641	87	165	26	3	24	90	.257	65	269	101	42-73
MAJOR LEAGUE TOTALS					1962	7583	1130	2087	395	37	297	1104	.275	817	3447	116	12 yrs

Kent Alan Hrbek   Born May 21, 1960 Minneapolis, MN
6'4   200 lbs   Batted left

YR	POS	TEAM	LG	FIN	G	AB	R	H	2B	3B	HR	RBI	AVG	BB	TB	OQ	RANK
1981	1B-DH	MIN	AL	7-7	24	67	5	16	5	0	1	7	.239	5	24	—	—
1982	1B	MIN	AL	7-7	140	532	82	160	21	4	23	92	.301	54	258	124	19-77
1983	1B	MIN	AL	5-7	141	515	75	153	41	5	16	84	.297	57	252	127	14-70
1984	1B	MIN	AL	2-7	149	559	80	174	31	3	27	107	.311	65	292	139	4-68
1985	1B	MIN	AL	4-7	158	593	78	165	31	2	21	93	.278	67	263	113	26-75
1986	1B	MIN	AL	6-7	149	550	85	147	27	1	29	91	.267	71	263	121	19-78
1987	1B	MIN	AL	1-7	143	477	85	136	20	1	34	90	.285	84	260	141	5-79
1988	1B	MIN	AL	2-7	143	510	75	159	31	0	25	76	.312	67	265	145	6-74
1989	1B-DH	MIN	AL	5-7	109	375	59	102	17	0	25	84	.272	53	194	140	—
1990	1B-DH	MIN	AL	7-7	143	492	61	141	26	0	22	79	.287	69	233	131	7-69
1991	1B	MIN	AL	1-7	132	462	72	131	20	1	20	89	.284	67	213	127	19-72
1992	1B	MIN	AL	2-7	112	394	52	96	20	0	15	58	.244	71	161	119	—
1993	1B	MIN	AL	5-7	123	392	60	95	11	1	25	83	.242	71	183	123	—
MAJOR LEAGUE TOTALS					1666	5918	869	1675	301	18	283	1033	.283	801	2861	130	9 yrs

Thomas Andrew Brunansky   Born Aug 20, 1960 Covina, CA
6'4   205 lbs   Batted right

YR	POS	TEAM	LG	FIN	G	AB	R	H	2B	3B	HR	RBI	AVG	BB	TB	OQ	RANK
1981	LF	CAL	AL	5-7	11	33	7	5	0	0	3	6	.152	8	14	—	—
1982	RF	MIN	AL	7-7	127	463	77	126	30	1	20	46	.272	71	218	127	14-77
1983	RF	MIN	AL	5-7	151	542	70	123	24	5	28	82	.227	61	241	108	38-70
1984	RF	MIN	AL	2-7	155	567	75	144	21	0	32	85	.254	57	261	113	28-68
1985	RF	MIN	AL	4-7	157	567	71	137	28	4	27	90	.242	71	254	111	33-75
1986	RF	MIN	AL	6-7	157	593	69	152	28	1	23	75	.256	53	251	100	52-78
1987	RF-DH	MIN	AL	1-7	155	532	83	138	22	2	32	85	.259	74	260	119	27-79
1988	RF	MIN	AL	2-7	14	49	5	9	1	0	1	6	.184	7	13	—	—
1988	RF	SL	NL	5-6	143	523	69	128	22	4	22	79	.245	79	224	128	15-58
1989	RF	SL	NL	3-6	158	556	67	133	29	3	20	85	.239	59	228	111	23-59
1990	RF	SL	NL	6-6	19	57	5	9	3	0	1	2	.158	12	15	—	—
1990	RF	BOS	AL	1-7	129	461	61	123	24	5	15	71	.267	54	202	115	25-69
1991	RF	BOS	AL	2-7	142	459	54	105	24	1	16	70	.229	49	179	96	55-72
1992	RF-1B	BOS	AL	7-7	138	458	47	122	31	3	15	74	.266	66	204	123	18-73
1993	RF	MIL	AL	7-7	80	224	20	41	7	3	6	29	.183	25	72	76	—
MAJOR LEAGUE TOTALS					1736	6084	780	1495	294	32	261	885	.246	746	2636	114	11 yrs

Gary Joseph Gaetti
Born Aug 19, 1958 Centralia, IL
6'0 180 lbs Batted right

YR	POS	TEAM	LG	FIN	G	AB	R	H	2B	3B	HR	RBI	AVG	BB	TB	OQ	RANK
1981	3B	MIN	AL	7-7	9	26	4	5	0	0	2	3	.192	0	11	—	—
1982	3B	MIN	AL	7-7	145	508	59	117	25	4	25	84	.230	37	225	99	55-77
1983	3B	MIN	AL	5-7	157	584	81	143	30	3	21	78	.245	54	242	100	46-70
1984	3B	MIN	AL	2-7	162	588	55	154	29	4	5	65	.262	44	206	87	58-68
1985	3B	MIN	AL	4-7	160	560	71	138	31	0	20	63	.246	37	229	93	60-75
1986	3B	MIN	AL	6-7	157	596	91	171	34	1	34	108	.287	52	309	124	15-78
1987	3B	MIN	AL	1-7	154	584	95	150	36	2	31	109	.257	37	283	103	50-79
1988	3B	MIN	AL	2-7	133	468	66	141	29	2	28	88	.301	36	258	138	11-74
1989	3B	MIN	AL	5-7	130	498	63	125	11	4	19	75	.251	25	201	94	51-67
1990	3B	MIN	AL	7-7	154	577	61	132	27	5	16	85	.229	36	217	87	62-69
1991	3B	CAL	AL	7-7	152	586	58	144	22	1	18	66	.246	33	222	86	63-72
1992	3B-1B	CAL	AL	5-7	130	456	41	103	13	2	12	48	.226	21	156	76	—
1993	3B-1B	CA/KC	AL	5/3	102	331	40	81	20	1	14	50	.245	21	145	95	—

MAJOR LEAGUE TOTALS   1745 6362 785 1604 307 29 245 922 .252 433 2704 101 10 yrs

Brook Wallace Jacoby
Born Nov 23, 1959 Philadelphia, PA
5'11 175 lbs Batted right

YR	POS	TEAM	LG	FIN	G	AB	R	H	2B	3B	HR	RBI	AVG	BB	TB	OQ	RANK
1981	3B	ATL	NL	5-6	11	10	0	2	0	0	0	1	.200	0	2	—	—
1983	3B	ATL	NL	2-6	4	8	0	0	0	0	0	0	.000	0	0	—	—
1984	3B	CLE	AL	6-7	126	439	64	116	19	3	7	40	.264	32	162	90	—
1985	3B	CLE	AL	7-7	161	606	72	166	26	3	20	87	.274	48	258	102	49-75
1986	3B	CLE	AL	5-7	158	583	83	168	30	4	17	80	.288	56	257	110	33-78
1987	3B	CLE	AL	7-7	155	540	73	162	26	4	32	69	.300	75	292	136	8-79
1988	3B	CLE	AL	6-7	152	552	59	133	25	0	9	49	.241	48	185	85	62-74
1989	3B	CLE	AL	6-7	147	519	49	141	26	5	13	64	.272	62	216	114	26-67
1990	3B-1B	CLE	AL	4-7	155	553	77	162	24	4	14	75	.293	63	236	116	23-69
1991	3B-1B	CL/OA	AL	7/4	122	419	28	94	21	1	4	44	.224	27	129	72	—
1992	3B	CLE	AL	4-7	120	291	30	76	7	0	4	36	.261	28	95	87	—

MAJOR LEAGUE TOTALS   1311 4520 535 1220 204 24 120 545 .270 439 1832 111 6 yrs

John Cornelius Ray

5'11   170 lbs   Batted both

Born Mar 1, 1957   Chouteau, OK

YR	POS	TEAM	LG	FIN	G	AB	R	H	2B	3B	HR	RBI	AVG	BB	TB	OQ	RANK
1981	2B	PIT	NL	4-6	31	102	10	25	11	0	0	6	.245	6	36	89	—
1982	2B	PIT	NL	4-6	162	647	79	182	30	7	7	63	.281	36	247	98	49-66
1983	2B	PIT	NL	2-6	151	576	68	163	38	7	5	53	.283	35	230	101	43-64
1984	2B	PIT	NL	6-6	155	555	75	173	38	6	6	67	.312	37	241	117	22-53
1985	2B	PIT	NL	6-6	154	594	67	163	33	3	7	70	.274	46	223	99	47-65
1986	2B	PIT	NL	6-6	155	579	67	174	33	0	7	78	.301	58	228	110	29-49
1987	2B	PIT	NL	4-6	123	472	48	129	19	3	5	54	.273	41	169	90	55-58
1987	2B	CAL	AL	6-7	30	127	16	44	11	0	0	15	.346	3	55	98	—
1988	2B-LF	CAL	AL	4-7	153	602	75	184	42	7	6	83	.306	36	258	108	39-74
1989	2B	CAL	AL	3-7	134	530	52	153	16	3	5	62	.289	36	190	93	54-67
1990	2B	CAL	AL	4-7	105	404	47	112	23	0	5	43	.277	19	150	88	—
MAJOR LEAGUE TOTALS					1353	5188	604	1502	294	36	53	594	.290	353	2027	102	8 yrs

Stephen Louis Sax

5'11   185 lbs   Batted right

Born Jan 29, 1960   Sacramento, CA

YR	POS	TEAM	LG	FIN	G	AB	R	H	2B	3B	HR	RBI	AVG	BB	TB	OQ	RANK
1981	2B	LA	NL	2-6	31	119	15	33	2	0	2	9	.277	7	41	91	—
1982	2B	LA	NL	2-6	150	638	88	180	23	7	4	47	.282	49	229	97	51-66
1983	2B	LA	NL	1-6	155	623	94	175	18	5	5	41	.281	58	218	97	49-64
1984	2B	LA	NL	4-6	145	569	70	138	24	4	1	35	.243	47	173	82	52-53
1985	2B	LA	NL	1-6	136	488	62	136	8	4	1	42	.279	54	155	94	49-65
1986	2B	LA	NL	5-6	157	633	91	210	43	4	6	56	.332	59	279	124	12-49
1987	2B	LA	NL	4-6	157	610	84	171	22	7	6	46	.280	44	225	90	55-59
1988	2B	LA	NL	1-6	160	632	70	175	19	4	5	57	.277	45	217	96	49-58
1989	2B	NY	AL	5-7	158	651	88	205	26	3	5	63	.315	52	252	105	38-67
1990	2B	NY	AL	7-7	155	615	70	160	24	2	4	42	.260	49	200	83	66-69
1991	2B	NY	AL	5-7	158	652	85	198	38	2	10	56	.304	41	270	103	46-72
1992	2B	CHI	AL	3-7	143	567	74	134	26	4	4	47	.236	43	180	79	71-73
1993	LF-DH	CHI	AL	1-7	57	119	20	28	5	0	1	8	.235	8	36	69	—
MAJOR LEAGUE TOTALS					1762	6916	911	1943	278	46	54	549	.281	556	2475	95	11 yrs

Scott Brian Fletcher Born Jul 30, 1958 Fort Walton Beach, FL
5'11 168 lbs Batted right

YR	POS	TEAM	LG	FIN	G	AB	R	H	2B	3B	HR	RBI	AVG	BB	TB	OQ	RANK
1981	2B-SS	CHI	NL	6-6	19	46	6	10	4	0	0	1	.217	2	14	—	—
1982	SS	CHI	NL	5-6	11	24	4	4	0	0	0	1	.167	4	4	—	—
1983	SS-2B	CHI	AL	1-7	114	262	42	62	16	5	3	31	.237	29	97	94	—
1984	SS-2B	CHI	AL	5-7	149	456	46	114	13	3	3	35	.250	46	142	83	61-68
1985	3B-SS	CHI	AL	3-7	119	301	38	77	8	1	2	31	.256	35	93	84	—
1986	SS	TEX	AL	2-7	147	530	82	159	34	5	3	50	.300	47	212	102	49-78
1987	SS	TEX	AL	6-7	156	588	82	169	28	4	5	63	.287	61	220	94	60-79
1988	SS	TEX	AL	6-7	140	515	59	142	19	4	0	47	.276	62	169	95	54-74
1989	SS-2B	TX/CH	AL	4/7	142	546	77	138	25	2	1	43	.253	64	170	89	58-67
1990	2B	CHI	AL	2-7	151	509	54	123	18	3	4	56	.242	45	159	80	69-69
1991	2B	CHI	AL	2-7	90	248	14	51	10	1	1	28	.206	17	66	63	—
1992	2B-SS	MIL	AL	2-7	123	386	53	106	18	3	3	51	.275	30	139	92	—
1993	2B	BOS	AL	5-7	121	480	81	137	31	5	5	45	.285	37	193	96	51-73

MAJOR LEAGUE TOTALS   1482 4891 638 1292 224 36 30 482 .264 479 1678 91 7 yrs

Ryne Dee Sandberg Born Sep 18, 1959 Spokane, WA
6'1 175 lbs Batted right

YR	POS	TEAM	LG	FIN	G	AB	R	H	2B	3B	HR	RBI	AVG	BB	TB	OQ	RANK
1981	SS	PHI	NL	3-6	13	6	2	1	0	0	0	0	.167	0	1	—	—
1982	3B-2B	CHI	NL	5-6	156	635	103	172	33	5	7	54	.271	36	236	94	58-66
1983	2B	CHI	NL	5-6	158	633	94	165	25	4	8	48	.261	51	222	92	56-64
1984	2B	CHI	NL	1-6	156	636	114	200	36	19	19	84	.314	52	331	141	6-53
1985	2B	CHI	NL	4-6	153	609	113	186	31	6	26	83	.305	57	307	137	8-65
1986	2B	CHI	NL	5-6	154	627	68	178	28	5	14	76	.284	46	258	105	30-49
1987	2B	CHI	NL	6-6	132	523	81	154	25	2	16	59	.294	59	231	116	24-59
1988	2B	CHI	NL	4-6	155	618	77	163	23	8	19	69	.264	54	259	115	26-58
1989	2B	CHI	NL	1-6	157	606	104	176	25	5	30	76	.290	59	301	137	12-59
1990	2B	CHI	NL	4-6	155	615	116	188	30	3	40	100	.306	50	344	144	6-63
1991	2B	CHI	NL	4-6	158	585	104	170	32	2	26	100	.291	87	284	143	7-52
1992	2B	CHI	NL	4-6	158	612	100	186	32	8	26	87	.304	68	312	146	6-49
1993	2B	CHI	NL	4-7	117	456	67	141	20	0	9	45	.309	37	188	107	42-77

MAJOR LEAGUE TOTALS   1822 7161 1143 2080 340 67 240 881 .290 656 3274 123 12 yrs

Brett Morgan Butler   Born Jun 15, 1957   Los Angeles, CA
5'10 160 lbs Batted left

YR	POS	TEAM	LG	FIN	G	AB	R	H	2B	3B	HR	RBI	AVG	BB	TB	OQ	RANK
1981	LF-CF	ATL	NL	5-6	40	126	17	32	2	3	0	4	.254	19	40	102	—
1982	LF	ATL	NL	1-6	89	240	35	52	2	0	0	7	.217	25	54	67	—
1983	LF	ATL	NL	2-6	151	549	84	154	21	13	5	37	.281	54	216	108	39-64
1984	CF	CLE	AL	6-7	159	602	108	162	25	9	3	49	.269	86	214	103	41-68
1985	CF	CLE	AL	7-7	152	591	106	184	28	14	5	50	.311	63	255	115	22-75
1986	CF	CLE	AL	5-7	161	587	92	163	17	14	4	51	.278	70	220	100	54-78
1987	CF	CLE	AL	7-7	137	522	91	154	25	8	9	41	.295	91	222	119	26-79
1988	CF	SF	NL	4-6	157	568	109	163	27	9	6	43	.287	97	226	133	11-58
1989	CF	SF	NL	1-6	154	594	100	168	22	4	4	36	.283	59	210	103	33-59
1990	CF	SF	NL	3-6	160	622	108	192	20	9	3	44	.309	90	239	119	25-63
1991	CF	LA	NL	2-6	161	615	112	182	13	5	2	38	.296	108	211	118	22-52
1992	CF	LA	NL	6-6	157	553	86	171	14	11	3	39	.309	95	216	133	14-49
1993	CF	LA	NL	4-7	156	607	80	181	21	10	1	42	.298	86	225	110	40-77

| MAJOR LEAGUE TOTALS | | | | | 1834 | 6776 | 1128 | 1958 | 237 | 109 | 45 | 481 | .289 | 943 | 2548 | 115 | 11 yrs |

Charles Theodore Davis   Born Jan 17, 1960   Kingston, Jamaica
6'3 195 lbs Batted both

YR	POS	TEAM	LG	FIN	G	AB	R	H	2B	3B	HR	RBI	AVG	BB	TB	OQ	RANK
1981	RF-CF	SF	NL	4-6	8	15	1	2	0	0	0	0	.133	1	2	—	—
1982	CF	SF	NL	3-6	154	641	86	167	27	6	19	76	.261	45	263	104	41-66
1983	CF	SF	NL	5-6	137	486	54	113	21	2	11	59	.233	55	171	95	51-64
1984	RF	SF	NL	6-6	137	499	87	157	21	6	21	81	.315	42	253	139	7-53
1985	RF	SF	NL	6-6	136	481	53	130	25	2	13	56	.270	62	198	118	24-65
1986	RF	SF	NL	3-6	153	526	71	146	28	3	13	70	.278	84	219	124	14-49
1987	CF	SF	NL	1-6	149	500	80	125	22	1	24	76	.250	72	221	115	26-59
1988	RF	CAL	AL	4-7	158	600	81	161	29	3	21	93	.268	56	259	110	35-74
1989	LF	CAL	AL	3-7	154	560	81	152	24	1	22	90	.271	61	244	116	24-67
1990	DH-LF	CAL	AL	4-7	113	412	58	109	17	1	12	58	.265	61	164	113	—
1991	DH	MIN	AL	1-7	153	534	84	148	34	1	29	93	.277	95	271	142	5-72
1992	DH	MIN	AL	2-7	138	444	63	128	27	2	12	66	.288	73	195	129	11-73
1993	DH	CAL	AL	5-7	153	573	74	139	32	0	27	112	.243	71	252	107	35-73

| MAJOR LEAGUE TOTALS | | | | | 1743 | 6271 | 873 | 1677 | 307 | 28 | 224 | 930 | .267 | 778 | 2712 | 118 | 11 yrs |

Von Francis Hayes   Born Aug 31, 1958 Stockton, CA
6'5   185 lbs   Batted left

YR	POS	TEAM	LG	FIN	G	AB	R	H	2B	3B	HR	RBI	AVG	BB	TB	OQ	RANK
1981	DH-LF	CLE	AL	6-7	43	109	21	28	8	2	1	17	.257	14	43	112	—
1982	RF	CLE	AL	6-7	150	527	65	132	25	3	14	82	.250	42	205	93	61-77
1983	RF	PHI	NL	1-6	124	351	45	93	9	5	6	32	.265	36	130	101	—
1984	CF	PHI	NL	4-6	152	561	85	164	27	6	16	67	.292	59	251	126	18-53
1985	CF	PHI	NL	5-6	152	570	76	150	30	4	13	70	.263	61	227	109	29-65
1986	1B-LF	PHI	NL	2-6	158	610	107	186	46	2	19	98	.305	74	293	135	6-49
1987	1B-CF	PHI	NL	4-6	158	556	84	154	36	5	21	84	.277	121	263	140	10-59
1988	1B-CF	PHI	NL	6-6	104	367	43	100	28	2	6	45	.272	49	150	124	—
1989	RF-1B	PHI	NL	6-6	154	540	93	140	27	2	26	78	.259	101	249	143	9-59
1990	RF-LF	PHI	NL	4-6	129	467	70	122	14	3	17	73	.261	87	193	126	17-63
1991	CF-LF	PHI	NL	3-6	77	284	43	64	15	1	0	21	.225	31	81	81	—
1992	RF	CAL	AL	5-7	94	307	35	69	17	1	4	29	.225	37	100	88	—

MAJOR LEAGUE TOTALS   1495 5249 767 1402 282 36 143 696 .267 712 2185 125   7 yrs

David Lee Henderson   Born Jul 21, 1958   Merced, CA
6'2   210 lbs   Batted right

YR	POS	TEAM	LG	FIN	G	AB	R	H	2B	3B	HR	RBI	AVG	BB	TB	OQ	RANK
1981	CF-RF	SEA	AL	6-7	59	126	17	21	3	0	6	13	.167	16	42	88	—
1982	CF	SEA	AL	4-7	104	324	47	82	17	1	14	48	.253	36	143	110	—
1983	CF	SEA	AL	7-7	137	484	50	130	24	5	17	55	.269	28	215	102	43-70
1984	CF	SEA	AL	5-7	112	350	42	98	23	0	14	43	.280	19	163	109	—
1985	CF	SEA	AL	6-7	139	502	70	121	28	2	14	68	.241	48	195	94	58-75
1986	CF	SE/BO	AL	7/1	139	388	59	103	22	4	15	47	.265	39	178	111	—
1987	RF-CF	BOS	AL	5-7	75	184	30	43	10	0	8	25	.234	22	77	98	—
1987	CF	SF	NL	1-6	15	21	2	5	2	0	0	1	.238	8	7	—	—
1988	CF	OAK	AL	1-7	146	507	100	154	38	1	24	94	.304	47	266	136	12-74
1989	CF	OAK	AL	1-7	152	579	77	145	24	3	15	80	.250	54	220	98	50-67
1990	CF	OAK	AL	1-7	127	450	65	122	28	0	20	63	.271	40	210	116	24-69
1991	CF	OAK	AL	4-7	150	572	86	158	33	0	25	85	.276	58	266	117	28-72
1992	CF-DH	OAK	AL	1-7	20	63	1	9	1	0	0	2	.143	2	10	—	—
1993	CF-DH	OAK	AL	7-7	107	382	37	84	19	0	20	53	.220	32	163	94	—

MAJOR LEAGUE TOTALS   1482 4932 683 1275 272 16 192 677 .259 449 2155 111   6 yrs

Jesse Lee Barfield   Born Oct 29, 1959   Joliet, IL
6'4   215 lbs   Batted right

YR	POS	TEAM	LG	FIN	G	AB	R	H	2B	3B	HR	RBI	AVG	BB	TB	OQ	RANK
1981	RF	TOR	AL	7-7	25	95	7	22	3	2	2	9	.232	4	35	—	—
1982	RF	TOR	AL	6-7	139	394	54	97	13	2	18	58	.246	42	168	105	—
1983	RF	TOR	AL	4-7	128	388	58	98	13	3	27	68	.253	22	198	113	—
1984	RF	TOR	AL	2-7	110	320	51	91	14	1	14	49	.284	35	149	121	—
1985	RF	TOR	AL	1-7	155	539	94	156	34	9	27	84	.289	66	289	136	6-75
1986	RF	TOR	AL	4-7	158	589	107	170	35	2	40	108	.289	69	329	138	3-78
1987	RF	TOR	AL	2-7	159	590	89	155	25	3	28	84	.263	58	270	105	46-79
1988	RF	TOR	AL	3-7	137	468	62	114	21	5	18	56	.244	41	199	104	45-74
1989	RF	TO/NY	AL	1/5	150	521	79	122	23	1	23	67	.234	87	216	117	20-67
1990	RF	NY	AL	7-7	153	476	69	117	21	2	25	78	.246	82	217	127	11-69
1991	RF	NY	AL	5-7	84	284	37	64	12	0	17	48	.225	36	127	111	—
1992	RF	NY	AL	4-7	30	95	8	13	2	0	2	7	.137	9	21	56	—

MAJOR LEAGUE TOTALS   1428 4759 715 1219 216 30 241 716 .256 551 2218 121   6 yrs

Jorge Antonio Bell   Born Oct 21, 1959   San Pedro de Macoris, DR
6'1   190 lbs   Batted right

YR	POS	TEAM	LG	FIN	G	AB	R	H	2B	3B	HR	RBI	AVG	BB	TB	OQ	RANK
1981	LF-RF	TOR	AL	7-7	60	163	19	38	2	1	5	12	.233	5	57	79	—
1983	LF-RF	TOR	AL	4-7	39	112	5	30	5	4	2	17	.268	4	49	96	—
1984	RF-LF	TOR	AL	2-7	159	606	85	177	39	4	26	87	.292	24	302	114	27-68
1985	LF	TOR	AL	1-7	157	607	87	167	28	6	28	95	.275	43	291	112	31-75
1986	LF	TOR	AL	4-7	159	641	101	198	38	6	31	108	.309	41	341	125	11-78
1987	LF	TOR	AL	2-7	156	610	111	188	32	4	47	134	.308	39	369	135	9-79
1988	LF	TOR	AL	3-7	156	614	78	165	27	5	24	97	.269	34	274	105	43-74
1989	LF-DH	TOR	AL	1-7	153	613	88	182	41	2	18	104	.297	33	281	113	27-67
1990	LF-DH	TOR	AL	2-7	142	562	67	149	25	0	21	86	.265	32	237	99	49-69
1991	LF	CHI	NL	4-6	149	558	63	159	27	0	25	86	.285	32	261	117	23-52
1992	DH-LF	CHI	AL	3-7	155	627	74	160	27	0	25	112	.255	31	262	96	56-73
1993	DH	CHI	AL	1-7	102	410	36	89	17	2	13	64	.217	13	149	72	—

MAJOR LEAGUE TOTALS   1587 6123 814 1702 308 34 265 1002 .278 331 2873 113   9 yrs

Patrick Sean Tabler Born Feb 2, 1958 Hamilton, OH
6'3 175 lbs Batted right

YR	POS	TEAM	LG	FIN	G	AB	R	H	2B	3B	HR	RBI	AVG	BB	TB	OQ	RANK
1981	2B	CHI	NL	6-6	35	101	11	19	3	1	1	5	.188	13	27	79	—
1982	3B	CHI	NL	5-6	25	85	9	20	4	2	1	7	.235	6	31	—	—
1983	LF-3B	CLE	AL	7-7	124	430	56	125	23	5	6	65	.291	56	176	114	29-70
1984	1B-LF	CLE	AL	6-7	144	473	66	137	21	3	10	68	.290	47	194	108	36-68
1985	1B-DH	CLE	AL	7-7	117	404	47	111	18	3	5	59	.275	27	150	89	—
1986	1B-DH	CLE	AL	5-7	130	473	61	154	29	2	6	48	.326	29	205	107	43-78
1987	1B-DH	CLE	AL	7-7	151	553	66	170	34	3	11	86	.307	51	243	107	41-79
1988	DH-LF	CL/KC	AL	6/3	130	444	53	125	22	3	2	66	.282	46	159	98	51-74
1989	RF-DH	KC	AL	2-7	123	390	36	101	11	1	2	42	.259	37	120	84	—
1990	RF-DH	KC	AL	6-7	75	195	12	53	14	0	1	19	.272	20	70	96	—
1990	RF-LF	NY	NL	2-6	17	43	6	12	1	1	1	10	.279	3	18	—	—
1991	DH-1B	TOR	AL	1-7	82	185	20	40	5	1	1	21	.216	29	50	82	—
1992	1B	TOR	AL	1-7	49	135	11	34	5	0	0	16	.252	11	39	76	—

MAJOR LEAGUE TOTALS | | | | | 1202 | 3911 | 454 | 1101 | 190 | 25 | 47 | 512 | .282 | 375 | 1482 | 107 | 5 yrs

Anthony Keith Gwynn Born May 9, 1960 Los Angeles, CA
5'11 185 lbs Batted left

YR	POS	TEAM	LG	FIN	G	AB	R	H	2B	3B	HR	RBI	AVG	BB	TB	OQ	RANK
1982	CF-LF	SD	NL	4-6	54	190	33	55	12	2	1	17	.289	14	74	105	—
1983	RF-LF	SD	NL	4-6	86	304	34	94	12	2	1	37	.309	23	113	102	—
1984	RF	SD	NL	1-6	158	606	88	213	21	10	5	71	.351	59	269	134	11-53
1985	RF	SD	NL	3-6	154	622	90	197	29	5	6	46	.317	45	254	112	27-65
1986	RF	SD	NL	4-6	160	642	107	211	33	7	14	59	.329	52	300	127	9-49
1987	RF	SD	NL	6-6	157	589	119	218	36	13	7	54	.370	82	301	152	6-59
1988	RF	SD	NL	3-6	133	521	64	163	22	5	7	70	.313	51	216	124	17-58
1989	RF	SD	NL	2-6	158	604	82	203	27	7	4	62	.336	56	256	127	15-59
1990	RF	SD	NL	4-6	141	573	79	177	29	10	4	72	.309	44	238	111	35-63
1991	RF	SD	NL	3-6	134	530	69	168	27	11	4	62	.317	34	229	116	25-52
1992	RF	SD	NL	3-6	128	520	77	165	27	3	6	41	.317	46	216	120	21-49
1993	RF	SD	NL	7-7	122	489	70	175	41	3	7	59	.358	36	243	133	13-77

MAJOR LEAGUE TOTALS | | | | | 1585 | 6190 | 912 | 2039 | 316 | 78 | 66 | 650 | .329 | 542 | 2709 | 126 | 10 yrs

Martin Glenn Barrett   Born Jun 23, 1958   Arcadia, CA
5'10   175 lbs   Batted right

YR	POS	TEAM	LG	FIN	G	AB	R	H	2B	3B	HR	RBI	AVG	BB	TB	OQ	RANK
1982	2B	BOS	AL	3-7	8	18	0	1	0	0	0	0	.056	0	1	—	—
1983	2B	BOS	AL	6-7	33	44	7	10	1	1	0	2	.227	3	13	—	—
1984	2B	BOS	AL	4-7	139	475	56	144	23	3	3	45	.303	42	182	102	42-68
1985	2B	BOS	AL	5-7	156	534	59	142	26	0	5	56	.266	56	183	90	67-75
1986	2B	BOS	AL	1-7	158	625	94	179	39	4	4	60	.286	65	238	99	56-78
1987	2B	BOS	AL	5-7	137	559	72	164	23	0	3	43	.293	51	196	87	69-79
1988	2B	BOS	AL	1-7	150	612	83	173	28	1	1	65	.283	40	206	86	61-74
1989	2B	BOS	AL	3-7	86	336	31	86	18	0	1	27	.256	32	107	86	—
1990	2B	BOS	AL	1-7	62	159	15	36	4	0	0	13	.226	15	40	68	—
1991	2B	SD	NL	3-6	12	16	1	3	1	0	1	3	.188	0	7	—	—

MAJOR LEAGUE TOTALS   941 3378 418 938 163   9 18 314 .278 304 1173   93   5 yrs

William Donald Doran   Born May 28, 1958 Cincinnati, OH
5'11   175 lbs   Batted both

YR	POS	TEAM	LG	FIN	G	AB	R	H	2B	3B	HR	RBI	AVG	BB	TB	OQ	RANK
1982	2B	HOU	NL	5-6	26	97	11	27	3	0	0	6	.278	4	30	78	—
1983	2B	HOU	NL	3-6	154	535	70	145	12	7	8	39	.271	86	195	113	31-64
1984	2B	HOU	NL	2-6	147	548	92	143	18	11	4	41	.261	66	195	104	37-53
1985	2B	HOU	NL	3-6	148	578	84	166	31	6	14	59	.287	71	251	124	19-65
1986	2B	HOU	NL	1-6	145	550	92	152	29	3	6	37	.276	81	205	112	26-49
1987	2B	HOU	NL	3-6	162	625	82	177	23	3	16	79	.283	82	254	110	34-59
1988	2B	HOU	NL	5-6	132	480	66	119	18	1	7	53	.248	65	160	104	38-58
1989	2B	HOU	NL	3-6	142	507	65	111	25	2	8	58	.219	59	164	92	48-59
1990	2B	HO/CN	NL	4/1	126	403	59	121	29	2	7	37	.300	79	175	140	—
1991	2B	CIN	NL	5-6	111	361	51	101	12	2	6	35	.280	46	135	111	—
1992	2B-1B	CIN	NL	2-6	132	387	48	91	16	2	8	47	.235	64	135	110	—
1993	2B-1B	MIL	AL	7-7	28	60	7	13	4	0	0	6	.217	6	17	—	—

MAJOR LEAGUE TOTALS   1453 5131 727 1366 220 39 84 497 .266 709 1916 108   7 yrs

Wade Anthony Boggs   Born Jun 15, 1958   Omaha, NE
6'2   190 lbs   Batted left

YR	POS	TEAM	LG	FIN	G	AB	R	H	2B	3B	HR	RBI	AVG	BB	TB	OQ	RANK
1982	1B-3B	BOS	AL	3-7	104	338	51	118	14	1	5	44	.349	35	149	124	—
1983	3B	BOS	AL	6-7	153	582	100	210	44	7	5	74	.361	92	283	150	1-70
1984	3B	BOS	AL	4-7	158	625	109	203	31	4	6	55	.325	89	260	124	18-68
1985	3B	BOS	AL	5-7	161	653	107	240	42	3	8	78	.368	96	312	145	3-75
1986	3B	BOS	AL	1-7	149	580	107	207	47	2	8	71	.357	105	282	151	1-78
1987	3B	BOS	AL	5-7	147	551	108	200	40	6	24	89	.363	105	324	171	1-79
1988	3B	BOS	AL	1-7	155	584	128	214	45	6	5	58	.366	125	286	170	1-74
1989	3B	BOS	AL	3-7	156	621	113	205	51	7	3	54	.330	107	279	143	3-67
1990	3B	BOS	AL	1-7	155	619	89	187	44	5	6	63	.302	87	259	122	16-69
1991	3B	BOS	AL	2-7	144	546	93	181	42	2	8	51	.332	89	251	140	10-72
1992	3B-DH	BOS	AL	7-7	143	514	62	133	22	4	7	50	.259	74	184	103	41-73
1993	3B	NY	AL	2-7	143	560	83	169	26	1	2	59	.302	74	203	102	40-73

MAJOR LEAGUE TOTALS   1768   6773 1150 2267 448 48 87 746 .335 1078 3072 138 11 yrs

Howard Michael Johnson   Born Nov 29, 1960 Clearwater, FL
5'11   178 lbs   Batted both

YR	POS	TEAM	LG	FIN	G	AB	R	H	2B	3B	HR	RBI	AVG	BB	TB	OQ	RANK
1982	3B-DH	DET	AL	4-7	54	155	23	49	5	0	4	14	.316	16	66	115	—
1983	3B	DET	AL	2-7	27	66	11	14	0	0	3	5	.212	7	23	—	—
1984	3B	DET	AL	1-7	116	355	43	88	14	1	12	50	.248	40	140	101	—
1985	3B	NY	NL	2-6	126	389	38	94	18	4	11	46	.242	34	153	101	—
1986	3B-SS	NY	NL	1-6	88	220	30	54	14	0	10	39	.245	31	98	121	—
1987	3B-SS	NY	NL	2-6	157	554	93	147	22	1	36	99	.265	83	279	131	13-59
1988	3B-SS	NY	NL	1-6	148	495	85	114	21	1	24	68	.230	86	209	129	14-58
1989	3B-SS	NY	NL	2-6	153	571	104	164	41	3	36	101	.287	77	319	159	5-59
1990	3B-SS	NY	NL	2-6	154	590	89	144	37	3	23	90	.244	69	256	114	31-63
1991	3B-SS	NY	NL	5-6	156	564	108	146	34	4	38	117	.259	78	302	145	4-52
1992	CF-LF	NY	NL	5-6	100	350	48	78	19	0	7	43	.223	55	118	104	—
1993	3B	NY	NL	7-7	72	235	32	56	8	2	7	26	.238	43	89	111	—

MAJOR LEAGUE TOTALS   1351   4544 704 1148 233 19 211 698 .253 619 2052 136 5 yrs

Keith Anthony Phillips   Born Apr 25, 1959   Atlanta, GA
5'9   155 lbs   Batted both

YR	POS	TEAM	LG	FIN	G	AB	R	H	2B	3B	HR	RBI	AVG	BB	TB	OQ	RANK
1982	SS	OAK	AL	5-7	40	81	11	17	2	2	0	8	.210	12	23	—	—
1983	SS-2B	OAK	AL	4-7	148	412	54	102	12	3	4	35	.248	48	132	87	—
1984	SS-2B	OAK	AL	4-7	154	451	62	120	24	3	4	37	.266	42	162	93	54-68
1985	3B-2B	OAK	AL	4-7	42	161	23	45	12	2	4	17	.280	13	73	109	—
1986	2B-3B	OAK	AL	3-7	118	441	76	113	14	5	5	52	.256	76	152	101	50-78
1987	2B-3B	OAK	AL	3-7	111	379	48	91	20	0	10	46	.240	57	141	96	—
1988	3B-2B	OAK	AL	1-7	79	212	32	43	8	4	2	17	.203	36	65	92	—
1989	2B-3B	OAK	AL	1-7	143	451	48	118	15	6	4	47	.262	58	157	100	48-67
1990	3B-2B	DET	AL	3-7	152	573	97	144	23	5	8	55	.251	99	201	106	39-69
1991	3B-2B	DET	AL	2-7	146	564	87	160	28	4	17	72	.284	79	247	121	23-72
1992	2B-RF	DET	AL	6-7	159	606	114	167	32	3	10	64	.276	114	235	121	21-73
1993	LF-2B	DET	AL	3-7	151	566	113	177	27	0	7	57	.313	132	225	132	14-73
MAJOR LEAGUE TOTALS					1443	4897	765	1297	217	37	75	507	.265	766	1813	111	7 yrs

Julio Cesar Franco   Born Aug 23, 1958 Hato Mayor, PR
6'0   160 lbs   Batted right

YR	POS	TEAM	LG	FIN	G	AB	R	H	2B	3B	HR	RBI	AVG	BB	TB	OQ	RANK
1982	SS-3B	PHI	NL	2-6	16	29	3	8	1	0	0	3	.276	2	9	—	—
1983	SS	CLE	AL	7-7	149	560	68	153	24	8	8	80	.273	27	217	90	58-70
1984	SS	CLE	AL	6-7	160	658	82	188	22	5	3	79	.286	43	229	87	57-68
1985	SS	CLE	AL	7-7	160	636	97	183	33	4	6	90	.288	54	242	96	56-75
1986	SS	CLE	AL	5-7	149	599	80	183	30	5	10	74	.306	32	253	100	53-78
1987	SS	CLE	AL	7-7	128	495	86	158	24	3	8	52	.319	57	212	112	35-79
1988	2B	CLE	AL	6-7	152	613	88	186	23	6	10	54	.303	56	251	110	34-74
1989	2B	TEX	AL	4-7	150	548	80	173	31	5	13	92	.316	66	253	132	10-67
1990	2B	TEX	AL	3-7	157	582	96	172	27	1	11	69	.296	82	234	117	20-69
1991	2B	TEX	AL	3-7	146	589	108	201	27	3	15	78	.341	65	279	133	12-72
1992	DH-2B	TEX	AL	4-7	35	107	19	25	7	0	2	8	.234	15	38	99	—
1993	DH	TEX	AL	2-7	144	532	85	154	31	3	14	84	.289	62	233	112	29-73
MAJOR LEAGUE TOTALS					1546	5948	892	1784	280	43	100	763	.300	561	2450	109	10 yrs

Peter Michael O'Brien   Born Feb 9, 1958   Santa Monica, CA
6'1   185 lbs   Batted left

YR	POS	TEAM	LG	FIN	G	AB	R	H	2B	3B	HR	RBI	AVG	BB	TB	OQ	RANK
1982	LF-DH	TEX	AL	6-7	20	67	13	16	4	1	4	13	.239	6	34	—	—
1983	1B-RF	TEX	AL	3-7	154	524	53	124	24	5	8	53	.237	58	182	90	57-70
1984	1B	TEX	AL	7-7	142	520	57	149	26	2	18	80	.287	53	233	116	25-68
1985	1B	TEX	AL	7-7	159	573	69	153	34	3	22	92	.267	69	259	115	23-75
1986	1B	TEX	AL	2-7	156	551	86	160	23	3	23	90	.290	87	258	128	7-78
1987	1B	TEX	AL	6-7	159	569	84	163	26	1	23	88	.286	59	260	110	37-79
1988	1B	TEX	AL	6-7	156	547	57	149	24	1	16	71	.272	72	223	113	28-74
1989	1B	CLE	AL	6-7	155	554	75	144	24	1	12	55	.260	83	206	109	33-67
1990	1B	SEA	AL	5-7	108	366	32	82	18	0	5	27	.224	44	115	85	—
1991	1B	SEA	AL	5-7	152	560	58	139	29	3	17	88	.248	44	225	96	56-72
1992	1B	SEA	AL	7-7	134	396	40	88	15	1	14	52	.222	40	147	93	—
1993	DH-1B	SEA	AL	4-7	72	210	30	54	7	0	7	27	.257	26	82	99	—

MAJOR LEAGUE TOTALS   1567 5437 654 1421 254 21 169 736 .261 641 2224 110   8 yrs

Donald Arthur Mattingly   Born Apr 20, 1961   Evansville, IN
6'0   175 lbs   Batted left

YR	POS	TEAM	LG	FIN	G	AB	R	H	2B	3B	HR	RBI	AVG	BB	TB	OQ	RANK
1982	LF-1B	NY	AL	5-7	7	12	0	2	0	0	0	1	.167	0	2	—	—
1983	RF-1B	NY	AL	3-7	91	279	34	79	15	4	4	32	.283	21	114	101	—
1984	1B-LF	NY	AL	3-7	153	603	91	207	44	2	23	110	.343	41	324	139	6-68
1985	1B	NY	AL	2-7	159	652	107	211	48	3	35	145	.324	56	370	142	4-75
1986	1B	NY	AL	2-7	162	677	117	238	53	2	31	113	.352	53	388	146	2-78
1987	1B	NY	AL	4-7	141	569	93	186	38	2	30	115	.327	51	318	135	10-79
1988	1B	NY	AL	5-7	144	599	94	186	37	0	18	88	.311	41	277	118	25-74
1989	1B	NY	AL	5-7	158	631	79	191	37	2	23	113	.303	51	301	124	14-67
1990	1B-DH	NY	AL	7-7	102	394	40	101	16	0	5	42	.256	28	132	83	—
1991	1B-DH	NY	AL	5-7	152	587	64	169	35	0	9	68	.288	46	231	99	51-72
1992	1B	NY	AL	4-7	157	640	89	184	40	0	14	86	.288	39	266	102	45-73
1993	1B	NY	AL	2-7	134	530	78	154	27	2	17	86	.291	61	236	113	27-73

MAJOR LEAGUE TOTALS   1560 6173 886 1908 390 17 209 999 .309 488 2959 124   9 yrs

Harold Craig Reynolds   Born Nov 26, 1960 Eugene, OR
5'11   165 lbs Batted both

YR	POS	TEAM	LG	FIN	G	AB	R	H	2B	3B	HR	RBI	AVG	BB	TB	OQ	RANK
1983	2B	SEA	AL	7-7	20	59	8	12	4	1	0	1	.203	2	18	—	—
1984	2B	SEA	AL	5-7	10	10	3	3	0	0	0	0	.300	0	3	—	—
1985	2B	SEA	AL	6-7	67	104	15	15	3	1	0	6	.144	17	20	61	—
1986	2B	SEA	AL	7-7	126	445	46	99	19	4	1	24	.222	29	129	67	—
1987	2B	SEA	AL	4-7	160	530	73	146	31	8	1	35	.275	39	196	86	71-79
1988	2B	SEA	AL	7-7	158	598	61	169	26	11	4	41	.283	51	229	100	50-74
1989	2B	SEA	AL	6-7	153	613	87	184	24	9	0	43	.300	55	226	101	46-67
1990	2B	SEA	AL	5-7	160	642	100	162	36	5	5	55	.252	81	223	96	51-69
1991	2B	SEA	AL	5-7	161	631	95	160	34	6	3	57	.254	72	215	91	59-72
1992	2B	SEA	AL	7-7	140	458	55	113	23	3	3	33	.247	45	151	87	68-73
1993	2B	BAL	AL	3-7	145	485	64	122	20	4	4	47	.252	66	162	90	61-73

MAJOR LEAGUE TOTALS   1300 4575 607 1185 220 52 21 342 .259 457 1572 93   7 yrs

Juan Milton Samuel   Born Dec 9, 1960 San Pedro de Macoris, DR
5'11   170 lbs Batted right

YR	POS	TEAM	LG	FIN	G	AB	R	H	2B	3B	HR	RBI	AVG	BB	TB	OQ	RANK
1983	2B	PHI	NL	1-6	18	65	14	18	1	2	2	5	.277	4	29	—	—
1984	2B	PHI	NL	4-6	160	701	105	191	36	19	15	69	.272	28	310	107	34-53
1985	2B	PHI	NL	5-6	161	663	101	175	31	13	19	74	.264	33	289	105	39-65
1986	2B	PHI	NL	2-6	145	591	90	157	36	12	16	78	.266	26	265	105	33-49
1987	2B	PHI	NL	4-6	160	655	113	178	37	15	28	100	.272	60	329	120	18-59
1988	2B	PHI	NL	6-6	157	629	68	153	32	9	12	67	.243	39	239	97	48-58
1989	CF	PH/NY	NL	6/2	137	532	69	125	16	2	11	48	.235	42	178	89	51-59
1990	2B-CF	LA	NL	2-6	143	492	62	119	24	3	13	52	.242	51	188	100	45-63
1991	2B	LA	NL	2-6	153	594	74	161	22	6	12	58	.271	49	231	104	40-52
1992	2B	LA	NL	6-6	47	122	7	32	3	1	0	15	.262	7	37	80	—
1992	RF-2B	KC	AL	5-7	29	102	15	29	5	3	0	8	.284	7	40	98	—
1993	2B	CIN	NL	5-7	103	261	31	60	10	4	4	26	.230	23	90	84	—

MAJOR LEAGUE TOTALS   1413 5407 749 1398 253 89 132 600 .259 369 2225 103   8 yrs

Spike Dee Owen

Born Apr 19, 1961 Cleburne, TX

5'9 165 lbs Batted both

YR	POS	TEAM	LG	FIN	G	AB	R	H	2B	3B	HR	RBI	AVG	BB	TB	OQ	RANK
1983	SS	SEA	AL	7-7	80	306	36	60	11	3	2	21	.196	24	83	65	—
1984	SS	SEA	AL	5-7	152	530	67	130	18	8	3	43	.245	46	173	82	63-68
1985	SS	SEA	AL	6-7	118	352	41	91	10	6	6	37	.259	34	131	93	—
1986	SS	SE/BO	AL	7/1	154	528	67	122	24	7	1	45	.231	51	163	77	77-78
1987	SS	BOS	AL	5-7	132	437	50	113	17	7	2	48	.259	53	150	88	68-79
1988	SS	BOS	AL	1-7	89	257	40	64	14	1	5	18	.249	27	95	97	—
1989	SS	MON	NL	4-6	142	437	52	102	17	4	6	41	.233	76	145	108	25-59
1990	SS	MON	NL	3-6	149	453	55	106	24	5	5	35	.234	70	155	101	42-63
1991	SS	MON	NL	6-6	139	424	39	108	22	8	3	26	.255	42	155	100	—
1992	SS	MON	NL	2-6	122	386	52	104	16	3	7	40	.269	50	147	114	—
1993	SS	NY	AL	2-7	103	334	41	78	16	2	2	20	.234	29	104	75	—

MAJOR LEAGUE TOTALS — 1380 4444 540 1078 189 54 42 374 .243 502 1501 92 5 yrs

Octavio Antonio Fernandez

Born Aug 6, 1962 San Pedro De Macoris, DR

6'2 165 lbs Batted both

YR	POS	TEAM	LG	FIN	G	AB	R	H	2B	3B	HR	RBI	AVG	BB	TB	OQ	RANK
1983	SS	TOR	AL	4-7	15	34	5	9	1	1	0	2	.265	2	12	—	—
1984	SS-3B	TOR	AL	2-7	88	233	29	63	5	3	3	19	.270	17	83	88	—
1985	SS	TOR	AL	1-7	161	564	71	163	31	10	2	51	.289	43	220	96	55-75
1986	SS	TOR	AL	4-7	163	687	91	213	33	9	10	65	.310	27	294	99	58-78
1987	SS	TOR	AL	2-7	146	578	90	186	29	8	5	67	.322	51	246	106	43-79
1988	SS	TOR	AL	3-7	154	648	76	186	41	4	5	70	.287	45	250	98	52-74
1989	SS	TOR	AL	1-7	140	573	64	147	25	9	11	64	.257	29	223	91	55-67
1990	SS	TOR	AL	2-7	161	635	84	175	27	17	4	66	.276	71	248	105	41-69
1991	SS	SD	NL	3-6	145	558	81	152	27	5	4	38	.272	55	201	101	42-52
1992	SS	SD	NL	3-6	155	622	84	171	32	4	4	37	.275	56	223	101	38-49
1993	SS	NY	NL	7-7	48	173	20	39	5	2	1	14	.225	25	51	85	—
1993	SS	TOR	AL	1-7	94	353	45	108	18	9	4	50	.306	31	156	109	—

MAJOR LEAGUE TOTALS — 1470 5658 740 1612 274 81 53 543 .285 452 2207 100 8 yrs

Willie Dean McGee   Born Nov 2, 1958   San Francisco, CA
6'1   175 lbs   Batted both

YR	POS	TEAM	LG	FIN	G	AB	R	H	2B	3B	HR	RBI	AVG	BB	TB	OQ	RANK
1982	CF	SL	NL	1-6	123	422	43	125	12	8	4	56	.296	12	165	96	—
1983	CF	SL	NL	4-6	147	601	75	172	22	8	5	75	.286	26	225	92	55-64
1984	CF	SL	NL	3-6	145	571	82	166	19	11	6	50	.291	29	225	101	40-53
1985	CF	SL	NL	1-6	152	612	114	216	26	18	10	82	.353	34	308	137	7-65
1986	CF	SL	NL	3-6	124	497	65	127	22	7	7	48	.256	37	184	93	42-49
1987	CF	SL	NL	1-6	153	620	76	177	37	11	11	105	.285	24	269	97	48-59
1988	CF	SL	NL	5-6	137	562	73	164	24	6	3	50	.292	32	209	101	41-58
1989	CF	SL	NL	3-6	58	199	23	47	10	2	3	17	.236	10	70	86	—
1990	CF	SL	NL	6-6	125	501	76	168	32	5	3	62	.335	38	219	120	23-63
1990	CF	OAK	AL	1-7	29	113	23	31	3	2	0	15	.274	10	38	89	—
1991	CF	SF	NL	3-6	131	497	67	155	30	3	4	43	.312	34	203	111	32-52
1992	RF-CF	SF	NL	5-6	138	474	56	141	20	2	1	36	.297	29	168	97	41-49
1993	RF	SF	NL	2-7	130	475	53	143	28	1	4	46	.301	38	185	101	52-77

MAJOR LEAGUE TOTALS					1592	6144	826	1832	285	84	61	685	.298	353	2468	105	10 yrs

Walter Kevin McReynolds   Born Oct 16, 1959   Little Rock, AR
6'0   205 lbs   Batted right

YR	POS	TEAM	LG	FIN	G	AB	R	H	2B	3B	HR	RBI	AVG	BB	TB	OQ	RANK
1983	CF	SD	NL	4-6	39	140	15	31	3	1	4	14	.221	12	48	86	—
1984	CF	SD	NL	1-6	147	525	68	146	26	6	20	75	.278	34	244	118	21-53
1985	CF	SD	NL	3-6	152	564	61	132	24	4	15	75	.234	43	209	93	50-65
1986	CF	SD	NL	4-6	158	560	89	161	31	6	26	96	.288	66	282	136	5-49
1987	LF	NY	NL	2-6	151	590	86	163	32	5	29	95	.276	39	292	114	27-59
1988	LF	NY	NL	1-6	147	552	82	159	30	2	27	99	.288	38	274	132	12-58
1989	LF	NY	NL	2-6	148	545	74	148	25	3	22	85	.272	46	245	120	17-59
1990	LF	NY	NL	2-6	147	521	75	140	23	1	24	82	.269	71	237	126	18-63
1991	LF	NY	NL	5-6	143	522	65	135	32	1	16	74	.259	49	217	110	33-52
1992	LF	KC	AL	5-7	109	373	45	92	25	0	13	49	.247	67	156	121	—
1993	LF	KC	AL	3-7	110	351	44	86	22	4	11	42	.245	37	149	101	—

MAJOR LEAGUE TOTALS					1451	5243	704	1393	273	33	207	786	.266	502	2353	119	8 yrs

Andrew James Van Slyke   Born Dec 21, 1960 Utica, NY
6'1 190 lbs Batted left

YR	POS	TEAM	LG	FIN	G	AB	R	H	2B	3B	HR	RBI	AVG	BB	TB	OQ	RANK
1983	RF-3B	SL	NL	4-6	101	309	51	81	15	5	8	38	.262	46	130	121	—
1984	RF-3B	SL	NL	3-6	137	361	45	88	16	4	7	50	.244	63	133	116	—
1985	RF	SL	NL	1-6	146	424	61	110	25	6	13	55	.259	47	186	118	—
1986	RF-1B	SL	NL	3-6	137	418	48	113	23	7	13	61	.270	47	189	121	—
1987	CF	PIT	NL	4-6	157	564	93	165	36	11	21	82	.293	56	286	126	16-59
1988	CF	PIT	NL	2-6	154	587	101	169	23	15	25	100	.288	57	297	141	9-58
1989	CF	PIT	NL	5-6	130	476	64	113	18	9	9	53	.237	47	176	100	40-59
1990	CF	PIT	NL	1-6	136	493	67	140	26	6	17	77	.284	66	229	130	14-63
1991	CF	PIT	NL	1-6	138	491	87	130	24	7	17	83	.265	71	219	128	17-52
1992	CF	PIT	NL	1-6	154	614	103	199	45	12	14	89	.324	58	310	145	7-49
1993	CF	PIT	NL	5-7	83	323	42	100	13	4	8	50	.310	24	145	114	—

| MAJOR LEAGUE TOTALS | | | | | 1473 | 5060 | 762 | 1408 | 264 | 86 | 152 | 738 | .278 | 582 | 2300 | 128 | 6 yrs |

Darryl Eugene Strawberry   Born Mar 12, 1962 Los Angeles, CA
6'6 190 lbs Batted left

YR	POS	TEAM	LG	FIN	G	AB	R	H	2B	3B	HR	RBI	AVG	BB	TB	OQ	RANK
1983	RF	NY	NL	6-6	122	420	63	108	15	7	26	74	.257	47	215	132	—
1984	RF	NY	NL	2-6	147	522	75	131	27	4	26	97	.251	75	244	131	13-53
1985	RF	NY	NL	2-6	111	393	78	109	15	4	29	79	.277	73	219	163	—
1986	RF	NY	NL	1-6	136	475	76	123	27	5	27	93	.259	72	241	138	4-49
1987	RF	NY	NL	2-6	154	532	108	151	32	5	39	104	.284	97	310	157	4-59
1988	RF	NY	NL	1-6	153	543	101	146	27	3	39	101	.269	85	296	160	1-58
1989	RF	NY	NL	2-6	134	476	69	107	26	1	29	77	.225	61	222	126	16-59
1990	RF	NY	NL	2-6	152	542	92	150	18	1	37	108	.277	70	281	139	9-63
1991	RF	LA	NL	2-6	139	505	86	134	22	4	28	99	.265	75	248	139	8-52
1992	RF	LA	NL	6-6	43	156	20	37	8	0	5	25	.237	19	60	108	—
1993	RF	LA	NL	4-7	32	100	12	14	2	0	5	12	.140	16	31	82	—

| MAJOR LEAGUE TOTALS | | | | | 1323 | 4664 | 780 | 1210 | 219 | 34 | 290 | 869 | .259 | 690 | 2367 | 141 | 7 yrs |

Philip Poole Bradley Born Mar 11, 1959 Bloomington, IN
6'0 185 lbs Batted right

YR	POS	TEAM	LG	FIN	G	AB	R	H	2B	3B	HR	RBI	AVG	BB	TB	OQ	RANK
1983	CF	SEA	AL	7-7	23	67	8	18	2	0	0	5	.269	8	20	—	—
1984	LF	SEA	AL	5-7	124	322	49	97	12	4	0	24	.301	34	117	101	—
1985	LF	SEA	AL	6-7	159	641	100	192	33	8	26	88	.300	55	319	123	14-75
1986	LF	SEA	AL	7-7	143	526	88	163	27	4	12	50	.310	77	234	125	13-78
1987	LF	SEA	AL	4-7	158	603	101	179	38	10	14	67	.297	84	279	120	25-79
1988	LF	PHI	NL	6-6	154	569	77	150	30	5	11	56	.264	54	223	110	29-58
1989	LF	BAL	AL	2-7	144	545	83	151	23	10	11	55	.277	70	227	117	21-67
1990	LF	BA/CH	AL	5/2	117	422	59	108	14	2	4	31	.256	50	138	91	—
MAJOR LEAGUE TOTALS					1022	3695	565	1058	179	43	78	376	.286	432	1557	119	5 yrs

Joseph Carter Born Mar 7, 1960 Oklahoma City, OK
6'3 215 lbs Batted right

YR	POS	TEAM	LG	FIN	G	AB	R	H	2B	3B	HR	RBI	AVG	BB	TB	OQ	RANK
1983	LF	CHI	NL	5-6	23	51	6	9	1	1	0	1	.176	0	12	—	—
1984	LF-1B	CLE	AL	6-7	66	244	32	67	6	1	13	41	.275	11	114	106	—
1985	LF	CLE	AL	7-7	143	489	64	128	27	0	15	59	.262	25	200	92	63-75
1986	RF-1B	CLE	AL	5-7	162	663	108	200	36	9	29	121	.302	32	341	117	24-78
1987	1B-LF	CLE	AL	7-7	149	588	83	155	27	2	32	106	.264	27	282	100	54-79
1988	CF	CLE	AL	6-7	157	621	85	168	36	6	27	98	.271	35	297	112	29-74
1989	CF	CLE	AL	6-7	162	651	84	158	32	4	35	105	.243	39	303	107	36-67
1990	CF	SD	NL	4-6	162	634	79	147	27	1	24	115	.232	48	248	95	54-63
1991	RF	TOR	AL	1-7	162	638	89	174	42	3	33	108	.273	49	321	119	25-72
1992	RF-DH	TOR	AL	1-7	158	622	97	164	30	7	34	119	.264	36	310	115	29-73
1993	RF-LF	TOR	AL	1-7	155	603	92	153	33	5	33	121	.254	47	295	109	33-73
MAJOR LEAGUE TOTALS					1499	5804	819	1523	297	39	275	994	.262	349	2723	107	9 yrs

Kirby Puckett
Born Mar 14, 1961 Chicago, IL
5'8 178 lbs Batted right

YR	POS	TEAM	LG	FIN	G	AB	R	H	2B	3B	HR	RBI	AVG	BB	TB	OQ	RANK
1984	CF	MIN	AL	2-7	128	557	63	165	12	5	0	31	.296	16	187	78	64-68
1985	CF	MIN	AL	4-7	161	691	80	199	29	13	4	74	.288	41	266	92	61-75
1986	CF	MIN	AL	6-7	161	680	119	223	37	6	31	96	.328	34	365	127	10-78
1987	CF	MIN	AL	1-7	157	624	96	207	32	5	28	99	.332	32	333	122	20-79
1988	CF	MIN	AL	2-7	158	657	109	234	42	5	24	121	.356	23	358	138	10-74
1989	CF	MIN	AL	5-7	159	635	75	215	45	4	9	85	.339	41	295	124	14-67
1990	CF	MIN	AL	7-7	146	551	82	164	40	3	12	80	.298	57	246	119	19-69
1991	CF	MIN	AL	1-7	152	611	92	195	29	6	15	89	.319	31	281	112	34-72
1992	CF	MIN	AL	2-7	160	639	104	210	38	4	19	110	.329	44	313	127	17-73
1993	CF-RF	MIN	AL	5-7	156	622	89	184	39	3	22	89	.296	47	295	112	28-73
MAJOR LEAGUE TOTALS					1538	6267	909	1996	343	54	164	874	.318	366	2939	115	10 yrs

William Augustus Hatcher
Born Oct 4, 1960 Williams, AZ
5'10 190 lbs Batted right

YR	POS	TEAM	LG	FIN	G	AB	R	H	2B	3B	HR	RBI	AVG	BB	TB	OQ	RANK
1984	LF	CHI	NL	1-6	8	9	1	1	0	0	0	0	.111	0	1	—	—
1985	CF-LF	CHI	NL	4-6	53	163	24	40	12	1	2	10	.245	8	60	88	—
1986	CF	HOU	NL	1-6	127	419	55	108	15	4	6	36	.258	22	149	86	
1987	CF	HOU	NL	3-6	141	564	96	167	28	3	11	63	.296	42	234	102	44-59
1988	LF	HOU	NL	5-6	145	530	79	142	25	4	7	52	.268	37	196	100	43-58
1989	LF-CF	HO/PT	NL	3/5	135	481	59	111	19	3	4	51	.231	30	148	79	56-59
1990	LF-CF	CIN	NL	1-6	139	504	68	139	28	5	5	25	.276	33	192	96	50-63
1991	CF-LF	CIN	NL	5-6	138	442	45	116	25	3	4	41	.262	26	159	91	—
1992	LF	CIN	NL	2-6	43	94	10	27	3	0	2	10	.287	5	36	—	—
1992	LF-CF	BOS	AL	7-7	75	315	37	75	16	2	1	23	.238	17	98	73	—
1993	CF	BOS	AL	5-7	136	508	71	146	24	3	9	57	.287	28	203	92	59-73
MAJOR LEAGUE TOTALS					1140	4029	545	1072	195	28	51	368	.266	221	1273	94	5 yrs

James Arthur Presley   Born Oct 23, 1961 Pensacola, FL
6'1 200 lbs Batted right

YR	POS	TEAM	LG	FIN	G	AB	R	H	2B	3B	HR	RBI	AVG	BB	TB	OQ	RANK
1984	3B	SEA	AL	5-7	70	251	27	57	12	1	10	36	.227	6	101	83	—
1985	3B	SEA	AL	6-7	155	570	71	157	33	1	28	84	.275	44	276	114	24-75
1986	3B	SEA	AL	7-7	155	616	83	163	33	4	27	107	.265	32	285	102	48-78
1987	3B	SEA	AL	4-7	152	575	78	142	23	6	24	88	.247	38	249	93	65-79
1988	3B	SEA	AL	7-7	150	544	50	125	26	0	14	62	.230	36	193	84	64-74
1989	3B-1B	SEA	AL	6-7	117	390	42	92	20	1	12	41	.236	21	150	89	—
1990	3B-1B	ATL	NL	6-6	140	541	59	131	34	1	19	72	.242	29	224	96	49-63
1991	3B	SD	NL	3-6	20	59	3	8	0	0	1	5	.136	4	11	—	—
MAJOR LEAGUE TOTALS					959	3546	413	875	181	14	135	495	.247	210	1489	98	5 yrs

Terry Lee Pendleton   Born Jul 16, 1960 Los Angeles, CA
5'9 178 lbs Batted both

YR	POS	TEAM	LG	FIN	G	AB	R	H	2B	3B	HR	RBI	AVG	BB	TB	OQ	RANK
1984	3B	SL	NL	3-6	67	262	37	85	16	3	1	33	.324	16	110	115	—
1985	3B	SL	NL	1-6	149	559	56	134	16	3	5	69	.240	37	171	78	62-65
1986	3B	SL	NL	3-6	159	578	56	138	26	5	1	59	.239	34	177	75	49-49
1987	3B	SL	NL	1-6	159	583	82	167	29	4	12	96	.286	70	240	110	35-59
1988	3B	SL	NL	5-6	110	391	44	99	20	2	6	53	.253	21	141	93	—
1989	3B	SL	NL	3-6	162	613	83	162	28	5	13	74	.264	44	239	103	36-59
1990	3B	SL	NL	6-6	121	447	46	103	20	2	6	58	.230	30	145	79	—
1991	3B	ATL	NL	1-6	153	586	94	187	34	8	22	86	.319	43	303	139	9-52
1992	3B	ATL	NL	1-6	160	640	98	199	39	1	21	105	.311	37	303	126	19-49
1993	3B	ATL	NL	1-7	161	633	81	172	33	1	17	84	.272	36	258	96	58-77
MAJOR LEAGUE TOTALS					1401	5292	677	1446	261	34	104	717	.273	368	2087	104	7 yrs

Danilo Tartabull   Born Oct 30, 1962   San Juan, PR
6'1   185 lbs Batted right

YR	POS	TEAM	LG	FIN	G	AB	R	H	2B	3B	HR	RBI	AVG	BB	TB	OQ	RANK
1984	SS-2B	SEA	AL	5-7	10	20	3	6	1	0	2	7	.300	2	13	—	—
1985	SS-3B	SEA	AL	6-7	19	61	8	20	7	1	1	7	.328	8	32	—	—
1986	RF-2B	SEA	AL	7-7	137	511	76	138	25	6	25	96	.270	61	250	121	18-78
1987	RF	KC	AL	2-7	158	582	95	180	27	3	34	101	.309	79	315	137	7-79
1988	RF	KC	AL	3-7	146	507	80	139	38	3	26	102	.274	76	261	140	9-74
1989	RF-DH	KC	AL	2-7	133	441	54	118	22	0	18	62	.268	69	194	126	13-67
1990	RF-DH	KC	AL	6-7	88	313	41	84	19	0	15	60	.268	36	148	122	—
1991	RF	KC	AL	6-7	132	484	78	153	35	3	31	100	.316	65	287	159	2-72
1992	RF-DH	NY	AL	4-7	123	421	72	112	19	0	25	85	.266	103	206	153	3-73
1993	DH-RF	NY	AL	2-7	138	513	87	128	33	2	31	102	.250	92	258	130	15-73
MAJOR LEAGUE TOTALS					1084	3853	594	1078	226	18	208	722	.280	591	1964	138	7 yrs

Robert George Deer   Born Sep 29, 1960   Orange, CA
6'3   210 lbs Batted right

YR	POS	TEAM	LG	FIN	G	AB	R	H	2B	3B	HR	RBI	AVG	BB	TB	OQ	RANK
1984	LF	SF	NL	6-6	13	24	5	4	0	0	3	3	.167	7	13	—	—
1985	LF-1B	SF	NL	6-6	78	162	22	30	5	1	8	20	.185	23	61	101	—
1986	RF	MIL	AL	6-7	134	466	75	108	17	3	33	86	.232	72	230	123	16-78
1987	LF	MIL	AL	3-7	134	474	71	113	15	2	28	80	.238	86	216	117	28-79
1988	RF	MIL	AL	3-7	135	492	71	124	24	0	23	85	.252	51	217	111	30-74
1989	RF	MIL	AL	4-7	130	466	72	98	18	2	26	65	.210	60	198	108	35-67
1990	RF	MIL	AL	6-7	134	440	57	92	15	1	27	69	.209	64	190	111	30-69
1991	RF	DET	AL	2-7	134	448	64	80	14	2	25	64	.179	89	173	107	40-72
1992	RF	DET	AL	6-7	110	393	66	97	20	1	32	64	.247	51	215	137	—
1993	RF	DE/BO	AL	3/5	128	466	66	98	17	1	21	55	.210	58	180	93	56-73
MAJOR LEAGUE TOTALS					1130	3831	569	844	145	13	226	591	.220	561	1693	110	7 yrs

Alvin Glenn Davis
6'1   195 lbs   Batted left

Born Sep 9, 1960   Riverside, CA

YR	POS	TEAM	LG	FIN	G	AB	R	H	2B	3B	HR	RBI	AVG	BB	TB	OQ	RANK
1984	1B	SEA	AL	5-7	152	567	80	161	34	3	27	116	.284	97	282	140	3-68
1985	1B	SEA	AL	6-7	155	578	78	166	33	1	18	78	.287	90	255	123	13-75
1986	1B	SEA	AL	7-7	135	479	66	130	18	1	18	72	.271	76	204	117	25-78
1987	1B	SEA	AL	4-7	157	580	86	171	37	2	29	100	.295	72	299	127	16-79
1988	1B	SEA	AL	7-7	140	478	67	141	24	1	18	69	.295	95	221	144	7-74
1989	1B	SEA	AL	6-7	142	498	84	152	30	1	21	95	.305	101	247	155	2-67
1990	DH-1B	SEA	AL	5-7	140	494	63	140	21	0	17	68	.283	85	212	128	8-69
1991	DH-1B	SEA	AL	5-7	145	462	39	102	15	1	12	69	.221	56	155	88	62-72
1992	1B-DH	CAL	AL	5-7	40	104	5	26	8	0	0	16	.250	13	34	92	—
MAJOR LEAGUE TOTALS					1206	4240	568	1189	220	10	160	683	.280	685	1909	128	8 yrs

Andres Jose Galarraga
6'3   235 lbs   Batted right

Born Jun 18, 1961   Caracas, Venezuela

YR	POS	TEAM	LG	FIN	G	AB	R	H	2B	3B	HR	RBI	AVG	BB	TB	OQ	RANK
1985	1B	MON	NL	3-6	24	75	9	14	1	0	2	4	.187	3	21	—	—
1986	1B	MON	NL	4-6	105	321	39	87	13	0	10	42	.271	30	130	107	—
1987	1B	MON	NL	3-6	147	551	72	168	40	3	13	90	.305	41	253	113	29-59
1988	1B	MON	NL	3-6	157	609	99	184	42	8	29	92	.302	39	329	144	6-58
1989	1B	MON	NL	4-6	152	572	76	147	30	1	23	85	.257	48	248	114	21-59
1990	1B	MON	NL	3-6	155	579	65	148	29	0	20	87	.256	40	237	100	44-63
1991	1B	MON	NL	6-6	107	375	34	82	13	2	9	33	.219	23	126	81	—
1992	1B	SL	NL	3-6	95	325	38	79	14	2	10	39	.243	11	127	92	—
1993	1B	COR	NL	6-7	120	470	71	174	35	4	22	98	.370	24	283	156	2-77
MAJOR LEAGUE TOTALS					1062	3877	503	1083	217	20	138	570	.279	259	1754	125	5 yrs

Vincent Maurice Coleman
6'0   170 lbs   Batted both

Born Sep 22, 1960   Jacksonville, FL

YR	POS	TEAM	LG	FIN	G	AB	R	H	2B	3B	HR	RBI	AVG	BB	TB	OQ	RANK
1985	LF	SL	NL	1-6	151	636	107	170	20	10	1	40	.267	50	213	90	55-65
1986	LF	SL	NL	3-6	154	600	94	139	13	8	0	29	.232	60	168	77	48-49
1987	LF	SL	NL	1-6	151	623	121	180	14	10	3	43	.289	70	223	97	48-59
1988	LF	SL	NL	5-6	153	616	77	160	20	10	3	38	.260	49	209	94	52-58
1989	LF	SL	NL	3-6	145	563	94	143	21	9	2	28	.254	50	188	93	46-59
1990	LF	SL	NL	6-6	124	497	73	145	18	9	6	39	.292	35	199	104	40-63
1991	LF	NY	NL	5-6	72	278	45	71	7	5	1	17	.255	39	91	100	—
1992	LF-CF	NY	NL	5-6	71	229	37	63	11	1	2	21	.275	27	82	107	—
1993	LF	NY	NL	7-7	92	373	64	104	14	8	2	25	.279	21	140	90	—
MAJOR LEAGUE TOTALS					1113	4415	712	1175	138	70	20	280	.266	401	1513	93	6 yrs

Oswaldo Jose Guillen
Born Jan 20, 1964   Oculare del Tuy, VZ
5'11   150 lbs   Batted left

YR	POS	TEAM	LG	FIN	G	AB	R	H	2B	3B	HR	RBI	AVG	BB	TB	OQ	RANK
1985	SS	CHI	AL	3-7	150	491	71	134	21	9	1	33	.273	12	176	78	72-75
1986	SS	CHI	AL	5-7	159	547	58	137	19	4	2	47	.250	12	170	65	78-78
1987	SS	CHI	AL	5-7	149	560	64	156	22	7	2	51	.279	22	198	76	79-79
1988	SS	CHI	AL	5-7	156	566	58	148	16	7	0	39	.261	25	178	74	70-74
1989	SS	CHI	AL	7-7	155	597	63	151	20	8	1	54	.253	15	190	71	66-67
1990	SS	CHI	AL	2-7	160	516	61	144	21	4	1	58	.279	26	176	83	67-69
1991	SS	CHI	AL	2-7	154	524	52	143	20	3	3	49	.273	11	178	74	72-72
1992	SS	CHI	AL	3-7	12	40	5	8	4	0	0	7	.200	1	12	—	—
1993	SS	CHI	AL	1-7	134	457	44	128	23	4	4	50	.280	10	171	79	—
MAJOR LEAGUE TOTALS					1229	4298	476	1149	166	46	14	388	.267	134	1449	74	7 yrs

Shawon Donnell Dunston
Born Mar 21, 1963   Brooklyn, NY
6'1   175 lbs   Batted right

YR	POS	TEAM	LG	FIN	G	AB	R	H	2B	3B	HR	RBI	AVG	BB	TB	OQ	RANK
1985	SS	CHI	NL	4-6	74	250	40	65	12	4	4	18	.260	19	97	100	—
1986	SS	CHI	NL	5-6	150	581	66	145	37	3	17	68	.250	21	239	93	43-49
1987	SS	CHI	NL	6-6	95	346	40	85	18	3	5	22	.246	10	124	75	—
1988	SS	CHI	NL	4-6	155	575	69	143	23	6	9	56	.249	16	205	85	58-58
1989	SS	CHI	NL	1-6	138	471	52	131	20	6	9	60	.278	30	190	106	30-59
1990	SS	CHI	NL	4-6	146	545	73	143	22	8	17	66	.262	15	232	96	51-63
1991	SS	CHI	NL	4-6	142	492	59	128	22	7	12	50	.260	23	200	98	45-52
1992	SS	CHI	NL	4-6	18	73	8	23	3	1	0	2	.315	3	28	—	—
1993	SS	CHI	NL	4-7	7	10	3	4	2	0	0	2	.400	0	6	—	—
MAJOR LEAGUE TOTALS					925	3343	410	867	159	38	73	344	.259	137	1321	96	5 yrs

Devon Markes White
Born Dec 29, 1962   Kingston, Jamaica
6'1   170 lbs   Batted both

YR	POS	TEAM	LG	FIN	G	AB	R	H	2B	3B	HR	RBI	AVG	BB	TB	OQ	RANK
1985	LF-RF	CAL	AL	2-7	21	7	7	1	0	0	0	0	.143	1	1	—	—
1986	LF-CF	CAL	AL	1-7	29	51	8	12	1	1	1	3	.235	6	18	—	—
1987	RF	CAL	AL	6-7	159	639	103	168	33	5	24	87	.263	39	283	96	59-79
1988	CF	CAL	AL	4-7	122	455	76	118	22	2	11	51	.259	23	177	91	—
1989	CF	CAL	AL	3-7	156	636	86	156	18	13	12	56	.245	31	236	86	60-67
1990	CF	CAL	AL	4-7	125	443	57	96	17	3	11	44	.217	44	152	86	63-69
1991	CF	TOR	AL	1-7	156	642	110	181	40	10	17	60	.282	55	292	113	33-72
1992	CF	TOR	AL	1-7	153	641	98	159	26	7	17	60	.248	47	250	94	62-73
1993	CF	TOR	AL	1-7	146	598	116	163	42	6	15	52	.273	57	262	105	36-73
MAJOR LEAGUE TOTALS					1067	4112	661	1054	199	47	108	413	.256	303	1671	97	6 yrs

Jose Canseco   Born July 2, 1964   Havana, Cuba
6'3   195 lbs   Batted right

YR	POS	TEAM	LG	FIN	G	AB	R	H	2B	3B	HR	RBI	AVG	BB	TB	OQ	RANK
1985	RF-LF	OAK	AL	4-7	29	96	16	29	3	0	5	13	.302	4	47	112	—
1986	LF	OAK	AL	3-7	157	600	85	144	29	1	33	117	.240	65	274	108	38-78
1987	LF-DH	OAK	AL	3-7	159	630	81	162	35	3	31	113	.257	50	296	103	49-79
1988	RF	OAK	AL	1-7	158	610	120	187	34	0	42	124	.307	78	347	154	3-74
1989	RF	OAK	AL	1-7	65	227	40	61	9	1	17	57	.269	23	123	136	—
1990	RF-DH	OAK	AL	1-7	131	481	83	132	14	2	37	101	.274	72	261	145	4-69
1991	RF-DH	OAK	AL	4-7	154	572	115	152	32	1	44	122	.266	78	318	141	8-72
1992	RF-DH	OA/TX	AL	1/4	119	439	74	107	15	0	26	87	.244	63	200	121	22-73
1993	RF	TEX	AL	2-7	60	231	30	59	14	1	10	46	.255	16	105	101	—
MAJOR LEAGUE TOTALS					1032	3886	644	1033	185	9	245	780	.266	449	1971	129	6 yrs

Michael Lewis Greenwell   Born Jul 18, 1963   Louisville, KY
6'0   170 lbs   Batted left

YR	POS	TEAM	LG	FIN	G	AB	R	H	2B	3B	HR	RBI	AVG	BB	TB	OQ	RANK
1985	LF	BOS	AL	5-7	17	31	7	10	1	0	4	8	.323	3	23	—	—
1986	LF-RF	BOS	AL	1-7	31	35	4	11	2	0	0	4	.314	5	13	—	—
1987	LF-DH	BOS	AL	5-7	125	412	71	135	31	6	19	89	.328	35	235	136	—
1988	LF	BOS	AL	1-7	158	590	86	192	39	8	22	119	.325	87	313	154	2-74
1989	LF	BOS	AL	3-7	145	578	87	178	36	0	14	95	.308	56	256	121	18-67
1990	LF	BOS	AL	1-7	159	610	71	181	30	6	14	73	.297	65	265	117	21-69
1991	LF	BOS	AL	2-7	147	544	76	163	26	6	9	83	.300	43	228	106	41-72
1992	LF	BOS	AL	7-7	49	180	16	42	2	0	2	18	.233	18	50	75	—
1993	LF	BOS	AL	5-7	146	540	77	170	38	6	13	72	.315	54	259	121	22-73
MAJOR LEAGUE TOTALS					977	3520	495	1082	205	32	97	561	.307	366	1642	124	5 yrs

Paul Andrew O'Neill   Born Feb 25, 1963   Columbus, OH
6'4   200 lbs   Batted left

YR	POS	TEAM	LG	FIN	G	AB	R	H	2B	3B	HR	RBI	AVG	BB	TB	OQ	RANK
1985	LF	CIN	NL	2-6	5	12	1	4	1	0	0	1	.333	0	5	—	—
1986	PH	CIN	NL	2-6	3	2	0	0	0	0	0	0	.000	1	0	—	—
1987	RF-LF	CIN	NL	2-6	84	160	24	41	14	1	7	28	.256	18	78	119	—
1988	RF	CIN	NL	2-6	145	485	58	122	25	3	16	73	.252	38	201	110	30-58
1989	RF	CIN	NL	5-6	117	428	49	118	24	2	15	74	.276	46	191	125	—
1990	RF	CIN	NL	1-6	145	503	59	136	28	0	16	78	.270	53	212	112	32-63
1991	RF	CIN	NL	5-6	152	532	71	136	36	0	28	91	.256	73	256	133	13-52
1992	RF	CIN	NL	2-6	148	496	59	122	19	1	14	66	.246	77	185	114	28-49
1993	RF-LF	NY	AL	2-7	141	498	71	155	34	1	20	75	.311	44	251	123	19-73
MAJOR LEAGUE TOTALS					940	3116	392	834	181	8	116	486	.268	350	1379	118	5 yrs

Steven Bernard Buechele

Born Sep 26, 1961 Lancaster, CA

6'2 190 lbs Batted right

YR	POS	TEAM	LG	FIN	G	AB	R	H	2B	3B	HR	RBI	AVG	BB	TB	OQ	RANK
1985	3B	TEX	AL	7-7	69	219	22	48	6	3	6	21	.219	14	78	79	—
1986	3B-2B	TEX	AL	2-7	153	461	54	112	19	2	18	54	.243	35	189	93	63-78
1987	3B-2B	TEX	AL	6-7	136	363	45	86	20	0	13	50	.237	28	145	87	—
1988	3B	TEX	AL	6-7	155	503	68	126	21	4	16	58	.250	65	203	109	37-74
1989	3B-2B	TEX	AL	4-7	155	486	60	114	22	2	16	59	.235	36	188	93	52-67
1990	3B	TEX	AL	3-7	91	251	30	54	10	0	7	30	.215	27	85	87	—
1991	3B-2B	TEX	AL	3-7	121	416	58	111	17	2	18	66	.267	39	186	110	—
1991	3B	PIT	NL	1-6	31	114	16	28	5	1	4	19	.246	10	47	106	—
1992	3B	PT/CH	NL	1/4	145	524	52	137	23	4	9	64	.261	52	195	104	36-49
1993	3B	CHI	NL	4-7	133	460	53	125	27	2	15	65	.272	48	201	112	36-77
MAJOR LEAGUE TOTALS					1189	3797	458	941	170	20	122	486	.248	306	1316	102	5 yrs

Kevin Lee Seitzer

Born Mar 26, 1962 Springfield, IL

5'11 180 lbs Batted right

YR	POS	TEAM	LG	FIN	G	AB	R	H	2B	3B	HR	RBI	AVG	BB	TB	OQ	RANK
1986	1B-LF	KC	AL	3-7	28	96	16	31	4	1	2	11	.323	19	43	139	—
1987	3B-1B	KC	AL	2-7	161	641	105	207	33	8	15	83	.323	80	301	123	18-79
1988	3B	KC	AL	3-7	149	559	90	170	32	5	5	60	.304	72	227	118	26-74
1989	3B	KC	AL	2-7	160	597	78	168	17	2	4	48	.281	102	201	109	32-67
1990	3B	KC	AL	6-7	158	622	91	171	31	5	6	38	.275	67	230	100	46-69
1991	3B	KC	AL	6-7	85	234	28	62	11	3	1	25	.265	29	82	97	—
1992	3B	MIL	AL	2-7	148	540	74	146	35	1	5	71	.270	57	198	99	53-73
1993	3B-1B	OA/ML	AL	7/7	120	417	45	112	16	2	11	57	.269	44	165	98	—
MAJOR LEAGUE TOTALS					1009	3706	527	1067	179	27	49	393	.288	470	1447	110	5 yrs

Benito Santiago

Born Mar 9, 1965 Ponce, PR

6'1 180 lbs Batted right

YR	POS	TEAM	LG	FIN	G	AB	R	H	2B	3B	HR	RBI	AVG	BB	TB	OQ	RANK
1986	C	SD	NL	4-6	17	62	10	18	2	0	3	6	.290	2	29	—	—
1987	C	SD	NL	6-6	146	546	64	164	33	2	18	79	.300	16	255	104	41-59
1988	C	SD	NL	3-6	139	492	49	122	22	2	10	46	.248	24	178	91	54-58
1989	C	SD	NL	2-6	129	462	50	109	16	3	16	62	.236	26	179	95	45-59
1990	C	SD	NL	4-6	100	344	42	93	8	5	11	53	.270	27	144	106	—
1991	C	SD	NL	3-6	152	580	60	155	22	3	17	87	.267	23	234	97	47-52
1992	C	SD	NL	3-6	106	386	37	97	21	0	10	42	.251	21	148	95	—
1993	C	FLA	NL	6-7	139	469	49	108	19	6	13	50	.230	37	178	89	71-77
MAJOR LEAGUE TOTALS					928	3341	361	866	143	21	98	425	.259	176	1345	95	5 yrs

William Nuschler Clark   Born Mar 13, 1964 New Orleans, LA
6'2   190 lbs   Batted left

YR	POS	TEAM	LG	FIN	G	AB	R	H	2B	3B	HR	RBI	AVG	BB	TB	OQ	RANK
1986	1B	SF	NL	3-6	111	408	66	117	27	2	11	41	.287	34	181	115	—
1987	1B	SF	NL	1-6	150	529	89	163	29	5	35	91	.308	49	307	143	9-58
1988	1B	SF	NL	4-6	162	575	102	162	31	6	29	109	.282	100	292	158	2-58
1989	1B	SF	NL	1-6	159	588	104	196	38	9	23	111	.333	74	321	165	3-59
1990	1B	SF	NL	3-6	154	600	91	177	25	5	19	95	.295	62	269	122	22-63
1991	1B	SF	NL	4-6	148	565	84	170	32	7	29	116	.301	51	303	143	5-52
1992	1B	SF	NL	5-6	144	513	69	154	40	1	16	73	.300	73	244	144	8-49
1993	1B	SF	NL	2-7	132	491	82	139	27	2	14	73	.283	63	212	117	31-77
MAJOR LEAGUE TOTALS					1160	4269	687	1278	249	37	176	709	.299	506	2129	142	7 yrs

Wallace Keith Joyner   Born Jun 16, 1962   Atlanta, GA
6'2   185 lbs   Batted left

YR	POS	TEAM	LG	FIN	G	AB	R	H	2B	3B	HR	RBI	AVG	BB	TB	OQ	RANK
1986	1B	CAL	AL	1-7	154	593	82	172	27	3	22	100	.290	57	271	113	30-78
1987	1B	CAL	AL	6-7	149	564	100	161	33	1	34	117	.285	72	298	128	15-79
1988	1B	CAL	AL	4-7	158	597	81	176	31	2	13	85	.295	55	250	111	31-74
1989	1B	CAL	AL	3-7	159	593	78	167	30	2	16	79	.282	46	249	107	37-67
1990	1B	CAL	AL	4-7	83	310	35	83	15	0	8	41	.268	41	122	109	—
1991	1B	CAL	AL	7-7	143	551	79	166	34	3	21	96	.301	52	269	125	20-72
1992	1B	KC	AL	5-7	149	572	66	154	36	2	9	66	.269	55	221	101	49-73
1993	1B	KC	AL	3-7	141	497	83	145	36	3	15	65	.292	66	232	122	21-73
MAJOR LEAGUE TOTALS					1136	4277	604	1224	242	16	138	649	.286	444	1912	115	7 yrs

John Martin Kruk   Born Feb 9, 1961   Charleston, WV
5'10   170 lbs   Batted left

YR	POS	TEAM	LG	FIN	G	AB	R	H	2B	3B	HR	RBI	AVG	BB	TB	OQ	RANK
1986	LF	SD	NL	4-6	122	278	33	86	16	2	4	38	.309	45	118	132	—
1987	1B-LF	SD	NL	6-6	138	447	72	140	14	2	20	91	.313	73	218	139	11-59
1988	1B-LF	SD	NL	3-6	120	378	54	91	17	1	9	44	.241	80	137	126	—
1989	LF	SD/PH	NL	2/6	112	357	53	107	13	6	8	44	.300	44	156	131	—
1990	LF-1B	PHI	NL	4-6	142	443	52	129	25	8	7	67	.291	69	191	129	15-63
1991	1B-LF	PHI	NL	3-6	152	538	84	158	27	6	21	92	.294	67	260	138	10-52
1992	1B-RF	PHI	NL	6-6	144	507	86	164	30	4	10	70	.323	92	232	154	5-49
1993	1B	PHI	NL	1-7	150	535	100	169	33	5	14	85	.316	111	254	150	3-77
MAJOR LEAGUE TOTALS					1080	3483	534	1044	175	34	93	531	.300	581	1566	142	5 yrs

Frederick Stanley McGriff   Born Oct 31, 1963   Tampa, FL
6'3 200 lbs Batted left

YR	POS	TEAM	LG	FIN	G	AB	R	H	2B	3B	HR	RBI	AVG	BB	TB	OQ	RANK
1986	DH-1B	TOR	AL	4-7	3	5	1	1	0	0	0	0	.200	0	1	—	—
1987	DH-1B	TOR	AL	2-7	107	295	58	73	16	0	20	43	.247	60	149	132	—
1988	1B	TOR	AL	3-7	154	536	100	151	35	4	34	82	.282	79	296	149	4-74
1989	1B	TOR	AL	1-7	161	551	98	148	27	3	36	92	.269	119	289	156	1-67
1990	1B	TOR	AL	2-7	153	557	91	167	21	1	35	88	.300	94	295	152	3-69
1991	1B	SD	NL	3-6	153	528	84	147	19	1	31	106	.278	105	261	154	2-52
1992	1B	SD	NL	3-6	152	531	79	152	30	4	35	104	.286	96	295	168	2-49
1993	1B	SD/AT	NL	7/1	151	557	111	162	29	2	37	101	.291	76	306	145	5-77

MAJOR LEAGUE TOTALS   1034 3560 622 1001 177 15 228 616 .281 629 1892 154 6 yrs

Mark David McGwire   Born Oct 1, 1963   Pomona, CA
6'5 215 lbs Batted right

YR	POS	TEAM	LG	FIN	G	AB	R	H	2B	3B	HR	RBI	AVG	BB	TB	OQ	RANK
1986	3B	OAK	AL	3-7	18	53	10	10	1	0	3	9	.189	4	20	—	—
1987	1B	OAK	AL	3-7	151	557	97	161	28	4	49	118	.289	71	344	147	4-79
1988	1B	OAK	AL	1-7	155	550	87	143	22	1	32	99	.260	76	263	128	17-74
1989	1B	OAK	AL	1-7	143	490	74	113	17	0	33	95	.231	83	229	128	12-67
1990	1B	OAK	AL	1-7	156	523	87	123	16	0	39	108	.235	110	256	139	6-69
1991	1B	OAK	AL	4-7	154	483	62	97	22	0	22	75	.201	93	185	108	38-72
1992	1B	OAK	AL	1-7	139	467	87	125	22	0	42	104	.268	90	273	162	2-73
1993	1B	OAK	AL	7-7	27	84	16	28	6	0	9	24	.333	21	61	210	—

MAJOR LEAGUE TOTALS   943 3207 520 800 134 5 229 632 .249 548 1631 135 6 yrs

Rafael Palmeiro   Born Sep 24, 1964   Havana, Cuba
6'0 175 lbs Batted left

YR	POS	TEAM	LG	FIN	G	AB	R	H	2B	3B	HR	RBI	AVG	BB	TB	OQ	RANK
1986	LF-RF	CHI	NL	5-6	22	73	9	18	4	0	3	12	.247	4	31	—	—
1987	LF-1B	CHI	NL	6-6	84	221	32	61	15	1	14	30	.276	20	120	129	—
1988	LF	CHI	NL	4-6	152	580	75	178	41	5	8	53	.307	38	253	121	18-58
1989	1B	TEX	AL	4-7	156	559	76	154	23	4	8	64	.275	63	209	104	42-67
1990	1B	TEX	AL	3-7	154	598	72	191	35	6	14	89	.319	40	280	120	18-69
1991	1B	TEX	AL	3-7	159	631	115	203	49	3	26	88	.322	68	336	141	6-72
1992	1B	TEX	AL	4-7	159	608	84	163	27	4	22	85	.268	72	264	115	29-73
1993	1B	TEX	AL	2-7	160	597	124	176	40	2	37	105	.295	73	331	138	8-73

MAJOR LEAGUE TOTALS   1046 3867 587 1144 234 25 132 526 .296 378 1824 123 6 yrs

Barry Lamar Bonds   Born Jul 24, 1964 Riverside, CA
6'1 185 lbs Batted left

YR	POS	TEAM	LG	FIN	G	AB	R	H	2B	3B	HR	RBI	AVG	BB	TB	OQ	RANK
1986	CF	PIT	NL	6-6	113	413	72	92	26	3	16	48	.223	65	172	115	—
1987	LF	PIT	NL	4-6	150	551	99	144	34	9	25	59	.261	54	271	118	23-59
1988	LF	PIT	NL	2-6	144	538	97	152	30	5	24	58	.283	72	264	145	4-58
1989	LF	PIT	NL	5-6	159	580	96	144	34	6	19	58	.248	93	247	128	14-59
1990	LF	PIT	NL	1-6	151	519	104	156	32	3	33	114	.301	93	293	166	1-63
1991	LF	PIT	NL	1-6	153	510	95	149	28	5	25	116	.292	107	262	164	1-52
1992	LF	PIT	NL	1-6	140	473	109	147	36	5	34	103	.311	127	295	211	1-49
1993	LF	SF	NL	2-7	159	539	129	181	38	4	46	123	.336	126	365	206	1-77
MAJOR LEAGUE TOTALS					1169	4123	801	1165	258	40	222	679	.283	737	2169	163	7 yrs

Roberto Martin Antonio Bonilla   Born Feb 23, 1963 New York, NY
6'3 210 lbs Batted both

YR	POS	TEAM	LG	FIN	G	AB	R	H	2B	3B	HR	RBI	AVG	BB	TB	OQ	RANK
1986	LF-1B	CHI	AL	5-7	75	234	27	63	10	2	2	26	.269	33	83	99	—
1986	LF-RF	PIT	NL	6-6	63	192	28	46	6	2	1	17	.240	29	59	94	—
1987	3B-RF	PIT	NL	4-6	141	466	58	140	33	3	15	77	.300	39	224	119	20-59
1988	3B	PIT	NL	2-6	159	584	87	160	32	7	24	100	.274	85	278	143	8-58
1989	3B	PIT	NL	5-6	163	616	96	173	37	10	24	86	.281	76	302	140	10-59
1990	RF	PIT	NL	1-6	160	625	112	175	39	7	32	120	.280	45	324	128	16-63
1991	RF-3B	PIT	NL	1-6	157	577	102	174	44	6	18	100	.302	90	284	148	3-52
1992	RF	NY	NL	5-6	128	438	62	109	23	0	19	70	.249	66	189	126	18-49
1993	RF-3B	NY	NL	7-7	139	502	81	133	21	3	34	87	.265	72	262	136	11-77
MAJOR LEAGUE TOTALS					1185	4234	653	1173	245	40	169	683	.277	535	2005	134	7 yrs

Robert Randall Thompson   Born May 10, 1962 West Palm Beach, FL
5'11 165 lbs Batted right

YR	POS	TEAM	LG	FIN	G	AB	R	H	2B	3B	HR	RBI	AVG	BB	TB	OQ	RANK
1986	2B	SF	NL	3-6	149	549	73	149	27	3	7	47	.271	42	203	95	40-49
1987	2B	SF	NL	1-6	132	420	62	110	26	5	10	44	.262	40	176	103	—
1988	2B	SF	NL	4-6	138	477	66	126	24	6	7	48	.264	40	183	106	36-58
1989	2B	SF	NL	1-6	148	547	91	132	26	11	13	50	.241	51	219	107	28-59
1990	2B	SF	NL	3-6	144	498	67	122	22	3	15	56	.245	34	195	95	53-63
1991	2B	SF	NL	4-6	144	492	74	129	24	5	19	48	.262	63	220	125	18-52
1992	2B	SF	NL	5-6	128	443	54	115	25	1	14	49	.260	43	184	113	30-49
1993	2B	SF	NL	2-7	128	494	85	154	30	2	19	65	.312	45	245	128	20-77
MAJOR LEAGUE TOTALS					1111	3920	572	1037	204	36	104	407	.265	358	1625	110	7 yrs

Ruben Angel Sierra   Born Oct 6, 1965   Rio Piedras, PR
6'1   175 lbs   Batted both

YR	POS	TEAM	LG	FIN	G	AB	R	H	2B	3B	HR	RBI	AVG	BB	TB	OQ	RANK
1986	RF-LF	TEX	AL	2-7	113	382	50	101	13	10	16	55	.264	22	182	106	—
1987	RF	TEX	AL	6-7	158	643	97	169	35	4	30	109	.263	39	302	101	52-79
1988	RF	TEX	AL	6-7	156	615	77	156	32	2	23	91	.254	44	261	102	47-74
1989	RF	TEX	AL	4-7	162	634	101	194	35	14	29	119	.306	43	344	136	7-67
1990	RF	TEX	AL	3-7	159	608	70	170	37	2	16	96	.280	49	259	107	37-69
1991	RF	TEX	AL	3-7	161	661	110	203	44	5	25	116	.307	56	332	127	18-72
1992	RF	TX/OA	AL	4/1	151	601	83	167	34	7	17	87	.278	45	266	109	35-73
1993	RF-DH	OAK	AL	7-7	158	630	77	147	23	5	22	101	.233	52	246	89	65-73
MAJOR LEAGUE TOTALS					1218	4774	665	1307	253	49	178	774	.274	350	2192	110	7 yrs

Gregory Scott Jefferies   Born Aug 1, 1967   Burlingame, CA
5'11   175 lbs   Batted both

YR	POS	TEAM	LG	FIN	G	AB	R	H	2B	3B	HR	RBI	AVG	BB	TB	OQ	RANK
1987	PH	NY	NL	2-6	6	6	0	3	1	0	0	2	.500	0	4	—	—
1988	3B-2B	NY	NL	1-6	29	109	19	35	8	2	6	17	.321	8	65	164	—
1989	2B-3B	NY	NL	2-6	141	508	72	131	28	2	12	56	.258	39	199	103	34-59
1990	2B-3B	NY	NL	2-6	153	604	96	171	40	3	15	68	.283	46	262	111	36-63
1991	2B-3B	NY	NL	5-6	136	486	59	132	19	2	9	62	.272	47	182	104	40-52
1992	3B	KC	AL	5-7	152	604	66	172	36	3	10	75	.285	43	244	101	47-73
1993	1B	SL	NL	3-7	142	544	89	186	24	3	16	83	.342	62	264	137	10-77
MAJOR LEAGUE TOTALS					759	2861	401	830	156	15	68	363	.290	245	1220	111	5 yrs

Jose Lind   Born May 1, 1964   Toabaja, PR
5'11   155 lbs   Batted right

YR	POS	TEAM	LG	FIN	G	AB	R	H	2B	3B	HR	RBI	AVG	BB	TB	OQ	RANK
1987	2B	PIT	NL	4-6	35	143	21	46	8	4	0	11	.322	8	62	106	—
1988	2B	PIT	NL	2-6	154	611	82	160	24	4	2	49	.262	42	198	89	55-58
1989	2B	PIT	NL	5-6	153	578	52	134	21	3	2	48	.232	39	167	76	57-59
1990	2B	PIT	NL	1-6	152	514	46	134	28	5	1	48	.261	35	175	86	58-63
1991	2B	PIT	NL	1-6	150	502	53	133	16	6	3	54	.265	30	170	87	51-52
1992	2B	PIT	NL	1-6	135	468	38	110	14	1	0	39	.235	26	126	69	49-49
1993	2B	KC	AL	3-7	136	431	33	107	13	2	0	37	.248	13	124	61	—
MAJOR LEAGUE TOTALS					915	3247	325	824	124	25	8	286	.254	193	1022	81	5 yrs

Ellis Rena Burks   Born Sep 11, 1964   Vicksburg, MS
6'2   175 lbs Batted right

YR	POS	TEAM	LG	FIN	G	AB	R	H	2B	3B	HR	RBI	AVG	BB	TB	OQ	RANK
1987	CF	BOS	AL	5-7	133	558	94	152	30	2	20	59	.272	41	246	99	57-79
1988	CF	BOS	AL	1-7	144	540	93	159	37	5	18	92	.294	62	260	129	15-74
1989	CF	BOS	AL	3-7	97	399	73	121	19	6	12	61	.303	36	188	125	—
1990	CF	BOS	AL	1-7	152	588	89	174	33	8	21	89	.296	48	286	123	15-69
1991	CF	BOS	AL	2-7	130	474	56	119	33	3	14	56	.251	39	200	101	48-72
1992	CF	BOS	AL	7-7	66	235	35	60	8	3	8	30	.255	25	98	107	—
1993	RF-CF	CHI	AL	1-7	146	499	75	137	24	4	17	74	.275	60	220	111	31-73
MAJOR LEAGUE TOTALS					868	3293	515	922	184	31	110	461	.280	311	1498	113	5 yrs

Ronald Edwin Gant   Born Mar 2, 1965   Victoria, TX
6'0   172 lbs Batted right

YR	POS	TEAM	LG	FIN	G	AB	R	H	2B	3B	HR	RBI	AVG	BB	TB	OQ	RANK
1987	2B	ATL	NL	5-6	21	83	9	22	4	0	2	9	.265	1	32	—	—
1988	2B-3B	ATL	NL	6-6	146	563	85	146	28	8	19	60	.259	46	247	117	24-58
1989	3B-CF	ATL	NL	6-6	75	260	26	46	8	3	9	25	.177	20	87	82	—
1990	CF	ATL	NL	6-6	152	575	107	174	34	3	32	84	.303	50	310	140	8-63
1991	CF	ATL	NL	1-6	154	561	101	141	35	3	32	105	.251	71	278	133	13-52
1992	LF-CF	ATL	NL	1-6	153	544	74	141	22	6	17	80	.259	45	226	110	31-49
1993	LF	ATL	NL	1-7	157	606	113	166	27	4	36	117	.274	67	309	128	19-77
MAJOR LEAGUE TOTALS					858	3192	515	836	158	27	147	480	.262	300	1489	126	5 yrs

William James Surhoff   Born Aug 4, 1964   Bronx, NY
6'1   185 lbs Batted left

YR	POS	TEAM	LG	FIN	G	AB	R	H	2B	3B	HR	RBI	AVG	BB	TB	OQ	RANK
1987	C	MIL	AL	3-7	115	395	50	118	22	3	7	68	.299	36	167	103	—
1988	C-3B	MIL	AL	3-7	139	493	47	121	21	0	5	38	.245	31	157	77	68-74
1989	C	MIL	AL	4-7	126	436	42	108	17	4	5	55	.248	25	148	81	—
1990	C	MIL	AL	6-7	135	474	55	131	21	4	6	59	.276	41	178	97	50-69
1991	C	MIL	AL	4-7	143	505	57	146	19	4	5	68	.289	26	188	89	61-72
1992	C-1B	MIL	AL	2-7	139	480	63	121	19	1	4	62	.252	46	154	85	70-73
1993	3B	MIL	AL	7-7	148	552	66	151	38	3	7	79	.274	36	216	90	61-73
MAJOR LEAGUE TOTALS					945	3335	380	896	157	19	39	429	.269	241	1208	88	5 yrs

Kenneth Gene Caminiti   Born Apr 21, 1963   Hanford, CA
6'3   200 lbs   Batted both

YR	POS	TEAM	LG	FIN	G	AB	R	H	2B	3B	HR	RBI	AVG	BB	TB	OQ	RANK
1987	3B	HOU	NL	3-6	63	203	10	50	7	1	3	23	.246	12	68	77	—
1988	3B	HOU	NL	5-6	30	83	5	15	2	0	1	7	.181	5	20	—	—
1989	3B	HOU	NL	3-6	161	585	71	149	31	3	10	72	.255	51	216	100	42-59
1990	3B	HOU	NL	4-6	153	541	52	131	20	2	4	51	.242	48	167	82	61-63
1991	3B	HOU	NL	6-6	152	574	65	145	30	3	13	80	.253	46	220	99	43-52
1992	3B	HOU	NL	4-6	135	506	68	149	31	2	13	62	.294	44	223	122	20-49
1993	3B	HOU	NL	3-7	143	543	75	142	31	0	13	75	.262	49	212	98	56-77
MAJOR LEAGUE TOTALS					837	3035	346	781	152	11	57	370	.257	255	1126	100	5 yrs

Craig Alan Biggio   Born Dec 14, 1965   Smithtown, NY
5'11   185 lbs   Batted right

YR	POS	TEAM	LG	FIN	G	AB	R	H	2B	3B	HR	RBI	AVG	BB	TB	OQ	RANK
1988	C	HOU	NL	5-6	50	123	14	26	6	1	3	5	.211	7	43	86	—
1989	C	HOU	NL	3-6	134	443	64	114	21	2	13	60	.257	49	178	113	22-59
1990	C-CF	HOU	NL	4-6	150	555	53	153	24	2	4	42	.276	53	193	95	52-63
1991	C	HOU	NL	6-6	149	546	79	161	23	4	4	46	.295	53	204	107	37-52
1992	2B	HOU	NL	4-6	162	613	96	170	32	3	6	39	.277	94	226	118	24-49
1993	2B	HOU	NL	3-7	155	610	98	175	41	5	21	64	.287	77	289	126	22-77
MAJOR LEAGUE TOTALS					800	2890	404	799	147	17	51	256	.276	333	1133	112	5 yrs

Roberto Alomar   Born Feb 5, 1968   Ponce, PR
6'0   184 lbs   Batted both

YR	POS	TEAM	LG	FIN	G	AB	R	H	2B	3B	HR	RBI	AVG	BB	TB	OQ	RANK
1988	2B	SD	NL	3-6	143	545	84	145	24	6	9	41	.266	47	208	106	34-58
1989	2B	SD	NL	2-6	158	623	82	184	27	1	7	56	.295	53	234	107	26-59
1990	2B	SD	NL	4-6	147	586	80	168	27	5	6	60	.287	48	223	101	43-63
1991	2B	TOR	AL	1-7	161	637	88	188	41	11	9	69	.295	57	278	112	35-72
1992	2B	TOR	AL	1-7	152	571	105	177	27	8	8	76	.310	87	244	128	13-73
1993	2B	TOR	AL	1-7	153	589	109	192	35	6	17	93	.326	80	290	134	12-73
MAJOR LEAGUE TOTALS					914	3551	548	1054	181	37	56	395	.297	372	1477	115	6 yrs

Mark Eugene Grace   Born Jun 28, 1964   Winston-Salem, NC
6'2   190 lbs   Batted left

YR	POS	TEAM	LG	FIN	G	AB	R	H	2B	3B	HR	RBI	AVG	BB	TB	OQ	RANK
1988	1B	CHI	NL	4-6	134	486	65	144	23	4	7	57	.296	60	196	125	16-58
1989	1B	CHI	NL	1-6	142	510	74	160	28	3	13	79	.314	80	233	146	7-59
1990	1B	CHI	NL	4-6	157	589	72	182	32	1	9	82	.309	59	243	116	29-63
1991	1B	CHI	NL	4-6	160	619	87	169	28	5	8	58	.273	70	231	107	36-52
1992	1B	CHI	NL	4-6	158	603	72	185	37	5	9	79	.307	72	259	129	17-49
1993	1B	CHI	NL	4-7	155	594	86	193	39	4	14	98	.325	71	282	132	15-77
MAJOR LEAGUE TOTALS					906	3401	456	1033	187	22	60	453	.304	412	1444	126	6 yrs

George Kenneth Griffey Jr   Born Nov 21, 1969 Donora, PA
6'3   195 lbs   Batted left

YR	POS	TEAM	LG	FIN	G	AB	R	H	2B	3B	HR	RBI	AVG	BB	TB	OQ	RANK
1989	CF	SEA	AL	6-7	127	455	61	120	23	0	16	61	.264	44	191	108	34-67
1990	CF	SEA	AL	5-7	155	597	91	179	28	7	22	80	.300	63	287	127	10-69
1991	CF	SEA	AL	5-7	154	548	76	179	42	1	22	100	.327	71	289	146	3-72
1992	CF	SEA	AL	7-7	142	565	83	174	39	4	27	103	.308	44	302	135	9-73
1993	CF-DH	SEA	AL	4-7	156	582	113	180	38	3	45	109	.309	96	359	162	3-73
MAJOR LEAGUE TOTALS					734	2747	424	832	170	15	132	453	.303	318	1428	136	5 yrs

YEAR	BTOR	YEAR	BTOR	YEAR	BTOR
1901	.614	1941	.680	1981	.627
1902	.611	1942	.619	1982	.675
1903	.544	1943	.591	1983	.670
1904	.508	1944	.602	1984	.665
1905	.510	1945	.598	1985	.680
1906	.516	1946	.629	1986	.687
1907	.503	1947	.641	1987	.715
1908	.490	1948	.689	1988	.653
1909	.505	1949	.697	1989	.647
1910	.524	1950	.727	1990	.657
1911	.612	1951	.673	1991	.668
1912	.599	1952	.635	1992	.655
1913	.577	1953	.663	1993	.697
1914	.557	1954	.651		
1915	.572	1955	.669		
1916	.563	1956	.694		
1917	.551	1957	.651		
1918	.560	1958	.644		
1919	.613	1959	.649		
1920	.667	1960	.663		
1921	.708	1961	.675		
1922	.682	1962	.666		
1923	.676	1963	.626		
1924	.695	1964	.633		
1925	.717	1965	.616		
1926	.686	1966	.605		
1927	.693	1967	.580		
1928	.678	1968	.559		
1929	.703	1969	.632		
1930	.721	1970	.643		
1931	.681	1971	.617		
1932	.699	1972	.573		
1933	.677	1973	.650		
1934	.702	1974	.626		
1935	.705	1975	.648		
1936	.749	1976	.610		
1937	.731	1977	.680		
1938	.738	1978	.650		
1939	.716	1979	.691		
1940	.702	1980	.673		

YEAR	BTOR	YEAR	BTOR	YEAR	BTOR
1876	.459	1916	.533	1956	.667
1877	.498	1917	.535	1957	.662
1878	.467	1918	.540	1958	.679
1879	.470	1919	.549	1959	.667
1880	.464	1920	.586	1960	.646
1881	.514	1921	.655	1961	.677
1882	.509	1922	.685	1962	.660
1883	.540	1923	.666	1963	.592
1884	.525	1924	.652	1964	.608
1885	.503	1925	.699	1965	.612
1886	.549	1926	.650	1966	.623
1887	.625	1927	.650	1967	.597
1888	.500	1928	.678	1968	.554
1889	.619	1929	.734	1969	.622
1890	.593	1930	.764	1970	.669
1891	.588	1931	.648	1971	.613
1892	.561	1932	.647	1972	.611
1893	.677	1933	.589	1973	.635
1894	.777	1934	.651	1974	.631
1895	.696	1935	.646	1975	.634
1896	.669	1936	.648	1976	.612
1897	.663	1937	.643	1977	.669
1898	.587	1938	.633	1978	.627
1899	.621	1939	.654	1979	.647
1900	.616	1940	.630	1980	.627
1901	.569	1941	.618	1981	.615
1902	.523	1942	.587	1982	.623
1903	.589	1943	.596	1983	.636
1904	.525	1944	.617	1984	.621
1905	.550	1945	.626	1985	.629
1906	.523	1946	.618	1986	.642
1907	.518	1947	.675	1987	.680
1908	.503	1948	.659	1988	.600
1909	.531	1949	.667	1989	.611
1910	.587	1950	.688	1990	.642
1911	.621	1951	.664	1991	.625
1912	.638	1952	.633	1992	.613
1913	.595	1953	.695	1993	.666
1914	.564	1954	.697		
1915	.546	1955	.686		

YEAR	BTOR

American Association

1882	.461
1883	.498
1884	.485
1885	.506
1886	.535
1887	.622
1888	.505
1889	.609
1890	.580
1891	.609

Union Association

1884	.468

Players League

1890	.671

Federal League

1914	.602
1915	.577

UNION ASSOCIATION

| 1884 | Fred Dunlap | 249 |

PLAYERS LEAGUE

| 1890 | Roger Connor | 167 |

AMERICAN ASSOCIATION

1882	Pete Browning	210
1883	Ed Swartwood	166
1884	Harry Stovey	184
1885	Pete Browning	180
1886	Dave Orr	157
1887	Tip O'Neill	224
1888	Harry Stovey	160
1889	Harry Stovey	157
1890	Cupid Childs	165
1891	Dan Brouthers	175

FEDERAL LEAGUE

| 1914 | Benny Kauff | 174 |
| 1915 | Benny Kauff | 180 |

AMERICAN LEAGUE

1901	Nap Lajoie	195
1902	Ed Delahanty	189
1903	Topsy Hartsel	162
1904	Nap Lajoie	189
1905	Elmer Flick	161
1906	George Stone	178
1907	Topsy Hartsel	159
1908	Ty Cobb	161
1909	Ty Cobb	191
1910	Ty Cobb	210

NATIONAL LEAGUE

1876	Ross Barnes	249
1877	Deacon White	189
1878	Paul Hines	165
1879	Charley Jones	184
1880	George Gore	178
1881	Cap Anson	190
1882	Dan Brouthers	188
1883	Dan Brouthers	180
1884	King Kelly	185
1885	Dan Brouthers	194
1886	King Kelly	214
1887	Dan Brouthers	170
1888	Cap Anson	180
1889	Fred Carroll	181
1890	Cap Anson	153
1891	Billy Hamilton	158
1892	Roger Connor	169
1893	Billy Hamilton	167
1894	Hugh Duffy	188
1895	Ed Delahanty	192
1896	Ed Delahanty	187
1897	Ed Delahanty	158
1898	Billy Hamilton	179
1899	John McGraw	200
1900	Honus Wagner	171
1901	Ed Delahanty	176
1902	Sam Crawford	157
1903	Roger Bresnahan	168
1904	Honus Wagner	187
1905	Cy Seymour	189
1906	Honus Wagner	165
1907	Honus Wagner	179
1908	Honus Wagner	196
1909	Honus Wagner	177
1910	Sherry Magee	175

AMERICAN LEAGUE			NATIONAL LEAGUE		
1911	Ty Cobb	196	1911	Honus Wagner	157
1912	Tris Speaker	192	1912	Heinie Zimmerman	159
1913	Joe Jackson	194	1913	Gavvy Cravath	171
1914	Eddie Collins	174	1914	Gavvy Cravath	168
1915	Ty Cobb	193	1915	Gavvy Cravath	173
1916	Tris Speaker	189	1916	Gavvy Cravath	153
1917	Ty Cobb	199	1917	Gavvy Cravath	159
1918	Ty Cobb	177	1918	Edd Roush	141
1919	Babe Ruth	214	1919	Heinie Groh	147
1920	Babe Ruth	281	1920	Rogers Hornsby	179
1921	Babe Ruth	253	1921	Rogers Hornsby	187
1922	Babe Ruth	188	1922	Rogers Hornsby	202
1923	Babe Ruth	266	1923	Rogers Hornsby	185
1924	Babe Ruth	233	1924	Rogers Hornsby	229
1925	Tris Speaker	169	1925	Rogers Hornsby	221
1926	Babe Ruth	239	1926	Hack Wilson	152
1927	Babe Ruth	230	1927	Rogers Hornsby	178
1928	Babe Ruth	209	1928	Rogers Hornsby	205
1929	Babe Ruth	183	1929	Rogers Hornsby	181
1930	Babe Ruth	215	1930	Hack Wilson	183
1931	Babe Ruth	220	1931	Chuck Klein	159
1932	Jimmie Foxx	213	1932	Mel Ott	176
1933	Jimmie Foxx	200	1933	Chuck Klein	187
1934	Lou Gehrig	200	1934	Mel Ott	168
1935	Jimmie Foxx	184	1935	Arky Vaughan	202
1936	Lou Gehrig	190	1936	Mel Ott	183
1937	Lou Gehrig	183	1937	Dolph Camilli	183
1938	Jimmie Foxx	190	1938	Mel Ott	185
1939	Jimmie Foxx	193	1939	Johnny Mize	185
1940	Hank Greenberg	180	1940	Johnny Mize	180
1941	Ted Williams	260	1941	Dolph Camilli	170
1942	Ted Williams	232	1942	Mel Ott	168
1943	Charlie Keller	170	1943	Stan Musial	177
1944	Bob Johnson	174	1944	Stan Musial	176
1945	Roy Cullenbine	151	1945	Tommy Holmes	169
1946	Ted Williams	235	1946	Stan Musial	179
1947	Ted Williams	223	1947	Ralph Kiner	175
1948	Ted Williams	199	1948	Stan Musial	202
1949	Ted Williams	204	1949	Ralph Kiner	189
1950	Larry Doby	151	1950	Stan Musial	167

AMERICAN LEAGUE			NATIONAL LEAGUE		
1951	Ted Williams	180	1951	Ralph Kiner	193
1952	Larry Doby	155	1952	Stan Musial	167
1953	Al Rosen	171	1953	Stan Musial	171
1954	Ted Williams	231	1954	Duke Snider	172
1955	Mickey Mantle	179	1955	Duke Snider	173
1956	Mickey Mantle	204	1956	Duke Snider	165
1957	Ted Williams	255	1957	Stan Musial	173
1958	Ted Williams	190	1958	Willie Mays	161
1959	Al Kaline	154	1959	Hank Aaron	167
1960	Mickey Mantle	160	1960	Frank Robinson	170
1961	Norm Cash	207	1961	Frank Robinson	162
1962	Mickey Mantle	205	1962	Frank Robinson	172
1963	Bob Allison	154	1963	Hank Aaron	176
1964	Mickey Mantle	182	1964	Willie Mays	175
1965	Carl Yastrzemski	160	1965	Willie Mays	187
1966	Frank Robinson	190	1966	Dick Allen	179
1967	Carl Yastrzemski	199	1967	Dick Allen	176
1968	Carl Yastrzemski	183	1968	Willie McCovey	174
1969	Harmon Killebrew	185	1969	Willie McCovey	213
1970	Carl Yastrzemski	189	1970	Willie McCovey	187
1971	Bobby Murcer	173	1971	Hank Aaron	197
1972	Dick Allen	201	1972	Billy Williams	175
1973	John Mayberry	153	1973	Willie Stargell	179
1974	Dick Allen	157	1974	Joe Morgan	163
1975	John Mayberry	166	1975	Joe Morgan	181
1976	Hal McRae	143	1976	Joe Morgan	196
1977	Rod Carew	164	1977	Reggie Smith	170
1978	Jim Rice	154	1978	Jeff Burroughs	175
1979	Fred Lynn	172	1979	Mike Schmidt	163
1980	George Brett	193	1980	Mike Schmidt	176
1981	Dwight Evans	165	1981	Mike Schmidt	202
1982	Dwight Evans	150	1982	Mike Schmidt	168
1983	Wade Boggs	150	1983	Mike Schmidt	161
1984	Eddie Murray	150	1984	Mike Schmidt	158
1985	George Brett	171	1985	Pedro Guerrero	175
1986	Wade Boggs	151	1986	Mike Schmidt	155
1987	Wade Boggs	171	1987	Jack Clark	190
1988	Wade Boggs	170	1988	Darryl Strawberry	160
1989	Fred McGriff	156	1989	Kevin Mitchell	184
1990	Rickey Henderson	175	1990	Barry Bonds	166
1991	Frank Thomas	176	1991	Barry Bonds	164
1992	Frank Thomas	169	1992	Barry Bonds	211
1993	John Olerud	181	1993	Barry Bonds	206

	OQ	PLAYER	YEAR	TEAM	LG
1.	281	Babe Ruth	1920	NY	AL
2.	266	Babe Ruth	1923	NY	AL
3.	260	Ted Williams	1941	BOS	AL
4.	255	Ted Williams	1957	BOS	AL
5.	253	Babe Ruth	1921	NY	AL
6.	249	Ross Barnes	1876	CHI	NL
	249	Fred Dunlap	1884	SL	UA
8.	239	Babe Ruth	1926	NY	AL
9.	235	Ted Williams	1946	BOS	AL
	235	Mickey Mantle	1957	NY	AL
11.	233	Babe Ruth	1924	NY	AL
12.	232	Ted Williams	1942	BOS	AL
13.	231	Ted Williams	1954	BOS	AL
14.	230	Babe Ruth	1927	NY	AL
15.	229	Rogers Hornsby	1924	SL	NL
16.	224	Tip O'Neill	1887	SL	AA
17.	223	Ted Williams	1947	NY	AL
18.	221	Rogers Hornsby	1925	SL	NL
19.	220	Babe Ruth	1931	NY	AL
20.	219	Lou Gehrig	1927	NY	AL
21.	215	Babe Ruth	1930	NY	AL
22.	214	King Kelly	1886	CHI	NL
	214	Babe Ruth	1919	BOS	AL
24.	213	Jimmie Foxx	1932	PHI	AL
	213	Willie McCovey	1969	SF	NL
26.	211	Barry Bonds	1992	PIT	NL
27.	210	Pete Browning	1882	LOU	AA
	210	Ty Cobb	1910	DET	AL
29.	209	Babe Ruth	1928	NY	AL
30.	207	Dan Brouthers	1886	DET	NL
	207	Norm Cash	1961	DET	AL
32.	206	Barry Bonds	1993	SF	NL
33.	205	Rogers Hornsby	1928	BOS	NL
	205	Babe Ruth	1932	NY	AL
	205	Mickey Mantle	1962	NY	AL
36.	204	Mickey Mantle	1956	NY	AL
37.	202	Rogers Hornsby	1922	SL	NL
	202	Arky Vaughan	1935	PIT	NL
	202	Stan Musial	1948	SL	NL
	202	Mickey Mantle	1961	NY	AL
	202	Mike Schmidt	1981	PHI	NL
42.	201	Dick Allen	1972	CHI	AL
43.	200	John McGraw	1899	BAL	NL
	200	Lou Gehrig	1930	NY	AL
	200	Jimmie Foxx	1933	PHI	AL
	200	Lou Gehrig	1934	NY	AL

RANK	OQ	PLAYER	YRS QUALIFIED
1.	218	Babe Ruth	15
2.	210	Ted Williams	13
3.	177	Lou Gehrig	14
	177	Rogers Hornsby	14
5.	176	Mickey Mantle	14
6.	174	Dan Brouthers	13
7.	173	Jimmie Foxx	14
8.	170	Ty Cobb	19
9.	169	Willie McCovey	9
10.	168	Johnny Mize	8
11.	166	Stan Musial	17
12.	164	Dick Allen	10
	164	Joe Jackson	9
14.	163	Barry Bonds*	7
	163	Pete Browning	9
16.	162	Mel Ott	18
17.	161	Tris Speaker	19
18.	160	Mike Schmidt	14
	160	Hank Greenberg	9
20.	159	Harmon Killebrew	12
	159	Hack Wilson	6
	159	Charlie Keller	6
23.	158	Willie Mays	18
24.	156	Ralph Kiner	9
25.	154	Frank Robinson	18
	154	Roger Connor	17
	154	Honus Wagner	17
	154	Ed Delahanty	13
	154	Billy Hamilton	11
	154	Fred McGriff*	6
31.	153	Willie Stargell	10
	153	Dolph Camilli	9
	153	Gavvy Cravath	7
34.	152	Hank Aaron	20
35.	151	Jack Fournier	6
	151	Dave Orr	5
37.	150	Duke Snider	9
	150	Frank Chance	5
	150	Benny Kauff	5
40.	149	John McGraw	6

*Active

PLAYER	SEASONS
Ty Cobb	15
Babe Ruth	15
Stan Musial	14
Mel Ott	14
Hank Aaron	13
Willie Mays	13
Ted Williams	13
Dan Brouthers	12
Lou Gehrig	12
Mickey Mantle	12
Tris Speaker	12
Jimmie Foxx	11
Frank Robinson	11
Mike Schmidt	11
Honus Wagner	11
Roger Connor	10
Rogers Hornsby	10
Cap Anson	9
Ed Delahanty	9
Harmon Killebrew	9
Willie McCovey	8
Johnny Mize	8
Dick Allen	7
Pete Browning	7
Dolph Camilli	7
Sam Crawford	7
Hank Greenberg	7
Joe Jackson	7
Nap Lajoie	7
Harry Stovey	7
Jesse Burkett	6
Eddie Collins	6
Elmer Flick	6
George Gore	6
Billy Hamilton	6
Harry Heilmann	6
Eddie Mathews	6
Willie Stargell	6

PLAYER	SEASONS
Ty Cobb	18
Mel Ott	18
Frank Robinson	18
Tris Speaker	18
Hank Aaron	17
Stan Musial	17
Eddie Collins	15
Willie Mays	15
Babe Ruth	15
Honus Wagner	15
Cap Anson	14
Sam Crawford	14
Jimmie Foxx	14
Rogers Hornsby	14
Mickey Mantle	14
Lou Gehrig	13
Mike Schmidt	13
Ted Williams	13
Dan Brouthers	12
Roger Connor	12
Harry Heilmann	12
Harmon Killebrew	12
Nap Lajoie	12
Billy Hamilton	11
Reggie Jackson	11
Bob Johnson	11
Al Kaline	11
Dick Allen	10
George Brett	10
Jesse Burkett	10
Ed Delahanty	10
Joe DiMaggio	10
Sherry Magee	10
Eddie Mathews	10
Harry Stovey	10
Paul Waner	10

SEASONS	PLAYER	POSITION
15	Eddie Collins	2B
15	Joe Morgan	2B
15	Babe Ruth	RF-LF
13	Hank Aaron	RF-CF
13	Willie Mays	CF
13	Stan Musial	LF-1B-RF-CF
12	Rogers Hornsby	2B-3B-SS
12	Mike Schmidt	3B
12	Honus Wagner	SS-RF
12	Ted Williams	LF-RF
11	Ty Cobb	CF-RF
11	Nap Lajoie	2B-1B
11	Mickey Mantle	CF-1B
11	Frank Robinson	RF-LF-1B-DH
10	Mickey Cochrane	C
10	Joe Cronin	SS
10	Eddie Mathews	3B
9	Yogi Berra	C
9	Lou Gehrig	1B
9	Willie McCovey	1B-LF
9	Arky Vaughan	SS
8	Earl Averill	CF
8	Home Run Baker	3B
8	Ed Delahanty	LF-CF
8	Carlton Fisk	C
8	Jimmie Foxx	1B
8	George Gore	CF
8	Billy Hamilton	CF-LF
8	Rickey Henderson	LF-CF
8	Tris Speaker	CF
7	Cap Anson	1B-3B
7	Ernie Banks	SS
7	Dan Brouthers	1B
7	Pete Browning	CF-LF-2B
7	Roger Connor	1B-3B
7	Sam Crawford	CF-RF
7	Joe DiMaggio	CF
7	Sherry Magee	LF-CF
7	Joe Medwick	LF
7	Willie Stargell	LF-1B
7	Carl Yastrzemski	LF-1B

LEADING DESIGNATED HITTERS

Players listed in these tables are OQ qualifiers who played at least half their team's games at the defensive positions indicated.

For some seasons, no catchers qualified for OQ ranking (3 at bats + walks per games played by team). The league leader (marked by an asterisk) is considered the catcher with the highest OQ who caught at least half his team's games.

1973	Frank Robinson	135
1974	Frank Robinson	134
1975	Billy Williams	115
1976	Hal McRae	143
1977	Jim Rice	146
1978	Rico Carty	131
1979	Willie Horton	105
1980	Hal McRae	114
1981	Greg Luzinski	137
1982	Andre Thornton	136
1983	Ken Singleton	130
1984	Mike Easler	134
1985	Gorman Thomas	117
1986	Larry Parrish	125
1987	Brian Downing	129
1988	Brian Downing	123
1989	Brian Downing	111
1990	Dave Parker	111
1991	Frank Thomas	176
1992	Dave Winfield	136
1993	Paul Molitor	135

FIRST BASE				SECOND BASE		
1901	Buck Freeman	150		1901	Nap Lajoie	195
1902	Charlie Hickman	145		1902	Jimmy Williams	136
1903	Harry Davis	130		1903	Nap Lajoie	159
1904	Charlie Hickman	132		1904	Nap Lajoie	189
1905	Harry Davis	135		1905	Danny Murphy	127
1906	Harry Davis	150		1906	Nap Lajoie	155
1907	Harry Davis	128		1907	Nap Lajoie	128
1908	Claude Rossman	136		1908	Nap Lajoie	131
1909	Jake Stahl	150		1909	Nap Lajoie	148
1910	Jake Stahl	132		1910	Nap Lajoie	191
1911	Germany Schaefer	129		1911	Eddie Collins	156
1912	Stuffy McInnis	129		1912	Eddie Collins	159
1913	Stuffy McInnis	128		1913	Eddie Collins	162
1914	George Burns	115		1914	Eddie Collins	174
1915	Jack Fournier	166		1915	Eddie Collins	174
1916	Wally Pipp	124		1916	Eddie Collins	142
1917	George Sisler	142		1917	Eddie Collins	133
1918	George Sisler	143		1918	Eddie Collins	136
1919	George Sisler	147		1919	Eddie Collins	129
1920	George Sisler	178		1920	Eddie Collins	144
1921	George Sisler	139		1921	Eddie Collins	117
1922	George Sisler	171		1922	Eddie Collins	114
1923	Frank Brower	138		1923	Eddie Collins	143
1924	Earl Sheely	124		1924	Eddie Collins	136
1925	Lou Gehrig	126		1925	Eddie Collins	138
1926	Lou Gehrig	155		1926	Max Bishop	122
1927	Lou Gehrig	219		1927	Tony Lazzeri	126
1928	Lou Gehrig	192		1928	Max Bishop	137
1929	Jimmie Foxx	181		1929	Tony Lazzeri	151
1930	Lou Gehrig	200		1930	Charlie Gehringer	134
1931	Lou Gehrig	190		1931	Max Bishop	130
1932	Jimmie Foxx	213		1932	Tony Lazzeri	136
1933	Jimmie Foxx	200		1933	Max Bishop	140
1934	Lou Gehrig	200		1934	Charlie Gehringer	151
1935	Jimmie Foxx	184		1935	Buddy Myer	136
1936	Lou Gehrig	190		1936	Charlie Gehringer	142
1937	Lou Gehrig	183		1937	Charlie Gehringer	148
1938	Jimmie Foxx	190		1938	Buddy Myer	138
1939	Jimmie Foxx	193		1939	Charlie Gehringer	147
1940	Jimmie Foxx	157		1940	Charlie Gehringer	133

FIRST BASE

1941	Jimmie Foxx	146
1942	Les Fleming	143
1943	Rudy York	157
1944	Nick Etten	149
1945	Nick Etten	139
1946	Hank Greenberg	167
1947	Roy Cullenbine	144
1948	Ferris Fain	124
1949	Eddie Robinson	119
1950	Walt Dropo	135
1951	Ferris Fain	149
1952	Ferris Fain	146
1953	Mickey Vernon	141
1954	Mickey Vernon	129
1955	Mickey Vernon	126
1956	Bill Skowron	132
1957	Vic Wertz	136
1958	Gail Harris	120
1959	Vic Power	104
1960	Roy Sievers	150
1961	Norm Cash	207
1962	Norm Siebern	147
1963	Norm Cash	142
1964	Bob Allison	164
1965	Norm Cash	150
1966	Boog Powell	155
1967	Harmon Killebrew	188
1968	Mickey Mantle	150
1969	Mike Epstein	167
1970	Carl Yastrzemski	189
1971	Harmon Killebrew	150
1972	Dick Allen	201
1973	John Mayberry	153
1974	Dick Allen	157
1975	John Mayberry	166
1976	Rod Carew	140
1977	Rod Carew	164
1978	Andre Thornton	146
1979	Bruce Bochte	130
1980	Jason Thompson	139

SECOND BASE

1941	Joe Gordon	119
1942	Joe Gordon	152
1943	Joe Gordon	134
1944	Bobby Doerr	160
1945	Snuffy Stirnweiss	145
1946	Bobby Doerr	123
1947	Joe Gordon	130
1948	Bobby Doerr	134
1949	Bobby Doerr	132
1950	Bobby Doerr	123
1951	Bobby Avila	111
1952	Bobby Avila	119
1953	Billy Goodman	114
1954	Bobby Avila	136
1955	Bobby Avila	114
1956	Nellie Fox	91
1957	Nellie Fox	121
1958	Pete Runnels	136
1959	Pete Runnels	134
1960	Pete Runnels	117
1961	Jerry Lumpe	100
1962	Jerry Lumpe	108
1963	Jerry Lumpe	101
1964	Don Buford	97
1965	Felix Mantilla	126
1966	Bobby Knoop	99
1967	Dick McAuliffe	136
1968	Dick McAuliffe	132
1969	Mike Andrews	136
1970	Dave Johnson	112
1971	Dave Johnson	123
1972	Rod Carew	118
1973	Rod Carew	137
1974	Rod Carew	143
1975	Rod Carew	148
1976	Bobby Grich	130
1977	Don Money	116
1978	Willie Randolph	111
1979	Bobby Grich	133
1980	Willie Randolph	135

FIRST BASE

1981	Eddie Murray	144
1982	Eddie Murray	147
1983	Eddie Murray	147
1984	Eddie Murray	150
1985	Don Mattingly	142
1986	Don Mattingly	146
1987	Mark McGwire	147
1988	Fred McGriff	149
1989	Fred McGriff	156
1990	Cecil Fielder	158

1991	Rafael Palmeiro	141
1992	Frank Thomas	169
1993	John Olerud	181

SECOND BASE

1981	Bobby Grich	150
1982	Bobby Grich	122
1983	Lou Whitaker	123
1984	Lou Whitaker	109
1985	Toby Harrah	136
1986	Tony Bernazard	114
1987	Willie Randolph	120
1988	Julio Franco	110
1989	Julio Franco	132
1990	Julio Franco	117

1991	Lou Whitaker	141
1992	Lou Whitaker	135
1993	Roberto Alomar	134

SHORTSTOP

1901	Kid Elberfeld	132
1902	George Davis	125
1903	Fred Parent	123
1904	Fred Parent	121
1905	George Davis	124
1906	Bobby Wallace	122
1907	Kid Elberfeld	114
1908	Bobby Wallace	118
1909	Donie Bush	130
1910	Donie Bush	124

1911	Steve Yerkes	102
1912	Donie Bush	115
1913	Jack Barry	110
1914	Donie Bush	116
1915	Ray Chapman	118
1916	Roger Peckinpaugh	109
1917	Ray Chapman	134
1918	Ray Chapman	132
1919	Roger Peckinpaugh	125
1920	Ray Chapman	117

THIRD BASE

1901	Jimmy Collins	135
1902	Bill Bradley	140
1903	Bill Bradley	145
1904	Bill Bradley	126
1905	Jimmy Collins	120
1906	Frank LaPorte	110
1907	Jimmy Collins	111
1908	Hobe Ferris	106
1909	Home Run Baker	141
1910	Home Run Baker	121

1911	Home Run Baker	141
1912	Home Run Baker	160
1913	Home Run Baker	158
1914	Home Run Baker	141
1915	Ossie Vitt	111
1916	Larry Gardner	125
1917	Home Run Baker	114
1918	Home Run Baker	124
1919	Larry Gardner	109
1920	Larry Gardner	109

SHORTSTOP

1921	Joe Sewell	121
1922	Chick Galloway	109
1923	Joe Sewell	150
1924	Topper Rigney	124
1925	Joe Sewell	111
1926	Joe Sewell	117
1927	Joe Sewell	108
1928	Joe Sewell	113
1929	Joe Cronin	117
1930	Joe Cronin	135
1931	Joe Cronin	130
1932	Joe Cronin	128
1933	Joe Cronin	126
1934	Luke Appling	109
1935	Luke Appling	127
1936	Luke Appling	146
1937	Joe Cronin	125
1938	Joe Cronin	142
1939	Joe Cronin	133
1940	Joe Cronin	130
1941	Joe Cronin	142
1942	Johnny Pesky	117
1943	Luke Appling	141
1944	Lou Boudreau	139
1945	Eddie Lake	147
1946	Johnny Pesky	127
1947	Lou Boudreau	123
1948	Lou Boudreau	160
1949	Eddie Joost	143
1950	Vern Stephens	120
1951	Eddie Joost	137
1952	Eddie Joost	134
1953	Phil Rizzuto	108
1954	Pete Runnels	114
1955	Harvey Kuenn	105
1956	Gil McDougald	125
1957	Gil McDougald	119
1958	Don Buddin	109
1959	Woodie Held	114
1960	Ron Hansen	115

THIRD BASE

1921	Larry Gardner	114
1922	Jimmy Dykes	107
1923	Willie Kamm	114
1924	Gene Robertson	106
1925	Willie Kamm	110
1926	Willie Kamm	113
1927	Sammy Hale	102
1928	Willie Kamm	116
1929	Marty McManus	109
1930	Marty McManus	122
1931	Red Kress	121
1932	Willie Kamm	109
1933	Mike Higgins	127
1934	Mike Higgins	130
1935	Harlond Clift	123
1936	Harlond Clift	136
1937	Harlond Clift	142
1938	Harlond Clift	148
1939	Red Rolfe	129
1940	Harlond Clift	130
1941	Harlond Clift	123
1942	Bob Estalella	137
1943	Mike Higgins	114
1944	Mike Higgins	132
1945	Oscar Grimes	127
1946	George Kell	119
1947	George Kell	118
1948	Ken Keltner	141
1949	George Kell	132
1950	Al Rosen	140
1951	Eddie Yost	134
1952	Al Rosen	148
1953	Al Rosen	171
1954	Al Rosen	151
1955	Eddie Yost	123
1956	Ray Boone	141
1957	Eddie Yost	112
1958	Eddie Yost	105
1959	Eddie Yost	148
1960	Eddie Yost	132

SHORTSTOP

1961	Woodie Held	122
1962	Tom Tresh	115
1963	Ed Bressoud	120
1964	Jim Fregosi	132
1965	Zoilo Versalles	117
1966	Dick McAuliffe	151
1967	Rico Petrocelli	121
1968	Jim Fregosi	109
1969	Rico Petrocelli	174
1970	Rico Petrocelli	124
1971	Leo Cardenas	113
1972	Danny Thompson	100
1973	Fred Patek	86
1974	Toby Harrah	109
1975	Toby Harrah	141
1976	Toby Harrah	118
1977	Rick Burleson	94
1978	Roy Smalley	122
1979	Roy Smalley	113
1980	Robin Yount	118
1981	Robin Yount	105
1982	Robin Yount	147
1983	Robin Yount	136
1984	Cal Ripken	134
1985	Cal Ripken	117
1986	Cal Ripken	116
1987	Alan Trammell	139
1988	Cal Ripken	127
1989	Jody Reed	116
1990	Alan Trammell	125
1991	Cal Ripken	143
1992	Travis Fryman	101
1993	Travis Fryman	126

THIRD BASE

1961	Brooks Robinson	97
1962	Al Smith	121
1963	Pete Ward	129
1964	Brooks Robinson	140
1965	Brooks Robinson	122
1966	Harmon Killebrew	165
1967	Brooks Robinson	123
1968	Ken McMullen	118
1969	Harmon Killebrew	185
1970	Harmon Killebrew	168
1971	Sal Bando	136
1972	Rico Petrocelli	118
1973	Sal Bando	137
1974	Sal Bando	126
1975	George Brett	118
1976	George Brett	132
1977	Toby Harrah	136
1978	Doug DeCinces	133
1979	George Brett	138
1980	George Brett	193
1981	George Brett	131
1982	Doug DeCinces	140
1983	Wade Boggs	150
1984	Buddy Bell	125
1985	George Brett	171
1986	Wade Boggs	151
1987	Wade Boggs	171
1988	Wade Boggs	170
1989	Wade Boggs	143
1990	Edgar Martinez	128
1991	Wade Boggs	140
1992	Edgar Martinez	150
1993	Robin Ventura	121

LEFT FIELD

1901	Mike Donlin	145
1902	Ed Delahanty	189
1903	Topsy Hartsel	162
1904	Kip Selbach	130
1905	Topsy Hartsel	154
1906	George Stone	178
1907	Topsy Hartsel	159
1908	Matty McIntyre	153
1909	Pat Dougherty	137
1910	Birdie Cree	136
1911	Birdie Cree	156
1912	Amos Strunk	121
1913	Duffy Lewis	111
1914	Tilly Walker	138
1915	Bobby Veach	141
1916	Joe Jackson	154
1917	Bobby Veach	150
1918	Joe Wood	124
1919	Babe Ruth	214
1920	Joe Jackson	167
1921	Babe Ruth	253
1922	Babe Ruth	188
1923	Ken Williams	176
1924	Ken Williams	150
1925	Al Wingo	152
1926	Goose Goslin	147
1927	Ken Williams	140
1928	Goose Goslin	171
1929	Al Simmons	156
1930	Al Simmons	174
1931	Al Simmons	176
1932	Al Simmons	130
1933	Bob Johnson	138
1934	Bob Johnson	138
1935	Joe Vosmik	138
1936	John Stone	138
1937	Bob Johnson	150
1938	Jeff Heath	138
1939	Bob Johnson	155
1940	Hank Greenberg	180

CENTER FIELD

1901	Dummy Hoy	130
1902	Jimmy Ryan	129
1903	Jimmy Barrett	143
1904	Chick Stahl	145
1905	Harry Bay	122
1906	Elmer Flick	148
1907	Sam Crawford	154
1908	Sam Crawford	154
1909	Sam Crawford	153
1910	Ty Cobb	210
1911	Ty Cobb	196
1912	Tris Speaker	192
1913	Ty Cobb	191
1914	Tris Speaker	173
1915	Ty Cobb	193
1916	Tris Speaker	189
1917	Ty Cobb	198
1918	Ty Cobb	177
1919	Ty Cobb	157
1920	Tris Speaker	181
1921	Ty Cobb	163
1922	Tris Speaker	185
1923	Tris Speaker	184
1924	Tris Speaker	144
1925	Tris Speaker	169
1926	Heinie Manush	147
1927	Earle Combs	136
1928	Red Barnes	127
1929	Earl Averill	137
1930	Earl Averill	135
1931	Earl Averill	151
1932	Earl Averill	143
1933	Dusty Cooke	124
1934	Earl Averill	152
1935	Earl Averill	123
1936	Earl Averill	157
1937	Joe DiMaggio	162
1938	Earl Averill	142
1939	Joe DiMaggio	177
1940	Joe DiMaggio	164

LEFT FIELD

CENTER FIELD

	LEFT FIELD			CENTER FIELD	
1941	Ted Williams	260	1941	Joe DiMaggio	179
1942	Ted Williams	232	1942	Walt Judnich	155
1943	Charlie Keller	170	1943	Stan Spence	128
1944	Bob Johnson	174	1944	Stan Spence	146
1945	Bob Johnson	126	1945	Bob Estalella	143
1946	Ted Williams	235	1946	Joe DiMaggio	141
1947	Ted Williams	223	1947	Joe DiMaggio	146
1948	Ted Williams	199	1948	Joe DiMaggio	152
1949	Ted Williams	204	1949	Larry Doby	126
1950	Hoot Evers	139	1950	Larry Doby	151
1951	Ted Williams	180	1951	Larry Doby	156
1952	Gene Woodling	141	1952	Larry Doby	155
1953	Gene Woodling	147	1953	Mickey Mantle	143
1954	Ted Williams	231	1954	Mickey Mantle	156
1955	Roy Sievers	130	1955	Mickey Mantle	179
1956	Ted Williams	189	1956	Mickey Mantle	204
1957	Ted Williams	255	1957	Mickey Mantle	235
1958	Ted Williams	190	1958	Mickey Mantle	188
1959	Jim Lemon	128	1959	Al Kaline	154
1960	Jim Lemon	131	1960	Mickey Mantle	160
1961	Rocky Colavito	161	1961	Mickey Mantle	202
1962	Harmon Killebrew	146	1962	Mickey Mantle	205
1963	Carl Yastrzemski	151	1963	Tom Tresh	141
1964	Boog Powell	175	1964	Mickey Mantle	182
1965	Carl Yastrzemski	160	1965	Tom Tresh	129
1966	Carl Yastrzemski	131	1966	Al Kaline	163
1967	Carl Yastrzemski	199	1967	Paul Balir	131
1968	Carl Yastrzemski	183	1968	Rick Monday	136
1969	Frank Howard	168	1969	Reggie Smith	144
1970	Frank Howard	169	1970	Reggie Smith	130
1971	Don Buford	154	1971	Bobby Murcer	173
1972	Carlos May	149	1972	Bobby Murcer	159
1973	Johnny Briggs	123	1973	Amos Otis	130
1974	Larry Hisle	125	1974	Ken Henderson	130
1975	Steve Braun	127	1975	Fred Lynn	158
1976	Roy White	124	1976	Fred Lynn	134
1977	Mitchell Page	144	1977	Larry Hisle	134
1978	Jim Rice	154	1978	Amos Otis	145
1979	Jim Rice	147	1979	Fred Lynn	172
1980	Ben Oglivie	140	1980	Chet Lemon	122

LEFT FIELD

1981	Rickey Henderson	138
1982	Dave Winfield	132
1983	Jim Rice	136
1984	Rickey Henderson	134
1985	Mike Young	125
1986	Jim Rice	127
1987	George Bell	135
1988	Mike Greenwell	154
1989	Rickey Henderson	134
1990	Rickey Henderson	175
1991	Rickey Henderson	129
1992	Rickey Henderson	148
1993	Rickey Henderson	146

CENTER FIELD

1981	Gorman Thomas	136
1982	Fred Lynn	135
1983	Lloyd Moseby	129
1984	Lloyd Moseby	126
1985	Rickey Henderson	149
1986	Kirby Puckett	127
1987	Kirby Puckett	122
1988	Kirby Puckett	138
1989	Robin Yount	139
1990	Ken Griffey Jr	127
1991	Ken Griffey Jr	146
1992	Ken Griffey Jr	135
1993	Ken Griffey Jr	162

RIGHT FIELD

1901	Socks Seybold	145
1902	Socks Seybold	141
1903	Sam Crawford	148
1904	Elmer Flick	152
1905	Elmer Flick	161
1906	Sam Crawford	130
1907	Ty Cobb	155
1908	Ty Cobb	161
1909	Ty Cobb	191
1910	Danny Murphy	134
1911	Joe Jackson	190
1912	Joe Jackson	186
1913	Joe Jackson	194
1914	Sam Crawford	157
1915	Joe Jackson	141
1916	Harry Heilmann	125
1917	Braggo Roth	125
1918	Harry Hooper	141
1919	Elmer Smith	123
1920	Babe Ruth	281

CATCHER

1901	Bill Clarke	94
1902	Harry Bemis	*110
1903	O. Schreckengost	* 96
1904	Joe Sugden	*103
1905	Lou Criger	*109
1906	Harry Bemis	*111
1907	Nig Clarke	*126
1908	Nig Clarke	*114
1909	Bill Carrigan	*121
1910	Ted Easterly	*121
1911	Oscar Stanage	83
1912	Jack Lapp	*110
1913	Bill Carrigan	*102
1914	Wally Schang	*128
1915	Ray Schalk	114
1916	Les Nunamaker	*135
1917	Ray Schalk	101
1918	Steve O'Neill	105
1919	Steve O'Neill	126
1920	Steve O'Neill	128

RIGHT FIELD

1921	Harry Heilmann	162
1922	Harry Heilmann	165
1923	Babe Ruth	266
1924	Babe Ruth	233
1925	Harry Heilmann	157
1926	Babe Ruth	239
1927	Babe Ruth	230
1928	Babe Ruth	209
1929	Babe Ruth	183
1930	Babe Ruth	215
1931	Babe Ruth	220
1932	Babe Ruth	205
1933	Babe Ruth	175
1934	Babe Ruth	164
1935	Pete Fox	125
1936	George Selkirk	136
1937	Wally Moses	127
1938	Ben Chapman	129
1939	Ted Williams	166
1940	Charlie Keller	144
1941	Jeff Heath	150
1942	Chet Laabs	149
1943	Roy Cullenbine	143
1944	Roy Cullenbine	139
1945	Roy Cullenbine	151
1946	Hank Edwards	137
1947	Tommy Henrich	134
1948	Tommy Henrich	143
1949	Vic Wertz	123
1950	Vic Wertz	138
1951	Vic Wertz	139
1952	Vic Wertz	146
1953	Vic Wertz	130
1954	Cal Abrams	128
1955	Al Kaline	155
1956	Al Kaline	135
1957	Jackie Jensen	130
1958	Rocky Colavito	176
1959	Jackie Jensen	140
1960	Roger Maris	152

CATCHER

1921	Wally Schang	131
1922	Steve O'Neill	128
1923	Muddy Ruel	109
1924	Hank Severeid	100
1925	Mickey Cochrane	115
1926	Luke Sewell	72
1927	Mickey Cochrane	133
1928	Mickey Cochrane	131
1929	Mickey Cochrane	129
1930	Mickey Cochrane	138
1931	Mickey Cochrane	152
1932	Mickey Cochrane	142
1933	Mickey Cochrane	166
1934	Mickey Cochrane	124
1935	Mickey Cochrane	142
1936	Bill Dickey	152
1937	Bill Dickey	166
1938	Rudy York	124
1939	Bill Dickey	135
1940	Frankie Hayes	125
1941	Frankie Hayes	119
1942	Bill Dickey	*108
1943	Jake Earley	111
1944	Frankie Hayes	103
1945	Frankie Hayes	108
1946	Aaron Robinson	*147
1947	Jim Hegan	* 94
1948	Birdie Tebbetts	105
1949	Birdie Tebbetts	98
1950	Yogi Berra	127
1951	Yogi Berra	121
1952	Yogi Berra	130
1953	Yogi Berra	133
1954	Yogi Berra	129
1955	Yogi Berra	119
1956	Yogi Berra	135
1957	Yogi Berra	114
1958	Sherm Lollar	126
1959	Yogi Berra	119
1960	Earl Battey	110

RIGHT FIELD

CATCHER

1961	Roger Maris	158	1961	John Romano	127
1962	Bob Allison	138	1962	John Romano	130
1963	Bob Allison	154	1963	Elston Howard	134
1964	Tony Oliva	142	1964	Elston Howard	124
1965	Rocky Colavito	142	1965	John Romano	*126
1966	Frank Robinson	190	1966	Bill Freehan	93
1967	Frank Robinson	181	1967	Bill Freehan	141
1968	Ken Harrelson	160	1968	Bill Freehan	139
1969	Reggie Jackson	178	1969	Bill Freehan	110
1970	Frank Robinson	149	1970	Ray Fosse	125
1971	Al Kaline	153	1971	Bill Freehan	128
1972	Reggie Smith	148	1972	Carlton Fisk	161
1973	Reggie Smith	149	1973	Thurman Munson	128
1974	Reggie Jackson	154	1974	Fran Healy	110
1975	Ken Singleton	145	1975	Gene Tenace	140
1976	Reggie Jackson	138	1976	Carlton Fisk	117
1977	Ken Singleton	155	1977	Carlton Fisk	142
1978	Ken Singleton	143	1978	Carlton Fisk	129
1979	Sixto Lezcano	157	1979	Darrell Porter	145
1980	Reggie Jackson	161	1980	Carlton Fisk	113
1981	Dwight Evans	165	1981	Jim Sundberg	113
1982	Dwight Evans	150	1982	Lance Parrish	126
1983	Dwight Evans	115	1983	Carlton Fisk	129
1984	Dwight Evans	146	1984	Lance Parrish	101
1985	Jesse Barfield	136	1985	Rich Gedman	122
1986	Jesse Barfield	138	1986	Rich Gedman	99
1987	Dwight Evans	154	1987	Matt Nokes	120
1988	Jose Canseco	154	1988	B J Surhoff	77
1989	Ruben Sierra	136	1989	Carlton Fisk	*125
1990	Jose Canseco	145	1990	Carlton Fisk	125
1991	Danny Tartabull	159	1991	Mickey Tettleton	141
1992	Tom Brunansky	123	1992	Mickey Tettleton	140
1993	Tim Salmon	139	1993	Chris Hoiles	156

FIRST BASE

1876	Cal McVey	138
1877	Deacon White	189
1878	Joe Start	147
1879	Joe Start	133
1880	Cap Anson	149
1881	Cap Anson	190
1882	Dan Brouthers	188
1883	Dan Brouthers	180
1884	Dan Brouthers	183
1885	Dan Brouthers	194
1886	Dan Brouthers	207
1887	Dan Brouthers	170
1888	Cap Anson	180
1889	Roger Connor	169
1890	Cap Anson	153
1891	Roger Connor	149
1892	Roger Connor	169
1893	Roger Connor	134
1894	Dan Brouthers	135
1895	Roger Connor	143
1896	Cap Anson	117
1897	Nap Lajoie	141
1898	Bill Joyce	130
1899	Fred Tenney	134
1900	Jake Beckley	124
1901	Joe Kelley	128
1902	Fred Tenney	147
1903	Frank Chance	156
1904	Frank Chance	141
1905	Frank Chance	168
1906	Frank Chance	162
1907	Tim Jordan	137
1908	Tim Jordan	128
1909	Dick Hoblitzel	137
1910	Ed Konetchy	140

SECOND BASE

1876	Ross Barnes	249
1877	Joe Gerhardt	115
1878	Johnny Peters	112
1879	Jack Farrell	107
1880	Fred Dunlap	133
1881	Fred Dunlap	143
1882	Fred Dunlap	111
1883	Jack Burdock	141
1884	Fred Pfeffer	152
1885	Fred Dunlap	117
1886	Fred Dunlap	120
1887	Fred Pfeffer	115
1888	Fred Pfeffer	117
1889	Hardy Richardson	122
1890	Hub Collins	129
1891	Cupid Childs	130
1892	Cupid Childs	159
1893	Cupid Childs	147
1894	Cupid Childs	136
1895	Bid McPhee	120
1896	Cupid Childs	150
1897	Cupid Childs	133
1898	Nap Lajoie	125
1899	Tom Daly	133
1900	Nap Lajoie	130
1901	Tom Daly	135
1902	Claude Ritchey	121
1903	Claude Ritchey	117
1904	Miller Huggins	131
1905	Miller Huggins	127
1906	Miller Huggins	126
1907	Ed Abbaticchio	121
1908	Johnny Evers	152
1909	Larry Doyle	134
1910	Johnny Evers	132

FIRST BASE

SECOND BASE

1911	Ed Konetchy	130		1911	Larry Doyle	154
1912	Ed Konetchy	130		1912	Johnny Evers	142
1913	Vic Saier	142		1913	Jim Viox	137
1914	Vic Saier	138		1914	Johnny Evers	127
1915	Fred Luderus	145		1915	Larry Doyle	134
1916	Hal Chase	141		1916	Larry Doyle	120
1917	Fred Luderus	120		1917	Larry Doyle	114
1918	Jake Daubert	133		1918	Lee Magee	119
1919	Fred Luderus	132		1919	Milt Stock	120
1920	Jack Fournier	127		1920	Rogers Hornsby	179
1921	Jack Fournier	140		1921	Rogers Hornsby	187
1922	Ray Grimes	162		1922	Rogers Hornsby	202
1923	Jack Fournier	156		1923	Rogers Hornsby	185
1924	Jack Fournier	158		1924	Rogers Hornsby	229
1925	Jack Fournier	160		1925	Rogers Hornsby	221
1926	George Grantham	141		1926	Rogers Hornsby	130
1927	Jim Bottomley	141		1927	Rogers Hornsby	178
1928	Jim Bottomley	164		1928	Rogers Hornsby	205
1929	Jim Bottomley	138		1929	Rogers Hornsby	181
1930	Bill Terry	155		1930	George Grantham	132
1931	Bill Terry	144		1931	Tony Cuccinello	118
1932	Don Hurst	154		1932	George Grantham	115
1933	Rip Collins	130		1933	Frankie Frisch	117
1934	Rip Collins	164		1934	Frankie Frisch	106
1935	Rip Collins	145		1935	Billy Herman	127
1936	Dolph Camilli	179		1936	Billy Herman	131
1937	Dolph Camilli	183		1937	Billy Herman	135
1938	Johnny Mize	179		1938	Lonny Frey	100
1939	Johnny Mize	185		1939	Lonny Frey	130
1940	Johnny Mize	180		1940	Lonny Frey	111
1941	Dolph Camilli	170		1941	Billy Herman	110
1942	Johnny Mize	155		1942	Lonny Frey	118
1943	Roy Sanders	134		1943	Billy Herman	133
1944	Frank McCormick	135		1944	Pete Coscarart	94
1945	Phil Cavarretta	164		1945	Eddie Stanky	129
1946	Stan Musial	179		1946	Eddie Stanky	142
1947	Johnny Mize	157		1947	Bill Rigney	104
1948	Johnny Mize	156		1948	Jackie Robinson	119
1949	Elbie Fletcher	123		1949	Jackie Robinson	153
1950	Earl Torgeson	139		1950	Eddie Stanky	142

FIRST BASE

1951	Gil Hodges	141
1952	Gil Hodges	151
1953	Gil Hodges	143
1954	Ted Kluszewski	166
1955	Stan Musial	151
1956	Joe Adcock	141
1957	Stan Musial	173
1958	Stan Musial	151
1959	Frank Robinson	155
1960	Frank Robinson	170
1961	Orlando Cepeda	145
1962	Bill White	129
1963	Orlando Cepeda	155
1964	Orlando Cepeda	147
1965	Willie McCovey	158
1966	Willie McCovey	168
1967	Willie McCovey	160
1968	Willie McCovey	174
1969	Willie McCovey	213
1970	Willie McCovey	187
1971	Lee May	137
1972	Hank Aaron	160
1973	Willie McCovey	176
1974	Tony Perez	121
1975	Willie Stargell	144
1976	Bob Watson	134
1977	Willie McCovey	133
1978	Steve Garvey	131
1979	Keith Hernandez	152
1980	Keith Hernandez	150
1981	Keith Hernandez	146
1982	Jason Thompson	156
1983	Darrell Evans	147
1984	Keith Hernandez	146
1985	Jack Clark	152
1986	Keith Hernandez	139
1987	Jack Clark	190
1988	Will Clark	158
1989	Will Clark	165
1990	Eddie Murray	155
1991	Fred McGriff	154
1992	Fred McGriff	168
1993	Andres Galarraga	156

SECOND BASE

1951	Jackie Robinson	153
1952	Jackie Robinson	154
1953	Red Schoendienst	133
1954	Granny Hamner	114
1955	Red Schoendienst	94
1956	Jim Gilliam	119
1957	Red Schoendienst	110
1958	Johnny Temple	121
1959	Johnny Temple	120
1960	Bill Mazeroski	99
1961	Frank Bolling	95
1962	Charlie Neal	102
1963	Jim Gilliam	117
1964	Ron Hunt	110
1965	Pete Rose	130
1966	Joe Morgan	135
1967	Joe Morgan	133
1968	Denis Menke	112
1969	Joe Morgan	122
1970	Joe Morgan	119
1971	Joe Morgan	122
1972	Joe Morgan	149
1973	Joe Morgan	152
1974	Joe Morgan	163
1975	Joe Morgan	181
1976	Joe Morgan	196
1977	Joe Morgan	148
1978	Bill Madlock	136
1979	Davey Lopes	132
1980	Joe Morgan	121
1981	Joe Morgan	127
1982	Joe Morgan	140
1983	Joe Morgan	127
1984	Ryne Sandberg	141
1985	Ryne Sandberg	137
1986	Steve Sax	124
1987	Juan Samuel	120
1988	Ron Gant	117
1989	Ryne Sandberg	137
1990	Ryne Sandberg	144
1991	Ryne Sandberg	143
1992	Ryne Sandberg	146
1993	Robby Thompson	128

SHORTSTOP			THIRD BASE		
1876	Johnny Peters	144	1876	Cap Anson	165
1877	Ezra Sutton	112	1877	Cap Anson	138
1878	Bob Ferguson	147	1878	Cal McVey	128
1879	George Wright	120	1879	Ned Williamson	157
1880	Tommy Burns	129	1880	Roger Connor	160
1881	Tommy Burns	116	1881	Jim O'Rourke	134
1882	Jack Glasscock	135	1882	Ned Williamson	133
1883	Tommy Burns	122	1883	Ezra Sutton	144
1884	Tommy Burns	100	1884	Ned Williamson	173
1885	Sam Wise	129	1885	Ezra Sutton	134
1886	Jack Glasscock	138	1886	Deacon White	107
1887	Sam Wise	144	1887	Billy Nash	127
1888	Ned Williamson	141	1888	Billy Nash	137
1889	Jack Glasscock	130	1889	Billy Nash	113
1890	Ed McKean	139	1890	George Pinkney	146
1891	Herman Long	130	1891	Arlie Latham	123
1892	Bill Dahlen	125	1892	Billy Nash	111
1893	John McGraw	135	1893	George Davis	144
1894	Bill Dahlen	144	1894	Bill Joyce	178
1895	Hughie Jennings	130	1895	Bill Joyce	152
1896	Bill Dahlen	159	1896	Bill Joyce	164
1897	George Davis	137	1897	John McGraw	141
1898	Hughie Jennings	144	1898	John McGraw	159
1899	Bobby Wallace	125	1899	John McGraw	200
1900	George Davis	116	1900	Charlie Hickman	122
1901	George Davis	128	1901	Sammy Strang	113
1902	Bill Dahlen	113	1902	Tommy Leach	136
1903	Honus Wagner	159	1903	Harry Steinfeldt	145
1904	Honus Wagner	187	1904	Art Devlin	128
1905	Honus Wagner	172	1905	Art Devlin	105
1906	Honus Wagner	165	1906	Harry Steinfeldt	147
1907	Honus Wagner	179	1907	Dave Brain	128
1908	Honus Wagner	196	1908	Hans Lobert	137
1909	Honus Wagner	177	1909	Art Devlin	120
1910	Honus Wagner	135	1910	Bobby Byrne	127

SHORTSTOP

1911	Honus Wagner	157
1912	Honus Wagner	140
1913	Al Bridwell	105
1914	Buck Herzog	107
1915	Honus Wagner	124
1916	Art Fletcher	107
1917	Rogers Hornsby	158
1918	Charlie Hollocher	133
1919	Rabbit Maranville	112
1920	Art Fletcher	101
1921	Dave Bancroft	123
1922	Charlie Hollocher	120
1923	Dave Bancroft	116
1924	Travis Jackson	102
1925	Dave Bancroft	118
1926	Dave Bancroft	117
1927	Travis Jackson	125
1928	Travis Jackson	109
1929	Travis Jackson	117
1930	Travis Jackson	119
1931	Woody English	118
1932	Dick Bartell	116
1933	Arky Vaughan	146
1934	Arky Vaughan	157
1935	Arky Vaughan	202
1936	Arky Vaughan	158
1937	Arky Vaughan	133
1938	Arky Vaughan	148
1939	Arky Vaughan	119
1940	Arky Vaughan	136
1941	Billy Jurges	111
1942	Marty Marion	112
1943	Arky Vaughan	123
1944	Buddy Kerr	100
1945	Marty Marion	102
1946	Pee Wee Reese	122
1947	Pee Wee Reese	133
1948	Pee Wee Reese	111
1949	Pee Wee Reese	124
1950	Pee Wee Reese	108

THIRD BASE

1911	Hans Lobert	119
1912	Heinie Zimmerman	159
1913	Heinie Zimmerman	142
1914	Heinie Zimmerman	116
1915	Heinie Groh	123
1916	Rogers Hornsby	144
1917	Heinie Groh	142
1918	Heinie Groh	138
1919	Heinie Groh	147
1920	Heinie Groh	122
1921	Frankie Frisch	128
1922	Milt Stock	103
1923	Pie Traynor	123
1924	Pie Traynor	105
1925	Pie Traynor	116
1926	Les Bell	139
1927	Chuck Dressen	116
1928	Harvey Hendrick	131
1929	Pinky Whitney	118
1930	Fred Lindstrom	138
1931	Pie Traynor	111
1932	Pie Traynor	114
1933	Pepper Martin	141
1934	Pepper Martin	107
1935	Stan Hack	132
1936	Stan Hack	121
1937	Pinky Whitney	126
1938	Stan Hack	136
1939	Cookie Lavagetto	120
1940	Stan Hack	131
1941	Stan Hack	141
1942	Stan Hack	141
1943	Bob Elliott	132
1944	Bob Elliott	139
1945	Whitey Kurowski	141
1946	Whitey Kurowski	139
1947	Whitey Kurowski	153
1948	Bob Elliott	152
1949	Sid Gordon	146
1950	Tom Glaviano	135

SHORTSTOP

1951	Solly Hemus	117
1952	Solly Hemus	128
1953	Solly Hemus	118
1954	Pee Wee Reese	128
1955	Ernie Banks	139
1956	Ernie Banks	134
1957	Ernie Banks	147
1958	Ernie Banks	150
1959	Ernie Banks	152
1960	Ernie Banks	143
1961	Ernie Banks	125
1962	Leo Cardenas	102
1963	Dick Groat	113
1964	Denis Menke	141
1965	Leo Cardenas	124
1966	Denis Menke	122
1967	Gene Alley	107
1968	Dal Maxvill	99
1969	Denis Menke	120
1970	Denis Menke	126
1971	Maury Wills	90
1972	Chris Speier	122
1973	Chris Speier	100
1974	Dave Concepcion	104
1975	Chris Speier	121
1976	Dave Concepcion	110
1977	Garry Templeton	104
1978	Dave Concepcion	113
1979	Dave Concepcion	113
1980	Garry Templeton	106
1981	Dave Concepcion	116
1982	Dickie Thon	105
1983	Dickie Thon	120
1984	Dave Concepcion	89
1985	Ozzie Smith	106
1986	Ozzie Smith	105
1987	Ozzie Smith	112
1988	Barry Larkin	118
1989	Shawon Dunston	106
1990	Barry Larkin	106
1991	Barry Larkin	143
1992	Barry Larkin	134
1993	Jeff Blauser	125

THIRD BASE

1951	Bob Elliott	123
1952	Bobby Thomson	123
1953	Eddie Mathews	165
1954	Eddie Mathews	170
1955	Eddie Mathews	168
1956	Eddie Mathews	141
1957	Eddie Mathews	149
1958	Ken Boyer	124
1959	Eddie Mathews	157
1960	Eddie Mathews	161
1961	Eddie Mathews	148
1962	Eddie Mathews	141
1963	Eddie Mathews	156
1964	Ron Santo	170
1965	Ron Santo	150
1966	Dick Allen	179
1967	Dick Allen	176
1968	Ron Santo	141
1969	Ron Santo	147
1970	Tony Perez	160
1971	Joe Torre	168
1972	Ron Santo	149
1973	Darrell Evans	167
1974	Mike Schmidt	162
1975	Mike Schmidt	148
1976	Mike Schmidt	154
1977	Mike Schmidt	157
1978	Ron Cey	137
1979	Mike Schmidt	163
1980	Mike Schmidt	176
1981	Mike Schmidt	202
1982	Mike Schmidt	168
1983	Mike Schmidt	161
1984	Mike Schmidt	158
1985	Graig Nettles	126
1986	Mike Schmidt	155
1987	Mike Schmidt	147
1988	Bobby Bonilla	143
1989	Howard Johnson	159
1990	Chris Sabo	125
1991	Howard Johnson	145
1992	Gary Sheffield	162
1993	Matt Williams	129

LEFT FIELD

1876	George Hall	197
1877	Charley Jones	156
1878	Tom York	153
1879	Charley Jones	184
1880	Abner Dalrymple	150
1881	Tom York	145
1882	Abner Dalrymple	127
1883	George Wood	133
1884	Jim O'Rourke	162
1885	Abner Dalrymple	148
1886	Hardy Richardson	165
1887	George Wood	130
1888	Jim O'Rourke	119
1889	Emmett Seery	137
1890	Billy Hamilton	141
1891	Billy Hamilton	158
1892	Billy Hamilton	148
1893	Jesse Burkett	155
1894	Joe Kelley	172
1895	Ed Delahanty	192
1896	Ed Delahanty	187
1897	Ed Delahanty	158
1898	Ed Delahanty	152
1899	Ed Delahanty	185
1900	Jesse Burkett	149
1901	Ed Delahanty	176
1902	Fred Clarke	156
1903	Mike Donlin	165
1904	Sam Mertes	130
1905	Jimmy Sheckard	135
1906	Sherry Magee	133
1907	Sherry Magee	161
1908	Sherry Magee	143
1909	Fred Clarke	137
1910	Sherry Magee	175

CENTER FIELD

1876	Lip Pike	161
1877	Jim O'Rourke	164
1878	Paul Hines	165
1879	John O'Rourke	161
1880	George Gore	178
1881	George Gore	142
1882	George Gore	145
1883	George Gore	150
1884	George Gore	156
1885	George Gore	176
1886	George Gore	176
1887	Paul Hines	129
1888	Jimmy Ryan	173
1889	Jimmy Ryan	145
1890	Mike Tiernan	150
1891	Bug Holliday	139
1892	Ed Delahanty	144
1893	Billy Hamilton	167
1894	Hugh Duffy	188
1895	Bill Lange	162
1896	Billy Hamilton	158
1897	Billy Hamilton	143
1898	Billy Hamilton	179
1899	Roy Thomas	137
1900	Billy Hamilton	146
1901	Roy Thomas	138
1902	Ginger Beaumont	146
1903	Roger Bresnahan	168
1904	Roy Thomas	148
1905	Cy Seymour	189
1906	Roy Thomas	133
1907	Ginger Beaumont	138
1908	Ginger Beaumont	117
1909	Tommy Leach	122
1910	Fred Snodgrass	153

LEFT FIELD

1911	Jimmy Sheckard	147
1912	Sherry Magee	126
1913	Sherry Magee	136
1914	George J Burns	146
1915	George J Burns	117
1916	Zack Wheat	146
1917	George J Burns	144
1918	George J Burns	126
1919	George J Burns	146
1920	Zack Wheat	138
1921	Austin McHenry	140
1922	Hack Miller	128
1923	Irish Meusel	116
1924	Zack Wheat	156
1925	Ray Blades	144
1926	Ray Blades	135
1927	Riggs Stephenson	141
1928	Chick Hafey	151
1929	Lefty O'Doul	168
1930	Lefty O'Doul	153
1931	Chuck Klein	159
1932	Lefty O'Doul	156
1933	Joe Medwick	132
1934	Chuck Klein	136
1935	Joe Medwick	149
1936	Joe Medwick	150
1937	Joe Medwick	176
1938	Joe Medwick	141
1939	Joe Medwick	133
1940	Jim Gleeson	134
1941	Joe Medwick	139
1942	Stan Musial	155
1943	Eric Tipton	141
1944	Augie Galan	162
1945	Jim Russell	128
1946	Del Ennis	131
1947	Ralph Kiner	175
1948	Stan Musial	202
1949	Ralph Kiner	189
1950	Ralph Kiner	163

CENTER FIELD

1911	Johnny Bates	135
1912	Dode Paskert	133
1913	Tommy Leach	139
1914	Jack Dalton	133
1915	Sherry Magee	124
1916	Benny Kauff	135
1917	Edd Roush	143
1918	Edd Roush	141
1919	Edd Roush	137
1920	Cy Williams	139
1921	Max Carey	125
1922	Cy Williams	135
1923	Cy Williams	146
1924	Cy Williams	153
1925	George Harper	135
1926	Hack Wilson	152
1927	Hack Wilson	160
1928	Hack Wilson	158
1929	Hack Wilson	157
1930	Hack Wilson	183
1931	Mel Ott	154
1932	Wally Berger	117
1933	Wally Berger	159
1934	Len Koenecke	149
1935	Wally Berger	139
1936	Wally Berger	126
1937	Herschel Martin	115
1938	Ernie Koy	122
1939	Frank Demaree	118
1940	Hank Leiber	133
1941	Pete Reiser	159
1942	Pete Reiser	139
1943	Augie Galan	144
1944	Johnny Hopp	149
1945	Goody Rosen	128
1946	Jim Russell	119
1947	Harry Walker	142
1948	Whitey Lockman	121
1949	Bobby Thomson	127
1950	Andy Pafko	151

LEFT FIELD

1951	Ralph Kiner	193
1952	Ralph Kiner	149
1953	Stan Musial	171
1954	Ralph Kiner	125
1955	Del Ennis	124
1956	Frank Robinson	141
1957	Wally Moon	134
1958	Harry Anderson	135
1959	Wally Moon	138
1960	Wally Moon	131
1961	Wally Moon	153
1962	Stan Musial	148
1963	Willie McCovey	154
1964	Rico Carty	159
1965	Willie Stargell	129
1966	Willie Stargell	160
1967	Tony Gonzalez	143
1968	Dick Allen	162
1969	Willie Stargell	156
1970	Rico Carty	176
1971	Willie Stargell	183
1972	Billy Williams	175
1973	Willie Stargell	179
1974	Willie Stargell	161
1975	Greg Luzinski	156
1976	George Foster	147
1977	George Foster	161
1978	Jeff Burroughs	175
1979	Dave Winfield	156
1980	George Foster	135
1981	George Foster	148
1982	Dusty Baker	127
1983	Jose Cruz	132
1984	Gary Matthews	145
1985	Pedro Guerrero	175
1986	Tim Raines	143
1987	Tim Raines	153
1988	Kal Daniels	150
1989	Kevin Mitchell	184
1990	Barry Bonds	166
1991	Barry Bonds	164
1992	Barry Bonds	211
1993	Barry Bonds	206

CENTER FIELD

1951	Willie Mays	123
1952	Stan Musial	167
1953	Duke Snider	166
1954	Duke Snider	172
1955	Duke Snider	173
1956	Duke Snider	165
1957	Willie Mays	171
1958	Willie Mays	161
1959	Willie Mays	152
1960	Willie Mays	149
1961	Willie Mays	155
1962	Hank Aaron	163
1963	Willie Mays	171
1964	Willie Mays	175
1965	Willie Mays	187
1966	Willie Mays	154
1967	Adolfo Phillips	146
1968	Willie Mays	158
1969	Jim Wynn	177
1970	Willie Mays	142
1971	Willie Mays	168
1972	Cesar Cedeno	153
1973	Cesar Cedeno	143
1974	Jim Wynn	152
1975	Jim Wynn	144
1976	Rick Monday	139
1977	George Hendrick	131
1978	Gene Richards	123
1979	Lee Mazzilli	134
1980	Cesar Cedeno	138
1981	Andre Dawson	150
1982	Leon Durham	150
1983	Dale Murphy	156
1984	Dale Murphy	154
1985	Dale Murphy	156
1986	Kevin McReynolds	136
1987	Eric Davis	160
1988	Eric Davis	144
1989	Eric Davis	157
1990	Ron Gant	140
1991	Ron Gant	133
1992	Andy Van Slyke	145
1993	Lenny Dykstra	148

RIGHT FIELD

1876	Dick Higham	134
1877	John Cassidy	152
1878	Orator Shaffer	163
1879	Jim O'Rourke	161
1880	King Kelly	133
1881	King Kelly	138
1882	Curry Foley	124
1883	King Kelly	106
1884	King Kelly	185
1885	King Kelly	151
1886	Sam Thompson	136
1887	Sam Thompson	160
1888	Mike Tiernan	148
1889	Mike Tiernan	167
1890	Oyster Burns	135
1891	Mike Tiernan	152
1892	Oyster Burns	149
1893	Sam Thompson	144
1894	Sam Thompson	169
1895	Sam Thompson	168
1896	Mike Tiernan	157
1897	Willie Keeler	157
1898	Elmer Flick	156
1899	Chick Stahl	153
1900	Honus Wagner	171
1901	Elmer Flick	157
1902	Sam Crawford	157
1903	Patsy Donovan	111
1904	Harry Lumley	132
1905	John Titus	148
1906	Harry Lumley	163
1907	Harry Lumley	130
1908	Mike Donlin	147
1909	Mike Mitchell	147
1910	Wildfire Schulte	129

CATCHER

1876	Deacon White	147
1877	Cal McVey	154
1878	Lew Brown	148
1879	Deacon White	140
1880	John Clapp	129
1881	Charlie Bennett	150
1882	Charlie Bennett	143
1883	Charlie Bennett	145
1884	Jack Rowe	141
1885	Charlie Bennett	161
1886	Charlie Bennett	*143
1887	Foghorn Miller	90
1888	King Kelly	161
1889	Buck Ewing	136
1890	Jack Clements	145
1891	Jack Clements	130
1892	Jack Boyle	70
1893	Jack Clements	122
1894	Wilbert Robinson	108
1895	Deacon McGuire	120
1896	Deacon McGuire	109
1897	Jack Warner	80
1898	Ed McFarland	113
1899	Ed McFarland	*142
1900	Ed McFarland	*111
1901	Deacon McGuire	*109
1902	Johnny Kling	110
1903	Johnny Kling	114
1904	Johnny Kling	84
1905	Roger Bresnahan	*137
1906	Roger Bresnahan	148
1907	Roger Bresnahan	*141
1908	Roger Bresnahan	151
1909	George Gibson	115
1910	George Gibson	103

RIGHT FIELD

1911	Wildfire Schulte	153
1912	John Titus	138
1913	Gavvy Cravath	171
1914	Gavvy Cravath	168
1915	Gavvy Cravath	173
1916	Gavvy Cravath	153
1917	Gavvy Cravath	159
1918	Al Wickland	140
1919	Ross Youngs	137
1920	Ross Youngs	159
1921	Ross Youngs	136
1922	Curt Walker	131
1923	Ross Youngs	129
1924	Ross Youngs	159
1925	Ki Ki Cuyler	154
1926	Paul Waner	151
1927	Paul Waner	160
1928	Paul Waner	158
1929	Mel Ott	171
1930	Babe Herman	169
1931	Babe Herman	136
1932	Mel Ott	176
1933	Chuck Klein	187
1934	Mel Ott	168
1935	Mel Ott	158
1936	Mel Ott	183
1937	Mel Ott	156
1938	Ival Goodman	140
1939	Mel Ott	184
1940	Mel Ott	144
1941	Mel Ott	155
1942	Mel Ott	168
1943	Stan Musial	177
1944	Stan Musial	176
1945	Tommy Holmes	169
1946	Phil Cavarretta	139
1947	Willard Marshall	134
1948	Enos Slaughter	138
1949	Stan Musial	181
1950	Del Ennis	136

CATCHER

1911	Chief Meyers	*120
1912	Chief Meyers	*147
1913	Chief Meyers	*124
1914	Roger Bresnahan	*135
1915	Frank Snyder	123
1916	Ivey Wingo	*105
1917	Bill Rariden	*121
1918	Mike Gonzalez	*111
1919	Ivey Wingo	*117
1920	Bob O'Farrell	*108
1921	Frank Snyder	*121
1922	Bob O'Farrell	139
1923	Bob O'Farrell	136
1924	Gabby Hartnett	*138
1925	Gabby Hartnett	*130
1926	Bob O'Farrell	121
1927	Gabby Hartnett	120
1928	Jimmy Wilson	93
1929	Jimmy Wilson	*116
1930	Gabby Hartnett	146
1931	Gabby Hartnett	*123
1932	Shanty Hogan	93
1933	Spud Davis	140
1934	Gabby Hartnett	129
1935	Gus Mancuso	99
1936	Gus Mancuso	106
1937	Al Todd	103
1938	Ernie Lombardi	145
1939	Harry Danning	122
1940	Harry Danning	118
1941	Harry Danning	90
1942	Mickey Owen	96
1943	Ray Mueller	116
1944	Ray Mueller	112
1945	Ernie Lombardi	*139
1946	Andy Seminick	*112
1947	Walker Cooper	135
1948	Walker Cooper	*118
1949	Roy Campanella	137
1950	Roy Campanella	137

RIGHT FIELD

1951	Enos Slaughter	116
1952	Enos Slaughter	131
1953	Carl Furillo	143
1954	Stan Musial	167
1955	Wally Post	142
1956	Hank Aaron	138
1957	Hank Aaron	154
1958	Hank Aaron	141
1959	Hank Aaron	167
1960	Hank Aaron	146

1961	Frank Robinson	162
1962	Frank Robinson	172
1963	Hank Aaron	176
1964	Frank Robinson	163
1965	Hank Aaron	159
1966	Hank Aaron	148
1967	Hank Aaron	164
1968	Hank Aaron	153
1969	Hank Aaron	176
1970	Hank Aaron	153

1971	Rusty Staub	143
1972	Jim Wynn	149
1973	Ken Singleton	157
1974	Reggie Smith	153
1975	Dave Parker	139
1976	Ken Griffey	138
1977	Reggie Smith	170
1978	Dave Parker	164
1979	Dave Parker	142
1980	Jack Clark	153

1981	Pedro Guerrero	130
1982	Pedro Guerrero	150
1983	Keith Moreland	132
1984	Chili Davis	139
1985	Dave Parker	146
1986	Darryl Strawberry	138
1987	Dale Murphy	163
1988	Darryl Strawberry	160
1989	Von Hayes	143
1990	Darryl Strawberry	139

1991	Bobby Bonilla	148
1992	Larry Walker	136
1993	Bobby Bonilla	136

CATCHER

1951	Roy Campanella	155
1952	Roy Campanella	124
1953	Roy Campanella	155
1954	Del Crandall	97
1955	Roy Campanella	151
1956	Stan Lopata	138
1957	Ed Bailey	133
1958	Del Crandall	115
1959	Del Crandall	103
1960	Ed Bailey	113

1961	Smoky Burgess	*123
1962	John Edwards	100
1963	Joe Torre	123
1964	Joe Torre	135
1965	Joe Torre	140
1966	Joe Torre	157
1967	Tim McCarver	135
1968	Tom Haller	122
1969	Johnny Bench	132
1970	Dick Dietz	157

1971	Dick Dietz	138
1972	Johnny Bench	163
1973	Joe Ferguson	139
1974	Johnny Bench	140
1975	Ted Simmons	141
1976	Ted Simmons	122
1977	Ted Simmons	143
1978	Ted Simmons	148
1979	Gene Tenace	141
1980	Ted Simmons	143

1981	Gary Carter	117
1982	Gary Carter	148
1983	Darrell Porter	125
1984	Gary Carter	135
1985	Gary Carter	135
1986	Gary Carter	118
1987	Benito Santiago	104
1988	Tony Pena	99
1989	Craig Biggio	113
1990	Darren Daulton	122

1991	Craig Biggio	107
1992	Darren Daulton	158
1993	Rick Wilkins	145

FIRST BASE
1882	Guy Hecker	115
1883	Ed Swartwood	166
1884	Harry Stovey	184
1885	Dave Orr	169
1886	Dave Orr	157
1887	John Reilly	120
1888	John Reilly	155
1889	Tommy Tucker	147
1890	Perry Werden	150
1891	Dan Brouthers	175

SHORTSTOP
1882	Bill Gleason	116
1883	Mike Moynahan	141
1884	Candy Nelson	133
1885	Frank Fennelly	144
1886	Frank Fennelly	125
1887	Oyster Burns	155
1888	Ed McKean	135
1889	Herman Long	109
1890	Phil Tomney	116
1891	Paul Radford	114

LEFT FIELD
1882	Mike Mansell	137
1883	Pete Browning	160
1884	Charley Jones	165
1885	Charley Jones	145
1886	Henry Larkin	152
1887	Tip O'Neill	224
1888	Harry Stovey	160
1889	Harry Stovey	157
1890	Spud Johnson	145
1891	George Van Haltren	137

RIGHT FIELD
1882	Ed Swartwood	179
1883	Tom Brown	116
1884	Ed Swartwood	130
1885	Tom Brown	143
1886	Ed Swartwood	135
1887	Fred Mann	113
1888	Chicken Wolf	118
1889	Oyster Burns	132
1890	Ed Swartwood	158
1891	Emmett Seery	144

SECOND BASE
1882	Pete Browning	210
1883	Pop Smith	126
1884	Sam Barkley	147
1885	Sam Barkley	119
1886	Yank Robinson	133
1887	Yank Robinson	143
1888	Yank Robinson	147
1889	Yank Robinson	115
1890	Cupid Childs	165
1891	Jack Crooks	115

THIRD BASE
1882	Hick Carpenter	148
1883	Jack Gleason	121
1884	Dude Esterbrook	136
1885	Bill McClellan	109
1886	Arlie Latham	125
1887	Denny Lyons	154
1888	Denny Lyons	139
1889	Denny Lyons	153
1890	Jimmy Knowles	117
1891	Denny Lyons	156

CENTER FIELD
1882	Oscar Walker	122
1883	Charley Jones	149
1884	Fred Mann	152
1885	Pete Browning	180
1886	Pete Browning	143
1887	Pete Browning	174
1888	Pete Browning	154
1889	Bug Holliday	139
1890	Rasty Wright	140
1891	Tom Brown	142

CATCHER
1882	Jack O'Brien	147
1883	Jack O'Brien	125
1884	Jim Keenan	*141
1885	Jocko Milligan	*109
1886	Fred Carroll	139
1887	Kid Baldwin	* 79
1888	Jim Keenan	*102
1889	Jack O'Connor	103
1890	Jack O'Connor	126
1891	Jocko Milligan	148

1884 UNION ASSOCIATION

1B	Lew Schoeneck	125
2B	Fred Dunlap	249
SS	Lew Say	93
3B	Jack Gleason	158
LF	Henry Moore	147
CF	Dave Rowe	136
RF	Orator Shaffer	189
C	Bill Krieg	105

1914 FEDERAL LEAGUE

1B	Fred Beck	109
2B	Duke Kenworthy	144
SS	Bill Louden	126
3B	Ed Lennox	159
LF	Chet Chadbourne	107
CF	Dutch Zwilling	136
RF	Benny Kauff	174
C	Art Wilson	146

1890 PLAYERS LEAGUE

1B	Roger Connor	167
2B	Yank Robinson	118
SS	Billy Shindle	121
3B	Bill Joyce	123
LF	Pete Browning	159
CF	George Gore	151
RF	Harry Stovey	136
C	Sy Sutcliffe	113

1915 FEDERAL LEAGUE

1B	Ed Konetchy	140
2B	Lee Magee	124
SS	Jimmy Esmond	107
3B	Mike Mowrey	117
LF	Claude Cooper	134
CF	Benny Kauff	180
RF	Steve Evans	135
C	Bill Rariden	120

Index

525